# The
# Windows 98

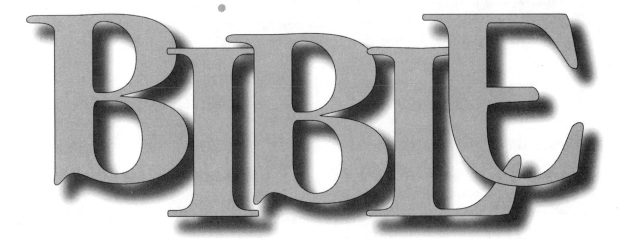

**FRED DAVIS · KIP CROSBY**

Peachpit Press

# The Windows 98 Bible

## by Fred Davis and Kip Crosby

**Peachpit Press**
1249 Eighth Street
Berkeley, CA 94710
(800) 283-9444
(510) 524-2178
(510) 524-2221 (fax)

Find us on the World Wide Web at: **http://www.peachpit.com**
Visit this book's Web site at: **http://www.winbible.com**

Peachpit Press is a division of Addison Wesley Longman

**Editor:** Corbin Collins
**Production Coordinator:** Kate Reber
**Compositor:** David Van Ness
**Index:** Ty Koontz
**Interior and Cover Design:** Mimi Heft

ISBN: 0-201-69690-8

0 9 8 7 6 5 4 3 2 1

Printed and bound in the United States of America

**Fred's dedication:**

To all those who,
in loyal fear,
in suffering and Service Packs,
frustration and sparse glory,
have used Microsoft Windows,
this book is dedicated,
with the hope that the Windows Bibles (all of 'em)
have blazed a trail for you and your computing.

**Kip's dedication:**

For Hilary,
who did so much to make this be this book,
with the greatest love.

# Table of Contents

. . . . . . . . . . . . . . . . . . . . . . . .

# Part 3: Advanced Windows 98 Techniques

## Chapter 13:  Optimizing Windows 98 Resources • **545**

# Part 4: Appendices

# Foreword

The last chapter of this book—one of the appendices, actually—has just been uploaded to the publisher, and in seven weeks exactly Windows 98 hits the store shelves. You, of course, are living in a world where that's already happened. In that world, you may be asking yourself a question we know all too well:

"What's this Windows 98 thing?!"

There are many answers to that question, and some of them are in here. But if we might be expansive for just a minute—Windows 98 is the end of an era, and the beginning. It's the end because (if we read the tea leaves right) Windows 98 is the last operating system that will ever be built on the Win32 core code. An immense chain of development that began with the 32-bit extensions to Win16, and persisted through all the revisions of Windows 95, has reached its highest point and logical conclusion in the Windows that this book is about.

On the other hand, the signs of a new awakening are all around us. In the last two years the price of a powerful Windows-compatible computer has fallen by half, sometimes by two-thirds. People by the millions are buying their first computers. Many are buying second and third computers for homes or offices, and connecting them to TV sets, digital cameras, or other computers. After decades of serving as the central artifact of Nerdvana, the personal computer has gone mainstream. The Internet has become a fact of all our lives as more and more computers are connected to it. And at this exact, yeasty juncture, what should arrive but a shiny new version of the world's most popular operating system.

Let's try that again: "What's this Windows 98 thing?!" It's what Windows 3.x never could have been. It's what Windows 95 always should have been. It's what will come pre-installed on your next computer. And because Windows 98 is all those things, it's also what we wrote this book about. We hope you like it.

*Fred Davis*　　　　　　*Kip Crosby*
*Berkeley, California*　　*Palo Alto, California*

*May 1998*

P.S. Be sure to visit **www.winbible.com**!

# Acknowledgments

While we worked on this book, a lot of other people did a lot of other work that made it possible. Some were friends and loved ones who contributed to the task in an amazing variety of ways. Many others have only a faint idea that we exist, if that, and yet … without them we wouldn't be quite where we are. Finally, whenever we can't shake the hands of the developers, we just have to thank the hardware and software.

Thanks to …

## The People

Donna and Joe Bradley
Ani and Richard Buckland
Paul Clapman
Corbin Collins
Flynn Crosby
Edwin Vivian El-Kareh
Tom E. Ellis
Maureen Forys
Paul Goldberg
Mimi Heft

Don Koijane
Frank McConnell
Sylvia Paull
Kate Reber
Scott Robinson
Erich Schienke
Karl Schmidtmann
Ondine Shugart
David Van Ness
John Woram

and the fine crews at:
Amazon.com
CDW
Microsoft PerOpSys
The Palo Alto NCA
Peachpit Press
and WombatNet

## The Software

We used a ton of software while we wrote this. A lot of it, we simply wrote about in the book. But there were a handful of programs that helped make this book as good as it is, because they did what was asked of them and came back for more. Our profound thanks for:

CompuPic 32 by Photodex, which has to be the most versatile graphics management tool known.

Microsoft Word, of course!

Paint Shop Pro by JASC, not just a paint program but a precision instrument that always leaves us smiling.

SnagIt 32 by TechSmith—one screen, one keystroke, one screenshot, no fuss. The best.

and, naturally …

Windows 98 itself.

## The Hardware

Goldrush: NCA-built Pentium tall tower, all-SCSI, Hewlett-Packard DAT tape, Windows NT Server 4.0, and it goes and goes and never quits.

Lucinda: homemade Pentium short tower, all-IDE, the fancy ATI TV card, half a dozen builds of Windows 98 from beta 1 to RC2 … and it never quit either.

Two Sony Trinitron monitors that get stared at for fourteen hours a day and never give us headaches.

# The Icons

 **New**  Indicates a brand-new feature in Windows 98.

 **Danger**  Flags potentially dangerous properties or behavior to watch out for.

 **Tip**  Points out useful tips and tricks.

 **Note**  Gives extra attention to unexpected or interesting aspects of the feature being discussed.

 **DOS**  Specifies a switch, option or error message related only to the DOS command line of the Registry Editor. [Registry only]

 **TweakUI**  Lets you know when you can use this powerful, automated, "underground" control panel instead of doing something more complicated.

 **xeH**  Warns you that Windows is using a special, potentially confusing, syntax to display or export Registry information. [Registry only]

# Part 1

## Mastering the Windows 98 Environment

# Part 1 At a Glance

# 1

# Windows 98: Why?

Somewhere in the world, in some placid back corner of a remote nation, the last tremors from the introduction of Windows 95 are just now dying down. The jaw-slackening quarter-billion dollar marketing blitzkrieg has long since been paid off by Microsoft's astounding revenues; the newspaper headlines, television news, radio talk shows, and office gossip have turned to fresher topics.

Now, suddenly, and with much less fanfare, there's Windows 98. Why? What does it do? Do we need it? Or is it, as jaded journalists would have it, only an incremental upgrade from 95, barely more than a Service Pack?

On the contrary, Windows 98—with its cleaned-up and speeded-up internals, its support for new ports and peripherals, and Internet-savvy user interface—is the most exciting, most versatile, and (probably) most stable consumer version of Windows in a long time. It is the version of Windows that, Microsoft hopes, will make *every* computer user into a 32-bit Windows user. And it might come close to succeeding.

That's why we've invested eleven months of curiosity, sweat, frustration, and sleep deprivation into this thousand-page book about Windows 98. Trust us—we wouldn't have done that for any Service Pack.

# What This Book Is About

Windows 98, after all, is a new version of Windows, the most popular and prominent operating system in all of computerdom. The changes that Microsoft has made to this important piece of software will dramatically change the way you work with your computer. Those who consider Windows 98 to be an "incremental upgrade" are basing their opinion primarily on the fact that Windows 98 looks—or can look, if you turn off the Active Desktop—almost exactly like Windows 95 (Figure 1.1). We're not revisiting the highly detailed paradigm shift that distinguished Windows 95 from Win 3.1.

All the more important, then, to get under the hood of Windows 98 and understand just how many improvements over Windows 95 it offers—and that's what this book will help you do. We're glad you chose it out of the dozens that have been written on the topic. As far as possible, we've based it on the final product and tried to describe the real world of Windows 98, based on hard experience with installations on several different machines. And we like to tell it like it is, so you can count on us to give you the straight scoop and sound advice.

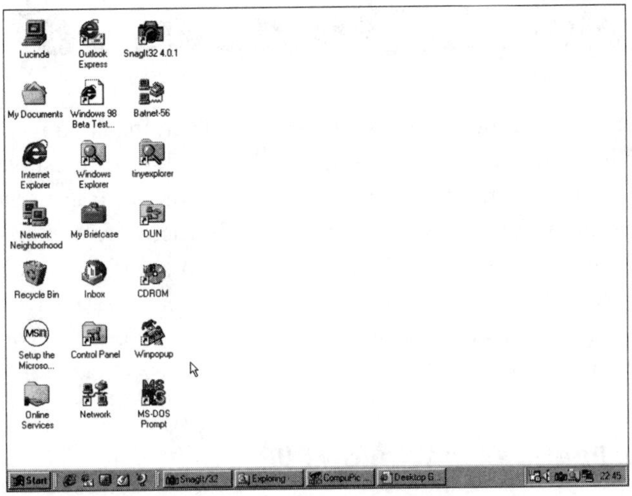

**Figure 1.1**

*Windows 98
Desktop (plain)*

How different is Windows 98? That depends on your perspective. It's still an operating system; much about it is evolutionary, not revolutionary. Most people will still be doing pretty much the same things with Windows 98 that they were doing with Windows 95 or even 3.1. It will be a little easier and prettier, but it won't fix your teeth, improve your serve, or turn your PC into a Mac. Although the much-touted Plug and Play feature has mostly been a success, you might still need to delve into the technical complexities of your hardware setup—new or old—when Windows 98 becomes part of your daily life.

On the other hand, we think Windows 98 is a big improvement over Windows 95. It's faster. It's much more Internet-aware. It fixes a giant list of pet peeves and annoyances that made many consumers less than satisfied with 95. It includes a whole bunch of new setup and diagnostic tools to make your computer easier to manage. And it's designed to wring the utmost out of the hardware you buy today, or tomorrow—but you can still run Windows 98 on a 486 and not feel like you need a new computer. (You may feel like you need a new disk, but that's normal.)

What a new version of Windows means to us, of course, is that we get to write a new book. And we hope you'll agree that *The Windows 98 Bible* is a big improvement over its predecessor, *The Windows 95 Bible*. It's almost twice as thick, and the difference is in the details; we go much deeper into Desktop controls, Internet management techniques, network setup, communications, the proper use of applets, and the vast amount of available shareware and freeware. This book also covers the Registry—the central, concealed, and highly mysterious database that stores every fact about your hardware and software and the way you want to run it. *The Windows 95 Bible* didn't cover the Registry, an omission we came to regret.

So, enough about us (for now) and on with the show!

# What's New in Windows 98?

 Building on the successes (and learning from the failures) of Windows 95, Windows 98 raises computing on a PC to a higher threshold in three important areas: features, performance, and ease of use. It integrates the operating system with the new, industrial-strength Microsoft Web browser, Internet Explorer 4.0. It also includes—by our count, not Microsoft's—13 new hardware-support features, 17 new optimization tools, 20 new applets, and a whole raft of Internet connectivity improvements above and beyond IE4. Let's just skim the new stuff:

## Table 1.1  New Features in Windows 98

| New feature | Significance |
| --- | --- |
| **ACPI**  (Advanced Configuration and Power Interface) | Takes system and power management away from the BIOS, where it's inflexibly burned into firmware, and gives it to Windows, which can vary priorities and power requirements according to system state. ACPI is the foundation of OnNow, a combined hardware/software feature that lets your computer "sleep" indefinitely, consuming minimal power, and then boot up immediately when you touch the controls. |
| **Active Desktop** | Adds a push client, delivering news, entertainment, and special-interest "channel" content, to the Desktop and the browser. |
| **AGP**  (Accelerated Graphics Port) | OS support for a special direct channel between the main CPU and the display subsystem, which will make screen graphics considerably faster when the AGP-compliant CPUs become available. |
| **APM**  (Advanced Power Management) 1.2 | Hot-swappable batteries and wake-on-modem-ring for laptops. |
| **Backup** | Enhanced tape backup support includes support for SCSI devices and many new formats. |
| **Broadcast Architecture** | Built-in support for various meldings of HTML, Explorer channel content, and broadcast television. |
| **CardBus** (32-bit PCMCIA support) | 32-bit performance for PCMCIA means that applications like video capture or hundred-megabit Ethernet will fit into little stainless-steel sandwiches that you can lose on your desk. Added support for 3.3-volt cards reduces the strain on your notebook's battery. |
| **DirectShow** | A unified playback engine for MPEG audio and video, .WAV, .AVI, and QuickTime—but not MIDI and not RealAudio. |
| **Disk Cleanup** | Available from the General tab of the Properties sheet for any hard disk, this utility offers a completely configurable way to get rid of Internet cache files, ActiveX and Java controls, Recycle Bin contents, and Windows temp files. If you want to go further than that, you can remove stale components and unused installed programs, and even convert your drive to FAT32, if it's not. |
| **Disk Compression** | DriveSpace 3 compression is supported and enhanced *on FAT16 drives only*. |

### Table 1.1 *(continued)*

| New feature | Significance |
| --- | --- |
| **Disk Defragmenter Optimization Wizard** | Speeds the load time of your favorite applications, not only by defragmenting, but by moving the apps you use most often to the most easily accessed cylinders of the disk. |
| **DVD** (Digital Video or Versatile Disc) | Resembling, but not compatible with, the likable but venerable CD, DVD uses more exacting laser technology and multilayer construction to put staggering amounts of data—up to 17GB—on a single two-sided disc. Drive transfer rates will permit seamless, skip-free full-motion video. It is probable, and manufacturers are certainly hoping, that DVD will do for desktop video and movies what the CD did for audio. |
| **Dynamic Display Setting** | All the on-the-fly video resets that made their debut in the Plus! Pack for Windows 95, and a few more, depending on how new your video hardware is. |
| **FAT32** | More efficient support for large hard disks. By making FAT entries longer, FAT32 allows smaller clusters on larger platters, reducing slack space and increasing data density, right along with meaningful data transfer. |
| **FAT32 conversion utility** | Reformats a disk from FAT16 to FAT32 on the fly and without removing data. This is an improvement over the FAT32 included in Windows 95 OSR2, which required the disk to be declared as FAT16 or FAT32 at the time of a fresh (data-destructive) format. |
| **FireWire** (IEEE 1394) | Your very own, flexible, six-wire digital fat pipe! Developed by Apple, this special high-speed bus allows the daisy-chaining of up to 63 devices with hot-swapping, has a transfer rate of 400Mbit/sec now and much more later, and can connect an immense variety of appliances to your computer, like digital camcorders, digital still cameras, and DVD players. *Note:* In these early days it seems as if computer marketers tend to call this FireWire and non-computer manufacturers prefer IEEE 1394, but they're the same thing. |
| **HelpDesk** | Connects the user to Microsoft's support center. |
| **Internet Connection Wizard** | Automated setup for Dial-Up Networking. Thank you, Microsoft! |
| **Internet Explorer 4.0** | HTML 4.0 support and an improved user interface that integrates the browser with the operating system. |
| **LDAP** (Lightweight Directory Access Protocol) | Integrates public directory search access into the Windows mail client, giving you—in essence—an Internet-wide "local" address book. |
| **Multilink PPP** (also called Channel Aggregation) | Lets you pair up communications links, such as modems or ISDN adapters, to double your effective throughput—ideal for remote LAN access. |
| **Multiple-display support** | Combines up to four physical monitors into a "continuous" virtual Desktop. |
| **Point-to-Point Tunneling Protocol** (PPTP) | Lets you set up secure links to Windows NT servers across the Internet. |
| **PowerToys** | A favorite download from the Microsoft Web site and considered indispensable by serious Windows 95 users, these quirky extras are incorporated into Windows 98 as respectable applets. |
| **Remote Access Server** | Windows 98 gets RAS handed down from big brother NT, and your SOHO peer-to-peer network acquires dial-up access. Hey, we can reverse-telecommute! |

**Table 1.1**  *(continued)*

| New feature | Significance |
|---|---|
| ***Start Menu Organizer Wizard*** | At last, a way to keep your Start Menu lean and mean without playing fifteen-puzzle in Explorer or poking around the Registry. (If you'd *rather* poke around the Registry, see Chapter 19.) |
| ***System File Checker*** | Checks your system files to make sure they all work, maintains a log file, and lets you restore configuration from the log file. In case of trouble, it helps you do things like extract single files from .CAB archives. An ideal tool for those times when an uninstaller doesn't work quite right. |
| ***System Update*** | Scans the Web for available driver files, compares their datestamps with the ones on your system, and downloads and installs updated copies of any drivers that have become obsolete. |
| ***Tuneup Wizard*** | Preset background scheduling for things like defragmentation, ScanDisk, and cleaning up cache files. |
| ***TV Viewer*** | A spiffy, graphical, integrated application that supports TV tuner cards. |
| ***USB***  (Universal Serial Bus) | Slower than FireWire (12 Mbit/sec) and cheaper, USB extends "Plug and Play down the cable" to as many as 127 devices per port, like monitors, controls, audio devices, modems, keyboards, mice, CD-ROM, tape and floppy drives, joysticks, data gloves, scanners, printers, digitizers, and further-out stuff like MPEG-2 video products and computer telephony—even ISDN. The serial port of the future with components available today, USB makes hardware installation a snap. |
| ***Web Integration*** | Divides your computing environment into three concentric segments—Internet, intranet, and local computer—all seamlessly accessible from your Windows desktop. |
| ***Win32 Driver Model*** (WDM) | By complying with the WDM, hardware and software developers will be able to write drivers that work with both Windows NT and Windows 98. This addresses the biggest shortfall of the Windows Compatibility Logo program, which was that too few developers wrote Windows 95 drivers and then had the energy to write completely separate drivers for WinNT. |
| ***Windows Scripting Host*** (WSH) | The Windows Scripting Host can automate any Windows functions and collaborate with JavaScript and VBScript, as well as extend function calls for scripts to create, read, write and delete Registry entries, create and modify Windows shortcuts, map network drives and printers, and retrieve and modify values stored in DOS environment variables. Microsoft at last provides a true and robust Windows batch language—with the puzzling omission of any way to create, read, write or delete disk files, scan directories or check version information?? |
| ***Windows Update*** | A Start Menu wizard that connects you to Microsoft's Web-based update site and automatically downloads new versions, patches and fixes. Requires a modem and a configured Dial-Up Networking connection. |
| ***Zero Administration for Windows*** (ZAW) | Helps corporate customers hold down management costs for Windows desktops by incorporating local and remote administrative tools into Windows 98 on the client side and WinNT 5.0 on the server side. Windows 98's client-side technology is called the Zero Administration Kit (ZAK). |

# What About the Software I've Got?

With so much that's new about Windows 98, it's nice to know that almost all the software written for Windows 3.1 and DOS will still run fine under the newest Microsoft OS. The tens of thousands of applications created for those older operating systems run the gamut from spreadsheets and word processors to shareware utilities and music software.

On the other end of the stick, Windows 98 has more Windows NT code in interesting places under the interface—which is a lot like slipping steel framing into a wooden house. This should make Windows 98 faster than Windows 95, more versatile, and more stable.

Ultimately, as Microsoft has promised for some time, the two versions of Windows will converge and any Windows you buy will have the NT kernel. At that point, the last remnants of Win16 (Windows 3.x) will be put out to pasture and the Win32 architecture will rule undisputed.

Is this a good thing? Almost certainly. Windows NT has offered distinct advantages for several years, but the main argument against running it was the overhead—the fact that not every processor you could buy in a retail computer could guarantee good performance with NT. Happily, those days are behind us, because any Windows computer you're likely to buy (new) today will have an Intel Pentium MMX, Pentium Pro, or Pentium II CPU, or some rough equivalent from Cyrix or AMD. Any of these processors will run WinNT with power to spare, so long as you don't skimp on the memory. The only adjustment necessary to a "consumer" version of WinNT would be greater patience with DOS games that play radical tricks with memory space or video palettes. (Although Microsoft's 3D Pinball, which is no tame game, runs fine on NT 4, so the situation isn't hopeless.)

Our crystal ball says that Windows 98 and the forthcoming Windows NT 5.0 will be truly worthwhile operating systems, and their successors—"Windows 2001" and NT 6—capable beyond belief.

# Why Do I Need to Read This Book?

Few computer users—not us and, we suspect, not you—were immune to the megabuck Microsoft blitz that launched Windows 95. Since you've gotten this far into this book, we're assuming that you, too, have been swept up in the cyclone of enthusiasm for 32-bit Windows. But even if the faith has yet to visit you, even if Windows 95 or 98 has been foisted on you by your boss, why just

**Figure 1.2**

*Windows 98 Desktop (personalized)*

tolerate it when you can actually put it to work for you? After all, if you suddenly had a Corvette in your driveway you wouldn't just use it to buy groceries. If you install the Windows 98 environment and an application or two, and stop there, you'll miss out on advances that have been called "the biggest change in the way we use computers since graphical user interfaces"[1]—advances that can help increase your productivity and creativity and even enhance your enjoyment of computing.

With a detailed understanding of the software and hardware resources that the environment offers, and with a command of the utilities that enable you to control and customize it, you can take full advantage of Windows. And as with any software product, it's the extras—the tips, the tricks, the little insights—that give you the incomparable pleasure of genuinely understanding and mastering your environment.

With Windows 98 (and, of course, this book) you can make your personal computer truly personal. You can customize your screen by selecting or designing icons, changing the colors of menus and buttons, and splashing the desktop with any pattern, from fleur-de-lis to flying toasters. Windows brings individuality to the forefront, so every system can reflect the personality and preferences of its user (Figure 1.2).

Once your Desktop suits you, you can begin digging down to the vast array of features and options contained—sometimes buried—in Windows 98. Armed with this book and a moderate amount of insatiable curiosity, you can learn the inner secrets that will let you optimize your system, your programs, and Windows 98 itself. That sports car is in your driveway; we'll teach you to rev up your engine, cover ground like never before, and have fun doing it.

---

[1]  Michael J. Miller, *PC Magazine,* September 9, 1997.

# What Is Windows Anyway?

And now for a little history.

## Stroking Genius

Every version of Windows belongs to a larger family of interfaces traceable to a parent source: Xerox Palo Alto Research Center, almost always called Xerox PARC. During the 1960s and 1970s, PARC was home to seminal work by computer scientists such as Doug Engelbart (inventor of the mouse and founder of the Bootstrap Institute), Alan Kay (inventor of the laptop, a long-time Apple Fellow, now at Walt Disney Imagineering), John Warnock (chairman of Adobe Systems and a designer of PostScript), Gary Starkweather (inventor of the laser print engine) and Larry Tesler (for years the Chief Scientist of Apple and now a developer of educational software). In a climate where intelligence was revered and money was irrelevant, a battalion of geniuses designed an incredibly comprehensive and detailed possible future for computing. In time, PARC and its ideas would revolutionize the industry.

Ironically, Xerox never reaped the fortune that they could (and should) have. In 1974 they introduced the Alto, now widely considered the first personal computer and at least ten years ahead of its time … in fact, an Alto would do things that your computer probably doesn't do *today*. But the Alto was so advanced that Xerox, selling a handful of them at $25,000 each, lost money on every one. (Many of them ended up in PARC's own network; the survivors are prized collector's items.) The Alto's successor, the Star Workstation, also failed—it did even more but cost more, too.

But the *ideas* had phenomenal staying power. Steve Jobs at Apple hired some of PARC's best engineers to create the brilliant, but mysterious, Lisa. Not many people who understood Lisa's unique interface were willing to part with $10,000 for the box, and so it languished on dealers' shelves. Apple took the design work and code base from the Lisa, combined it with concepts and designs by Jef Raskin, Steve Capps, and others—and created the quite phenomenal Macintosh. PARC's vision of computing, refined and made affordable, finally reached "the rest of us."

The Mac's success catalyzed an industry-wide move to GUIs. UNIX led the way as Sun Microsystems developed OpenLook and the Open Software Foundation created Motif. Steve Jobs' third try, the awesomely elegant NeXT, ran NeXTStep, a GUI so powerful that the software survived when the hardware went out of production. IBM, trying to recapture the lead in the PC market, introduced a new hardware architecture (the barely remembered PS/2) and a GUI operating system, the OS/2 Presentation Manager and Workplace Shell.

The Commodore Amiga ran its own graphical AOS; the Atari ST, a fierce competitor of the Macintosh, ran GEM, one of the most flexible GUIs ever written. In less than ten years, the GUI took over computing.

## The Proclamation

During all this time Microsoft was not sitting still. (Big surprise!) In September 1981—the *month after* the IBM PC was *introduced*—work began on a project called Interface Manager, which would permit an Intel-based computer to open several programs at once, each in a separate "window." Inaugurating a long-standing policy of preannouncing software, Microsoft proclaimed in 1983 that Windows 1.0 would be available shortly. "By the end of 1984," Bill Gates assured the pundits, "Windows will be operational on 90 percent of computers running MS-DOS."

This was breathtaking optimism. Making a multitasking OS run on an Intel processor of the early eighties was the next door down from impossible. Hundreds of thousands of lines of C code were written, programmers slept on their carpets for months, and only the profits from MS-DOS and Apple II applications kept Microsoft financially solvent. The Mac, running a more polished GUI on a more appropriate CPU, arrived in 1984 and stole Microsoft's thunder-to-be. Not until November 1985 would Windows 1.03 ship in quantity, and it was some of the least stable software ever offered for retail sale.

No matter. A month earlier Intel had introduced the 80386, its first processor with virtual machines, flat memory space, and protected mode that worked. Here was the CPU that would run Windows—and Microsoft had the bit in its teeth. Version numbers climbed to 2.0, 2.1, and 2.2, then Windows/286 and Windows/386. A small, but highly advanced and influential, community of programmers began developing third-party Windows applications.

In the spring of 1990 Microsoft released Windows 3.0, frankly the first version that made real concessions to the consumer market. It was still far from perfect, but a seductive interface, broad hardware support, and unprecedented ease of use took it over the hurdle from cult preoccupation to mainstream environment. Applications development reached escape velocity as major developers realized that "Windows versions"—of course in parallel with "DOS versions"—of their programs would be critical to their bottom line. Day-in-day-out users soon understood that tweaking the .INI files was a nightmare, the dreaded UAE (Unrecoverable Application Error) in one program could lock the whole system, and it was slow on anything but the very fastest 386DX or a 486; but Windows had made its mark at last, selling about 7 million copies. This version introduced many of the features and concepts that remain today in Windows 98.

Microsoft was on the back stretch and would not be denied. Less than two years after Win 3.0 came Windows 3.1. In the technical evolution of Windows, 3.1 represented a minor step forward: its GUI was almost identical to that of 3.0. It was somewhat kinder to system resources, and fatal memory overlaps—renamed General Protection Faults, GPF's—could halt an offending program while the rest of the system kept going. Supplied games included a colorful Solitaire (which Microsoft ingenuously claimed was meant to "make users comfortable with drag-and-drop,") and the instant classic Minesweeper. Was this enough improvement to make Windows truly ubiquitous? Probably not on its own; but 3.1 arrived at the same time as Intel's "clock-doubled" DX2 processor and the beginnings, only the beginnings, of inexpensive RAM and disk space. 3.1 running on a 486DX2/66, with 16MB RAM and a 340MB disk, was the top-line spec of the day and a power user's feast. When 3.1 was upgraded to Windows for Workgroups, with software for a small peer-to-peer network in the same box, the die was cast.

Windows 3.1 and 3.11 were a success so huge that even Microsoft tired of it and wished, just the way they had with DOS, that somehow it would falter and stop. The 3.x installed base soared to over 50 million users by August 1995, when Windows 95 was launched. Even now, two years later, 3.1 has been hustled off the market but Windows for Workgroups is still sold and supported. Microsoft is very firm that, just as DOS 6.22 is the "last DOS," Windows for Workgroups is the "last Win16" and its days are numbered. (A plan to release one more revision of Win16, to be called Windows Classic or Windows 3.5, was allegedly scrapped as recently as 1996. It's fascinating that one of the text setup files for Microsoft Office 7.0—nominally a full 32-bit suite—contains the message "This program requires Windows 3.5 or higher," suggesting that if 3.5 had ever appeared, it would have included a hefty portion of Win32s.)

## The Heir Apparent

So Windows 98 enters the fray with four very hard jobs in sight. It must be a strong, flexible, client-side OS for networks with Windows NT servers. (This is actually the easiest of its tasks since Windows 95 was already pretty good at that.) It has to keep the Microsoft installed base loyal and satisfied during a time of tremendous volatility spurred by the Internet. It must be perceived as a meaningful and attractive upgrade from Windows 95. And—if Microsoft is lucky—it will be the version of 32-bit Windows *that finally convinces the Windows 3.x user base to abandon Win16.*

It's a tall order, but Microsoft numerology suggests it's not unreasonable. Back when Windows 95 was the eagerly awaited "Chicago," it was also sometimes called Windows 4.0. Windows 98 is Windows 4.1, but the resonance is far greater that you might expect from a point-one upgrade. We suspect that, just as both 3.0 and 4.0 introduced a new architecture and interface, the "minor" improvements in 4.1 as in 3.1 are the gateway to universal adoption—or so Redmond must hope.

Will it work? Is Windows 98 the "right stuff" that can at last displace and replace one of the world's most popular operating systems—*another version of Windows itself?*

We'll just have to see.

## Okay, So What's Windows NT?

Something quite, and not quite, different.

Several years ago, IBM outlined a series of design principles intended to give all their computers—smallest to largest—a common interface and method of operation. In perennial IBM style, they christened it System Application Architecture Common User Access, a name so unwieldy that even its acronym is too long. Non-IBM programmers balked at its unbending rules and heavy overhead, and nicknamed it "Blue Glue," which was rarely a compliment.

But Microsoft saw advantages and bought in. Microsoft and IBM, like Spain and Portugal in the Middle Ages, had divided the world once between PC-DOS and MS-DOS; now they would do the same with OS/2 Presentation Manager and Windows. Presentation Manager 1.*x* and all the versions of Windows 2 shared an appearance dictated by SAA CUA. The collaboration deepened and parallel versions of OS/2 appeared: IBM OS/2, for IBM desktop machines with the Microchannel hardware bus, and MS-OS/2, for computers with Intel processors and more conventional buses.

OS/2 was, and is, formidable. It was designed with literally industrial strength and security, meant for banks and hospitals and airlines. It was thoroughly 32-bit at a time when Windows was 16-bit. It escaped the limitations of the old FAT file system with its own allocation scheme, HPFS, which used large disks much more efficiently. Early versions were flawed—the "DOS compatibility box," OS/2's 16-bit DOS prompt, was so slow it was nicknamed the "DOS penalty box"—but corporations, especially, saw its merit and were willing to wait for the bugs to shake out. OS/2 users tend to be fanatically loyal, and even today can buy a retail version updated with full Internet connectivity.

IBM and Microsoft seemed to have reached fruitful common ground, but when there are two kings on one board, every game becomes chess. In 1991 the long-standing joint development efforts, which ten years earlier led to the creation of DOS and the PC standard, were severed—and so was the codebase of OS/2, in a process scrutinized by squads of lawyers. Microsoft had designed much of the original, common OS/2; they wasted no time repossessing their portion of it and reworking it so that it appeared even more similar to Windows.

The result, Windows NT (for New Technology) 3.1, looked like Windows 3.1, but the similarity stopped at the skin. Besides being the inheritor of MS-OS/2 and Microsoft's LAN Manager, WinNT could claim a family relationship with DEC (Digital Equipment Corporation) VMS, with Steve Jobs' NeXTStep, and with some versions of UNIX. The rugged filesystem, called NTFS, was based on IBM's HPFS but was rewritten by Microsoft to eliminate one or two significant flaws in the way that pointers to files were stored on the disk.

The release of two versions, "plain" NT and NT Advanced Server (NTAS), put the computing world on notice that Microsoft intended to become a player in the network and enterprise operating systems market, which had until then belonged almost exclusively to companies like Novell, Artisoft, IBM, and various UNIX vendors. NT promised to be a strong competitor, but the handwriting on the wall was that it would run both "native" Windows NT applications (32-bit software specifically designed for NT) and existing 16-bit Windows 3.1 applications. A Windows network, running NT at the server and Windows for Workgroups at the workstation, was seamless; other vendors' networks had to run Windows on top of the network OS, on top of DOS, which could be complex to set up and time-consuming to maintain. In later versions, to underscore the point, "plain" NT was called NT Workstation and Advanced Server became just NT Server.

When Windows 95 came along, it took a step closer to the 32-bit world of WinNT; the two operating systems used many of the same internal programming codes, called application programming interfaces (APIs). Windows NT can also run applications designed for Windows 95, and because Windows 95 programs are based on the 32-bit API, they run faster on Windows NT than do Windows 3.1 programs.

Windows NT offers several advantages over Windows 95. Windows 95 is a hybrid 16-bit/32-bit system; NT is a fully developed 32-bit operating system, with better overall performance and broader capabilities. (NT runs Win16 programs in a subsystem called WOWEXEC, the Windows on Windows Executive, which is a "Windows box.") Windows 95 and 98 can run only on a single Intel processor; Windows NT can run on more than one processor and on non-Intel processors. By using two or more CPUs simultaneously and installing NT to control them, you can build a powerful desktop or server system at relatively low cost. At one time, Microsoft made "ports" of Windows NT available for the PowerPC chip, the MIPS 4000-series chip, and the DEC Alpha chip—all state-of-the-art RISC processors with higher performance than competing Intel CPUs; today the Intel Pentium Pro and Pentium II are the most popular chips for high-performance applications, and Microsoft has discontinued the PowerPC and MIPS flavors of NT. The combination of strong multithreaded architecture and the ability to run on multiple processors makes NT suitable for a broad range of demanding applications, such as engineering workstations, Web or database servers, and even parallel super-computers.

In the summer of 1996 Microsoft delivered Windows NT 4.0 Server and Workstation, which present the Windows 95 Desktop on the screen and hide the 32-bit NT "steel" behind it. You can sit down at a 32-bit Windows computer and literally not know whether you're running 95 or NT 4, unless you know what to look for in the Start Menu or Control Panel. This family resemblance makes it especially easy to set up and maintain networks with NT on the server and 95 or 98 on the workstations. NT 4.0 is the power behind Microsoft's steeply rising share of network "seats."

By the summer of 1999, Microsoft should deliver Windows NT 5.0, which will incorporate many of Windows 98's interface goodies and also be able to handle a broader range of network sizes—in the industry jargon, be more "scalable." Until recently, NT has competed with other LAN operating systems for market share; NT 5 will be the Microsoft operating system that competes with UNIX to supply the very largest network customers, such as banks, stock exchanges, insurance companies, and airline and hotel reservation systems. In October, 1997 Bill Gates said he was "betting the farm" on the release of NT 5 and called it the most significant OS delivery in the history of Windows.

# So, You're Upgrading?

Naturally, Windows 98 users come at this shiny new operating system from several different angles. You're either upgrading from a different operating system, from a different kind of computer, or from no computer at all. Read on for a few quick tips that will help you introduce yourself to Windows 98 from the perspective of what you know already.

## To Windows 98 from Windows 95

You're in Toyland with a flashlight. For you, the big news is the melding of the operating system with your Internet access, and your ability to run your Desktop like a Web page—that is, with single clicks and hyperlinks. Internet Explorer 4 is much more tightly integrated with Windows 98 than IE 3 was with Windows 95; the Active Desktop gives you a good selection of push content without forcing it on you.

*Figure 1.3*

*Layered taskbar*

Check out the slick two-layer sliding Taskbar (Figure 1.3) that lets you get back to the Desktop without minimizing all your running tasks.

Try out the new integrated apps like WebTV (Figure 1.4), Chat, and NetMeeting, as well as applets and tools like the System File Checker, Maintenance Wizard, and DirectShow. Windows 98 is the most full-featured upgrade ever, but you will have to prowl around and find all the new pieces.

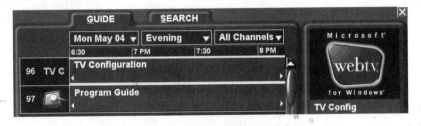

*Figure 1.4*

*WebTV*

## To Windows 98 from Windows 3.x

Windows 98 is more than a face-lift of Windows 3.1, and in fact, the two don't have a lot in common other than running your Win16 software.

To use Windows 3.1, you interact with both Program Manager and File Manager. Program Manager's colorful icons are just aliases—that is, you can't manipulate them to control the program files they represent. The icons act as buttons that give you access to the actual files, but you can't delete an icon and delete the file it stands for. To work with actual files in Windows 3.1—say, to clean up a directory or copy a file to a floppy disk—you have to fire up the File Manager, a file-browsing utility so weak and unintuitive that power users often resort to the DOS command line instead.

Shortcut to
CDROM

*Figure 1.5*

*Shortcut*

Windows 98 has two kinds of icons, one of which is called a Shortcut (Figure 1.5). A Shortcut is the closest thing to a Win 3.1 icon, but it's also a real file with the extension .LNK. If you highlight a Shortcut and hit Alt Enter, you'll bring up the Shortcut's Properties, in the same way that Alt Enter in Windows 3.1 brought up an icon's Program Item Properties. (As you get used to the Windows 98 interface, you can also right-click on a Shortcut and pick Properties from its Context Menu.) A Shortcut will have a small boxed arrow in its lower left corner and its icon title will say "Shortcut to…" (Figure 1.5).

You can turn off both those features with TweakUI—see Chapter 13 and please get a little experience with Windows 98's standard interface before you start using radical Windows tool kits!

**Online Services**

**Figure 1.6**

*Folder on desktop*

**Recycle Bin**

**Figure 1.7**

*Recycle Bin*

An icon *without* a Shortcut arrow, on the other hand, is actually the file or folder that it represents, and if you delete the icon you've also deleted the file or folder. But you'll find it very convenient to drag files that you're working on to the Desktop and keep them within reach (Figure 1.6).

If you delete something you actually wanted, don't worry, because Windows 98 has a Recycle Bin (Figure 1.7)—like the Macintosh Trash Can, although renamed on the advice of Microsoft's legal department. If something ends up in the Recycle Bin you can get it back out.

Compared to Win 3.1, Windows 98 has a richer interface reminiscent of the Macintosh or of IBM's OS/2. The design of almost every component has changed, altering not only the look and feel, but the way you operate your computer. Program Manager and its Siamese twin, File Manager, have been replaced by interface triplets: My Computer, the Taskbar, and the Windows Explorer. Unlike the twins, the triplets are independent—each one gives you a unique and stand-alone way to work with your computer and change the way it works.

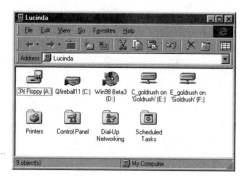

**Figure 1.8**

*My Computer*

My Computer, as its name suggests, presents the warmest, fuzziest way to view your system (Figure 1.8). It is organized into a system of file folders that represent directories. Inside those folders are icons, which represent programs, data, and other files. Inside My Computer, you can double-click on a drive's icon to view the contents of that drive and double-click on a folder to open up that folder.

Once you're used to My Computer, give the Explorer a try (Figure 1.9). The Explorer could be described as the Windows 3.1 File Manager on steroids, and is probably the best place for a 3.1 user to start, because it will look somewhat familiar. At least you'll spot icons. The alias icons in the Windows 3.1 File Manager were tiny and not very informative; the Explorer dishes up a more powerful system of managing files, letting you choose from a variety of icon sizes and displaying the actual icons for applications and many data files. It only takes a glance to identify what's what.

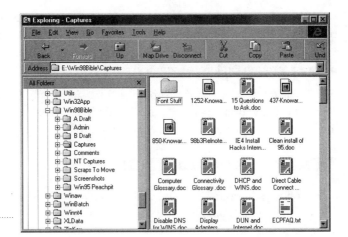

**Figure 1.9**

*The Explorer*

Finally, hit that great big button labeled **Start** at the bottom left-hand corner of your screen, and get friendly with the Taskbar—the Windows power user's favorite way to get things going. When you push on that puppy, you pop up a cascading array of menus that can resemble a maze, depending on how many files and folders you've created (Figure 1.10).

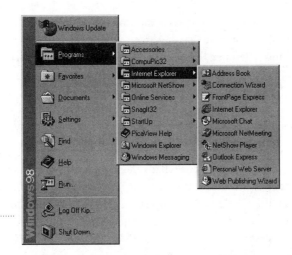

**Figure 1.10**

*Cascaded Start menu*

Your mouse hand can quickly learn its way through the maze, and the Start button could become your favorite starting place. The Taskbar gives you out-of-the-way, single-click icons for all your running applications, and as you get used to it, you'll start spending much less time in "Alt-Tab hell."

When you do use (Alt)(Tab), you'll find it's much nicer—it includes a parade of icons so that you'll know instantly whether to go through the loop forwards or backwards.

An animated message pops up when you install Windows, pointing to the Start button and inviting you to click on it. But we don't recommend the Start button for Windows 98 beginners; start with My Computer and progress through Explorer as you feel more comfortable.

 When that animated arrow starts to drive you mad, which should take about one day, you can banish it with TweakUI. Or install any application in your Startup group, which will also turn it off.

## To Windows 98 from DOS

Start with My Computer and take it slow. Remember that as far as the interface goes, you're jumping forward fifteen years, which is roughly a geologic era in computer time. Read the sections on My Computer, the Explorer, and the Taskbar above.

You'll want to pay some attention to some key concepts that got their start with Windows 3.*x* or 95:

**The Clipboard.** With this invisible tool you can transfer text or graphics from one program to another—only one piece at a time. Highlight something and press Ctrl C; the highlighted object stays where it is but a Copy (thus, C) goes to the Clipboard. If you want to remove it from where it is, press Ctrl X (think X-out); it vanishes from where it was and goes to the Clipboard instead. Then, by pressing Ctrl V (think down-arrow or push-down) you can Paste the contents of the Clipboard wherever the cursor is. The longer you use this, the more it becomes second nature, until eventually it's just part of your typing; in this paragraph every occurrence of the words "the Clipboard," after the first one, was pasted in with Ctrl V.

 The only tricky thing about the Clipboard is that, every time you send something to it, you wipe out what's there already. If you're working with several pieces of text that you don't want to lose, the best approach can be to keep one on the Clipboard and insert the others with your program's macro or glossary facility. Alternatively, you can keep multiple Clipboards with the Windows accessories ClipTray or ClipBook Viewer; but the Clipboard tends to work best if you don't make it too fancy.

 If you're familiar with the DOS version of Microsoft Word, just think of the Clipboard as a fancy Scrap that can jump from one program to the next.

**Long Filenames.** You can say goodbye to BUDGET08.XLS and its brethren. All 32-bit versions of Windows support names up to 255 characters long for files and folders, including spaces, so go ahead and call that file August Budget.XLS.

You don't want to go wild with this—Windows' own cache-file folder, "Temporary Internet Files," is probably stretching it—but it's a tremendous advantage to have even ten or twelve characters instead of eight available for a filename. Also, the more you use Windows, the more you'll realize that you rarely type a *whole* filename; mostly you just type the first letter, or click on the file's name or icon.

## *More On Long Filenames*

In parallel with whatever long filename you select, 32-bit Windows maintains an 8.3 filename for use by DOS and 16-bit Windows. It tries to be intelligent about how it does it, but the system isn't very flexible; it lops off everything after the sixth character of the filename and uses a ~ (tilde) and a number for the last two. This means that if you had a file called August Budget.XLS it would translate to AUGUST~1.XLS, and a file called August Payroll.XLS would translate to AUGUST~2.XLS. At times, this behavior can be inconvenient.

If you're working entirely within 32-bit Windows, it doesn't matter, because you'll never see the short filenames. But if you're going to be using these files on another computer that runs DOS or Windows 3.*x*, or on your computer with a 16-bit Windows application, you want to make your filenames unique within their first six characters. In our example, you could use the names Aug Budget.XLS, which would translate to AUGBUD~1.XLS, and Aug Payroll.XLS, which would translate to AUGPAY~2.XLS.

If you don't like the tilde-and-number extension—and a lot of people don't—you can force Windows to use this only when it's needed to resolve conflicts in filenames. *But be sure you understand the importance of backing up the Registry first!!* See Chapter 17.

**Drag-and-Drop.** Since its beginnings, Windows has offered a feature called Drag-and-Drop, which means that you can "drag" any object from one place—or folder, or icon—to another by clicking on it, holding down your left mouse (or trackball) button, and dragging it to a destination. Once a file is an icon on the Desktop, Drag-and-Drop it onto a Printer icon to print it. Drag-and-Drop a file from one folder to another in Explorer. There are even applications that will let you Drag-and-Drop objects onto toolbar buttons. (If the use of the word *object* in this way causes some confusion, don't worry; it started as a programmer's term, and you'll understand it better the more you use Windows.)

The best way to get practice in Drag-and-Drop—okay, okay, Microsoft's right!—is to go into your Programs\Games folder and start a game of Solitaire, which lets you "drag" the cards from one stack to another. You'll find you can play a more relaxed game if you go into Game\Options in Solitaire and clear the Timed Game, Status Bar, and Outline Dragging checkboxes.

**OLE (Object Linking and Embedding).** This is the advanced technology that operates behind the scenes in Windows to, for example, make Shortcuts work. Basically it's the machinery underneath two processes that are quite fundamental to Windows. *Object linking* is a connection between two objects (or more) in the background, so that when you click on the Shortcut, the program (or whatever) that it's linked to opens. *Object embedding* is a connection between multiple objects in the *foreground,* which makes one object appear to be part of another. You can use embedding to, among other things, put automatically updating Excel spreadsheets in the middle of your Word documents.

OLE is not something that you see, as itself, in Windows. (The Windows 3.*x* Object Packager, which was the closest OLE ever came to being an application, has no equivalent in Win9*x*.) But it's working tirelessly behind the scenes to save you time and keystrokes, in both Windows itself and most of your Windows programs.

## To Windows 98 from a Macintosh

Start with My Computer, which bears an uncanny resemblance to the Macintosh interface. This comes as no surprise to Mac aficionados, who know that … how can we put this tactfully … as the Windows and Macintosh interfaces mature, they become more alike.

After you use a Mac, the thing you'll probably like best about Windows 98 is the application software rather than the operating system itself. Mainstream software is developed for Windows first and the Mac later, and the Windows version often has a richer feature set. The performance of standard *office* applications—word processors, spreadsheets, PIMs—will probably be better on a Windows box than on the Mac. It is still true in general that compute-intensive graphics applications will run better on a Mac, and Photoshop in particular is a *lot* better on a Mac.

There are a few things you need to know about Windows before you really start clawing your jeans:

*Extensions are important.* Windows looks at the file extension—the one to five letters after the dot in the filename—to decide what program to open the file with. On the Mac, meanwhile, the association between the file and its program is tucked into the file header. Mac filenames don't need extensions and generally don't have them. Windows files do; if you have a file whose name ends in .TXT and you click on it, Notepad will open it. If a file's name ends in .DOC and you click on it, Word will open it, unless you don't have Word or Office installed, in which case Wordpad will open it. *If the file doesn't have an extension, Windows will not know what to open it with and will ask you.*

Worse yet, Windows 9x defaults to hiding the extensions of what it calls "common file types," so that a file can actually have an extension and just *look* like it doesn't. To understand more about this, look in the **View\Folder Options\File Types** tab of Explorer.

*Your mouse has two buttons and you need them both.* Clicking the left button brings up a menu called the Action menu; the right button brings up the Context menu. They overlap in function to an extent that you'll probably find irritating at first, but practice will help.

Too many Windows users—whether or not they were Mac users originally—make the mistake of using left-click or left-double-click almost exclusively, when right-click contains a significant part of the functionality. Play with right-click in unlikely places (like the Desktop) until you always remember that it's available.

Now for some short tips:

A Shortcut is *effectively* the same thing as an alias.

You don't have Eject Disk in software … sorry. You have to push the button.

Windows doesn't have a Preferences folder. Preferences are set for each application within that application. Unfortunately the option isn't always on the same menu, but ninety per cent of the time you'll find it under either File or Edit. If you don't find Preferences, look for Options.

Windows' nearest equivalent to a DA folder is the **Start Menu\Programs\Accessories** folder.

Programs that are Inits on a Mac are most likely to be in the Windows Control Panel. Actually, the Mac and Windows Control Panels are fairly similar.

The Chooser splits into two sections. For Printer control, look in **Start Menu\Settings\Printers** or **Control Panel\Printers,** or just select your printer from within the application you're using. For network configuration, right-click on **Network Neighborhood** and pick **Properties. File and Print sharing** is a button on the Configuration tab of the Network Properties sheet; see Chapter 10, "Networking."

The **Shut Down** button is at the bottom of the Start Menu, or you can use Alt F4 .

Overall, in comparison to a Mac, the most generally true thing about Windows is that it probably makes you go through one or two more steps to accomplish any given action. But Windows can be run very quickly by a skilled user. Have faith.

### Windows 98 on Your First Computer

About two-thirds of this book is written just for you; that's why we tried to cover everything. Let us know if we succeeded!

# A Few Words About System Resources

Let us say this: Windows 95 and 98 have *enormous* appetites for system resources—processor cycles, RAM and disk space. Of those, RAM is the most important, and disk space probably the least.

If you've bought a new computer with Windows 98 pre-installed, you probably don't have to worry too much, since almost any computer you can buy at retail today will have 16 MB of RAM and a Pentium processor running at 100 MHz or better. We might suggest specifying a minimum clock rate (processor speed) of 133 MHz, and definitely not *less* than 16 MB of RAM—in fact, if you're the kind of person who runs several applications at the same time, go for 32 MB.

If you already have your computer and you're upgrading, you might have a

- 286: 32-bit Windows can't run on a 286, and it wouldn't even if it could.

- 386, 486DX/25, 486DX/33, 486DX2/50: Microsoft once claimed that Windows 98 would run on these processors, then backed off. Since Windows Classic—see page 13—never became available, we can only recommend sticking with 3.11 or 95. A new computer is cheaper than you think—it'll cost you less than you paid the last time.

- 486DX/50: These were real aristocrats, but rare. Some people claim to have made Windows 98 run on this chip, but officially, it will not.

- 486DX2/66, 486DX4/100 and up, Pentium 60, 66, 75 or 90: With enough RAM you can manage it. You won't be wild about the performance, but you can stand it while you save up for something newer.

- Pentium 100, 120, 133: Things start to get good. The performance isn't neck-snapping but it isn't frustrating either. 32MB of RAM isn't a bad idea; you'll be hitting the swapfile a lot less often.

- Pentium or Pentium MMX 166 or better: Windows 98 and your computer are a marriage made in heaven.

- Pentium Pro or Pentium II, Deschutes, IBM/Cyrix 6x86, AMD K6: 98 would be fine, or had you considered running NT?

If you use full-screen graphics, computer-aided design (CAD), animation programs, or full-motion video, double the RAM requirements given above. As of this writing, if your motherboard has four SIMM slots, you can install 64 MB without spending too much; now that 16 MB SIMMs aren't top-of-the-line, they're cheap.

# What's in the Box?

Windows 98 is a retail software product, sold either on its own or bundled with a computer system. According to our latest information from Microsoft, Windows 98 will be sold at retail in only two versions:

- A CD-ROM full version that does not require you to have an earlier version of Windows already installed.

- A CD-ROM upgrade version that requires you to have installed Windows 3.x or 95, and will ask you to insert the Windows 95 CD (or one or more Windows 95 floppies) during installation.

The version is identified on the box when the product is sold at retail. The term "full version" is confusing but merely means it's the version for people who have never installed earlier incarnations of Windows. Whichever version you buy, Microsoft uses the extra space available on the CD-ROM to add information, such as the Windows 98 Resource Kit (an excellent technical reference), some demos, and some visual treats, such as full-motion video clips.

Floppy-disk versions (either full or upgrade) will be available from Microsoft, but you'll need to buy the CD, fill out a coupon in the box, and mail it in with a handling charge. These versions will be less complete than the CD versions and will ship on 80 to 100 diskettes.

The prices of the full and upgrade versions differ significantly. The upgrade version carries a street price of $80 to $90. The full version can cost $200 or more because you aren't given the price break for already being a Windows owner. Obviously, the CD-ROM upgrade version is the best value, because you get the extra goodies at the low price. Don't overzealously wipe out your old Windows installation in anticipation of the new one, because the upgrade version checks for existing Windows components before it installs Windows 98.

Most computer manufacturers will preinstall Windows 98 on the hard disk of a system as part of a so-called bundle. The same doesn't hold for dealers, however; if they include bundled software, it may not have been preinstalled. Because of its popularity and value, Windows 98 is frequently bundled with other products, such as mice, multimedia upgrade kits, and software programs. Whether you buy straight from the computer maker or from a dealer, your copy of Windows 98 should contain a set of installation disks or a CD-ROM and a slim user guide, *Introducing Microsoft Windows 98*; and there will probably be a green-and-white or blue-and-white, fancy-looking, Microsoft Certificate of Authenticity sealed in with the user guide.

## *Alas, Poor Plus!*

When Microsoft's product developers met to plan Windows 95, they filled a whiteboard with all sorts of great ideas. Many of those ideas were erased when it became apparent that, had they all been incorporated into the grand totality of Windows 95, it would not run on a 386 system. The Microsoft marketing department viewed the millions of 386 computer users running Windows 3.1 as a profitable upgrade market, so they leaned on the techies to yank a few things and make a lean, mean Windows 95 able to run on a 386. The leftover features that would require a 486 or larger processor were repackaged as a separate CD, Microsoft Plus! for Windows 95, which made Microsoft its cut of $49.95 retail—neatly bumping the street upgrade price of 95 plus Plus! to about $130.

But times have changed, and Microsoft has given up on anything slower than a fast 486. (As we mention, if you want to keep your 386, consider sticking with Windows 3.11.)

Most of the features of Microsoft Plus! have been incorporated into the basic Windows 98, including data compression, screen font smoothing, full window drag, task scheduling, and the Internet Setup Wizard and Extensions. Many other new components and utilities have been seen, so far, on Microsoft's Web site (**www.microsoft.com**) or as part of the Internet Explorer 4.0 Commemorative CD. What the distribution version of Windows 98 finally contains may depend on the outcome of the current holy war over the browser being, or not being, part of the operating system. We are sure, however, that Windows 98 in its release version will have more features than any previous version of Windows. There will also be a Windows 98 Plus! Pack.

Many computer makers place their labels on Windows when they bundle it with their systems. In those cases the manuals and software are usually identical to what Microsoft has produced, despite the change on the cover. However, sometimes the software has been modified by the manufacturer. This can affect how your system operates, particularly if the setup program has been altered.

For the remainder of this book, we refer to the installation software, whether on floppy disks or on CD-ROM, as the Windows installation disks. Keep those disks handy even after you've installed Windows. As we point out later in the book, you may need them from time to time.

# What's Ahead for Windows

Windows 98 will be one of three retail versions of Windows, the other two being Windows NT 5.0 Server and 5.0 Workstation. Windows 98 shares the codebase of Windows 95 and is essentially a beefed-up version of the earlier product. NT Server and Workstation have quite different core code—NT is a cousin of UNIX, Win9x isn't—and are almost identical internally; the main difference is that the Server package comes with more stuff in it.

Microsoft has said for some time that, as Win9x and WinNT mature, they will converge internally. As we've mentioned, this is already happening with Windows 98, which is more NT-ish than its predecessor. But various tea leaves suggest that the next consumer version of Windows (Win2001?) will be based on the NT core code.

This would signal the end of Win16 programming as we have known it. "Win2001" will probably run Win16 software (if it does) in a "Windows box" subsystem, as NT does now. This would make Win2001 and its contemporary version of NT Workstation very similar products; indeed, they might be identical, except that the consumer version would have more games, graphics programs and fun stuff, while the corporate version could be packed chock-full of connectivity hooks and groupware. Microsoft Outlook Express, in Windows 98, is a big clue to what we can expect from the corporate Windows client operating system of the near future.

The benefits of this strategy to Microsoft are formidable, as always. One operating system kernel and one body of code, with proper extensions, could run in every computing environment from an elementary-school classroom to the farthest-flung enterprise-level network. Experts on computing have maintained for years that system integration on this scale would never be possible; but it's our experience that, once Microsoft decides it wants something, it's only a matter of time.

# 2

# The Windows 98 Interface

The Windows 98 interface is a spiffed-up version of the interface you may already recognize from Windows 95. It uses many of the same metaphors, objects and tools, but it differs in one crucial way: It makes room for, and takes terrific advantage of, the central place of the Internet in today's computing experience.

# The Windows 98 Desktop

So far as Windows 98 is concerned, when you're at your computer, you can be one of three places. You might be on your local computer, which is the box you can see on or under your desk—and which probably has a name, but we won't presume to ask. If your computer is connected to another computer, whether to a server or just another workstation, then you're on your local network, which Windows 98 (bowing to contemporary corporate slang) calls your *intranet* or your *local intranet zone.* And if your computer is connected to an Internet Service Provider (ISP) through anything from a humble 28.8 modem to a T3 fiberoptic cable, then you're on the *Internet,* the worldwide network of networks.

Past versions of Windows have presented these three layers of computing experience with different tools, giving you access to your local machine through the Desktop, the Start Menu and the Taskbar; to your local network through Network Neighborhood; and to the Internet through Internet Explorer. In Windows 98 all those tools still exist, but they're more clearly part of a unified whole. Windows now encourages you to think of your individual computer, your local network, and the Internet as three concentric parts of one whole—one big computer, which covers the world, and of which you use as much as you need at any given time.

The new switches and controls are mostly contained in three places: Folder Options, Internet Explorer (which is vastly more important and central than it was in Windows 95) and the totally new Active Desktop. Because this book is organized in approximately the same way as Microsoft's concentric view of computing, we'll treat these new elements in the Internet section, right after the chapter on Networking. In this more basic chapter, we'll introduce the classic Windows Desktop to those of you who haven't seen it before—or need a refresher.

## The Local Desktop

The Windows 98 Desktop, your virtual desk, is an attempt to make running a computer program as intuitive as working with paper and pencil. It's not a concept original to Windows; a desktop is the dominant metaphor of almost all graphical user interfaces, or GUIs. As we saw in Chapter 1, several important GUI operating systems have fallen by the wayside, so that today's most successful and prevalent GUIs are 32-bit Windows, the Macintosh OS, and the UNIX GUI called X Windows. Which one of these you like best is a matter of taste, but frankly, these days they're more alike than different.

The Windows 98 GUI was designed to mirror everything on your desk—including, in some cases, the clutter. What you see is what you've got: the full-screen background is your desktop, and windows and icons represent items you work with every day, such as papers (documents), filing drawers (volumes), file folders (folders), and tools (applications). Icons in Windows 98 can also depict devices such as printers, fax machines, your Internet dial-up connection, and audio and video controls. Windows 98 expands the look and feel of a desktop to accommodate anything you can reasonably do with a computer.

An obvious advantage of the desktop metaphor is easy orientation. If you get lost, just click your way back to the desktop, where you can view your tools, rearrange documents, and assemble a familiar setting to solve thorny problems. Windows 98 lets you arrange the desktop almost any way you like, so you can organize the Windows environment to suit your personal preferences, no matter how idiosyncratic. In fact, sometimes we think Windows 98 was designed to satisfy the needs of those with weird tastes. To make the most of your design options, become familiar with the main components of your desktop, described below.

## Windows, Menus, Icons, and Dialog Boxes

The Windows 98 interface is constructed of four main types of building blocks: windows, menus, icons, and dialog boxes. Both Windows 98 and the software programs that run on it use those four elements to communicate with you and to help you operate your computer.

**Windows.**  As its name suggests, the window is the most basic building block of the Windows 98 environment. A window visually defines a work space on the computer display and can be manipulated in various ways; you can move, shrink, expand, and (usually) change the dimensions of a window. You can rearrange windows on the screen just as you would shuffle papers on an actual desktop, and that's why the Windows computer screen—with its layers of windows and icons—is called the Desktop.

**Menus.**  Most computer programs and applications use menus to present commands. Microsoft's programming guidelines encourage (Microsoft-ese for "force") application developers to present commands in standard ways, so you'll find File and Edit menus at the left-hand end of the menu bar in most Windows programs. Not only that, those menus often contain the same or similar commands from program to program. Even the keyboard shortcuts that activate commands on the menu are fairly consistent; for example, the Exit command—Alt F X —is the same in almost every Windows program. If menus are your favorite way to control a computer, you'll probably gravitate to the Windows 98 Start button, which takes menus to the extreme, allowing you to access your entire system (or as much of it as you like) from one tree of menus.

My Computer    LaserJet 4P

(D:)    Compose.xls

**Icons.**  Icons are small, neatly organized pictures that represent elements of your computer system. Sometimes intuitive, sometimes obtuse (depending on the artist's talent), icons can represent programs, documents, files, folders (sometimes called directories), storage, devices, and special controls. Ideally, the meaning of an icon is obvious. For example, the icons for computers, printers, disks, and documents are literal representations of those items (Figure 2.1).

**Dialog Boxes.**  Dialog boxes, the most interactive element of the Windows 98 user interface, are like New York taxicab drivers: they talk back. Dialog boxes relay or request information in.one of three basic ways. One variety simply delivers a message, such as "The operation was completed successfully." Another common dialog box asks you to make a yes-or-no choice—for example, "Save Changes Before Quitting?" The most complex (and often annoying) kind of dialog box presents an almost bewildering array of options, which in turn may include tabbed menus that bring up even more dialog boxes, like the Russian doll within a doll. A dialog box with index tabs can present you with a bewildering array of options (Figure 2.2).

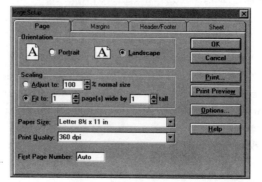

**Figure 2.2**

*Tabbed dialog box*

If a dialog box contains a title bar, you can move the box to a different spot on the screen either by grabbing the title bar with the mouse and dragging the dialog box to its new location or by using the dialog box's Control menu: type Alt Spacebar M and move the box with the arrow keys. You can move among the pages of a tabbed dialog box by clicking on each page's tab, which becomes the title when the page opens.

**Getting To The Point.** Windows 98 is designed so that windows, menus, icons, and dialog boxes can be manipulated best with some sort of pointing device—most commonly a mouse, but also a trackball, touchpad, joystick, or even a pen and tablet. As you move your device, a small pointer, usually shaped like an arrow, appears on the screen and echoes the motions of the pointing device. When the pointer changes its shape or orientation, it's letting you know that it can be used for a special task (Figure 2.3).

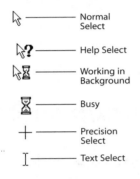

Normal Select

Help Select

Working in Background

Busy

Precision Select

Text Select

*Figure 2.3*

*Cursors*

You can use a mouse to activate objects on your computer screen; first point to an item on your screen, then click or double-click on it. Clicking is simple: just give the left mouse button a quick push. Double-clicking means just that: two quick clicks of the mouse in rapid succession. (If you're left-handed and want to swap the buttons, or to adjust the period of time between the two clicks, use the Buttons tab of Mouse\Control Panel.)

Once you've pointed and clicked, you can drag an item around the screen. Dragging involves a series of actions: point to something on the screen, press and hold down the left mouse button, and "drag" whatever you have thus grabbed to its new location. Finally, release the mouse button to drop the repositioned object into place.

*Figure 2.4*

*A pop-up menu*

In Windows 9x the right mouse button, which was a useless appendage in previous versions of Windows, enables you to perform actions on objects throughout the interface. For example, to rename a file—in this case, the file is the object—select it with the left button, then click on it with the right button, which brings up a pop-up menu (Figure 2.4). The pop-up menu in this example features standard commands used to manipulate files, including the Rename command.

In this book the menu that pops up when you click the right mouse button is called the Context menu, which is its official name, or simply the right-click menu.

**Keyboard Commands.** You can manipulate windows, menus, icons, and dialog boxes from the keyboard. In fact, Microsoft has made sure you can operate everything in Windows 98 without a pointing device. Experienced DOS users and proficient typists may find it faster to issue many Windows commands from the keyboard rather than take their hands off the keyboard to use the mouse. That's why this book includes keyboard equivalents for all the commands we mention.

The rest of this chapter gives you a closer look at windows, icons, menus, and dialog boxes. If you're an experienced Windows user, you can skip to the next chapter—you probably know these tricks by now. If you're new to Windows, by all means read on. Consider this your orientation to computer life.

# Windows: Applications and Documents

Windows 98's heavily revised interface is still haunted by remnants of an old scheme for displaying windows—originally developed by IBM—called MDI, for Multiple Document Interface. MDI was developed to create a standard look for programs and to provide a way for applications to display many documents within one window.

The MDI system displays a document only inside the main window of the application or program that created the document. The application window defines the screen; document windows—called child windows—are found within the application window. In other words, if you create a document in WordPerfect, you can open that document's window only inside the main WordPerfect window. The old MDI system was developed when a document was created by only a single application. For example, word processors created word-processing documents, and paint programs created graphics documents. Nowadays, technologies such as OLE allow a single document to contain data from several applications.

32-bit Windows displays a document in its own window, independent of the application that created the document. With the release of Windows 98, Microsoft has begun to discourage the use of the MDI in favor of what it feels is a more intuitive interface, one that places both documents and applications in their own separate windows. Someday, all Windows applications will abandon the MDI, but for the time being, you'll probably see a mixture of the old and the new schemes.

Figure 2.5 shows a Windows 98 desktop. The main components of the interface are identified.

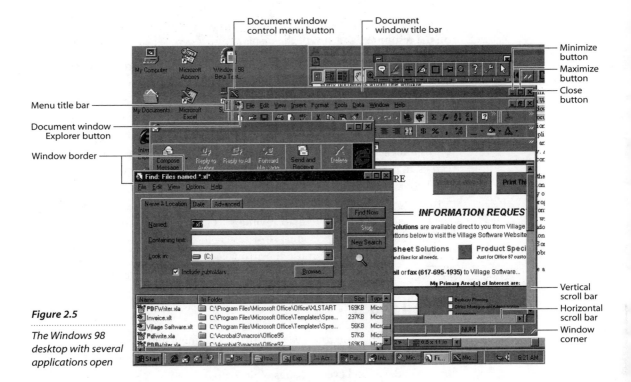

Document window control menu button

Document window title bar

Minimize button

Maximize button

Close button

Menu title bar

Document window Explorer button

Window border

Vertical scroll bar

Horizontal scroll bar

Window corner

**Figure 2.5**

*The Windows 98 desktop with several applications open*

## Moving and Resizing Windows

You can move any application window and the new Windows 9*x* independent document windows around on the desktop and position them any way you like, even with portions moved off the screen. The older, child document windows, however, can be moved around only within the parent application window to which they belong. Windows 98 helps mitigate this limitation by enabling you to move any type of window with a mouse: grab the window's title bar by pointing at it and pressing down on the mouse button, drag the window to a new location (its outline will move as you drag it), and release the mouse button when the window is positioned at the desired location. To abort the move at any time, press the (Esc) key before releasing the mouse button.

For the most part, the new independent document windows look and behave much the same as application windows.

To reposition just one edge of a window, move the cursor to whichever of the four sides you want to move; the pointer changes into a two-headed arrow when it's on target. Then simply drag the window border with the mouse. You can also grab a window corner (especially the one at the bottom right, distinguished by a special "grip" pattern) to lengthen or shorten two adjacent sides at the same time. To abort a resizing, press the (Esc) key before releasing the mouse button. The minimum size for any window is a small chunk of the title bar, about two inches wide by half an inch tall, but this varies depending on the resolution and size of the display.

Windows can also be moved or resized with the cursor control, or arrow, keys. To select an application window, press [Alt][Tab] to cycle through application windows until you reach the one you want. When you have selected a window, issue the appropriate command (Resize or Move) from the window's Control menu, as described later in this chapter. The pointer changes shape into a four-headed arrow. If you have selected Move, pressing any arrow key causes an outline of the window to move accordingly. When the window has reached its new position, press [Enter]. If you have selected Resize, use an arrow key to select a window border. For example, press the [↑] key to select the top window border. To grab a window corner, press two of the arrow keys together; for example, pressing [↓][→] selects the lower right-hand corner of the window. Then you can use the arrow keys to resize the window; press [Enter] when you're done. To abort the moving or resizing process, press [Esc].

## Scroll Bars

Scroll bars enable you to move contents of a window into view when the window is too small to display all its contents at once. Application windows, document windows, and even sections of dialog boxes can have scroll bars. Scroll bars usually appear only when they might be needed; if you alter the contents or dimensions of a window so that everything inside it can be viewed on one screen, the scroll bar usually disappears. The scroll bar will reappear when you add items to a window so that it can no longer display all its contents at once.

The vertical scroll bar appears along the right-hand side of a window, and the horizontal scroll bar at the bottom of the window. The position of the button in the scroll bar provides a visual indication of your location in the document; that is, if the button is in the middle of the scroll bar, the window you're looking at is in the middle of the document. The length of the button relative to the length of the scroll bar gives you a clue as to the document's approximate length, so that if the button is about half as long as the scroll bar, the window you're looking at is about half the length of the document.

You can scroll the contents of a window in several ways:

- Grab the scroll button in the middle of the bar and drag it with the mouse. To move to the top of the window's contents, drag the scroll button to the top of the vertical bar. To get to the bottom of the window, drag the scroll button down the bar. This will not move the window contents until you release the button.

- Click on the arrow buttons on either end of the scroll bar to move the contents up or down in small increments.

### Table 2.1 Common Conventions for Keyboard Scrolling

| Keystroke | Scrolls |
|---|---|
| ↑ | Up one line. |
| ↓ | Down one line. |
| Page Up | Up one screen. |
| Page Down | Down one screen. |
| Ctrl Page Up | One screen to the left. |
| Ctrl Page Down | One screen to the right. |
| Home | To the beginning of the line. |
| End | To the end of the line. |
| Ctrl Home | To the beginning of the document. |
| Ctrl End | To the end of the document. |

- Hold the mouse button down, while pointing at one of the arrow buttons at the ends of the scroll bar, to scroll the contents continuously, slowly.

- Click on the scroll bar itself, in between the scroll button and the appropriate arrow button, to move the window's contents one windowfull at a time.

- Hold the mouse button down while pointing at the scroll bar itself, between the buttons, to scroll the contents continuously, quickly.

- With some applications, you can scroll using the keyboard. Table 2.1 lists the common conventions for keyboard scrolling.

## Folder Windows

In earlier versions of Windows, an application window almost always contained a running program, and document windows were displayed within the application window. As mentioned earlier, Windows 98 now allows documents to occupy their own independent windows that behave like application windows. To add more confusion, Windows 98 has introduced a new type of window called a folder window. The folder window has the status of an application window; it's definitely a daddy or a mommy window, not a child window. That's because a folder window performs a powerful function: it enables you to view and organize the contents of your computer. When they are minimized, folder windows are represented by small file folder icons (Figure 2.6).

**Figure 2.6**

*A folder window that contains file folder icons*

Folder icons and folder windows represent the directories on storage devices such as floppy-disk drives, hard-disk drives, CD-ROM drives, and network servers. When you double-click on a folder icon, it opens to display the contents of the directory it represents. (No, Virginia, this is not a novel concept. Macintosh users will experience déjà vu because this is the way the Mac has always worked.)

# Menus

The WIMP—window, icon, mouse and pointer—interface model of Windows 98 is so smoothly integrated that it can be hard to tell which components are most important. But in general, the more comfortable you are with any application (and the more agile you become with the mouse), the more you'll find yourself using the menus. 32-bit Windows actually has two types of menus: *Control menus,* which offer one method of controlling the windowing interface, and *application menus,* which give you access to commands for programs.

## Title Bars and Control Menus

You can find the name of a window and other information about it (including the generating application) in the title bar at the top of every standard window. The Windows 98 Title Bar is a luminescent, shaded bright blue that really stands out from the gray and white of the standard Windows environment. If you open more than one window, the title bar of the active window—the window you most recently selected—appears in a different color or intensity from the title bars of the dormant windows, usually a medium gray. Of course you can change these colors, and just about every color in Windows, with the Appearance tab of Control Panel\Display Properties; just remember that, if you go too wild and end up with something you can barely read, the default color set is saved as Scheme, Windows Standard. (See Chapter 3 for more detail on this, along with the rest of Control Panel.)

**Figure 2.7**

*Minimize, Maximize and Close*

A    B    C

At the right end of a window's title bar, you'll see three small buttons: the Minimize button, the Maximize button, and the Close button (Figure 2.7). These buttons are created with a special set of artifacts called a *graphic screen font;* see "Marlett the Starlet" in Chapter 8. Pressing the Minimize button shrinks the window down into a button on the Taskbar, just like selecting the Minimize command from the Control menu, discussed later in this chapter.

The Maximize button is "two-faced." If the active window occupies less than the full screen, the button looks like Figure 2.7a, and clicking it enlarges the window to fill the entire screen; this is equivalent to the Maximize command on the Control menu. If the active window occupies the entire screen, the button looks like Figure 2.7b, and clicking it restores the window to its original size; this is equivalent to the Restore command on the Control menu.

The rightmost button on the title bar is the Close button (Figure 2.7c) which closes the window and, if it's an application window, quits the application.

**Image8* [1:1]**

*Figure 2.8*

*Typical title bar*

The left end of the window's title bar (Figure 2.8) contains the Control menu, also called the System menu. In Windows 98 this menu is represented by a small icon, just to the left of the application name or document title, which varies with the type of window:

- Application windows are represented by miniature versions of their application icons.

- Independent document windows are designated by small versions of their file icons.

- Folder windows display an icon of an open folder.

The Control menu icons clue you in about the window you are viewing. To pull down the Control menu, click once on its small icon, or press Alt Spacebar. If the window contains a DOS session, there's no icon, so just press Alt Spacebar. The Control menu contains commands that enable you to move, resize, and close windows, and it's particularly well suited for keyboard users; mouse handlers can accomplish most of these tasks in other ways. For example, you can shrink an application window down into an icon either by clicking the window's Minimize button or by typing Alt Spacebar N. To expand the window to fill the entire screen, press the Maximize button or press Alt Spacebar X. The Control menus of most application windows include the commands shown in Table 2.2.

To close an application window, double-click on its Control menu button, choose Close from the Control menu (Alt F4), select Exit from the File menu (Alt F X), or click on the window's Close button at the upper right-hand corner.

## Table 2.2  Common Control Menu Commands for Windows

| Menu Command | Keystroke | Description |
|---|---|---|
| Restore | Alt Spacebar R | Restores window to previous size. |
| Move | Alt Spacebar M | Enables you to move window using arrow keys. |
| Size | Alt Spacebar S | Enables you to resize window using arrow keys. |
| Minimize | Alt Spacebar N | Reduces window to icon on Taskbar. |
| Maximize | Alt Spacebar X | Enlarges window to full screen. |
| Close | Alt F4 | Closes window; quits if it's an application. |

Application windows that contain DOS sessions can also include the menu selections shown in Table 2.3:

**Table 2.3  Common Control Menu Commands for Windows That Contain DOS Applications**

| Menu Command | Keystroke | Description |
| --- | --- | --- |
| Edit | Alt Spacebar E | Displays a cascading menu with Mark, Copy, Paste, and Scroll. |
| Settings | Alt Spacebar T | Displays dialog box that enables you to toggle the toolbar. |

 **If you're running a full-screen DOS session, you can still press** Alt Spacebar **to bring up the Control menu.**

## Child Document Windows

What's in a child document window depends on the nature of a program or an application. For example, in a child document window for Microsoft's Word for Windows, you find word-processing documents, whereas Adobe Photoshop uses child document windows to display image files.

Child document windows share the menu bar of their so-called parent application window. If you select a command from a menu, it usually affects the contents of the active document window. To activate a document window, click on it anywhere, or press Ctrl Tab repeatedly until the window is selected. When more than one document window is open, the active one displays a different-colored title bar and appears in front of any overlapping document windows.

**Table 2.4  Common Child Window Control Menu Commands**

| Menu Command | Keystroke | Description |
| --- | --- | --- |
| Restore | Alt - R | Restores document window to its previous size. |
| Move | Alt - M | Enables you to move document window with arrow keys. |
| Size | Alt - S | Enables you to resize document window with arrow keys. |
| Minimize | Alt - N | Reduces document window to an icon within the application window. |
| Maximize | Alt - X | Enlarges document window to the full size of the application window. |
| Close | Ctrl F4 | Closes document window. |
| Next | Ctrl F6  or Ctrl Tab | Switches to next document, regardless of whether it is a window or a minimized document icon. |

The Control menu buttons in parent applications and child document windows have some similarities and some differences. The icon in the center of a button is smaller in a document window and changes to reflect the window's contents. To get to a document window's Control menu, click on its button or press [Alt][–]. Control menus sometimes contain special commands for particular applications, but almost all Control menus for document windows contain the commands shown in Table 2.4.

The button for a child document window's Control menu is positioned at the left end of the document window title bar. If you press the window's Maximize button or double-click on the window's title bar—or if you issue the Maximize command from the keyboard by typing [Alt][–][X]—the document window expands to fill the entire application window, and a number of changes occur (Figures 2.9 and 2.10).

**Figure 2.9**

*Before Maximize*

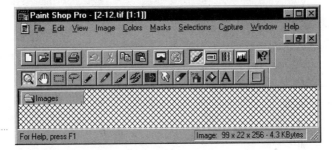

**Figure 2.10**

*After Maximize*

When a document window is maximized, it loses its own title bar; as a result, the document window title is usually incorporated into the application window title bar. Other changes occur when you maximize: the document window's Control menu appears at the left end of the menu bar, and the Restore button, which we saw as Figure 2.7b, is at the right end of the menu bar. If you click on the Restore button, the document window shrinks back to its previous size.

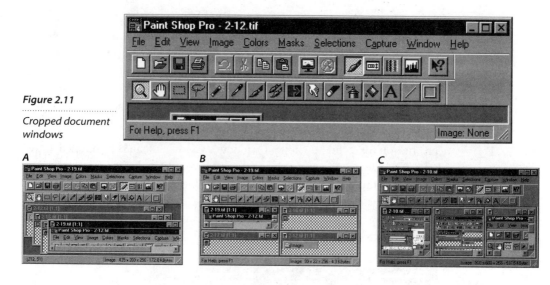

**Figure 2.11**

*Cropped document windows*

Oops! A big problem with the old MDI is that child windows sometimes get cropped by parent application windows (Figure 2.11). When this happens, their scroll bars and other controls can be out of reach. To view the portions of a child document window that are out of sight, you can use the scroll bars, or you can move and resize the document window itself.

But there's an easier solution. Many, if not most, Windows applications provide commands that automatically arrange the document windows inside the application window; generally, there are three such commands:

- The Cascade command arranges all document windows so they fit inside the application window, overlapping except for their title bars (Figure 2.11a).

- The Tile Horizontally command arranges all the document windows inside the application window as horizontal strips, without overlapping (Figure 2.11b).

- The Tile Vertically command arranges all the document windows inside the application window as vertical columns, without overlapping (Figure 2.11c).

Any one of these will bring all the child document windows into partial view, so that you can select the one you want and, if necessary, issue other commands to bring it to the front and maximize it. If you Cascade you will probably have to click on the title bar of the document you want, to bring to the front, or shuffle the document windows by pressing Ctrl F6 .

Keyboard equivalents for document windows are not as common, or as well defined, as the ones for application windows. In *some* Windows applications, the keystroke for Tile Vertically is [Shift][F4], Cascade is [Shift][F5], and Tile Horizontally is [Shift][F6]. These are worth trying, because they're handy where they exist. Unfortunately, they were most common in Windows 3.1 applications and have been fading away slowly since 1992; only a few 32-bit Windows programs offer them.

Even if you have only one window open, the Tile command can prove useful. For example, if the scroll bars of a document window are out of reach because that window is cropped by an application window, issuing the Tile command resizes the document window so that it fits entirely within the application window, revealing all the controls.

To close a document window within an application window, double-click on its Control menu button, choose Close from the Control menu ([Ctrl][F4]), select Close from the File menu ([Alt][F][C]), or click the Close Window button. At this point a dialog box may appear to ask if you want to save any changes before closing the window—in other words, the changes you've made since you last saved.

**Bear in mind that some file operations are "changes" to Windows applications but not necessarily to you. If you save a Microsoft Word file, then check its statistics with the Statistics tab of File Properties, and then Close, Word will prompt you again to save your changes—although as far as you're concerned, there aren't any. The simple act of checking Statistics altered something in an "invisible" part of the file that Word maintains along with the formatting instructions; it didn't change anything in the visible document, so you can abandon the changes and be no worse off. If you can't remember whether you made *real* changes since your last save, go ahead and save when you're prompted; with today's fast disks it takes almost no time, and often it rescues that one tiny but important edit that you forgot you made.**

## Application Menus

Menus display the primary commands for operating Windows and its applications. This à la carte system enables you to issue a command simply by clicking on the Menu Bar (immediately below the Title Bar) and selecting a choice from the menu that drops down. They're also informative because they present the commands and options for an application in an organized fashion that makes it easy for you to browse. Menus offer an incomparable advantage over a command-driven environment like DOS, in which you have to recall the exact spelling or syntax of a command to issue it. In addition to commands, menus can contain lists of open files or windows, font styles, and the names of cascading menus, which in turn reveal further choices.

*Figure 2.12*

*Menu bar*

To make this movable feast possible, Windows uses two types of menus: Control menus and Application menus. Control menus, like the menu that you can drop with [Alt][Spacebar] are generic and change little from application to application. Application menus, however, are the command centers of Windows programs and contain the basic tools to operate each application. Because Microsoft has rigorously encouraged developers to standardize the layout of the command structure, you'll find that you can use many of the same commands—such as [Alt][F][X] to exit—for almost any Windows application. Application menus are found on the menu bars of virtually all application windows, and although they vary widely from program to program, the two at the left are usually a File menu followed by an Edit menu (Figure 2.12).

The menu bar shows the names of menus from which you can select commands. Menus can be pulled up or down, depending on their length and the available space on the display (Figure 2.13).

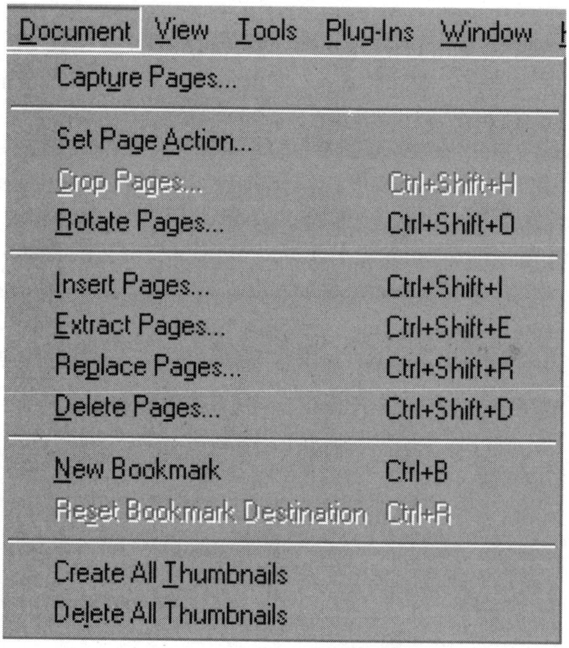

*Figure 2.13*

*Menu bar with Document menu pulled down*

Selecting a menu with a mouse is easy; you can either pop it up or pull it down. To pop it up, point to the name on the menu bar and click once. Point to an item on the menu and click once again to select it. Alternatively, you can use the pull-down method familiar to Macintosh users: point to the menu, hold the mouse button down, drag the mouse to an item (which is then highlighted), and release the button to select the item. Pulling a menu up works the same way: just point and drag up instead of down.

 **If you use menus Macintosh-style—click, hold and drag—moving the mouse pointer off the menu and letting the button come up will dismiss (a fancy word for "cancel") the menu. If you use menus Windows-style—click, let up, slide and click again—you'll have to move the mouse pointer off the menu and click on the background to dismiss it.**

## No Mousing Around: Menus and Keyboard Commands

The mouse is not always the fastest way to work in Windows 98. You can use the [Alt] key in combination with other keys to select frequently issued commands without having to take your fingers off the keyboard. To access a menu, press the [Alt] key (or [F10]), followed by the underlined letter in the menu's name. Then select an item by typing the underlined letter in that item's name. For example, to quit a program, use the standard [Alt][F][X] command: [Alt] accesses the menu bar, [F] selects the File menu, and [X] chooses the Exit command on the menu. In those rare cases when the menu names do not include an underlined letter, you can press [Alt] to select the menu bar and then use the [→] or [←] key to highlight the name of the menu you wish to select. Similarly, once the menu is open, you can use the [↑] and [↓] keys to highlight a menu item and then press the [Enter] key to select the item. To deselect a menu and return to the application, click anywhere outside the menu or press [Alt] (or [F10]). To close the menu but remain on the menu bar ready to select a different menu, press [Esc].

Sometimes a command is placed directly on the Start menu. In this case, you can press [Ctrl][Esc] to reveal the Start menu and then type the underlined letter in a menu option to select it.

Menus also follow certain other conventions:

- Items appear dim on a menu ("grayed out") to indicate that a command or an option is not available at the time. Often you need to take another step, such as selecting text for formatting, before the command can be applied.

- Menu items are often followed by key combinations which are the keyboard shortcuts for the option.

- A menu item preceded by a check mark means this choice is already in effect. To turn the item off and remove the check mark, reselect the command. To toggle the item on and off, just keep selecting it.

- An ellipsis (...) following any menu item means that by selecting that item you'll pop up a dialog box.

Any menu item with a small triangle (arrowhead) at its left or right points to a cascading menu. If you choose this item, a submenu appears offering additional choices, which can be selected in the same way as regular menu items (Figure 2.14).

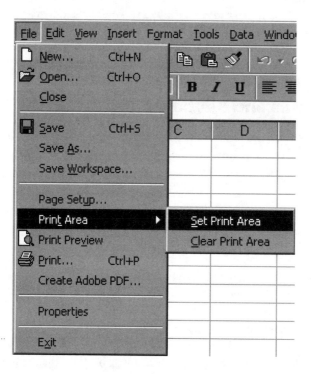

*Figure 2.14*

*Cascading menu*

**Don't forget right-click!** If you're exceptionally agile with the mouse, you may be bothered that, in order to pull down a menu, you have to travel to the menu bar. If toolbars are docked next to the menu bar, it's not much of an improvement. Many Windows applications recognize that as an annoyance, and reproduce the most useful menu commands on the right-click menu— because, while left-click only works at the menu bar, right-click works *anywhere* in your document. For example, Microsoft Word offers an in-document right-click menu that will let you Cut or Copy (with text selected), Paste, or format Font, Paragraph, or Bullets and Numbering.

# Icons

Icons defy any one definition because they can represent a hodgepodge of materials and functions, including applications, documents, disk files, directories, and special controls. Every Windows program contains one or several unique icons, and developers seem to strive for individuality in their icon designs. Although icons should give you some visual clue as to what they represent, sometimes creativity gets out of hand.

Icons often represent programs and data files. Sometimes icons act like buttons. Clicking or double-clicking on an icon usually activates it. For example, to open a folder on the Windows 98 desktop, double-click on its folder icon.

Microsoft has created seven primary types of Windows 98 icons:

- Application icons.

- Child document icons.

- Folder icons.

- File icons.

- Help icons.

- Network and Internet icons.

- Volume icons.

You'll also encounter many other types of icons in specific applications.

## Application Icons

One of the most common types of icon, the application icon, represents a program that is stored somewhere on one of your accessible mass storage devices—whether it's a hard disk, a floppy disk, a network server, or an Internet application server. Double-clicking on an application icon causes Windows 98 to load the program's code into memory so that Windows can execute—in other words, run—the program (Figure 2.15).

Windows 9*x* can create two kinds of application, document, folder, volume or network icons. One of them is the actual icon, and one of them is called a Shortcut. They look quite similar:

The Shortcut, as we've noted, has a small curved black arrow superimposed on a white square box in the lower left corner. The "real" icon doesn't. The title below the Shortcut starts out reading

   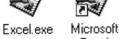

Findfast.exe   Excel.exe   Microsoft Excel   Inbox

*Figure 2.15*

*Application icons*   *Shortcut icon*   *Inbox icon*

"Shortcut to…" and the name of the application or document, unless you have re-titled the icon, or you might have suppressed the "Shortcut to…" and the boxed arrow with switches on the Explorer tab of TweakUI—in which case the "real" icon and the Shortcut would look identical.

 Since the two kinds of icon have exactly the same effect, it might seem academic which is which. Not so! and here's why: If you delete the Shortcut, you're deleting a tiny (less than 1K) pointer file which you can easily re-create. If you delete the "real" icon, you're deleting the *physical, actual application file, folder or document.* Admittedly, you're only sending it as far as the Recycle Bin, and you can get it back out; but we recommend against taking that kind of risk until you're an experienced Windows user. Leave your icon settings at the Windows defaults so that you always know what effect a deletion—accidental or otherwise—might have.

 Since Windows tries to take fanatical care of system integrity, you might expect that there are some "real" icons you can't delete from the Desktop, and you're right. They're called System icons and they include My Computer, Network Neighborhood and the Recycle Bin. For some reason, though, the Inbox (Windows Messaging) icon *can* be deleted from the Desktop *and doesn't* go to the Recycle Bin. If you delete it anyway, you'll have to reinstall Windows Messaging, and you stand a fair chance of losing all your previously received e-mail and faxes when you do. Tiptoe around your Inbox when you're cleaning up your Desktop.

Windows 95 and 98 let you create and move application icons almost anywhere in the interface—including the Desktop. This is part of the "OS/2 heritage" of 32-bit Windows and is a radical change from Windows 3.*x*, whose application icons were found almost exclusively in the Program Manager shell. In Windows 3.*x*, also, when an application window was minimized, its application icon appeared at the bottom of the screen. In Windows 9*x*, on the other hand, minimized applications shrink to become Taskbar buttons.

## Child Document Icons

A document icon can represent one of two things. In Windows 98, document icons usually represent actual document files, such as a text file or a graphics file. If you minimize a child document window within a parent application's window, it appears as a miniature document Title Bar, containing its document icon, the beginning of the document's title, and the three appropriate control buttons—Restore, Maximize and Close (Figure 2.16). Although child document icons (and their corresponding document windows) often do represent traditional documents such as word-processing and paint files, they can designate anything the individual program designers wish—within reason, that is. Microsoft encourages Windows developers to adhere to certain guidelines.

Figure 2.16

*Child documents*

You can minimize an active child document window into a document icon by clicking on the Minimize button or by typing [Alt][–][N]. The child window implodes into the mini-Title Bar and generally takes its place along the bottom of its parent application window. You can move document icons freely within the parent window by dragging them with a mouse (or by typing [Alt][–][M] and using the arrow keys), but you can't move them outside the boundary of the parent application's window onto the desktop. (OK, try it and see what happens!)

## Getting an Icon Back Into a Document Window

If you shove a child document icon almost completely under the edge of the parent window, and then try to break it loose with [Alt][–][M], it may not work—the four-headed Move pointer will rove freely as you press the arrow keys, but the icon won't follow suit.

Here are two ways to explode the icon back into a document window:

1. Double-click on the icon, or click once on the icon to pop up the Control menu, then choose Restore from the menu. From the keyboard, use [Ctrl][Tab] to cycle through the document icons; when the one you want is selected, issue the Restore command by typing [Alt][–][R]—or, usually, [Alt][–][Enter] since Restore is the choice at the top of the menu.

2. To maximize the document icon so that the resultant document window fills the entire application window, click once on the icon to pop up the Control menu, and choose Maximize from the menu. Or double-click on the icon to restore it to a window, then press its Maximize button if needed. From the keyboard, select the document icon (use [Ctrl][Tab] to cycle through the document icons), then type [Alt][–][X] to issue the Maximize command.

# Volume, Folder, and File Icons

Icons, icons, icons. You also need to know about three other major types of icons—volume, folder, and file icons—which are all used to represent the contents of your system (Figure 2.17).

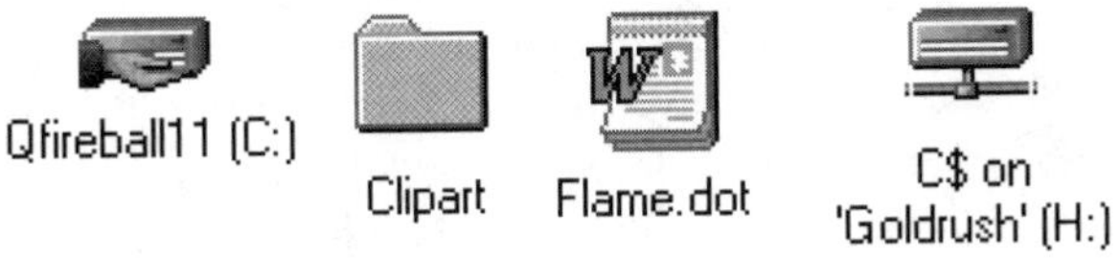

Figure 2.17

*A volume, a folder, a file, and a share icon*

 Qfireball11 (C:)             C$ on
                      Clipart    Flame.dot    'Goldrush' (H:)

Volume icons represent the storage volumes that Windows recognizes as being connected in or to your computer. Commonly, you find volume icons for a floppy disk, a hard disk (or a hard-disk volume partition), a RAM disk, a Zip or SyQuest drive, a CD-ROM drive, and a network volume. Volume icons appear in the My Computer folder and usually depict the type of storage device they represent, whether removable (a floppy disk, Zip/SyQuest disk, or CD-ROM) or fixed (a local or network hard disk, or a RAM disk). Volume icon titles include a generic name, or the volume label if there is one, and are always followed by the DOS drive letter in parentheses, like (A:).

A volume icon title on a network may point to a drive on another, connected, computer; this is called a *network share*. For example, if the icon shows a T-connector below the volume and the icon title reads **C$ on 'Goldrush' (H:)**, (Figure 2-17) that means "This is an icon for a shared drive, physically in a computer called Goldrush, which Goldrush calls C: and this computer calls H:." If a shared drive is inaccessible for any reason, the icon and title stay in My Computer but the icon is covered with a red X. For more on this, see pages 403 to 406 in Chapter 10, "Networking."

**If a volume or folder icon is displayed in the palm of a hand (Figure 2-17d) it indicates a share from the opposite perspective; that is, a resource that physically resides on the local computer but is made available to other computers on the network. Folder icons normally represent directories and subdirectories; you'll recognize them on screen as yellow file folders. Keep in mind that every folder is tied to the storage volume that contains the directory the folder represents. An open file folder icon represents an open file folder; likewise, a closed file folder icon stands for a closed file. Such literal-mindedness!**

Windows 9*x* introduces another type of document icon, called a file icon. This icon appears within file folder windows. File icons let you know which application created the document file represented by the icon. For example, Windows 98 gives every document created by Word a file icon that is similar to Word's own application icon. This makes it easy to identify a document file created by Word; it also lets you know that opening that icon will cause Word to load, so you can edit the file's contents.

## Other Icon Types

In addition to document file icons, you'll also run across a variety of other file icons, such as application icons, font icons, and system component icons (Figure 2.18). Something almost always happens when you double-click on one of these icons. If it's a volume, a window opens to reveal the contents of that storage device. If it's a folder, a window displays the contents of the directory or subdirectory represented by that folder icon. If it's an application program, the program runs. If it's a document icon, the program that created the document will be launched, with the document already loaded into it.

Agentsvr.exe

Copperplate Gothic Bold

Internet Explorer

*Figure 2.18*

*Application, font and component icons*

# Dialog Boxes

Windows 98 uses dialog boxes to make you work. They request information that it needs to complete an action, or present you with important messages.

## Confirmation Boxes

Often a dialog box presents an option related to a command or a procedure that you initiated by choosing a menu item, and gives you a checkpoint: you're asked to click a Yes button to carry out the task, or to click No to decline it, or to bail entirely with the Cancel button (Figure 2.19).

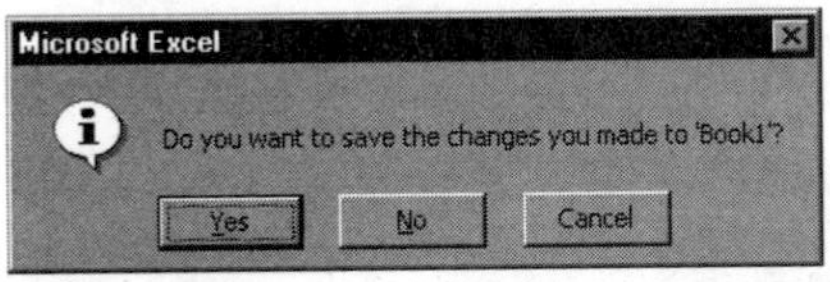

**Figure 2.19**

*Dialog box to confirm command (1)*

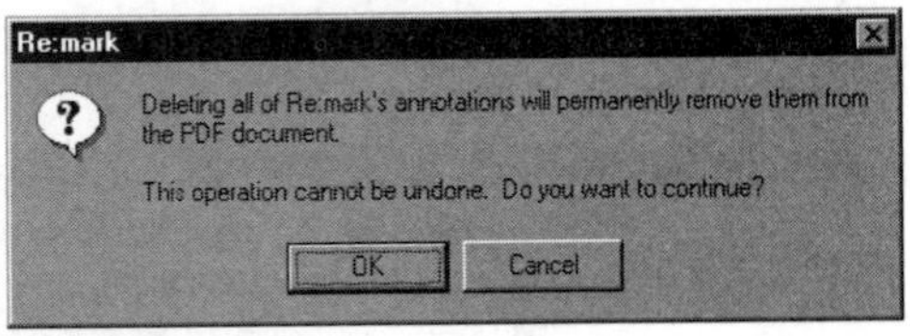

**Figure 2.20**

*Dialog box to confirm command (2)*

A simpler version of the same dialog lets you choose OK to execute the command or Cancel to decline it (Figure 2.20).

## Alert Boxes

Some dialog boxes—also called alert boxes—display warnings and cautionary information. These dialog boxes aren't completely consistent; they vary from one application to the next. Here are Acrobat Exchange and Microsoft Excel both telling you they can't find a file, but Acrobat uses a question mark (Figure 2.21) while Excel uses an exclamation point (Figure 2.22).

**Figure 2.21**

*Dialog box to alert user (1)*

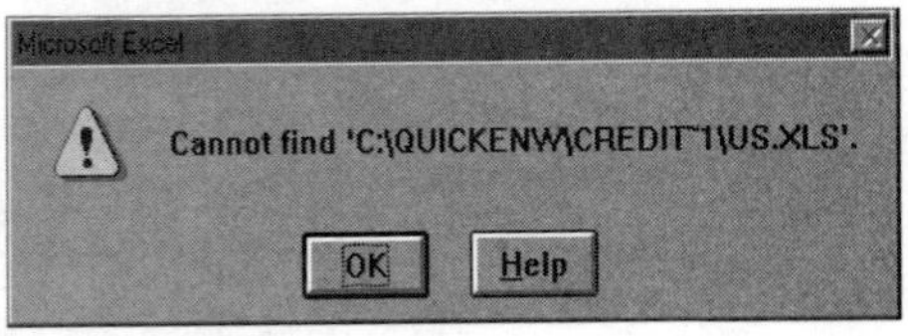

**Figure 2.22**

*Dialog box to alert user (2)*

## Caution Boxes

Windows also tends to use an exclamation point when you're trying to do something it doesn't think you should (Figure 2.23)

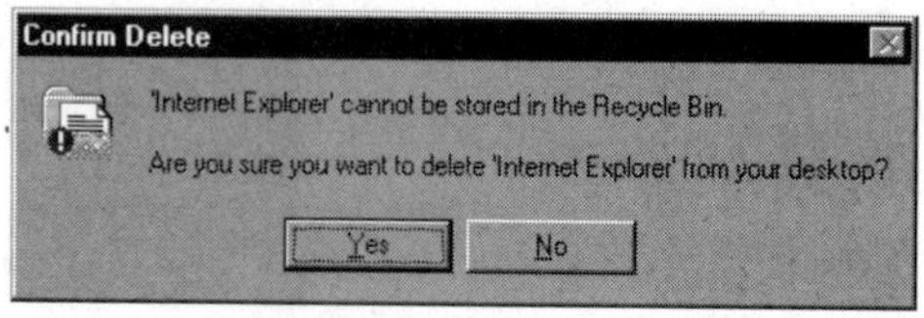

**Figure 2.23**

Dialog box to caution user

## Problem Boxes

Finally, there's a dialog announcing that something has gone seriously wrong—by Windows' standards if not yours—which is adorned with a white X superimposed on a red circle. There are two varieties. If Windows is complaining about something you can fix, like a discon-nected peripheral, this dialog generally includes a Retry button (Figure 2.24).

**Figure 2.24**

Problem dialog with Retry button

If Windows is complaining about something you *can't* fix, like a crashing program, the alternative to Close will be Details instead (Figure 2.25a). If you click the Details button you get a bunch of arcane geekspeak which will rarely be of much help (Figure 2.25b)

**Figure 2.25a**

Problem dialog with Details button

**Figure 2.25b**

Problem dialog with Details open

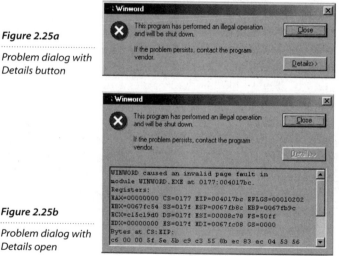

# Summary

This chapter introduced you to the building blocks of the Windows 98 graphical user interface. Most of these elements—windows, icons, and dialog boxes—are all too familiar to users of previous versions of Windows (not to mention Macintosh crossovers). Windows 9x spruces up those features and adds a few more as well—sort of like a face-lift plus a hair implantation. You get the picture.

All in all, though, the changes make it easier not only to look at the screen, but to figure out how to use what's there. You can probably understand them best by glancing at the Upgrade Alerts we've scattered throughout this chapter, which are hints about how to take advantage of the new interface developments. Remember that these innovations don't stop at the edges of Windows 98 itself; they reach out to become part of all the applications, utilities, and other items that you encounter in your Windows wanderings.

Buckle your flight belt! In the next chapter, we'll show you how to take the controls of the Windows 98 environment—not only to work on your own computer, but to cooperate effectively on your network and navigate the wild, woolly Internet. In Windows 98, Microsoft has created an operating system that does it all with equal ease.

# 3

# Navigating Windows 98

Windows 98 includes four tools for operating Windows and Windows applications while you navigate the world of computing. Three of these—My Computer, the Explorer, and the Taskbar—were introduced in Windows 95, the first consumer version of 32-bit Windows. The fourth, Internet Explorer, was a separate program until its most recent version became an integral part of Windows 98.

# Local Navigation

My Computer, the Explorer, and the Taskbar replace the Program Manager and the File Manager found in Windows 3.x. Good riddance, if you ask us. Those artifacts were each severely limited, yet to operate your system you needed to use them both in intricate collaboration. The weird functional division, with each Manager doing most but not quite all of the job, was the single most criticized feature of older versions of Windows.

Microsoft responded by making each of the three "local" tools functional enough on its own to enable you to run your computer. Reading this chapter will help you determine which tool to use, but in most cases there's no one right choice. Ultimately, your decision will be based mostly on personal preference.

**My Computer** uses icons to depict the elements that make up your computer and its software—including documents, applications, the printer, and Windows 98 itself—in what is called an object-oriented view. You can look at My Computer to scan and access the entire contents of your computer. Of the three "windows," My Computer bears the closest resemblance to the Macintosh Finder and offers Macintosh users the easiest way to approach Windows 98.

The **Explorer** offers the most literal representation of what's on your system. This souped-up file browser presents a hierarchical view of your storage devices, folders, and files, and offers you a nice choice of perspectives, from the icon-oriented "almost-My-Computer" to a full detail view like the Windows 3.1 File Manager on steroids. Former Windows 3.1 users will probably gravitate to the Explorer while they're getting a handle on Windows 98.

The **Taskbar** offers the most concentrated functionality. Its push-button control center places an almost staggering array of commands and options at your fingertips. So long as you're running 32-bit Windows applications, you'll find the Taskbar resting at the bottom of your screen, ready to spring into action whenever you need it—a far faster and more intuitive task switcher than the old Alt Tab keystroke. Power users who push operating systems to the limit tend to use the Taskbar in preference to other tools.

Of course, all three of these tools are available whenever you're running Windows. If it takes you a while to decide which one you're most comfortable with, no harm done—and when you're a really adept Windows user, you'll switch among all three as they meet your needs.

# Getting Around the World

When the ARPAnet, ancestor of the Internet, began in 1965, no one could have dreamed of computing in the nineties. When electronic mail crept into American corporations in the eighties, few would have foreseen e-mail software in shrink-wrapped boxes on retail store shelves. And when the World Wide Web was first proposed and implemented in 1991—yes!—it would have taken a clairvoyant crackpot to imagine www.wantyourbucks.com splashed all over TV commercials, cereal boxes and glossy newspaper inserts. Yet so it has become, and no computer is an island.

Let's face it: Today, if you spend any sizable amount of your day sitting at a desk in front of a computer, that computer spends some sizable amount of its day talking and listening to other computers. Windows 98 is one of the world's first operating systems that seamlessly incorporates the tools your computer will need to communicate—Fax for fax, Outlook Express for e-mail, and Internet Explorer for Web browsing. (Microsoft Voice for text-to-speech, and Microsoft Dictation for the other way around, aren't part of Windows 98, but we have … ah … played with them. Look forward to them rounding out the set in a year or so.)

Of this veritable arsenal of programs that ties you into the Big Buckyball, Internet Explorer has garnered the most press—not because it's an unparalleled product, but because it's become controversial. Is a Web browser properly part of the operating system? We say yes, and here's why: *Internet Explorer is just one more channel to connect you to a network,* although it's a whopping big network. If you were an experienced user of Windows 3.1, you probably remember the publicity and curiosity that greeted the version of Windows called Windows for Workgroups. That version included the tools and utilities to set up a small network in the same box with the operating system for the single computer. If you had Windows for Workgroups, individual computers, and inexpensive network adapters and cables, you could set up a network. Because it was a "peer-to-peer" network that didn't need an extra computer dedicated as a server, it was affordable and relatively simple to maintain.

Windows 98, the spiritual inheritor of Windows for Workgroups, operates on the same principle; with a modem, a cable, and an ISP (Internet Service Provider) account, you can connect to a network of networks. In the same way that Windows for Workgroups was a "network operating system," Windows 98 is an "Internet operating system."

Microsoft realizes that not everybody wants or needs a completely Web-centric interface. Windows 98 gives you several options for the degree of integration—or, more exactly, separation—between Explorer and Internet Explorer. You can run Windows 98 with the "classic" Windows 95/NT 4 interface, in which case Internet Explorer 4 will behave as a freestanding but highly compatible Web browser. You can go to the other extreme and create an interface that's written completely in HTML and works with single-click throughout, so that it's literally difficult to tell whether you're on the Web or not. Or you can pick from a menu of options that will let you choose the Web-like features you prefer and ignore the others—which is what we believe most Windows 98 users will eventually do.

In this chapter we're going to examine all the Windows 98 navigation tools, and their strengths and weaknesses in running your local computer. We'll take another look at some of them, especially My Computer and Internet Explorer, in the chapters on Networking and on the Internet.

# The Windows 98 Taskbar

The Taskbar is like one of those leather tool cases electricians strap onto their hips in an attempt to carry the entire shop around with them. Like a virtual wraparound belt, the Taskbar provides a compact way to get at myriad tools and services. The Taskbar is normally found along the bottom of the screen and serves as the resting place for minimized windows. You'll notice that the Taskbar is often visible while you are running applications, which makes it handy to switch quickly from one window to another. The Taskbar also includes the powerful Start button, which provides a grab bag of shortcuts for getting to almost anywhere in your system (Figure 3.1).

*Figure 3.1*

*The basic taskbar*

Microsoft's own tool of choice for accessing 32-bit Windows is obviously the potent Start button. After all, when the Start button logo was used as a motif for the Windows 95 launch—in both live stage shows and TV commercials—it was backed by the Rolling Stones' "Start Me Up." Microsoft had paid a formidable $12 million for the rights, in the first third-party agreement ever reached for the use of a Stones song. Clearly Microsoft meant the Start button, with its proudly flying Windows banner, to signify the start of something big.

The Start button and Taskbar, which appear by default as a horizontal band across the bottom of the screen, are the Windows navigational tools you'll probably find yourself using the most, especially once you become familiar with Windows 98. Even more robust than its counterpart in Windows 95, the Taskbar has become an application-style toolbar with overlapping, sliding layers—so that, even though it takes up only a quarter-inch band of your valuable screen real estate, it can be used to control your running programs, your entire Desktop, anything in your System Tray, and the whole spectrum of your Internet access.

In line with the have-it-your-way attitude behind the design of Windows 98, you can move the Taskbar if you like. Click on any blank space left on the Taskbar, hold down the mouse button, and drag the Taskbar to any edge of the screen: top, bottom, or either side. When the Taskbar borders the top or the bottom of the screen, it maintains its horizontal orientation, but if you drag it to either side, the Taskbar becomes vertical. A vertical Taskbar provides more room for stacking icons but also truncates names (Figure 3.2). Once you are familiar with what your icons represent, however, this can be a good way to stuff more into your Taskbar.

**Figure 3.2**

*Turn the taskbar on end to stuff more icons into it*

On the other hand, if you want a comprehensive view of your Taskbar's contents, you can use the double-headed arrow cursor to pull it up or out and "unpleat" the toolbars. We recommend that if you do, though, you click the **Taskbar Options** tab of **Start Menu\Taskbar Properties** and check the **Auto hide** box, so that the expanded Taskbar will slither demurely out of sight until you want it.

Many commands and options that you can access from the Start button provide shortcuts to operations we cover in greater detail later in this chapter. We'll begin with an overview of the Start button's basic submenus and their functions.

It can be a real drag holding the mouse button down while you drag your pointer through a complex array of cascading submenus. Guess what? You don't need to. With Windows 98, you simply click on the Start button once and then let your mouse pointer hover for a moment over each menu item to bring up its submenu; the same technique works for the submenu. Once you've pointed your way through the menu maze to the item you want, click once more to select it. The overgrown, multipane Win95/NT 4 Start Menu was a nightmare that had mouse pointers skipping over it like rocks on water, desperately trying to select before the array collapsed. No more! The Windows 98 Start Menu remains in a single vertical column, and if it gets too tall for the screen, it becomes a scrolling menu with arrows at the ends (Figure 3.3).

**Figure 3.3**

*Scrolling Start Menu*

Got something on your Start Menu that you wish was on your Desktop? Vice-versa? Want to get rid of something that an uppity app put on your Start Menu during the installation? (Microsoft Office would be a *lovely* example.) You can now *drag items off the Start Menu* and drop them wherever you like. As an item is dragged off the Start Menu it turns into a Shortcut. Or you can drag any object onto the Start button to *add* it to the Start Menu.

## Programs

The first Start menu selection you notice is the **Programs** submenu. Here you see additional submenus, each representing a program or a group of programs that has been installed on your system. By default, you find submenus for items such as the Windows 98 **Accessories** (more on these in Chapter 5), **Multimedia** (covered in Chapter 12), and the **Startup** folder (which lists programs that should be started automatically by Windows 98 when you boot it up). See Figure 3.4.

*Figure 3.4*

*The Start submenus*

The Programs menu also contains icons for running specific applications or utilities. On a new installation of Windows 98, you find icons for the MS-DOS prompt (see Chapter 4), the Microsoft Network online service, and usually, at the bottom of the menu, an icon for the powerful Explorer utility, which we cover later in this chapter.

To start one of those programs, highlight its menu entry and click. This quick-click action was introduced in Windows 95 and is designed to make the environment easier for novices. You don't have to worry about folders or volumes or even double-clicking—just highlight an entry in the Start menu, click once, and you're on your way.

Right-clicking any Program, Favorite or Document on the Programs menu
will bring up its Context menu (Figure 3.5).

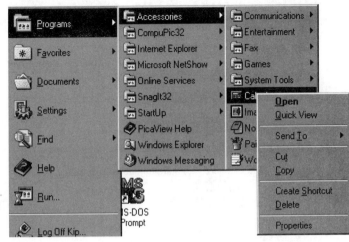

*Figure 3.5*

*Start menu Program
Context menu
(right-click)*

## Favorites

The **Favorites** submenu accomplishes three things: It continues the relentless
integration of Internet content into your operating system, it gives you a place
to look for software updates automatically, and it makes the My Documents
folder easier to get to. For various reasons, we're not wild about some of the
implications of this submenu, but we'll explain those as we get to them.

The first Favorites option, **Channels,** is your system's doorway into what's
called *push content.* Channels are like regularly updated Web sites except that,
instead of displaying their updated content whenever you visit the Web site,
they "push" the updated content down the wire *to* you as soon as each update
is completed. Naturally, you're not completely defenseless here—you do have
to enter into an agreement with the push provider to receive the push content.

It sounds great, and it may *be* great, but to us it's not above suspicion. Looking
at the list of push providers supplied with Windows 98—which includes
Disney, Warner Brothers, *The Wall Street Journal*, CBS, and ESPN, as well as
(naturally!) MSN—we have to assume that multinational mega-business is
seizing on this opportunity to mold the Web into an updated form of television, which they understand much better and can control more effectively. To
those of us who embraced the Web because it *wasn't* television, because it
wouldn't flood our living rooms with commercials, because we loved the
thrill of the chase and detested the drone of the network schedule, most of all
because we understood that stale content was *our problem* and *we* could fix it...
Enough ranting! You may well find channel content rewarding (certainly for
news, as even we concede) and you won't know till you try it.

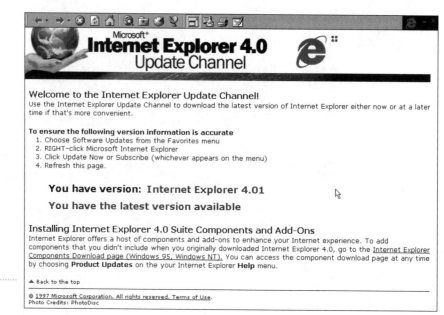

*Figure 3.6*

*Internet Explorer
update page*

**Links** is another copy of the Links toolbar up above. Mmm, that means you can get to this in three places—on the Toolbar, on the Taskbar, and on the Start Menu. Does it feel like Microsoft has an agenda working here?

**Software Updates** is potentially the most exciting option in Favorites. When software developers first discovered the Web, they rushed to post patches, drivers, and enhancements on their sites, making them readily and quickly available to interested users without the intervention of (expensive) support techies. The second phase of this process, using a technology which Microsoft calls Active Setup, involves your browser going up on the Web, hunting for updates to your installed applications, automatically downloading only the pieces that are newer than what you have, and installing them in the same pass (Figure 3.6). If Active Setup is implemented intelligently and with enough respect for user preference, it could be deliverance from Service Pack hell. To the grumble of "It also makes everybody into a beta tester," we reply that Microsoft did that years ago and where were you? At the moment, the only application that has Active Setup ready and waiting is Internet Explorer, but that will change—soon.

**My Documents** is Microsoft's traditional and indiscriminate bucket for document files that you, the user, create. Look at the number of folders that are required for a default Windows installation, and then you only get one for yourself. Assuming you were clueless or slothful enough to let all your business correspondence, recipes, spreadsheets, Web .GIFs, and yard-sale flyers get tossed into a single folder, can you imagine the mess you'd be in? Microsoft already puts dubious ideas in your head by insisting that no amount of RAM

**Figure 3.7**

*The Documents submenu*

can ever be too much; it has no business teaching you bad habits of document management. Learn to make folders for projects and for categories of documents, in tree structures that make sense to you. (Of course there's no harm in keeping the My Documents folder as the root of all the more specific folders you make yourself.)

# Documents

The Documents submenu lists the document files you've most recently opened, up to the last 15; through this menu, Windows 98 makes it easy for you to start working where you left off. You don't have to locate a particular folder to recall items you handled recently. Think of the Documents submenu as a bookmark for your system (Figure 3.7).

 The Documents submenu lists only documents that you open directly from within a folder, by double-clicking on their icons. If you first start a program and then load a document data file, that file's name will not appear on the Documents submenu.

 **Of course, there are limits to any good thing. Maybe you've been writing a letter to your steadily-more-significant-other while your boss thinks you're sweating over a proposal. The luscious missive is safely on a floppy in your pocket, but what about the icon and title on the Documents submenu? You can do two things. If this is a one-shot deal, go to Start Menu\Settings\Start Menu, pick the Start Menu Programs tab and click the Clear button under Documents menu.**

 If you want to cover your tracks *totally*—and you have TweakUI installed on your computer—open it, pick the Paranoia tab, and check the Clear Document history at logon box. For extra peace of mind, click the Clear Selected Items Now button.

# Settings

**Figure 3.8**

*The Settings submenu*

The **Settings** submenu provides quick access to five of the main configuration options for the Windows 98 environment.

**Control Panel** enables you to alter the appearance and behavior of Windows 98.

**Printers** lets you install new printers, change the configuration of existing printers, and view currently spooled print jobs.

**Taskbar & Start Menu** lets you alter the behavior of the Taskbar (Figure 3.8)—or, at least, of its non-Internet portion.

 **The Documents menu's Clear button (which you can drive yourself to distraction looking for) is on the Start Menu Programs tab of Taskbar Properties.**

**Folders & Icons** is the same dialog as View\Folder Options from the menu bar.

**Active Desktop** (which should be called "And Now For Something Completely Different") is the series of options that can make your Windows interface into a local Web page, as follows:

**View as Web Page,** a toggle, turns your whole Desktop into an HTML document. See "Internetting Your Interface" later in this chapter.

**Customize my Desktop …** opens the Web tab of the Display Properties Control Panel. If "View as Web Page" is toggled on, the "View my Active Desktop as a web page" box is checked.

**Update Now** brings your subscriptions (hyperlinks to optional Channel content) into synch with the latest information available on the Microsoft server.

All of these options are discussed later in this chapter.

**Find.** The Find submenu brings up five flavors of the Windows 98 Find utility, which tracks down missing objects.

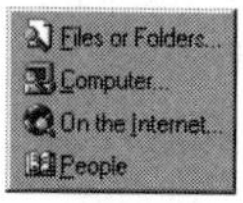

**Find Files or Folders** enables you to search disk and network volumes for a particular set of files or folders by name, date, or content.

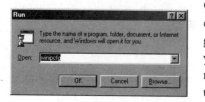

*Figure 3.9*

*The Find submenu*

**Find Computer** enables you to search for a particular network resource, such as a file server (Figure 3.9).

**Find on the Internet** launches Internet Explorer.

**Find People** lets you look for names and addresses in your choice of your local Windows Address Book, if you've set one up for yourself, or several Internet-based free directory services.

**On the Microsoft Network** enables you to search for a resource on Microsoft's own online service.

We'll be taking a closer look at the Find utility later on in this chapter.

**Help** and **Run**—two additional Start menu items—provide functions that we discuss in detail later in the book. The Help item brings up the Windows 98 context-sensitive help system, which includes an online reference to all the major functions and features of the environment. We provide help on Help in Chapter 5. The Run item brings up a dialog box that enables you to run a program by typing its name—useful when you can't find the program in the Start menu's submenus (Figure 3.10). We cover the Run command in Chapter 4.

*Figure 3.10*

*The Run dialog box*

# The Task List

Besides providing a handy spot for the Start button, the Windows 98 Taskbar also functions as a task list—that is, Windows 98 uses the Taskbar to keep track of all open application windows. The list is displayed as a series of horizontal boxes, each containing the title of an application window, a miniature version of its application icon, and in some cases the name of a related open document or data file.

If you've worked with previous versions of Windows, you'll see that the Windows 98 Taskbar combines the Task Manager program and the application icons that used to appear at the bottom of the screen in the Program Manager. When a program's application window is minimized, it no longer shrinks to an icon on the Windows desktop, as it did in Windows 3.*x*; now the window is minimized on the Taskbar. Instead of bringing up a separate Windows Task List to switch between running programs, you now use the Taskbar, which is similar to the push-button channel controls on a radio. Click on the Taskbar entry for a particular program, and its application window is immediately brought to the "top" of the desktop.

 **The old Task List hotkey, ⌨Ctrl ⌨Esc, now brings up the Start Menu. You could use the old Windows Task List to shut down a program, but that's one thing that gets more complicated in Windows 98. If you want to shut down a *running* program, right-click on the Taskbar and click Close. But to terminate a *non-running* program—this *is* Windows we're talking about—hit ⌨Ctrl ⌨Esc ⌨Delete to open Close Programs, pick the offending hunk of code from the list, and click the End Task button. If you're teetering on the brink of a crash (which you generally are if Explorer's the program that's not running) you can Shut Down from here, too.**

 When you're in Close Programs, if you hit ⌨Ctrl ⌨Alt ⌨Delete *twice,* you Shut Down instantly. This can be handy if your pointing device is frozen, *but,* first of all you'll lose any unsaved data in any running applications, and second, when Windows comes back up it will insist on running a full ScanDisk with a surface check. In today's world of multigigabyte drives, that can definitely mean it's time to go out for lunch.

## The System Tray

![System Tray icons 8:51]

***Figure 3.11***

*The System Tray*

The final piece of the Windows 98 Taskbar is the System Tray. This small region at the right end of the Taskbar provides useful information about system events. It also serves as a standard location for hardware controls, such as the volume control for a sound card installed in a Windows 98 system (Figure 3.11). Finally, it's where your running Clock lives.

The System Tray can be used for a variety of tasks: for example, it can alert you to incoming e-mail messages, indicate battery power level on a notebook or a portable computer, and provide a modem-line monitor for the Windows 98 Remote Access Services. (See Chapter 10 to find out more about all the cool networking and communications features that have been built into Windows 98.)

**Juicy tips:**

- **Let your mouse pointer hover over the Clock and you pop up the day and date. You can set the format with Control Panel\Regional Settings Properties\Long date style.**

- **Double-click on the Clock and you bring up Date/Time Properties, which lets you set the date, the clock, and the time zone.**

- **Right-click on the Clock and you bring up a menu with Taskbar Toolbar selection, Adjust Date/Time (which is Date/Time Properties), Cascade, Tile and Minimize Windows, and Taskbar Properties (the same one on Start Menu\Settings).**

- **If you don't want a Clock at all, go to Taskbar Properties, pick the Taskbar Options tab and uncheck Show clock.**

## Advanced Taskbar: Getting to the Net, or Not

All of the above has been a discussion of the local, or classic, Taskbar in a direct line of inheritance from other versions of 32-bit Windows. But the complexity that swamped the poor, honest Toolbar—as you'll see when we look at the Explorer in detail—has overtaken the Taskbar too, even if not to the same degree.

The familiar "hit it and get it" Taskbar, with one button for each of your running applications, is as robust as ever … and we're grateful, believe me. But it's now only one layer of several, the others being:

**Quick Launch.** Single-click access to programs you *don't* have running. The installed defaults are Internet Explorer (no surprise), Outlook Express (e-mail client), Show Desktop (single-click to the Desktop no matter how much is sitting between you and it), and View Channels, which connects you to a special Web site called IEChannelGuide.com. We'll discuss these at length elsewhere. You can also add others.

**Desktop.** Windows 98 gives you a Desktop Taskbar that reproduces every icon and title on your Desktop; since you probably have lots too many objects on your Desktop to fit across the bottom of your screen, it scrolls left and right with scroll arrows.

With all due respect to Microsoft, such as that may be, this is an artifact from the 800-Pound Gorilla School of Design. We can find no way to set the order of the icons on the ribbon; if you leave the icon titles turned on, it takes forever to scroll through the ribbon; when you turn them off, the ribbon is more compact, but duplicate icons on your real Desktop—like folders, drives, Help icons, or generic document or program icons—are indistinguishable on the ribbon. Nice try, but the Show Desktop button on Quick Launch is a much better deal.

 **To minimize all your open applications at once and get back to the desktop, right-click anywhere on the Taskbar that is not a button and select Minimize All Windows.**

**Address** and **Links.** These two toolbars are discussed in the Explorer section in Chapter 16; since they appear by default on the Explorer Toolbar, they're turned off by default on the Taskbar, but it's easy enough to reverse the order if you decide you prefer these toolbars on the bottom of your screen rather than the top.

 Yes, you can make Taskbar toolbars! And we can think of some, like Printers, that would be genuinely handy. Right-click on any blank area of the Taskbar, select **Toolbars\New Toolbar...**, and you'll get a Tree pane dialog. Pick any one of your local folders or resources, or type in an Internet address (URL). If you want to create a toolbar for a URL, though, be sure you're connected to the Net when you start.

 **If you don't like the top-to-bottom order your Taskbar toolbars are in, you can shuffle or undock them. Open the Taskbar right-click menu and make sure Show Title is turned on (checked). Left-click on the title area of the toolbar, drag it—the cursor will change to the Move four-headed arrow, and the toolbar will follow the pointer till you drop it where you want it.**

 No matter how elaborate your arrangement of toolbars, the Start button and the System Tray will sternly stand guard at the ends. It's a comfort.

# Control Panels

Like a film director in the editing room, you can use **Control Panels** to manipulate what goes into your Windows 98 environment, from sounds to sights and keyboard options to time settings. This is your chance to play the all-powerful computerist—with the Control Panels, you can configure and customize Windows 98 to your nerdliest delight.

Windows 98 already comes with an array of default Control Panels, which cover your basic needs; if you install optional applications in Windows, such as Exchange, or certain hardware options, such as a joystick or PCMCIA card, you'll install Control Panels along with them. Some third-party software vendors and hardware manufacturers—mostly the ones that are really good at Windows—also supply Control Panels as part of the installation software. Here's a brief description of some typical Control Panels:

- **32-bit ODBC** (Open Data Base Connectivity). This is Microsoft's way of giving you access to data in a database, without caring which program you're in. We're not sure why Microsoft made this a default Control Panel; it's horribly complex and generally useful only to programmers and administrators.

- **Accessibility Options.** Enables you to configure Windows 98 to be more easily operated by individuals with physical disabilities.

- **Add New Hardware.** Brings up the Windows 98 hardware auto-detection and installation wizard. This Control Panel enables you to install new hardware and device drivers.

- **Add/Remove Programs.** Enables you to install new software programs, remove existing programs—if they were installed with Windows' full knowledge and consent—and selectively install and remove optional portions of Windows 98.

- **Date/Time.** Enables you to set the system's date and time and adjust the settings for location and time zone. (As noted, you can get to this more easily by double-clicking on the Taskbar Clock.)

- **Display.** Enables you to control all aspects of your Windows 98 display configuration, including video drivers, resolution, background patterns, color schemes, power management, hardware palettes, screensavers, and Web compatibility. This is also one of several places where you can set Folder Options. Advanced Display Properties, a new button on the Settings tab, lets you install a new graphics adapter or monitor and configure your graphics subsystem for optimal performance.

- **Fonts.** Displays currently installed typefaces and provides the controls for installing or removing typefaces.

- **Internet.** Provides the settings for Internet Explorer, also accessible from IE's View\Internet Options menu.

- **Game Controllers.** Lets you install and configure a pad controller, joystick, flight yoke, data glove, or just about anything (or things) you can attach to the computer.

- **Keyboard.** Enables you to fine-tune your key delay, repeat rate, and cursor blink rate, and select a language and layout.

- **Microsoft Exchange Profiles.** Enables options for the Microsoft Exchange mail and fax program.

- **Microsoft Mail Post Office.** Lets you create an e-mail post office in your computer.

- **Modems.** Provides controls for the installation and configuration of modems attached to your system.

- **Mouse.** Enables you to fine-tune your mouse's operation, including tracking speed, double-click speed, cursor scheme, pointer "trails," and right- or left-handedness.

- **Multimedia.** Provides a control center for audio recording and playback, video playback, MIDI configuration, and audio CD playback. The Advanced tab is Multimedia's equivalent of the Device Manager in System.

- **Network.** If you have a network, this is where you configure your network adapters, client software and logon, file and print sharing, computer network name, and level of access control. Note that if you have an Internet provider account, and your modem is configured to run the standard Internet protocol called TCP/IP, the modem will be in here as a network adapter called Dial-Up Adapter.

- **Passwords.** Enables you to set your Windows (and other) passwords, configure Remote Administration, and set global defaults for User profiles.

- **PC Card (PCMCIA).** Provides socket control, memory range configuration and sound effects for your PC Card drive. This is installed as a default on portable computers but is available for any computer that accepts PC Cards, portable or not.

- **Power Management.** Lets you specify time-to-power-down of the monitor and disk for a standalone computer or workstation, a server, or a laptop. You can also define custom configurations.

- **Printers.** Similar to the Printers item in Start Menu\Settings, enables you to install, configure, and manage printers, including your fax printer.

- **Regional Settings.** Enables you to control the display of formats for currency, date, time, and other items.

- **Sounds.** Enables you to attach sounds to specific system events, and to save specific groups of sounds as schemes.

## *Go Not Where Ye Need Not Go*

Windows sets Performance parameters dynamically and almost always brings them closer to perfection than you can by hand. You'll rarely need to alter the **Performance\Advanced** settings; **File System\Troubleshooting** in particular should be left to experts.

**Performance\Performance status\System Resources** typically shows that your computer's resource pool is between 75% and 95% free. Ah, you think, what an improvement over Windows 3.*x*, where System Resource percentages used to dip into the teens and twenties ... probably just before the computer locked up. Well, it's true that memory usage in Windows 9*x* is considerably improved, but Microsoft also cheated by moving the goalposts. Free memory now is not the percentage of total memory but the percentage left after Explorer loads.

- **System.** Provides access to advanced system features, including the *Device Manager,* which is the Windows 98 hardware configuration tree; *Hardware Profiles,* which lets you run the same computer in multiple configurations—for example, a docked and undocked laptop; and *Performance,* which lets you set defaults for the filesystem, graphics hardware acceleration, and virtual memory (swapfile).

- **Telephony.** This, it would seem, is a Control Panel that's being saved for later. (There are many such blind alleys in Windows 98, especially in the Registry.) The Dialing Properties tab is the same tab you reach with the Dialing Properties button in Modems Properties. Under Telephony Drivers, clicking on Unimodem Service Provider brings up Modems Properties too; if you have a network and click on WAN.TSP, you'll be told it can't be configured "at this time." The Telephony Control Panel will probably become more important when TAPI (Telephony Applications Programming Interface) descends from the heights of Windows NT and reaches the client desktop; at that time it may replace the Modems Control Panel completely.

- **TweakUI.** This roguish collection of utility tabs, written by "rebellious Microsoft programmers" and long supplied through Microsoft's Web site with *total* denial of responsibility, is—if you ask us—an absolute necessity for a 32-bit Windows system. If you're working in a big corporation, your IS manager might not let you have it; if you do install it, you might want to learn more about Windows before you use it extensively; but if you use it wisely, it gives your interface a flexibility that no seasoned Windows user would pass up. Wherever TweakUI can help you do something otherwise difficult or impossible with the Windows interface, we'll plonk down one of these: .

- **Users.** This Control Panel will set up new User Profiles on the computer, so that each person who uses it can have an individual Desktop and distinct rights to use software. This is naturally most useful in the corporate setting, but don't overlook the possibilities for sharing a computer at home; it's no accident that the User icon in Control Panel looks like two children…

All of those options are described in more detail as we progress through *The Windows 98 Bible*. Once you're familiar with them, you will be able to exercise near-complete (and gratifying) control over your computing environment.

Users of previous Windows versions will notice several differences in the Control Panels feature. Windows 3.*x* treated all control panels as subsections of a single program, called the Control Panel. In Windows 9*x*, the Control Panels (notice the plural) exist as independent programs and can be executed directly. Another difference is that the Control Panels offer a broader range and more depth in controlling configuration parameters than was possible in previous Windows versions. Finally, many functions of the old Windows Setup have been replaced by function-specific Control Panels, such as Display. Not only is this design cleaner, it's more compact and lets you find things more easily.

# Shutting Down the Windows 98 System

After you've finished your work, it's vital to shut down the environment properly before you hit the power switch and call it a day. In Windows 3.*x*, this meant closing the Program Manager, which terminated the Windows

*Figure 3.12*

*The Shut Down dialog box*

environment and left you at a DOS prompt. Because DOS is now part of Windows, and Windows is what you terminate to stop using the computer, you encounter a few new wrinkles in the shutdown procedure.

The **Shut Down** option itself is located at the bottom of the Start menu. Selecting this option brings up the Shut Down dialog box (Figure 3.12).

The Shut Down dialog box provides you with four choices:

- Shut down the computer?

- Restart the computer?

- Restart the computer in MS-DOS mode?

- Close all programs and log on as a different user?

Selecting the first option tells Windows to close all of your running programs. (Don't worry—if you haven't saved your data, the editing program prompts you to do so.) The program then clears the Windows 98 desktop and displays a message that the computer is ready to be turned off.

Selecting the second option produces the same results as the first, except that instead of telling you it's safe to turn off the computer and waiting, the program reboots the computer automatically. If Windows 98 is the default operating system, you return to Windows 98 (this process is commonly referred to as a "warm boot").

Selecting "Restart the computer in MS-DOS mode" forces Windows 98 into a special MS-DOS compatibility mode with most of the Windows drivers and Registry support not loaded. This is desirable when you run a tricky DOS program, such as a game, that has proven to be incompatible with DOS application support within Windows 98. You'll learn more about MS-DOS mode, and how to configure it, in Chapter 4.

Finally, the "Log on as a different user" option is something you'll see only if you've set up User Profiles. Windows 98, through its user account feature, can be set up to maintain multiple, independent configurations of the desktop for different users—a feature we'll show you how to use in Chapter 6.

# An Object-Oriented View of Your Computer

Now that you're familiar with the basic features of Windows 98, it's time to explore *objects*, one of the most powerful concepts behind the operating system. The Windows 98 interface is what is commonly referred to as an object-oriented interface. Computer scientists and other purists contend that Windows 98 doesn't really qualify as a true object-oriented system because it is not designed to let you program with objects. That's true for programmers. But for users of Windows 98, the system definitely looks like an object-oriented interface—at least there are graphical objects on screen that represent the hardware and software components of your system.

Windows 98 is designed to act as a natural extension of your physical work space, with objects that represent familiar tools hiding the complexities of the underlying hardware and software. Fundamental to the look and feel of Windows 98 is the Desktop. As part of the object-oriented design, the Desktop itself is an object, just as your real desk is an object in your office, along with paper, pencils, and card files. You work in the Windows 98 environment by opening objects and displaying them on the desktop. For example, to edit a word-processing document, you first open the folder in which it is stored, then open the document file. Windows 98 then loads the appropriate tool and displays the document on the desktop for editing. The entire operation is like opening a file cabinet, removing a folder, and opening the folder on your desk. Computers are finally simulating reality.

In another design shift, Windows 98 helps you move your focus away from applications, such as word processors and spreadsheets, so that you can concentrate on the documents you are handling. This heightened emphasis on both documents (rather than applications) and objects makes the document one of the most important objects and concepts in Windows 98. Documents are represented by a much wider variety of icons than in previous versions of Windows. Windows 98 enables you to start applications, and even to load documents into running applications, by double-clicking on document icons.

This major shift away from applications and toward documents is powered by Windows 98's use of OLE—Object Linking and Embedding—a powerful software standard that includes a set of rules for applications and documents to share information. With Windows 98 OLE, you can create a single document that contains data generated by several applications. For example, a single document file can contain text created by a word processor, graphics designed with a paint program, and a table generated by a spreadsheet. And by means of a powerful (but quirky) interface mechanism called Scraps, you can actually keep snippets of data from individual files, then drag and drop them at will throughout the Windows 98 interface.

# My Computer

What's the use of an object-oriented interface without a bevy of objects? That's the point behind the Windows 98 interface—you interact with it by manipulating numerous objects that appear on the screen. Windows 98 organizes these objects by grouping them into larger objects, so some objects represent just a single item—like a document—whereas other objects, such as file folders, contain many other objects. The metaphor is that of a desktop—the primary object in Windows 98—which incorporates the rest of "your" objects, whether they are physically on your system or connected to your computer through a network.

In the upper left-hand corner of the Windows 98 Desktop sits My Computer, an object that contains all the other objects on your system—as distinct from, say, objects you access via a local area network, which would be found inside

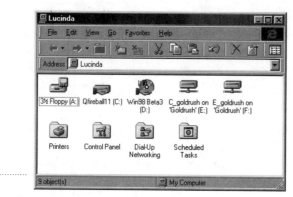

*Figure 3.13*

*My Computer*

the Network Neighborhood icon. Double-click on My Computer for an eagle's-eye view of what's on your system (Figure 3.13).

When you select My Computer, a window pops up containing a variety of icons. These include volume icons, which represent the mass storage devices attached to your computer, and several special-settings folder icons, which contain Control Panels and other items related to the configuration of your system. Typical volume icons include:

- **Floppy-disk drives** which have a drive letter in parentheses, whether or not there's a disk in the drive, and whether or not the disk in the drive has a label (a volume name).

- **Hard-disk drives.** If your hard disk has been given a volume name, then that name will appear in My Computer, along with a drive letter in parentheses; if there is no volume names, just the drive letter will appear.

- **CD-ROM drives.** If the drive is empty, just the drive letter will appear. If the drive has a CD in it, the volume track of the CD will appear as the drive name.

- **Syquest, SyJet, Zip, Jaz** or other high-capacity **cartridge drives,** which will be called 'Removable Disk' with a drive letter in parentheses, whether or not there's a disk in the drive, and whether or not the disk in the drive has a volume name.

- **Network drives** that have been mapped to your computer. These will be called [*share name*] on '[*name of remote computer*]' with a drive letter in parentheses; the icon will be similar to the ordinary icon for that type of drive, except that a network T-connector (like a T-connected plumbing pipe) appears at the base.

- **Printers folder.** This contains all your connected printers, local or remote, and an Add Printer icon that lets you set up a new printer. The icon for the default printer (the printer currently selected to print to) will include a white checkmark on a black circle, which will jump from icon to icon if you change defaults. Icons for shared local printers will be held in the upturned hand; icons for shared remote printers will include the T-connector.

- **Control Panel folder.** This is just another way to get to Start Menu\Settings\Control Panel as discussed above.

- **Dial-Up Networking** folder. This contains one icon for each Dial-Up connection configured on your computer, and an icon called Make New Connection that lets you set up more.

- **Scheduled Tasks** folder. With the Task Scheduler and the Add Scheduled Task Wizard, you can schedule normal system maintenance— like backup or disk defragmentation—to take place daily, weekly or monthly at your chosen time, when the computer boots, or whenever it has nothing else to do. The Wizard gives you a list of all the programs on your Start Menu to choose from, and the option to browse for others.

 If a resource on your computer is able to be shared by other computers on the local network, its icon will be held in an upturned hand, as if it's being politely offered to the rest of the network.

# Grappling with Device Objects

An icon representing a printer connected to your computer's parallel port is a particular case of something called a *device object*, which represents a peripheral hardware device attached to your system. You can manipulate a device object icon as you would other objects in Windows 98.

Device objects bring controls to the Desktop that are intrinsic to the devices they represent. For example, printers maintain a print queue that contains the pending print jobs requested by applications you are running. To view the print queue, you can double-click on the icon that represents the printer, which brings up a window displaying the contents of the queue (Figure 3.14).

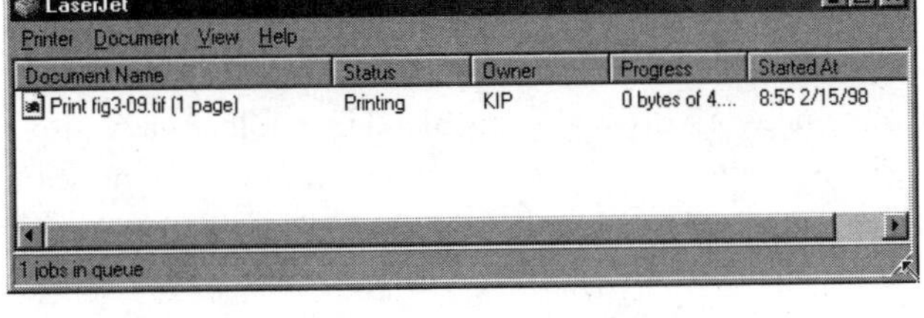

| LaserJet | | | | |
|---|---|---|---|---|
| Printer  Document  View  Help | | | | |
| Document Name | Status | Owner | Progress | Started At |
| Print fig3-09.tif (1 page) | Printing | KIP | 0 bytes of 4.... | 8:56 2/15/98 |

1 jobs in queue

*Figure 3.14*

*Right on cue*

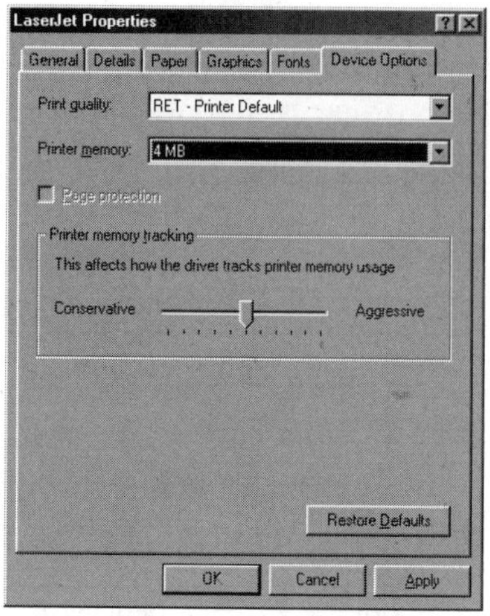

**Figure 3.15**

Examining the Device Options properties for a device object

The window displayed when you open a device object icon is a "folder view on steroids"—customized for the kind, brand, and model of device you're viewing. For example, in addition to displaying the print queue, a printer object window typically contains the menu options you need to control your printer. As shown in Figure 3.15, the Properties command on the Printer menu brings up a tabbed dialog that contains numerous controls specific to your printer, including network port, capture and spool settings, options for paper handling, graphics, font protocol, and device resolution and memory management. Windows 98 assumes that your printer has the standard amount of installed memory; if you add hardware memory to your printer, click the **Device Options** tab of **Printer Properties** and set Printer memory to the new value. Windows 98 can use the extra memory to improve printing speed.

# Folder Views: Your Window on Objects

Normally, if you double-click on any of the icons in My Computer, Windows 98 opens a new window displaying the object's contents. For example, if you double-click on a volume object, you see a window displaying all the folders and files stored in that particular volume. This type of window is commonly called a folder view, and it's a key visual tool in the Windows 98 interface.

Folders are software containers in which collections of icons are stored, and folder views are windows that display the same collections of icons. Several types of icons open up to display folder views, including volume icons and folder icons. My Computer itself opens into a folder view, as do all the volume and folder objects within My Computer—including, for example, the settings folders for the Windows 98 Control Panels (Figure 3.16).

Folder views make it easy to view and work with hard disks and other storage devices. That's because data on a mass storage device—be it floppy disk, hard disk, or network drive—is organized by a folder view into a hierarchical, branching pattern so that you can let your eyes do the searching. The root folder (sometimes called the *root directory*) of the drive may have any number of subfolders branching from it. These subfolders, in turn, may contain additional subfolders of their own, forming a pattern reminiscent of a tree with many branches.

*Figure 3.16*

*Viewing the
contents of a folder*

The Windows 98 folder view was designed to present a neat hierarchy of your
storage volumes. For example, when you first open a volume icon, you are
presented with a view of the volume's root folder. Included in that view are
any file icons located in the root folder, as well as icons representing additional folders that branch from the root. Double-clicking one of those folders
opens a new window displaying a folder view of its contents. This view may
include additional nested folders, files, or a combination of both (Figure 3.17).

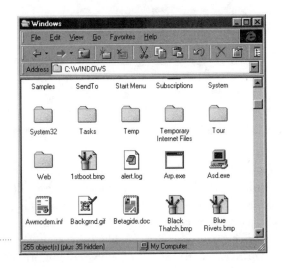

*Figure 3.17*

*Easy navigation*

The folder view concept of Windows 98 makes navigating your disks and
other storage volumes a snap. Simply double-click, and you've moved up or
down the tree. Every folder and file in the Windows 98 interface is part of the
hierarchical file system.

## Custom-Designed Folder Views

Windows 98 enables you to customize your folder views to create a desktop that suits your needs, tastes, and whims. You can adjust the way icons are displayed, prod the system into displaying more information, or change your method of navigating through folders. You can even enable a special toolbar to use in a folder view window.

## Changing the View Style

Want to change the size and style of the icons inside your folder view windows? As you've noticed, Windows 98 displays the folder view contents using large icons that are easy to read but tough on your screen real estate (Figure 3.18).

*Figure 3.18*

*The Default folder view*

These mega-icons don't provide more information about what they represent than smaller icons could. After a while you may long for a denser presentation, and we suggest that intermediate users—those of you ready to handle having more objects squeezed into the folder view—select **Details** from the **View** menu, and check out the view. It's like going from the *Weekly Reader* to the *New York Times*: expect to see considerably more information about each object's size and type; its free space, if it's a volume; and the last time it was modified (Figure 3.19).

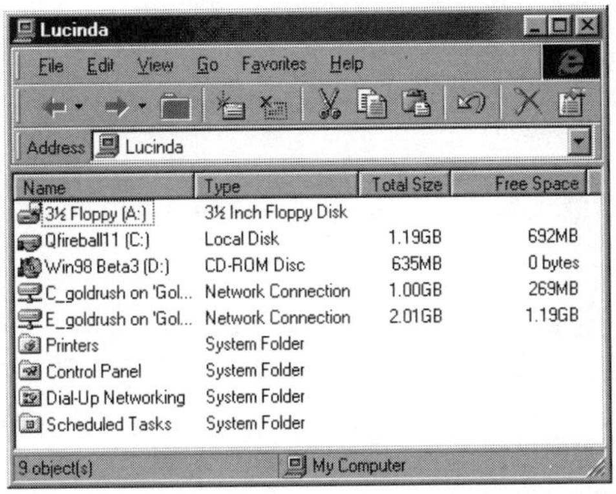

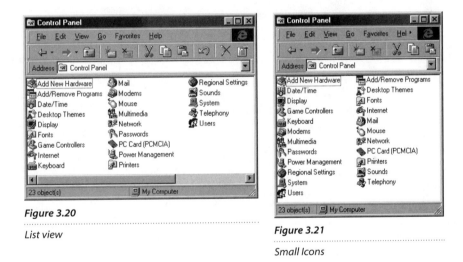

**Figure 3.19**

The Details view

Want another view option? Try one of these:

- **List.** Sorts the icons from left to right (Figure 3.20).

- **Small Icons.** Sorts the icons from top to bottom (Figure 3.21).

**Figure 3.20**

List view

**Figure 3.21**

Small Icons

## Hello, Toolbar

Because the Toolbar offers shortcuts for a variety of handy commands, it can be useful in a folder view window. Normally, folder view windows hide the toolbar for two sensible reasons: to reduce clutter, and to clear up as much viewing space as possible. But by turning on the toolbar, you can sacrifice a little space and gain push-button access to frequently used functions. For example, you can click on one button to connect to a network drive, or click on another to change your style of view to **Small Icons, List,** or **Details.**

*Figure 3.22*

*Toolbar in the folder view*

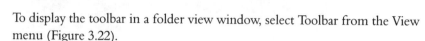

To display the toolbar in a folder view window, select Toolbar from the View menu (Figure 3.22).

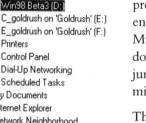

*Figure 3.23*

*The toolbar's drop-down list box*

If you, the intermediate to advanced computerist, feel particularly nimble, you can take advantage of the toolbar's Address field—a drop-down list that provides a treelike overview of your entire Windows 98 system, including My Computer and all open folder windows. This system tree makes it easy to jump from directory to directory with a minimum of clicking (Figure 3.23).

The Toolbar architecture of folder view windows is one "feature" which has most radically changed between current and previous versions of 32-bit Windows—and, in our view, not much for the better. Windows 98's passion for awareness of the Internet means that—even in the so-called "Windows classic style"—much of the toolbar functionality we were accustomed to in Windows 95 has changed substantially or disappeared.

Windows 95/NT 4 had one "Toolbar," which always contained the system tree drop-down list box, along with a selection of buttons which were specific to the nature of the folder view window. For example, the toolbar in folder view windows of My Computer and Network Neighborhood contained buttons for connecting to and disconnecting from a network. There were some complaints about the "inconsistency" of the specialized controls—it might, for example, have been reasonable for the network drive mapping and disconnect buttons also to exist in Control Panel—but in general the context-sensitive controls were welcomed.

In Windows 98, fewer specialized controls are available and Microsoft feature bloat strikes once more as one Toolbar becomes three:

The Toolbar buttons, now known as the **Standard** Buttons, include Back, Forward, Up, Cut, Copy, Paste, Undo, Delete, Properties, and Views. **Back** and **Forward** have drop-down lists of Back-to-where and Forward-to-where, in case you've been cruising around a lot. **Up, Cut, Copy, Paste, Undo, Delete,** and **Properties** have their traditional functions; if you're not familiar with those, look on pages 108–109. The **Views** button condenses the standard options, Large and Small Icons, List, and Details, into a drop-down menu, and adds "as Web Page." If you click on the Views button repeatedly, you'll loop through all the available views.

If the Standard Buttons have icon titles, like "Cut" and "Copy," below them, they take up a lot of room; in fact, at the default 800x600 resolution, they may not fit in the full width of the screen. Pull down **View, Toolbars**, and uncheck **Text Labels**; the width of the iconbar will shrink by about half.

The system tree drop-down list box is now called the **Address Bar,** which is puzzling, but consistent with the Explorer's rapid drift toward the architecture and conventions of the Internet Explorer. The way it works hasn't changed, though. Are we approaching the day when individual hard disks will have URLs?

The third and new bar, the **Links Bar,** gives you pushbutton access to the Internet; the five buttons installed as defaults are **Best of the Web, Channel Guide, Customize Links, Internet Explorer News,** and **Internet Start.** Unsurprisingly, all of these are aliases for URLs at either `microsoft.com` or `msn.com`; Microsoft, having discovered that MSN is a tepid draw as a pay-for-play service, still has it available as a cattle chute to the Internet. Once you install Windows 98, you'll do a lot of clicking and dragging and dropping before your personal Internet profile isn't dominated by Microsoft.

## A Change of View

The explosion of folder view options in Windows 98 makes the menu structure deeper, more complex, and inevitably more confusing. By default, Windows 98—like Windows 95—creates a new window for each new folder view. If you're cruising through many folders, the screen can quickly become overrun with hordes of open windows. In both versions of Windows 9*x*, you can change this default to display a single window that depicts only the contents of the currently opened folder; but the path to the option is quite different (Figure 3.24):

| | | |
|---|---|---|
| *Windows 95* | View\Options, Folder tab, click one of two buttons in **Browsing options** | Alt S or Alt N |
| *Windows 98* | View\Folder Options, General tab, click Custom, click Settings, click one of two buttons in **Browse folders as follows** | Alt M or Alt W |

*Figure 3.24*

*Changing the viewing behavior*

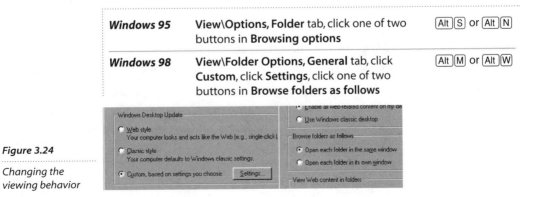

Although the single-window viewing approach spares you from window clutter, it makes your place in the overall tree structure harder to remember. That's why it's a good idea to turn on the Standard Buttons toolbar when you use this viewing method. With the toolbar in place, you can use the Up One Level button and the drop-down list box to locate your position in the folder tree and to jump quickly from folder to folder.

# How to Find Anything

Microsoft definitely went overboard in providing a cornucopia of techniques to accomplish each navigational task. We've already surveyed several methods of finding your way through folders and directories, and believe it or not, more are coming. All this flexibility can drive you crazy, which is why we encourage you to keep reading this book.

*Figure 3.25*

The Find submenu

Although folders can help you organize data, they can also make finding a particular file or other object a daunting task, especially on a fully loaded system. With this unhappy scenario in mind, Microsoft included a powerful search utility with Windows 98. The Find utility can streamline your computing life considerably; it makes it easy to put your finger on files, folders, and even other computers across a network, without having to click your way through mountains of nested folders.

To summon the Find utility, go to the Taskbar's **Start Menu** and select **Find.** From the short submenu that pops up, select whatever type of object you're seeking (Figure 3.25).

The **Find** submenu lets you send out a search party for five types of objects:

- **Files or Folders...** Specific files or folders on a local or networked drive.

- **Computer...** Other computers on your network, so you can tap into their resources, like storage volumes, printers, and other peripherals.

- **On the Internet...** This is another way of launching Internet Explorer with the URL defaulted to the Microsoft All-in-One search engine page. It's enough to make us think that the Microsoft advertising slogan, "Where do you want to go today?" should really be, "How do you want to go to Microsoft today?"

- **People...** A custom search tool that lets you enter someone's name, e-mail address, snail-mail address, phone number, or "Other" in your choice of the Windows Address Book or several of the free, public online directory services.

- **On the Microsoft Network...** Files, programs, or device drivers located on the Microsoft Network online service.

Let's look at each of these in more detail:

## Finding Files or Folders

You'll use the **Files or Folders** option more often than any of the others, so if you're skimming, slow down and pay special attention. Select Files or Folders from the Find submenu to bring up a tabbed dialog box containing three pages: **Name & Location, Date,** and **Advanced.** The first page enables you to search for an object based on its name, its text contents, and its location in your system. Use this page if you know the object's name; enter the name, or any part of it, into the **Named** box and click the **Find Now** button (Figure 3.26).

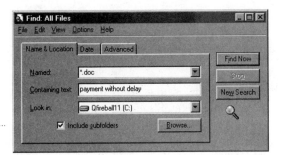

*Figure 3.26*

*The Find Now button*

By default, the Find utility searches for a file, folder, or text string on the hard disk you used to boot Windows 98, but you can expand the search to include all your volumes; select the **My Computer** option in the **Look In** drop-down list box. This tells the Find utility to search every volume in the My Computer folder, which should contain every volume currently attached to your system, networked or not.

The **Containing text** dialog—which was moved from the Advanced tab to Name & Location for the newest release of Windows—enables you to search for files that contain a specific word or fragment of text. This is a great feature because it lets you find files just by remembering words, names, or other bits of text, which can be case-sensitive if you prefer. But watch out—this option takes by far the most time to complete its search.

If you have more than one hard disk in your own computer, you might not know which disk your sought-after file is on; but you still don't want to make the Find utility tromp all over your CD drive and your network shares. It's time for the neat intermediate option called **Local hard drives,** which searches—of all things—every fixed disk in your local computer, and that's all.

Once the Find utility's detective work is done, it displays its results in a folder view window that gets tacked onto the bottom of the Find dialog box (Figure 3.27). You can then manipulate the contents of this folder view as you would with any other folder.

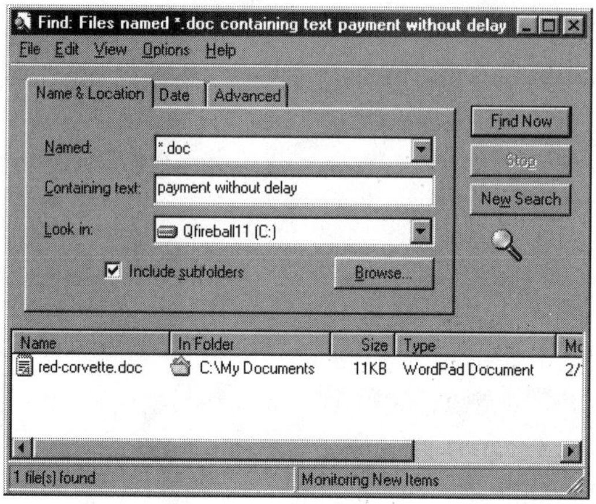

*Figure 3.27*

*The results window from a string-based search*

The search results window is now a fully functional folder view. For example, you can open a data file by double-clicking on its icon, and you can drag and drop objects from the search results window into other folder views or onto the Windows 98 desktop. You can also save the results of your search.

## The Date Tab

Knowing an object's name makes finding the object easier, but it's not the only way to track down what you're searching for. For example, you can also find an object based on its date and time stamps. Windows 98 stamps each file with three dates and times: the time of file creation, of the last modification, and of the last access. For example, if you know that you were working with a particular file earlier this morning, but you can't remember if you edited it, and now you can't find it—and you say "How likely is that?" and we reply, "Likely to drive you bananas,"—you can use the **Date** tab of the Find dialog box to round up all the files that have changed during this time period (Figure 3.28).

You can also use the Date tab to search for file objects that fall within a range of dates. Or you can look for objects that were changed within a specific number of days or months.

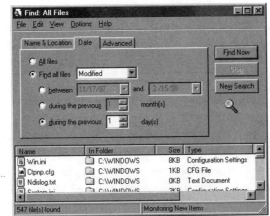

**Figure 3.28**

*The results window from a date-confined search*

## The Advanced Tab

If you want to search through your system with a fine-tooth comb, click the **Advanced** tab in the Find dialog box. The Advanced tab enables you to search for a file object based on several criteria:

- **Of type.** Enables you to find all the objects of any type listed in the View\File Types dialog, such as all the animated cursors.

- **Size is.** Enables you to find an object of less than, greater than or equal to a specific file size.

You can combine options to narrow your search. For example, to look for all the Word documents containing the word "Microsoft," you would first specify **Word document** in the **Of Type** drop-down list box, then enter the word "Microsoft" in the **Containing Text** box and click on the Find Now button (Figure 3.29).

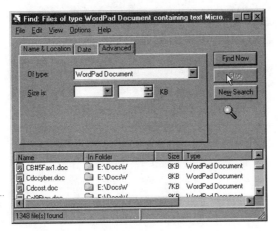

**Figure 3.29**

*The Advanced page of the Find utility*

When Windows 98 is handling document categories, it refers to a Microsoft Word file as a WordPad file. This is a consequence of overlapping Registry settings between WordPad and Word for Windows 6.0; see Chapter 17.

Once you've completed searching for a particular object, you can begin a new query by clicking the **New Search** button. This resets all the search criteria so you can start afresh.

## Finding Objects on Other Computers

If you are overly curious, work for the CIA, or are a network administrator, you may need to look for an object that's located on another computer connected to yours over a network. That's when you need to select **Computer** from the Find submenu.

When you choose Computer, you bring up a relatively simple dialog box with only a single field: Named. If you know the name of the computer or other network resource, enter it into the **Named** field and click on the **Find Now** button. (What you key in here, as distinct from, say, Map Network Drive, doesn't have to be festooned with backslashes and isn't case-sensitive.) The Find utility searches your network for a computer or a resource with that name. The results are displayed in the same tacked-on folder view window you see in the Find Files or Folders dialog box. You can open and view the contents of any of the found resources—such as shared network volumes or printers—by double-clicking on their icons (Figure 3.30).

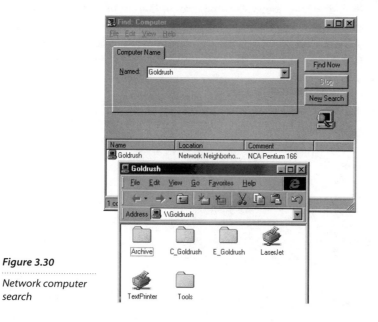

**Figure 3.30**

Network computer search

## On the Internet

As noted, this is simply a way of launching Internet Explorer and pointing it to the search engine pages of **microsoft.com** or the Microsoft Network.

## People

 This is a front end to the Windows Address Book or to your choice of well-established Internet directory services including Four11, Bigfoot, InfoSpace Home and Business, SwitchBoard, Verisign (for digital security ID's), and WhoWhere. If you get one or more "hits," they accumulate in a drop-down box common to the other tasks of the Find dialog (Figure 3.31). Once you have a hit, you can click the Properties button to display the full Windows Address Book entry; click Delete to remove the entry from the list of results; or, if it's a hit from an Internet directory service, click **Add to Address Book** to do just that.

*Figure 3.31*

*Start Menu\People Four11 search results*

 If you click Delete on a Windows Address Book entry, you *permanently* delete that entry from the Windows Address Book, whereas if you Delete an Internet directory entry, you simply remove it from the list. At least Windows does warn you.

## The Windows Address Book

 When you're trying to hunt down the neat apps and applets bundled into the vast goodie basket that is Windows 98, put the **Windows Address Book** near the top of your list. This capable contact manager (Figure 3.32) offers a forest of tabs that let you enter personal information, comments, multiple e-mail addresses, home and business Web pages and snail-mail addresses, conferencing information, and digital ID's. It integrates smoothly with Microsoft's NetMeeting conferencing software and with Outlook Express, the medium-weight e-mail program that comes bundled with Windows 98. About the only thing it won't do is scheduling—if you want that as part of the package, you'll need to install the full Microsoft Outlook that ships with some versions of Microsoft Office—but, even as a pure Rolodex, the Windows Address Book is much too good to languish unused on your disk.

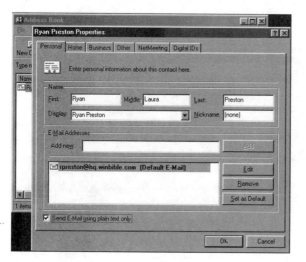

**Figure 3.32**

Address Book main screen

 The one irritating limitation of Find People is that, while it will query most of the established Internet directory services, it does it one service at a time; to query a different service you have to start another search. If you want an industrial-strength people-finding utility that will scamper out and look all over the Net in a single pass, we strongly recommend **NetFerret** by FerretSoft LLC. This well-written set of search utilities will hunt through Web sites, e-mail directories, FTP sites, IRC channels, address and telephone databases, and USENET newsgroups, looking for just about whatever you can imagine; and since it integrates itself fully with your Find menu, it's quick and easy to use. Time-limited demos of all the pieces are downloadable from `http://www.ferretsoft.com/netferret/`, and the modules can be purchased individually or in various Value Packs, but the best deal by far is the whole kaboodle for $50.

## Microsoft Network

Surprise, surprise! Leave it to Microsoft to give itself a pitch in every niche. The last option in the Find submenu, **On the Microsoft Network,** lets you search for a specific piece of software or other resource on Microsoft's online service. If you've already signed up for the Microsoft Network, Windows 98 automatically connects you to the service when you select this Find option. Once it successfully connects to Microsoft Network, this Find option uses the search facilities of the online service to locate specific resources, such as an elusive printer driver or an online database.

# The Windows 98 Explorer

So far in this chapter, we've described how the Taskbar can provide you with quick, push-button access to frequently used documents, programs, and utilities. For Macintosh expatriates, we've reviewed the My Computer icon, which deftly presents a Macintosh-like system for working with Windows. We've saved the trickiest—and most sophisticated—tool for last. That's the **Explorer,** a file-browsing utility that presents all the elements of your computing environment in a treelike hierarchy so that you can easily see the structure of the information on any storage device.

Of all the parts of the Windows 98 interface, the Explorer is the most Darwinian—it evolves with every succeeding version of Windows. Some of its features, such as a split-window view with the tree on the left side and the contents window on the right, trace their ancestry to the old Windows 3.1 File Manager, although you'll soon realize that the Explorer is much more powerful than File Manager.

As Windows 95 developed into Windows 98, Explorer changed its interface again. Explorer, the local file browser, and Internet Explorer, the Microsoft Web browser, began converging, swapping pieces of their controls, and looking more similar. The clear intent is that, working within a single interface and control set, you should be able to access *any* computer resource—from your own computer's floppy drive to the whole Internet—as if it were part of one seamless whole. This is an audacious idea and a genuine example of the overused phrase "paradigm shift." It's engaged the attention of the highest levels of the United States Government and sparked legal action against Microsoft for purported antitrust violation. Whatever else this means, it does prove that the Net as an information carrier is entering a maturity (or let's say adolescence!) comparable to that of television or radio; it also means that Microsoft, in its ongoing relationship with those of us discerning enough to choose 32-bit Windows as an operating system, expects to deliver a torrent of channel content and software upgrades through a robust Net connection.

Nonetheless, Microsoft is savvy enough to realize that not every potential Windows 98 user is a certified Net-aholic. (Not to mention that, if every Windows user went up on the Web at the same time, the resulting packet storm would probably bring the Net to a halt.) So the newest Explorer has almost too much flexibility; depending on the options you select, it can be something almost (but not quite) like the familiar Windows 95 Explorer, or almost (but not quite) like Internet Explorer 4.0. In this chapter, we'll begin by describing Explorer in its most "classic" (Windows 95-like) aspect, then describe the optional features that can make it more browserish.

## How to Explore

The Explorer enables you to browse effortlessly through every folder in your system or network, by combining a treelike map of available resources with a custom folder view pane. Both Explorer elements—the tree and the folder view—share a single window on the Windows 98 desktop; a movable split bar separates the tree from the folder view (Figure 3.33).

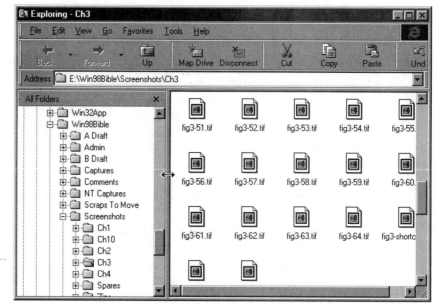

*Figure 3.33*

*The Windows 98 Explorer (note split control)*

To view a resource, click on its icon in the tree on the left side of the Explorer window. You can look at the icon's contents in the folder view on the right side of the window. As you move through the tree on the left side (try tapping the Down Arrow key) the folder view on the right is updated automatically.

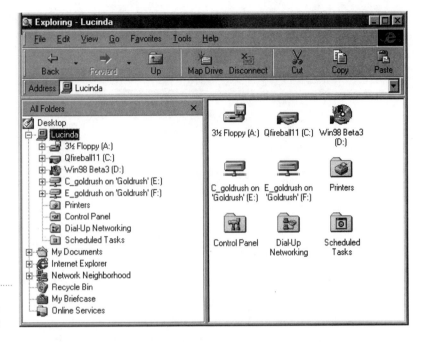

*Figure 3.34*

*Viewing the My Computer folder's object tree branch*

This enables you to jump from resource to resource without digging through a bunch of folders, as you have to do with My Computer.

The Explorer's tree is upside down; its root is at the top, with everything else branching off below. At the base of the Explorer's object tree is the Windows 98 desktop—your starting point for the entire Windows 98 interface. Branching from this root are the folders and other resources you can access in Windows 98, such as the My Computer folder, complete with volumes, Control Panels, and all the other items it normally contains (Figure 3.34).

Each branch of the Explorer's object tree can be expanded or collapsed to broaden or narrow the scope of what you see. By default, only top-level resources, like the Desktop and My Computer icons, are shown in the tree. To expand a branch—and thus delve deeper into the system's hierarchy—click on the small plus sign next to the branch's name, or tap the gray Plus key. To collapse a branch, click on its minus sign, or tap the gray Minus key. A branch without a sign signifies a top-level branch that contains no additional folders nested within it.

## Exploring Other Resources

The Explorer's object tree can contain everything, from directory folders and files inside those folders to Resource icons representing objects like Control Panels or the desktop. Because the Explorer's folder view window can display the contents of just about any resource you encounter, you can take advantage

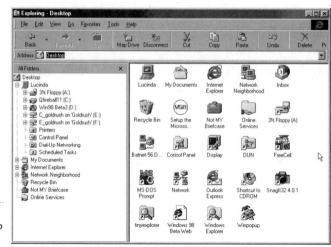

**Figure 3.35**

Examining the
Windows 98 desktop
from the Explorer

of the Explorer to scrutinize everything in your system, from the Fonts folder
to the desktop itself (Figure 3.35).

In addition, the Explorer's folder view pane is fully functional; you can
manipulate each object within the contents pane as if you were working with
a normal folder view window. For example, if you're viewing the contents of
the Control Panels folder, double-clicking on any Control Panel will bring it
up (Figure 3.36).

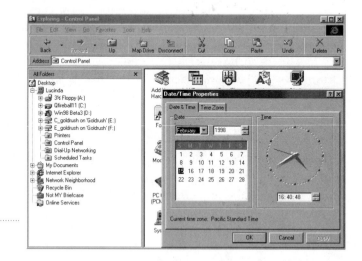

**Figure 3.36**

Expanding the
Explorer view

If you're connected to a network, its resources can also be viewed with the
Explorer. Select **Network Neighborhood** and expand it into an open
branch. You'll see a list of computers in your network work group or domain.

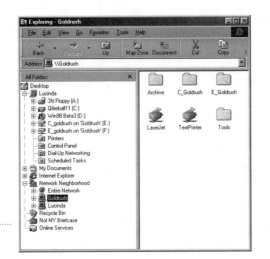

**Figure 3.37**

Viewing network
shares in Explorer

To view the contents of their shared resources, select computers in the object
tree and expand branches as necessary (Figure 3.37).

## Changing Explorer Views

The way the Explorer displays items in the contents pane can be customized
like any normal folder view window. You can tell it to use either large or small
icons or to display contents in list form; just click on the Views button until
the pane contents are arranged the way you want them. The Explorer also features the same multipurpose toolbar that is found in traditional folder view
windows. Notice the similarity between the Explorer's object tree and the tree
displayed in the drop-down list box of the Address Bar (Figure 3.38). If you're
starting to like the Windows 98 interface, you'll see this as one more example
of its flexibility; if you're not warming up to it, you're probably complaining

**Figure 3.38**

Comparing Explorer
and folder view
object trees

that—here as elsewhere—there are too many different ways to accomplish the same thing. Inside an operating system as complex as 32-bit Windows, there's ample support for both views.

All of the configuration options described previously are available from the Explorer's **View** menu. In fact, aside from the separate object tree, nearly every other major Explorer function is identical to that of the normal folder view. This design feature arises from a planned consistency among the four interface tools—the Explorer, My Computer, the Taskbar, and Internet Explorer—that allows you to manipulate the interface in similar ways.

# Manipulating Objects

Now that we've surveyed the ways in which Windows 98 lets you view objects in your system, the next step is to begin working with the objects themselves. As we mentioned earlier, Windows 98 treats each software and hardware resource in your computer as an individual object. For example, a file stored on your hard disk is a file *object*, and the directory in which it is stored is a *folder object,* or "folder" for short. Folder objects are containers that hold collections of other objects. The Windows 98 desktop is itself an object, and peripheral hardware devices are represented by device objects.

Most objects perform unique functions; that's why every object bears a unique name. Objects are visually identified by icons that specify the type of object—what kind of file it is, what kind of disk or printer it is, whether it's local or on the network.

 **If you want to find out more about an object than its icon and title tell you, right-click on it to bring up the Context Menu, go to the bottom of the menu (usually), and click Properties to open its Properties sheet, which lists specific characteristics of the object, such as its name, its size, its location on the system, and the dates it was created and last modified. If the object is a file object, its Properties sheet will also display—and let you set—its Attributes, which are *Read-only* (whether or not the file can be modified), *Archive* (used mostly by backup programs), *Hidden* (whether or not the file will be listed in My Computer and Explorer), and *System,* which is used only by the operating system. Since most files don't need to be, and can't be, System files, the System checkbox is generally grayed out.**

# First Drag, Then Drop

The best way to manipulate objects is to drag and drop them with the mouse. Because objects represent items such as files and programs and devices connected to your computer, dragging and dropping lets you move, start, close, and otherwise mess around with things on, in, and connected to your computer. For example, you can drag the onscreen icon of a file and drop it into the Recycle Bin to delete the file. This mirrors the act of crumpling a piece of paper and tossing it into the trash.

Not only is the drag-and-drop concept meant to make it easier to learn the system, it's also a handy way to get things done. Often the quickest way to perform a task is to drag an icon and drop it somewhere else. Dragging and dropping is just what it sounds like: you "grab" an object with the mouse—place the mouse pointer over an icon and hold down the left mouse button—then drag the object to its destination and drop the object by releasing the mouse button (Figure 3.39). While you drag the object, it will "ghost" (be displayed in paler colors) to indicate that it has no permanent location; when you drop it, it gets its full colors back.

**Figure 3.39**

*Drag and drop*

Although the drag-and-drop process is fairly straightforward, the same action can cause entirely different results, depending on what you drag and where you drop it. For example, if you drag a file icon from one folder to another on the same drive, your action moves the file. If you drag that same icon to a folder on another volume, your action copies the file instead of moving it. But there's a wrinkle: if you drag an application icon somewhere, your action creates a shortcut, instead of moving or copying the application. You can perform this same sort of drag-and-drop operation on folders, too. But watch out—when you drag and drop a folder, the entire contents, including any nested folders and their contents, are affected.

Normally Windows 98 moves an object in response to your performing a drag-and-drop operation. Sometimes you may want to copy an object instead—that is, make a duplicate and place it in a different folder. To tell Windows to copy an object instead of moving it, hold down the Ctrl key during the entire drag-and-drop operation, provided the items are on the same disk. A new copy of the object appears in the destination folder, and the original remains in place (Figure 3.40).

Debug.exe    Edit.com

**Figure 3.40**

*Copying an object*

Those two drag-and-drop procedures—move and copy—can be used in virtually every part of the Windows 98 interface, with a few exceptions. Some objects, such as the volume objects in My Computer, should never be moved, and Windows 98 does its best to restrict this kind of drag-and-drop operation.

**Windows doesn't expect you to know whether an object is being moved or copied or a shortcut created—but you do have to be observant to tell. If an object is being moved, the mouse pointer that's "pushing" it will be the same as your ordinary mouse pointer (Figure 3.41a). If it's being copied, the mouse pointer will have a small box at its tail with a plus sign in it (Figure 3.41b). And if a Shortcut is being created, the small box at the pointer tail will have a Shortcut arrow in it (Figure 3.41c). Since drag-and-drop behaves differently depending on the context in which it's done, you'll probably want to experiment with the [Shift] and [Ctrl] keys while you watch the pointer change. Oh, yes, and a barred circle—the international symbol for "forbidden"—superimposed on the icon you're dragging means "You can't drop this here" (Figure 3.41d).**

*Figure 3.41a*

*Move-and-drop pointer*

*Figure 3.41b*

*Copy-and-drop pointer*

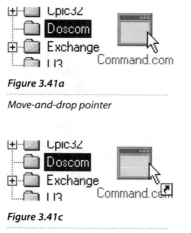

*Figure 3.41c*

*Drop-and-shortcut pointer*

*Figure 3.41d*

*Forbidden drop pointer*

# Digging Deeper into Drag and Drop

The simplest use for drag and drop is moving and copying files between folders. By creating folders for different topics and placing related files in each folder, you're practicing good housekeeping and creating an informational structure for your system. Because Windows places few restrictions on how you organize things, you can drag and drop to your heart's content. Of course, there may be some unexpected results, so keep reading.

**Figure 3.42**

*A drag-and-drop operation across volumes*

When you drag and drop an object across volumes, Windows 98 copies the object instead of moving it. For example, dragging a document icon from its folder on a hard disk and dropping it onto a floppy-disk drive makes a copy (Figure 3.42).

You can, however, override this behavior and force Windows 98 to move instead of copy the file. First select the file with the left mouse button, then hold down the [Shift] key while you perform the drag-and-drop operation. This places the file in the destination volume and deletes the original from the source volume.

Drag and drop is particularly handy when you move objects onto icons that represent device objects. For example, if you drop a file object onto one of the printer objects in the Printers folder, Windows 98 interprets this action as a request to print the document. Windows loads the application that created the file and instructs that application to print the document. Finally, Windows closes the application, and the document prints in the background using the Windows print spooler. Similarly, you can drag the same file and drop it onto a fax object to send the document out as a fax.

Microsoft has gone out of its way to make drag and drop pervasive throughout the interface. For example, you can drag icons and drop them into some dialog boxes, as you'll find out later in this book.

## The Recycle Bin

**Figure 3.43**

*The Recycle Bin*

These are politically correct times, even for operating systems. In Windows 98, you don't delete objects—you recycle them. Actually, the concept's not new, just the terminology: what's known as the Trash on a Macintosh is called a Recycle Bin in Windows 98, making enough of a difference to keep the Apple lawyers at bay. The Recycle Bin is technically a folder object, but it has a special purpose: if you want to delete an object, just drag it to the Recycle Bin and drop it onto the Bin's icon (Figure 3.43).

If you're bent on a course of mass destruction and deletion, you can drag a folder full of stuff to the Recycle Bin. But be warned: if you drag a folder to the Recycle Bin, you are also dragging any nested folders that reside within the first folder. Also, Windows 98 doesn't let you put certain things in the Recycle Bin, including device objects and configuration folders. Basically, icons for objects that represent either hardware or important system software components can't be thrown out—at least not without a lot of extra effort.

Well, Kip and Fred can't tell you where people go when they die, but we can tell you where objects go when you've condemned them to death by dropping

*Figure 3.44*

*Recovery action*

them into the Recycle Bin. They don't go far at first; the icons have simply been moved from their old locations into the Recycle Bin's folder, and the objects represented by the icons are still intact. If you change your mind about deleting them, you can double-click on the Recycle Bin's icon to open its folder, then drag the objects back to their original locations, giving them a reprieve and returning them to active duty (Figure 3.44).

Be forewarned, however, that icons don't stay in the Recycle Bin forever; if you don't do anything, the objects they represent are ultimately deleted. The Recycle Bin dedicates a percentage of each volume's storage space to recently deleted objects; the default is 5%, which on any modern drive is probably at least 50MB, so you should have space for quite a few days' deletions. Nonetheless, as this limit is approached, older objects are permanently deleted to make space for newer ones. This means that the more recently you threw out an icon, the more likely you are to be able to retrieve it from the Recycle Bin.

  Files that have been deleted in MS-DOS Mode, at a DOS command prompt, or by a DOS application do *not* go into the Recycle Bin. They get zapped as soon as you delete them.

Files in the Recycle Bin are actually stored in one or more subfolders of a hidden folder called Recycler. Access to Recycler is controlled by the Registry. Leave these folders alone; emptying the Recycle Bin with the **File\Empty Recycle Bin** command will delete the files and update the Registry information, too.

You can control the Recycle Bin's behavior by calling up its Context menu. (Almost every object in Windows 98 has a similar pop-up menu offering a list of commands and options specific to that object.) Point to the Recycle Bin and click the *right* mouse button, then select **Properties** from the menu. The resulting dialog box features a page containing the overall configuration options, and includes tabs that enable you to set recycling options individually for each storage volume connected to the system (Figure 3.45).

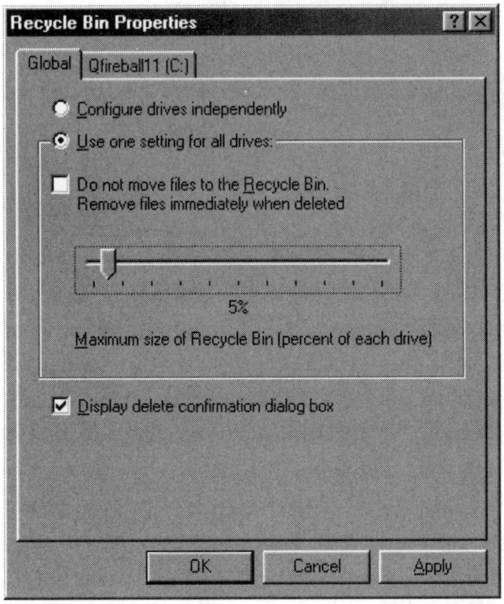

**Recycle Bin Properties**

Global | Qfireball11 (C:)

○ Configure drives independently
◉ Use one setting for all drives:

☐ Do not move files to the Recycle Bin.
   Remove files immediately when deleted

5%

Maximum size of Recycle Bin (percent of each drive)

☑ Display delete confirmation dialog box

OK      Cancel      Apply

*Figure 3.45*

Configuring the
Recycle Bin

If it's time to take out the trash, you can check a box that forces the Recycle Bin to purge files immediately. If you're a person who has trouble making up your mind, a slider control enables you to specify how much space is set aside for recoverable files on your hard disk, setting a limit on your indecisiveness. Finally, you can either set these options globally, so they control the recycling on all your storage devices, or choose a different recycling schedule for each storage volume.

## What's in an Object?

Each object has unique properties related to its function. For example, each file object has a unique name that corresponds to a specific disk file located in one of a system's volumes. Similarly, each folder object contains a corresponding subdirectory name. Device objects each control the connection and configuration of a particular device.

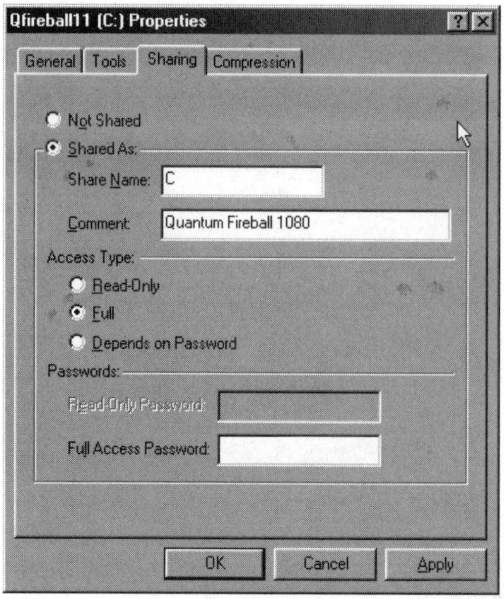

**Figure 3.46**

Properties sheets

Windows 98 provides a Properties dialog box, specifically called a *sheet* in Microsoft-ese, for each object in a system. Each Properties sheet contains information about its object—in the same way that a driver's license or a police record contains information about a person. These sheets also display Control Panels that enable you to select options related to the object. For some objects, such as file objects, the Properties sheet is relatively simple and has only a single tab, usually called *General* and providing basic information like the object's file name and size. Device objects, at the other extreme, often have extensive Properties sheets with multiple tabs, covering configuration parameters including device and file system type, used and free space, various maintenance indicators, and (on a network) the device's share status and access level (Figure 3.46). For both files and devices, 32-bit Windows makes it easy to change parameters that were almost inaccessible under earlier network operating systems.

To view an object's Properties sheet, point at the object and click on it with the right mouse button; this pops up a menu called the **Context,** or right-click, menu. Then select **Properties,** which is usually at the bottom of the menu.

**Figure 3.47**

Printer Context menu

Quite a few objects provide items in their Context menus that give you quick access to frequently used options. A printer object, for example, may place controls on its Context menu that enable you to pause the printer or purge its queue. It's handy to be able to tweak an object's most useful properties without having to open a Properties sheet (Figure 3.47).

Once you've explored enough Context menus, you're bound to notice that each one contains commands that replicate drag-and-drop operations, including copy, move, delete, and, in some cases, print. Yet again Microsoft has provided more than one way to accomplish the same task. If you prefer menus to drag-and-drop, remember that clicking on an object with the right mouse button brings up the object's Context menu.

## Object Face-Lifts

Once you've gotten the hang of viewing an object's properties, you'll probably want to do some cosmetic surgery. The most direct way to change the way an object looks or performs is to bring up the object's Properties sheet. Device objects, in particular, can be modified. (Figure 3.48).

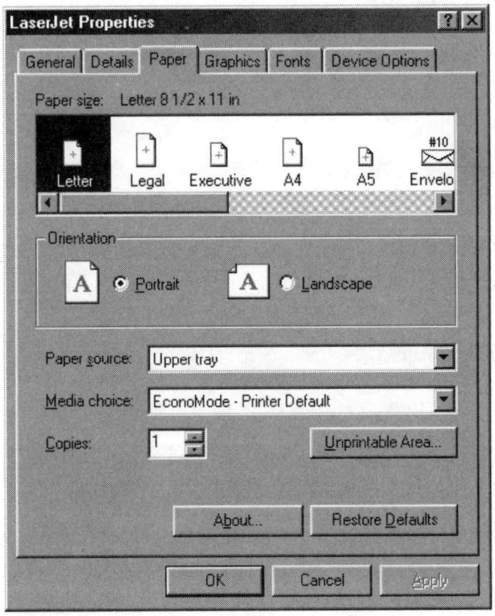

**Figure 3.48**

Changing the properties of a device object

But what about a simple operation like renaming an object? Windows 98 offers three ways to do this. The first, and simplest, method is to select the object's icon with the mouse pointer, then reselect the object (click once) with the mouse pointer positioned directly over the title. The title field changes into an editable field, highlighted and framed, and you can alter the text at will (Figure 3.49).

**Figure 3.49**

Editing the title text of an object

You can also edit an object's title by selecting **Rename** from the object's Context menu. If the object is located in a folder, you can perform the Rename function a third way; by highlighting the object in the folder view window and selecting **Rename** from the folder window's File menu.

### Don't Touch That Object!

Although it's OK to mess up the objects, a few objects in Windows 98 should be off-limits unless you know exactly what you're doing. Most of these critical system objects reside in the Windows 98 folder on your boot disk (probably called something like c:\windows or c:\win98). Some of the objects lurking within this main Windows folder are very sensitive.

For example, the System folder contains the core of the Windows 98 operating system, including the 32-bit code that makes up the interface. The System folder and surrounding folders should not be renamed, or Windows will not be able to find critical systems and will most likely crash. Nor should you delete any file objects from within these folders unless you are absolutely certain what role they play in the system. Accidentally deleting the wrong file can leave Windows 98 unbootable, forcing you to reinstall the operating system from scratch.

# Shortcuts

Shortcuts work the way the little programs called macros do—they let you circumvent normal routes to get to frequently used functions. Windows 98 includes Shortcut icons that work like buttons. Clicking on a Shortcut icon is like clicking on the object that the Shortcut icon represents.

**Figure 3.50**

*Freecell shortcut*

For example, if you crave quick access to the all-important Freecell game, you can create a shortcut to it (Figure 3.50) on the Windows 98 desktop. When you double-click on the Freecell shortcut icon, Windows 98 uses a special pointer inside the shortcut to track the original program down. Windows then opens the original program just as if you had opened it directly from within its folder.

You can create a shortcut to any object in the system. Especially handy are shortcuts to frequently used storage volumes. By placing those shortcuts on the Windows 98 desktop, you don't have to use an interface browser like My Computer. Instead, you can open the volumes directly via their desktop shortcuts. The same can be done for file, folder, or device objects, and these shortcuts can be placed anywhere on your desktop or in a folder.

## Creating a New Shortcut

Hey, this is Windows, so you'd expect to find several techniques for creating shortcuts. The first and easiest method is to select an object with the mouse, pop up the object's Context menu with a right-click, and select Create Shortcut. This creates a shortcut to the object, in the same folder as the original program. You can then move the shortcut anywhere you like—usually to the Desktop or, if your Desktop is cluttered, to a folder on your Desktop—and it remembers where its original resides (Figure 3.51). Notice that the sheet keeps track of the complete path to the object's file. This is why you can move shortcuts around your system at will: Windows 98 can always extract the location of the original from the Shortcut's properties.

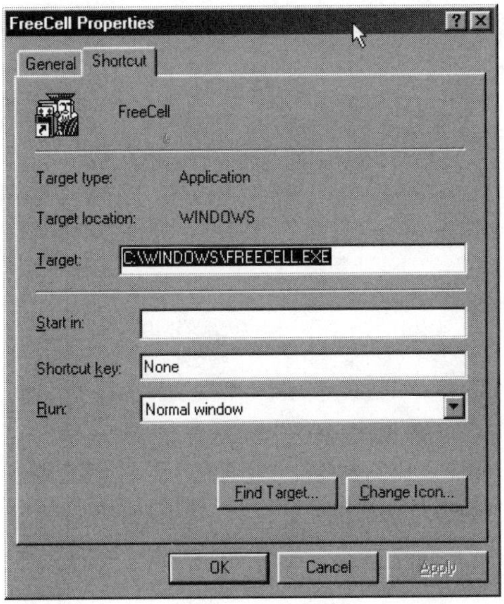

**Figure 3.51**

Shortcut properties

Another way to create a shortcut is to select the original object and drag it to a new location with the right (not the left) mouse button. Using the right mouse button during a drag operation causes Windows 98 to prompt you with

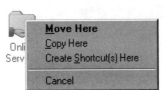

**Figure 3.52**

Right-click drag-and-drop

a small menu when you attempt to drop the item at its new location. Menu choices include **Copy Here, Move Here,** and **Create Shortcut Here.** Selecting the latter tells Windows 98 to create a new shortcut to the object at the target location (Figure 3.52).

# Managing Shortcuts

Once a shortcut is created, you can move it virtually anywhere within the confines of your Windows 98 system. Should you ever need to locate the original object, you can use the shortcut's Properties sheet to track down the original. Point to the shortcut with the mouse and click on the right mouse button to bring up the shortcut's Context menu, then select **Properties.** Next, click on the **Shortcut** tab to bring the second page of the sheet to the front. To bring up the folder view containing the original object, click the **Find Target** button. Up pops a folder view of the object's folder (Figure 3.53). But note that Windows doesn't highlight the target—it figures it's done enough for you by opening the folder.

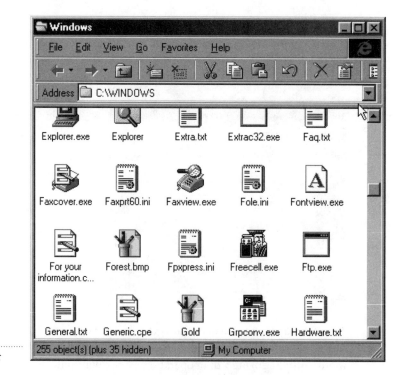

*Figure 3.53*

*Finding a target*

# Repairing Broken Shortcuts

Taking shortcuts—like leaping over crevasses—can sometimes be dangerous. Certain changes to an original object, if Windows can't keep track of them as they're made, break the link between it and its shortcut. For example, if you create a shortcut to a document and then either rename the document or move it to another folder, the shortcut might not be able to locate the original.

Shortcut to
General.txt

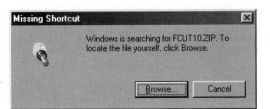

*Figure 3.54*

*"Best Guess"
shortcut*

Windows 98 does make an attempt to reestablish broken shortcut links, but it is limited to searching on the volume that held the original when the shortcut was created. If it can't find the file that the shortcut originally pointed to, it opens the local file that most closely matches the Properties of the original (Figure 3.54).

When it comes to repairing a broken shortcut, Windows 98 provides you with several options. The first and probably easiest option is simply to recreate the shortcut. Locate the original and then use one of the techniques we mentioned earlier to create a new shortcut. If you're not sure where the original was moved, use the Windows 98 Find utility to track it down.

Alternatively, bring up the shortcut's Properties sheet and enter the new file and directory information directly onto the Shortcut page. The shortcut is reestablished when you exit the sheet.

Finally, while Windows 98 is searching for the original (Figure 3.55) as part of its attempt to reestablish the link, you can click on the Browse button in the Missing Shortcut dialog box to bring up a simple file-browsing window. You can then click your way to the original's folder and reestablish the link manually.

*Figure 3.55*

*Missing Shortcut
dialog box*

# Fancy Fingerwork

Now that we've covered the basics of operating Windows 98, let's take a moment to relax and forget about all those fancy GUI (graphical user interface) advances like Taskbars and Explorers. It's time to regress. It's time to do what they did in the good old days of DOS: acquire some mind-blowing skills that will amaze your hacker friends, impress your boss, and limber up your fingers. We're going to provide you with enough keyboard shortcuts and insider tricks to let you fly through Windows 98 (see Table 3.1). If you take the extra time to memorize a few keyboard commands, you can save yourself from clicking through menus and dialog boxes, and instead get right to the point.

## Table 3.1  Keyboard Shortcuts

| Keystroke | Command |
|---|---|
| F1 | Start the Windows help system. |
| F2 | Rename an object. |
| F3 | Start the Find utility. |
| F4 | In the Explorer, display the drop-down list box that contains a system tree; in an Open or Save dialog box, display the Look In list. |
| F5 | Refresh the view or contents of a window (use if a disk's or folder's contents have changed since the window was opened). |
| F6 | Move the focus between the tree portion of the Explorer window and the contents portion. |
| F10 | Switch to menu mode. |
| Shift F10 | Display Context menu for selected object. |
| Ctrl A | Select all. |
| Ctrl C | Copy an object. |
| Ctrl V | Paste an object. |
| Ctrl X | Cut an object. |
| Ctrl Z | Undo last action. |
| Ctrl G | Choose the Go To command in the Explorer. |
| Delete | Mark a selected object for deleting by placing it in the Recycle Bin. |
| Shift Delete | Delete the selected object instantly, without first placing it in the Recycle Bin. |
| Ctrl Tab | Move forward through pages in dialog boxes. |
| Ctrl Shift Tab | Move backward through pages in dialog boxes. |
| Alt Enter | Display the Properties dialog box of an object. |
| Backspace | Go to the parent folder. |
| * on numeric keypad | Expand the entire Explorer tree under the current selection. |
| + on numeric keypad | Expand only the currently selected branch of the Explorer tree. |
| − on numeric keypad | Collapse the currently selected branch of the Explorer tree. |
| → | Expand a selected branch of the Explorer tree; if it's already expanded, step down to the first child folder. |

### Table 3.1  (continued)

| Keystroke | Command |
|---|---|
| ← | Collapse a selected branch of the Explorer tree; if it's already collapsed, step up to parent folder. |
| Ctrl arrow key | Scroll the Explorer tree without changing the current selection. |
| Ctrl Esc | Move the focus to the Taskbar and display Start menu. |
| Esc or Ctrl Esc | Move the focus to the Taskbar (use Tab and then Shift F10 to access Context menus for objects; use Tab and arrow keys to switch among tasks; use Tab to go to the desktop). |
| Alt Tab | Switch to the next running application. |
| Alt M | Minimize all open windows and move the focus to the desktop. |
| Alt S | When no windows are open and no items are selected on the desktop, display the Start menu (use arrow keys to select menu commands). |
| Win R * | Bring up the Run dialog box. |
| Win M | Minimize all open windows. |
| Shift Win M | Undo the Minimize All command. |
| Win F1 | Help. |
| Win E | Start the Explorer utility. |
| Win F | Use the Find utility to locate files or folders. |
| Ctrl Win F | Use the Find utility to locate a computer resource. |
| Win Tab | Cycle through the buttons on the Taskbar. |
| Win Break | Display System Properties dialog box. |
| Ctrl drag | Copy a file into another folder on the same storage volume (instead of moving it). |
| Ctrl Shift drag | Create a shortcut. |
| Alt double-click | Display the Properties sheet (dialog box) of an object. |
| Ctrl right-click | Show any alternate choices on an object's Context menu. |
| Shift double-click | Explore the selected object; if there is no Explore command for the selected object, issue the default action for the object (typically, Open). |
| Shift click the Close button | Close a folder and all its parent folders. |
| Shift insert a CD | Bypass the AutoPlay function for audio CDs and CD-ROMs. |

*Note: The Win key—which sports a small Windows icon—was originally available only on Microsoft Natural keyboards but has been showing up on better compatibles.

# Internetting Your Interface

All the above applies to the Windows 98 Explorer in "classic" mode, meaning as close to the Windows 95 Explorer as you can get. It's also possible to make the Windows 98 Explorer into something closely resembling Internet Explorer 4.0. However, since Microsoft passionately wants Windows to suit everyone who might use it, they've made it possible to go from one to the other in nearly imperceptible gradations.

Having tried it both ways, we think you'll be happiest with something in between the two extremes—at least while you're settling in to a new operating system. So we'll cover the new features one by one and let you take your pick.

## Toolbars

We've already mentioned the three-for-one Windows Toolbars—the **Standard Buttons, Address Bar,** and **Links Menu.** Here are the Explorer defaults for all three:

**Standard Buttons.**  **Back** takes you back to the locations you visited recently in Explorer, with the most recent first. If you want the map of where it's going, click on the little downward-pointing triangle next to the icon; the drop-down list will show your most recent nine locations. (The buffer in the icon has room for a lot more locations than that, so you're not stuck if you try to go back past nine. You will, though, eventually hit the rear wall of your travels, at which point the Back arrow will vanish.)

**Forward,** not unreasonably, retraces Back. This means that, if you're at your most recent destination, the Forward arrow has nowhere to go, so it's grayed out.

**Up** takes you to the parent object of the one you're sitting on, in either the Tree or the Contents pane. If you're sitting on a folder, Up jumps you to the drive object; from a drive it jumps you to My Computer; from My Computer it jumps you to the Desktop and grays itself out, having no place above that to go.

**Map Network Drive** and **Disconnect Network Drive** let your local computer attach and detach your network drive shares. These aren't installed on your system unless it's networked, and they also don't appear by default; you have to pull down the **View** menu, click **Folder Options...,** click the **View** tab, go to the **Advanced settings** dialog and check **Show Map Network Drive** button in toolbar.

**Cut,** as usual, sends a copy of an object to the Clipboard and removes it from the original location. If the object you're removing is particularly important or if it has stuff (like subfolders) underneath it, cutting it won't make it vanish immediately, but will make its colors turn paler, as if it were being dragged. Only when you paste it into another location will it disappear from the place where it was cut. It's sort of a keyboard drag-and-drop.

**Copy** creates a copy of the highlighted object on the Clipboard, up to a point; it'll copy any file or folder (and the folder we tested with contained 50MB) but not a drive, not even a floppy. It's true that, if you tried to copy all of C: to the Clipboard, you'd encounter formidable overflow...

**Paste** takes the contents of the Clipboard and pastes it to the highlighted location, with some smarts in the process; if you have a folder in the Paste buffer and paste it to another folder, the pasted folder becomes a subfolder of the target folder. Also, if you have a file highlighted called *object.obj* and you hit Copy and Paste without moving—thus threatening to create two objects with the same name in the same folder, a filesystem no-no—the pasted copy is named "Copy of *object.obj*" to forestall the collision.

**Undo** undoes whatever boneheaded thing you just did. By the way, as we'll keep telling you, the keyboard equivalent for Undo is Ctrl Z.

**Delete** asks you for permission to send whatever's highlighted to the Recycle Bin. Consistent with the Delete function elsewhere, Shift Delete asks you for permission to blow it, or them, away entirely. Like Copy, Delete will work on a file or folder but not a drive.

**Properties** opens the Properties sheet of the highlighted object. In the Contents pane it will create a Properties sheet for highlighted multiple objects, but since that only contains the information that all objects have in common, it's not terribly informative. (You can't highlight multiple objects in the Tree pane.)

**Views,** on successive clicks, cycles through the four Contents pane views—**Large Icons, Small Icons, List, Details.** If you want to get to one particular view, use the drop-down list, although it's not clearly faster than successive clicks.

**Address Bar.** The **Address Bar,** when used with local data, gives you the full path (one might stretch and say the URL) of the device or folder you have highlighted in the Tree pane. It's handy if the folder you're examining in the Tree pane has scrolled out of sight, but since it completely refuses to jump the fence and give you the full path of any object in the Contents pane, it seems underpowered.

If you hit the drop-down arrow in the Address Bar, what you get is no more than a copy of the Tree pane—and not even the whole thing, but just the top eleven-plus lines.

**Links Bar.** As Windows 98 arrives in your computer, the **Links Bar** contains five buttons:

**Best of the Web** takes you to the Best of the Web site at `home.microsoft.com`, which changes weekly and features sites selected for educational and entertainment value. It's nowhere near as feisty as Yahoo!'s Weekly Picks, but the sites do have merit.

**Channel Guide** connects you to the Microsoft Active Channel Guide, with several picks daily of channels for News & Technology, Sports, Business, Entertainment, and Lifestyle & Travel.

**Customize Links** takes you to a local page, supplied by an Internet Explorer .DLL, that explains how to beef up and rearrange Internet Explorer and the Links Bar until they suit you.

**Internet Explorer News** takes you to, guess what, the Microsoft Internet Explorer home page.

**Internet Start** (Figure 3.56) is the Microsoft "personal content" page with news and stock quotes; you can customize it.

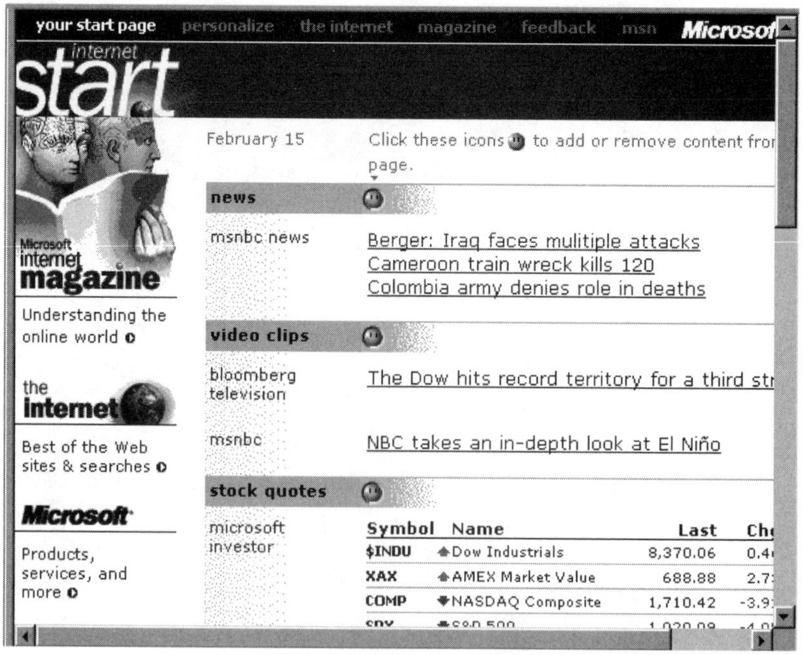

*Figure 3.56*

Internet Start page

While you're working within the Links Bar, your Standard Buttons become Internet Explorer controls: **Back** with a drop-down, **Forward** with a drop-down, **Stop, Refresh, Home, Search, Favorites, History, Channels, Fullscreen, Mail** and **Print**. See Chapter 16, "Your Own Private Internet," for more detail.

> If you don't like the top-to-bottom order your Explorer toolbars are in, you can shuffle or undock them. Left-click on the title area of the toolbar, drag it, the cursor will change to the Move four-headed arrow, and the toolbar will follow the pointer till you drop it where you want it.

 **Explorer Bars.** The Explorer Bars are alternative left-pane contents for the Explorer or Internet Explorer. In Explorer you get, by default:

**Search.** Connect to your search engine of choice—although you can have `home.microsoft.com` or the "Provider-of-the-day" if you're allergic to decisions—and plonk it in the left pane. This way you can have your search engine in the left pane, your search target in the right pane, and not have to keep flicking your back and forward arrows all the time.

**Favorites.** The same as menu-bar Favorites or Start Menu\Favorites, but if you're (for example) methodically working your way through your saved list of Civil War Web sites, it can be handy to have it sitting in a pane where it's persistent, rather than on a pop-up or drop-down menu where it's not.

**History.** Your history of visited locations, in a tree-structured format more highly organized than the old Internet Explorer History pane. It looks like Figure 3.57, with the day as the top-level icon, the Web domain names as the next level down, and the URLs of the individually visited pages as the bottom level. If you Explored any of the HTML on your local computer, its URLs are

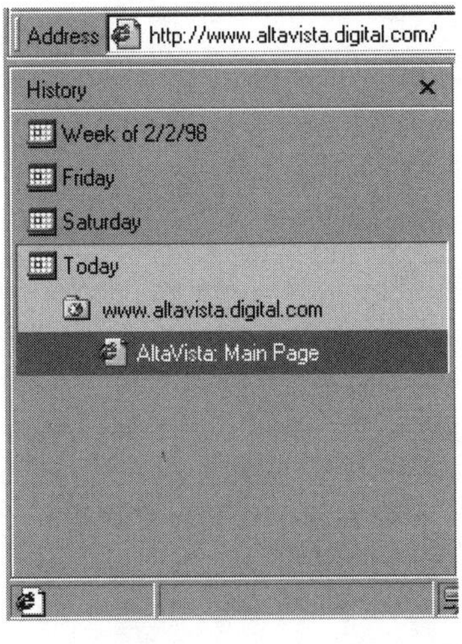

*Figure 3.57*

*Internet Explorer history*

in here too. Naturally, almost all of the URLs get truncated by the split bar, but when you hover your pointer you get the whole string in a Tooltip drop box.

 **Channels.** If you run the Active Desktop there isn't much point to having your Channels Explorer Bar enabled, since it's only a duplicate; but if you run the Classic Desktop, this is a nice place to keep your Channels.

 **If you find the Channel Bar or Channels Explorer Bar hard to read, there's a third choice of format—as always! \Channels is a subfolder of \Windows\Favorites, and each Channel category is a subfolder of \Channels. Switch back to the Tree-pane Explorer, cruise to \Windows\Favorites\Channels, and select Large Icons view (Figure 3.58) This is no unmixed blessing, since some Channel icons put garish commercials for themselves in the margin of the Contents pane.**

**All Folders.** This is the classic Explorer Tree pane with all your local stuff on it … and, incidentally, if you *lose* the Tree pane, this is where you get it back.

**None.** This makes the left pane go away. But then, so does the Close button in the top corner of the left pane, which is quicker.

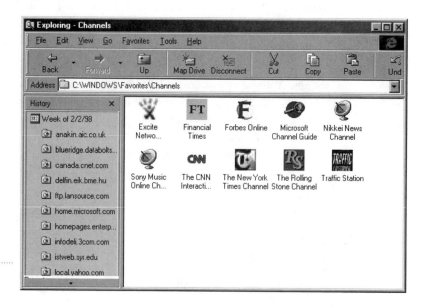

*Figure 3.58*

*Channel folder
Large Icons view*

# Turning On the Internet Features

The features that engage the Internet compatibility in Windows 98 are buried in several submenus of the Start Menu and the Explorer. Simply turning on the Active Desktop is a one-click pony, but if—as we suspect—you insist on picking and choosing among these prospective changes, the situation becomes more complex.

## Marked-Down Markup

The vast majority of the World Wide Web (except for what's Java, which involves programming) is written in a language called HTML: Hypertext Markup Language. For the historians among us, HTML began as a small specialized subset of something much bigger and more stuffy, called SGML, or Standardized General Markup Language, which IBM had a lot to do with.

In 1989, while Tim Berners-Lee was a software engineer at CERN—the European Particle Physics Laboratory in Geneva, Switzerland—he was trying to solve some of the problems scientists faced when they collaborated across the Net. One of the most important was that, while scientists tend to do lots of work involving graphs and illustrations, the Net of the pre-nineties displayed only plain text. Lack of graphical capability was a chokepoint in what was otherwise becoming, for the world scientific and academic community, a truly fabulous toy. (Okay, okay, people shared plenty of work too, but the Web never would have taken off if it hadn't been fun.)

Berners-Lee basically invented three things: HTTP, the Hypertext Transfer Protocol, which moved hypertext data from computer A to computer B without messing it up; HTML, a set of universal formatting instructions in plain text for the data being transferred; and the concept of the URL, Uniform Resource Locator, an address that would let your computer (computer B) go out and grab any piece of hypertext from anywhere on the Net (computer A) so long as everybody followed the rules.

Simple, clean, stingingly pure genius. Frankly, we hope Tim Berners-Lee gets a Nobel Prize for that while he's around to enjoy it. The same old text and bitmaps went racing around the Net, but now people had … *Web pages*. In the middle of 1993, there were fifty Web servers. By the end of 1994 there were 1,500. Today we couldn't begin to guess, but it's an absolute fact that the Web's model of information handling has come to dominate the universe of personal computing.

Along comes Microsoft, in its swashbuckling style, and pops the question: Do you want Web style to dominate your *personal* personal computer? And it's not an easy question. Read on.

# Activate the Desktop, Captain!

As we've noted, when you click on **Start Menu\Settings\Active Desktop,** you get three options: **View as Web Page, Customize my Desktop,** and **Update Now.**

When you click on View as Web Page, something amazing happens. (Windows always has worked hard behind the scenes.) The *entire interface* of your computer, instead of being the usual compiled code, switches over to HTML. You're clicking a button that says to Windows, "Rewrite the entire visible portion of the operating system in a different language, but keep it looking exactly the same." Talk about a show-stopper!

Actually, the show is a little *slower,* because HTML isn't as fast as Windows' other coding; it's what's called an *interpreted language,* meaning that every time you click on something that changes the interface, Windows has to re-read the instructions before it makes the change. (This is also part, but only part, of what makes Web pages appear slowly when you're browsing.) We have to say, though, that for an HTML interface the performance is adequate.

The advantage of restructuring the interface in HTML is that any other piece of HTML, from the Web or anyplace else, can become part of your Desktop just by sticking itself in the middle. With compiled code, that's harder to do; a compiled program is a sealed, seamless unit that can't (usually) be altered from the keyboard. HTML is a piece of running text that can be edited or rearranged at will, like a document.

Let's watch the HTML editing process happen. Click on **Start Menu\Settings\Active Desktop\Customize my Desktop;** Display Properties pops up with the Web tab selected. Internet Explorer Channel Bar, the Windows 98 default, should be checked; check it if it's not. Then check **View my Active Desktop as a web page** and **Apply,** and you'll see the Channel Bar appear, both in the preview screen on the Web tab and on the real screen behind the Properties sheet.

The Channel Bar, like any other group of hyperlinks on a Web page, is a group of icons that conceal hyperlinks to other Web sites—the channel content sites of Microsoft and its partners. Right now, it's the only thing on your Desktop that points to resources that aren't local; everything else is either on your computer or on your hard-wired network, which is what "local" means in this context.

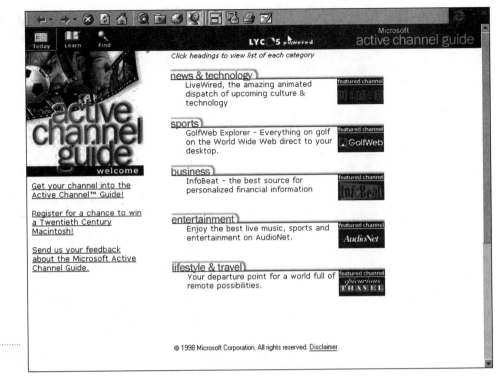

**Figure 3.59**

Microsoft Active
Channel Guide

This (Figure 3.59) is an invitation from Microsoft to visit the Active Desktop Gallery and download more hyperlinks (called *subscriptions*) for your Channel Bar. At this writing there are about a thousand available, with the cheerful assurance from Microsoft that "We're adding new Active Desktop items all the time!" Some of the subscriptions offered are The Weather Channel, ESPN SportsZone, the Microsoft Investor ticker, Fortune's personal stock chart, the AudioNet Jukebox, entertainment news from Paramount and Sony … the list goes on and, no doubt, on. If you want to go to Microsoft's Web-hosted repository of subscriptions, click Yes here.

 If something about the existing roster of Channels leaves you cold, you can publish your own Channel on the Microsoft Web content site, `http://www.iechannelguide.com`.

## The New Active Desktop Item Wizard

If you want to create a Channel Bar hyperlink and add it to your local system manually, we wish we could give you solid instructions, but in the time it's taken us to write this book, Microsoft has completely changed the format of the Active Channel Guide and the Channel management hyperlinks at least

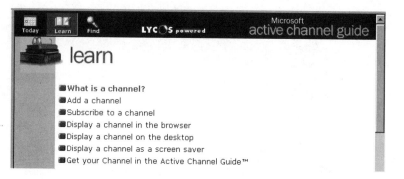

**Figure 3.60**

Microsoft Active
Channel Guide
Learn tab

three times. As of *right now,* here's what the Contents pane looks like (Figure 3.60). From the Active Channel Guide navigation bar, click the **Learn** tab. Your mileage may vary.

## Active Desktop Recap

Ultimately, because your Desktop is speaking the same language as all the Web content streaming onto its disk, your computer has become a Web participant of a kind that never existed before. Certainly it's not a Web server, fully occupied with pumping content out onto the Net. On the other hand, it's more tightly coupled to the Web than a computer running an old-style browser, a "viewer" program. Maybe we should call it a Web node.

## Local Control

You can control the Channel Bar without resorting to the Start Menu or Control Panel. The Channel Bar as it appears on the Desktop is borderless, but if you move your mouse pointer over it, it grows a gray border with two controls at the top: a drop-arrow and a Close button (Figure 3.61).

The drop-down menu is **Customize my Desktop**—that is, the Web tab of Display Properties—and **Close.** Both Close from the menu and the Close button dismiss the Channel Bar, but they don't uncheck View as Web Page; you're still running the HTML interface.

## Updating Automatically

The **Update All Subscriptions** dialog refreshes your Channel content. Active Desktop channels are constantly updated on the Microsoft or MSN servers, and as they are, the static copies on your own local disk become obsolete. (It's the price you pay for not having a full-time connection to Microsoft, but, hey …) The Update Subscriptions dialog keeps track of the channels you subscribe to and, when you log on to the Channel server, downloads the newest material for those channels.

**Figure 3.61**

On-mouse-over
channel bar controls

Don't assume that, because a channel arrives by default on the Windows 98 Channel Bar, you have all the local widgets you need to run it. Clicking on PointCast, for example, will take you to the PointCast Web site, where you'll receive instructions for downloading several megabytes of ActiveX controls and executables. Of course you *did* buy that 56K modem?

## Feature Creep

Now that you understand the principles behind the Active Desktop, you need to decide which ones you want—because you can pick and choose, although your options are sometimes limited.

Reach Folder Options any one of the several possible ways: **View\Folder Options** from the Explorer menu bar, **Settings\Folders & Icons** from the Start Menu, or the **Folder Options** button on the Web tab of Display Properties, which you can reach from either Control Panel\Display or Active Desktop\Customize my Desktop. All roads lead to Redmond! You're at the sheet now, right?

The General tab of Folder Options includes a dynamic preview and three click-options for Windows Desktop Update: **Web style, Classic style,** and **Custom.** The problem begins because, of the descriptions for the three options, only the one for Custom tells you anywhere near what you're going to get.

**Web style:** When the description says "Your computer looks and acts like the Web (e. g., single-click)" that "(e. g., single-click)" is masterfully sneaky and opaque. Here's what you get, so far as we can tell:

**Desktop:** The full-house Active Desktop, with a default Windows 98 logo and slate-blue background. We've seen some versions with a black background, which makes the Channel Bar (which is also black) look even slicker, but when the whole screen area is black, the contrast is hard on your eyes.

**Icons:** The icons themselves don't change, but the icon titles become underlined hyperlinks that default to white. The maximum contrast and the underlining make the titles as heavy as the icons; the Desktop looks cluttered.

**Pointer:** A standard mouse pointer over fallow Desktop turns into the universally known index-finger-pointing hand when the pointer moves within focus of a hyperlink. Right-click still works everywhere, thank heavens.

**Selection:** How do you single-click to select when you already single-click to execute? Well, you bring the mouse pointer to the object you want to select, and you let it linger there for a fraction of a second, till the highlight jumps to the object—no click needed. (Microsoft calls this behavior "hovering.") Well done, but one more thing to make the interface feel slightly reluctant; is this what Microsoft means when they say "acts like the Web?"

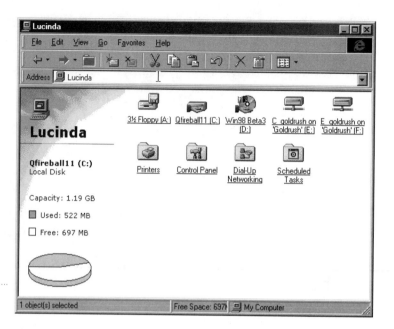

**Figure 3.62**

Drive object Web view

**Explorer Tree pane:** No change, because in fact, the Tree pane is *already* single-click to open, even in Classic style. Since the "styling" of the pane doesn't change, the pointer doesn't become a Web pointer and the object titles aren't underlined—good thing, since the tree would look really cluttered if they were.

**Figure 3.63**

Contents pane Web view of a graphics file

**Explorer Contents pane:** Of the whole environment, probably the best payoff. The blown-up icon in the top left corner can seem bulky if it's a plain folder, but the My Computer icon does well; My Computer also benefits from the page-like left margin of the pane, used to display the capacity, used and free space of any selected storage volume (Figure 3.62). If any graphics file is selected, the left margin makes room for a faithful thumbnail (Figure 3.63). Our only complaint is that, as noted, the Address bar gives the address of the selected object in the Tree pane, not of the selected object in the Contents pane—which violates the true spirit of a URL.

The Web-compatible Contents pane is really made for Large Icons view. If a file icon is highlighted, its full filename, file type, date and time modified, and size are in the pane margin anyway. The Small Icons and List views with so much underlining are hard to read, and the Details view for a folder with a lot of files takes up a ridiculous amount of room.

**Classic style:** As Classic as you can get, which may still leave you pining for some features of the Windows 95/NT 4 interface. Even if you've set Windows Desktop Update to **Classic style,** dropped the View menu again, and unchecked **as Web page**—yes, you may have to do both—you are still stuck, for example, with the swooshy "Net-ready" toolbars and Taskbar.

**Custom:** Definitely the way to go if, like us, you find the new OmniExplorer (note to Microsoft: You use that term, you pay us for it) interface to be an unsettling mixture of attraction and distraction. The Settings tab of Folder Options\Custom looks like Figure 3.64 and is quite a panel, actually, so let's discuss the options:

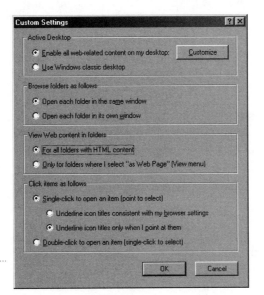

*Figure 3.64*

*Folder Options Custom settings*

### Active Desktop Region.

**Enable all web-related content on my desktop.** This should be labeled "Switch to HTML interface," a more straightforward description of what it does. The Customize button looks promising but is only yet another path to the Web tab of Display Properties.

**Use Windows classic desktop.** What you get isn't the Windows classic desktop, but this is the best place to start if you don't want a local environment that looks like a Web page.

### Browse folders ... Region.

**Open each folder in the same window.** This has one object—to reduce the number of open folders and therefore the amount of clutter on the Desktop. Objects are displayed in a window; if you click on one object within the window, that object opens in a child window that takes the place of its parent.

**Open each folder in its own window.** If you click on one object within a window, that object opens in a child window that spawns from, and overlaps, its parent. This makes it somewhat easier to trace your path through computing life, and it's handy if you want to examine lots of objects in the same folder, but it can leave you with a virtual haystack of windows to clean up by hand. Overall, you may prefer this method, especially since the Show Desktop button on the Taskbar makes it easy to tunnel through the mess with one click.

### View Web content ... Region.

**For all folders with HTML content.** This should read "Convert all folders *into* HTML content." If you click this, you can modify the folder's content, styles, and colors just as if you were writing HTML, because you are. My Computer and Control Panel are exempt; they're HTML already, and read-only.

**Only ... where I select "as Web Page".** You might *think* that if you highlight a folder or a Contents pane object, then click this button, it would convert the view of *only* this folder's Contents pane into the Web content view, leaving the others alone. We might think it was meant to be that way, too; but at the moment, clicking this button puts *all* folders across all drives into Web view, and unclicking it returns them to their former state, whatever it was.

### Click items ... Region.

**Single-click to open ... Underline icon titles consistent with my browser settings.** Naturally enough, this makes scant sense unless you know where Internet Explorer's underline settings are. In Internet Explorer, go to **View\Internet Options,** click on the **Advanced** tab, and look for **Browsing\Underline links,** where you'll find three choices: **Always, Never,** and **Hover.** In other words, you can have Internet Explorer show hyperlinks as always underlined, never underlined, or underlined only when your pointer is near them. If you then choose this item in Custom Settings, the behavior of your local links on the Desktop, in the Explorer Contents Pane, or elsewhere, will exactly match the setting for Internet Explorer.

Before you start thinking that it would be scary to have Internet hyperlinks with no underlining at all, bear in mind that the colors of visited and unvisited links can be set to suit yourself, and that the mouse pointer over a link still changes to the pointing finger. In short, there's still plenty to indicate a link even without underlining, and we think that if you set Internet Explorer's **Advanced\Browsing** option to **\Underline links\Never,** you'll like the clean appearance. Try it for your Web-cruising first, and if you prefer it, use this option to match up your Web and local environments; you'll banish underlined links from your computing experience.

**Single-click to open … Underline icon titles only when I point at them.** To continue the thought, this says "Set my Desktop and Explorer to \Underline links\Hover even if my Internet Explorer is set to something else." This will be the option for you if you want to keep the Web's classic appearance but cut down on underlining locally.

You notice what you can't say here? "Give me single-click, underline *everything* on the Web, and underline *nothing* on the Desktop." Sorry!

**Double-click to open …**

This is the way Windows has always worked. It's not as slick as single-click, but it does have the merit of positive action. Or you might have double-click so firmly embedded in your thumb or fingertip that you'll just *never* get it out of there.

Even after you have your Active Desktop set up, you won't want it on all the time—trust us. Here's the fastest way to switch back and forth. Right-click on the Desktop, click Active Desktop on the Context menu, and:

*Active to Classic:* click **View as Web Page** to uncheck it.

*Classic to Active:* click **View as Web Page** to check it.

# Summary

If you didn't read this chapter, you are missing out on vital features new to Windows 98, and you have some questions to answer, of which the most important is "The Web is a nice place to visit but do I really want to live there?" Worse yet, unless you're up to speed with the material in this chapter, whole vast meadows and mesas of this book won't make a lot of sense. Go back right now and read about the four new interface tools—My Computer, the Taskbar, the Explorer, and Internet Explorer—and learn how they can help you move around, look at the stuff in your computer, and manipulate just about anything you want. It's important to be able to find things like folders and documents; if you don't know how, you can waste a lifetime (or more) looking for lost files. For keyboard crazies, we offer great shortcuts for getting where you want to go (today) without using the new graphical user interface tools it took Microsoft programmers years to develop.

# 4

# Ready, Set, Run!

Windows 98 comes even closer than its predecessor, Windows 95, to being the universal operating system. It will run applications created for three platforms—32-bit Windows, 16-bit Windows, and DOS—as robustly (well, mostly) as any operating system ever written for those platforms. You can confidently use everything from programs written in the early 1980s for a text-based operating system—MS-DOS—to the very latest 32-bit applications developed for Windows NT and used on high-end workstations and servers. This flexibility, which allows you to use over fifteen years' worth of software developed for Intel *x*86-based computers, is unprecedented in the history of computing. The comparatively minor tradeoff is that, if you mean to use all or even most of the power inherent in the newest Windows interface, you've got some learning to do.

# Jump Start

No matter what type of application you run—Win32, Win16, or DOS—Windows 98 offers many ways to start a program. There's the *nouvelle,* object-oriented way we discussed in preceding chapters: you double-click on an object, and Windows 98 figures out how to present that object to you. If you've clicked on an application, Windows 98 runs it. If the object represents a data file, Windows 98 loads the appropriate application together with the file, ready for you to edit.

Of course, since we're talking about Windows, there's more than one way to start a program. You can start applications using any of Windows 98's three main interface tools: the **Taskbar, My Computer,** or the **Explorer.** Each provides its own way to get at the objects on your system. Perhaps the most convenient is the Taskbar, with its primal Start button—an excellent place to begin our tour.

## Hit Start

Nested within the many branches of the **Start Menu** are entries for virtually every application you have installed on your PC. To launch an application, find the appropriate Start menu item and click (Figures 4.1 and 4.2).

There are entries for the bundled Windows 98 mini-applications, as well as for system maintenance tools such as the Backup program. Windows applications installed after Windows itself create custom Start menu entries as part of the installation process.

*Figure 4.1*

*The Start menu*

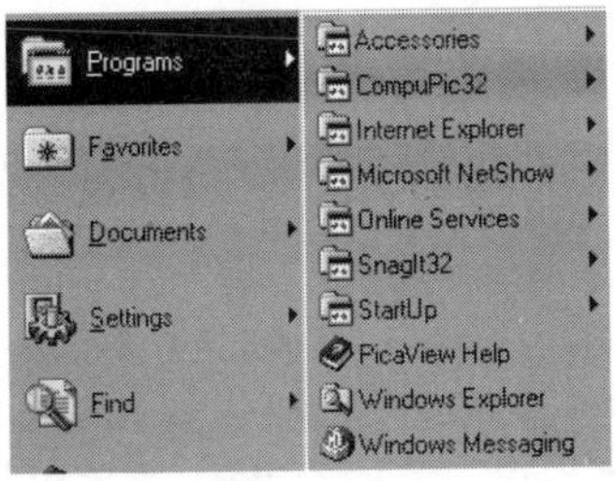

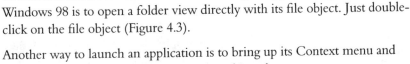

**Figure 4.2**

The Programs
submenu

When Windows 98 is first installed, application program entries are arranged together under the **Programs** submenu. In Chapter 6, you'll learn how to customize this menu structure, as well as modify other aspects of the Start button's behavior.

## Use a Folder View

red-corvette....

**Figure 4.3**

Launching from
a file object

The second most common method of starting an application program in Windows 98 is to open a folder view directly with its file object. Just double-click on the file object (Figure 4.3).

Another way to launch an application is to bring up its Context menu and select the Open item. When you open an object that represents a program, Windows 98 runs it. You can also start an application by creating a Shortcut to its file object and clicking on it to run the program. Mini-tip: Keep Shortcut icons on your Desktop for the applications you use most frequently, so you can get to them quickly. This method gives you flexibility, because you can move the Shortcut anywhere you like.

**Figure 4.4**

Drag-and-drop a
Shortcut

If your Desktop gets crowded, park related Shortcuts in a folder (Figure 4.4). Here we see a text file Shortcut's "ghost" being dragged to a newly created Desktop folder called Text Files. When the highlight shifts to the Text Files folder, simply unclick the left mouse button, and the Shortcut will "drop" into the folder, vanishing from the Desktop.

Finally, you can take advantage of the object-oriented nature of Windows 98 to bring up an application by double-clicking on an associated data file. For example, if you double-click on a Windows bitmap (.BMP) image, Windows launches the Paint accessory with the file preloaded and ready for editing (Figure 4.5).

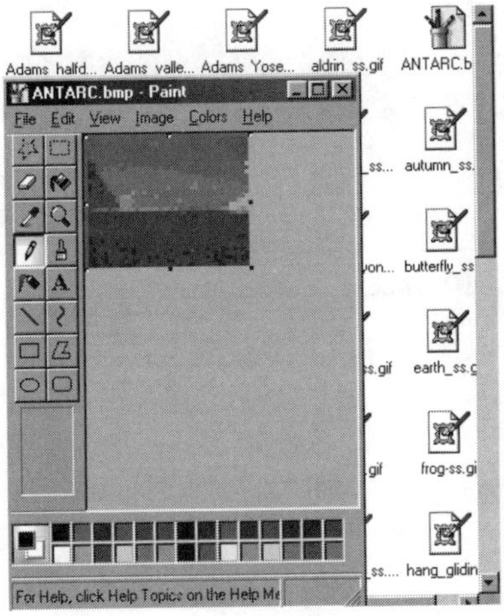

**Figure 4.5**

Paint with an
image loaded

## Instant Files

Windows 98 enables you to create a new document file without having to load the corresponding program first. Use the Windows right-click menu system to create new data files for most Windows applications, just as if you were grabbing a fresh, blank sheet from a pad or a book of forms. First click the right mouse button while the cursor is hovering inside a folder view (which can be the Windows desktop) and open the **New** submenu. You see a list of data file types, as well as more common entries, such as folders. Select **WordPad Document,** for example

*Figure 4.6a*

*New menu at desktop*

(Figure 4.6a), and Windows 98 creates a new document in the current folder view. You can rename the document (Figure 4.6b), and Windows 98 loads it into WordPad, ready for your input.

If an application you launch is an MDI program—that is, if it opens document

*Figure 4.6b*

*Newly created data file*

windows within its own application window—you can drag and drop to open data files for editing. Drag a data file from its folder view and drop it onto the title bar of the target program's application window (Figure 4.7). If the program is maximized, click on its Restore button—or select Restore from the System menu—and resize the window so that you can see both the folder view of your data files and the application's title bar.

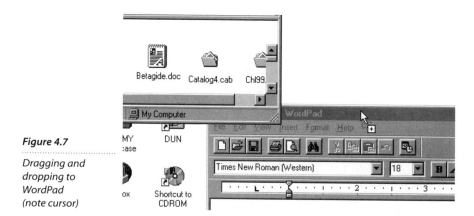

*Figure 4.7*

*Dragging and dropping to WordPad (note cursor)*

## Launching Applications from an MS-DOS Command Prompt

As part of its support for DOS applications, Windows 98 provides a Start menu item—the **MS-DOS prompt**—that brings up a DOS command prompt, indicating that DOS is running. The $\boxed{\text{Alt}}\boxed{\text{Enter}}$ keystroke will toggle between full-screen DOS and a DOS window ("DOS box") on the Windows 98 desktop.

*Figure 4.8*

*Starting an application from a command prompt*

Virtually all DOS commands are supported during an MS-DOS command prompt session. You can also launch both DOS and Windows application programs directly from a command prompt (Figure 4.8). To do so, you use the DOS Change Directory command cd\, then enter the name of the program's folder. To start Eric Isaacson's ZIPKEY from the root directory of the drive, for example, you would first type cd\zipkey and press the $\boxed{\text{Enter}}$ key to enter that folder, then type zipkey 2 (where **2** is a parameter that governs the way the program runs) and press $\boxed{\text{Enter}}$ to run the program.

A launched DOS program takes over the command prompt and maintains control of a session until it has finished executing. It then returns you to the command prompt. In contrast, when you launch a Windows program, Windows 98 only loads the program into a window before returning you to the command prompt.

Two convenient ways to start a program have been part of every 32-bit version of Windows: typing the program's name at the MS-DOS command prompt, and using the **Start** command in conjunction with the MS-DOS command prompt.

# The Run Dialog Box

The final way to launch an application directly is to select **Run** from the Start menu. This brings up a **Run Application** dialog box, into which you can enter the pathname of any application you'd like to launch (Figure 4.9). If the program is in a folder that Windows knows about (that's *on the path*) you can simply type the name of the program, as we have here.

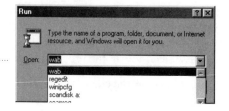

**Figure 4.9**

The Run application dialog box

If the folder's not on the path, you type the path to the program files into the **Open** field. For example, to launch Word from the Run Application dialog box, the pathname is typically something like `c:\winword\winword.exe`. Then you click on the OK button, and Windows 98 launches the program.

Windows 98 maintains a list of programs that have been launched recently from the Run Application dialog box. This means you can repeat a Run operation without reentering the entire pathname. Simply expand the drop-down list box—part of the Open field—and click on the matching entry (Figure 4.10).

**Figure 4.10**

The list of recently launched applications

Since the Run Application list box has the potential to contain sensitive information (it is, after all, a consecutive list of every program you've recently launched with the Run command), you might find it handy to clear it occasionally. Use the top command of the **Paranoia** tab of TweakUI.

To locate an application, use the **Browse** dialog box, which you can bring up by clicking on the **Browse** button in the Run Application dialog box (Figure 4.11). The Browse dialog box provides you with a wealth of information. For starters, it includes a folder view of your desktop; you can navigate this view

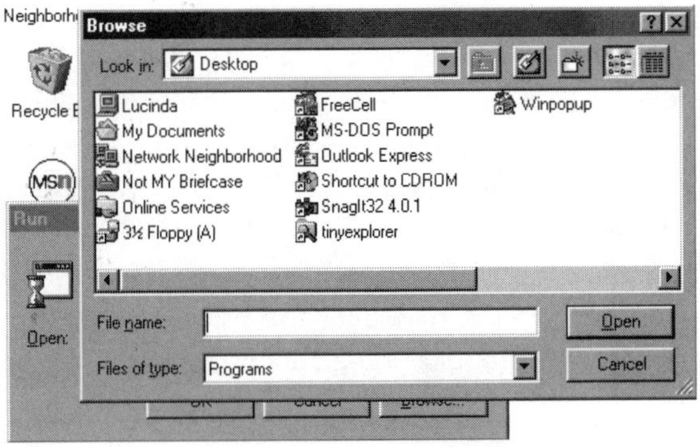

*Figure 4.11*

*The Browse dialog box*

as you would any other. You can also perform maintenance tasks, such as creating a new folder, by using the right mouse button to bring up the view's pop-up menu. Finally, a drop-down list box labeled **Look In** enables you to switch among volumes, including network drives. If you know what kind of file you're trying to find, you can select its type from the **Of Type** dialog box (which is set to **All Files and Folders** by default).

When you are already working (or playing) on your computer, you can access the Browse dialog box by double-clicking on folder icons. For example, in order to find Word—located in this example in the WinWord folder on the C: volume—first open the **My Computer** folder, then the volume storing the Word program. Finally, burrow through the folder structure until you find the folder containing the Word program files (Figure 4.12).

Selecting the WinWord icon causes Word to fill in its file name automatically. Clicking on the Open button returns you to the Run Application dialog box, with the complete pathname now stored in the Open field. Click once more, this time on the OK button, and Word is launched.

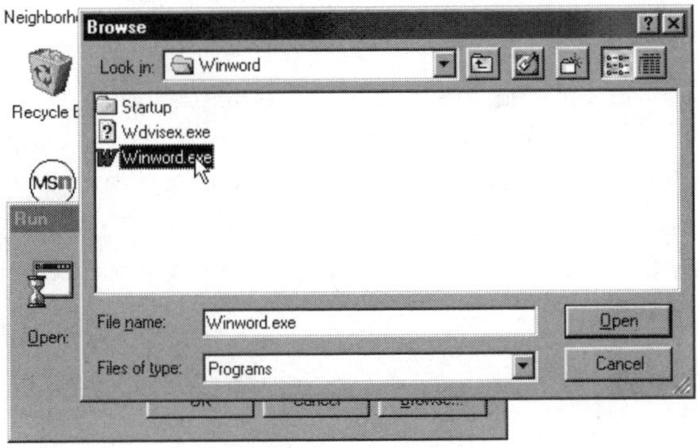

*Figure 4.12*

*Selecting an application program with the Browse dialog box*

## The Documents Submenu

**Figure 4.13**

*The Documents submenu*

Though the integration is smooth enough that you might not notice, this approach to launching a program incorporates the once-revolutionary notion of object orientation into interface design. 32-bit Windows enables you to launch a program through the data file type associated with it. Because the data—rather than the application that was used to create it—is the focus, you have a more direct approach to your work. In other words, Windows is beginning to work more like you do, focusing more on content and less on technique.

Having learned the trick of launching programs by association, 32-bit Windows leverages this knowledge by remembering which data files you used most recently. Windows 98 maintains a list of up to 15 of those files ready for access in the **Documents** submenu of the Start Menu (Figure 4.13) with your most recently used data file at the top of the menu. You can click on it to bring up the appropriate editing tool (such as Word or Excel), then load the file automatically.

Only data files that are opened directly—by clicking on the filename and letting Windows use OLE to open the application—are listed in the Documents submenu. If you load the application and then use File Open or the File drop-down list to open a data file, the file will not be listed in the Documents submenu.

## Programs A-Go-Go

Once you start a program with Windows 98, myriad opportunities are available to you. Any application will let you create, open, save, and close data files. You can also multitask to your brain's full extent, and copy and paste with the Windows 98 Clipboard. How much you can do depends on the range of your application.

OLE—Object Linking and Embedding, the technology that (for example) lets you insert a spreadsheet or graph into the middle of a text document—is a powerful mechanism for sharing data among applications, but is not always built into software programs. When you shop for Windows software, look for programs that support OLE. Products that exploit this technology offer more flexibility and are more intuitive to use.

# File Operations

Most applications use the procedures developed by Microsoft for opening, saving, and closing files. Read on for more details.

**Open.**  To load a data file into a running Windows application, select **Open** from the File menu. The application presents you with a dialog box showing

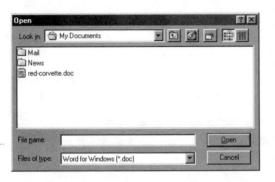

a folder view of available data files and folders (Figure 4.14).

We're using WordPad as an example, and if this dialog box looks familiar, that's because it's used by the Browse function of the Run Application dialog box. In fact, aside from its title (which changes from one program to the next), this dialog box is universal to all Windows 98 applications. It incorporates several powerful features.

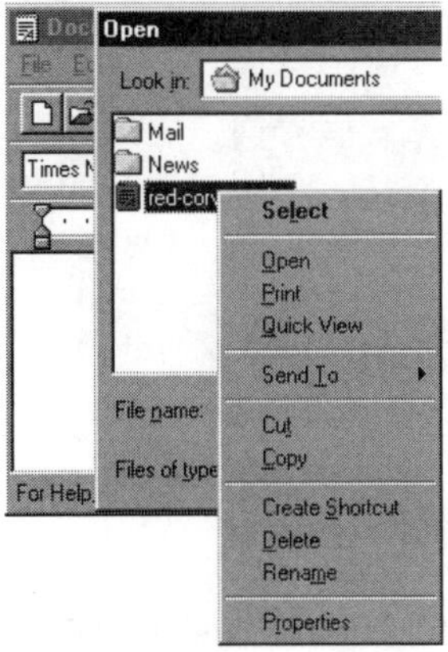

*Figure 4.14*

*The Open dialog box*

First, the folder view itself is fully functional. You can copy, rename, delete, and create new files and folders just as you would in a view opened from a volume icon. Click the right mouse button to open the view's pop-up menu, then select the desired action (Figure 4.15).

*Figure 4.15*

*Open dialog context menu*

The Open dialog box also provides a limited version of the folder view toolbar (Figure 4.16). It includes an **Up One Level** button for navigating "upward" (closer to the root) in the folder hierarchy, as well as buttons for selecting **List** or **Details** view (no Large Icons view is provided). A **Create Folder** button creates a new folder within the currently selected folder view. A **View Desktop** button climbs to the "top" of the filesystem tree and puts the Desktop in the Look In field. Applications more tightly integrated with Windows offer additional buttons, like **Look In Favorites**, **Add To Favorites**, **Preview**, or **Commands and Settings.**

*Figure 4.16*

*The WordPad toolbar*

Microsoft is somewhat playing with our heads here. On the WordPad toolbar there's a button, showing some objects on an old-fashioned desk blotter, called **View Desktop**; as noted, it puts the Desktop in the Look In field, giving you the loftiest possible view of your filesystem. On the Windows 98 Taskbar there's a button, exactly the same one, called **Show Desktop**—but what *it* does is minimize all your running applications at one click and show you the Desktop. Conceptually, they're … the same thing … sort of. However, the *effect* is quite distinct, since one just climbs to a different perspective on the filesystem, while the other one (which we actually like a lot) makes your whole, cluttered workspace topple like a bulldozed movie set.

To make navigating across volumes easier, the **Look In** drop-down list box provides access to all your PC's attached volumes, including network drives. Click on the list box and select the desired volume; the folder view is updated automatically to reflect the new volume's contents (Figure 4.17).

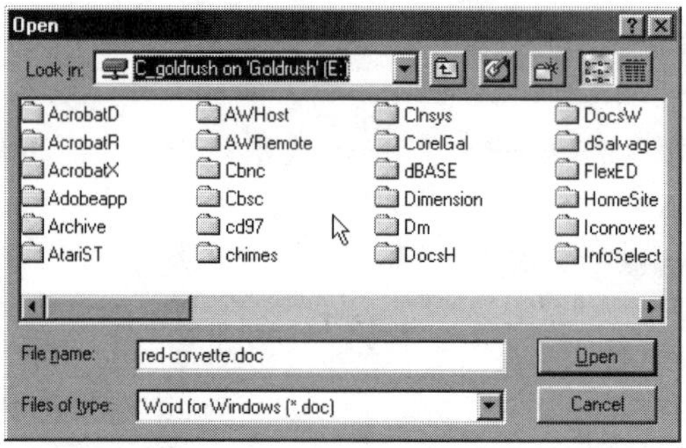

Finally, a **Files of type** drop-down list box filters the information in the folder view to display only data file objects that meet certain criteria—for example, Word documents. By default, this list box displays the file type of the application that presented the dialog box; for example, in Microsoft Word the list box is set to display Word files. (In WordPad the list box is set to display "Word for Windows" files, which is hilarious, because when Windows itself sees a "Word for Windows" file, it calls it a WordPad file.) However, you can override the default type and either broaden or narrow the search based on options presented in the box.

To open a data file, first use the navigational tools of the Open dialog box to locate the appropriate folder, then select the desired data file and click on the **Open** button. The application loads the data file, and you're on your way.

**Save.**  Saving a file is similar to opening one. In fact, when you select **Save As** from the File menu of an application, you see the same dialog box as when you select **Open,** except that a **Save** button replaces the **Open** button and a generic file name is proposed (Figure 4.18). Otherwise the two dialog boxes are identical, and you can perform the same navigational and maintenance chores in either by right-clicking to bring up the Context Menu for the folder view.

*Figure 4.17*

*A fully functional folder view*

**Figure 4.18**

The Save As
dialog box

To save a new data file in a Windows 98 application, select either **Save** or **Save As** from the File menu. If this is the first time the data has been saved, it has no name or a generic name, and the **Save As** dialog box appears regardless of which of the two menu items you chose. Type a name into the **File name** field and click the **Save** button. Windows 98 supports file names of up to 255 characters; it warns you if you exceed this limit or if you enter unacceptable punctuation.

If you're saving a file that has already been stored to disk, Windows 98 does not prompt you with the Save As dialog box unless you specifically choose it. If you select Save, Windows 98 assumes that you wish to save the data to the existing file, updating its contents.

The same thing happens with a so-called empty data file. You create an empty file by choosing the **New** menu option in a folder view, then double-clicking either on the data file itself or on the **Open** menu item within the application. Selecting **Save** does not bring up the Save As dialog box because, even though the new data file object is empty, it already exists as a file object on a volume.

Normally you want to save a file under the name you first assigned it. Sometimes, however, you want to change the name of a file. For example, you might keep several revisions of the same document by saving them under different file names. Fortunately, virtually all File menus in Windows applications provide the Save As option. Selecting **Save As** brings up the Save As dialog box so that you can enter a new file name, although the current one is proposed (Figure 4.19).

**Figure 4.19**

Selecting the Save
As menu item

**Close.** If you use an application based on the older, MDI interface, you'll discover a third universal File menu option: **Close.** Close tells the application to remove the currently selected data file from memory and close its disk file. Close is useful when you work with multiple documents simultaneously. As you finish with a document, you can close it to free up memory and unclutter the application window. Microsoft suggests that Windows 98 applications not use MDI but instead place documents in independent windows, eliminating the need for a Close command on the File menu.

Older applications, especially Win16 applications written for Windows 3.1, can't access the new common dialog boxes for opening and saving data files. Those applications use an older, text-based dialog box familiar to users of 16-bit Windows. Most of the old-style dialog boxes include a Help button; click on it or press the [F1] key for further instructions.

# Win32 Applications

32-bit operating systems were developed specifically to take advantage of today's 32-bit microprocessors. Windows NT, Mac OS, UNIX, and Linux are all uncompromisingly 32-bit. But Windows 98, like Windows 95 before it, has to bend over backwards to provide Win16 compatibility; so it makes its living as a hybrid operating system, designed partly for 16-bit systems, partly for 32-bit systems. Windows 98 can run newer 32-bit programs, but still contains several core components from its Win16 heritage, and runs almost all 16-bit Windows software perfectly.

Win32 programs, the latest and greatest, can take advantage of large amounts of RAM and can handle sophisticated tasks involving, for example, audio, video, or graphics editing. If you're running a performance-hungry type of application, a Win32 program will probably work better than its Win16 counterpart.

Win32 programs also run—in most cases, better—under Windows NT, so any investment you make in these more advanced applications will continue to pay off if you upgrade to NT Workstation or NT Server.

Win32 applications are better integrated with Windows itself and can take control of the Desktop directly. For example, an electronic mail application can use a custom icon in the Taskbar's notify area to alert you when a new message has arrived. There's no doubt about it: a Win32 version of an application will incorporate the latest code from the vendor, will work as smoothly as possible under Windows 98, and will help you get the most out of your computer.

# How Do I Know?

Armed with the knowledge above, you walk into a retail software store, pick up a shrink-wrapped box, and wish you had Superman's X-ray vision to help you see through the cardboard. "Oh, yes, sir or ma'am," the salesdroid assures you blandly, "that's the very latest version." But, assuming you want 32-bit, how can you be sure that's what you're buying?

To begin with, retail software stock is *probably* 32-bit just because it's so fresh. Software retailers, operating on thin margins in a viciously competitive industry, give shelf space only to programs that don't linger on the shelves; inventory turnover and restocking are rapid. Besides, power users have an irritating habit of asking for the newest version of anything for a week before it arrives, so having new versions in stock is a certified path to extra profits. (Power users are people you want in your store, early and often.)

**Figure 4.20**

Windows 95
compatibility logo

Your next line of defense is Microsoft's own *Logo Compatibility Program.* When Windows 95 appeared in the stores, in August 1995, its look-alike version of Windows NT was waiting in the wings. In preparation for a smooth launch, Microsoft was determined to have a broad selection of solid 32-bit programs available to purchasers. So it offered a sizable incentive to software developers; any pure Win32 program that ran cleanly on *both* Windows 95 *and* Windows NT 4.0 could print the logo shown in Figure 4.20 on its box, and buyers—especially corporate buyers—would plunk down lots of money for it.

When Windows 98 appeared, the logo was updated to that shown in Figure 4.21.

But the principle stands; it certifies untroubled operation. So look for either of these logos, and you'll know you're 32-bit-clean.

**Figure 4.21**

Windows 98
compatibility logo

Your final protection is your own common sense. Does the box say "System requirements: Windows 3.1 or higher?" Does it say "Compatible with Windows and Windows 95?" How about "Runs with all versions of Microsoft Windows?" These are Win16 applications with packaging cleverly updated for a Win32 audience and, oddly enough, they can be excellent bargains once you understand what you're buying. A Win16 program that retailed for $50, $70 or $100 when it first appeared may be on sale now for $30 or less—and work well for you in an application that doesn't need 32-bit muscle. If you need to put three or four hundred names into a mailing list manager that will print labels for your holiday cards, you can *easily* get by with a Win16 program, and save yourself serious money. The rule about 32-bit major applications (above) doesn't say, and doesn't mean, that *every* piece of software on your system has to be Win32.

### *Don't Run Lots of Win16*

Unfortunately, there's one thing 16-bit Windows can't do that WOWEXEC can't do either—and that's let two applications share the CPU while they're both running. Any Win16 program needs complete control of the CPU in order to do anything. When two or more Win16 programs are running, WOWEXEC has to work like a square-dance caller, telling one "dancer" to stay in place and the next one to move along.

If you're running only one or two Win16 programs, WOWEXEC won't burn up a lot of machine cycles doing this kind of arbitration. But if you're running several, poor WOWEXEC spends almost as much energy directing traffic as it does providing memory and services to the program that's currently running. The result under WOWEXEC is the exact result you remember from Windows 3.*x*—your performance goes down the tubes. And, unlike most Windows performance bottlenecks, this one can't be overcome with more RAM. It's purely a question of slicing the CPU thinner with a faster and faster knife.

The upshot here is that the programs you use most often, whether your word processor, spreadsheet, personal information manager (PIM), presentation program, e-mail client, or Web browser, should be Win32 versions. Make it a rule to purchase the 32-bit version of any program you use more than twenty to thirty per cent of the time. This strategy has its price, but remember that 32-bit Windows software is an investment with a long future.

Microsoft did not control the programming of Win16 programs by independent companies as firmly as it laid down the 32-bit law a few years later. Some Win16 applications do things that WOWEXEC doesn't expect them to—or the other way around. The usual result is that these programs refuse to run under Windows 95 or 98.

A next-to-undocumented utility called MKCOMPAT sits in the System directory of Windows 95 or 98 systems, and gets overwhelmingly ignored because Microsoft never mentioned what it was good for. It convinces reluctant Win16 applications to run under Windows 9*x* the good old-fashioned way … by lying to them.

# Win16 Applications

From 1991 to 1995, all the software you could buy for Windows was Win16 software—that is, 16-bit applications designed for Windows 3.1 and 3.11. Naturally, there's as much Win16 software as DOS software out there today, since 16-bit Windows spurred the development of thousands of applications used by millions of people.

Win16 applications gain some 32-bit Windows look and feel when they run under the new environment. However, in many ways a Windows 3.1 program is still a Windows 3.1 program. For example, the more common dialog boxes don't look any different than they did under Windows 3.1, and many applications still use the old MDI interface system, which places documents in child windows within application windows. But applications like Microsoft Word 6.0 and 2.0, Microsoft Excel 5.0 and 4.0, and the 16-bit Windows versions of Corel Draw, WordPerfect, Lotus Approach, *etc., etc.,* remain elegant and powerful programs that still meet every need of the SOHO (small office, home office) user.

The excellence of the Win16 software base has Windows developers in a pickle. It was fairly easy, after all, to convince Windows 3.*x* users that upgrading from DOS to Windows application software was worth their time and money; there's not much use giving your computer a shiny new operating system and not buying the apps to go with it. But when the consumer market was urged to upgrade from Win16 to Win32, it wasn't quite as enthusiastic … especially when the developers promised that Win32 code would be a lot faster, and then it wasn't. (It was, and is, more stable, but the blunt truth is that if you want Win32 to go faster, you upgrade your hardware.)

Therefore, 32-bit Windows does a particularly effective job of making 16-bit Windows software feel comfortable. On any given computer, all Win16 applications are supported by a single VDM called WOWEXEC—Windows on Windows Executive or, sometimes, Win16 on Win32 Executive. It's reasonable to call WOWEXEC a Virtual Windows Machine, although that's not a term that Microsoft ever uses.

To keep a crashing Win16 application from bringing down the Win32 software in its vicinity, WOWEXEC runs in dedicated address space separate from all other user-level processes. It emulates a PC in software, just the way a DOS VDM does, and serves as a bilingual "gatekeeper," converting Win16 APIs and messages to and from Win32. Then the Win32 subsystem executes the translated calls. The worst you can say about this contraption, day in and day out, is that it imposes a lot of overhead and makes Win16 software slower than it might be; on the other hand, WOWEXEC does a better job of being 16-bit Windows than Windows 3.11 ever did. If a 16-bit Windows application crashes with a General Protection Fault (GPF) while it's running in WOWEXEC, it's probably poorly written software.

# Windows 98 and MS-DOS: Family, After All

Windows and DOS started out with a love-hate relationship that has mellowed over time, because neither party can get out of it. Windows is an operating system designed and optimized for the needs and the hardware of the twenty-first century. If your computer is powered by a fast 486 or a Pentium—or, absolutely, by the latest Pentium Pro or Pentium II—then 32-bit Windows is the *only* operating system that will connect with every one of its subsystems, put all the pedals to all the metal, and let you accomplish the phenomenal array of tasks that people feed to their computers today. A truly fast computer running only DOS is, to put it kindly, not all there.

On the other hand: The Windows that fills up a CD-ROM in 1998 began as a small and very hypothetical Microsoft project called the Interface Manager in 1982. Over eighty programmer-years, slippery with midnight oil and spilled free Coke, were consumed before Windows 1.0 even emerged as a retail product in late 1985. Since then Windows has gone through ten major version changes in thirteen years, and its development cost—that we can swear to—has been at least $10 billion. Possibly a lot more. You don't make $10 billion selling lemonade, but you *do* make it selling MS-DOS. Especially, you make it selling a copy of MS-DOS with every "IBM-compatible" computer that goes out every factory door ... whether it ever gets loaded on the disk or not. And MS-DOS, old and brittle as it may be, is entitled to ask where this young whipper-snapper Windows would ever have come from without all that money.

So Windows takes good care of DOS for old times' sake. Windows takes good care of DOS *applications* because, of the world's 150 million PC users, almost half still use DOS as their primary operating system and don't necessarily want to throw out all their software, at least not this minute. Even as a main platform, 32-bit Windows *cannot* take over the world unless it makes it easy for people to run DOS applications from time to time; this is especially true of accounting systems and other corporate software with potentially giant data files, either because the conversion of the data would be a huge costly job, or because there isn't equivalent 32-bit Windows software yet—or if there is, it's expensive. Therefore, Microsoft built full DOS compatibility—two flavors of it!—into Windows 95 and improved it materially in Windows 98.

To maintain this compatibility, Microsoft had to make certain compromises in 32-bit Windows, but the situation is improving. In Windows 98's DOS you cannot use long file names—ones longer than "eight-dot-three"—because, although Microsoft originally intended to incorporate this capability, it discovered that a longer file name would create incompatibilities with (i. e., break) DOS and older Windows programs. Compatibility was given priority over other design considerations.

In Windows 98 DOS, a long-named file is still handled according to its "DOS-compatible" eight-dot-three filename, but Windows maintains both names in parallel tables, and if you issue the `dir` command in a DOS box, the listing of a long-named file contains both names, like this:

```
19AWIN~1 DOC 220,160 10-19-97 12:35p 19aWin98Bible.doc
```

Another improvement in Windows 98 DOS's handling of long-named files surfaces in the **copy** command, where DOS will let you get away with a long filename—after a fashion:

```
copy a:jul98bud.xls c:July 98 Budget.xls
```

will result in a file called **July 98 Budget.xls** in whatever folder you were pointing to on your C: drive. Of course that's its Windows name; DOS will call it **July98~1.xls.**

# The START Command

Windows 98 introduces the **start** command, a DOS equivalent of the Windows run command, which it inherits from Windows NT. Start will run a Windows program in a DOS box; if you type

```
start notepad
```

Windows will start a copy of Notepad. It also respects the associations that you or your programs have stored in File Types; if you type

```
start july98~1.xls
```

Windows will start a copy of Excel with `July 98 Budget.xls` loaded into it—always assuming that you have Excel installed and that Excel is associated with the file type **.XLS.**

**start** has some cool command-line switches that let you specify how Windows displays an application once it is loaded. For example, if you want to load a program now but don't plan to use it until later, you can load it in a minimized state, so that only its Taskbar button is visible on the screen.

Here are some variations on the **start** command:

- `start winword` Starts Word (a Windows application) and returns control to the command prompt.

- `start doom` Starts Doom (a DOS game) in its own window.

- `start /m pbrush` Starts the Paintbrush program minimized.

- `start /max notepad` Starts the Notepad program maximized.

- `start /r sol` Starts the Solitaire game restored (windowed).

By default, after Windows launches a Windows application from the DOS command prompt, the prompt returns to the Desktop. However, you can tell Windows to suspend the command prompt until the launched application has quit by adding /w to the end of a **start** command line.

# DOS Applications

All versions of 32-bit Windows, beginning with Windows 95, provide extensive support for DOS applications. Windows NT 4 has a powerful command-line mode called CMD that amounts to 32-bit DOS. Windows 98 builds on both of these to supply an improved protected-mode environment, most importantly, for DOS games. You can run these applications in (at least one of) three ways:

- In a Windows window.
- Full-screen DOS within Windows.
- In MS-DOS mode.

**DOS Windows ("DOS boxes").**  If you want to use other applications at the same time—including other DOS windowed programs—you can run a DOS program in a window on the Windows 98 desktop. This mode lets you make full use of the Windows 98 Clipboard for transferring data. A new toolbar providing one-click access to frequently used functions is available for windowed DOS applications. And to improve the way you view text in a windowed DOS application, Windows 98 can automatically adapt the screen font based on the size of the window itself.

You can use multiple DOS applications simultaneously. For example, you can run a lengthy DOS telecommunications session in the background while you play a DOS game in the foreground. Instead of running only one application at a time as does MS-DOS, Windows 98 lets you open dozens of applications at the same time. The applications can run either full screen or windowed on the desktop, and you can switch among them at will.

**Full-Screen DOS.**  If you want to give your whole screen to a DOS application, you can run in full-screen DOS mode; your application looks just the way it would in native DOS, while the Windows 98 desktop and Taskbar—along with everything else that's happening, including running Windows applications and other DOS sessions—"hides" in the background. When you want to shrink your DOS program in the foreground to a window, just hit Alt Enter and the program will become one window among several. Meanwhile, all your Windows services and peripherals (like your CD-ROM drive) are still available in background.

**MS-DOS Mode.**  Full-screen DOS is a virtual DOS machine (VDM) relying on Windows file and print services, the Windows installed driver set, and settings in the Windows Registry to communicate—both within the computer and with the outside world. This provides very good DOS compatibility with minimal disruption to the way your computer is working.

Certain finicky, mostly older, DOS programs refuse to rely on Windows services and memory management. A program like this, most likely, either won't run in the same computer with anything in protected mode, or insists on making all the extended memory in the computer subject to its own rules. Such a program can run in **MS-DOS Mode,** which lets you clear Windows almost completely out so the program can run in a configurable and genuine DOS rather than in a VDM.

Naturally, to unload Windows from memory, you have to reboot the computer. Close all your running applications—especially Microsoft Exchange or Windows Messaging and anything that depends on them—click the **Start** button, pick **Shut Down** from the Start Menu, and when you see this screen:

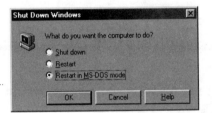

***Figure 4.22***

*Windows 98 Shut
Down Dialog*

select **Restart in MS-DOS mode.** When the computer comes back up, you'll be running MS-DOS 8.0, and Windows will be present in your machine only as a mute, woozy stub. While here, please observe the following local customs:

You can only run one program at a time. This is DOS, remember?

You can't switch windows. There are no windows.

 If you hit [Ctrl][Alt][Delete] *once, even once,* you will reboot the computer; so don't try popping up the Task Manager.

You don't have Windows drivers or Registry services. This means that, if you need anything while you're here like access to your CD-ROM drive, your remote disks, or your network printer, you'll have to load appropriate real-mode drivers through CONFIG.SYS or AUTOEXEC.BAT—possibly along with a third-party memory manager to make them all fit. Eighties computing at your fingertips!

 The caution about network resources also applies to anyone trying to access resources attached to *your* computer. If you reboot into MS-DOS mode, your computer will "cease to exist" as a networked device, and network requests attempting to pass through it will end up in a black hole.

 You'll sometimes see MS-DOS mode referred to as Single MS-DOS Application (SMA) mode.

**Advanced DOS in Windows.** We'll say much more about the uses of DOS boxes, and the fine-tuning of MS-DOS mode and virtual DOS machines, in Chapter 14, "Windows 98 and DOS."

Windows can't close a DOS application in the same quick, clean ways it closes a Windows application. If you have a proper DOS window open, with the cursor sitting at the C:\ (or other) prompt, Windows can close it because it "knows" that the DOS window's area of memory doesn't contain any unsaved data. But when you have a DOS application running with a data file open, Windows has no way of telling whether the latest information in that data file has been written to disk—or whether it's "unsaved" and likely to be destroyed when the DOS window is closed.

### Shutdown Warning Dialog Box

When you try to close a DOS application by double-clicking on the Close Window button or the System menu icon, Windows tells you this (Figure 4.23).

**Figure 4.23**

Shutdown Warning dialog

If you know that all the data in your DOS application's file has been saved to disk, go ahead and click **Yes** to close it. If you're not sure that all your work is safe, click **No** and then exit the DOS program with its usual command. Depending on how you started the program, either the DOS window will vanish when the program closes, or you'll be left with a DOS window at a prompt, which you can then close by double-clicking on the Close Window button.

# Multitasking with Windows 98

One of the most powerful features of Windows 98 is its support for multitasking—the ability to do more than one thing at a time. With Windows 98, you can run more than one program at once and switch among those programs at will.

Multitasking enables your computer to mirror the richness and variety of your work. Instead of focusing on a single task at a time—as you are limited to doing with DOS—you can open multiple applications concurrently, each providing a specific tool or function. The net result is a more natural working environment. Unless you are the head of a large corporation—in which case your desk may be dramatically bare for effect—your real desk probably serves as the resting place for multiple ongoing jobs. On one side is that stack of unfinished reports. At the top is a copy of a memo you were reading. On one corner is a letter to your congressperson, while sitting center stage is the latest stock report from Wall Street.

Similarly, multitasking enables you to keep lots of things open at once on your virtual desktop. You probably have your fax and e-mail programs handy, certainly the tools for your current project are open, and someone down the hall just sent you an incredulous network message. Pop everything up off the Taskbar, and you get the picture (Figure 4.24).

## Opening Multiple Applications

In practice, each time you launch a program from the Start menu or open a data file in a folder view, you are multitasking. Windows 98 folder views are considered application programs, so just by navigating the Windows 98 interface, you tap into its multitasking capabilities.

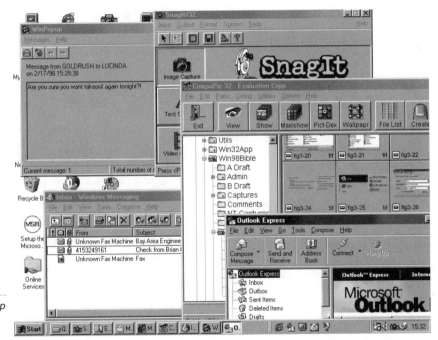

*Figure 4.24*

*Windows 98 desktop with multiple applications open*

However, opening multiple applications is only the tip of the multitasking iceberg. Windows 98 also allows applications to operate simultaneously, letting you continue to work in one application—called the *foreground task*—while a complex, time-consuming operation (like a print job) takes place in another application in the *background*.

This sleight of hand is accomplished by dividing up the amount of processing time available on your PC. By giving each application a slice of the computer's processing capacity, and switching quickly between applications behind the scenes, Windows 98 creates the illusion that more than one thing is happening at once. In reality, Windows is simply moving from one task to the next every few milliseconds.

This enables you to do more with your computer in a given length of time, because you no longer have to wait for an application to finish a complex procedure before continuing. Now, instead of going for coffee while that hundred-page report is printing, you can switch to another running application—or open a new data file for editing—while the print job continues to churn away in the background. Luckily, thanks to the amount of time and head-scratching required to understand the Windows environment, the overall effect of Windows on world coffee production has been slight.

## Printing in the Background

The Windows 98 interface remains responsive even when multiple applications are performing heavy processing in the background. You can continue to navigate folders, open other applications from the Start menu, and perform virtually any other task while your computer chugs away on other, invisible jobs. But while Windows is masterful at allocating resources, it can only work with the resources your computer makes available. If multitasking in Windows pushes your computer close to the limits of what it can do, you're going to notice that your foreground task is slow. This is why, when people upgrade to a new version of Windows, they often also upgrade—or even replace—the computer it runs on.

## Switching Applications

Windows 98 makes it easy to exploit its multitasking capabilities by providing a running list of open applications on the Taskbar. This task list includes full-blown programs, like Word, as well as the folder views you use to navigate the Windows 98 interface.

To switch to a different application, click on its entry on the Taskbar. The application appears at the top of the desktop. Do the same for applications that have been minimized. Although you can't see their application windows, you can always locate them by looking at the bottom edge of your screen—or side edge, if you've moved the Taskbar. A simple click on a program on the Taskbar restores that application's window and places it at the top of the desktop pile (Figure 4.25).

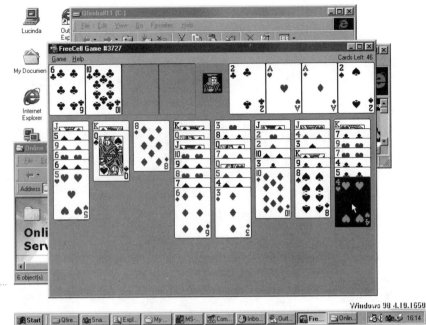

**Figure 4.25**

Switching between applications with the Taskbar

# The Windows 98 Clipboard

Under Windows, no application is an island. That's because Windows 98 provides bridges that enable applications to communicate with one another in powerful ways. The best-known of those bridges is the ubiquitous Windows Clipboard.

Based on a concept borrowed from the Macintosh—to give credit where credit is due—the Windows 98 Clipboard is a sort of universal scratch pad. Data copied to the Clipboard from one application becomes available to any other application. Text, graphics, and more complex amalgamations (even whole files) can all be copied to the Clipboard. If you want to copy worksheet data from Excel, for example, into a document you are writing in Word, you use the Clipboard as the go-between. The Clipboard doesn't care that Word and Excel use different data formats; it acts as a neutral depository and translator that can be filled with, and transmit, virtually any kind of data regardless of its source.

**Cut, Copy, and Paste.** To place data on the Windows Clipboard, you use an application's Edit menu. For example, to copy a range of cells from an Excel worksheet to the Clipboard, you highlight the cells in Excel and select Copy from the Edit menu. (Or click the Copy button on the toolbar, or hit Ctrl C. As usual, there's more than one way to get where you're going in Windows.) The cells are then placed on the Clipboard.

To insert that data into another application, you use that application's Edit menu. For example, to insert the data into Word, you switch to Word's window and select Paste from the Edit menu, click the Paste button on the toolbar, or hit Ctrl+V. The data is pasted into the current Word document, where it can be formatted and integrated with the document text for printing (Figure 4.26).

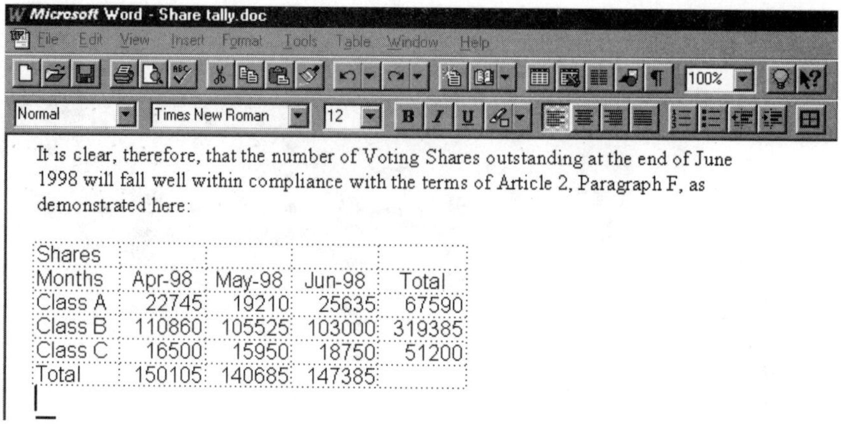
Microsoft Word - Share tally.doc
File Edit View Insert Format Tools Table Window Help
100%
Normal
Times New Roman
12
It is clear, therefore, that the number of Voting Shares outstanding at the end of June 1998 will fall well within compliance with the terms of Article 2, Paragraph F, as demonstrated here:
Shares
Months Apr-98 May-98 Jun-98 Total
Class A 22745 19210 25635 67590
Class B 110860 105525 103000 319385
Class C 16500 15950 18750 51200
Total 150105 140685 147385

***Figure 4.26***

*Copying and pasting from Excel to Word*

Suddenly Windows 98 becomes more than a cluttered desk—it's a United Nations that works. Not only can you run multiple applications concurrently, but you can also share data among them virtually at will.

A third choice, cutting data, can be made by selecting Cut from the Edit menu, clicking the Cut button on the toolbar, or hitting Ctrl+X. Cutting actually removes the data from a file as it places it on the Clipboard. If you cut a range of cells from an Excel worksheet, the data ceases to exist in the worksheet, and is present only on the Clipboard. Novice Windows users generally prefer copying to cutting, because cutting destroys the data in the original, leaving the data only in the Clipboard and in any applications into which it is pasted. Once you're an old hand with these keystrokes, though, you'll have no fear of using whichever one is most appropriate for the job.

**The Windows Clipboard management keystrokes were actually changed between Win16 and Win32. Ctrl+x for cut, Ctrl+C for copy, and Ctrl+V for paste were borrowed from the Macintosh interface, which is conceded to have gotten this right. The old cut Shift+Del, copy Ctrl+Ins, and paste Shift+Ins still work.**

If you do something awkward with cut, copy, or paste, always remember that other, nearly universal Windows "oops!" key—Ctrl Z, which Undoes the last thing (or, with repeated presses, several things) you did. Personally, we find that the fastest response to an accidental Ctrl X cut is an immediate Ctrl V paste, which sticks the information back where it was but leaves a copy on the Clipboard.

There are a happy few 32-bit Windows applications that implement the nonstandard, but delightful, Ctrl Y as Redo—that is, as the key that undoes an Undo. You can't really know how much you'd love to have this until you mean to hit Ctrl Z four times, and instead you hit it five times, three paragraphs of deathless (oh yeah?) prose vanish and you ... can't un-Undo it. We think that, if more applications' Edit menus included Ctrl Y as Redo, the world would be a nicer place. We have spoken.

Once a piece of data is on the Clipboard, incidentally, it stays there until you reboot your computer or replace the data with another piece. One limitation of the Clipboard is that you can't see what's on it except by pasting a copy into a document. If you suddenly realize that you had five pages of a Word document on your Clipboard, and you've just accidentally overwritten it with a percent sign, try undoing your last edit with Ctrl Z and see if that also undoes the replacement of the Clipboard's contents. It should.

**Hot Links with DDE.**  Although cutting, copying, and pasting are powerful mechanisms for sharing data, they can become tedious, especially with data that frequently gets replaced. For example, if you generate a monthly report in Word that includes worksheet data pasted from multiple Excel data files, updating that information manually can become a real chore.

Fortunately, 32-bit Windows provides a mechanism for automating Clipboard exchanges. By means of Dynamic Data Exchange (DDE), you can instruct Windows 98 to update data automatically, copying and pasting it into a document whenever it is changed in the original file. When you update the original, DDE searches out and updates each pasted link.

To use DDE, first copy the data from the source file to the Clipboard. In the scenario just mentioned, this would mean highlighting cells in the Excel worksheet and selecting **Copy** from the Edit menu. Next, switch to Word and select **Paste Special** from the Edit menu, then **Paste Link** and **Formatted Text (RTF)** from the Paste Special dialog.

Selecting *Paste Link* (as opposed to Paste) tells Windows 98 to establish a DDE link between the two data files. Instead of merely pasting the data, Windows establishes a dynamic link between the cells in the Excel worksheet and their pasted equivalents in the Word document. Now, whenever the data in the

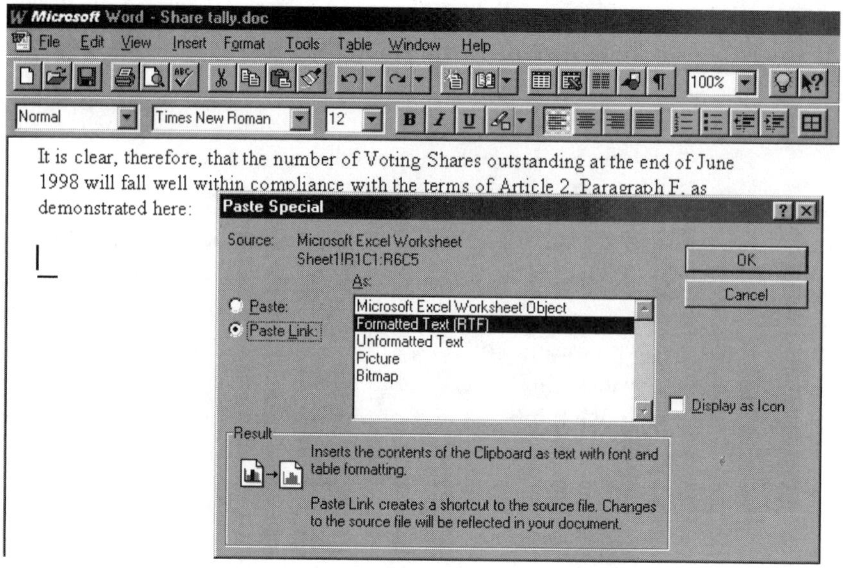

**Figure 4.27**

*Using DDE to establish a dynamic link*

Excel file is updated, all of the references to it in the Word document will be updated automatically as soon as you open the Word document (Figure 4.27).

Keep a few caveats in mind when you work with DDE:

- Data you copy to the Clipboard must be part of a file that has been saved to disk; using data from a new, unsaved document or worksheet is not allowed.

- DDE links are sensitive to the location of the source file. If you move a file, you will likely break any links made to its data. If you accidentally break a link, try moving the file back to its original location.

- Data that is placed on the Clipboard is generic; once pasted into another application, it loses its original characteristics. This means that when you paste Excel data from the Clipboard into a Word document, the data ceases to be Excel data and is converted into raw text. And although DDE may be able to update this pasted raw text automatically, the data itself cannot be manipulated with worksheet commands; it is text and nothing more.

**Working With the Clipboard: Cliptray.** If you're the meticulous type, you might want to manipulate the Clipboard's contents—especially when you're preparing to insert data into a sensitive document. If you inadvertently paste your lumber company's confidential profit-and-loss statement into the staff newsletter, your future there will not be bright.

Fortunately, Windows 98 provides a great new mechanism for working with the contents (at least the text contents) of the Clipboard. The Cliptray, a

Windows 98 accessory program (Figure 4.28), seems to replace the venerable Windows applet called the Clipboard Viewer; we say *seems to* because, at this writing, it's part of the Windows 98 Resource Kit, but we can easily see it ending up in the Accessories folder of the Windows 98 retail version.

The Cliptray is unusual in that there is no single master screen that encompasses a bunch of options. This applet defaults to a muted, handsome icon in the System Tray, and when you double-click it, you get the thing in Figure 4.29.

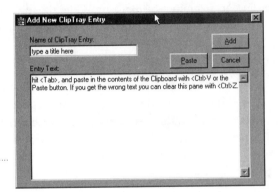

**Figure 4.29**

*Add New Entry
dialog*

By making it as easy as possible to add new entries, the Cliptray combines the effortlessness of the Clipboard with the unlimited capacity of Scraps. Pop it up and follow the directions below to add an entry. Piece of cake.

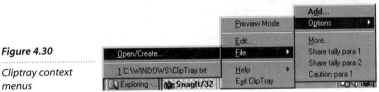

**Figure 4.30**

*Cliptray context
menus*

But the Cliptray is like a Leatherman tool; it doesn't look like much till you unfold it (Figure 4.30). Right-click—which is, increasingly, the gold key to the System Tray in general—on the icon and you'll discover ways to:

- Create multiple Cliptray files, each with an unlimited number of entries.

- Edit the entries in Cliptray files.

- Shuffle the order of the entry stack in a Cliptray file.

- Preview the entries in a Cliptray file, if it helps you remember which one's which; or turn Preview off if you want your entries to be less visible.

Cliptray goes far beyond the old Clipboard Viewer to offer approximately the muscle of AutoText in Microsoft Word—or, if you go back this far, to the old

*Figure 4.31a*

*Figure 4.31a*

*Cliptray Edit/Insert
menu (single item)*

*Figure 4.31b*

*Cliptray Edit/Insert
menu (multiple
items)*

Glossary function in Word for DOS. Let's start by highlighting this text, sending it to the Clipboard, and creating a Cliptray entry:

Put the highlighted text on the Clipboard with Ctrl C.

Double-click on the Cliptray icon to pop up the **Add New Clip Tray Entry** dialog. Type a name in the **Name...** field, hit Tab, and paste in the Clipboard's contents with the **Paste** button or Ctrl V. You can clear the buffer with Ctrl Z, or if you're satisfied with what you have, click **Add** to save the entry and open another blank form. When the form is blank, the **Cancel** button turns to **Close**. (Ah, Visual Basic, let me count thy ways.) Hit the **Close** button and your first entry becomes part of the CLIPTRAY.TXT file. Right-click on the Cliptray icon.

At the bottom of the Context Menu you'll see the name of the entry you just created (Figure 4.31a) which, of course, can be more descriptive than "Entry 1." Click that name once and the text of the entry is transferred to the Clipboard, the menu vanishes, and the entry is ready to paste into the underlying (or any) document with Ctrl V. Go ahead and add a second item, then right-click the icon again (Figure 4.31b).

This menu can display one entry, or as many as 99; the default maximum is 20. To open the settings dialog, click **More...** (Figure 4.32):

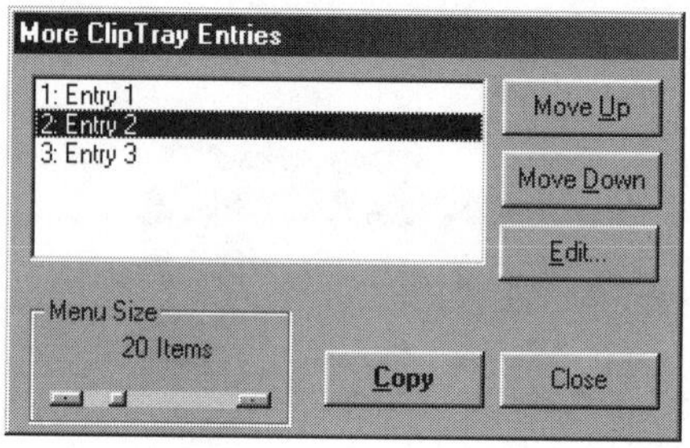

*Figure 4.32*

*Cliptray settings
options*

This dialog is headed **More ClipTray Entries** because, should you have more entries in a single Cliptray file than will fit on the Context Menu, you can still get to them all from the scrolling list box in here. Entries are numbered, and you can jump to an entry by typing its number. Options are:

- **Move Up:** Move the highlighted entry up in the stack. Its number will decrease.

- **Move Down:** Move the highlighted entry down in the stack. Its number will increase.

- **Edit:** Open the Cliptray Editor for the current highlighted entry (see below).

- **Menu Size:** Use the slider to set the number of Context Menu entries from 1 to 99.

- **Copy:** Send the current highlighted entry to the Clipboard.

- **Close:** Poof!

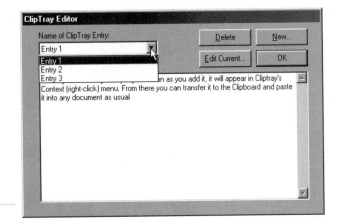

**Figure 4.33**

*Cliptray Editor*

Typical Windows—you can reach the Cliptray Editor (Figure 4.33) from either the **Edit** button in Settings, or the **Edit...** line on the Context\Options Menu. The **Name of ... Entry** field will default to whatever entry was highlighted in the parent dialog, but you can reach any entry in the file through the drop list (shown). The entry text is scrollable, if need be, but not editable from here. Options are:

- **Delete** the current entry. You'll be asked for confirmation.

- **New...:** Open the **Add New Clip Tray Entry** dialog.

- **Edit Current...:** Open the *actual* Cliptray editor, which looks just like the Editor, except with different buttons (Figure 4.34).

- **OK:** If you got here from **Edit...** line on the Context\Options Menu, this pops back to **More ClipTray Entries.** If you got here from the **Edit** button in Settings, the Editor vanishes.

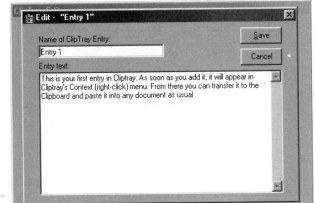

**Figure 4.34**

*Cliptray Editor editor*

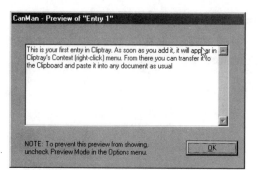

*Figure 4.35*

*Entry preview box*

If you have **Options\Preview Mode** checked and you click an entry's line in the Context Menu, the text of the entry pops up in a Preview box (Figure 4.35). Here again the text is scrollable but not editable. What's not obvious (well, it wasn't to *us*) is that the Preview box pops up *and* the text goes to the Clipboard at the same time, so you don't have to click twice. The NOTE almost makes it sound like Microsoft wishes you wouldn't turn this on.

*Figure 4.36*

*Open/Create Cliptray file*

**Options\File\Open/Create...** pops open a typical file dialog (Figure 4.36) which lets you either open one of your existing files—in fact it proposes the name of the last one you created—or make a new one by typing a new name and clicking **Open.** If you type the name of a new file, you'll be prompted for confirmation (Figure 4.37).

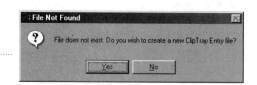

*Figure 4.37*

*New File confirmation*

 Incidentally, Microsoft fixed the file format problem. The Clipboard Viewer created proprietary .CLP data files, which it but few (if any) other programs could open. A Cliptray entries file is plain text, the format straightforward;

you could write one in Notepad if you wanted to. The only disadvantage is that Cliptray uses the limited character set of a system font, whereas the Clipboard Viewer could work with the OEM text font for displaying oddball characters.

As you can probably tell from the space we've devoted to it, we like Cliptray a lot. Unlike the old Clipboard Viewer, it really delivers speed and productivity in proportion to extra keystrokes; the investment in disk space is tiny, and the presentation is elegant. If you install it, you'll use it … speaking of which, we tested this on Windows 95 and Windows NT 4 and it seems to work fine!

## Object Linking and Embedding

Although the Windows Clipboard and DDE are able to link your data regardless of which application created it, these mechanisms do have their limitations. Fortunately, Windows 98's Object Linking and Embedding (OLE) provides a more sophisticated mechanism for sharing data among applications.

**In-Place Editing.**  By using OLE, an application can continue to edit its data after that data has been pasted into another application's file. Called *in-place editing,* the feature enables you to work with information that has been transferred into a host, or "container," document. Data pasted with OLE is called an *embedded object;* you can use **Paste Special** to paste OLE objects into files, as well as to exchange data through DDE.

When you double-click on an embedded object, Windows 98 interprets this as a request to edit the object in place and searches the system for an appropriate "server" application to handle the editing chores. Once found, the server application essentially takes over the application window of the "client" application—the one in which the embedded object and its container document reside—providing all the necessary tools and menu options to edit the data (Figure 4.38).

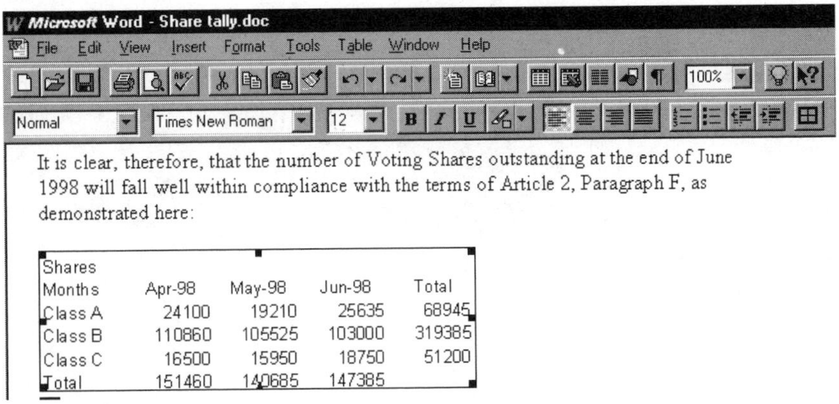

**Figure 4.38**

*In-place editing: Excel spreadsheet embedded in Word*

To see in-place editing in action, open Excel, an OLE-aware application. Copy a range of cells to the Clipboard, using the Copy command on the Edit menu. Now launch Word, another OLE-aware application. When you select Paste Special from the Edit menu, instead of selecting **Formatted Text** as you did before, select **Microsoft Excel Worksheet Object**. Click on the **OK** button, and the data is pasted into Word as an embedded object—in other words, as a live spreadsheet (Figure 4.38).

If you subsequently double-click on the embedded Excel data, the Excel program takes over the Word application window, and you gain access to all of Excel's menus and toolbars. It's as if you were editing the data in Excel itself—and that's because you are.

The advantage of in-place editing is obvious. You can see exactly how changes made to the data affect the overall container document, and this in turn makes it easy to format the information precisely.

**Embedding With an OLE Server.**  In-place editing makes it easy to change information that has been embedded as an OLE object. In fact, you don't even need to edit the data in the original OLE-capable application and then Copy/Paste Special it into your final document; you can use the **Insert Object** command in Word to—for example—start a fresh Excel spreadsheet in the middle of your Word page. Start by selecting **Microsoft Excel Worksheet** from the Object Type list (Figure 4.39).

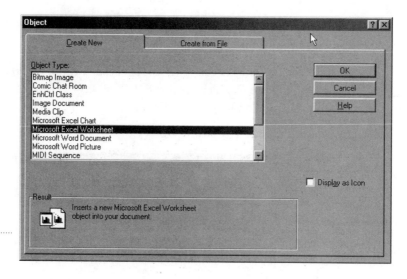

*Figure 4.39*

*Insert Object Type dialog*

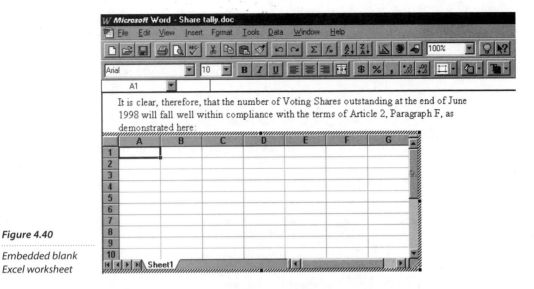

*Figure 4.40*

*Embedded blank
Excel worksheet*

Click **OK** and the Excel worksheet is embedded in the Word page (Figure 4.40). Note that you have a Microsoft Word title bar, but Excel toolbars and drop menus.

When you're done editing, simply click outside the border of the worksheet to put away the Excel controls and return control of the document to Word— but with the ability to edit the worksheet at any time (Figure 4.41). Excel can act as the OLE server *without* running in the foreground, which means that you can edit the worksheet without seeing Excel on your Taskbar.

| Shares | | | | |
|--------|--------|--------|--------|--------|
| Months | Apr-98 | May-98 | Jun-98 | Total |
| Class A | 24100 | 19210 | 25635 | 68945 |
| Class B | 110860 | 105525 | 103000 | 319385 |
| Class C | 16500 | 15950 | 18750 | 51200 |
| Total | 151460 | 140685 | 147385 | |

*Figure 4.41*

*Finished embedded
Excel worksheet*

**Scraps.** One of the most useful features of the Windows 98 interface is its level of support for OLE. Although previous versions of Windows supported OLE operations such as drag-and-drop embedding and in-place editing, Microsoft has expanded OLE support in 32-bit Windows by making folder views OLE aware. Since each folder view is a potential OLE container, you can drag and drop or copy and paste snippets of data into folder views just as if you were embedding the data into another program.

These miscellaneous pieces of data—called **Scraps** in Windows 98—sport their own icon, which can be manipulated just like any other desktop object (Figure 4.42).

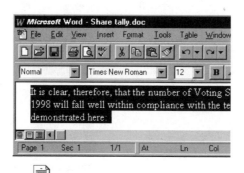

*Figure 4.42*

*Scrap dragged from Microsoft Word*

*Figure 4.43*

*Renaming a scrap*

You can use Scraps in a number of productive ways. To begin with, you can store interesting data items as Scraps without having to create an entire data file (Scraps take up less disk space than most data files). You can drag Scraps from folder to folder, delete them using the Recycle Bin, and rename them with more descriptive titles (Figure 4.43).

You can use the Scraps mechanism as a scratch pad for data. Simply drag the data from an OLE application onto the desktop for later use, in its own application or another one. The advantage of using Scraps, instead of the Clipboard, is that you don't lose the data in the Scrap if you accidentally copy something else onto the Clipboard and overwrite its contents.

Scraps also make it easy to copy multiple individual data items for later use. Whereas the Clipboard holds only one item at a time, you can create dozens of Scraps and later drag them back into applications as desired. If you simply double-click on a Scrap, the application that created it will start up and display it—as a *foreground* OLE server.

# Quitting Programs

After you load and save files, embed objects, and drag Scraps until your fingers hurt, only one task is left undone: quitting an application. Windows 98 offers three ways to shut down an application.

The first and quickest way to quit an application is to click on the Close Window button in the upper right-hand corner of the application window. This is the button that contains the little X and sits next to the Minimize and Maximize buttons on the window's title bar.

You can also select Exit from the application's File menu (see Figure 4.44). Virtually all Windows applications include an Exit item on this menu, although on occasion a developer takes the liberty of calling it something else (like **Close**, which shouldn't be confused with the **Close** option of an MDI application).

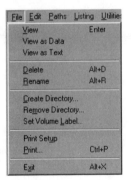

**Figure 4.44**

The Exit menu item

Finally, you can double-click on the application's **System** menu icon. This is the one that contains a miniature of the program's icon. It's located in the upper left-hand corner of the application window, right next to the program's title in the title bar. You can also open this menu with a single click and select Close, but double-clicking is quicker.

Whatever technique you employ, the application interprets the command in the same way. It closes any open data files—prompting you to save any changes first if you haven't already done so—and then closes its application window, shutting itself down.

# Summary

Several features have been added to Windows to make it easier to start programs, to run them, and to use them either by themselves or in conjunction with data contained in other programs. Through its Clipboard, DDE, and OLE, the Windows 98 operating system enables you to integrate all the information on your computer, whether it was generated by DOS, Windows 3.1, Windows 98, or Windows NT, downloaded from an online service, or captured off the Web. More than that, the multitasking capability of Windows 98 makes it possible for you to work on more than one program at once, so you can send messages to your home office, for example, while working on a spreadsheet. All this computing power, much of it reserved for corporate mainframes and minicomputers as recently as ten years ago, is now truly at your fingertips, thanks to 32-bit Windows.

# 5

# Toys, Games, and Pocketknives

To succeed, an operating system needs to be witty, wise, useful, enjoyable, addictive, sexy, and stimulating. Of course, to a true nerd, an operating system is all this and more—it's a way of life. But the rest of us are likely to seek all those qualities from the programs written for an operating system, not from the system itself. That's why Microsoft has always bundled a variety of little programs with Windows—so you can have fun (or do business) with it right out of the box. The programs range from a skeletal word processor to a paint program, a calculator, an automatic phone dialer, and a handful of games. Naturally, Microsoft also makes full-fledged shrink-wrapped equivalents of many of these applets, and wouldn't mind if the Windows mini-versions whetted your appetite for them.

# A Lightweight Software Sampler

The programs that came with Windows 3.1 were simple enough for even a novice to learn quickly, but not terribly powerful. The Windows 95 accessories, being 32-bit, were much more capable and in some cases (like WordPad and Paint) rivaled freestanding, separate applications with their sophistication. Windows 98 takes the cake—or, more exactly, gives *you* the cake—with the most comprehensive bundle of utility software ever included with a retail operating system.

Let's start with an overview (Table 5.1), since there's so much new software in Windows 98 that we've had to split it over several chapters.

To turn you on to what you can do with Windows 98, Microsoft has bundled a cornucopia of basic programs with your package. These miniature applications, or applets (which Microsoft calls Accessories), lack the power and range of their full-featured, commercial counterparts but still provide some functions. You can write a memo to your boss, draw a picture of your house, or

## *How to Get There*

**Figure 5.1**

*The Accessories submenu*

On the Programs submenu of the Start button is a submenu called Accessories. Click on it once to access almost all the Windows 98 applets (Figure 5.1). Of course, Windows isn't quite as consistent as we might like, so every time we discuss an applet, we'll start out by giving you the full path to it on the default Windows menus.

### Table 5.1  Overview of Windows 98 Applets

| Applet | Where to find Details |
|---|---|
| **Accessibility Options:** If you have impaired hearing or vision, or any reason to type in a non-standard way, these can compensate wonderfully for your computer's unyielding hardware design. Keyboard modifications, extra alert sounds or onscreen messages, high-contrast and magnification for your display, keypad control of the mouse, and support for alternative input devices can all make your console a pleasanter place to spend time. | Appendix B, "Accessibility Options" |
| **Backup** is a barebones version of the award-winning Seagate (Arcada) Backup Exec retail product, and compared to crusty old Microsoft Backup, it's the dawn of a whole new day. The licensed Seagate product backs up to parallel-port, SCSI, and IDE/ATAPI drives, in about fifteen currently popular tape formats including QIC, Travan, SCSI DAT, DC 6000, and DLT. The higher-capacity formats on that list will store up to 70GB per tape. You get a Backup Wizard too. It's NT's turn to be jealous. | Chapter 15, "Tips, Tools, and Troubleshooting" |
| **Briefcase.** The Briefcase is a file synchronization utility to assure that if you're working with multiple machines—a desktop and a laptop, say—you end up with the right copies of the right files on the right computer. An applet that many people play with but few master, Briefcase is worth the investment of any road warrior's time. | Chapter 5, "Toys, Games, and Pocketknives" |
| **Calculator.** Even though this is as old as the hills, it's one of the finest Windows applets—and the Windows 98 version has been through another round of debugging. The Standard view is an ordinary four-function calc with square root, percentages and memory; the Scientific view, with four bases, trig, inverse and hyperbolic functions, and statistics, is neck-and-neck with a powerful handheld. Right-click help means that, if you've never seen a "dms" key before, the definition is two clicks away. Put a Shortcut to this on your Desktop and we guarantee you'll use it. | Chapter 5, "Toys, Games, and Pocketknives" |
| **CD Player** offers the standard audio CD controls—play, pause, skip, loop, shuffle, stop—and the ability to create, but not save, playlists. Turn on the Toolbar, which defaults to off. One unusual feature is a choice to play just the first few seconds of each song. | Chapter 12, "Multimedia" |
| **Character Map.** An oldie but goodie, the Character Map lets you insert any character from any installed font into the document you're working on—not exactly with a single click, but easily enough that it's worth doing. | Chapter 8, "Fonts" |
| **ClipTray.** The Clipboard—at long last!—becomes a fully interactive, ready-and-waiting, file-based clip server, not only a neat toy (which it is) but an AutoText function for any program that will accept Clipboard Paste. Five stars! | Chapter 4, "Ready, Set, Run!" |

### Table 5.1 (continued)

| Applet | Where to find Details |
|---|---|
| **Compression Agent** takes hard disks that have *already been compressed* with DriveSpace 3 (that part is important) and gives them another squeeze, to a user-selectable threshold of pain. *NOTE: DriveSpace 3 is not compatible with FAT32.* Whaddayawant, oxide flakes? | Chapter 13, "Optimizing" |
| **Dial-Up Scripting** gives Dial-Up Networking its own scripting language, automating the most complex Internet and intranet negotiation into single-click connection, and making the Windows 98 DUN (finally) as powerful as its big cousin, Windows NT Remote Access. | Chapter 11, "Communications" |
| **Direct Cable Connection** is a Wizard that walks you through connecting two computers with a parallel or serial cable, then automates fast data transfer. Note that ordinary printer or modem cables don't have the right pinouts for this; you need what computer retail stores usually refer to as a "Laplink-style cable." | Chapter 11, "Communications" |
| **Disk Cleanup** offers you a structured way to get rid of your binary dust bunnies—unused applications, optional components, browser cache files, stale ActiveX and Java controls, and temp files. Nice of Microsoft to help you get rid of this, since they gave you most of it. You can also run the FAT32 Converter from here. | Chapter 13, "Optimizing" |
| **Disk Defragmenter** gives you the same options that the Wizard does—to shuffle your program files for optimum performance, and to run ScanDisk along with Defrag—but here you select them manually. On a badly fragmented drive *Defrag can be slow,* and if you turn on Show Details, it's even slower. | Chapter 13, "Optimizing" |
| **Disk Defragmenter Optimization Wizard** is a Defrag with a difference—not only does it make sure your files are in contiguous clusters, but it puts the applications you use most often on the parts of the disk that can be most quickly reached and read. | Chapter 15, "Tips, Tools, and Troubleshooting" |
| **DriveSpace 3** is the disk compressor from Windows 95, and probably works as well as it did before. *NOTE: DriveSpace 3 is not compatible with FAT32.* | Chapter 13, "Optimizing" |
| **DVD Player.** When you get tired of watching TV (see **TV Viewer**) Windows will show you movies! The forthcoming 17GB disk capacity will make future versions of Windows and Microsoft Office a snap to install—no more shuffling CD's. Intel, meanwhile, fantasizes about the middle-class home of the future, with one computer per room. | Chapter 12, "Multimedia" |

**Table 5.1**  (continued)

| Applet | Where to find Details |
|---|---|
| **FAT32 Converter** converts the filesystem on your hard disk from the old FAT16 cluster pattern, compatible with DOS and earlier versions of Windows, to FAT32, compatible with (so far) Windows 98 and late Windows 95. The Converter is a major timesaver since it allows the filesystem to be converted while your data stays in place; the earlier version of FAT32 required a reformat for installation. *Note:* Don't bother to install FAT32 if you're looking for speed, since even Microsoft admits that it's—if anything—slightly slower than what it replaces. It will save you bucketfuls of disk space, though. | Chapter 13, "Optimizing" |
| **FrontPage Express** is a limited, but slick and useful, "lite" version of FrontPage 97, Microsoft's retail Web site editor. You get almost all of the HTML editing capability and most of the templates and bots of the full product, but no frame support, no in-line spellcheck, and no tools for image editing, resizing, or mapmaking. The server-side extensions are also absent. Still, the Express version is more than adequate for light page creation, editing, and quick touchups. | Chapter 16, "Your Own Private Internet" |
| **Games: FreeCell** is a card game that had to wait for 32-bit power, then became one of the most addictive forms of solitaire in the history of computing. If you're anything like us, you'll play it too much and uninstall it in disgust, then put it back on. | Chapter 5, "Toys, Games, and Pocketknives" |
| **Games: Hearts** is a faithful and attractive rendition of the game so often played in English country houses. Introduced in Windows 95, this was one of the earliest networked multiplayer computer games; if you're not connected to a like-minded network, you can ask the game to supply three opponents. | Chapter 5, "Toys, Games, and Pocketknives" |
| **Games: Minesweeper** is a diabolical turnaround of a treasure hunt—a *don't*-find-the-bomb game. For those who are intent on beating it, Minesweeper seems never to lose its allure. | Chapter 5, "Toys, Games, and Pocketknives" |
| **Games: Solitaire,** Microsoft's sneaky way of teaching us all to drag-and-drop, is a different kind of fun than FreeCell—you play for points that accumulate for good moves, but decline over time. Even those who have been playing Solitaire since Windows 3.x will pop up a copy occasionally. | Chapter 5, "Toys, Games, and Pocketknives" |
| **Help Desk:** The Web-based problem report filing mechanism that delivers your System Troubleshooter results to Microsoft. | Chapter 15, "Tips, Tools, and Troubleshooting" |
| **HyperTerminal:** A licensed terminal and file transfer program, it's the slimmed-down version of HyperAccess by Hilgraeve. HT is bewildering to set up and somewhat quirky to use, but rewards you with bulletproof connections and some of the fastest dial-up file transfers ever seen in captivity. | Chapter 11, "Communications" |

***Table 5.1*** *(continued)*

| Applet | Where to find Details |
|---|---|
| ***Inbox Repair Tool*** automatically repairs corruption in the Personal and Offline folders (.PST and .OST files) of Microsoft Exchange. | Chapter 15, "Tips, Tools, and Troubleshooting" |
| ***Internet Connection Wizard*** will help you get connected to the Net if you're not. If you have no ISP, it'll point you to a Microsoft-supplied list of ISPs local to you; if your ISP account is already established, it helps you set up Dial-Up Networking. | Chapter 16, "Your Own Private Internet" |
| ***Kodak Imaging,*** formerly the Wang Imaging viewer launched by the Microsoft Fax utility, comes into its own as a nearly universal image viewer; it displays images from digital cameras and scanners, opens graphics files in a plethora of standard formats, offers TWAIN32 compliance, and is still always ready to show you your incoming faxes. As a bonus, it doesn't crash nearly as often as its brittle predecessor. | Chapter 11, "Communications" |
| ***Media Player,*** the core of Windows' multimedia capabilities, is a simple but universal front end to every variety of playback, from Windows Video to MIDI, from MPEG to CD audio. To play back a file, pop it up manually; if a document contains a compatible sound or image file, Media Player appears and plays it automatically. | Chapter 12, "Multimedia" |
| ***Microsoft Chat:*** A lighthearted, NetMeeting-compatible chat client that (naturally) invites you to log on to the Microsoft Network chat server. Bizarre avatars, but pushbutton convenience. | Chapter 11, "Communications" |
| ***Multilink,*** also known as Channel Aggregation, lets multiple inexpensive modems and cheap POTS lines be multiplexed together into bargain-basement copper "fat pipe." Eat your heart out, ISDN! | Chapter 11, "Communications" |
| ***Multiple display support*** spreads a single giant Desktop over two, three, or four monitors and graphics adapters, Macintosh-style. | Chapter 12, "Multimedia" |
| ***Net Watcher*** is a tidy monitoring applet that monitors network connections, shared objects, or shared resources. With appropriate network setup, you can install Net Watcher on a workstation and use it to administer the entire network, server included. | Chapter 10, "Networking" |
| ***NetMeeting,*** a corporate killer app for those who can meet its demands, offers application and Clipboard sharing, whiteboard, chat, file transfer, videoconferencing, Internet phone calls, and "intelligent" audio and video stream control. It ties directly into Microsoft Exchange, Outlook or Internet Explorer. Fast Ethernet will suffice if you're deploying NetMeeting for intranet use; when you want to send your teleconferencing out into the big world, you're looking at a dedicated T1 or big piece of a T3. | Chapter 16, "Your Own Private Internet" |

***Table 5.1*** *(continued)*

| Applet | Where to find Details |
|--------|------------------------|
| **NetShow:** The NetShow that ships with Windows 98 is the client, an ActiveX control poised to receive sound, video, IP multicast and file transfers. Ultimately, the Windows 98 NetShow client will team up with its matching pieces in Microsoft's Internet Information Server (IIS) and deliver an enhanced TV signal called Broadcast Services … to what kind of a box? Your guess is as good as ours. | Chapter 16, "Your Own Private Internet" |
| **Notepad,** one of the oldest Windows applets, is showing its age. Even the 32-bit version won't open a text file bigger than about 60K. More irritating yet, the control set isn't standard Windows—Find is not Ctrl F, Select All is not Ctrl A, word-wrap is still a manual toggle, and you can't close a file without exiting. But it's brutally simple, and it's … what we've got. | Chapter 5, "Toys, Games, and Pocketknives" |
| **Outlook Express,** the replacement for Internet Explorer 3.0's Internet Mail and News, offers full-featured Internet e-mail with a choice of POP3, SMTP and IMAP4 protocols—and superb integration with Internet Explorer. Unless you really crave contact management, scheduling, mail and news all in a single application, we'd say that Outlook Express and the Windows Address Book may be a better deal than the "big" Outlook in Microsoft Office. | Chapter 16, "Your Own Private Internet" |
| **Paint** looks just like the Windows 95 version, except for minor shuffling of the drop-down menu items; but it's now an ActiveX server, creating images to be embedded in other documents, and MAPI-compliant so you can send images through Outlook mail or Exchange fax. On top of that, it's a spiffy paint program—although its file handling is very limited; it reads and writes .BMP format and reads .PCX format. | Chapter 5, "Toys, Games, and Pocketknives" |
| **Personal Web Server** is a small, local, but capable Web server that can run as a background task with minimal resources. Not intended as a full-dress server for a live Internet site—because it lacks the robust authentication you need—PWS is still a fine choice for alpha-testing site code, for hosting a small intranet, or just for running as an alternative to a traditional browser. | Chapter 16, "Your Own Private Internet" |
| **Phone Dialer** gives you a standard telephone keypad, call logging, and eight numbers of speed dialing, without a lot of fuss. It also handles requests for dial-out by other DDE-compatible applications. | Chapter 11, "Communications" |
| **QuickView** is an add-on to almost every file's right-click menu. If the file you click on is a document or graphic, QV will do its best to display it; an executable file will have its technical file information extracted and listed; any other kind of file will have its contents dumped. A few kinds of files, like Shortcuts, can't be QuickViewed, and neither can files that are currently open in applications. | Chapter 5, "Toys, Games, and Pocketknives" |

## Table 5.1 (continued)

| Applet | Where to find Details |
|---|---|
| **Resource Meter** is a thermometer for Windows—it tells you when your computer's about to freeze. We've had this hapless applet since Windows 3.1, but the Windows 98 version is prettier, and so much more optimistic. It minimizes to the System Tray, which is useful; right-click to exit. | Chapter 13, "Optimizing" |
| **ScanDisk,** now available in your choice of character-based or GUI, is still checking disks for integrity (with optional surface scan) and repairing or locking out any defects it may find. Windows 98 runs it automatically when your computer boots up after an "improper" shutdown, or when it encounters a hard error. | Chapter 13, "Optimizing" |
| **Scheduled Tasks Folder** is the upgrade for System Agent, first introduced in the Windows 95 Plus! pack and often called the best applet in it. Clicking Add Scheduled Task starts the Scheduled Task Wizard, which lets you pick a program to run automatically, then specify when and how often to run it. The Tuneup Wizard calls on this to run ScanDisk, Defrag, and Cleanup, but you'll think of a few more uses for it. | Chapter 5, "Toys, Games, and Pocketknives" |
| **Sound Recorder** lets you record, edit, and play back Windows digital audio files, as well as embed them in documents. If you need a smaller file you can convert between 8-bit and 16-bit, mono and stereo, at any sampling rate from 8KHz to 48KHz. | Chapter 12, "Multimedia" |
| **System File Checker** scans your system files for errors, compares them against benchmarks, logs the errors, and backs up your configuration. **BONUS** At long last, the ability to extract single files from the Windows installation folders!! | Chapter 15, "Tips, Tools, and Troubleshooting" |
| **System Information Utility.** Go ahead, expand the whole tree, and marvel at what unfolds. All your IRQs, DMA channels, memory ranges, driver revisions, loaded modules … everything about your hardware and software you could want to know, and on top of that, a gutsy toolkit. The more you learn about SysInfo, the less use you'll have for Device Manager, REGEDIT, and SYSEDIT. | Chapter 15, "Tips, Tools, and Troubleshooting" |
| **System Monitor,** a neat adaptation of Windows NT's Performance Monitor, lets you track any number of system performance parameters—filesystem, disk, network, memory, or adapters—and display them as line, bar, or numeric charts. If you're on a network and have the Remote Registry service enabled, you can monitor other computers on the network. | Chapter 13, "Optimizing" |
| **System Troubleshooter** integrates the Windows Help engine with Internet Explorer to help you troubleshoot common Windows problems by stepping through debugging trees, then connecting you to the Microsoft Knowledge Base, and finally helping you compose a Windows problem report that can be submitted to a Microsoft support engineer. | Chapter 15, "Tips, Tools, and Troubleshooting" |

## Table 5.1 (continued)

| Applet | Where to find Details |
|---|---|
| **TuneUp Wizard** lets you schedule defragmentation, disk scanning and file cleanup at any time and with any frequency you like, then runs the tuneup automatically in the background. | Chapter 15, "Tips, Tools, and Troubleshooting" |
| **Update Manager** automatically downloads and installs (with veto power from you) any operating system updates you need from Microsoft's Web site. | Chapter 15, "Tips, Tools, and Troubleshooting" |
| **Volume Control**, sitting in your System Tray, is really two controls. Click once and you get a single slider that controls the volume for whatever audio you're recording or playing back, and a checkbox for Mute. Click twice and you get a panel of separate sliders to control volume and balance for WAV audio, MIDI output, CD audio, PC speaker, line-in, and microphone, in any combination you need. If you have a Sound Blaster or compatible sound card you can enable bass and treble sliders too. | Chapter 12, "Multimedia" |
| **Web Publishing Wizard** lets you save your newly created HTML and graphics files directly to a Web server without the bother of going through separate ftp. | Chapter 16, "Your Own Private Internet" |
| **WebTV For Windows** is a complete control and scheduling center for a TV tuner card in your computer. | Chapter 12, "Multimedia" |
| **Windows Address Book** is a contact manager with ample space for personal information, work information, e-mail and Web addresses, and the half-dozen phone numbers that we all seem to have these days. The WAB serves as a digital verification utility and integrates nicely with Outlook Express e-mail and the NetMeeting teleconferencing software. This can serve very well as the contact side of your PIM if you use something else—either Schedule+ or a third-party product—for timekeeping. | Chapter 5, "Toys, Games, and Pocketknives" |
| **Windows Scripting Host** is the robust batch language that Windows has always needed, incorporating both the JavaScript and VBScript engines that first appeared in other Microsoft products. A true programming language for system administrators, WSH supports subroutines and functions, variables and arrays, true if/else statements, flow-control statements that allow looping, and functions that can be called by scripts, as well as tools to create dialogs and other interactive automation. But Microsoft omitted any functions that would allow scripts to work with hard disk files, probably because a WSH script that accessed the disk directly could be devastating if launched with malicious intent. | Chapter 11, "Communications" |
| **WinPopup** is a minimal, but handy, peer-to-peer message-passing utility—a visible intercom of sorts—for those times when e-mailing across the network is just too formal. It also sends and receives broadcast messages. | Chapter 10, "Networking" |
| **WordPad,** the Microsoft entry-level word processor, is capable and cute but—now that Word has moved on and left it—less of a draw than it was in Windows 95. | Chapter 5, "Toys, Games, and Pocketknives" |

calculate how long it will take to pay off the mortgage, while you become more proficient with this new version of Windows.

You'll find more than ever in this grab bag of appetizing applets: besides the traditional word processor, paint program, and calculator, Microsoft has included a briefcase for packing and porting your data when you're on the road, a graphics program, a multitude of enjoyable, time-wasting games, and help on an assortment of topics. Windows 98 also comes with a character map, discussed with Fonts in Chapter 8; specialized applets for voice, fax and data communications, which we cover in Chapter 10; and multimedia, covered in Chapter 12.

Some of the specialized applets, such as the Backup and Disk Defragmenter programs, the System Monitor, and the System Information Utility, are really system maintenance and optimization tools. You can find out more about them in Chapter 13, "Optimizing," and Chapter 15, "Tips, Tools, and Troubleshooting."

# Productivity Applets

Here we discuss some of the applets designed to help you accomplish your goals effectively.

## The Briefcase

Default path: `Desktop\My Briefcase`

Your Briefcase

**Figure 5.2**

The Briefcase

This utility (Figure 5.2) can be a lifesaver if you have both a laptop and a desktop system and want to coordinate the information you keep on both computers. Without the Briefcase, it can be all too easy to lose track of which is the most recent version of a file. You can thus commit one of the mortal sins of computing: accidentally copying an older version of a file over a newer version, wiping out any of the changes you've made to the new version.

Road warriors will love the Briefcase because it makes it easy to transfer data from laptop to desktop, and vice versa. The Briefcase is a special folder for people who regularly switch between computers and don't want to spend extra time copying files from one system to another. Designed to ease the process of taking data with you when you leave the office, the Briefcase uses the date and time stamp assigned to each file to track and, when necessary, synchronize two copies of the same file.

**A Sample Scenario.** So you're leaving for Taiwan in the morning, and you need to massage the latest sales figures on the plane. Drag and drop those files into the Briefcase—it's called packing your Briefcase—and then drag the Briefcase icon onto a disk or across a network connection to your notebook computer.

En route, you can open the Briefcase as you would any folder view and work on the contents at will. When you return to your office, simply reverse the process: move the Briefcase back to the desktop, either with a disk or across a network connection, and open the Briefcase folder. Windows 98 compares the contents of the Briefcase to the original files on your desktop. If there are any changes, Windows asks you whether you want to update the originals. You can either update the originals file-by-file, or the entire contents of the Briefcase at once. In either case, the original files are replaced with the revised files in the Briefcase folder.

**My Briefcase.**  Did you notice? Even if you wear shades to work, it would be hard to miss the icon on the Desktop called My Briefcase. This is your Starter Briefcase, which you are free to rename anything you like; use the menu that pops up when you click the right mouse button. You can also create other Briefcases by selecting Briefcase from the New submenu of any folder view's right-click menu.

Lots of people have trouble packing before a trip. To help you pack your Briefcase, Windows 98 includes a helpful wizard utility. If you want the Briefcase Wizard to help you pack, double-click on My Briefcase. The wizard presents you with a series of dialog boxes that lead you through the packing process, making sure you have everything you need for the files you select, and that it's neat and tidy. Clicking on the Finish button dismisses the Wizard and returns you to a folder view of the Briefcase's contents.

My Briefcase's folder view sports a toolbar, and the folder's contents are displayed in Details view. The Status field lets you know whether a particular Briefcase entry is current on your desktop system (Figure 5.3).

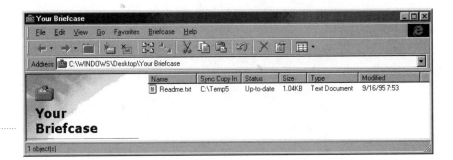

*Figure 5.3*

*Default Briefcase folder view*

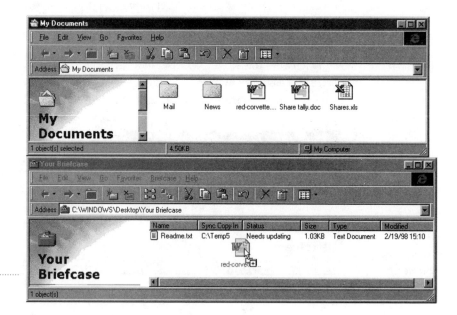

*Figure 5.4*

*Briefcase folder
view before
synchronization*

If the Status field reads "Up-to-date," the file in the Briefcase matches the
original. If the field reads "Needs updating," your Briefcase version no longer
matches the original (Figure 5.4).

**Working with a Briefcase.**  To add new files to a Briefcase, drag them
from their folders and drop them into the Briefcase's folder view (Figure 5.5).
Close the folder view, and the Briefcase is ready to travel. Typically, you drag
the Briefcase to a disk icon (which moves, as opposed to copies, the
Briefcase—this is normal). Then you remove the disk from your desktop PC,
load it into your notebook, drag the Briefcase from the disk drive's folder
view, and drop it onto your notebook's desktop. Again, Windows 98 moves
the Briefcase when you drag and drop; this type of folder is almost never
copied. You can also use a network or a Direct Cable connection to drag and
drop the Briefcase into your notebook (see Chapter 11).

*Figure 5.5*

*Briefcase
drag-and-drop*

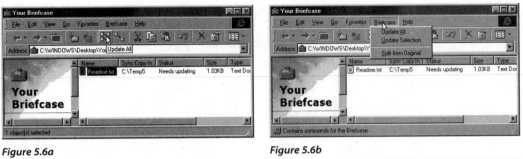

**Figure 5.6a**

Briefcase toolbar options

**Figure 5.6b**

Briefcase menu options

**Synchronizing the Data.** Once you're back home, it's time to unpack your Briefcase. Open the folder view and check out the Status field. If it indicates that files need to be updated, click the Update All button on the folder view's toolbar (Figure 5.6a) or select Update All from the Briefcase menu (Figure 5.6b).

The controls are:

- **Update All.** Updates every file in the folder.

- **Update Selection.** Updates highlighted files.

- **Split from Original.** Breaks the OLE connection between the two copies of the file. (drop menu only).

Windows 98 prompts you with a scrolling list of all the files that need to be updated (Figure 5.7). It's all one big shuffle: the left side of the dialog box contains icons for the files in the Briefcase, the icons on the right side represent the originals, and the arrows in between the icons tell you which way the update will go. If an arrow points to the original, the original will be updated, and vice versa.

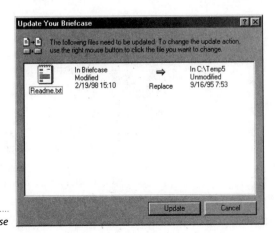

**Figure 5.7**

Updating a Briefcase

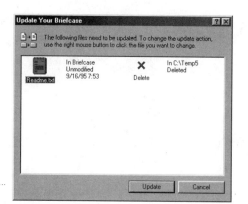

**Figure 5.8**

*Impossible update*

If one of the copies of a file has been deleted—either the original or the Briefcase version—then a red X is placed between the two icons (Figure 5.8). This is to warn you that your only copy will be deleted to "synchronize" with its match.

 *Don't synch phantoms!* Be warned: if you click the Update button, both your copies will be deleted.

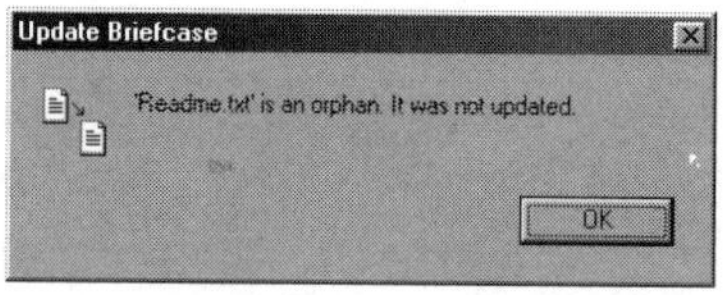

**Figure 5.9**

*Orphan warning*

If one of the copies of a file has been deleted and you *don't* try to Update, the remaining copy is called an *orphan,* and the OLE link is broken. Windows warns you about this (Figure 5.9).

Conveniently, you have the option of updating files how and when you like. Right-click while the cursor is over a particular entry to bring up a Context Menu with an **Update** option that enables you to change the default update action on the fly. You can change the direction of the update arrow, or if you prefer to procrastinate, you can select the Skip option to bypass synchronizing that particular file (Figure 5.10). And if a file's been marked for deletion,

you can undo that command or create a new copy of the file, either in the original location or in the Briefcase.

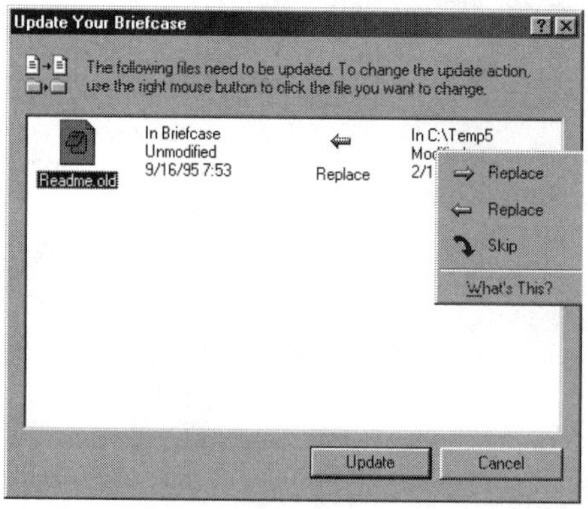

Once you're happy with the way your entries are arranged, click the **Update** button, and the files are automatically updated. If you're not an all-in-one-fell-swoop kind of person, you can synchronize files one at a time: select a single entry in the Briefcase folder view,

**Figure 5.10**

*Overriding defaults*

then click on the **Update Selection** button. Once the files are updated, the Status field changes to reflect their new state.

**From Port to Port.** Yes, Virginia, you can use Briefcase to transport your files between any two computers running Windows 98. Whenever you need to bring your files to a remote computer and keep the copies on both systems current, use a Briefcase as your data carrier.

 Oops! There's a loophole in the Briefcase system. What if you change both your Briefcase copy and your original file, independently? You'll freak out the Update mechanism, unless the program used to create the files was OLE-aware. OLE features a revision-reconciliation mechanism that cross-checks alterations in both files against an original benchmark. But if the application isn't OLE-aware, you get to reconcile the two files yourself—manually.

# Calculator

Default path: `Start Menu\Programs\Accessories\Calculator`

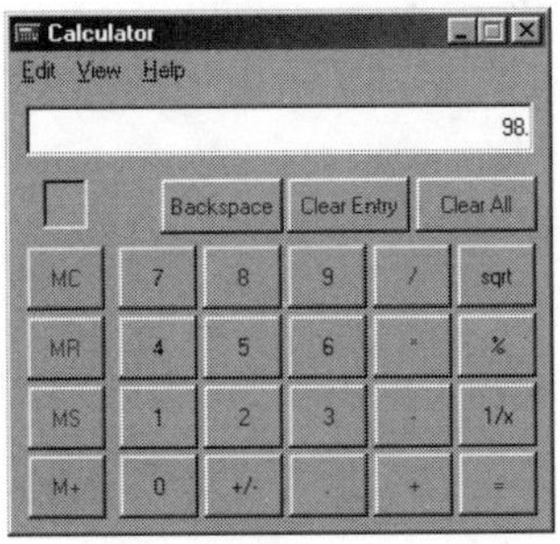

**Figure 5.11**

Calculator

One of the most straightforward Windows 98 applets, Calculator looks a lot like its real-life counterpart. It displays a simple onscreen keypad simulating a traditional seven-function calculator with memory. You can either click on the virtual calculator buttons with the mouse pointer or enter values directly from the numeric keypad on your computer keyboard (Figure 5.11).

**Scientific Mode.** If you want to get fancy with your calculator and do something like convert a large number into a binary or octal numeric system, you can switch to Scientific mode from the View menu. In Scientific mode (Figure 5.12), Calculator can perform a variety of complex numeric and statistical manipulations—it's as powerful as a scientific hand-held calculator, if not as portable.

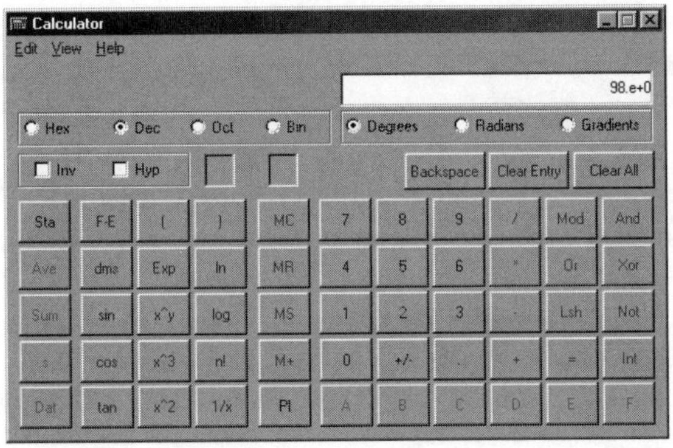

**Figure 5.12**

Calculator in Scientific mode

These are the Scientific mode features:

| | |
|---|---|
| **Bases** | Binary (base 2), octal (base 8), decimal (base 10), hexa-decimal (base 16) |
| **Data entry** | Hex keypad, 0–9 and A–F; four-function memory |
| **Trigonometry** | Sine, cosine, tangent; expression in degrees, radians or gradients; degree-minute-second conversion; hyperbolic functions |
| **Logarithms** | Logs, natural logs |
| **Exponents** | $x^2$, $x^3$, $x^y$, scientific notation with toggle |
| **Statistics** | Mean, sum, standard deviation |
| **Boolean operators** | AND, OR, XOR, NOT |
| **Special functions** | Inverse; factorials; reciprocals; times-pi; left-shift; integer; modulus; nested calculations |

To get help on any function, right-click the key and click on **What's This?** The keyboard equivalent will be listed along with the Help.

 Oddly enough, Calculator has a square-root key in Standard view but not in Scientific view, where you have to hit **Inv** and **x ^ 2**.

Once you've obtained your results, you can use the ubiquitous Edit menu to copy them into the Clipboard. They can then be pasted into another application.

# Notepad

Default path: `Start Menu\Programs\Accessories\Notepad`

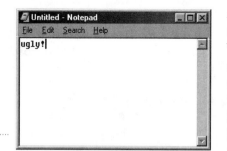

A relic from Windows 3.1, Notepad (Figure 5.13) is included with Windows 98 only because many applications still load it to display ReadMe or Setup files during installation. To call it a simple text editor would be an understatement. Notepad is limited to working with raw ASCII text files smaller than 60K, allows only one monospaced font at a time, and does a rotten job of handling special characters. You can't even underline, boldface, or italicize words. Notepad does let you `Ctrl` `X` Cut, `Ctrl` `C` Copy, `Ctrl` `V` Paste, and `Ctrl` `Z` Undo, and you can search for a particular text string—although with the `Alt` `S` `F` command left over from the old DOS text editor, rather than the Windows standard `Ctrl` `F`. The only mildly special feature left in Notepad is that `F5` sticks the

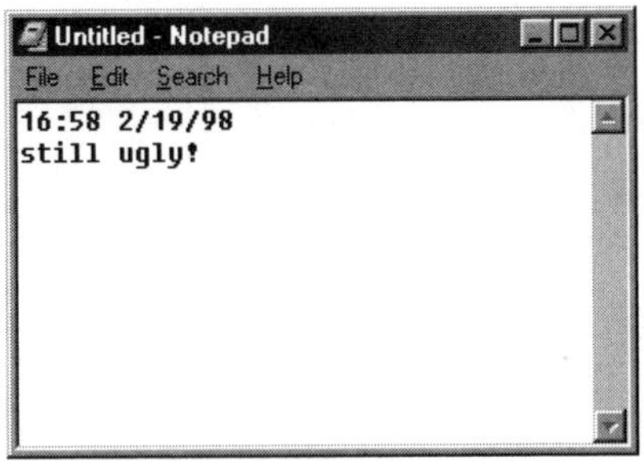

**Figure 5.14**

Notepad with
inserted date

system time and date into your file
(Figure 5.14). For this Microsoft bothered to write a 32-bit version?

The only reason left to use Notepad is
that it forces you to save every file as
plain ASCII text, and doesn't wrap
lines unless you tell it to, so it's a
good emergency editor for (small!)
system files or source-code files.

## Super NoteTab

"No problem," you say, "I'll just use WordPad." But if you're editing raw ASCII, WordPad is perilously too much, just as Notepad falls annoyingly short. Unless you tell it not to, WordPad saves its files with Word for Windows 6.0 formatting, which makes total dog food out of your system files. To keep the formatting out of your file, you have to pull down **File, Save As, Save as type,** and select **Text Document;** and if you forget and hit the Save toolbar button just once, your file is corrupt.

We recommend one of two ways out. The first is the Windows System Configuration Editor, **SYSEDIT,** which automatically opens up your AUTOEXEC.BAT, CONFIG.SYS, WIN.INI, SYSTEM.INI, and whatever other system files you were editing during your previous session, lets you edit them, and definitely saves them as ASCII text. The Windows installation doesn't put SYSEDIT on a menu, but you can enter **sysedit** in the **Run...\Open** dialog of the Start Menu.

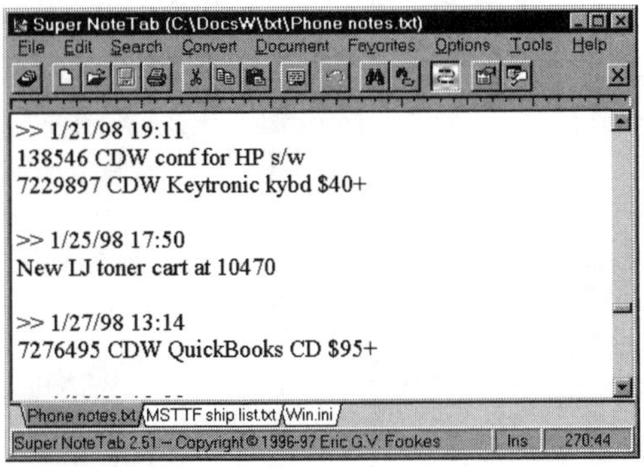

**Figure 5.15**

Super NoteTab

The second—which makes a great endless notepad as well as a spiffy multi-file ASCII editor—is **Super NoteTab** by Eric G. V. Fookes in Geneva, Switzerland (Figure 5.15). This amazing editor will open multiple files and arrange them in a tabbed dialog so you can switch back and forth instantly; for you Notepad freaks, F5 inserts the system time and date (think about phone messages); it has an exhaustive set of toolbar and menu controls and has won shareware awards by the bucketful … except that it's not shareware, it's free! When you're not using it, it minimizes to your System Tray, which is *the* way to keep an applet handy without using up your valuable Desktop. You can download the latest version from **http://www.unige.ch/sciences/terre/geologie/fookes/notetab.htm**. If you insist on paying, Eric also offers a shareware version called **NoteTab Pro** that adds HTML tagging and highlighting; it costs US $5.00 and outperforms programs costing ten times as much.

# Paint

Default path: `Start Menu\Programs\Accessories\Paint`

If you provide the inspiration, Windows 98's **Paint** applet (Figure 5.16) provides the tools. Paint is a virtual art studio complete with easel, paints, paint-

brushes, pencils, and something handy for the budding artist: an eraser. Using a mouse and Paint's tool palettes, you can create a masterpiece in mere seconds. With the help of the Clipboard (or OLE), you can export your art into other applications, such as WordPad.

Paintings and other graphic images you create in Paint are technically referred to as *bitmaps*. A bitmapped graphic image is actually composed of many tiny dots, or pixels, just the way images are composed on your computer. This is in contrast to vector

*Figure 5.16*

*The Paint applet*

graphics—used by, for example, PostScript and AutoCAD—which are images built from a series of mathematical expressions that represent the strokes, lines, and objects contained in the image.

**Basics.** When you first open the Paint applet, you see what every budding Picasso must face: a blank sheet of paper—in this case, virtual paper. This is your drawing surface, which you can resize and adjust as you like. To draw on this surface, you use the mouse. A typical movement is to drag a selected tool across the surface. The Paint tools are arranged in a palette on the left side of the application window; another palette at the bottom of the window offers

you a selection of colors. If you don't like the location of the palettes, you can drag them anywhere else on the desktop (Figure 5.17).

By far the most popular of the Paint tools is the brush. As its name implies, the brush is a freehand drawing tool that lets you add paint directly to the drawing surface. You select the brush icon from the tool palette and drag it across the drawing

*Figure 5.17*

*Paint with
floating palettes*

surface. Depending on your dexterity, the resolution of your mouse, and the quality of your monitor,

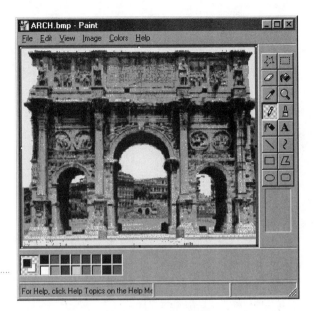

**Figure 5.18**

*Painting with the brush*

you'll find the brush either cumbersome or elegant. With practice, you should be able to produce pleasing results (Figure 5.18).

If you are familiar with using a real paintbrush or drawing pencil, you'll probably complain that drawing with a mouse is like trying to draw with a bar of soap. Don't despair; in Chapter 7 we'll discuss graphics tablets with styluses that not only feel like brushes, but are pressure sensitive. The brushes splay like real ones when used with sophisticated paint programs.

**Figure 5.19**

*Paint sprayer*

You can alter brush size and shape by selecting icons in the lower portion of the tool palette. This region is context-sensitive—that is, the options change depending on what tool you have selected. For example, if you switch from the brush to the paint sprayer, the options change from brush sizes and shapes to spray patterns (Figure 5.19).

Other painting devices include a fill tool for painting enclosed regions with a particular color; a pencil for performing precise drawing operations; an eraser for clearing a particular region of the drawing surface; a tool for drawing straight lines; shape-creation tools (for example, for rectangles, ellipses, and polygons); and a tool for adding typed text to your image (Figure 5.20).

**Colors.** Paint uses black as the default drawing color and white as the default background color. Changing colors is easy, though. Select a color—red, for example—

**Figure 5.20**

*Painting, drawing, and boundary tools*

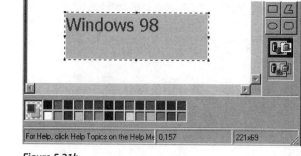

*Figure 5.21a*

*Changing foreground*

*Figure 5.21b*

*Changing background*

from the color palette by clicking on that color with the left mouse button. From now on, all your tools will use red paint. An indicator on the left end of the color palette changes to reflect your current color selection (Figure 5.21a). You can change the background color by clicking on a color palette entry with the right mouse button (Figure 5.21b).

If you want to create your own colors, select **Edit Colors** from the **Colors** menu. Toward the bottom of the Edit Colors dialog box (Figure 5.22), you'll see a large button labeled **Define Custom Colors >>.** Clicking this expands the dialog box to show you Paint's color mixer (Figure 5.23).

*Figure 5.22*

*Edit Colors*

You can mix your own colors using three methods. The simplest is just to click in the multicolored spectrum to select a new hue. If you'd rather mix colors by number, you can define colors with two color systems. The first, the "rainbow box," lets you mix amounts of red, green, and blue—the primary colors. The second, the vertical bar growing paler toward the top, lets you specify hue,

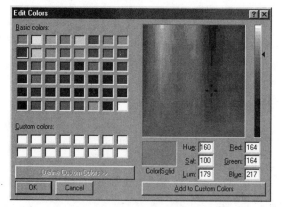

*Figure 5.23*

*Color mixer*

**Figure 5.24**

A custom color

saturation, and luminance. You can create any color with either method, or by combining both. When you're done, click on the **Add to Custom Colors** button, and your new shade is available on the palette (Figure 5.24).

**Special Tools.** Paint has only one special effect—a paint sprayer—but it provides many special tools. You can, for example, magnify a part of your art or alter sections of it without affecting the rest of the drawing.

*Magnifier.* The **Magnifier,** through the **View\Zoom** menu, enables you to zoom in on a specific portion of your drawing. At the same time, you can look at a thumbnail view of the selected portion to see how your changes play out at their real size (Figure 5.25). By selecting **View\View Bitmap** or Ctrl F you can see the image at real size on an otherwise blank screen (Figure 5.26).

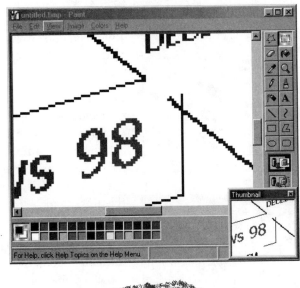

**Figure 5.25**

Magnifier with thumbnail

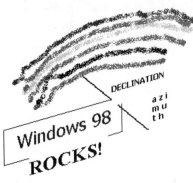

**Figure 5.26**

Bitmap view without controls

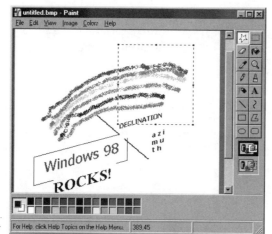

**Figure 5.27**

Rectangular selector

**Figure 5.30**

Edit menu

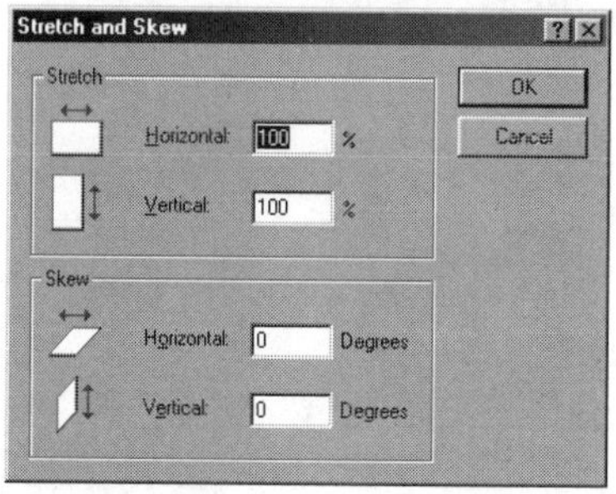

**Figure 5.28**

Stretch and skew

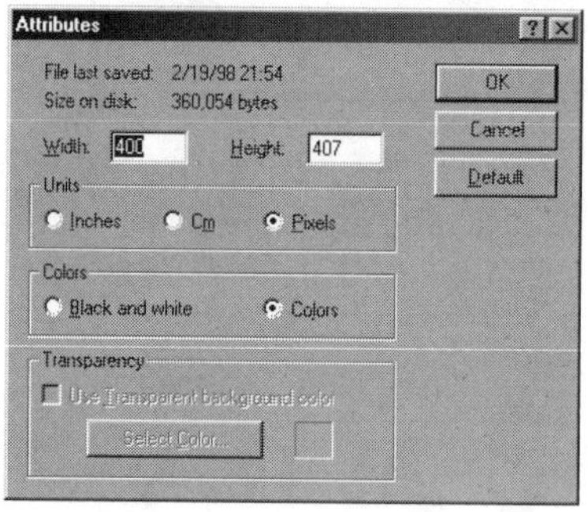

**Figure 5.29**

The Attributes
dialog

*Selector.* The **selection tool** enables you to select a specific region of your drawing for further editing. For example, to copy part of your drawing to the Clipboard, select the region with the selection tool and then use the Edit menu's Copy command.

The normal selection tool lets you drag a rectangular selection box over a particular region (Figure 5.27). But if you don't want to be boxed in, a free-form tool enables you to define a region using freehand drawing.

*Distortions.* Once you've selected a target region of a drawing, you can copy things to it from the Clipboard. You can also flip, rotate, stretch, and skew the region. The Image menu makes this all possible with dialog boxes of options (Figure 5.28).

*Attributes.* To change settings that affect an entire drawing, select the Attributes option from the Image menu. You can define the height and width of a drawing in screen pixels or other units, and indicate color or grayscale on opaque or transparent background (Figure 5.29).

**Edit Menu.** **Copy To** on the **Edit** menu (Figure 5.30) enables you to copy a selected region of a drawing to a separate disk file. **Paste From** allows you to paste an existing graphic image into your drawing.

**File Menu.** Several options on the **File** menu are similar to those in applets such as WordPad. Those include the ubiquitous **Open, Save,** and **Save As**; **Print** and **Print Preview**; **Send** via mail or fax; and a special item for making your current drawing the Windows 98 wallpaper (you'll learn more about wallpaper in Chapter 6).

# QuickView

Default path: `right-click, select QuickView`

**Figure 5.31**

*QuickView window*

QuickView, a licensed third-party applet, is handy for taking a one-click look at that mystery file. Highlight any file, right-click it, and chances are that QuickView will appear on the menu. Select it and here's what you get, with the most common file types:

| File Type | What QuickView Shows |
| --- | --- |
| .386 (device driver) file, .BIN (binary) file, .COM file | MS-DOS Executable Technical File Information (tabular) |
| .BMP (Windows bitmap) image | Thumbnail image |
| .DAT file | varies |
| .DBF (dBase database) file | Can't do it! |
| .DLL (dynamic link library) file, .CPL (Control Panel) file | Windows DLL Technical File Information (tabular) (Figure 5.31) |
| .DOC (Word, WordPad) file | Thumbnail document |
| .EXE file, .SYS file (but not MSDOS.SYS, which is text) | Windows or MS-DOS Executable Technical File Information (tabular) |
| .GIF (Compuserve bitmap) image | Can't do it! |
| .HLP (Windows help) file | Literal file dump (junk) |
| .HTM, .HTML file | HTML text |
| .INF (installation) file | Plain text (readable) |
| .INI (initialization) file | Plain text (readable) |
| .JPG (JPEG) image | Can't do it! |
| .LOG file | Plain text (readable) |
| .MID (MIDI audio) file | Literal file dump (junk) |
| .PPT (PowerPoint) file | Can't do it! |
| .RA, .RAM (RealAudio) file | Literal file dump (junk) |
| .TXT (ASCII) file | Plain text (readable) |
| .WAV (Windows audio) file | Can't do it! |
| .WK1 (Lotus 1-2-3), .WQ1 (Quattro Pro) file | Thumbnail document |
| .XBM image | Literal file dump (junk) |
| .XLS (Excel spreadsheet) file | Thumbnail document |
| .ZIP (archive) file | Can't do it! |

From this list you'll see that QuickView is frustrating at least as often as it's useful, but when it works, it's decidedly better than no viewer at all.

# Scheduled Tasks Folder

Default path: `Start Menu\Programs\Accessories\System Tools\`
`                 Scheduled Tasks`

Scheduled Tasks is a beefed-up successor to the System Agent that shipped with the Windows 95 Plus! pack. With it, you can schedule any Windows task to take place at any time and at almost any interval.

 Once you load Scheduled Tasks, it appears as a mini-icon in the System Tray and can be clicked from there.

Scheduled Tasks uses the Internet Explorer interface but has a special, additional header bar with five buttons:

- **Name** is the name of the task to be run at the scheduled time.

- **Schedule** gives the start time and interval of the task and the first day it will be run.

- **Next Run Time** gives the next start time and day that the task will be run.

- **Last Run Time** gives the most recent time and day that the task finished running.

- **Status** tells you that the scheduled task is running.

**Adding a Scheduled Task.**    Double-clicking **Add Scheduled Task** opens the Scheduled Task Wizard, which begins by showing you a list of the most common programs you might want to run according to a fixed schedule … and, for some reason, their version numbers (Figure 5.32). If you

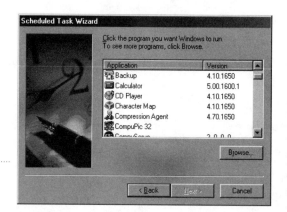

*Figure 5.32*

*Scheduled Task Wizard opening screen*

can't find the application you want to schedule, click the **Browse...** button and go into Explorer.

Once you've selected the program to run, click **Next.** Type a name in for the task; the name of the program is proposed as a default, but you can use something longer to remind yourself of why you're setting it up. The scheduling options are **Daily, Weekly, Monthly, One time only, When my computer starts,** and **When I log on.** Click an option and click Next.

The current time will be proposed as the **Start time,** but you can adjust it with the spin buttons or by typing in a new value. Use the ⟶ key to switch from hours to minutes. When you're done setting the time, Tab to **Start date** and fill in the date fields, again using the arrow keys to switch between fields—or use the drop-down button to pick the date from a monthly calendar. (You can change the month with the arrow buttons to the left and right of the calendar title.) Click **Next.**

On the last page, Windows will confirm the task name and scheduling and offer a blank checkbox. If you check this box, the Scheduled Tasks Properties sheet will open as soon as you click Finish; you can use this to make additional settings and add comments.

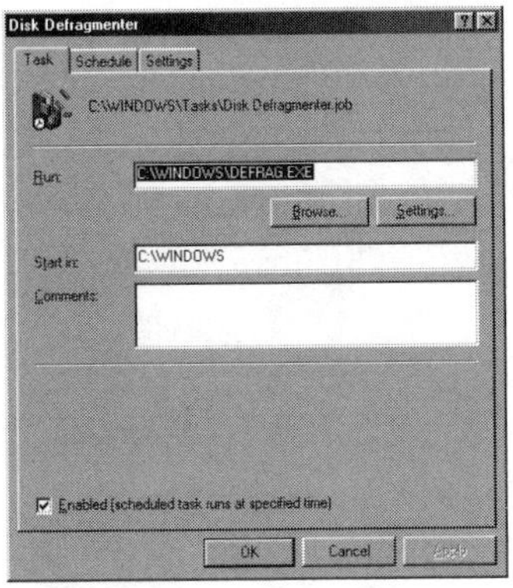

**Figure 5.33**

Properties Task tab

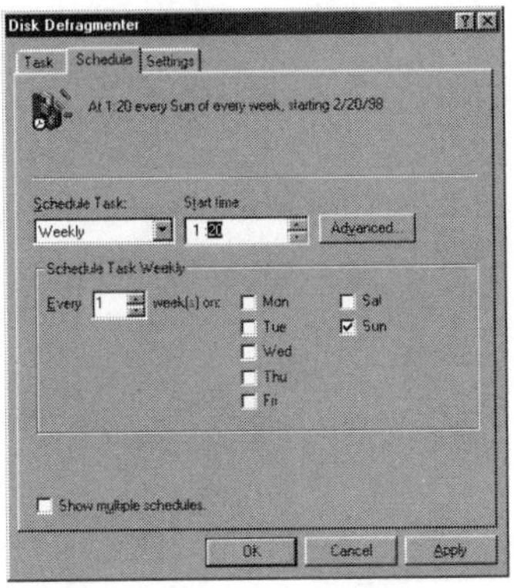

**Figure 5.34**

Properties Schedule tab

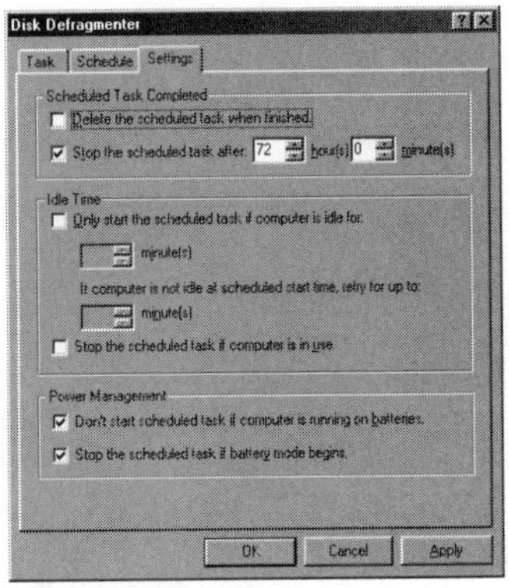

**Figure 5.35**

Properties Settings tab

**Scheduled Tasks Properties.** The Scheduled Tasks Properties sheet (Figure 5.33) has three tabs: **Task, Schedule** and **Settings.**

**Task** includes the path of the application to be Run, the path that the application should Start in, a box for Comments, and a checkbox (checked by default) to Enable or disable the task.

**Schedule** (Figure 5.34) presents a Schedule Task dropbox, a Start Time with spin buttons, a Schedule Task dialog whose contents will vary according to how the Schedule Task dropbox is set, and a checkbox (blank by default) to Show multiple schedules. There's also an **Advanced...** button which we'll get to in a minute.

**Settings** offers options to Delete the task when finished, Stop the task after it executes for a given length of time, relate the task to the onset or duration of idle time, and manage power for laptops. (Figure 5.35)

**Enabled Checkbox (Task tab).** Any task whose **Enabled** checkbox is checked will run as scheduled. Any task whose Enabled checkbox is cleared will not run; its Schedule and Next Run Time will be listed as "Disabled" in the task list, and the clock face in its icon will be replaced with a white X on a red background.

**Schedule Task (Schedule tab).** Note that the Schedule Task dropbox gives you an option, **When idle,** that the Wizard doesn't include.

**Multiple Schedules Checkbox (Schedule tab).** When **Show multiple schedules** is checked, it becomes possible to set up more than one schedule—for example, **Weekly** and **At logon.** Use the New button to set up an additional schedule, the Delete button to delete one or more of the existing ones.

 If you check this checkbox, set up more than one schedule for one task, and then uncheck the box, the multiple schedules remain in effect. The next time you open the Schedule tab, the box will be checked.

**Advanced... Button (Schedule tab).** Wow! We need **Advanced** schedule on top of it all? Here's what the Advanced Options (Figure 5.36) do:

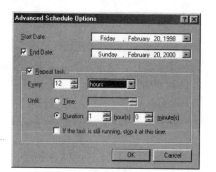

*Figure 5.36*

Advanced Schedule options

- **Start Date** sets the start date. Use ⬅ and ➡ to jump between day, month, date and year; ⬆ and ⬇ to increment or decrement any of them.

- **End Date,** if the checkbox is checked, lets you specify the last time the task will be run using the same options as Start Date.

- **Repeat task,** if the checkbox is checked, lets you specify how often to repeat the task, for how long or until when, and lets you set an absolute time to stop the task even if it's running at the time.

**Context Menu.** Right-clicking on any scheduled task gives you a Context Menu with two special options: **Run,** meaning run the task once immediately, and **End task,** if the task is running and you want to end it immediately. There's also the usual **Cut, Copy, Delete** and **Rename,** as well as **Properties,** which pops up the Scheduled Tasks Properties sheet.

# Windows Address Book

Default path: `Start Menu\Programs\Internet Explorer\Address Book`
Fast access: `Start Menu\Find\People`

If there's any competition for Greatest Rookie Windows Applet, the brand-new Windows Address Book has to be a serious contender. This integrated, middleweight contact manager is fully attuned to the realities of modern life and work. (You mean there's a difference?)

The Windows Address Book uses the Explorer interface to store a useful amount of information about each contact, then hooks its database into Outlook Express for e-mail or into NetMeeting—or a third-party application—for conferencing. This is the Address Book default first screen (Figure 5.37):

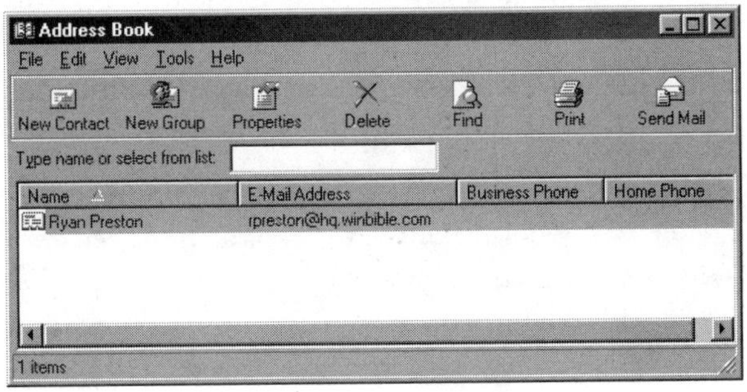

*Figure 5.37*

*Windows Address Book*

**Toolbar.** The Toolbar is straightforward:

- **New Contact** (or Ctrl N) opens a blank Contact record for you to fill in.

- **New Group** (or Ctrl G) allows you to sort contacts into Groups for list-based e-mailing or conferencing.

- **Properties** opens the selected record; it's grayed out unless a record is highlighted.

- **Delete** erases the selected record; you're prompted for confirmation, and the option is grayed out unless a record is highlighted.

- **Find** uses LDAP, the Lightweight Directory Access Protocol, to search in the local Address Book or in any one of several Internet directories. This is the same dialog you reach from Find\People on the Start Menu. If you're searching by name in the local Address Book, it's faster to use the "Type name or select" incremental pick-box that's part of the Toolbar.

- **Print** (or Ctrl P) prints the selected record or records, or all records, in your choice of three formats: Memo, Business Card, or Phone List.

- **Send Mail** opens a blank Outlook Express mail message, with the Send To box filled in with the selected person, people, or group.

**Record Properties Sheet.** The Record Properties Sheet has five tabs: **Personal, Home, Business, Other,** and **Digital IDs.** If NetMeeting is installed there's also a **NetMeeting** tab (Figure 5.38).

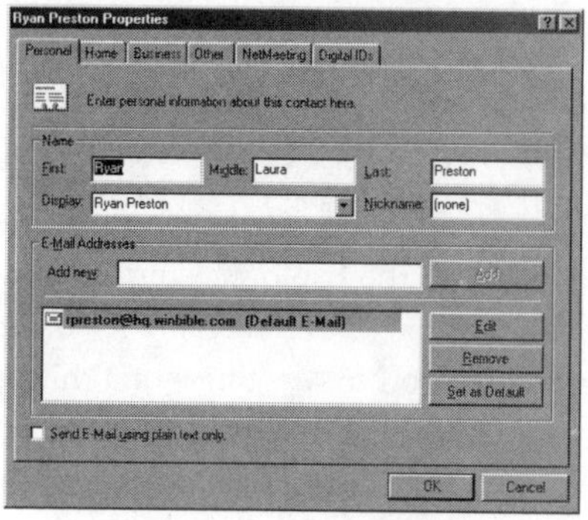

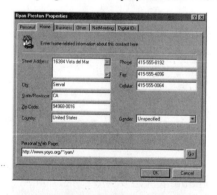

**Figure 5.38**

*Record Properties Sheet*

On the **Personal** tab there are regions for Name and for E-Mail Addresses. As you fill in First, Middle and Last name, the Display field fills in with what you're typing; but actually, the Display field drop-box gives you a choice of First, Middle and Last name, or Nickname if any, or Company off the Business tab, if any.

In the E-Mail Addresses region, you can key in an address and hit Add. If this contact has more than one e-mail address, you can pick one with the Set as Default button to tell Outlook Express to use that address when it sends mail.

**Plain Text.** The checkbox **Send E-Mail using plain text only** (blank by default) allows for a discrepancy; Outlook Express can embellish its messages with fonts and formatting, but many competing e-mail programs won't know what to do with the formatting instructions on receipt. Since e-mail sent by one program can display as unutterable garbage when opened by another, it's only polite to check this box unless you know your recipient also uses Outlook Express (see Chapter 16).

**Home Tab.** The Home tab (Figure 5.39) gives you room for home address, home phone and fax numbers, and cell phone number, as well as **Gender** (which can be listed as "Unspecified" if this would be inappropriate for your database) and **Personal Web Page.**

**Figure 5.39**

*Home tab*

**Business Tab.** The Business tab (Figure 5.40) gives you room for company name, business address, job title, department name, office location, office phone and fax numbers, and pager number, as well as **Business Web Page.**

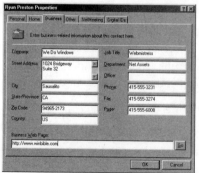

**Figure 5.40**

*Business tab*

The Street Address field in Home or Business, and the Notes field in Other, are free-form, and you can hit ⏎Enter⏎ between lines to break them. In any *other* field, if you hit ⏎Enter⏎, you'll close the Properties sheet.

**Go Buttons.**    The Go buttons (Figure 5.41) load Internet Explorer to take you to the Personal or Business Web address.

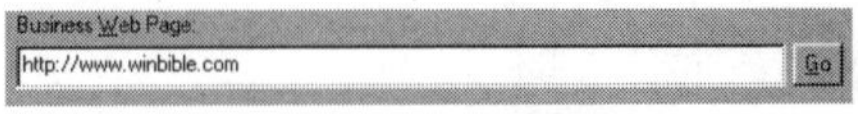

Business Web Page:
http://www.winbible.com    [Go]

**Print Formats.**    The three output formats are:

- **Memo** prints everything on the Home and Business tabs.

- **Business Card** prints everything on the Business tab, and the Home phone numbers.

- **Phone List** prints all the phone numbers on both tabs.

**Other Tab.**    The Other tab includes a Notes field and a Group Membership field, which is grayed out unless this individual is part of a group or groups (see below).

**NetMeeting Tab.**    If you chose to install NetMeeting as part of Windows, the NetMeeting tab (Figure 5.42) offers space for conferencing information. In the Conferencing E-Mail field you can put one or several e-mail addresses that are configured for teleconferencing over the Net.

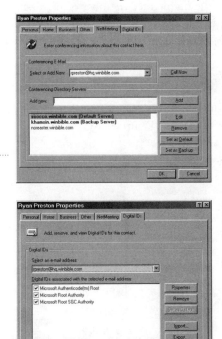

This works just like the E-Mail Addresses dialog on the **Personal** tab, and lets you enter any number of directory servers. The first server you enter will be designated the Default Server and the second will be designated the Backup Server, but you can override these selections with the **Set as Default** and **Set as Backup** buttons.

*Figure 5.42*

*Conferencing directory servers*

**Digital IDs Tab.**    The **Digital IDs tab** shows you which Digital IDs installed on the system are associated with the selected e-mail address.

*Figure 5.43*

*Digital IDs tab*

***Figure 5.44***

*Group Properties*

**Group Properties.**  Pulling down File\New Group or hitting `Ctrl` `G` at the Explorer screen brings up the Group Properties sheet (Figure 5.44). To begin a new Group, type in a group name.

While a Group is being established there are four options:

- **New Contact** lets you add a new individual record directly from the Group Properties sheet.

- **Select Members** (Figure 5.45) lets you add records from the existing list to the new group. Highlight the record to add in the left pane, click the **Select->** button to copy the record name to the right pane.

- **Remove** removes the highlighted member or members from the group. You can't remove the last member; if the composition of your group completely changes, add the first of the new ones before you remove the last of the old ones.

- **Properties** opens the Properties sheet of the highlighted individual.

When you finish creating a new Group it will appear in the left pane, as a branch of the Address Book tree (Figure 5.46).

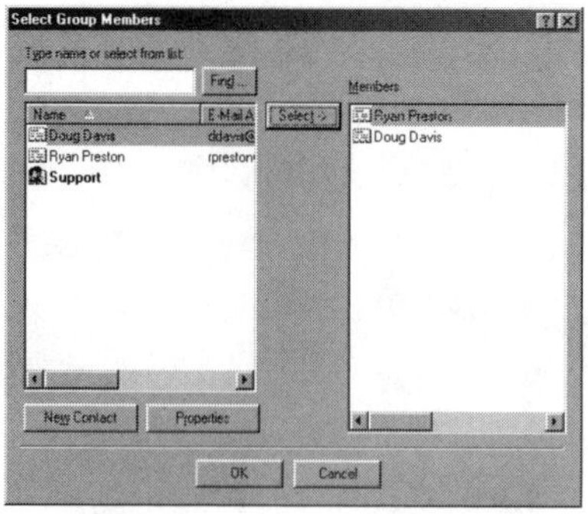

***Figure 5.45***

*Select Group Members*

***Figure 5.46***

*Group branch*

**Menu Options.** Most options on the Windows Address Book pull-down menus will be familiar from general Windows practice, but there are a few we need to describe:

| Option | Description |
| --- | --- |
| *File\Import* | Brings data into the Windows Address Book from Eudora, Microsoft or Netscape address books, or comma-delimited text files. The text file option isn't incredibly useful since there's no information on the allowed field names, field length, or specification for the header, if any. You can also import files in the vCard digital business card format. |
| *File\Export* | The range of export formats is more limited: Microsoft Exchange address book, comma-delimited text file, or vCard. Guess you're stuck if you want to export to … that other browser. |
| *View\Sort By* | If **Sort By** is set to **Name and First Name**, names in the list are displayed as **<firstname> <lastname>** and the **Type name** list finds by first name. If **Sort By** is set to **Name and Last Name**, names in the list are displayed as **<lastname>, <firstname>** and the **Type name** list finds by last name. If Sort By is set to anything other than Name, the First Name/Last Name choice is grayed out but "sticky"—that is, the last setting you made is locked until you set Sort By to Name again. |
| *Tools\Accounts* | Lets you customize the list of Internet directory services that are available to the Find command. |
| *Tools\Options* | Lets you decide whether to make Windows Address Book available to Outlook and other applications. If your information is shareable, Outlook stores it; if not, the Address Book stores it. The choice to share data is grayed out unless Outlook is installed. |
| *Tools\Send Mail* | Starts an Outlook Express message to the highlighted record or records. |
| *Tools\Internet Call* | Starts a NetMeeting session; if NetMeeting has not been set up, it starts the Setup Wizard. |

**Summary.** If you're coming to the Windows Address Book from a free-standing contact manager like ACT!, Maximizer, or Goldmine, you'll immediately notice a lack of certain features. For example, there are no timers, there's no call logging, there's no integral editor for paper documents, and there's only one note field per person. Even so, the Address Book is a tantalizing early clue to the nature of contact management in a cyber-centered world. We recommend, at least, playing with it long enough to understand what it might do for you. Using the Address Book and Outlook Express might help you decide to adopt Outlook, Microsoft's real Swiss army knife for phone jockeys.

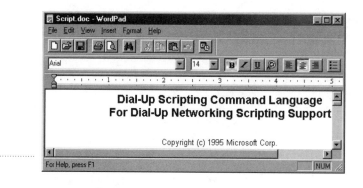

*Figure 5.47*

*WordPad*

# WordPad

Default path: `Start Menu\Programs\Accessories\WordPad`

Not as modern or powerful as Microsoft Word, Windows 98's WordPad nevertheless does what a basic word processor should do, and it's a snap to use. You can't run a spell checker or create a macro with WordPad, but you can create a document, save it, and print it (Figure 5.47).

WordPad was introduced in Windows 95 to replace the Write applet that was included with Windows 3.1. Write was a robust program, but had limited formatting choices, and created, edited and read only its own .WRI file format, which was shared by nothing else. It became popular mostly for documenting Windows applications, since it was the one word processor that any Windows user was almost guaranteed to have.

When WordPad appeared, it was hailed as a big improvement over Write. It allowed elaborate formatting and could read Word files directly. Unfortunately, WordPad has its file format in common with Word for Windows 6.0 and Word for Windows 95 (also known as 7.0), so that WordPad's files are no longer compatible with a version of Word you can buy today. The bottom line is that Windows 98 offers you a choice, according to file size, between two editors— Notepad and WordPad—both of which are obsolete. We suspect that some Windows 98 users, like many Windows 95 users, will end up digging out their Windows 3.1 diskettes and reinstalling Write as their lightweight word processor.

**Formatting Text.** When you format text with WordPad, the complete range

*Figure 5.48*

*The Font dialog box*

of Windows 98 fonts is available to you. You can also center, justify, and perform other feats of typographic dexterity by using convenient menu commands, dialog boxes, and toolbar buttons (Figure 5.48).

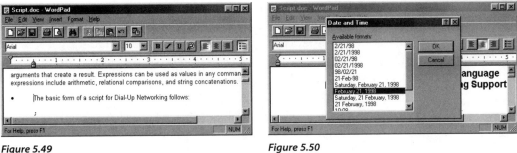

**Figure 5.49**

List bullet

**Figure 5.50**

Insert date and time

WordPad also supports advanced features such as bulleted lists, and it enables you to insert the current date and time into a document (Figures 5.49 and 5.50). You can access those functions on WordPad's menus and toolbar buttons. A more limited subset of commands is available on the right-click menu.

**Figure 5.51**

Tab stop on ruler

WordPad is up to speed on tabs. To create new tab stops, click on the WordPad ruler bar. You see a tab stop indicator wherever you just clicked. You can drag the tab stop across the ruler bar to adjust its position precisely (Figure 5.51).

Unlike big brother Word, WordPad allows only left tabs, not right or decimal. There are also no tab leaders. The only adjustment you can make in the **Format\Tabs** dialog is the tab stop position.

**Clipboard Maneuvers.** WordPad provides a perfect chance to practice with the Clipboard. If you highlight a region of text and click the **Copy** button or select **Copy** from the **Edit** menu, WordPad places a copy of the text on the Clipboard. Similarly, click **Paste** to insert the Clipboard's contents into a document where the cursor is positioned.

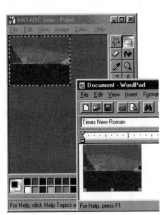

**Figure 5.52**

Pasting graphics
into WordPad

To spruce up WordPad documents, you can use the Clipboard to paste in graphics. Anything created and selected in the Paint applet or another paint program will work (Figure 5.52).

Because WordPad is an OLE-aware application, it can exchange OLE data with other applications and with the Windows 98 operating system. To see this feature in action, highlight a region of text in WordPad and drag it to the Windows 98 desktop. The text data is turned into an OLE Scrap, which can be dragged back into WordPad or into another OLE-aware application.

**Saving Data.** Whenever you save a document, WordPad automatically stores it in Word 6.0 format. You can also save data in four other formats: as raw text, MS-DOS text-with-layout, Unicode (16-bit) text or Rich Text Format (RTF). Saving a document as anything *other than* a Rich Text or Word 6.0 file means you lose all formatting and graphics but can transfer data to other programs. Rich Text format, like Word 6.0 format, retains formatting and graphics which you can transfer into any other Microsoft word processor. Make your format choice when you save data; use the **Save As** dialog box (Figure 5.53).

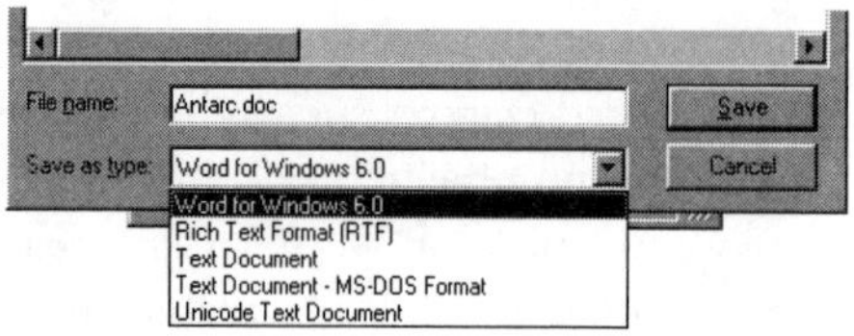

*Figure 5.53*

*The Save As dialog box in WordPad*

WordPad can only save formatting information—such as fonts, justification, and pasted graphics data—if you use the Word 6.0 or Rich Text format. The Text Document format produces a file with ASCII text, which drops all formatting and graphics information.

## Saving Your ASCII

We recommend against using WordPad to edit any system file—for example, an .INI, a .SYS, or a .BAT file—because the text formatting and other technical data embedded in Word and Rich Text files will corrupt system files and make your computer choke. If you want to avoid crashing your whole system, always double-check that system files have been saved as plain ASCII text. Better yet, use Notepad or Super NoteTab (see earlier in this chapter) to edit system files with no risk of damaging them.

**Preview and Print.** Once you've completed your masterpiece, WordPad makes it easy to preview and print the document. A Print Preview mode shows you how your document will look on paper by providing a bird's-eye view of each virtual page, displaying the text exactly as it will appear when printed (Figure 5.54).

You can zoom to Print Preview to see details of a particular region of a document and even to view two pages side by side. By default, Print Preview displays the current page. You can use the scroll bars to navigate around a single page or to access any other page in the document.

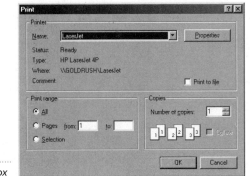

*Figure 5.54*

*Print Preview mode (two-page)*

To bring up Print Preview, either click on the Print Preview button on the toolbar or select Print Preview from the File menu. Once you have finished previewing your document and are ready to print, WordPad offers several options.

Click on the **Print** button (or select Print from the File menu) to bring up the standard Windows 98 Print dialog box. From this box you can select a printer, specify the type of paper and the handling of graphics and fonts, and indicate how many copies you'd like to print (Figure 5.55).

*Figure 5.55*

*The Print dialog box*

Most of the Print dialog box items are self-explanatory. Once you've set the number of copies, specified which pages to print, and selected a printer, clicking the Print button sends the data to the Windows 98 print spooler and returns you to WordPad.

**A Custom Fit.** You can customize WordPad as you can most Windows 98 applications. For example, you can activate the toolbars with the View menu, and you can control the way data is displayed by using the Options dialog box.

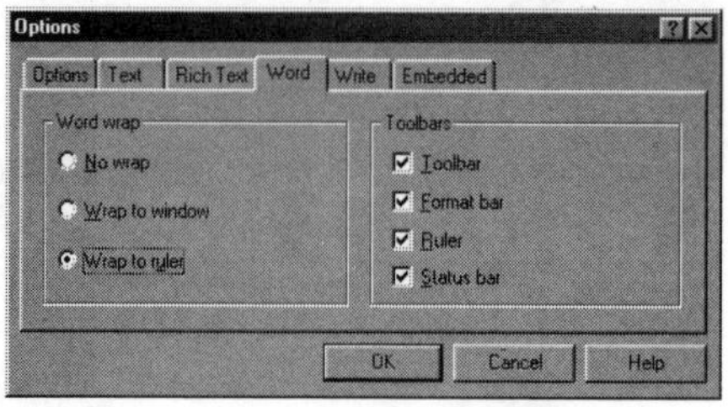

**Figure 5.56**

The Options dialog box

To open this box, click on Options on the View menu.

Here you'll find one of WordPad's neatest features, the ability to select separate word wrap and toolbar settings for each type of file that WordPad can edit (Figure 5.56).

# Windows 98 Games

No operating system would be complete without distraction for the weary worker, and Windows 98 is no exception—in fact, it's a shining example. On the Games submenu, you'll find four unique and challenging games designed to appeal to your lighter side while you're taking a break from number crunching. Some, like Solitaire, are notoriously addictive holdovers from Windows 3.1. Others, like Freecell, made their debut on Windows NT, Windows 98's big brother. All are guaranteed to entertain.

There's one serious problem with the game applets: if you get too entertained around work, your boss could accuse you of improper use of company assets or some other hideous crime against bureaucracy. Don't worry; just tell the boss that these games are actually mouse training utilities, an important educational component of the system, and that they allow you to get familiar with Windows 98 without risking damage to mission-critical work files. (We suggest that for maximum effectiveness you say something as close to that as possible; it's a line we've polished and perfected for years.)

## Freecell
Default path: `Start Menu\Programs\Accessories\Games\Freecell`

One of the most mesmerizing computer card games ever written, Freecell (Figure 5.57) was first introduced on Windows NT. It's as simple in concept as it is diabolical to play.

The key to the game is the row of eight "cells" below the menu bar. The four on the right are the "home cells," which you gradually move all the cards to, starting with the aces. The four on the left are the "free cells," which you can use to store inconvenient cards—but only one per cell, and only temporarily. You win when you make four stacks of cards on the home cells; one for each

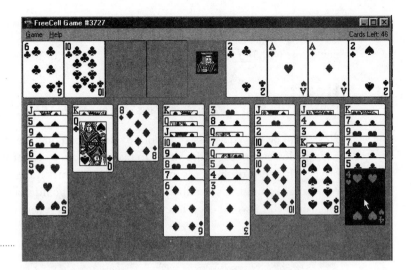

*Figure 5.57*

Freecell

suit, stacked in order of rank. You lose when you realize, with creeping dismay, that every remaining possible move requires one more free cell than you have …

The mad brilliance of Freecell is that there are no hidden cards, and that therefore, *in theory,* you can win any and every game—provided you make exactly the right moves. Fred suspects this rumor might be a plot to keep you plugging away until you crash or your machine does; Kip, forever the optimist, remains hopeful but has spent far too many hours playing Freecell.

**Freecell Hints.**  Before you move the first card of a new game, make sure you know where the aces are. Generally speaking, the higher your aces or

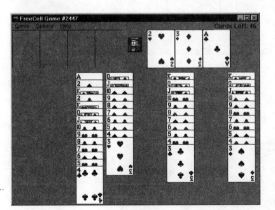

*Figure 5.58*

A tough game

deuces are in the stacks, the more difficult the game will be; Figure 5.58, winnable from this position, is the toughest game Kip ever remembers winning, and he took the screenshot as a souvenir. Look at the top of the left-hand column.

If you have more than one free cell, and a column with only one card in it, move the card up to the free cell and leave the column empty. As practice will demonstrate, you can do amazing moves with one empty column.

If the game's title bar starts to blink, there's only one legal move left. (Good luck finding it.)

There are 32,000 distinct games of Freecell. For the practiced player, the games with higher numbers are too easy. Sharpen your skills by selecting a new game with F3 , then playing one with a three- or four-digit number.

# Hearts

Default path: **Start Menu\Programs\Accessories\Games\Hearts**

Hearts can be played across a network by more than one player. The player with the lowest ending score wins. To play, you pass three cards to the next player. The value of the cards in your hand determines how many points you earn in each round. It's possible to gain or lose a large number of points in this game; you need to experiment to get the hang of it (Figure 5.59).

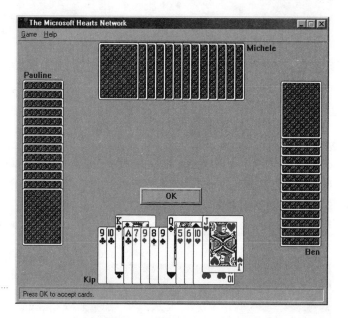

*Figure 5.59*

*Hearts in action*

When you begin a game of Hearts, you can choose either to become the dealer or to join an existing game. Only one player can act as the dealer; all the other players join the game by connecting to the dealer's system (Figure 5.60).

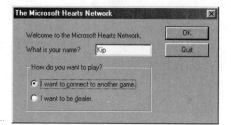

*Figure 5.60*

*Starting Hearts*

If you want to play the game solo against the computer, Windows 98 provides three artificial opponents. To play solo, choose to be dealer, then press F2 (or select **New** from the **Game** menu) to start a new game.

## Minesweeper

Default path: `Start Menu\Programs\Accessories\Games\Minesweeper`

**Figure 5.61**

Minesweeper

Minesweeper has been part of Windows since 3.1, and if it ever disappears, the howls of rage will lift the sky. No matter how many hours people play this game, it proves riveting time after time. That's because the consistent challenge is always mixed with an element of surprise.

The object of Minesweeper is to locate all the mines in a virtual mine field without uncovering (and thus detonating) any of them. To do this, you click on the squares of a grid over the mine field. As you uncover a "safe" square, it tells you how many mines are buried in the surrounding eight squares (Figure 5.61).

The number provided by a safe square helps you guess which of the surrounding squares are most likely to contain mines. You can avoid those squares as you continue to uncover more safe squares. If you accidentally uncover a mine, however, all of the mines in the mine field detonate, and you lose. To win, you have to uncover all the safe squares without detonating a mine. You are timed, so you can rate yourself on both speed and level of difficulty.

To adjust Minesweeper's settings, including how difficult you want to make it, pull down the Game menu. To start a new game, click on the smiley-face icon at the top of the Minesweeper window.

## Solitaire

Default path: `Start Menu\Programs\Accessories\Games\Solitaire`

Few computer games are as notorious as Windows Solitaire. Another holdover from Windows 3.1, Solitaire has a highly addictive nature that has provoked

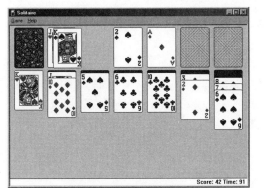

**Figure 5.62**

Solitaire

many a Windows user's wrath over the years. It's simply a hard game to walk away from. For many early adopters of Windows, Solitaire was the only reason for having a (flaky) graphical user interface on their computers.

Solitaire is a virtual version of the old single-person card game (Figure 5.62). You play Solitaire by dragging cards between stacks in an effort to produce ordered piles of alternating colors. Windows Solitaire includes a shuffle deck, as well as spaces in which to place the ace from each suit to build to foundations—solitaire-speak for the way you sort the deck in a session.

The game offers numerous options. Do you want to draw one or three cards at a time from the shuffle deck? Do you want to score Vegas style, normal style, or no style? Should your score depend on how quickly you play, or not? You can even choose from a dozen colorful card backs to brighten up your Solitaire display. Use the Game menu to set up the game the way you like it.

 **Unless your computer has a very slow video adapter, don't check Outline dragging.** It speeds up game play slightly but impairs the realism.

# Summary

Everything about Windows 98 was planned to make it easy for the first-time user to adjust to computing in general. That's why miniature versions of real computer programs were included with Windows 98. All of those applets, as they are called, offer some benefit, although once you've gotten the hang of them, you'll understand their limitations as well. However, you may never get tired of the games Microsoft has included; Solitaire, Hearts, Freecell, and Minesweeper have become addictions for millions of Windows users. All in all, whether you're working or playing, Windows 98 offers something to suit your every mood.

# Part 2

## Living with Windows 98

# Part 2 At a Glance

# 6

# Personalizing Windows 98

People like to customize. You pick out your own clothes, decorate your home according to your own tastes, and enjoy your right to add any amount of salt and pepper to your plate. At work you arrange your desk into your own personal chaos, placing critical elements—like the coffee mug—within easy reach. In life, your individuality shows through in everything from the colors you wear to the order of your credit cards in your wallet.

Those fun-loving software engineers up at Microsoft made it possible for you to express your individuality by customizing the Windows 98 interface. You can, for example, change the color of your desktop from the default seaweed green to a more pleasant pastel, a shocking psychedelic, or even a graphic image (tip: you don't want to make it too graphic). You can also customize application windows by painting their elements different colors or by altering the fonts.

Although some customization options exist merely for pleasure, others have a more practical side. For example, you can modify the contents of the Windows 98 Start menu itself, placing items you use a lot within easy reach. Even the Taskbar's behavior can be customized. And in true Windows 98 fashion, you can make all those changes easily, by responding to the appropriate dialog box and moving objects with the ubiquitous drag and drop.

If you're like us, the first thing you'll do is run right out and substitute colors in the Windows 98 interface. Everybody's taste in colors is different, and virtually every visual element can be recolored to suit your personal whim, including the desktop, dialog boxes, and application window controls. Indeed, it almost seems as if Microsoft intentionally made the default background for Windows 98 an obnoxious shade of green to challenge users to come up with better combinations on their own. Which brings us to the most forgiving aspect of this tweaking: When you blunder into a color scheme that you can't live with for a whole minute (and we've all done it at least once), you can change it back and start over very quickly.

# Display Properties

To change the colors of onscreen items, you use the Display Properties control panel. To view this panel, select Start Menu\Settings\Control Panels, then double-click on the Display icon. You can also click with the right mouse button on any open area of the Windows 98 desktop, then select Properties from the pop-up menu. In either case, you're presented with the Display Properties control panel (Figure 6.1).

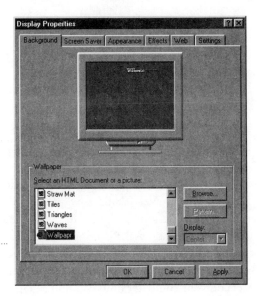

**Figure 6.1**

The Display
Properties control
panel

Like most control panels, the Display Properties panel presents its information in a tabbed dialog box. On most pages, a miniature, blank computer screen sits ready to show you your changes before you apply them. Like a film director—or an omniscient digital artist—you can scroll through page after page of options, fine-tuning the image on the preview screen until you achieve your desired effect.

## Background

**Figure 6.2**

The Live Wire
pattern

The first page of the dialog box, **Background,** enables you to alter the surface of your desktop by applying patterns or wallpaper. For example, if you click the **Pattern...** button and select **Live Wire** from the Pattern list box, Windows 98 adds a series of black, zigzag lines over the current background color (Figure 6.2).

Similarly, if you select the **Argyle** image from the Wallpaper list box and pick Tile from the Display dropbox, Windows 98 covers your screen with an image

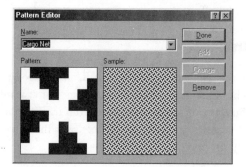

**Figure 6.3**

Browsing for wallpaper

reminiscent of a gaudy argyle sock. Yes, it's true: Beau Brummell is alive and well and living in Windows 98.

You can use virtually any graphic image as wallpaper, including anything you create yourself with the Paint applet. Windows 98 provides you with over thirty wallpapers; some, like Autumn Leaves, Cars, and Blue Rivets, will be nostalgic favorites with the Windows 3.1 contingent, while others are newer. If you don't like what you see in the list box, click on the Browse button. Up pops the **Browse for Background Files** dialog box. You can navigate through the folders on your computer until you find a graphic design that you like (Figure 6.3). Once you've located the desired graphic, you can either center it on the desktop or have Windows 98 tile the image, filling the entire background with the design.

Windows 98 also provides about thirty patterns for your selection. You can't use imported graphic images as patterns (although you can as wallpaper), but

**Figure 2.2**

Tabbed dialog box

you can alter existing patterns—even create new ones—with the **Pattern Editor,** a special pixel-editing dialog box. To edit an existing pattern, select its name from the Pattern list box and click on the **Edit Pattern** button. Up pops the Pattern Editor (Figure 6.4).

With the Pattern Editor, you can manipulate individual pixels in the **Pattern** field and preview your changes in the accompanying **Sample** field. Once you finish, click the **Done** button, and the Pattern Editor asks you if you want to save the changes. Click on **Yes,** and the pattern is updated. You can also save your creation as a completely new pattern by typing a new name into the Name field before clicking on the Done button.

In the Windows 98 world, wallpapers override patterns. For example, if you select the Autumn Leaves wallpaper and tile it, then select Thatches as a pattern, don't be surprised if all you see is Autumn Leaves. Because patterns are designed to work with only solid-color desktops, a pattern always takes a back seat when a graphic is in use.

## Color Schemes

Wallpapers and patterns are only part of the picture. Click on the **Appearance** tab, and you see a dizzying array of colorization options. It's enough to make Ted Turner turn seaweed green with envy (Figure 6.5).

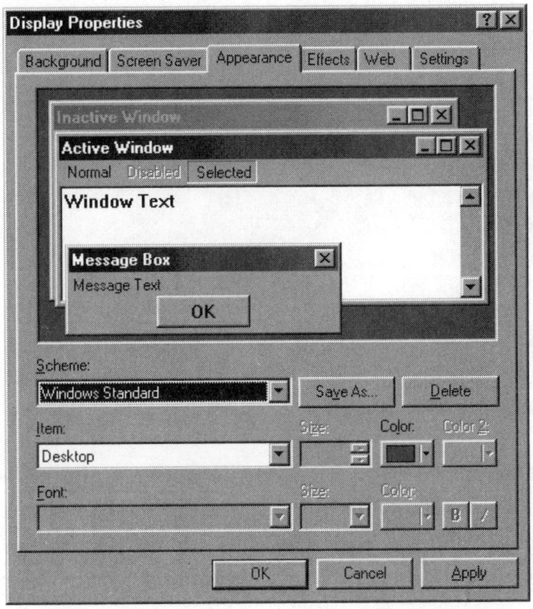

**Figure 6.5**

The Appearance tab

The first thing you notice is the **Scheme** list box. Windows 98 lets you either colorize each item separately or use predefined color schemes that alter more than one item simultaneously. Each sample scheme, like Desert or Lilac, is supposedly color-coordinated, but we have to wonder who coordinated Eggplant and with what. And some of the most vivid schemes from Windows 3.*x*, like Rugby, have vanished. On the other hand, if you crave post-industrial stimulation and wish these corporate pastels would go away, try High Contrast Black.

If, in the end, you share our distaste for most of the canned combinations, you can select the one that comes closest to being palatable, then customize its individual elements. For example, let's say you like the Rainy Day scheme but find the jet-black background a tad depressing (no use getting suicidal—Windows isn't your whole life, after all). First select the Rainy Day combination using the **Scheme** list box, then select Desktop from the **Item** list box. Skip two spaces to the right of the Item list box and click on the dropbox called **Color**; you're presented with a choice of white, black, and 18 colors. (You don't want a white Desktop, it gets dirty in no time.)

Still not satisfied? Click on the **Other...** button at the bottom of the list to bring up a custom color-selection dialog box. Here you can pick from forty-eight standard colors, or define the color of your dreams (Figure 6.6). You can perform this fine-tuning on virtually every visual element in the Windows 98 interface, from application window title bars to the background color of menu items (which is blue by default).

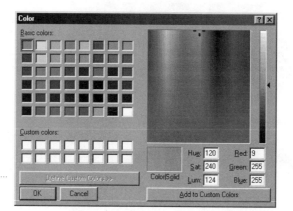

*Figure 6.6*

*Coloring your desktop*

**Are you hunting all over the beautiful Northern Lights display of the custom color panel, only to find that most of your custom colors end up as charcoal gray? Their luminance (brightness) is probably very low; it may even be zero. Go to the tall thin column at the right of the color panel, use your mouse pointer to grab the black left-pointing triangle, and slide it up to the middle of the column. In the sample box labeled Color/Solid, which is the color you've *really* mixed, you'll now see something very close to the color pinpointed by the crosshairs of the color panel. Only when you master the delicate interplay of the color panel and the luminance column will you appreciate Windows' dazzling ability to present every sliver of hue that your monitor and video card can produce.**

## Text

You can also alter the text used in specific areas of the interface; for example, icon titles. When you select a text element from the Item list box, additional list boxes become active. You can change point size, the color of some items, and other characteristics, such as boldfacing and italicizing (Figure 6.7).

**Figure 6.7**

*Modifying item fonts*

Although the Appearance page previews your changes by simulating application windows and dialog boxes, it doesn't represent some items, like the text used in icon titles. To see changes to those items, either you can close the Display Properties dialog box by clicking on the OK button, or you can leave the dialog box open on the desktop and bring up the changes manually by clicking the Apply button. You can use the Apply button from all the Display Properties pages, as you can in almost all other dialog boxes throughout Windows 98.

## Screensavers

Screensavers are like graffiti artists—they take over what's on your screen when you're not watching. Basically, a screensaver is a specialty program that displays an animation sequence on your PC's screen when the computer is idle.

Originally designed to prevent phosphor etching by images that stayed on the screen for a long time, and the subsequent "ghosting" that was burned into the screen permanently, screensavers have long outgrown that purpose. Newer screens don't use the antiquated cathode-ray tube (CRT) technology that suffers from ghosting. Screensavers, meanwhile, have remained a big hit as "canvases" for many creative animations that clever artists have devised.

Your choice of screensaver can reflect your personality, whether whimsical (the **After Dark** series from Berkeley Systems), humorous (**Opus and Bill** of Bloom County/Outland fame), artistic (Microsoft's **Scenes**), or witty (build your own screensaver by filling a Flying Toaster module with flying quotes). You can also get motivational screensavers, religious screensavers, and psychedelic screensavers that can be controlled by a MIDI keyboard. A friend of Fred's is designing a Grateful Dead screensaver, and who knows, a classical composers screensaver might be available by the time this book is published. Briefly, screensavers have become varied and popular accessories.

Windows 98 provides about a dozen screensavers for your pleasure. (The ones whose names begin with **3D** depend on a special graphics model called OpenGL; they're spectacular, but will work best if you have a powerful graphics card.) Click on the **Screen Saver** tab in the Display Properties dialog box, and you're transported to screensaver central. Here you can also access Windows 98's screensaver controls (Figure 6.8).

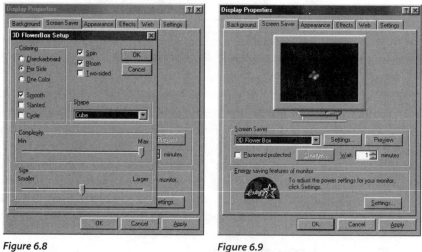

*Figure 6.8*

*The Screen Saver page*

*Figure 6.9*

*Screensaver trailers*

The Screen Saver list box on the Screen Saver page offers a variety of screensavers, including the ever-popular Flying Windows. Select a name from the Screen Saver list box, and a miniature computer screen comes to life with a preview of that screensaver in action (Figure 6.9).

Want to see how the screensaver will really look on your screen? Click on the **Preview** button; your screen goes blank, then the animation takes over.

To stop the preview, simply move the mouse or press any key on the keyboard. Indeed, any screensaver—constantly monitoring the mouse and keyboard in the background—knows enough to vanish the minute it feels your touch. The world will know you're back at work and ready to earn that paycheck!

Another screensaver control is the **Wait** field, which lets you specify how long Windows 98 waits before bringing up the screensaver. If you set the value to ten minutes with the spin buttons, and don't touch your computer for that long, Windows 98 kicks in the screensaver.

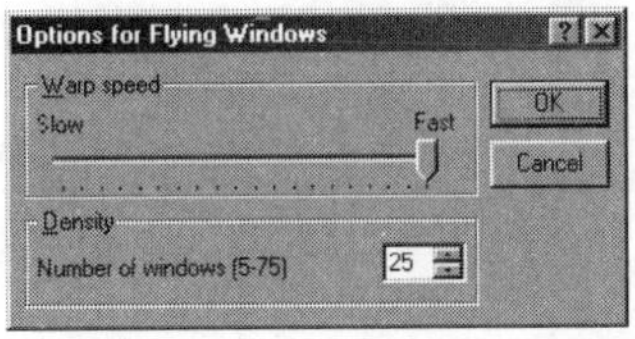

*Figure 6.10*

*Settings for a screensaver*

Some screensavers have other controls as well. For example, with the Flying Windows screensaver, you can adjust the speed at which the windows fly across your screen, as well as the density of windows (Figure 6.10). Other screensavers include settings specific to their animation. To adjust the controls on a screensaver, select it, then click on the Settings button.

**Screensaver Security.** If you're concerned about others snooping in your computer while you're away from your desk, you can use your screensaver as a lock. This makes it impossible for people to turn off the screensaver and

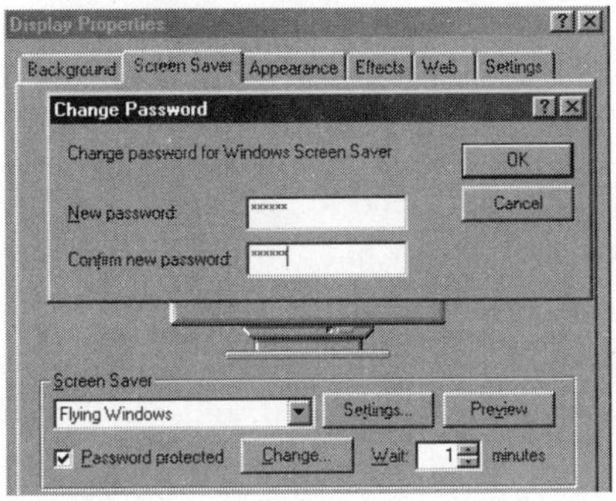

*Figure 6.11*

*Adding a password*

browse through your computer files, unless they know your password—or they shut down your system and reboot it before the screensaver can take over. To add or change a password, click on the **Password Protected** checkbox and then on the **Change** button. This brings up the **Change Password** dialog box (Figure 6.11).

One welcome change from the previous version of Windows is that in Windows 95, some screensavers had their Password Protected checkbox in their Settings dialog—in which cases, the Password Protected checkbox on the main Screen Saver tab was grayed out. No longer: in Windows 98 the Password Protected checkbox is always on the Screen Saver tab.

*Figure 6.12*

*Screensaver password prompt*

Once you've entered and confirmed your new password, click on OK. Your password is now in effect. When you return to your PC and your screensaver is on, you are prompted with a dialog box and must reenter your password before the screensaver stops its animation sequence (Figure 6.12).

**Energy Star Monitors.** Finally, for the eco-conscious among us, Windows 98 supports the new Energy Star power-saving monitors (Figure 6.13). If you have this type of monitor, you can set up Windows 98 so that after a specific period of inactivity, the monitor goes into standby mode or shuts itself off. For more about this, see the next chapter.

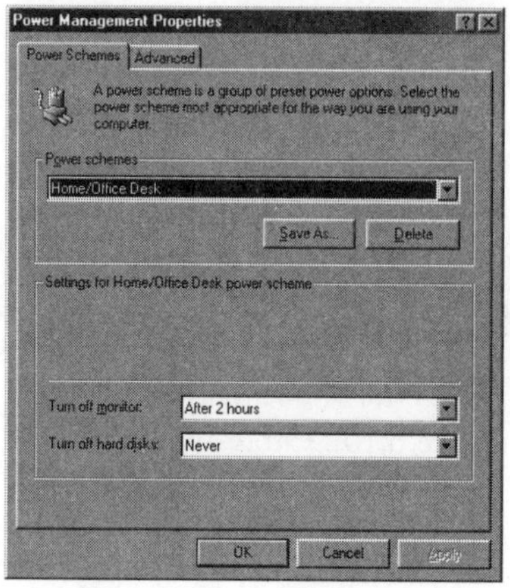

*Figure 6.13*

*Power settings dialog*

Although you can use the Windows 98 Screen Saver page to control the settings of most screensavers, a few products, such as **After Dark for Windows** from Berkeley Systems, "feature" proprietary interfaces. We advise you to test-drive a commercial screensaver before you purchase it, to see how difficult it is to set up and change the controls.

# Customizing the Taskbar

Continuing in the spirit of any-which-way-you-want, Microsoft encourages you to customize the Windows 98 **Taskbar.**

The Taskbar is something people tend to love or hate. Some users will want to make the ultimate customization and get rid of it altogether. If you love it, you'll want to make sure it's always available, and you'll rejoice that you can even adjust its appearance. If you want to tweak your Taskbar heavily, you can control how items appear in the Start menu, and whether the System Tray (the small indented section at the right-hand end of the Taskbar) contains a tiny clock. To exercise your options, select **Start Menu\Settings\Taskbar,** or move the mouse pointer over an unoccupied region of the Taskbar; right-click, and select **Properties** from the Context Menu. This opens the Taskbar Properties dialog.

*Figure 6.14*

*Taskbar and application windows*

The first option of the Taskbar Options tab, **Always on Top** (Figure 6.14), defines how the Taskbar interacts with application windows. If the checkbox is marked, the Taskbar remains visible above any open application window, even if they both occupy the same region of the desktop.

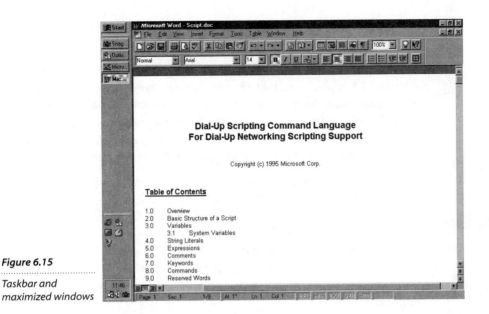

**Figure 6.15**

Taskbar and
maximized windows

This setting also controls the way maximized application windows appear on your screen. If Always on Top is selected, maximized applications use the top edge of the Taskbar as the bottom boundary of their application windows (Figure 6.15).

If you disable the Always on Top feature by clicking on the checkbox to clear the mark, the Taskbar behaves like any other application window. If it's currently selected, it's on top; if another window is selected, the Taskbar takes second place and may be covered over (Figure 6.16). A maximized window

**Figure 6.16**

Obscured Taskbar

sets its lower boundary at the very bottom of the screen, not at the top edge of the Taskbar.

 Having your Taskbar Always on Top most often creates problems with Windows 3.1 applications that are programmed to occupy the entire screen when maximized. There's rarely anything earth shattering happening in the Status Bar of a Windows 3.*x* application, but it can be annoying to not see what you expect. If you still run a lot of Win16 programs, experiment with either unchecking Always on Top or checking Auto Hide (see below)

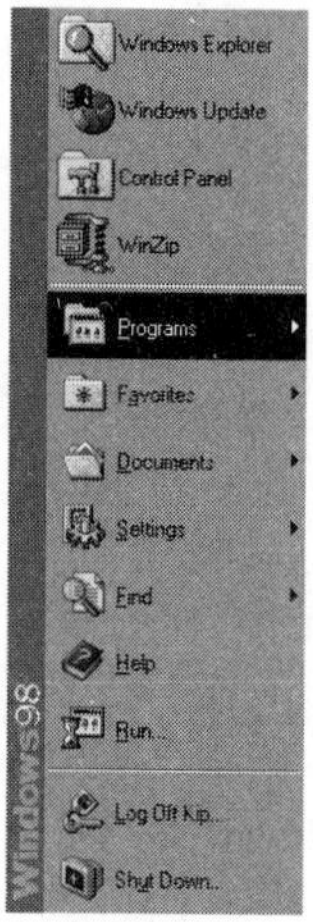

What if you can't decide whether you want the Taskbar on top all the time or not? There's a compromise: choose **Auto Hide,** which keeps the Taskbar hidden till you call it. You make it reappear by touching the mouse pointer to the Taskbar's (concealed) top edge. This gives you the best of both worlds; you get to use the maximum amount of desktop real estate for application windows, yet you can quickly access any of the Taskbar's riches simply by dragging the pointer to the bottom of the screen—where you'd take it to access the Taskbar in any case.

*Figure 6.17*

Start Menu with large icons

Normally you want to keep the Taskbar Always on Top because the Taskbar is such an integral part of the Windows 98 interface. If, however, you decide to disable the feature—for example, to increase the amount of window space for a maximized application—you can still view the Taskbar without having to minimize any windows. Press Ctrl Esc on your keyboard, and the Taskbar pops up over whatever application is currently filling the screen.

Another Taskbar option, **Show Small Icons,** enables you to change the size of the icons that appear in the initial Start menu. When this option is disabled (the default setting), the Start menu displays large, easily identifiable icons for the first tier of entries (Figure 6.17); if you enable it, you get the smaller but less legible icons common to the Start Menu's nested submenus (Figure 6.18). If you don't have much screen real estate, and especially if you own a laptop, this option may prove useful.

*Figure 6.18*

Start Menu with small icons

Finally, the **Show Clock** option enables you to control the Notify area of the Taskbar. When this feature is enabled, a small digital clock is displayed showing the current time. To find out what the date is (in case you've been working too hard), position the mouse pointer over the clock.

# Messing with the Start Menu

All things start with the Taskbar. So if you want to change the contents of the Start menu, go to the Taskbar Properties sheet's other tab, called Start Menu Programs.

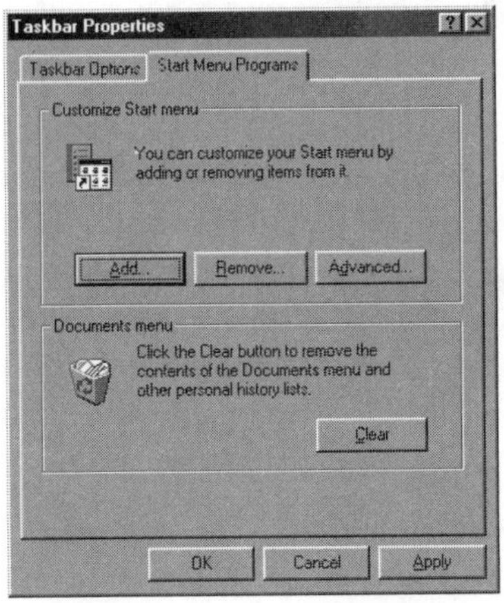

To access the Start Menu Programs page, first bring up the Taskbar's Properties dialog box by selecting **Start Menu\Settings\Taskbar & Start Menu...** or by clicking the right mouse button on the Taskbar and selecting **Properties** from the Context menu. Next click on the **Start Menu Programs** tab (Figure 6.19), and in the region called Customize Start Menu you'll see three buttons: **Add, Remove,** and **Advanced.**

*Figure 6.19*

*Tweaking the Start Menu*

## Adding a Program

No doubt you'll want to add your own programs to the Taskbar. To add a new program to the Start menu, click on the **Add** button. A friendly Add Program Wizard pops up. This wizard is like a tour guide; it shows you around a strange place. The first page of the wizard presents a diagram of the procedure you follow to add a new program to the Start menu. First you enter the pathname into the program's disk file (Figure 6.20).

If you don't know the pathname, click on the **Browse** button to bring up the standard Windows 98 Browse dialog box (Figure 6.21). Use the navigational buttons to move through the folders on your computer until you find the program's disk file.

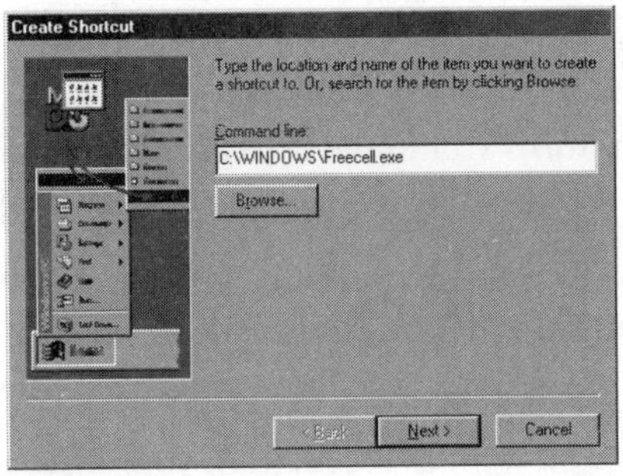

*Figure 6.20*

*Adding a program*

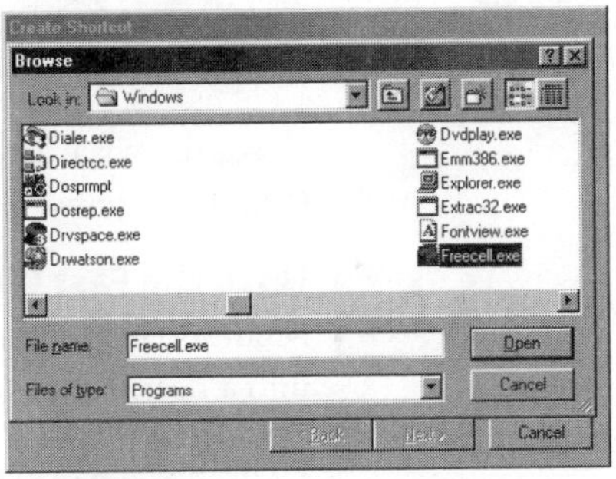

*Figure 6.21*

*Browse dialog*

Once you find the program, highlight it with the mouse pointer and click on **Open.** You're returned to page one of the Add Program Wizard, with the pathname automatically inserted into the Command Line field.

Now click on the **Next** button to move to **Select Program Folder,** which is page two of the Wizard. You see a list of folders that looks somewhat like the tree pattern in the submenu of the Start menu. You can deposit your newly created shortcut into any of these folders by clicking on one of them, or you can create a new folder by clicking on the **New Folder...** button.

Your new folder will be located in the currently selected folder. For example, if the Programs folder (the equivalent of the Programs submenu of the Start

menu) is highlighted, clicking New Folder creates a folder within the Programs folder (and thus a new submenu under Programs), which Windows will name **Program Group (n),** but which you can rename (Figure 6.22).

*Figure 6.22*

*Renaming a created folder*

After you either select or create a folder, click on the **Next** button to bring up a page called **Select a Title for the Program**—although what you're actually doing, as the instructions for the dialog tell you, is picking a name for the *Shortcut* and not the program itself (Figure 6.23). Windows will propose the obvious name; for example, if

you just added a shortcut for accessing WordPad, it suggests the title WordPad. Feel free to indulge yourself with something more descriptive, however, and enter something like Big, Bad Text Editor. You have this latitude only with Windows programs—you can't choose your own name or icon for a DOS program.

*Figure 6.23*

*Naming the shortcut*

Finally, clicking the **Finish** button closes the wizard and returns you to the Start Menu Programs page. Congratulations! You've just added a new program to your Start menu.

**Now, The Fast Way.** You can also drag-and-drop a Shortcut onto the Start Menu or any submenu, although if you want to install a new program deep into a nested submenu, it does require some dexterity with your pointer.

First, find the program you want to access from your Start Menu and create a Shortcut to it; the best way is probably by right-clicking the highlighted program file, selecting **Create Shortcut** from the Context menu, and picking up the Shortcut from the bottom of the list. Drag the Shortcut onto the Desktop, then from the Desktop to the Start Menu button.

If you simply drag it to the Start Menu button and drop it, it will appear at the top of the Start Menu, "above the line" in the special area where newly installed programs create their icons. On the other hand, if you drag it to the Start button and hold it there for a second, the Start Menu will pop up, and by holding the left button down and dragging the Shortcut, you can create this program's icon in any submenu of the Start menu.

## Removing a Program

Of course, what is built must occasionally be torn down. Programs, once installed, tend to fall out of favor with their users. New versions come along; old versions are reinstalled into new locations. Whatever the reason, the time will come when you need to prune an overgrown Start menu, and this is when you'll need the **Remove** button.

Clicking on Remove brings up the **Remove Shortcuts/Folders** dialog box, which you can use to exterminate existing Start menu entries selectively. For example, to remove the entry for the Explorer (which is part of the Programs folder by default), highlight the entry in the provided tree view and click on the Remove button (Figure 6.24). A dialog box asks you to confirm the deletion operation; if you click on Yes, the selected shortcut or folder is removed.

You can remove as many folders and shortcuts as you like from within this dialog box. Once you finish pruning, click on the Close button to return to the Start Menu Programs dialog box.

*Figure 6.24*

*Removing a Start Menu entry*

Take care when pruning your Start menu entries. Although Windows 98 protects itself by letting you modify only entries that are part of the Programs submenu (you can't, for example, remove the Find or Help items), you can still do a lot of damage if you prune the wrong entry. You wouldn't want to have to recreate the entire contents of the Accessories submenu because of an errant mouse click.

 **Again, The Fast Way.** You can remove any item from the Start Menu by dragging it off the Start Menu and onto the Desktop, where it becomes a Shortcut. From the Desktop you can drag the shortcut anywhere else you like, or delete it.

## The Advanced Button

Good things come to those who persevere. Clicking on the **Advanced** button on the Start Menu Programs page brings up an Explorer view of the entire Start Menu folder hierarchy (Figure 6.25).

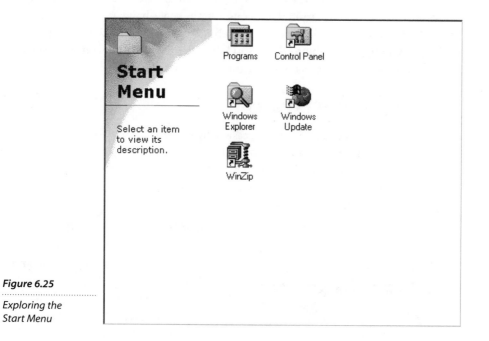

*Figure 6.25*

*Exploring the Start Menu*

The panel on the left side of the window displays a tree view of the entire Start menu structure. On the right you see the entries in each submenu. The only submenu displayed is Programs, but a click of the mouse on the Programs plus sign reveals all the other nested submenus (Figure 6.26).

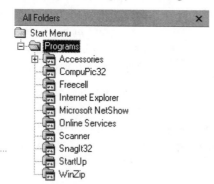

*Figure 6.26*

*Revealing the submenus*

If any other icons besides the Programs folder are displayed, they're Shortcuts that appear on the Start Menu above the Programs group, or "above the line." Applications, and especially Microsoft applications, have an annoying habit of depositing their icons here when they really belong on the Programs menu or one of its submenus. We recommend that you frequently prune non-essential icons from this area, to keep your Start Menu from growing taller than your screen.

If your Start Menu is turning into a skyscraper and you can't find anything you want to remove, bring the height under control by clicking the **Taskbar Options** tab and checking the box for **Show small icons in Start menu.** This reduces the height of the Start Menu by more than a third.

This Explorer view gives you the power to directly control other folder and Explorer views. Adding a new program to a particular submenu is easy—possibly, depending on your mouse agility, easier than dragging the Shortcut directly onto the submenu.

For example, to add a new program to the Communications submenu, open the folder view that contains the program, then click on the **Advanced** button to bring up the Explorer view of the Start menu's contents. Expand the Start menu Explorer view tree until you see the Communications folder, then highlight it. Finally, drag the icon for the new program from its folder view and drop it into the Communications folder (Figure 6.27).

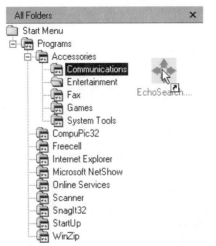

*Figure 6.27*

*Adding a program with Drag and Drop*

You've just created a shortcut to the new program by adding it to the Communications folder. Now when you close the Explorer view and click on OK on the Start Menu Programs page, a new menu entry for the program is added to the Start menu's Multimedia submenu.

# Multiple Users

You can customize your Windows desktop to your heart's delight. But what if you share your computer with other people, people whose taste in wallpaper runs to Rivets when you'd prefer Dilbert on a surfboard?

Microsoft has provided a solution to the problem of several people sharing the same computer: multiple desktops, which make it easy to share a PC among several users. Each desktop is maintained in a User Profile and protected by a password. Each person who uses the system stores his or her own, private settings for elements—such as desktop wallpaper and color schemes, icon positions, and even network connections—as part of his or her user profile, which starts up when that user enters his or her password.

*Figure 6.28*

*The Family Logon dialog box*

When you boot up a multiple-desktop system, a Family Logon dialog box asks you to select your name and enter your password (Figure 6.28). Windows 98 uses this information to identify which user profile it should load.

For example, if the name entered is Emily, then Emily's profile gets loaded, and the desktop is configured accordingly. If the name entered is Charlotte, then Charlotte's desktop gets loaded. Changes made to the desktop by one user are restricted to that particular user's profile; other desktops are unaffected. Individuals can customize their working environments without stepping on each other's toes.

## Setting It Up

To set up a computer to run with multiple desktops, open **Start Menu\ Settings\Control Panel,** then double-click on the **Passwords** icon to open the Passwords Properties control panel. Next, click on the **User Profiles** tab to bring forward that page of the Properties sheet.

To set up multiple user profiles, click the **Users can customize...** radio button (Figure 6.29). This will deactivate the other available radio button, **All users...use the same preferences....** In the **User profile settings** region below, the **Include desktop icons...** and **Include Start menu...** checkboxes become active.

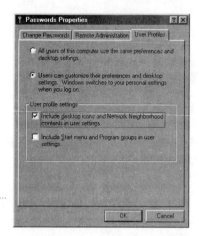

*Figure 6.29*

*User profiles properties*

**Include desktop icons...** tells Windows 98 whether to save the overall desktop arrangement—that is, icon spacing, colors, and any network connections—as part of each user profile. If you uncheck this box, all the users of this computer will see the same Desktop icons and Network Neighborhood contents, no matter what other individual settings they save in their user profiles. **Include Start menu...** tells Windows 98 whether subsequent changes to the Start menu affect all the Desktops, if the box is cleared, or only one, if it's checked.

When you're through defining the user profiles, click on the **OK** button to save the changes.

# Working with User Profiles

When your PC reboots for the first time after you set up multiple desktops, you're prompted with your first Logon dialog box. Unless you were previously connected to a network, both the user name and password fields are blank. To create a new profile, simply type in a name—for example, your first name or an abbreviation of your first and last names—and a password.

If this is the first time you've logged onto the PC since setting up multiple desktops, Windows 98 asks you to confirm your password. Simply retype it and press (Enter). The next thing you see is the Windows 98 desktop. Congratulations! You've created a user profile.

In reality, the password is optional. If you don't want to use one, press (Enter) and then (Enter) again when Windows asks you to confirm the password. This can speed the log-on process. Also, if you tend to forget passwords (Fred even lost one Internet account because he couldn't remember his password), it might be a good idea just to keep an open computer.

Now go ahead and rearrange the desktop to your heart's content. Change colors, move icons, even rename a few things. Next, select Log Off [*your name*] from the Start menu, confirm (Figure 6.30), and your computer will look as if it's shutting down and restarting.

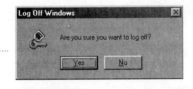

**Figure 6.30**

*Multi-user log off confirmation*

 Note that this is a different series of steps from those used in Windows 95; now there's no Shut Down Windows menu option called *Close all programs and log on as a different user.* The result is the same, although the process isn't.

Suddenly you're right back where you started: at the Logon prompt. Now try entering a different user name and password to log on as that user. Again you're asked to verify the password, but this time when the desktop loads, none of your changes—the ones you made when operating under the other user profile—are visible. Where'd they go?

Don't panic—this is a feature, not a bug. Windows 98 has stored your settings as part of your user profile. It then loaded a default profile for the new user you just created. Your days of multi-user desktop anguish are finally over.

The default profile for each user is based on how your system is set up before you create multiple desktops. So if you want to change any aspect of the desktop for all users—for example, if you want to set up a network connection—do it before launching the multiple-desktop option. Then when each user creates a new account, that person will have the options you've included as part of the default desktop.

# Date and Time

Setting up your system's date and time is fun, because Microsoft designed a slick front end for this otherwise mundane task. The Date/Time Properties control panel provides a useful clock and calendar (Figure 6.31). To bring up the control panel, select **Start Menu\Settings\Control Panel,** then double-click on the **Date/Time** icon.

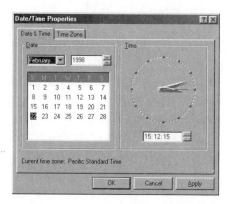

**Figure 6.31**

The Date/Time Properties control panel

On the **Date & Time** tab, a miniature calendar—with a dropbox for the month and spin buttons for the year—can be used to set the current date. If you're curious, you can examine future calendars well into the next century; some Windows third-party software may have problems with the Year 2000, but Windows 98 itself will be fine until December 2099, when your great-grandchildren will presumably have upgraded to a newer version of Windows. Simply change the year and month fields to see the desired calendar.

A large analog clock shows the current system time in minutes and seconds. To set the time, edit the field directly below the analog clock, either by typing a new entry or by selecting a section of the field and clicking on the spin buttons.

**Figure 6.32**

Setting the time zone

You can also use the Taskbar to get to the Date/Time Properties control panel. Double-click on the digital clock at the right end of the bar.

The second page of the Date/Time Properties control panel enables you to specify your time zone. Select the zone from the drop-down list box, or easier still, click on your part of the world on the accompanying map (Figure 6.32).

# Regional Settings

If you're a transcontinental Windows user—or if you just have a pen pal in another country—open **Start Menu\Settings\Control Panel\Regional Settings** and check out the Properties sheet. The Regional Settings Properties control panel helps you bring your system, and the information it produces,

into compliance with a particular country's currency and measurement standards.

The first tab of the sheet, titled **Regional Settings,** provides a template for settings that vary based on geographic location. Like the time zone tool mentioned previously, the Regional Settings page contains both a list box and a map of the world (Figure 6.33). Either select your location from the list or click on the appropriate map location.

**Figure 6.33**

Regional settings

On the **Number** page you can specify everything from the placement of decimal points to a choice of measuring system, English or metric (Figure 6.34). Use the **Currency** page to choose a currency symbol—for example, a dollar or a pound sign—as well as more esoteric functions, such as how many numbers make up a digit group (Figure 6.35). Finally, the Time and Date pages enable you to define formats for numerical entries. For example, you can choose a date separator (normally a forwardslash) and can specify your preferred style for a.m. and p.m.

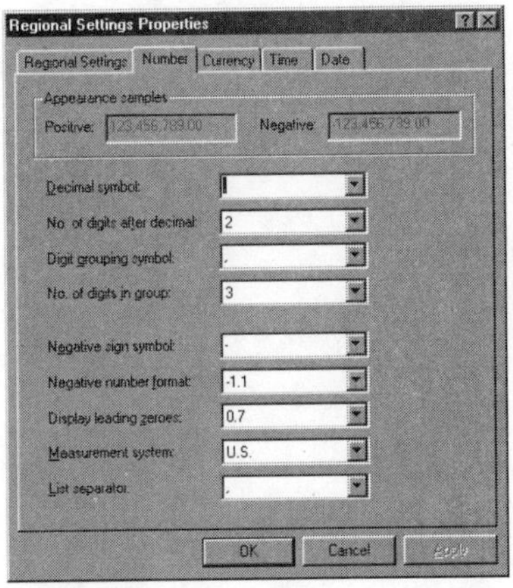

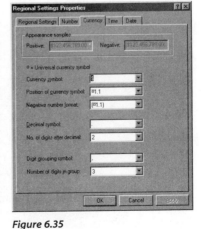

**Figure 6.34**

The Number page

**Figure 6.35**

The Currency page

# Summary

Windows 98 gives you a variety of options for dressing up your desktop to match your every mood. Some controls are even useful, providing you with shortcuts to frequently used programs and functions. For the first time, people who share a computer can customize their own desktops, by designing their own backgrounds, adding wallpaper, choosing their own screensavers, and rearranging the Taskbar and other controls. Finally, Microsoft has added features for those who are specially challenged—and for anyone who finds the features handy.

# 7

# Of Displays, Mice, and Keyboards

Computers used to be faceless; to communicate with them you had to punch cards with patterns of rectangular holes representing binary instructions, then send the cards down a chute into the card reader. If the computer returned any information to you, it appeared on a long, dimly printed sheet of paper that spewed forth from a clattering Teletype machine. We've come a long way from that to the Windows 98 graphical user interface, which combines a CRT (or flat screen) display, a mouse or other pointing device, and a keyboard into a smoothly functioning whole that enables you to have direct two-way communication with your computer.

This chapter presents an overview of the Windows 98 display system, including display cards, monitors, and Windows-compatible display driver software; pointing devices, primarily mice, but also trackballs, styluses, and pens; and the venerable keyboard, which (in sharp contrast to some devices) has survived relatively unchanged since the invention of the mechanical typewriter in the last century.

# Display Systems

A good display system shows off the Windows 98 environment and Windows applications to their best advantage. Your display system includes three components: the monitor—which is the hardware that you see—the display card, which is hardware that you don't see, and the display driver, which is software. The display driver enables Windows to exploit the capabilities of the display card. The display card—also called the graphics adapter or the video card—affects the quality of your display more than the monitor itself does, because the display card controls resolution, number of colors, and amount of visible flicker. The monitor must be compatible with the display card, since output signals from the latter vary.

Not only does Windows 98 sport an improved graphics engine, it also includes a universal display driver that handles generic display tasks. This means that display manufacturers no longer need to provide complete drivers. All they need to include are mini-drivers that inform Windows 98 about the capabilities of their display devices.

 As a result you see better performance (because the universal driver speaks the same 32-bit language as does Windows 98), and manufacturers have an easier time making the performance and features of their display cards accessible to

Windows. (For previous versions of Windows, each driver's generic display commands and hardware-specific instructions were the manufacturer's responsibility. Small separate drivers written by dozens of manufacturers were much more likely to cause conflicts on your system than today's universal 32-bit Windows driver.)

Windows 98 includes a slew of new minidrivers for displays that existed when Windows 98 was shipped. If your display is included, Windows automatically replaces your older driver with a new minidriver during the upgrade process. If Windows 98 doesn't know about your display, it will load and run a driver that it believes to be hardware-compatible, which may be the Windows 95 driver, the Windows 3.1 driver, a current driver for another monitor by the same manufacturer, or (as a last resort) the generic VGA driver, which will at least let you see what's going on while you search for something better. However, the Monitor tab of the Display Properties sheet gives you access to the Upgrade Device Driver Wizard, which will search for an optimized driver that gives you the best performance. If you have access to the Internet, a major online service, or a bulletin board service (BBS), you can probably find a Web page or forum hosted by the manufacturer of your display. The manufacturer's Web page will usually include a hyperlink titled something like "Support" or "Downloads" where you'll find the latest drivers along with downloading and installation instructions.

## Font Sizes

All Windows drivers that provide resolutions of at least 640x480 pixels can display either large or small fonts to accommodate monitors of varying sizes. Using larger fonts improves the legibility of text, whereas smaller fonts minimize the amount of room required by windows and menus on the desktop.

Because Windows 98 incorporates DOS, you don't need DOS display drivers—another improvement over earlier versions of Windows. The Windows 98 universal driver enables you to run DOS graphics programs in a window, display colors more accurately, and select fonts of different sizes for DOS windows.

## Graphics Performance

 If you play games on your computer, you have good reason to get excited about Windows 98. Microsoft worked closely with hardware vendors to establish a new standard, DirectDraw, which accelerates the speed and increases the video quality of games. The results of this collaboration are published in the Windows 98 Game Software Development Kit, which software developers use to create accelerated versions of their games.

The DirectDraw driver is only half the story, though. You also need a graphics accelerator card incorporating the proper hardware acceleration element. As this is being written, most cards from respected name-brand manufacturers—certainly including ATI, Diamond Multimedia, ELSA, Matrox, Number Nine, and STB—provide built-in DirectDraw driver support, many of them at highly affordable prices. You do need to ask your dealer about a card's features, though, and there's absolutely no substitute for reading the latest magazine or Web reviews of graphics cards immediately before you buy. With graphics coprocessor development at fever pitch, and new cards entering the market almost daily, buyers can look forward to a doubling in performance *every six months.*

The net result? With Windows 98 games and the correct hardware, you'll see up to four times more detail than you did in the long-gone Windows 95 era; twenty or more times as much as was possible with typical DOS games run under Windows 3.1. The action is stunningly quick and the experience nearly comparable to a high-end arcade game.

## Display Standards

Of all the systems in your computer, perhaps none has changed more during the 12-year history of Windows than the video subsystem. This means that Microsoft had a special problem when they tried to create video drivers for every card that might be installed on a computer running Windows 98.

Since the advent of Windows 3.0 in 1990, Microsoft has done its best to accommodate all the major display standards of the IBM-compatible universe. The Windows 98 installation disks provide a startling variety of display drivers for almost every kind of VGA monitor and a few earlier ones. A few outdated display card standards will make you work harder, but can still be accommodated; no driver is included, for example, for the original IBM CGA (Color Graphics Adapter) display, which can still be found on older systems, especially laptops and portables. However, you can use your CGA display with Windows 98 if you obtain a CGA display driver from the Windows Driver Library, available from Microsoft on disk, through the company's online support system, or on most commercial online services.

In the early 1980s Hercules developed its own monochrome display card to challenge IBM's display cards. The original Hercules monochrome adapter, with a resolution of 720x348, displayed high-quality text as well as high-resolution monochrome graphics; it garnered the support of most leading developers, as well as users of spreadsheets, desktop publishing programs and Computer Aided Design (CAD) applications.

In 1984 the IBM Enhanced Graphics Adapter (EGA) replaced the CGA and emerged as the most popular display card for the IBM PC. The earliest EGA configuration included a puny 64K of display memory, which allowed only four colors to be displayed at once—no better than CGA. But the final EGA specification permitted up to 256K of on-card memory, which allowed 16 simultaneous colors at a resolution of 640x350 pixels; most EGA adapters were built this way, and a few, which used "tweaked" nonstandard circuitry, could display 64 simultaneous colors. Because EGA uses rectangular pixels, and 32-bit Windows was designed for the square pixels of VGA (described next), Windows distorts images on EGA displays. Although almost everyone now buys the higher-resolution VGA displays, EGA displays are still common on older systems, including 286s and even a few 386s.

The introduction of the IBM PS/2 in 1987 brought the new Video Graphics Array (VGA) display architecture, which is now the industry standard. Unlike the earlier CGA and EGA displays, which use digital signaling techniques to control the number of colors on a monitor, VGA monitors employ analog signaling and can potentially display millions of colors. Most older and some current but bargain-basement VGA display cards, because of data-bit limitations, attain only a fraction of this potential; they display either 16 or 256 colors. VGA cards capable of displaying 32,000 colors (which Windows calls High Color) or over 16 million colors (called True Color) are now common, and many new computers come equipped with them.

Pixel resolution measures the number of spots of light on a monitor. A resolution on a VGA display of "640 by 480" (also called "standard VGA" or just "VGA") indicates that each line contains 640 pixels—or *picture elements*—and that the monitor displays 480 lines of pixels. "Standard VGA" resolution is 640x480 pixels—about 30 percent higher than the resolution of a standard television set. However, a TV image often looks more realistic than the graphics on a VGA computer display, because TVs have better color-depth resolution.

## Crunching VGA Numbers

*Color-depth resolution* refers to the number of bits, or *levels,* of color information that each pixel can display. If each pixel can display 4 bits, only 16 colors can be displayed simultaneously on the screen. The reason is that each bit is a binary number (that is, it can be either 0 or 1) so 4 bits yields 16 possible combinations, ranging from binary 0000 (0) to binary 1111 (8+4+2+1 = 15).

Now: An absolutely rock-bottom VGA card, capable of displaying 640x480 pixels at 16 colors, needs

$640 \times 480 = 307{,}200$ pixels on the screen

and, at four bits per pixel, needs

$4 \times 307{,}200 = 1{,}228{,}800$ bits of video memory,

but there's eight bits to a byte and it's easier to think in bytes, so

$1{,}228{,}800/8 = 153{,}600$ bytes of video memory. This is called the *frame buffer* and is the amount of memory needed to hold one full screen of video at 4-bit depth. Because a VGA card also needs memory for functions like paging and control, the minimum VGA card requires 256K of memory.

So far it may seem as if we haven't gotten very much for a complete revision of the video hardware architecture. After all, the "old" EGA adapter also required 256K of memory and could display 16 or even 64 colors, although with not quite as many pixels. Add this comparison to the fact that the earliest VGA cards were very slow, and you'll understand why many people thought VGA was a step backward—another doomed IBM standard that only IBM would ever adopt, just like the Microchannel bus.

But VGA had one real ace up its sleeve; it was very, very extensible. It was comparatively easy to turn VGA into a "Super VGA" with more resolution and deeper color. And that was destined to happen … after a few false starts.

**TIGA.** In the late 1980s Texas Instruments introduced two high-performance graphic coprocessor chips (the TMS32010 and TMS32020) as a basis for a display card technology called TIGA (Texas Instruments Graphics Architecture) which the company hoped would overtake VGA. TIGA was capable of screen resolutions of 1,024x768 pixels and higher. Several manufacturers produced such cards, including the Hercules Graphics Station and the NEC Graphics Engine, but TIGA was expensive—as much as $1,000 per card—and the mass market never embraced it.

Windows 98 doesn't directly support TIGA, but you can use the standard Windows 98 VGA driver or a Windows 3.1 TIGA driver. If you install Windows 98 over a previous version of Windows, Setup keeps the previous TIGA driver. If you install Windows 98 from scratch, Setup installs the standard VGA driver. Either way, you still get good results from the TIGA adapter.

**8514/a.** IBM, meanwhile, always understood that VGA wouldn't meet everybody's video needs. In 1987, along with the IBM VGA, they introduced a card called the 8514/a as a "professional quality" graphics adapter for PS/2 computers. The 8514/a provided 256 simultaneous colors from a palette of 262,400, at a resolution of 1,024x768—a useful step above VGA—but its architecture had five serious drawbacks: its displays were interlaced, which meant lower video quality; its refresh rate was a flickery 44 Hz; it worked only with the Microchannel bus, essentially meaning only in a PS/2; IBM never published the standard, making it impossible for other manufacturers to produce compatible hardware; and, fatally, 8514/a was incompatible with VGA. Thus, if you wanted to produce a VGA image, you needed separate VGA circuitry—on either a board, an add-in card, or the motherboard—to pass the image on to the 8514/a display card and through to your monitor. This meant, in essence, doing the work of one graphics adapter with the cost and complexity of two, and it was a hugely unpopular solution.

 **If you use a VGA card to pass a VGA signal through to an 8514/a card, Windows 98 may be unable to detect the memory used by the VGA adapter. You need to keep Windows from using the memory address areas used by the VGA adapter. To do this, use the EMMExclude= statement in the [386Enh] section of your SYSTEM.INI file. For example, the statement line EMMExclude=C400-C7FF locks out the area that usually causes the memory conflict. If your screen blanks out when you are running a DOS session with an 8514/a card, you can sometimes retrieve the display by typing MODE CO80 at the invisible DOS prompt. This forces the display into color 80-column mode and can cause it to reappear.**

**XGA.** In 1990 IBM introduced its XGA (Extended Graphics Array) display card, which had three modes: a 640x480 256-color mode with relatively high performance, a 640x480 65,536-color mode, and a mode with 256 colors at an extended resolution of 1,024x768. This time IBM revealed everything about the architecture in hope of making XGA an open standard.

But the XGA, though advanced in certain ways, was too little and too late. Like the 8514/a, the XGA interlaced the display; like the 8514/a, the XGA was made available only for the Microchannel bus. Worse yet, it required a 386 or 486 CPU when there were still plenty of 286s working for a living. Some third-party developers offered noninterlaced XGA-compatible cards for the ISA and EISA buses, but these were scarce, and competed with noninterlaced TIGA display cards that offered resolutions and performance rivaling those of XGA. Microsoft itself drove the last stake through XGA's heart; when Windows 3.0 was introduced in 1990, its most effective resolution was 800x600, which an XGA card wouldn't produce. In due time IBM introduced a card capable of 800x600, called XGA/2, which is nearly a museum piece today.

XGA did have some virtues. It was designed with bit-mapped graphics in mind, so it provides better Windows performance than does the 8514/a card, which was developed for CAD packages and therefore optimized to draw vectors (lines) rather than bitmaps. And, since XGA was one of the earliest accelerated graphics cards, it had an internal command set that serves as the core of the instruction set for most of today's accelerated display hardware.

## *What's an Interlaced Display?*

While we're mentioning interlaced displays, we'll tell you to beware of them. In an interlaced display, the electron gun of the monitor's video tube creates an image by writing every other line on the screen and then returning to the top of the screen to fill in the empty lines, in effect *interlacing* the empty and the written lines. Thus an interlaced 1,024x768 display system is really a 1,024x384 display that scans the face of the video tube twice. This double passage causes a noticeable flicker, which varies depending on how quickly your eyes react to images, how close you are to the screen, and whether fluorescent lighting is present (such lighting produces its own flicker, which can accentuate the screen flicker).

The flicker can be so pronounced that it causes eyestrain and headaches. Companies that sell interlaced displays typically try to combat this by using longer-persistence phosphor in the monitors, making the screen image more durable. However, long-persistence phosphors introduce other problems: they can make the screen appear dim, or leave ghostlike trails of former images when you move a window, an icon, or another object.

Interlacing is often found in monitors with resolutions of 640x480 or greater, especially older models. Fortunately, most current monitors are noninterlaced, so you shouldn't encounter this problem if you buy new equipment. Do read the manual while you're setting up, though, because some new monitors—especially large expensive ones that display very high resolutions on large screens—can be set for either noninterlaced or interlaced video modes. In such a case, you want to be sure you're using the noninterlaced settings.

**Monochrome and Grayscale VGA.** When VGA was introduced in 1987 and had yet to become an industry standard, compatible monitors and adapters were produced by only a few manufacturers and were quite expensive. To make the new architecture attractive at the low end of the market, some companies marketed *grayscale VGA,* which used the 4-bits-per-pixel VGA standard to display 16 shades (or brightnesses) of gray on a monochrome monitor. Grayscale VGA display cards were often identical to 16-color display cards; only the monochrome monitors were different, and considerably less expensive than color monitors.

You can run a grayscale VGA display with the default Windows 98 VGA driver; these monitors are no longer guaranteed to be Windows-compatible, but the standard VGA driver will run any device that meets the VGA specification. When the 16-color VGA palette is displayed in grayscale, many of the resulting brightnesses appear similar, making it difficult to discern individual grays. To correct this, go to **Control Panel\Display Properties,** select the **Appearance** tab and the **Scheme** drop-down list, and pick High Contrast White. Then, using the Item and Color lists, lighten or darken individual elements until you have your own grayscale color scheme. Use the **Save As…** button to save it as Grayscale VGA.

In the long run, though, remember that color adds information. The ability to run Windows 98 in color is worth the price of an upgrade to a VGA color monitor. Besides, monochrome VGA display cards will often also drive color VGA displays, in which case you need to upgrade only your monitor.

Don't confuse Grayscale VGA with *Monochrome VGA,* which provides 1-bit color for strictly monochrome displays, such as the ones found on laptops. In previous versions of Windows, laptop users with LCD displays were offered several color schemes created expressly for LCD screens; unfortunately, in Windows 98 those seem to have disappeared. Also, the new graduated color fill of the Windows 98 title bar makes it less likely that any Windows 98 scheme will work well in a 1-bit environment. You can look for a laptop-specific video driver in the Windows Driver Library at `ftp.microsoft.com` or on the Web page or online forum of your laptop's manufacturer.

**VESA to The Rescue.**  The lack of almost any industry standard beyond VGA's basic 640x480 resolution allowed the makers of video boards to do what computer manufacturers usually do: explore higher levels of perform-ance with serious sacrifice of compatibility. Graphics adapter makers were careful to duplicate VGA as a foundation for the new boards they designed, while they added a happy anarchy of resolution levels and operating frequen-cies. Anyone who was messing with high-resolution video in the early nineties will remember the instant migraine of the phrase, "Upgrade your video driver."

These extended VGA cards became known generally as "Super VGA." The VGA part was a standard, while the "Super" was a blindfolded leap. Every "Super VGA" card would operate at 800x600 resolution, and many at 1024x768, but only if you had the exact right monitor, the appropriate version of the video BIOS—which the manufacturer had to mail to you, since it was a chip—as well as special drivers for DOS and that week's revision of the high-resolution Windows driver, which you got sometimes from Microsoft but more often from the makers of the video card. Then, every time you shifted to a new resolution, the position of the image might change drastically, forcing you to tweak the image size and positioning controls on your monitor, if you had any. Unless you could change the image positioning on the fly, the new driver might be useless.

If all of this sounds unbearably awful, you can thank the people who made it go away; Microsoft's programmers, for the 32-bit Windows universal video driver, and Jim Schwabe of NEC, who founded VESA, the Video Electronics Standards Association. VESA hammered out the Discrete Monitor Timing standards and the VESA BIOS Extensions (VBE) which, together, do things like guarantee that the image will be in the right place on the screen and that software will be able to cope with high-resolution video modes. VESA is now an internationally respected computer standards body, still working hard to improve the compatibility of high-resolution video, so that when you go to the computer store, walk down one aisle and find the monitor of your dreams, and walk down another aisle to discover a fabulous price on the newest Windows accelerator card, you don't have to worry about whether they'll work together. Lucky you!

## Bits Per Pixel (Continued)

Naturally, four-bit color had a brief day in the sun. Super VGA rapidly defaulted to 8 bits per pixel, which yields 256 colors and is the lowest color depth that Windows 98 will support. 8 bits per pixel is fine for text and diagrams—it gives an especially good black on white—but if you're trying to reproduce any kind of multicolored, realistic image, it falls down seriously. 16 bits per pixel can yield more than 64,000 colors, and by optimizing a computer's color palette, you can display images on a 16-bit display with only a slight loss of color quality. At this writing, even inexpensive video cards will achieve 16 bits per pixel at a decent refresh rate. To achieve a color image as realistic as a photograph, you need to use 24 bits per pixel, which devotes 8 bits each to the three primary colors of light—red, green, and blue—and can yield more than 16 million colors.

The more pixels to be transmitted to the screen, and the higher the number of colors to be displayed, the more memory will need to be installed on the adapter. The display card must contain enough memory to address all the pixels on the display multiplied by the number of bits of color resolution per pixel. Thus, to drive a display with a given number of pixels, an 8-bit-per-pixel Super VGA card requires twice as much memory as does a 4-bit-per-pixel VGA card, and a 24-bit True Color card requires at least three times the memory of an 8-bit card—probably more, since additional memory on display cards permits faster screen redrawing.

Video memory is a separate and sometimes painful subject. Most adapters require video RAM—also called VRAM—which isn't the same kind of RAM you use to expand the memory of your computer system. VRAM chips can read and write simultaneously (they have one port for each) and run at considerably higher speeds than standard computer RAM, but they cost a lot more. A few years ago, some manufacturers split the memory on their cards, using one screen's worth of VRAM as a fast caching framebuffer and standard, less expensive DRAM for the bulk of their memory; these cards offered good performance at attractive prices but were rarely found in the ranks of the real screamers.

# Graphics Accelerators

"Now wait a minute," we hear you saying, "here these guys are, talking about 16 and 24 bits, and yet I see ads for 64-bit and 128-bit video cards. If 24 bits gives me 16 million colors, how many colors would I get out of 128 bits?"

Hold on! Before you fire up the Windows Calculator, which would probably overflow anyway, let us explain that you're talking about apples and oranges—especially if you like your apples really red and your oranges absolutely orange. *Bits per pixel,* which we were talking about earlier, describe color depth. But when somebody starts talking about a 64-bit or 128-bit video card, they're referring to *internal bus width,* one aspect of the card's hardware design—which we now have to discuss.

Most modern video cards (meaning the ones produced in the past few years) are *graphics accelerator cards,* which means that they speed up graphics by providing their own video processing power. Windows 98 is a graphical user interface; its graphics kernel, called the GDI (Graphics Device Interface), is responsible for drawing all the images on your screen, both text and graphics, while Windows runs. Much of your system's performance depends on its ability to execute Windows graphics instructions.

A standard VGA card, by definition, has no processing power of its own; it serves merely as a framebuffer for your display, and forces your computer's CPU chip to perform all the GDI instructions. The higher the resolution of your display, and the more colors in the image, the greater the work your CPU has to do. A graphics accelerator card can speed up much of your Windows 98 environment by shifting this responsibility away from the CPU. Boosting processor speed also contributes to graphics performance, and graphics accelerators often perform best with high-speed CPUs.

Over the years, many different design strategies have been used for graphics accelerators, with varying success—but these are the main varieties:

**Accelerated graphics cards.** The modern descendants of the VGA card, accelerated graphics cards include fixed-function circuitry that performs Windows graphics operations, unloading these tasks from the CPU chip and improving overall system performance while it speeds up the transfer of graphics information to the display card. Rather than transfer an entire image to the card, the CPU sends only the graphics instructions. Examples of accelerated graphics cards include many that use chips from S3, from ATI, and from Weitek. Although the chips are not programmable, they take over the toughest graphics processing tasks and are inexpensive compared with fully programmable coprocessors.

**Coprocessor cards.** These cards contain a programmable (rather than fixed-function) on-board processor that takes over many of the graphics operations normally performed by the CPU chip. The earliest type of graphics accelerators, coprocessor cards, were exemplified by the 8514/a, TIGA, and XGA cards discussed earlier in this chapter; many of them offered unusual features, such as NTSC video output, but they were quite costly and never migrated from the "professional" high end into the mainstream. Windows 98 no longer supports these cards.

**Bus-cycle accelerators.** These cards use fixed-function circuitry to halve the number of bus cycles that a CPU must complete to perform graphics operations. The Chips & Technologies 82C453 chip uses this approach, but few others ever did.

Another graphics acceleration strategy, no matter what kind of on-card accelerator chip it uses, focuses on the width and speed of the bus between the video card and the CPU. There are two types of accelerated-bus video in common use today, and a third one just entering production:

**VESA local bus video.** Often called "VL-bus" for short, this strategy integrates the display card into the local bus of the CPU chip, bypassing the expansion bus to achieve high data transfer speeds. VL-bus cards had a special double-length edge connector that was pure murder to insert and remove, and no more than three VL-bus cards could be installed in one VL-bus motherboard. The design's performance was gratifying, but it had many quirks, and is almost a thing of the past.

**Bus-mastering video cards** take advantage of 32-bit buses to offer advanced capabilities. The principle is great; the hardware took three tries to get right. *EISA bus-mastering,* pioneered by Compaq and a few other manufacturers, was a double-length version of the original ISA bus, and found much more use in disk controllers than in video, in the days before video throughput mattered so much. *Microchannel* bus-mastering, like all other Microchannel hardware, worked well enough in the IBM PS/2 computers where it lived. Finally Intel came up with the *PCI* (Peripheral Component Interconnect) bus, which combines some features of bus-mastering with some features of VL-bus, and which took over the world of commodity computing right along with Pentium systems. If you buy a graphics adapter today, its architecture will be PCI, unless your computer's motherboard only has ISA slots, in which case you can still buy an ISA version of some cards, but you'll sacrifice a lot of performance.

The third and newest type of video bus acceleration, **AGP** or Accelerated Graphics Port, we discuss on page 236.

**Pixel Blasters.** All of these designs have taken wildly different approaches to the task at hand, and it's ironic to look around now and realize that the job is still so simple. The one and only thing an accelerated card has to do is move the color data around within the card, so it can get coded and decoded and RAMDAC'ed and all that other stuff, and out to the monitor. Now, if your card was operating with 16 bits per pixel, and the internal bus width of the card was also 16 bits, the card would be pulling one pixel—one 16-bit block—of program color data across the bus at a time.

About ten years ago, video engineers began experimenting with something called *bit block transfer* (or "bitblit" for short) which was a way of stuffing more than one data pixel across the bus with each tick of the bus clock. Until recently a typical high-end graphics accelerator card, probably working with 16-bit data pixels, would have a 32-bit internal bus to accommodate two pixels per tick. Number Nine (a consistently innovative company) introduced the first 64-bit card, and the race was on as other vendors rushed competing cards to market. Number Nine retaliated by introducing the first 128-bit card, the Imagine 128, once again raising the bar for video acceleration. Naturally, these wider buses are barely keeping pace with fatter bit blocks—the latest accelerator cards offer video modes with 32 bits per pixel—but the ability to transfer two or four bit blocks per clock tick is still one of the most important factors in the performance of contemporary computer video.

Another, of course, is a frightening amount of sheer processing horsepower. One example will show you why; say you've got your video card jacked up to True Color, you've got your twenty-inch monitor (we didn't mention money here) set at 1,024x768, and you're running real-time full-motion video at 30 frames a second. Okay—start with the number of pixels on the screen, which is

$$1,024 \times 768 = 786,432$$

For True Color, every pixel needs 24 bits, which is three bytes, so

$786,432 \times 3 = 2,359,296$ bytes $= 2.25$ megabytes *per framebuffer,* and believe me, you've got more than one running. Then multiply that by thirty frames, that is, thirty framebuffers every second, and you're talking ...

*67.5 megabytes of data* pouring onto your display screen *every second.* That is a jaw-dropping data transfer rate, for anything. It's why digital video clips aren't very long. It's also why full-motion video usually isn't full-screen, and why it drops frames occasionally, even so. This is why people are excited about DVD (digital video disk), which will hold enough data for a full-length movie at 30 frames a second, real soon now. But to sum up: If you're hunting for the fastest RAM, the fastest digital-to-analog conversion, and the fastest real-time data handling in history, look into a good high-end video card. And we haven't even thought about ...

**2-D and 3-D.**  There was a time when all graphics cards were 2-D, just the way all television was black-and-white, and all telephones were wired to a wall jack. It worked, but it was *bo-ring*. Then came home theater, flip-phones, Doom, Quake, and z-buffering.

Z-buffering is a method of allocating graphics resources so that a flat, screen-based image *seems to* have a **z-axis**—a visual axis that runs toward and away from you, and promotes the illusion of depth. Z-buffering, and the perspective scaling that goes with it, makes a 3-D graphics card very, very complicated, even relative to what we were talking about so far. 3-D cards (and the best 2-D cards) also pull other tricks far beyond the scope of this book, like texture mapping, hardware rendering, and various kinds of compression.

There are video cards today with good 2-D *and* 3-D performance, but they're expensive—if not breathtakingly so, at least pricey enough to make you stop and think. We recommend that, before you buy a video card, you decide whether 2-D or 3-D performance is most important to you. If you're a gamer or you do rendering, then you'll think primarily of 3-D. If you mostly run applications, play with bitmaps, and might dabble in a little video, go for high-performance 2-D. It's not a black-and-white decision; many cards that offer stellar performance in one will be at least middle-of-the-pack in the other.

We remind you again that, before you buy any graphics adapter, it's absolutely imperative to read reviews—the latest ones you can get your hands on. We could say nice things now about particular cards and chipsets, which would be materially obsolete by the time this book reaches bookstore shelves. If you've got a Web browser, you can view manufacturers' home pages to compare product specifications and prices. Many of those home pages also include links to electronic magazines (and electronic versions of printed magazines, such as *Windows Magazine*) that rate products. Use those links to compare offerings from different manufacturers.

**Accelerated Graphics Port (AGP).**  Coming soon to a computer near you—on your own desk, if you're lucky: the Accelerated Graphics Port, which is thoroughly supported by Windows 98.

AGP addresses a problem that was addressed—but not really solved—by VL-bus and PCI cards. All these bits are whipping around the inside of the graphics adapter, like confetti in a Cuisinart. But the computer's PCI bus, on the way from the CPU to the video card, isn't nearly as fast as what's happening inside the card. The bus becomes a bottleneck, wasting much of the sophistication that's been lavished on the video chipset.

AGP is a special expansion bus, designed by Intel and based on the industry standard PCI design, but potentially four times as fast. It uses an incompatible (naturally) connector design and imposes tight design restrictions on matching components. Originally, Intel intended AGP for computers that used the Pentium Pro CPU, with its exceptionally fast cache and floating-point processor—a combination born to run 3D graphics.

The Pentium Pro never became what Intel hoped it would, although it's still an unusually nice processor, but AGP is here to stay. This architecture offers graphics adapters something they've been begging for: dedicated and even *pipelined* access to main memory. With AGP, if an accelerator chip is madly engaged in texture mapping or alpha blending and runs out of its on-card memory, it can reach out over a fast dedicated link to use main memory for video functions.

To design AGP, Intel took the latest revision of the PCI specification and added four innovations:

- Pipelined memory that eliminates wait states.

- Separate address and data lines on the bus to allow interleaving of transactions, to keep the pipeline packed full and minimize waste of bus cycles. Data in the pipeline is prioritized so that the most important information gets where it's going first.

- A special transfer mode that can load data on the interface twice each clock cycle—so that although the actual clock speed of the AGP bus is 66 MHz, the same as the PCI bus, AGP effectively operates at 133 MHz. With 32 bits transferred per clock cycle, potential throughput approaches 500MB per second.

- Freedom from a lot of the main computer's concerns. AGP doesn't go near the level-2 cache. It isn't involved in non-graphic I/O. It doesn't share the system's PCI or ISA peripheral buses or the memory bus. It's a 32-bit rifle barrel extending from the graphics accelerator on one end to the microprocessor and glue logic on the other.

Not much AGP hardware is currently available, and we'll probably have to wait for the next round of fundamental board design to see if it can live up to these mouth-watering specs. But considering the immense care that Intel devoted to the hardware bus design, and the prominence that Microsoft gives to AGP support in Windows 98, it's clear that the video subsystem will be much more important to the computers of the near future than it has been so far.

## Scan Rates

A computer display has two scan rates:

- Horizontal scan frequency, also called the *screen draw rate*.

- Vertical scan frequency, also called the *frame rate* or *refresh rate*.

To display a particular resolution, a monitor must be able to accommodate the matching horizontal scan frequency. To display the 800x600 resolution of a SuperVGA card, for example, a monitor must support at least a 35 kHz horizontal scan rate; to display a 1,024x768 resolution, the monitor needs to support at least a 49 kHz horizontal scan rate. Some display cards offer a range of scan rates; for example, SuperVGA is offered with horizontal scan rates ranging from 35 to 48 kHz. The higher the horizontal scan rate, the faster the pixels can be drawn on the screen; therefore, as a rule of thumb, the better the quality of the display and the greater the stability of the image.

These are the scan rates that generally work best with the following resolutions:

- 320x200 (CGA) has one fixed frequency, 15.575 kHz.

- 640x350 (EGA) has one fixed frequency, 23.1 kHz.

- 640x480 (VGA) works best with a scan rate of 31.5 kHz.

- 800x600 (SuperVGA) works best at 35 to 48 kHz.

- 1,024x768 (SuperVGA) works best at 48 to 72 kHz.

The vertical scan frequency, or refresh rate, is the rate at which a monitor redraws the screen image from top to bottom. The more quickly the screen can be redrawn, the less flicker you'll see on the monitor, because the interval between redraws is shorter and your eyes are less likely to perceive it. The standard vertical scan frequency is 60 Hz, which means the screen is redrawn 60 times per second. Newer display cards support higher vertical scan rates, typically 72 Hz, the standard in Europe. High-end cards support up to 200 Hz. Higher vertical scan rates create a more stable image, contribute to display quality, prevent eyestrain and fatigue—and, of course, cost more money.

## Video Problems

Many manufacturers build graphics adapters that offer unique features or resolutions not supported by Windows 98. Sometimes a display card will work up to a point—even a standard VGA card can run in more than a dozen modes, and some of them are guaranteed to cooperate—but a specific combination of settings isn't supported by the Windows 98 universal driver. And some drivers contain lurking bugs that produce inexplicable problems only with certain applications. In this case contact the graphics card vendor and make sure you have the most recent version of the appropriate display driver. Card manufacturers typically distribute updated drivers in their forums on commercial online services, such as CSi (CompuServe) and America Online, as well as on their own Web pages and electronic bulletin boards.

You might encounter another problem if you have one of those older VGA cards that require an update of their RAMDAC chips. The RAMDAC is the digital-to-analog converter that changes the digital information in your computer's memory (or on the card's memory) into the analog video signal that the card sends to your display. If your RAMDAC is too old, you may have problems switching between full-screen DOS sessions run from within Windows. In some cases the screen goes blank when you try to make the switch. If this happens, update the RAMDAC or treat yourself to a new graphics adapter.

## Expanding the Desktop

Okay, so you've got all these hyperactive pixels. What do you do with them?

**Be It Resolved.**   Having more pixels on tap lets you run Windows at a higher resolution and work with a larger desktop. A resolution of 800x600 pixels—the standard for SuperVGA and the default for Windows—increases the area of your desktop by more than 50 percent compared to VGA's standard resolution of 640x480 pixels (Figures 7.1 and 7.2).

*Figure 7.1*

VGA desktop:
640x480 pixels at
8 bits

*Figure 7.2*

SuperVGA desktop:
800x600 pixels at
16 bits

The difference between these two desktops is far greater than what is suggested by grayscale screenshots on tree slices. Increasing your screen resolution to 800x600 pixels gives you more room to display windows, icons, and other onscreen paraphernalia. It also makes for a much more pleasant, and more sustainable, viewing experience. When the Windows video standard was first declared to be 800x600, it was roundly criticized as making too many demands on hardware, but time has proven the wisdom of the choice.

**Screen Fonts and Font Spacing.** With either a VGA or a SuperVGA display, Windows uses 96 pixels to display each inch of a document. Thus, on a SuperVGA display of 800x600, you can view almost the entire width of an 8½ x 11-inch page (800 divided by 96 is almost 8.5).

As you move to a higher resolution at the same screen size, the images in your Windows display appear to shrink. On a small monitor, this shrinking can make menus, window titles, dialog boxes, and other interface components difficult to read. To compensate, you can go to Control Panel\Display Properties, select the **Settings** tab, click the **Advanced...** button and pick the **Large Fonts** option from the Font Size drop-down list. This makes Windows use 120 pixels, rather than 96, to display each inch of the document—in effect making the font 25 percent larger.

## *Application Font Spacing*

The name **Large Fonts** is misleading since this option scales other interface components besides fonts. Windows itself, having been written with Microsoft's object-oriented programming tools, maintains fairly smooth relationships between things like fonts, buttons, dialogs, and windows for drop-down lists. But in third-party Windows software written with other toolkits, components can scale haphazardly. In practice this often means that legends overflow the objects they're sitting on, fonts are cropped and messages are truncated.

This is ugly but not usually mission-critical. If you find it happening with applications you use frequently, you'll have to decide for yourself whether the benefits of Large Fonts are worth putting up with their occasionally obtrusive effects.

**Big Screens.** A better alternative, if you don't mind the investment, is to buy a new monitor big enough to accommodate increased resolutions comfortably. The default VGA resolution of 640x480 was specified at a time when 13-inch monitors were commonplace and a 14-inch monitor (which 640x480 is ideal for) was a distinct step up. For the default Windows resolution of 800x600, we recommend at least a 15-inch display; this gives roughly the same component sizes as 640x480 on a 14-inch monitor. For a resolution of 1,024x768, a 17-inch or larger display is appropriate.

Monitors are measured diagonally, so increasing the size by even an inch adds significant area to a display. Stepping up to a 15-inch monitor from a 14-inch one increases the display area by around 20 percent; going from 14 to 17 inches adds 50 percent more space.

Prices of large displays are coming down as 15" and 17" monitors become the norm. At $250 to $450 for a 15-inch unit and $450 to $750 for a 17-inch unit, large monitors can be worth the investment, not only to give you a bigger Desktop, but for the sheer comfort of a big, clearly detailed screen while you run applications all day. For desktop publishing, graphics editing, and Web development, you may even want a 19", 20", or 21" monitor, although these currently begin at about $850 and go up to several thousand dollars. If you're buying a whole new system, either make sure it comes with a 17" monitor or see how much the dealer wants for an upgrade from 15" to 17"—probably not more than $200.

Furthermore, accelerated graphics adapters are now sophisticated enough to deliver both high resolution and deep color with no sacrifice in performance. It wasn't very long ago that, if you were running any resolution higher than 640x480 with any more than 256 colors, even a highly recommended display card could be painfully slow. Those days are over and a mid-price, name-brand 2-D card will run acceptable High Color or even True Color at 1,024x768. If you have *any* doubts about your current graphics adapter, replace it along with the monitor; a mismatch between your old card and your new monitor may produce flicker, screen distortion, or a short, fat image that takes up only part of the screen.

Finally, while you're shopping, remember that you want a noninterlaced display! After all, you're spending this money to make computing easier on your eyes. Insist on the following three components:

- A display card capable of generating a video signal that produces a non-interlaced display.

- A monitor that can display noninterlaced video and that has a high enough vertical scan frequency (refresh rate) to work with the display card.

- A software configuration for the display card that works with non-interlaced video.

 If both your display card and your monitor support a noninterlaced signal but are older, you may be able to obtain noninterlaced video if you adjust jumpers or DIP switches on the card or set a switch on the monitor.

**Virtual Desktops.** You can use a special software trick to create several virtual desktops, in effect multiplying the desktop real estate available through your display. The technique works by letting you set up several desktops, complete with document icons and shortcuts to applications and folders, and then quickly switch between them. A smart way to use this feature would be to organize desktops by project or by the type of work—personal documents on one desktop, for example, business documents on another, and games on a third. Several commercial utilities provide this feature, including Symantec's Norton Navigator and Starfish Software's Dashboard 98.

## Display Drivers and How They Work

Windows cannot use any piece of hardware—a so-called device—without a software component called a driver. A driver translates commands between Windows and the device. If you press keys on a keyboard, for example, the keyboard driver tells Windows what command you are issuing. Similarly, a driver translates commands from Windows to the display.

In the days of pre-Enhanced video, display drivers were a simple matter. Under DOS, you might need one driver for each application you ran and one for the operating system itself, but you were only driving one of three kinds of video: IBM's Monochrome Display Adapter (MDA) or Color Graphics Adapter (CGA) or the Hercules Graphics Card (HGC). Since, at that time, microcomputer users rarely bought new monitors, it was easy enough for application developers to include the three required video drivers with their software. These were humble and simple times, fondly remembered.

EGA, the Enhanced Graphics Adapter, seriously tilted the applecart and IBM's VGA knocked it clean over. We've discussed the tumultuous days of SuperVGA, TIGA, 8514/a, XGA, XGA/2, and a couple we didn't even mention, like PGA (a super-EGA) and MCGA (a mangled low-end VGA). People who stayed abreast of Windows 2.x, 3.0 and 3.1 during the Video Troubles learned a lot more than they really wanted to know about video drivers.

16-bit Windows tried to solve this problem; it didn't require applications to perform direct addressing of each type of display card. Instead, all programs addressed a Windows graphics kernel called the GDI (Graphics Device Interface), which remained the same regardless of the display hardware installed. To make a card compatible with Windows, the manufacturer simply provided a device driver that translated GDI instructions to the display card. The 16-bit Windows GDI worked tolerably well, although it tended to run out of memory and freeze about once a day; but manufacturers discovered that, even when they were writing to a standard software interface, it was tricky to write a driver that made use of every hardware feature on the card.

Windows 95 materially enhanced video stability with two strategic changes. First, the 32-bit GDI was more robust. Second, Microsoft began providing the whole cornucopia of video drivers with Windows itself, and keeping a running record of what drove what by periodically issuing the Windows Hardware Compatibility List (HCL) which is available in the form of a Windows Help file, or in plain text, from Microsoft's Web site. When you installed a video driver, you could use Windows Display Properties to find out which other drivers (if any) were functionally or exactly equivalent.

Now, Windows 98 takes the whole concept of hardware-specific drivers a giant step further. Almost all displays—like modems and printers before them—are now controlled by a single, universal display driver, supplemented (if at all) by minidrivers which the manufacturer provides. (These minidrivers, which are plain text files with the extension .INF, are much easier to create and debug than the old, compiled Windows .DRV files.) Thus, the field of future video products is wide open; as long as you have a Windows 98 minidriver for any future type of display, you'll be able to use it.

When you install Windows 98 over an earlier version of Windows, the Setup program examines your previous drivers, detecting the presence of hardware devices if your computer and the devices support Plug and Play. (Plug and Play, supported by all versions of 32-bit Windows, is a feature that enables bidirectional communication between your computer and its installed hardware devices.) Windows 98 Setup then installs any updated versions of the necessary hardware drivers and, during this process, removes any incompatible drivers or components.

If your computer supports Plug and Play and you later add another piece of hardware, Windows 98 will know that you've connected a device. Furthermore, once Windows identifies the device, it can often choose a software minidriver from its own collection of .INF files and go on to use the device. With the intelligence of Plug and Play, Windows 98 makes it less likely that you will have to deal with drivers, especially if you have fairly new equipment.

**Changing Display Drivers.** If you've got older equipment that isn't supported by the Windows 98 universal driver—what Microsoft terms "legacy" hardware—you may have to do a little more work.

With the generous list of display drivers it supplies, Windows 98 can work with most of the display products on the market. For example, the universal driver supports 800x600 16- and 256-color resolutions on most SuperVGA cards—such as those produced by ATI, Cirrus Logic, Everex, Genoa, Orchid, Paradise, STB, and Trident—and on other cards compatible with the SuperVGA standard set by VESA. In other words, the vast majority of standard video cards will find a driver ready and waiting under Windows 98, together with fonts and any other details necessary to complete the configuration. It's all done automatically.

## *Not Plug and Not Play*

But what if your computer *doesn't* support Plug and Play? Well, you're missing out on a lot, but you do have options. Plug and Play—often seen abbreviated as "PnP"—for your computer is part of a chip (or two-chip set) called the BIOS, that sits in sockets on the motherboard. Since these chips are socketed, they're replaceable.

Almost all BIOS chips are made by one of three companies: American Megatrends (also called AMI), Award, or Phoenix Technologies. You can tell which manufacturer's BIOS your computer has by watching the text that appears on the screen—character-mode text, usually light gray or white on a black background—*before* the full-color Windows logo takes over. Then fire up your browser, or grab the phone, and read on:

**American Megatrends** supplies BIOS chips only for AMI-manufactured motherboards, which can be a problem, because there are plenty of non-AMI motherboards that use AMI BIOSes. If you have one of those, you'll need to know who made your motherboard, which can be much more difficult to dig up than who made your BIOS. At any rate, try the AMI Web site at `http://www.amibios.com/enduser.html`.

**Award Software** supplies its BIOS chips through Unicore Corporation, whose URL is `http://www.unicore.com/` or call 1 800 800-BIOS (2467). Unicore also sells BIOSes by MR, AMI and Phoenix, which makes it a one-stop shop.

**Phoenix Technologies** supplies its BIOS chips through Micro Firmware; try the Web site at `http://www.firmware.com/` or call 1 800 767-5465 (1 405 321-8333 outside the U. S.).

Note: Remember that replacing the BIOS involves opening the case, whether it's done by you or by your support person. Therefore, if you hunt down a BIOS upgrade only to find that it's inordinately expensive—like over $100—you might want to consider swapping out your motherboard instead. Just remember that any new motherboard has to accommodate the CPU *and* the memory you already have. If you start talking about upgrading those too, you're on the slippery slope to replacing your computer.

A few cards, after you install Windows 98, will boot to the standard VGA drivers and use nothing else. You may need to obtain a driver from your card's manufacturer to be able to use it with Windows 98. Here's the procedure:

Open the Display Control Panel. Either open **Start Menu\Settings\Control Panel** and double-click on Display, or, to jump straight to the Display Properties sheet, right-click on a blank spot on the desktop, then click on Properties on the pop-up menu.

Click on the **Settings** tab, then on the **Advanced...** button. You're in your Display Hardware Properties sheet (Figure 7.3), which indicates what type of display card is installed, what type of monitor you have hooked up, which

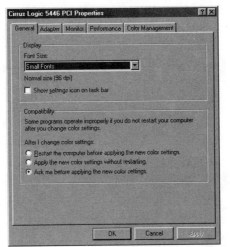

**Figure 7.3**

The Display
Hardware Properties
sheet

font size you have installed, and how much acceleration you have turned on—if you're running as standard VGA, probably none.

Select the **Adapter** tab and click on the **Change…** button next to the adapter type description. This brings up the Upgrade Device Driver Wizard, and here you can sigh deeply; by "automating" this procedure for Windows 98, Microsoft made manual device driver selection much more difficult than it was under Windows 95. Click **Next.**

Click the button that says **Display a list of all the drivers,** etc. Click **Next.** The Wizard will come up with a list of locally available drivers known to be compatible with your adapter (Figure 7.4), and most likely you'll pick one of those.

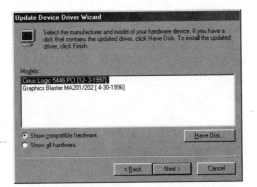

**Figure 7.4**

The Show
Compatible
Hardware dialog

If you have a disk from the adapter manufacturer that contains drivers you think may work (tip: this does *not* mean Windows 3.0 or 3.1 drivers), click **Have disk…** Windows 98 instructs you to insert the disk containing the new driver into the floppy drive. (If the driver is stored elsewhere, use the [Backspace] key to delete A:\. Then enter the path to the new display driver.) Once you've inserted the driver disk into drive A or indicated the path to the driver files, Windows Setup reads the files and copies them onto your hard disk.

If you follow the instructions and Windows says there are no drivers on the disk—meaning that there's a Windows 3.0 or 3.1 .INF file, or no .INF file, on the disk—or if you don't have a disk, click the **Show all hardware** button (Figure 7.5).

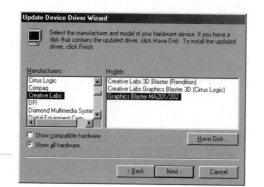

**Figure 7.5**

The Show All Hardware dialog

In the left pane of the dialog box, scroll to your display card's manufacturer. If you don't find the manufacturer, either there's a new video card in your near future, or you're willing to put up with running in Standard VGA.

Then, in the right pane, try to find your display card's model. If you don't find the model, you can pick another model from the same list that has the same processor, but *we don't recommend that*—which means you don't get to blame us if you blow up your adapter or, worse, your monitor.

If the display card model you select needs a Windows 98-compatible driver that isn't installed on your system, Windows asks you to insert the Windows CD-ROM or one of the installation diskettes. Windows Setup then reads the device driver from the disk and recognizes the new display driver when you restart your system.

If your display card type isn't listed, but the manufacturer is, contact the manufacturer to get an updated driver, if it's available; try searching on the Web for the manufacturer's name or the card's model number—sometimes model or chipset numbers, like "7548 PCI," give tight search results on the Web. Most manufacturers of display cards make Windows 98 drivers, which may give you access to special features of the card, like support for higher resolutions or more colors. In the meantime, you can use the generic Windows VGA driver.

What if you *can't* use the generic VGA driver? What if your card is so—ah—special that it doesn't have the VGA or VESA specification built in as a baseline? There are two possibilities:

- Your card is an 8514/a. As we write, IBM hasn't released an 8514/a driver for Windows 98, but they may have by the time you read this. Go find another computer with Web access (since yours won't boot) and log onto `http://www.ibm.com` to see if the driver is available.

- Your card is *not* an 8514/a, is *not* VGA or VESA-compatible, and is *not* anything Windows 98 ever heard of. Accept our sympathy, contact the manufacturer, and hope for an updated driver; but frankly, you're far enough out on the crumbling edge that your quickest remedy is probably a trip to the store for a video card. When you're buying, take the old card with you so that the vendor can help you select a replacement for the appropriate bus.

**Color and Resolution Changes.**  If your monitor can display more than one resolution, you can change the monitor's configuration. You can do this on the fly—that is, without closing the applications you're running—if your display card and driver support Plug and Play. Otherwise, you need to restart Windows before making your changes.

Using the Display Control Panel, you can change the number of colors displayed on your monitor, as well as the resolution and the font size. To change a display configuration manually, follow these steps:

Open the Display Control Panel. Either open **Start Menu\Settings\Control Panel** and double-click on **Display,** or, to jump straight to the Display Properties sheet, right-click on a blank spot on the desktop, then click on **Properties** on the pop-up menu.

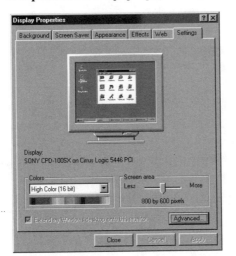

*Figure 7.6*

*The Settings tab of the Display Properties sheet*

Click on the **Settings** tab (Figure 7.6). To change the color depth, drop down the list in the **Colors** region and choose the color depth you wish to display; your choices are **256 Colors,** which is 8 bits per pixel, **High Color (16 bit)** which gives 65,536 colors, and **True Color (24 bit)** which gives 16 million colors. An exotic video card may provide a 32-bit option, but you didn't buy one of those by accident.

Not all of these options may be available, because some cards (and some drivers) support particular color depths only at specific resolutions. For example, a card might be capable of 65,536 colors at a resolution of 800x600 but only be able to display 256 colors when the resolution is increased to 1,024x768. If an option isn't available, it's grayed out.

To change the resolution, click on the **Screen Area** slider bar and move it to the right or the left; the resolution you have chosen appears below the slider bar. For a garden-variety 15" or 17" monitor, your choices are 640x480 (VGA), 800x600 (Windows default), or 1,024x768. For a 19", 20", or 21" monitor you may find additional choices listed, such as 1280x1024 or 1600x1200. Start with 640x480 if you have a 14" or smaller monitor, 800x600 if you have a 15" monitor, and 1,024x768 if you have a 17" or 19" monitor. Remember that increasing resolution may force you to decrease color depth.

To change the font size, click on the **Advanced...** button. Choose from the Font Size drop-down list box; your choices are **Small Fonts** for 96 pixels per inch (which Windows calls "100%"), **Large Fonts** for 120 pixels per inch,

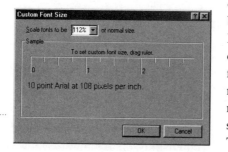

or **Other...** for a custom font size between 20% and 500% (Figure 7.7). Incidentally, "To set custom font size, drag ruler" is an opaque instruction for a spiffy effect; it means "Put your mouse pointer anywhere inside the ruler, hold down the left button, and slide the pointer back and forth." Try it, it's cute.

*Figure 7.7*

*Custom Font Size dialog*

The **Show settings icon on task bar** checkbox is a definite plus. When it's checked, you have a small icon in your System Tray which will pop up a menu of resolutions and color depths; with this, you can choose video settings and not bother going all the way into Display Properties. (Recreational tuners of Windows 95 will recognize the QuickRes Powertoy, now neatly built in.) Whether your computer reboots after you pick from this menu will depend on the following setting.

**Compatibility** accommodates your monitor's ability to shift its scan rates. Older monitors (or adapters) need to be rebooted to change resolution and pixel depth; newer Plug and Play hardware can adjust itself with a momentary shiver, like crossing the sound barrier. **Restart the computer,** etc., means that the computer will be rebooted and the new color settings will be applied at video power-on. **Apply the new color settings,** etc., means that resolution and pixel depth (and the monitor's synchronization) will change on the fly. The puzzling third option, **Ask me before applying**

**the new color settings,** seems to assume that your computer will sometimes need to reboot, sometimes not, and you'll know the difference.

Click on OK, and your changes are accepted.

 The Display Properties\Advanced Properties\General tab isn't the only place to adjust font size. Increased font sizes are a feature of some Windows 98 predefined color schemes. Go to the **Appearance** tab of Display Properties, choose a color scheme with a name followed by the words (**large**) or (**extra large**), and the size of window titles and commands will automatically increase.

## Display Ergonomics

Three factors determine how easy your monitor is to use and how safe it is: the quality of the video monitor, the quality of the graphics adapter, and the way you set everything up.

Be sure you have plenty of time when you select a monitor. A good dealer will have anywhere between six and a dozen monitors running and available for scrutiny, all connected to the identical (or at least comparable) middle-of-the-pack graphics card. Sit down at this Wall of Video and do the following:

- Adjust the image on each monitor until it's as good as you can make it. It's not fair to compare monitors in random states of tune; a monitor that looks second-rate may be top-quality but poorly adjusted. Besides, then you'll know how intuitive the controls are and how configurable the monitor is.

- Take a small tape measure and measure the diagonals of the screens. You're not buying the spec sheet; you're buying what you're looking at.

- Does the screen have an anti-glare treatment, and is it a good one? Some monitors have a tiny grid etched into the screen glass, which gives it a frosted appearance. We dislike this surface because it reduces the sharpness of displayed images, and it's harder to clean. Better glare-reduction methods involve coating the screen glass with fused quartz, or with a coating called OCLI. These treatments are usually available only on higher-priced monitors.

- Hunt for some of your favorite applications and run them. The best screens to test with are the screens you know best.

- Open the Accessories menu, go to Games and play Solitaire, which is a wonderful monitor test. The colors should be achingly brilliant. When you drag-and-drop the cards, motion should be smooth and edges remain crisp, with no ghosting.

- If you can find the QuickRes Powertoy, or any other method of setting color depth and resolution on the fly, try a few settings. *Don't try the most extreme resolution or refresh rate.* It's not nice to set fire to other people's hardware.

- Consider the monitor's dot pitch—the size of the dots on the monitor that create the pixels. Generally, the smaller the dot pitch, the clearer and sharper the images on the display. .25 millimeters dot pitch is super-sharp, but likely to be expensive. .26 dot pitch is, increasingly, available at a competitive price. .28 dot pitch is about the coarsest you'll want to live with. We recommend avoiding any monitor with a dot pitch greater than .28 millimeters.

- Finally, if nobody squeaks at you for doing it, turn the monitors off and back on, one by one. As you turn each monitor on, notice the effect on the monitors to either side. Less effect means better shielding, although it can be difficult to tell which monitor has the good shielding—the one you just turned on or the one next to it. Give each monitor a few seconds to warm up, then make sure that the color settings and image geometry are *exactly* what they were when you turned the monitor off. A monitor that can't hold its settings is not one you want to live with.

Now find a salesperson, and explore the two or three monitors you like best. Find out which graphics adapter(s) those monitors are running with. Discuss the uses that this monitor will see the most of, and ask if this graphics adapter is the most appropriate choice, or whether there might be a better one. Make sure that both the monitor and the adapter you buy are noninterlaced, at least at their most useful resolutions. Pay attention to refresh rates; your prospective monitor and display card should work together at high vertical scan frequencies to minimize flicker. The salesperson may think you're a pain in the rump, but will also realize (with luck) that a knowledgeable customer who goes away satisfied is likely to be a repeat customer.

Now—*ack!*—it's between you and your wallet. If you're anything like us, the monitor you like will cost more than you were planning on spending. Remember these things:

- Because Windows displays text as graphics, the quality of your display affects both text and graphics applications. A high-quality display minimizes flicker and distortion, both of which can lead to eyestrain and headaches.

- A monitor, especially a good one, is a long-term investment. If you buy equipment that conforms to durable industry standards—like a PCI-bus video card, for example—your monitor may outlast your computer, or even last you through two or three. Video standards are substantially more settled than they were in the late eighties; the monitor you buy now may easily serve you for five years or longer.

- A top-quality monitor is a pleasure for your eyes, every time you use your computer. If you walked into the store looking for a 15" monitor, don't rule out a 17" that takes your breath away. If there's one monitor on the Wall of Video that looks miles better than the rest, buy it!

A word about pricing is in order here. Monitor prices vary widely, and it's our observation that neither the least nor the most expensive displays are worth what they cost. A cheap monitor may be cheap for a monitor, but it's an expensive mistake. On the other end of the scale, the most costly monitors of a given size overlap the price range of the next size up. For example, we noted that the current price range for acceptable-to-great 15-inch monitors is $250 to $450. Fine, but it's possible to spend as little as $175 or as much as $700. If you ask us (and you are), $175 is much too much to waste on a bogus 15" monitor when you can get a much better one for $250. On the other hand, any 15" monitor you shell out $700 for may be awe-inspiring, but for that price you can get a 17" unit that's nearly as impressive. So, to reiterate, shop defensively and *don't hurry*. It's also perfectly okay to identify the monitor of your dreams in person, then poke around on the Web for the lowest price by mail. Just make sure you know in advance what the shipping cost will add to the order.

## Saving a Bundle

Always remember to ask about the monitor when you buy a bundled system—because it just happens that, when retailers assemble blue-chip specials and try to beat the competitor's prices, the monitor is a favorite place to cut a corner. But you don't want a cheap monitor when you're buying one separately, so there's no reason to buy one as part of a bundle. If you ask the salesperson what kind of monitor comes with the system, and the answer is something that you've never heard of or read a review of, go do the Wall of Video tour, then ask brightly "How much for an upgrade to that one?" Upgrading a bundled system is one of the least expensive ways to get a top-quality monitor.

Actually, this tactic is dying out as more and more retailers (following the lead of Apple and Compaq) advertise system prices without monitors, so you get to pick whatever one you want, anyway. A generous retailer will give you a few bucks off the price of any monitor you select, if you buy it on the same ticket with the computer.

## Product Recommendations

What, you want us to do *everything?* Well, this time we can't. When you're selecting a monitor—or, more exactly, a monitor-and-card combination—there is no substitute for informed personal experience. The monitor you buy has to pass the test of *your* eyes, fingers, and tape measure, none of which we have at our disposal.

 **Having said that, though, we can give you an alphabetical list of the manufacturers whose hardware has earned reputation through time—the names we think of when we think "quality." If we were going out to buy a monitor today, we'd look first at Eizo (also known as Nanao), Iiyama (also known as IDEK), MAG, Mitsubishi, NEC, Nokia, Princeton Graphics, Sony, and Viewsonic. Also, Hewlett-Packard monitors are rarely sold separately, but go right ahead and buy one as part of a Hewlett-Packard bundled system.** *There are other good monitors.* **There are other monitors as good as the ones on this list. But with a monitor, as with a graphics adapter, you really don't know enough to go shopping until you've read the latest reviews.**

## When It's Not Your Monitor

So far we've assumed that you're buying your own monitor, for your own computer, on your very own desk. Sometimes you're replacing your computer at work, and Purchasing won't authorize a new monitor along with it. Sometimes you're buying a computer for yourself, and the monitor in a different month.

If you're stuck with an interlaced display, or a display with a low refresh rate, you can do several things to minimize jittery video. First, keep away from fluorescent lighting. Fluorescent lights emit a pulsation of their own that can exaggerate the monitor's flicker. If your office is lit by fluorescent ceiling panels, get an incandescent desk lamp; the more stable light from this lamp will mask the cycling of the fluorescent light.

Sometimes display cards and monitors can be reconfigured to work with a higher refresh rate or in a noninterlaced mode; check your manual. Another trick is to select a color scheme in the Control Panel that consists of all solid colors, rather than dithered colors or patterns. Solid colors appear more stable on a display. Dithered colors are made by combining tiny dots of different colors that your eyes perceive as one color; naturally, they look less saturated than solid colors.

How you position your monitor also affects the ergonomics of your system. The most troublesome problem is glare; set up your monitor to avoid light from a window or an artificial source. If you can't reposition your monitor, a so-called anti-glare filter that fits over the screen might be helpful. Quality varies widely, however, so test the filter first to be sure it allows a clear view of the monitor screen.

The best place to position your monitor is slightly below eye level. Your eyes should rest naturally on the monitor's surface, so you don't need to crane your neck up or down. Many computer desks are designed so that the monitor is high enough only when placed on top of the system unit. If your computer has a tower case, or if you prefer not to place your system unit underneath your monitor—which we can understand if you ever take the case off—you may need to put the monitor on a stand to boost it. (Fred uses old phone books; Kip sits his monitors on top of heavy plastic diskette drawers.) A swivel base is a good accessory for a monitor because it enables you to fine-tune the viewing angle. However, don't use it to tilt your monitor steeply upwards as a substitute for placing the monitor at the proper height.

The most controversial issue related to ergonomics of display systems concerns VDT emissions. Video monitors, like television sets, emit various forms of energy, ranging from electromagnetic radiation to high-pitched sound waves. The scientific jury is still out as to whether these emissions pose significant health hazards, but emotions run high on the issue. Some people feel the emissions are dangerous because, potentially, they could cause cancer and birth defects. Others say that less radiation is emitted than can typically be measured from a bedside electric alarm clock.

Personally, we believe the danger from most monitors is minimal, especially assuming recent manufacture. The only ones we consider potentially dangerous are monitors produced in the early 1980s and some large-screen color monitors built before 1986. (You probably aren't using either one today, unless you're a collector. Early-eighties monitors conforming to the MDA and CGA standards are totally obsolete; mid-eighties large-screen color monitors cost thousands of dollars and were never a mainstream product.) Public awareness of the potential health threat of VDT emissions, and the possible onslaught of product liability lawsuits, have prompted most monitor manufacturers to increase the shielding on their monitors, which reduces emissions. If emissions are a concern for you, look for monitors that adhere to the Swedish National Council for Meteorology standards, most often referred to as MPR II, which set limits on the amount of very low frequency (VLF) and extremely low frequency (ELF) radiation a monitor can emit. In the near future, monitors made with materials that do not produce emissions will replace cathode-ray tube monitors; the color LCD and transistor-matrix screens used in many laptop computers are already made of such materials.

Finally, if you have a relatively new machine or are in the market for one, you can be a good citizen of the world by selecting a monitor that complies with the Environmental Protection Agency's Energy Star guidelines. If your computer is also Energy Star-compliant, it can minimize the amount of power your system consumes by powering down the monitor (and any other Energy Star-compliant components) when the system has been idle for a while—for example, when you run off to a meeting or lunch.

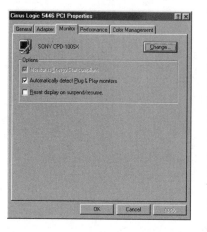

Windows 98 supports Energy Star. To see how, go to Control Panel, then Display Properties, click on the **Settings** tab, then on the **Advanced...** button. You're in your Display Hardware Properties sheet. Click the **Monitor** tab, which provides checkboxes to specify whether your monitor complies with the Energy Star and Plug and Play guidelines. (Normally Windows checks the Energy Star checkbox during the install routine, and on some monitors—including this one—

*Figure 7.8*

*Monitor Settings dialog*

the option is checked *and* grayed out, meaning that it's permanent. If it's not grayed out, you can override it, if you prefer; it doesn't work anyway unless your monitor is compliant.) Finally, the checkbox titled **Reset display on suspend/resume** is blank by default, and only works if Windows 98 installed the **Suspend** option on the Start Menu of your computer, which probably means it's a laptop. (Figure 7.8).

 Not *all* your display settings are in Display Properties, and the one that's missing is one you'll particularly want to find—when your monitor seems to black out at random. One of the newer Control Panels is called Power Management. Its property sheet, Power Management Properties (which we'll discuss elsewhere) has a top tab called **Power Schemes.** Of the Power Schemes that Windows 98 supplies, the default is called **Home/Office Desk,** and one of its settings is "Turn Off Monitor: Every 15 minutes." Aha! Go to the Turn Off Monitor drop-down list, which offers automatic shutdown delays from one minute to five hours, and set it to either a long period or "Never." Power Management Properties is a sterling example of good citizenship, but it goes too far if you'll let it.

## What the Future Brings

Because custom device drivers can extend the video reproduction power of Windows independent of the VGA standard, and because so many PC users now have Windows, Windows fosters the development of new graphics products for Intel-based and compatible computers. Advanced displays that can attain resolutions as high as 2,048x2,048, previously unavailable to all but a few PC users, are now built by several manufacturers—thanks to the advent of Windows' uniform graphical driver model. As a result, more graphics display systems are being introduced now than at any other time in the history of the PC.

New high-end display cards and monitors can display realistic images of photographic quality on the screen, as well as full-motion video. With Windows 98, PC owners can achieve the level of video quality once reserved for Macintosh users. Leading Macintosh manufacturers, like TrueVision and Hitachi RasterOps, have introduced high-quality PC graphics cards, monitors, video interfaces and editing systems whose capabilities are breathtaking. Most of this gear is still too costly for home or recreational use, but it's inexpensive enough to revolutionize professional video production.

For home and play, the most common integration of television signal into computers will be so-called "video in a window" cards, which are flirting with the magic sub-$100 price level. They are popular for multimedia applications because they enable input from a TV cable, video disk player, laserdisk player, VCR, or even your favorite game deck (!) to be displayed in a movable window. Vendors such as ATI, AVerMedia, Matrox and STB have begun to build TV circuitry directly into graphics adapters or add-on cards; some of these offer features like still capture, clip capture, pan and zoom. Windows 98 accommodates these cards handsomely with the new TV Viewer applet (see Chapter 13).

Expect improvements in display technology to go hand in hand with advances in sound and video compression, which will eventually (although not soon) make real-time videoconferencing standard for homes as well as businesses. New forms of communication are evolving—for example, real-time chat conferences and workshops at Internet sites—which allow people around the world to discuss any topic in the world. Microsoft is at the forefront of these developments with the inclusion of NetMeeting in Windows 98; Intel's ProShare is also a strong and popular contender.

As for video monitors, expect them to be replaced by flat-screen color monitors, a spinoff of the technology used in active-matrix display panels found on high-end laptops. Flat-panel color displays provide exceptionally sharp images and virtually no flicker; they are also lighter and easier to set up than cathode-ray tube monitors, and eliminate the potential risk of VDT emissions. Right now, almost a dozen manufacturers of high-end monitors have begun producing flat-screen displays, but at $2,000 to $3,000 for a 14-inch or 15-inch unit, they're not mainstream purchases yet. NEC makes a 20-inch flat-screen display, the LCD2000 XtraView, that sells for (gulp) $8,000. ... By the time you read this, magazine and Web reviews of these units will have appeared for about six months, and of course we urge you to read them.

# Mice and Other Pointing Devices

Pointing devices include many types of hand-held objects, from the well-known mice and trackballs to graphics tablets, pens, touchpads, touch screens, joysticks, flight yokes, data gloves, and (primarily on laptops) trackpoints. A few years ago, fewer than 10 percent of PCs were pointer-controlled; the installation of Windows on over 100 million computers worldwide has made the mouse into a default component for new systems and a nearly universal add-on for older computers. Logitech leads in mouse sales, with roughly 40 percent of the market, but Microsoft has produced durable and comfortable high-end mice for many years, and recently introduced the IntelliMouse—which adds a wheel for scrolling to the usual two buttons.

Of all the types of pointing devices, the mouse is still the most commonly used, with the trackball (which needs less room) coming up strongly behind it. For some applications, especially graphic arts and CAD, either a graphics tablet with a stylus or a pen stylus that you use on your desk provides a natural way to work with Windows. But the variety of "finger-driven interfaces" is incredible, and people tend to be highly partisan about their favorites—not only favorite pointing devices, but favorite manufacturers.

## Pointing Device Ergonomics

Your choice of a pointing device should be based on ergonomic concerns as well as on the functioning and features of the hardware itself. Your first decision is whether to use a mouse or a non-mouse. After over forty years of hands-on computer experience between us, Fred finds the mouse the easiest to operate, while Kip is a fanatic for trackballs. (He's talking about a massive, sensitive trackball, not the pea-sized, almost useless type that comes built into many laptops.) Pens, like their real counterparts, can cause writer's cramp. If you choose a pen, keep in mind that the thicker the stylus, the easier it is to hold for long periods. One recent addition to the pointer scene is a finger-activated pad or touchpad, manufactured by Alps and Cirque under the name Glidepoint. Like the housing of a trackball, the pad doesn't move; instead, you slide your finger on the pad to move the cursor on screen. Tap once and you've clicked; tap twice to double-click. Touchpads typically also have two or more buttons as part of the housing around the pad surface.

Another new type of pointing device is the *trackpoint*. You may have seen one; a trackpoint looks like a pencil eraser that got stuck in the middle of a keyboard. IBM pioneered those devices a few years ago in its ThinkPad laptops, and a number of other major laptop manufacturers have adopted this pointer as well, including Toshiba and Canon. You move the cursor by pushing the trackpoint in the direction you want the cursor to go. While almost anything is easier to push around than a mouse on an airplane tray table, skillful use of a trackpoint takes practice; some people find them skittish, while others think they're absolutely intuitive and natural. If your laptop is equipped with a trackpoint and you're wishing for one on your "big" computer too, IBM makes a nice full-size keyboard with a trackpoint in it.

Light pens and touch screens are intended for special applications, such as information kiosks and other dedicated systems. Although those pointers work with Windows, we don't recommend them for the average user. Holding a light pen to your screen for long periods of time can tire your arm. Touch screens require you to use your finger, which is also fatiguing, and the screens smudge easily.

The placement of your mouse is important. Having to reach too far forward for it can strain your shoulder. Reaching up for the mouse can tire your arm; it should be level with the height of your elbow or slightly lower. If using the mouse tires your finger or wrist, you can switch the mouse to your other hand, using the Mouse Control Panel to swap the mouse buttons.

If your wrist often tires, you may want a wrist-cushioning product, which also helps prevent carpal tunnel syndrome. The wrist pad, a rectangular bar of foam covered with a soft fabric, elevates your wrist to the height of the mouse. Mouse pads with integral wrist support are slightly less comfortable.

## Mice

The mouse was invented more than 20 years ago by Doug Engelbart, a researcher at Tymnet. Engelbart's first mouse was made of wood, supported by wheels, and topped by a tiny red button. (At the same time, he demonstrated a five-key chording keyboard; the idea was to operate the mouse with one hand, and the keyboard with the other, all the time. Mice took off, chording keyboards didn't, and the awkward result is still with us today.) The mouse was a component of many famous early microcomputers, including the Xerox Alto and the Apple Lisa, but didn't roar until 1984, when Apple's Macintosh served notice to industry and users alike that this beneficial little device was destined for desktops all over the world.

What makes a mouse? Despite their variations, all mice are held in the hand and are moved to control the corresponding movements of a pointer on the computer screen. Macintosh mice have one or two buttons; PC mice have two, three or many buttons. And usually each mouse has a tail—a cord connecting it to the computer—although cordless mice are scampering around more desktops than ever.

Mice differ widely in physical appearance, but each contains an internal tracking mechanism that interprets the mouse's movements for the computer. All mice track movement by recording horizontal and vertical motions, whether they employ a mechanical, an optomechanical, or an optical mechanism.

A mechanical mouse, like a Microsoft Mouse, contains a rolling ball that moves everywhere the mouse does. The ball, turned by friction against the mouse pad, turns two rollers positioned at right angles to each other inside the mouse body; one roller records vertical motion, and the other tracks horizontal motion. Both rollers drive mechanical encoders that send the horizontal and vertical signals to the computer. The mouse driver software translates those signals into X and Y coordinates and matches those coordinates to the location of the pointer on the screen.

Optomechanical mice, such as those built by Logitech and Apple, contain the same type of ball and roller as do mechanical mice. The rollers of an optomechanical mouse are connected to optical encoders, which use light to send signals to the computer which are translated to the pointer position on the screen. Logitech maintains that optomechanical mice are more durable than strictly mechanical ones, with lifespans of 300 miles of mouse movement, as opposed to the 50 to 100 miles of movement provided by a Microsoft mouse.

An optical mouse, like a Sun workstation mouse, operates only with a special pad coated with a reflective surface and printed with a rectangular grid. As you move the mouse over the pad, photosensors inside the mouse decode the reflections of the grid lines into horizontal and vertical movement. Mouse Systems' Optical Mouse is an example of this species. Because optical mice don't contain moving parts, they are reputed to be more reliable and accurate than other types of mice. On the other hand, if you lose the special mouse pad—or sometimes even turn it the wrong way—you're incapacitated.

## Trackballs

Now imagine flipping your mouse over and adding a drop of growth hormone to its rolling ball. Presto! You've got a trackball. The unit housing the trackball is stationary; to move the pointer on the screen, you roll the ball with your fingers. Trackballs require less desk space than do mice, and they allow you to perform coarse operations, like menu selection, more quickly and with less hand movement. (Trackballs are used in video games for lightning-fast cursor control.) Some people insist that you get more exact positioning with a mouse, especially for drawing programs and CAD; others retort that trackball precision comes with practice, and trackball speed is unbeatable. Whether a mouse or a trackball is more comfortable to use—especially for long periods—is strictly up to the individual.

## *Trackball Advice*

The earliest trackballs had their buttons where mouse buttons are; side by side at the front of the device. Some trackballs are still laid out this way, and we don't recommend them. You end up trying to move the trackball and click the buttons with the same two fingers, which means that in order to click the buttons you lift your fingertips off the ball, which is a nuisance, and kills your accuracy.

The newest, ergonomically brilliant trackball designs assign the two tasks to distinct fingers. With the Logitech Trackman Marble or Genius EasyTrak, you click with your fingers as usual, but roll the ball with your thumb. The Kensington Expert Mouse and newer Kensington Orbit take the opposite tack—the buttons are at either side of the ball, so that you left-click with your thumb, roll the ball with your first two fingers, and right-click with your ring finger or pinky. For a skilled user, it's like playing a one-handed musical instrument.

A trackball with a large ball may also appeal to you if, like many people, you have a slight tremor in the tips of your fingers. The ball of the trackball, if it's large enough, tends to damp out the unwanted minute motions, while many users believe that the body of a mouse tends to amplify them.

# Graphics Tablets

Graphics tablets, or digitizing tablets, are the most precise and also the most expensive pointing devices. A standard graphics tablet measures 12x12 inches, but both larger and smaller models are also available. An electromagnetic sensor is embedded in the tablet's surface; to move the pointer on your screen, you slide either a stylus or a puck across the tablet.

Artists find that a pen-shaped stylus provides the most natural drawing tool. Some sophisticated drawing programs support graphics tablets with pressure-sensitive styluses; when you press harder against one of these tablets, your brush stroke thickens as it would if you were actually painting. A pen-shaped stylus from Wacom also includes an eraser on the top, so that you can erase and feather digital lines. Cordless pens from several manufacturers combine technologies to give you the freedom of an untethered drawing device. The puck, most often used with CAD applications, is shaped somewhat like a mouse and contains cross hairs for precise cursor placement.

Graphics tablets can be expensive, depending on size, resolution, controls, and cordlessness. The smallest tablets, which make great toys or teaching tools, measure 4x5 to 5x7 inches and cost as little as $100; you might look, for example, at the Genius Kids Designer. For a "standard" size professional digitizing tablet, at 6x8, 12x12, or 12x18 inches, expect to pay $300 to $700. The largest digitizing tablets generally available (at the moment) are 36x48 at $1200 to $1600; a few larger ones have very serious prices. The best manufacturers in this business—CalComp, Kurta, Summagraphics, and Wacom—are very aware that the livelihoods of serious graphic artists and CAD users depend on what they build.

## About Plug and Play

Windows 98 supports Plug and Play for mice and other pointing devices, and Windows' new drivers eliminate the need for DOS mouse drivers. In addition, you can connect your pointing devices to the serial ports (COM1 through COM4) or to the dedicated mouse port, if your computer has one.

## You Say You Want Your Resolution

The sensitivity of a mouse determines its resolution. The level of movement a mouse tracking mechanism can detect and transmit to the computer is translated into resolution measured in points per inch (ppi). If the resolution of a particular mouse is 200 ppi, for example, its tracking mechanism can detect movements as small as 1/200 inch, the typical resolution of a bargain basement mouse. Microsoft's and Logitech's offerings claim resolutions of 400 ppi. In general, the higher the resolution of a mouse, the more control you have over its behavior. For work such as drawing, photo retouching, or layout, a high-resolution mouse provides an absolutely necessary degree of control.

In most early mice, a direct one-to-one ratio existed between the resolution in ppi of a mouse and the pixels on the screen. If your mouse device driver uses a one-to-one ratio and your mouse has a resolution of 200 ppi, the pointer on screen moves 200 pixels each time you move the mouse an inch.

Newer mice let you change the ratio of ppi to pixels from the regular one-to-one standard, varying the resolution and either increasing or decreasing the mouse's tracking speed. Beginning mouse users usually prefer slower tracking speeds, since at those speeds the mouse is less sensitive to unpracticed movements. Experienced users usually prefer higher tracking speeds, because they don't have to move the mouse as much to travel a given distance.

Windows 98 also provides ballistic tracking, also called ballistic or non-linear gain. With this speed-sensitive feature, the faster you move the mouse, the farther the cursor travels on the screen. Some users find non-linear tracking an impediment; they prefer an undistorted, direct correlation between mouse and pointer movements.

# Pointing Device Product Overview

From the hundred or so pointing devices available on the market, we've selected a few to describe. These have been chosen because they offer good performance and an assortment of special features at reasonable prices.

**Mice: Top Brands.**  Here we cover some mice that are at the upper end of the quality spectrum.

*Microsoft:*  **IntelliMouse.** The Microsoft IntelliMouse adds a brand-new control to (between, to be exact) the traditional buttons—a vertical, textured wheel that automatically scrolls the screen. No more sitting with your mouse pointer on the arrow tab of a scroll bar, or wondering which component of the scroll bar to grab to get where you're going the fastest. As an added benefit, when you press the Ctrl key, the Wheel turns from an "up-down" scroll command to an "in-out" zoom command—subtle testimony to the emerging three-dimensional quality of computing.

**Microsoft Mouse.** The classic Microsoft Mouse is available in serial, PS/2-style PDP (Pointing Device Port), InPort, and bus versions. It sports a clean design and fits comfortably into either palm—it's one of the few mice that makes serious accommodation for left-handed people. The ball is positioned slightly forward of center, can be removed easily for cleaning, and grips most flat surfaces with a good amount of traction. A Microsoft Mouse should be good for 50 to 100 miles of mouse travel, which is the equivalent of about ten years of everyday use.

This mechanical mouse boasts a resolution of 400 ppi. It also offers ballistic tracking with a wide range of tracking speeds, from exceedingly fast to excruciatingly slow. With the ballistic control turned up high, you can cover an entire VGA screen using only one square inch of desk space—but at that rate you'll need a lot of concentration to control the cursor.

*Logitech:*  Logitech is the overall leader in mouse sales, offering many models to fit a variety of needs and budgets. The centerpieces of Logitech's mouse line are the **MouseMan**, a 400 ppi ballistic mouse that comes in designer colors, and the new **MouseMan Plus**, which takes the MouseMan's advanced ergonomic design and adds a center scroll/zoom wheel to compete with the Microsoft IntelliMouse. If you want the very latest in Windows navigation combined with ultra-cool design and Logitech durability, here it all is.

The large size of the MouseMan or Plus makes it a handy hand rest, and because the mouse ball is positioned toward the rear, it's easy on your wrist to position the cursor. A symmetrical design lets you use whichever hand you're most comfortable mousing with, and you can easily switch hands if one hand needs a break. The MouseMan is also offered in a serial version that includes both 9- and 25-pin connectors as well as an adapter that plugs into a PDP mouse port. The MouseMan has three buttons and includes a Windows software utility that enables you to assign the buttons to macros or keystrokes. MouseMan is $45—in OEM packaging, as little as $25 if you're lucky—and MouseMan Plus is $55, on the street.

On the cutting edge of mouse design is Logitech's three-button Cordless **MouseMan Pro**, a radio mouse. Most other cordless mice employ an infrared beam, which can be interrupted by objects on your desk. The radio design ensures continuous transmission to the receiver from anywhere up to six feet away; Hyperjump software assigns commonly used Windows commands to single clicks. At $60, this is one classy rodent—like something from the product collection of an art museum.

In addition to the MouseMan line, Logitech offers **SurfMan**, a three-button hand-held … er … radio-controlled remote pointing device designed for fully laid-back Web surfing with either hand. The case design is, you might say, advanced, and the price is $90. In the same case, but with different internals, Logitech also makes **TrackMan Live!**, a battery-powered cordless radio controller for computer-driven presentations; the 30-foot range is notable, as is the fact that it doesn't need to point toward what you're controlling. TrackMan Live! street-retails for $120. Either of these will work as a normal, roll-on-the-pad cordless mouse when you need one.

Logitech's **Magellan 3D Controller** is at—heck, it *is*—the high end of the mouse spectrum. This nine-button mouse, designed for high-end CAD applications, is the only mouse that provides full three-dimensional positioning with six degrees of freedom. In 1993 a Magellan was used to control a robot during a NASA Shuttle mission, and the company now proudly refers to it as "space-proven." At about $600, Magellan is less costly than a "real" 6D device from one of the boutique VR companies, but you may have a hard time buying one—Logitech hasn't decided to let it all the way loose into retail channels. Check it out on the Mice and Trackballs page of `http://www.logitech.com`.

For those who lament the passing of the **Logitech Kidz Mouse**, no longer produced, we can only suggest that the Logitech **First Mouse** and **First Mouse Plus** are solid, no-nonsense mice that—at a street price of only $25 to $30—will do well in a budget system for a grade-schooler or anyone else. The First Mouse is a standard two-button mouse; First Mouse Plus adds the scroll/zoom wheel.

*IBM:* **Scrollpoint Mouse.** Just can't decide between a mouse and a trackpoint? Now you don't have to! The new IBM Scrollpoint Mouse has a trackpoint-like device tucked between its two buttons, to be used for scrolling, highlighting, or clicking. Slightly less expensive than the Microsoft IntelliMouse, but competing closely with it on features, the Scrollpoint

Mouse is otherwise a basic but well-executed two-button mechanical design with 400 ppi resolution and a claimed "travel life" of over 600 miles. You can buy it in black or white, but so far only with a PS/2 connector; IBM, as usual, is marketing under the umbrella of its own product line and has this positioned primarily as a ThinkPad (laptop) accessory.

*Mouse Systems:* **PC Point Pro**, **ProAgio**, and **Optical Mouse.** In 1982 Mouse Systems was the first company to make mice for the PC. It's still a big cheese in the mouse market with products like its PC Point Pro, a Plug and Play three-button mouse with an unusually high base resolution of 420 ppi.

One of the company's more esoteric offerings is the ProAgio mouse, a five-button mouse that offers some snazzy features. For one thing, a small button on the side is programmed to switch between applications; it enables you to access the Task Manager without using the function keys. The ProAgio also has a unique SmartScroll feature: when you press a button while moving the mouse, the cursor scrolls at a uniform speed.

The Optical Mouse is a three-button mouse available in a serial version with a PS/2 adapter. Because it's optical, it has no moving parts to break or wear out, but you must use it with the reflective grid-lined mouse pad, included in the package. The Optical Mouse can be made to emulate a two-button mouse in Windows by sliding a small switch on the back of the mouse. Its base resolution is only 300 ppi, but the highly tuned UltraRes ballistic driver helps make up for that. The Optical Mouse has long been popular even as a high-end product, but now, at $50 street, is no more expensive than mechanical mice of comparable quality.

**Bargain Mice.** You are most likely going to use your mouse frequently with Windows 98, so investing in a good-quality mouse that fits your hand makes a lot of sense. If you are budget conscious, however, bargain mice abound—some are offered for as little as $10. It might be worth keeping a couple of these mice around as spares in case your main mouse goes down for repairs.

*IMSI:* The **Pet Mouse**, a serviceable low-cost mouse, sells for $19 to $25 on the street and enables you to switch between Microsoft and Mouse Systems compatibility modes, which both run with Windows 98.

**Mousepads.** The average **mousepad** is a mouse mattress. With a little patience you can score one free, and it's worth it. Some are better than others, if you can see that far down. A mousepad's main excuse for being is interior decoration—a fact bravely confronted by Adriaan van der Hek in Utrecht, the Netherlands, whose Virtual Mousepad Museum is on the Web at `http://www.expa.hvu.nl/ajvdhek/index.html`. Now you can look at nice mousepads without having to own them.

*3M:* What you need instead is a **Precise Mousing Surface** (hey, *we* didn't name it) by 3M. This rugged, washable piece of plastic, with a fifties-retro shape and exotically microtextured finish, is everything you need to keep your mouse rolling; since it's a sixteenth of an inch thick and weighs nothing, it's totally great to tuck into your laptop case, but you'll want one anywhere you use a mouse. It's purple, it's $10 on the street, and it may take some hunting—3M doesn't market these the way they do Post-Its.

**Trackballs.** Kind of like an upside-down mouse.

*Logitech:* **TrackMan.** This is one of the most ergonomically designed track-balls for right-handed users, but the placement of the buttons makes it awk-ward for left-handers. The rolling ball is placed on the left side, with three buttons to the right of it, so you can keep your hand fully opened; the thumb manipulates the ball, and the fingers are free to click buttons. The TrackMan is available in both serial and bus versions and is compatible with the Logitech mouse driver included with Windows 98.

**TrackMan Marble.** Still a thumb-operated trackball, but substantially differ-ent in layout from the TrackMan, the TrackMan Marble is an opto-mechanical device that has to be tried to be believed. Some gamers swear by it. With fewer moving parts than other trackballs, it needs cleaning less often, a big plus.

*Kensington:* **Expert Mouse.** Despite its name, Kensington's flag ... er ... mouse is an industrial-strength trackball. Half of its 2-inch, billiard-ball-like ball protrudes from the unit. The Expert Mouse is a high-end product—list about $130, street $100, sale about $70—and available in serial, PS/2, and bus versions. The stability of the large ball and the solid feel and durability of the unit have earned it popularity among Macintosh users. (Macintosh users, my foot, says Kip. I've had an Expert Mouse connected to my Windows boxes for years, and I wouldn't have anything else.) Kensington enjoys a good reputa-tion for warranty repairs, if you need them.

**Orbit.** A narrower and lighter cousin of the Expert Mouse, the Orbit needs less room and is significantly less expensive ($60 street) yet retains the won-derful stability of that great big ball. The royal-blue ball and tapered case are very cool-looking—and the ball is held in by tabs, so that if you should knock the Orbit off your desk, the ball won't roll underneath with the dust bunnies.

*Microsoft:* Microsoft has introduced a trackball with the IntelliMouse's scroll-ing wheel incorporated. Just to keep things lively, they're both called **IntelliMouse** and they both retail for the same price—about $80—so, if you're ordering online or by mail, be sure you specify the right one!

*Mouse Systems:* **PC Trackball II.** This three-button trackball has an innova-tive, dome-shaped design, with the buttons placed at the base of the dome, just below the ball. This makes it comfortable to move the ball with two fingers

while resting your thumb on the left or right button. The PC Trackball is economical ($40 street) and available in a serial version with a PS/2 adapter.

**Keyboard and Pointer Combinations.** If you've got a cluttered desk or
a small computer stand that doesn't have enough room for either a mouse or a
trackball, then you might be interested in a keyboard that comes with its own
pointing device.

*Qtronix:* The **Scorpius 95** keyboard, with 104 keys (including Windows keys)
and an integrated trackball, requires the same amount of space as a standard
101-key keyboard. The ballistic trackball—conveniently located just to the
right of the [Enter] key—has a resolution of 200 to 6400 dpi; it can be removed
for cleaning, which solves one problem of earlier trackball keyboards. Street is
$50 to $60, which is like buying a trackball and getting a keyboard free, but this
keyboard is *not* easy to find. To get one, you may have to bug your vendor.

*IBM:* If you'd like a keyboard with a trackpoint, IBM's offering is called,
guess what, **the IBM Enhanced Keyboard with TrackPoint.** This features
IBM's buckling-spring key technology, which gives more definite tactility than
rubber-dome keys, as well as the same trackpoint they use in the ThinkPad
laptops; there's also a PS/2 mouse port in the keyboard itself, Macintosh-style.
It's available in black, IBM model number 13H6705, or white, IBM model
number 92G7461, for about $130. (You'll need those model numbers if you
ever hope to find one.)

*ALPS/Cirque:* If you're a devotee of one-finger exercise, both Alps and
Cirque make keyboards with integral **Glidepoint** touchpads for $70 to $120.

**Laptop Pointing Devices.** PC laptops were introduced, frankly, without
mice in mind—it was enough of a struggle just to build a decent portable keyboard. Then Apple introduced the PowerBook, originally with a small trackball located below the keyboard, and now with a built-in touchpad. PC
vendors have quickly followed suit, and now most laptops include an integral
pointing device, whether a trackball, a touchpad, or an eraser-head trackpoint
built into the keyboard. If you've got a laptop without a built-in pointer, the
still-seething computer industry has graciously granted you several options.

*Microsoft and Logitech:* The Microsoft **Ballpoint** and Logitech **TrackMan
Portable** are two surprisingly similar miniature trackballs in semicircular
cases, which clip to the left or right side of your laptop's keyboard—making
them equally convenient for either hand. To use them, you grasp the device
between thumb and palm, moving the trackball with your thumb and pressing
buttons along the sides of the device with your fingers.

Logitech makes a three-button mouse, built short, wide and light with a short
cord, called the **MouseMan for Notebooks**; it's both serial and PS/2-compat-
ible, but at $50 street, it's a hair more expensive than the "real" MouseMan.

*Fellowes:* **MousePen.** The MousePen from Fellowes Manufacturing, now sold by Questec, is a mouse substitute with a distinctive design. It's shaped somewhat like a pen, with small buttons that are equivalent to regular mouse buttons, and ends in a pea-size ball. The MousePen is a ballistic mouse that comes in three versions: a battery-powered cordless infrared model, a professional three-button model that controls cursor speed and works with either a PS/2 or serial port, a slightly cheaper serial-only model, and a children's model called the **Computer Crayon.** Street prices range from $80 for the Cordless MousePen Pro PC to about $15 for the Computer Crayon.

### The Cult of the MousePen

The MousePen is like a religious cult: either you love it or you don't know about it and don't miss it. Its small following consists mainly of laptop users, who claim you can easily use the MousePen on your leg when you are cramped into an airline seat without enough room to maneuver a traditional mouse. Some desktop users like it because it feels more like a pen—an attribute we have a hard time appreciating as a benefit. The MousePen's detractors say that using it is like trying to write with a ballpoint pen on waxed paper because the small ball doesn't always make firm contact with the surface below and tends to skip.

Fellowes does supply two additional balls with the MousePen to correct the skipping problem that occurs with the regular ball. Those other balls have a rougher, more textured surface that solves the skipping problem but creates a cleaning problem: the balls pick up dirt and dust almost as well as a small vacuum cleaner.

*ALPS/Cirque:* Finally, if lightweight and portability are at the top of your list, check out the external versions of the Alps or Cirque **Glidepoint** touchpads. At $50 to $70 (maybe less on sale) they cost as much as a pricey mouse, but they're almost as convenient as a built-in touchpad, and weigh next to nothing.

## The Mouse Control Panel

Microsoft combined all the Windows 98 mouse configuration options into one Control Panel. It's easy to set up your mouse to suit your working style. The Mouse Control Panel has three tabs:

- **Buttons.** On this tab you can change the configuration of the mouse buttons and set the double-click speed.

- **Pointers.** On this page you can change the appearance of the mouse pointer or insertion point to go with specific actions. You can also save a custom configuration.

- **Motion.** Here you can customize mouse speed and choose whether to display mouse trails.

Rodent *aficionados* from the days of Windows 95 will notice that the **General** tab has vanished, which means that you can no longer switch mouse drivers through the Mouse Control Panel, but only through **Add New Hardware.** Most contemporary mice are Plug and Play and will be detected on a restart anyway. See "Changing Mouse Drivers" on page 269.

### Switch-Hitting Buttons and Adjusting Double-Click Speeds

Windows recognizes only two mouse buttons, although many mice include three or more buttons. One button is the primary button; you use it for most of your clicking, double-clicking, and dragging. Windows 98 uses the secondary button to display a pop-up menu of commands related to whatever was clicked on and to perform special dragging operations. When you're in an application, the action of this button depends on the application. In Microsoft Word, for example, you can use the second button to see pop-up menus for selected text.

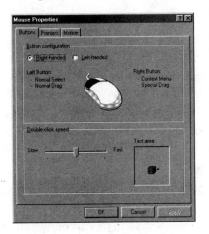

The Buttons tab of Mouse Properties enables you to choose which button is your primary button; the left button is the default. If you're left-handed, you might want to click on **Left-handed,** to make the right mouse button the primary button (Figure 7.9).

Another option on this page enables you to change the interval between the two clicks of a double-click. If you're a slow clicker, your computer might interpret a double-click as two separate clicks. Use the slider bar and the Test Area in the Double-Click Speed box to change the double-click speed. Move the slider bar toward Slow or Fast, then double-click in the Test Area box to try it out. If you click too slowly, nothing happens, and you should move the slider bar towards Slow. But when you double-click at the correct speed or faster, the jack-in-the-box pops up (Figure 7.10). Double-click again, and the jack-in-the-box goes back into its box.

*Figure 7.9*

The Button page of the Mouse Control Panel

*Figure 7.10*

The Double-Click Speed test area jack-in-the-box

Scurrying for mouse supremacy, some vendors have produced mice with three and four buttons. In fact, three-button mice abound in the UNIX world. Very few Windows programs, however, support more than two buttons, although some mice include drivers that enable you to set up the third button as a function key for a frequently issued keystroke sequence or macro.

Utility programs and drivers included with third-party mice that have two or more buttons enable you to assign commands to the second and third mouse buttons. For example, assigning your third button the function of the Enter key enables you to click OK quickly in a dialog box. Some drivers, such as

Kensington's Thinking Mouse driver, even allow chording—that is, you can assign a function to two buttons clicked simultaneously. Chording effectively increases the number of buttons on a mouse and can make short work of complicated tasks, since you can assign more than one action to a chord. For example, you can save and close a document and quit an application with only one click.

**The Pointers Tab.** Windows 98 enables you to change the look of pointers and cursors. The Windows Standard choice is okay, but why pass up the look of 3-D Pointers, with their graceful shading? Besides the 3-D scheme, four others are available: Animated Hourglasses with animated color cursors, Windows Black with silhouettes, Windows Inverted with hourglasses that look like photographic negatives, and Windows Standard. The last three of these have alternative schemes with pointer shapes in slightly larger or extra-large sizes. To change the scheme of your cursors quickly, select a scheme from the Scheme drop-down list box on the Pointers page of the Mouse Properties dialog box, then click on Apply or OK (Figure 7.11).

*Figure 7.11*

The Pointers tab of Mouse Properties

To change the shape of one pointer, click on the name of the pointer and then click on Browse. Locate a cursor file and click on Open. To make Windows truly your own, you can create images in or import them into some paint programs and save them in a cursor file (with a .cur extension). Save the file to the Windows Cursor folder so it's easy to find. Then select that file to obtain a new pointer shape.

If you change the look of your pointers or cursors, you can save them as a scheme under whatever name you like. (If you have children in the house, they might want to create their own schemes of mouse pointers using cartoon characters or original creations.)

*Figure 7.12*

The Mouse Control Panel's Motion page

**Of Pointer Speeds and Trails.** Some mouse drivers give you the ability to change mouse resolutions. To take advantage of this option, check out the Motion tab of Mouse Properties. To alter the tracking speed, adjust the **Pointer speed** option (Figure 7.12).

Why would you want to alter the one-to-one ppi-to-pixel ratio? Let's say you barely have any desk space in which to move your mouse around. To reduce the amount of space you need, just increase the tracking speed. Speeding up the tracking mechanism enables you to cover large distances on the screen by moving the mouse only a little. This is useful for actions such as menu selection and dialog box navigation. Slowing down the tracking speed, on the other hand, gives you more precise control over your mouse, which is useful when you perform fine detail work.

If you have a slower LCD screen, you've probably found that your pointer gets lost sometimes, especially if you move the mouse or trackball too quickly. The **Pointer trail** option offers some relief. Showing pointer trails is a little like having a strobe light on as you move your pointer; you see momentary shadows indicating where the pointer was, making your pointer easier to follow. To show pointer trails, check the **Show pointer trails** box and then use the slider bar to adjust the length of the trails. Since the changes take place immediately, you can try them out, fine-tuning the trail length to fit your liking.

## Changing Mouse Drivers

If you change mice, you may also need to change drivers. Most newer mice support Plug and Play, which means Windows 98 should be able to detect the type of mouse you've attached and then ask you to insert the disk that contains the driver. If not, you can choose the select-from-list option of the Add New Hardware Wizard on the Add New Hardware Control Panel to detect or change the driver.

Windows 98 provides "Standard" mouse drivers that support the following mice:

- HID (Human Interface Device)-compliant mouse.

- InPort Adapter mouse.

- Standard Bus Adapter mouse.

- Standard PS/2 Port mouse.

- Standard Serial mouse.

All of which together covers 90 percent of what's out there, at least this week. Windows 98 also supplies drivers for newer pointer models by Alps (touchpad), BTC, Cherry, Chicony, Compaq (trackball), ELO TouchSystems (touchscreen), Focus, Forward, Genius, ITAC Systems, Jing Mold, Kensington (serial trackball), Key Tronic, Logitech, MaxiSwitch, Microsoft (mostly serial stuff), Monterey, NMB, Ortek, Rainbow, Samsung, SUH,

Texas Instruments, and Toshiba (trackpoint). Any of these not specified otherwise is a USB (Universal Serial Bus) mouse. If your mouse is none of the above, you may need to dig up the OEM driver diskette or contact the manufacturer for a device driver.

To select a non–Plug and Play mouse driver by hand, pick the select-from-list option of the Add New Hardware Wizard, and then do just what you'd do for a graphics adapter or keyboard; pick your manufacturer from the left pane, then your model from the right pane. If your manufacturer or model isn't listed, you need to click the **Have Disk...** button and insert the OEM driver diskette in drive A:, or change the path to wherever else you have a copy of the driver.

## Connecting Your Mouse

Mice and other pointing devices are attached to your system in one of three ways, depending on the type of mouse:

- A serial mouse is connected to a COM port.

- A bus mouse is connected to an add-in card that plugs into a slot inside the system. It can also be connected to a special port on a notebook computer.

- A Pointing Device Port (PDP) mouse is connected to a mouse port on the system unit.

The serial mouse/COM port connection is the most common arrangement. Serial mice are usually less expensive than bus mice because they don't require a port card supplied with the mouse. The disadvantage of a serial mouse is that it uses one of your COM ports. Some systems have only one or two COM ports, which may already be in use by an external or PC Card modem, a printer, or another serial device. If that's the case, you have to get either a serial card with more COM ports, or a bus mouse.

 Mouse Systems makes a serial card called the **Com-5 Card** which can be set to nine IRQs—between IRQ2 and IRQ15—and offers extended addressing. It needs a 16-bit ISA slot, and street price is around $29. This is especially handy to use with Windows 98. Fire up the Microsoft System Information Utility, check the Resources\IRQs key to find out which IRQs are unused in your system, and check the Resources\I/O key to find out which address ranges are free; then set up the card to match.

Also, because both mice and COM ports can be configured for either 9-pin or 25-pin connectors, you have to match your COM port with your mouse connector pins. Most serial mice include adapters that work with either 9-pin or 25-pin adapters. If yours doesn't, you might need to get the appropriate serial port converter, available in most computer stores.

The bus mouse does not require a COM port because it attaches directly to its own connector on an add-in card. This add-in card takes up a slot inside your system. You may have an available slot, but if you have other peripherals, you may not have a free hardware interrupt request line (IRQ), which enables your system to communicate with hardware devices. If you run out of serial ports, add-in slots, or IRQs, you may have to disconnect something to attach your mouse. You can use the Microsoft System Information Utility described in Chapter 16 to investigate the status of your system's IRQs.

The InPort mouse interface card comes with the bus version of the Microsoft Mouse, which is the most common bus mouse in use. Other companies, such as MicroSpeed, also offer InPort interfaces for InPort-compatible devices. The InPort card is a small card with one chip. It contains three jumper blocks: one to configure the card for a normal slot or for Slot 8 of XT systems, another to tell your system whether this is the primary or secondary InPort card (you can attach two), and a third to set the hardware interrupt used by the InPort card at either 2, 3, 4, or 5.

## IRQ Starvation

Why is it that, when the ISA architecture was handed down from on high, its humble servants were granted only sixteen IRQs? Something to do with it being a 16-bit bus. If a device reassures you that it can be set to "IRQ 2, 3, 4, 5, or 7," that's not a lot of help, since IRQ 2 is the default for network adapters, 3 and 4 give you room for a mouse and modem, and 7 belongs to the printer, leaving only 5, which was once the rarely-used second parallel port but today is probably the sound card. Any modern, useful serial add-on device should offer you at least two choices from IRQ 10, 11, 12, and 15.

The Pointing Device Port (PDP) is the best alternative—a built-in mouse connection. The PDP is built into the motherboard of IBMs, Compaqs, and other systems. If you have a PDP, simply plug your mouse into it. It's usually located next to the keyboard connector on the back of the system unit. The PDP is gaining popularity among systems manufacturers; all PS/2s use it, and PDP input devices are manufactured by companies such as IBM, Microsoft, Mouse Systems, Logitech, Calcomp, Kensington, and MicroSpeed.

Some mice, such as the Logitech models, can be connected in more than one of the ways just mentioned. Check the documentation to see if an adapter is available that allows a mouse to be used with a different connector.

# Keyboards

The keyboard still plays a major role in a substantially mouse-controlled environment. You need a keyboard for data entry, and many commands are issued more easily and more quickly from a keyboard than from a mouse, because you don't have to remove your hands from the keyboard to reach for the mouse.

In fact, you don't even need a mouse to run Windows; almost every command can be issued from the keyboard. This capability gives Windows an edge over the Macintosh, which is almost totally mouse-dependent. With Windows you can have the best of both worlds—keyboard and mouse—using each input device when it is the more efficient or merely when it suits you.

### Shameless Connector

We can't begin this section without a plug for Kip's favorite plain old keyboard, the Key Tronic Lifetime Designer. The action is satin-smooth and slightly stiff, not reluctant; it has two [Win] keys, two [Alt] keys, two [Ctrl] keys, a drop-menu key, and an oversize [Backspace]; it's semi-gloss black, which is quite nice if you *don't* like looking at the keyboard; and the "Lifetime" in the name *refers to the warranty*. $60 list and about $45 street, meaning that for the price of two cheap, rattly, rollover-and-die keyboards, you can have this top-of-the-line black slab for as long as you need it. If you're a serious (or even halfway) writer/typist, you absolutely want to try one of these.

## Keyboard Ergonomics

In spite of all this debate about VDT emissions from the monitor, the keyboard may actually pose the biggest health hazard associated with your computer. Use of the keyboard has been proven to cause a variety of hand and wrist injuries, known collectively as repetitive stress injuries (RSI).

The two most common of those injuries, *tendinitis* and *carpal tunnel syndrome*, are caused by poor typing habits and an improper work setup. If you pound on the keyboard while typing or type for a long time in an awkward position, you can place too much stress on your muscles and connective tissues. You can also hurt yourself by repeating the same motion over and over without resting the tendons in your wrists and hands. Repetitive motion can lead to chronic swelling of the tendons, or tendinitis, with symptoms ranging from numbness to severe pain.

Prolonged repetitive motion causes excessive stress on the tendons that pass through a small area of the wrist known as the carpal tunnel. When the tendons become so swollen that they press on the nerves going to the hand, carpal tunnel syndrome results. This condition can make it impossible to type or use your hands for almost anything. An operation to alleviate the pain or paralysis caused by repetitive hand motion has become one of the most common surgical procedures in the United States, but is costly and often ineffective. Prevention is the best recourse!

The best preventive measures are to take frequent short breaks from typing, and to position your keyboard and your body properly. You are typing too long without a rest if your fingers remain slightly curled when your hands are relaxed—a sign of tight tendons. During your breaks, stretch your fingers gently—press your hands flat against a wall—or squeeze a small ball or hand-gripper. Position your keyboard so that it is level with your wrists; typing with your wrists flexed too far forward or bent too far back can damage them.

Fortunately, many new ergonomic keyboards have built-in wrist rests, and their designs make typing more comfortable in other ways, too. A split keyboard is an especially nice improvement for those with wide shoulders, although it can take a little while to get used to the setup. Once you do, however, you may never willingly give it up and type on a standard keyboard again.

Another hazard to avoid is cradling the phone between your ear and your shoulder while you type; get a headset instead. (The Nady EasyTalk TH-45, a stereo telephone headset with a headset/handset switch, a mute button and two volume controls, is available at better office supply stores and some computer retailers for less than $80. If you've only ever used a headset with a single earpiece, the EasyTalk will be a revelation.) Also, don't place the heels of your hands on the desktop and bend your wrists up so that your fingers can reach the keys.

You can adjust the height of your keyboard itself or adjust the height of your chair in relation to the keyboard. Aim to place the keyboard slightly lower than your elbow. Most desks are 29 inches tall, which is considered about 3 inches too high for comfortable typing. You can sometimes remedy this height problem by getting a keyboard tray that attaches to the underside of the desk. (This is usually easier than sawing 3 inches off the legs of the desk.) Look for a keyboard tray that includes a built-in wrist rest, such as those made by 3M or Sunway. Unfortunately, a solid, non-resonating keyboard tray with an angle adjustment, wide enough for a 101-key keyboard and a trackball, is likely to cost $250, but you'll use it for years and probably save your wrists a lot of grief.

# Keyboard Device Drivers

Windows 98 provides "Standard" keyboard drivers that support the following keyboards:

- AT-style, 84 to 86 keys.

- AT&T 301 and 302.

- Standard 101-key or 102-key (U.S. and non-U.S.).

- Microsoft Natural.

- Olivetti 101 and 102 A.

- Olivetti 83-key, 86-key, and M24 102-key.

- PC/XT-style 83-key and 84-key.

There are also drivers for newer keyboard models by Acer, Alps, BTC, Cherry, Chicony, Focus, Forward, Fujitsu, Jing Mold, Key Tronics, MaxiSwitch, Microsoft, Monterey, NMB, Ortek, Rainbow, Samsung, Sejin, Silitek and SUH. Most of these are USB (Universal Serial Bus) keyboards. If your keyboard is none of the above, you may need to dig up the OEM driver diskette or contact the manufacturer for a device driver.

To select a non-Plug and Play keyboard driver by hand, pick the select-from-list option of the Add New Hardware Wizard, and then do just what you'd do for a graphics adapter or mouse; pick your manufacturer from the left pane, then your model from the right pane. If your manufacturer or model isn't listed, you need to click the **Have Disk...** button and insert the OEM driver diskette in drive A:, or change the path to wherever else you have a copy of the driver.

# The Keyboard Control Panel

The Keyboard Control Panel is similar to the Control Panels for other devices, such as the mouse; it combines all the keyboard options into one tabbed sheet. The Keyboard Properties sheet has two tabs:

- **Speed.** Enables you to set the character repeat and delay speeds and specify how quickly you want the cursor to blink. (Cursors blink, for example, when you're inserting text into a word-processing application. Blinking offers a simple visual cue that helps you locate the cursor.)

- **Language.** Enables you to choose a keyboard language so that you can access the characters of a foreign language. Also enables you to change the layout of the keys.

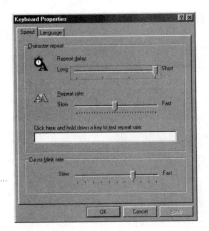

**Figure 7.13**

The Speed tab of the Keyboard Control Panel

**Speed Options.** Speed, the first tab of the Keyboard Properties dialog box (Figure 7.13), offers two character-repeat options. The **Repeat delay** option enables you to set the amount of time between when you begin holding down a key and when the character it represents begins repeating. The **Repeat rate** option enables you to set the rate at which the character repeats. The **Cursor blink rate** option gives you the ability to set the speed at which the cursor blinks.

You might want to increase the interval before a key repeats if you're heavy-handed or are a novice at typing. If the key repeat delay is set at too short an interval, you're likely to type double or triple letters when you intend to enter a single letter.

To change the amount of time that elapses before a key repeats itself, drag the **Repeat delay** slider bar to the left to lengthen the time delay, or to the right to shorten it. To adjust the rate at which the key repeats once it gets going, use the **Repeat rate** slider bar. To test your settings, click in the Test box, then press any alphanumeric key on the keyboard.

You can also change the **Cursor blink rate.** As you type in a word-processing or other type of application, the cursor blinks to indicate where your next typed letters will go. Some people find that a cursor blinking at a fast rate makes them feel frenetic and tense, while others find that if it blinks too slowly, they lose sight of the cursor altogether. To change the rate, drag the **Cursor blink rate** slider bar one way or the other. The cursor animation to the left of the slider bar indicates the current blink rate.

**Altering Keyboard Languages and Layouts.** Windows 98 enables you to change your keyboard layout to that of another country, making available different characters and symbols. You can also change the layout from a standard QWERTY layout to the more efficient (but less common) Dvorak

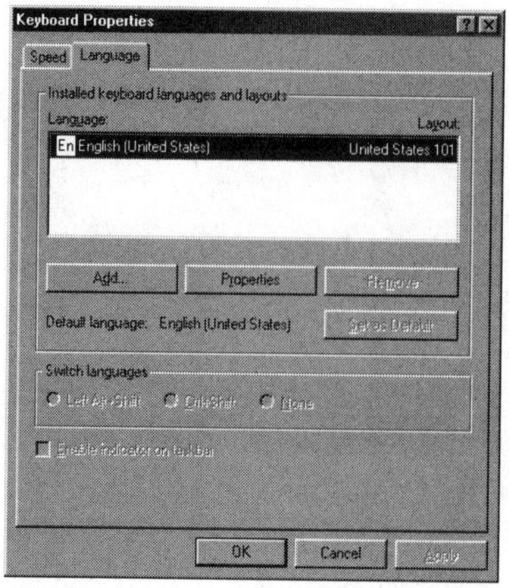

**Figure 7.14**

Language tab
of the Keyboard
Control Panel

arrangement. Both settings are located on the Language tab, the second tab of Keyboard Properties (Figure 7.14).

The current keyboard language and layout are highlighted on the Language page. You can change the keyboard language to one that uses characters from another alphabet, such as Swedish or French. You can also select other versions of English, such as Canadian English. You can install more than one keyboard language, but you can use only one at a time. However, you can switch keyboard languages quickly by using your own keyboard macro or by clicking on the keyboard language indicator on the Taskbar.

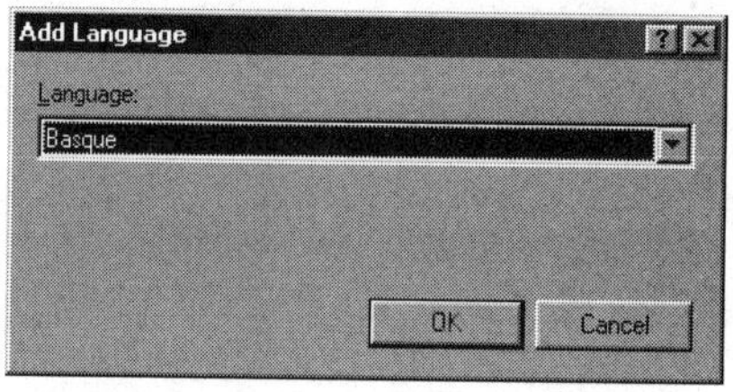

**Figure 7.15**

Add Language tab
in the Keyboard
Control Panel

To add a keyboard language, click on the Add button and select a language from the Language drop-down list box. Have your Windows 98 installation disks or CD-ROM on hand, because you will be asked to install the language from the correct disk. Follow the instructions, and Windows 98 loads the correct files automatically (Figure 7.15).

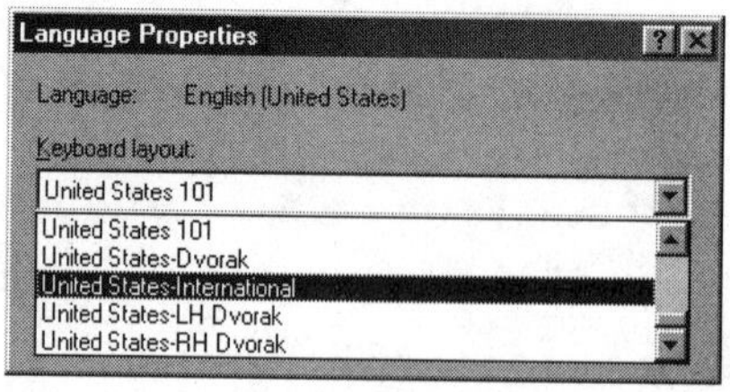

**Figure 7.16**

Language Properties
tab of the Keyboard
Control Panel
(with Options list
dropped)

Changing your keyboard layout is as easy as selecting a new keyboard language. Select the language for which you want to change the keyboard layout, then click on the **Properties** button to see the Language Properties dialog box. Select a layout from the Keyboard Layout drop-down list box, then click on **OK.** Again, be prepared with the appropriate Windows 98 disk or CD-ROM so you can install the desired layout (Figure 7.16). To remove an installed language and layout combination, select the option you want to delete and click on **Remove.**

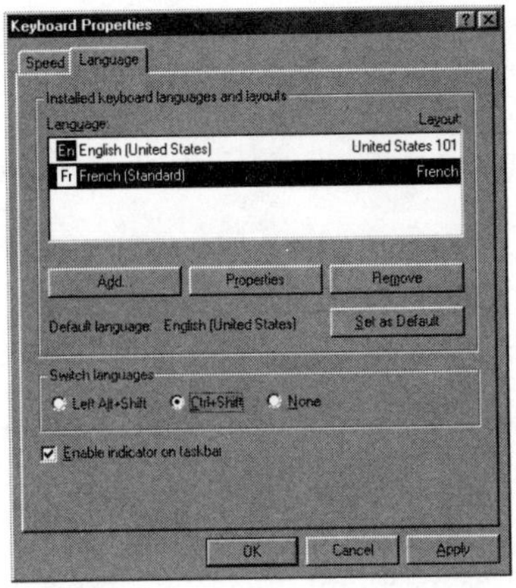

**Figure 7.17**

Language Properties tab with multiple languages installed

You can switch between layouts quickly either by using a keyboard shortcut (a macro) or by clicking on an indicator on the Taskbar. You can select a preset shortcut, either Left Alt Shift or Ctrl Shift, from the Switch Languages options on the Language page. You can also choose **None** to disable both preset short-cuts (Figure 7.17).

Some people find it handier to use the Taskbar to switch between languages. If you check **Enable indicator on taskbar**, a square appears beside the clock on the Taskbar showing an abbreviation of the name of the keyboard language you are using. (You can find the same indicator on the Keyboard Properties sheet in the **Installed keyboard languages and layouts** region.) What's more, if you position your pointer over the language indicator, you see the full name of the language, such as *English (United States)*. Click on the indicator to bring up a list of the languages you have installed. To switch to a particular language, click on its name in the list.

**The Dvorak Keyboard Layout.** One of the goals of Windows 98 is to boost your computing productivity. However, in light of the demands Windows 98 places on your system—and on you—it often seems as if the reverse were true. The standard keyboard, similarly, enhances productivity, but at quite a cost. The learning curve can be steep, and for some, insurmountable—or at least not worth the effort of discarding the hunt-and-peck method. In any case, the layout of the standard keyboard that comes with most computers was intentionally designed to slow you down. In fact, the layout of your keyboard is one of the most antiquated elements of your computer interface.

Standard keyboards use what is called the QWERTY layout (named after the first six keys on the top row of the keyboard), designed between 1868 and 1872 by Charles Sholes, one of the inventors of the typewriter. In the cockeyed QWERTY layout, frequently used keys were placed at opposite ends of the keyboard, so that moving type bars were less likely to collide and jam the action. For the sake of sales, Sholes also arranged the letters so that the word TYPEWRITER (which was used in demonstrations) could be typed quickly, using only the top row. The result has been slowing typists down for a century and a quarter.

Jammed keys are hardly a concern on computer keyboards, and jammed fingers are an everyday burden. It's time to explore the alternative to the QWERTY keyboard: the Dvorak keyboard. Named after its inventor, efficiency expert August Dvorak, this layout places the most commonly used keystrokes on the so-called *home row,* the middle row of letters.

Dvorak's research demonstrated that almost 70 percent of commonly used words—about 3,000—can be typed from the home row of his keyboard. By comparison, only 120 commonly used words can be typed from the home row of a QWERTY keyboard. As a result, your fingers would travel only 1 mile during a typical day of typing on a Dvorak layout, whereas the fingers of an average typist would cover 16 miles on a QWERTY keyboard. Because the fingers do less traveling, accuracy has been shown to improve by almost 15 percent, and typing speed by 20 percent.

Despite its many advantages, the Dvorak keyboard, which was patented in 1936, has remained obscure; its followers are few and far between, although devoted. Some Dvorak proponents must have influenced Microsoft, however, because Windows 98 provides the ability to remap your keyboard to the Dvorak layout.

Open the Keyboard Control Panel and click on the **Language** tab. Select a language, click on **Properties,** and then select **United States-Dvorak** from the drop menu of the Keyboard Layout section (Figure 7.16). Once you select that option, your keyboard is reconfigured in the Dvorak layout whenever you run Windows. The Dvorak layout rearranges the keyboard as shown in Figure 7.18.

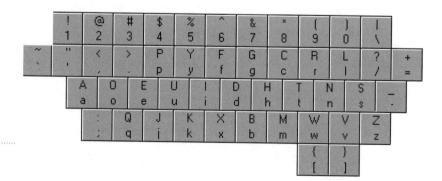

**Figure 7.18**

United States-
Dvorak option

If your conversion to the Dvorak layout is permanent, you will probably want to rearrange the keycaps on your keyboard as well. Most keyboards allow you to pull the keycaps off directly (pull gently, or obtain a keycap-puller tool from your dealer). Then replace them according to the layout depicted in Figure 7.18.

 There are also special Dvorak layouts optimized for the left hand only and the right hand only. These are illustrated in Appendix B, "Accessibility Options."

If you're just learning to type, want to learn the Dvorak layout, or want to improve your typing skills, several typing tutorial programs support the Dvorak keyboard layout as well as the QWERTY layout. Our recommendation is **Mavis Beacon Teaches Typing,** an excellent Windows typing program for both QWERTY and Dvorak layouts from Mindscape in Novato, California. The program is both educational and entertaining and can be used by adults and kids. A clever feature is the program's ghostlike guide hands, which show you how to type correctly (Figure 7.19).

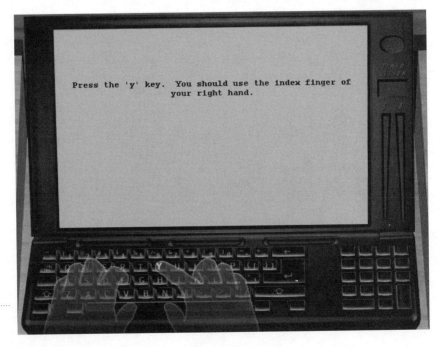

*Figure 7.19*

*Ghostly guiding hands*

For more information about the Dvorak keyboard layout, contact the Dvorak International support group at P.O. Box 44, Poultney, VT 00764, (802) 287-2343 or DvorakInt@aol.com.

# ANSI Characters

You may occasionally need to include special characters in a document—such as accented letters and foreign currency symbols—that are not represented by keys on the keyboard. Those characters are often referred to as ANSI characters, named after the ANSI character set, a set of 256 characters and symbols specified by the numbers 0 through 255.

If you need to enter a special character from the keyboard, first determine its ANSI numeric code. Table 7.1 lists the standard ANSI character codes, but because those values can vary by typeface, you may need to refer to the documentation for your font package. You can use the Character Map also to figure out which key combination to press (see Chapter 8).

## Table 7.1  Standard ANSI Character Codes

| ANSI Value | ANSI Character | ANSI Value | ANSI Character | ANSI Value | ANSI Character | ANSI Value | ANSI Character |
|---|---|---|---|---|---|---|---|
| 32 | (space) | 54 | 6 | 76 | L | 98 | b |
| 33 | ! | 55 | 7 | 77 | M | 99 | c |
| 34 | " | 56 | 8 | 78 | N | 100 | d |
| 35 | # | 57 | 9 | 79 | O | 101 | e |
| 36 | $ | 58 | : | 80 | P | 102 | f |
| 37 | % | 59 | ; | 81 | Q | 103 | g |
| 38 | & | 60 | < | 82 | R | 104 | h |
| 39 | ' | 61 | = | 83 | S | 105 | i |
| 40 | ( | 62 | > | 84 | T | 106 | j |
| 41 | ) | 63 | ? | 85 | U | 107 | k |
| 42 | * | 64 | @ | 86 | V | 108 | l |
| 43 | + | 65 | A | 87 | W | 109 | m |
| 44 | , | 66 | B | 88 | X | 110 | n |
| 45 | - | 67 | C | 89 | Y | 111 | o |
| 46 | . | 68 | D | 90 | Z | 112 | p |
| 47 | / | 69 | E | 91 | [ | 113 | q |
| 48 | 0 | 70 | F | 92 | \ | 114 | r |
| 49 | 1 | 71 | G | 93 | ] | 115 | s |
| 50 | 2 | 72 | H | 94 | ^ | 116 | t |
| 51 | 3 | 73 | I | 98 | _ | 117 | u |
| 52 | 4 | 74 | J | 96 | ` | 118 | v |
| 53 | 5 | 75 | K | 97 | a | 119 | w |

## Table 7.1 (continued)

| ANSI Value | ANSI Character | ANSI Value | ANSI Character | ANSI Value | ANSI Character | ANSI Value | ANSI Character |
|---|---|---|---|---|---|---|---|
| 120 | x | 154 | | 188 | G | 222 | π |
| 121 | y | 155 | | 189 | H | 223 | ß |
| 122 | z | 156 | | 190 | I | 224 | à |
| 123 | { | 157 | | 191 | ¿ | 225 | á |
| 124 | \| | 158 | | 192 | À | 226 | â |
| 125 | } | 159 | | 193 | Á | 227 | ã |
| 126 | ~ | 160 | | 194 | Â | 228 | ä |
| 127 | | 161 | ¡ | 198 | Ã | 229 | å |
| 128 | | 162 | ¢ | 196 | Ä | 230 | æ |
| 129 | | 163 | £ | 197 | Å | 231 | ç |
| 130 | | 164 | ¤ | 198 | Æ | 232 | è |
| 131 | | 165 | ¥ | 199 | Ç | 233 | é |
| 132 | | 166 | \|- | 200 | È | 234 | ê |
| 133 | | 167 | § | 201 | É | 235 | ë |
| 134 | | 168 | ¨ | 202 | Ê | 236 | ì |
| 135 | | 169 | © | 203 | Ë | 237 | í |
| 136 | | 170 | ª | 204 | Ì | 238 | î |
| 137 | | 171 | « | 205 | Í | 239 | ï |
| 138 | | 172 | ¬ | 206 | Î | 240 | D |
| 139 | | 173 | - | 207 | Ï | 241 | ñ |
| 140 | | 174 | ® | 208 | D | 242 | ò |
| 141 | | 175 | ¯ | 209 | Ñ | 243 | ó |
| 142 | | 176 | ° | 210 | Ò | 244 | ô |
| 143 | | 177 | ± | 211 | Ó | 245 | õ |
| 144 | | 178 | ¤ | 212 | Ô | 246 | ö |
| 145 | ' | 179 | ‹ | 213 | Õ | 247 | ÷ |
| 146 | ' | 180 | ´ | 214 | Ö | 248 | ø |
| 147 | " | 181 | µ | 215 | ¥ | 249 | ù |
| 148 | " | 182 | ¶ | 216 | Ø | 250 | ú |
| 149 | • | 183 | · | 217 | Ù | 251 | û |
| 150 | – | 184 | … | 218 | Ú | 252 | ü |
| 151 | — | 185 | / | 219 | Û | 253 | ý |
| 152 | | 186 | Ø | 220 | Ü | 254 | þ |
| 153 | | 187 | » | 221 | ¥ | 255 | ÿ |

Once you determine the ANSI numeric code for the character you want to type, make sure your computer's numeric keypad is active. (Usually, a light on the keyboard glows to indicate that the keypad is active; and pressing Num Lock toggles the keypad on and off.) Hold down the Alt key while you type the ANSI code on the numeric keypad; using the numbers on the top row of the keyboard doesn't work. Be sure to include a zero in front of the code number.

For example, to type the copyright symbol, locate its ANSI code, which for most typefaces is 169, and hold down Alt while typing 0169. When you release the Alt key, the copyright symbol appears. If you don't use the zero, Windows interprets the code as for the computer's built-in character set, which contains many of the same characters as the ANSI set but varies by manufacturer. Sound complicated? Now you know why Microsoft created the Character Map utility.

 ANSI characters that are typed into a Windows document (or pasted into a document from Character Map) may not be interpreted properly if you open the document later with a DOS application. Also, remember that not every font uses the same character set.

# Summary

The display, the mouse, and the keyboard are the hardware interface between you and your computer—the elements that physically enable you to interact with Windows. All three directly affect the performance of Windows 98 and of your system as well.

The display system consists of a Windows driver, a display card, and the display itself (usually a video monitor). All three components are critical to the performance of your system: the display card controls the resolution and the number of colors that can be produced, the monitor needs to match the output signal of the display card, and the Windows display driver enables you to take advantage of the display card's capabilities.

In addition, Windows graphics accelerators can take some of the graphics load off a system's CPU. The devices range from simple software drivers to fixed-function graphics cards and sophisticated graphics coprocessor cards. A promising area of graphics acceleration involves local bus systems that bypass the computer's expansion bus to provide the display card with direct access to the CPU chip.

The mouse and other pointing devices enable you to manipulate onscreen objects, issue commands, select text, and perform other functions. Although the mouse is an important part of a graphical interface, Windows 98 is not completely dependent on it; you can operate the system with a keyboard alone.

Even with a mouse, you also need a keyboard for data entry. Often a keyboard enables you to issue commands more quickly than you can with a mouse, because you don't have to remove your hands from the keyboard.

Daring folks and efficiency maniacs (and perhaps those who suffer from repetitive stress injuries or other disabilities) can also avail themselves of Windows' capacity to convert the standard keyboard layout into the more efficient Dvorak layout. If you do, though, you're breaking from the pack, and other people who use your Dvorak-configured computer might think they are on the verge of a nervous breakdown.

# 8

# Fonts

Of all the amazing things designed at Xerox PARC in the seventies, one great leap forward stands out; the ability to match what you see on your screen with what comes out of your printer. From the wild ferment of that blue-sky lab came the Alto full-page monitor, the laser print engine, font rasterization, and the smarts to tie everything together. From that in turn sprang WYSIWYG ("what you see is what you get"), the Macintosh user interface, Adobe's PostScript system of computer typography, and a whole, unprecedented field called desktop publishing.

As a result, the whole equation between computing and printing has been turned around. In the days of hulking mainframes, the computer printer was a way of talking—and listening, pun intended—to the vastly important computer. The printer was probably a rackety Teletype that ground out line after line of faint dot-matrix print on a carpet of fragile yellow paper. What a difference today! when high-resolution lasers, dye-sublimation printers, and Linotronic imagesetters deliver pristine sheets of press-quality output … and oh, yeah, they do need computers hung off them to drive them.

In this chapter we'll talk about fonts, a lot, and (less, but somewhat) about page-description languages. In Chapter 9, we'll talk about printers and printing. So let's get going on:

- Adobe PostScript—Type 1 fonts, Type 3 fonts, and the PostScript language.

- Microsoft/Apple TrueType fonts.

- Hewlett-Packard cartridge fonts and PostScript firmware.

- Bitstream and other third-party soft fonts.

- Windows native raster and vector fonts.

- Font management—native Windows 98, and third-party utilities.

- Other page description—HTML, Adobe Acrobat, and WYGIWYG.

- The Microsoft/Apple TrueType Open specification.

- The Microsoft/Adobe OpenType specification (which is *not* the same thing).

# PostScript

It all began with PostScript, which sounds backwards, but truth knows no sequence.

PostScript—the world's premier page-description language—was invented by John Warnock and Chuck Geschke, founders of Adobe Systems, and developed jointly with Apple. In 1985 it was announced to the world, both as a free-standing page-description language and as the internal language for Apple's LaserWriter printer. It proceeded to transform computer-driven publishing in the way that Gutenberg's movable type revolutionized manuscript printing.

PostScript is a language for describing the way a page (or any part of a page) looks, by exactly defining the positions of the dots that any output device—from a printer to a typesetting machine—puts on the page. From these dots, PostScript can assemble any character in any font, as well as any picture, chart, or other graphic you want to insert into your document. It also uses sophisticated pixel-shifting (called *hinting*) and grayscaling of edges (called *anti-aliasing*) to remove "jaggies" (ragged edges) from printed characters. Through a special export method called **Encapsulated PostScript** (EPS), images in PostScript can be inserted into non-PostScript documents. As a result, printer output looks as if it had been professionally typeset; matching PostScript screen output looks as good as the hardware will let it—see "Right On the Dot" in Chapter 9 for our lament about monitors. Today PostScript has become the standard for most serious desktop publishers.

## PostScript Fonts

When most people say "PostScript fonts," what they mean is "PostScript Type 1 fonts." These are *outline fonts,* which means that the code going from the computer to the printer—or to any device that prints from the PostScript language—is a set of mathematical instructions telling the printer how to draw the outlines of the characters, then fill them in. This mathematical character description goes to a magical engine in the printing (or plotting, or typesetting, etc.) device, called the *PostScript interpreter.* The interpreter turns the Type 1 outline code into input for the *rasterizer,* which creates the language that tells the printer where to put what dots to create the characters. (If this all sounds like it takes lots of hardware horsepower, you're darn right, and that's why PostScript printers typically have more memory—and maybe faster processors—than non-PostScript printers.)

The beauty of this is that, within the "shell" of the mathematical character description, if you want to change the appearance of the font, the PostScript driver only needs to tweak a few numbers! PostScript fonts can be scaled, rotated, stretched, and otherwise manipulated with no decrease in quality. In a graphics program, you can turn a typeface character into a graphic element, then add color or patterns, change the size or height of its parts, and exercise other options. The appearance of a PostScript font varies only with the resolutions of the devices on which it's printed.

The standard family of 35 PostScript fonts includes the following:

- Avant Garde: Book, BookOblique, Demi, DemiOblique.
- Bookman: Demi, DemiItalic, Light, LightItalic.
- Courier: plain, Bold, BoldOblique, Oblique.
- Helvetica Narrow: plain, Bold, BoldOblique, Oblique.
- Helvetica: plain, Bold, BoldOblique, Oblique.
- NewCenturySchlbk: Bold, BoldItalic, Italic, Roman
- Palatino: Bold, BoldItalic, Italic, Roman.
- Symbol.
- Times: Bold, BoldItalic, Italic, Roman.
- Zapf Chancery: MediumItalic.
- Zapf Dingbats.

Those fonts are built into all PostScript printers (except the earliest, pre-Plus Apple LaserWriters). You can do quite a bit with these, but if you need other PostScript fonts, they can be downloaded into printer RAM or stored on the printer's disk to minimize print times. (Tip: Trying to whittle down print times is inseparable from using PostScript, and if printing with PostScript is part of your everyday life, you will accumulate a whole bag of tricks to do it.)

So far we're still talking about Type 1 fonts. *Type 3 fonts,* which can be scalable but are mostly bitmaps, skip a step in the encoding process and go straight to the rasterizer. Because they don't pass through all the stages of the PostScript interpreter, they can't be hinted (we'll get to hinting in a while) so they don't look as good in some sizes. On the other hand, they print more efficiently in small sizes than Type 1 fonts, because it takes less time to send a little bitmap than a whopping Type 1 outline. Windows 98 lets you balance your use of Type 1 and Type 3 fonts, elegantly; see **Threshold to switch…** under "PostScript Printer: Fonts Tab" in Chapter 9.

## PostScript Screen Fonts

So you're printing with Type 1 fonts and, naturally, you want the fonts on your screen to look as much like your print fonts as possible. Big problem! Monitors don't have PostScript interpreters in them. (*Your* monitor doesn't. Adobe poured a king's ransom into a technology called Display PostScript that generated the same fonts for screen and printer, but only the elegant-unto-death NeXT computer ever made it work.) Enter one of the neatest font utility programs ever written—Adobe Type Manager, or ATM, which does three things:

- Creates bitmapped screen fonts compatible with the Type 1 (*not* Type 3) fonts your print job is using.

- Makes it possible to use Type 1 fonts on non-PostScript printers.

- Corrals, organizes and generally manages your Type 1 *and* your TrueType fonts.

If you use Type 1 fonts on a Windows computer, ATM will make your life a lot easier. The version current at this writing, Adobe Type Manager Deluxe 4.0, is available at better software retailers or by mail for about $65.

## PostScript Triumphant

In the late Eighties, Type 1 fonts were the top of the heap. On the elegant Apple LaserWriter, they looked about as good as a 300-dot-per-inch font was ever going to—*and* they were scalable, which meant that if you were printing from a Macintosh, you had effortless access to an almost unlimited repertory of point sizes. Those of us wrestling with non-PostScript laser printers—this is Kip talking, not Fred, who was editor of *MacUser* at the time—had to use PCL bitmap fonts and "build" or compile a separate set of bitmaps for *each* typeface *and* point size we wanted to use. A font compile for an entire typeface routinely took all day or overnight; the resulting bitmaps ate up a LaserJet's limited memory like a famished cat gobbling sardines.

No question: Type 1 was *numero uno*. Adobe had found The Way. They would be the kings of the hill forever.

Oh, yeah?

# TrueType

Adobe's font specifications in the original PostScript were a classic example of the Right Thing at the right time. Digital fonts escaped from hopeless confusion to an accessible common standard; equally, a versatile font description language emerged just when the laser printer made such a thing imperative. Adobe knew that they were sitting on a gold mine, and possibly more than one, depending on how effectively the PostScript language and its applications could be leveraged.

Adobe released the PostScript language itself, and the Type 3 font specification, but the Type 1 specification—less memory-intensive and more flexible—

remained proprietary. It included a bunch of exotic math called *hinting,* which corrected imperfections in certain parts of letters (like thin vertical and diagonal stems) and made fonts on paper look more type-like. Secrecy for hinting was Adobe's ace in the hole; it meant that no one would ever reverse-engineer a perfect PostScript interpreter, because the math for hinting could never be included.

Microsoft, Apple, and IBM pondered Adobe's ultimatum. All three wanted to build fundamental font scaling code into their operating systems; none wanted to pay Adobe's stiff price for the Type 1 specification, or to concede that Adobe held the keys to digital font technology on the desktop. Microsoft developed an elaborate and buggy PostScript clone called TrueImage; Apple developed its own clone, like Type 1 but based on subtly different math; and IBM finally did pay Adobe a small fortune to incorporate real Type 1 into OS/2.

Microsoft and Apple swapped what they had developed, and Microsoft got the better deal—not for the first time or the last. Microsoft's TrueImage was so internally weird that, finally, no one ever used it for anything. Apple's TrueType, in Microsoft's hands, became a sword that sliced apart the digital-font deadlock. Its core font set—Times Roman, Helvetica, and Courier—had been developed with obstinate precision and was impressive. Its architecture beat Type 1 hollow by having screen fonts that automatically matched print fonts. TrueType became part of MacOS in May 1990 and of Windows 3.1 in April 1991, while Microsoft shoveled money at font developers.

The Windows 3.*x* TrueType never compared with the Mac's System 7 TrueType, because the Mac ran the 32-bit rasterizer that TrueType had started with. The Windows 16-bit adaptation was nowhere near as good; sometimes characters would appear on the screen and not on the paper—or on neither. But Windows TrueType *mostly* worked, and Microsoft knew what it always knows: That if a product *mostly* works, drums and bugles will do the rest. Microsoft released TrueType Font Packs that, for $30 to $50 street, competed with Adobe Type 1 font sets costing hundreds, maybe thousands, of dollars. Even Microsoft was flabbergasted at the way the Font Packs flew off retailers' shelves.

Wounded Adobe snarled and fought back. In 1990 it released Adobe Type Manager for the Mac, and then for Windows; ATM automated the installation and embedding of Type 1 fonts, and made sure the print fonts had screen fonts to match. Then it released the ultra-secret Type 1 specification to the public. (The intellectual property had lost some of its prodigious value when Bitstream, a rival font developer, cracked the Type 1 hinting code and then released an ATM clone called FaceLift.) TrueType, it was said, was inelegant, barely adequate for home and office. People who *knew* fonts and typography, who lived by them, would use—and pay for—superior Type 1 fonts and ATM.

Well, fine. Until Windows 95, and Windows NT 3.1, showed up with a 32-bit TrueType rasterizer—and the sword of Redmond struck once more.

# What's The Difference Anyway?

Partly because of their volcanic mutual history, TrueType and PostScript have been portrayed as the Hatfields and McCoys of typography. Actually, they're more like cousins who sneak behind the barn to kiss. PostScript fonts are drawn using *Bézier curves,* which are very demanding while they're being drawn, but they represent font curvature as exactly as (currently) possible. TrueType fonts are drawn using *quadratic splines,* which produce less exact curves but can be drawn relatively quickly. The difference between the two, in architecture or in effect, is not huge, and it's perfectly possible to substitute one font type for the other, or even convert them back and forth. Whether you like the results, of course, is up to you.

So, which one should you use? That's up to you and your hardware. If you have a PostScript printer, you'll naturally use Type 1 fonts. If you have almost any other kind of printer, from dot-matrix to the latest LaserJet, TrueType fonts offer advantages you may want to look at—and the addition of Adobe Type Manager will let you run TrueType and Type 1 fonts in seamless combination. Since PostScript still dominates desktop publishing, DTP products for Windows often come bundled with ATM, either "free" as a sales incentive, or at minimal extra cost.

Ultimately the choice isn't easy, because each system has its strengths and weaknesses. TrueType is included free with Windows 98, which certainly makes it attractive. If your output is destined for any kind of professional imagesetting, PostScript is more entrenched and still maintains a clear advantage. And most people who have experience with both font types will concede that Type 1 fonts *do* look better on the page—at the lofty level where the difference becomes important.

Performance can also be an issue. TrueType, with its simpler math, prints faster to non-PostScript printers such as Hewlett-Packard LaserJets; PostScript soft fonts work better with PostScript printers, because the printer and system fonts are similar. Type 1 fonts still do need to be downloaded to the printer and interpreted on their way to the page, a time-consuming process unless it can all be performed in RAM. (For a description of the Windows 98 controls that speed up downloading, see "PostScript Printer: PostScript Tab" in Chapter 9.) Both products do an admirable, but understandably slow, job of printing on dot-matrix and inkjet printers.

Whichever standard you select, you can feel good about its future. Type 1 fonts are available in great profusion from Adobe—who invented them, after all—and from painfully respectable companies like AGFA Compugraphic, Bitstream, Casady and Greene, Letraset, Monotype, and URW. (We've put a vendor list at the end of this chapter.) Many of them are still more expensive than their TrueType equivalents, but fonts in general are becoming more affordable.

TrueType fonts, as the 32-bit Windows standard architecture, are also in no danger. The Microsoft TrueType Font Packs that did bloody battle with Adobe's Type 1 are now only sold to the educational market, but you can always start with the fifty-plus Windows 98 standard typefaces and then, as the mood strikes, pick up free additions—from Microsoft's, Letraset's, and Bitstream's Web sites, among others. Eventually you'll want to round out your library by acquiring some of the excellent commercial font sets available, and probably an organizer utility (see pages 314–315).

## Taking the Hint

Both TrueType and PostScript are based on outline fonts, and both use some form of hinting. But they implement it in different ways, and the differences are important. Hinting adjusts the outline of a character so that the component strokes are better aligned with the dots on a printer or the pixels on a monitor; this compensates for the discrepancies that occur when gently flowing outlines are converted to grid-like bitmaps. It's a typographic equivalent of digital-to-analog conversion (DAC) which your computer has to do in other places (notably the video adapter) and for a lot of the same reasons.

This process greatly increases the legibility of the text, especially when small type is displayed on your monitor or on a 300 dpi laser printer; 300 dpi was the standard resolution for mass-market lasers from 1985 to 1993, which makes Adobe's contemporary protection of its hinting perfectly understandable. At the time of this writing, the resolution of a top-end commodity printer is either 1200x1200 (laser) or 1440x720 (piezo inkjet) and at that level, hinting becomes optional if not completely irrelevant. There are just so many more pixels available for mimicking the fit of each smooth curve.

Even so, both common types of outline fonts are still hinted. PostScript hinting is contained in the PostScript rasterizer—the coding that converts the outline of the font into a bitmap for screen display or printer output. Type 1 fonts contain hints that tell the rasterizer how much to distort the outlines of all the characters in a typeface to adjust them for low-resolution output devices. There are two disadvantages to this, although they may be more potential than actual: first, every character in the font gets the same set of tweaks applied to it, and second, if your rasterizer happens to be in firmware rather than software, you can't update your hinting algorithms without swapping chips in the printer. (Fun!)

TrueType incorporates its hints into the typeface file, so that each character in the typeface can contain its own hints. Software that displays TrueType on screen can be more efficient, because it doesn't need to calculate hinting on the fly; it just reads the hinting information contained in the typeface. TrueType, also, has two comparative drawbacks. First, once the typeface is created, hinting cannot be improved; second, top-of-the-line TrueType fonts must be hand-hinted by programming each character, and that (according to a designer for one of the smaller top-quality font houses in the Vendors' List) is "an [expletive] nuisance." You the user are spared the nuisance, but you'll find that hand-hinted TrueType fonts aren't cheap.

The bottom line in the TrueType versus PostScript debate is this: At the resolutions prevailing for typesetters, print shops, and desktop publishing services, hinting is irrelevant, and PostScript is the standard. If all you need is a straightforward and inexpensive (tending toward free) way to make your laser printer produce attractive documents, TrueType is the ticket. Because of its approach to hinting, TrueType can look good at comparatively low resolutions—for example, on 300 dpi laser printers, 640x480 laptop screens, and 800x600 SuperVGA monitors, which are disappearing from PC retail channels, but remain staples of the PC user base.

## Outline Fonts and Device Independence

Oddly enough, now that we're through saying PostScript is vastly superior to TrueType for typesetting and high-end DTP, we have to consider the one way in which it may not be—the elusive dream of device independence.

In theory, a line of characters is a line of characters, no matter whether you print it at 300 dpi, 1200 dpi, or 2540 dpi. But printing the same file at those three resolutions means entrusting it to hardware devices whose internal logic may be quite different—a Linotronic imagesetter doesn't "think," pardon the term, the way an Apple LaserWriter does. Still, all devices have to deal with the problem of fractional pixels, and the difference arises from how they may do it.

When an outline font goes through an interpreter and rasterizer, any character comes out with an absolute width computed from the outline and hinting math. What if your capital I comes out *exactly* 27.2 device pixels wide? Bitmapping hardware can't handle fractional pixels, so the printer firmware rounds up the character spacing, making the character 28 pixels wide *on that device,* which (let's say) is a 600 dpi laser printer. Move that file over to a 2540 dpi typesetter, the same character is exactly 115 device pixels wide as it sits, there's no rounding up, and the capital I is fractionally—infinitesimally—narrower on the typesetter than on the laser. Spread that tiny uncertainty, which makes word-wrap a crapshoot, over hundreds of thousands of characters and … every PostScript type house has stories about jobs that came out half a page too long, with their layouts ruined. Some application software (mostly by Adobe) tries to head this off at the pass, by applying sophisticated in-line corrections. But so long as the PostScript interpreter insists on applying the same hinting to every character of a given font, we live in fear.

TrueType insists that compatible applications relate to it in a fine-grained way. TrueType communicates the exact pixel rounding error of each character to the program; the program sums the rounding errors and corrects for them at the end of each line. Some minor errors in word-wrap could occur between one line and the next, but there's no way for rounding error to gain momentum blindly, like a snowball down a mountain. Today TrueType isn't quite the equal of PostScript for precise page description; tomorrow, if the interpreter specification keeps improving, TrueType may turn the tables. The other possibility is that the OpenType specification (see discussion near the end of this chapter) may make this whole argument a thing of the past.

## TrueType and PostScript: Summary

In short, while TrueType and PostScript are both admirable technologies, choosing between them is something you'd almost rather not do. There isn't a lot to be said against TrueType for general-purpose document production; it was designed for that, and it excels at it. However, if you plan to do serious desktop publishing, you want access to the enormous library of professional-quality Type 1 PostScript typefaces—and that means installing Adobe Type Manager. If you have ATM installed on your computer, and a modern printer that can interpret both PCL and PostScript at decently high resolution, you're ready to do almost any kind of computer-based typography.

# The Third Force: Device Fonts

TrueType and PostScript between them have grabbed so much of the limelight that a respectable third alternative, the *device font,* has been overshadowed. Device fonts have several advantages in specific situations, most of them involving upgrades, limited memory, or both. There are three kinds of device fonts:

- **Font SIMMs.** Made by Hewlett-Packard, Lexmark, Epson, NEC, and other companies, these fit in a printer's extra memory slots. Currently, almost all of them are PostScript upgrades for printers that didn't originally have PostScript installed. If you have a printer that only speaks PCL, and you want PostScript too, a PostScript SIMM at $300 to $600 (street) can be much more cost-effective than replacing your printer. If you're buying a new printer, though, the most economical choice is to buy one that speaks both PostScript and PCL out of the box.

- **Printer soft fonts** are fonts on diskette or CD with installation utilities that send the fonts directly into the printer's (rather than your computer's) memory. If you have ample printer memory, these can speed up printing considerably, since you don't need to send the fonts to the printer in advance of the document every time you print.

- **Font cartridges** or ROM cartridges. These are rugged plastic brick-like units, with gold-striped card connectors at one end, that fit into the cartridge slots of some LaserJets or compatible printers; they work best for semi-automated repetitive production of a few document types. Hewlett-Packard made most of them, under names like ProCollection, Great Start, TextEquations, or Forms, Etc. As far as we can find out, these are no longer manufactured, but they don't wear out (unless you push the edge connector into the slot and pull it out about a thousand times) and Windows 98 does provide drivers for these and their matching screen fonts, if you have them.

Windows 98 will use any of these device fonts, if you install them in a way that Windows understands, and will list them in the font selection dialog of any of your applications. It will *not* list them in the **Windows\Fonts** folder that you open with Control Panel\Fonts.

Now you've had a tour of every kind of font you can print with—or, at least, print attractively with—so let's take a look at typography.

# Typography

For the discipline of typography, computers have been good news and bad news. They took the world of fine printing—which, in the days of cold lead type and heavy presses, was anything but portable—and transported it to millions of desktops, where it enjoyed a startling rebirth. On the other hand, they took the *vocabulary* of typography, turned it upside down, and shook it enthusiastically. It was old when that happened, and it will never recover.

## Face, Style, and Font

For traditional printers, the terms *typeface, type style,* and *font* all meant distinct and useful things. *Typeface* could describe the face—literally the flat part that struck the paper—of a piece of type, and it was extended from there to mean all the faces in one set of characters, so that one spoke of a Times *typeface* or a Goudy *typeface.* Within this, it was correct to discuss a Roman *face* or an Italic *face,* but those were in no way the same thing. Times Roman meant that the *face* was Times, and the type was Roman because its stems (principal strokes— we'll get to stems in a minute) were vertical.

A *font* was literally an upper and lower case of type, with letters, ligatures, accents, and everything needed to print with full variety, but all one face and all one size. In the days before CD drives, printers might not have very many typefaces—since each face in its full range of fonts would be very expensive and bulky—but he might say he had a "Roman pica font," that is, an upper and lower case of (roughly) 12-point vertical type.

Type style in the age of lead was intimately related to what the printer printed. If he spoke of a particular face as being book or poster, he did so because he used it to print books or posters. Because most printers owned too few faces to be worried about global similarities, any formally defined use of *style* as a printing term is relatively recent—the 1913 *Webster's Unabridged Dictionary,* for example, doesn't include it.

In the days of Linotype, five styles were generally recognized:

- **Serif** typefaces have short lines, called serifs, that extend at angles from the ends of letters. Now called Roman, as in Times New Roman (TrueType), and if you look back at the original meaning of the term "Roman," it had come quite a distance.

- **Sans serif** faces (French for "without serifs") have their endings and corners cut blunt, without any flaring. Sans serif faces were comparatively rare in the days of cold type, because a serif protected the individual (expensive, and soft) characters against nicking. Now called Swiss and meaning faces like Arial, Small Fonts, MS Sans Serif, and Helvetica.

- **Modern** stylized fonts and typefaces are usually for headlines and signage, usually sans serif, and austere in character.

- **Decorative** faces are highly embellished, for ornate display and symbols, in contrast to Modern.

- **Script** faces resemble cursive writing, sometimes called *calligraphic.*

Computers splashed down in the middle of all this, and you're living with the resulting mess. Font and face will never be untangled again, but once you consider the original meaning of font, you'll realize that "outline font" is subversive and "scalable font" is a hopeless oxymoron. Once upon a time, Roman and Italic weren't the same font—we mean face—but today they are. Nowadays people talk about "display fonts" and think they're saying "display faces" which means Modern and Decorative mixed together. What "style" used to mean is now encompassed by Microsoft's term "font family," and poor "style," shorn of its purpose, wanders around meaning whatever people want it to—which usually isn't much. For computer users, a typeface is a font, and both terms refer to the general design of a group of characters … whether Arial, Courier, or Palatino, UltraLight, Halbfett or Black.

# A Glossary of Type

Now, Windows 98 cares nothing about all this, and you can understand fonts quite well from the Windows perspective without plunging into most of this terminology (Table 8.1). But if you have any sense of the fine-grained discipline that typesetting was and still is, you'll find more enjoyment in the truly amazing possibilities of desktop publishing. Let's take time for a few words.

## Table 8.1  A Glossary of Typography

| | |
|---|---|
| *arm* | A horizontal, or upward-oblique, stroke free at one or both ends; the horizontal of a T or an F, or the upper diagonal of a K. |
| *bar* | A horizontal stroke enclosed by two verticals; the horizontal in H or A. |
| *bowl* | Any curve that completely encloses a white space. |
| *color* | An even relationship of light and dark over the entire page, created first by the design of individual letters in the font, and then by proper tracking and leading. Sloppy spacing results in distracting light- or dark-looking blotches on the page. |
| *counter* | White space bounded by any curve, including a bowl. |
| *cross stroke* | A stroke free at both ends but fully crossing another stroke; horizontal of a t or –. |
| *em* | The width of a piece of type whose width is equal to its height; an **m.** Both an em and an en vary directly with their type size. |
| *en* | The width of a piece of type whose width is half of its height; an **n.** The average width of all lowercase letters of a given font. |
| *fixed font* | A font in which each character takes up an equal amount of horizontal space. Now almost a relic; before the typewriter and after it, each character occupies its proper width. |
| *kerning* | Trimming away the white space next to an individual letter to make it fit more closely—at most, even overlap—with the previous or following letter. |
| *leading* | The thickness of a strip of metal (or space) that pushes typefaces further apart vertically. Type set without leading is *set solid.* In digital typography, leading can be negative. |
| *pica* | A measure of type size. Nowadays 12 points; but the pica is older than the point, and used to be slightly taller than it is now. |
| *point* | $\frac{1}{72}$ of an inch. |
| *proportional font* | A font in which each character takes up horizontal space in proportion to its width; an I is narrower than an M. |
| *serif* | A stroke, usually horizontal, bounding the end of a stem, arm or tail. |
| *set* | The absolute width of a piece of type. |
| *side bearing* | The part of a piece of type that extends past the typeface at the left or right. Adding both the side bearings to the width of the typeface gives the set. When characters are kerned, this is negative. |

***Table 8.1*** *(continued)*

| | |
|---|---|
| *size* | The absolute height of a piece of type. |
| *tail* | The diagonal of a Q or R or the lower diagonal of a K. |
| *tracking* | Opening or closing letter spacing over a whole line or more, to give the line the right color. |
| *typeface* | The part of a piece of type that strikes the paper. |
| *weight* | The amount of vertical thickness in the characters of a typeface. In one face, the font with the thinnest stems might be called Light, then Book, Medium, Demi-Bold, and finally Bold being the thickest. |

There are many other terms in typography that date from the age of solid metal. You don't need to use them all, or even know them all; but if you look at them, you begin to grasp the way in which people thought about metal type while they set it and printed from it. Some of the inherent richness and complexity of typography will become clear to you. These words may influence and, we hope, improve the ways you use digital type.

## *More Typographic Terms*

If this vocabulary fascinates you, you can find lots more of it. Try the enjoyably tongue-in-cheek tutorial at **http://www.microsoft.com/typography/glossary/content.htm**; or use a search engine to search on **typography and glossary**, or **typesetting and glossary**.

# How Windows Does All This

Windows matches and manages fonts in two ways. First, it identifies fonts according to their family—Roman, Swiss, Modern, Script, or Decorative— and relies on those specifications when it installs fonts, and when it maps fonts to the screen and to the printer. Windows also relies heavily on the PANOSE font-matching system, which we'll get to in the section on the Fonts Folder later in this chapter. Finally, it adds a few terms to its type description language. You'll need to know *type width,* which describes whether the width of all the characters in a typeface has been condensed or expanded (shrunk or stretched) for a distinctive look; *font style,* Microsoft's synonym for *type style,* which describes characteristics such as bold, italic, and regular; and *font effects,* which refers to "extra-typographic" attributes such as underline, strikethrough, and color. Microsoft also uses the term *type track* to mean the same thing as *tracking*—the overall control of space between characters.

# A Triad of Fonts

Windows classifies fonts into three categories, based on how they're drawn for display or printing. For *outline*—TrueType or PostScript—fonts, the outline of a character is drawn by the interpreter and then filled in, or rendered, by the rasterizer. This gives the tremendous flexibility we've already discussed but also adds a lot of overhead, which is coped with by coprocessors in printers and on video cards. For its own internal purposes, Windows doesn't need that flexibility and would rather not shoulder that overhead.

The other two types of fonts—raster and vector—are carried over from Windows 3.0. *Raster fonts* are stored as bit-mapped images in specific point sizes; they look good only in those sizes, and can't be scaled or rotated. They're rarely required for printing, but Windows 98 uses them for screen display. Raster fonts are sometimes used to display your work on screen if you choose a printer font that has no screen font. Windows 98 also uses raster fonts to display text in menus, toolbars, and icon titles—items that you generally don't change or pay much attention to.

*Vector fonts* are drawn on the screen or for the printer by means of a mathematical description of the typeface design. Originally employed by pen plotters, these fonts were used by pre-Windows 3.1 applications requiring fonts that could be resized and rotated. Better options have made vector fonts largely unnecessary, but to provide backward compatibility (and because you never know when you're going to have to send output to a plotter) they remain.

Here's a rundown of the physical types of fonts that work with Windows 98:

- **Device fonts.** Fonts built into a printer or plugged into it via a card or a cartridge, such as the cartridges that plug into Hewlett-Packard LaserJets.

- **Soft fonts.** Software-based fonts for a printer. These fonts are installed on the hard disk and downloaded to the printer as needed. Soft fonts usually must be loaded into a system with their own installation program.

- **Printable screen fonts.** Screen fonts that can also be printed.

## TrueType And Windows 98

With the advent of Windows 98, TrueType—the Leatherman of digital typography—reaches a maturity that rewards a decade of hard work. Say goodbye to the hassles of matching screen fonts and printer fonts; TrueType's universal page-description language provides fully scalable and rotatable typefaces that appear the same on screen as on the printed page and print identically on almost all printers, from dot-matrix printers to high-resolution imagesetters. TrueType can convert its fonts to PostScript, or to Hewlett-Packard's PCL, for printing—all automatically and behind the scenes.

TrueType also bridges platforms by offering unified computer typography for the Macintosh and Windows. If you use TrueType fonts in a Windows document, you can transfer the document to a Macintosh, or vice versa, and its appearance won't change.

**Basic Typefaces.** One of the best parts of Windows 95 was its all-purpose collection of 14 TrueType typefaces. Microsoft made a good thing strikingly better: Windows 98 Setup automatically installs more than 50 TrueType fonts on your computer and gives you instant access to them (see Table 8.2).

## Table 8.2  Windows 98 Standard TrueType Fonts

| Font Name | Filename | Description | Copyright |
|---|---|---|---|
| Abadi MT Condensed Light | abalc.ttf | A clean, vertical sans serif font, legible and versatile. | Monotype |
| Arial | arial.ttf | The classic Helvetica clone. | Monotype |
| Arial Bold | arialbd.ttf | | Monotype |
| Arial Black | ariblk.ttf | | Monotype |
| Arial Italic | ariali.ttf | | Monotype |
| Arial Bold Italic | arialbi.ttf | | Monotype |
| Large Arial | larial.ttf | Note: The *Large* fonts don't appear separately in the Fonts folder. | Monotype |
| Large Arial Bold | larialbd.ttf | | Monotype |
| Large Arial Italic | lariali.ttf | | Monotype |
| Large Arial Bold Italic | larialbi.ttf | | Monotype |
| Book Antiqua | bkant.ttf | A TT interpretation of the PostScript standard Palatino. | Monotype |
| Calisto MT | calist.ttf | A book face, something like Times but older-looking. | Monotype |
| Century Gothic | gothic.ttf | Modern—i. e. thirties—sans serif with thin strokes. Lots of air. A headline font. | Monotype |
| Century Gothic Bold | gothicb.ttf | | Monotype |
| Century Gothic Italic | gothici.ttf | | Monotype |
| Century Gothic Bold Italic | gothicbi.ttf | | Monotype |
| Comic Sans MS | comic.ttf | The Microsoft Chat font; a blackboard take on Tekton. | Microsoft |
| Comic Sans MS Bold | comicbd.ttf | | Microsoft |
| Copperplate Gothic Light | coprgtl.ttf | Serifs, unflashy elegance, an expensive lawyer's business card. | URW |
| Copperplate Gothic Bold | coprgtb.ttf | | URW |

**Table 8.2** *(continued)*

| Font Name | Filename | Description | Copyright |
|---|---|---|---|
| Courier New | cour.ttf | The IBM Selectric will live forever. | Monotype |
| Courier New Bold | courbd.ttf | | Monotype |
| Courier New Italic | couri.ttf | | Monotype |
| Courier New Bold Italic | courbi.ttf | | Monotype |
| Large Courier New | lcour.ttf | | Monotype |
| Large Courier New Bold | lcourbd.ttf | | Monotype |
| Large Courier New Italic | lcouri.ttf | | Monotype |
| Large Courier New Bold Italic | lcourbi.ttf | | Monotype |
| Impact | impact.ttf | Sans serif, thick verticals, urgent; think of European posters from the forties and fifties. | Monotype |
| Lucida Console | lucon.ttf | An angular, chiseled update of Letter Gothic; severely beautiful, and easy to read. | B & H / Monotype |
| Lucida Handwriting Italic | lhandw.ttf | Lucida's romantic side, loose-coupled and looking like felt-tip, but nothing lost in balance or line. | B & H / Monotype |
| Lucida Sans Italic | lsansi.ttf | Sans-serif, skinny, and would be austere, but the handprinted look of the bowls and counters relaxes it. | B & H / Monotype |
| Lucida Sans Unicode | lsansuni.ttf | More formal than the italic. If you need a Unicode font (see page 308) this is the one supplied with Windows. | B & H / Monotype |
| Marlett | marlett.ttf | A screen graphics font. See page 303. | Microsoft |
| Matisse ITC | matisse_.ttf | Remember the way Matisse drew hips and shoulders, primal and flippant at the same time? This font uses those curves. Designed by making paper cutouts, then scanning them. | ITC |
| News Gothic MT | nwgthc.ttf | A "bookish" sans serif book font, lighter than Arial. Designed in 1908, but doesn't look its age. | Monotype |
| News Gothic MT Bold | nwgthcb.ttf | | Monotype |
| News Gothic MT Italic | nwgthci.ttf | | Monotype |
| OCR A Extended | ocraext.ttf | The classic character-recognition font, with the bent comma and the rectangular zero. | Monotype |

## *Table 8.2* *(continued)*

| Font Name | Filename | Description | Copyright |
|---|---|---|---|
| Symbol | symbol.ttf | A shapely upper- and lowercase Greek alphabet, standard serif numerals, and a few logical operators. | Monotype |
| Tahoma | tahoma.ttf | Still more formal than Lucida Sans, and faintly European-looking, like old HP Line Printer. A scalable screen font. | Microsoft |
| Tahoma Bold | tahomabd.ttf | | Microsoft |
| Tempus Sans ITC | tempsitc.ttf | A classically proportioned font with ragged stems and thick ends, as if the pen had dragged slightly on the paper. The designer calls it "punk roman." | ITC |
| Times New Roman | times.ttf | There may not always be a Fleet Street, or even an England, but there will always be Times Roman. Sculpted strokes and pin-sharp serifs make it one of the world's most readable book faces. | Monotype |
| Times New Roman Bold | timesbd.ttf | | Monotype |
| Times New Roman Italic | timesi.ttf | | Monotype |
| Times New Roman Bold Italic | timesbi.ttf | | Monotype |
| Large Times New Roman | ltimes.ttf | | Monotype |
| Large Times New Roman Bold | ltimesbd.ttf | | Monotype |
| Large Times New Roman Italic | ltimesi.ttf | | Monotype |
| Large Times New Roman Bold Italic | ltimesbi.ttf | | Monotype |
| Verdana | verdana.ttf | Maybe more relaxed than Tahoma, but its cousin, at least. Reminiscent of the type in the London Underground. | Microsoft |
| Verdana Bold | verdanab.ttf | | Microsoft |
| Verdana Italic | verdanai.ttf | | Microsoft |
| Verdana Bold Italic | verdanaz.ttf | | Microsoft |
| Webdings | webdings.ttf | An odd collection of glyphs, everything from modes of transportation to the controls of a tape recorder. | Microsoft |
| Westminster | westm.ttf | The definitive science-fiction font, so ugly it's cute, begging to be printed in green on black. | Eraman / Type Solutions |
| Wingdings | wingding.ttf | Look here first if you need a glyph, from an astrological sign, to a sizzling bomb, to a coffeepot, to a Celtic cross. How did we live without these? Did we, ever? | Microsoft |

(We include the copyright information in the preceding table so that, if you like a font from a particular developer, you can use the Font Vendors list as a pointer to its Web site or catalog.)

Now, minor complaints could be made. The only calligraphic font included is Lucida Handwriting Italic, and although that's beautiful, it's a brush font; since Monotype/Agfa supplied most of the fonts for Windows 98, we wouldn't have minded a return visit from Monotype Corsiva, probably the most elegant TrueType calligraphic font ever widely distributed. And the Webdings, while up-to-the-minute, are really no substitute for Monotype Sorts. As for the celebrated Lucida fonts by Bigelow & Holmes, do we really get only four? What happened to the rest of the ones from the TrueType Font Packs? (We had to dig for the answer to this; see page 342.) But this is carping, considering versatile new fonts like Calisto, Comic Sans, and Tahoma. Whereas Windows 95 did barely more than implement the original TrueType core fonts, Windows 98 supplies the core of a proper font library.

## Marlett the Starlet

Ever wondered what Marlett is good for? It's no use for printing! And yet when you see its character map, it looks so familiar …

Marlett is the 32-bit Windows screen font, and Windows 98, 95, and NT 4.0 need it in order to run. It's primarily found on button faces, like the thick low bar of the Minimize button, the overlapping panes of the Restore button, the fully opened window of the Maximize button, and the question mark that you click on for context-sensitive Help.

The diagonal stripes that make the lower right corner of a pane look rough and "grabbable" are also here, as are the black triangles for scroll bar controls, drop-down list buttons, and spin buttons. Marlett, together with the 3-D DLLs, gives 32-bit Windows its sculpted and embossed appearance that contrasts so favorably with the flattened look of previous Windows versions.

**If You're Pole-Vaulting from Win16.** When you upgrade from Windows 3.1, documents you created previously should appear exactly as they did before you got Windows 98. If you find yourself using a document created with a program (or in an environment) that was TrueType-clueless, you can open it, select it with Ctrl A, and pick a TrueType font from the application's font list.

**.FOT File Farewell.** If you've been following font evolution, you may remember that in Windows 3.*x*, each TrueType font required two files to make it whole—a .TTF file and a .FOT file. The .TTF file contained the font code, while the .FOT file was just a bunch of pointers. The location of the .TTF file was stored partly in the .FOT file and partly in WIN.INI, yet another one of the lightheaded Win16 arrangements that made it next to impossible to find anything. In Windows 98, font information (such as location) is no longer stored in far-flung control files, but in the Registry. (For more information on the Registry, see Chapter 17.)

Let's go to the special place where your fonts live—the **Windows\Fonts** folder—and take a look at them.

## The Fonts Folder

In a significant improvement to Windows' internal organization, TrueType font files no longer live in your **Windows\System** folder, mixed in with your thousand or so DLLs and Visual Basic controls. Instead, they're installed in the **Fonts** subfolder of the main Windows folder, predictably called Windows, unless you changed its name during Setup.

The Fonts folder is special because:

You open it, in single-pane My Computer view, by double-clicking on Control Panel\Fonts.

The fonts really are installed, rather than just copied. In any other folder, a TrueType font's icon title is `<filename>.ttf`. If you drag the same file into the Fonts folder—and it's not already there—the icon title changes to the real name of the font. This correlation lives in the Registry.

 **This incidentally gives you a great method for installing fonts quickly. Hunt down your TrueType files anywhere they are on your computer—or network—select them, and drag-and-drop them into the Fonts folder. Bingo, they're installed. If you don't want a lot of duplicate font files hogging your local disk space, just create shortcuts to them instead of making copies ... naturally bearing in mind that, if you create shortcuts to fonts on a non-local network drive, you'll need mapping to that drive in order to print with those fonts.**

It doesn't show all your fonts, even if you have **Folder Options** set to **View all files.** Set **View** to **Large Icons** and count the icons with a red **A** on them; these are the Windows system fonts, the non-TrueType fonts, and you'll see about half a dozen. Now go to **Start Menu\Find\Files or Folders...,** point the **Look in** dialog at \Windows\Fonts, and tell it to look for **\*.fon**—of which there are about twenty! Your Fixedsys fonts (\*fix.fon), System fonts (\*sys.fon), and Terminal fonts (\*oem.fon and Dosapp.fon), don't show in Control Panel\Fonts because you have no control over them; Windows decides when to use them. We'll talk about the system fonts, and where they appear, later in the chapter.

It *does* show all your TrueType fonts, whose icon is a blue TT on a document page. It does *not* show PostScript, PCL, or other kinds of fonts, which you have to install and manage with third-party utilities. To identify which fonts are TrueType, many applications use the TT symbol as the mini-icon for TrueType typefaces in lists. The applets bundled with Windows, such as WordPad and Paint, follow this convention.

You can display a page of samples (Figure 8.1) for any font that the Fonts folder recognizes, by double-clicking on its icon, or right-clicking and selecting **Open** from the Context Menu. This page opens:

The page lists the name, orientation and type of the typeface, version number, file size, and copyright, and shows the full character set (except for Unicode) in one size, as well as all or part of a sample sentence in a range of sizes.

*Figure 8.1*

*TrueType Font Properties sheet*

The **File** menu has an **Install New Font…** choice that brings you into the good old Windows Font Installer.

The **View** menu offers **List Fonts By Similarity,** which can be useful if you need to substitute fonts (see "Screen Fonts, Printer Fonts, and Substitution" on page 318). You may be wondering, "similar to what?" In the **List Fonts by Similarity To** list box, you answer that question yourself; the similarity is to a font you select, which must be another font installed in, and managed by, your Fonts folder.

**View** also includes **Hide Variations,** which suppresses display of the icons for variants like bold and italic, leaving only the core font icon visible.

Unfortunately, the Hide Variations option seems both zealous and arbitrary. When you turn it loose on the Windows 98 default font set, it truncates Lucida Sans Unicode Italic to Lucida Sans Unicode, hiding the probably useful fact that the Italic is the only variant you have installed. On the other hand, Copperplate Gothic Bold and Light, and Arial and Arial Black, persist as separate icons. These oddities probably arise because font "variations" are determined by their PANOSE information (see "Windows 98 and PANOSE Matching" later in this chapter).

Finally, **View\Folder Options** has an extra tab called **TrueType** which offers you a checkbox, **Show only TrueType fonts in the programs on my computer.** It's a nice choice, but we can't imagine using it, since even non-PostScript people have fonts in their printer firmware, and it seems pointless to give them up. Once you check this box you will have to reboot your computer, which is a surprise, given that this must be a Registry setting and should take effect immediately; also, when you come back up and open the Fonts folder, you'll find the previous system fonts visible after all.

## Font Installing Tips

If you open a folder that contains a lot of fonts, it's going to take a while for Windows 98 to enumerate and display the contents of the folder (see Figure 8.2). Don't click wildly because you don't get an instant response. A counter on the screen indicates what percentage of the data has been retrieved.

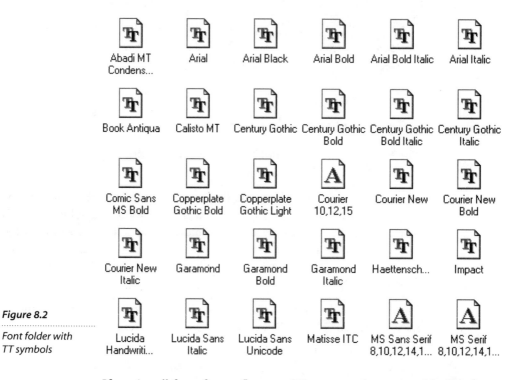

*Figure 8.2*

*Font folder with TT symbols*

If you install fonts from a floppy, a CD, or any other removable disk that might not be available when you want to use those fonts, make sure the option **Copy fonts to Fonts folder** is checked. Your system can access fonts directly from a removable disk, but access is slower, and you have to keep the disk in place just about all the time. Hard disk space is amazingly cheap; use it lavishly to make your life easier.

The **Network** button in the Add Fonts dialog box opens the **Map Network Drive** dialog so you can map to other drives that might be sources of fonts. Why would you use fonts stored on another system instead of dragging the font files directly into the folder? Because instead of seeing the file names of the fonts (for example, COURBI.TTF for Courier New Bold Italic), you see the genuine font name.

Either way, since TrueType and system font information is stored in the Registry and updated in real time, you can preview and use fonts as soon as you install them, without having to shut down and restart your system.

## Supercharge Your Properties

The one thing that seems lame about font control under Windows 98 is the Font Properties sheet, which has a General tab with the same old MS-DOS file information, file dates, and attribute checkboxes. Ah! But what you, the font maven, need is the OpenType Font Properties Shell Extension, TTFEXT.EXE, which you can download from the Microsoft Typography Web site, **http://www.microsoft.com/typography**—we can't give you a more precise URL than that, because downloadable files on the Microsoft site wander around incessantly. This turns the Font Properties sheet into a ten-tab monster that could keep you mesmerized for hours. Since it also refers to tools and initiatives that are very new, it also asks more questions than it answers … which of course means that we get to answer them.

**General** is the same General tab you had before, exactly as useful as it wasn't.

**Embedding** tells you which class of font embedding—*installable, editable, Print & Preview,* or *restricted license*—is allowed for the particular font you're looking at. See "TrueType Font Embedding" below, but in a nutshell, this establishes whether a TrueType font that's part of a document can become part of a remote system's software along with the document.

**Char Set/Unicode** tells you which DOS and Windows code pages and, beyond that, which Unicode character ranges, can be completely satisfied by the character set of the font. If you look at an old-standby font like Courier New, which contains 327 characters, you'll find that it comprises seven code pages—English and European—and two Unicode ranges. Look at the 1775 characters of Lucida Sans Unicode, which is a real Unicode font, and you'll begin to get the idea. See the next section, called "What's Unicode Anyway?"

**Statistics** gives you the font version number, the create and modify file dates, the number of characters in the font, and whether or not the font incorporates kerning and bitmaps.

**Hinting/Font Smoothing** tells you what point size ranges of this font will be hinted, or smoothed (if you have Font Smoothing turned on), or both, and whether Windows will use the generic settings or the settings embedded in the font code.

**Names** gives you the font name, font family name, font vendor name, and copyright and trademark information.

**OpenType Layout Tables** are only found in OpenType—not TrueType—fonts. See the discussion of OpenType at the end of the chapter.

**Links** gives you live URLs (or at least tries) for the font vendor, font designer, and the Microsoft Typography site. Hyperlinks! On a Properties sheet! What's the world coming to!

**Description** gives a paragraph or so of background on the font, the designer, and the circumstances of the design. Many of the older fonts don't have this, but try News Gothic MT or Tempus Sans ITC.

**License** is the license information embedded in the font, if there is any.

## What's Unicode Anyway?

Unicode is one of the least-known, most hazily understood, yet potentially most influential initiatives undertaken by software developers at the turn of the century.

In most books about computing (including this one) the default character set is referred to as "7-bit ASCII"—00h through 7Fh, 0 through 127—or as "8-bit ASCII," 00h through FFh, 0 through 255. **ASCII** is the acronym for *American Standard Code for Information Interchange* ... meaning that, for decades, the core character set in computing was developed by (and, largely, for) English-speaking people who used the Latin alphabet and a set of Teletype control codes. In retrospect, it's amazing how long we all made the 7-bit and 8-bit character sets serve that purpose.

7-bit ASCII accommodated English and not much more. The eighth bit was added and, over time, extensions were proposed. French, Spanish, German and the Scandinavian languages needed accented letters, a few mathematical symbols crept in, then a graphics set or two, and one result was the PC Multilingual character set, DOS code page 850, which you can see in Appendix G.

When it came time to add Cyrillic, Mandarin, Japanese, Hangul, and a few other languages, chaos ruled. The Principle of Least Coordination, also known as the "bag on the side approach," guaranteed that the information architects for each national language would develop their character drivers independently. Japanese *kanji* and other ideographic languages needed "double-byte," or sixteen-bit, character encoding already. Cyrillic and Arabic were separate, but pressing, issues.

In 1991 the Unicode Consortium, based in San Jose, California, began the construction of a universal sixteen-bit character set that would serve the needs of information systems *worldwide*. 8-bit ASCII had 256 characters; each additional bit would double the number, so 16 bits would offer 64K distinct codes. In the current Unicode set, version 2.0, 47,398 of the codes have been allocated; not all of them are written characters, because many control codes are also needed to accommodate (for example) languages written right to left, or vertically. It will take years to allocate the rest—this is a titanic job, and haste is not advised, since this set has to be as inclusive and functional as 65,536 characters can possibly make it. The first 256 Unicode characters—also called "ISO Latin 1" or Hewlett-Packard Symbol Set 0N—are a lot like 8-bit ASCII.

If you use the Windows Character Map or an application's Insert Symbol menu command to insert a character that your keyboard doesn't offer, the **Shortcut** (so to speak!) listed as Alt +four digits is in Latin 1 Unicode. You have to use the numeric pad for the four digits.

32-bit Windows works by mapping DOS or ANSI code pages (for English, Windows 3.1 ANSI, page 1252, and MS-DOS U.S, page 437) to Unicode internally. All TrueType fonts are supposed to map to some portion of Unicode; how big a portion, as we've seen, depends on the extent and purpose of the particular font. Ultimately—although not soon—the world's language drivers for computer displays and printers will all be part of a single, coordinated series.

## Windows 98, Unicode, and Language Support

Having Unicode fonts for multiple languages on your system is one thing; gaining access to them is another. You can enable Windows 98 Multilanguage Support in any (or all) of five modules:

- Baltic (Estonian, Latvian, and Lithuanian)

- Central European (Albanian, Czech, Croatian, Hungarian, Polish, Romanian, Slovak, and Slovenian)

- Cyrillic (Bulgarian, Belarusian, Russian, Serbian, and Ukrainian)

- Greek

- Turkish

Open **Control Panel\Add/Remove Programs,** click the **Windows Setup** tab, and check the **Multilanguage Support** checkbox. To install all five modules, click OK. To install any subset, click **Details,** check the boxes for the module(s) you want to use, and click OK. Have the Windows 98 CD in your CD-ROM drive, because Multilanguage Support isn't supplied with the floppy-disk version. Windows will copy additional DLLs and drivers to your system, as well as font patch files that "bolt on" to your installed TrueType fonts to provide support for more code pages.

With Multilanguage Support installed, you can write text in any language that the module contains, switch keyboard layouts, observe language-specific sorting and formatting rules, cut, copy and paste with the Clipboard, and save language-specific RTF files. (What you *can't* do is change the language of compiled applications; if you want Russian legends, drop-down menus, and Help in Excel, you need a Russian copy of Excel.) Then see "Altering Keyboard Languages and Layouts" in Chapter 7 for instructions on how to make your working language and keyboard layout instantly switchable.

Once Multilanguage Support is installed, you can turn it on and off locally with the special language indicator on the Taskbar or with the `Ctrl` `Shift` or `Shift` `Left Alt` key combination. It's worth mentioning that both `Ctrl` `Shift` and `Shift` `Left Alt` are useful keyboard shortcuts for certain applications—we personally couldn't do without `Shift` `Left Alt` `↑` and `Shift` `Left Alt` `↓` to "walk paragraphs" or "walk table rows" in Microsoft Word—so you may have some priorities to observe.

## TrueType Font Embedding

Font embedding addresses two questions about document portability—and tries to strike a balance between them. The first is "How can we make sure that a document that we format, and then transfer or send to a second computer, will end up looking the same on both computers—even though they may not have the same fonts installed?" The second is "How can we attach fonts to documents, and then distribute the documents, without just giving the fonts away?" The answer is to attach the fonts, but also attach a level of permission that governs how the fonts can be used by the recipient. Microsoft has devised four levels of TrueType font embedding, ranging from open to highly restrictive; which level of embedding to attach is left up to the font developer.

Developers who want the world to see their fonts (and vice-versa) can set their font embedding status to *installable*. A document that embeds a TrueType font as installable contains a readable, writable, and detachable copy of the font itself. When such a document is sent to another user, the recipient can freely edit the document and view or print it; insert the font into documents created by other applications on the recipient's system; and, usually, install the font permanently on the target computer, as if that user had purchased the font.

An installable font can be used in any TrueType-aware Windows application that supports font embedding, like Microsoft Word 97 or PowerPoint 97. The TrueType fonts included with Windows 98 are set to installable embedding status. This is advantageous when compared with the read-only status of many commercially available font packs.

A developer who doesn't want a TrueType font to be distributed at random can develop it with *editable* embedding. This allows a document to be edited, viewed and printed in the proper typeface when it's transferred to another computer. The font is bound to the document; it can't be used in any other document, and it leaves the computer when the original document does. Many vendors sell TrueType fonts with the embedding status set to editable, allowing documents to be freely exchanged, but protecting the developer's ability to sell more copies of the typeface.

The third level, *Print & Preview,* enforces the restrictions of editable embedding but also sets the document to read-only. The document can be read on the remote computer with the proper font and layout, but nothing about it can be changed by the recipient.

*Restricted license* embedding isn't embedding at all; the font can't be merged with the document in any way. Even applications that support font embedding don't let you embed a restricted typeface into a document. If you work with one of these fonts and you have to transmit a document to something like an imagesetter, you have three choices:

- Send the necessary .TTF file along with the document, and make sure it gets removed from the receiving device when printing is finished.

- Buy a second copy of the font to install on the receiving device.

- Substitute an embeddable font for the restricted font.

Relatively few TrueType fonts have this level of restriction, although most PostScript fonts do. Some developers who exercise this restrictive choice get around the "send to an imagesetter" problem by licensing the .TTF file for a specific, small number of computers. If you find that you can't embed a font and it's a hassle, consider complaining to its developer about heavy-handedness.

## Windows 98 and PANOSE Matching

Windows 98 determines font similarity using the PANOSE Typeface Matching System, a font classification strategy developed to battle confusion and help with font substitution. PANOSE assesses a font's design, including its serifs, proportions, contrast, stroke variations, arm type, letterform, midline, and x height, and assigns a number to it.

 PANOSE isn't an acronym; it's a mnemonic device. The uppercase letters **P, A, N, O, S,** and **E,** along with the lowercase letters **a, b, e, g, k, m, o, q, s,** and **t,** include enough shapes to comprise and define the important features of any given typeface.

PANOSE information is embedded as part of the font data, and controls the order of entries in the similarity list; any font with PANOSE information is a candidate to be listed in the **List Fonts by Similarity** box. After it reviews PANOSE characteristics, Windows 98 returns a diagnosis of **Very similar, Fairly similar, Not similar,** or **No PANOSE information available.**

## TrueType Font Caching

Every TrueType character starts as an outline and goes through the rasterizer, which creates a solid character called a *rendered bitmap.* Each time you use a certain size of a particular TrueType font, Windows creates a bitmap set of all the characters in that font and size, but is smart enough not to throw it away later. Instead, those rendered bitmaps are stored in a font cache for the remainder of your Windows session—or until the font cache is full. The first time you use a particular font during a session with Windows, you'll notice that font taking a little longer to display and print. Every time after that, Windows will retrieve copies of the cached bitmaps, to give you quicker display and printing time when you reuse any TrueType font. But nothing good lasts forever; when you shut down that Windows session, the cache is flushed.

TrueType's performance has improved materially from each version of Windows to the next. In Windows 3.1, if you used a plethora of fonts and a multitude of sizes within a single document, you could easily believe that your computer had frozen solid. The 32-bit rasterizer included in Windows 95 gave dramatically superior font handling speed, and the Windows 98 rasterizer has been hand-tuned to improve performance once again. (When Microsoft throws another bucketful of money at its ongoing projects, TrueType is standing there with open arms. As we've noted in the discussion of Unicode, and as you'll see when we discuss TrueType Open, Microsoft considers scalable and embeddable character sets to be a crucial—maybe *the* crucial—incentive to the spread of Windows computing throughout the world.)

If you're shooting for a record in *Guinness* and get anywhere near the practical limit of a thousand fonts in one document—Microsoft's "The Registry will eat anything" notwithstanding—you'll probably notice a slowdown in display and printing speed. The font cache, overloaded with rendered bitmaps, has bulged past available RAM and is frantically spilling out to swapfile ... ironically, because the fonts came off the disk to begin with. This problem occurs with all Windows fonts, not just TrueType, and in fact TrueType isn't the worst offender; but your performance won't take the hit that it did with earlier versions of Windows. (Nothing could be as slow as sending a trainload of raster fonts to an old PCL laser printer, with a separate file for each typeface and point size.)

# Character Map, and Other Utilities

Sooner or later, you'll be typing a letter or an address with accented characters in it, and you'll confront a problem: How do you get to the characters that aren't easy to reach with the keyboard? It's not quite worth installing Multi-language Support, you can't remember the arcane Alt (NumPad) codes, and let's say you're working with an application that doesn't have an Insert Symbol command. Welcome to an oldie but goodie, the **Character Map** accessory, which lets you easily view the characters of any font installed on your system. It also enables you to copy and paste characters into a document. It's in **Start Menu\Programs\Accessories\Character Map** (Figure 8.3).

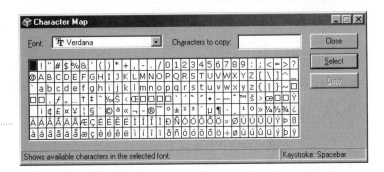

*Figure 8.3*

Character Map window with Verdana typeface

The Character Map window contains a grid displaying the current subset of all the characters in the currently selected typeface. Above the grid is a drop-down list box labeled **Font,** which you can access by pointing or by pressing Alt F. (If the Font field is highlighted, you can also navigate the list with the arrow keys.) From this list, select a typeface to display in the grid. You don't have to stick to classic alphabets; Figure 8.4 depicts a Windows 98 TrueType typeface called **Webdings,** which is made up of symbols and dingbats.

As you'll notice, the Character Map is one-size-fits-you; there's no way to either maximize it or drag it larger. The characters displayed in the grid are minute. Your choices are:

To see an enlarged view of an individual character, hold down the mouse button while pointing at the character (Figure 8.4).

To rove around the entire font in enlarged view, press Tab to move the cursor into the character grid, then use the arrow keys to navigate through the grid.

*Figure 8.4*

Inspecting a dingbat

To copy a character that you want to paste into another application, double-click on it, click the Select button, or press Alt S. Whatever your method, the character you select is placed in the **Characters to copy** field at the top of the Character Map window. When you've finished picking characters, click on the **Copy** button or press Ctrl C to transfer the contents of the Characters to Copy field onto the Clipboard. When the characters are on the Clipboard, switch to your document and choose **Paste** or press Ctrl V.

 There are two reasons for your characters to change typefaces on the fly. If you have characters waiting in the Characters to Copy field and you switch fonts in the Font list, the selected characters will follow your choice in the Font list. If the characters are transformed when you paste them, it's because the base font of your document is different from the font you had selected in the Font list. To reset the characters, highlight them and select the correct font from within the application.

 **To quit Character Map, press Esc, and the window will vanish. Sorry, you still can't print the Character Map or—better yet—a list of characters with their codes. But, as noted earlier, you can print font samples from the Fonts folder.**

## Font Organizers

If you're really into typefaces, you might want a serious font utility to help you view and organize your collection. We suspect that anybody who would try all four of these will end up buying more than one.

**Printer's Apprentice** ($25) and **FontReview** ($10) by Bryan Kinkel are two great TrueType font organizers and explorers. Printer's Apprentice makes elegant use of tabbed dialogs and sliders to show you everything about a font, whether on the single-character or the character-set level; it'll also install—even from CD—and uninstall fonts. (If you want to say "How'd he *do* that?!" a few times, hit Ctrl K to open the Keyboard window, which makes Character Map look lame. Tip: The keys work.) FontReview is an upgraded replacement for the dialog that opens when you double-click on a font in the Fonts pane; it also adds an Install choice to the Context Menu. Cruise by the Lose Your Mind Development Web site at **http://www.igi.net/~btkinkel/down01.htm** and download a time-limited demo of either or both.

Bitstream's **Font Navigator** ($40 list, but sometimes bundled at a discount) will work with both TrueType and Type 1, show you font samples and extended information, demonstrate special effects like rotated and reversed, let you define font catalogs and groups, drag-and-drop install and uninstall fonts, and find duplicates even over a network. Curiously, when it installs fonts it won't copy to the Fonts folder, which it claims is "not required." True, but…. Otherwise, this is a real Swiss army knife with a copious Help file, so download a thirty-day demo from **http://www.bitstream.com/fontnav/trial.htm**.

Finally, for sheer depth of information about your font library, **Typograf** by the German team of Alexander and Matthias Neuber is unbeatable. Typograf does a lot of the stuff the others do, but also offers a database of font structure including full PANOSE information, IBM and Windows font metrics, TrueType file structure, a full-screen character map with ANSI *and* Unicode values in decimal *and* hex, a typography timeline…. Invest $35 and get back data that font wonks have sweated to extract for years. As a bonus, Typograf handles your TrueType, Type 1, Windows raster, and printer fonts all in the same display pages, keeping track of whether or not they're installed. If Font Navigator is a Swiss army knife, Typograf is a tray of scalpels. Surf posthaste to `http://www.neuber.com/typograph/` and, less than a megabyte later, you'll be in font heaven. (If you're like us, you'd pay thirty-five bucks just for the key to the encrypted manual.)

(FontShow, which we recommended in a previous edition of this book, is no longer available because Rascal Software ceased development of retail products at the end of 1997.)

## TrueType In The PostScript World

As we've tried to make clear, there's every reason to be happy with TrueType for a multitude of purposes. But if dealing with type is part of your profession, you will sooner or later have to assemble a job in PostScript—from a rough or trial that was done in TrueType. When this happens, you'll want some insight into the familial but uneasy relationship between the two major scalable-font architectures.

### Table 8.3  *PostScript Equivalents of TrueType Fonts*

| TrueType Font Family | PostScript Font Family |
|---|---|
| Arial | Helvetica |
| Arial Narrow | Helvetica Narrow |
| Book Antiqua | Palatino |
| Bookman Old Style | Bookman |
| Century Gothic | Avant Garde |
| Monotype Corsiva | Zapf Chancery |
| Courier New | Courier |
| Monotype Sorts | Zapf Dingbats |
| Symbol | Symbol |
| Times New Roman | Times Roman |

One issue that *has* become less vexing in the last few years is the correlation of names between TrueType and PostScript fonts, because increasingly, both have (nearly or exactly) the same name. Table 8.3 lists Windows TrueType font families and their PostScript equivalents that happen to have different names. Each font family includes a regular, italic, bold, and bold italic typeface.

The design of a typeface cannot be copyrighted; only its name is protected by copyright law. Because of this, the Helvetica design is called Arial in Windows, whereas some vendors call it Swiss.

# Installing PostScript Fonts

PostScript fonts are still installed in the WIN.INI file, which—unfortunately—makes the installation table a contributor toward that file's 64K limit. Use Adobe Type Manager (ATM) to install and manage your PostScript fonts, as you always have. ATM Deluxe version 4 is compatible with Windows 98, and will manage both TrueType and PostScript fonts seamlessly. Once the PostScript fonts are installed, you can use them freely in your applications.

If you don't have ATM, you can install your PostScript fonts manually by adding the appropriate lines to WIN.INI. Here's how: Windows looks for PostScript font listings in the WIN.INI [*Printer,Port*] sections. The listings refer to each style of a typeface, with one line per font, and include the full path and the name of the font file or (usually) two files: *<fontname>*.PFM, the metric spacing information, and *<fontname>*.PFB, which contains the font outlines themselves.

The PFM is crucial; without it, the font would not be listed in the ATM Control Panel or in any application. The PFB is not crucial if you don't print the file yourself (for example, if you send it to a commercial printer who has that font). With just the PFM file, you can select a font, and get a good enough idea of the spacing that you can lay out your page. Table 8.4 shows a sample of lines from the WIN.INI file.

The font names in WIN.INI aren't very intuitive; the examples in Table 8.4 include Bauhaus Heavy, Light, Medium, and Bold. **softfont1** is Bauhaus Heavy, and so on.

### Table 8.4  PostScript Font Listings in the WIN.INI File

```
[PostScript,LPT1]       Section heading. There's one for every port you specify.
softfonts=15            Number of fonts installed.
softfont1=c:\psfonts\pfm\bhh_____.pfm,c:\psfonts\bhh_____.pfb
softfont2=c:\psfonts\pfm\bhl_____.pfm,c:\psfonts\bhl_____.pfb
softfont3=c:\psfonts\pfm\bhm_____.pfm,c:\psfonts\bhm_____.pfb
softfont4=c:\psfonts\pfm\bhb_____.pfm,c:\psfonts\bhb_____.pfb
[....]
```

**PostScript Management Tips.**  The underscores following letters in the font names are crucial, because font names must contain eight characters before the extension.

Some applications, such as Corel Draw, install fonts into your system and update the WIN.INI file, and don't tell you about it. Be very careful about telling a big, hungry program to "install all fonts" and then leaving your system unchaperoned; we have personally watched a brand-name publishing application try to install over 1,300 fonts on one computer, truncating WIN.INI and (shudder!) corrupting the Registry with key overflow. Sure, it's tempting to have a CD's worth of fonts just a few clicks away, but we (who know) recommend you keep your system mean and lean by installing only the ones you actually use. Installing fonts as you need them is straightforward.

To install a large group of fonts at one time, first place them all in the same directory. You can then select the entire group with Ctrl A.

If you're running an older version of Adobe Type Manager (anything earlier than 4) be sure you don't check the box in the \Windows\Fonts Folder Options that hides all the non-TrueType fonts in your applications. If that box is checked, you won't be able to locate the PostScript fonts.

**Printing on Multiple Systems.** It's hard to find two computer systems that have the identical set of fonts installed, which often gets in the way of printing a document identically on different computers. Although WYSIWYG provides a visual correlation between what you see on your screen and the output from your printer, that's still *your* screen and *your* printer. All too often, in your office, the carefully formatted document you prepared on your own system will look mangled when you print it out on your co-worker's local printer.

Typeface troubles can also emerge when you send a disk to a PostScript service bureau for output, unless the service bureau already owns the fonts you used—or you send the fonts along with the job, which is an added hassle and a potential copyright violation, because few commercial Type 1 typefaces are licensed for more than one machine.

An easier (and legal) solution for the service bureau problem is to create a Print-to-Disk file, also called a PostScript or dot-PS file. You route all the information you would have sent to your printer—including graphics, and data—into one file that you can usually put on a disk and take anywhere, especially to a service bureau. Once you set up the "port" for this type of print job, it's no different than printing any other job on your computer, except that the file you end up with gets downloaded to a printer elsewhere. This approach offers many benefits:

- You can proof the print file on your own PostScript printer before you send the file to the service bureau.

- You can save money, because service bureau staff don't have to open and print the original file.

- Printing to a file is particularly easy with Windows 98.

- You don't violate copyright laws, because the font information is included in your PostScript files, not sent separately as a usable font.

To perform this useful transmogrification, select FILE: as the output port for your print job. FILE:, as already described, accepts all the data that would have gone to the printer and stores it in the file you designate. You can print to a file by clicking on the icon for your own local printer and checking the **Print to file** checkbox, or you can create an icon specifically for the output device you want. For example, you can install a printer driver for your neighbor's color printer and target it to file, and you can do the same for your service bureau's imagesetter—although you'll need to know what model it is.

Once you determine which printer you're going to use, select its icon and choose **Properties** from its Context menu. Click on the **Details** tab, and from the **Print to the following port** drop-down list, select **FILE:**.

 **Mixing Architectures?** "Some people get away with it," you grumble. Yeah, some people get away with jumping motorcycles over flaming barrels, too. Although TrueType and PostScript typefaces are roughly equivalent in a general way, subtle design discrepancies exist between the two architectures. Furthermore, spacing can vary so much between comparable fonts that line lengths—and therefore line breaks, page lengths, and word wrap—are completely out of control. We've heard the horror stories, read the advice on the Net, tried a few tests ourselves, and this is Kip and Fred's Word From On High: When you're preparing pages for publication, *do not mix TrueType and PostScript fonts in the same job, ever!!*

## Screen Fonts, Printer Fonts, and Substitution

Whenever you use a printer firmware font, like a ROM cartridge or SIMM, it's worthwhile to obtain the matching screen font from the manufacturer. The printer font is essential for quality output; the screen font controls the appearance of characters on screen.

What happens when your screen and printer fonts don't match? If you print matter in a particular screen font but do not have the corresponding printer font, your laser printer may react by reproducing the screen font in what resembles a crude dot-matrix style. If you're still using an old dot-matrix printer, then screen fonts and even plotter fonts may be acceptable. Your printer may also substitute one of its built-in fonts for the screen font.

If, on the other hand, you use a printer font but do not have the corresponding screen font, then Windows substitutes whichever screen font, plotter font, or TrueType font most closely matches the printer font. To determine which font to use, Windows compares characteristics such as available characters, pitch, font family, height, width, and weight. Although what you see may not exactly equal what you get, Windows still tries its best to match onscreen line and page breaks and other formatting to printer output.

If you want to override Windows 98's choices of substituted fonts, use the Font Substitution table; refer to "PostScript Printer: Fonts Tab" on pages 380–381. This only works for PostScript printers.

**Screen Inches.**  When is an inch not an inch? When it's a *screen* inch, or as some people call it, a *logical* inch.

Before we discuss the Windows System fonts, turn to page 369 and read "Right On the Dot," our discussion of monitor resolution. You'll see that with typical hardware, your screen displays at about 70 to 110 pixels per inch—dpi. Windows screen fonts don't relate evenly to those resolutions; the Small Fonts set is encoded at 96 dpi, the Large Fonts set at 120 dpi. For the two currently most common monitor sizes, 15" and 17", see Table 8.5.

### Table 8.5  Screen Font Sizing Conversions

| Font Set DPI | Monitor Size | Resolution | Screen DPI | Conversion |
|---|---|---|---|---|
| 96 (Small) | 15" | 800x600 | 71 | 96/71 = 1.35 |
| 120 (Large) | | | 71 | 120/71 = 1.69 |
| 96 (Small) | | 1024x768 | 91 | 96/91 = 1.05 |
| 120 (Large) | | | 91 | 120/91 = 1.32 |
| 96 (Small) | 17" | | 85 | 96/85 = 1.13 |
| 120 (Large) | | | 85 | 120/85 = 1.41 |
| 96 (Small) | | 1280x1024 | 107 | 96/107 = 0.90 |
| 120 (Large) | | | 107 | 120/107 = 1.12 |

*Font Set DPI* is either the 96 dpi of the Small Fonts set or the 120 dpi of the Large Fonts set. *Monitor Size* is nominal; what matters here is that a 15" monitor screen is typically 11.25" wide and a 17" monitor screen is roughly 12" wide. *Resolution* is one of the three resolutions you'd be likely to run with that screen size. *Screen DPI* is the number of horizontal pixels divided by inches of real screen width. *Conversion* is the font set dpi divided by the screen dpi.

The point here is that, ordinarily, a font on the screen is bigger than the same font on paper. If you look at a 96 dpi character on a 71 dpi screen, it's actually about one and a third times as tall as it "should" be. This is a Good Thing, since your eyes are typically farther from your computer screen than they are from your book or newspaper, so the magnification is useful. How useful? Set your resolution to 1024x768 if you have a 15" monitor, or to 1280x1024 if you have a 17" monitor, set Small Fonts in Display Properties, and try to read your screen. That ratio is about 1 to 1, and you won't like it for very long.

At some places, in our System Fonts section or elsewhere, you may have to bear in mind that what you're looking at or reading about is a magnified screen inch, rather than a physical inch.

 Darn it, that 1 to 1 ratio might be handy if you were a graphic designer or something. If you want to try it, take the screen DPI of your monitor from the table or figure it out the way we did, then set your screen font to Custom in Display Properties and use the slider to match the font DPI to the DPI of your screen. Who knows where enlightenment resides?

**System Fonts.** The ascent of Lucida Console, Marlett, Tahoma, and Verdana as application and operating system screen fonts is an early clue to a new direction; before long we will see versions of Windows that use TrueType every time they need a font. Windows 98 hasn't made that leap, though, and includes all the standard raster fonts for displaying the text of icons, menus, dialog boxes, window titles, and other system components. System and screen fonts that are displayed in the **Fonts** folder have an icon of a document page with a red A on it; not all of the System fonts are displayed or listed in the Fonts folder or in Explorer, and the only way to find them all is to call a directory at a command prompt.

The raster fonts in Table 8.6 are included with Windows 98.

### Table 8.6  Windows 98 Standard Raster Fonts

| Font Name | Font Characteristics | Filenames |
|-----------|---------------------|-----------|
| Courier* | Fixed-width serif, reminiscent of a typewriter font | COURE.FON, COURF.FON |
| MS Serif | Proportional, in the Times tradition | SERIFE.FON, SERIFF.FON |
| MS Sans Serif | Fixed-width serif, less elaborate than Courier | SSERIFE.FON, SSERIFF.FON |
| Small Fonts | Proportional, optimized for sizes under 9 points | SMALLE.FON, SMALLF.FON |
| Symbol | Proportional math symbol font | SYMBOLE.FON, SYMBOLF.FON |
| System | Used for menus, dialogs, and other elements of the interface | VGASYS.FON, 8514SYS.FON |
| Fixedsys | Fixed-width, Windows 2.x system font, provided for compatibility | VGAFIX.FON, 8514FIX.FON |
| Terminal | Fixed-width, for tabular displays in telecommunications, and for Write files and Clipboard Viewer text | VGAOEM.FON, 8514OEM.FON |
| Dosapp | CP 437 font set for windowed DOS sessions | DOSAPP.FON |

* Windows may use the raster font, COURx.FON, or the TrueType font, COURxx.TTF, as a Courier System font. So far as we can tell, though, the default scalable System font in Windows 98 is Lucida Console, LUCON.TTF. See "Fonts and DOS Applications" on page 323.

### Table 8.7  Windows Standard Raster Font Series

| Letter | Device | Horizontal by Vertical Resolution | Aspect Ratio |
|--------|--------|-----------------------------------|--------------|
| A | CGA display | 96 by 48 dpi | 2:1 |
| B | EGA display | 96 by 72 dpi | 1.33:1 |
| C | Printer | 60 by 72 dpi | 1:1.2 |
| D | Printer | 120 by 72 dpi | 1.66:1 |
| E | VGA display | 96 by 96 dpi | 1:1 |
| F | 8514/a display | 120 by 120 dpi | 1:1 |

There are two stories here (Tables 8.7 and 8.8). The *E.FON and *F.FON files, from Courier through Symbol, appear in the Fonts folder and are all part of the following series.

Only the E and F files are included in the Windows 98 distribution; the A through D files are obsolete Windows 3.*x* or 2.*x* files. Even so, there is material here for the contemporary student of Windows. Remember the remark in the Displays section that CGA/EGA pixels (and therefore character cells) were rectangular, but that VGA and 8514/a pixels were square? The resolutions of the A and B versus the E and F fonts will bear this out. Furthermore, if you've experimented with screen font sizes in Display Properties, you'll recall that Small Fonts are 96 dpi—the E set—and Large Fonts are 120 dpi, the F set. If you pick the Custom screen font in Display Properties, you segue from a raster to a scalable font which is presumably TrueType.

Now, so far as screen font *sizes* are concerned, the newer .FON files each contain several sizes, the older files have one.

### Table 8.8  Windows Standard Screen Font Sizes

| Font Name | Filenames | Font Sizes |
|-----------|-----------|------------|
| Courier | COURx.FON | 15, 12, and 10 *characters per inch* |
| MS Serif | SERIFx.FON | 8, 10, 12, 14, 18, and 24 *points* |
| MS Sans Serif | SSERIFx.FON | 8, 10, 12, 14, 18, and 24 *points* |
| Small Fonts | SMALLx.FON | 2, 3, 4, 5, 6, and 7 *points* |
| Symbol | SYMBOLx.FON | 8, 10, 12, 14, 18, and 24 *points* |
| System | *xxx*SYS.FON | 9 *points* in VGA, 11 *points* in 8514 |
| Fixedsys | *xxx*FIX.FON | 9 *points* in VGA, 11 *points* in 8514 |
| Terminal | *xxx*OEM.FON | 9 *points* in VGA, 11 *points* in 8514 |
| Dosapp | DOSAPP.FON | *Character-cell sizes* of 4x6, 5x12, 6x8, 7x12, 8x8, 8x12, 10x18, and 12x16 |

Windows can scale raster fonts to even multiples of the provided sizes; for example, the Symbol, MS Serif, and MS Sans Serif sets don't include a 16-point or a 20-point font, since those can be scaled from the 8 and the 10. However, because these fonts are black on white only (hence no grayscaling) and have no font metric data (hence no hinting) larger sizes will appear with jagged edges. You can print with raster fonts if their resolution and aspect ratios closely match those of your printer (an aspect ratio is the relationship of the height to the width of an object). To determine what horizontal and vertical ratios your printer is capable of producing, and match it with the closest raster font, you may need to consult your printer manual.

**Control Files.**  The Fixed and OEM fonts—and the TrueType fonts assigned to windowed DOS sessions—are listed in the Registry under **HKLM\[....]\CurrentVersion\fontsize**, but their font assignments are scattered all over good old SYSTEM.INI (Table 8.9) and WIN.INI (Table 8.10). Doesn't it make you nostalgic?

### Table 8.9  SYSTEM.INI Control for Fixed and OEM Font Sets

| Font Set | SYSTEM.INI Header | Setting |
|---|---|---|
| Small | [boot] | oemfonts.fon=vgaoem.fon<br>fixedfon.fon=vgafix.fon<br>fonts.fon=vgasys.fon |
| Large | [boot] | oemfonts.fon=8514oem.fon<br>fixedfon.fon=8514fix.fon<br>fonts.fon=8514sys.fon |
| Both | [boot.description] | woafont.fon=English (437) |
| | [386Enh] | woafont=dosapp.fon |
| | [NonWindowsApp] | TTInitialSizes=4 5 6 7 8 9 10 11 12 13 14 15 16 18 20 22 |
| | [TTFontDimenCache] | see below |

If any ancient Windows fonts such as Tms Rmn remain, Windows 98 replaces them with the MS Serif and MS Sans Serif fonts by remapping them in WIN.INI, where you'll also find the settings for Font Smoothing and for the **Show only TrueType fonts...** checkbox on the TrueType tab of View\Folder Options.

### Table 8.10  WIN.INI Control for Raster and TrueType Fonts

| Font Set | WIN.INI Header | Setting |
|---|---|---|
| Raster | [FontSubstitutes] | Helv=MS Sans Serif<br>Tms Rmn=MS Serif<br>Times=Times New Roman |
| TrueType | [TrueType] | FontSmoothing=0 (off) or 1 (on)<br>TTOnly=0 (off) or 1 (on) |

**Fonts and DOS Applications.**  Now, and only now, are we prepared to understand how DOS sessions in Windows use System fonts, and how we can select those fonts through the Properties sheet.

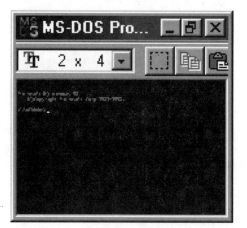

*Figure 8.5*

*Minimal DOS box*

Without even hacking the font list (see below) you can select from over twenty raster and TrueType fonts to display the character-based DOS applications you run from within Windows 98. Since the metrics of the selected font determine the size of the resulting DOS window, you can select type sizes that let you run several DOS applications at once in full view, or keep a single window open without obscuring the rest of

*Figure 8.5*

*Minimal DOS box*

your Windows screen. The smallest DOS window, generated with the TrueType 2x4 font, is this big (Figure 8.5) and only a hamster could read the type, but this window would be fine if you're running a long process that will give you substantial or colorful notice that it's finished. On the other end of the scale, a DOS window generated with the TrueType 13x22 font is roughly full screen of a 17" monitor.

The 32-bit Windows DOS window is a nice place, so let's explore it. If you haven't made an MS-DOS Prompt shortcut for your desktop yet (which we recommend) go to **Start Menu\Programs\MS-DOS Prompt** and launch one from there. The first thing you'll probably notice is the toolbar (Figure 8.6) with its buttons from left to right.

*Figure 8.6*

*DOS Box toolbar*

**Font and window size.** This drop-down list lets you set the size of your DOS window font and, implicitly, of the window itself. You can leave it at **Auto** or set it to a font size from a vast range; the ones with the TT at the left are Lucida Console, while the others are raster fonts. If you drop this list and pick a different font size, the window will auto-rescale to match.

**Mark** a screen region for the Clipboard.

**Copy** to the Clipboard.

**Paste** from the Clipboard.

Go to borderless **Full Screen.** These four aren't involved with fonts, so we'll discuss them in Chapter 14, "Windows 98 and DOS."

Pop up the **Properties sheet** with the Program tab at the top. Fonts is the next one over.

**Background.** See Chapter 14.

**Font.** Pop up the Properties sheet with the Fonts tab at the top. If you pick **Font size,** then **Font preview** shows you a small section of the resulting DOS window, and **Window preview** shows you a DOS window scaled to this metric, as it will appear against your whole Desktop (Figure 8.7). With **Available types** you can pick **Bitmap only** and restrict the choice to the eight raster fonts contained in DOSAPP.FON, pick **TrueType only** and restrict the choice to Lucida Console in the sizes from the TTInitialSizes= list in SYSTEM.INI, or pick **Both font types** and have them all. Why not?

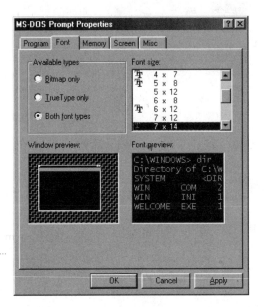

*Figure 8.7*

*MS-DOS Prompt Properties dialog box*

 Your choice of fonts depends on which video grabber file you use. Note that CGA fonts used with DOS applications can simulate a CGA display inside a window, regardless of the actual type of display you use.

**Vector Fonts.** Vector fonts, which contain mathematical instructions for composing fonts by drawing straight or curved outlines, were originally used by pen plotters, which drive a pen to draw characters or graphs on paper. Many newer plotters, such as the HP DesignJet, will plot using TrueType or Type 1 fonts anyway. Previous versions of Windows have included three vector

## *Editing [TTFontDimenCache]*

[TTFontDimenCache] seems to be a list of TrueType font sizes that Windows caches permanently to have available quickly for the MS-DOS Prompt. The abridged list looks like this:

```
0 4=2 4
[....]
0 15=9 15
0 16=10 16
0 18=11 18
[....]
0 22=13 22
```

The number in *the first column* is always zero, and we don't know what it represents, but we encourage you to leave it zero for additional entries. The number in *the second column* always equals the one in the fourth column, but we think this is just convenience for the programmer; the numbers in the second column (and possibly in the fourth) only need to be consecutive. The numbers in *the third and fourth columns* are, what ho, the character-cell sizes of the TrueType fonts in the **Font size** list, without the times-sign; so, for example, "=13 22" in TTFontDimenCache is the origin of "13 x 22" in the Font size list.

Say you want to add Lucida Console 8 x 16 to your repertoire of DOS window fonts. Simply add an additional line to the table, and edit the sequence in the second column, so that the table reads:

```
[....]
0 15=9 15
0 16=8 16
0 17=10 16
0 18=11 18
```

and the next time you boot, 8 x 16 will become an available font size. We have made this work, and seen it documented on the Net; at this writing, the `microsoft.com` Web site contains no trace of it. Your mileage may vary, and as usual, we strongly suggest that you back up your SYSTEM.INI before you modify it.

font files: ROMAN.FON, MODERN.FON, and SCRIPT.FON. If our experience is anything to go by, Windows 98 installs only MODERN.FON.

Before TrueType and ATM, vector fonts were the only scalable fonts available for Windows, and some developers used them to create large characters and special type effects, such as rotated text. If you need to drive an older pen plotter with Windows 98, MODERN.FON should still work, but we recommend using TrueType for scalable fonts on any device that accepts them.

### Table 8.11  Printer and Font Compatibility

| Printer | TrueType Fonts | Raster Fonts | Vector Fonts |
|---|---|---|---|
| HP LaserJet-compatible | Yes | No | Yes |
| PostScript | Yes | No | Yes |
| Dot matrix | Yes | Yes | Yes |
| Pen plotter | Possibly | No | Yes |

Table 8.11 identifies the font architectures that work with different printer types in Windows 98.

**Changing System Fonts.**  When Windows 98 Setup installs raster and TrueType fonts, it decides for itself which fonts to use for display, and which to use for printing. You can print with "display" fonts, though, and display with "print" fonts, as long as you understand the capabilities of your hardware.

To change the fonts used in your system programs and listings, choose **Settings** from the Start Menu and select **Control Panel\Display.** You can change fonts using two tabs in Display Properties:

The **Appearance** tab lets you change fonts in message boxes, title bars, button captions, and other parts of the Windows interface. Click on individual components (such as window parts) to change them; the name of the component appears in the **Item** field and, if there's a font associated with the component, the Font drop-down list becomes active. The default font for most Windows components is MS Sans Serif 8, but if you want to be cutting-edge, try Lucida Console 9. Avoid script fonts.

### Table 8.12  Font Size Settings in Display Properties

| Size | Percentage | Dots/screen inch | Suitability |
|---|---|---|---|
| Minimum | 20% | 19 | Unreadable |
| Smallest on list | 75% | 72 | Readable |
| Small Fonts | 100% | 96 | Usable |
| Large Fonts | 125% | 120 | Comfortable |
| Largest on list | 200% | 192 | Huge |
| Maximum | 500% | 480 | Unusable |

The **Settings** tab lets you change the font of icon titles and change the size of things like dialog box text. Table 8.12 shows some possible values.

Windows would like you to think that this is all done with a single TrueType font, but we suspect that you may get one of several fonts depending on the scaling percentage. If you choose a display font equivalent to 7 points or smaller, Windows 98 automatically substitutes the Small raster font for TrueType. (At that size you'd be hard put to tell the difference between the two.) Small Fonts is, of course, the E (VGA) set, and Large Fonts is the F (8514/a) set. The others probably all are a TrueType font; the Sample box mentions (and displays) Arial, but the font used as an example may be settable somewhere.

Be careful; when you play with system fonts, make sure that you can reverse what you do. Settings that are livable within Windows itself may cause strange effects in some of your applications.

## Removing Fonts

 No matter what else you have in mind, do not *ever* delete:

**MS Sans Serif.**  If this isn't available, Windows substitutes a font which can make some onscreen items difficult to read.

**Marlett.**  We don't want to think about the carnage if you blow this away. Microsoft says that if it's corrupted, "numbers or garbled characters appear in place of controls," skirting the question of whether these non-appearing controls still work.

**8514***xxx***.FON**, **DOSAPP.FON**, and **VGA***xxx***.FON**. These are the Large and Small Fonts and DOS raster sets. If you remove them, Windows will either refuse to boot, or start booting but crash with a GDI fault.

It is true that these files are elaborately protected, so much so that we couldn't test for consequences because we couldn't delete or rename them even at the DOS level. Even so, it's our job to assume that everything bad that can happen to a computer eventually will. If you ever need to reinstall these files from the Windows 98 CD, you'll find the Small Fonts, MS Serif, and MS Sans Serif in the MINI.CAB file; those will at least get you booted into Windows. See "Using the EXTRACT Command to Browse CAB Files" in Chapter 15.

To remove a font, select its icon in the Fonts folder and choose Delete from the File menu or from the pop-up menu. You can also drag the icon to the Recycle Bin or a Recycle Bin shortcut. If you want to uninstall a font but keep it on the hard disk, drag (or cut and paste) it to another folder on your local or network drive.

Beware of going overboard deleting fonts. Unlike previous versions of Windows, Windows 98 doesn't give you the option of keeping uninstalled fonts on your hard disk. As soon as you empty the Recycle Bin or it empties itself, the fonts are gone.

Some documents that you print may use fonts that are not installed in your system. This can happen if you receive a document from someone else or if you remove a font that was previously installed. In such cases, Windows does its best to substitute a font that approximates the missing one. If the missing font is TrueType, Windows can make a better substitution, because it can call on TrueType to render the character. And if TrueType fonts are embedded in a document, you can print it properly without having to substitute fonts.

# Fonts, Languages, and the Future

To anyone interested in computer typography, few things are more fascinating than the future of page-description languages. Certainly they have one, but what could it be?

## A Focused Deconstruction of HTML, PostScript, and Acrobat

One of the greatest promises and traps of computerdom is the premise that as soon as something *can* be done, it *must* be done; or, to put it another way, that the possibility of doing something (with a computer) is itself the excuse—even the imperative—to do that thing. Okay. We can now control the *exact* placement (and color, if color) of any sub-minuscule dot of toner on a page of indefinite size. Because we can, should we? If we should, how much effort should we devote to doing so?

We can put muscle behind this question with a tiny comparison of three of the most popular languages on the Net—HTML, PostScript, and Acrobat. Let's examine a minimal job of page description and see what it takes to accomplish all three ways. Could I have a "Hello, world" in 24-point Times Roman bold, please?

# Hello, world

Thank you. There's the output we're looking for. What if we wanted to do it in HTML, PostScript, or Acrobat?

**HTML.**   It's often said that any darn fool can be simple but it takes a genius to be really simple. If anything on the Net is simple genius, it's HTML—the markup language that took over the world—and thank you, Tim Berners-Lee and company! Let's not bother sizing the font explicitly; let's stick to the old, quick, *fun* kind of HTML:

```
<!doctype html public "-//ietf//dtd html//en//3.0">
<html>
<head><title>Hello, world</title></head>
<body bgcolor="#FFFFFF">
<h1 align="left">Hello, world</h1>
</body>
</html>
```

Seven lines of code and less than 200 bytes, even with setting the background white instead of the default gray. Now, what do we give up in exchange for the simplicity? We settle for WYGIWYG—what you get is what you get. Most immediately, the text isn't specified as 24-point; it's just a top-level header that happens to come out as roughly that. If you stick to elementary HTML, there's not a lot of flexibility, and if you build on the more recent extensions, the simplicity (which is the point here) vanishes. Let's enjoy the HTML example for what it is: page description that you can write in Notepad and sight-read, as congenially as walking barefoot on a warm beach.

**PostScript.** Flexibility? Ultimate. Put that little ol' black dot anywhere you precisely please. But something's happened to the code; it's 100 lines, almost 2500 bytes, and the (abridged) file doesn't look all that readable:

```
%!PS-Adobe-3.0
[13 lines....]
bd/a{currentpoint}bd/c/curveto ld/d/dup ld/e/eofill ld/f/fill
    ld/tr/translate
ld/gr/grestore ld/gs/gsave ld/j/setlinejoin ld/L/lineto ld/M/moveto
    ld/n
[16 lines....]
[{300 /languagelevel where{pop languagelevel 2 ge}{false}ifelse
{1 dict dup/WaitTimeout 4 -1 roll put setuserparams}
{statusdict/waittimeout 3 -1 roll put}ifelse
}stopped cleartomark
[49 lines....]
10.84 783.66 translate 72 600 div dup neg scale
0 0 transform .25 add round .25 sub exch .25 add round .25 sub exch
    itransform translate
%%IncludeFont: Times-Bold
[200 0 0 -200 0 0]/Times-Bold MF
(Hello, world)660 822 MS
showpage
[7 lines....]
%%EOF
```

Of several scary things about this file, the most obvious is that the text "Hello, world" is on the ninetieth line. Everything before that was either device setup or drawing instructions. Can you imagine how much code this would become if we ever changed the font, or the point size, or inserted a graphic? Now you understand why PostScript printers need fast raster processors and abundant RAM—the endless string of page-description language goes zipping through like fishing line off a reel.

PostScript teeters on the outer edge of human legibility. Yes, it is possible to compose this and key it in by hand—but probably not frivolously, not in Notepad, and not without wishing for utility software. Automation begins to dominate composition as page description heads for the sealed box of ...

**Acrobat.** A great language, truly, and a great idea; PostScript compiled into a file that, when opened by a reading program, displays a fully composed PostScript page on screen and sends it to your printer. The compiler is a transmitting machine, the reader is a receiving machine. Our "Hello, world" has become an encapsulated binary file of just over 1,500 bytes, passed between machines.

There is no such thing as "writing Acrobat by hand." Some utilities exist that allow limited editing of the compiled file, but the efficient way to make changes in Acrobat code is to edit the PostScript source and give it to the compiler again. Just as page composition became page description, page description now becomes page programming.

All three of these page presentation methods need significant resources to support them—a computer of course, probably a printer, and then either a graphical browser, or a PostScript viewer, or a copy of the Acrobat Reader. Nothing much there to influence a choice. Really, when you select your methods for page description and typography, your talisman will be *involvement.* How much do you crave the feeling of warm sand on your toes? How ready are you to straddle a shining seamless machine? And don't take the computer as your oracle; it just follows your lead as you walk or ride. Think about how you're going, not about whether you've gone too far.

## The TrueType Open Specification

When you look at the future of scalable fonts, one thing you're looking at is **TrueType Open**—a bold and rigorous attempt to give (or, okay, sell) outline font technology to the whole world. Unicode was the foundation, but Unicode at its roots is only a map; it specifies which character goes where, in the vast number of possible positions. TrueType Open will fill in the map and create a universal character set.

TrueType Open is an extension of TrueType that relies on the same fundamental mechanism and simply makes more room. Although we rely on TrueType to draw characters, its elements are letters, numerals and punctuation marks called *glyphs.* These take account of format as well as content. A and A are "the same letter," but A is the glyph called "uppercase letter A in Times New Roman," and A is the glyph called "uppercase letter A in Lucida Sans." Applications use character codes to call for characters; TrueType maps the character codes to internal tables that tell it what glyphs to produce.

Glyphs can represent combinations and alternative forms of characters. For example, if you type the characters "f" and "l," you type two characters, but the best representation of that on the page would be the ligature "fl," which is a single TrueType glyph. TrueType Open uses deeper mapping (and more tables) to fulfill requirements that don't occur in Latin alphabets; some Arabic characters, for example, take different forms at the beginning, middle, or end of a word, so an Arabic font will need one glyph to represent each form of a single character. A table in TrueType Open fonts provides information about possible glyph substitutions.

A group of related glyphs is called a *script*, which may be used by one or more languages. Latin, Arabic, or Thai are scripts. Depending on how broadly a single font supports Unicode, it may use a single script—like Comic Sans, which uses only Latin—or it may use many scripts; if you have the OpenType Font Properties Shell Extension installed (and we hope you do by now) go to the Properties of Lucida Sans Unicode and click the **CharSet/Unicode** tab for an example. A subset of a script that accommodates only one language is called a *language system;* for example, the Latin script is used to write English, French, or German, but special requirements for text processing in each language belong to the language system, not the script. Each script contains a unique character set, but each language system may not. A font developer can work from information specific to a script, to a language system, or to both.

A TrueType Collection (TTC) uses a single file structure to deliver several OpenType fonts when the combined fonts have many glyphs in common. By "shrinking down" multiple fonts to their smallest common glyph set, Collections can save significant file space, especially in some Asian languages.

Ultimately, Microsoft hopes, TrueType Open as an implementation of Unicode will bring the benefits of TrueType font technology to every significant written language in the world.

## The OpenType Specification

**OpenType** (TrueType Open 2.0) is the waking moment of the dream that has hovered over this entire chapter. TrueType and Type 1, those kissing cousins, have overcome the objections of their families and are getting married.

The OpenType font format is a superset of the TrueType and Type 1 formats; an OpenType font can have Type 1 outlines only, TrueType outlines only, or both. The Type 1 data can be rasterized by a Type 1 rasterizer like Adobe Type Manager, if you have that installed, or converted for rasterization by the TrueType rasterizer. The burning question is whether Windows will incorporate a native Type 1 rasterizer, and the answer from both Microsoft and Adobe is a firm "Well, maybe." (Presumably Adobe is after a premium price for Type 1 technology, as usual.) OpenType will also include subsetting, compression, and a protocol for embedding fonts in HTML documents. This will make it an ideal font format for Web sites, but on the other hand, HTML version numbers may start looking like PostScript version numbers.

OpenType will seamlessly support the TrueType and Type 1 fonts you already own. Native OpenType fonts will support advanced typographic features like ligatures and alternate glyph forms. Adobe will convert their existing library of Type 1 fonts to OpenType, and both Microsoft and Adobe will throw money at developing and promoting new OpenType fonts—although, as Adobe puts it tartly, "This initiative does not imply that fonts will be free." Naturally not, but we'd bet they'll be cheaper than Type 1 fonts have historically been.

Without comment or judgment of any kind we republish this question and reply from the Adobe OpenType FAQ:

**Q:** Does this mean MS is capitulating to Adobe in the font wars? Does this mean Adobe is capitulating to MS in the font wars?

**A:** Both companies see this as a mutually beneficial agreement, and as being beneficial to customers as well. The decision to work together came from a desire to provide the best solution for customers, and to provide an environment for future joint innovations.

*"Let me give you a hint,"* says the Cheshire Cat's grin, fading slowly into the twilit sky …

## A Few Thoughts on Buying Fonts

That old saw about competition being good for the customer has rarely been more true than in the matter of digital type. Before we turn you loose on a strictly personal and subjective list of favorite foundries, let us share some of our thoughts on building up a personal font library … something we've both done, to say the least.

Get your feet wet gradually. Fonts in and of themselves are valuable only for abstract beauty; using fonts intelligently requires you to build your skills in composition, layout, appropriateness, and document production. It takes time and thought simply to make good use of the fifty-six standard faces that ship with Windows 98.

When you buy fonts, you generally get what you pay for. (Old saw #2.) Hand-hinted TrueType fonts from boutique foundries can be as much as $100 each; usable, attractive fonts from reputable designers can be less than a dollar each, if you buy font families and collections. But shareware TrueType, and TrueType fonts on no-name $10 CDs, are mechanically hinted—or not hinted at all—and they look it. Here as elsewhere, a computer makes the production of ugliness quicker and easier than ever before. If you like type, you'll find that investment pays regular dividends; "personal" font sets from Adobe, Bitstream and Monotype are more than worth the modest cost.

Having said that, we'll promptly make an exception to it. Many of the world's better digital foundries, large and small, promote themselves by periodically making fonts—especially new ones—available for downloading. Free fonts are generally display faces, and you may have to put up with an occasional crippled character set, but with discretion and dedication, you can assemble a respectable type library just by hanging around Web sites. That's one reason we put nice fresh URLs in this list of font foundries, the other reason being that the Web is a great place to look at type before you buy it.

Don't worry too much about buying Type 1 fonts or TrueType fonts, because nowadays, when you buy a type CD you usually get both. Only a few meticulous foundries still restrict themselves to Type 1 only; their reasons are generally that Type 1 is still the standard for commercial digital typography, or that top-quality hand hinting is much more difficult on a TrueType font than on a Type 1 font. Both of these contentions are loads of fun to debate but, in the last analysis, probably true.

CDs of "locked" type, whose fonts you can peruse on the disc and then purchase one by one as you need them, are strictly for professionals. Adobe Type on Call, at about $50 list for 2,300 encrypted typefaces, has a certain allure, but the unlocking keys for the font families are $70 to $200 each—at which point the real size of your commitment becomes apparent. (If you're going to use a lot of typefaces, it's cheaper to buy Adobe Font Folio, which is the full Adobe Type 1 library ready to use for about $7,200 street.) When you're ready to take this route, don't overlook the Agfa/Monotype Creative Alliance CD set; for $25 list, it includes over 6,000 fonts, and—if you take advantage of periodic promotional specials—the unlocking keys are $20 each or less.

When do you have to worry about hinting? Remember what hinting is; it's an arcane kind of math that lets blocky pixels build up attractive diagonal strokes and properly tapering stems and serifs. The more, and smaller, pixels that are assembled into a letter, the less of this adjustment is necessary. If your printer's resolution is 300x300 or 360x360 dpi, hinting matters a lot; if resolution is 600x600 or 720x720, it matters much less; and if resolution is 1200x1200 or better, hinting makes no difference.

Always install (or drag, or shortcut) new fonts into the Windows\Fonts folder, or you'll lose track of them. And remember that, in spite of Microsoft's blathering about unlimited Registry space, you can't install more than about 1,000 fonts on a single computer. In fact, if you install more than a few hundred, you'll take a performance hit that you may find unacceptable.

That 1,000-font limit, which is a rough guide rather than an exact value, arises because all scalable font names in the Windows 98 Registry are under the key HKLM\SOFTWARE\Microsoft\Windows\CurrentVersion\Fonts, and no single Registry key can contain more than 64K of name and value data. Microsoft's *Windows 95 Resource Kit* stated that unlimited fonts could be installed in 32-bit Windows, a canard that has been bouncing around ever since, and it isn't true and never was.

**Places to Read About (And Look At) Fonts.**   To begin with, you need to know the territory, and fascinating terrain it is. PostScript is one of the beloved languages of the Net—although we've never been sure whether that's because the results are so good, or because the programming is so gnarly. For a quick education in fonts, typography and page description, try the following:

`http://www.will-harris.com/type.htm`. *Typofile,* an e-zine by longtime word-processing and DTP guru Daniel Will-Harris.

`http://www.cs.indiana.edu/docproject/programming/postscript/post script.html`. Peter Weingartner's great *First Guide to PostScript,* about as gentle as any introduction to a page-description language could possibly be.

`http://jasper.ora.com/compfont/foundry.htm`. The Web's front end to the USENET newsgroup *comp.fonts.* Tip: `jasper.ora.com` can be hard to get through to, but keep trying.

`http://www-cgrl.cs.mcgill.ca/~luc/postscript.html`. Luc Devroye's incredibly useful page of links to PostScript resources on the Net.

`ftp://wilma.cs.brown.edu/pub/comp.lang.postscript/faq.txt`. The PostScript FAQ at Brown University, maintained by Jon Monsarrat, who generously provided us with the core of our Font Vendors list.

`http://jasper.ora.com/comp.fonts/internet-font-archive`. Plenty of fonts to download, even more to look at. Maintained by Norman Walsh.

`http://www.truetype.demon.co.uk`. The biggest and *best* TrueType site on the Web, and the only one that goes after TrueType with the comprehensiveness and granularity that seem routine in the world of PostScript. The history, the glossary, the spec, the math, the mysteries, and the future—Laurence Penney has done a sterling job of bringing everything together and forcing it to make sense.

`http://www.microsoft.com/typography/default.htm`. The Microsoft Typography site: a first-class resource for TrueType, okay for PostScript, and one of the few places on the Web (so far!) with info on OpenType and TrueType Open. Free fonts, and lots of Properties extensions for font editing and embedding. There's also a great tutorial on typography.

### Places to Buy Fonts (and Sometimes Get Them Free)

**Adobe Systems**
1585 Charleston Road, Mountain View, CA 94039
1 650-961-4400
`http://www.adobe.com`

- With the huge number of third-party Type 1 vendors, in recent years Adobe has specialized in creating its own "Adobe Originals"—high-quality fonts, some of which are their renditions of classic faces (Adobe Garamond) and some of their own devising (Stone, Utopia ...) Also, of course, many utilities including Type Manager Deluxe and Type Reunion.

- Adobe Type Basics CD: 65 fonts, $120 street. 35 of these fonts are the "PostScript standard set," so this CD is a good deal if you want to run PS fonts with ATM on a non-PostScript printer, less so if you already own the standard set in firmware.

**AGFA Compugraphic**
90 Industrial Way, Wilmington, MA 01887
1 800-424-TYPE (8973)
1 508-658-5600
`http://www.agfahome.com/agfatype/pstype/main.html`

- High quality, for the designer, comprehensive. For the Creative Alliance CD, see Monotype.

**Bear Rock Technologies Corporation**
4140 Mother Lode Drive, Suite 100, Shingle Springs, CA 95682-8038
1 800-232-7625 (toll free in continental US)
1 530-672-0244
`http://www.bearrock.com`

- Specialists in bar code fonts.

**Bitstream**
Athenaeum House, 215 First Street, Cambridge, MA 02142
1 800-522-3668 US and Canada
31 20 5200 300 Europe
1 617-497-6222 worldwide
`http://www.bitstream.com`

- Some of the least expensive high-quality TrueType fonts.

- Bitstream 500 Font CD: 500 PS Type 1 and TrueType fonts ($50 list)

- Bitstream TypeShop: the entire Bitstream Typeface Library in Type 1 format, over 1,000 fully hinted and kerned fonts, on an unlocked CD-ROM ($695 list)

- Bitstream Font Navigator 3 font organizer and manager ($40 list, trial downloadable)

### Callifonts

P.O. Box 224891, Dallas, TX 75222

1 972-504-8808

- Has a really nice-looking set of calligraphy typefaces. No e-presence that we can find.

### Casady and Greene

22734 Portola Drive, Salinas, CA 93908-1119

1 800-359-4920 in the US

1 408-484-9228

1 408-484-9218 FAX

`http://www.casadyg.com/c&g/products/flf/description.html`

- Fluent Laser Fonts and the Glasnost Cyrillic font in Type 1 and TrueType. Excellent Web site.

### Castcraft

3645 W. Chase Avenue, Skokie, IL 60076

1 888-89FONTS (893-6687)

`http://www.castcraft-software.com/homepage.html`

- The Optifont family of Type 1 and TrueType fonts.

### Castle Systems

Jason Castle, 1306 Lincoln Avenue, San Rafael, CA 94901-2105

1 415-459-6495

`castlesys@earthlink.net`

`http://home.earthlink.net/~castlesys`

- Cyrillic and nice display fonts, Type 1 and TrueType.

### Deniart Systems

P.O. Box 1074, Adelaide Station, Toronto, ON Canada M5C 2K5

1 800-725-9974 sales

1 416-941-0919

1 416-941-0948 FAX

`sales@deniart.com`

`http://www.deniart.com`

- Really wild display and symbol fonts, Type 1 and TrueType.

### DigitEyes TypeArt Library

1 800-BUY-TYPE (289-8973)

1 604-602-0331 outside North America

`http://www.typeart.com`

- Type 1 and TrueType. Amazing variety of styles; grunge, deco, glyphics, blackletter.

### DS Design

1157 Executive Circle, Suite D, Cary, NC 27511
1 800-745-4037 in US
1 919-319-1770
1 919-460-5983
`sales@dsdesign.com`
`http://www.dsdesign.com`

- Children's handwriting and art fonts. Also a *lot* of Web design and animation tools.

### Ecological Linguistics

P. O. Box 15156, Washington, D. C. 20003
1 202-546-5862

- Specializes in non-Roman alphabets.

### Emigre

4475 D Street, Sacramento, CA 95819
1 800-944 9021
1 916-451-4351 FAX
`http://www.emigre.com`

- Over 70 faces, all TrueType and Type 1 ATM compatible, almost all "must haves" for graphic designers. Call for a free catalog. *Note:* Emigre's license for TrueType fonts is restricted (see *Restricted license embedding* on page 311) and *does not permit* use in any document format that requires duplication of the font, such as Adobe PDF or Bitstream TrueDoc.

### The Font Company

12629 North Tatum Boulevard, Suite 210, Phoenix AZ 85032
1 800-442-FONT (3668)
1 602-998-9711

### FontHaus USA

1375 Kings Highway East, Fairfield CT 06430, USA
1 800-942-9110 toll-free
1 203-367-1993
1 203-367-1860 FAX
`http://www.fonthaus.com`

- A major "one-stop shop" and vendor for their own and other people's fonts; all Type 1, some TrueType

### Fonts Online (Alphabets Inc.)

`http://www.fontsonline.com/html/catalog.html`

- Type 1 and TrueType. Very cutting-edge.

**FontWorld, Inc.**
1746 Ocean Avenue, Brooklyn, NY 11230
1 718-252-1121
1 718-252-1120 FAX
`support@fontworld.com`
`http://www.fontworld.com`

• Multilanguage fonts, especially Middle Eastern.

**GarageFonts**
P.O. Box 3101, Del Mar, CA 92014
1 619-755-4761
1 619-755-4761 FAX
`http://www.garagefonts.com`

• Esoteric display faces.

**House Industries**
`http://www.houseind.com/showcase.html`

• Custom fonts and custom type.

**Image Club Graphics**
(a division of Adobe Systems)
833 Fourth Avenue Southwest, Suite 800, Calgary, AB, Canada T2P 3T5
1 800-661-9410 North American orders
1 800-387-9193 North American catalog requests
1 403-262-8008 Technical support and outside North America
`http://www.imageclub.com`

**International Typeface Corporation (ITC)**
228 East 45th Street, 12th Floor, New York, NY 10017
1 212-949-8072
1 212-949-8485 FAX
`info@itcfonts.com`
`http://www.esselte.com/itc/fonts/index.html`

• Type 1 and TrueType. Everything! A huge selection. *U&lc* magazine; articles online.

**Jack Yan & Associates**
*through* Precision Type, Inc.
47 Mall Drive, Commack, NY 11725
1 800 248-3668
1 516-543-5721 FAX
`http://www.jyanet.com/jyafonts.htm`

• A definite focus on elegance.

### Letraset USA/Esselte
40 Eisenhower Drive, Paramus, NJ 07652
1 800-343-TYPE (8973)
1 201-845-6100
`http://www.esselte.com/letraset/productshowcase/index.html`
- Fontek and DesignFont faces. Type 1 and TrueType.

### Linguists Software
P. O. Box 580, Edmonds, WA 98020-0580
1 206-775-1130
1 206-771-5911 FAX

- Specializes in non-Roman alphabets (Farsi, Greek, Hangul, Kanji, etc.).

### Mainz Workshop
Andrew Meit, 6500 Cypress Road, #309, Plantation, FL 33317
`http://members.aol.com/MainzWrks/private/ManzWrks.html`
- Calligraphic fonts with lots of character; Fontographer specialist.

### MindCandy Design
1712 E. Riverside, Suite 86, Austin, TX 78741
1 512-448-3955
1 512-448-3760 FAX
`http://www.mindcandy.com/typemenu.html`
- Esoteric display faces.

### Monotype Typography, Inc.
985 Busse Road, Elk Grove Village, IL 60007-2400
1 800-666-6897
1 847-718-0500
`sales@monotypeusa.com`
`http://www.monotypeusa.com`

- A biggie. Designed many of the fonts for Windows 98 and for the Microsoft TrueType Font Packs.
- Monotype/AGFA Creative Alliance CD 8.0: about 6000 fonts on two CD's, Type 1 and TrueType ($25 list) Fonts are locked, contact Monotype to purchase.
- Monotype Font Packs, 15 to 57 typefaces, $40 to $90 list.

### NIMX Foundry
Dallas, TX
1 800-688-NIMX (6469)
`http://members.aol.com/nimx001/index.html`
- Gutsy display faces and dingbats, Type 1 and TrueType.

### P22 Type Foundry

P. O. Box 770, West Side Station, Buffalo, NY 14213-0770

1 800-P22-5080

1 716-885-4482

`http://www.p22.com`

• Historically inspired display faces, good looking site. Type 1 and TrueType.

### Prototype-TypeO

2318 N. High, #9, Columbus, OH 43202

`http://www.prototype-typeo.com`

1 614-447-8103

1 614-447-8104 FAX

• Extremely out-there display faces.

### Page Studio Graphics

3175 North Price Road, # 1050, Chandler, AZ 85224

1 602-839-2763

`http://www.primenet.com/~pixymbol/psgcatal.html`

• Specialize in symbols fonts such as ASL, Braille, highway signs, Mac icons, keyboards, and others.

### Psy/Ops Type Foundry

481 Mississippi Street, San Francisco CA 94107-2927

1-888-PSY-FONE (779-3663)

1 415-285-8820 international & SF orders/inquiries

1 415-285-6069 FAX

`http://www.psyops.com/html/home.html`

• Text and display, alluring and polished.

### Ragnarok Press

POB 140333, Austin, TX 78714

1 800-797-TYPE (8973)

`http://www.ragnarokpress.com/scriptorium`

• Display, art, fantasy, archaic and arcane.

### Software Complement

8 Penn Avenue, Matamoras, PA 18336

1 717-491-2492

1 717-491-2443 FAX

`http://www.digitalid.com/company.html`

• Specializes in creating logo fonts and "digital identity."

### SynFonts

Synstelien Designs, 1338 North 120th Plaza, #9, Omaha, NE 68154

`http://www.synfonts.com/index.html`

- Display fonts, nice site.

### t-26 Digital Type Foundry

1110 North Milwaukee Avenue, Chicago, IL 60622-4017

1 888-T26-FONT (826-3668)

1 773-862-1201

1 773-862-1214 FAX

`t26font@aol.com`

`http://www.t26font.com/pages/intro.htm`

- Modern and postmodern fonts, Type 1 and TrueType, European character sets, painfully cool site.

### The Font Bureau, Inc.

326 A Street, Suite #6C, Boston, MA 02210

1 617-423-8770

1 617-423-8771 FAX

`info@fontbureau.com`

`http://www.fontbureau.com/cgi-bin/index.cgi`

- Comprehensive font library, Type 1 only.

### The Hoefler Type Foundry, Inc.

611 Broadway, Room 815, New York, NY 10012-2608

1 212-777-6640

1 212-777-6684 FAX

`info@typography.com`

`http://www.typography.com`

- Display, poster and text faces. Upscale.

### Tiro TypeWorks

PO Box 3346, Vancouver, BC, Canada V6B 3Y3

1 604-669-4884

`http://www.portal.ca/~tiro/`

- Historically inspired text faces. Elegant! Type 1 only.

### Treacyfaces/Headliners

`http://www.treacyfaces.com`

- Comprehensive selection, designer-oriented. Type 1 and TrueType.

**URW**

4 Manchester Street, Nashua, NH 03060

1 603-882-7445

- High-quality fonts at low prices. Creators of the top-of-the-line font creation and editing software called Ikarus.

**Y and Y Software**

45 Walden Street, Concord, MA 01742-2513

1 800-742-4059 North America only

1 978-371-3286

1 978-371-2004 FAX

`http://www.yandy.com`

- Type 1 fonts for TeX; Font Metric Manipulation Package for DOS with lots of interesting utilities; Lugaru's Epsilon TeX editor.

 *Note* on **Lucida**: The four Lucida fonts supplied with Windows 98 are part of a widely used and admired series, created by Bigelow & Holmes. These were sold as part of the Microsoft TrueType Font Packs, but have been hard to find since the Font Packs left retail channels. You can buy some of them from Y and Y, and some from Monotype, in Type 1; commercial TrueType versions should be available from Monotype by the time you read this. Meanwhile, if you still have the Microsoft Font Packs, hang on to them.

Many more font vendors exist. Look in magazines and other sources. Check the Usenet newsgroup comp.fonts. Look in *U&lc*, published by ITC, for long lists of vendors.

Thanks to Jon Monsarrat, `jonmon@alum.mit.edu`, maintainer of the PostScript FAQ at Brown University, for allowing us to incorporate the Font Vendors list from that document in this one.

# Summary

Whereas the developers of Windows 3.1 concentrated on improving computer output by introducing TrueType fonts, the developers of Windows 98 placed more emphasis on high-quality typography. Microsoft has also introduced easier and quicker ways to install fonts, print fonts, view fonts, and even remove them. Desktop publishing is as painless as it's ever been. The next chapter describes parallel improvements made to the printing process with Windows 98.

# 9

# Printing

If ever there was a dud prediction about the future of computing, it was the paperless office. A computer without a printer is like a full coffee pot without cups. Today you can buy a greater profusion of computer printers than ever before, from fold-up ink-jet portables that weigh a couple of pounds, to dry-ink color flatbeds that bring near-photographic quality to your desktop at home, to departmental workgroup printers that spit out documents as quickly as floor-standing copiers. Oh, and how many dots per inch would you like? 600? 720? 1200? 1440? Suddenly, everybody loves to print!

Recognizing the importance of printing, Microsoft streamlined the process with Windows 95, offering true background printing, two-way communication between the printer and the computer, automatic deferred printing, metafile spooling, Extended Capabilities Port (ECP) support, and Image Color Matching. Printer setup—especially network printer setup—was easier, faster, and more flexible with Windows 95 than it ever was with Windows 3.*x*.

Windows 98 takes everything that was new about printing in Windows 95, and puts extra muscle behind it. On the surface, you won't notice a lot of changes, aside from some polished details in the interface. But down below, where the bits churn and carouse, the Windows 98 printing model has been significantly beefed up. Guess how? With a big jolt of Windows NT! The upshot for you, and your digital printing press, will be added control over printing and more time than ever to get on with your other work.

The other side of the coin, naturally, is that increasing sophistication makes printing, and printers, a complicated subject. So, even though we've already discussed **Fonts** in a separate chapter, we've divided this chapter into halves. The first half talks about the ways Windows 98 manages printing and gets the dots onto the paper; the emphasis is on the many ways that *you* can configure, instruct, and refine Windows' printing capabilities. The second half discusses printer hardware more specifically, talks about how Windows controls each *type* of printer, and explains why you might want one printer rather than another.

With Windows 98 you control all print-related functions from one central location, the Printers folder.

# The Printers Folder

To open the folder, select **Start Menu\Settings\Printers** (which is a short-cut to the Printers folder). You can also open the Printers folder by double-clicking on the **Printers** icon on the Control Panel. The Printers folder (Figure 9.1) contains an icon for each printer installed on your system, both local and networked.

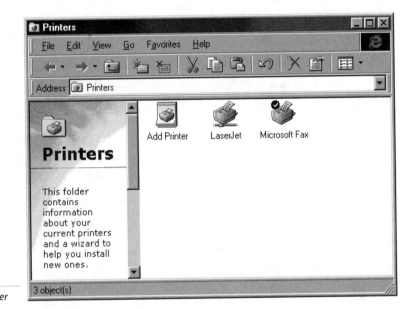

*The Printers folder*

You can view and change information in the Printers folder in several ways. First, no matter which view you have enabled, you can see which printer is the current default; the default printer's icon will include a white check mark on a small black circle.

This folder also contains the **Add Printer** icon; double-click on it to start the Add Printer Wizard, which helps you install a new printer.

## Changing Properties

Through the printer objects in the Printers folder, you can examine and change printer properties. Select a printer and choose **Properties** from the File menu, or click the right mouse button on a printer icon and choose **Properties** from the Context menu; the Properties sheet for the highlighted printer pops up. The contents of the tabs vary slightly depending on the printer model, but for a generic laser (an HP LaserJet 4P) there are six—

**General, Details, Paper, Graphics, Fonts,** and **Device Options**—and they include the following controls:

- **General** gives you a space for a comment (like "This is the printer in the supply room") and lets you choose a separator page, if the printer is set up for batch-mode network printing. The **Print Test Page** button is also here.

- **Details** are the port and spooling settings for the printer. You select a port to print to if the printer is connected to the local computer, or a network share to print to if the printer is connected to another computer on the network. (If the printer is attached to your computer which is also part of a network, you'll have an extra tab called Sharing so that you can set up network sharing for your local printer. See Chapter 10 for more about network shares.) You can add or delete a port, select from the installed drivers, or add any new driver from the Windows 98 driver list or an OEM diskette. Capture settings are important when you're using Windows 98 as the client side of a non-Windows network operating system, like Novell NetWare. Spool settings, which we'll get into in detail later, govern the location and format of data waiting to be sent to the printer.

- **Paper** lets you set form size, orientation, and source, number of copies, and (if the printer will control this) print density. No matter what kind of printer you have, there's an Unprintable Area... button, which lets you define the page margins on which the printer cannot or should not print; this is generally important for lasers but not important (i. e., set to all zeroes) for continuous-form printers. When you're finished with your run of nonstandard forms, click the Restore Defaults button to set the form back to Letter size, Portrait orientation and the default paper source.

**Windows always gives you a generous selection of paper sizes to choose from, but sooner or later, you'll be printing a party invitation on the odd paper from the fancy store.... At the right-hand end of the Paper Size dialog, past all the envelopes, there's a Custom icon that leads to a dialog called User-Defined Size. You can define a form size ranging from the mildly ludicrous—half an inch by an inch, say—to the maximum form size your printer is capable of, as defined in its minidriver.**

All User-Defined Sizes are measured in your choice of .01-inch or .1-millimeter steps; Unprintable Areas, in your choice of .001-inch or .01-millimeter steps. This is an improvement over Microsoft's original form size increment, the *twip*, which was $\frac{1}{1440}$ inch ... seriously.

- **Graphics** lets you pick graphic output resolution, dithering method (the way that modulated colors or grays are built up from dots), and the intensity, defaulting to halfway between the darkest and the lightest. You can also choose between raster and vector graphics for object printing, if your hardware will support both.

- **Fonts** lets you tell Windows that your printer has a supplementary font cartridge installed. The buttons in the TrueType fonts region let you specify what format your TrueType fonts are sent to the printer in; see Chapter 8 for a full explanation, because this gets complicated. If you have an Install Printer Fonts... button, it opens a dialog to let you specify which permanent (soft) fonts should be downloaded from the local disk into the printer's memory before printing begins. (This does *not* apply to ordinary printing from Windows with TrueType fonts, which are managed by the Windows universal driver.)

- **Device Options** is the dialog for every special feature not covered on the other tabs, which means it varies considerably from one printer model to the next. Look here for escape codes, extended character mapping, alternate codepages, resolution hinting, installed memory, page protection, memory tracking, etc.

Whenever you install a new printer, click on Device Options and examine the settings to make sure they really correspond to what's in the printer. Windows goes to great lengths to make features available; Device Options may give you access to printer features that you've never used because you didn't know how to get to them—or didn't know they existed! Conversely, if you have an older printer that isn't capable of Plug and Play bidirectional communication, you may have added memory or another paper tray, but Windows may not "see" it and won't use it. In that case, you'll need to update the appropriate Properties tab by hand, so Windows 98 knows about the change. You can explore your options by right-clicking on any dialog title and choosing **What's This?** for an explanation about that option. If you modify printer settings, print a test page to make sure you haven't inadvertently created an incompatibility or other type of problem. Above all, bear in mind that when you alter a printer's

## More Than One at Once?

Believe it or not (also known as "This sure surprised us") you can select and examine more than one printer at once. Click on the first printer, then—just the way you would with any other file object—hold down the Ctrl key and click on one, or more, additional printers. If you then pull down the **File** menu, you'll see that some options have vanished and some are grayed out, but several remain active ... and **Properties** is probably the most useful. If you select multiple printers and click Properties, the Properties sheets for all the printers will open, cascaded. This makes it easy to compare network printers, for example, and make sure that they're set up the same way, or in complementary ways. It could also be handy (although we shudder to think why) to select all printers with Ctrl A and **Purge Print Documents** from all your network queues with one click.

settings through its Properties sheet, you set its behavior with *every* application that prints to it. This may not be what you had in mind if, for example, you want to produce a particular effect in Microsoft Word. To configure a printer for (and from) one application, what you want to use is that application's Printer Setup command.

## Print Queues

Yet another way to unearth information about a printer is to double-click on its icon to open its print queue. The queue shows any files that are waiting to print or that you've printed offline. When there are files waiting to print, the print queue puts a small printer icon in the System Tray next to the clock … which, unfortunately, is nearly indistinguishable from the Microsoft Fax status icon. Finally, the print queue gives you the power to rearrange jobs before they print—handy if you want to advance your own documents in a network print queue when nobody else is looking. (For shame!)

## Print It Later!

Windows 98 supports deferred printing, whether you use an application designed for Windows 98, for older versions of Windows, or for DOS. You can get the document you're working on ready to print to a specific printer, and Windows 98 will store documents as printable files—containing all the information the particular printer needs to print the files—on your hard disk.

Go to **Start Menu\Printers** or **Control Panel\Printers.** Highlight the printer you'll want to print on later. Then do one of two things:

If the printer is your local printer, select **Pause Printing** from the File menu or the printer's right-click menu, before you start to print. If you send the job "to the printer" with the **File\Print** option, the dialog will remind you that the printer is paused, and the file will spool to disk. The next time your computer is docked or connected to your desktop printer, pull down the menu again, uncheck **Pause Printing,** and the spooled file will begin printing.

If the printer is a network printer, choose **Use Printer Offline** from the File menu or the printer's right-click menu. The printer's icon dims. Go through the normal steps of printing the document. The print job enters the queue; you can see it if you double-click on the dimmed icon. When you are ready to print, return to the printer's Properties menu and uncheck **Use Printer Offline**. The job begins printing automatically.

 **Pause Printing** and **Use Printer Offline** will never appear on the same menu. Don't confuse **Use Printer Offline** with **Work Offline,** which is an option about Web browsing. See Chapter 16, "Your Own Private Internet," but we do wonder why Microsoft thinks Web browsing is work. …

You can only use these options if spooling is enabled. Right-click on the printer, open the Properties sheet, select the **Details** tab, click the **Spool Settings** button, and in the dialog box, click **Spool print jobs so program finishes printing faster.** Make sure that **Spool data format** is set to EMF (Enhanced Metafile, see below) or your printing will be much slower.

## Bidirectional Communication

Windows 98 talks to your printer, and your printer can talk back—if it supports bidirectional printing. With bidirectional communication, Windows 98 can learn from the printer such things as what fonts are available, how much memory it has, and whether it needs paper. Because the printer can communicate with Windows 98, setup is easier, and if a problem arises, the printer can identify it and let Windows know about it. Any printer capable of bidirectional communication also supports Plug and Play, which makes installation and configuration a snap.

Unfortunately for the world's millions of printer users, no practical way exists to retrofit older printers with either Plug and Play or bidirectional communication. If you don't need a printer right now, you're out of luck until it's time to buy a new one. At that time you'll likely want to look for a model that incorporates both.

## Enhanced Metafile Spooling

Windows 98 quickly spools all print jobs, other than PostScript jobs, in a format called Enhanced Metafile (EMF). EMF data is produced by the GDI print interface, and is much denser and more efficient than data in the printer driver's so-called "raw" format; thus, the spooling takes less of your computer's processing power, so you don't feel sluggishness in your foreground tasks. After the EMF is created, Windows hands control of the foreground back to you.

EMF data goes to the 32-bit Windows *preemptive spooler.* This spooler, "compatible with"—meaning appropriated from—the Windows NT print subsystem, is one of the Windows 98 components clearly more advanced than its counterpart in Windows 95. While you're working away in foreground, the spooler is having an intense conversation with the printer driver, handing over chunks of EMF just as fast as the driver can process them—but no faster. The driver translates EMF to the printer's native language, feeds it smoothly out the port, and the print job reaches the printer more quickly, so printing can start sooner. It's like having two computers at once, one working with you while the other one supervises the print job.

Windows 98 uses the new 32-bit spooler for print jobs from DOS programs as well. DOS output isn't converted to EMF, so the process is slower than it would be from a Windows application, but it's much smoother than DOS printing from any previous version of Windows. If you regularly print from both DOS and Windows programs, you may notice that Windows 98 can arbitrate conflicts between DOS and Windows print queues, enabling them to spool data for the printer simultaneously without jamming the printer port.

## Extended Capabilities Port Support

An Extended Capabilities Port (ECP) can accommodate various I/O ranges and IRQ and DMA settings; you can tailor its parameters to meet your needs. An ECP improves printing speed, especially when the device at the other end is also ECP. Windows 98 provides ECP support, which you can set up with the Device Manager, providing Windows 98 has detected the ECP port on your computer. If the software has not detected the ECP port, you may be able to correct the problem by going into Control Panel and forcing the Add New Hardware Wizard to run a detection of Plug and Play devices.

## Image Color Matching

Color discrepancies are an aggravation in desktop publishing. Image Color Matching (ICM) does a lot to relieve that problem. Developed by a consortium of hardware vendors and standards setters (including Microsoft, Kodak, Apple, Sun, and Silicon Graphics), ICM enables applications to print the same colors as they display. It does this by establishing color profiles based on international color standards for software and hardware. The result is color that is consistent among applications, hardware devices, and platforms. The first version of ICM was released by Microsoft as part of Windows 95.

ICM 2.0, the Windows 98 version, has the earlier version as its core but has been improved and refined in several ways. The biggest news is that 2.0 is scalable; it provides a level of color support to Microsoft Word, for example, that a Word user will typically need, while for Adobe Photoshop it goes all-out. This lets the new version of ICM be more effective than the old one, with less overhead. 2.0 will also support a broader range of bitmap formats, color palettes, and color models. A lot of this is primarily of interest to programmers who write to the Windows graphics management API, but in due time the benefits will reach us all.

How can you take advantage of ICM? Buy software and hardware that conform to it. Because ICM is built into Windows 98, it's up to software and hardware vendors to make the standard meaningful. Many will, particularly manufacturers of scanners and color printers, following the lead of desktop publishing and graphics developers who incorporate one or more color-matching schemes.

# Printers and Memory

Just as Windows 98 itself benefits from RAM added to your computer, Windows printers can work faster if you install extra memory in them. For one thing, high-res printing is a lot like high-res video: the more dots you have on the page, the more memory it takes to hold them, whether your "page" is paper or glass.

Now, naturally there's a difference, or more than one. First, whereas with video a whole "page" arrives on the screen in about a seventieth of a second—depending on the refresh rate,—a typical laser printer has several seconds to write a full page. Second, a printer leaves the white space on the page alone, whereas video has to write every dot. Third, for reasons too technical to go into here, color on a printed page doesn't require the voluminous memory of a video screen's pixel depth.

### Table 9.1  Printer Memory Requirements

| Resolution | Memory per letter page, full coverage |
|------------|----------------------------------------|
| 300x300 dpi | .9MB |
| 360x360 dpi | 1.3MB |
| 600x600 dpi | 3.6MB |
| 720x720 dpi | 5.2MB |
| 1200x1200 dpi | 14.4MB |
| 1440x1440 dpi | 20.8MB |

On the other hand, as we've mentioned in Chapter 7, printers operate at much higher resolutions than monitors! You can easily figure out a printer's memory needs: if you have a 300 dpi printer and you print a square inch of solid black, that requires 300 x 300 = 90,000 bits = 11 Kb of RAM, almost exactly. As the resolution and the page size increase, these numbers go ballistic, as Table 9.1 demonstrates.

Now: Printers don't generally have to hold a full page—full framebuffer, if you like—in memory at any one time. But printers use RAM to store other things besides the page bitmap, like fonts and control code, and if your printer is generously endowed with RAM, printing will be substantially faster. Unless you have at least two megabytes of RAM in your laser printer, consider adding more. The Windows driver will cooperate by monitoring the amount of free memory in the printer, retaining and reusing fonts that have already been downloaded, as space allows; this also saves time.

Don't try to fake out your printer by overestimating the amount of installed memory; the printer driver could send too much data to the printer and provoke an Out of Memory error. Some people assume that all the installed memory is available, but this isn't always the case. Many printers use some of that installed memory to store macros, drivers, and system information, so not every byte is free. On the Properties sheet of some laser printers, the Device Options tab includes a field called **Reserved printer memory** that gives you this amount; otherwise, the printer's user manual can tell you how to determine the amount of available memory.

## Printers and Virtual Memory

Virtual memory is another useful trick—it's a way of managing a block of disk space to substitute for additional RAM in your printer. Manipulating virtual memory can speed up printing, free up memory for other Windows applications, and alleviate potential printer problems. Since the vast majority of printers equipped to manage virtual memory also happen to speak PostScript, we discuss this under "PostScript Virtual Memory," on page 384.

# Installing a Printer

For the old hands in the audience, we'll give a summary first.

## Adding a Printer

To install a printer, double-click on the Add Printer icon in the Printers folder. The Add Printer Wizard steps you through installation by asking simple questions, usually one per dialog box. The first dialog box (Figure 9.2) asks how your printer is connected (Local versus Network, defaulting to Local). Answer by clicking the appropriate button, then click **Next.**

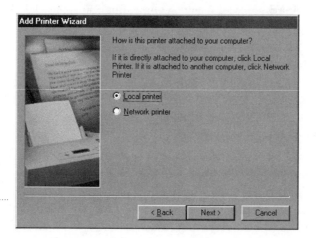

*Figure 9.2*

*Printer connection dialog*

In the next dialog, you choose the make of your printer from a list of manufacturers. Windows 98 includes drivers for over 1300 printers—we didn't count them, but that's what Microsoft says! When you click on the name of a

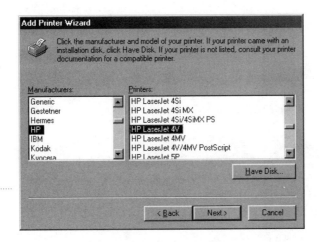

**Figure 9.3**

*Printer manufacturer dialog*

manufacturer at left, a list of the printers it manufactures appears at the right (Figure 9.3).

If you don't see the name of your printer, there are two possibilities; it's too old or it's too new. If it's old, all we can say is that the daisywheels and some of the less standard dot-matrix printers are among the missing, and we're sorry, but you need a new printer. If it's fresh out of the box, check to see whether the accessory kit includes a disk or a CD-ROM with a printer driver. If it does, click on the **Have Disk** button and follow the instructions. When you select the Have Disk option, Windows 98 asks you to insert one of your printer's disks or its CD-ROM during installation. The overwhelming likelihood, though, is that your printer has a Windows 98 driver ready and waiting.

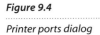

**Figure 9.4**

*Printer ports dialog*

The next dialog (Figure 9.4) asks you to select a port for your printer. Chances are that, unless you're connecting something like an Apple LaserWriter to your PC, your printer is a parallel printer, and it's connected to LPT1:, which is likely the only physical parallel port on your system. (The hardware interrupt that once allowed the connection of a second printer now belongs to your sound card.) If your printer supports Plug and Play, you skip this step altogether.

## Configuring a Port

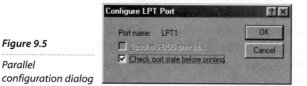

*Figure 9.5*

*Parallel configuration dialog*

In rare cases you'll want to configure the port. If you're connecting to a parallel port (Figure 9.5), **Spool MS-DOS print jobs** is grayed out here, but when you finish installing the printer you can check or uncheck it through the Details tab of the printer's Properties sheet. The other option is **Check port state before printing,** which is checked and we suggest you leave it that way. If you're connecting to a serial (COM) port (Figure 9.6), you open a port Properties sheet resembling that for a modem; just match its settings to the ones contained in your printer's manual. **Advanced...** lets you tweak your UART buffer states, if the UARTs in the ports are 16550A spec or better, which can improve performance ... and with a serial printer you want all the performance you can get. **Restore Defaults** is a fast way of setting port parameters to 9600, 8-N-1, and Xon/Xoff, which might be just what your printer wants. If you have any doubts about this process, see "Choosing a Printer Port," below.

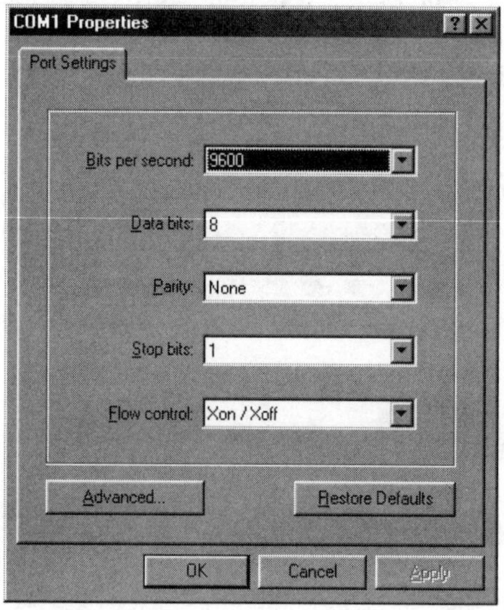

*Figure 9.6*

*Serial configuration dialog*

# Naming the Printer Object

Finally (Figure 9.7), you're invited to name your printer—the driver name is suggested, since the printer object has to have a name—and asked whether you want to designate it as the default printer. (When you name a printer, you can be creative or pragmatic; either add a little office levity, or make the name useful by including the location or resolution of the printer or the type of stationery it contains.) Click **Next,** print a test page if you like, and click **Finish**.

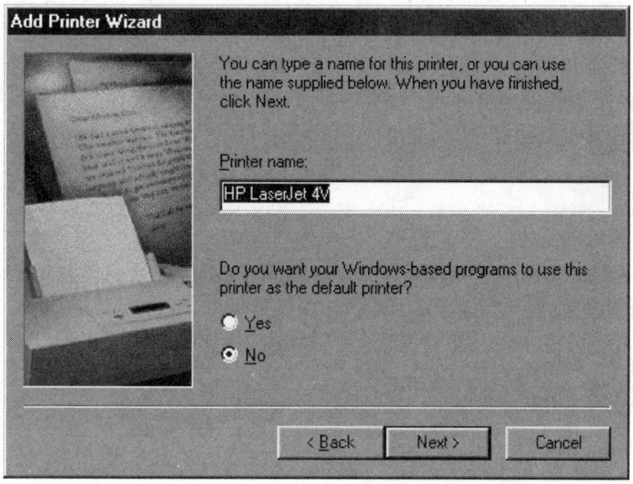

*Figure 9.7*

*Finishing printer setup*

## A Bit of Prevention

At this point Windows 98 may need to copy appropriate files from the distribution disk. If you're installing from a CD, make sure the disk is in the drive before you click **Next**. Windows 98—for that matter, Windows 95—has been known to choke if it can't copy printer files from the CD; if that happens, you may or may not have to restart your computer, but you'll certainly have to repeat the printer installation.

If Windows 98 already has a printer driver for the printer model you're installing, a dialog box asks whether you want to keep or replace the existing driver. This usually happens when you reinstall a printer driver or when you add a printer that uses the same driver as a previously installed printer. If you're not sure where the driver file is but you know it's somewhere on your computer or network, you can Browse the drives and directories connected to your system.

If you choose to replace a driver, be forewarned; all printers that use the driver you're replacing will switch to the new one as well.

HP LaserJet
4V

**Figure 9.8**

New printer icon

# Finishing and Testing

A new printer icon (Figure 9.8), labeled with the name you chose, appears in the Printers folder. (Notice the "printer-with-T-connector" icon identifying a network printer—which Windows knows because the parallel port we attached it to was a network share. See Chapter 10, "Networking.") You can print to it right away. Later in this chapter we give you some tricks to speed up your send and setup times.

When you install a printer, Windows 98 sets up the printer driver for the configuration it expects—that is, the printer's configuration when it came out of the box. That's why you should check out the new printer setup as soon as you install the driver, particularly if you've upgraded the printer in any way. To see how Windows set up the printer, open the Properties sheet by right-clicking on the new printer icon in the Printers folder, and choosing Properties from the Context menu (Figure 9.9).

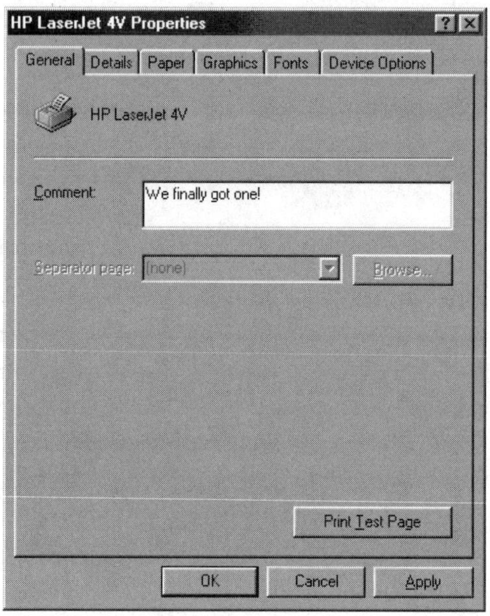

**Figure 9.9**

Printer Properties

If you've added memory to a printer, be sure to specify the installed amount of memory in the **Device Options** tab; Windows can't use memory it can't see. We'll discuss available options later in this chapter, but remember that you can always extract more details about an option by clicking with the right mouse button, then clicking on **What's This?**

# Choosing a Printer Port

These are the designations that Windows uses when it routes information to be printed:

- LPT1:, LPT2:, and LPT3: specify parallel ports.

- COM1:, COM2:, COM3:, and COM4: designate serial ports.

- EPT: refers to an EPT port.

- FILE: tells Windows not to use a port at all but to send output to a disk file. When you select this option, Windows prompts you for the name of an output file each time you print. If you install a printer to FILE: it will have a special icon of a printer and turning arrow pointing to a diskette.

Unless your PC is part of a network, your printer is probably connected to one of its LPT, or parallel, ports. Some printers, however, are connected to COM, or serial, ports, and others, such as the IBM Personal Page Printer, are connected to EPT ports through an add-in card and a driver (loaded by the CONFIG.SYS file) that sets up the port. If you're on a network, the method you use to connect to a printer depends on the network (see Chapter 10, "Networking").

**Parallel Ports.** The default settings for the parallel ports of most PC systems are shown in Table 9.2. (PC) means a standard computer with a PCI, VL or ISA bus and probably an Intel CPU; (PS/2) means an IBM PS/2 computer with a Microchannel bus.

## Table 9.2 Default Settings for Parallel Ports

| Port Name | Default Interrupt (IRQ) | Default I/O Address (PC) | Default I/O Address (PS/2) |
|-----------|-------------------------|--------------------------|----------------------------|
| LPT1 | 7 | 0378h | 03BCh |
| LPT2 | 5 | 0278h | 0378h |
| LPT3 | 7 | 03BCh | 0278h |

These are the parallel port addresses and ranges that Windows 98 installs as part of Basic Configuration 0000. For a full explanation of Basic Configurations and how they work, consult Chapter 15, "Tips, Tools, and Troubleshooting."

If you can't find a configuration that eliminates the conflict, click on Change Setting and reassign the port address range for the printer. Or change the addresses of the device that's causing the conflict with your printer. Check that device's documentation and change its I/O port addresses or interrupts accordingly.

**Serial Ports.** Printing through a serial port is considerably slower than printing through a parallel port. However, some printers, such as label and envelope printers, provide only serial interfaces. If your printer is connected to a serial port, the port should conform to the default I/O port and interrupt settings used by Windows 98. Although it's possible to change some of Windows' I/O port and interrupt settings, do so only if it's absolutely necessary. It's a better idea to configure your port to match Windows' default settings than to change Windows' settings to match an aberrant hardware configuration. In any case, Windows 98 usually assigns the best settings for your hardware, especially if the hardware is Plug and Play. Table 9.3 shows the default settings for the serial ports of both PCs and PS/2s. (PS/2s use IRQ3 for every serial port beyond COM1 because they can make the same IRQ work for more than one port—which is called *splitting an interrupt.* PCs can't do that.)

### Table 9.3  Default Settings for COM Ports

| Port Name | Default Interrupt (IRQ) | Default I/O Address (PC) | Default I/O Address (PS/2) |
|---|---|---|---|
| COM1 | 4 | 03F8h–03FFh | 03F8h–03FFh |
| COM2 | 3 | 02F8h–02FFh | 02F8h–02FFh |
| COM3 | 4 (PS/2: 3) | 03E8h–03EFh | 3220h–3227h |
| COM4 | 3 | 02E8h–02EFh | 3228h–322Fh |

These are the serial port addresses and ranges that Windows 98 installs as part of Basic Configuration 0000. For a full explanation of Basic Configurations and how they work, consult Chapter 15, "Tips, Tools, and Troubleshooting."

To view and change COM port settings, double-click on Control Panel\System and click on the **Device Manager** tab. Then choose **Ports,** select a device, and click on the **Properties** button (or double-click on the name of the device). To change settings, click on the **Port Settings** tab. This brings up the COM port controls that will be familiar from the Add New Printer Wizard. Check your printer's manual to see what port configuration the printer requires; the most common settings are 9,600 baud, no parity, 8 data bits, and 1 stop bit, with hardware handshaking.

Handshaking, also called flow control, modulates the flow of data to the printer and prevents the computer's print buffer from overflowing. Some serial printers use Xon/Xoff (software) handshaking, which is the Windows default, but most do it in hardware. In any case, don't disable the handshaking option for a serial printer, because print buffers can fill up quickly when you print from Windows 98. (Printer output with nowhere to go, like water from a half-blocked garden hose, can end up in odd places—like all over your screen.)

**Timeout Settings.**  Printer time-outs specify the amount of time that Windows will wait before telling you about a printer problem. To set time-outs, right-click on the icon of the desired printer in the Printers folder, then choose **Properties** from the Context menu. The Timeout settings (Figure 9.10) are at the bottom of the **Details** tab.

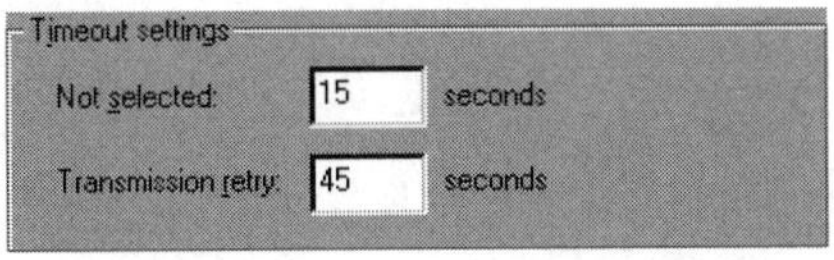

*Figure 9.10*

*Timeout settings*

You can only change these values on a local printer; in other words, you can only set them from the computer that the printer is physically attached to.

The first time-out option, **Not selected,** sets the number of seconds Windows 98 waits after sending data to a printer for the printer to respond that it is powered-on and able to print. After the specified number of seconds has elapsed with no response, a dialog box appears, telling you that the printer is offline. The default of 15 seconds allows plenty of time for the printer to wake up and respond. If you see that dialog box, it may indicate that your printer is improperly connected, turned off, or suffering from some technical malady. Most modern printers have small LCD or LED displays that report error codes, so at a time like this, look for one.

The second time-out setting, **Transmission retry,** specifies the number of seconds that the printer can work without notifying Windows that it's finished processing data that has been sent to it. After this amount of time elapses with no response, you see a dialog box declaring that your printer cannot accept any more data. The default settings are 90 seconds for PostScript printers and 45 seconds for all others, and they're sufficient unless you print a complex document that contains many graphics and different typefaces. In that case, the printer can take significantly longer to process each chunk of information; this is particularly true for PostScript printers, which may require a **Transmission retry** setting of several hundred seconds to prevent unnecessary warning messages from appearing on your screen.

Bear in mind, though, that a PostScript printer has two *other* adjustable timeouts on the PostScript tab of its Properties sheet, called *Job timeout* and *Wait timeout.* Refer to the definitions on page 376.

Unless you print complex PostScript graphics, you can probably leave the Timeout settings alone, particularly if your printer supports bidirectional communications. If either of the two dialogs described here appears often, experiment with the configuration of other printer settings—such as memory and font types—before adjusting the Timeout settings.

**When You Need More Ports.**  PCs usually come equipped with only one parallel port, LPT1:, and two serial ports, COM1: and COM2:. Most PC systems can accommodate up to three parallel ports and four serial ports, but these days, physical accommodation is not the issue—not compared to the dire shortage of IRQs, also called *hardware interrupts* or *interrupt request lines* (for which "IRQ" is an acronym, sort of). In the hardwired scheme of things, you'll find that LPT1: is IRQ7, COM1: is IRQ4, and COM2: is IRQ3— assignments that date from the original, eight-bit IBM PC architecture of 1981. Then other greedy bus riders, like your sound card, network adapter, floppy drive, and keyboard, get into the act, and before you know it, a free IRQ is about as likely as a free hundred-dollar bill.

However, if you need more—for example, so you can connect multiple local printers or serial devices such as modems and mice—you can purchase add-in cards that supply extra ports. These can take some calling around to find, but they certainly don't cost a lot.

- **Extra parallel ports**: Koutech Systems makes two add-in cards with bidirectional parallel ports, the KW-508F-1 with one port for about $24, and the KW-508F-2 with two ports for about $30, street. These can be set to any port from LPT1: through LPT6: (!) and to IRQ3, 4, 5, 7, 9, 10, 11, 12, or 15. This sounds like a lifesaver if you have another parallel device besides your printer, like an external tape backup drive or Iomega Zip drive. If you have trouble finding a vendor (we did) call Koutech at 1 562 699-5340.

- **Extra serial port**: We've mentioned the Com-5 Card by Mouse Systems, which gives you one serial port on IRQ2, 3, 4, 5, 7, 10, 11, 12, or 15. This card is about $30 street, and seems to be widely available, but you can call Mouse Systems at 1 510-656-1117 for a vendor name. If you need more than one more serial port, Koutech makes cards with two (their KW-509S-2) or four (their KW-535-4) but these, unlike the Mouse Systems card, aren't configurable beyond COM4.

All you need to know now is which ports and which IRQs are available on your system, and you can find that out with the Device Manager or the Microsoft System Information Utility, described in Chapter 16. If you have no available IRQs—"Gee," Kip says scratching his chin, "all I've got left is IRQ9,"—you might seriously consider getting a second computer, a couple of cheap Ethernet adapters and a crossover cable.

**Installing a Printer Twice.** Even if you have only one printer, you may want to install it more than once. Additional configurations can be used for the same printer when you want it to behave differently depending on what you send to it. This is useful if your printer has more than one personality (for example, a Hewlett-Packard printer that can be either a PCL or a PostScript printer). If you print mostly in portrait mode from your word processor and in landscape mode from your spreadsheet, for example, you can set up two printer icons—one for each orientation—so that you never have to change the settings.

You could also add your Hewlett-Packard LaserJet twice to the Printers folder, configuring it once for LPT1 and the second time to send output to a disk file. This trick is handy when you use a printer connected to another system. Your "second" printer could be a friend's that has better resolution or duplexing capabilities, or it could be at a service bureau, where you can get higher-resolution output, color, negatives, or other qualities you can't squeeze out of your own desktop printer.

To install a printer a second time, repeat the steps of the first installation but change the appropriate elements of the configuration, and give the printer a different name when you're prompted for it. Because the drivers will have been installed already, you shouldn't be prompted to insert any disks.

## Removing a Printer

To delete a printer, open the Printers folder, select the icon of the printer to be banished, and choose Delete from the File menu. You can also right-click on the icon and choose Delete from the Context menu. We wish everything about Windows was this easy.

*Figure 9.11*

*Default printer deletion dialog*

If you delete the default printer, you won't be asked for confirmation, but you will be notified afterwards (Figure 9.11).

If the printer you delete required support files that nothing else on your system uses, you'll be asked if you want to remove them (Figure 9.12).

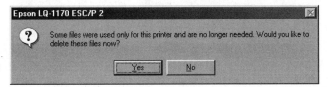

*Figure 9.12*

*Support file deletion dialog*

# Printing from Windows Applications

With most Windows programs, you print a document directly from the File menu or by clicking on a Print button. Some programs include a separate Print menu, but most install the Print command on the File menu. Consequently, for the vast majority of Windows applications, the keyboard sequences [Alt][F],[P] and [Ctrl][P] are still the easiest ways to begin a print job when you're inside the document you want to print.

However, if the document isn't open, you can print it by dragging it either onto a shortcut to your printer or onto a printer icon in the Printers folder; you can also use the Send To command on the Context menu. (The Context menu pops up when you click with the right mouse button on just about anything in the Explorer or My Computer. Shortcuts to printers and other destinations can be added to the Send To menu by dropping them into the Send To folder inside the Windows folder.) You can send multiple documents to the printer with either drag and drop or the Send To command.

## Appearance

The appearance of a printed document is affected by these factors:

- The fonts and formatting options you choose from within an application.

- The ability of your printer to print the fonts and formats you've chosen.

- The use of special drivers to achieve certain kinds of output. For example, many presentation graphics packages use a printer driver that redirects graphics to a modem for transmission to a slide service bureau. Fax modem software often works in a similar way; instead of sending a document to a printer, it redirects the output—fonts, graphics, and all—to a fax modem.

TrueType fonts (or PostScript fonts installed on your system with Adobe Type Manager) provide the best match between the typeface you see on the screen and the printed version. If you don't use TrueType, it may take some tweaking to print documents the way you want them to look.

Most Windows applications provide a Printer Setup command on the File menu, which lets you choose a printer and configure that printer's driver. The command and its location vary from application to application. You might find Printer Setup on the File menu, as part of the Print command (click on Options or Printers), or under Page Setup.

Changing the printer is meant to be as easy as changing a TV channel, and on the surface it is. When you choose Printer Setup, you see a list of all installed printers. Select a printer from the list, and Windows designates it as your active printer. The catch is that that printer becomes the default printer for all applications. Switching printers is so easy, though, that it takes little effort to do so on a regular basis.

# Printing from DOS Applications

DOS applications used to bypass Windows at printing time, even when you ran the DOS programs from within Windows. When you printed from WordPerfect for DOS inside a Windows session, for example, the job would be sent directly to the printer port that you selected from WordPerfect.

Windows 98, however, controls the printer ports for both Windows and DOS applications, even though DOS applications can't take advantage of all the printing features offered by Windows 98. An important exception is the Windows 32-bit spooler and print queue, which DOS programs take advantage of to eliminate potential conflicts with Windows programs.

If you have trouble printing from a DOS application, make sure it works with the type of printer you are using. You need to select the printer (and possibly install a printer driver for the printer) from the DOS application; DOS programs do not respond to choices made in Windows.

To allow a DOS document to take advantage of Windows fonts, you must transfer it to a Windows application. Once it's there, the document can be reformatted in one of these three ways:

- Many Windows applications, such as Microsoft Word, Corel WordPerfect, and Lotus Ami Pro, can read the file formats of DOS word-processing applications, including formatting commands for items such as boldface and page margins. If you cannot directly open a document created by a DOS program, you may be able to go back into the DOS program and save the document in another format that your Windows word processor understands, such as RTF (Microsoft's Rich Text format).

- The next-best choice is to save your DOS document as a text-only file, then open it in the handiest Windows text editor. For example, WordPad— or even the 16-bit Write applet, if you still have that—can open plain text files and perform considerable formatting.

- If all else fails, express yourself vividly, then resort to cutting and pasting information from a DOS application in a Windows DOS box into a

Windows application. This option requires the most fussing and reformatting, but it may be your only choice if your DOS application doesn't let you save "text only" or save text at all. This method, tedious as it certainly is, can transport virtually anything from a DOS application into a Windows application for formatting and printing. (For more information about how DOS applications behave in Windows, see Chapter 15.)

Windows 98 includes the Print Troubleshooter, a Help section for those all-too-frequent printing problems. Click on a specific question, click on a possible answer, and hopefully you'll find a solution. It's worth a try and is more convenient than calling Technical Support.

Windows 98 makes network printing—network *anything*—so simple that you might want to switch to it for that reason alone. If you've got a small office and you're looking at the cost of installing Windows 98, balance that against the savings of sharing one workgroup printer, one scanner, and one tape backup across the whole network.

Because we don't like to split topics across chapters, which would make you jump all over the place hunting for things, we discuss network printing in Chapter 10, "Networking."

# Managing Print Queues

A print queue monitors all current print jobs sent to a given printer and handles requests for "emergency" changes in print order. If you control numerous output scenarios (multiple printers, several stationery types, people who think their bad planning constitutes a crisis worthy of your attention), you'll be happy to have control over the print queue.

Let's take an insane, but typical, situation. You issue three print orders: WordPad is to print a draft document on a 24-pin printer! Paintbrush is to send a drawing to a LaserJet! Excel is to print a graph on a plotter! You can execute all those operations simultaneously and let the Windows GDI and preemptive spooler work for a living while you knock off a quick game of FreeCell. Everything will print; that's what computers are for.

## Queue Contents

You can view any printer's queue by double-clicking on that printer's icon in the Printers folder. A small printer icon near the right side of the Taskbar indicates an active print queue; double-click on the icon to see what's in the queue (Figure 9.13).

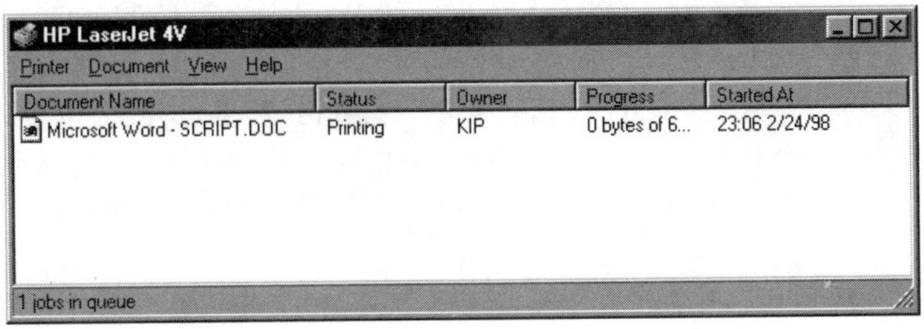

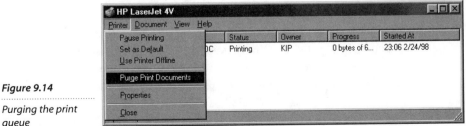

**Figure 9.13**

*An active print queue*

Each entry in the print queue contains the title of a print job (usually the name of the application and the document being printed), the size of the file in kilobytes, the percentage of the file that has been printed (if it's still printing), the "owner" of the job, and the time and date it was sent to print. Jobs are listed in the order in which they will be printed.

You can change the order of files in a queue except for the first file listed (unless that printing job has not yet commenced). To make a change, select the item, drag it to a new position in the list, and release the mouse button. It's easy to imagine a use for this feature: suppose your boss is leaving for the airport and suddenly needs a copy of the document at the end of the list.

## Pausing and Purging Jobs

From the menus in the Printers window you can pause or cancel a particular print job or purge all print jobs. Use the following commands from the Printer menu to change all print jobs in the queue globally:

- **Pause Printing.** Temporarily stops all print jobs.

- **Purge Print Documents.** Removes all jobs from the queue permanently (Figure 9.14).

**Figure 9.14**

*Purging the print queue*

To control the print queue on a per-job basis, use the following commands from the Document menu:

- **Pause Printing.** Temporarily keeps a document from printing.

- **Cancel Printing.** Makes that print job go away.

A check mark next to the appropriate Pause Printing command indicates that either a job or an entire queue is paused. When you want printing to resume, click again on the command to clear the check mark.

 Note that you can use the Pause Printing command only if spooling is enabled on your computer. For more on how to enable spooling, see the section later in this chapter called **Changing Print Speed.**

Whether you can pause a print job on a network print queue depends on the network software and the control it offers to the individual workstation. Some network software builds in limits so that individuals can't mess with another user's files; as a result the network runs more smoothly. See Chapter 10, "Networking."

If you delete a print job that is in the middle of printing a graphic, you may need to reset your printer or toggle it off and on. Otherwise the printer can get hung up waiting for an End of File command that never arrives.

## Spool Files

The printing process creates temporary spool files. In Windows 98, creation and naming isn't always straightforward, but the process is carried out behind the scenes; you don't have to get involved. Here's how it works: When you print using Enhanced Metafile spooling (which is the default), .TMP files are created. Those files do not go to the printer; instead, they are sent to your system, telling it to process the information and keep it away from your immediate work space. This enables you to return to work immediately. Later, the same information goes into a spool, or .SPL, file, which is sent to and understood by the printer. In addition, another file, called a shadow file (.SHD), keeps a tracking record of the spooling process. If you send RAW data to the printer, you get only .SPL files, no temporary or shadow files.

Spool files are located in the **Windows\spool\Printers** folder. Temporary files are usually located in the **\Temp** subdirectory of the main Windows folder.

Normally Windows 98 deletes spool and temporary files (but not shadow files) automatically after they have been printed. If your system crashes or is shut down in the middle of a print job, however, you may wind up with leftover temporary files. If this happens, check for the leftover files and delete them. If you want to print them first, copy them to your printer port. For example, if your printer is connected to LPT1, go to a DOS prompt (go to the Start button, choose Programs, and click on MS-DOS Prompt) and type

```
copy c:\win98\temp\~spl????.tmp lpt1:
```

This assumes that the Temp variable specifies the `C:\Win98\Temp` directory.

### Trash In the Shadows

When you print using EMF format (the default) and the print spooler is set to **Start printing after first page is spooled** (also the default) .SHD files are only deleted when you restart Windows 98. If you rarely reboot your computer (also the default) and you print a lot, you could pile up enough of this trash to have an impact on your disk space—and in a very out-of-the-way place.

You could reboot your computer every couple of days, and that's not a bad idea, since it gives you nice fresh memory allocation. You can also set the spooler option to **Start printing after last page is spooled**, which makes printing take a bit longer, but means that a print job's .SHD file gets deleted as soon as the last of the job leaves the spooler.

# Changing Print Speed

At long last Windows isn't just faking it; it's actually multitasking. Multitasking has become a reality for Windows 98, unless you have some old drivers that aren't compatible with this marvelous feature. (So remove those drivers and find some that run in protected mode!)

Processing and printing speeds partially depend on your setup. For example, if your computer spools to a network server, it makes a difference whether that server is running Windows 98 or some other software. A server running Windows 98 or Windows NT usually provides networked users with good performance on their own computers while printing is taking place, because the server handles most of the processing needed for printing. On the other hand, if the server uses NetWare, much of the processing happens before it goes to the network—that is, on your own computer.

Other factors can affect print speed as well. To explore your options, open the Printers window, select your favorite printer, and choose **Properties** from the File menu. Click first on the **Details** tab and then on **Spool Settings,** and some choices appear.

Select **Spool print jobs so program finishes printing faster** if it's your priority to return to your next task within seconds. Whether you choose **Start printing after last page is spooled** or **Start printing after first page is spooled** depends on how fast you want to get back to work and how much disk space you can devote to the process; the quicker, the more disk space. By choosing **Print directly to the printer** you'll get pages through the printer as quickly as possible, but until printing is complete, your foreground application will run slowly—if at all. Table 9.4 sums up your choices.

### Table 9.4  Printer Output Options

| Spooling option: | Impact on foreground | Impact on disk space | Impact on disk duration | Data type |
|---|---|---|---|---|
| **Spool print jobs...: Start printing after last page is spooled** | Minimum | Maximum (whole job spooled before printing) | Shorter (files deleted at end of job) | EMF or RAW |
| **Spool print jobs...: Start printing after first page is spooled** | Medium | Medium (job goes to printer as spooling continues) | Longer (some files persist till Windows restarts) | EMF preferable |
| **Print directly to the printer** | Maximum | None | None | RAW |

In practice, there are two things to remember. Unless you're printing big documents with loads of graphics, the difference in time between **Start...after first page** and **Start...after last page** is negligible. And if you're tight enough on disk space to worry about Windows spool files, then you should clean off your disk or get a bigger one, because your Windows performance and flexibility is taking a hit in all sorts of other ways too.

If you want to disable Enhanced Metafile spooling for a particular printer, go to the printer's Properties sheet, click the Details tab, then click on Spool Settings. Choose RAW from the **Spool data format** drop-down list to disable EMF spooling, then click on OK. (You can also set data type to RAW by clicking **Print directly to the printer** and clicking on OK, but that will bypass the spooler and force your computer to manage the print queue in the foreground.) The requirement for raw printer output, prevalent in the days of 16-bit Windows printer drivers, has almost vanished today; so long as the Windows 98 universal driver will provide 32-bit support to your printer, or you can dig up the right Windows 98 or 95 .INF file, you'll never remotely need to worry about this.

# Right On the Dot

When you first install Windows 98, the Add Printer Setup wizard asks you to enter the name of the printer or printers connected to your system, either directly or across a network. At that point Windows 98 installs the appropriate driver for each device.

The proper driver, meaning the proper set of routines to communicate between the printer and Windows, implements the concept of WYSIWYG—meaning that, *in theory,* the images that emerge from the printer are identical to those that you create on a monitor. But with present-day hardware you can't take this too literally. To begin with, although color printers are improving in quality while their price drops, most of the computers running Windows 98 and 95 are connected to color monitors and black-and-white printers. The computer magazines on the newsstands may be trumpeting "Don't ever buy another black-and-white printer," but we're talking about what you're printing on today, not what you're lusting for in your next round of upgrades.

More to the point, sadly, is that hundreds of excellent printers on the market now will print at a resolution, and in sizes, that monitors can't touch. Here's why: Screens are the wrong shape. The visible area of a high-end 15" monitor is just short of eight and a half inches *high* and about eleven and a quarter inches *wide.* It would do a passable job of displaying a full, letter-size page … *if* you turned it sideways. And monitors that can turn sideways, while they offer tremendous advantages, have never become popular enough to sell side by side with "regular" monitors. So, you ain't got the space.

Worse yet is the problem of resolution. Say you're running Windows at 800x600 on that fifteen-inch monitor, which means that you're spreading 800 pixels over that same eleven and a quarter inches. That's 71 pixels to the inch, 71 dpi, a dot pitch that a nine-pin dot-matrix printer could beat in the early eighties. "Hold on," you say, "I'll jack up the resolution." Fine; switch to 1,024x768 on a 15" monitor and you're at 91 dpi. Not even as good as a fax. You want to go higher? Can you still read your icon titles? Is your video card starting to screech? You ain't got the resolution either. (Back in the days when laser printers boasted of 300 dots per inch, Xerox made a prototype monitor with 300-dot-per-inch resolution—but not at a price that you or I wanted to pay.)

A monitor is just that—a *monitor,* a way of keeping track of what's going on. It offers only a rough preview of what will finally appear on the printed page. And WYSIWYG should be called YWYMLTG—You Wish Your Monitor Looked This Good.

Sigh!!

# Printer Drivers, Continued

Once your printer is successfully installed, you shouldn't have to deal with printer drivers, unless you change a printer's setup options. Everything that your printer's driver will do is matched by a control on your Printer Properties sheet; set the Properties, you set the driver. Having skimmed Properties settings in the summary above, we will now dig deep and come up with fistfuls of mesmerizing detail. Right-click on the Printer icon and choose Properties from the Context menu.

We're not about to cover every Properties setting of every printer make and model, because this isn't *The Windows 98 Printer Bible.* (If that's a book you'd like to see, though, tell us so in this book's area at `http://www.peachpit.com`, or send e-mail to our editors at `tell@peachpit.com`.) The layout of the Printer Properties sheet varies, but you still see many of the same controls from one driver to the next. Printer Properties sheets offer the selections in Table 9.5.

### *Comply At Your Peril*

The Add Printer Wizard dialog and the Details\New Driver\Select Device dialog are almost the same, but not quite. The onscreen instructions for the Select Device dialog begin this way:

**Click the Printer that matches your hardware, and then click OK. If you don't know which model you have, click OK.**

One could be forgiven for thinking that this means "If you don't know both the manufacturer and model of the printer you're installing, pick the manufacturer, click OK, and let Windows take care of the rest." Hah! We're not sure what Microsoft was trying to say here, but if you follow those instructions, Windows simply installs the driver for the model at the top of the model list for the manufacturer you selected. Unless that was what you wanted (unlikely) you have to specify manufacturer and model too, so make sure you know which model you have, even if that involves poking around your printer manufacturer's Web site.

## Table 9.5  Printer Properties

| Tab | Dialog | Explanation |
|---|---|---|
| **Color Management (Color printers)** | | |
| | Profiles... | ICM (Image Color Matching) stores its parameters in files called Profiles. To set up a printer according to a different set of color priorities, simply open the Color Management tab and click on a different Profile. Unfortunately, ICM 2.0 didn't go the whole route and let us match a monitor and a printer by setting them to the same Profile file; if you try to do that, you get a grouchy warning |
| **Details** | | |
| | Print to port | Tells the printer which port to send output to. Can be a physical port, a network share, a phantom port for fax output, or a file |
| | Add port | Adds any of the above to the list of available ports |
| | Delete port | Deletes any of the above from the list of available ports. This attempts to delete the port from the global list, not just the list for a particular printer; if the port is in use by any device, you won't be able to delete it |
| | Print using driver | Selects a driver for this printer from the list of all available installed drivers. This is actually of limited use, since one printer is unlikely to run with the driver for another one; what you probably need is the button next to it |
| | New driver | Opens a Select Device dialog that looks, and works, a lot like the Add Printer Wizard—but the instructions are crucially different; see "Danger Zone" below. Once you select the printer, click OK if the driver is on the Windows CD, or Have Disk if you have a driver diskette |
| | Capture port | Connects a logical, not physical, printer port to a capturing (spooling) device on a network. *Device* can only be LPT1: through LPT9: and can't conflict with any physical parallel port on the computer. *Path* has to be a computer or sharename. Refer to the sections on Novell net works in the Windows 98 Resource Kit |
| | End capture | Stops network spooling; uncouples the logical port from the capturing device |
| | Timeout settings | See "Timeout Settings," page 359. If one or both of these is grayed out, your printer has fixed timeout settings |
| | Spool settings | See "Changing Print Speed," page 367 |
| **Details (parallel printer)** | | |
| | Port settings | *Spool MS-DOS print jobs* lets you select or deselect the Windows print spooler when you print from DOS applications; our advice is to leave this checked unless it causes problems. Either way, the data type will be RAW. *Check port state before printing* tells Windows to check for Port Ready signal before it starts sending data |

**Table 9.5** *(continued)*

| Tab | Dialog | Explanation |
|---|---|---|
| **Details (serial printer)** | | |
| | Port settings | Set the baud rate, data word, parity, stop bit, and handshaking. You'll need the printer manual for this, and see "Serial Ports" on page 358 |
| **Device Options (Dot matrix driver)** | | |
| | Print quality | Proportion of dot dithering (overstruck dots) usually given as high, medium or low. Dot overstriking gives darker print, smoother edges and slower printing. See **Graphics\Resolution** |
| **Device Options (Generic driver)** | | |
| | Printer model | Enter the name of the printer. With this sheet and the manual you can define a minidriver from scratch, although probably not with every feature of the hardware |
| | Begin job | Enter the escape code that begins the print job (sometimes called Reset or Start Print). To edit this and the following three fields, see "Escape Codes" in Appendix H |
| | End job | Enter the escape code that ends the print job (sometimes called Job Separator) |
| | Paper size | Enter the escape code for paper size (sometimes two codes, height and width) |
| | Paper source | Enter the escape code for the appropriate paper feed device, e. g. tractor or sheet feeder— but you can only use one |
| | Mapping: On screen | Shows the equivalency between the 8-bit ASCII character code (0 to 255) and the matching character in the Windows code page. To edit this and the next field, see "Extended Character Mapping" in Appendix G |
| | Mapping: On printer | Shows the equivalency between the highlighted character in the Windows code page and the character that will be printed. You can edit this field |
| | Mapping: Character mapping | Lets you choose mapping. *TTY custom* lets you define mapping for characters with ASCII codes between 128 (80 hex) and 255 (FF hex). You can also choose a *code page*, or mapping table maintained in background by your system; see "Code Pages" in Appendix G, or the Windows 98 Resource Kit |
| | Add new model | Define an additional printer through this Properties sheet. You *can* run two or more printers through the same Device Options tab dialog, but remember that they'll be connected to the same port. It would be nice to define multiple Generic printers and stick with one icon per printer, but see "You Can't Have Twins" in Appendix G |
| | Remove current model | Remove this printer. |

## Table 9.5 (continued)

| Tab | Dialog | Explanation |
|---|---|---|
| **Device Options (Laser driver)** | | |
| | Installable options | Settings for vendor-installed hardware options like extra trays, envelope feeders, duplexing; virtual memory settings, if available, may be here too—see "Printers and Virtual Memory" later in this chapter. Hardware memory is more likely to be in **Printer memory** |
| | Print quality | Controls dot dithering or dot anti-aliasing, which produces smoother edges on fonts and solid areas of graphics. Hewlett-Packard calls this RET (Resolution Enhancement Technology); IBM/Lexmark calls it PQET (Print Quality Enhancement Technology) |
| | Print density | Toner coverage per unit area. Usually given as light, medium or dark |
| | Printer features | If parameters like RET, grayscaling, and toner coverage aren't set in **Print quality** or **Print density,** they'll be set here |
| | Reserved printer memory | Memory excluded from printer data area and reserved for macros or other user-defined controls |
| | Page protection | Reserves memory, usually one page, as an output buffer for printing complex documents; generally requires additional hardware memory, and is grayed out unless the printer has enough |
| | Printer memory | Installed hardware memory in KB or MB. On some printers, called **Available printer memory** |
| | Printer memory tracking | The printer driver's comparison of available printer memory with the estimated amount needed to print the next document in the queue. *Conservative* tracking will allow the document to be printed if enough printer memory is definitely available, but may wrongly prevent a document from being printed. *Aggressive* tracking will allow the document to be printed if enough printer memory *may* be available, but may also permit printer overflow |
| **Fonts** | | |
| | Cartridges | Highlight the cartridge or cartridges that are installed in your printer's cartridge slot/s, to make their fonts available to applications |
| | Install Printer Fonts... | Copy soft fonts of various types into an HP (or compatible) laser printer's memory. *This is not the Windows font installer and it has nothing to do with TrueType.* See "Installing HP Fonts" in Chapter 8 |
| | TrueType fonts | Lets you choose to download TrueType fonts as outlines (vector fonts) or bitmaps (raster fonts) or print them as graphics. For the advantages of each, see "TrueType Fonts" in Chapter 8 |
| (Generic driver) | Font codes | Enter the escape codes that select a font pitch, or turn a character attribute on and off. To edit the fields on this tab, see Appendix G |

## Table 9.5  (continued)

| Tab | Dialog | Explanation |
| --- | --- | --- |
| **Fonts**—continued | | |
| (PostScript printers) | TrueType fonts | Set priority for, and substitution in, the relationships between built-in (printer firmware) fonts and TrueType fonts. See "PostScript Printer: Fonts Tab" below |
| **General** | | |
| | Comment | Anything special about this printer, like where it is, what it's connected to, or what kind of paper stock it's supposed to be loaded with. Any Comment you enter here appears in the Comment column of Explorer Details View |
| | Print test page | Prints a test page |
| (local printers only) | Separator page | Prints identifying pages, sometimes called "banner pages," between documents; these can include the name of the user, the name of the document, or other information. A *full* separator is a graphical page and can include any Windows metafile (.WMF) graphic selected with the **Browse...** button. A *simple* separator is a page of plain text |
| **Graphics** | | |
| | Dithering | Patterning that overlaps dots to create colors (or grays) between the colors (or grays) in the hardware palette. Click *None* to turn dithering off, *Fine* at resolutions less than 300 dpi, *Coarse* at resolutions 300 dpi or higher, *Line art* if your graphic has sharp edges, or *Error diffusion* if your graphic has soft edges (e.g. a photograph) |
| | Intensity | Darkness in graphics, analogous to **Print density.** The scale from 0 (darkest) to 200 (lightest) seems backwards |
| | Mode | Choose between sending graphics elements to the printer as raster (bitmap) data or as vector (outline) data |
| (Color printers) | Color... | The color control settings for non-PostScript color printers hide out here. Before you change these, right-click on the descriptions and look at **What's this?** |
| (laser printers) | Resolution | Dots-per-inch that graphics are printed at. Because laser printers print coarse resolutions by combining multiple dots of the default size, resolution starts out at maximum dpi (single dot pitch) and goes down by halves, so: 1200 dpi, 600 dpi, 300 dpi, 150 dpi, 75 dpi. No known laser will print at all these resolutions, but all will print at some of them. |
| (dot-matrix printers) | Resolution | Dots-per-inch expressed as separate horizontal and vertical values, like 180x180 or 120x72. Relative to the way lasers do it, dot-matrix printers work backwards: single dot pitch is the *minimum* resolution, and finer resolutions are produced by overlapping (dithering) dots in one or both directions. For example, a dot-matrix printer with a native dot pitch of 180 dpi would have a "coarse" resolution of 180x180, a "medium" resolution of 360x180, and a "fine" resolution of 360x360. |

**Table 9.5** *(continued)*

| Tab | Dialog | Explanation |
|---|---|---|
| *Graphics*—continued | | |
| (PostScript printers) | Halftoning | Lets you choose between the printer's native halftone settings, and custom frequency and angle settings. |
| (PostScript printers) | Special | Gives you the choice, through checkboxes, of printing a negative image of the original document, a mirror image, or both at once (there's an icon to guide you) |
| (PostScript printers) | Scaling | Lets you scale output size from 25% to 400% of the original document, in 1% increments |
| (color PostScript printers) | Color control | Lets you choose between the printer's native color settings and Image Color Matching (ICM). ICM is configurable; see the dialog under **Choose…method…** For an explanation of ICM, see "Image Color Matching," page 350 |
| *Paper* | | |
| | Size | Gives you a name and an icon (sometimes inaccurate) for each form type and size the specific printer can handle, or lets you define your own size. A red barred-circle over a paper icon means that you can print on that icon's size only if you change some other setting on the Properties sheet or on the printer |
| | Source | Every paper handling method available from the specific printer, like *Tractor, Bin 1, Manual feed*, or whatever. A red barred-circle icon next to a Source means that the option requires hardware (envelope feeder, e. g.) that isn't installed. If you try to set Size and Source to an impossible combination, Windows will warn you |
| | Orientation | Portrait (print along the short edge) or landscape (print along the long edge). Some high-end printers support *Rotated landscape*, which inverts the page along the long axis |
| | Duplexing | *Flip on long edge* prints double-sided in book format; *flip on short edge* prints double-sided in steno-pad format. This will only appear if duplexing hardware is installed |
| | Type | Plain, preprinted (forms) letterhead, glossy, transparency. Called **Media choice** for a printer that will print foils |
| | Output bin | Select output bin, and select face-down or face-up output |
| | Layout | Print one-up, two-up, four-up |
| | Copies | Default number of copies for the printer to print. This can be overridden by the *Number of copies* setting within applications |
| | Unprintable area | The blank margin where the printer can't print; set to the printer's default, in thousandths of an inch. Usually a quarter of an inch for lasers, a tenth to a sixth of an inch for dot-matrix, on each edge |

## Table 9.5 (continued)

| Tab | Dialog | Explanation |
|---|---|---|
| **Paper**—continued | | |
| | About... | Revision numbers of the minidriver and universal driver (to let you know if you need a newer one) |
| | Restore defaults | Set everything back to the default defined by the printer |
| **PostScript (PostScript printers)** | | |
| | Output format | Gives you the choice of PostScript output in five different formats. See "PostScript Printer: PostScript Tab" below |
| | Header | Lets you choose to download the PostScript header (also called the preamble) with the document, or immediately, or to skip it. See "PostScript Printer: PostScript Tab" below |
| | Error information | Leave this unchecked unless you're having printing problems. If your PostScript isn't printing right, check this to produce printed diagnostics for yourself or your support. You may need a degree in Cryptic Languages to understand the messages; have your printer manual and PostScript reference manual handy |
| | Timeout values | *Job timeout* sets how long, in seconds, the printer will wait for starting data before it cancels a job. *Wait timeout* sets how long, in seconds, the printer will pause for additional data before canceling a job that has started. Setting either of these to 0 lets the printer wait indefinitely |
| | Advanced... | Set language level, bitmap compression, data format and reset (Ctrl)(D). These are said to be optimized, and if you want to change them, grab your printer manual. Note that UNIX networks may not accept (Ctrl)(D) as a printer reset |
| **Sharing (Printers on networks)** | | |
| | Not Shared / Shared As | A printer *not shared* receives print data only from the computer it's physically connected to; the rest of the options are grayed out. A printer *shared as* requires, of the next three options, at least the name |
| | Share Name | The resource name of the shared printer, which will appear to other computers on the network as \\**computername\printername.** Windows proposes the Manufacturer name from the Select Device dialog, but you can name it anything (unique) that you like |
| | Comment | Any Comment you enter here is private and does *not* appear in the Comment column of Explorer Details View—although the Help says it does |
| | Password | The string that other users will be required to key in before they can print to this printer |

## A Parable

Once upon a time there was a very busy master named Bit. Bit had two servants who were just as busy, named Letter and Dot.

Letter was a real aristocrat. He traced his ancestry hundreds of years, past the great Line and Chain, back to the Linotype and even Typecase. He wasn't the easiest to get along with, being edgy and stiff; and he moved at a stately pace. But he printed beautiful pages and, as everyone admitted, he was a character.

Dot was, well, Dot. She bounced around doing a little of everything, made noise, and was jealous of Letter and his beautiful pages. "He's just a bunch of old *sticks,*" Dot said pouting. "I can do that too."

"Of course you can, Dot," Bit said absently. "You just need to practice." Dot was very young and when she made some of her letters, like g's and j's and y's, Bit could barely tell what they were.

Years passed. Dot grew up. Letter got older. Bit worked faster and faster. The day came when Bit sent for Letter and said "I beg your pardon, but I must ask you to make your beautiful pages more quickly."

Letter was graven and gray. "I cannot, my lord," he muttered. "I can do no more than I have always done." And Bit was speechless, but Letter was right, and left. Bit groaned, to himself as he thought, "What do I do now?"

"Hey, *pssst,*" said Dot, who appeared out of nowhere. "Watch this!" And in no time she silently made a beautiful page much more beautiful than Letter's best.

Bit was thunderstruck. "How'd you do *that?*"

"Practice," said pretty Dot. "I got faster. Just like you!"

*Moral: Every Dot has her day.*

# Paradigm Shift

In the dozen years since the world first saw Windows, computer-driven printing has been totally transformed. Windows 1.03, the very first retail version of Windows in 1985, did have a driver for the original Hewlett-Packard LaserJet that appeared in the same year; but even Windows 3.1, in 1992, shipped with *lots* more impact-printer drivers than laser drivers. In Windows 98, the victory of the bitmapped printers is *almost* complete; you'll find a driver for your dot-matrix printer, if it's not too old and arcane, but the lasers and inkjets have the run of the place.

Nor was the struggle for supremacy confined to hardware. In the chapter on **Fonts,** which we hope you've already read, we chronicled the dot-eat-dot battle among Adobe's PostScript, Microsoft/Apple's TrueType and HP's Intellifont to become the letter of the law. Today the dust has settled, and you can get great results from either TrueType or Type 1. Most people will admit that Type 1 fonts *do* look slightly better on the page. They also still cost more. TrueType fonts, meanwhile, are simply everywhere—so much so that Microsoft has nearly stopped selling them as a separate product, and when Microsoft stops selling something, you *know* everybody's got it. You can use Type 1 fonts on a whole bunch of PostScript printers, TrueType fonts on almost every other printer in sight, or get one of the real aristocrats—including Hewlett-Packard M-series LaserJets—that will handle PCL or PostScript at the flip of a control code.

The questions remain:

- What are the primary types of printers available today?

- What are their advantages and drawbacks?

- And what support for them is included in Windows 98?

Why, we were only waiting for you to ask.

## Printer Support

A two-tiered device-driver model enables Windows 98 to support almost every imaginable model of printer. The first tier is an umbrella driver, aptly called the universal driver, which covers most types of printers. The second tier is made up of a huge number of minidrivers specific to models not covered by the universal driver. The minidrivers, usually written by printer manufacturers but conveniently shipped with Windows 98, are go-betweens that speak with both the printer and the universal driver, which in turn communicates with Windows itself.

 **If your Windows 98 CD or disks don't contain a driver for your printer, the printer manufacturer should be able to supply you with one. If the printer doesn't already include a driver, it might be just a phone call away; most manufacturers maintain a Web page or electronic bulletin board service (BBS) so that you can download current drivers, and many have forums on one or more of the major online services, such as CompuServe.**

The universal printer driver UNIDRV.DLL supports resolutions of up to 600 dpi. This driver also supports most non-PostScript page-description languages, covering TrueType and Intellifont scalable fonts, monochrome HP GL/2, generic text printing, Epson ESC P/2 raster graphics, and most dot-matrix formats. PostScript printers are another species and use PSCRIPT.DRV as a universal driver.

If you're somewhere out in printer hinterland and can't get the correct driver for your printer, try installing the driver for an older model of the same printer, or a printer that's similar to yours. You may not be able to take advantage of all your printer's features, but you might get by until you obtain the correct driver. If that fails, try setting up your printer to mimic a more common variety; see "Secretly Compatible Printers" in Appendix H.

 Minidrivers written for Windows 98 also work with the Windows NT 4.0 universal printer driver, so you don't need separate versions if you work in a mixed network environment.

## Bundled Drivers

The printer drivers included on the Windows 98 installation disks fall into six main categories:

- PostScript lasers.

- Non-PostScript lasers, mostly Hewlett-Packard LaserJets and compatibles.

- Dot-matrix.

- Ink-jets.

- Pen plotters.

## PostScript Printers

The PostScript font and printing technology, like TrueType, provides scalable outline fonts that can be printed in any size (although some applications stop at 127 points), rotated to any angle, and printed on a wide variety of output devices. The first PostScript laser printer, the Apple LaserWriter, included 17 fonts; the next version, the Apple LaserWriter Plus, came with 35 fonts ever afterwards referred to as the "PostScript standard font set." One reason you can set up almost any PostScript printer as an Apple LaserWriter Plus is that its firmware usually includes at least the same 35 fonts.

The advantage of a PostScript printer is the ready availability of high-quality compatible fonts; you can download PostScript fonts from companies such as Adobe and Bitstream. The one drawback of PostScript fonts beyond the "standard 35" is that, because they include custom installation utilities, you can't use the Windows PostScript driver to install them.

Once you do install additional PostScript fonts, you'll need Adobe Type Manager to scale them on screen. Otherwise, you'll have to get by with specific fixed sizes of screen fonts; unless you have a gigabyte of memory, install only those sizes you plan to use. To take full advantage of your PostScript fonts, you should definitely buy ATM; the current version, Adobe Type Manager Deluxe, manages both PostScript and TrueType fonts, includes 30 bonus Type 1 fonts, and is a major bargain at $65 street.

## The PostScript Driver

The Windows 98 PostScript driver, PSCRIPT.DRV, supports Level 2 PostScript, Image Color Matching 2.0, control over the format of your output, version 4.2 PostScript Printer Description (PPD) files, reporting of available printer memory, and installable device options. Some older PostScript printers require a printer-specific support file ending in .WPD. Windows 98 still supports those files for the sake of compatibility, but they've been superseded by PPD files, which serve essentially the same purpose.

## PostScript Properties

The **Fonts** tab of a PostScript printer's Properties sheet (Figure 9.15) will let you print with native PostScript fonts, TrueType fonts, or a definable mixture of both, and perform conversion tricks on the fly to change the looks of your fonts or speed up the printing process. Click on the Fonts tab of Properties to access these options:

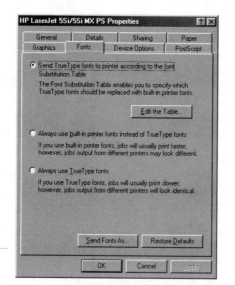

*Figure 9.15*

*PostScript printer: Fonts tab*

- **Send TrueType fonts to printer according to the font Substitution Table.** Substitutes built-in printer fonts for TrueType fonts. Although this accelerates print speed, printed output may not exactly match screen fonts. You can **Edit the Table...** by clicking the button. The list at the top specifies the resident font that will be substituted for the TrueType font in the document; if there's any substitution you don't like, highlight the line, then pick an alternative font from the drop-down list. Your choices are limited; if all the alternatives are far-fetched, Windows proposes you "Send [the TrueType font] As Outlines."

- **Always use built-in printer fonts instead of TrueType fonts**. Gives you less control, but more speed; causes the same screen font discrepancies as does the previous choice.

- **Always use TrueType fonts.** Sometimes you really do want to use the fonts that Windows specifies in the document. Print speed slows down, but the fonts you choose match the ones you print—even when you use different printers, since the fonts in use are resident in the computer, not in the printer.

You can also control how fonts are sent to the printer. Click on the **Send Fonts As...** button to access the following options:

- **Send TrueType Fonts as** offers four choices. *Outlines* (Type 1, scalable) are a good choice for larger type sizes, because documents print more quickly if large fonts are sent as outlines; the time needed to download large bitmap files to the printer becomes a significant part of the job time. *Bitmaps* (Type 3, mostly fixed-pitch) are the most efficient way to send small TrueType font sizes, because it takes less time to download small bitmaps than to rasterize their outlines. *Type 42* is a way of converting TrueType fonts into spline-based scalable font code that can be read directly by a PostScript interpreter; it gives cleaner printing than either Type 1 or Type 3, but in order to use these fonts, your printer's interpreter needs to supply the rasterizer. Consult your manual. *Don't Send* means that you don't want any TrueType fonts at all, you're going to do the job with either resident or downloadable PostScript fonts.

- **Threshold to switch...** specifies the size, in pixels, at which the PostScript driver will stop downloading Type 3 bitmaps and start downloading Type 1 outline fonts. All very precise, except that the threshold value is in dpi, and what you probably care about is point size, and point size is fixed and dpi is a moving target, and.... The default value is 100 pixels, because Microsoft says that at 300 dpi resolution, it starts to be more efficient to download outlines for font sizes over 24 points; $24/72$ (points) $= \frac{1}{3}$ (of an inch) $= 100/300$ (dpi). Following that logic, we suggest that if you're printing at 600 dpi you set this value to 60, and if you're printing at 1200 dpi you set it to 0, which means that only outlines will be sent.

- **Favor system TrueType fonts...** lets you globally set a chunk of the Substitution Table by specifying that, if a TrueType and a PostScript font have the same name, the TrueType font should always be used. This is handy, but to guarantee the results of checking this box, you'll need to be entirely familiar with your respective font sets.

- **Send PostScript fonts as** gives you the option of downloading your PostScript fonts, or not. *In Native Format* sends the fonts to the printer ahead of your document data. *Don't Send* means that you don't want any PostScript font information off the computer's disk, because the fonts for the job are already either resident in the printer's firmware or downloaded into its memory.

The PostScript tab (Figure 9.16) enables you to choose one of five PostScript output formats: regular, portable, encapsulated, archive, or PJL archive.

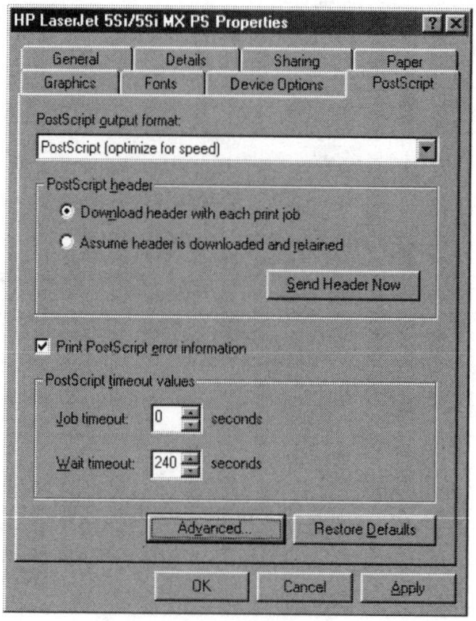

*Figure 9.16*

*PostScript printer: PostScript tab*

**PostScript (optimize for speed)** is the regular option, which you use when you print directly to a PostScript printer.

**ADSC (optimize for portability)** is output formulated according to the Adobe Document Structuring Conventions (ADSC), which will be readable by the widest variety of PostScript interpreters. Use this option when you're saving a file to print to another printer.

**Encapsulated PostScript (EPS)** is a file format that can be imported into documents by, and printed from, another program such as a word processor.

This can only be saved as a print-to-file, and Windows warns you to set your printer port to FILE: (which you presumably have set up) before you save it.

**Archive format** saves all the PostScript data for printing the pages in a compressed format optimized for storage.

**PJL archive format** is an alternative archive format that includes all the job language commands for a specific printer.

**Header** lets you choose to download the PostScript header (also called the preamble) with the job, or immediately, or to skip it. You want this choice because the header is, after all, one more thing to download to the printer, and under certain circumstances it's a waste of time. Download the header *with the job* if you're printing one document and you can't be sure that the header is in memory. Download the header *immediately* if you're about to print a whole string of documents, so you want to get the header into place and forget about it. *Skip* downloading the header if you know that your printer has the header in firmware, or that printer memory hasn't been reset since the last time the header was installed. (Tip: Skip downloading the header only if you're printing to a local printer.)

The **Error Information** printing feature is helpful for diagnosing PostScript problems, if [*sic!*] they occur; and you can boost **PostScript time-out values** if your document contains complex graphics or your printer is slow. See the table on page 376.

Finally, you can examine and modify data transmission settings by clicking on the **Advanced...** button, which opens the Advanced PostScript Options dialog (Figure 9.17). When you install your printer, Windows 98 optimizes these settings to provide the best possible performance and compatibility, but you *can* change them, if you have wizardliness.

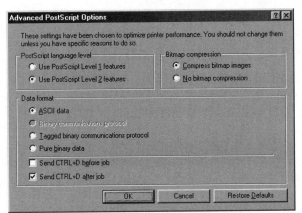

**Figure 9.17**

*Advanced PostScript properties*

**PostScript Virtual Memory.** Virtual memory is almost a necessity for PostScript printers, because their transient needs for vast blocks of code paging can overwhelm almost any amount of RAM.

How much virtual memory do you have in your PostScript printer? If it's not somewhere in the Device Options tab of the Properties sheet, it's almost a state secret. To find out, you need to download TESTPS.TXT—usually located in the \Win98\System folder—to your printer. Open a DOS window and type

```
copy \win98\system\testps.txt lpt1:
```

and press [Enter]. Substitute the name of your Windows folder if it's not Win98, and the name of the port connected to your printer, if it's not LPT1. TESTPS.TXT contains a PostScript program that prints a page showing several of your printer's settings, including how much virtual memory it uses.

 For TESTPS.TXT to work, your PostScript printer must support the *sccbatch* operator. Most of them do, but not all.

Some PostScript printers, such as the Apple LaserWriter NTX and LaserWriter Pro 630, can receive a memory transplant in the form of a hard disk installed in the printer. This yields many megabytes of virtual memory, and it's quicker to have the disk space in the printer than in the computer.

## Hewlett-Packard LaserJet and Compatible Printers

The Hewlett-Packard LaserJet and compatibles are, by far, the most commonly used printers with Windows. The HP LaserJet family includes printers made by Hewlett-Packard, as well as dozens of compatibles made by other manufacturers, all of which employ a page-description language called HP PCL, for Hewlett-Packard Printer Control Language. LaserJet and compatible printers can use TrueType fonts, font cartridges, downloadable soft fonts, and vector screen fonts—but not raster screen fonts.

If you use an HP PCL printer, TrueType should be your first choice of font. The universal driver is optimized to print TrueType characters, so this is one of the best ways to take advantage of the speed of Windows 98 printing.

**HP Models List.** HP LaserJet printers fall into one of the following five categories, which HP compatibles usually emulate as well:

- **HP LaserJet 4000 series.** Potent, broadshouldered workgroup printers, with 17 pages per minute, a 100-MHz processor, 4MB memory, *both* HP PCL 6 and PostScript Level 2, 600-sheet paper capacity, a 10,000-page toner cart … and all of this is in the base model, the 4000 ($1200 street). There are four other 4000 models, each more feature-laden than the one before, the top of the line way under two grand. Get thee to **http://www.solutionjet.hp.com/LJ4000/** and take a long, awestruck look.

- **HP LaserJet 6 series**. Now that the "big" LaserJets are the 4000 series, the most muscular Sixes—squarely targeted at SOHO and workgroup use—are the 6P and 6MP, with eight pages per minute, a 24-MHz processor, 128-level grayscale, and two standard paper sources for $700 to $900 street. Meanwhile, HP has again fallen prey to multi-model disease and produced a 6Pse, a 6Pxi, a 6L, a 6Lse and a 6Lxi; for specs on these go to **http://www.hp.com/peripherals/printers/lj6/**.

- **HP LaserJet 5 series.** These models offered faster processors than the equivalent series 4 models, as well as a faster print engine (six pages per minute instead of four) and a second paper tray as a standard feature. This printer's flashiest feature is an infrared port for wireless printing, which comes in handy when you can't string a printer cable. Infrared transmission depends on a direct line of sight, so your printer and your computer need to be able to see each other for this to work. The inheritor to the gutsy 4 Plus, the 5N ($1400 street), packs in 12 ppm, all kinds of network interfaces and administration tools. The currently available 5-series models also include the Color LaserJet 5 and 5M—what more can we say but "the LaserJets of color printing?" The 5Si MX and 5Si NX, at up to 24 ppm, are two of the most formidable departmental or companywide printers ever made. All the high-end 5Si and Color LaserJets are $2,500 to $5,000 street, but you won't buy another printer for a long, long time.

- **HP LaserJet 4 series.** Improved and expanded printing options with, at long last, true 600 dpi resolution (in most models), 120 levels of gray, many internal scalable fonts (both Intellifont and TrueType), bidirectional communications, a high-speed RISC processor, and automatic I/O switching (useful when you print in different formats—for example, in both PostScript and PCL). The original 4 was found wanting in some ways and quickly replaced with the 4 Plus, a true great. Another series 4 that became a legend in its time was the 4V, the only LaserJet yet that would do 600 dpi, 16 ppm, *and* 11"x17" pages; you can still get one for about $1800 street. But the comic relief of the 4 series was the forgettable 4L, which flatly violated the HP Way by being built to a price instead of a standard, and became the first LaserJet ever to leave a bad taste in owners' mouths.

- **HP LaserJet III series.** Improved on the previous models by adding its own set of non-TrueType scalable fonts, called Intellifonts; adding an image-enhancement mode that prints more realistic grayscale images, such as photographs; and offering Resolution Enhancement Technology, which smooths fonts and graphics. Available cartridge and soft font versions of the scalable Intellifonts still don't offer the universal compatibility of TrueType fonts. Built like an armored Mercedes limo, the last of the 300-dpi LaserJets was also the best, and when you find one for sale today it may cost as much as a new SOHO laser. The 4-ppm IIIp, a real sweet spot, was called "the best printer HP ever built" by dazzled magazine reviewers. All the virtue of the Series III was told twice over by the massive IIID duplexing laser, still sought after on the secondhand market.

- **HP LaserJet II.** In a streamlined and handsome case, the Series II improved on the LaserJet Plus design by allowing two font cartridges to be used simultaneously—and by having a proper parallel interface. Its slightly different PCL escape codes, for functions such as selecting the paper tray, were more consistent internally but annoyingly different from the PCL of the original LaserJet and Plus. The IID would print two sides of a page in one pass (duplexing) and improved on the Series II design by allowing bitmapped fonts to be rotated. The IIP, a smaller and lighter 4-ppm printer based on the Canon LX engine, was the first laser that people bought to take home instead of to the office. All in all, the clever and robust II Series made the laser printer into a prudent purchase and a mainstream commodity.

- **HP LaserJet Plus.** An upgrade of the original LaserJet. Still limited to one font cartridge but worked with downloadable soft fonts—although with less than 400K RAM available, you couldn't look forward to downloading very many. The Canon CX engine was bulletproof; the firmware had all kinds of tricks in it … if you could puzzle out the PCL that turned on the tricks. When the LaserJet Plus first appeared, it was still a serial printer, but a Centronics parallel upgrade kit followed shortly.

- **HP LaserJet.** The original HP laser printer used only a single font cartridge and didn't work with downloadable soft fonts. Its command language, HP PCL, was like nothing previously encountered. The LaserJet was cumbersome, it was huge, it was arcane, it cost five thousand bucks, and none of this mattered; because it did the most beautiful text printing anyone had ever seen, quickly, on cut sheet paper, *and* without any racket. O brave new world of silent, scarlet, cursive light!

 The LaserJet 4 series began the practice of adding **M** or **MX** as a suffix meaning "PostScript-capable" to printer designations, e. g., 4M Plus, 4MV, 4Si MX.

# Ink-Jet Printers

Once upon a time the world of printing was divided firmly into two camps. Lasers were silent, elegant, quick, and produced breathtaking output, but the up-front cost was a stopper. Dot-matrix printers were cheap and versatile, output quality was presentable if not exactly presentation, and the speed at best wasn't too bad—but the noise would send your pets scurrying under the couch. There had to be a middle way; no more expensive than dot-matrix, or not much, with the silence of a laser, and output quality somewhere between the two. Enter the ink-jet.

Canon's ink-jet technology depended on precisely sized droplets of liquid ink, forced down hair-fine tubes and onto the paper; dot-matrix in essence, but hammerless. Early ink-jet printers had a raft of problems, including print-head clogging, output that smeared if it was handled too soon, and a tendency to curl the paper—but the design had such obvious promise that the world was patient. Incremental improvement over many years has made ink-jet a world-class printing method, with high resolution, great saturation, and nearly dry output. Many of them are so quiet that the only noise comes from the paper handling, not the printing.

At the low end of the market, the ink-jet has been so successful that it forced the laser to fight back. Personally, we don't think much of under-$500 lasers, but they are plentiful, and ink-jets are the reason why; not many (or not enough) people would willingly spend $1000 to $1200 for a laser when they could get almost indistinguishable output from an ink-jet at half that price. At the other end of the scale, ink-jets compete with midrange lasers feature for feature, and triumph over them with versatility. The superb Hewlett-Packard 1600C and 1600MC color ink-jets are $1400 to $1900 street—and worth it. Few lasers will ever match a good ink-jet's ability to print silhouette-sharp monochrome one minute, and riotous color the next.

In the SOHO range of $300 to $600, ink-jets almost own the market, which provokes our one reservation about them. A typical ink cartridge contains an ounce or two of ink and will cost $20 or more—which makes the per-page cost of ink-jet printing quite high. A laser toner cartridge at $90 will print *lots* more pages than three ink-jet carts at $30 each. If it's time for you to decide between a new ink-jet and a new laser, bear one thing in mind; you'll probably keep this printer long enough that the laser will be distinctly more economical over its lifetime.

If you're planning to use your new ink-jet printer for both color and mono-chrome printing, make sure that both color and black cartridges are available, and that they're easy to swap—or, better yet, can all remain installed at once. Ink-jets with *only* color cartridges print black by combining all the colors, and cause remarkable shortages of green … in your wallet. And the pricey pseudo-black (called "composite black") isn't even that good; the best you can hope for is an extremely dark brown or violet.

## "Dry Ink Jet" Printers

Alps Corporation, a venerable maker of hardware from floppy drives to touchpads, has introduced Micro-Dry print technology, which is (at this writing) the first fundamentally new way for a printer to work since the invention of the high-resolution ("bubble") ink-jet.

These fascinating color printers are ink-jets … except they're not, because the ink is dry when it goes on. The brilliant color is claimed to be fade-proof and completely non-smearing; Alps says that Micro-Dry output on plain old laser printer paper is as good as the output of a high-end color ink-jet on special (expensive) glossy proof paper. The samples we've seen from Alps certainly bear this out. Standard ink colors are CMYK (cyan, magenta, yellow, black) and a finishing ink; four metallic inks and white are also available.

If the MD1000 ($350 street) weren't one of the finest color printers available today, it would be almost irresistible just as a toy, but a printer capable of photo-realistic color at 600x600 and 600x1200 resolution is no toy, even if it will print T-shirts. It also makes stunningly saturated color transparencies. The only limits that you might find annoying are an 8"x10" maximum image size and a 100-sheet paper capacity.

The MD2300 ($700 street) is two printers in one. Using the same Micro Dry cartridges as the MD1000, it delivers identical output, which is fine for proofing and goofing. Take out the Micro Dry cartridges, snap in the Photo cartridges, load the printer with glossy paper, and—so says Alps although we haven't seen this—you'll achieve photo-quality, continuous-tone printing that rivals the output of professional dye-sublimation printers costing thousands of dollars.

The MD4000 ($600 street) combines the MD print engine with a 600x600, 24-bit, single-pass scanner, in one device as compact as a medium-size printer that weighs less than 15 pounds. With all the advantages of the MD1000 plus an 8"x13" maximum image size and integrated scanning, this has to be a top contender for the title of Ultimate Image Tweaking Machine.

Our sole concern about the Micro Dry printers (as with all ink-cartridge printers) is cost of consumables, but since the Alps cartridges are street-priced at about $7 per color for Micro Dry and about $11 per color for Photo, we're cautiously optimistic. If color is your priority—and especially if you also have a laser or ink-jet for everyday monochrome printing—you owe it to yourself to evaluate these printers.

# Dot-Matrix Printers

Dot-matrix printers once dominated the world of personal computers. Many have been replaced by low-priced lasers and ink-jets, especially for use with Windows. But the millions of dot-matrix printers still around are fully supported by Windows 98.

Dot-matrix printers print each character as an accumulation of small dots. Early dot-matrix printers had print heads with nine pins that created the matrix of dots. Then came 24-pin print heads, with their greater graphics resolution. Both types of printers support TrueType; the typefaces look ragged on nine-pin printers, but the output from a high-end 24-pin printer rivals that of an ink-jet; it just takes longer to put on the page.

The major drawback of dot-matrix printers is the noise they make. As the print head moves across a page, the pins are hammered onto the paper, squashing dots of ink off the intervening ribbon. One printer doing bold or doublestrike is enough to make you leave the room; if several are competing in your office, you might have cause for a noise-violation inspection from OSHA. The hammering does have one advantage, though; it makes short work of the multipart forms commonly used by accounting software. No matter how alluring lasers and ink-jets become, dot-matrix printers and multipart forms will keep each other alive.

Dot-matrix printers work with their own built-in device fonts, which are usually limited selections of ugly typefaces. The printers also work with TrueType and with raster and vector screen fonts. Windows 98 creates the bit-mapped image of a TrueType font and sends it in graphics format to the printer. Because graphics print so slowly on some dot-matrix printers, you might try using the less pleasing but speedier built-in fonts whenever looks don't count and you've got a long document to print.

*Figure 9.18*

*Dot-Matrix printer graphics properties tab*

The Graphics Properties tab for dot-matrix printers usually lets you specify your graphics resolution in dots per inch (Figure 9.18). As resolution increases, so do both the print quality and the time required to produce a page. To print drafts choose a low resolution; use the maximum resolution only for final copies. Many dot-matrix printers support a high-resolution graphics mode, which can double the normal graphics resolution (see **Graphics\Resolution** in Table 9.5 on page 374). Because Windows sends TrueType fonts to dot-matrix printers as graphics, the high-resolution mode improves the appearance of TrueType fonts and graphics. The gain in resolution, however, comes at the expense of speed.

The Setup dialog for a dot-matrix printer may also contain settings for paper size and paper feed (either tractor or single sheet). Automatic paper feed is available only on Fujitsu dot-matrix printers. If your printer supports font cartridges or soft fonts, click on the Fonts button to install them. Examples of such printers are some 24-pin models manufactured by Epson and NEC.

Some dot-matrix printers can also print in color, with a multicolored ribbon. Windows 98 supports those printers with a universal color support library, DMCOLOR.DLL. Windows installs this color library only if you tell Windows you are using a Citizen color printer, although some other brands of printer are compatible with the Citizen.

Some dot-matrix printers—especially the IBM Proprinter X24, the Epson MX-80, and a few 24-pin models from Okidata—are sensitive about how data flows from the Windows spooler. Short pauses can cause those printers to hic-cup, which can halt the printing process or turn the output to Martian garbage.

If that happens, disable the spooler. Right-click on the printer's icon in the Printers folder, and choose Properties. Click on the **Details** tab in the sheet, click **Spool Settings**, and in the Spool Settings dialog box, click on **Print directly to the printer.** Then click on OK to close the dialog boxes. If you still encounter problems, access the Connections dialog box through the Printers icon and redirect your printer output to a disk file by designating FILE as the port, as described earlier in this chapter. To print the file, copy it to a printer port (LPT1, for example) from the DOS command prompt, using the DOS COPY command.

## 24-Pin Dot-Matrix Printers

If you're going to use a dot-matrix printer with Windows 98, a 24-pin printer provides more attractive text and graphics than do the older, nine-pin models. However, 24-pin printers vary considerably; they print at different resolutions and with different aspect ratios. (An aspect ratio is the ratio between the number of vertical dots and the number of horizontal dots that constitute an image.)

For example, the Epson 24-pin and the IBM Proprinter 24 series can print at resolutions of 120x180 dpi (with an aspect ratio of 1:1.5), 180x180 (1:1), and 360x180 (2:1). Others, like the NEC 24-pin, provide a resolution of 360x360. The printer's 180x180 resolution is best for printing raster screen fonts because they use a 1:1 aspect ratio. A 180x180 screen font is available from Epson if you really need one.

If Windows 98 doesn't provide a driver for your 24-pin dot-matrix printer, you may be able to set it up as an Epson printer or as an IBM Proprinter, provided that the printer emulates one of those two models. This may require you to flip some DIP switches on your printer to change its emulation mode, so check the manual.

## Nine-Pin Dot-Matrix Printers

Nine-pin dot-matrix printers are the dinosaurs of the printer world, but Windows 98 does its best to maintain compatibility with them. Like their 24-pin cousins, they print at different resolutions and with different aspect ratios. The Epson nine-pin and the IBM Proprinter typically print at an aspect ratio of 1.67:1. The Epson nine-pin driver supports these resolutions: 120x72 (aspect ratio of 1.67:1), 120x144 (1:1.2), and 240x144 (1.67:1). You can print raster screen fonts using the D font set (120x72 dpi) with the 120x72 and 240x144 printer resolutions. The D font set can also be used at half-point sizes (for example, 12.5 points) with the 240x144 printer resolution.

All the nine-pin dot-matrix printers supported directly by Windows 98 use the UNIDRV.DLL driver library. Citizen printers also require the DMCOLOR.DLL "universal" color driver file from the \Windows\System folder.

# Other Printers

Although most printers fall into one of the categories we just discussed, Windows 98 also supports a host of others. Table 9.6 lists the printer drivers, soft font installers, and printers supported by the Windows 98 installation disks. All the printers listed require the UNIDRV.DLL library file. The TTY.DRV driver is provided as a way to send plain text to the printer port and can be used as a driver of last resort.

The Canon LBP-8 Mark III and Mark IV printers use their own outline font technology. Those two printers work with Windows vector screen fonts, as well as their own internal fonts. The Canon series II and III laser printers do not directly support TrueType fonts. To print TrueType fonts on those printers, you must treat the fonts as graphics or as bitmaps, both of which print more slowly than the native fonts. See "TrueType Fonts" in Chapter 8.

IBM's Laser Printer 4019 can use TrueType fonts, its own internal device fonts, vector fonts, and IBM downloadable fonts and font cards. To install the IBM fonts, use the Windows font installer; open **Control Panel\Fonts,** pull down the **File** menu and select **Add New Font**. If this process is new to you, walk yourself through it with Chapter 8, "Fonts," pages 304–307.

## Table 9.6  Printer Drivers Requiring Soft Font Installers

| Printer Driver | Soft Font Installer | Supported Printer |
| --- | --- | --- |
| LBPIII.DRV | CAN_ADF.EXE | Canon LBP-4 |
| LBPII.DRV | CAN_ADF.EXE | Canon LBP-8 II |
| | CAN_ADF.EXE | Canon LBP-8 III |
| PG306.DRV | SFINST.EXE | Hermes H 606 |
| IBM4019.DRV | SF4019.EXE | IBM Laser Printer 4019 |
| | SFINST.EXE | Olivetti PG 306 |
| | SFINST.EXE | Triumph Adler SDR 7706 |

## Pen Plotters

Pen plotters are often used with computer-aided design (CAD) programs to create schematic diagrams, architectural drawings, and other documents that it's desirable to have a pen draw. A plotter is also handy for creating overhead transparencies for presentations. Plotters work with their own built-in device fonts, and with Windows vector fonts, but not with TrueType or raster fonts.

When you print documents on a pen plotter, you sometimes have to experiment with margin settings from within your application. You can also try flipping on the plotter's Expand switch, which increases the plotting area but can decrease the quality of the output. Refer to your plotter's documentation for more information on using hardware settings to adjust margins.

The plotters in Table 9.7 all use the HPPLOT.DRV pen plotter driver supplied with Windows 98. Many other plotters can emulate HP plotters. Refer to a plotter's documentation to see if you need to flip a DIP switch to put the plotter in HP emulation mode.

### Table 9.7  Hewlett-Packard and Compatible Pen Plotters

| | | | |
|---|---|---|---|
| AT&T 435 | HP 7470A | HP 7475A | HP 7550A |
| HP 7580A | HP 7580B | HP 7585A | HP 7585B |
| HP 7586B | HP ColorPro | HP ColorPro with GEC | HP DraftPro |
| HP DraftPro DXL | HP DraftPro EXL | HP DraftMaster I | HP DraftMaster II |

# Buying a Printer

To capitalize on the Windows 98 graphical environment, you need more than a good screen display; you should also have a good graphics-capable printer. Because Windows sends everything on a page to the printer, including typefaces, as graphics, a graphics-capable printer is important.

Windows 98 works with over a thousand printers, because Microsoft is haunted by a memory; the early versions of OS/2, which were plagued by printer drivers that didn't work. This delayed delivery of the system and angered users who couldn't get it to print properly. Microsoft is determined not to repeat that mistake, for both marketing and functional reasons: you don't want to make the customer mad, and it's important for a visually oriented system to generate visually attractive output.

If you're buying a new system along with Windows 98, which calls out for a fast computer and no skimping on the RAM, you're not likely to welcome the extra expense of a new printer. But if you are in the market for a printer and know that a good percentage of your computing time will be spent using Windows, the next few sections offer some pieces of advice—in descending order of importance, depending on your commitment to WYSIWYG.

## Get a Windows Driver

Before you buy a printer from any source, make sure that a Windows driver for it is readily available. Windows 98 lists hundreds of printers that it supports—at installation, and thereafter in the list you can also peruse by going to **Start Menu\Printers**, double-clicking on the **Add Printer** icon, and clicking **Next** twice. If you are purchasing a printer to use with Windows 98, make sure that either Windows lists the printer, or the manufacturer will promise that a current driver is supplied in the box. Any new printer that does not supply either a Windows 98 driver, or compatibility with an existing Windows 98 driver, should be avoided; manufacturers are notorious for letting their support hotlines promise nonexistent drivers "real soon now," and then taking their own sweet time to write them. Given the overwhelming popularity of Windows, it's safe to say that you'd probably be very happy with one of the printers it already supports.

As for making a very old printer work with Windows 98, you take your chances, and we hope you understand that buying a printer at a garage sale involves a degree of risk. But since we have a secret liking for legacy hardware—most of which was unsophisticated, but also rugged, by today's standards—we'll lend a hand. Take a look at Appendix G.

## Go Laser!

If you're buying a new printer (oh, go ahead) and you can spend at least $500, we recommend you buy a laser printer, especially given today's bargain street prices for Windows-compatible lasers from Epson, Hewlett-Packard, Lexmark (formerly IBM's printer division), NEC, and other manufacturers. Lasers are quick and quiet; they print on inexpensive plain paper with long-lasting, easily installed sealed toner cartridges; and they're the world's best printers for monochrome graphics. Almost any name-brand laser today will give you 600 dpi and six pages (of text) per minute. Furthermore, you can add a bushel of features and still not drive the price out of sight. Want a high-resolution graphics printer on a budget? The Brother HL-1060 prints 1200x600 dpi graphics and costs $700 street. Want camera-ready text *and* high output? Take a look at the Lexmark Optra S 1250—1200x1200 text and 12 ppm for $1,000. Need a printer for a demanding workgroup? That $1,000 will buy an NEC Superscript 1260N, network-ready and boasting a 60MHz Adobe PrintGear imaging processor. And if you're looking for a jack-of-all-trades SOHO laser that will last about forever, check out the 8-ppm Hewlett-Packard LaserJet 6Pse for $800—complete with a CD-full of publishing advice and utilities.

It's official. You can now get print-studio laser quality or workgroup laser speed at what, two years ago, was a personal laser price. Combine that with the unprecedented range of printing support built into Windows 98, and you might go for a new printer even if you keep your old computer.

## Buying a Laser

When you shop for a laser printer, look for the following features:

- Make sure the printer has at least 2MB of memory or the ability to expand to that point. If you plan to print PostScript graphics, you need 2MB to 3MB or more, depending on the printer. With any less, printing graphics is hopelessly slow, and print jobs with complex graphics sometimes stop in the middle—or, worse, go bananas and start spewing pages of stuff that only a printer could understand. Some newer printers from HP and other manufacturers use proprietary memory encoding ("memory enhancement") to use less hardware memory more efficiently, even for PostScript printing; look for these if you're on a budget.

- Make sure the printer has download capabilities, so it can load fonts from your computer or another external source.

- Look for a speed of at least 8 ppm (pages per minute), unless you really don't mind waiting. 6 ppm should be fast enough for a single user who doesn't print lots of pages. The 4-ppm laser is basically obsolete. Everybody wants faster and cheaper, and these days you can get both in the same box, except at the lowest of low prices.

- Shop around. Laser printers are more similar than different internally, yet prices for comparable products can vary considerably. A printer with a particular laser engine—the system's most important component—may cost several hundred dollars less than a different machine with the same engine. Before you buy a laser printer through mail order or at one of the computer superstores, research the components that go into that particular unit; preparation can make the difference between a good deal and no deal at all.

## Ink-Jets Rule!

Okay, wait a minute. Suppose it doesn't bother you if a page takes ten seconds to print instead of five; and you'd never blast your way through a ream of paper in an afternoon, but you print a few sheets a day, every day; and a grand is a lot of money. But most of all, you need versatility. You like to print in sizes besides letter and legal. And you crave color. Welcome to the world of the ink-jet.

The new, modern, jump-hoops-and-fly-loops ink-jet printer is epitomized by the Hewlett-Packard DeskJet 1000Cxi, which prints six pages a minute monochrome. And three pages a minute color. And 600 dpi either way. *And* any sheet size to 13"x19". *And* all for less than $500 street. Feel better? The millennium has come; for as little as $200 and almost never more than $600, you'll find an ink-jet to serve your every (low-volume) printing need. An Epson Stylus, Hewlett-Packard DeskJet or Lexmark ColorJet makes an ideal printer for a starter system.

If you venture into the high end of ink-jetdom, you'll find printers that will do the impossible … or so you thought. The Epson Stylus Color 3000 ($2,000 street) prints 1440x720 color graphics at anything up to C-size—17"x22"—or on banners. The Fargo Signature CD ($1,100 street) prints high-res, high-color artwork on CDs and their cases. The rule of thumb is simple: Anything a laser *won't* do, an ink-jet probably will. And the big winner here is you.

## Picking a Color Printer

Choosing a color printer, like other equipment decisions, is application-driven—based on the principle of WYGDOWYWTDWI (What You Get Depends on What You Want to Do with It). The two major applications most likely to demand color printing are graphic design and desktop presentation. For design work you want a printer that can handle large pages, so you can print full-size drawings with room around the edges for annotations and instructions. For presentations, large size isn't crucial, but you want a printer that can create high-quality overhead transparencies. You can buy a desktop (or almost) color printer today that will print almost anything, from a T-shirt to a CD to process color. So shop till you drop—and insist on seeing samples.

## Beyond Good Looks

If you're not titillated by fancy print options, you can keep your old printer and still appreciate some improvements. But a printer that takes complete advantage of Windows 98 will support cutting-edge advancements like bidirectional communication and the Extended Capabilities Port. Some printers are also fax machines, scanners, and copiers, and would probably even take phone messages with a little prodding—although modems already do that. We haven't seen one yet that makes coffee.

# Summary

Almost every Windows print feature has been improved in Windows 98, accelerating print speed and giving you greater control over the process. Printer control is centralized in a Printers folder, and added features include two-way communication between the printer and the computer, enhanced support for network printing, driver support, and support for almost every printer in existence. Although you don't have to fiddle anymore with bare-metal technicalities of printer setup, Windows 98 provides a host of options to help you control aspects such as speed, font conversion, queue arrangements, deferred printing, and printers shared on a network.

# 10

# Networking

In Chapter 2 we introduced you to Windows 98's concept (and Windows NT's concept) of concentric computing—the fact that Windows gives you the tools to operate your own computer, and to connect to practically any other computer in the world, depending on which part of the toolkit you use. To recap:

- You might be on your local computer, which is the box that your monitor and keyboard are physically connected to, and just using plain old Windows 98. That situation has been covered in most of the chapters so far.

- You might want to connect your local computer to one other computer with a cable, for which Windows 98 offers you the Direct Cable Connection utility; all you need is Windows, the two computers, and what your local computer retailer probably calls a "null modem" or "Laplink-style" cable. For a more robust and permanent connection, use the Network utilities with two inexpensive Ethernet adapters and a crossover cable (under $100 for the whole kaboodle) to create a two-computer peer-to-peer network—a truly delightful configuration for those times when a single computer, whatever its horsepower, leaves you obscurely unsatisfied. ("Hey, Oscar! We need two more IRQ's over here! And where's that other modem?") This material is covered in Chapter 11.

- If your computer is connected to other computers, whether to a server or to other clients running Windows 98, then you're on your local network, which Microsoft (bowing to contemporary corporate slang) calls your *intranet* or your *local intranet zone,* and Windows 98 refers to as the Network Neighborhood. This material is covered in this chapter.

- Finally, if your computer is connected to an Internet Service Provider (ISP) through anything from a humble 28.8 modem to a T3 coax cable, then you're on the *Internet,* the worldwide network of networks. For this, Windows 98 reserves its most formidable single component— Internet Explorer 4.0. You'll find this material in Chapter 16, "Your Own Private Internet."

This chapter gives you an overview of Windows 98's hardwired networking components, protocols, and conventions. Most of them work quite well and they'll all merit your close attention, because you're likely to use them before long. We include remarks about Windows NT when we have to, but only then. In Chapter 11, we discuss installing and configuring a modem, the HyperTerminal software program for basic communications tasks, Dial-Up Networking, the Direct Cable Connection, and other applets. Installing and configuring Dial-Up Networking is discussed in detail in Appendix C, "Dial-Up Networking Without Tears."

Necessarily, this chapter trades depth of consideration for breadth of outlook. When you finish it, you'll know what Windows networking is and how to make it work; you may not know, for example, every last thing that would make you comfortable with setting up a network of your own. We're driven to make this compromise because Windows networking, like the Registry and a few other topics, is something that could be treated exhaustively only in a book of its own. If *The Windows 98 Networking Bible* is a book you'd find truly useful, leave us a note in the guestbook of our Web site or e-mail us at `tell@peachpit.com`.

# Why Networks?

Computing is like politics—its power belongs in numbers. When you connect a personal computer to other computers, through a network or any other type of communications link, you multiply its capabilities. And if you make the right connections, you can gain access to information that would otherwise be unavailable to you—just the way you would in politics. That's the biggest reason for the popularity of computer networking in recent years.

The second reason is that, in the last two decades, network architecture has been turned upside down. In the sixties and seventies, to participate in a computer network, you needed a terminal (which probably cost as much as a powerful desktop computer does now) and a connection to a minicomputer or a mainframe computer, which required a carefully climate-controlled room of its own, plus a full-time network administrator to reboot that megalithic computer regularly. Translation: In the sixties and seventies, a computer network was something you might be part of, but it was not something you could set up on your own, and assuredly it was not anything you could afford.

In the eighties, a profound reversal took place. Networks stopped being single computers distributing their energies to a bunch of terminals (which were called "dumb terminals" for good reason) and began being voluntary associations of independently powerful, small, relatively cheap computers. In the old days, with the computer at the center, every new, additional terminal *diluted* the power of the network. Once desktop computers were combined into networks, every new, additional computer *increased* that power. The networks grew more powerful as they grew larger … and each network began touching the edges of others …

Improvements in the tools for connecting computers helped to catalyze explosive growth in the personal computer industry. With the introduction of faster modems, ISDN lines, improved cabling technologies, and better software for making connections, networking became not only worthwhile, but imperative.

Connecting your computer to others extends your reach literally worldwide, and offers one of the greatest advantages of a networked environment; the ability to share resources. (A resource is anything, like a disk, a printer, or a modem, that can be shared by people connected to the network.) All of this access and power is built into Windows 98; you just provide the hardware.

This chapter describes how to use Windows 98 with a peer-to-peer network—that is, a network all of whose computers are running Windows 98 and being used as workstations—as well as how to use it with a network server running Windows NT. We also describe its support for several other popular network operating systems. We introduce the Network Neighborhood, which enables you to view and control network components, as well as Windows 98's ways to share your computers' resources and protect your network's security.

Windows 98 expands on Windows 95's built-in support for the most popular commercial networks, including, of course, Microsoft's LAN Manager, Windows for Workgroups, and Windows NT Workstation and Server. The following networks are also supported by Windows 98:

- Novell NetWare (3.11 and later, which can also communicate with any version of NetWare 2).

- Banyan VINES (5.52 and later).

- DEC Pathworks (installed as a protocol).

- FTP Software's NFS Client.

- SunSoft PC-NFS (5.0 and later).

Windows 98's built-in support enables you to use those networks without having to fine-tune every network configuration file on every networked computer. Some tweaking is still required, however, to get things working right, and this chapter helps you to set up everything with a minimum of bother.

# Using The Network: Basics

You can mouse your way from one computer to another, in a Windows 98 peer-to-peer network, without going through a server—or even having one. Windows 98's **Network Neighborhood** enables you to stroll through your own workgroup or any other workgroup in your organization. If you have permission, you can search another computer on your network for information or resources as easily as you can search your own hard disk.

# Browsing the Network

Network Neighborhood provides a consistent interface for browsing the network, no matter what type of network you're running. You can even place shortcuts to network resources on your desktop; if you frequently use the same network printer, for instance, or open a particular folder on a remote computer, you can set up an icon on your desktop to make that resource one-click-available.

To see what network resources are available to you, double-click on the Network Neighborhood icon or, if an Explorer window is open, select the Network Neighborhood folder (Figure 10.1).

*Figure 10.1*

*Network neighborhood*

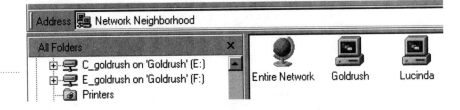

To examine resources outside your workgroup, click on **Entire Network.** To access the resources or contents of a particular computer or workgroup, double-click on its icon.

Similarities among Network Neighborhood, My Computer, and the Explorer are no accident; both Network Neighborhood and My Computer are derived from the Explorer. To prove it, press Shift as you double-click on either Network Neighborhood or My Computer, and the Explorer window will open. The window displays a folder view and an overall, hierarchical view of your computer which makes the Explorer a favorite with us.

If you can't find something on your network, either you're looking in the wrong place, or you might not have privileges to access that resource. For more information, see *Searching for Network Resources* later in this chapter. You may also need to contact your network administrator, or the person whose resource you want to access.

# Connecting to Network Resources

Windows 98's ease of use has leaped ahead of previous versions. Not only is it easier to connect to a network; it's also simpler to use the resources and information available from other networked computers.

When your computer is part of a network, Windows 98 can connect you automatically each time you turn on your machine; all you need to provide is a password. This ability, called *unified logon,* means a network user can log onto all available networks simply by logging on to Windows. Unified logon also permits network administrators to coordinate use of Windows 98 with access to the network.

The first time you start Windows 98 on a network, Windows displays a log-on dialog box for each network client on your computer. Then Windows automatically stores the passwords you have entered in a password cache. Subsequent log-ons retrieve passwords from the cache, so you can connect to networks without having to type your passwords each time.

Once you're on the network, you can use any resources, such as printers and computers, that are connected to the network and shared, provided you have the appropriate level of access. To use a resource, locate it and select it with Network Neighborhood (or the Network Neighborhood portion of an Explorer window). Then click on whatever computer and folder you want to open. If you want to work with a file, select it, then copy it, open it, or run it as you would any file on your own computer.

**Figure 10.2**

*Exploring a network resource*

If the resource is a folder, printer, or disk, right-click on it; this brings up the Context menu, where you'll find options galore (Figure 10.2). If the resource is a folder, you can map it as a network drive so you can reach it more easily from any Explorer window. If the resource is a printer, you can open and view its print queue.

 Computers connected to a network are available only when they are turned on. If a computer is turned off, then it doesn't appear in the Network Neighborhood, and you can't see or access any resource that it contains.

## Mapping Network Drives

You can always use Network Neighborhood to look at other computers on the network, but it may be more convenient to *map* a remote drive. (A *remote drive* is a hard disk on a computer attached to yours through a network. A *local drive* is a drive on your own computer.) Mapping a network drive assigns a local drive letter to it, so that the same drive can be C: on its own computer and, say, F: as far as you're concerned. Once a drive has been mapped, you can have Windows 98 remap it whenever you log onto the network, making access more convenient when other conditions change. Once you map a drive, pre-Windows 9x applications can find it and open files on it. (Applications built for Windows 95 and 98 are savvy enough to find remote drives even if they haven't been mapped.)

 If you'd rather describe a remote drive with something more descriptive than a letter, you can give it a share *name* instead (Figure 10.3).

*Figure 10.3*

*Contents of a named remote drive*

To map a remote drive, locate it in Network Neighborhood in the Explorer, then right-click on the name of the drive. Choose **Map Network Drive** from the Context Menu. By default, Windows offers the first available unused drive letter for the mapped drive, but you can pick another one. Any drive that has been mapped before will propose its previous names (Figure 10.4).

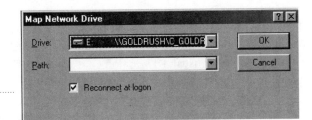

*Figure 10.4*

*Mapping a network drive*

You can also map a network drive by clicking the **Map Network Drive** button that appears in the Explorer and on other toolbars. You type the network server name and path in the dialog box, using UNC syntax. (See page 421, but for example, to connect to the server **baby** and the shared directory **face,** you enter the name \\**baby\face.**) Then choose a letter to assign to the drive.

If this procedure seems rather DOS-oid, keep in mind the one benefit of using the Map Network Drive dialog box: since it stores pathnames, you can quickly map a network drive by choosing it from the Path drop-down list box, which beats having to find and select the drive in the Explorer.

 It's even easier to map the drive with a toolbar button (Figure 10.5). But the **Map** and **Disconnect Drive** buttons aren't defaults; you have to pull down the **View** menu, click **Folder Options...**, pick the **View** tab, and check the box for **Show Map Network Drive button in toolbar.** If you're on a network, it's easily worth it.

**Figure 10.5**

*Mapping a network drive using buttons*

You can make the mapping of any drive persistent—that is, you can have it automatically restored each time you start Windows 98—by checking the **Reconnect at Logon** checkbox in the Map Network Drive dialog box.

## Printing across a Network

The most commonly used function of any network—whether it consists of two computers or 20—is sharing a printer. Windows 98 makes it easy to switch among printers.

Use the **Add Printer Wizard** to set up a network printer. Open the Printers folder located in the My Computer window, and double-click on the **Add Printer** icon. Choose Network Printer when the Add Printer wizard appears, then set up the printer as usual. (If you don't already know the network path to the printer, click on the Browse button to help you locate it.) Once a printer is installed as a network printer, you can control access to it using the printer's Properties sheet. Right-click on the printer's icon to display its Context Menu, click **Sharing...**, and fill in the appropriate fields.

You can also use Network Neighborhood to install a network printer. Locate the printer on the network, right-click to display its Context Menu, and choose Install; the Add Printer Wizard will pop up.

# New Printing Convenience

Windows 98 simplifies the process of using networked printers with *point and print, remote print-queue control,* and *deferred printing.*

**Point and print** allows you to print to a network printer simply by selecting it. If the local computer lacks the appropriate printer drivers, Windows 98 (or Windows NT Server or Novell NetWare) automatically copies the driver from the remote computer and sets it up locally. All you have to do is drag a document and drop it onto the printer in Network Neighborhood; Windows 98 fires up the Add Printer Wizard, installs and sets up the driver, and prints the document.

**Remote print-queue control** enables you to cancel, pause, and resume printing from a remote computer; you can even rearrange the order of print jobs in a queue. (This depends on appropriate access privileges, which your network administrator determines.) You open the queue for a network printer through the Printers window; choose **Start Menu\Settings,** then **Printers,** then double-click on the icon of your selected printer (Figure 10.6). You control the printer by choosing commands from the Printer menu. To pause or cancel printing of an individual document, select it in the queue and choose the appropriate command from the Document menu. To leapfrog your document to first place in the queue, select it and drag it to the top of the list. (If any of these manipulations don't work, you may not have permission to modify the print queue.)

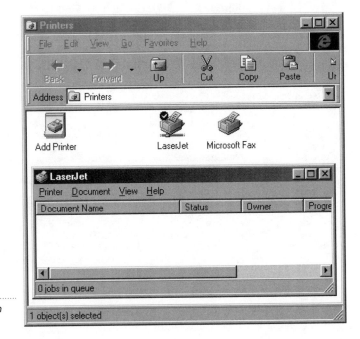

*Figure 10.6*

*Printer with Open Queue*

In some cases you can receive feedback from the printer. An ECP—Extended Capabilities Port—enables bidirectional communications between a printer and a computer. If your system includes an ECP, your printer can notify you, for example, when the paper has jammed, or when the print tray needs paper.

With **deferred printing,** you can queue print jobs when your printer is temporarily disconnected from the network. This feature is a boon for laptop users; you no longer need to rely on the limited capacity of your human memory to determine what needs to be printed once you are back in the office. Instead, while you're not connected to the network printer, you can designate documents to be printed and have Windows 98 store the print jobs in a queue on your computer. When you reconnect your computer to the network, Windows 98 sends deferred print jobs to the network printer automatically.

## Searching for Network Resources

To search for remote files, folders, computers, Web resources, and even names and addresses, you can use the newly enhanced Find command in several ways:

If you're "starting" from scratch, click on **Start Menu\Find.**

If you have some idea where your target is located, right-click on its drive or folder in the Explorer, then choose **Find** from the Context Menu.

When you're shooting from the hip, put your mouse pointer on the Desktop and hit the ⟨F3⟩ key.

All of those methods open the Find dialog box (Figure 10.7). How you opened it will determine the initial contents of the **Look in** field.

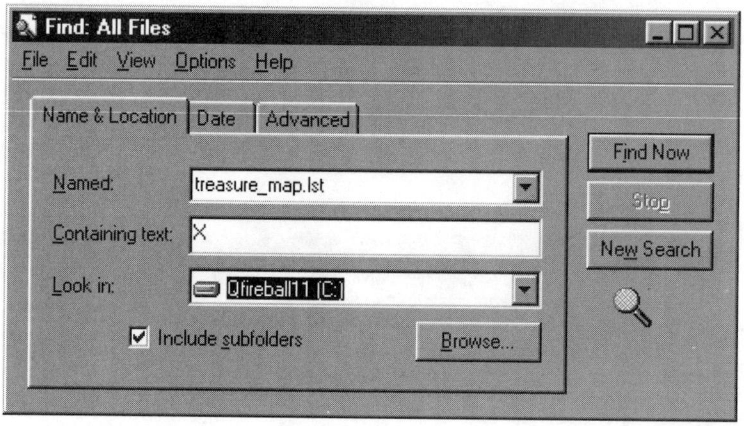

**Figure 10.7**

The Find dialog box

With Find open, you can continue your search in a variety of ways. The simplest way is to enter the name of a file, a folder, or another resource; if you don't know the exact spelling, you can enter just part of the name.

When you click on **Find Now,** Windows 98 searches the resource described in the **Look in** field for any file or folder whose name contains the text you entered. Click on **Browse** to search through a list of available folders, drives, and desktop objects.

The Find dialog offers powerful features for finding files and folders. With the Date Modified tab, you can narrow a search based on the date of file creation, modification, or last access. If you don't know a file's name, but know its file type or likely size, you can use the Advanced dialog to have Windows 98 search for those attributes. If you want to find computers, Web pages, or names and addresses, you can use similar methods, each with a slightly different Find dialog. (If you can't find a computer, it could be that you're not networked to it, or not authorized to access it.)

 Folks who like the search conventions of older Windows or DOS can still specify target file names with wild-card characters; use the asterisk (*) for any string, and the question mark (?) for any character. For example, *kip\*.\** locates all files whose names begin with the three letters **kip,** and *??fred.msg* locates files whose names contain any two characters followed by **fred.msg.**

# One on One

The peer-to-peer network included with Windows 98 is good news for small groups who want to engage in straightforward activities like sharing files, printers, and modems. If you want to connect fewer than a dozen computers, the cheapest and least complicated choice is sitting on the Windows CD you already have. No additional software is required.

A peer-to-peer environment does away with the central server—the muscle-bound computer that stores and disburses hefty programs, databases, and the like. Each computer in a peer-to-peer network is both a client and a server. For example, your computer is a client when you instruct it to use a network printer. It's a server when someone copies a file from a shared folder onto your hard drive. You might think of a client-server network as a wagon wheel, with one central hub (the server) and many spokes (the client workstations). A peer-to-peer network is more like a wagon train drawn into a circle of individual, more or less equal workstations.

Setting up a peer-to-peer network requires cards and cables. First you install a network interface card (or "NIC" or "network adapter") in each computer; since the majority of PC-compatible network adapters that you can buy today are Plug and Play, Windows 98 will detect that you've installed them and install the necessary software drivers for you. Then you connect the cards with cable—either coaxial cable, which looks like cable-TV cable, or twisted-pair cable, which resembles phone cord; you can buy either type in lengths from three feet to a hundred feet or more, with the connectors ready-installed on the ends. Finally, go to the Control Panel, click on the Network icon, name your new network and its computers, and set the levels of access and sharing for everything you've connected. In comparison with earlier, DOS-based network operating systems—which could take days to set up, even for a small network—this is positively fun, and almost guaranteed to work when you're finished.

Being cheap, easy to install, and as easy to use as Windows itself, a Windows 98 peer-to-peer network has a lot going for it. The one potential drawback is lackluster performance at times of heavy load. What if everyone on the network wants to use a database located on your hard drive just when you're trying to work on a spreadsheet on the same drive? You may find your program slowing down because of the network access taking place in the background.

Despite performance issues, though, peer-to-peer networks are adequate and cost-effective for most small groups. If you want everyone on your network to have access to a single large file—a client database, for example—you can set up a "dedicated workstation" whose only job is serving that file to the network users. You can also introduce a separate computer running Windows NT Workstation to provide file, print and intranet services for up to ten Windows 98 clients (at least at this writing; check the latest version of `http://www.microsoft.com/ntworkstation/info/ntlicensing.htm` for details).

# Microsoft's Networking Vocabulary

Let's take a break for a vocabulary workout (see Table 10.1). Actually configuring a Microsoft network is much easier if you understand, for example, that "bindings" are unrelated to your skis and "layers" have nothing to do with a birthday cake. This glossary, while not exhaustive, contains most of the terms you're likely to run into while you're specifying, shopping for, or bolting together a small or medium-size network; we put it here so you wouldn't have to flip back and forth to an appendix. The definitions contain terms in **boldface** that are pointers to other definitions.

## Table 10-1 Networking Glossary

| Term | Definition |
|---|---|
| **10 Base 2** | Quarter-inch **Ethernet** coaxial cable, also called "thinnet" or "cheapernet." Uses **BNC connectors** and has adapters with integral transceivers. Can be run for up to 600 feet before a repeater is needed. |
| **10 Base 5** | The original 0.4-inch **Ethernet** coaxial cable, also called "thicknet" or (sarcastically) "firehose." Uses adapters cabled to separate transceivers with **AUI connectors.** Can be run for up to 1500 feet before a repeater is needed, but is difficult to install and rarely used today. |
| **10 Base F** | A fiberoptic implementation of 10-Mbit Ethernet for very long ranges, up to 6,500 feet. |
| **10 Base T** | Unshielded Twisted Pair (UTP) Ethernet wiring, using Category 3 or better UTP. Can be run for up to 300 feet before a repeater is needed; not as rugged as coax, but cheap, therefore common. |
| **100 Base T4** | An IEEE standard for Fast (100-Mbit) Ethernet that uses four pairs of Category 3, or better, cables. |
| **100 Base TX** | An IEEE standard for Fast Ethernet that uses two pairs of Category 5 cables. |
| **100 Base VG** | An IEEE standard for Fast Ethernet, like 100 Base T but adding the ability for the network to deliver data according to priority. Originally developed by Hewlett-Packard. |
| **active star** | A **star topology** network with an active hub or repeater at the center. See **passive star.** |
| **adapter** | A card that plugs into a computer's hardware bus and provides a connector on the backplane for network cabling. The adapter provides services at the **physical** and **data link** levels of the network; every computer on the network needs one. |
| **Address Resolution Protocol (ARP)** | A protocol for translating the **IP address** of a node to its hardware or **MAC address.** |
| **American Standard Code for Information Interchange (ASCII)** | The standard character set for computing in English. Exists in two flavors: *7-bit* or *flat* ASCII, which comprises 128 characters of 7 bits each, and *8-bit* ASCII, which comprises 256 characters of 8 bits each. The characters that are in the 8-bit set but not in the 7-bit set are called *high-ASCII* or the *top half of ASCII.* For an explanation of ASCII as a manifestation of cultural imperialism, see "What's Unicode Anyway?" in Chapter 8. |
| **application layer** | The seventh or top layer of the **network data model,** containing user controls for services such as opening, closing, reading and writing files, network resource access, e-mail, file transfer, remote file access and remote job execution. |
| **ARCNET** | One of the first LANs ever invented; uses a **star topology** and delivers about a quarter to half the throughput of 10-Mbit **Ethernet.** Old, slow, inexpensive and robust, ARCNET still accounts for a sizable fraction of the LAN installed base, and Windows 98 includes both generic and manufacturer-specific ARCNET support. |
| **Asynchronous Transfer Mode (ATM)** | A **packet-switched** method of transmitting data that delivers fixed-length, 53-byte **packets** at data rates from 1 Mbit/sec into the gigabit range. Now being implemented by telephone companies as the successor to **leased-line** transmission. Versatile, fast, and not quite here yet. |

## Table 10.1 (continued)

| Term | Definition |
| --- | --- |
| **Attachment Unit Interface (AUI)** | A 15-pin interface between a network **transceiver** and a network **adapter** card. |
| **backbone** | One continuous linear wire, tapped into with a cable from each client or server computer, and terminated at both ends to prevent spurious signal from reflections. The original "information superhighway." |
| **baseband** | Communications that use unmodulated digital pulses. Cheaper than **broadband** but with less range. See **Token Ring, CSMA/CD.** |
| **binding** | The process that relates layers; in particular, the process that links the driver for the network adapter to the driver for a particular communications protocol. Since your system is likely to have more than one adapter—probably a NIC and a modem at least—and more than one protocol in force, there will be multiple bindings. |
| **b-node (broadcast)** | A communications mode in which **NetBIOS names** are resolved to the equivalent **IP addresses** by enthusiastically broadcasting the NetBIOS name as a whole bale of **UDP datagrams** until the device with that NetBIOS name replies with the IP address. This works crudely, but well enough, on small NetBIOS networks; but it generates so much packet noise that, although b-node traffic *can* be routed, it usually isn't. Compare **p-node, m-node, h-node.** |
| **bridge** | A device that connects two or more networks or network segments and transfers frames between them, operating at the **data link layer** and forwarding frames only if they meet criteria stored in the bridge. A bridge is more generic than a **router** (also faster) because it's protocol-independent, which reduces overhead. Compare **router.** |
| **British National Connector (BNC)** | A coaxial connector commonly used for Ethernet; also called a **T-connector.** |
| **broadband** | Communications that use modulated digital pulses encoded at transmission and decoded on receipt. Faster, more versatile and with longer range than **baseband**, but more expensive. |
| **brouter** | A bridging router that operates at the **data link layer**, but transmits packets instead of frames and can manage multiple lines. |
| **browse** | To view the folders, files, user accounts, computers, groups and domains available on a network, and make subsets of this resource list available to users who request them (for example, through Network Neighborhood) |
| **bus topology** | A topology in which all computers are connected by **T-connectors** to a terminated **backbone.** Contrast **ring topology, star topology.** |
| **Carrier Sense Multiple Access/ Collision Detection (CSMA/CD)** | A protocol in which, if **packets** are being transmitted over a network segment and the segment becomes busy, the transmitter waits a random length of time before retrying. If two transmitters send at the same time and packets collide, both transmitters wait a random length of time before retrying. **Ethernet** works this way; the built-in random pauses are most of the reason that Ethernet throughput takes a steep dive when networks are heavily loaded. 100-Mbit Ethernet is equipped with extra intelligence to avoid these slowdowns. |

**Table 10.1** *(continued)*

| Term | Definition |
|---|---|
| **Category 3 (Cat-3)** | A type of **unshielded twisted-pair** cable used to carry 10-Mbit **Ethernet,** 25-Mbit **ATM**, or 100-Mbit **100Base-VG**. Now considered mildly obsolete for new installations. See **100Base-T4.** |
| **Category 5 (Cat-5)** | A type of **unshielded twisted-pair** cable used to carry ATM or 100-Mbit Ethernet. The contemporary standard for new installations. See **100Base-TX.** |
| **Channel Service Unit/Data Service Unit (CSU/DSU)** | Devices that connect an internal network to an external digital circuit (for example, a T1 line). One digital equivalent of a modem. |
| **client** | *Hardware:* A computer that requests data, programs or services from a central computer called a **server**. In the Windows world, used as a rough synonym for **workstation**, a term which means something very different in the context of scientific computing. *Software:* A program that reaches out over a network to obtain information requested by the user (e. g., an e-mail client) |
| **coaxial cable** | One of the two major types of network cabling, the other being **twisted-pair**. Coaxial cable conducts signal in one direction through a wire down the center of the cable, which is covered with a thick insulating sheath, which is covered with a cylindrical wire braid that conducts signal in the other direction, and finally has an outer sheath of more insulation. Coax is generally blue, black, orange or yellow, fairly stiff, and expensive, but rugged. Compare **twisted-pair.** |
| **Compressed Serial Line Internet Protocol (CSLIP)** | A more efficient version of **SLIP** with compressed packet headers. |
| **Connectionless** | Said of data transmission in which different packets take different routes, depending on available bandwidth. Each packet contains information that permits the message to be reassembled at the receiving point. Examples are **IP** and Novell **IPX.** |
| **Connection-Oriented** | Said of data transmission in which an explicit connection is set up before packets are transmitted, then broken after the last packet. Packets are sent in sequence but may contain error-correcting code. Examples are **ATM, ISDN, frame relay, X.25, TCP, FTP, HTTP, Novell SPX** and **Dial-Up Networking.** |
| **Copper Distributed Data Interface (CDDI)** | Like **FDDI**, but for unshielded **twisted-pair** instead of optical fiber. Rivals FDDI in speed and is cheaper, but the maximum run length is about 300 feet. |
| **Data Link Control (DLC)** | An IBM standard protocol manager and device driver competing with Microsoft's **NDIS.** |
| **data link layer** | The second layer of the **network data model**, containing the code to assemble messages, regulate their flow, correct message errors, check link validity, and maintain transmission integrity. Traffic on this layer is divided into frames and independent of protocols. |

## Table 10.1 (continued)

| Term | Definition |
|---|---|
| *datagram* | A block of data created and managed by the **UDP**. See **User Datagram Protocol**. |
| *domain name server (DNS)* | A specialized **name server** that maintains the list of correlations between domain names (like winbible.com) and their associated IP addresses. Thanks to DNS, e-mail that you send in care of a domain name will actually arrive at the correct computer; this function is absolutely crucial, so installations that depend on it usually have two or more computers running domain name service, to prevent any interruption. See "WINS, DHCP, DNS, and the LMHOSTS File" on page 433. |
| *Dynamic Host Configuration Protocol (DHCP)* | The Microsoft-originated, but not Microsoft-exclusive, protocol that "leases" **IP addresses** to individual **NetBIOS** computers as needed. See "WINS, DHCP, DNS, and the LMHOSTS File" on page 433. |
| *Ethernet* | A set of networking protocols, developed originally by Bob Metcalfe at Xerox PARC. The installed base of Ethernet runs primarily at 10Mbps; 100Mbps Fast Ethernet is now competitively priced and increasing in popularity. It connects up to 1,024 nodes and can run on a wide variety of cable types. See **10 Base T, 10 Base 2, 10 Base 5,** and **fiberoptic.** |
| *External Data Representation (XDR)* | The **presentation layer** protocol used by **NFS.** |
| *Fiber Distributed Data Interface (FDDI)* | An ANSI standard **token-passing** network with a 100-Mbit data rate over **fiberoptic** cabling, and a range of about 6,500 feet. Mostly used for **backbones** and internetwork **bridges;** expensive, but like all optical architectures, offers gratifying performance. Compare with **CDDI.** |
| *fiberoptic cable* | Glass fiber cabling, transmitting data as pulses of coherent light. Expensive, but offers awe-inspiring speed, high bandwidth, very low data loss, minimal power requirements, and compactness; it also shrugs off interference and features highly secure transmission. Can be run for over 6,000 feet before a repeater is needed, making it *the* cable for networks that tie together multiple buildings. |
| *File Transfer Protocol (FTP)* | A connection-oriented protocol that allows remote login and file transfer over **TCP/IP** networks. Operates at the higher layers of the **network data model** and so can be used as an application. A command-line, character-mode ftp is included with Windows 98. See "FTP Explorer" in Chapter 16. |
| *firewall* | A mechanism, in hardware and software or just software, that prevents unauthorized access to a network from outside the network. Optionally, it can block access to selected external sites from within the network. |
| *frame* | A group of data bits terminated with flags at each end and transmitted with a fixed or variable block size. The basic unit of serial data transmission, the frame is handled by the **data link layer.** Compare **packet,** although the two are sometimes confused. |
| *frame relay* | A **connection-oriented, packet-switching** protocol used for wide-area networks and internetwork bridges; most efficient for very long hops over leased lines. The advantage is that multiple data types, like voice, data, and video, can be carried concurrently, although frame relay may not be the most efficient protocol for any single data type. The disadvantages are a comparatively inefficient variable packet length and the need for dedicated lines. **ATM** is theoretically and practically superior to frame relay and may be poised to replace it. |

**Table 10.1** *(continued)*

| Term | Definition |
|---|---|
| *gateway* | A device connecting two or more dissimilar networks, converting protocols and data formats on the fly as required. Operates at the higher layers of the **network data model**. In modern practice, a gateway usually has one side connected to a hardwired local network and the other side connected to the Internet. |
| *gigabit Ethernet* | An adapter and hub architecture with a theoretical throughput of 1 Gbit (1,000 Mbit) per second. Under development by major manufacturers at this writing, but not yet available. |
| *h-node (hybrid)* | An architecture in which a NetBIOS client computer performs name resolution first by querying a **NetBIOS name server (p-node)** and then, if this is unsuccessful, by performing a broadcast (**b-node**). Since the majority of resolutions will be performed by the NBNS, this approach conserves traffic compared to b-node; but since the client retains the ability to perform a broadcast, it isn't stuck for an IP address if the name server goes down, the way it would be in pure p-node. The opposite of **m-node**; also compare **b-node, p-node.** |
| *hub* | A repeater with multiple ports, used in **star topology** networks. Can be active (amplifying) or passive (connecting). By accommodating different cable types, a single hub can become a bridge between dissimilar networks. See **switching hub, MAU.** |
| *HyperText Markup Language (HTML)* | The language in which Web documents are written; flat **ASCII**, easy to write, versatile. See "Marked-Down Markup" in Chapter 3 and "What You Get Is What You Get" in Chapter 8. HTML used to be more fun before people gummed it up with **Java**, although Java itself is probably a Good Thing. |
| *HyperText Transfer Protocol (HTTP)* | The **connection-oriented** protocol used between **Web servers** and Web browsers (clients) to transmit documents (pages) written in **HTML.** |
| *Integrated Services Digital Network (ISDN)* | A scalable digital telecommunications standard combining a data (D) channel for control with a variable number of 64-Kbit bearer (B) channels for transmitting information. In its most elementary form, called Basic Rate, an ISDN line comprises a D channel controlling two B channels for 128-Kbit nominal throughput assuming use of both channels. ISDN went into widespread use in the mid-nineties, with heavy telephone company promotion, but since the ISDN standard had been established several years earlier, ISDN is now nearly obsolete for many network uses. At this writing it looks as if competing technologies, using either TV coax cable or good old **twisted pair**, may leapfrog it in the broader marketplace. |
| *Internet Protocol (IP)* | The routing half of TCP/IP, a **connection-oriented** transport protocol that wraps sequential packetized data with the network information needed to guide it to its recipient. See **IP Address, TCP.** |
| *Internet[work] Packet Exchange (IPX)* | The **connectionless** message routing protocol of Novell NetWare, providing services at the **network layer** of the **network data model.** 32-bit Windows supplies an IPX client. See **SPX, IPX/SPX.** |
| *IP (Internet Protocol) Address* | The 32-bit address of a **TCP/IP** server or workstation. Depending on the network's particular configuration and the number of hosts, the 32 bits can be variously split between the network address (netid) and the host address (hostid). |

**Table 10.1** *(continued)*

| Term | Definition |
|---|---|
| *IPX/SPX* | Internetwork Packet Exchange/Sequenced Packet Exchange; the complete suite of native data transmission protocols for Novell's NetWare, usually spoken of as such, although strictly speaking the two are separable. See **IPX, SPX**. |
| *Java* | Yet another universal computer language, the BASIC of the nineties, currently so popular that you'd think nothing like it had ever existed before. Actually, it's a cousin of C++ heavily optimized to be portable from one platform to another, and it seems to have a great future in elaborate Web content and in embedded systems. |
| *leased line* | A telecommunications channel leased from a provider for exclusive use. Compare **switched line**. |
| *MAC (Media Access Control) address* | The six-byte address hard-coded into a **NIC**. See also **ARP**. |
| *m-node (mixed)* | An architecture in which a NetBIOS client computer performs name resolution first by performing a broadcast (**b-node**) and then, if this is unsuccessful, by querying a **NetBIOS name server (p-node)**. Since the majority of resolutions will be performed by the NBNS, this approach conserves traffic compared to b-node, but not as efficiently as it would if the server were queried first. The opposite of **h-node**; also compare **b-node, p-node**. |
| *Multipurpose Internet Mail Extensions (MIME)* | Extensions to the **SMTP** format that allow it to carry multiple types of data, such as binary files. |
| *Multi-station Access Unit (MAU)* | A central **hub** in a **token-ring** network. |
| *name server* | A network server that keeps track of the relationship between a resource's global name (for example, its hostname) and its IP address or other physical location in the network. See **domain name server; NetBIOS name server.** |
| *NetBIOS name server (NBNS)* | A computer set up as a server to supply **NetBIOS** name resolution requested by hardware clients. In a Microsoft network this is usually a **WINS** server, but it doesn't have to be. |
| *network adapter* | See **adapter**. |
| *Network Basic Input/Output System (NetBIOS)* | The **transport layer** of the standard networking protocol for Microsoft DOS networks. Now largely replaced by the more versatile **NetBEUI**, but supported by Windows 98 for compatibility. |
| *Network Basic Input/Output System Extended User Interface (NetBEUI)* | The **transport layer** of the standard networking protocol for Microsoft Windows networks. Because NetBEUI is not routable—that is, it's not compatible with the way a router dispatches data—it's almost always used for small, hardwired peer-to-peer or server-based networks, which Microsoft calls *workgroups* and the rest of the world calls *local area networks*. If your Windows network is large enough to need a routable protocol, you can choose between **IPX/SPX** and **TCP/IP**. |
| *Network Control Blocks (NCBS)* | The data **frames** used for interrogation and acknowledgment by **NetBEUI**. |

### Table 10.1 (continued)

| Term | Definition |
|------|-----------|
| *network data model* | A model that specifies how dissimilar computing devices can and should exchange data over a network by adhering to common protocols. The seven layers of the standard model comprise definitions for every aspect of network access, point-to-point communications, and network hardware and software compliance. See **OSI Reference Model**. |
| *Network Driver Interface Specification (NDIS)* | A device driver specification developed by Microsoft and 3Com that allows one network adapter to be used with several **protocols** simultaneously. |
| *Network File System (NFS)* | A UNIX-based distributed file system developed by Sun Microsystems, NFS offers compatibility across protocols and between operating systems; it has become an industry standard. See **External Data Representation**. |
| *network layer* | The third layer of the **network data model**, containing the code to route and switch messages between network segments and whole networks, including telephone networks. Traffic on this layer is divided into packets and depends on protocols. |
| *NIC* | See **adapter**. |
| *OSI Reference Model* | The seven-layered **network data model** comprising the layers: (1) **physical layer**, (2) **data link layer**, (3) **network layer**, (4) **transport layer**, (5) **session layer**, (6) **presentation layer**, and (7) **application layer**. See **network data model** and the individual definitions. |
| *packet* | A string of data bits enclosed by control information including the addresses of the data's source and destination, handled by the **network layer** of the **network data model**. Because each packet includes the information that "tells" the network where it's "going," as well as the instructions for reassembling individual packets into a coherent message, the packets can travel from their source to their destination by multiple paths, as internetwork capacity becomes available; this technique is called *packet switching*. Because packetized data is "self-sufficient" in this way, packet switching is **connectionless**, and one destination can receive data from several sources—for example, your e-mail, your incoming Web browse, and your chat—all at the same time. Compare **frame**; see **TCP, IP**. |
| *passive star* | A **star topology** network with a "dumb" connector at the center. See **active star**. |
| *physical layer* | The first layer of the **network data model**, containing the code that sends and receives bits (pulses) over wires, cables, or other network transmission media (for example, microwave or infrared wireless) without interpreting the bits. |
| *p-node (peer-to-peer)* | An architecture in which a NetBIOS client computer performs name resolution by querying a **NetBIOS name server**. By confining the majority of resolutions to exchanges between the client and the NBNS, this approach conserves traffic compared to b-node; but if the name server goes down, the client is bereft of an IP address until the server comes back. Compare **b-node, h-node, m-node.** |
| *Point-to-Point Protocol (PPP)* | A much enhanced **SLIP** that provides several different methods for connecting over a serial network. Currently the default protocol for consumer dial-up Internet accounts. |

## Table 10.1 (continued)

| Term | Definition |
|---|---|
| *presentation layer* | The sixth layer of the **network data model**, containing the code that mediates between computer systems that use different internal data formats, like character sets or numeric formats. Also handles encryption and decryption. |
| *protocol* | A set of rules that specify the packet or frame format, timing, sequencing, and error correction for transmitted data. Before transmission begins, the protocol must be agreed on by the sending and receiving computers. A protocol can involve more than one layer of the **network data model**; see **NetBIOS, NetBEUI, TCP/IP, PPP, SLIP, CSLIP**, and **IPX/SPX**. |
| *repeater* | A device which accepts incoming signal, cleans it, amplifies it, and rebroadcasts it. See also **hub**. |
| *RG-58* | The standard coaxial cable for thin **Ethernet** (thinnet, cheapernet) |
| *ring topology* | A topology in which all computers are connected consecutively in a loop. See **token passing**; contrast **bus topology, star topology**. |
| *RJ-11* | The most common standard for telephone (and modem and fax machine) plugs and modular jacks. This format can accommodate six wires but is typically wired for only two or four. |
| *RJ-45* | A modular plug and jack similar to RJ-11, but with eight wires. The standard cable for **twisted-pair Ethernet** (10 Base T) |
| *router* | A device that connects two or more networks or network segments and transfers packets between them, operating at the **network layer** and forwarding packets only if they meet criteria stored in the router. A router is more specialized than a **bridge**, because it operates with specific protocols and recognizes network addresses; therefore it can route data more efficiently. Compare **bridge**. |
| *Sequenced Packet Exchange (SPX)* | The data formatting protocol of Novell NetWare, which cooperates with IPX and provides services at the **transport layer** of the **network data model**, guaranteeing the integrity of messages. 32-bit Windows supplies an SPX client. See **IPX, IPX/SPX**. |
| *Serial Line Internet Protocol (SLIP)* | An early serial-bit relative of TCP/IP that allows the use of Internet protocols over dial-up lines. Superseded first by the more efficient CSLIP and then by the more versatile PPP. 32-bit Windows supplies a SLIP client, which it refers to as "Unix Connection." |
| *session layer* | The fifth layer of the **network data model**, containing the code that manages the dialog between networked computers and the timing of data exchange. Since this layer controls the **transport layer** directly beneath it, these two layers are sometimes merged for efficiency. |
| *shielded twisted pair (STP)* | **Twisted pair** with metal shielding to minimize cable noise from interference. Compare **UTP**. |
| *Simple Mail Transfer Protocol (SMTP)* | The **TCP/IP** protocol governing interchange of electronic mail and operating at the highest layers of the **network data model**. **MIME** (which see) is a series of extensions to this. |

**Table 10.1** *(continued)*

| Term | Definition |
| --- | --- |
| **Simple Network Management Protocol (SNMP)** | A protocol monitoring and controlling network activity by collecting data from agents embedded in network devices, then transmitting that information to a management console. |
| *star topology* | A way of laying out a network with an individual cable running from each computer (client or server) to a central hub or connector. The advantage is that one problematic computer can be easily isolated; the disadvantage is that a hub or server failure will bring down the whole network. Contrast **bus topology, ring topology.** |
| *subnet mask* | A 32-bit ID that, when overlaid on an **IP address,** allows the local host computer to "see" only the routing information for the local network. Because it hands some of the responsibility for Internet routing to the local hosts, it's an important factor in keeping **DNS** routing tables as small as possible, although they're still too big for comfort. |
| *Switched Ethernet* | An **Ethernet** network controlled by a high-speed switching **hub** and guaranteeing the full 10-Mbit Ethernet bandwidth to each user, rather than distributing it over the network. A common upgrade to **10 Base T** because only the hub needs to be replaced. |
| *switched line* | A temporarily assigned line for dial-up connections. Compare **leased line.** |
| *Switched Multimegabit Data Service (SMDS)* | A high-speed **connectionless** packet-switched communications service offered by telephone providers for inter-connecting LANs in widely separated locations and with a variety of networking technologies. Data rates are scalable from 56 Kbits to 45 Mbits. |
| *T-connector* | The classic T-shaped connector for Ethernet coax; the "crossbar" of the T includes two sockets for the cable, while the "stem" is a **BNC connector** that latches to the **adapter.** |
| *T1* | T for **twisted pair,** *1* for first-level multiplexing. A digital link capable of transmitting at 1.55 Mbits over two twisted pairs, useful for high-volume Internet connection or remote internetwork connection. Normally sold by telco providers, and so not cheap; often split into narrower channels and sold as *fractional T1.* |
| *T2* | A digital link capable of transmitting at 6.3 Mbits; four times the capacity of T1. |
| *T3* | A digital fiberoptic link capable of transmitting at 45 Mbits; twenty-eight times the capacity of T1. |
| *T4* | A digital link capable of transmitting at 274 Mbits over coaxial cable, fiberoptic cable, or waveguide; 168 times the capacity of T1. |
| *telnet* | A **TCP/IP** client that lets a freestanding computer emulate a moderately dumb text terminal on a remote computer; a packetized **connectionless** fake of a **connection-oriented** dedicated link. |
| *terminal server* | A server functioning both as a client of a single (robust) network connection and as a server to several local computers, remote computers, or subnetworks. The traditional method of connecting a local network to the Internet. |

**Table 10.1** *(continued)*

| Term | Definition |
|------|------------|
| ***terminator*** | A resistor that sits on the end of a (typically **Ethernet**) network main cable or **backbone** and provides the impedance to prevent phantom signals from echoing back down the cable. |
| ***token passing*** | A network data transmission method that uses an empty **frame**, called a *token*, as a bin on a conveyor belt. Any computer that wants to send data waits for an empty token to come by on the "belt," then fills that token with a destination address and all the data that it can hold, and returns it to the "belt." Meanwhile, the receiving computer (which is constantly examining the traffic on the "belt,") sees and grabs the token with its own destination address, empties the token, and returns it to the belt. This slightly more disciplined alternative to **packet switching** naturally appealed to IBM, which invented the method; but the need for every network client to examine every token creates tremendous overhead and has prevented this from becoming a true high-performance architecture. Used in **Token Ring** and **FDDI** networks. See also **star topology**, **MAU**. |
| ***Token Ring*** | The IBM implementation of the **token-passing** data model, with star topology and a data rate of 4 Mbit or 16 Mbit. Windows 98 provides support for Token Ring from IBM and from such "compatible" manufacturers as Compaq, DEC, and Madge. |
| ***transceiver*** | A small, moderately intelligent piece of hardware that helps a network **adapter** exchange data with the main network cable, and also provides electrical isolation. In the original **Ethernet** specification, the transceiver is connected to the adapter by a short cable; a modern transceiver is more likely to be built into the adapter. |
| ***Transmission Control Protocol (TCP)*** | The control half of TCP/IP, a **connection-oriented** transport protocol that manages the exchange of sequential data and guarantees the integrity of messages. See **IP**. |
| ***transport layer*** | The fourth layer of the **network data model**, containing the code that manages data delivery between networked computers, detects lost packets in the data stream, and makes sure data received matches data sent. This layer and all the ones below it are sometimes collectively called **transport services**. |
| ***twisted pair*** | Two 22-gauge copper wires each coated with plastic, then twisted around each other and covered with more plastic (**unshielded twisted pair**, UTP) or metal braid and plastic (**shielded twisted pair**, STP). Just robust enough, just versatile enough, easy to install, and impossibly cheap, twisted pair stitches together the world of communications— starting with the piece that runs from your telephone or modem into the wall jack. |
| ***Uniform Resource Locator (URL)*** | An attempt, incomplete but promising, at a uniform naming—and, implicitly, locating—convention for objects on the Internet, where *object* is the generic term for a resource accessible from a client computer through **TCP/IP**. The term is popularly used to mean a Web address in the format `http://www.sitename.dom/page.html`, but there are other possibilities, including `ftp://ftp.sitename.dom` for straight file transfer without the HTML interface. Eventually this scheme will, in theory, be extended to all servers, peripherals, files and documents on the Net; who'd like to bid on the index server for *that*? |

**Table 10.1** *(continued)*

| Term | Definition |
| --- | --- |
| **Universal Naming Convention (UNC)** | A naming scheme used by Windows to identify a network share, or part of one, with the syntax \\*machinename*\*sharename*\*path*\*filename*. Watch out for that double backslash, you need it. Now, as to *why* UNCs have backslashes and URLs have forward slashes … |
| **unshielded twisted pair (UTP)** | **Twisted pair** with only plastic sheathing. Its resistance to electrical and radio-frequency noise is minimal, but it's as cheap as cable gets, and since it's made entirely of stranded copper and soft plastic, it's about as flexible as string—a big plus when you're running cable in a room or building that wasn't designed for it. |
| **User Datagram Protocol (UDP)** | A **connectionless** transmission protocol that creates blocks of data, numbers them for reassembly, and shoves them off down the wire. It doesn't negotiate with the receiver before it sends, it doesn't ask for acknowledgement of receipt, and it doesn't perform error correction. On the other hand, if you're working in a context where you can assume an intrinsically low error rate, UDP puts more message (and less envelope) down a given wire in given time than practically any other protocol. Contrast **TCP**; see also **datagram.** |
| *uuencode, uudecode* | A protocol for encoding binary data (like images) into flat **ASCII** so it can be sent over a network link and remain intact, then be decoded at the other end. An older competitor to **MIME**, but uuencoded data travels as visible text in the body of an e-mail message, where it looks like the ravings of a maladjusted printer. |
| *Web server* | An Internet server equipped with server-side software for the World Wide Web, and connected to a high-bandwidth network link, typically a T1 or T3. Such a server will have a top-level **URL** of http://www.sitename.dom/ and will send documents in **HTML** to its clients—that is, computers browsing it with their Web browsers. It's possible to send files as well as HTML pages from a Web server, but generally, if you anticipate heavy demand for files, you set up your Web server to redirect the request to an **ftp** server.<br><br>Whether you need a whole server for your Web pages is a matter of anticipated demand and economics. A minimal Web server, with its attached T1 line, currently costs about $2,000 a month without extras. If that won't be cost-effective for you, you can buy a piece of someone else's server, at a monthly rate usually based on either megabytes of disk space or number of transactions (hits). |
| *Windows Internet Naming Service (WINS)* | The Microsoft network service that maintains a database resolving **NetBIOS** node names into **IP addresses,** and may (or may not) collaborate with **DHCP.** See "WINS, DHCP, DNS, and the LMHOSTS File" on page 433. |
| *X.25* | An elderly, **connection-oriented, packet-switching** interface specification governing the opening of circuits, exchange of data, and closing of circuits between private terminals (or local networks) and large public data communications networks. Maximum data rate is 64 Kbits. The international standard for the protocol suite defines only the **physical layer, data link layer,** and **network layer** of the **network data model;** standards for the layers above those vary with the individual implementation. |

# Getting It Together

From the glossary, you'll infer that setting up a computer network confronts you with a tremendous number of choices, depending on:

- The number of computers in the network.

- The variety of computer types in the network.

- The variety of architectures in the network.

- The desired (or existing) cable type or types.

- The desired speed of response.

- The necessary data handling capacity.

- The geographical area covered by the network.

These factors can encompass almost infinite variety. A minimal network can be two computers, each with a NIC, and connected by a single cable; that's what's sitting in front of Kip as he writes this, with one computer running Windows 98 and the other running Windows NT 4.0. Throw in a few hubs and a wiring closet, and you can connect all the computers on a floor—or in a building—into a "real" network. Add some leased lines, fiber pipes, or wave-guides, and your network can span a continent, which is handy if you're a bank, insurance company, or manufacturer. Finally, the Internet—which must comprise every network architecture and operating system so far known—covers the globe and is still one network, if you look at it right.

Microsoft introduced its first network operating system, a version of Windows 3.*x* called Windows for Workgroups, in the early 1990s. As computer networks proliferated, it became obvious that no single operating system could run all of them; so now Microsoft sells three (see Table 10.2).

Depending on your needs, you can mix and match Windows 98, NT Workstation, and NT Server on a single network, equipping each computer with the Windows version that will do the job most economically. Microsoft will be happy to discuss the several schemes they offer for licensing networks.

Since a network of almost any size can run Windows, it stands to reason that the Windows network drivers are compatible with every popular architecture, including ARCNET, Token Ring, and Ethernet; if you're buying a new network today, the hardware will probably be some kind of fast Ethernet. Similarly, every version of Windows will run on a computer with a 486

### Table 10.2  Microsoft's Three Operating Systems

| | |
|---|---|
| **Windows 98** | Primarily sold as a single-user operating system, 98 also includes all the "bits" to set up a small peer-to-peer network that can share disks, printers, modems, or other costly peripherals. |
| **Windows NT Workstation** | The basic version of Windows NT, more expensive than Windows 98 but considerably cheaper than NT Server, can be used as a client of NT Server or as the operating system on a server whose clients are running Windows 98. Used on the server, NT Workstation adds elaborate and potent features to a network with Windows 98 clients; used as a client, NT Workstation runs programs significantly faster than 98, or so Microsoft claims. Finally, NTFS—the NT-only file allocation system—uses disk space more efficiently than either FAT16 or the new FAT32. Note that if you run NT Workstation as a server operating system, the number of clients will be limited by the Microsoft license. |
| **Windows NT Server** | NT with all the administrative tools, security features, redundant disk safety methods—mirroring, striping, and volume spanning—and lots of extra goodies. You *can* run this as a bulletproof client operating system, but it's meant for servers of medium-to-large corporate networks. Server isn't cheap, partly because Microsoft wants lots of money for it, mostly because it wants very powerful computers to run on. For most networks smaller than a continent, NT Server is competing vigorously against Novell's NetWare; IS managers are still deciding whether, on the very largest networks, Server can haul the freight as well as modern versions of UNIX. Support for huge networks will be beefed up in the next (or next two) versions of NT. |

processor, even if you'd realistically want something faster to guarantee acceptable performance; Windows 98 is obliging on a 133 MHz Pentium (a processor already so old that you can hardly buy one) and snappy on anything faster. NT, as noted, wants all the horsepower it can get. In a networked environment, realistic minimum RAM is 16 MB for Windows 98 and 32 MB for either version of NT. Specialized NT server configurations can profit from a gigabyte of RAM or more and, of course, elaborate arrays of disks.

This chapter, sticking closely to Windows 98, will discuss small peer-to-peer networks as a way of introducing principles of networking and showing you the Windows network controls. Again, you can *probably* use the information in this book to set up a Windows-98-only network of two to four computers, but because any network is so variable in the details of its hardware and software, we can't guarantee your results. Your best asset in setting up a Windows network is someone who's done it before and done it right. Such people are easily retained, by the hour or by the job, and we encourage you to go find one.

# Setting Up a Network

Network setup with Windows 98 is, literally, as simple as it could be. For a peer-to-peer network, setup doesn't need to be complicated; if you're using Windows 98 on the clients in a server-based network, the tough stuff gets handled in the (more elaborate) setup of Windows NT on the server.

Go to **Start Menu\Settings\Control Panel** and double-click on **Network.** You'll see a Properties sheet with three tabs (Figure 10.8):

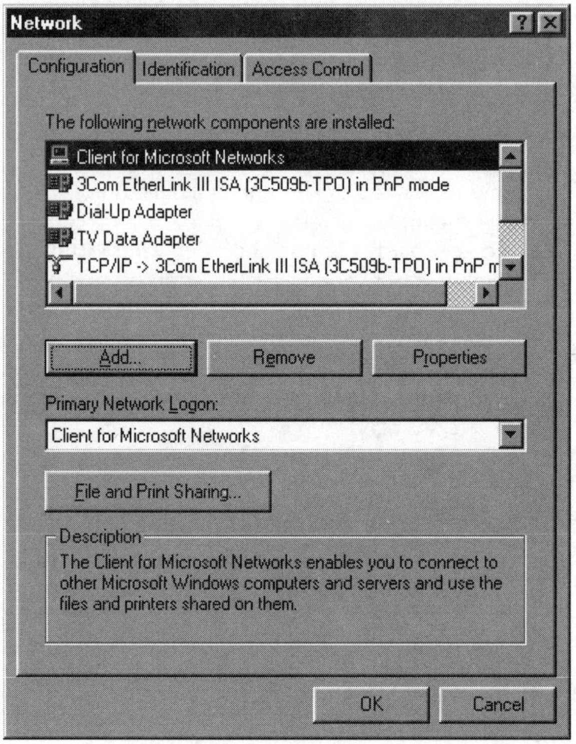

*Figure 10.8*

*The Network control panel: Configuration tab*

The **Configuration** tab lets you install and remove network components, pick a logon sequence, and invoke file and print sharing. We'll discuss these things in detail later in the chapter, but let's do some groundwork with basic definitions.

In Microsoft's networking dialect, the word *component* can mean four things; a *client,* an *adapter,* a *protocol,* or a *service.* We'll define these things here, then discuss them in greater detail later in the chapter.

# Clients

The **client,** following the definition of a software client in the glossary, is a small program that establishes communication with other computers and with resources—like disks and printers—stored on the network. It also provides authentication to the network and, in order to do that, monitors your logon behavior. Windows 98 supplies these clients (see Figure 10.9 and Table 10.3).

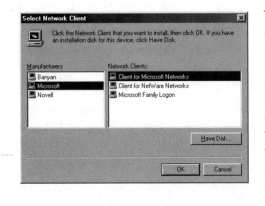

*Figure 10.9*

*Select Network Client dialog*

You can also use the Have Disk option to install network clients provided by your network operating system vendor; for example, the 32-bit Banyan client. For the newest information on network clients, read the NETWORK.TXT file in your **\Windows** directory, or search on the name of your network operating system and the word **client** in the Support section of the Microsoft Web site.

## Table 10.3  Network Clients

| | | |
|---|---|---|
| ***Banyan*** | Banyan DOS/Windows 3.1 Client | A 16-bit client for Banyan VINES, which Windows 98 will run under WOWEXEC. |
| ***Microsoft*** | Client for Microsoft Networks | Puts up a logon window with blank spaces for the username and password. |
| | Client for NetWare Networks | This is the *Microsoft* client for Novell networks. Whether you use this or the Novell client will depend on whether your application software expects to find the full NetWare shell or just the NetWare low-level calls. |
| | Microsoft Family Logon | *new*  Puts up a list of users entitled to log on to the computer; you select yourself from the list and type in your password. |
| ***Novell*** | Workstation Shell 3.*x* [NETX] | The real-mode NETX client that connects NetWare 3.0 through 3.12 to Windows. Use this client or the one below if you need full Novell shell compatibility. |
| | Workstation Shell 4.*x* [VLM] | The Virtual Loadable Module that connects NetWare 4.0 and above to Windows. |

# Adapters

An *adapter* is a NIC, of course, but Microsoft uses the word to mean much more than that (Figure 10.10). In Microsoft-ese an **adapter** can be:

* Any network adapter, whether PCI, VL-Bus, ISA/EISA, or PCMCIA. Windows 98 supports all popular network architectures.

* Any modem, whether internal, external, or PCMCIA, and whether analog, ISDN, or ATM. Confusingly, most modems are classified as Dial-Up Adapters but a few (mostly ISDN) are listed with the network adapters, so you'll have to look in both lists.

* Any infrared (IrDA) connecting device.

* Any TV tuner card, which Microsoft—anticipating the convergence of TV and Internet channel content into video multicasting—calls a "TV Data Adapter."

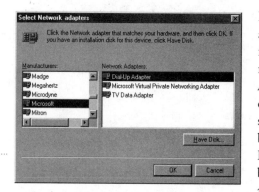

In the general case, an adapter is any physical object you install inside your computer to connect it to one or more networks. Although most adapters are cards that plug into PCI or ISA slots on the computer's motherboard, it's also possible that your NIC will be part of the motherboard chipset and run a cable to a BNC, AUI or RJ-45 connector on a bracket. Notebooks use PCMCIA adapter cards, also called PC cards, as big as thick credit cards; you can even get PC cards that combine a NIC with a dial-up modem, which are pricey, but save you a precious slot. Less common—but handy when you need one!—are parallel port adapters, primarily for pre-PCMCIA laptops but appropriate for desktop machines as well; these are inherently slower than other adapters and, as a result, may not work well with faster network protocols.

*Figure 10.10*

*Select Network Adapters dialog*

# Protocols

A *protocol* is a set of rules for data transmission that two computers agree on before they begin exchanging data. For a more comprehensive definition, see page 418. Windows 98 supplies these protocols (Figure 10.11 and Table 10-4).

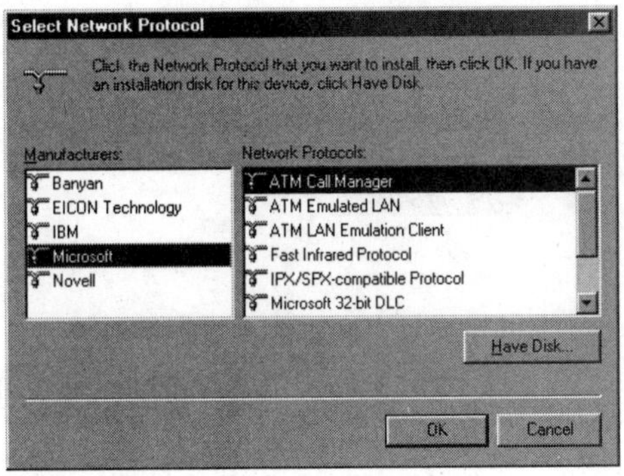

**Figure 10.11**

*Select Network Protocol dialog*

## Table 10.4  Network Protocols

| **Banyan** | Ethernet | Protocol for VINES network and Ethernet adapters |
| | Token Ring | Protocol for VINES network and token-ring (IBM or compatible) adapters |
| **EICON Technology** | ISDN Interface | Protocol for EICON ISDN adapter |
| **IBM** | DLC | To run Windows 98 on a real IBM network you can install this instead of the IBM LAN Support drivers. |
| **Microsoft** | ATM Call Manager ATM Emulated LAN ATM LAN Emulation Client | This and the next two are part of the ATM support (see page 411) built into Windows 98 and Windows NT 5.0. A component of the forthcoming NDIS 5. Full installation will require these three components, the Client for Microsoft Networks, TCP/IP, and an ATM hardware adapter. |
| | Fast Infrared (FIR) Protocol and Microsoft Infrared Transfer | A high-speed (4 Mbit/sec) upgrade of the IrDA file transfer utility, with a point-and-click front end |
| | IPX/SPX-compatible Protocol | For use on a network combining 32-bit Windows with Novell NetWare 3.*x* |
| | 32-bit DLC | Protected-mode client |
| | 16-bit DLC | Real-mode client |
| | NetBEUI | The default protocol for a Windows local network |
| | TCP/IP | The default protocol for connecting to the Internet |
| **Novell** | IPX ODI | For use on a network combining 32-bit Windows with Novell NetWare 4.*x* |

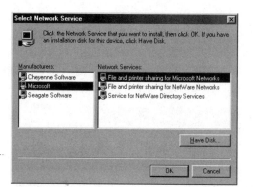

*Figure 10.12*

Select Network
Service dialog

## Services

In Windows-ese, a *service* is something like a client, except that it runs in the
background and it's an integral part of the operating system. The Windows 98
Service menu (Figure 10.12) is restricted to those services that a client computer or member of a peer-to-peer network will typically need; if you're setting up a server-based network you'll discover (once again) that Windows NT,
which has services by the bucketful, is meant to handle the heavy stuff. These
are the Windows 98 network services:

Cheyenne Software ARCserve Agent. This is the control service for
Cheyenne tape backup; like the Seagate Software Backup Exec Agent, it's
available in Windows 98 because, no matter what kind of network you have,
your tape backup device will probably be installed in a client computer.

File and printer sharing for Microsoft and Novell networks. You can also install
these with the **File and Print Sharing...** button on the Configuration tab.

Service for NetWare Directory Services. Novell's Directory Services are a
mapping for keeping track of objects and resources—files, printers, or what
have you—in such a way that the user making the request doesn't need to
know which server the object or resource is physically attached to. NDS is
awesomely sophisticated and Microsoft has yet to develop any comparable
service within Windows; Windows 98's ability to run as a client of NetWare
and tap into NDS makes the combination of the two operating systems a
compelling proposition. Microsoft, meanwhile, is slated to introduce its comparable, native "locationless" directory service with Windows NT 5.0.

Seagate Software Backup Exec Agent, the control service for Seagate tape
backup. See above. Previous versions of this software were known as Arcada
Backup Exec.

Remote Procedure Call Print Provider. By installing this, you can manage print queues and retrieve print batch accounting and job status information from a Windows NT server with your Windows 98 client. Windows Setup doesn't install this automatically, but if you'd find it useful, you can add it to your list of installed services by clicking **Add\Service\Add\Have Disk**, browsing to your Windows CD, and entering the path **\tools\nettools\rpcpp**.

Simple Network Management Protocol (SNMP). Install this if you want your Windows 98 client to be monitored by a management console for a Windows NT server-based network. Add it to your list of installed services by clicking **Add\Service\Add\Have Disk,** browsing to your Windows CD, and entering the path **\tools\nettools\snmp.** You'll need to reboot after you install this. Note that only the agent (client) software is supplied with Windows; the management console itself is typically a third-party product like Hewlett-Packard's OpenView, Cisco's CiscoView, or Eicon's WAN Services for Windows NT. Some SNMP consoles require dedicated hardware in the client computers, some don't.

## Add/Remove Buttons

Adding and removing clients, protocols, adapters, and services is not for the faint of heart, but there are times when you have to do it, and other times when it's optional but makes sense. You'll need to add an adapter through this dialog, for example, if it's not a Plug and Play device; after you've installed it, Windows has to know about it. On the other hand, if you have protocols installed that you're not using—say that IPX/SPX has mysteriously appeared in the Installed list and your network isn't running NetWare—it makes sense to remove the surplus protocols, which will conserve memory, improve performance, and (in our experience) make your client computer slightly more crash-resistant.

Even so, be especially careful with the Remove button. When you hit it, the network component highlighted in the Installed list is gone; there is *no* confirmation dialog. And what if it was a third-party component that was installed off a diskette? And that diskette happens to be … right here yesterday but where did it go?

# Component Properties

By component properties, we refer to;

- Client properties.

- Adapter properties.

- Protocol properties.

- Service properties.

- Primary network logon dialog.

- File and print sharing.

- Computer name.

- Workgroup name.

- Description.

## Client Properties

The Client Properties sheet (Figure 10.13) has one tab, **General,** which offers three options.

**Logon validation** decides which computer your logon is validated by. If your Windows 98 client computer is attached to a Windows NT server, it's possible—but optional—to have your logon information transmitted over the network and validated by the server. To have your validation work this way, check the **Log on to Windows NT domain** checkbox, then fill in the **Windows NT domain** field with the name of the domain you're attached to. If you

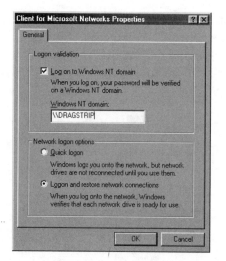

*Figure 10.13*

*Client Properties sheet*

want your validation to take place on the client (your own) computer, leave these blank.

**Network logon options** lets you choose when your network drives are reattached. If you click **Quick logon,** Windows logs you on to the network and performs the network drive mapping—so you can still see the drives in Network Neighborhood—but skips attaching the drives until you call for a file or folder from one. You'll probably prefer this option if you do most of your work on your local disk, or if you have some *huge* number of network drives and no good reason to be attached to them all. Otherwise, if all you have is a local disk or two and a couple of network drives, **Logon and restore network connections** is only slower by a couple of seconds. It's also worth noting that if you have **Quick logon** clicked, it applies to *disks* only; you may have to attach to (for example) your network printer by hand, whereas if you click **Logon and restore...,** the printer connection will be restored along with the drives.

## Adapter Properties

The Adapter Properties sheet always has two tabs, Driver Type and Bindings. Depending on the exact kind of adapter it is, it may have a third tab, Advanced, and a fourth, Resources.

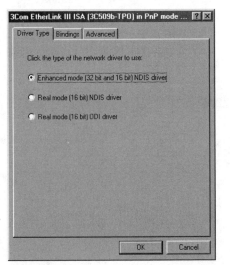

*Figure 10.14*

*Adapter Properties sheet, Driver Type tab*

**Driver Type** (Figure 10.14) gives a choice of physical hardware drivers.

The **Enhanced mode (32 bit and 16 bit) NDIS driver** is always present; it's the default Windows NIC driver, and Windows makes it available to every NIC that can use it. If you can use this driver, we recommend it, since protected-mode operation offers the best performance. (See page 417 for a detailed definition of NDIS.)

The **Real mode (16 bit) NDIS driver** operates in conventional memory and will not be as fast as the Enhanced mode driver, but if you're using a very old NIC, it may be your only option. You might want to consider installing a newer (but still inexpensive) card that can use the Enhanced mode driver.

The **Real mode (16 bit) ODI driver** is the one you'll need if you're running Windows 98 on workstations and Novell NetWare on the server.

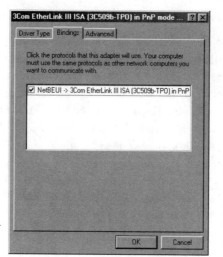

**Figure 10.15**

*Adapter Properties sheet, Bindings tab*

The **Bindings** tab keeps track of the links between the hardware driver for the NIC and the driver for a communications protocol. Through the magic of NDIS, one adapter can be driven by more than one protocol, so the Bindings dialog for a given adapter may link it to multiple protocols, with a checkbox and a line in the dialog window for each (Figure 10.15). You can temporarily disable a protocol by unchecking the checkbox, without actually removing the protocol from the configuration. (You'll be prompted to reboot afterwards.)

The **Advanced** tab lets you instruct the Windows hardware driver about the settings—such as network address, number and size of buffers, and frame location—that are specific to the NIC (Figure 10.16). Generally speaking, the newer the NIC, the fewer of these settings there will be, until a true Plug and Play NIC may have none at all.

The **Resources** tab lets you set the values of resources (such as the I/O address range) that the NIC will require *from the computer* (Figure 10.17). You can twiddle these in Device Manager too, but you wouldn't necessarily know that manual settings were required in both Control Panel\Network and Control Panel\System, so Windows puts it all on one Properties sheet and

**Figure 10.16**

*Adapter Properties sheet, Advanced tab*

**Figure 10.17**

*Adapter Properties sheet, Resources tab*

makes sure you'll see it. Again, a true Plug and Play NIC manages its resource channels in background and won't have this tab.

A pound sign (**#**) in the parameter field means that the hardware setting and the setting in the Properties sheet are identical, which is what you want. An asterisk in the parameter field means that the setting in the Properties sheet overlaps with the established setting for another device, which is *not* what you want; use a different setting.

# Protocol Properties

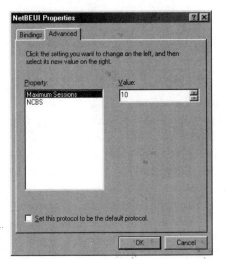

Following are the protocol properties.

**NetBEUI.**  The **Bindings** tab for NetBEUI will generally include the Client for Microsoft Networks, if you have that installed, and File and Printer Sharing, if you have that enabled. The **Advanced** tab has three settings:

**Maximum Sessions** refers to the number of connections to remote computers that can be supported simultaneously. The Windows default is 10. Some applications and network situations will require this number,

*Figure 10.18*

*Protocol Properties sheet for NetBEUI*

the number of NCBs, or both to be set higher; unless the documentation hands you a value, you'll have to find it out by experimentation.

**NCBS** (Network Control Blocks) are the number of NetBIOS commands that can be used. Here too, the Windows default of 12 is a minimum.

The **Set ... default protocol** checkbox guarantees that this protocol will be used whenever no protocol is specified. If you have this protocol bound to the NIC, you don't really need to worry about checking this box.

**TCP/IP.**  Ah, TCP/IP! The lusciously dangling, gold-plated keys to the Internet! Has anything (other than adolescent interpersonal crises) ever cost us more sleep? In all fairness, we need to define some terms first; and don't start whimpering "But you already did that."

***WINS, DHCP, DNS, and the LMHOSTS File.***  The Internet begins, in a sense, with *DNS*—domain name service—which converts Internet domain *names* to their corresponding *numbers*. A domain is part of the Internet naming hierarchy, and domain names exist because they're easier to remember than IP addresses, the same way your name is easier for most people to remember than your phone number.

So the Net talks to people about names, but communicates internally with numbers. You hand a name to your local server, and the computer needs to know what number goes with that, madly looking it up like directory assistance while you wait.

Once upon a time—back about 1990—this was easy. The domain name server had a table installed on disk, and when you gave it the name, it looked up the corresponding address, and sent the query on its way. Then the Internet exploded. What had been a cozy way for civil servants and academics to swap information became … well, you know! And in 1998, with the master DNS table occupying whole disk arrays, *DNS still works the same way.* We can only hope that something replaces it for good before it starts to collapse.

One problem with DNS is that it uses *static mapping,* which means roughly that a particular computer always has the same IP address. Originally this was fine, because the number of possible IP addresses was much bigger than the number of computers trying to use them. Today the world's running out of IP addresses and computers are snapping for them like sharks. DNS, which locks away IP addresses for computers even if they aren't on the Net, is … impolite. Not to say wasteful.

The Internet Engineering Task Force (IETF), including Microsoft, got busy developing methods of allocating IP addresses *dynamically,* so that a computer logging on to the Net would always have the IP address that it needed, but could log off and hand that address to another computer—making the available pool of addresses stretch to cover more computers.

The result was … we interrupt this text to direct your attention to the sidebar titled "Exactly What I Say It Means."

### Exactly What I Say It Means

Before we go any further, we need to know that the word *domain* means two significantly different things, depending on who's using it and when. When the Net says *domain* they mean a particular segment of the Internet naming hierarchy. When Microsoft says *domain* they mean an administrative group of computers, serviced and supervised by a computer running NT Server and designated as the *domain controller.* Sometimes, though, Microsoft starts talking about name service on Internet hosts, and then it uses *domain* the way the Net does, sort of.

When Microsoft took *domain,* a word whose meaning the whole Net agreed on, and used it to describe something just different enough to be totally confusing, the screams echoed for miles. However, we're stuck, and when the word *domain* is used in the next few paragraphs, we just hope the meaning is clear from the context! Now return to reading where you left off.

The result was … an Internet-blessed specification called *Dynamic Host Configuration Protocol* (**DHCP**) which manages a range of IP addresses and, on request, doles them out to client computers that need them. This is different from DNS in two (pertinent) ways:

A client computer doesn't always have the *same* IP address. It does have an IP address that no other computer is using at the moment, which amounts to the same thing.

The client computer gets the IP address along with a *lease,* which is the period of time that it can expect to keep that IP address without saying anything. If the client leaves the net before the lease period expires, it gives up the address. If it needs the IP address for longer than the lease period—which it probably won't, because the default lease period is four days—it can ask to lease the address again.

In order to run DHCP on a Microsoft network, you need a computer running Windows NT Server and with the DHCP Server service installed. To find out more about DHCP, look it up in one of the *Resource Kits,* or search on the Net for a copy of the official Internet document called RFC 1541.

Next, there's **WINS,** the *Windows Internet Naming Service.* WINS maintains a database of available IP addresses on a local disk, and doles them out to clients. WINS *can* get its IP addresses via DHCP, but it doesn't have to; it can simply collect the addresses that are defined on the Network Properties sheets of the individual clients, and deal them out as needed. Like DHCP, WINS attaches timed leases to addresses; like b-node (see page 412) WINS is meant for a NetBIOS environment, but because WINS is much more versatile and less noisy than broadcasting, it can be routed between subnetworks and used for internetwork communication. If you want to know the IP address and lease period of an individual client attached to a WINS server, you can run WinIPCfg on it (see pages 456–458).

To run WINS on a Microsoft network, you need a computer running Windows NT Server and with the WINS Server service installed, but it can be the same one that's running DHCP.

 *Note* the advice, often given by Microsoft to its larger customers, that "WINS is not forever." The problem is that WINS, being Microsoft-specific and NetBIOS-only, isn't much like DNS; in some ways, it's a confined attempt to invent DNS over again. At this writing, any Windows-based NetBIOS network that wants to connect to the Internet has to do it through a gateway running DNS and maintaining a hosts file (see below).

WINS will be replaced by a more powerful inheritor called *Dynamic DNS* (**DDNS**) which will similarly lease out IP addresses from local databases, *but also be DNS-compliant,* so that a local network can conserve IP addresses and yet merge seamlessly with the Internet. So far as we know, the *client* side of DDNS is part of the release version of Windows 98. The *server* side won't appear until the release of Windows NT 5.0.

That said, what happens if the WINS or DHCP server blanks out for a minute? **Anyone designing a network, no matter how robust it's meant to be, should consider what the failure of any component or components will mean to the network as a whole, and plan to forestall or minimize the consequences of the failure.** <rant mode off>. Therefore, although a well-constructed and configured NT server with protected power is extremely hard to kill, you still need to prepare for the worst.

Take a tip from a DNS server. A computer that correlates Internet domain names with IP addresses does it by maintaining a file, called the hosts file, that's just a long, rigorously formatted list of both. In the same way, a Windows NetBIOS name server—which correlates *NetBIOS computer* names with IP addresses—does it by maintaining a file called the LMHOSTS file. (The LM stands for *LAN Manager*, an early Microsoft server operating system.) You can configure your network so that, if the normal source of IP addresses (be it a WINS or a DNS or a DHCP server) is unreachable for any reason, the client computer will snag an IP address out of the LMHOSTS file instead. This makes it tricky to browse across a router between subnetworks, but within any given subnetwork, maintenance of the LMHOSTS file is easy. You can edit it with Notepad or any other ASCII editor that won't add formatting, meaning *not* Wordpad or MS-Write.

 To make use of either hosts or LMHOSTS, you'll need to click **Enable DNS** in the DNS Configuration tab of the Protocol Properties sheet for TCP/IP.

To configure a server, you need more than this book, but start with the section in your *Resource Kit* called **Network Technical Discussion: TCP/IP Protocol.** As soon as you've installed TCP/IP on a Windows 98 computer you'll find a sample hosts file, called HOSTS.SAM, and a sample LMHOSTS file, called LMHOSTS.SAM, in your Windows folder. (You can rename these to HOSTS and LMHOSTS and use them, but Microsoft discourages you from doing that, since they're so heavily commented that they'll be slow. On the other hand, since the comments are highly informative, do look at these before you roll your own.)

The LMHOSTS file is meant to *stay* in your Windows folder, too, because the Registry key **HKLM\System\CurrentControlSet\Services\VxD \MSTCP\LMHostFile** says that that's where it is. If you want to put the file somewhere else, you'll have to hack the Registry to match.

The last question here is, what if you don't have DHCP, WINS, DNS, NBNS, or any other kind of server-based resolution? You are with the innocents, and the hand of Microsoft is extended above you; your network will get its local IP addresses through a hidden dynamic scheme called **Autonet Addressing** or (in the Registry) **IP Autoconfiguration.** Windows automatically pulls an IP address from the series *10.nnn.nnn.nnn* and assigns it to the first computer on the network, then "walks" through the network and assigns an ID to each computer in turn, making sure there are no collisions with the ones already assigned. Autonet addressing allows you to run a TCP/IP network without either a DNS or a WINS server, and actually—since it's enabled by default— without even thinking about it.

## You Can't Do That in This Country

IP addresses in the series *10.nnn.nnn.nnn* are uncommon in the United States but you may find them in intranets in large corporations or other countries. If you do, we recommend against using Autonet addressing; set up a WINS server instead, which will override it. If you need to disable Autonet addressing *explicitly,* go into REGEDIT, go to **HKLM\System\CurrentControlSet \Services\VxD\DHCP\DHCPInfonn** (where *nn* is the adapter number) and add a DWORD key of **IPAutoconfigurationEnabled** with a value of 0. And you'll have to do this to every single workstation, oh joy.

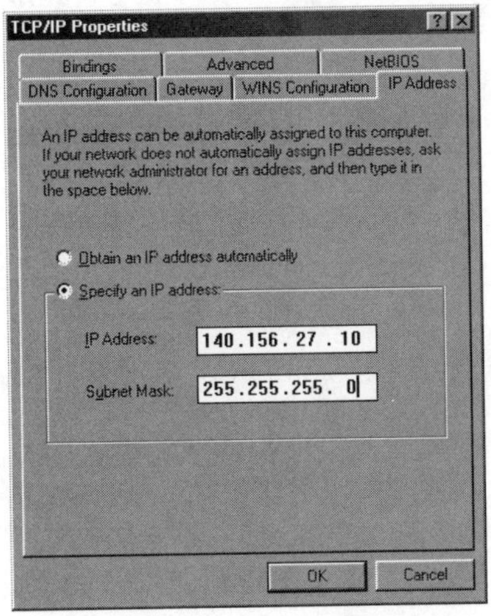

*Figure 10.19*

*Protocol Properties sheet for TCP/IP: IP Address tab*

**IP Address Tab.** If you're working with Ethernet adapters in a pure Windows network that includes a router, TCP/IP will be your protocol of choice, and the Properties sheet is (wouldn't you know it) much more complicated than the one for NetBEUI. But the seven tabs are worth examining in sequence because, all together, they hold the keys to Windows' implementation of the primary Internet protocol.

The first tab visible is the **IP Address** tab, which gives you two choices:

If you click **Obtain … automatically,** it means that the computer you're using has no fixed IP address of its own; when you connect to the network, a DNS server will give you a temporary address for the duration of the connection, a WINS server will "lease" you one dynamically, or Windows will hand you an Autonet address (see page 437). Comparatively, WINS and Autonet are more efficient ways of connecting; by allowing the address of each node to be pulled from a pool of addresses and used as needed, they keep (scarce) IP addresses from falling idle while they're bound to unused computers. The **Specify...** option will be grayed out.

If you click **Specify ... address,** you'll need an IP address and subnet mask from your network administrator. Fill in the fields, noting that Windows fields for IP addresses are arrow-between-boxes, *not* tab-between-boxes. Click OK.

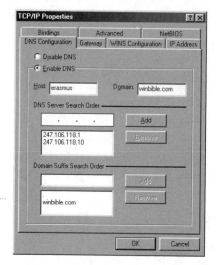

*Figure 10.20*

*Protocol Properties sheet for TCP/IP: DNS Configuration tab*

*DNS Configuration Tab.* The next tab is the **DNS Configuration** tab, which lets you enable DNS, or not. The only reason to **Disable DNS** is that you have a completely self-contained network running NetBEUI or IPX/SPX. If you connect with any network (or provider) that has a DNS server or servers, though, you'll need to configure DNS, and here's how:

Click **Enable DNS.**

Fill in **Host** with the local name of the server and **Domain** with the Internet domain name. That is, if your server's network name is erasmus.winbible.com, *erasmus* is the Host name and *winbible.com* is the Domain name.

In **DNS Server Search Order,** fill in the IP addresses of your DNS servers, as usual using the ⊡ key to jump between fields. Enter the IP addresses in the order you want them to be searched for, and click **Add** after each one; the first one you enter will remain at the top of the list, and so on down.

**Domain Suffix Search Order** is a matter of convenience and can be left blank; it tells Windows what to append to the domain name that you enter. On the assumption that most of the time you'll enter the full domain name, the first suffix should be . (a period). Then click **Add,** type in the contents of the Domain field, and click **Add** again. That way, if you enter *erasmus.winbible.com,* the suffix table will simply append the dot and find what you typed, but if you just enter *erasmus,* the suffix table will append the dot, look for *erasmus.,* not find it, jump to the next entry, look for *erasmus.winbible.com* and find it.

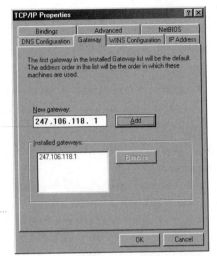

**Figure 10.21**

Protocol Properties
sheet for TCP/IP:
Gateway tab

*Gateway Tab.* The next tab is the **Gateway** tab, which lets you specify the IP address of the computer (or computers) providing the point of contact between your local network and the Internet—in other words, being a router. The gateway machine can also be the DNS server, and often is, since modern hardware can easily juggle both functions without becoming overloaded. Fill in the **New gateway** field just the way you filled in the DNS Server Search Order field, and click **Add.** If you want your computer to attempt sending through more than one gateway (assuming you have them), you can install multiple gateways and your messages will go to them in the listed order.

*WINS Configuration Tab.* The **WINS Configuration** tab lets you specify the IP address of the computer (or computers) handling Microsoft's Windows Internet Naming Service, which is one method of dynamically distributing IP addresses to local computers or dialup connections. There are three options:

**Figure 10.22**

Protocol Properties
sheet for TCP/IP:
WINS Configuration
tab

**Disable WINS Resolution.** If you click **Obtain ... automatically** on the **IP Address** tab, and then click this, your network will get Autonet IP addresses (see page 437) or addresses from the LMHOSTS file (see page 433).

**Enable WINS Resolution.** Click this if your workstations get their IP addresses from the database maintained by a WINS server or servers. Fill in the **WINS Server Search Order** field just the way you filled in the DNS Server Search Order field, and click **Add.** Fill in **Scope ID** with the NetBIOS scope ID that identifies the set of computers—for example, the workgroup—that you want this WINS server to talk to. (Even Microsoft admits that this is a rarely invoked restriction, but if properly used, it's a security feature; NetBIOS computers with the same scope ID talk only to each other, preventing strangers from walking in and checking out your network.

For details, see the *Windows 98 Resource Kit,* or the document "Microsoft Windows 95 Technical Notes: Browsing and Windows 95 Networking," available from the Microsoft Web site. We can't give you an exact URL because, like most Microsoft white papers, this seems to hop around.)

**Use DHCP for WINS Resolution.** Click this if your workstations get their IP addresses from a WINS database dynamically replenished by a DHCP server.

 Any NetBIOS scope ID that you set for a given computer is transmitted as part of the packets of information that originate from that computer. If the scope ID of the receiving computer doesn't match the scope ID of the sending computer, the receiving computer will ignore the incoming packets. Only computers that have the same scope can communicate with each other, and unless you set scopes carefully, you can exile big hunks of your own network to the outer darkness. This is why explicit scope IDs are avoided.

 Windows 98 allows up to twelve WINS servers, compared to the Windows 95 maximum of two.

 Since DHCP is a standard Internet specification rather than a Microsoft proprietary protocol, you can buy DHCP server software that runs on several platforms. For a pure Microsoft network, though, DHCP Server, DHCP Manager, and DHCP Relay Agent are Windows NT administrative utilities, so one computer on your network will need to run Windows NT Server.

*WINS And DNS: The Mystery.* In Windows NT, on the WINS Address tab of the TCP/IP Properties sheet, there's a checkbox for *Enable DNS for WINS Resolution.* That box used to be in Windows for Workgroups, too, but in Windows 9*x* it's gone. Where'd it go, and what was (is) it for anyway? After all, WINS resolving NetBIOS names and being backed up by the LMHOSTS file seems to be in a parallel universe to DNS.

Ah, but: There are times when a computer receiving its IP address via DHCP needs to shake hands with a computer running DNS, and *WINS has to act as the intermediary.* DNS is baffled by DHCP, but can talk to WINS, which can also talk to DHCP.

The invention and ascendancy of DHCP makes communication between WINS and DNS more important—so much so that, in Windows 9*x*, the relationship is enabled all the time and there's no "front-panel" way to turn it off. We can't imagine why you'd want to, but we're too busy to wonder about such things, so we'll just give you the Registry hack to do it.

Go to **HKLM\System\CurrentControlSet\Services\VxD\MSTCP** and find the string value **EnableDNS,** which should be 1. Set it to 0. The usual precautions about hacking the Registry apply; see Chapter 19 *now* if you don't

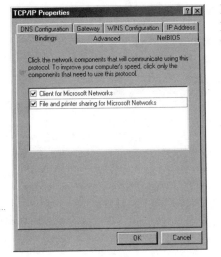

*Figure 10.23*

*Protocol Properties
sheet for TCP/IP:
Bindings tab*

know what that means. Once
**EnableDNS** is set to zero, the channel *between* WINS and DNS is turned
off. DNS in *general* remains active, and
can only be turned off with **Disable
DNS** on the DNS Configuration tab.

*Bindings Tab.* The TCP/IP **Bindings**
tab is much like the Adapter Bindings
tab. As usual, you can use this to turn
off any clients or sharing you aren't
using, which can improve performance. If your local network uses
TCP/IP only to connect to the
Internet—and you aren't firewalled—
you may want to make sure TCP/IP

File and Printer sharing is unchecked, to prevent inquisitive lurkers from
browsing your assets.

*Advanced Tab.* As we go to press, we have not been able to figure out exactly
what the TCP/IP **Advanced** tab does. As soon as someone tells us, we'll put
it on the Web site.

*NetBIOS Tab.* The TCP/IP **NetBIOS** tab lets you run NetBIOS applications over TCP/IP without the overhead of installing NetBEUI.

*Figure 10.24*

*Protocol Properties sheet for TCP/IP:
Advanced tab*

*Figure 10.25*

*Protocol Properties sheet for TCP/IP:
NetBIOS tab*

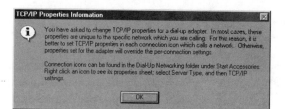

**Figure 10.26**

*TCP/IP Dial-Up Adapter Warning*

**Dial-Up Adapter Setup.** 32-bit Windows considers the device you use to make a dial-up connection to be a network adapter, pure and simple. Sometimes, as with an ISDN adapter, that's obvious, and sometimes, as with an external modem, it can seem faintly weird. Conceptually, though, it's absolutely consistent with Microsoft's stance that "there's only one computer network in the world and you choose how much of it to use."

To the TCP/IP Properties sheet, a dial-up adapter is the same as any other network adapter; you install it, you assign a server IP ID for it to connect to, you set any other necessary parameters, and that's it. The problem is that, ordinarily, you'll probably want your TCP/IP dial-up adapter to connect to several IP addresses, which are more appropriately configured through Dial-Up Networking. The IP address assignment in TCP/IP Properties overrides whatever is configured in Dial-Up Networking; Windows wants to make sure you realize that, thus the warning message.

If you have some reason, whether personal or corporate, to hard-wire your modem to a single IP address, then set it up here. If not, set it up in Dial-Up Networking and leave this tab blank.

## Service Properties

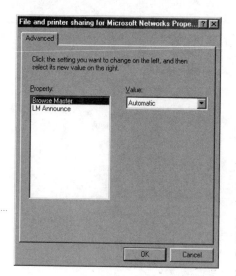

**Figure 10.27**

*Service Properties sheet for File and Printer Sharing: Advanced tab*

Services have Properties less often (and you will make use of them less often) than some other networking components. The two listed here, **Browse Master** and **LM Announce,** are worth examining for the insight they give into Windows networking methods.

When a computer on a Windows network scans the inventory of what's available to the network, that process is called *browsing,* and the inventory is called the *browse list.* One computer in each Windows network, called the **Browse Master,** takes responsibility for maintaining the browse list and sending a copy to any computer or application that asks for it. The list of computers and devices in Network Neighborhood, for example, is a copy of the browse list. The browse master isn't always the same computer; computers on the network are constantly trading this responsibility back and forth depending on which version of Windows they have installed, how long they've been running without interruption, and where their NetBIOS names fall in the alphabet. The process of deciding which computer should become which browser is called a *browser election,* and they occur frequently—using up machine cycles that would otherwise expire while you decide which keys to put your fingers on.

In larger, server-based networks, browsing is crucially important, and a whole hierarchy of *master, backup, preferred,* and *possible* browsers can be established through the Windows NT Browser service to make sure it gets done. Windows 98 takes a more relaxed attitude and, for peer-to-peer networks, makes browser elections possible but not mandatory. The **Browse Master** property can be set to:

**Automatic** if you want the browser on your network to be routinely elected. This is the safest option, because if one computer leaves the network for any reason, a browser election will quasi-instantly force another computer to pick up the browse master's job. It's also the default.

A computer with this property set to **Disabled** will *never* become the browse master. This is useful for computers with limited free memory, computers connected to the network by dial-up links, or computers that are very busy being things like fax servers; some computers just don't have the resources or reliability to serve as browse masters, and they shouldn't be asked.

A computer set to **Enabled** is a thorny proposition, depending on the rest of your settings. To set one computer on the network to **Enabled** and all the others to **Disabled** is risky in the extreme, since if the browse-master-for-life loses power or otherwise leaves the network, everybody else's file sharing, network printing, and Network Neighborhood vanishes until it gets back. If you *prefer* but don't *insist* that one particular computer should be the browse master, leave that one set to **Enabled** and the others set to **Automatic;** your formally promoted pet will have priority in any elections, but if it has to step outside for a minute, any of the others will take over for it.

**LM Announce** is a relic; the LM here, as in **LMHOSTS,** stands for *LAN Manager.* Microsoft LAN Manager was Microsoft's first operating system for server-based networks—at least the first one that anyone saw in the real world—and it became, or begat, several other operating systems, such as 3Com's 3+Open, DEC's Pathworks, and IBM's OS/2 LAN Server, as well as Windows NT itself.

When computers running LAN Manager exchange messages, they don't do it the same way that Windows browsers do. If you set **LM Announce** to *Yes*, it means that your Windows computer can and will exchange messages with client computers running LAN Manager.

Unless there *are* computers running LAN Manager on your network, leave **LM Announce** set to *No.* Otherwise, your computer will spend time making announcements to LAN Manager clients that don't exist, and some things—notably shutting down the computer—will become much slower.

## Primary Network Logon Dialog

You can set this to establish which of the available logon procedures will be given the highest priority. Depending on what you've installed, one or more of these will be available:

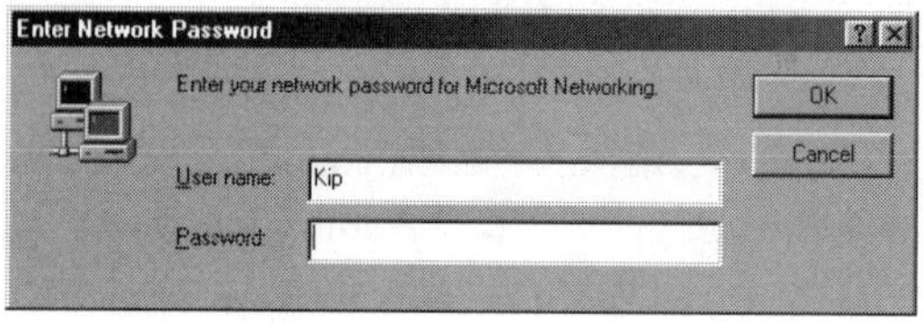

*Figure 10.28*

*Client for Microsoft Networks Logon dialog*

**Client for Microsoft Networks.** **Client for Microsoft Networks** is the client that will give you the most comprehensive access immediately; you log on to the entire network with a single password. Naturally, you only want to be logged on to the entire network if you're definitely connected to it; if you're not, you probably want to use **Windows Logon** instead. But **Client for Microsoft Networks** is a prerequisite when you install some other Windows networking features (see below).

**Microsoft Family Logon.** **Microsoft Family Logon** is your best choice if you have several users logging on to a single computer and you want to make it easy. When you combine the menu-driven Family Logon with user-definable desktops and user-level access to network resources, it literally gives the computer a different personality for everyone who uses it.

*Figure 10.29*

*Microsoft Family Logon dialog*

**Windows Logon.** **Windows Logon** logs you onto your local session of Windows 98 (Figure 10.30). Even if you're using only Windows 98 peer-to-peer networking, you'll find this handy when your notebook computer is disconnected from the network, and you don't want Windows to spend time searching for network components.

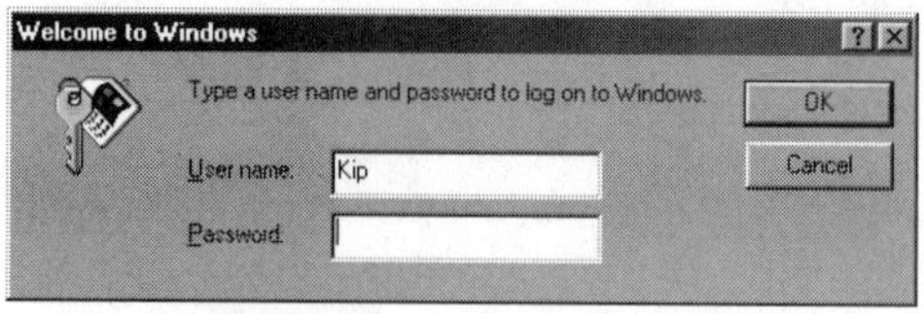

*Figure 10.30*

*Windows Logon dialog*

**Other Clients.**  The protected-mode **Microsoft Client for NetWare Networks** can be set up to serve as a file and print server for other computers on NetWare networks, using the user account databases already in place. *Note* that only user-level security is available. If most of the users who will share resources are running NETX, VLM, or Client for NetWare Networks, install File and Printer Sharing for NetWare Networks; if most of the users are running Microsoft clients, install File and Printer Sharing for Microsoft Networks, which will give you the option of share-level security.

If for some reason the 32-bit Microsoft Client doesn't suit your needs, you might explore the Novell Client32 for Windows 98, which is Big Red's version of the same thing. The reasons to pick one over the other are honestly beyond the scope of this book, but you do need to make an informed choice.

**Novell Workstation Shell** version 3.*x* (NETX) and version 4.*x* (VLM). Attention, performance freaks; these are *real-mode clients* and will cause drag on your throughput. Since both the Client for NetWare Networks and the Services for NDS run in protected mode while they provide real-mode hooks, the only excuse to run these is an application picky enough to require "real Workstation Shell." Whichever one you're using, install the appropriate Novell DOS client first, then add the matching client from Network Properties\Add\Client\Novell. *Note* that nobody, not even Novell, thinks running the NETX shell with Windows 98 is a great idea, so if you must run Workstation Shell, at least try to run the VLM version.

## File and Print Sharing

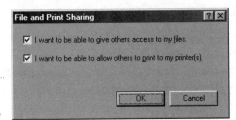

The **File and Print Sharing** button is a shortcut to installing the **File and printer sharing for Microsoft Networks** service. Check the upper checkbox if you want to share files over the network; check the lower one if you want to enable network printing. There are three additional requirements:

- Client for Microsoft Networks must be running.

- File and Printer Sharing for NetWare Networks *cannot* be installed; you have to choose between them.

- File and Printer Sharing with user-level security must be authenticated by a Windows NT server acting as domain controller. (You can get around this by selecting share-level security.)

# Identification

What's in a name? Every networked computer running Windows 98 must be part of a workgroup (see "Microsoft's Networking Vocabulary," above) and must also be assigned a name, which Windows will use to identify that computer on the network.

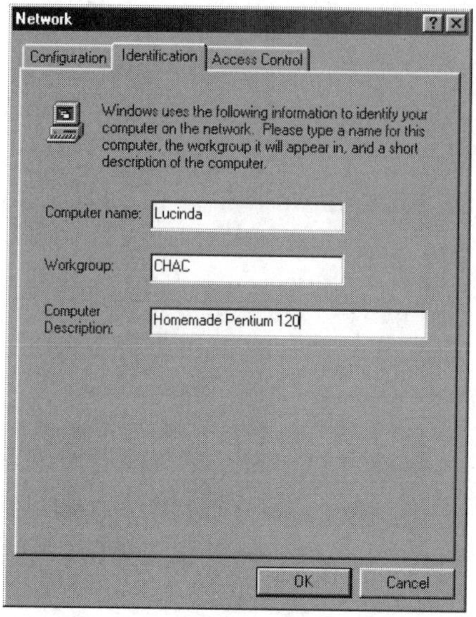

**Figure 10.32**

Network
Identification tab

## Computer Name

If you don't enter this name when you're prompted for it during Windows 98 installation, you can do it at any other time (unless your network administrator has restricted this ability). Double-click on **Control Panel\Network,** or right-click on the **Network Neighborhood** icon on the desktop and select **Properties** from the Context Menu; then click the **Identification** tab.

Enter a name for your computer. This name must be unique on the network; it can be up to 15 characters long, with no blank spaces; and it can contain only letters, numbers, and these special characters: ! @ # $ % c & ( ) - _ ' { } . ^ (We've met networks that were called all those things in a row, but this is a book for a general audience.)

It would be neat if, when you clicked on **OK** of the Identification tab, the icon title of My Computer on the desktop changed to match. It doesn't, but you can certainly do that by hand; highlight and Ctrl C the computer name in its field, go up to the My Computer icon, click-pause-click on the title and paste the name in with Ctrl V.

## Workgroup Name

The workgroup uses the same naming conventions as the individual computer. It doesn't need to be unique, but it needs to be the same on every computer; and once you establish a workgroup, you can only change the workgroup name by changing the name on every computer.

 If all the computers in your local network are running Windows 9x, then your network is a workgroup, and you have complete control over its name through the Identification tabs on the individual computers. If any computer in your local network is running Windows NT, your workgroup may also be included in a *domain* for which the NT computer is the *domain controller,* and changing the workgroup name may be more complicated. Consult your sysadmin or the *Resource Kit* for your version of Windows NT.

## Description

This should be a short comment to help people know which computer this is—like "Homemade Pentium 120," or "Sally's office," or "fax server." The description will show up in Network Neighborhood Properties, and in the Windows NT Server Manager, if you have one.

The Windows computer name, workgroup name, and domain name are required by your Windows environment, regardless of what is or isn't required by any existing network environment (for example, NetWare).

# Access Control

## Introduction

Windows 98 can protect shared resources on networked computers, and prevent unauthorized access to the entire network, with security available on two levels: *share level,* in which you create a password for each shared resource you want to restrict, and *user level,* in which you create a password for each user who needs to access shared resources.

**Share Level.** With *share-level* security, you determine what is shared, and you specify a password for each shared resource. Users type a password each time they want to access a specific resource, such as a folder or a printer. Share-level security is like keeping information in a series of safes; a user has to know the right combination to open each one.

Share-level security is the only type available for peer-to-peer networks running on Windows 98, Windows 95, and Windows for Workgroups.

 *Share* is used by alpha-geek-wannabes as a synonym for *shared resource,* typically a drive or folder on a network server.

**User Level.** *User-level* security, sometimes called *account-based* security, is like having a security badge; you flash it once to enter a restricted area, then you're free to wander around. With user-level security installed, a user types only one password to gain access to all the shared resources on a network.

You can install user-level security only on a network that includes one or more Windows NT or Novell NetWare servers. User-level security requires a centralized and protected list of users, their privileges, and their passwords, as well as validation and other tools that only a client-server network is equipped to offer. Strictly speaking, user-level security is outside the realm of Windows 9x.

When you try to use a shared resource protected by user-level security, Windows 98—the client—provides your password to the server. Either the server verifies that you're a known person, and can use the resource according to the rights assigned to you, or it tells the client, and thus you, to get lost. With the added flexibility of server-based security, you can share resources among any combination of individuals or workgroups on the network, and different computers on the same network can use different types of security.

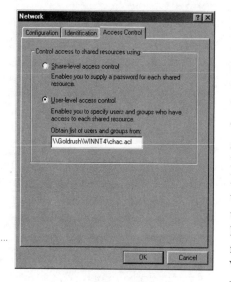

*Figure 10.33*

*The Access Control tab*

Double-click on **Control Panel\Network,** or right-click on the **Network Neighborhood** icon and select **Properties** from the Context Menu; then click the **Access Control** tab.

This shows user-level access enabled and the path to the Access Control List, or ACL, stored on your NT or NetWare server. Windows 98 refers to the ACL automatically when a user tries to share a resource. User-level security enabled with Client for Microsoft Networks requires a Windows NT server or domain to validate user accounts; with Client for NetWare Networks, a NetWare server must be available.

 Share-level security is not available for NetWare networks.

# Sharing a Resource

To share your system's resources, first make sure that sharing is enabled on your computer. (If your computer has user-level sharing, it was probably enabled or disabled by an administrator when your computer was added to the network.)

To check the sharing status of your computer, and enable it if it's disabled, click into **Control Panel\Network\Configuration\File and Print Sharing,** and make sure the appropriate boxes are checked (Figure 10.31 on page 445). Once sharing is enabled on your computer, you can grant or deny access, item by item. Drives and folders that you declare shareable are then shared automatically, unless you turn off all sharing through the File and Print Sharing dialog.

Here's how to share a folder or a drive:

In the Explorer, right-click on the folder or drive you want to share, and choose Sharing from the Context Menu. The Properties sheet for the resource appears with the Sharing tab visible.

Click **Share As**, then specify how you want to share the resource. If your computer is set up for share-level security, the Properties sheet looks like the one in Figure 10.34, enabling you to choose the kind of access you want.

If your computer is set up for user-level security, the Properties sheet looks like the one in Figure 10.35. Use this dialog to modify your list of users and their access privileges.

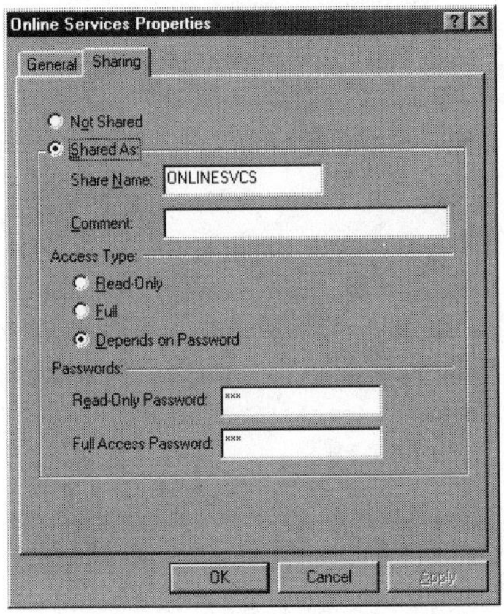

*Figure 10.34*

*A Folder Properties dialog box with share-level security*

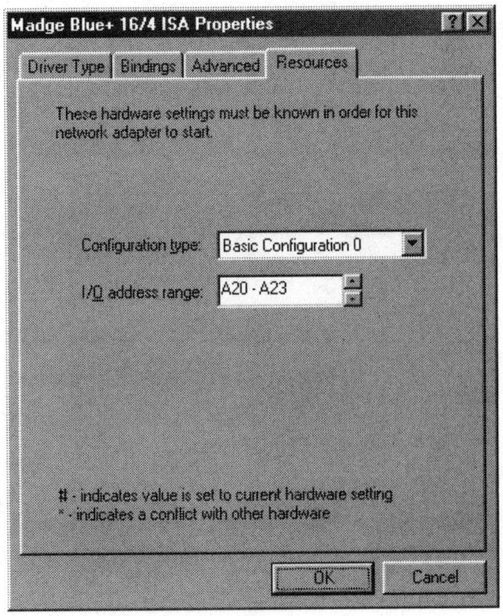

*Figure 10.35*

*A Folder Properties dialog box with user-level security*

To restrict access to any shared resource, you must create one or more passwords. In user-level security, there will be one password per user, so control of access to individual objects will be defined by control of rights. In share-level security, each object can have two passwords, one for full access—which grants all rights to the object that a standalone user would have—and one for read-only, which allows users to open or copy files in a folder, but not to change or delete files in the folder, or add files to the folder. The **Depends on Password** option will let users switch access types by switching passwords.

Remember that if a drive or a folder is shared, all of its contents (including subfolders) are shared as well. You can't restrict access to a folder if its parent folder is shared (Figure 10.36). You can, however, leave the parent folder unshared but share individual subfolders (Figure 10.37).

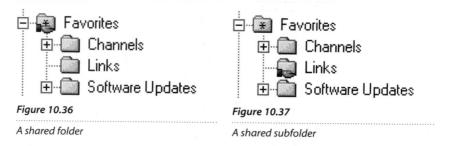

**Figure 10.36**

A shared folder

**Figure 10.37**

A shared subfolder

Because you can share subfolders of an unshared parent folder, the folder structure of shared resources often appears different on remote computers than it does on your computer. That's because subfolders move up a level on a remote display when the parent folder is not shared. As a result, your carefully crafted hierarchy of folders and subfolders may travel far over the network, only to turn into anarchy on the recipient's screen.

# Network Security

Windows 98's handy Properties sheets and dialogs store all kinds of information about a resource and allow you to modify many attributes. Each resource, from a folder to a disk drive to a printer, has a Properties dialog unique to itself. A little savvy and you'll be customizing your resources with abandon.

## Security and Network Properties

To look at a resource's Properties sheet, right-click on its icon in the Explorer, My Computer, or the Desktop, then choose Properties from the Context menu. Properties dialogs vary wildly from one item to the next, but almost all have at least two tabs, organized by the kinds of information they contain. For network use, we're interested in the Sharing tab of a folder's Properties dialog, which will let you share resources, assign a resource a descriptive name, or restrict access to the resource with a password.

## Assigning a Resource Name

When you share a resource, you can assign it a special name for sharing on remote computers. It will appear when other users select Details from the View menu.

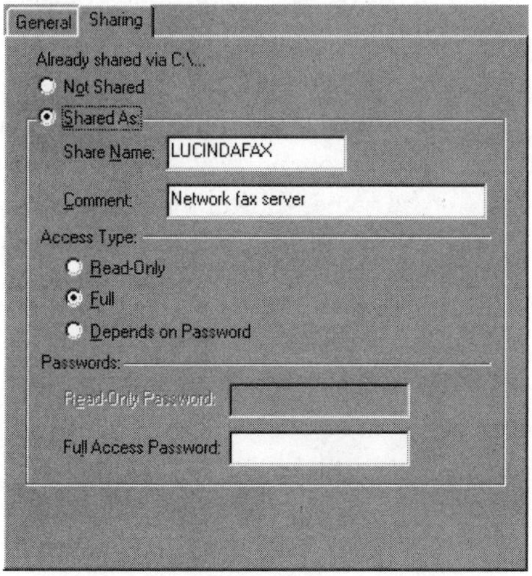

**Figure 10.38**

Setting up a
Share Name
in Properties

To assign a resource name, right-click on the resource's icon in the Explorer, then choose Sharing from the Context Menu. On the Sharing page, type a name for the resource in the Share Name box (Figure 10.38). You can also add a one-line comment that remote users will see when they select Details from the View menu.

Thoughtfully used, resource naming can save time and minimize frustration for people sharing your folders. For example, the folder name Ch1EdSch5-98 might make perfect sense to you, but your co-workers would probably appreciate seeing Chap1, Editing Schedule for May '98.

 You can assign a resource name, assign passwords, and restrict access to any shared resource on your computer, but not to shared resources on remote computers, even if you have full permission to access those resources.

 You can share an object quietly, hiding it from the Network Neighborhood browsing list. Simply append a dollar sign to the end of the object's share name; for example, *Doom* becomes *Doom$*. It's a good way to hide your games folder from the casual busybody. Others can share the folder only if they know it's there; they have to choose **Map Network Drive** from the Tools menu in the Explorer, then enter the exact pathname in the Map Network Drive dialog box. For more information about drive mapping, see *Mapping Network Drives* on page 404.

### Down To Our Last Dollar

Having said that, we'll point out that it's important to keep your share names from becoming unruly, especially if some of them don't show. If you right-click on **Network Neighborhood**, click on **Map Network Drive…**, and click on the drop arrow at the right-hand end of the **Path** field, you'll get a drop-down list of proposed UNC's to be mapped to the appropriate drive letter (Figure 10.39). The problem is that those proposed UNC's are based on what the network drive share names *have been* in the past. If, in the meantime, you've gone into **My Computer**, right-clicked on the icon for that drive, opened its Properties sheet, and filled in a *new* share name … well, then the share names in Drive Properties and in Map Network Drive Path won't be the same.

When they aren't, depending on whether the client or the server authenticates your logon, you can see some bizarre dialogs, of which the least misleading is probably "Network path not found." This can be hard enough to puzzle out anyway, and if—thanks to a dollar-signed share name—one of the mismatched shares is *invisible*, it's worse. Sharing drives is serious business, kids. We're not saying don't do it. We're just saying, be careful.

**Figure 10.39**

*Historical drive mapping list*

While we're discussing *gotcha!*'s that you're likely to get got by, don't forget that sharing isn't persistent when it's re-established. In English that means that, if you have user-level security running and you switch to share-level—or the other way around—your existing shares are stripped off, and they all have to be set up again. This isn't quite as bad as a misaligned share name, but it can be disconcerting when you switch security levels, and a few of your computers vanish because they aren't shared any more. The real point here is that you should switch security levels infrequently, with ample warning to your users, and only after deep consideration.

## Assigning Passwords

Passwords are used for shared resources when share-level security is in place. If no password is in force, anyone with access to the network can open a shared resource. By assigning passwords, you can limit the community of people who can see or change your files. Remember that you, in turn, can assign passwords and restrict access only to resources located on, or attached to, your own computer. Full access to a resource on a remote machine doesn't include the right to change the access password.

You assign passwords using a shared resource's Properties sheet. In the Explorer, right-click on the resource, then choose Properties from the Context menu. Click on the Sharing tab and type the passwords you want to use.

To assign one password to several folders at the same time, drag with the right mouse button in the Explorer to select a group of folders, then choose Sharing from the Shortcut menu. The password you type on the Sharing page applies to all the folders you selected.

## Managing Network Printing and Other Resources

Windows 98 controls every printer through its own queue, and you can inspect the queues of printers on a network as easily as checking out your local printer; double-click on any network printers icon to see that printer's queue. The information in a network's print queues can give you an idea of which printer will be available first.

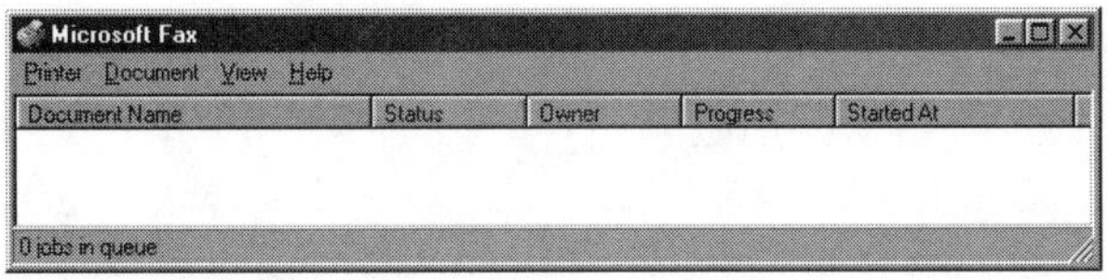

**Figure 10.40**

A print queue

If you have administrative privileges for a printer, you can right-click on any print job to pause, resume, or cancel it, or use the commands on the Print menu to stop or start the printing of all jobs at once. You can also rearrange the order of print jobs in a queue by highlighting jobs you want to move, then pressing the up and down arrow keys to reposition them.

When you print to a network printer, a printer icon appears next to the clock in the Windows 98 taskbar and remains for as long as the print job is pending or printing. When the print job is completed, the icon disappears. This little device enables you to monitor print job status without getting up to check the printer.

## Network Tools

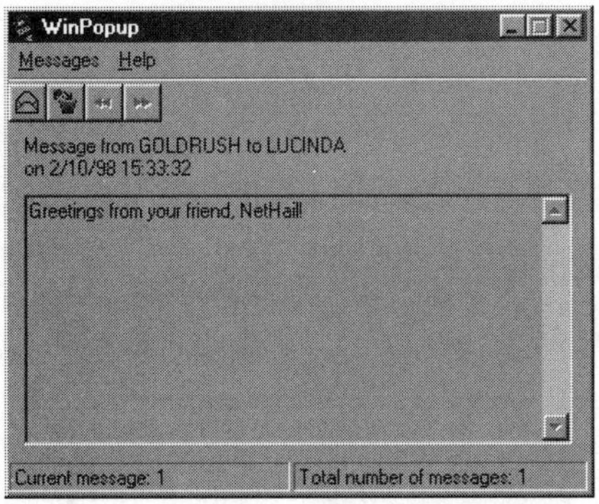

**Figure 10.41**

WinPopup in action

When you're managing a network, you never seem to have quite enough tools and utilities to do it with.

**WinPopup.**  WinPopup is a little applet that you can use to send a broadcast message, to one person or to a whole workgroup. WinPopup can also display received messages from other users on your network, or from a printer when your print job is done. With WinPopup, you can send messages from computers running Windows for Workgroups, Windows 95, and Windows 98, and receive them from Windows NT, Windows 9*x*, LAN Manager, and Windows for Workgroups servers and clients. Like the Clipboard, it's not fancy, but it's perennially useful.

To send a message:

Click the Send button on the toolbar; select **Messages\Send;** or hit Ctrl S to open the Send Message dialog.

Click to specify whether to send the message to a specific **User or computer** or to a **Workgroup**. Then type the recipient's name. Some defaults, such as the current workgroup, may be proposed.

Type a message, and then click on OK.

To page to the previous or next message, click the Previous or Next button on the toolbar; select **Messages\Previous** or **Messages\Next;** or hit Ctrl P or Ctrl N.

If you're at the first or last message one of these will be grayed out. This is important, because WinPopup only displays one message in each dialog pane, so if you have a big stack, you'll be keeping your place in it with the status bar information and the states of your arrow buttons.

To discard a message, click the Discard button on the toolbar; select **Messages\Discard;** or hit Ctrl D to delete the current message without confirmation.

To discard *all* messages, select **Messages\Clear All,** or hit Ctrl C to clear the stack; you'll be asked to confirm.

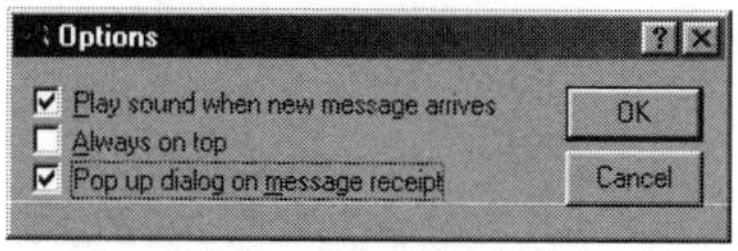

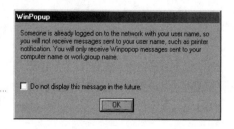

*Figure 10.42*

WinPopup options

Select **Messages\Options** or hit Ctrl O to pop up the Options dialog with three choices: **Play sound when new message arrives,** default checked; **Always on top,** default cleared; and **Pop up dialog on message receipt,** default cleared. Actually, the "dialog" that pops up "on message receipt" is WinPopup itself—you have to have it loaded in order to get messages at all, so this box just controls whether or not WinPopup jumps out of the Taskbar when a message arrives.

*Figure 10.43*

WinPopup multiple login warning

If you're logged in to more than one computer on the network at once, WinPopup only sends your personal messages to the computer where you've been logged in the longest, but at least it warns you.

## NeTHail

One of the biggest nuisances about inter-computer messaging on a Windows network with an NT server is that you can't deploy WinPopup network-wide; it's one of those irksome little 16-bit programs that NT won't condescend to run. Aren't we lucky that there's **NeTHail** by Oleg V. Toropov, which amounts to an NT version of WinPopup, only better:

Because it was written with discipline as well as skill, this utility is exactly what it needs to be. It's easy to install, tiny (at least by NT standards), intuitive to operate, and free for noncommercial or educational use. Commercial licensing is $10 per seat or $149 per unlimited site. Pick up an evaluation copy at `http://www.geocities.com/SiliconValley/Bay/1999/NT_Hail.html` or e-mail the author at `torus_ot@geocities.com`.

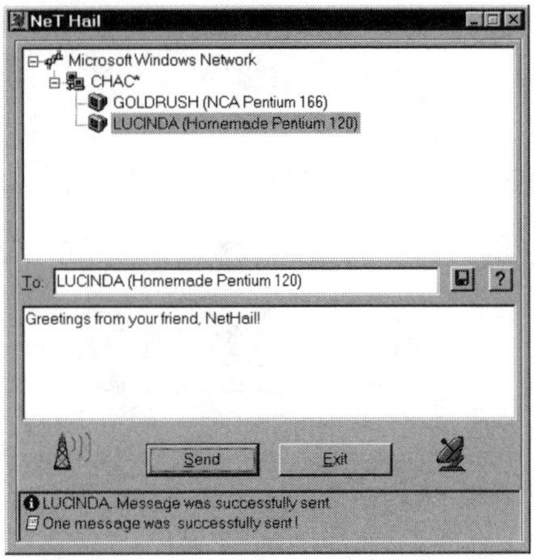

**Figure 10.44**

*NeTHail*

**Net Watcher.** Like a spy satellite, Net Watcher shows everything that's happening on a network, from connections with peer computers to the sharing of resources. *Note* that you must have File and Print Sharing enabled in order to use this tool.

Net Watcher is buried in **Start Menu\Programs\Accessories\System Tools** (Figure 10.45). If you need it and it's not there, you can install it through Control Panel\Add/Remove Programs\Windows Setup\Accessories; click on the Details button, check Net Watcher, and install it.

Net Watcher lets you choose three views of network activity from its View menu: *By Connection, By Shared Folders,* and *By Open Files.*

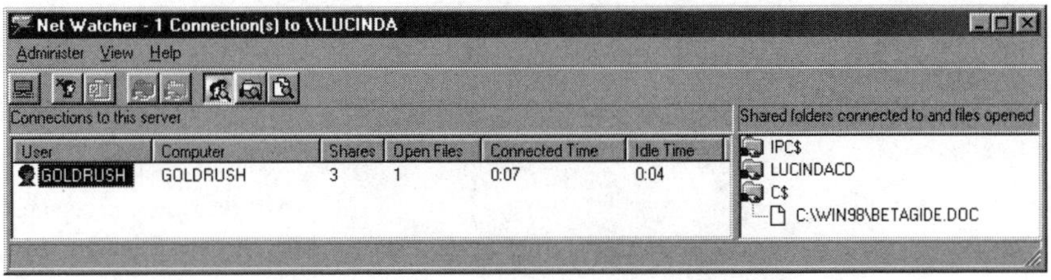

**Figure 10.45**

*Net Watcher By Connection*

**By Connection** shows you which users are connected to at least one resource on your computer. If you select a user's name from the User column, you can see what resources and files that user is accessing.

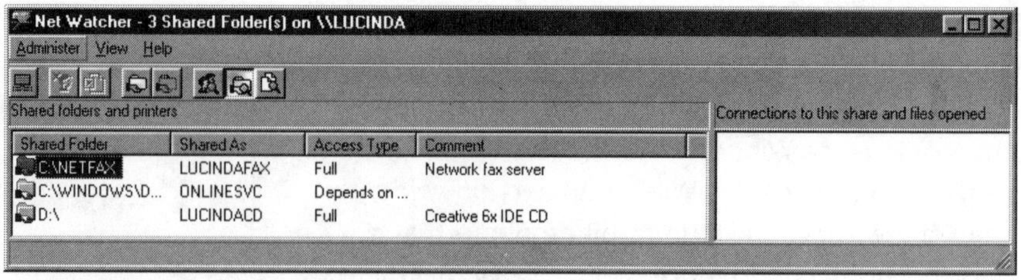

**Figure 10.46**

Net Watcher By
Shared Folders

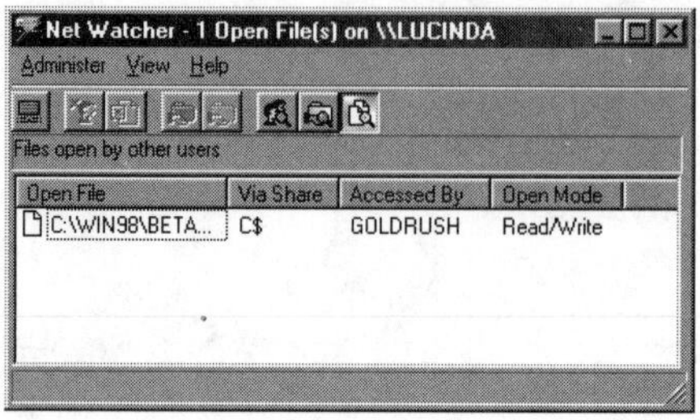

**Figure 10.47**

Net Watcher By
Open Files

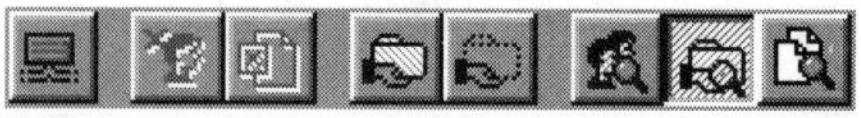

**Figure 10.48**

Net Watcher toolbar

**By Shared Folders** lets you select each resource you are sharing, and see which users are connected to it.

**By Open Files** lists all files that are open and shows who is using each file.

The Net Watcher toolbar gives pushbutton convenience. Naturally, some buttons will be available and some will be grayed out, depending on which view is active. From left to right the buttons are **Select server, Disconnect user, Close file, Add share, Stop sharing, Show users, Show shared folders,** and **Show** [open] **files.**

*Remote Network Administration.* You can use Net Watcher to disconnect users, to share or stop sharing resources, and to modify sharing properties. Choose a view from the View menu, select a resource you want to modify or a user you want to disconnect, and choose a command from the File menu or use the toolbar buttons.

If you are on a client-server network, you can use Net Watcher to locate and connect to servers. From the Administer menu choose Select Server and then either type in the name of the server you want to view or choose one from the Browse list.

**WinIPCfg.** How in heck do you pronounce *that?* Don't bother, just use it. In these days of total-immersion Internet, WinIPCfg can save your skin.

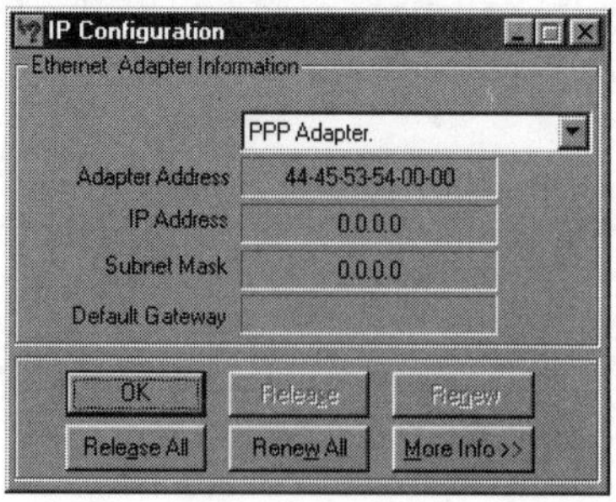

**Figure 10.49**

WinIPCfg Default
view

To start with, WinIPCfg hands you the six-byte MAC address for each adapter installed in your system, which can be almost impossible to discover otherwise; and its IP address, of which the same is true, if it's dynamically assigned. But the treat comes when you click the **More Info>>** button and find out everything you could possibly know

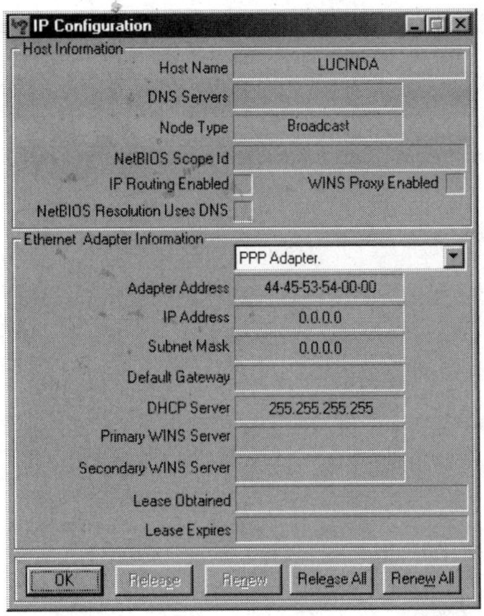

**Figure 10.50**

WinIPCfg Full view

about your TCP/IP adapter, including its WINS server and lease information (Figure 10.50). And you can obtain this information for every adapter in the system, dial-up, pop-in, or hardwired!

WinIPCfg is unusual for a dialog of its type; you can click the **More Info>>** button to go from the default to the full view, but once you're in the full view, there's no going back. You have to close WinIPCfg and relaunch it.

WinIPCfg has four commands:

- **Release** releases the IP address of the currently selected adapter (returns it to the pool of addresses)

- **Renew** reaches out to the address pool—whether that's a DHCP or WINS server, an LMHOSTS file, or Autonet—and refreshes the IP address of the currently selected adapter.

- **Release All** does the same thing as *Release,* but for every adapter in the computer.

- **Renew All** does the same thing as *Renew,* but for every adapter in the computer.

Now, why? Say you've got a laptop attached to your company network. After lunch you have to go to the branch office and take the laptop with you, but remain attached to the network. Simple! Before you detach the laptop from the headquarters network, run WinIPCfg and click **Release,** to give the laptop's IP address back to the local pool. When you get to the branch office, attach to the network and click **Renew,** to request a fresh IP address from the branch office server. And believe us, if you didn't have WinIPCfg, this would be a knuckle-busting nuisance.

 You can get most of the same information from **ipconfig /all** (see below) at a DOS prompt, but you don't have the pushbutton commands.

**TCP/IP Utilities.**   These TCP/IP utilities run in a DOS box, and are mostly for use when you connect to UNIX and other non-Microsoft hosts. The tools are installed automatically when you install the TCP/IP protocol, and they only work if you do.

| Command | Purpose |
| --- | --- |
| *arp* | Displays and modifies the MAC (IP-to-Ethernet) address translation tables. |
| *ftp* | Transfers files to and from a node running ftp service. The prompt is ftp>, and quit gets you out. |
| *ipconfig* | Displays configurations of local IP adapters. You might want to use WinIPCfg instead. |
| *nbtstat* | Displays protocol statistics and current TCP/IP connections using NetBIOS over TCP/IP. If you use it without switches, displays the list of switches. |
| *netstat* | Displays protocol statistics and current TCP/IP connections. |
| *ping* | Verifies connections to a remote host or hosts. If you use it without switches, displays the list of switches. |
| *route* | Manually controls network routing tables. If you use it without switches, displays the subcommands PRINT, ADD, DELETE, and CHANGE, and examples. |
| *telnet* | A bare-bones but robust telnet client. If you type telnet or start tel net at the DOS prompt, pops up in a window resembling Notepad's. |
| *tracert* | Determines the route taken to a destination. If you use it without switches, displays the list of switches and their parameters. |

These are arcane enough that, if you need to use them, you probably know how already; but if you need a refresher, they're well documented in the *Resource Kit* for Windows 98, 95 or NT.

 Bear in mind that, since you're visiting the world of Real Computers©, most of these commands and switches can be case-sensitive.

**System Monitor.**   Since performance is eternally a network issue (and we don't mean having too much of it!) we encourage all network administrators to get comfortable with the Windows System Monitor in **Start Menu\ Programs\Accessories\System Tools.** It's not as broadshouldered as the awesome NT Performance Monitor, but it can still tell you where your bottlenecks are. You'll find System Monitor discussed in Chapter 17, "Tips, Tools, and Tech Support."

### If You Need More

Plow as we might, we've only scratched the surface here. Windows TCP/IP is a hugely complicated subject, about which this book is not *the* book. We unhesitatingly recommend *MCSE: TCP/IP Study Guide*, by Todd and Monica Lammle and James Chellis (Network Press/SYBEX, 1997: ISBN 0-7821-1969-7). Last we looked, you could buy this at **Amazon.com**, and maybe your boss will reimburse you.

# Summary

The fully graphical and completely scalable network architecture of Windows 98, bolstered by the optional server-based resources of Windows NT, has finally resulted in quick, affordable, and relatively straightforward computer networking for the common man and woman. Resources, such as hard disks, removable-media drives, tape backups, and printers, can be made substantially more cost-effective by connecting them to, and sharing them in, a Windows network. Learning the terms and setting the priorities for constructing a larger network can be time-consuming, but Microsoft has made a comprehensive effort to provide you with the tools and the information you'll need.

# 11

# Data
# Communications

Those of us who have made a living by pulling and pushing data over the telephone network (emphatically including Kip and Fred) have a special reason to remember September 11, 1940. On that day, at a meeting of the American Mathematical Society in Dartmouth, New Hampshire, the famous mathematician and circuit scientist George R. Stibitz used a Teletype to communicate with the Complex Number Computer—really a fancy relay-and-vacuum-tube calculator—at Bell Labs in Murray Hill, New Jersey. He sent a problem to the calculator over a phone line, and it sent back the answer.

The audience was impressed, and rightly so, because this was the world's first demonstration of remote computing—of what, in mainframe days, became known as *remote job entry* and swept the globe. With every succeeding generation of computers, this exchange of information has become relatively more important, until today almost every desktop computer has a piece of twisted-pair extending from its backplane to a phone jack.

*Data communications,* or *telecommunications* if it involves the phone system, covers any connection between two or more computers that requires a dedicated ("hardwired") connection or a modem, telecommunications software, and a telephone line. Communications encompasses an incredible spectrum of activities, from sending and receiving mail and faxes to remote networking, from playing games over a modem with a friend across town to electronically traversing the world on the Internet. But no matter what, your computer is talking to another personal computer, a mainframe, a large information service such as the Microsoft Network or America Online, or an Internet service provider.

In this chapter, we discuss installing and configuring a modem; the Hyper-Terminal dial-up program for basic communications; Dial-Up Networking, the Windows dial-up connector for Internet servers and online information services; Direct Cable Connection, which enables you to create a network connection to another computer using just a serial or parallel cable; the Windows Phone Dialer, and other applets. In Windows 98, automation of routine communications tasks is made much easier with Dial-Up Scripting and the Windows Scripting Host. This version of Windows offers a more robust suite of tools for connection-oriented communications in general.

This chapter does *not* include any material on cabling computers together using NetBIOS, NetBEUI, IPX/SPX, or TCP/IP, which is covered in

Chapter 10, "Networking." Using Internet Explorer 4.0 and Outlook Express for mail, news, and to surf the net is covered in Chapter 16, "Your Own Private Internet." Installing and configuring Dial-Up Networking is discussed in detail in Appendix C, "Dial-Up Networking Without Tears." Finally, for the sorry demise of Microsoft Fax, see "A Note On Fax."

# COM Ports and Windows 98

COM ports are serial communications ports—ports that transmit and receive one bit of data at a time—that are either built into your system's motherboard or supplied on add-in cards plugged into the computer's expansion bus. You met them incidentally in the chapter on Printers, but they become much more important when you start talking about moving data. Most communications software works with your computer's COM ports, although specialized applications—particularly fax programs—can talk to printer ports. Windows 98 sets up your COM ports automatically to work with your Windows-compatible software, searching through your system's BIOS chips to detect proper base I/O addresses and hardware interrupts (IRQs) for installed ports.

Most computer systems, except older notebook computers, include at least two COM ports, which are assigned the system names COM1 and COM2. A system that adheres to the IBM and DOS standard architecture can contain up to four COM ports—if you're careful about which ones you try to use at the same time—but you can have more if you're able to use nonstandard IRQs; see, for example, the description of the Mouse Systems Com-5 Card in Chapter 7. Windows, which can use nonstandard IRQs automatically through Plug and Play, allows you to define up to nine serial ports (COM1 through COM9) and automatically assigns a modem to one of them when you install the modem.

You usually access COM ports through either 9-pin or 25-pin male (pins-out) connectors on the backplane of a system unit. Some adapter cards, such as internal modems, use the COM port internally and simply provide a standard telephone-jack connector on the bracket at the back of the computer. If you're not sure what type of connectors you have or how they're defined, you have a few choices:

Refer to the documentation included with your hardware. It may be a bit dry, but after all, you paid someone to write it.

Go to **Start Menu\Programs\Accessories\System Tools** and open the
Microsoft System Information tool, which has three very useful screens (see
Figures 11.1 thru 11.3).

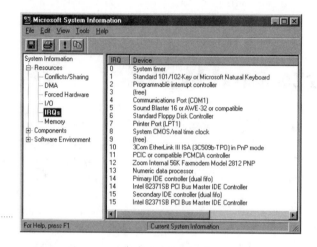

*Figure 11.1*

*IRQ list*

At **System Information\Resources\IRQs**, you find a list of all the IRQs in
the system and what's using them (Figure 11.1). In this particular case, pardon
the pun, IRQ3—which would normally belong to COM2/COM4—is free
because there's no second serial port. IRQ9, ordinarily reserved for the network
adapter, is free because Windows has put the Plug and Play NIC on IRQ10.

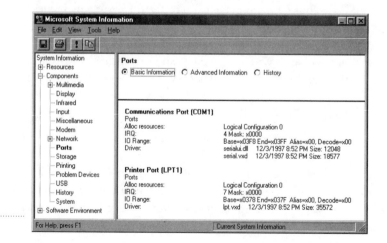

*Figure 11.2*

*Ports Basic list*

At **System Information\Components\Ports**, this (Figure 11.2) is a list of
useful information about all installed ports, including which configuration
they're part of, what their reserved IRQs and I/O ranges are, and what driver
files they use. Table 11.1 shows the standard interrupts and base I/O addresses
used by the COM ports on an ISA bus system.

## Table 11.1  Default Settings for COM Ports

| Port Name | Default ) Interrupt (IRQ | Default I/O Address (PC) | Default I/O Address (PS/2) |
|-----------|--------------------------|--------------------------|-----------------------------|
| **COM1** | 4 | 03F8h–03FFh | 03F8h–03FFh |
| **COM2** | 3 | 02F8h–02FFh | 02F8h–02FFh |
| **COM3** | 4 (PS/2: 3) | 03E8h–03EFh | 3220h–3227h |
| **COM4** | 3 | 02E8h–02EFh | 3228h–322Fh |

These are the serial port addresses and ranges that Windows 98 installs as part of Basic Configuration 0000. For a full explanation of Basic Configurations and how they work, consult Chapter 15, "Tips, Tools, and Troubleshooting."

Ports
- ○ Basic Information   ● Advanced Information   ○ History

```
Communications Port (COM1)
Ports
Registry Key:          HKEY_LOCAL_MACHINE\enum\BIOS\*PNP0501\0A
Alloc resources:       Logical Configuration 0
IRQ:                   4 Mask: x0000
IO Range:              Base=x03F8 End=x03FF Alias=x00, Decode=x00
Forced resources:      None
Boot resources:        Logical Configuration 0
IRQ:                   4 Mask: x0000
IO Range:              Base=x03F8 End=x03FF Alias=x00, Decode=x00
Filtered resources:    Logical Configuration 0
IRQ:                   0 Mask: x0010
IO Range:              Base=x0000 End=x0000 Min=x03F8 Max=x03FF Alias=x00, Decode
                       Logical Configuration 1
IRQ:                   0 Mask: x0008
IO Range:              Base=x0000 End=x0000 Min=x02F8 Max=x02FF Alias=x00, Decode
                       Logical Configuration 2
IRQ:                   0 Mask: x0010
IO Range:              Base=x0000 End=x0000 Min=x03E8 Max=x03EF Alias=x00, Decode
                       Logical Configuration 3
IRQ:                   0 Mask: x0008
IO Range:              Base=x0000 End=x0000 Min=x02E8 Max=x02EF Alias=x00, Decode
Basic resources:       Logical Configuration 0
IRQ:                   0 Mask: x0010
```

**Figure 11.3**

Ports Advanced list

If you need to know more than that, click the **Advanced Information** button and find out more than you ever wanted to (Figure 11.3). Actually this is handy if you need the Registry information about the port, which is immensely hard to find in the Registry itself.

**The one serial device that almost every computer has is a mouse/trackball/touchpad, and if you have a choice of which COM port to install it on, COM2 is probably your best bet. Why? Because, as the table above shows, COM1 and COM3 share IRQ4, while COM2 and COM4 share IRQ3. These days we'd bet on anybody's computer having three serial devices, but it's less likely to have four, which gives your pointing device—which must work uninterruptedly—a better chance at an IRQ of its very own. (Of course, if you're installing a Plug and Play modem, Windows will make this decision and your modem will probably be thrilled with IRQ12.)**

Windows detects conflicts between devices that try to use the same IRQ and, in general, mediates them. If there are conflicts between Plug and Play peripherals, Windows will resolve them, probably by kicking one device to a higher IRQ; in the days before 32-bit Windows, the IRQs above 9 were rarely accessible, but as Table 11.1 shows, Windows 98 uses them all the time. If you have a conflict between *non*–Plug and Play peripherals, Windows will tell you about it, but you need to reassign interrupt settings for the ports by hand. You do this with **Control Panel\System\Device Manager** (Figure 11.4).

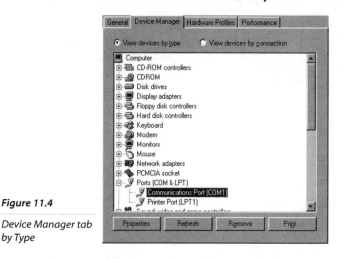

**Figure 11.4**

*Device Manager tab by Type*

If you look at the **by Type** tab, highlight the port (Figure 11.4), and click **Properties**, you'll get four tabs:

**General** is notable, in this case, only because in the **Device status** region you want to see the phrase "This device is working properly." If you see an error message and something about "(Code *xx.*)," then you'll need to figure out what's not working; the list in Appendix E, "Device Manager Error Codes," may help. Bear in mind we're debugging the *port* here and not whatever's attached to it.

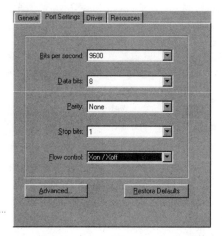

**Figure 11.5**

*Port Settings tab*

In **Port Settings** (Figure 11.5) there are definite gotchas: the Windows default for **Bits per second** is 9600, and for **Flow control** is Xon/Xoff. Consult your modem docs if in doubt, but in general, for almost any serial port made in the last three years, *BPS* should be set to about twice the nominal speed of the modem; try 38400 for a 14.4, 57600 for a 28.8 or 33.6, and 115200 for a 56K. (If you have an internal modem, Windows will set this automatically.) *Flow control* should be set to Hardware. As with all communications settings, your mileage may vary, so test thoroughly after changing them.

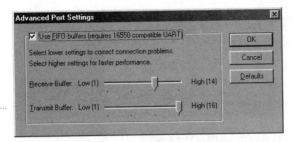

**Figure 11.6**

Port Settings
Advanced dialog

The **Advanced...** button of Port Settings (Figure 11.6) has sliders for the FIFO buffer size. Again, for any reasonably modern port, the **Use FIFO buffers** box should be checked, since the UART (control chip) in the port will be at least a 16550. The defaults on the sliders are about right for everything; push them higher if you're very sure of your connection quality. When the dialog says "Select lower settings to correct connection problems," it does *not* mean line noise, so before you start sliding these around to fix a flaky connection, listen to your line and make sure it isn't noisy.

**Driver** is of interest here only if you want to update the driver file.

**Figure 11.7**

Device Manager
Resource settings

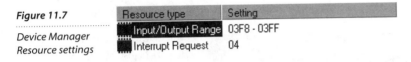

In Resources, as an example, the standard resource settings for COM1 should look like this (Figure 11.7). If Use automatic settings is checked and the Conflicting device list says "No conflicts," there are no problems here. Otherwise, hasten to Chapter 15, "Tips, Tools, and Troubleshooting."

 Don't leave the Device Manager without a peek at the best part. Highlight Computer at the top of the tree and click Properties.

**Figure 11.8**

Device Manager
Computer Properties

This gives you almost all the same information as the Microsoft System Information tool, but more concisely, and with less work to get to it. We'll discuss this Properties sheet more thoroughly in Chapter 15, "Tips, Tools, and Troubleshooting."

# Modem Installation

Windows 98 handles modems like any other hardware peripherals. If an internal modem is installed when you run Setup (or if an external modem is connected and turned on), Windows 98 configures the modem automatically.

## Installing Hardware

If you have already installed Windows 98, you'll have to add the modem by hand. Turn your computer off, install the modem, restart the computer, then install the device driver software through the Install New Modem wizard, as follows:

Double-click on the **Modems** icon in the Control Panel, then click on the **Add** button in the Modems Properties General tab. The Install New Modem dialog will ask whether you want to install a **PCMCIA modem card** or **Other**. Pick Other or refer to "Installing a PC Card Modem," below. Click **Next.**

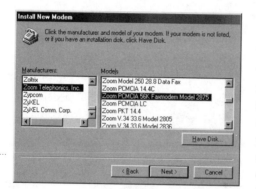

**Figure 11.9**

*The Install New Modem wizard*

Follow the directions in the **Install New Modem** dialog. The wizard can usually discern what type of modem you have; if it can't, you can go back and select your modem from a list (Figure 11.9). If the model you've installed doesn't appear on the list, either you can install drivers from the modem manufacturer by clicking on **Have Disk**, or you can install generic drivers that work with most modems.

At the top of the **Manufacturers** list, under (Standard Modem Types), there are entries for setting up hardwired serial or parallel communications with Dial-Up Networking. We're not sure exactly how these differ from setting up the same communications with Direct Cable Connection (below), but you might want to try both.

## Installing a PC Card Modem

Don't insert the card yet! At the Install New Modem dialog, pick **PCMCIA modem card**. Click **Next**.

Insert the card. The Add New Hardware Wizard will bring up the standard driver search dialog. Click **Next.**

Click **Search for the best driver for your device...** and click **Next.**

Pick the locations you want to have searched, including a floppy, your hard disk, the Windows CD, or the Microsoft Windows Update service. Click **Next.**

When driver installation is complete, click **Finish**, and when the main dialog appears with "Your modem has been set up successfully," click **Finish** again. Your PC Card device should now be a bonafide modem in the Modems list, installed on a specified serial port; you can run diagnostics on it as usual (see below).

The PC Card Services mini-icon will appear in the System Tray. Click on it once to bring up a button saying **Stop** [type of] **PCMCIA Card Modem**, and click the button before you eject the card. Right-click on it to bring up the PC Card Properties sheet, which shows you socket status and lets you tweak PC Card settings; for details, see "The PC Card Control Panel" in Chapter 13, "Optimizing."

The Properties of an installed PC Card modem will remain accessible even when the card is undocked.

On some, if not all, PC Card modems, the **Call preferences** and **Error control** options of Connection Properties are grayed out.

## Configuring the Modem

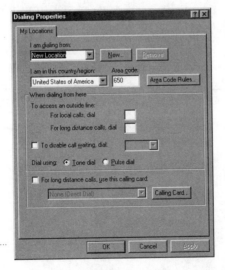

After your modem is installed, the Dialing Properties dialog opens (Figure 11.10). It has one tab, **My Locations**, which accepts the characteristics and calling card options of whatever phone you want to use to place calls. For example, if you connect via modem from your home phone, which has Call Waiting, you might want to disable the feature for business calls. These are your choices:

**I am dialing from**. The default is **New Location**, but you can replace this name, and you can also use the **New...** button to set up Dialing

*Figure 11.10*

*Dialing properties*

Properties pages for several different telephone lines.

**I am in this country/region** lets you pick from a list of countries from Afghanistan to Zimbabwe and including INMARSAT and International Freephone. Once you make this selection, Windows knows what country code to use.

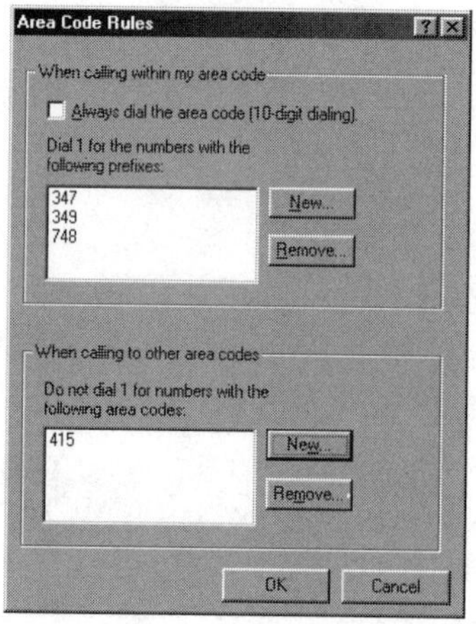

**Figure 11.11**

*Area Code Rules*

Once you fill in **Area code** with the local three-digit area code, Windows will—by default—*not* dial it when it occurs in the Address Book. If you don't want this behavior to be absolute, you can tune it with the **Area Code Rules** dialog (Figure 11.11) which makes room for exchanges that need a 1 to be dialed with them; for area codes that aren't local but don't need to be dialed (permissive dialing) and for the infuriating always-dial-ten-digits situation, which the whole world is probably headed for eventually.

This option is available only for the United States, Canada, and the English-speaking Caribbean.

In the **When dialing from here** region, you can enter your outside-line prefixes for local and long-distance calls; your string to disable call waiting—the drop menu offers **\*70**, **70#**, and **1170**, but you can enter anything else—and whether this line uses tone dial or pulse.

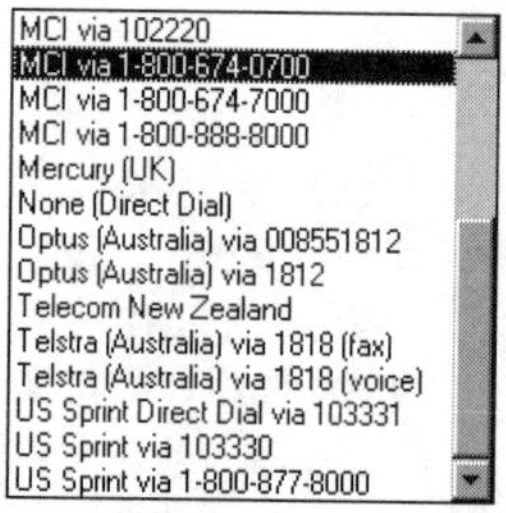

**Figure 11.12**

*Calling Card types*

Finally, the **Calling card** options conceal amazing depth. As soon as you check the **For long distance calls...** box, you can pick from a pop-up list of calling card types (Figure 11.12).

Click the **Calling Card...** button to open the Calling Card settings dialog (Figure 11.13) and enter the PIN and access codes for this calling card.

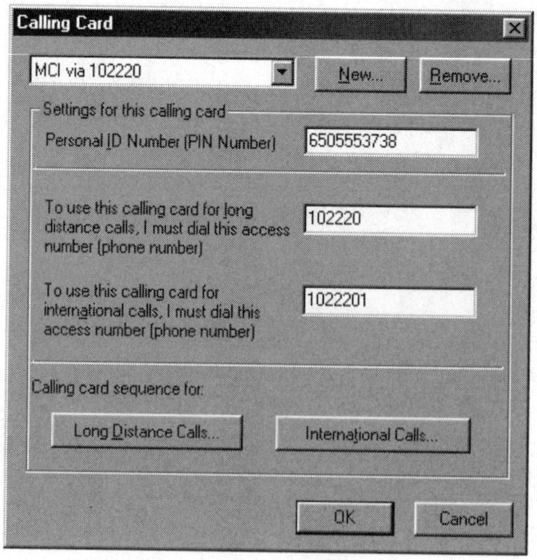

**Figure 11.13**

*Calling Card settings*

*Figure 11.14*

*Calling Card scripting*

If you have a type of card that wasn't in the pop-up list, you can use the **New...** and **Remove...** buttons to define a new card type. Then, by using the buttons under **Calling card sequence for**, you can set up sequences of actions and responses using a kind of scripting language (Figure 11.14).

## Modem Diagnostics

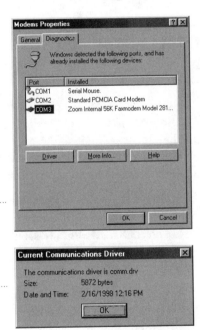

The **Diagnostics** tab of Modems Properties (Figure 11.15) tells you whether your modem is healthy. Actually, it reports on all the serial devices in your system, but doesn't tell you much about anything but the modems.

You can highlight the port name and double-click on it, which will do absolutely nothing, since all the action is through the three buttons shown in Figures 11.17 thru 11.19.

*Figure 11.15*

*Modems Diagnostics*

**Driver** shows what you see in Figure 11.16. Interestingly enough, this is *not* the same information you get when you go into Device Manager, highlight the modem, click **Properties**, select the **Drivers** tab, and click **Driver File Details**—which says the loaded drivers

*Figure 11.16*

*Current communications driver*

are SERIAL.VXD and VMM32.VXD, also known as VCOMM.VXD. What we *think* this means is that COMM.DRV is part of the Windows API, the side that the software talks to, while the .VXD files are the actual physical device drivers ... which, of course, Microsoft says don't exist any more because they were all replaced by a single universal driver. Maybe they're virtual virtual device drivers.

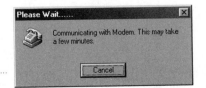

**More Info...** puts up a fancy sign (Figure 11.17) but the interrogation of the modem usually takes only a few seconds. If the modem doesn't answer the query, you'll

*Figure 11.17*

*Please Wait*

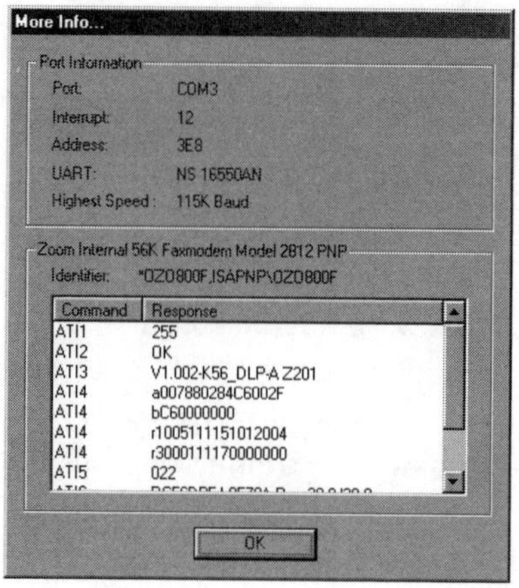

**More Info...**

Port Information
| | |
|---|---|
| Port: | COM3 |
| Interrupt: | 12 |
| Address: | 3E8 |
| UART: | NS 16550AN |
| Highest Speed: | 115K Baud |

Zoom Internal 56K Faxmodem Model 2812 PNP
Identifier:    *OZO800F\ISAPNP\OZO800F

| Command | Response |
|---|---|
| ATI1 | 255 |
| ATI2 | OK |
| ATI3 | V1.002-K56_DLP-A Z201 |
| ATI4 | a007880284C6002F |
| ATI4 | bC60000000 |
| ATI4 | r1005111151012004 |
| ATI4 | r3000111170000000 |
| ATI5 | 022 |

[ OK ]

*Figure 11.18*

*Modem Polling response*

get a box that says "Couldn't open port" or "Modem not communicating." (If the Please Wait lasts a long time, hit [Ctrl][Alt][Delete] to pop up the Task Manager and see if the process has gone off its rails.) After poking around, it comes up with Figure 11.18.

You will need the original docs for your modem, probably bolstered with considerable intuition, to figure out what your modem replied to Windows' queries, but ordinarily that's beside the point; if all these values look reasonable, either the modem works, or you should be able to go through the output line by line and figure out where the discrepancy is. A **Print** option here would be extra-useful, alas …

 The "Identifier" just above the list of commands and responses is this device's hardware enumerator from HKEY_LOCAL_MACHINE in the Registry, which can be handy if you have a REGEDIT window open and you're trying to find out what's attached to what.

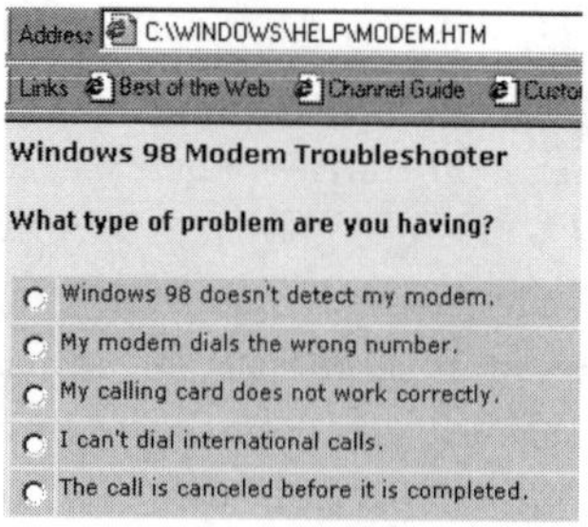

Address [ C:\WINDOWS\HELP\MODEM.HTM ]
Links [ Best of the Web ] [ Channel Guide ] [ Custo ]

**Windows 98 Modem Troubleshooter**

**What type of problem are you having?**

○ Windows 98 doesn't detect my modem.
○ My modem dials the wrong number.
○ My calling card does not work correctly.
○ I can't dial international calls.
○ The call is canceled before it is completed.

*Figure 11.19*

*Modem Troubleshooter (detail)*

**Help** opens Internet Explorer and a useful local Web page called the Windows 98 Modem Troubleshooter (Figure 11.19) which you can use to zero in on your problems by eliminating possibilities one at a time.

# Buying and Maintaining Hardware

The kind of modem or digital connection you choose will depend very much on the services available in your area, your taste in hardware, and your budget for monthly access. It's also an important choice, because if you're like most of us, from now on you'll spend more and more time on the Net. Therefore fearlessly we say: *A 33.6K or 28.8K modem working alone will not cut it.* Such devices should be Multilinked or bonded (see page 490) put out to pasture with e-mail-only systems, sold in yard sales, or given to your favorite cause.

## What Should You Connect With?

Top-rated **56K modems** are available, as we write, for less than $150. Previously, the one you picked depended on whether your service provider supported the US Robotics x2 technology, or Rockwell's K56flex, or both; now that the emerging ITU-T 56K standard has been promulgated, new firmware should be available in "universal" 56K modems soon.

**Bonding modems** are available at either 112K (two channels of 56K) or with one channel of 56K plus the ability to "bond in" the bandwidth of the modem you already have.

**ISDN**, giving 64K on one channel or 128K on two, is probably available from your local phone company; it requires special installation and its charges accrue by the minute, so that many early adopters have concluded that the performance increase isn't worth the bother.

**Cable modems** deliver multimegabit throughput, orders of magnitude faster than any analog modem—but the technology is young, availability is uneven, and the price varies wildly. Also, if you live in an apartment or condo, you may be told that you don't have the "right kind" of cable to support a modem.

Satellite **mini-dishes** like DirecPC are an interesting possibility especially if you live in an area with scant alternatives. Watch out for the costs—they can creep up on you.

**T1**, whole or fractional, gives crystalline high-speed throughput, but requires special installation and special hardware at your end; it also costs so much that it's hard to justify unless you spend most of your life on the Net and get paid doing it.

*x*DSL technology will eventually make all this academic, delivering Web content over plain old phone wire with the speed and snap of television. Unfortunately, at this writing it's years away, and even the standards are still being hammered out.

# Changing Settings

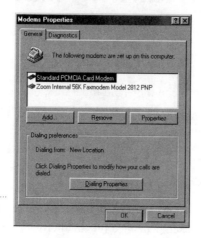

To change the settings of your modem after initial setup, open the **General** tab of Control Panel\Modems Properties (Figure 11.20). This Properties sheet shows you which modem and location are active (or selected).

Most of the options in the Modem Properties sheet require no configuration. **Add** adds a new modem and **Remove** removes the highlighted modem; bear in mind that, while adding a modem is generally automatic, removing one is always a manual process. The **Properties** button

**Figure 11.20**

*Modems Properties General tab*

brings you to the few settings you might want to tweak (Figure 11.21, 11.22):

**General\Speaker volume** controls the speaker in the modem, not in or connected to your computer. Although this is a slider, it offers only four settings. We recommend that you leave this at the lowest audible setting rather than turn it off, since if your modem is having trouble connecting, your ears are your most formidable diagnostic tool.

**General\Maximum speed** should ordinarily be set to a number about twice the rated speed of your modem—and if you have an external modem, your computer's serial port should be set to the matching speed; see page 466. You'll want to run your modem at its fastest speed when possible, but if you often encounter problems—such as corrupted files, garbage on the screen, or dropped connections with commercial online services—you may want to try

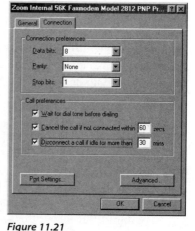

**Figure 11.21**

*Specific Modem Properties General tab*

**Figure 11.21**

*Specific Modem Properties Connection tab*

forcing the modem to run at a slower speed, which can make the connection more robust, although of course everything runs more slowly. Note that some older Windows telecommunications programs allow you to set the modem speed from within the program. You can check the **Only connect at this speed** checkbox if you'd rather redial for the fastest possible connection, rather than settling for any old connection you get; make sure that this option is supported by both your modem and the remote site.

**Connection\Connection Preferences:** Almost all the data connections you're likely to make today are **Data bits 8**, **Parity None**, and **Stop bits 1**, so set those as the defaults. If you need to set different values for one particular connection, you can override the defaults with the particular communications software you're using, like Dial-Up Networking.

**Connection\Call Preferences:** The **Wait for dial tone before dialing** checkbox is normally checked, but you can uncheck it to help you connect in special situations. For example, some central voicemail systems warn you of waiting messages by making the dial tone into a stutter tone or high-pitched whine, and although *you* realize that's still a dial tone, your modem doesn't. If you uncheck this box, the modem will dial anyway. You might also want to uncheck it if you have to dial manually.

**Cancel the call if not connected within *nn* secs** and **Disconnect a call if idle for more than *nn* mins** are useful if you're making an automated connection or if, for any reason, you want to make a connection and leave it running unobserved. If you're paying for time to either your Internet service provider or your telephone company, and you leave your modem connected overnight by accident, it can cost you a bunch ...

**Connection\Port Settings...** (Figure 11.6) gets you to the same dialog as Device Manager\Properties\Port Settings, with the same defaults, thank heavens. *Note,* though, that in Device Manager you get to this with the button called **Advanced...** and in Modem Properties\Connection you get to it with the button called **Port Settings...**, so it's not you that's confused, it's Windows.

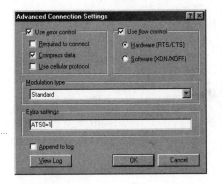

**Connection\Advanced...** (Figure 11.23) has a whole bunch of options, any of which you're likely to set once and forget about, and most of which you'll never need:

**Use error control: Required to connect** forces what's called a *reliable connection,* for better success rates with indifferent line quality. Not all modems can enforce this. **Compress**

*Figure 11.23*

*Advanced Connections Settings*

**data** turns on the hardware (not the software) data compression, but again, you have to be sure that the modems at both ends know how to speak the language. **Use cellular protocol** is for wireless modems.

**Use flow control: Hardware** uses an acknowledgement called RTS/CTS (Ready to Send/Clear to Send) to make the stream of data start and stop, and prevent overruns. **Software** uses an older acknowledgement called Xon/Xoff, which doesn't always work. Of the two, RTS/CTS is clearly preferable, but it has to be built into the modems at both ends; these days it usually is, but check your modem docs if you're not sure.

 You can use the checkboxes to turn error control and flow control completely off, but we don't recommend it!

*Figure 11.24*

*Modulation types*

Non-standard (Bell, HST)
Standard
V.23 (Minitel)

Modulation type has three choices (Figure 11.24) and Standard is what you're likely to need. As for Non-standard, Bell is the *'way* old Bell 103A type for 300 baud modems, while HST (High Speed Technology) was a proprietary architecture that US Robotics—now part of 3Com—used in its fastest modems between 1986 and the early nineties. If you have an HST, you already realize it. V.23 (Minitel) enables Windows communications to run on the French Minitel national intranet.

Extra settings is a plain-text field; anything you put in here will be transmitted intact to your modem, so if you need to send commands that aren't included in the standard Windows controls, this is the place for them.

Append to log saves all new session statistics to the files \WINDOWS\MODEMLOG.TXT; the View log button opens this file in Notepad. This can be useful for connection debugging, should you be stuck with doing any. The file \WINDOWS\[*modemname*].LOG may be involved here too.

 The interesting thing about MODEMLOG.TXT is that it tells you which section of which .INF file (minidriver) the modem is using. This can be hard to find out otherwise.

## Dialing Properties

Once you've finished setting up your modem, you can access the Dialing Properties dialog (Figure 11.10) with the button on the Modems Properties General tab.

## Hardware Summary

All your Windows 98 communications software—Outlook Express, HyperTerminal, and Phone Dialer—uses the modem settings recorded in Modems Properties; you don't need to tweak settings for each program. You may still need to adjust modem settings for applications that don't take advantage of the Windows 98 universal modem driver, such as older communications programs you used with Windows 3.1.

You may need to change connection settings to match a remote computer's. Any changes you make to those settings in the Modem Control Panel become, or at least affect, the default settings for Connections in all applications. If you need to change settings for a specific Connection, change them from within the program you use to connect to the remote computer. HyperTerminal, for example, saves settings for individual Connections.

# HyperTerminal

Default path:  **Start Menu\Accessories\Communications\**
              **HyperTerminal**

A licensed terminal and file transfer program; the slimmed-down version of HyperAccess by Hilgraeve. HyperTerminal is a rudimentary piece of telecommunications software that allows you to communicate with another computer to exchange files, or to connect to an external source of information in pre-Internet format, such as an electronic bulletin board service (BBS) or a public library.

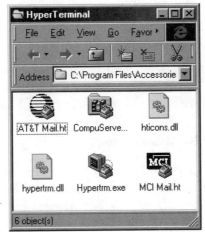

*Figure 11.25*

*The HyperTerminal folder*

HyperTerminal has the reputation of being somewhat fearsome to set up, but it's much more approachable if you're already accustomed to Dial-Up Networking, because it works like a cross between Dial-Up Networking and telnet. Start with the folder (Figure 11.25) which contains the main HyperTerminal file icon—that is not a Shortcut, so don't delete it—along with two DLL files, one an icon library and one for Properties sheet magic, and the three default connections supplied with the program.

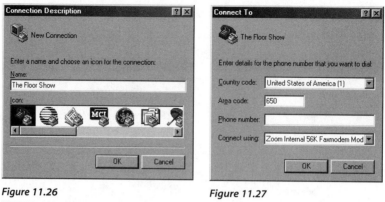

**Figure 11.26**

Connection Description dialog

**Figure 11.27**

Connect To dialog

The bad news is that, just as with DUN, you have to create a separate Connection for every number you want to call. The good news is that setting up a Connection isn't difficult. The first time you open the HyperTerminal program, you create a new Connection automatically; key in a name (Figure 11.26), pick an icon, and click **OK**.

The **Connect To** dialog comes up with the country code, area code and chosen modem pulled from Modems Properties; HyperTerminal is integrated with Windows 98, which means that as we've mentioned, once you install your modem you don't need to configure communications software separately. Key in the phone number (Figure 11.27) and click **OK**.

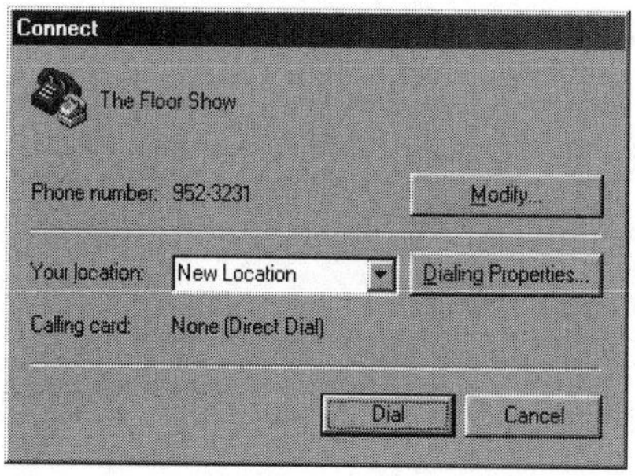

**Figure 11.28**

Connect dialog

The next thing you'll see is the **Connect** dialog (Figure 11.28), and you can simply dial from here by clicking the **Dial** button; but until you're thoroughly familiar with HyperTerminal, you might as well take a look at the **Modify...** and **Dialing Properties...** buttons, both of which conceal surprises.

## Configuration and Settings

Click the **Modify...** button, and the Properties sheet resembles much that we've already seen, with three exceptions; the **Redial on busy** checkbox, the **Configure...** button (Figure 11.29) and the **Settings** tab (Figure 11.30).

Click the **Configure...** button, and the Properties sheet looks like—in fact, it is—Windows 98's own Modems Properties, but HyperTerminal has added an interesting **Options** tab. **Bring up terminal window before** or **after dialing**

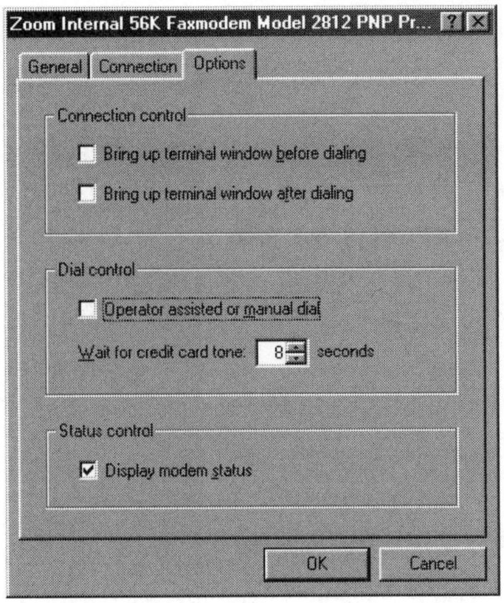

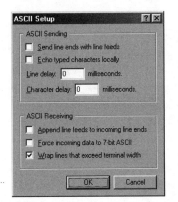

**Figure 11.29**

*Specific Modem Properties Options tab*

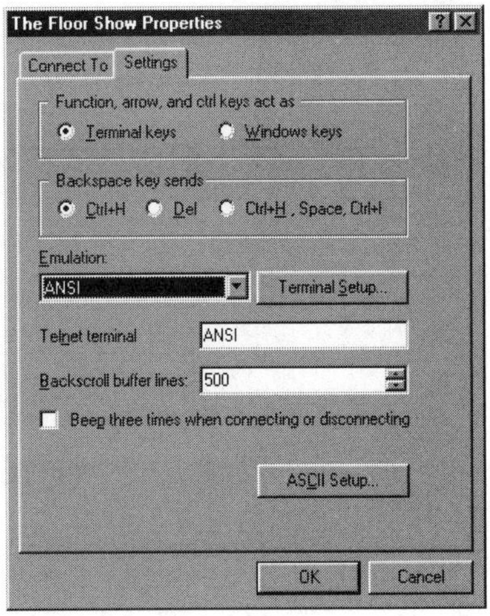

**Figure 11.30**

*Connection Properties Settings tab*

are useful when you need to command the modem or log in directly from your keyboard. **Operator assisted or manual dial** helps out when a hotel operator or receptionist stands between you and an unassisted connection. **Wait for credit card tone** sets the delay to enter a credit card number before the computers negotiate. **Display modem status**, if checked, parks a modem icon with blinkenlights in the System Tray.

Click the **Settings** tab to discover a wealth of terminal settings. You can set up your function, arrow, Ctrl, and Backspace keys to behave the way they do under Windows, or the way they do on the terminal you're emulating. Your computer can emulate eight different common terminal types, or default to **Auto detect** and do its best to match what's expected of it. If you set **Emulation** to any specific terminal type, you can use **Terminal Setup...** to set things like the cursor attributes, although exactly what you can set depends on the specific terminal. The **Telnet terminal** type can be different from the base terminal type—seems like gilding the lily to us, but someone somewhere will need it—and you can enable audible connect and disconnect. Finally, click on **ASCII Setup** and configure your delays and formatting for exchanging text. (You'll want to connect to the host and see what you get, or they get, before you start making these adjustments. In general, the defaults will work fine.)

**Figure 11.31**

*ASCII Setup dialog*

All in all, this is one smart program for a dumb terminal!

## Dialing Properties

HyperTerminal makes only one change to Windows' standard **Dialing Properties...**, but it's useful; the **Dial as a long distance call** checkbox. "What," you might ask dizzily, "is the difference between that and **Always dial the area code** under **Area Code Rules**?!" Answer is—**Always dial...** dials the area code and phone number, but HT's **Dial as...** dials *1 and* the area code and phone number. The difference will become apparent when you (say) take your laptop outside your usual area code, want to call home, and have to dial the 1. Dial-Up Networking also has this feature, but it should be available everywhere in Windows.

## Connecting with Another Computer

HyperTerminal, like most Windows apps and applets, gives you multiple ways to do anything. Once you've set up a Connection, you can dial it by double-clicking on its icon in the HyperTerminal folder, then run it from the Toolbar (Figure 11.32).

*Figure 11.32*

*Toolbar*

The Toolbar buttons are **New** Connection, **Open** Connection, **Call**, **Hang up**, **Send** file, **Receive** file, and Connection **Properties**. (If you haven't opened a Connection from the folder yet, some of these buttons will just get you a blank New Connection.) Double-click on a Connection icon, click **Call**, and when the Connect dialog box appears, click on **Dial**.

To redial a connection that's already open, choose **Connect** from the Call menu to open the Connect dialog box. You can also enter modem commands manually. Click on Cancel in the Connect dialog box, and type the modem commands in the HyperTerminal window, just as you would with any other terminal program.

## Getting Comfortable

When you connect, it's quite likely that the font or screen size at the remote end will need adjusting. Click **Font...** on the **View** menu and pick from a limited selection of fixed-pitch and TrueType fonts, including the original Windows Terminal and Fixedsys fonts. To resize the window after a font switch, pull down **View** again and click **Snap**.

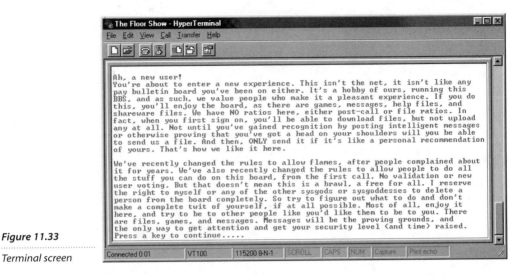

*Figure 11.33*

Terminal screen

A screenful of text will look about like Figure 11.33. You can type commands as you would with any terminal program.

## Sending and Receiving Files

You can send and receive files using HyperTerminal.

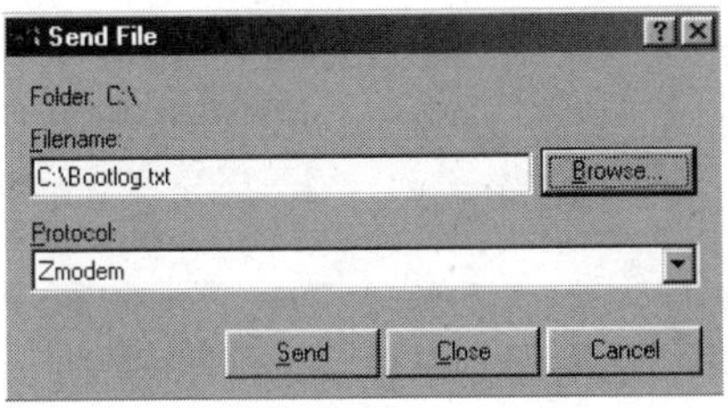

*Figure 11.34*

Send File dialog

**Sending.** To send a file, make any necessary arrangements at the remote end; then click the **Send** button on the Toolbar or pick **Send File** from the Transfer menu. The Send File dialog appears (Figure 11.34).

Fill in the name of the file to be sent. You can send a group of files by using wild-card characters (asterisks or question marks) to specify files; for example, to send all the files in a directory called Upload, type \Upload\*.* in the Send File dialog box. Pick your protocol from the drop menu (Figure 11.35).

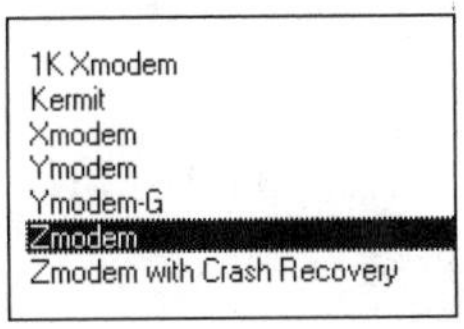

*Figure 11.35*

Protocol options

**Protocols.** HyperTerminal's protocol options are a mix of the meritorious and the desperate; are you looking for fast file transfer or just trying to match what's out there? Naturally, both computers have to be running the same protocol. Your choices are:

• **Xmodem** and **1K Xmodem**. Older standards that are widely supported. Xmodem sends 128 characters at a time, then waits for confirmation that the data arrived intact before it sends the next chunk. 1K Xmodem is faster because it sends 1,024 characters at a time. The shortcoming of these older standards is that you can't easily send multiple files; each file must be manually given a name at the receiving end.

- **Ymodem** and **Ymodem-G**. More advanced versions of Xmodem. They support multiple file transfers. Ymodem-G is fast because it sends one block after another without waiting for confirmation that the data arrived intact. Use Ymodem-G only when you have an error-free connection over a dedicated line—such as a null-modem cable—rather than over a temperamental phone line, which could result in a corrupted transfer or broken connection.

- **Zmodem**. Zmodem is fast, has great error detection and correction, and supports multiple files. It's the protocol of choice, if you have a choice. **Zmodem with Crash Recovery** adds the ability to resume interrupted transfers at the point where they broke.

- **Kermit**. A transfer protocol designed for, and ported to, many different platforms. Originally widely used for communicating between mainframe computers and desktop machines.

We recommend that you use Zmodem when you can, Ymodem or Kermit as your next choice, and Xmodem only if unavoidable. If none of these protocols is compatible with the remote computer, you'll need commercial telecommunications software which supports the remote computer's protocols.

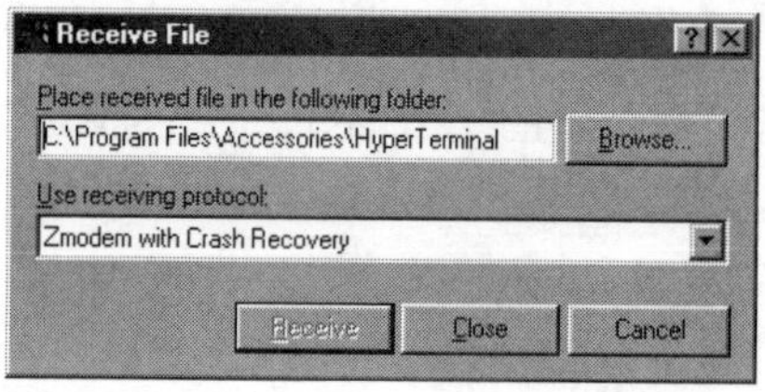

*Figure 11.36*

*Receive File dialog*

**Receiving.** To receive a file, make your arrangements, then click the **Receive** button on the Toolbar or pick **Receive File** from the Transfer menu. The Receive File dialog appears (Figure 11.36).

Fill in the name of the folder to which the file should be downloaded.

When you use Zmodem, you don't need to set up a Receive explicitly; as soon as you tell the remote computer to start sending data, your computer will start receiving (Figure 11.37).

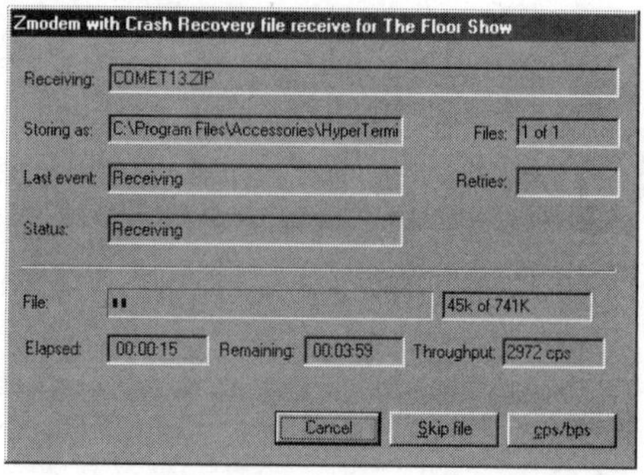

*Figure 11.37*

*File Transfer dialog*

*Figure 11.38*

*Saving a connection*

The Floor
Show.ht

*Figure 11.39*

*Connection icon*

**Logging Off.** If you're working with a Connection that you've already made and saved, simply log off and close HyperTerminal. If you're in a New Connection that you started from scratch, it's not a Connection yet (even though it worked) but something called a *session file*; when you try to close it, you'll be prompted to save to disk (Figure 11.38). The saved session file becomes a Connection with the extension **.ht** and acquires its own icon (Figure 11.39). This is the real file, so if you delete it, you'll have to set up the Connection over again.

**Receiving Calls.** Windows 98's version of HyperTerminal receives calls more smoothly than its predecessors. To answer an incoming call from another computer, open the Connection for the remote computer—which you must have already set up—and dismiss the Connect dialog by clicking on Cancel. Then pull down the **Call** menu and select **Wait for a Call**. HyperTerminal will wait until the next call, then pick up the phone.

**Quirks.** HyperTerminal is good at what it does, but even the current version perpetuates some annoying quirks and shortcomings. Almost *anything*—even using the Terminal Window to query or command your own modem—will make it think it's "connected," although the modem's not online. If you want to integrate your terminal client with your Web browser, use a scripting language, or set up an unattended session to receive data, you'll need to evaluate a more sophisticated program, such as pcAnywhere, ProComm, QModem Pro, or Hilgraeve's own "pro version," HyperACCESS. HyperTerminal, in the tradition of Microsoft communications applets, seems to have been deliberately held back to sidestep any competition with full-featured retail telecommunications programs. Still, it's miles better than 16-bit Windows Terminal.

 If you feel like sticking with HyperTerminal, bear in mind that Hilgraeve updates it periodically and makes it available free—as HyperTerminal Private Edition—on its Web site, **www.hilgraeve.com**. The Private Edition downloadable directly from Hilgraeve generally has a richer feature set than the version bundled with Windows.

# Dial-Up Networking

Default path: **My Computer\Communications\Dial-Up Networking**

Ah, DUN! For those of us who live or die by the Net, Dial-Up Networking (Figure 11.40) has to be considered 32-bit Windows' single greatest gift to our daily lives. Give Windows another generation or two, and nobody will even *remember* that setting up TCP/IP on an Intel box used to be an absolute bed of nails.

*Figure 11.40*

*Dial-Up Networking folder*

## Where to Look: Installation and IP

We're trying to keep things convenient, but if we start repeating ourselves, this chapter will go on forever. Therefore: Installing Dial-Up Networking and setting up new connections through the Make New Connection Wizard is covered in Appendix C, "Dial-Up Networking Without Tears." (DUN is no bed of nails, but it can stick you with a pin once in a while.) We've covered TCP/IP in Chapter 10, so if you need help with the IP setup for Dial-Up Networking, look in the **TCP/IP** section and particularly at "IP Address Tab" on page 437.

## Configuring DUN

Any Windows 98 computer can be a Dial-Up Networking client, connecting to a network via its modem (or modems) and telephone lines.

**Making Friends.** Use dial-up networking when you're at home, or on the road with your laptop, and you want to connect to your network server or office computer. Connect to the Internet through a dial-up service provider. Your servers can be any computer running Windows 98 or 95 Dial-Up Server, Windows NT Remote Access Service (RAS, rhymes with *jazz*), Novell NetWare Connect, or UNIX configured for dial-up. To communicate with the network, the client (that is, your computer) must be running the same network protocols as the server. Depending on the server's configuration, once you connect, you may be able to use network resources as if you were on-site. (We describe how to configure your Windows 98 computer as a dial-up server later in this chapter; it's the simplest and cheapest way to add dial-up capability to your network.)

Dial-Up Networking is only for connecting as a node on a network. To connect to a commercial online service or to a BBS, use HyperTerminal or another connection-oriented communications program.

**Dial-Up Networking**

*Figure 11.41*

*Dial-Up Networking folder icon*

**Are You There Yet?**  If Dial-Up Networking has been installed on your system, it appears as a folder in **My Computer** (Figure 11.41), or in **Start Menu\Programs\Accessories\Communications**. If it doesn't appear in either of those places, you need to install the software through **Control Panel\Add/Remove Programs** and set up a Connection; go to Appendix C. But let's assume that it's properly installed in My Computer, and proceed.

**Overall Settings.**  As its claim to fame, Dial-Up Networking is almost completely connection-based—it lets you set up an icon, loaded with properties and settings, for each connection you intend to complete. This orientation is so overwhelming that it's easy to overlook DUN's *general* settings, those that apply by default to every separate connection you make. Let's look at those first.

*Figure 11.42*

*Dial-Up Networking toolbar*

If Windows were completely consistent, you could right-click on the Dial-Up Networking folder icon, pick Properties from the Context Menu, and open a General Properties sheet. That's not the way it works this time. When you open the Dial-Up Networking folder and look at the toolbar (see Figure 11.42), you'll see that two icons and a drop menu have been added to the default toolbar. The left icon, **Create**, is a duplicate of the **Make New Connection** icon below it. The right icon, **Dial**, is only active when one of the Connection icons below it is highlighted. But pull down the **Connections** menu, click **Settings…**, and the General Properties sheet (Figure 11.43) will appear.

Most of these settings are either improved from Windows 95, or completely new.

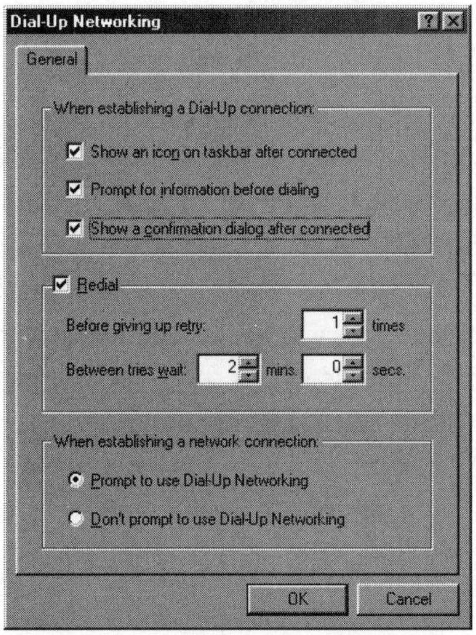

*Figure 11.43*

*Dial-Up Networking General Properties*

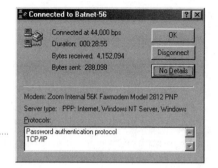

**Figure 11.44**

*Connection Status dialog*

**Show an icon on taskbar after connected** puts an arcane little icon in the System Tray to show that you're connected. If you let your pointer hover over it, you get a mini-report of bytes received, bytes sent, and speed; if you double-click it, you get the **Connected** dialog (Figure 11.44, shown with Details turned on); and if you right-click it, a mini-Context Menu pops up offering **Status**—the Connected dialog—and **Disconnect**. (Unfortunately, Microsoft didn't go quite far enough here, because the icon only sits in the System Tray *while* you're connected. Windows NT 4's equivalent RAS icon lives in the System Tray whether you're connected or not, and you can use it to connect with, which is much handier.)

**Prompt for information before dialing**, if it's checked, brings up the **Connect To** dialog to prompt you for your username and password. If it's unchecked, this step is skipped and DUN dials straight through, trusting to luck that the username and password of the last successful logon will also be correct for the current one. If you always (or mostly) use DUN to log on to the same business network or Internet provider, uncheck this and save yourself a few clicks.

**Show a confirmation dialog after connected** is primarily an easy way into the Dial-Up Networking Help, for people who still need a hand with connecting and being online. It's friendly, but after a day or two of experience you'll find you don't need it.

The **Redial** options let you set the number of times to retry a failed connection, and the length of time (in minutes and seconds, or just minutes or just seconds), to wait between retries. Setting this to the shortest interval your phone line will accept is a good way to get through to a busy provider.

**Prompt/Don't prompt to use Dial-Up Networking** reminds you to dial up if you're working remotely, or will just keep DUN out of the way if you're accessing local network resources and don't need a phone connection.

**Batnet-56**

**Figure 11.45**

*Dial-Up Networking Connection icon*

**Connection Icon.** If your Connection has been set up, your Dial-Up Networking folder will have an icon in it that looks like Figure 11.45, and conceals a lot of information. As in HyperTerminal, this is *not* a Shortcut, and if you delete it you will have to set up the Connection over again. (Of course you can make a Shortcut from it by dragging it onto the Desktop, and if you're going to use your Internet connection a lot, that's an excellent idea.) Right-click on the icon and select **Properties** from the Context Menu.

# Connection Properties

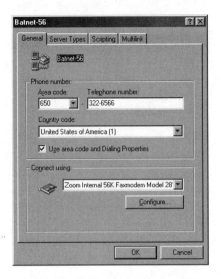

*Figure 11.46*

*Connection Properties*

**Connection Properties** (Figure 11.46) has four tabs: **General**, **Server Types**, **Scripting**, and **Multilink.**

**General Tab.** In **Area Code**, the drop menu gives you the choice of the area code selected in Dialing Properties, or a blank. If you're dialing within your local area code, select the blank, or see **Use area code…** below.

Telephone number is the number for this Connection. If you want to change it *permanently*, change it here. To change it for one call, change it in the Connect To dialog.

Unchecking Use area code… grays out the Area Code and Country Code fields. If this Connection is from a non-portable computer and to a server that can be seven-digit-dialed, uncheck it.

**Connect using** puts the installed modem or modems in its drop-menu. The Configure… button is another way of getting to Specific Modems Properties, which (from here) includes the same Options tab that Hyper-Terminal does (Figure 11.29). The two **Bring up terminal window** options are especially handy when you're logging into an older server that requires you to log on by hand.

*Figure 11.47*

*Server Types tab*

**Server Types Tab.** Server Types (Figure 11.47) covers the negotiation with the server you're dialing up.

Type of Dial-Up Server offers five choices: CSLIP, NRN (IPX/SPX), PPP, SLIP, and Windows 3.1/3.11. For general definitions of all of these except Windows 3.*x*, see the Networking glossary. Broadly speaking: PPP is the protocol that modern 32-bit Windows uses, but it can also be a UNIX protocol, as are SLIP and CSLIP. NRN is the client application for Novell's Remote Node Service (RNS). If you're dialing into an Internet service provider, your Server Type is included somewhere in the setup materials they sent you, but these days, almost all commodity Internet connections are PPP anyway. If you're logging in to any other kind of private or commercial server, you'll have to ask the sysadmin what type it is.

Potential source of confusion: In Dial-Up Server, if you have that installed, **Type of Dial-Up Server** means the type your computer *is* when people dial into it. In Connection Properties, **Type of Dial-Up Server** means the type of server (remote computer) your computer is dialing *into*. They don't have to be the same, and in fact probably aren't.

It's not clear at this writing whether Windows 98's Dial-Up Networking will talk to Novell's PPPRNS, the recent replacement for RNS. We suggest hunting around Microsoft's or Novell's Web sites if this becomes an issue for you.

### Advanced Options

**Log on to network** is checked and, for almost all applications, should stay that way. Uncheck this only if you have a hardwired connection to a network and don't dial in, or if you perform a separate manual login procedure. (All server types)

**Enable software compression** is safe to leave checked, because Dial-Up Networking will work with the other computer to arrive at a compatible type of compression; if there isn't one, the data is transmitted uncompressed. (PPP only)

**Require encrypted password** and **Require data encryption** are Microsoft-specific security options at the discretion of the server administrator. (PPP only)

**Record a log file...** records connection statistics in the file \WINDOWS\[*connectiontype*]LOG.TXT. If you're debugging, also consult \WINDOWS\[*modemname*].LOG. (All server types)

**Allowed...protocols** have to be previously installed, of course, and vary by server type (see Table 11.2).

Protocols not allowed are grayed out.

## Table 11.2  Allowed Protocols by Server Type

|            | NetBEUI | IPX/SPX | TCP/IP |
|------------|---------|---------|--------|
| *CSLIP*    | No      | No      | Yes    |
| *NRN*      | No      | Yes     | No     |
| *PPP*      | Yes     | Yes     | Yes    |
| *SLIP*     | No      | No      | Yes    |
| *Win/NT 3.x* | Yes   | No      | No     |

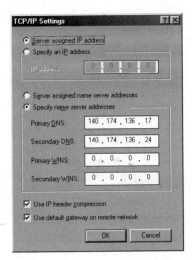

*Figure 11.48*

*Connection TCP/IP Settings*

**TCP/IP Settings** (Figure 11.48) sets the local computer's IP Address and the DNS and WINS server addresses for this particular connection. Any address can be specified ("hardcoded") by your computer, or assigned by the server or servers. For a full explanation, see the section on TCP/IP in Chapter 10, "Networking," but remember that *connection parameters set in Dial-Up Networking override any settings made in the Network Control Panel for the Dial-Up Adapter.* See Figure 10.26.

**Use IP header compression** can stay checked unless your sysadmin or Internet provider tells you to uncheck it. **Use default gateway...** says that, if more than one computer on the remote end could receive your data, you don't care which one does. You can generally leave this checked too.

**Scripting Tab.** The **Scripting** tab takes Dial-Up Scripting, a Windows NT-originated method of automating complex logons by writing and running script files, and ties it in with Dial-Up Networking. This technique matured, in a separate applet called the Dial-Up Scripting Tool, through various versions of Windows 95 and the Plus! Pack; in Windows 98 it goes mainstream.

The name of the file to be executed goes in the **File name** field.

*Figure 11.49*

*Scripting tab*

**Edit** pops up the selected script in Notepad, a good place for it, since these files are flat-ASCII and not large.

**Browse** lets you hunt for script (★.SCP) files on disk, starting in the **Accessories** folder. Windows includes four template scripts: CIS.SCP for Compuserve, PPP-MENU.SCP for a PPP connection with a login menu, SLIP.SCP for a plain SLIP connection, and SLIPMENU.SCP for a SLIP connection with a login menu. These have to be modified before they're run, and in any case aren't real run-time scripts, but are heavily enough commented to be mini-tutorials.

**Step through script**, if checked, executes the script one line at a time with pauses, to make debugging easier; you can pin down the lines that malfunction.

**Start terminal screen minimized** keeps the terminal window out of your way if you need to key in responses to intermittent prompts.

For commands, syntax, and sample scripts, see the MS-Word or WordPad file **Script.doc** in the \WINDOWS folder.

**Multilink Tab.** Multilink, one of Windows 98's innovations, allows you to devote multiple modems to a single task and take advantage of their combined throughput. Considering that combining two or three inexpensive 56K modems might give you the throughput of dual ISDN B-channels (see page 415) and spare you the per-minute charges, Multilink sounds like a great deal—and it is, within limits. There are a few gotchas.

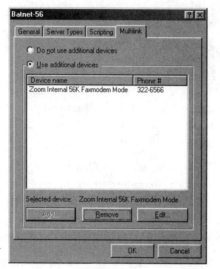

Multilink works only with Dial-Up Networking and with PPP, not with SLIP, CSLIP, or any other communications software.

Multilink was originally designed for ISDN adapters and, while it does work with analog modems, Microsoft admits that performance of parallel analog connections my be degraded by data flow errors.

You need one phone line for each modem. The practicality of this, naturally, is between you and your telco. Imminent hardware technology will allow the second line to be temporarily released for voice traffic, then rejoin the communications session.

*Figure 11.50*

*Multilink tab*

Whatever's at the other end of the wire also has to be configured for Multilink. We're not sure how popular this approach (with substantial up-front hardware cost) will be among ISPs, but we'd wager that Multilink will emerge as a solution better suited for business than for the Net. Rumor has it that in ISP use, Multilink connections can be made on a single account but will count as multiple logins, for those who get charged per login.

Clearly, Multilink isn't as universally applicable as one would wish, but if you're in a situation where you can use it, here's the procedure:

Click the **Use additional devices** button. "Additional" means "in addition to the modem that's already set up for this connection," so the primary device won't be listed here.

Click **Add**. Pick the additional modem from the drop-down list and fill in the phone number you want it to dial. Tip: If you're setting this up for an ISP and the modems you're combining have different maximum speeds, remember that your ISP may want modems of different types to dial different numbers.

Click **OK** on the Edit dialog. The newly combined modem will appear in the **Device name** list. Click **OK** on the Properties sheet.

Multilink is now set up, and the next time you dial out with this connection, both modems will dial—first the primary, then the secondary. If our experience is anything to go by, count on extensive testing and the involvement of technical support on the remote end.

**Doing It In Hardware.** The advantage of a Multilink connection is that it can use the ordinary analog modems in our systems or scrapboxes. But rather than use Multilink, you can boost your throughput with a partial hardware upgrade—a new modem with special technology that allows it to "bond" with, and enlist the help of, the modem already in your computer.

At this writing, the leading provider of bonding modems is Diamond Multimedia, which installs its Shotgun technology in two different products. The SupraExpress 56 modem will cooperate with whatever modem you already have while it performs the channel mastering; the SupraSonic II modem offers two 56K channels on one card, for throughput of 112K in theory and, probably, 88K to 96K in the real world. These are K56flex devices, so if you combine a single-channel Shotgun modem with an existing X2 modem, the most you'll get is 56K+33.6K = about 90K theoretical tops, 72K real. We haven't tested a SupraSonic II yet, but it could be an attractive alternative to ISDN.

## Tweaking DUN

Okay, you midnight bit blasters. It's time you knew the truth. There are settings that make Dial-Up Networking go faster, and *Windows won't let you get to them.* Obviously this is an insult, a flagrant violation of the Hacker Ethic, and a waste of online time. These are some of the settings:

**MTU (Maximum Transmission Unit)** is the maximum size (in bytes) of the data packet that can be transmitted over a given network architecture. Windows 98's default is 1,500 bytes, the same as Ethernet default. Unfortunately, the MTU of the TCP/IP for an Internet provider's server is typically much smaller—576 bytes is a good first try—and so, every time Windows connects to your ISP, the two computers have to agree on a value for MTU, *all over again.* You'd be a lot better off to set it and forget it.

**RWIN (TCP Receive Window)** is the amount of data that the host computer can send without receiving an acknowledgement and update from the target computer. Without getting technical here, let's just say that the Windows 98 default RWIN is 8192 bytes, which is too big, because the Windows 98 default MTU is too big, and the two numbers are related. If you set your

MTU to the appropriate value, then set your RWIN to a lower-than-standard multiple of the revised MTU, you can wring every drop of performance out of your Internet connection.

**TTL (Time To Live)** is the length of time, in seconds, that an Internet (IP) data packet is allowed to survive without reaching its destination. (The TTL value is part of the packet.) If TTL expires, and the packet is still in transit, it gets axed. This keeps the Net from being ankle-deep in stale packets. Unfortunately, the Windows 98 and 95 default TTL value is 32 seconds, and these days the Internet is so big that 32 seconds often isn't long enough. Tip: the Windows NT 4.0 default TTL value is 128 seconds, which sounds a *lot* more serious. Now, you can *change* your TTL value in Windows 98 … if you want to hack the Registry.

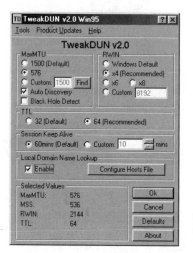

**TweakDUN.** Enter TweakDUN (Figure 11.51), a fine and stealthy applet that lets you configure all this stuff with a few clicks—not only MTU, RWIN, and TTL, but a raft of other Internet mysteries. It doesn't guess, either, but establishes optimum MTU by dialing up a server and querying it (Figure 11.52).

TweakDUN is developed by Casey Patterson at Patterson Design Systems. Version 2.0 is a "Windows 95" program but works fine with Windows 98, Windows 95, and Windows NT 4.0— we tested it with all three. You can get it from **http://www.pattersondesigns.com/tweakdun/** or from **http://www.buydirect.com**, and *it is not shareware,* but requires a credit-card payment of $15.00 before downloading, with various options to protect the buyer. We think TweakDUN would be worth fifteen bucks just for the context-sensitive help and the Windows Help file, which is an education in itself; but we've also seen it improve performance significantly.

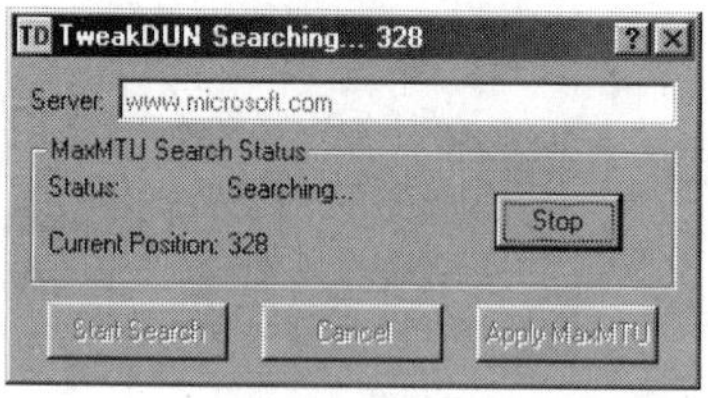

*Figure 11.51*

TweakDUN

*Figure 11.52*

TweakDUN host query

# Internet Access with Dial-Up Networking and TCP/IP

This section is a thumbnail treatment of configuring TCP/IP for Internet access, and probably resembles the material you received (or will receive) from your Internet service provider. For more detail on TCP/IP and its inner workings, see Chapter 10.

Acronyms such as **TCP/IP**, **PPP**, **SLIP**, **CSLIP**, and **DNS** are defined in the **Networking Glossary** on pages 411 through 421.

If you connect to the Internet exclusively through an online service such as the Microsoft Network or AOL/WorldCom/CompuServe Interactive, your protocols have already been set up by the installation software, and you can skip this section.

The UNIX and Windows NT networks that form the backbone of the Internet use TCP/IP protocols for Internet communications. If you use an Internet service provider, you dial its PPP or SLIP server, which connects to you through modems, and is connected directly to the Internet through a leased line. You can also use TCP/IP across your own network to communicate with a dedicated server, called a *gateway server,* that is directly connected to the Internet.

## Configuring TCP/IP: Are You There Yet?

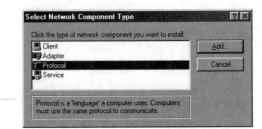

*Figure 11.53*

*Installed TCP/IP*

Did you install TCP/IP when you installed Windows 98? Open the Network Control Panel. Scroll down the list of installed components on the Configuration page. If TCP/IP appears on the list with an arrow pointing to the Dial-Up Adapter or to another network adapter (Figure 11.53), then TCP/IP is installed on your computer.

If TCP/IP is not on your system, install it by clicking on **Add** in the Network Control Panel to open the **Select Network Component Type** dialog (Figure 11.54).

*Figure 11.54*

*Select Network Component Type*

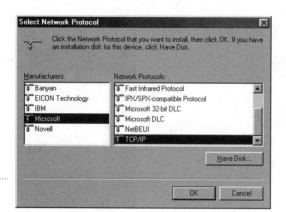

*Figure 11.55*

*Select Network
Protocol*

Select **Protocol** and click **Add** to open the Select Network Protocol dialog box. Select **Microsoft** and **TCP/IP** for Manufacturer and Network Protocol, respectively (Figure 11.55). Then click **OK**. You may need to have your Windows 98 installation CD or floppies on hand.

After you install the protocol, scroll through the list of installed components on the Configuration tab of Network Properties, to verify that the protocol is listed. Windows 98 automatically configures TCP/IP to work with any network adapters on your system, including Dial-Up Networking if it was previously installed. You see a TCP/IP entry for each of the network adapters you have installed. You'll need to configure each adapter with its own TCP/IP settings.

## Configuring For Your ISP

Before you connect to the Internet, your computer will need to recognize Internet domain names. See page 434 for more about the Internet's Domain Name System (DNS). Because some providers assign your Internet Protocol (IP) address "dynamically"—that is, automatically—you may not need to configure your Dial-Up Adapter with a specific IP address. Contact your provider to determine whether your address will be static (hardcoded) or dynamic.

For each Dial-Up Networking connection that uses TCP/IP, open the Dial-Up Networking window, select the **Connection** for your Internet service provider, right-click to bring up the Context Menu, and choose **Properties.** Click the **Server Types tab** for the connection, make sure that Type of Dial-Up Server is set to **PPP...**, check the **TCP/IP** box in Allowed Network Protocols, then click on **TCP/IP Settings...** (Figure 11.56). We've discussed these options more generally under "Server Types Tab" on page 487, but here we'll deal specifically with setting up for an ISP:

If the service provider assigns an IP address that links dynamically to a domain name, select **Server Assigned IP Address**. Otherwise, select **Specify an IP**

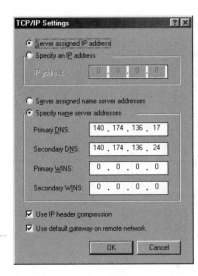

**Figure 11.56**

*Server Type TCP/IP settings*

**Address** and enter the address. Do the same for the primary and secondary DNS addresses, which will *probably* be specific rather than dynamic. It's unlikely that an Internet provider server will involve WINS addresses, for reasons we discuss on page 435. Click on **OK.**

If you connect to the Internet through a local network server, you can adjust the IP and DNS settings through Control Panel\Network. See the directions under "IP Address Tab," "DNS Configuration Tab," and "Gateway Tab" in the **TCP/IP** section of Chapter 10, "Networking." If your LAN gateway server is running Dynamic Host Configuration Protocol (DHCP), it will assign those addresses dynamically and you don't need to set them yourself.

# Dial-Up Server

Default path: **Start Menu\Accessories\Communications\Dial-Up Networking\Connections Menu\Dial-Up Server**

Are you a Net party animal? Was Microsoft Chat the third thing you set up on your computer, after DUN and Internet Explorer? Well, now the whole Net can have twenty-four-hour access to *you!* Just install Windows 98's Dial-Up Server and clean up that desktop; company's coming! (Dial-Up Server is also an easy way to share resources, and to dial into your office computer when you're on the road or at home.)

### Who Put These Warez in My FTP Folder?

Remember that "anyone can dial in and use your computer" means exactly what it says. If you install Dial-Up Server on a computer that matters to you, create passwords to control access, and be sure to change them frequently. You can implement your security at the *user level,* which requires a separate password for each user, or at the *share level,* which requires one password for each shared resource. Your decision affects some dial-up sharing options. See Chapter 10, "Networking," for a more detailed explanation of security levels.

## Configuring Dial-Up Server

From the **Connections** menu of Dial-Up Networking, choose **Dial-Up Server** to bring up the dialog box. If multiple modems are installed, you'll get a tabbed dialog with one tab per modem (Figure 11.57).

Click on **Allow Caller Access**, then click on **Password protection** and enter the password that will allow access to your computer. If you have user-level security on your machine, click on **Add**, then enter the names of authorized users. Click on **OK.**

Click on Server Type (Figure 11.58). You can select PPP for Windows 98 and Windows NT 3.5 to let Win32 users log in, Windows NT 3.1 and Windows for Workgroups to let Win16 users log in, or Default to let any Windows user log in. (Only clients running Windows 3.1 or newer can log into a Dial-Up Server.)

To improve performance, leave Enable software compression checked, and Dial-Up Server will negotiate compatible compression or transmit the data uncompressed. If you check Require encrypted password, only users who have checked the matching box on the Server Types tab of Dial-Up Networking Connection Properties will be able to log in. Click on OK.

*Figure 11.58*

*Server Types dialog*

Click OK in the main dialog. Any changes you've made have no effect in a currently open Connection, but once you enable caller access and the line is free, Windows 98 monitors the modem and picks up calls. Dial-Up Server minimizes to the System Tray when active.

You can disconnect a user in one of two ways; either click on **Disconnect User** in the Dial-Up Server dialog box, or unplug the phone line into your modem!

# Direct Cable Connection

Default path: `Start Menu\Accessories\Communications\`
`Direct Cable Connection`

Direct Cable Connection, or DCC, is a near-instant "adapterless" network protocol that lets you network two Windows 9*x* computers by connecting them with a parallel or serial cable. Once connected, the two computers can share resources, although more slowly than through a modem or Ethernet connection. DCC is especially handy when you don't have a modem or a PC Card adapter for connecting a portable computer to a desktop or another portable.

## Too Public?

When you're thinking about installing Direct Cable Connection, remember Microsoft's First Law of Network Access: If you can see it, you can mess with it. DCC basically gives you network access to the machine on the other end of the cable, but without the precautions and restrictions that are built in to Microsoft's more elaborate connectivity—which makes DCC a "smoking gun," to quote one of our senior technical advisers, because if the machine on the other end is itself part of a network …. DCC is simple and powerful, but to be used cautiously.

## Cables

By far the most common type of parallel port on desktops today is either the "unidirectional" (4-bit) or the "bidirectional" (8-bit) port. To connect two computers with DCC and these port types, all you need is a so-called "Laplink-style parallel" cable which you can buy for about $10 at any good computer retail store. Microsoft recommends the DirectParallel cable from Parallel Technologies; look in Windows Help under **Direct Cable Connection: ordering cables** for contact information, or browse to `http://www.lpt.com`.

Desktop computers built after 1995 may have an ECP (Extended Capabilities Port); laptops with Intel SL low-power chipsets may have an EPP (Enhanced Parallel Port). Both of these port types have distinct pinouts and need special cables for use with DCC. You'll have to discuss this with your vendor.

You can also run DCC with a Laplink-style serial cable, but unless you have to (see below), you won't want to, because a serial DCC connection gives about one-tenth the performance of a parallel connection.

# Configuring DCC

DCC is a quick (plug, plug, click, click) and dirty (no error correction) way of tapping one computer into another computer's resources, even if the guest computer is fairly brainless at the time. Fred, for example, was setting up Windows 98 on a computer whose Ethernet adapter wasn't working yet, so he created a DCC to a second computer with a CD-ROM drive, put the Windows CD in the drive, accessed it as a "network share" even though there was no network, and finished Windows Setup.

To use DCC, you assign **host** status to one computer and **guest** status to the other computer. Both computers must be running one or more similar network protocols, primarily NetBEUI, and must have different names. Once you connect the computers, the guest computer can access other computers on the host's network using NetBEUI, but not TCP/IP. The guest computer can also print to any network printer if the host has enabled printer sharing. (See the **Gotchas** section regarding DCC and IPX/SPX.)

**Are You There Yet?**  Open **Start Menu\Programs\Accessories\ Communications** and see if Direct Cable Connection is one of the items on the menu. If not, it's not installed. Double-click on **Control Panel\ Add/Remove Programs**, click the **Windows Setup** page, and select **Communications** from the list of components. Click on the **Details** button, check the box for **Direct Cable Connection**, and click **OK.**

**Setup.**  To set up a DCC:

1. Decide which computer is the host (the computer with resources to be accessed) and which is the guest (the user logging in).

2. On the host computer, open the Network Control Panel; click the **File and Printer Sharing** button and make sure both boxes are checked. Also make sure that the host computer is running NetBEUI, and if not, add it. Use the **Sharing...** option of the Context Menu to create network shares for the resources that you want to make available to the guest computer; otherwise, it won't be able to "see" them.

3. On the guest computer, open the Network Control Panel; make sure NetBEUI is installed, and if not, add it.

4. Connect the two computers using a Laplink-style parallel or serial cable. Parallel connections are faster, but cables are limited to 15 feet in length; if the cable is longer, the data bits vanish before they reach their destination. Serial cables can be longer, but the connection is slower than a parallel connection.

5. If you want to print from the guest computer to a network printer, you need to install the appropriate printer drivers on the guest computer.

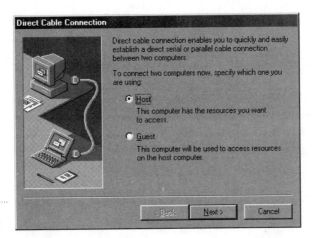

**Figure 11.59**

*Direct Cable Connection wizard*

The first time you open Direct Cable Connection, the Direct Cable Connection wizard (Figure 11.59) helps you specify and configure both the host and the guest computers. You need to run the wizard on both computers.

**Running DCC.**  When you're ready to connect, start DCC on the host computer by choosing Direct Cable Connection from the Communications submenu. Click on **Listen** and the host will put this up (Figure 11.60).

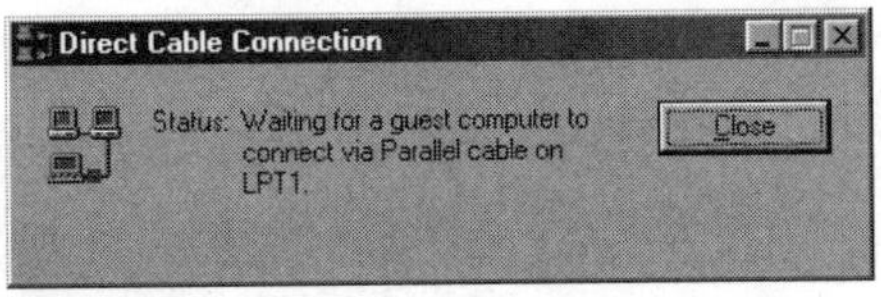

**Figure 11.60**

*Waiting DCC host*

Then start DCC on the guest computer. The two machines should connect. (If they don't, check your cable to make sure it's plugged into the correct ports.)

Later, if you need to make changes in the DCC configuration of either the host or the guest, click on the **Change** button in the Direct Cable Connection dialog box. When you're finished working with the two computers, click on **Close** to disconnect them.

**What About NT?**  Windows 98 and 95 have DCC, but Windows NT doesn't, probably because accessing the ports at the bare-metal level violates NT's rules for hardware protection. If you need to hard-wire a Windows 98 box to an NT 4.0 or 3.5*x* machine, there are some workarounds:

You *can* connect a 9*x* computer to an NT computer by using DCC on the 95 side, RAS configured for direct connection on the NT side, and a serial cable. The procedure has been documented and well illustrated by Frank J. Kime at Purdue University; it's too long to reproduce here, but the URL is `http://www.cs.purdue.edu/homes/kime/directcc/directcc.htm`.

You can use HyperTerminal on both machines, and a serial cable.

You can install Ethernet adapters in both machines, enable NetBEUI or TCP/IP, and use an RJ-45 crossover cable. This is the most involved option but gives you the best error correction, the most flexibility, and the best performance.

You can install third-party software like Traveling Software's LapLink or Symantec's pcAnywhere, which work with parallel as well as serial connections.

**Gotchas.** There are a few well-known gotchas with Direct Cable Connection:

- Make sure the parallel ports on both computers are the **same type**.

- You can't run **DCC and DUN** on the same computer at the same time.

- It may or may not be possible to use DCC to connect a Windows 9$x$ computer to a **Windows 3.1/3.11** computer.

- Transmission speeds will **vary wildly** and transmission of compressed files, such as .ZIP files, may be very slow.

- Don't try to run DCC with **IPX/SPX**. You can connect, but you're unlikely to see the shared resources on the host.

- Disable **LM Announce** on both the host and the guest computers; it's useless anyway unless some of the computers on your network are running LAN Manager, and it will make your DCC connection take an eternity to close. See page 443 in Chapter 10, "Networking," for details.

- **Browse Master** on the host should be set to Enabled; see page 442 in Chapter 10.

- If the two computers try to connect across a parallel cable, and both put up the message **LPT Parallel cable disconnected**, make sure that both computers are running the same version of DIRECTCC.EXE and its support files. There's anecdotal evidence that the version from the original Windows 95 won't handshake with the version from OSR2, and our test showed that the version from OSR2 won't connect successfully with the one from 98.

**Other Resources.** Direct Cable Connection is nowhere near as famous as the renowned Dial-Up Networking, but there is one excellent Web page devoted solely to DCC. Without this page, this section would have been a lot longer—or, more likely, shorter. Browse to `http://www.tecno.demon.co.uk/dcc.html` at Electronic Design Laboratory in Bristol, UK, who deserve resounding cheers for this public service.

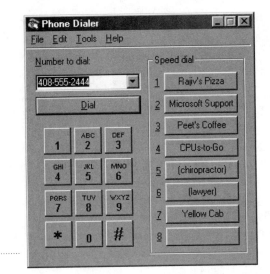

*Figure 11.61*

*Phone Dialer*

# Phone Dialer

Default path: **Start Menu\Accessories\Communications\Phone Dialer**

If your modem is bored, make it dial your voice calls with Phone Dialer (Figure 11.61) which gives you a standard telephone keypad, call logging, and eight numbers of speed dialing, without any fuss. It also handles requests for dial-out by other DDE-compatible applications.

## Options

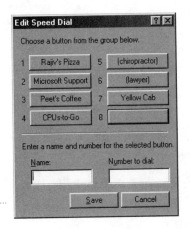

*Figure 11.62*

*Edit Speed Dial*

The only option on the **File** menu is **Exit**. Phone Dialer saves your Speed Dial entries in \WINDOWS\DIALER.INI and your successfully completed calls in \WINDOWS\CALLLOG.TXT, but you can't choose other filenames.

The **Edit** options are the usual **Cut, Copy, Paste** and **Delete** for the contents of the *Number to dial* field and **Edit Speed Dial** (Figure 11.62).

If you click a button that's already programmed, the contents of the button are displayed ready to edit; if you click a blank button, the *Name* and *Number to dial* fields are cleared. When you're done, don't forget to save changes.

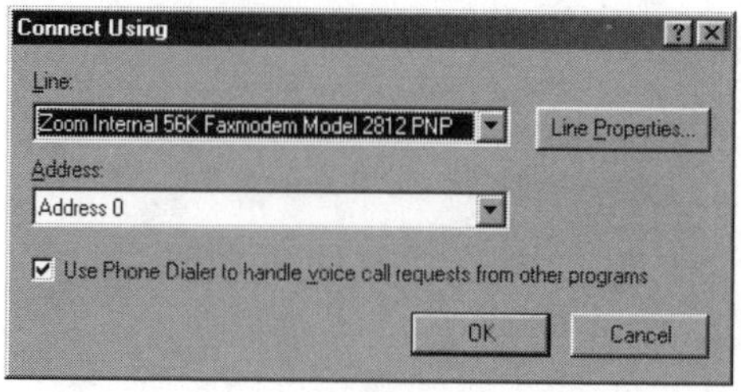

**Connect Using** dialog box:

Line:
Zoom Internal 56K Faxmodem Model 2812 PNP

Line Properties...

Address:
Address 0

☑ Use Phone Dialer to handle voice call requests from other programs

OK    Cancel

**Tools\Connect Using** (Figure 11.63) sets up your dial-out and phone line.

**Line** means Modem, with a drop list if you have more than one, and **Line Properties** takes you to Specific Modem Properties. **Address** supposedly allows for your modem dialing out on more than one line. If you check **Use Phone Dialer...**, Phone Dialer will dial out every voice call requested by another program.

*Figure 11.63*

*Tools Connect dialog*

**Tools\Dialing Properties** pops up the usual Dialing Properties sheet.

**Tools\Show Log** opens the Call Log and gives you the choice of logging incoming calls, outgoing calls, or both.

 The only odd thing about **Help** is that context-sensitive help, rather than launching from the usual question mark button in the Title Bar, is a Help menu item called **What's This?**

## Pad Dial

You can dial from your numeric keypad (although Phone Dialer won't automatically turn [Num Lock] on), or you can point and click. The number will appear in the *Number to dial* field as you enter it. When you finish, click **Dial** or hit [Enter] or [Alt][D] to dial out.

 The *Number to dial* field keeps a stack of the last eleven numbers you dialed. It's smart enough not to keep redials; it's too dumb to reject non-numeric input. You can get to this stack by clicking the drop list or [Alt][↓][↓], but double-clicking a number in the stack won't dial—you have to left-click the number and hit **Dial**.

## Speed Dial

Click once on a programmed button and it pastes the number into the *Number to dial* field and dials out. Click once on a blank button and the Program Speed Dial dialog pops up (Figure 11.64).

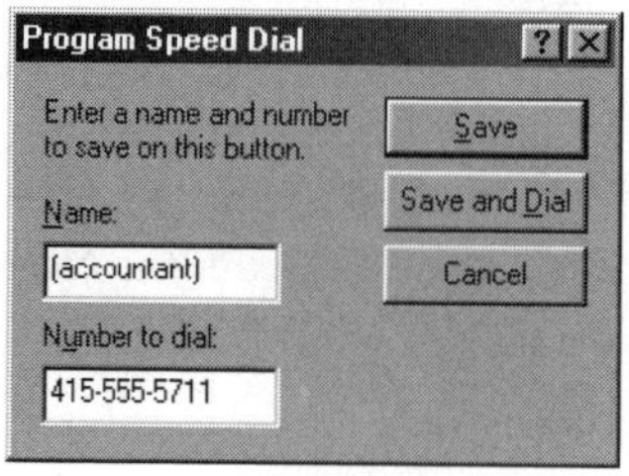

**Program Speed Dial** dialog box:

Enter a name and number to save on this button.

Save

Name:
(accountant)

Save and Dial

Cancel

Number to dial:
415-555-5711

Once you fill in the name and number, you can just **Save**, or **Save and Dial** simultaneously.

*Figure 11.64*

*Program Speed Dial*

## Connecting

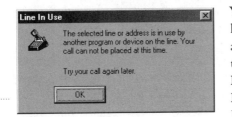

*Figure 11.65*

*Dialing*

"Dialing Unknown" and "Name to place in call log: Unknown" (Figure 11.65) mean that this number was entered by hand, so there's no name to associate with it in DIALER.INI. You can type in the name to paste into the call log. If the number was dialed with a Speed Dial button, the name on the button will appear here. "New Location" and "using None" will vary according to whether you've named your location in Dialing Properties, and whether you're using a calling card; to change these settings, see pages 469–470.

## Not Connecting

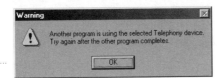

*Figure 11.66*

*Line in use*

You'll see this (Figure 11.66) if the line you're trying to call out on is already in use, *or* if the number you're trying to call is busy and you have **Redial** turned off in **Dial-Up Networking\Connections\Settings**. If you have **Redial** turned on, the Dialer will redial the set number of times.

*Figure 11.67*

*Device in use*

This (Figure 11.67) can mean exactly what it says: that another program, like Dial-Up Networking or HyperTerminal, is using the modem you're trying to dial out with. It can *also* mean that the modem you're trying to use isn't responding or isn't installed, so if you see this warning, run Modems Diagnostics, check your connections, and look in your PC Card slots.

## After Connecting

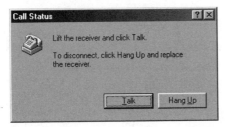

*Figure 11.68*

*Call status*

As soon as you connect (Figure 11.68), pick up the phone and click **Talk**. When you're done, click **Hang Up**.

# Windows Scripting Host

Default path: `\Windows\WSCRIPT.EXE; Windows 98 Resource Kit\WSH.HLP`

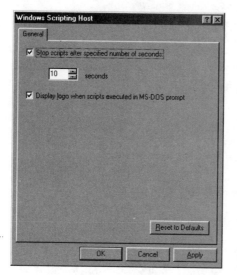

**Figure 11.69**

*Windows Scripting Host, GUI mode*

The Windows Scripting Host is the robust scripting tool that Windows has always needed, incorporating both the JavaScript and VBScript engines that first appeared in other Microsoft products. Both a GUI version (WSCRIPT.EXE, Figure 11.69) and a character-mode version (CSCRIPT.EXE) are supplied as applets.

A true programming language for system administrators, WSH supports subroutines and functions, variables and arrays, true if/else statements, flow-control statements that allow looping, and functions that can be called by scripts, as well as tools to create dialogs and other interactive automation. But Microsoft omitted any functions that would allow scripts to work with hard disk files, probably because a WSH script that accessed the disk directly could be devastating if launched with malicious intent.

Writing scripts at this level means writing JavaScript or VBScript. Since this book is primarily for Windows users, rather than Windows programmers or systems administrators, we reluctantly declare the Windows Scripting Host to be outside the current scope. (If you'd be really interested in **The Windows 98 Scripting Bible**, we'll … find someone who would really like to write it. Let us know.) But we'd never leave you high and dry, so:

- Both versions of the Scripting Host applet are in your \WINDOWS folder.

- The readily available documentation is the Windows Scripting Host Administrator's Guide. In the *Windows 98 Resource Kit,* open WSH.HLP and click on "Administrator's Guide, about."

- Two pertinent Web sites are `http://www.microsoft.com/MANAGEMENT/WSH.htm`, and `http://www.microsoft.com/scripting`. (Remember that Microsoft's URLs are notoriously volatile, but these look like they'll last for a while.)

# Telephony Properties

Telephony, in the context of computing, refers to the general case of what you can do with dial-out and dial-in. In Windows 98, it's an outline rather than a reality; it takes the form of the Unimodem driver, which is the force behind Dial-Up Networking and Dial-Up Server, and of NDISWAN TAPI (Telephony Application Programming Interface) which is the driver to link wide-area networks into the telephone system.

There isn't as much TAPI in Windows 98 as there will be in versions down the road; of what there is, the majority is under the hood and out of sight. But to Microsoft, TAPI is a centerpiece of the next century's global networking, and they want you to know about it. So if you'll pardon a slight handwave, we'll refer you to `http://www.microsoft.com/communications/telephony.htm`, the Microsoft Comprehensive Platform for Telephony Solutions, and `http://www.microsoft.com/windows/tapi/default.htm`, the TAPI Homepage. They're both worth a look.

# A Note On Fax

At this writing, the future of faxing in Windows 98 is totally confused. We know there will be a solution, but we're willing to bet it won't please everybody.

In our discussion of Outlook Express in Chapter 16, we note that Microsoft Exchange—the Exchange *client,* also known as Windows Messaging—is not part of Windows 98. Outlook Express is its nominal replacement. But the Windows 95 Fax applet, which integrates itself into Windows Messaging, won't run with Outlook Express.

On our current Windows 98 CD, there's a file called AWFAX.EXE. (Never mind the folder path since it's undoubtedly different on your CD; just do a Find File.) This is the latest version of the Fax applet, and it will run on your system *if:*

- You have Microsoft Outlook, *not* Outlook Express, installed, or

- You're upgrading from Windows 95 and you have the Microsoft Exchange client installed, or

- You're upgrading from Windows 95 and you have Windows Messaging installed.

If none of the above is true, then you need to buy and install the "real" Microsoft Outlook, which is about $90 street as a standalone product, or less if you buy it bundled with MS-Office. But before you go to the trouble and expense of installing Outlook and convincing the Fax applet to work with it, you should know that Microsoft considers AWFAX.EXE to be unsupported software, which means it's very difficult to get help. Microsoft's short-term fax solution for Windows 98 is uninspiring, to put it mildly.

In the long run we may be somewhat better off. Our best information is that, by the time the retail distribution of Windows 98 is available, a special "lite" version of Symantec's WinFax will be bundled with it. Depending on how tightly WinFax is integrated with the Windows 98 core code, this could be an excellent solution, but we want to try it before we buy it.

 In an early clue to a new direction, we installed a beta of Outlook 98 downloaded from Microsoft's Web site, and the first thing it did after setting itself up was install a fax service. Maybe, ultimately, Microsoft will just shift fax capability from the operating system core to Outlook, but right now, your guess is as good as ours.

# Summary

Windows 98 incorporates many new features that make networking and data communications as seamless as possible. Setup hassles are minimal for most telecommunications and network hardware and software, and Windows 98 adds new options for controlling communications. Much of Microsoft's strategy for the future of telephony remains in active development, and will appear only in future Windows versions, including the forthcoming NT 5.0. That's a nice way of saying that if you try to implement telephony with Windows 98, you may find it doesn't have all the pieces you need.

Microsoft, no less than the rest of us, is running to stay in sight of a moving target. Burgeoning local access, the popularity of the Internet, and innovations like digital cellular communication and caller-ID all point the way to a thickly wired, dimly understood future. Windows 98 provides compatibility with the Internet, one of the few things in the computing world that's far bigger than Windows itself. Windows versions to come will, we expect, give you the tools for many more creative uses of the telephone network.

# 12

# Multimedia

In the three years since the previous edition of this book, perhaps no single computer technology has changed—and grown—as much as the explosion loosely called "multimedia." When Windows 95 first appeared, *multimedia* was still in teddy-bear pajamas, and (unless you had *lots* of money) basically meant a slow CD-ROM drive, a sound card, and thirty-buck speakers.

Listen up, sleepyhead. Everything's happening at the turn of the century. Your humble computer is about to become a home theater, an arcade console, a 24-hour newsfeed, and the listening room of a stereo store. Are you ready for Total Immersion Hack? Can you deal with a computer in every room? Is your subwoofer bigger than your TV set? The new high times—44.1 KHz—are here.

# Are You There Yet?

Well, not entirely. Some of the pieces you'll need, like the DVD drive, the TV tuner card, and the MPEG-3 decoder, are still … ah … undergoing shakedown, which is a way of saying that you can buy the components, but maybe not (yet) whole systems equipped with them. The software bits, though, are all installed in Windows 98 and waiting.

The "basic" multimedia components of today are standard on all but the cheapest computer systems available at retail—even "business" systems. CD-ROM drives are climbing in speed as their prices drop; budget-price computers are equipped with 20x or 24x drives, while high-end systems sport 32x drives, as fast as the hard disks of a few years ago. Sound cards are available in profusion, led by highly refined entries from Creative Labs and Ensoniq, but in many cases the sound "card" has shrunk to a chip on the motherboard, a sure sign that it's here to stay. And the tinny gamers' speakers of yesteryear have been replaced (many of them literally) by quality stereo systems with subwoofers, from companies like Advent, Altec Lansing, Cambridge Sound Works, Sony, and Yamaha. The combination of fast Internet access, high-speed CD drives, wavetable sound, and 3-D accelerated video (discussed in Chapter 7) has spawned a network gamer's culture that would have been unimaginable three years ago. Internet videoconferencing is poised to invade, not only corporate offices, but the SOHO market as well. And you can barely imagine what multimedia computing promises to do for entertainment …

## Windows 98 and Multimedia

Windows 98 has been designed to take maximum advantage of all this stuff—and it's easy to guess why. The industry has tried everything—twenty years of refinement and increased performance, prices that tumble till you think they can't any more, reams of hype, and the fostering of entire subcultures—and still, *over half* the population of the advanced industrial countries *does not* own a computer. There are millions of people in the world who could afford a computer, but have never felt compelled to buy one.

"Okay," says the computer industry, "the easy sales are gone. The tech-heads have all bought their computers, and some of them are buying more; but given the bang we deliver for the contemporary buck, we can't count on replacement sales to keep us at takeoff power. To reach the rest of the world, we have to make the computer as ubiquitous as the TV, the boom box, and the phone."

And the rumble came forth from the labs: "So we'll make the computer *into* the TV, the boom box, and the phone." And they did; and lo, they saw that it was good. Thus, this chapter.

## What Bits Do You Get?

Windows 98's Entertainment menu comprises an odd mix of the old and the new, to accommodate the full spectrum of likely hardware. Some of the applets are crufty and stale, some are so advanced they're still wet, and there's hardly anything in the middle. Let's just say that the Start Menu\Entertainment group reflects the currently rapid and uneven development of multimedia itself.

So, without further ado: the applets.

# CD Player

Default path: `Start Menu\Programs\Accessories\Entertainment\`
`CD Player`

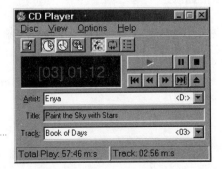

*Figure 12.1*

*CD Player
(toolbar on)*

Windows 98 provides a built-in player for audio CDs that works like a good one-shot CD player. Since it hasn't been updated since NT 4, it can't touch the latest high-quality shareware players; furthermore, if you leave it configured with the defaults you'll probably never see most of it. But it's not a bad applet (Figure 12.1).

To open CD Player:

Insert an audio CD into your CD drive. Windows AutoPlay detects it and starts playing it.

Click **Start** and choose **CD Player** from the Entertainment menu.

## Toolbar

*Figure 12.2*

*CD Player toolbar*

From left to right the buttons are: **Edit Playlist**, **Display Track Time Elapsed**, **Display Track Time Remaining**, **Display Disc Time Remaining**, **Random Track Order** (shuffle) **Continuous Play**, and **Intro Play** (play first *n* seconds of each song, settable). Most of these are duplicated on the menus. **Continuous Play** is defined as "Start [disc] over once last track is done playing," and you can combine it with Random Track Order or Intro Play or both.

## Playlist

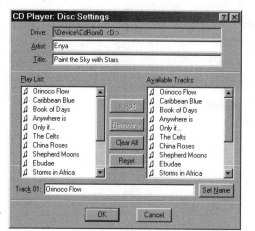

To create a playlist for a CD, choose **Edit Play List** from the **Disc** menu. CD Player opens the Disc Settings dialog to let you enter artists, titles, and tracks for the playlist (Figure 12.3).

By default, all tracks on a disc are on the playlist. To remove a track, select it on the list and click **Remove**.

*Figure 12.3*

*Creating a playlist*

You can also rearrange the order in which tracks are played by selecting the track or tracks you want to move, releasing the mouse button, clicking, dragging, and dropping within the playlist. The changes take place immediately. If you want to change the playlist for only a single session, go into the Preferences dialog and uncheck **Save Settings on Exit.**

**Figure 12.4**

*Display Track Time Remaining*

**Figure 12.5**

*Display Disc Time Remaining*

## Options

**Display Track Time Remaining** counts down by seconds from the full duration of the track.

**Display Disc Time Remaining** counts down by minutes and seconds from the full duration of the disc.

## Preferences

**Figure 12.6**

*Preferences*

**Figure 12.7**

*Small Font*

**Preferences** (Figure 12.6) sets program options, rather than play options. **Stop CD playing...**, **Save settings...**, and **Show tool tips** all default to checked. **Intro play length** sets the length, in seconds, of the song excerpt played when **Intro play** is selected.

Large Font is shown as the selected **Display font.** Given that the only available timer display colors are gray-olive on black, it's hard to see why anyone would choose barely legible Small Font (Figure 12.7).

## The Problems

The Microsoft CD Player is, as they say, long in the fangs. It takes up a lot of screen real estate when being tweaked; while it's running, it takes up a whole Taskbar slot. This combination of resource greed and low functionality is not compelling. But the big problem, today, is that it makes you type all your own playlists.

Kip, who has (probably) a four-foot stack of audio CDs, and Fred, who has more, are firmly agreed that keying in playlists is robotic, lame, and a poor use of time. Luckily, with CDDB, you mostly don't have to do that any more—and when you do, you can at least share the wealth with your fellow audiophiles. So why did Microsoft, the company doing more than any other to integrate the Net into your operating system, stick us with an audio player that's not Internet-aware? Ack phfffttt!

**Wait a Sec, What's CDDB?** CDDB, the CD Database, is the brilliant collaboration of Ti Kan and Steve Scherf. It's a *giganormous* playlist with entries for artists, album names, and tracks, keyed to eight-digit hexadecimal ID numbers. All you have to do—*if* you have the right CD player—is be connected to the Net, slip a CD into the drive, and *bam!* your CD client software logs onto CDDB, finds the playlist for the CD that you're playing, downloads it to your local database, and it's yours with no wear on the fingers. The worst you may have to do is click on a menu item that says "Query CDDB."

Okay, but what if your CD client scouts CDDB and *doesn't* find the playlist you need? Then you do barely more than you would anyway; you key in your artist, title, and tracks, and the next time your Net connection's lit up, you pick a musical category, and click on "Submit to CDDB." Now you have your playlist, and so does anybody else who needs it. A very big database gets built very quickly. If you want to know more, which we certainly did, browse to `http://www.cddb.com`.

## The Solution

**CD-Valet** by Greg Leichner. Okay, there are tons of shareware CD players; we've tried about a dozen, and liked most of them. But the award-winning CD-Valet, like Super NoteTab (Chapter 5) and INFTool (Appendix A), has the double-barreled wow factor that puts it first across the line.

CD-Valet is totally CDDB-aware, naturally. (You need either SMTP or MAPI support installed.) When in use, it minimizes to the System Tray and looks like a tiny CD. If you want rack-style controls, you can have them (Figure 12.8) but they take up far less space than Microsoft's CD player.

*Figure 12.8*

*CD-Valet rack controls, actual size*

Please note that the diminutive panel crams in track title, track timing, Play, Pause, Stop, Track Forward, Track Back, Eject, a spin-button volume control, and auto-hide.

**Running CD-Valet.** The CD icon in the System Tray, though tiny, is versatile. Click it during play, the music pauses, and a black double-bar appears on the icon. Click it again and the music starts. (Perfect for those incoming phone calls.) If the CD has finished, the icon will show a black Stop square. And if there's no disc in the drive, the icon is covered with a red X. "All very traditional," we hear you muttering, "and what's he raving about?" Right-click the icon.

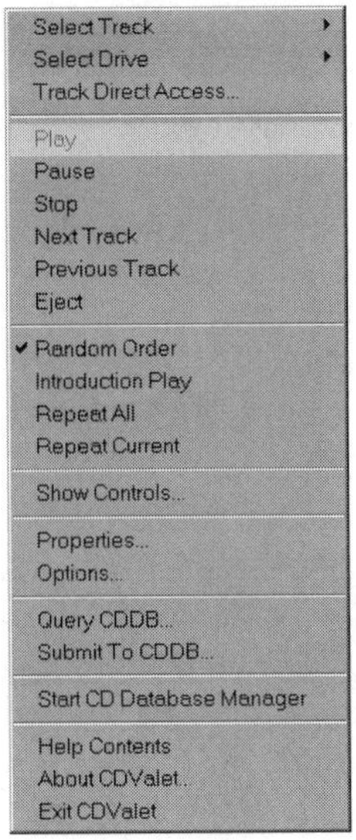

Select Track ▸
Select Drive ▸
Track Direct Access...

Play
Pause
Stop
Next Track
Previous Track
Eject

✔ Random Order
Introduction Play
Repeat All
Repeat Current

Show Controls...

Properties...
Options...

Query CDDB...
Submit To CDDB...

Start CD Database Manager

Help Contents
About CDValet...
Exit CDValet

**Figure 12.9**

CD-Valet Context
Menu

How's *that* (Figure 12.9) for a Context Menu? Isn't that the most hypertrophied right-click you've ever *seen?* And believe us, there's plenty underneath: Properties, Options, and Help, too. The only things lacking are a front-panel track slider (it's in Track Direct Access) and maybe a corkscrew.

CD-Valet is some of the best evidence yet that truly polished and integrated multimedia demands innovation in software as well as hardware. It's available for either $10.00 or $15.00 depending on method of payment, and upgrades are free. Browse to `http://www.ghlsoftware.com` and download an eval copy that has the CDDB access set to time out after thirty days—which is irrelevant since you'll be a CD-Valet registered owner within about ten minutes. Four stars!

# DVD Player

Default path: `Start Menu\Programs\Accessories\Entertainment\ DVD Player`

## The Good News

Having at last seen DVD (Digital Versatile Disc) properly implemented, we are blown away by it. The unsupported idea made us think diffusely of TV-on-a-platter, of a mere format shift that would doom VHS tape in much the same way that audio CDs mortally wounded the audio cassette. One more fancy laser player to stick in a half-height bay.

Now we've seen it and we will be honest: DVD gives a whole new gloss and immediacy to the idea of the "moving picture." It's not TV; it has no raster lines, no artifacts, no flicker—if your monitor's good enough to keep up—and no blur. Its clarity is easily that of 16-millimeter film, if not quite the equal of a real Hollywood movie. When you see a great film transferred to DVD, something like a black-and-white Hitchcock thriller or an epic from the most expansive days of Technicolor, you'll remember the hair-raising thrill of your first encounter with the real thing. You'll also realize that "real movies" on garden-variety color TV are permanently pathetic.

Computer art on DVD is breathtaking, too. When your DVD-equipped computer plays back an animation disc or game disc, it's *just* playing back—not blowing out zillions of polygons while it tries to create the images all over again. Let another computer do the rendering, and take all the time it needs; then slap the output onto a gleaming piece of plastic, and let your own computer reproduce it as easily as music from an audio CD. Take our word, there are dimensions here that you're unlikely to experience in any other way.

Your next computer *needs* a DVD drive. It's true that the technology is still somewhat volatile, and you might want to wait a couple of months while the specifications firm up and some of the hot air leaks out of the prices. But don't deprive yourself of the DVD experience for too long; of all the new applications of computer power to entertainment, it produces some of the most exciting results.

## The Bad News

DVD drives are much like TV tuner cards; there are many different kinds, of which only a few were able to work with the beta versions of Microsoft's player software. The DVD drives we tried were able to work fine with their *own* players running under Windows 98, but they wouldn't work with the *Microsoft* player. And since the Microsoft player would only condescend to run on a computer that had compatible hardware installed, we were never able to run it, which meant no pretty pictures of the dialogs for you.

This is unfortunate, but not a total sacrifice. Most name-brand DVD drives come with application software, highly polished and quivering with anticipation, right in their boxes. Whether you run Microsoft's player or a third-party player will probably make little practical difference; and besides, the retail version of Windows will absolutely support more different DVD drives (and TV tuner cards) than the betas did. So don't let your appetite for Windows 98 keep you from splurging on DVD, and don't let the thought of new DVD hardware interfere with your upgrade to Windows 98. They're both too good to pass up!

# Interactive CD Sampler

Default path: **Start Menu\Programs\Accessories\Entertainment\ Interactive CD Sampler**

 Whaddayamean, Stack Fault? This has loopily, messily crashed on our test system every time we've tried to run it. We hope the release version works better for you.

# Media Player

Default path: **Start Menu\Programs\Accessories\Entertainment\ Media Player**

Media Player is a tool for playing multimedia data files; it'll also play audio CDs, but not in any inspiring way. The Media Player in Windows 98, like the one in Windows 95, lets you play AVI files, and you can copy selections from a CD or a multimedia file to the Clipboard, then paste them into another document.

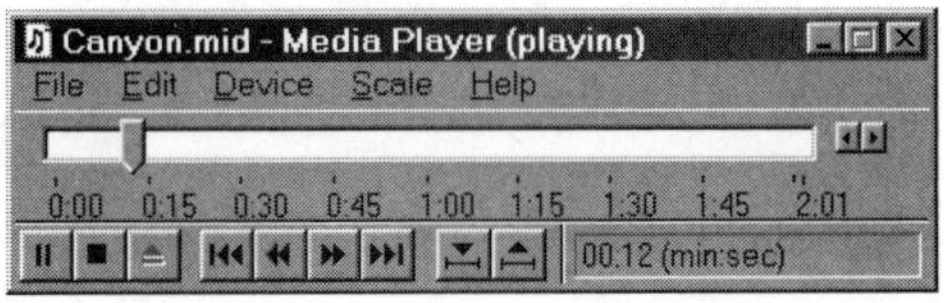

**Figure 12.10**

*Media Player in action ("long" time scale)*

Media Player presents a simple application window, recalling the controls on a VCR or a CD player (Figure 12.10). You can use the slider to scroll through a multimedia file. Nine buttons are available for manipulating files. The title bar of the window tells you which device or file is active and whether it is playing, paused, or stopped.

To operate a device or play a file with Media Player, open the file with the File Open command or with one of the commands on the Device menu. The Device menu lists the multimedia file types available on your system.

When you load a file, a numeric scale appears above the slider (Figure 12.11). The scale displays one of two measurements, Tracks or Time. The Tracks scale (Figure 12.12) applies to simple devices that organize information into tracks. For example, an audio CD player displays the number of cuts on a compact disc.

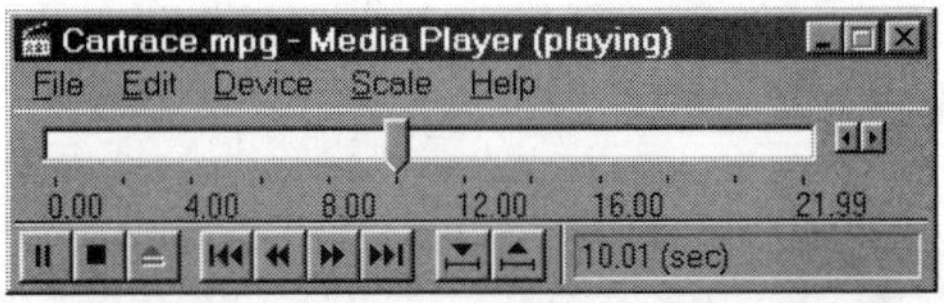

**Figure 12.11**

*Media Player Time scale ("short" scale)*

The Time scale is divided into time intervals scaled to the length of the media file. You can slide the slider to start playing the file at a particular time.

**Figure 12.12**

*Media Player Track scale*

The Track scale is divided into, guess what, tracks. You can slide the slider to start playing any track at any point. (The arrow keys will slide the slider too, but the delay introduced by the CD seek time makes it awkward to use them.) Use the "full forward" and "full back" buttons to hit the track marks.

| File Type | 98 Player | 95 Player |
|---|---|---|
| SoftMPEG, .MPG, .MPC | All | Some |
| Video: .AU, .AIF/F, .AIFC | All | Some |
| VfW: .AVI | All | All |
| WinSound: .WAV | All | All |
| MIDI: .MID, RMI | All | Some |
| QuickTime: .QT, .MOV | All | All |
| CD Audio | All | All |

## Improvements

Windows 98 has exactly the same interface as the Windows 95 version, but will play more file types.

## The Future

Like many of the applets that have persisted through several versions of Windows, the Media Player is worth keeping around because of its undemanding versatility. (It's a lot better than Notepad, which we doubt we'll ever be totally rid of either.) But Media Player isn't the future of Windows' built-in media playback, which—as multimedia in computing quickly becomes a bigger deal—is earning a lot more attention from Microsoft. *Media playback* in Windows 98 means not only WebTV and the DVD Player, but WaveTop, DirectShow, NetShow, and DirectX in general.

Given the pitch of multimedia ferment at Microsoft and elsewhere, some of these technologies will be folded into others and some of these names will be obsolete by the time you read this. The official "meaning" of the NetShow file extension .ASF has already shifted from ActiveMovie Streaming Format to Advanced Streaming Format. We're just working with what we've got!

*Figure 12.13*

MPEG Video in Media Player

For example, it's possible to open an MPEG video file in Media Player (Figure 12.13), but if you click on the MPEG file's name in a folder, Windows 98 uses the DirectShow player to open it (Figure 12.14).

All in all, we think the Media-Matic approach of Media Player is worth keeping around for a while; but Microsoft is likely to develop much more sophisticated playback engines for specific types of audio and video files. Stay tuned.

*Figure 12.14*

MPEG Video in DirectShow Player

# NetShow

Default path: **Start Menu\Programs\Microsoft NetShow**

**Figure 12.15**

Streaming Video in
NetShow Player

NetShow (Figure 12.15) is a highly specific
solution to a problem posed mostly by
corporate intranets, but here and there
throughout the wider Net: How do you run
short-to-medium video or audio sequences
whenever required, over your existing network wiring? Say you've got twisted-pair
going to every workstation; certainly you
don't want to add coax all over your building
just so people can watch TV. On the other
hand, there are situations—say, if everybody needs driving directions to next
morning's meeting—when the form and content of a brief video clip are ideal.
Enter NetShow, your Inter-intranet-video-on-not-very-demanding-demand.

## Controls

**Figure 12.16**

Player with Simple
Controls

**Figure 12.17**

Player with No
Controls

Depending on how you're using NetShow—meaning, essentially, how much
control the viewer is meant to have—you can use a Properties setting to run it
in one of three modes. Figure 12.15 shows it with **Full** player controls (home,
end, skip, play/pause, stop and slider) as well as a timer and menus. The next
notch down is **Simple Controls** (Figure 12.16) which leaves off the skip,
fast-forward and rewind options. Finally, you can elect **No Controls**, which
gives you menus but no buttons (Figure 12.17).

 In order for skip, fast-forward and rewind to work, the file needs to have
markers (Figure 12.18) embedded in it. See **Markers** under **Properties.**

**Figure 12.18**

Control Panel of file
with marker

## Menus

**File Menu.** **Open File…** opens a browse box for a file on the local disk or network. **Open Location…** lets you type in the URL of a file on a NetShow server, although oddly, it doesn't keep a drop-down Run list. **Close** closes the file; **Exit** closes the player. **Properties** is a whole box of tricks we'll get into in a minute.

**Go Menu.** You can **Go** to the NetShow home page, the NetShow update-and-FAQ page, or any of your last five files or locations.

**View Menu.** **Always On Top** "floats" NetShow above all other objects on the Desktop, which could be handy for demos. **Play Settings…** opens the Settings tab of Properties; **Statistics** opens the Statistics tab of Properties. **Markers** are enabled only if the running .ASF file contains markers embedded when it was created; see "Using Markers" in the Help file.

**Help Menu.** Not only the usual **Contents** and **Help About**, but a **Troubleshooting Guide** which suggests that even now a few bugs may lurk.

## Properties

The Properties tabs for a particular NetShow file will vary depending on the file type, the way the file was created, the amount of embedded information, and possibly other factors. At a minimum, you might only find General and Advanced. We've tried to illustrate all of them here, but your mileage may vary.

**General Tab.** General information about the presentation as intellectual property.

**Details Tab.** Technical information about the file, like its source (this one came from a Web page) duration, bandwidth, and image size.

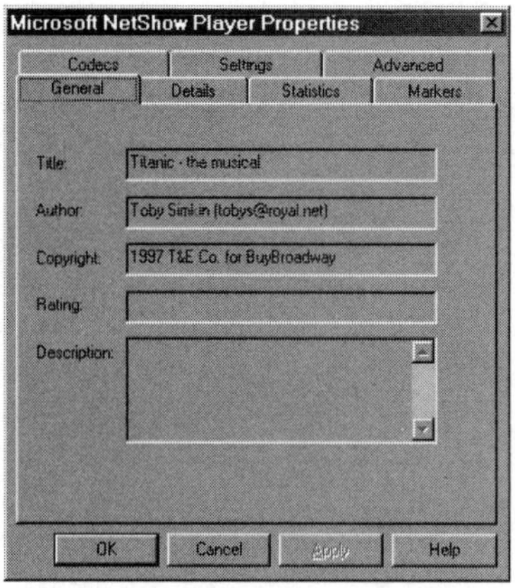

*Figure 12.19*

*NetShow Properties General tab*

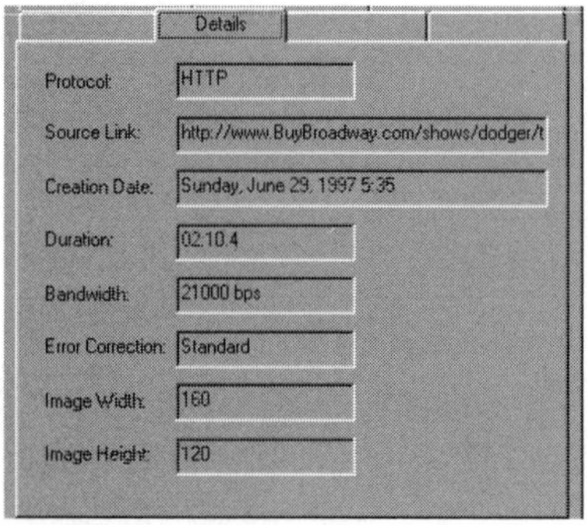

*Figure 12.20*

*NetShow Properties Details tab*

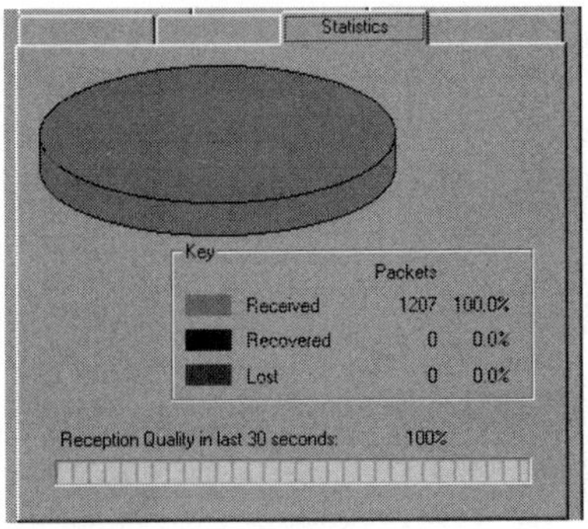

**Figure 12.21**

*NetShow Properties Statistics tab*

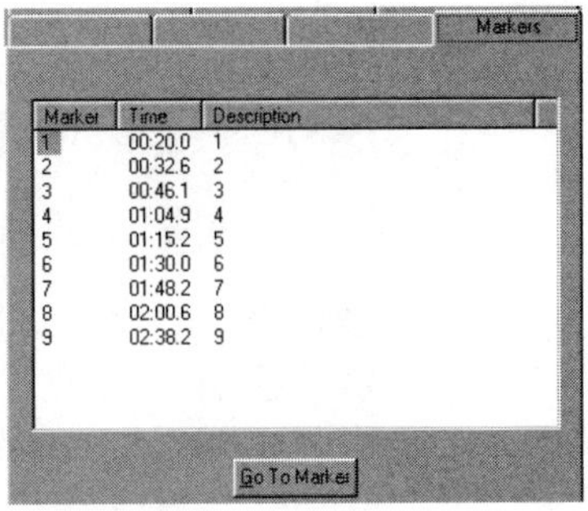

**Figure 12.22**

*NetShow Properties Markers tab*

**Statistics Tab.** File Transmission Quality: If you're getting NetShow content over the Internet or from your local disk, this tab doesn't mean much, but if your content is coming over an intranet and you start dropping frames, this can help indicate the degree of contention on the network.

**Markers Tab.** Markers are "stops" in a NetShow presentation. Without them, you can't jump back and forth in the file—you can only play it straight through, pause it, or restart it.

**Codecs Tab.** *Gotcha!* There are all kinds of codecs (coding/decoding algorithms) that can be involved in the creation of NetShow content—Microsoft, Intel, Cinepak, and Vivo are only a few—and you may or may not have the appropriate codecs on your particular system. Microsoft proudly proclaims that NetShow is "codec-independent" and that you can play back a content file without having all its fundamental codecs installed, but troubleshooting gossip on the Net strongly suggests otherwise.

**Settings Tab.** These settings are for demos and unattended running. You can play the file any fixed number of times, or indefinitely, and rewind at the

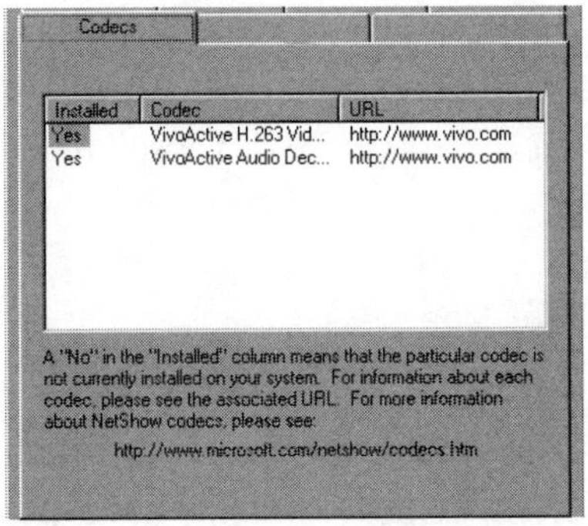

**Figure 12.23**

*NetShow Properties Codecs tab*

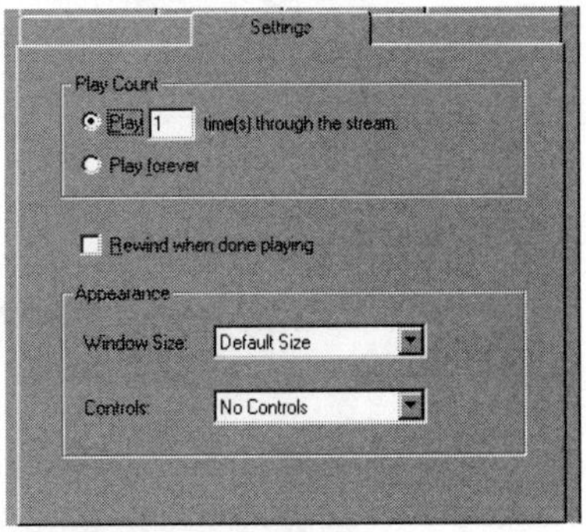

**Figure 12.24**

*NetShow Properties Settings tab*

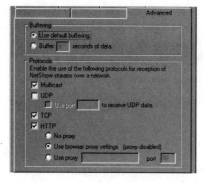

*Figure 12.25*

*NetShow Properties Advanced tab*

end of play, or not. **Window Size** can be **Default, Half,** or **Double,** and **Controls,** as discussed, can be **Full, Simple,** or **None.**

**Advanced Tab.** You can set buffering duration here (although the default is usually fine for a clean connection) and set the stream protocol or protocols to **Multicast, UDP, TCP,** or **HTTP.** Default protocols, which presuppose that you'll get your NetShow content off the Web, are Multicast, TCP, and HTTP, but if you're pulling content from an intranet server, you'll have your NetShow clients configured to match protocols available from the server.

## Troubleshooting

**No Audio.** If you're playing an AV file and getting only video, or playing an audio file and getting nothing, start the file again, open **Properties,** click the **Codecs** tab and look under **Installed.** For every entry in the left-hand column that says "No," you're missing a codec and—no matter what Microsoft says—a missing codec can lose you a channel. Go get the codec from the developer's Web page, install it, and try again.

If all the entries in the left-hand column say "Yes," then use Device Manager and System File Checker to troubleshoot your sound card.

**Low Stream Quality.** If you get frequent buffering or dropout in audio or video, start the file again, open **Properties,** click the **Statistics** tab and look for high Packets Recovered, high Packets Lost, or low Reception Quality. If you have these problems, they arise from some bogosity in your network link, and you should complain to your sysadmin. (Nicely.)

**Jerky Motion.** Can you spell *bandwidth?* We knew you could. The pipe between your computer and the server isn't wide enough for what you're receiving, and some of the content is getting stuck at the edges. There isn't much you can do about this, unless you're in a position to demand—or install—a fatter pipe.

## NetShow Summary

We like NetShow a lot, and much of our satisfaction is related to its maturity; the version we're working with is 2.0, so compared to most of the newer Windows 98 multimedia, it isn't exactly wringing wet. Microsoft promises to release the beta of 3.0 soon, and we look forward to it, although we won't have it in time to include here.

The whole notion of audio and video over TCP/IP—whether done with NetShow, with RealAudio and RealVideo, with the various MPEGs, or even with MIDI for audio-only—adds incredible richness to the networked experience. If developers take care to provide a balanced product like NetShow, they can add that color and depth without making inordinate demands on resources. The current NetShow has a few rough edges, but as a whole, it truly works.

# Sound Recorder

Default path: **Start Menu\Programs\Accessories\Entertainment\ Sound Recorder**

*Figure 12.26*

*Sound Recorder*

You can use Sound Recorder (Figure 12.26) and any Windows-compatible sound card to record sound files to disk, then edit them and play them back. You can also generate simple effects, making sounds louder or faster, adding echoes, or mixing two or more sounds together.

Sound Recorder is in the same pickle as Media Player; if you click on a WAV file's name in a folder, Windows 98 uses the DirectShow player to open it (Figure 12.27). This is too bad, since Sound Recorder is a much more versatile file handler.

*Figure 12.27*

*WAV Audio in DirectShow Player*

Sound Recorder works with standard Windows digital audio files in the .WAV format, no matter what sound hardware was used to record them. Since Sound Recorder is an OLE server application, you can use it to embed sound files into or link sound files to compound documents. In general, Sound Recorder is limited in its capabilities, but handy; we haven't noticed much change between the Windows 98 version and the Windows 95 version, and that in turn was only slightly enhanced from Sound Recorder in Windows 3.x. For serious digital sound editing, you'll want a full-featured shareware or commercial program like Voyetra's Digital Orchestrator Pro (yum!).

## Controls

Sound Recorder's five buttons control the recording and playing of sound files. Symbols familiar from a tape deck or VCR denote **Rewind**, **Fast Forward**, **Play**, and **Stop**; the button with the red circle is **Record**. (The Record button is dimmed if you don't have a sound card installed.)

To play a file, open it and click on the **Play** button. As the file plays, the sound's waveform is displayed graphically in the Sound Recorder window. Click on **Stop** to halt play, and **Play** again to resume where you left off; unlike Stop on CD Player or NetShow, this Stop doesn't automatically rewind to the beginning.

To move to a specific place in a sound file, slide the slider. For greater precision, use the arrow keys to move in .1-second increments, or click on the slider slot to take 1-second steps. As you scroll or step through a sound file, the **Position** box reports your current location, while **Length** contains the total length of the file, in seconds. **Rewind** and **Fast Forward** jump you to the beginning or end of the file, and no, you can't click Fast Forward and Play at the same time; you have to do that with the **Effects\Increase Speed** command.

Keyboard shortcuts for Sound Recorder are useful for fine tuning (see Table 12.1).

### Table 12.1  Sound Recorder Keyboard Shortcuts

| Keyboard | Sound Recorder Button |
|---|---|
| End | End of file (Fast forward) |
| Home | Start of file (Rewind) |
| →, ↓ | Move .1 second forward in file |
| ←, ↑ | Move .1 second back in file |
| Page Down | Move 1.0 second forward in file |
| Page Up | Move 1.0 second back in file |
| F1 | Help |

## Recording

Sound Recorder can record a new file, record over an existing file starting at any point in it, or record new material starting at the end of a file. To record a new sound file, choose **New** from the File menu and click on the **Record** button. When you finish, press Stop, then save the new sound file. Remember that .WAV files, being uncompressed, are huge; recording may be cut short if the program runs out of memory.

 To figure the size of a .WAV file, remember that each bit in the signal is a bit in the file. Huh? Okay, look: It's like figuring color depth. If you're recording 8-bit mono signal, you need one byte (8 bits) of file space for 8 bits x 1 channel of signal. At 11.025 KHz, you need 11,025 bytes—about 11KB—to record one second of signal. Now multiply by four to record at CD quality (44.1 KHz), by two to record at 16 bits depth instead of eight, and by two again to record two channels (stereo). You have a whopping 176KB of file for each second of signal, which means that six *seconds* of CD-quality stereo music takes up just over 1MB of disk space.

To start recording in the middle of a sound file, scroll to the desired location and click **Record**. The new material records over and erases the remainder of the original file. Sound Recorder will let you scroll to the end of the original file and append new recording, but not all hardware supports this feature.

**Sampling from CD-ROM.** Sound Recorder will record samples from audio CDs. Insert a CD into the CD-ROM drive; when the part you want to record starts playing, click **Record**. Sound Recorder records 60 to 70 seconds of audio at a time, depending on available memory and the bit depth of the file; you can continue to record by clicking again on Record. Then edit the sample you've captured, if you like, and save it as a .WAV file. Using the Sound Control Panel, you can attach the file to a Windows action. Opportunities for fun are limited only by your imagination.

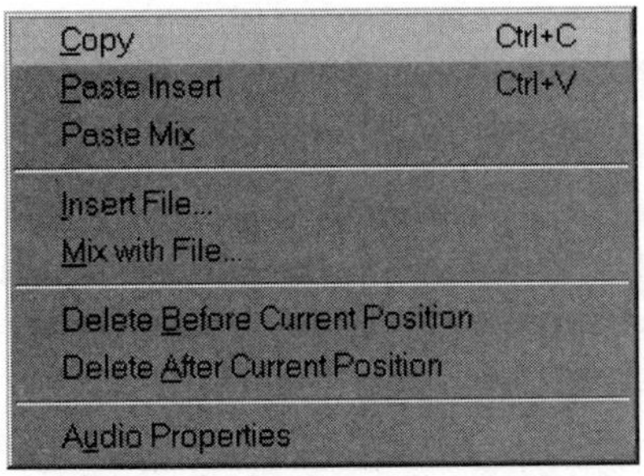

**Figure 12.28**

*Sound Recorder Edit menu*

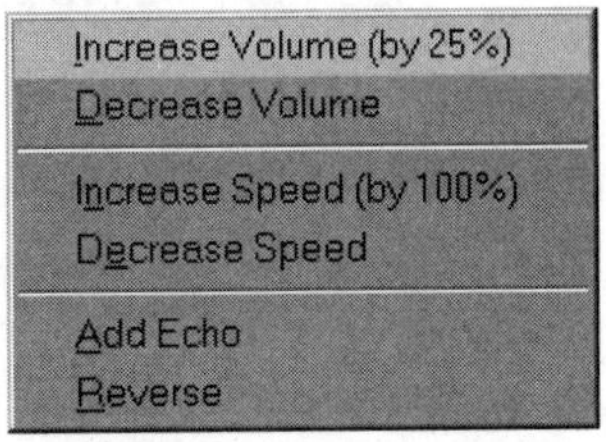

**Figure 12.29**

*Sound Recorder Effects menu*

**Edit and Effects Menus.** Sound Recorder's **Edit** and **Effects** menus (Figure 12.28–29) offer these commands:

- **Edit\Copy** copies the current file to the Clipboard.

- **Edit\Paste Insert** inserts the contents of the Clipboard into the current sound file. The insertion increases the length of the current file, because the two sounds don't overlap.

- **Edit\Paste Mix** mixes the contents of the Clipboard with the current file, dubbing the sounds in the two files together. The length of the resulting file is the length of the current file or of the insertion, whichever was longer.

- **Edit\Insert File** inserts a second sound file anywhere into the current sound file.

- **Edit\Mix with File** mixes a second sound file with the current file.

- **Edit\Delete Before Current Position** erases from the beginning of the sound file up to the current playing position, as specified in the Position box.

- **Edit\Delete After Current Position** erases from the current playing position to the end of the sound file.

- For **Edit\Audio Properties**, see below.

- **Effects\Increase Volume** increases the volume of the sound by 25 percent.

- **Effects\Decrease Volume** decreases the volume of the sound by 25 percent.

- **Effects\Increase Speed** speeds up the playback of the sound by 100 percent, signaling this fact by cutting the values in the Position and Length boxes in half.

- **Effects\Decrease Speed** slows down the playback of the sound by 50 percent (in other words, one Decrease undoes the effect of one Increase).

- **Effects\Add Echo** produces a simple digital reverb effect.

- **Effects\Reverse** reverses the file bit order so that the sound plays backward.

To use any of these commands, open a file and choose a command from the Edit or Effects menu. The command applies to the entire file. You can layer the effect of any command except Reverse by choosing it two or more times. If you want to add an effect to just a portion of a file, you have to copy the sound file, chop it up into smaller files, and apply the effect to one file at a time.

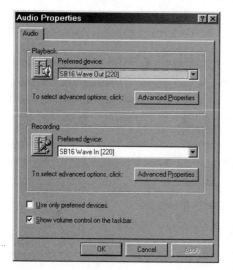

*Figure 12.30*

*Audio Properties*

**Audio Properties.** Audio Properties lets you set the preferred installed devices for recording and playback, restrict recording and playback to the use of *only* those devices, and show the Volume Control "on the taskbar," meaning in the System Tray.

Advanced Properties (for playback or recording) optimizes for head-phones or for about ten speaker setups, from laptop to home theater; lets you set scope of hardware acceleration to one of four levels; and lets you set sample rate conversion quality to one of three levels, with better being slower.

**Save or Revert.** Make changes to a sound file, then audition it by pressing the **Play** button. If you like the new sound, save the changes. If you aren't

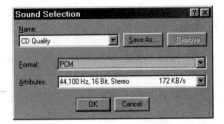

*Figure 12.31*

*Format Selection dialog*

happy with the audition, you can undo the changes you've just made by choosing the **Revert** command from the File menu.

**Save File Formats.** The three Windows default sound file formats are 44.1KHz 16-bit stereo, called "CD Quality;" 22KHz 8-bit mono, called "Radio Quality;" and 11KHz 8-bit mono, called "Telephone Quality;" but Sound Recorder saves in a startling variety of file formats, even though it won't play them all back (see Table 12.2).

## Table 12.2  Sound Recorder Save As formats

| File Type | Sampling Range | Bit Depth, Channels |
| --- | --- | --- |
| CCITT A-Law | 8KHz > 44.1KHz | 8-bit, mono or stereo |
| CCITT u-Law | 8KHz > 44.1KHz | 8-bit, mono or stereo |
| DSP Group TrueSpeech | 8KHz | 1-bit mono |
| GSM 6.10 | 8KHz > 44.1KHz | mono |
| IMA ADPCM | 8KHz > 44.1KHz | 4-bit, mono or stereo |
| Lernout & Hauspie CELP | 8KHz | 16-bit mono |
| Lernout & Hauspie SBC (3 formats) | 8KHz | 16-bit mono |
| Microsoft ADPCM | 8KHz > 44.1KHz | 4-bit, mono or stereo |
| Microsoft G.723.1 | 8KHz | mono |
| MPEG Level-3 (.MP3) | 8KHz > 24KHz | bit depth varies, mono or stereo |
| PCM (Windows default) | 8KHz > 48KHz | 8-bit or 16-bit, mono or stereo |
| VivoActive G.723.1 | 8KHz | mono |
| VivoActive Siren | 16KHz | mono |
| Voxware MetaSound (AC* files or streaming) | 8KHz > 22KHz | mono |
| Voxware MetaVoice (RT* files or streaming) | 8KHz | mono |

For most of the formats in Table 12.2, you can (read: have to) create your own file type extensions with the **Save As...** dialog.

# Volume Control

Default path: **Start Menu\Programs\Accessories\Entertainment\ Volume Control**

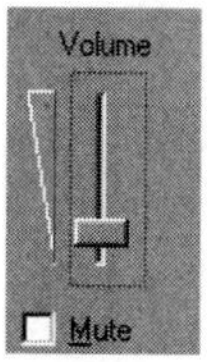

**Figure 12.32**

Volume Control (universal)

The Volume Control applet is one of the better Multimedia controls; it hasn't changed much over the years—at least not on Windows' own initiative—but it doesn't need to, either. It has two modes; the one-size-fits-all slider that adjusts the volume level of your entire system (Figure 12.32) and the Volume Control panel (Figure 12.33), a "volume mixer" controlling the volume and balance of each sound component on your system individually. The master volume control, by default, iconizes as a small speaker in the System Tray. It's a quick way to turn down (or mute) whichever component happens to be making noise. To open the single slider, *single*-click on the Speaker icon in the System Tray.

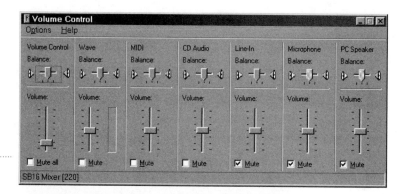

**Figure 12.33**

Volume Control (Playback Panel)

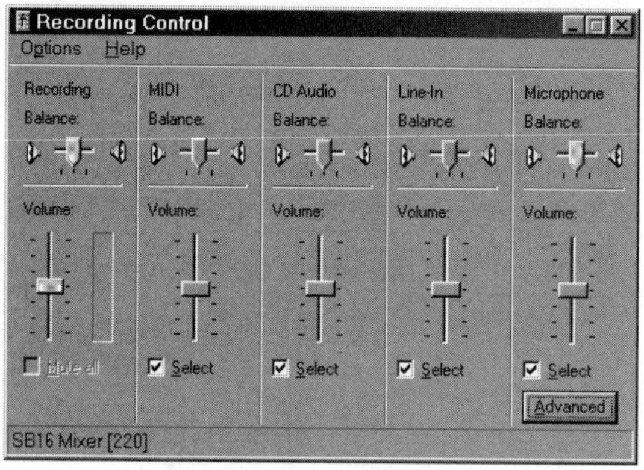

**Figure 12.34**

Volume Control (Recording Panel)

The Volume Control gives you control over individual components that record or play sound, such as microphones, line inputs, WAV or MIDI output, or a CD-ROM drive. The applet also includes a master control. To open the panel, *double*-click on the Speaker icon in the System Tray.

# Standard Controls

The panel's balance controls are like the ones on a stereo tuner. Move a horizontal slider to the left, and more sound comes from the left speaker. If the sound is in stereo, you may hear only parts of it. The volume controls are vertical; the higher the slider, the louder the sound. To mute a device, check its **Mute** box; when you uncheck the box, the sound comes back at the level preset by the volume slider.

The unenhanced Volume Control panel has seven sets of controls:

- Master volume control (same as the all-in-one slider).

- Wave (.WAV) playback.

- MIDI playback and record.

- CD audio playback and record.

- PC Speaker playback (the driver must be installed and, by default, isn't).

- Microphone input record and playback.

- Line input record and playback.

You don't have to have all of your installed devices in the Volume Control panel, and you can select the ones to appear by checking and unchecking boxes in **Options\Properties**. Once you set up a device the way you like it, you may want to remove it from the panel so that its settings aren't changed accidentally.

# Third-Party Controls

The exact appearance of the Volume Control depends on what sound card or devices you have installed. The standard panel without add-ons looks like Figure 12.33, but, for example, having a Sound Blaster card installed adds an **Advanced** button (Figure 12.35).

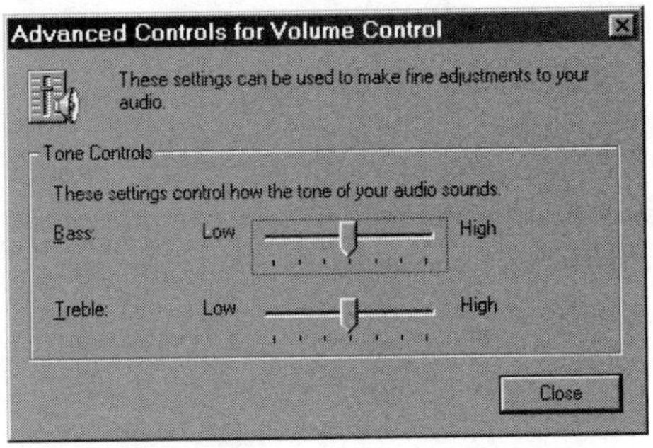

***Figure 12.35***

*Volume Advanced button*

The Advanced button opens to a separate dialog with tone controls (Figure 12.36).

***Figure 12.36***

*Volume Advanced controls (Sound Blaster)*

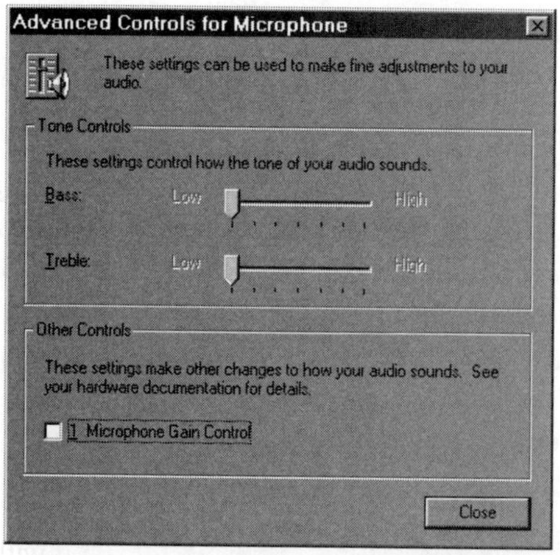

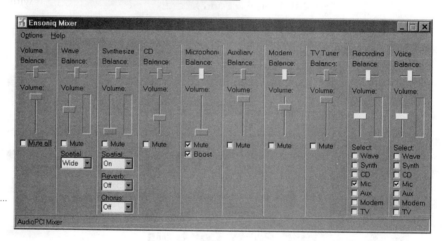

**Figure 12.37**

Microphone
Advanced controls
(Sound Blaster)

**Figure 12.38**

Volume Advanced
controls (Ensoniq)

There are also advanced microphone tone and gain controls (Figure 12.37).

The panel for an Ensoniq card is even more elaborate (Figure 12.38).

The Volume Control may have compatibility problems with mixers installed on your computer, such as the one included with your sound card, and others whose origins will remain forever mysterious. You might want to go to Control Panel\Multimedia, click on the **Devices** tab, open the **Mixer Devices** branch and look at all the mixers you have. Choose the one(s) you like best, and on the Properties sheets of the others, click **Do not use Mixer features on this device**. Redundant drivers are then out of your way, but if you need one, you can get it back without reinstalling it.

# WaveTop

Default path: **System Tray**

We'll say as much about WaveTop as we can, but the rest is up to you. Unlike NetShow, which already sports a certain polish, and WebTV, which is complete but basically broken, WaveTop is an engaging puzzle that's missing a few pieces; thus, the holes in the screenshots. Even in its incomplete state, and even though we're not wild about push, WaveTop looks to us like next week's great toy.

We're not sure what it is, but it's fun! Actually, WaveTop is a cable-based browser that uses spare bandwidth at your local PBS television station (of all places) to deliver push content, cleverly interspersing it with downloads from a dedicated cache server. If you're saying, "You mean something halfway between Internet Explorer and WebTV?" you've got it.

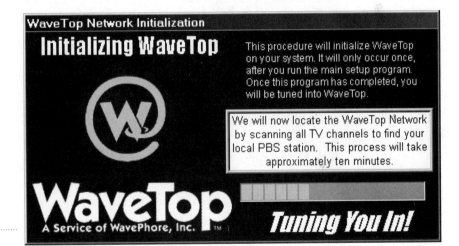

**Figure 12.39**

WaveTop setup

## Installation

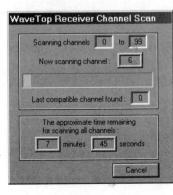

**Figure 12.40**

WaveTop channel scan

Since you're installing something you've never seen the like of, WaveTop is careful to explain what it's doing (Figure 12.39).

First it scans channels looking for your PBS carrier (Figure 12.40).

Then, after ten minutes of scanning and a few more of dire-sounding disk access, it presents you with something like Figure 12.41.

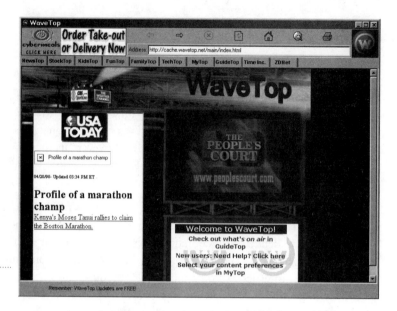

**Figure 12.41**

WaveTop main
screen

## Main Screen

WaveTop's main screen (Figure 12.41) lets you branch to several arenas of specialized push, like NewsTop (real-time news updates), StockTop (investment advice), TechTop (articles, reviews, and the usual gossip), and the two you care most about—MyTop and GuideTop.

## MyTop (Start Page)

MyTop (Figure 12.42) is a personalized front end, resembling the Microsoft Internet Start Page, which helps you keep track of which services (channels? publications?) you're subscribed to.

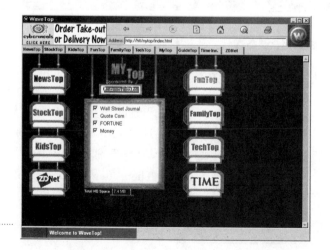

**Figure 12.42**

MyTop

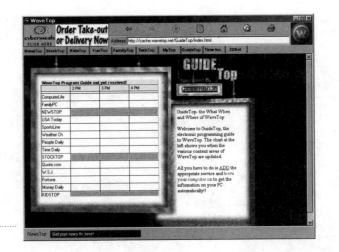

*Figure 12.43*

*GuideTop*

### GuideTop (Channel Guide)

GuideTop (Figure 12.43), which we rather wish they'd called WaveGuide, is—so to speak—WaveTop's preview channel, telling you when the channel content was (or will be) updated. The screenshot would be more convincing if the grid had any entries, but see prior remark about missing pieces.

### How It Stays Up

Even from this meager overview, it's obvious that WaveTop is sustained by a robust variety of banner ads. This is the future of the Net, in many ways, and while nostalgic old-timers may be upset, the Net might never have been accepted by the general population if it couldn't participate wholeheartedly in commerce. Love it or sniff at it, WaveTop is tomorrow's Net and we'll be interested to see what it makes of itself.

# WebTV for Windows

Default path: `Start Menu\Programs\Accessories\Entertainment\`
`WebTV for Windows`, or `QuickLaunch toolbar`

TV on a computer has been such a Holy Grail that, now that it's here, a lot of experienced micro users have trouble believing it. "Full-screen, full-motion video?" they say, remembering too well the days when video either ran in a tiny box or dropped frames left and right. "You're kidding." Not at all; the Windows 98 TV viewer, now called WebTV for Windows, combines with a stunning new generation of hardware to deliver digitized TV.

**Figure 12.44**

Full-screen WebTV
with controls

And, like many techno-miracles, now that it's here it seems so obvious. You
can have full-screen (Figure 12.44) for your favorite sitcom.

Of course you can make the controls go away until you want them, then bring
them back with a keystroke or wiggle of your mouse. Or, if you're using your
computer for other things too, you can have TV-in-a-box (Figure 12.45),
which is handy for glancing at elections, small wars, or minor-league sports.

**Figure 12.45**

Vidwindow
(with apologies
to ReBoot)

# Preparation

Here's how to prepare WebTV for Windows:

**Hardware Setup.** Assuming you have an appropriate video/TV adapter or add-in TV tuner card installed (see "Hardware" below), all you theoretically need to do is connect the TV coax cable to the tap at the back of the card. If you need to do more, refer to the manufacturer's Web page, hotline support, or—always an option—the manual.

**Software Setup.** We're not sure at this point whether WebTV for Windows will be installed with Windows 98 automatically, or only if it finds compatible hardware installed, or whether you'll have to do it yourself. If the latter, you'll find WebTV for Windows on the **Windows Setup** tab of Control Panel\Add/Remove Programs, at the bottom of the list—it's an entry to itself, not part of Multimedia. While you're installing WTW, you might also want to install WaveTop (see earlier in this chapter) if you like push content.

**Scanning for Channels.** Before it can deliver TV to your desktop, WebTV for Windows needs to create a local database of channel and signal information, and determine which channels your hardware can receive correctly. It does both by polling your cable provider. To scan:

Launch WebTV for Windows from the Start Menu.

Pull down the Toolbar with the F10 key.

Highlight the channel number in the black box at the upper left. Key in **96** and hit Enter.

You're now in WebTV channel 96, **TV Config**, and Figure 12.46 will appear.

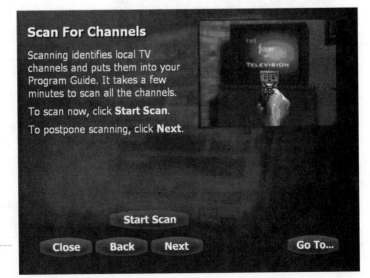

*Figure 12.46*

*Scan for Channels screen*

**Figure 12.47**

Scanning into
database

Click **Start Scan**. The scan begins (Figure 12.47) and takes several minutes.

When the scan is finished, you can return to WebTV or fetch your listings; ordinarily you won't have to scan again.

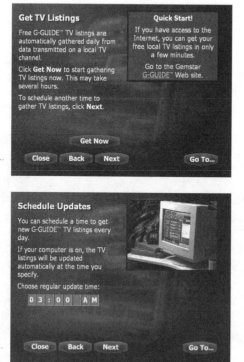

**Figure 12.48**

Get Listings screen

**Figure 12.49**

Schedule Updates

**Fetching listings.** You need the local listings from the Gemstar database to fill the slots in your Program Guide. Click **Go To…**, pick **Get TV Listings**, and you'll see this screen (Figure 12.48).

From here you have two quite distinct choices:

**Download** your listings over the TV cable. It really can take several hours, as the legend says, but the advantage is that it can be done automatically at a set time (Figure 12.49).

Naturally, your computer has to be on at the time you set to fetch listings. But that's okay—Windows 98 doesn't really like it when you turn your computer

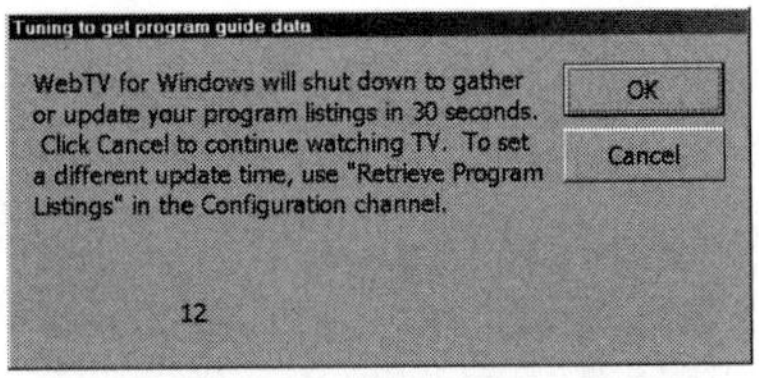

**Figure 12.50**

Scheduled update
advisory

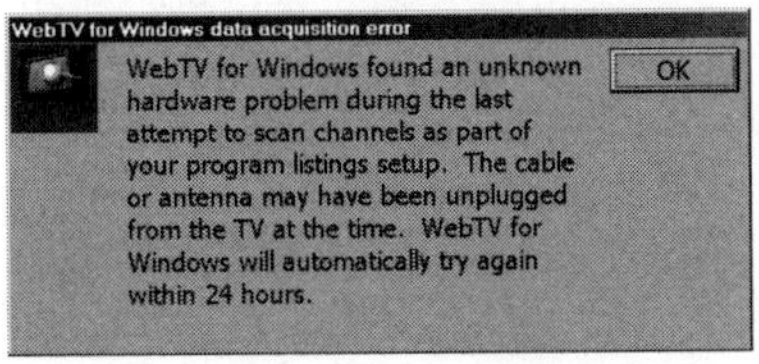

**Figure 12.51**

Acquisition error

off anyway (joke). Should you be
watching TV at the time the update is
scheduled to start, WebTV warns you
politely (Figure 12.50).

When the preset update process fails, as
it sometimes does, WebTV reports an
acquisition error (Figure 12.51). At this
point, instead of waiting for WebTV to
crash again at some random time, we'd
rather do a manual update.

Which brings us to the second choice:

**Click on the G-Guide hyperlink** in the Quick Start sidebar to download
the listings from the Microsoft Broadcast Web server (Figure 12.52).

**Figure 12.52**

Web-based schedule
updates

You'll need to set this up by filling in your ZIP code and the name of your
cable provider, but once that's done, you can update your program listings
in less than five minutes. If you don't want to fetch interactively you can
set up Dial-Up Networking to contact the Web site at a predefined time
(Figure 12.53).

**Figure 12.53**

Web-based
automatic updates

Having tried both methods
of updating, we find the
Web-based option vastly
preferable, especially since
you can log on, update
listings, and log off without being anywhere near
your computer.

*Figure 12.54*

*WebTV for Windows icon*

# Running It

From your Desktop, double-click on your WebTV icon (Figure 12.54). After a splash screen that covers a short delay, you'll pop into full-screen TV at whatever channel you were last watching. Your mouse pointer will be visible but you should be able to park it off-screen.

**Toolbar.** To bring up the toolbar, hit $\boxed{\text{F10}}$, press and release an $\boxed{\text{Alt}}$ key, or move your mouse pointer toward the top of the screen (Figure 12.55)

*Figure 12.55*

*WebTV toolbar*

Above the line, left to right:

- Channel changer. This is non-optimal; you can only move through the channels consecutively. The up arrow goes to higher numbers, etc.

- The channel number, call letters and network affiliation. If this doesn't match the channel you're watching, talk to your cable provider.

- The Interactive TV button, which only works if you have something like Intel Intercast installed.

- Standard Windows Restore and Close buttons which, please note, are the only remotely Windowsy aspect of the full-screen interface. This toolbar is attractive enough, but obviously inherited from WebTV when Microsoft bought the company.

 **If you want to go from, say, channel 20 to channel 9 with a click, pass your pointer over the channel number to highlight it, type in the new channel number, hit** $\boxed{\text{Enter}}$**, and you'll jump. This isn't documented and it isn't terribly intuitive, but it works.**

Below the line, left to right:

- Program **Guide** button. Flips you from your TV screen to your program listings (see below).

- **Settings**. This (Figure 12.56) does less than you'd think; it controls which channels appear in your channel roster, if for some reason you want fewer channels to flip through than the maximum number available. *But* you can also turn on closed captioning, which is handy for accessibility and for silent watching.

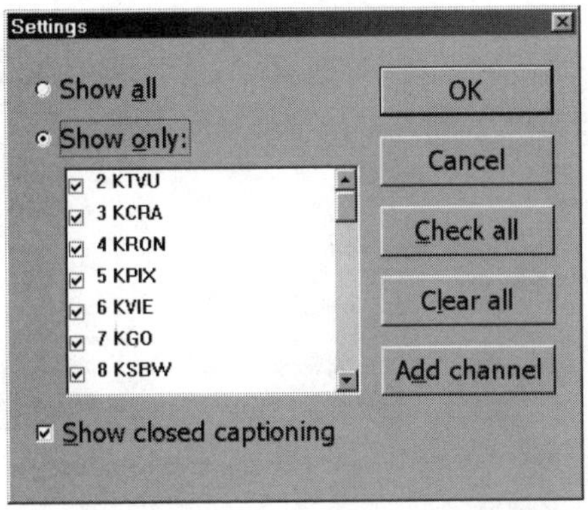

*Figure 12.56*

*Settings dialog*

- **Help** turns on the Help, which is in HTML, like the rest of this interface.

- **Add** is the grace that saves the consecutive channel changer. Click Add when you're watching a favorite channel, and you add a button that jumps directly to it (Figure 12.57). When you're watching a channel that already has a button created, the Add button becomes a **Remove** button … which you'll need, because (gotcha!) you can only have four buttons for favorites, although the toolbar would accommodate several more.

*Figure 12.57*

*Playing favorites*

**Watching a Window.** When you flip between window and full screen, or between full screen and the Program Guide or Configuration channels, the part of the screen being filled will briefly turn magenta or blue. This is interesting, but normal.

Watching a window is good and bad news. It's comfortable, it lets you combine watching with other tasks, it adds color and motion to your Desktop, and it reasserts the Windows—rather than the WebTV—interface. Finally, thanks to blazingly fast modern video chipsets, you can have a window running in the background and you'll hardly notice its impact on your foreground task. The nicest part of WebTV isn't "watching TV on your computer," but having video as one peer-to-peer element of your application mix.

On the other hand, it's not obvious how to get to the controls (click in the viewing area) and they're the WebTV controls, which try to scale to the smaller space and don't do very well. Overall, watching a window is probably the most useful viewing mode as long as you leave everything alone, but is much less satisfactory as soon as you want to change settings.

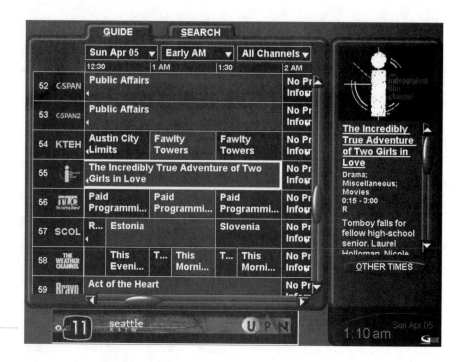

**Figure 12.58**

Program Guide

## Program Guide

The Program Guide, Channel 97, is one of the best parts of WebTV, because it does for your TV viewing what a computer usually does for a repetitive task—automates, streamlines and organizes it.

The two tabs, **Guide** and **Search**, give you time-based and category-based perspectives on available programs. (Your Guide tab will only look like this if your listings are up to date.)

**Guide Tab.** The left-hand section of the **Guide** screen (Figure 12.58) is a scrolling channel preview list; whatever program is highlighted in the preview list (note the thicker white border at channel 55) will be featured with a description—and maybe a hyperlink—in the right-hand section. Above the description and title, for many shows, will be a live "mini-screen" of the high-lighted show. Below it will appear one or maybe two buttons: **Watch**, which will jump you straight to full-screen video, and **Other Times**, which will tell you when the show is being broadcast again.

**Figure 12.59**

Select Day
drop menu

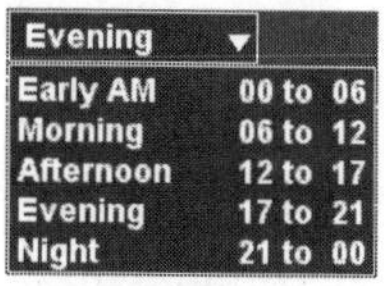

**Figure 12.60**

Select Time
drop menu

The drop-boxes just under the Guide tab let you select from the days with locally available listings (Figure 12.59), pick the part of the day whose listings you want to see (Figure 12.60), and choose between listings for all valid channels or just for your toolbar Favorites (Figure 12.61).

**Figure 12.61**

Select Channels
drop menu

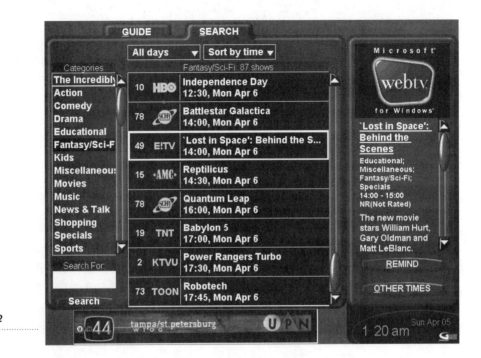

**Figure 12.62**

*Search tab*

**Search Tab.** The **Search** tab (Figure 12.62) keeps track of shows by category. Its organization is somewhat gloppy, but it does a lot.

**Figure 12.63**

*Category time filter*

On the left, the **Categories** dialog gives you a preset list of show categories, which also includes (at the top) whatever is highlighted on the Guide tab. Below that is a Web-style Search box; key in your keyword and submit.

Once you pick a Category, all the shows in it will be listed in the center section; the default is to list shows for all days in the local database, but you have choices (Figure 12.63).

You can see **All** shows, what's **On now**, or the shows for any day in the database. If you want to be alerted to a show you want to watch later, click the **Remind** button (Figure 12.64).

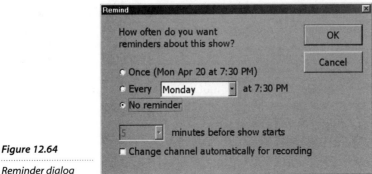

**Figure 12.64**

*Reminder dialog*

## Video In/Out

We'll just mention that WTW allows you to reserve one channel (usually 95) as a video In/Out channel for fun (or work, if you prefer) like AVI playback and video capture. The way you set this up will be highly hardware-specific, so we can't say much about it here.

## Hardware

Making your computer receive television capitalizes on the fact that, by owning a SuperVGA monitor, you already own most of an exceptionally well-made small-to-medium TV set. (Once you watch a clean cable signal or, better yet, digital video on your computer, you'll know that your monitor is a much more exacting device than your TV.) So all you need is a TV tuner and cable tap, which—in these amazing days—can fit on your video card in a metal case no bigger than a pack of gum.

TV cards are currently made by ADS, AITech, ATI, Hauppauge, Matrox, and STB, among others, and with more manufacturers poised to jump in. You can buy anything from an adapter that converts your existing video card to receive TV, to a first-class SuperVGA card with a TV receiver, FM receiver, video input and output, and some of the most confusing cables you've ever seen. Plan on spending from about $100 to well over $400, depending on how many things you want the card to do.

The cards most often used with pre-release versions of Windows 98 were the ATI All-in-Wonder ($170 street this week) and All-in-Wonder Pro ($330 street) and we have to say that these are both breathtaking devices whose performance will tempt you to immoderate language. With either of the All-in-Wonders, you can be crunching on a spreadsheet one minute, playing Riven or Mechwarrior the next, and watching CNN the next, knowing you got a deal the whole time. The refresh rate and color saturation are excellent in any context, and ATI's own Rage II+ and Rage Pro chipsets just do not choke. Our only caution is that the All-in-Wonder Pro, with 8MB VRAM, requires an AGP slot that your motherboard might not have, but the 4MB All-in-Wonder is plain PCI and should be compatible with most system boards made in the last two or three years. Whether you're specifying a new computer or upgrading your old one, either of these cards is a handsome investment.

While we're discussing making your monitor into a TV, you might be interested in ADS' Superscan 2 card, which will do just the opposite—make your TV into a monitor. It's all just bits, guys!

# The Future of Hardware

The itching point of the near future will be that, while your 15-inch monitor makes a very nice TV, it's a 15-inch TV and, get serious. Luckily, some large LCD monitors are in beta as we write, leading to fantasies of a 36-inch Sony Trinitron flatscreen on a pedestal, said pedestal containing a video-optimized computer with CD and DVD drives, a 24GB A/V-rated hard disk, and an IR port for the remote. The satellite dish will be installed unobtrusively on the back of the flatscreen. The pieces for this exist *now;* the sleekly assembled, irresistible totality will arrive at a showroom near you before long.

# WebTV Summary

WebTV for Windows is the first attempt to bring video to commodity Wintel computing at the operating-system level. It deserves praise for that, for being fun, and for being adequately stable. Full-screen, full-motion video was so recently a dream and is now a fact—not yet a cheap fact, but nowhere *near* as expensive and gnarly as it was. You can look at WebTV and understand that video, before long, will follow the lead of the sound card and shrink to an ASIC or two on the motherboard.

Having said that, we have a nagging feeling that WebTV—in its actual, 0.99 reality—got out of the barn too soon. If the interface is jarringly un-Windows-like, that's a matter of taste; but it is *slow,* and made slower by trying to do terribly fancy things with overburdened HTML. If WebTV works out of the box for you (which, in fairness, it did for us) it's tolerably easy to configure, but if something goes wrong, it can be infuriating to troubleshoot. The software is the only component in Windows 98 that ate all our test machine's system resources and locked it up; and, while we're talking about resources, WebTV isn't real light on disk space either. And we cannot believe the lack of elementary features like a dedicated volume control.

WebTV is the same old Microsoft story; even as you wrestle with 1.0, you dream of 2.0. In this case, we'd settle for 1.1 with improved controls and better screen scaling. But in the meantime, sad to say, you might prefer the TV console software that comes with your tuner card.

# Summary

Convergence of hardware and software has combined with a major push (pardon the pun) by the industry to make new computers more necessary by making them more versatile. The result is a captivating emphasis on multimedia, in which Microsoft enthusiastically takes part—but with uneven results. This strange assembly of something old (CD Player, Media Player, Sound Recorder), something new (NetShow, DVD Player), something borrowed (WaveTop), and something blue (WebTV for Windows) proves that, for the foreseeable future, Redmond is married to the idea of distributable content.

# Part 3

## Advanced Windows 98 Techniques

# Part 3 At a Glance

# 13

# Optimizing Windows 98 Resources

The performance and capabilities of your Windows 98 environment ultimately depend on two things: the selection of your hardware and the configuration of your software.

In the three years since Windows 95 was introduced, the capability of ordinary, retail computer hardware has taken amazing leaps. In the average machine, clock speed has doubled, from 100MHz to 200MHz; typical RAM has also doubled, from 16MB to 32MB; and whereas in 1995 a pre-built, package-deal computer's hard disk held between 540MB and 1.1GB, today you can expect to find 2GB to 4GB of disk space in even the least expensive computers. (These bigger disks are also faster, because they spin faster, their electronics are more efficient, and their bits are closer together.) Finally, in the same length of time, graphics and sound hardware have improved almost beyond recognition.

Add it all up and you'll find that, even for $1,000 to $1,400, you can enjoy a computer of unprecedented power and flexibility. The shame of it is that, because Windows 98 arrives pre-installed on so many machines—and 32-bit Windows in general has a reputation for being bizarrely complicated—too many computer users never change, or even inspect, the myriad of Windows performance settings. This is too bad, because every copy of Windows 98 offers a comprehensive set of tools that lets you tailor your operating system to take maximum advantage of your nice new (or nice old) computer.

# What's "Optimizing" Anyway?

So far as Windows 98 is concerned, there are three kinds of optimizing:

- **Optimizing by installation.** Of course this covers buying enough processor, memory, and disk space to begin with! But there are choices that you can make about optimizing your installation of Windows, such as whether to install the FAT32 filesystem or (*or,* not *and*) DriveSpace 3, whether to use Compression Agent, where to look for the newest and best drivers, and how to manage virtual memory.

- **Optimizing by configuration.** After your Windows 98 installation is complete, you can go to work with Control Panels like **Add/Remove Programs**, **Power Management**, and **TweakUI** to make your computer's behavior suit your taste and operating style.

- **Optimizing by housekeeping.** Even if you've created the ideal installation, an installed copy of any version of Windows is not a static thing—

for better or for worse. Temp files stack up in out-of-the-way folders; shareware programs accumulate in the folder tree under Program Files; your disk becomes fragmented, which impairs performance by lengthening file access time. Windows 98 offers more and better housekeeping tools than any previous version of Windows, and it needs them, too.

## Do I Need All This Stuff?

There are two ways of looking at that. The first is that Windows 98 does its best to optimize itself during the installation process, and generally does an adequate job. At a minimum we would recommend looking into, and enabling, automatic execution of Windows housekeeping utilities like **Disk Cleanup** and **Disk Defragmenter**, which will help Windows stay as snappy as it was when it was originally installed.

On the other hand, few—if any—operating systems have ever offered the degree of flexibility that Windows 98 does right off the disk. (At the cost of jaw-dropping code bloat and a sometimes frustrating interface, it's true, but both of those are firmly in the Windows tradition.) If you take the time to understand how the main components of your computer work together, and optimize them to meet the significant demands made by Windows 98, you can create a system that fits you like a *Star Trek* uniform, answers your every whim, stays easy to navigate, and never skips a beat—a system, in other words, that feels like an extension of yourself. There is a learning curve here; you will spend time and energy creating the perfect computer, just as you would perfecting any other appliance you spend a lot of time with. *However,* you already have this book, which is a terrific start on the process.

Ultimately, you choose how much to optimize your computer, just as you do to optimize your car. If you buy a car, drive it off the lot, use the right grade of gasoline, change the oil often enough, and keep it clean, you'll probably be satisfied with it for as long as you own it. On the other hand, if your life revolves around thinner head gaskets, different rear axle ratios, and metalflake paint jobs, you can do things like that to a computer, too. And computers don't need to pass smog tests when they're finished!

## The Compatibility Myth

Windows 98 runs on "IBM PC and compatible" systems, but no single standard really exists for "IBM PC compatibility." Profound differences exist among the systems described as IBM PC compatible; even IBM itself has produced machines that are, in many ways, incompatible with each other. The only real tie that binds those systems is their ability to run the DOS operating system, which is now scarcely available for sale.

### *Your Framistat Has the Wrong Number of Tracks Per Pixel*

Installing Windows 98, in and of itself, makes it easier to run programs and add peripheral devices, because 32-bit Windows provides a compatibility buffer between your computer's hardware and your applications. Still, we don't have all the answers for ourselves and we can't promise them to you. Some of your problems may be insurmountable; you might have to purchase some new hardware before you can run Windows 98. This section is about doing that intelligently, and making the outlay well worth it.

So, within the last five years, a new term has come to the fore: *Wintel*, which is shorthand for "Intel-powered computer running Windows." That's an excessive generalization—the new computer you buy with Windows installed may have a CPU made by Intel, AMD, or IBM/Cyrix—but it's a better description of the platform paradigm than "IBM PC compatible," a term almost twenty years old and functionally meaningless. Try taking some relative's original IBM PC XT and installing an Ultra/DMA hard disk, a 64-bit PCI video card, a CD-ROM drive, and 32MB of memory.

The term "Wintel" doesn't describe a standard for hardware compatibility in the way that the phrase "IBM PC compatible" used to. The good news is that most Windows-compatible hardware shares a level of common understanding that was never really possible with DOS alone. Windows 98, by means of universal virtual device drivers and minidrivers (.INF files), establishes a "language" through which different hardware devices can communicate with different software applications. This means you no longer have to go through the agony of separately configuring each application to run on your hardware setup, as was often the case with DOS. A glance at the Microsoft-produced Help file called the *Windows 98 Hardware Compatibility List* will show you the lengths that Windows will stretch to support older hardware. Incompatibilities are not as common as they were with earlier versions of Windows, and when they arise, they can more easily be resolved.

This isn't to say that your troubles are over. Because of the wide spectrum of "PC-compatible" hardware, almost every computer system is configured differently, making it difficult to identify hardware incompatibilities. If you run into problems, your three best resources are:

- The vendor who sold (or manufacturer who made) your computer

- The Web sites of the makers of your hardware and software components

- This book, especially the chapter on Troubleshooting.

## The Most Efficient Optimizing Tool: Money

Of course, the quickest way to get a computer optimized for Windows 98 is to buy one! It's not a cheap solution—although it's getting cheaper—and you probably don't want to replace your computer every time you upgrade your operating system, although the industry would love it if you did. Let's suppose for the moment, though, that the advent of Windows 98 has you jazzed into admitting that your old 386 or 486, with the 8MB of RAM, the fourteen-inch monitor, and the overflowing disk, can no longer be what you expect a computer to be. For people in your position, we'll discuss what to look for in new hardware; then, for those with existing computers that only need a brush-up to be Windows 98-appropriate, we'll talk about upgrading.

# Getting a New Computer

When you have a chance to buy a whole new computer, you want to concentrate on the components that have the biggest effect on performance—which are, in *about* this order: CPU, processor cache, RAM, disk, and video adapter. Naturally, while you're buying a new computer, you'll have lots of other things to think about—like the monitor—but those aren't part of "optimization" as we mean it in this chapter.

## *A Bag of Prevention*

When you get a new computer, do yourself the biggest imaginable favor. Take all the booklets, leaflets, cards, and CDs that you find in the various boxes, and put them on the table. Remove all the stuff that you probably won't use or that has no direct relation to the computer, like the free trial CDs for online services and the tent-cards for discounted magazines. Organize the rest—emphatically including the booklets for the motherboard, modem, and monitor, leaflets about the hard disk, CD drive, and I/O ports, and your Windows OEM CD—and seal it all in a Ziploc bag, which you then label something like COMPUTER EMERGENCY BAG. Put it where you can find it again. In a perfect world, you would never need this bag. This is not that world, and you'll be glad to have it, more than once.

## Central Processing Unit (CPU)

The central processing unit, or CPU, is your computer's brain. Because the CPU chip actually runs your programs and operating system, it has substantial impact on your system's capabilities and performance.

**What and How.** CPU chips are distinguished from other, less powerful chips by the fact that CPUs can do the following:

- Perform arithmetic and logical operations.

- Decode special instructions.

- Issue electrical signals that control other chips.

Intel CPUs, the overwhelming favorite of the commodity computer industry, have gone through a long period of evolution. The 8088 and 8086 CPU chips developed by Intel in the late 1970s were used in the original IBM and Compaq PCs between 1981 and 1984, and they operated in what is called *real mode*. In real mode the operating system can directly access only 1 megabyte of memory, and DOS was originally designed to work only in this mode … which seemed like a good idea at the time, because one megabyte was as much memory as many large, expensive business computers featured. Even IBM's first hard-disk-equipped PC, the 1984 IBM PC XT, had only 256K of RAM installed, so there seemed to be plenty of room for growth. Windows 3.0 offered a special real mode that allowed it to operate using an 8088 or 8086 chip and one megabyte of memory.

Then a fatal misstep was made. The "top" 384K of the one-megabyte 8086 address space was reserved for the video BIOS and video paging RAM, and *that block could not be moved.* It was "hardwired" into the IBM memory map, leaving the "lower" 640K for programs and data. After all, Bill Gates himself is reputed to have said that 640K of RAM was plenty for anything you'd want to do with a computer (snickers Kip, whose system for this project sported 256MB).

The limitations of real mode spawned a torrent of affliction for programmers and designers, haunt DOS to this day, and cause many of the memory-management headaches you experience when you configure Windows. Briefly, they meant that any time your operating system wanted to use *more* than 640K of RAM, it had to leap over the reserved video block—like jumping a fence with a motorcycle—and start counting memory addresses again at the one-megabyte boundary. Worse yet, the 384K of reserved memory was divided into six blocks of 64K each, called Upper Memory Blocks (UMBs), and under certain circumstances (related to what kind of video adapter and system bus you had) one or more UMBs of the "video" memory *could* be used by programs, subject to irritating restrictions.

If you succeeded in jumping the fence and reaching the strange land above one megabyte, you had to deal with two rival addressing schemes—one called *expanded memory* (EMS) and the other called *extended memory* (XMS)—which only matter any more when you're setting up address space for DOS applications under Windows, so we discuss them in Chapter 14, "Windows 98 and DOS." Finally, the first 64K block *above* the one-megabyte boundary is known as the HMA (High Memory Area) and, with both Windows 3.0 and 3.1, you could tune your applications for top performance only by knowing whether individual programs could or could not run when part of DOS was stored in the HMA. For programmers who had to hack their way through these mazes, the words "memory addressing" became inseparable from the words "brain-dead."

In 1984 Intel introduced the 80286 chip (286 for short) which included *protected mode,* which protects memory addresses above one megabyte from the conflicts that result when several applications try to access that memory at the same time. A processor running in protected mode can safely address memory above one megabyte. Windows 3.1 did away with real mode and ran only in protected mode, meaning that it ran only on a 286 processor or better. But the 286 had, and still has, a dirty secret; it could jump *from* real mode *into* protected mode, but not back into real mode, unless you turned the processor off and back on. Programmers who used colorful synonyms for "memory addressing" came up with pyrotechnic equivalents of "protected mode"—especially after Microsoft muscled in with yet *another* memory handling technique, the *DOS Protected Mode Interface* (DPMI), which allowed DOS applications to access protected-mode memory. Again, see Chapter 15 for details.

In 1986, Intel caught the brass ring, with the i386 processor and its *virtual mode*. A superset of protected mode, virtual mode creates almost any number of self-contained virtual DOS machines that appear to be individual 8086-based systems, each with its own 640K of memory. (Notice that the magic 640K is still around? Unless we want to completely give up on DOS compatibility, we'll never be rid of it.) Whenever you see the letters VDM in relation to Windows, it's a reference to virtual DOS machines.

Actually, *everything* in Windows 98 taps the processor's virtual mode to run multiple virtual machines. Without getting absurdly technical, let's outline the process this way:

- Each DOS session runs in its own VDM window (Figure 13.1). The default Windows 98 DOS VM has a moderately advanced configuration, with DOS in the HMA, but no use made of UMBs. 584K free out of a possible 640K is enough to run most normal DOS programs, but in Chapter 15 we'll find out how to free up yet more DOS memory when necessary.

*Figure 13.1*

*Output of*
***mem/c*** *command*
*in DOS VM*

If a DOS program running in a VDM stops executing, Windows is able to shut down that VDM without damage to other running processes. It is *not* possible to write a data file to disk from within a crashed VDM, and when Windows closes out a stopped VDM, it warns you that you will lose unsaved information.

- Through the magic of WOWEXEC, the Windows on Windows Executive, existing 16-bit Windows 3.*x* applications all run in the System Virtual Machine (the primary Windows VM) and all share a common pool of resources in a process called *cooperative multitasking*. In cooperative multi-tasking—which would be more understandable if it were called "serial multitasking"—any running program can have full control of the CPU and available resources for as long as it chooses, while other programs in memory "cooperate" by remaining idle until their turns come for control of the CPU. As you'll remember if you ever ran Windows 3.1, this alloca-tion scheme worked well enough *unless* a rogue program got the CPU and memory in a death-grip and wouldn't let go—at which point the hourglass appeared on your screen, it wouldn't go away, you got tired of waiting for Windows to resolve the situation, and you rebooted to clean up memory.

  This method of executing programs was appropriate for the hardware and software of the early 1990s, when Windows 3.1, the 486DX CPU, and 30-pin SIMM memory were the order of the day. It had clear-cut limitations then, and it does now, when Windows 98 essentially runs a copy of Windows 3.*x* inside itself so that Win16 applications will find exactly the environment that they expect. It's still possible for a rogue 16-bit Windows program to lock up the entire 16-bit resource pool, but when that happens, Windows 98 can generally keep resulting damage confined within the WOWEXEC.

- 32-bit programs designed for Windows 95 and NT are written for *preemptive* multitasking—in which multiple 32-bit applications can access the CPU at the same time, but Windows doles out the timeslices that keep them running smoothly. Like Win16 programs, they all run within the System Virtual Machine; *unlike* a Win16 program, each Win32 pro-gram is assigned a unique, non-overlapping block of memory and system resources. Windows 9*x* is much more hardware-intensive than Windows 3.*x*, but in a way that makes 32-bit programs nearly crashproof—they can't step on each other's resources.

Just to finish the set, we'll mention that Windows NT takes the safest possible path and can set up a separate VM for *any* program that requires one—whether it's a DOS, Win16, or Win32 program. This is why NT rarely crashes com-pletely, and why its processor and memory requirements are gargantuan.

**Selecting a CPU.** How much processor is enough for you? Why, as much as you feel like paying for! Remember, folks, *a fast computer is more fun than a slow one*. In Chapter One we talked about what processors *would* and *wouldn't* run Windows 98; Table 13.1 shows some more detailed recommendations about processor selection, based on what kinds of applications you plan to use, and on your budget.

## *Table 13.1  Processors*

| Type | MHz | Maker | Comments |
|---|---|---|---|
| **486DX** | 50 | Intel | A rarity, but a real prize; a 50-MHz processor that required peripheral components to run at the same speed. At the time, such components were expensive and hard to produce. Many 486DX/50 motherboards could accommodate 16MB of RAM, and this combination will run Windows 98, not very fast, and not officially. |
| **486DX2** | 66 | Intel | Since it was "clock-doubled," this CPU gave almost exactly the performance of a DX/50, but could use cheaper 33-MHz motherboard logic. Will also run Windows 98, not in an inspiring way. |
| **486DX2** | 80 | AMD | A rare chip; we haven't tested it with Windows 98. |
| **486DX4** | 100, 133 | Intel, AMD | These were "clock-tripled," with the CPU running at three times the speed of the peripheral logic. The 100's will give about the performance of a slow Pentium; the AMD 133 is an inconsistent chip with compatibility problems. |
| **Pentium** | 60, 66, 75, 90 | Intel | These will run Windows 98 and make you wish for something faster. |
| **Pentium** | 100, 120, 133, 150 | Intel | If these have enough RAM they will run Windows 98 without making you feel the need of an upgrade. |
| **Pentium** | 166, 200, 233 | Intel | Performance enough for anybody, assuming you have enough RAM that running multiple applications won't put you into the swapfile. |
| **Pentium MMX** | 166, 200, 233 | Intel | As above. The jury is still out as to whether this round of MMX extensions materially speeds up graphic-intensive operations, but we know they don't hurt. |
| **6x86MX** | PR200 | IBM/Cyrix | Roughly the performance of a Pentium MMX 233, and cheaper. We anticipate that the PR200 and PR233 will be fully Windows 98-compatible. |
| **Pentium Pro** | 180, 200 | Intel | A great, somewhat overlooked chip whose full-clock level 2 cache was both its secret weapon and its downfall. A Pro-based computer is absolutely a Windows NT machine; its performance with Win16 code is poor. |
| **K6** | 233 | AMD | More advanced architecture and a fatter on-chip cache make the K6 233 conclusively faster than the Pentium MMX with the same clock rate. |
| **6x86MX** | PR233 | IBM/Cyrix | Roughly the performance of a Pentium II 233, and cheaper. Definitely try NT with this one. |

## Table 13.1 (continued)

| Type | MHz | Maker | Comments |
|---|---|---|---|
| *Pentium II* | 233, 266, 300 | Intel | Plenty of these have been—and will be—sold with Windows 98 and 95 installed, but we'd suggest that (if your vendor will cooperate) you also try NT Workstation and see which you like better. |
| *6x86MX* | PR266 | IBM/Cyrix | With careful selection of the motherboard and peripheral components, can be one of the world's true screamers. We'd suggest NT from the start. |
| *Pentium II* | 333 | Intel | At the moment, and we do mean moment, this would seem to be the fastest Windows CPU you can buy. Available at premium prices from the guys who like to be in front when the checkered flag drops—think Compaq, Dell, Gateway, Hewlett-Packard, Micron, and NEC. These are NT boxes pure and simple. |

**Tomorrow's Processors.** What's ahead in the processor race? It only gets better. First of all, some quiet R&D—rummaging and deduction—in the southern extremity of Silicon Valley suggests that the existing Pentium II design starts gasping for electrons at about 400 MHz. (We can't tell you this, but one of the 400 MHz Pentium IIs was water-cooled.) All the better, then, that Intel will shortly introduce its 32-bit "Deschutes" and 64-bit "Merced" chips, which will expand on the form factor of the Pentium II, but pack a *whole* lot more punch. As we write, Intel is sternly proclaiming that Merced is intended "for workstation- and server-class computers only." Uh-huh. So far as we can remember, Intel has said that about every new chip they've introduced since the 486DX. We can only surmise that, if you want a Merced-based computer, you won't have a hard time buying one.

Nonetheless, the Pentium II is expensive to make, and Merced will be too. Other manufacturers are coming up with awe-inspiring CPUs for less money; we think particularly of IBM/Cyrix' MediaGX chip which, by combining traditionally non-CPU functions (like audio, video, game ports, and PCI and USB buses) right into the central processor, makes it easier to build a full-featured multimedia computer at a bargain-basement price. Intel is not about to concede this potentially huge market segment, and has just announced a competing, low-priced, highly integrated CPU called Celeron.

Packaging design is another fascinating avenue of speculation. The AMD K6, IBM/Cyrix 6x86MX, and Intel Pentium are all so-called *Socket 7* chips—big flat packages that attach to the motherboard with a dense grid of gold-plated pins out the bottom of the package. (The Pentium Pro socket, of the same type but bigger, is *Socket 8.*) The Pentium II took a sudden ninety-degree turn—literally—and sticks straight up off the motherboard, in a plastic case called the Single Edge Contact (SEC) Cartridge. An SEC Cartridge looks like a small black candy bar, and mates with the motherboard through an edge connector that fits in a special slot called Slot One.

The SEC Cartridge design is the intellectual property of Intel, who would presumably be upset if any other manufacturer copied it … but, in an industry as competitive as this, enforcing proprietary standards isn't always the way to sustain your lead. Some microprocessor builders are shouting *Socket 7 isn't dead!* while others snarl *We'll build a Slot One processor that doesn't look like yours!* and Intel, narrow-eyed, retorts *Wait till you see Slot Two!* All in all, with unrelenting appetite for performance blossoming into a wild round of innovation, the time between now and the turn of the century promises to be a golden age of microcomputing.

**The System Bus.** The *system bus* provides an electrical highway over which the CPU transmits instructions. It operates at very high speed and extends only from the CPU to satellite processors called "the chipset" or "the glue logic." The glue logic, in turn, connects to slots that accept add-in cards for memory, peripherals, and other hardware options; these are collectively called the *peripheral bus*.

Since the advent of the IBM PC's 8-bit *ISA* (Industry Standard Architecture) bus in 1981, several microcomputer peripheral bus schemes have arrived, been trumpeted as improvements, then—for the most part—disappeared much more quietly. We reminisce about them in the **Upgrading Computers** section. If you buy a new computer today, though, it will have some combination of 16-bit ISA and 32-bit or 64-bit *PCI* (Peripheral Component Interconnect) slots; these are, ironically, the oldest and the newest of the PC-compatible peripheral buses. PCI, an awesomely sophisticated standard developed primarily by Intel, will shortly be the only peripheral bus in new Wintel computers—later this year, when manufacturers begin producing computers to a Microsoft-promoted specification called PC 98, ISA slots will no longer be included.

**Clock Rate.** Ah, the days of the 286 were so simple! 8 MHz processor, 8 MHz system bus, 8 MHz main RAM, and no need for processor caching or any of that fancy stuff. It was a blissful accord that collapsed (roughly) when we noticed that with a 33 MHz CPU going four times as fast as its system bus and main RAM, the CPU spent a lot of time doing nothing.

Today's system bus is still struggling to keep up. Typical system bus clock rate is 66 MHz, which is, of course, not nearly as fast as today's fast CPUs. This is why, when you talk about system clock rate, you also mention *multipliers,* which are the ratios between the CPU's internal (quoted) speed and the system bus speed. So, for example, if you're running a Pentium 133 chip on a 66 MHz bus, the multiplier is $133/66 = 2$. If you run a Pentium 200 on the same bus, the multiplier is 3.

Computer performance depends on a lot of things, but increased system bus speed is a Big Win. A minimal step-down of the processor speed, corresponding to a low multiplier, makes a faster computer. In the past few years, system bus speeds have crept upwards to 66 MHz, 75 MHz, and 83 MHz—superficially a weird number, but it's 166 with a multiplier of 2, 250 with a multiplier of 3, and 333 with a multiplier of 4, all of which are useful-sounding processor clock rates. As we write, the very first Socket 7 motherboards with 100 MHz system buses are becoming available. Of course, with a 100 MHz system bus, it would be nice to have 100 MHz main RAM, but only RDRAM and SDRAM will achieve it; EDO RAM and its variants are left in the dust. (For an explanation of RAM varieties, see *System RAM* below.)

Overall, making a faster system bus is one of the grand challenges of computer design. The faster a bus is, the more likely it is to make ghastly electrical noises and run at an unstable frequency. The next time you're shopping for a new computer, ask your retailer about bus speed and multiplier, and remember that CPU clock rate is only part of the story.

## Memory Configuration

Memory ranks second only to the CPU as a crucial factor in the performance of your system. Memory chips take one of two forms: RAM or ROM.

**Read-Only Memory (ROM).** *Read-only memory* chips are a form of solid-state memory—*solid-state* meaning that, unlike disk-based memory, they have no moving parts—whose contents cannot be altered after they're created. ROM chips contain the BIOS (Basic Input/Output System) instructions that control the start-up and fundamental functions of computer hardware, and also contain diagnostic programs. Most versions of the BIOS produced within the past few years are compatible with Windows 98, and therefore don't pose operating problems. Other ROM chips are found in the motherboard glue logic, and on the add-in adapter cards that control disk drives, video displays, and other peripherals.

**Random-Access Memory (RAM).** The term RAM, short for *random-access memory,* describes memory chips that can be filled with data, then emptied, then filled again at fantastic speeds. In fact, most chip-based memory empties itself a little too enthusiastically, and its contents have to be refreshed several hundred times a second. Because of this constant rewriting, this kind of memory is called *dynamic RAM,* or DRAM for short. The other kind of chip-based memory, called *static RAM,* is nonvolatile—so long as it has power, it holds its information without being refreshed—and very fast, but much more expensive than DRAM and used only where the price can be justified. (Your computer's settings in the so-called "CMOS," like the time and date and hard-disk parameters, are stored in static RAM powered by a battery.

The computer can refresh its own "memory" from these settings every time it boots, unless the battery goes flat.)

Under Windows 98, *RAM* in general can mean three things. It can mean the *processor cache,* which is the area for transient storage of the CPU's work in progress, and is usually static RAM. It can mean the *system RAM* or *main RAM*, which is the computer's main workspace, and holds data that you enter or recall from a storage device, so that you can manipulate it.

The third kind of RAM, called *virtual memory,* is a special disk file that Windows 98 uses to fool your system into thinking it has more system RAM than it really does. All three of these types of memory are discussed in this chapter.

**Processor Cache.**  Windows 98 uses a variety of complex memory-management techniques, which cause your system to access RAM frequently. Ordinary RAM modules can't keep up with the tempo of your Windows environment and its applications, but your *processor RAM cache* (also referred to as *Level 2 cache*) takes up the slack and can materially improve system speed. Basically, your processor uses the external RAM cache to store information that's being transferred either to or from the system, or *main,* RAM. The processor RAM cache serves as a high-speed holding area for the processor; it doesn't add to the amount of RAM available to your programs.

The processor cache is made up of fast static RAM that can accept data from fast CPU chips at nearly their full speed, then hand the cached information to slower main RAM. Static RAM is expensive and power-hungry, but a little of it goes a long way. The earliest processor caches, on fast 386DX machines, were 64K or 128K; 486DX, DX2 or DX4 machines had 128K or 256K; pre-MMX Pentiums seemed to like 256K, while both the Pentium Pro and Pentium II have various sizes of level 2 cache right in the chip—keeps the signal paths nice and short. With the advent of reasonably priced multi-processor computers, which Windows NT is already equipped to run, level 2 caches of 1MB or more will arrive quickly. Merced's planned level 2 cache is rumored to be 4MB.

 Sizing a processor cache is a fine art. If a level 2 cache is too small, a fast CPU will waste processor cycles while it starves for data. If the cache is too large, the processor will waste cycles browsing through cache space that never gets filled from main RAM. The lengths of time involved here are infinitesimal, but we're at the level where such quantities matter. Furthermore, optimum cache size depends not only on CPU type and speed, but on the amount of ·installed main RAM. (In a 1996 test on a Pentium 166 computer with 32MB main RAM, a 256K cache gave *better* performance than a 512K cache. When main RAM was increased to 64MB, both cache sizes performed equally.)

In modern processors, between the level 2 cache and the CPU core, there's *another* cache called the *level 1 cache, internal processor cache,* or *instruction cache.* The level 1 cache is insanely fast, and right on the silicon die next to the CPU. IBM produced a version of the 386 chip that contained a level 1 cache and was used in certain PS/2 computers, but the first generally used chip with a level 1 cache was the Intel 486DX, with 8K of instruction cache. As tiny as that cache seems today, it was one of the most important reasons why the 486 was faster than the 386. Since then, level 1 caches have grown in step with level 2 caches; plain Pentiums and Pentium Pros have 16K, a Pentium MMX or Pentium II has 32K, and today's champion is probably the AMD K6 with 64K.

Years of benchmark testing have shown that the combination of a level 1 and level 2—internal and external—RAM cache yields the best overall perform-ance. Not all processor RAM caches work equally well, since different manu-facturers use different schemes for caching memory, so you may want to test the systems or refer to published tests to see which computers offer the best performance for Windows 98.

In general, RAM caches do offer significant advantages with Windows 98; constant transfers of 32-bit code place a heavier burden on the memory subsystems of your PC than earlier versions of Windows did. A level 2 cache of at least 256K, and possibly as much as 1MB, will have a substantial positive impact on performance. When in doubt, go with as much cache as you can afford.

**System RAM (Main RAM).**  If you run Windows applications exclusively, you only need to know two things; how much system RAM you have, and that it isn't enough. However much memory you have, Windows will manage it for you.

RAM is at a crossroads. Microprocessors are now so much faster than main memory that, unless wizardry is applied, the processor spends too much of its time waiting for data. How can we speed up main memory? Static main RAM would cost too much for commodity computers. Level 2 caches are a good interim solution, but they're complex, expensive, require extra components, and take up space. RAMBUS main memory—boasting five times the speed of current DRAM—is the elegant answer but won't be available in quantity for at least another year; also, the first round of RAMBUS chips is likely to go into video adapters, which need fast RAM even worse than the motherboard does. The near-term fix is several exotic types of memory enhanced from the original DRAM specification.

There are lots of acronyms flying around when you discuss RAM, partly because some of them refer to memory *types* while others refer to *form factors,* and that's why we have Table 13.2.

## Table 13.2  Memory Types and Form Factors

| Memory Types | | |
|---|---|---|
| **RAMBUS** | | Also **RDRAM**. An improved architecture and 64-bit memory bus will make main memory transfers so fast (up to 500MB per second) that Level 2 cache will—finally!—be superfluous. Available sometime in 1999, but only in redesigned motherboards. |
| **SDRAM II** | | Also known as **DDRRAM** (double-data-rate RAM) because it's SDRAM twice as fast. Available sometime in 1998. |
| **SDRAM** (Synchronous DRAM) | | DRAM with a clocked (pulse-timed) interface, very fast and (unlike EDO RAM) doesn't care whether fetches are contiguous or not. SDRAM operates at 50 to 150 MHz correlated to system bus speed. Beginning to appear in commodity computers in Spring 1998. |
| **EDO DRAM** (Extended Data Out) | | Like DRAM, but makes the assumption that when data is fetched from it, the fetches will be from consecutive addresses. EDO RAM is about ten per cent faster than page mode DRAM—say 30 MHz. Generally available, as we write this; but inherent limitations in this architecture mean that it will never be as fast as SDRAM. A faster variant called **BEDO** (Burst Extended Data Out) may buy it some time, but SDRAM is expected to overtake it quickly. |
| **FPM** (Fast Page Mode) **DRAM** | | DRAM that speeds up access by being designed for overlapping fetches. Capable of 25 MHz on a good day. Seldom found in new computers. |
| **DRAM** (Dynamic RAM) | | "Plain old" RAM, the kind that's ruled the roost since the days of the Apple II. Installed in Wintel boxes until the mid-1990s. Tops out at roughly 8 MHz—the original ISA bus speed. Obsolete. |
| Form Factors | | |
| **DIMM** (Dual Inline Memory Module) | 200-pin | So far, confined to high-end server and workstation memory. This will probably become the commodity computer standard form factor, but we have no idea when. |
| | 168-pin | Easier to install than SIMMs and don't have to be installed in pairs—in essence they *are* pairs of SIMMs back-to-back. Available in 8MB to 256MB. |
| **SIMM** (Single Inline Memory Module) | 72-pin | A wider bus than the original, to accommodate faster memory transfer rates. Available in 1MB (rare) to 128MB. For Pentium-based computers, must be installed in pairs. |
| | 30-pin | The first form of RAM in which all eight or nine bits of the byte were one physical piece. Available in 256K to 16MB, but most IBM-compatibles used 1MB or 4MB. Obsolete. |

 Although the issue of *parity* in Wintel memory is fading slowly, it still has some relevance, and both parity and non-parity memory are widely available. *Parity* memory has nine bits to the byte, with the ninth bit being a check (error-correcting) bit; it's used in older Wintel computers. *Non-parity* memory has eight bits to the byte, and is used in new Wintel computers and all Macintoshes. A SIMM or DIMM described as [some number] "x8,"

"x32," or "x64" is non-parity memory; one described as [some number] "x9," "x36," or "x72" is parity memory. We'll say more about replacing and mixing memory types in the section on **Upgrading Computers.**

If you're still trying to support certain DOS applications, you may have to know whether they require either expanded or extended memory, and how to configure the Windows "DOS boxes" that they run in. If you can't make them run in DOS boxes, you may be able to run them in MS-DOS mode, but only one at a time. See Chapter 14, "Windows 98 and DOS," for details.

## Disk Subsystem

**Disk Types.** There are three basic types of hard disk available in new computers today (see Table 13.3), and you need to know which one you're getting.

### Table 13.3  Types of Hard Disks

| | |
|---|---|
| **Ultra/DMA** | The newest variant of IDE is the first one that offers performance roughly equal to a good SCSI drive—and capacity to burn, with inexpensive drives up to 8.4GB. Most new motherboards with embedded disk controllers are Ultra/DMA-compatible. Sometimes called **U/IDE.** |
| **EIDE (IDE-2, ATAPI)** | Stands for *Enhanced Integrated Drive Electronics.* EIDE drives are mildly obsolete, but often found in pre-built retail systems because they're inexpensive, have reasonable throughput under light loads—the kind of loads you'd typically find in a desktop or laptop computer—and don't need separate controllers, which makes them still less expensive. In any one computer you can install up to four IDE devices, which might include not only a hard disk or two, but a CD-ROM drive and a tape backup. EIDE drives still take a back seat to SCSI in raw performance. |
| **SCSI, SCSI-2, SCSI-3, UltraSCSI, UltraSCSI-2** | Stands for *Small Computer Systems Interface* and was originally developed for the Macintosh; the original specification has been eclipsed by a plethora of supersets. Compared to IDE devices, SCSI devices are longer-lasting, more rugged, and offer higher performance under heavy (read *server*) loading; they're also more expensive, in part because they're marketable as premium goods, but mostly because they require separate controllers which are also not cheap. Any one SCSI controller can have at least seven devices attached to it, not only hard disks, but CD-ROM drives, DAT and DLT tape backups, scanners, removable-media drives, and all manner of exotic peripherals; and you can install more than one controller per computer. Computers sold as servers and workstations, for which minimal downtime matters more than minimal price, favor SCSI components overwhelmingly. The emerging tendency to build disk controllers into the motherboard may make SCSI more affordable. |

If you're buying a new hard disk, don't forget to find out how fast it spins, which along with the amount of data that flows through the heads (called the *transfer rate*) is the primary indicator of disk subsystem performance. Once upon a time, all hard disks spun at 3600 RPM; today, only the most cost-conscious new disks are that slow. A typical name-brand retail disk spins at 4500 or 5400 rpm, with high-capacity high-end drives reaching 7200 rpm, and a very few, expensive server/workstation drives playing king-of-the-hill at 10,000 rpm. The hard disk, like that ubiquitous pink bunny, just keeps going and going …

 Prior to development of SCSI and IDE disks, IBM-compatible computers used other types of hard disks which are no longer available new; we discuss these in the next section.

# Upgrading Your Existing Computer

When you upgrade a computer it is vital that you observe *the Rules*:

1.  **These instructions are for desktop or tower computers only.** If your laptop or notebook needs upgrading, send it to the manufacturer.

2.  **Buy an anti-static wrist strap, know how to use it, and use it.**

3.  **Locate the documentation for any motherboard, hard disk, I/O card, or adapter whose settings you plan to change.** If you can't find the manual or data sheet, don't start pulling jumpers. If you start pulling jumpers and discover that one or more of them are glued down, stop, put the other jumpers back the way they were, and call your vendor.

4.  **Write down the parameters—heads, cylinders, sectors, precomp and landing zone—for any hard disk you remove or replace.** Tip: They should be on the big label on the drive casing. If they're not, log onto your drive manufacturer's Web site, go to the Support section, and look up the drive's name or model number.

5.  **Don't get carried away**. If you find yourself tempted to throw away everything but the case, it's time for a new computer. (Unless the case is a stainless-steel full tower.)

6.  **Your mileage may vary**, and we cannot accept responsibility for anything that may happen to you or your computer because you, of your own free will, decided to take any or all of our advice.

## Holding the Bag

Remember the Bag of Prevention? If you have that, you should have all the documentation you need to upgrade any part of the computer—and it's all in one place. We *told* you it was a good idea. Oh, and when you're done with that slip of paper that has all the information about your hard disk, put that in there. Put the bag away along with the anti-static strap.

# Upgrade CPUs

This book's predecessor, *The Windows 95 Bible,* was both enthusiastic and informative on the topic of chip-swaps—of buying a CPU especially configured to fit in your existing motherboard's processor socket, but to run at a higher clock rate. In principle this is easy: You turn off the computer, unplug the power connector to the chip fan, pry the old CPU out of its socket with a tool you find in the new CPU's box, banish the old CPU, orient the new one properly to the socket, press it in gently *gently* and—assuming this is a Socket 7 processor—push down the wire lever that locks the CPU's pin grid into the socket. It doesn't take any longer to do this than to read about it. (This is a description of a generic procedure and should not be substituted for any specific instructions included with your new processor. We have enough dead CPUs on our conscience, thank you.) The worst that may happen is that you'll have to pull the fan off the old chip and install it on the new one, but most upgrade chips have new, integral fans anyway.

# The Alternative

There's just one problem here. Times have changed, and so have prices, and so has the technology. Upgrade processors are made by many fine companies—Intel, Kingston and Evergreen come to mind—and they cost $200 to $400. This is an amount that would, or would nearly, buy a new *non*-upgrade CPU *and* a Socket 7 motherboard *and* a 16MB or 32MB DIMM. It's also an amount that could make you think, hmm, maybe the budget would accommodate $700 to $900 for a whole new computer, if I used my old monitor.

"Hang on," we hear you saying, "I can get an upgrade processor for $98." Not for *Windows* 98, you can't. The upgrade CPU for under a hundred bucks typically makes a mid-range 386 into a mid-range 486, or a low-end 486 into a high-end 486. In the context of Windows 98, this barely justifies spending the money and popping the case.

Let's look at a pertinent example. Intel makes an OverDrive processor that replaces a plain Pentium 100, 133 or 166 with a Pentium MMX 200. From our reference standard mail-order dealer, this chip is $270. From the same dealer on the same day, a "regular" non-OverDrive Pentium MMX 200 is $150. The $120 difference would buy a Socket 7 motherboard ... even a rather nice one, with serial and parallel ports and IDE taps. Toss in another $90 for a 32MB DIMM, and you've got most of a new computer ... in contrast to the OverDrive, which buys you a chip and a fan.

We're not saying that a motherboardectomy is the solution for everybody—or even that an upgrade processor is yesterday's silicon. Some people aren't thrilled by the idea of gutting a computer all over the dining room table.

But Fred and Kip, after having done this a couple of dozen times between them, can report routinely satisfying results. A board swap takes time and care, teaches you a lot about your computer, and can save you money.

**A Few Hints.** We're *not* going to walk you through an entire board swap. This isn't that book, and if you're unfamiliar with this procedure, you need more detail and background than we can give you here. We also assume that you have screwdrivers, needlenose pliers, tweezers, and maybe a quarter-inch hex socket on a handle. Unplug the computer power cord, monitor and printer cables, and anything else connected to the backplane.

Now, here are a few of the things we always run into, and how to get around them:

- For Pentium owners only: Do you even need a new board? Dig the board manual out of your Bag of Prevention. Many Socket 7 motherboards accommodate CPUs from 75 MHz to 200 MHz, by having bus rates and multipliers selectable with jumpers. If you have (say) a 100 MHz through 133 MHz Pentium CPU in one of these boards, go get a regular—not OverDrive—200 MHz Pentium chip, pop out the old chip, pop in the new one, and re-set the motherboard jumpers for the higher clock rate. Cheap! Quick! Grin-inducing!

- Can you keep some or all of your old RAM? Many motherboards have RAM slots for both short and long SIMMs, or both long SIMMs and DIMMs. *However,* some boards recognize both types of memory at once, and some make you choose one or the other. Similarly, some boards will let you mix parity and non-parity memory and let it all function as non-parity; some won't. If you intend to reinstall old RAM in a new board, be sure to talk it over with your vendor.

- How much RAM do you intend to install? The Windows 98 "sweet spot" is 32MB, and personally we don't see much point in going beyond twice that … not and sticking with 98, at least. If you do plan to install more than 64MB, be careful to buy a motherboard whose Level 2 cache will talk to all your RAM; some boards (regardless of cache size) leave memory above 64MB uncached, which can impair performance. If this is an issue for you, browse to **http://www.tomshardware.com/mainboard.html** and read the comparative reviews of available motherboards.

- Before you buy the motherboard, make sure you know what kind of hard disk you have. Most of today's motherboards are equipped with embedded controllers for **Ultra/DMA**, or **EIDE**, or both, backward-compatible. If you have an EIDE disk, it will generally work flawlessly with a new motherboard. If you have an **IDE** disk, the motherboard logic may be too fast. Kip did this with a 1997 motherboard, a 1994 IDE-1 disk, and

Windows 95 OSR2, which every so often bombs out with a blue screen and says that disk writes can't be completed—the disk just can't keep up. Either buy a new disk or resign yourself to the existing motherboard.

- If your old motherboard is VL-bus, and you have a compatible video card, disk controller, or whatever, stop and think. VL-bus is *gone,* and once you replace the motherboard, you will have to replace every VL-bus peripheral card along with it.

- Any board you buy today will have a mix of ISA and PCI slots, and unfortunately, the trend is toward fewer ISA slots. If your existing computer has a whole bunch of ISA cards in it, like a modem and a sound card and a SCSI controller and a bus mouse, make sure the new board has enough ISA slots for everything you still want. You may be able to toss one port card because parallel-and-two-serial are on the motherboard. If your computer has an ISA video adapter, splurge on a new PCI video card instead; your video performance will be tons better, and you'll free up a precious ISA slot.

- When you buy the motherboard, try to score a few of the white plastic dart-shaped spacers that keep the board propped off the steel backplate. The techies in the back room don't have enough of these and may not want to give you any, so beg. While you're at it, see if you can get a few jumpers.

- If the CPU you buy doesn't come with a fan, buy a fan. Get the right one for the size and thickness of your CPU, and make sure it has ball bearings, not sleeve bearings. Don't skimp. Once the fan is installed, you want it to last, because replacing it is a nuisance. (See note on PC Power & Cooling under "Power Supply.")

- You'll need a *small* top-quality flashlight with a narrow head, that takes two AA or AAA batteries. Don't skimp on this either; if you've never had one of the $8 metal ones, this is your excuse.

- Speaking of that backplate: If you have a tower case, and you value your sanity, *don't* try to extract the old motherboard and insert the new one with the chassis still intact. The motherboard attaches to a piece of sheet-metal that is held into the rest of the chassis, usually, with two hex-head screws and two locking tabs. Pull the peripheral cards and set them aside; remove the screws, swing the motherboard out on its backing plate, unhook the tabs, and lay the motherboard and backplate down on your work surface.

- While the motherboard is out, you can get at both sides of the drive bays; ordinarily you can only reach one, since the installed backplate blocks the other. Make sure your drives are held in by screws at both sides, which don't need to be (and shouldn't be) brutally tight, but they should hold the drives firmly. Also, while the chassis is apart, vacuum it out—the power supply and electronic components attract dust like nobody's business.

- As you disconnect the old motherboard, take notes of what connected to what, and how. Remove the SIMMs and put them in an anti-static bag if you're going to reuse them.

- The settings on the new motherboard aren't necessarily correct for the CPU you bought with it—unless you went to a very nice retailer who set the jumpers while you waited. With the new board still in its box or lying on its anti-static bag, grab the manual and check the settings for your processor against the actual jumper positions on the board. There may be thirty to forty jumpers; you should verify them all but, with luck, you'll reset half a dozen at most. You'll need the flashlight.

- Removing the old motherboard: One of the connectors holding the board to the backplate will be, instead of a "dart," a screw run through a solder-edged hole in the board and tightened into a metal standoff, which in turn threads into the backplate. This is a ground. Locate and remove that screw, then squeeze the barbs of the white nylon darts with needlenose pliers, and wiggle the board off the darts one by one. Don't lose any of the darts.

- Fastening the new board: How many darts you can use will depend on how closely the hole pattern of the board matches the slot pattern of the backplate, but at a *minimum,* find places for five darts—one at each corner and one close to the center—and the ground. The more darts the better, which is why you got extras. You need to prevent the board from sagging and shorting against the backplate.

- Install the CPU, the fan if it's separate, and the RAM. If the connectors from the power supply to the board will reach, connect them; these connectors, labeled P8 and P9, are locking connectors and moderately difficult to seat correctly. When they're properly seated they'll be flush against each other and won't wiggle. The black wire of P8 should be next to the black wire of P9.

- When you've reconnected everything you can without reattaching the backplate, swing the backplate up, hook in the tabs, make sure everything clears, and tighten the bolts.

- Your next problem is that, working with a motherboard and case that have never met before, you have to connect the lights and switches of the case—like the reset light and switch, the turbo light and switch (if there is one), the power light, and the speaker wire—to the motherboard.

All these connectors are usually paired square pins in a row on the front (forward) edge of the board, and the drawing in the manual will tell you which pins are which. Meanwhile, the wiring in the case is *usually:*

| Light or Switch | Wiring |
| --- | --- |
| Hard disk (red) LED | Red/white |
| Keylock | Blue/white |
| Power (green) LED | Green/white |
| Reset switch | Gray/gray |
| Speaker | Red/black |
| Turbo (yellow) LED | Yellow/white |
| Turbo switch* | Orange/white/black |

* Many newer chipsets have no step-down from full CPU clock rate. If you install a motherboard with one of these chipsets in an older case with a turbo switch, the switch may reset the speed LCD on the front panel but will have no effect on the actual speed.

- IDE devices: Most new motherboards have two IDE connectors side by side. Each connector can have two devices in sequence on the same ribbon cable, one called the **master**, the other called the **slave**. (Which is which can be set with jumpers on the individual devices.) If you have two IDE devices with very different characteristics and transfer rates—for example, a hard disk and a CD drive—do *not* make them the master and slave on the same connector. Instead, make each one the master on its own connector. If you have two hard disks, or two CD drives, or (maybe) a CD drive and a backup tape drive, you can set those as master and slave on the same cable.

- When it comes time to connect the floppy drive and parallel and serial ports to the taps on the motherboard, you'll wonder how anybody ever got all those parts on there. Pin 1 of the connectors *will* be marked, but you'll need the flashlight to see the silkscreened legends on the board. Pin 1 of the ribbon cable is marked with a colored stripe or spatter.

- From now on, just reverse the uninstallation. Reconnect all ribbon cables and four-pin power cables to drives. Don't forget the power cable to the chip fan. Seat all the cards in their slots, bolt the brackets to the chassis, and connect any cables to cards that have them—for example, a sound card or PCMCIA controller.

- Whether you replace the case at this point is up to you. Personally, we fire up the computer without the case the first time, for two reasons; first, because it's easier to see or hear something like a non-spinning chip fan; second, because there always seems to be one connection that we stupidly forgot, and with the case still off, we can reconnect it quickly. On the other hand, a computer running without its case has poor ventilation and RF shielding, probably violates FCC rules, and poses increased risk to you, your small children, and your pets.

- Reconnect the keyboard, the pointing device, and the monitor. Turn on the monitor. Turn on the computer. If it boots, you're home! and think of all you've learned. If it doesn't, you'll be learning even more.

## Recommendations

Okay! You now have some idea of what's involved in a motherboard-level upgrade. Again, it's not a quick job, but you can install *as many state-of-the-art components as you want*—a sharp contrast to a chip swap, which turns your computer into a sort of jalopy with a bigger engine and the same old bald tires. Now we'll make a few remarks about upgrades, relative to performance, reliability, and bang-for-the-buck.

Necessarily, these are highly personal recommendations, based not only on our own preference, but on the usual inventories of our preferred vendors. These aren't the only good parts in the world, and you may find others that suit you perfectly; on the other hand, working exclusively from this list may not leave you with an optimal combination. Your best move will be to read this chapter, visit a few of the URLs we include, and then go to your retailer for further consultation. Also bear in mind that, the computer industry being what it is, our advice may be slightly dusty when you read it. Again, go talk to your vendor, who can show you parts that don't even exist when we're writing this.

**Power Supply.** For some reason, when people sketch out a motherboard swap, they hardly ever consider replacing the power supply. We wish they would! A power supply that fails slowly can provoke all manner of hangs and blue screens that look like software glitches but aren't. A power supply that fails abruptly can electrocute the rest of your computer, including your nice new motherboard. And it would be one thing if a garden-variety PS was generally reliable, but even the ones in brand-new, pre-built retail systems are sort of awful. (Most builders pay $20 or $25 for the power supply *and* the case, so what would you expect?) It's downhill from there as the fan-cooled PS slowly fills with gritty dust, which makes it run hotter and can even cause a short circuit.

Lose these headaches! Go first-class all the way with a power supply from PC Power and Cooling in Carlsbad, California. The best available, miles better than anything you can buy in a corner-store case, these Silencer and Turbo-Cool power supplies start at about $70, and don't cost more than $130 unless you get really exotic. One of Kip's Silencers started life in a 286 and has lasted through four motherboards in nine years—okay? The Web site at **http://www.pcpowercooling.com** is packed with drawings and dimensions to help you decide which power supply you need, and then you can order by toll-free phone. PCP&C also makes top-quality chip fans, thermosensing alarms, and awesome (pricey) cases.

**The Processor.**   For an *inexpensive system* we like Socket 7—the Pentium MMX, IBM/Cyrix 6x86MX, or AMD K6. Some people say the IBM processor runs warm, but it also has great performance. Don't buy any pre-MMX Pentium chip, which will be obsolete by the end of 1998. Don't bother with any processor slower than 200 MHz—the difference in price between a 133 MHz chip and a 200 MHz chip is $50 or less, well worth it.

The *Pentium Pro* (Socket 8) is a processor we adore for its elegance even while we cringe at its real-world shortcomings. For technical reasons, it won't go faster than 200 MHz. It demands the fastest RAM you can get, which ain't cheap, or easy to find. It will address 4 GB of RAM, but for any amount of RAM less than 512 MB, you can build a computer around a Pentium II with less trouble and for less money. It's *totally pointless* to run Windows 98 on a P-Pro, which executes 16-bit code indifferently and only warms up to NT. The Pro also deserves a SCSI disk subsystem, and … You can see where this is going. If you insist on building a personal Socket 8 computer—a passionate, not reasonable, decision—we hear nice rumors about the Tyan Tacoma (S1672) motherboard.

When *power is everything,* build a system around a Pentium II processor with a carefully selected motherboard, SDRAM at least, lots of cache, and an Ultra/DMA or UltraSCSI disk. You can still get dragstrip performance by buying a processor at one step *under* the highest clock rate—for example, a 300 MHz CPU will be materially less expensive than a 333 MHz part, for only slight real-world difference—but *any* Slot One processor is lots more money than a Socket 7. The preferred peripheral chipset is Intel's 440LX or, in 1999, the much faster 440BX. Tip: When you're buying parts for this one, make sure they don't start costing more than a whole new computer …

**Multiprocessor Computers.**   Like many people, we sometimes dream of owning a Ferrari F40. We also know that an actual real F40, which drinks a Niagara of high-octane gas, is so noisy that the driver needs earplugs, and perennially stalls in traffic, would turn that dream into a nightmare in the first five minutes.

Multiprocessor computers, at their current state of evolution, remind us of that. You'll have to run Windows NT or UNIX; Windows *9x* is single-CPU-only. The second processor will provide real-world performance gains of about 40% to 60%, *only* with software that actually executes 32-bit multithreading, which is scarce. Multiprocessor is a big deal to build, and not as big a deal when it's finished.

You can buy motherboards that accept dual Pentium MMX, dual Pentium Pro, or dual Pentium II. Please—don't go there. If you really *need* a multi-processor computer (which is like saying "If you really *are* entering the 24 Hours of Le Mans,") start fresh and talk to Hewlett-Packard about a very lovely box called a Kayak.

**The Motherboard.  Buy a brand-name motherboard**. A reputable manufacturer will have advantages like telephone support, a well-maintained Web site, and downloadable flash BIOS upgrades. Besides, this is the most important component in your system, so why shop on price to save thirty bucks? At the moment, the best-known and best-liked brands are Abit, ASUS, ECS, Gigabyte, Intel, Shuttle, Supermicro, and Tyan. Quality and perform-ance of board models can vary considerably even within one manufacturer's lineup, so we recommend reading the product reviews on the Tom's Hardware Web page (above).

**The System Bus.**  VL-bus having come to the aforementioned sad end, you have the choice of all-PCI or mixed ISA/PCI, and we recommend the latter—at least for a while. There are just too many top-quality ISA cards still available or useful, like the Creative Labs AWE64 or AWE32 sound cards, or the new 56K modems. On the other hand, you'll certainly want a PCI video card, disk controller (if it isn't embedded), and network adapter. Until the PC 98 specification mandates all-PCI, make sure your new board has more than one ISA slot.

**Bus Clock Rate.**  Motherboards in current retail stock have bus clocks of 50, 55, 60, 66, 75, 83, and 100 MHz—but not every board has every clock rate available. If you want to play on the straight and narrow, this year's standard bus clock is 66 MHz, and next year's will be 100 MHz. If you like to play wide and wicked … A 133 MHz CPU with a bus clock of 66 and a multiplier of 2 is as fast as a 150 MHz CPU with a bus clock of 50 and a multiplier of 3. A 166 MHz Pentium with a bus clock of 83 and a multiplier of 2 is easily the equal of a typically configured 200 MHz Pentium. Unlike chip overclocking, this doesn't burn up the CPU. We're not telling you to *do* anything with this information, but we wouldn't want you to live in ignorance of it.

**Memory Configuration.**  Memory is the key to sparkling Windows 98 performance. RAM is like all good things in life—friends, wealth, leisure time, and computer music; you can never have too much.

**Processor Cache.**  Don't decide this in isolation. The optimum level 2 cache size depends on your CPU type, CPU speed, motherboard, bus clock, and amount and type of installed main RAM. Having said that, we suspect that for *most* configurations you can build with this week's retail parts (that's the week of March 9, 1998) you'll get near-optimum results from either 256K or 512K—so see if your vendor will help you test both. A high-end Pentium II has its own 512K. With a Pentium Pro it's not your problem, since (depending on the chip clock rate) there's 256K, 512K or 1MB right on the chip.

**System RAM.**  How low can you go?

- **8 megabytes**. Yes, Windows 98 runs in eight meg. Or maybe it walks.

- **16 megabytes**. You'll be comfortable if you're running two or three applications, and none of them is anything ravenous like Photoshop or Corel Draw. Occasionally you'll find yourself bogged down in the swapfile and have to close some stuff.

- **24 megabytes**. Same as above, but you can run larger programs.

- **32 megabytes**. Probably the ideal for a real-world application mix, and the maximum size for really cheap memory—at this writing, two 16MB long SIMMs cost about $80, or a 32MB DIMM costs less than $100. We recommend this as a minimum for any computer that will see a lot of use.

- **64 megabytes**. For the industrial-strength SOHO or business machine, where you want your Taskbar permanently loaded for bear ... with, say, your word processor, spreadsheet, PIM, e-mail, Web browser, Dial-Up Networking, graphics program, audio player, chat applet, and a couple of Explorers. This is as much memory as it makes sense to install with Windows 98, and—providing your motherboard has four long SIMM or two DIMM slots—64MB costs only $90 or so more than 32MB. (Which is astounding to certain journalists who would, er, rather not talk about how long they've been buying RAM—or at what prices.)

**Disk Subsystem.**  Windows 98, like any graphical operating system, consumes RAM and disk memory more quickly than does character-based DOS. One screen in character-based DOS has a capacity of 2,000 (80x25) characters or 16,000 bits, whereas a Windows 98 screen—depending on its color depth and as we found out in Chapter 7—can contain many megabits of data. Add multimedia capabilities, and your data storage requirements skyrocket. Animation files consume up to 30 screens of graphics for every second of animation, and even compressed sound files—like the .MP3 format we discuss in Appendix H—require a megabyte of disk storage for every minute of digitized speech or music. The economy of character-based information, whether on your screen or on your disk, is gone forever.

Windows makes demands that go beyond graphical data storage, multi-megabyte applications, and high-color screen displays, to include a cohort of software components that work together to create the environment. Both system RAM and system storage are taxed to their limits. A full installation of Windows 98 with Internet Explorer 4 will occupy over 100 megabytes of disk space, and popular Windows 98 applications like Word, Excel, Outlook, and Quicken can each consume 30 megabytes or more. When you factor in data files and virtual memory, it's obvious why the 350- or 540-megabyte disk that seemed ample for 16-bit Windows will barely contain Windows 98.

Earlier in this chapter, in "Getting a New Computer," we talked about the three types of hard disk you were likely to buy at retail today—**SCSI**, **Ultra/DMA**, and **EIDE**. Now, let's consider the drive types you might have in an older computer (see Table 13.4).

### Table 13.4  Older Computers' Drive Types

| Drive Type | Comment | Works with Win98? |
|---|---|---|
| **IDE (IDE-1)** | Stands for *Integrated Drive Electronics.* The first non-SCSI 3.5-inch drives, these launched a second revolution in disk capacity and price. They're moderately slow by today's standards, but you may be able to combine them with a new motherboard if you use a separate IDE controller. | Maybe |
| **ESDI** | Stands for *Enhanced Small Device Interface* and was an attempt to breathe new life into the aging ST-506 (MFM) architecture by doubling the bus width and doubling, or tripling, the data transfer rate. Produced by only a few computer (CDC, Compaq, IBM) and drive (Fujitsu, Maxtor, MiniScribe, Seagate) manufacturers, ESDI drives were large, heavy, and expensive, but were the drive of choice for demanding applications until SCSI unseated them.<br>    If you keep this disk you'll have to keep your motherboard too; there are no new ESDI controllers or motherboards. | Maybe |
| **RLL** | Stands for *Run Length Limited,* a hardware strategy to increase the capacity of MFM disks by 50% while changing as little as possible about the basic disk design. Great theory combined with skimpy development time resulted in temperamental and often unreliable drives—but RLL, after some trips back to the drawing board, became the ancestor of IDE. | No |
| **MFM** | Stands for *Modified Frequency Modulation* and were the first hard disks produced for microcomputers, provoking a revolution in the accessibility of programs and data. Compared to later drives they were heavy, fragile and finicky, but have long since been forgiven since they made the "serious" small computer a reality. They are now obsolete. | No |

MFM and RLL drives are too small *and* too slow for 32-bit Windows, as well as incompatible with most other hardware you can buy today. ESDI is frozen in time. The best strategy, if you're buying a new motherboard, is to combine it with a new EIDE or (preferably) Ultra/DMA disk; the commonest and most economical capacities range from 2.1GB to 8.4GB, at prices from $150 to $400. A SCSI disk with a PCI (or embedded) controller may give you even better performance but will cost more.

**It's Not Fake Anything, It's Real Virtual Memory.** Total installed main RAM often falls short of what's required by the combination of applications you've loaded. When that happens, 32-bit Windows takes advantage of available memory by playing various tricks—starting with Windows programming languages which, by default, create programs that load only part of themselves into memory at a time. A spreadsheet program, for example, might load only the data-entry portion of the program while you're entering numbers, leaving the graphics portion unloaded until you switch to constructing charts. It might also load only one immediate area of the data file you're working with, rather than the entire file. Those software manipulations, however, only make the most of a finite resource. You have a fixed amount of system memory, and sooner or later, you're going to reach its end.

Windows 98 prepares for this inevitability by reserving a portion of your hard disk as a temporary scratch pad, for those times when the total system memory required overflows the available physical RAM. This scratch pad is known formally as *virtual memory* and informally as *paging file* or *swapfile*. Windows 98 temporarily swaps segments of code and data to and from the hard disk, freeing RAM for use by programs. This background optimization lets you run more applications and load bigger data files than you possibly could within system RAM.

Your computer pays for this by trading speed for memory. When a program swaps part of itself, or of the data it's handling, between RAM and a disk, the slower speed of the disk drive makes the program seem sluggish. Performance will be better if the system contains enough RAM to store the entire program and data file. Most programs designed for memory swapping are smart enough to monitor their supply of RAM, and not swap to disk unless they run out.

Windows 98 automatically provides memory for all running applications. The applications themselves are oblivious to the creation of virtual memory; they simply ask for program and data space, and the operating system gives it to them. Windows itself decides whether to allocate the memory from free physical RAM, or to swap code and data from an idle program to disk, creating free physical RAM that in turn can be allocated.

The scheme used to create virtual memory is an ingenious one, based on a Least Recently Used (LRU) algorithm that determines which programs should be swapped to disk first. Typically, the least active program—for example, a spreadsheet program that has been minimized to the Taskbar and is not receiving input—is the first to be swapped out. Windows copies the program's memory pages (the contents of locations in physical RAM that the program occupied) to a paging file on the hard disk, then marks those emptied locations in physical RAM as free and usable. Windows can then allocate those pages to another program and satisfy its request for memory.

When the swapped-out program becomes active again and needs its pages back, Windows 98 retrieves those pages from the paging file and copies them back into memory—making room, if necessary, by swapping yet other inactive pages to disk. This happens over and over again as applications are promoted or demoted by the LRU algorithm, based on the amount they are used.

On a heavily taxed system—meaning any Windows computer with less than 256MB of RAM—the hard disk can be accessed almost constantly just for management of the paging file. This is the best reason to invest in a speedy hard disk, and to maintain it by regularly running the Disk Defragmenter.

The Windows 98 virtual-memory subsystem is much improved over prior versions and requires almost no tuning. If you keep your disk defragmented and test it periodically with the ScanDisk utility, Windows takes care of the rest. (Just ask it! Go to **Control Panel\System**, pick the **Performance** tab and see what it says.)

But if you can't resist the urge to meddle, the Windows 98 virtual-memory subsystem *is* accessible from the Performance tab. Click on the **Virtual Memory...** button to bring up the Virtual Memory dialog (Figure 13.2).

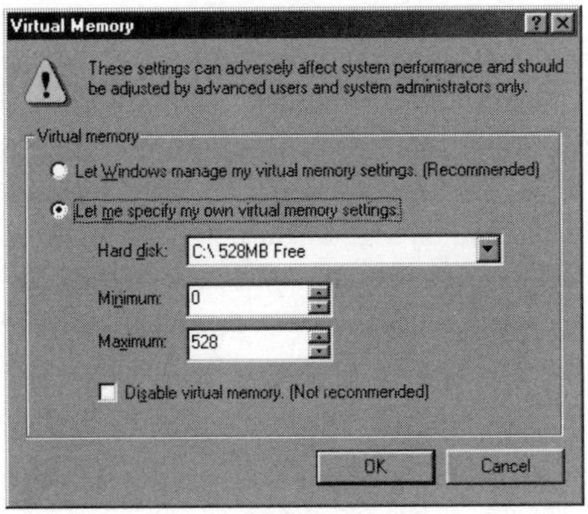

*Figure 13.2*

*System Virtual Memory dialog*

This dialog tells you snidely that when it comes to configuring virtual memory, Windows 98 usually knows best. Unless you're absolutely certain you want to tinker with this feature, you're better off leaving the **Virtual memory** region set to its default, which is **Let Windows manage my virtual memory settings**.

You might want to change your virtual-memory target drive *if* the hard disk that boots up your computer isn't the fastest drive in your system. Windows 98 invariably selects your boot drive as the location for its paging file. If this drive isn't your fastest—if, for example, you normally boot from an IDE drive, but also have a high-performance SCSI disk attached to your system—

you may want to tell Windows to write its paging file to the SCSI drive, and improve virtual-memory performance thanks to the SCSI drive's higher overall throughput.

To change the target drive for the Windows paging file, click on the button labeled **Let me specify my own virtual memory settings**; then select the desired drive from the **Hard Disk** drop-down list (Figure 13.3).

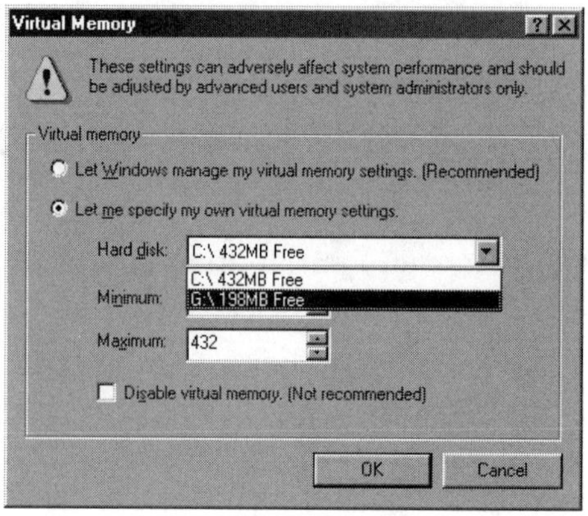

*Figure 13.3*

*Selecting a paging drive*

You may also want to fine-tune the size of your system's paging file. For example, if you want to force Windows 98 to allocate a minimum amount of paging file space, enter a value into the Minimum field. This ensures that Windows 98 grabs that amount of space at start-up, instead of expanding the paging file dynamically as demand dictates. The result can be better overall virtual-memory performance, especially in RAM-starved systems.

There are only three reasons to shut down Windows 98's virtual-memory system completely; for diagnostic purposes, to conserve power on a notebook computer by minimizing disk activity, or to watch your computer's performance go completely down the tubes. If any of these apply, click on the **Disable virtual memory** checkbox. As the dialog says, this isn't recommended; you severely limit Windows' ability to deal with tight memory situations and, in extreme cases, can crash your system.

It's our experience that Windows' dynamic management of virtual-memory settings is thoroughly satisfactory, and you'll gain little or nothing by forcing Windows to accept a manual reconfiguration. Don't fix what isn't broken.

 Both permanent and temporary swapfiles still exist in Windows 98, but you don't have to decide which to use; Windows chooses one or the other and even bounces back and forth. Also, for the first time, a swapfile doesn't have to be a locked, contiguous block of space—it can be a plain old fragmented file.

## *High-Pressure Swapfile*

Having said that, we'll let you in on something we tried with our own test system. We're not recommending that *you* do this, because we haven't pounded on the arrangement long enough to rule out disaster. On the other hand, it saves space on your boot drive and—for a reason we'll get to in a minute—doesn't hurt performance and may even help it. And Microsoft says it's okay.

Follow the directions for making a compressed partial drive in the section "Applying DriveSpace to Part of a Drive" under "DriveSpace 3," below. Start with uncompressed space about twice the size of your system RAM. When the compressed drive is created, DriveSpace will roughly double this amount.

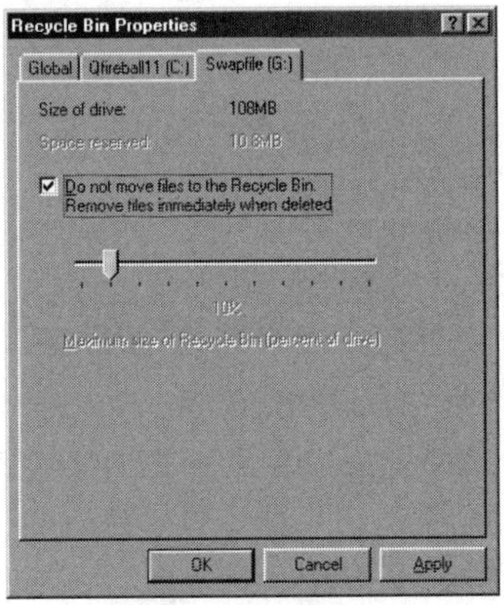

You don't want a Recycle Bin on your paging-file drive. Right-click on the Recycle Bin, pick **Properties**, and on the **Global** tab, click **Configure drives independently**. Then select the tab for the new compressed drive and check the **Do not move files...** checkbox. Most of the tab will gray out (Figure 13.4). Click **OK**.

By this time, Windows may already have created a Recycle Bin on the compressed drive—it depends on exactly when you do what—but just look at the new drive in

**Figure 13.4**

*Disabling a Recycle Bin*

Explorer. Once you've checked the **Do not move files...** checkbox, you can delete the Recycle Bin if there is one, and it won't be created again.

Go to **Control Panel\System**, select the **Performance** tab, and click the **Virtual Memory** button. In the **Virtual memory** region, click **Let me specify my own virtual memory settings**.

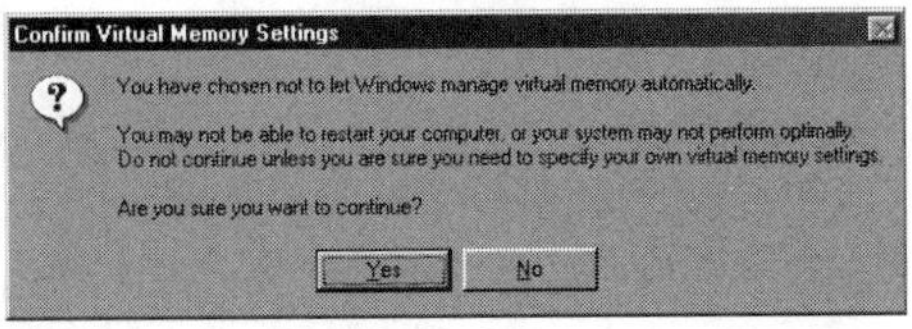

**Figure 13.5**

*Virtual Memory Warning dialog*

Select the new drive from the **Hard disk** drop-down list, set **Minimum** to *half* the drive size, and **Maximum** to the *full* drive size. Click **OK**. You'll be warned (Figure 13.5). Click **OK** again.

The new WIN386.SWP file will be created on the compressed drive, and the old one will be deleted from the boot drive. The next time you look in the **Virtual memory** region, the setting will have reverted to **Let Windows manage my virtual memory settings**, but the paging file will remain on the compressed drive.

If this strikes your fancy, please, don't try it on a mission-critical machine. On the other hand, it's well known that putting the paging file on a *physical* drive other than the boot drive improves 32-bit Windows performance—and if that advantage extends to *logical* drives as well … We can only offer the opinion of our NT guru: "It wouldn't. Or it shouldn't. But it might."

# Race Ready: The Tools, The Tweaks, The Tricks, The Traps

Okay, we've spent all your money. Now we'll tell you about Windows 98's choice collection of performance tools, available without dropping another dime. Whether or not you've ever tuned a piano, or a fish, you sure can tune a computer.

## DriveSpace 3

Default path: `Start Menu\Programs\Accessories\System Tools\`
`           DriveSpace`

 NOTE: DriveSpace 3 is not compatible with FAT32.

As we've mentioned, Windows 98 and all those feature-rich Win32 applications take up one heck of a lot of disk space. It's as unavoidable as death and taxes, and running out of disk space can strike with less warning than either one.

**Genuine Phantom Disk Space.**  Fortunately, just as you can sometimes stave off death or (less often) taxes, Windows 98 can help you defer a disk-space crisis with DriveSpace, the Windows 9*x* disk compression technology. In a nutshell, DriveSpace compresses a portion of your hard disk so that it can hold more data; the new, compressed portion of the disk appears to the computer (and to you) as another mass storage device—complete with its own drive letter and directory structure—but is in reality a hidden file stored on the original, or *host*, hard disk. Because the DriveSpace hidden file appears as a real drive volume, it's easier for applications to interact with it. For example, you can move or copy files to a DriveSpace volume using drag-and-drop just as you would between real hard disks; and the File Open dialogs in application programs can't tell the difference between a DriveSpace volume and a physical disk.

When you copy a file to a DriveSpace volume, it is automatically compressed by an algorithm that removes redundant characters and blank spaces in the file's contents, replacing them with symbolic codes that are more compact than the sequences they represent. The new, compressed file becomes part of the DriveSpace hidden file. A physical disk that stores 1GB of uncompressed data can, instead, store a DriveSpace 3 volume that contains 1.8GB to 2.2GB of compressed data. It's like getting a bigger hard disk for free.

**The Microsoft Uncertainty Principle.**  Why "1.8GB to 2.2GB?" Because there's no way to determine exactly how much data a particular DriveSpace volume can hold. It depends partly on the mix of file types you store there; documents, programs, worksheets, and graphics all vary in their degrees of

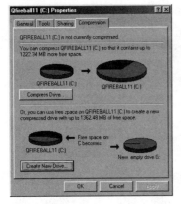

**Figure 13.6**

Compression Properties of
uncompressed drive

**Figure 13.7**

Compression Properties calculation

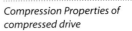

**Figure 13.8**

Compression Properties of
compressed drive

"compressibility." Plain ASCII text can hardly be compressed at all; ordinarily, there's no repetition (redundancy) in it. The other end of the spectrum is probably a bitmapped graphics file, which contains long runs and repeated patterns of ones and zeroes and can frequently be compressed to five or ten per cent of original size.

To allow for this uncertainty, as well as purely mechanical factors like the size and type of the disk holding the compressed file, Windows 98 offers an estimate instead of a number when it reports free space on a particular DriveSpace volume. In practice, you may or may not get that much data to fit on the volume. Compression is an inexact science, and DriveSpace can't resist optimism when it estimates potential free disk space. In our test of a 1GB drive, DriveSpace promised "up to" 1.22GB more free space (Figure 13.6) and by its own calculations (Figure 13.7) produced 1.047GB (Figure 13.8).

Three things are worth noting:

- DriveSpace 3's original prediction was less than 17% optimistic, making it far more accurate than earlier versions of DriveSpace.

- An overall compression ratio of 2.13 to 1 is distinctly worthwhile.

- This compression was accomplished using the Standard, and least ambitious, algorithm. The other two, HiPack and UltraPack, are available—from here—using Compression Agent (see "Compression Agent," below)

The burning question is—considering both storage and performance, can we make the most efficient use of disk space with uncompressed FAT16, with DriveSpace-compressed FAT16, or with FAT32? We're collecting benchmarks, and we'll summarize the results for you when we've got them all.

**Applying DriveSpace to the Whole Drive.** You create and manage DriveSpace volumes with the DriveSpace applet, which is located in **Start Menu\Programs\Accessories\System Tools\DriveSpace**. If this is the first time you're running DriveSpace, you're presented with a window similar to the one in Figure 13.9.

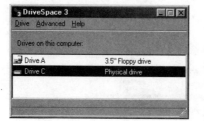

The **Drives** listing includes all physical disk drives on your PC. DriveSpace cannot create a compressed volume on a network drive, or on what it considers a simulated volume.

**Figure 13.9**

*The DriveSpace Applet*

Do you want to compress the entire contents of a drive, or to create a new, empty DriveSpace volume that occupies only part of a drive? To compress an existing disk drive, DriveSpace creates a *volume file* that takes up the drive's entire capacity (subject to certain limitations). As DriveSpace compresses the drive, it moves existing file and directory information into the volume file, compressing the information in the process. DriveSpace then swaps drive letters around, so that the newly created DriveSpace volume appears to be the original hard disk, only fatter, while the original drive acquires a new drive letter.

For example, if you compress drive D:, the newly created volume file is assigned the drive letter D. The original, or *host,* drive is assigned a different drive letter that doesn't conflict with other drives on your system, and one of two things will happen:

If the volume size is 1GB or less, for all practical purposes it ceases to exist as a storage volume. You can still access it, but it will appear to be completely full, which is exactly so: the DriveSpace volume file is occupying almost the entire original drive.

If the volume size is greater than 1GB, any space over 1GB will remain as uncompressed space available on the host drive.

## It Came from Outer Space

Compressing an entire drive is *dangerous* for one reason. If you ever have to reinstall Windows, you—woops!—won't be able to read the DriveSpace volume file while you're doing it, which effectively means that you're hosed. For one thing, your (shudder) Registry files are in there. If you're installing DriveSpace on a new computer and you want to maximize disk space, *install Windows first* if it's not, then use the remaining free space to set up a DriveSpace partition. You'll get almost the same amount of free space, and with your Windows folders uncompressed, your disaster recovery is unimpaired.

**Precautions.** Before compressing an existing drive, back up your data, then run ScanDisk on the drive. DriveSpace runs its own check for errors on your drive before compressing it, and is particularly good at recovering from errors encountered during the compression process. But when your data is on the line, there's no substitute for prudence. Back it up before you compress.

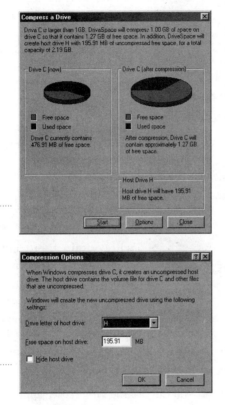

**Figure 13.10**

Compress a Drive dialog

**Figure 13.11**

Compression options

**Starting.** To compress an existing drive, highlight it in the list of available drives and select **Compress...** from the **Drive** menu to open the **Compress a Drive** dialog, which shows "before" and "after" shots of your drive's capacity (Figure 13.10). Because this drive is larger than 1GB, only the first 1GB will be compressed.

The **Drive C (after compression)** chart represents DriveSpace's estimate of free space to be created.

Clicking on the **Options** button brings up the **Compression Options** dialog. This dialog box allows you to fine-tune the DriveSpace process (Figure 13.11). The **Drive letter of host drive** drop-down list box lets you assign a drive letter to the host drive; the **Free space on host drive** field enables you to specify how much of the original drive should be left uncompressed. On a physical disk less than 1GB in size, by default DriveSpace leaves 2MB uncompressed, and on a larger disk everything over 1GB, but you can increase this value. Finally, the **Hide host drive** checkbox tells DriveSpace to hide the original drive from application programs and My Computer. If you've compressed an entire physical disk, this completes the illusion that the new DriveSpace volume is indeed the original, and prevents you from accessing the host drive instead of the new DriveSpace volume.

When you're ready to begin the compression process, click on the **Start** button of **Compress a Drive**. DriveSpace displays a progress indicator until it's finished, then tells you to reboot your system so that the new configuration can take effect.

**Applying DriveSpace to Part of a Drive.** Compressing an existing drive moves that drive's data onto a new DriveSpace volume. Creating an empty DriveSpace drive does exactly the opposite; it allocates some of your hard disk's free space to a new, empty volume, which is assigned its own drive letter independent of the original. You can access it just as you would any other drive.

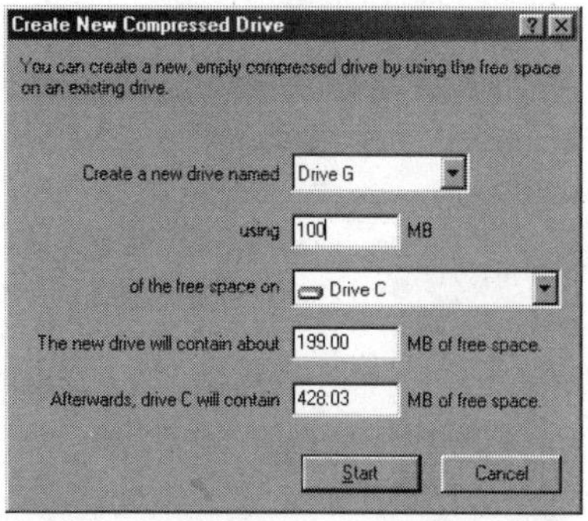

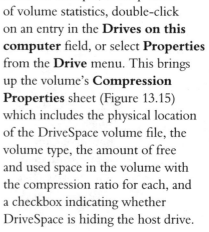

**Figure 13.12**

*Create New Compressed Drive dialog*

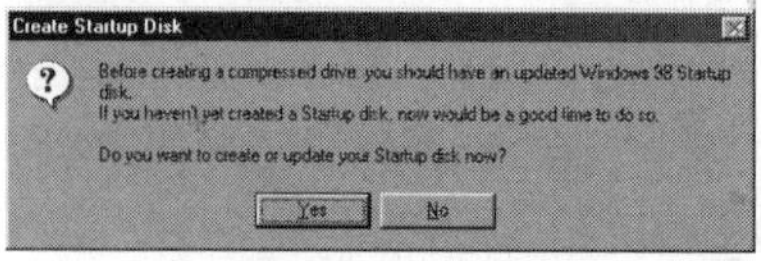

**Figure 13.13**

*Create Startup Disk*

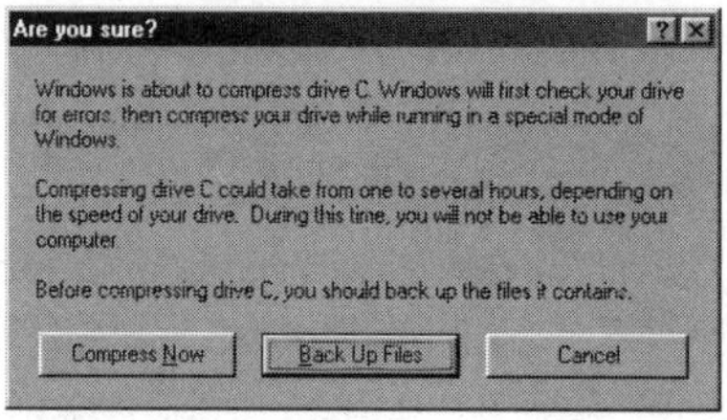

**Figure 13.14**

*Confirm Compression/ Optional Backup*

To create a new, empty DriveSpace volume from part of an existing drive, highlight the name of the appropriate drive, and select **Create Empty** from the **Advanced** menu. The **Create New Compressed Drive** dialog (Figure 13.12) appears and lets you specify the exact dimensions of the new volume.

For example, to create a 100MB DriveSpace volume with the letter G, select that drive letter from the **Create a new drive named** list box, specify 100 in the **using** field, and select Drive C from the **of the free space on** list box. The other fields—**The new drive will contain about** and **Afterwards, drive C will contain**—are completed automatically with DriveSpace's own estimates. Click on the **Start** button, and DriveSpace will suggest that you create a Startup Disk (Figure 13.13)

Finally, it will confirm and offer you a chance to back up your data (Figure 13.14) before it creates a volume to your specifications.

**Volume Maintenance.** You can use the DriveSpace applet to perform maintenance tasks on a DriveSpace volume. For example, to keep track of volume statistics, double-click on an entry in the **Drives on this computer** field, or select **Properties** from the **Drive** menu. This brings up the volume's **Compression Properties** sheet (Figure 13.15) which includes the physical location of the DriveSpace volume file, the volume type, the amount of free and used space in the volume with the compression ratio for each, and a checkbox indicating whether DriveSpace is hiding the host drive.

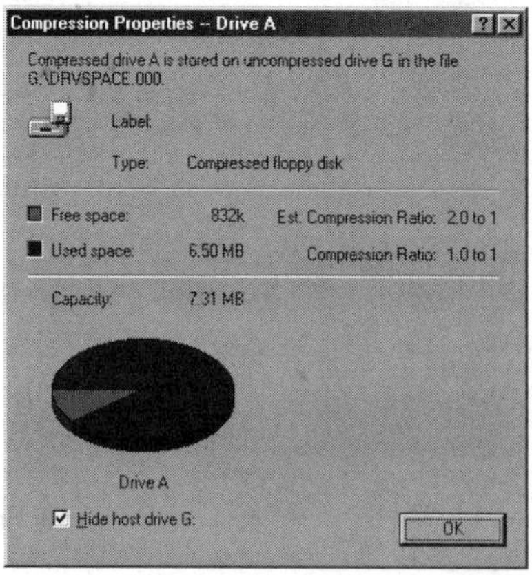

**Figure 13.15**

*Properties of a compressed drive*

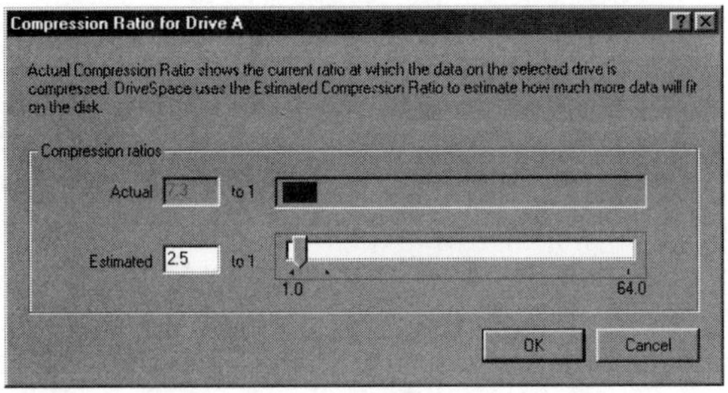

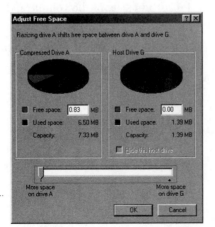

**Figure 13.16**

Changing the estimated compression ratio

You can adjust the estimated compression ratio for a DriveSpace volume, which governs how much free space Windows 98 reports for that volume when you browse in My Computer or the Explorer. (You might want to do this, for example, if you intend to store highly compressible data on the volume, and can afford to make the estimate more optimistic.) To change the estimated compression ratio, highlight the volume in the **Drives** field and select **Change Ratio** from the **Advanced** menu. This brings up the **Compression Ratio for Drive** dialog box (Figure 13.16). To adjust the ratio, move the slider control in the desired direction.

 The Actual Compression Ratio bar here is less useful than it might seem, because its relationship to the Estimated Compression Ratio slider is tenuous. "Actual" Compression Ratio is the packing of data *already on the disk,* and we know from experience with Compression Agent that that number is suspect. Estimated Compression Ratio is DriveSpace's best guess at how much more data will fit, and is much closer to the 2 to 1 that DriveSpace can be counted on to deliver. Our advice is to ignore everything but the Estimated Compression Ratio, and not push that much beyond 2.5, no matter what you intend to copy or save to the volume.

**Figure 13.17**

The Adjust Free Space dialog

You might sometimes need to adjust the size of a DriveSpace volume— for example, when you require more free space on the host drive, and so need to shrink the volume's hidden file. As long as you have enough free space in a DriveSpace volume to allow for a loss in overall size, you can adjust the balance between the host and the volume file. Highlight the volume in the **Drives** field and select **Adjust Free Space...** from the **Drive** menu to open the Adjust Free Space dialog (Figure 13.17).

When you move the slider to the right, the host drive gains free space. Move it to the left, and the DriveSpace volume increases in size. Click **OK**, and the changes take effect immediately.

**Removing a DriveSpace Drive.** If you want to uncompress a DriveSpace drive or delete a DriveSpace volume, you need to find a place for important data that you've stored under DriveSpace, but that won't fit on the physical disk once it's uncompressed. This is no easy task with a large volume. Before you commit to creating a particularly large compressed drive, make sure you can transfer your data from the DriveSpace volume to some sort of warm or hot backup, like a tape drive, a well-endowed file server over a network connection, or even rented remote server space.

Once your data is safely copied, you have two choices:

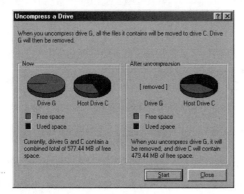

*Figure 13.18*

*Uncompress dialog*

Delete some or all of the data from the DriveSpace volume, then **uncompress** it. This is the less disruptive choice, but it takes longer. Highlight the volume in the Drives field and select **Uncompress...** from the **Drive** menu; the dialog will show you the current state of the volume and compare it to the state after uncompression (Figure 13.18)

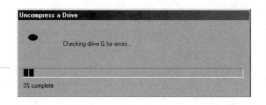

*Figure 13.19*

*Uncompress error checking*

Click **Start** and DriveSpace will begin error-checking the host drive (Figure 13.19) and begin the uncompression itself.

## Will You Go into Withdrawal?

Windows says that while DriveSpace compresses or uncompresses, it "goes into a special mode" that looks to us like Standard VGA with a black background and probably intends to conserve memory. In spite of all it can do, the conversion between states amounts to a complete disk rewrite—maybe more than one—and will take between an hour and six hours in either direction.

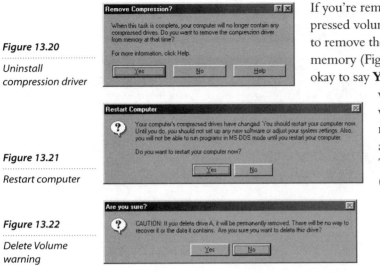

**Figure 13.20**

Uninstall
compression driver

**Figure 13.21**

Restart computer

**Figure 13.22**

Delete Volume
warning

If you're removing your last compressed volume, DriveSpace will offer to remove the compression driver from memory (Figure 13.20). It's perfectly okay to say **Yes**, since even if you'll be working with compressed volumes again soon, reloading the driver is almost instantaneous. Then you need to reboot (Figure 13.21)

Your other choice is to delete the DriveSpace volume file—not the host drive—by highlighting it in the Drives field and selecting **Delete...** from the **Advanced** menu. DriveSpace displays a dialog box (Figure 13.22) warning you of the dire consequences of your action.

 Once you delete a DriveSpace volume, any data stored on the volume is lost forever. Be *absolutely certain* you've transferred everything important before proceeding.

**DriveSpace Miscellaneous Options.** **Drive\Upgrade** applies DriveSpace 3 compression to a drive already compressed with Windows 95's DriveSpace 2 or the earlier DriveSpace or DoubleSpace for DOS.

**Drive\Format...** removes all data from a DriveSpace volume. You get a warning before you start, and a message when formatting is complete, but (unlike the normal Format dialog) no progress indicator. The end product of this operation is a blank DriveSpace disk, which you still have to uncompress separately.

 The ordinary Windows Format command won't format a DriveSpace disk.

**Advanced\Mount** establishes a connection between the DriveSpace volume file—which Windows calls a *compressed volume file* or *CVF*—and the drive letter that names that file to the system. Unless the volume is mounted, you can't access the volume file's contents. See **Automatically mount new compressed drives** in **Advanced\Settings....**

**Advanced\Unmount** breaks the mounting connection. If your host drive is hidden, unmounting it and remounting it unhides it.

**Advanced\Change Letter** changes the drive letter for host drives and for drives created by Create Empty.

**Figure 13.23**

*Disk compression settings*

**Advanced\Settings...** gives you Compression Agent-style control entirely within DriveSpace (Figure 13.23). You can choose among HiPack, complete standard compression, standard compression when the drive reaches a settable percentage full, and no compression. This is also the hiding place of the **Automatically mount new compressed drives** checkbox, which is checked, and that's probably the way you want it.

 Why on earth would you run DriveSpace with **No compression?** Because you're an optimizer unto your very soul. Even with compression turned off, DriveSpace improves cluster sizing and performance, and without compression, it doesn't steal CPU cycles.

**Advanced\Refresh** refreshes the volume table in the DriveSpace applet.

**Don'ts in DriveSpace.** There are, naturally, a few ways to get into major trouble on a computer running DriveSpace. If you follow these handy tips, you'll avoid most of them. *Don't:*

- Run DOS games in MS-DOS mode on a DriveSpace drive, or you'll run out of memory.

- Delete the DRVSPACE.00*x* file on the host, since it contains your files. If you try, here's what you get (Figure 13.24).

**Figure 13.24**

*Volume File deletion warning*

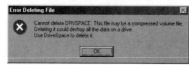

- Delete the DRVSPACE.BIN file, which is the Windows real-mode DriveSpace driver. (Actually, this is less of a worry than you'd think. For one thing, you have two or three copies of it; one in the root directory, one in \WINDOWS\COMMAND, and—as part of the fileset for the Emergency Startup Disk—one in \WINDOWS\COMMAND\EBD. Also, if the Microsoft KnowledgeBase is to be believed, DRVSPACE.BIN barely has time to yawn and stretch in the morning before its functions are taken over by the *really* important protected-mode driver, DRVSPACX.VXD.)

- Use any other compression program on the disk.

- Forget to monitor disk integrity. Use Scheduled Tasks to ScanDisk regularly!

- Set your estimated compression ratio higher than your real one.

- Compress your whole hard drive.

**Addenda: DriveSpace and DOS.**  There are more DriveSpace tricks (groans of "Say it isn't so") that become especially important when you spend time in DOS inside Windows. Rather than go on any longer, we refer you to the Disk Compression page of Gordon Fecyk's invaluable Low-Nonsense Windows 95 FAQ at `http://www.orca.bc.ca/win95/faq11.htm`. Much of the information here seems still applicable to Windows 98, and besides, it is a great site.

**The Future of DriveSpace.**  We wish we were clearer about this, but at the moment we're reading tea leaves. The only information that we have from Microsoft concerning DriveSpace 3 is, to quote from Russell Borland in the Microsoft Press *Introducing Windows 98:* "We don't plan to make further modifications to DriveSpace." Phrasing like that tickles our antennas with its delicate ambiguity; does he mean "We're not going to rework DriveSpace to handle FAT32, but you can count on enduring compatibility with FAT16," or does he mean "We're not bothering with refinements and upgrades because the next version of Windows will kill DriveSpace in a dark alley?"

Realistically, we suspect the latter. Microsoft has a long history of making pronouncements that sound like "As a service to our customers, we're taking this program/utility/applet away, rather than making people get rid of it themselves." On the other hand, we'd be glad to be wrong. DriveSpace 3 is a robust, feature-rich product that delivers astonishing gains in disk capacity with *no* tradeoff—overall—in performance. Those of us who bear faded scars from the bloodlettings of first-generation, third-party disk compression salute DriveSpace as the definitive version that works, always assuming a few elementary precautions.

## Compression Agent
Default path: `Start Menu\Programs\Accessories\System`
`Tools\Compression Agent`

Compression Agent takes hard disks that have *already been compressed* with DriveSpace 3 (that part is important) and gives them another squeeze, to a user-selectable threshold of pain. The options are **HiPack**, which is the highest compression that can be applied without adversely affecting performance, and **UltraPack**, which is the highest level of squish that you can get, but makes the files take longer to read.

 DriveSpace 3 is not compatible with FAT32.

To test Compression Agent, we made a special 1.44MB floppy of various types of small files—recycled browser cache files, to be exact. The root directory contained 208 files. The largest file was 13KB, the smallest file was 1KB, with a heavy bias toward the smaller sizes. Disk free space was 512KB, which is the minimum necessary volume free space for running DriveSpace 3.

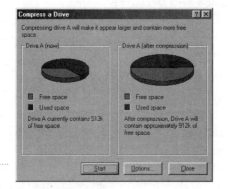

*Figure 13.25*

*DriveSpace dialog*

**Testing DriveSpace.** DriveSpace promised us (Figure 13.25) that free space would increase from 513KB to 912KB, for a gain of 78%. Free space actually increased to 1MB, a gain of 100%.

Time required for DriveSpace compression was 29 minutes, 27 seconds.

*Figure 13.26*

*Compression Agent dialog*

**Testing HiPack.** HiPack (Figure 13.26) didn't promise us anything in advance, but produced 68KB of additional free space, for a gain of 6.6% over DriveSpace.

Time required for HiPack compression was 13 minutes, 54 seconds.

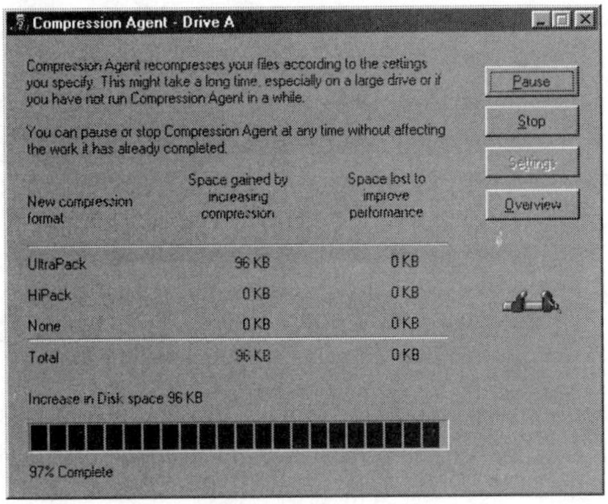

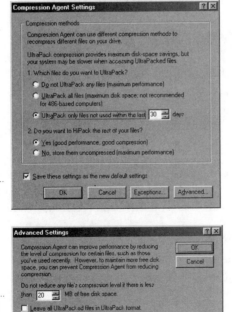

*Figure 13.27*

*UltraPack dialog*

**Testing UltraPack.** UltraPack (Figure 13.27) produced 96KB of additional free space, for a gain of 8.6% over HiPack.

Time required for UltraPack compression was 14 minutes, 1 second.

*Figure 13.28*

*Compression Agent settings*

*Figure 13.29*

*Compression Agent Advanced settings*

**Custom Settings.** The **Settings** button of the Compression Agent dialog opens a **Settings** dialog (Figure 13.28) that lets you choose what proportion of your files should be UltraPacked, HiPacked, or left alone, and whether files not used within a settable number of days— minimum 1, default 30, and maximum 999—should be UltraPacked. This maintains a balance between a lower overall level of compression, for better performance, and a higher level, which conserves disk space.

The **Advanced** button of Compression Agent Settings opens a dialog (Figure 13.29) that prevents global decompression from making too many inroads into your free space. Files will be decompressed only until a settable value—from 0MB to 2GB with a default of 20MB—of minimum free space is reached. (Could this be the value that Disk Cleanup uses for "low on disk space?")

If you check the **Leave all...** checkbox, only HiPacked files will be uncompressed globally, which is handy if all your UltraPacked stuff is deep archival material that you never look at.

**Exceptions.**  The **Exceptions** button of Compression Agent Settings opens a list box that lets you define individual files, folders, and file types for which a particular (overriding) compression method should be used. This is handy if you want to say, "HiPack my whole drive, except UltraPack all my graphics files," or "Compress everything except my Word documents and Excel spreadsheets."

**A Few Hints.**  If you want to use Compression Agent but keep the impact on performance to a minimum, use Exceptions to keep your .EXE and .DLL files from being compressed. Also, don't compress .ZIP files (which are sometimes .EXE files too); if you try, you'll lose the time that Compression Agent spends evaluating the files, and it eventually decides to leave them alone anyway.

Before you start to uncompress a diskette (guess how we found this out) go into Compression Agent Advanced Settings and set the minimum free space for uncompression to 0 MB. Otherwise, the Agent will go through its paces with no change to the diskette, then tell you with a straight face, "I'm sorry, I couldn't uncompress any files because there was less than 20 MB of free space on the disk." Really, Windows, you ought to know enough to check the volume size first!

Microsoft is right: Don't try to UltraPack a drive in a computer with a 486-class CPU. Not only could the process take overnight or longer, but we've heard rumors that if system resources are particularly tight on a 486 computer, UltraPack may simply never finish. If so, your filesystem won't suffer—we hope—but aborting the process after a lot of hours is no fun. For a gain in space of 8% to 10% over the more tractable HiPack, it's hard to see how this could be worth the frustration.

You need a strategic approach to make the best use of DriveSpace and Compression Agent. Run Disk Cleanup before either of these, so you don't waste time compressing cruft. Start full-drive compressions and decompressions before you leave work or go to bed. Above all, remember that a voluminous decompression will take *at least* as long as the compression that preceded it.

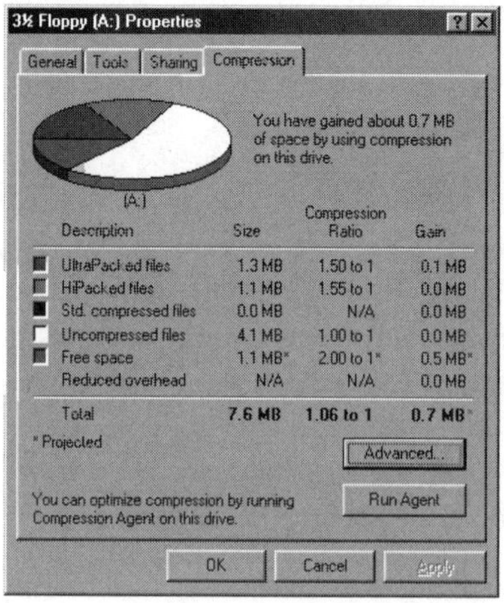

**Figure 13.30**

Test diskette
compression
properties

**The Last Analysis.**  After almost an hour of squishing bits into a glob that only Windows 98 could ever recognize, DriveSpace and Compression Agent produced results on our test diskette that are unspectacular, cryptic, and alarmingly vague (Figure 13.30).

It's hard to believe that the total file space and the total "projected" free space add up to 7.6MB, when we know that the original uncompressed diskette had 928KB of files and 512KB of free space.

When we ran Compression Agent, HiPack and UltraPack between them allegedly added 164KB of free space, but when we ran the Agent again to reverse the process, it concluded that 280KB of free space had been lost.

On the Properties sheet, the compression ratio for HiPacked files is 1.55 to 1 and for UltraPacked files 1.50 to 1, but during the process, we saw much higher ratios for both.

After three different types of compression have been applied to 928KB of files, how can "Uncompressed files" (the white part of the pie chart) still account for 4.1MB?

When we took this diskette out of drive A, put in a normal uncompressed diskette, and tried to read it, the computer blue-screened, black-screened, and rebooted spontaneously. Okay, so we were experimenting with a beta operating system at two-thirty in the morning, but behavior like that is unnerving.

We like DriveSpace, a lot, but our consensus on HiPack and UltraPack is that they don't interest us until they can give us statistics that are consistent, if not meaningful.

# FAT32

Default path: `Start Menu\Programs\Accessories\System Tools\`
`           Drive Converter`

Unlike DriveSpace, which plays tricks with compression and slack space, FAT32 installs an entirely new—and significantly more space-efficient— filesystem that radically decreases cluster size. By doing so, it alleviates the most wasteful aspect of FAT16 and brings the FAT filesystem into sync with the modern world of multi-gigabyte drives. The complete rationale for FAT32 is beyond the scope of this book, but a boiled-down version will put across the central ideas.

**The Past of FAT16.** The FAT file system in DOS 1 used 12-bit file allocation table entries for floppy disks—the only disks it knew about—and floppies today still use a 12-bit FAT. DOS 2, the first version of DOS that supported hard disks, allowed 16-bit FAT entries for hard disk sectors. Since each sector was described by a 16-bit value, there could be 65,536 distinct sectors; each sector contained 512 bytes, so 65,536 sectors yielded 32MB—the limit of DOS physical partition size from DOS 2.0 to DOS 3.3.

This was no particular problem as long as most commodity hard disks, like Seagate's ST4038, had a maximum size of 30MB. But in about 1987, technical improvements made 40MB disks possible at attractive retail prices. The whole world leapt at the disks, then discovered they could run DOS on them only if they divided the space into two partitions. Nobody much cared for this.

The short-term fix, first implemented in Compaq DOS 3.31 and MS-DOS 4.0, was to increase the length of the sector table, so that instead of 65,536 *sectors,* one disk volume (or partition) could comprise 65,536 *clusters.* (Actually, ten fewer than that, but this rarely matters.) A cluster is an arbitrary unit of disk space, made up of a fixed number of contiguous sectors. The original DOS 2.0 cluster was four sectors (2 KB) and was primarily a dodge to reduce the overhead of handling small pieces of disk space. But, as disk sizes ballooned and the number of clusters remained fixed, the individual cluster was allowed to grow to make up the difference. Each cluster jumped in size from 2KB, to 4KB, to 8KB, to 16KB, and finally to 32KB. 64K clusters of 32KB each makes a maximum disk size of 2GB. In *theory,* FAT16 could accommodate 64K clusters of 64KB each for a maximum disk size of 4GB, but it happens that in Windows 9*x,* a cluster size of 64KB runs into other limits we won't go into.

Clearly, FAT16 is doomed, and for two intractable reasons. The first is that 2GB maximum partition size, when many or *most* new disks today are bigger than 2GB, and people don't like partitioning disks any more than they ever did.

The second, called *slack space,* is the bane of large volumes. No piece of data, no matter how small, can occupy *less* than one cluster. A file one byte long occupies—uses up—one cluster. A file one cluster *plus* one byte long uses up two clusters. If your FAT16 filesystem uses 32KB clusters (which it does if your disk is over 1GB), the *slack* or empty space in your disk clusters can waste 20% to 40% of your disk space.

"Hang on," says the skeptic, "the only end-of-cluster space that gets wasted is the end of the last cluster in the file." To which we say (because we keep the Skeptic around just so we can jump on him) that many of the files on your disk are smaller than one cluster, and *most* are smaller than two clusters. Take a look at your browser cache files, your memos, your e-mail messages, and even your spreadsheets. The majority are smaller than 64KB.

Sorry, FAT16. Your time's up.

**FAT32's Promise.** You might want to bear in mind that, in an orderly world, FAT32 would be called FAT28, because the FAT descriptor is 28 bits wide; the last four bits are reserved—why, we know not yet. Even a 28-bit FAT entry length is enough to make a gargantuan difference in capacity. (Trust us on the arithmetic here. It would take a lot of space.)

Whereas FAT16 can have no more than 64K clusters per partition, FAT32 can have over 268 *million.* And, naturally, if you can have so many more clusters, each cluster doesn't have to be so huge. Remember that FAT16 "maximum disk size of 2GB" with 64K clusters of 32KB each? For a 2GB disk, FAT32 can have 512K clusters, and shrink the cluster size back down to 4KB. So long, slack space!—or most of it, anyway.

FAT32 is the answer to the brave new world of huge disks. In fact, FAT32 doesn't even bother to handle partitions below 512 MB; you can create a 512 MB partition with FAT16 and 8KB clusters, so there's no need to get exotic.

The FAT32 *maximum* partition size, meanwhile, is two terabytes (2TB). If you're like most of us, you've never met a terabyte; they live in mainframe disk farms and military supercomputers. A terabyte is 1,024GB, and it will be a while before you have one of your own. We're off the hook in the cluster crunch.

**FAT32's Problems.**  Yeah, right. There's a catch, and not a pretty one.

The problem with FAT16 may be the 16, but the problem with FAT32 is the *FAT*—as in, obese. FAT16 and FAT32 are functionally (nearly) identical; and maybe they shouldn't be, because FAT32 is inflated to the point where we're not sure it makes sense.

First, the self-evident: A 16-bit FAT entry is two bytes. A 32-bit FAT entry is four bytes. With that in mind, let's go back to those two 2GB disks:

|  | Cluster size | Clusters | FAT entry/cluster | FAT size |
|---|---|---|---|---|
| 2GB disk, FAT16 | 32KB | 64K | 2B | 128KB |
| 2GB disk, FAT32 | 4KB | 512K | 4B | 2048KB (2MB) |

So, in exchange for dropping back to a minimum cluster size, FAT32 shows up with a file allocation table sixteen times as big. Disk space is cheap, and a 2MB FAT is still only one-tenth of one per cent of a 2GB volume; superficially this tradeoff seems acceptable. But again, two problems lurk in the depths.

The first is that the FAT gets referred to constantly—to such an extent that any improvement in speed is worthwhile. Therefore, ordinarily, the FAT that your computer uses for lookups isn't the one on disk, *but a copy in RAM.* And whereas 2MB of disk space is trivial, 2MB of RAM is not—at least in what it implies. Think about 16MB of RAM for a 16GB disk, which you can buy today. Rock and a hard place. You either use up a sizable fraction of your system RAM to maintain a FAT copy for fast access, or you accept the penalty of doing FAT lookups from disk. Either way, your performance will take a hit that you won't comfortably live with ... which brings us to the second problem.

Microsoft knows that many systems won't willingly dedicate 16MB or more of RAM to a fast FAT copy. So when a FAT32 volume gets to 8GB—and the FAT itself to 8MB—the cluster size doubles. At 16GB it doubles again. At

32GB it doubles again and … we're right back to those 32KB clusters that we did all this to be rid of. Does FAT32 offer advantages that are worth the squandering of disk space? Read on and decide.

What *we* think is: FAT32 is exactly like getting a higher credit line on your platinum card. It doesn't get you out of debt; it just postpones your problems and makes them worse. *What we need is not a fatter FAT but a more efficient filesystem lookup architecture.*

Which FAT32 is not. And we're about to prove it.

**Faceoff!**   For this test, we installed the excellent WinBench 98 test suite from Ziff-Davis Benchmark Operations (ZDBOp). We then converted our test machine's disk to DriveSpace 3, ran the Business Disk WinMark 98 test suite, unconverted it to its original FAT16, ran the suite again, converted it to FAT32, and ran the benchmarks one last time. We are deeply grateful to Ziff-Davis Labs for making this test suite freely available; information in compliance with the license to publish these results is in Appendix I.

All figures in Table 13.5 are in KB of data transferred per second, for a "businesslike" mix of file types, with the figure next to "Entire Suite" being

## Table 13.5   Kip and Fred's FAT Test

|  | DriveSpace 3 | FAT16 | FAT32 |
|---|---|---|---|
| **Entire Suite** (KB/sec) | 796 | 793 | 690 |
| **Spreadsheet/Database** | 781 | 741 | 659 |
| **Word Processing** | 989 | 951 | 758 |
| **Publishing** | 721 | 711 | 624 |
| **Web Browsers** | 679 | 886 | 880 |
| **Task Switching** | 1020 | 1110 | 842 |
| **Disk free space** (MB) | 1477 | 477 | 665 |

### Same table normalized to FAT16

|  | DriveSpace 3 | FAT16 | FAT32 |
|---|---|---|---|
| **WinBench Suite** (FAT16 = 1) | 1 | 1 | 0.87 |
| **Spreadsheet/Database** | 1.05 | 1 | 0.89 |
| **Word Processing** | 1.04 | 1 | 0.8 |
| **Publishing** | 1.01 | 1 | 0.88 |
| **Web Browsers** | 0.77 | 1 | 0.99 |
| **Task Switching** | 0.92 | 1 | 0.76 |
| **Disk free space** (FAT16 = 1) | 3.1 | 1 | 1.39 |

the average of all the file type scores underneath it. "Disk free space" is the amount in MB of free space after conversion of a 1.2GB IDE disk which was somewhat more than half full.

The conclusions worth noting are that:

- DriveSpace 3 won the overall speed test—by a hair, but genuinely. One of the more cherished arguments of the past few years has been "disk compression helps performance because it means you transfer fewer bits" versus "disk compression hurts performance by adding overhead for file compression and decompression." One test certainly won't bring on consensus, but this one bolsters what we've always thought; that high-quality host-type compression offers substantial benefit without exacting much (if any) penalty.

- DriveSpace 3 more than tripled the volume free space—turning less than .5GB to about 1.5GB—and almost doubled the total volume space, from 1.2GB to about 2GB.

- FAT32 took an average performance penalty of thirteen per cent relative to FAT16, and was much worse in task switching, where it forfeited almost a quarter of FAT16's performance. The only category in which FAT32 drew level with FAT16 was in Web Browsers, where the two—puzzlingly—both beat DriveSpace hands down.

- FAT32 made no difference in total volume space, since it performs no compression. It recovered 665 − 477 = 188MB of disk space. This seems to imply that, on a 1.2GB drive, FAT32 reclaimed about fifteen per cent of the total area, which is impressive, because slack space exists only at the ends of files, not in empty clusters. In other words, the reclaimed space wasn't fifteen per cent over the whole disk, it was thirty per cent of the full half of the disk.

- The three conversions—FAT16 to DriveSpace 3, DriveSpace 3 back to FAT16, and FAT16 to FAT32—took between seven and eight hours total, not counting time for benchmarking.

**The Future of FAT32.** We wish we could be optimistic that, as disk volumes grow, FAT32 will come into its own and provide increasingly attractive means for conserving disk space and performance. Unfortunately, on present evidence, just the opposite is likely. If FAT32 retains its 4K cluster size, the 32-bit FAT will gobble system resources and become so vast that lookups will start (in this context) taking forever. If cluster size grows, so that FAT size can stay roughly constant, we've only returned to a bargain that's failed us once; FAT32 will waste the same proportion of a 32GB disk that FAT16 does of a 2GB disk. Other aspects of the way FAT32 works, which would be difficult or tedious to discuss here, make this solution look even more bleak.

Scanning the event horizon, we declare FAT32 to be "the Year 2000 Problem nobody's thought about yet."

**What About NTFS?** Windows NT's NTFS filesystem, dauntingly elaborate and nearly bulletproof, is—as usual with NT—secure in the assumption that there's always more horsepower. Would it be a better choice for the disks of the future than FAT32? Briefly, yes and no, but it looks promising. Let's take a look at NTFS' cluster sizes in Table 13.6.

## Table 13.6  NTFS Cluster sizes

| Partition Size | Sectors/Cluster | Cluster Size |
|---|---|---|
| 512MB or less | 1 | 512 bytes |
| 513MB–1GB | 2 | 1K |
| 1025MB–2GB | 4 | 2K |
| 2049MB–4GB | 8 | 4K |
| 4097MB–8GB | 16 | 8K |
| 8193MB–16GB | 32 | 16K |
| 16,385MB–32GB | 64 | 32K |
| 32GB or more | 128 | 64K |

On cluster size, NTFS competes with FAT32 only up to a partition size of 4GB. From 4GB to 8GB—a size range pertinent to new computers today—NTFS jumps to an 8KB cluster while FAT32 continues with the 4KB cluster. Above that, jump for jump, NTFS clusters are twice the size of FAT32 clusters. But big clusters, while lamentable, can be a fair price for other strengths.

NTFS has excellent (and transparent) disk compression that can be used so long as the cluster size is 4KB or smaller—in other words, on any partition up to 4GB. Disk compression for FAT32 doesn't exist yet, and it's an open question whether it will. In any case, NTFS compression works without phantom drives and host files, and does much less violence to the workings of the filesystem than DriveSpace.

Finally, NTFS' signal virtue is the nature of the filesystem itself. It isn't a linked list like FAT; a file's location on an NTFS disk is contained in its directory entry. It isn't a flat file like FAT, but a proper, hierarchical, tree-structured index. We suspect that with large volumes, it offers higher performance than FAT32. And because NTFS is transaction-based and keeps logs, it has built-in ability to recover from disaster by rolling back to previous states. Yes, it's complicated, and yes, advanced information about it is hard to find. But it's been proven on big, mission-critical systems for years—and it's the most capable filesystem that Microsoft has developed yet.

*Dear Microsoft: Every time we complain that Windows 9x is a pig for disk space, you say "The hardware will catch up." Every time we ask why Windows 9x can't have the NTFS filesystem, you say "NTFS makes too many demands on the hardware." The truth is that, while you waited for the hardware to "catch up," disk size and performance blew past you and sent you into the poison ivy. Next time, make up your cotton-pickin' minds and give us a filesystem we can live with.*

**FAT32 Converter.**   Now that we've said all that, do you want to convert your disk to FAT32? We'll tell you the good news and bad news up front. Good news: The Converter is a major timesaver since it allows the filesystem to be converted while your data stays in place; the version of FAT32 in Windows 95 OSR2 required a reformat for installation. Bad news: If you convert your disk to FAT32 and ever want to convert it *back,* you have two choices. One is to reformat the drive, because there is no FAT32-to-FAT16 converter from Microsoft. The other is to get yourself a copy of *Partition Magic* V3.0 ($60 street) by PowerQuest, which will convert FAT32 to FAT16 and do lots of other nifty disk-type things; browse **http://www.powerquest.com** for the whole list.

But okay. Supposing you know that FAT16 will only create a 2GB partition even if you use DriveSpace, and you've got a brand-new 6.4GB Ultra/DMA drive, and you really want to format it all in one piece with FAT32's elegant, space-saving 4KB clusters. Here's how it works:

From Start Menu\Programs\Accessories\SystemTools, select **Drive Converter (FAT32)**. "After the conversion," says the Wizard enticingly, "you gain additional disk space and your programs start faster." Click Details to open Drive Converter Help, or click Next.

*Figure 13.31*

Select drive for conversion

Select the drive you want to convert (Figure 13.31)

A dialog warns you that antivirus software may be running, seemingly whether there is any or not. If there is, you should bail out of the conversion and **reboot without the antivirus software.**

## Good Intentions

*Watch out!* Installation of FAT32 alters the formats of the master boot record and partition table. Your antivirus software almost certainly will not recognize these changes and may consider them unauthorized or dangerous. If you reboot and the antivirus program "repairs" the changes by rewriting them to FAT16 formats, your disk data's permanently inaccessible.

**Figure 13.32**

*Start conversion*

The Converter also checks for incompatible software—software already on the disk that may not run correctly under FAT32—which you also have to decide what to do about. Click **OK** for the off-you-go dialog (Figure 13.32), and when it says, "might take a few hours," they aren't kidding! Click **Next.**

The computer will reboot, not actually into MS-DOS mode, but into a special, exhaustive character-mode Scandisk. When this finishes, it goes into what looks like MS-Defrag but lasts a lot longer, because it resizes every cluster and writes out the 32-bit FAT.

**FAT32 Warnings.** The Drive Converter Help lists potential pitfalls, which we abridge heavily and summarize here:

- To return to FAT16 you'll have to repartition and reformat. This isn't quite true (see above) but it carries some weight by being Microsoft's official opinion.

- If your drive is compressed you'll have to uncompress it. MS says "most" compression software is incompatible but nothing about what's compatible.

- A removable disk in FAT32 format won't be readable under other operating systems. Er … Neither will a *nonremovable* disk.

- The conversion may turn off your computer's suspend feature.

- After the conversion, you can't uninstall Windows 98 because nothing else will read the disk. Actually, you could probably uninstall 98 and install 95 OSR2, but that would be a tutorial in existential despair.

- If the Drive Converter finds installed software that won't run with FAT32, it will admonish you and make you contact the program's developer about a compatible version.

- After the conversion, you can't dual-boot with any other version of Windows, except 95 OSR2. (The Help text implies that you can dual-boot with 95 SR-1, but we wouldn't bet your payroll records on it.) Earlier versions of Windows can access a FAT32 drive over a network.

# Disk Cleanup

Default path: `Start Menu\Programs\Accessories\System Tools\`
`Disk Cleanup`

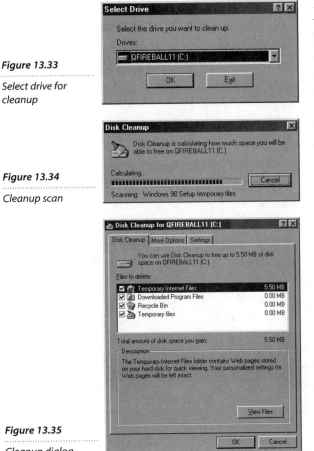

**Figure 13.33**

*Select drive for cleanup*

**Figure 13.34**

*Cleanup scan*

**Figure 13.35**

*Cleanup dialog*

Disk Cleanup offers you a structured way to get rid of your binary dust bunnies—unused applications, optional components, browser cache files, stale ActiveX and Java controls, and temp files. Begin by selecting a drive (Figure 13.33) and Disk Cleanup will scan its contents (Figure 13.34)

When the scan is finished, Cleanup offers you a three-tab dialog (Figure 13.35).

The **Disk Cleanup** tab offers reclamation at its most elementary level: Temporary Internet (browser cache, other than cookie) files, Downloaded Program (ActiveX and Java, *not* shareware) files, Recycle Bin (deleted-but-not-gone) files, and the scratch files in your \TEMP or \WINDOWS\TEMP folders. By default all categories are included, but you can exclude files from Cleanup by unchecking their boxes.

The **More Options** tab leads to **Windows components**, **Installed programs**, and **Drive conversion** choices. **Windows components** and **Installed programs** both go to the standard Add/Remove Programs Control Panel; in fact, if you're struck by the error of your ways, you can add programs here too. **Drive conversion** is the FAT32 Converter.

The **Settings** tab has one checkbox, which is checked by default and which triggers Disk Cleanup "if this drive runs low on disk space." Nothing is said about the granularity at which Disk Cleanup should run, or about what exactly "low on disk space" might mean.

# Disk Defragmenter

Default path: `Start Menu\Programs\Accessories\System Tools\`
`Disk Defragmenter`

You can maintain rewarding performance of any disk subsystem by defragmenting your disk on a regular basis, and Windows 98 gives you a fine set of tools for the job.

In almost any filesystem based on a file allocation table, a single file can be written into several non-contiguous spaces on a disk. This means that space for files doesn't have to be "pre-allocated" before the files are written, which makes a FAT filesystem relatively fast and flexible. But after you rewrite and erase thousands of files during prolonged use of your hard disk, files become fragmented and many small fragments become dispersed on the disk surface. This makes the FAT more complex and less efficient; it also makes file read and write operations slower, because the disk heads spend more time moving and less time handling data. Windows 98's Disk Defragmenter utility reunites file fragments, allowing them to be read more quickly, and creating larger areas of contiguous free space on your disk.

**Pre-Op.** Before you defragment your hard disk, it's a good idea to delete unnecessary files. This frees up some of your system's disk space, giving Disk Defragmenter more room to sort file sectors, while it reduces the number of files to be evaluated and repaired. Good candidates for deletion are the files identified by the Disk Cleanup utility; at the very least, clean out your hundreds or thousands of browser cache files, most of which are so small that they can't be fragmented anyway. You can generally delete word processing and spreadsheet backup files, which often have the extension .BAK.

## *Dupeless*

The disk cleanup devoutly to be wished, of course, is the intelligent elimination of duplicate files, which are to any Windows computer as ants to a picnic. But you can't just rampage around terminating multiple copies of files with the same name, primarily because DLL's don't always work the way they should.

Enter *Dupeless,* another free and fine utility from ZD/PC Magazine, that uses warm fuzzy logic to tell you which files really are and aren't duplicates, then lets you be smart about which ones you delete; it's also extremely fast. ZD's URLs, like Microsoft's, perennially wander around, but browsing to **http://www.zdnet.com** and searching on **dupeless** will probably get you there.

How serious is this? Well, Kip's primary computer has been running for a couple of years and has 22,000 files on it, which is *already* a problem. Running Dupeless disclosed that over 4,000 of them were unnecessary ...

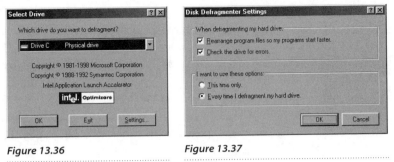

**Figure 13.36**

Selecting a drive to defragment

**Figure 13.37**

Defragmentation options

**Starting.** When you first start Disk Defragmenter, you can let it select your boot drive, or you can select a different drive in the drop-down list box (Figure 13.36).

The Windows 98 version of Disk Defragmenter is more flexible, and more concerned with performance, than prior versions. While it sorts fragments, it sorts files, putting your most-used applications on the most accessible tracks of the disk. It'll also defragment DriveSpace host files, although we shudder to think how a DriveSpace file can be fragmented in the first place! (Must be quantum clusterdynamics.)

The **Settings** dialog (Figure 13.37) lets you decide whether you want your program loading optimized, and whether you want Disk Defragmenter to run Scandisk too. These options can apply to this run or all runs, including the ones managed by Scheduled Tasks.

**Figure 13.38**

Disk Defragmenter status bar

**Watching.** Click **OK** on Settings and click **OK** on Select Drive. Disk Defragmenter will begin defragmenting the contents of the selected drive; you

**Figure 13.39**

Disk Defragmenter Details (detail)

can monitor its progress by watching the status bar (Figure 13.38), or you can click the **Show Details** button to watch an animated, full-color map of the defragmentation process (Figure 13.39).

**Figure 13.40**

Disk Defragmenter legend

If you're baffled by the dance of the cute little blocks, you can click **Legend** (Figure 13.40)

*Figure 13.41*

*Stopping Disk Defragmenter*

You can run Disk Defragmenter with other applications open. You can ask it to pause at any time by clicking the **Pause** button, which simply puts **(paused)** in the title bar and changes the Pause button to **Resume**. To abort the process—for example, if you need to do something horribly disk-intensive immediately—click **Stop**. Disk Defragmenter warns you that it hasn't finished and asks you to confirm your choice, pick a different drive, or resume (Figure 13.41). Don't worry, because you can stop Disk Defragmenter at any point during its process without ill effects.

### Defrag Tips

- The length of time needed for defragmentation will be longer if you haven't run Disk Defragmenter in a while—which is one good reason to schedule it with Scheduled Tasks.

- Defragmenting any drive takes a long time.

- Defragmenting any FAT32 drive takes an *incredibly* long time. (You didn't think all those tiny clusters were free lunch, did you?)

- Defragmenting any drive with Show Details turned on takes even longer.

- The **Check Drive for Errors** checkbox should always be marked. Defragmentation is serious business, during which the most minor error in your disk's allocation tables can turn your hard-earned data into digital sludge.

## ScanDisk

Default path: **Start Menu\Programs\Accessories\System Tools\ ScanDisk**

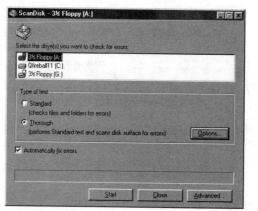

*Figure 13.42*

*ScanDisk*

ScanDisk, now available in your choice of character-based or GUI (Figure 13.42), is still checking disks for integrity (with optional surface scan) and repairing or locking out any defects it may find. Windows 98 runs it automatically when your computer boots up after an "improper" shutdown, or when it encounters a hard error.

## Look On My Works, Ye Mighty, And Despair

The **Automatically fix errors** checkbox should be marked *unless* you believe—on the strength of, for example, a blue-screen warning—that your disk is having trouble writing correctly. Firing up a drive that's doing bad writes and turning it loose with Scandisk can do damage that you don't want to know about. Of course, if you suspect that your disk subsystem is misbehaving in *any* way, you've already taken a full backup or two or three.

From the main menu, you can select a drive and pick your test: **Standard**, a logical test that checks the integrity of the directory structure, or **Thorough**, which combines that with a physical test of the disk surface, whose extent you can set. You can run Scandisk with other applications open.

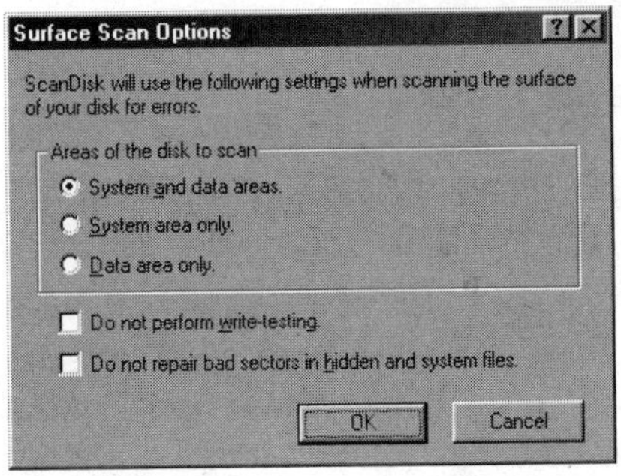

*Figure 13.43*

*Thorough Test Options dialog*

**Surface Scan.** The Surface Scan Options (Figure 13.43) let you select the following:

- **Areas...\System and data:** Test the entire disk. This is the default.

- **Areas...\System only:** Test only the system area. The Help says, perhaps too modestly, that "Scandisk usually cannot repair errors in the system area" and that you'd be wise to brace for a new disk, since physical damage to the system (inner) tracks is often irreparable.

- **Areas...\Data only:** If you know that you have file corruption and want to trace its origin, confine testing to the data area and save some time. Scandisk can "lift" data from bad (or going-bad) sectors, transfer it to a better neighborhood and update the FAT, but can't guarantee that the data isn't corrupt after it's rewritten.

- **Do not perform write-testing:** See above. Unless this box is checked, Scandisk reads each sector and writes it back as a verify pass.

- **Do not repair...hidden and system files:** Ordinarily, you'd care much more about the integrity of a file than about its exact location, if you had to choose! But there are yet a few programs—mostly ancient games and copy-protected DOS applications—that will run only if certain key files occupy specific locations on the disk. These files usually have the Hidden, Read-only and System attributes set. If you run such software, you'll have to check this box before you run Scandisk.

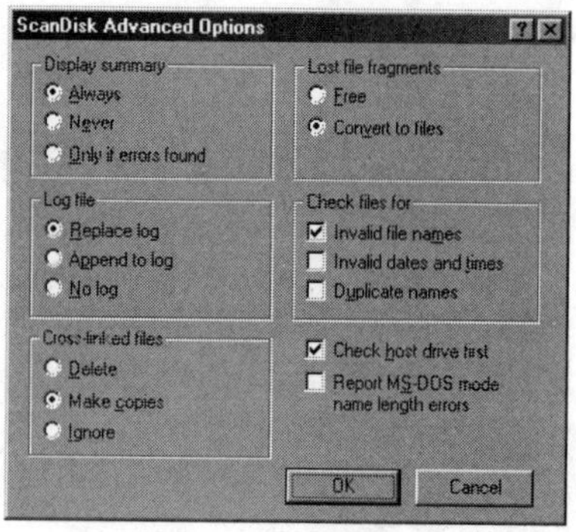

**Figure 13.44**

Advanced Options dialog

**Advanced Options.** You'll never need most of these, except that naturally, we're talking about hard disks, so you might.

The Advanced Options (Figure 13.44) are:

- **Display summary\Always:** Always end a Scandisk run with a results summary. **\Never:** Skip the summary. **\Only if errors found:** Summarize only if the run detected errors.

- **Log file:** SCANDISK.LOG is a small ASCII file (you *hope* it's small) that Scandisk creates for every run; it includes the date and time of the run, the test type, the drive tested, and the error summary. You can open it in Notepad. **\Replace log:** By default, each new run's file overwrites the previous one. **\Append to log:** Maintain a running log of consecutive tests. We like this one best since, if your drive is starting to get weird, logged errors that persist through several scans can be highly informative. **\No log:** Oh, come on. A full Windows installation takes 100MB, and you can't spare the room for a tiny logfile?

- **Cross-linked files**—correct only in the plural, since you can't have just one—are files whose FAT entries have the same cluster or clusters listed in them; they're lying on top of each other, so to speak. The whole point of a FAT is to prevent this from happening, so you have problems, plural. The biggest problem is that cross-linked files are both at risk—any repair will, in general, save one file and doom the other, and the doomed one will be the one you desperately needed. **\Delete:** Go ahead, if you must, but you're not giving Scandisk a chance. **\Make copies:** Makes multiple copies of the cross-linked clusters and patches them into each damaged file, a heroic and underrated technique. You may end up with several files all of which are garbage, but this is your best shot at getting your data back, at least within Windows. If you have fabulous luck, you may be able to cut and paste the multiple files into something useful. **\Ignore:** Do not *ever* ignore a cross-linked file. The right-click Help says "If you try to use or delete cross-linked files, the data in them may become further damaged," but in our experience, you're a lot worse off if you don't take steps right away.

- **Lost file fragments** are pieces of file that exist on the disk, but have no corresponding FAT entries, so they're wandering around with amnesia. **\Free:** Delete the fragments and convert them to empty data space. **\Convert to files:** This converts file fragments to files in the root directory, named FILE*nnnn*.CHK, the way DOS CHKDSK used to do it. Mostly these are junk, and it's a nuisance to go in and delete them by highlighting. *But!* Almost by definition, these are files (or pieces) that were open when the system crashed … in other words, the report you were slaving on last night when the lights went out. You would rather have that information in *some* form than not at all. The NT Guru remembers "ten thousand times when those files were useless" and the one time that one of them opened as an undamaged Microsoft Word document—to gasps of relief from the onlookers.

- **Check files for\Invalid file names:** Both this and **\Invalid dates and times** suggest problems with the FAT, but a file with illegal characters in its names, date or time can also be evidence of virus infection. If we were you (and we have been), we'd leave this checked; if Scandisk reports an error of any such kind, run it a second time, then run your anti-virus software of choice. **\Duplicate names:** This is definitely FAT damage, and serious too, but not likely at all. Given that checking this box slows Scandisk down a *lot,* we don't bother.

- **Check host drive first:** This is misleading and should be called "Check host drive," period. For a DriveSpace disk, the only prudent choice is to have Scandisk check the volume file for logical errors *and* the host drive (physical disk) for hard errors, like deteriorating sectors. If this box isn't checked, Scandisk checks only the volume file, which isn't enough diligence.

- **Report…name length errors:** At this point, we have no idea.

## Resource Meter

Default path: `Start Menu\Programs\Accessories\System Tools\`
`Resource Meter`

The Resource Meter (Figure 13.45) will keep track of your system resources and your USER and GDI heaps (see "Heap Space in Windows 98," below) and give you at least some warning that your computer is running out of memory. It minimizes to the System Tray, which is useful; right-click to exit.

**Figure 13.45**

*Resource Meter*

We've had this hapless applet since Windows 3.1 days, when it got itself a bad name because it was so often inseparable from heaps of trouble. The Windows 98 version is prettier, and rarely has dire shortages to report. Yes, USER and GDI are still sometimes bottlenecks to Windows operations; but even in Windows 95 they rarely filled your machine with glue, and some incremental improvements to heap management have been made in Windows 98.

## System Monitor

Default path: `Start Menu\Programs\Accessories\System Tools\`
`System Monitor`

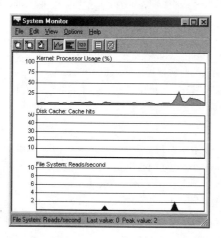

Windows 98 users don't have to be jealous of NT's Performance Monitor and its spiffy charts! System Monitor (Figure 13.46) lets you track any number of system performance parameters—file-system, disk, network, memory, or adapters—and display them as line, bar, or numeric charts. If you're on a network and have the Remote Registry service enabled, you can monitor other computers on the network.

**Figure 13.46**

*System Monitor*

**Toolbar.** Toolbar buttons are: **Add** process, **Remove** process, **Edit** process, **Line** charts, **Bar** charts, **Numeric** charts, **Start** logging, **Stop** logging.

**Menu Options.** Table 13.7 lists menu options.

## Table 13.7  Menu Options

| File | Connect... | Fill the field with the name of another computer on the network, and that computer will be monitored. |
|------|-----------|------|
| | Start Logging | Start logging data for the processes that have been added to the monitor window. |
| | Stop Logging | Stop all logging. |
| | Exit | Quit System Monitor. |
| Edit | Add Item... | Add graph space for another process to the monitor window. |
| | Remove Item... | Remove the graph of a running process. |
| | Edit Item... | Presents a list of running processes. Highlight one and click **OK** to open a dialog and edit the chart color, whether the y-axis of the chart scales to accommodate the data (**Automatic**) or is fixed, and, if fixed, what the y-axis maximum **Value** will be. Note that this dialog, called **Chart Options**, is not the same thing as **Options\Chart**. |
| | Clear Window | Clear all data from the window, leave the charts. |
| View | Toolbar | View or hide the toolbar. |
| | Status Bar | View or hide the status bar—which you want, because it reports dynamically with the title and Last and Peak values of the last chart you clicked in. |
| | Hide Title Bar | Actually, Hide Every Bar; it stashes all the information at the edges and displays the charts in a tastefully thin frame. Hit Esc to resume normal view. |
| | Always on Top | Keep System Monitor on top of other running applications. |
| | Line Charts | Display default line charts (Figure 13.47a) |
| | Bar Charts | Display bar charts (Figure 13.47b) |
| | Numeric Charts | Display numeric charts (Figure 13.47c) |
| Options | Chart | Use a slider (Figure 13.48) to adjust the update interval of the charts, with a minimum of one second, default of five seconds, and maximum of one hour. |

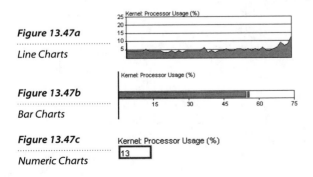

**Figure 13.47a**

Line Charts

**Figure 13.47b**

Bar Charts

**Figure 13.47c**

Numeric Charts

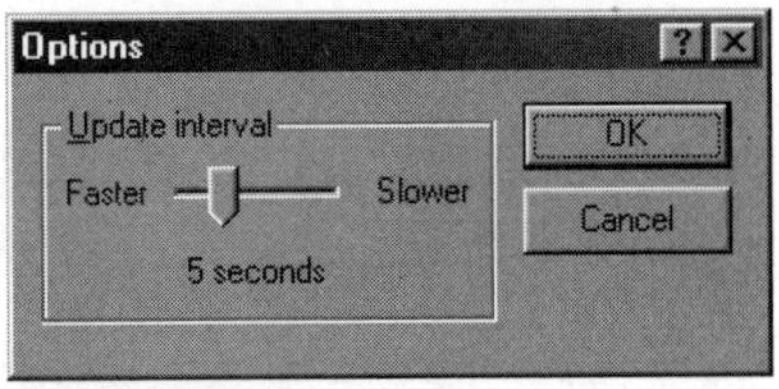

**Figure 13.48**

Chart Update slider

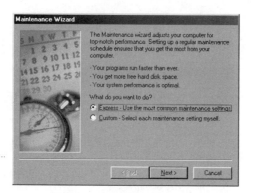

*Figure 13.49*

*Maintenance Wizard*

## Maintenance Wizard

Default path: `Start Menu\Programs\Accessories\System Tools\`
`              Maintenance Wizard`

The Maintenance Wizard opening screen (Figure 13.49) is a front end to Disk Defragmenter, Scandisk, and an expanded Disk Cleanup. There are two options:

- **Express** includes the three standard functions and lets you run them between midnight and 3 a. m., noon and 3 p. m., or 8 and 11 p. m. You can also keep prior settings for the individual utilities, but can't change them from here.

- **Custom** lets you use the same global settings as Express, or reconfigure the individual utilities on the fly. You can also modify your Startup group, temporarily or permanently, with checkboxes.

**Disk Cleanup in Maintenance Wizard.** This Disk Cleanup (Figure 13.50) has only one tab but broader choices; besides the standard **Temporary Internet Files**, **Downloaded Program Files**, **Recycle Bin**, and **Temporary files**, it includes **Temporary Setup Files**, **Old Scandisk files in the root folder** (.CHK files), and **Windows 98 Setup temporary files**—however arcane those distinctions may be. There's no running total of recoverable disk space, but the extra file types in this Disk Cleanup and extra tabs in the freestanding one make them about equally useful.

*Figure 13.50*

*Disk Cleanup in Maintenance Wizard*

*Figure 13.51*

*Maintenance
Wizard Run Mode*

**Run Mode.** Once you have Maintenance Wizard configured to your liking, it launches with this mini-dialog (Figure 13.51) that lets you run the utilities immediately, or jump into the full Wizard to change settings.

# File System Settings

The Windows 98 32-bit filesystem keeps all of Windows 95's benefits—like long filenames—and improves on them incrementally. From the few documents available to us, it's hard to tell what attributes of the 32-bit Windows filesystem are specific to Windows 98, but let's say this; even in the nominal "FAT16" filesystem, most of the actual data handling is performed by 32-bit protected-mode code. A cryptic comment in *Introducing Windows 98,* "File system components implemented as 32-bit protected-mode device drivers ... leverage existing driver technology first implemented in Windows NT," again suggests that Win98 has slaked its thirst at the deep well of the NT codebase.

To access Windows 98 file system settings, go to **Control Panel\System**, select the **Performance** tab, and click on the **File System...** button to open the File System Properties sheet (Figure 13.52).

*Figure 13.52*

*File System
management*

## Hard Disk Tab

Windows 98 does a good job of managing its filesystem generically for optimal performance, but recognizes that computers serve various purposes that will benefit from distinct filesystem configurations.

**Disk Priority Optimization.** For a standalone computer or a workstation with a local drive, you can configure Windows 98 to balance disk I/O demands with other tasks; this optimizes performance for applications you run from your own hard disk. Select **Desktop computer.**

For a portable computer, you can tell Windows 98 to tune disk activity to minimize battery drain. Few things put more of a strain on notebook batteries than disk I/O, so Windows' ability to minimize this strain is a real benefit. Select **Mobile or docking system.**

For a file or print server on a network, you can configure Windows 98 to favor disk and network I/O over other system tasks. If other workstations rely on your system for file and printer service, use this option for the best network throughput. Select **Network server.**

**Read-Ahead Optimization.**   This sets the size of the read-ahead buffer used when applications ask Windows to do data fetches. You can disable read-ahead by clicking **None** or select 4KB, 8KB, 16KB, 32KB, or 64KB **(Full)** but the default is **Full** and, in our estimation, you should leave it there unless you're running Windows on a computer with almost no RAM.

## Floppy Disk Tab

Windows checks the box that says **Search for new floppy disk drives each time your computer starts.** What, you keep installing more and more of them? What this means is "Check the contents of the disks in the floppy drives when you boot, just in case you need to use one." Sometimes this is handy for laptops or for diagnostics; it makes less sense for computers that routinely boot from a healthy hard disk, and if you uncheck the box, Windows will come up more quickly.

The conservative position, on the other hand, is to leave this checked, just in case your disk abruptly and absolutely won't boot; but in our experience, that very rarely (if ever) happens with no warning at all.

## CD-ROM Tab

If your installed CD-ROM drive operates at anything from 4x to 32x—which is most of them—set **Supplemental cache size** to **Large**, set **Optimize access pattern** to **Quad-speed or higher**, and forget them both.

If your drive is a 3x, 2x, or 1x, the defaults may make the drive choke. First, set **Optimize access pattern** to the setting that matches your drive, click **Apply,** and test with a CD. If you still have problems, ratchet **Supplemental cache size** back from **Large**, one notch at a time until everything is copasetic.

Might we mention that a 16x IDE CD drive is currently about $50, and you can install one in less than half an hour?

## Removable Disk Tab

Checking the **Enable write-behind caching...** checkbox makes disk operations faster, but removable disks can't always cope with it. If the drive is a floppy, or a pseudo-floppy like a Syquest or Zip, leave this unchecked. If it's a cartridge hard disk, like a Jaz, SyJet or SparQ, follow the manufacturer's recommendation or just try checking it.

One problem here is that the setting applies to *all* removable disk drives indiscriminately, so if your system contains one such drive that can handle write caching and one that can't, you have to accommodate the one that can't by unchecking the box.

## Troubleshooting Tab

All of these settings are unchecked by default, and any of them can play heck with Windows performance. In order to use any of them effectively, you need information outside the scope of this book. We suggest you experiment with these only under the guidance of professional technical support.

(Yeah, yeah, we know … "Disable your synchronous buffer commits and call me in the morning.")

# Graphics Settings

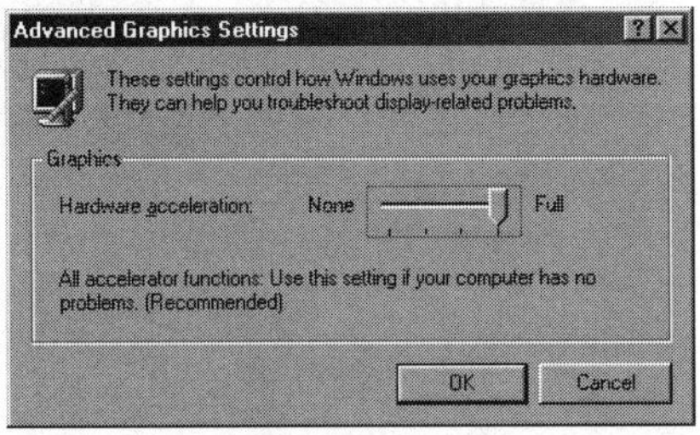

*Figure 13.53*

*Graphics Settings*

The Advanced Graphics Settings (Figure 13.53) control the extent to which your graphics adapter uses its accelerator functions. Unless the card is old by the standards of 32-bit Windows, **Full** acceleration is unlikely to cause video problems.

The slider notches are **No**, **Basic**, **Most**, and **Full** acceleration. Each position has context-sensitive help. If you think your graphics card is giving you grief, try ratcheting this back, but don't forget to hunt for a new driver on the manufacturer's Web page, which may solve everything. On the other hand, if your adapter isn't in the Windows 98 Hardware Compatibility List, the simplest solution may be a new adapter; there are a few cards around that simply won't run 32-bit Windows.

# Caching

The Windows 98 installable file caching subsystem, like its predecessor in Windows 95, is self-tuning and maintained automatically; you never need to fiddle with configuration switches. To anyone who remembers hand-optimizing SMARTDRV in 16-bit Windows—an ordeal that seemed to require chalked pentagrams and a powdered bat—Windows 98's completely self-sufficient VCACHE is blessed relief. Since you'll never meet it, which is exactly the point, we at least wanted you to realize how hard it's working for you.

# Heap Space in Windows 98

Now for the bad news: the GDI heap and the USER heap still exist. Windows 98—with its virtual memory, 32-bit file systems, and dynamic disk caching—is even now burdened with the 16-bit memory limitations imposed by holdovers from Windows 3.1, creating barricades to greater memory use. GDI and USER, two 64K chunks of RAM, contain graphics or interface components in use by the Windows applications you're running. If you try to involve more components than either of the two heaps can hold, your system can freeze or crash. The 64K heap limitation is inseparable from the System Virtual Machine held over from Windows 3.1, which we discussed in this chapter's section on the Central Processing Unit (CPU) and WOWEXEC; even if your system has ample RAM and virtual memory, you're hostage to applications that consume too much of your GDI and USER heap space. To escape from this constraint, you have to install Windows NT.

The Graphics Device Interface module, GDI.EXE, uses the GDI heap to store the handles and pointers to graphics objects such as brushes, pens, bitmaps, buttons, and other graphic regions that make up the Windows graphical interface. Programs that use complex toolbars or perform many graphics manipulations can quickly consume this 64K.

The USER heap is used by the window-management module USER.EXE to store components of the user interface, including the windows themselves. Each time you open a window, you eat up some of the USER heap. The two heaps together are called your *system resources;* each application you start usually consumes between 5 and 10 percent of your free system resources, and each open folder or Explorer view also consumes a few percentage points. If you find your system's performance taking a dive that you can't explain otherwise, use Resource Meter to check your free heap space—and the old 16-bit Windows rule applies; once any of the numbers are much below 50%, close all programs, Shut Down and restart.

Windows 98 does alleviate heap bottlenecks considerably, compared to previous versions by moving many interface components into spacious 32-bit heaps. Still, so long as 32-bit Windows has to maintain compatibility with existing 16-bit applications, it will share some heap characteristics of Windows 3.1. In practice you'll find that you can do a lot more with Windows 98 than you could with Windows 95 or 3.1 before you run out of system resources.

# Summary

The performance of Windows 98 and the applications you run within it ultimately depends on the quality of your components. Microsoft tries to make Windows compatible with as much as possible of the varied hardware available today, but even that only assures a baseline level of performance. If you want the optimum, perforce, you tweak.

Select components by considering the mix of applications you use and your performance criteria for your system. Because Windows 98 makes greater demands on your system's hardware than previous versions did, you'll want the fastest processor, memory, and disk that you feel able to afford. Be generous to Windows and it will return the favor.

# 14

# Windows 98 and DOS

Since its genesis, Windows has had a symbiotic relationship with DOS. Windows and DOS used to be sold separately, but starting with Windows 95, the two have been combined into a single product. Although Windows 98 includes both Windows and DOS in the same box, the two operating systems are not integrated seamlessly; instead they maintain mutual support, sometimes uneasily.

DOS came first. Years later Windows was built on top of the DOS foundation, which complained. The first few versions of Windows could not run without DOS, which Windows needed to access the computer's hardware. Over the years, Microsoft has worked quietly in the background to lessen Windows' dependence on DOS; with each successive release, Windows has gained more power to control PC hardware directly by means of device drivers.

To give Windows the power that DOS formerly held closely, Microsoft systematically replaced DOS-based functions with native virtual device drivers (VxDs), which are a key component of Windows. A VxD creates a virtual device that always looks the same to Windows and Windows applications. The manufacturer of a hardware peripheral, such as a video adapter, creates a minidriver (.INF file) that interprets the physical features of the hardware in a language that the Windows VxD can understand.

Windows 98 consolidates many VxDs into larger, more comprehensive "universal drivers" that control more and different types of hardware than did Windows 95 or 3.*x*. VxDs control everything from mice to CD-ROM drives to sound cards, improving compatibility and helping make Windows 98 hardware-independent. Think of Windows 98 and its applications as running on a giant virtual computer system, which is translated as necessary into your specific hardware configuration.

Though it may be more virtualized, Windows 98 is no more a "completely new 32-bit operating system" than was Windows 95. The marriage of convenience between DOS and Windows has changed dramatically over the years, but there's still enough DOS lurking within Windows 98 to be worth an entire chapter of this book. So, without further ado …

# DOS: The Big Picture

DOS still boots your computer in real mode and prepares it to run Windows 98. Once Windows 98 is running, it maintains DOS in memory to serve as a subsystem mostly related to compatibility with other Windows and DOS applications. The DOS code executes in a Virtual DOS Machine, or VDM.

Windows 98, in the form of a Virtual Machine Manager or VMM, holds the keys to your PC's processor and hardware. VMM itself is a 32-bit, protected-mode operating system. (*Protected mode* is the full 32-bit mode available on 386 and larger processors. *Real mode* is the 16-bit processor mode used by DOS and designed for 286 and older chips. Windows 3.0 and 3.1 can be forced to run in real mode; Windows 95, 98 and NT can't.) Once the VMM takes charge, it creates a number of virtual DOS machines, which emulate complete 8086-based PCs tailored to run DOS applications (Figure 14.1). The VDMs are the most important supports for DOS compatibility in 32-bit Windows.

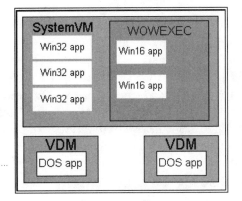

*Figure 14.1*

*How Windows 98 sees your PC*

One Windows virtual machine, the *System VM,* contains the 16-bit portions of Windows 98's window management (USER) and graphics (GDI) subsystems; all 16-bit Windows programs operate inside this VM, which they naively perceive as a running copy of Windows 3.1. The VMM also creates one VDM for each DOS program—which it, of course, perceives as a running copy of DOS—so you can run multiple DOS applications simultaneously and even multitask them.

VDMs inherit the state of the computer after DOS has booted it up, but prior to VMM taking control. This means that if you load DOS device drivers or terminate-and-stay-resident (TSR) programs that take up part of the 640K of DOS application memory, that memory is reduced by an amount reflected in any VDM. However, each VDM also gains the benefits of whatever driver or TSR program consumed the memory. In any case, you can still use your old device drivers; if they're loaded during the initial, real-mode phase of start-up, their capabilities will be available to any VDMs you create to run DOS applications during Windows sessions.

# Boot Action

In Windows 98, the previous system files IO.SYS and MSDOS.SYS are combined into a new, more powerful IO.SYS, along with a few Windows-98-specific device drivers—like HIMEM.SYS and IFSHLP.SYS. Loaded automatically as part of IO.SYS, these drivers pave the way for the protected-mode VMM while they provide Windows 98 with critical links to the real-mode world of DOS.

The real-mode component of the operating system doesn't automatically load COMMAND.COM, as DOS did. Instead it searches for an AUTO-EXEC.BAT file. If it finds one in the root directory of your hard disk, it loads COMMAND.COM (a command interpreter script) and uses COMMAND.COM to process the file. If it fails to locate an AUTOEXEC.BAT file, it doesn't load COMMAND.COM. Windows 98 doesn't need a command interpreter; the VMM takes over as soon as IO.SYS paves the way for it. Windows 98 makes the start-up process more automatic than previous versions did—and makes DOS less visible in the bargain.

Despite its disappearing act, however, DOS is still very much a part of Windows 98. When Windows 98 runs in protected mode, it communicates constantly with a virtualized copy of DOS running in a VDM. Most of the time Windows 98 transmits commands from running applications—for example, any API calls made to DOS's INT21h interface—to this virtual DOS. Once DOS has processed a request, Windows 98 receives and interprets the results. In other cases Windows 98 relies directly on DOS—for example, to create and manage the critical PSP (Program Segment Pointer) structures used by all DOS and Windows applications.

# Real-Mode Device Drivers and TSRs

To make a DOS device driver available to Windows 98 VDMs, you add a DEVICE= entry to CONFIG.SYS. Similarly, to make a specific TSR program coexist with your DOS applications and command prompts, you add a reference to it to AUTOEXEC.BAT. Working from protected mode, Windows 98 uses the pre-Windows real-mode environment created by IO.SYS, CONFIG.SYS, and AUTOEXEC.BAT as the model for each new VDM it creates. Every DOS application or command prompt can gain access to those device drivers and TSRs from within Windows 98, so long as the VDM is able to give up the RAM that they occupy. Previous Windows versions, back to 3.1, handled DOS configuration in exactly the same way; in this context, the boot process for Windows has changed only cosmetically.

## Device Driver Collisions

The ability to define global VDM parameters at boot time is a blessing, but can also be a curse. You cannot load a DOS device driver into a single VDM; to change one VDM, you have to make a global entry in the CONFIG.SYS file, which affects all your VDMs.

This poses a problem if not all your drivers coexist peacefully. As any seasoned DOS/Windows veteran knows, combining more than a few DOS device drivers on a system can lead to memory conflicts, load-order discrepancies, and total frustration with DOS memory management. Because Windows 98 uses the DOS model of Windows 3.1, you may have to spend extra time tuning CONFIG.SYS to make a complex configuration sing harmony on your PC.

The same is not true, however, for TSRs, which you *can* load into specific VDMs.

## Virtual Device Drivers

The situation isn't quite as grim as we make it sound. Windows 98 tries to handle DOS configuration issues by supplying 32-bit virtual device drivers (VxDs) that supersede common drivers and TSRs. VxDs, or native 32-bit Windows device drivers, are the building blocks of the Windows 98 operating system. They are particularly flexible because they support both Windows and any DOS applications running under Windows.

VxDs improve performance and use less memory than the equivalent drivers and TSRs. Because VxDs are 32-bit and run in protected mode along with Windows 98's own code, they are faster than real-mode DOS drivers, which must be run in a VDM. In addition, because almost all VxDs exist in protected mode, they consume little or no conventional memory. VxDs also provide Expanded Memory Specification (EMS) memory support and DOS Protected Mode Interface (DPMI) services. Many formerly separate VxDs have been combined into the new and "universal" VMM32.VXD, the core of the Windows 98 VMM.

VxDs have gradually taken over from 16-bit drivers to such an extent that—unless you run very old hardware or software—use of real-mode drivers is confined to situations that don't arise very often. An

### Virtualizing the Virtual Machine

 Of course, the driver that *exists* may be one thing, whereas the driver an application thinks it's looking at—or for—is another. If your modem wants to cozy up with COMM.DRV, then by golly, VMM32.VXD will find a way to look like COMM.DRV, at least to your modem.

The only problem with this is that "which" driver you're running may depend on where you look, because certain Properties listings may report the real-mode .DRV while others report the protected-mode .VXD, but they're both talking about the same thing. See "Modem Diagnostics" in Chapter 11 for an example.

example would be the MSCDEX driver on the Windows emergency diskette, which installs real-mode support for your IDE or SCSI CD-ROM so that, if necessary, you can reinstall all or part of Windows from the CD.

### Installing Virtual Drivers

Unlike DOS device drivers and TSRs, VxDs are installed automatically when you add a new hardware device. The installation is handled either by a third-party setup program or by Windows 98 itself. Typically, hardware supported by Windows 98 relies on corresponding VxDs on the Windows 98 CD or diskettes, while devices supported by third-party software have VxDs supplied on disks provided by the manufacturers.

# The Windows 98 Command Prompt

Past and present DOS users will appreciate that the DOS command prompt has persisted into Windows 98. GUIs such as Windows were designed as richer and simpler interfaces, but they can't compete with the DOS command line for speed; few GUI users can rival a touch-typist already familiar with DOS commands.

Aware of this, Microsoft has always included some form of command prompt shell with Windows, available either full-screen or in a window. Thanks to DDE and OLE, the command prompt acquired features specific to Windows, such as the ability to copy and paste data between a windowed command prompt and the Clipboard—something you couldn't do with DOS alone.

32-bit Windows takes the command prompt to new heights of flexibility with toolbars, TrueType fonts, and a Start command.

### The Toolbar

*Figure 14.2*

*The Windows 98 Command Prompt toolbar*

If you work with DOS applications regularly, you're likely to love the Windows 98 Toolbar. This enhancement of the VDM interface lets you jump to common functions that integrate data from a DOS application into a Windows application, and to control how an application behaves when it is in the background. The Windows 98 command prompt toolbar resembles the toolbars in Windows 98 folder views (Figure 14.2). Each item on the toolbar features a pop-up description of itself, or ToolTip, which you can bring up by pointing to the item's button.

The drop-down list at the left $\boxed{\text{T}\ \ 7 \times 11\ \blacktriangledown}$ is the **Font** dialog, which lets you set the size and type of the font you want to run in this DOS window. See "Fonts and DOS Applications" in Chapter 8. From there rightward, the buttons are:

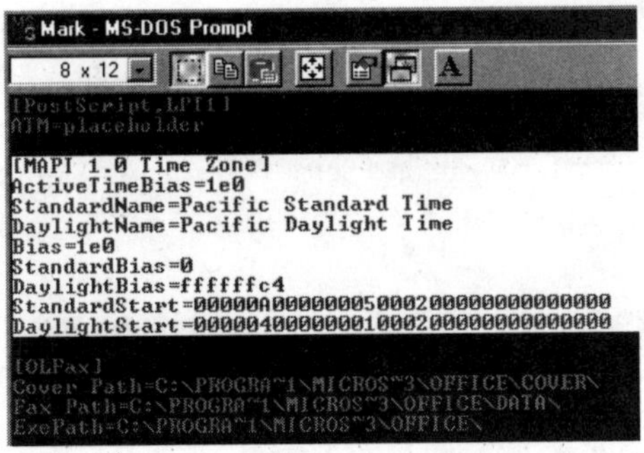

**Figure 14.3**

Marking data

**Mark** switches the DOS window into data marking mode. Click on the button to change the window's cursor into a block, which enables you to highlight (in reverse video) a region of text or graphics by using the [Shift] and Arrow keys or left-click-and-dragging with the mouse. (Figure 14.3)

**Copy** lets you send the highlighted data to the Clipboard.

**Paste** inserts the contents of the Clipboard at the cursor in the DOS window. Most DOS programs and command prompts work with the Windows 98 paste mechanism, but you can paste only text, not graphic data formats.

Some older DOS programs are incompatible with the Windows default method of pasting. For those applications, Windows 98 provides an alternative method that is slower but more likely to work. Refer to the **Misc** tab under "Starting Programs from a Command Prompt," below.

**Full screen** opens a full, borderless DOS character-mode screen of the DOS window. You'll be in the same screen mode—Default, 25 line, 43 line, or 50 line—in full screen that you have set for the window with **Properties\Screen\Initial size**.

**Properties** opens the DOS window's Properties sheet at the Program tab. You can learn more about the properties of DOS programs later in this chapter.

**Background** controls the multitasking behavior of DOS programs. When you click this button "down," it tells Windows to keep running a program even when its window is in the background and another program is running in the foreground. If the Background button is "up," Windows 98 suspends this program's execution in favor of the application in the foreground. With the button "up," you conserve your computer's processing power, because you aren't giving CPU time to a program that isn't in use.

**Font**—yes, the controls at the two ends of the Toolbar have the same name—opens the DOS window's Properties sheet at the Font tab. See "Fonts and DOS Applications" in Chapter 8.

## System Menu

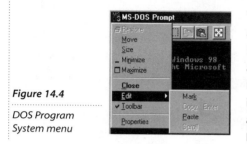

**Figure 14.4**

DOS Program
System menu

You can access all the DOS button commands from a DOS application window's System menu, by clicking the tiny icon at the upper left. Like Windows applications, DOS applications include System menus when they run as windows. Menu items include the standard Move, Size, Minimize, Maximize, and Restore, as well as a submenu with Mark, Copy, Paste and Scroll commands (Figure 14.4).

# MS-DOS Prompt Properties

You can start both DOS and Windows programs from a Windows 98 command prompt; enter the DOS path to the file you want to run, and press (Enter). When you launch a DOS program, it takes control of the command prompt's window, switching it to full-screen mode if necessary. A Windows program, on the other hand, loads into its own application window, ready to respond to other commands while it leaves the DOS prompt running. To launch a DOS program in its own window, you can use the Windows 98 Start command, which we discussed in Chapter 4.

Windows 98 maintains a Properties sheet for each DOS application in a system. The property sheets are roughly analogous to the Program Information Files (PIF) found in Windows 3.1, but with a few new twists. The breadth and depth of the configuration options have been expanded, and you now access information by means of the right mouse button pop-up menus rather than via a separate PIF editor program.

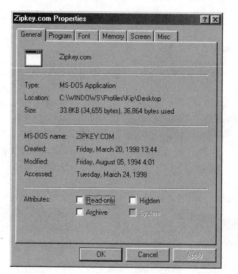

To access the properties of a DOS application, highlight the program's icon in a folder view, then click on the right mouse button and select Properties from the resulting pop-up menu. This brings up the Properties dialog box (Figure 14.5).

**Figure 14.5**

The Properties
dialog box

## General Tab

The **General** tab provides basic file information:

- Its current icon and Windows name.

- Its file type, system location, net size, and "used" size (including slack space)

- Its MS-DOS (8.3) name, and the dates it was created, last modified, and last accessed.

- Attributes checkboxes for setting Read-only, Hidden, Archive, and System.

### *Everything But What You Think*

**Read-only** doesn't mean you can't delete the file; it just earns you a warning and confirmation if you try. **Hidden** doesn't conceal the file from Explorer view, but it does make the icon paler. **Archive** is used mostly as a switch to tell backup programs whether a file is "clean" (identical to the copy last backed up) or "dirty"—modified since last backup and thus in need of being backed up again. **System** refers to core operating system files that are written to reserved inner tracks of the boot drive, and for almost all files, this box is grayed out; a file can't be declared a System file unless it really is one.

DOS icons and Shortcuts have a General tab; DOS applications and command-line prompts don't.

## Program Tab

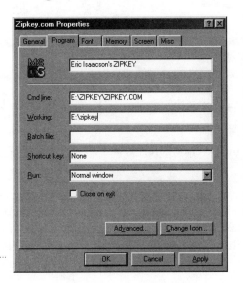

The **Program** tab allows you to define the basic configuration of a DOS program. In the first field, next to the assigned icon, you can enter a title for the program; the contents of this field appear in both the title bar and Taskbar entry of the running program, after you close it and open it again. So, for example, you can pay tribute to an admired shareware author (Figure 14.6).

**Figure 14.6**

*Program tab*

**Cmd line.** The **Cmd line** field contains the DOS path to the program file; for example, the Windows 98 EDIT program will have a Cmd line field that reads:

C:\WIN98\COMMAND\EDIT

assuming that WIN98 is the name of your Windows 98 folder.

**Working.** The **Working** field specifies a working folder for the program. This becomes the DOS current directory value, a DOS variable that determines where default file actions take place. If you know you will be accessing files contained in a specific folder while you use a program, setting its Working field to the desired directory makes sure that files are created, opened and closed in the right location. If the Working field is blank, it's quite likely that the program will refuse to open, claiming that it "can't find" a component that's sitting in the same folder.

**Batch file.** The **Batch file** field can contain the name of a batch file to be run after a program's VDM is created. You can use this to load memory-resident software into a VDM before the application itself loads. For example, to load DosKey (the Windows 98 command line recall stack) into a VDM, you create a batch file that calls DosKey, then put the full path to the batch file into this field. Windows will load DosKey into the VDM when it is first created, then load the application or command prompt.

**Shortcut key.** The **Shortcut key** field will assign a keyboard shortcut to a DOS program. Valid shortcuts combine Ctrl, Shift, and Alt with a number or letter. To assign the shortcut Ctrl Alt E to the Windows 98 EDIT program, for example, select this field, put the cursor ahead of the word **None,** and hold down those three keys. This adds the new combination to the field (Figure 14.7).

*Figure 14.7*

*Shortcut key field*

Shortcut key: | Ctrl + Alt + D|

Windows will assign Ctrl before Shift and Shift before Alt regardless of the order of your keystrokes.

In this field (and maybe elsewhere?) Windows interprets Win [*letter*] as Ctrl Alt [*letter*].

**Run.** The **Run** drop-down list lets you specify how a program's window is displayed. If you select **Minimized,** the program appears on the Taskbar at start-up. Select **Maximized** and the program launches in a maximized window, usually one that occupies the full width of the screen. The default, **Normal Window,** displays the program in a nonmaximized window.

**Close on exit.**  **Close on exit** defaults to checked, and tells Windows 98 to close the DOS window when the program stops running, which is usually what you want.

You may want to uncheck this box, for example, if you want to take a snapshot of a DOS program's output after it finishes running. Clearing this checkbox saves the last screenful of information in the window (Figure 14.8) and adds the word **Finished** to the title bar. A Finished MS-DOS program can be closed by clicking on the title bar's Close button, with no nagging from Windows.

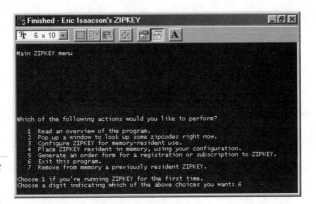

*Figure 14.8*

*Freezing the output from a DOS program*

**Advanced.**  This button opens a dialog that's an education about DOS-in-Windows all by itself—and gives you wizardly powers over the DOS environment. It's more complicated conceptually than the other Properties dialogs, so we'll discuss it later in this chapter, in the section called **Advanced DOS Configuration Topics**.

**Change icon.**  Every version of Windows since 3.0 has allowed users to assign icons to DOS programs. Those icons represent the programs in Shortcuts on the Desktop, and appear on the running program's Taskbar and System menu. To get you started, Windows 98 provides a number of predefined icons in the PIFMGR.DLL file (Figure 14.9).

To select an icon for a program, click the **Change icon...** button to bring up the Change Icon dialog. Select a new icon from the scrolling pane and click **OK**.

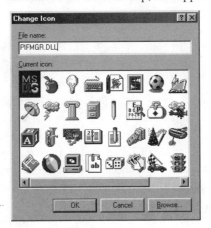

*Figure 14.9*

*PIFMGR.DLL*

Icon libraries other than PIFMGR.DLL are the two classics, SHELL32.DLL and MORICONS.DLL. The somewhat puzzling SHELL.DLL and URL.DLL are keyed to associations in the Registry.

## Font Tab

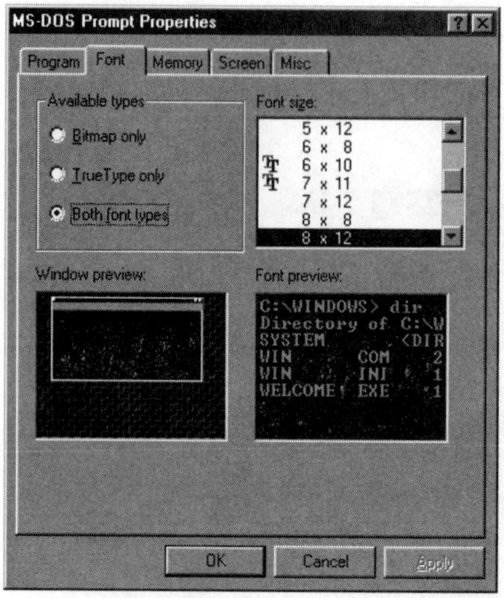

*Figure 14.10*

*Font Properties*

Clicking the **Font** tab brings up the Font Properties dialog (Figure 14.10). Windows 98 lets DOS diehards use scalable TrueType fonts to display DOS information on the desktop—with considerable flexibility.

Select the type of font you want to use—bitmap, TrueType, or both—as well as a default font. A long list of font sizes allows you to fine-tune text display, and an auto-sizing feature computes window size from text point size. (Yes, this does mean that selecting a particular font sticks you with a matching, fixed window size, but you can choose from so many fonts that this isn't much of a bother.)

 Windows 98 still won't let you resize a DOS box by dragging the corner, but there's a better-than-nothing option. Leave the **Font Size** list set to **Auto;** you can use the title bar's Maximize and Restore buttons to flip the DOS window between two sizes, and the font will scale to match. If you set the Font Size list to a specific font, using the Maximize and Restore buttons will do the usual annoying thing—flip the DOS window between two *positions*.

There's more, but we won't use up space here, since it's covered extensively (and with hacks) in the "Fonts and DOS Applications" section of Chapter 8, "Fonts."

## Memory Tab

Even though the 640K memory "limit" still lurks in Windows, the **Memory** tab (Figure 14.11) will let you alleviate the problem by messing around with the memory parameters of a DOS program's VM. You can specify how much conventional, EMS, XMS, or DPMI memory to give the VDM, set its environment specification, define the level of memory protection surrounding it, and give it rights to the high memory area (HMA). And, since this *is* Windows, almost every one of these settings has a gotcha.

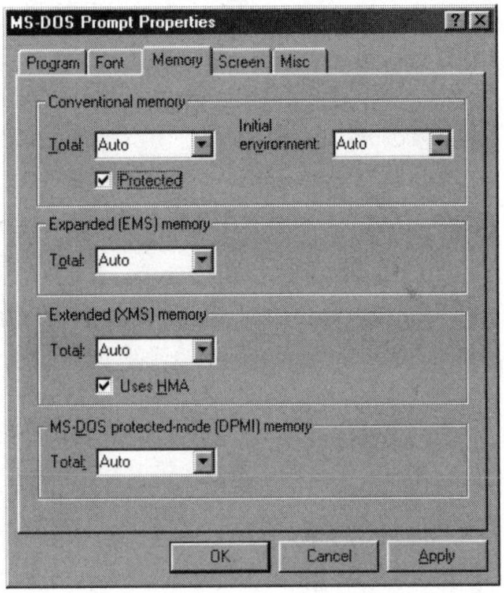

*Figure 14.11*

Memory
configuration

The **Total** field for each type of memory is set to **Auto**, which means Windows 98 dynamically determines how much of each type of memory an application requires. Windows does an acceptable job of estimating how much memory an application requires by monitoring the application's behavior as it loads. Usually, you should leave these parameters alone; when you change them, it will *not* be for entertainment. Therefore, our discussion of the contents of individual fields will concentrate on when and why to enter specific values.

We hope you don't remember all of these heroic attempts to put DOS memory back together again, most of which blossomed like strange, toxic flowers during the last half of the eighties. If you're starting to get an acronym headache, hang on for "DOS Memory Types and Memory Management," at the end of the chapter. We put it at the *end* of the chapter to make it easier to skip!

**Conventional Memory.**  When asked for advice on investment, Mark Twain is reputed to have said, "Buy land; nobody's making any more of it." Anybody who ever pushed the envelope with a DOS computer knows exactly what he meant, but by now we've bought all the conventional memory we're going to, and nobody's making any more of it.

Of all the amounts settable on the Memory tab, conventional memory values are the least manageable. On a "clean" system, with a minimum of real-mode drivers installed, you can expect roughly 605K of conventional memory to be available; but as we mentioned earlier in the chapter, the amount of available conventional memory in a Windows 98 DOS virtual machine is diminished by the quantity of TSRs and device drivers you load at boot-time. To see how much conventional memory is available on your system, use the **mem** command, as we did in Chapter 13.

**Mem**, in its "Conventional" row and its "Used" column, reports the amount of memory taken up by drivers loaded in CONFIG.SYS and AUTOEXEC.BAT. This is memory lost to the DOS virtual machine, and the conventional memory Total setting cannot give it back; the value reported by **mem**, next to "Total under 1 MB" and underneath "Free," is the maximum amount you can put in the Total field. DOS and your pre-Windows configuration—not Windows 98—determine the upper limit on VDM conventional memory.

Our advice: Leave the conventional memory Total field set to **Auto**, and if your application needs more memory than the VDM can provide, find a Windows application that will do the same job. It pains us to say that; once upon a time, we encouraged people to rely on third-party memory managers. But the complexity of memory management under 32-bit Windows makes us wonder whether any developer can do that job better than Microsoft itself.

 The **Protected** checkbox doesn't mean that you can borrow protected-mode memory to use as conventional memory. Wouldn't that be lovely! It means "Check this box if you think your gnarly old DOS app might do something your memory needs to be protected *from.*" Activating protection can slow down an application, so it's best to leave the box cleared unless you're sure a program end-runs around Windows to change DOS directly.

**Initial Environment.**  **Initial Environment** is another relic of pre-Windows DOS configuration. Environment space is the "scratch" memory used by the DOS command interpreter, COMMAND.COM, to store environment variables, like the DOS path, and the SET statements defined in AUTOEXEC.BAT and other batch files. If you know this value (expressed in bytes) is insufficient for some task, you can increase it; you might want to do this, for example, when you launch a DOS command prompt planning to assign new SET variables, increase the length of the path, or modify the prompt. If any DOS program crashes frequently or displays the message "Out of Environment Space," you should definitely increase the value.

If the **Initial Environment** field is set to **Auto**, Windows 98 uses the size of the environment in the pre-Windows DOS configuration as the size for the VDM … and there's the gotcha. First of all, what *was* that? Default environment space varied from one version of DOS to the next. Secondly, no matter what it was, it wasn't enough. One of the most worthwhile performance hacks in Windows 3.*x* was to increase the size of the environment space.

Guess what—you're about to play by Windows 3.*x* rules again. The maximum value for this field is 4,096 bytes, but for any DOS program behaving erratically, half of that is a good place to start. Do three things:

From the drop-down list of **Initial Environment**, pick **2048**.

Use SYSEDIT to add the line

```
SHELL=C:\COMMAND.COM C:\ /E:2048 /P
```

to your CONFIG.SYS file. (If you didn't have a CONFIG.SYS, make one, but you probably had at least a zero-byte file for compatibility.)

and in SYSTEM.INI under the heading [NonWindowsApp] (where your
TTInitialSizes= variable probably is) add

CommandEnvSize=2048

and restart your computer. You now have enough environment space to keep
almost any frisky DOS application from straying, at the cost of a tiny amount
of conventional memory.

**Expanded (EMS) Memory.** Ah, EMS. Who remembers that once upon a
time it was called LIM EMS, for Lotus-Intel-Microsoft Expanded Memory
Specification? Some mistakes are hard to bury, but you can at least try to
change their names.

An older DOS program may be set internally, with charming vagueness, to
use "all available" EMS memory. Windows 98, faithfully complying with a
request made in ignorance, tries to service the DOS with as much as 16MB of
the stuff. In a virtual-memory frenzy, the operating system clears its decks for
the demand by frantically shuffling data from memory to disk, paging out
portions of other programs. Your system slows to a crawl. The DOS app
meanwhile, experiencing the rare but notorious "topless memory problem,"
may panic as it confronts an amount of EMS memory beyond anything it was
programmed to accept.

If you load an EMS DOS application and notice a significant slowdown, a tor-
rent of disk activity, or the program freezing, use the drop-down list in the
EMS **Total** field to assign a fixed maximum of EMS memory to the program.
Try something between 2048 (2MB) and 8192 (8MB).

You might not be running any DOS programs that *need* EMS memory. If you
aren't, you can try running without it. From the drop-down list of **Expanded
Memory**, pick **None**; then use SYSEDIT to add the line

NoEMMDriver=TRUE

to SYSTEM.INI under the heading [386Enh], and restart your computer. Bear
in mind that disabling the EMS driver through the global CONFIG.SYS is an
all-or-nothing proposition; if you do it, the **Expanded (EMS) memory** region
of your Memory tab turns to Figure 14.12 and no matter *what* needs expanded
memory, it won't get it outside of MS-DOS mode. If you click **Details...**, a
dialog helpfully explains that this
arises from the NoEMMDriver=TRUE
line in SYSTEM.INI, and that you
should remove it.

*Figure 14.12*

*Memory Properties
with EMS disabled*

## *Here Be Tygers*

We're trying to improve conventional memory context by getting rid of the memory allocation called the *page frame*. This is a 64K block of upper memory that the EMS specification uses as a staging area to shuffle data between conventional memory and the memory above 1MB, no doubt cursing the intervening block of video memory the whole time.

The question is whether this is worth doing—or whether EMS handling in Windows 98 has changed past recognition. In Windows 95, it could be advantageous to add `DEVICE=EMM386.EXE` to your CONFIG.SYS, with an argument of either `FRAME=NONE` or, if that didn't work, the slightly less efficient `NOEMS`. The problem here is that Windows reads CONFIG.SYS before it reads IO.SYS (see below) and you can't load EMM386.EXE unless HIMEM.SYS is resident ... so the computer boots, reads CONFIG.SYS, gets told to load EMM386.EXE, realizes that HIMEM.SYS isn't there, reports that it can't load EMM386.EXE, and then reads IO.SYS and loads HIMEM.SYS too late. Okay ...

so the answer is to load HIMEM.SYS and EMM386.EXE in CONFIG.SYS in that order. *Except it isn't.* If we use CONFIG.SYS to load HIMEM.SYS and EMM386.EXE with either `FRAME=NONE` or `NOEMS`, we end up with 30KB to 40KB less conventional memory than we have if we just leave everything alone. IO.SYS seems to load HIMEM.SYS more efficiently—either that, or loading HIMEM.SYS in CONFIG.SYS loads it twice. It would appear that in Windows 98—especially now that the DOS memory optimization utility MEMMAKER is no longer available from the \OLDMSDOS folder— playing with manual settings for EMS and XMS management is a game with diminishing returns.

**Extended (XMS) Memory.** **Extended (XMS) memory** was designed from the start to be a rough-and-ready, straightforward scheme for referencing and accessing memory. Just start counting at the one-megabyte boundary and keep going till you reach a habitable planet! Like most things intended above all to be simple, XMS slowly became hideously complicated, and Windows has to live with the results—which it does as well as it can up to a point, and then bails out by suggesting MS-DOS mode. Many of the complexities belong to the rank, dripping world of DOS games.

When the 80386 came along, one of the ways to run it was to divide it into multiple VDMs, any of which *individually* posed no threat to the hegemony of DOS compatibility, because it confined itself to offering the same 640KB as a playing field. Game programmers, panting after gobs and gobs of memory, wanted to run the '386 in its alternate mode, which offered acres of flat memory space, like a Motorola 680x0. Of course, any strictly DOS-compatible program looked at that and fainted.

A whole family of addressing schemes sprang up to give games (and a few other programs, like large databases) access to flat memory. Collectively they were called *DOS extenders,* and several of them became the foundations of nice software. As a group they had three big problems. First, any specific application was tied to the particular extender it was written with. Second, the extenders ran only on the '386, which was awkward in the days when those were expensive. Third, they gave Windows fits, because when Windows runs a DOS program, Windows expects it to *act* like one.

The DOS extenders, and the schemes they implemented, have faded now as programming tools—but the games that depend on them still lurk in software collections, and some of them (*SimCity* by Maxis, *Chuck Yeager's Air Combat* by Electronic Arts, *Falcon AT* by Spectrum Holobyte, *King's Quest III* by Sierra Online, *Links 386* and *Mortal Kombat II* by Acclaim, and *Wing Commander II* and most other games by Origin) are classics. There are particular problems with games that use a memory scheme called Virtual Control Program Interface (VCPI) which is enough to make Windows head for the hills. Many of these games can only be run within MS-DOS mode.

If you want to make your pet DOS game run in Windows 9x, browse to **http://support.microsoft.com** and look up KnowledgeBase article Q132994 for game titles A through H, Q132995 for game titles I through Q, or Q132996 for game titles R through Z.

XMS is Windows' default specification for memory above one megabyte, managed by the Windows driver HIMEM.SYS, one of the most important files in your system—without it, Windows won't run. HIMEM.SYS is automatically loaded at boot-time by IO.SYS, and Windows keeps a spare copy of the file to put on the Emergency Startup Disk whenever you make one. The downside of HIMEM.SYS' close integration with the system is that you can't fine-tune it to make optimum use of memory; unlike EMM386.EXE, it has no relevant switches.

When a DOS application needs XMS, Windows would prefer that it use Microsoft's own, mature "DOS extender-compatible" memory model, called **DPMI** (see below). But there are still some programs that will agree to access XMS memory in a way that Windows can tolerate. If you notice that an application is taking a long time to load or causing a lot of disk activity, limit **Total XMS memory** to no more than 8192 instead of using Auto.

Checking the **Uses HMA** checkbox tells Windows 98 that this program is entitled to use the High Memory Area, which is the first 64K of extended memory, from 1024KB to 1088KB. Windows 98 usually loads the bulk of DOS into the HMA, and you can make this space available to other programs only by adding the line DOS=LOW to your CONFIG.SYS file and forcing DOS into "the lower 640."

Unless you're using one of the few programs that could occupy the HMA, like an older Novell requester, leave this box unchecked. The impact on conventional memory, and thus performance, of loading DOS low is not something to take lightly.

**MS-DOS protected-mode memory.** The wrangle between law-in-this-town DOS extenders and the chilly bureaucracy of Windows' protected mode was finally settled by the **DOS Protected Mode Interface (DPMI)** which amounts to a treaty between two philosophies of memory management. A DOS application can operate with a DOS extender, it says, if it promises to work entirely within protected mode, where it can be prevented from stepping on areas of memory that belong to the operating system or to hardware management. It's the equivalent of saying, "We'll let you into the Saturday night game, sonny, once you learn how to play poker." The three standard extended memory management interfaces of today are XMS, DPMI, and VCPI; Windows heavily favors DPMI, tolerates XMS, and will have nothing to do with VCPI.

Like XMS, DPMI can be set explicitly or left at **Auto**, but there's a difference; DPMI can't be set to "None." You're either going to let Windows manage protected-mode memory for this DOS program, or agree to a DPMI set-aside of at least 1MB. Windows is the sheriff of protected mode and isn't about to be caught without a badge.

## DPMI is Extended, Not Expanded

The *Windows 95 Resource Kit* refers to DPMI memory as "... memory, which Windows 95 automatically provides as *expanded* memory for MS-DOS-based applications that require it to run ..." and goes on to counsel the need for a reserved page frame. This goes against both the literature and our experience, and is wrong; DPMI memory is protected-mode *extended* memory and doesn't care a hoot about paging. The quickest proof is that, if EMS memory is turned off in Memory Properties, a value for DPMI memory can still be entered and will stick. If DPMI were actually *expanded* memory, disabling EMS would turn DPMI off too. Unfortunately, the Net is the world's fastest-talking liar, and this glitch in the Resource Kit has been copied to a frightening number of Web pages.

## Screen Tab

With the Screen tab, you can design the onscreen appearance of DOS programs (see Figure 14.13).

**Usage.** **Usage** defines how Windows 98 displays a program overall. The **Full-screen** button displays the program as a DOS-like, character-mode full screen. The **Window** button displays it in a window on the desktop.

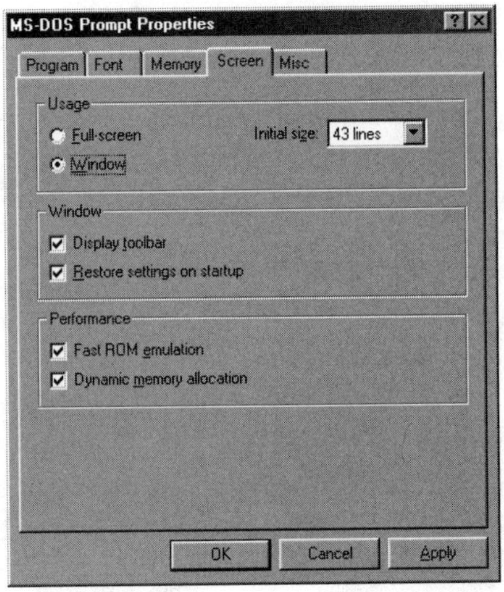

**Figure 14.13**

Screen tab

**Initial size** determines how many lines of text the VDM displays at a time—standard EGA/VGA 25, extended VGA 43, or extended VGA 50.

Some **Usage** settings are "stickier" than others. If you're in Window mode, for example, you can click **Full-screen**, click **OK**, and the display will instantly expand to full-screen. If you want to change the number of lines on the screen with **Initial size**, you'll have to click **OK**, close the DOS box, and open it again. Using **Initial size** to change the number of lines of text also changes the size and shape of the window on the Desktop. You may need to experiment a bit to get what you want.

**Window.** Window controls the appearance of a DOS program running in a window. **Display toolbar** toggles the toolbar underneath the window's title bar. **Restore settings on startup** tells Windows to restore the original DOS window configuration when a program ends. This changes interface settings, such as the number of lines and the font, back to the values you originally set.

**Performance.** The two **Performance** parameters control program interaction with video hardware. **Fast ROM emulation** tells Windows 98 to emulate your display adapter's ROM code, which is slow, with VxDs, which execute more quickly. This boosts the performance of programs that write large amounts of text to the screen. Some older DOS applications object to this; if you notice that a program has trouble writing text to the screen, uncheck this box.

**Dynamic memory allocation** tells Windows 98 to allocate video memory to the program as needed. When the program switches from text to graphics mode, Windows 98 "steals" memory from other processes to answer program requests for more video memory. When the program reverts to text mode, Windows makes the "borrowed" memory available to other programs.

Checking this box enables Windows to manage video memory more carefully, but under certain conditions it can create more overhead than it saves; uncheck it if you notice lagging performance in DOS programs that switch between text and graphics modes, Disable this function, also, if you notice display corruption when a program switches from one mode to the next.

## Misc Tab

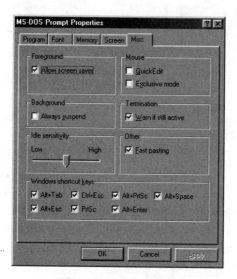

*Figure 14.14*

Misc tab

The **Misc** tab (Figure 14.14) holds everything that wouldn't fit somewhere else, from the mundane (Mouse QuickEdit) to the arcane (Idle Sensitivity).

**Foreground\Allow screen saver**, when checked, allows Windows 98 to start a screensaver when a DOS program is running in the foreground. If you have problems with video or other corruption in a program when the screensaver comes on, disable this function.

If you check **Mouse\QuickEdit**, mouse action over the contents of a DOS window marks the contents for subsequent copying to the Clipboard. The tradeoff is that you disable mouse support for the DOS application. Keep this checked when you're doing lots of marking and copying from DOS; uncheck it if your DOS program requires a mouse.

**Mouse\Exclusive mode** does just the opposite; with this box checked, only the DOS program receives mouse input. You can't use the mouse with Windows. *Watch out!* If you enable this for a DOS task that doesn't *know* about mouse support—like, say, a command prompt—you will lose your mouse pointer completely. (Okay, we'll take you out of your misery; [Alt] [Esc] pulls the focus off the DOS box and gives you back your mouse pointer, so you can click the Properties toolbar button and turn this off.)

**Background\Always suspend** denies this program the use of system resources when it's in the background.

**Termination\Warn if still active** controls whether Windows 98 warns you if you try to close a windowed DOS application with the **Close Window** button or the System menu's **Close** command, rather than with its own menu or keyboard commands.

If you try to close the DOS program from Windows, and **Warn if still active** is checked, Windows 98 displays a dialog advising you to close the program directly. If it's unchecked, Windows 98 attempts to close the program by terminating its VDM. DOS programs other than command prompts don't appreciate having their virtual machines yanked out from under them, so we suggest you leave **Warn if still active** checked, or risk losing data. Some DOS utilities that ship with Windows 98 support the Close Window function and can be closed with the title bar's X button; try the one you're interested in, and if it closes normally, it's safe.

**Idle sensitivity\Low > High** lets you control allocation of system resources to "idle" DOS programs. If a DOS program is waiting for keyboard input to continue processing, it's continually polling the keyboard for input, but doing nothing else. Windows 98 calls this "running in an idle loop" and punishes such programs by reducing the amount of CPU time devoted to them.

Move the **Idle sensitivity** slider toward **High**, and Windows clamps down on such programs the moment it detects they're looping. Move the slider toward **Low** and Windows is more generous, letting programs race around the loop for a while before lowering their CPU priority.

Try lowering the Idle Sensitivity value to improve the performance of some CPU-hungry DOS programs—like games—if you notice them running sluggishly. Just remember that while a DOS application is Windows' favored task, other running programs may slow down or stop altogether.

Windows 98 has two techniques for inserting data into a DOS application, and when **Other\Fast pasting** is checked, uses the faster one. Some older DOS programs are incompatible with this method; if you have trouble pasting Clipboard data into a particular DOS program, uncheck this box.

**Windows shortcut keys** are keyboard commands that execute Windows 98 standard functions. The ones that are checked will be reserved for Windows' use while a DOS program is running. (For example, if the **Alt+Tab** checkbox is checked, Windows will continue to use that keystroke for task switching even if a running DOS program ordinarily uses Alt Tab for something else.) To allow DOS to override Windows' use of a command, clear its checkbox.

# Advanced DOS Configuration Topics

Everything in this chapter so far has concerned the ways Windows 98 accommodates DOS programs that will run within it. It's a tribute to Windows' flexibility, and to the robustness of modern programming languages, that most of them will.

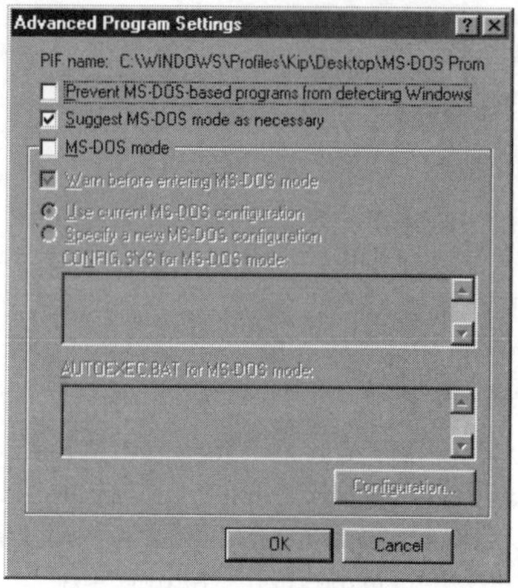

*Figure 14.15*

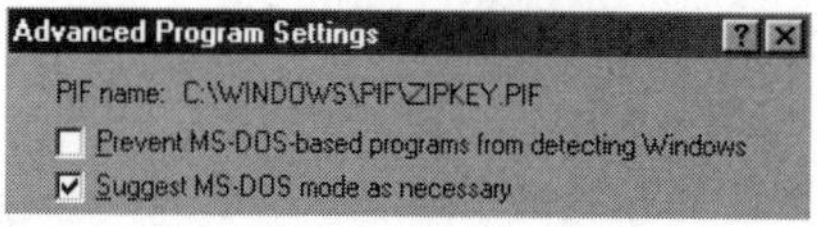

*Advanced Program Settings dialog*

But there have been DOS programs for almost twenty years, and for that entire time, programmers have been striving for the highest possible performance in what they write. They are no more to be criticized for this than are racing-car engineers. It's still true that programming hacks like VGA hardware palette resets, direct memory access, VCPI compatibility, and what used to be called "end-runs around the BIOS" can create situations that are impossible for Windows to adapt to.

When that happens, you reach for the **Advanced** button at the bottom of the **Program** tab (Figure 14.15) to bring up a highly configurable pure DOS environment within Windows—MS-DOS Mode.

The **Advanced** button is rich with possibilities that fall into four broad categories. To begin with, you can stop short of leaving Windows with the top two checkboxes (Figure 14.16).

## Adaptive Options

*Figure 14.16*

*Adaptive options*

**Prevent MS-DOS Programs from Detecting Windows** fakes out older DOS programs that have been programmed to quit running when they share memory space with Windows. If you check this box, Windows 98 disguises itself, so that the DOS program believes it occupies a straight DOS environment; it's analogous to the SETVER utility, which was used in later versions of DOS to convince applications they were running in earlier ones. You're not *in* MS-DOS mode, but Windows is making the application think you are.

**Suggest MS-DOS Mode as Necessary** means that Windows is trying to launch a program as a DOS task and has decided that MS-DOS mode is the only possible environment. Read on for more about this.

## MS-DOS Mode

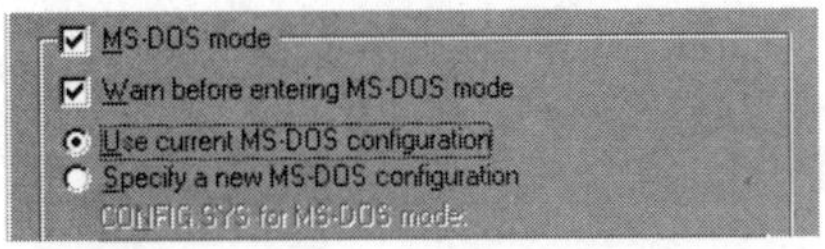

*Figure 14.17*

*MS-DOS Mode with global configuration*

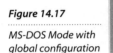

Check the **MS-DOS mode** checkbox if you want this DOS application to run outside of Windows; see below for details. By checking this box (Figure 14.17) you also turn on the checkbox and button beneath it:

If you check **Warn before entering MS-DOS mode**, Windows 98 will remind you what's about to occur when you launch the program. You'll want to keep this checked.

Leave **Use current MS-DOS configuration** clicked if you know, or believe, that your existing DOS configuration with its values for FILES=, BUFFERS=, STACKS=, and the rest of your AUTOEXEC.BAT and CONFIG.SYS provides an environment in which this program will run well.

### IO.SYS Autoconfiguration

If you don't *have* values for some fundamental system parameters in your CONFIG.SYS, it's because IO.SYS has taken over part of the job that CONFIG.SYS used to do. Unless it's overridden by CONFIG.SYS, IO.SYS will add these to your environment:

```
FILES=60
FCBS=4
BUFFERS=30
LASTDRIVE=Z
STACKS=9,256
```

as well as the usual paths for the Windows TMP and TEMP variables, which you shouldn't have to change. But if you need more FILES= or STACKS=, which are the two of these settings most likely to cause trouble, use a custom MS-DOS mode configuration with an appropriately higher value in CONFIG.SYS.

## Customizing MS-DOS Mode

**Figure 14.18**

MS-DOS Mode with program-specific configuration

There are certain programs—mostly old ones and especially DOS games—that expect a customized environment. Some wanted their own program directory to come first in the DOS path; some used batch files to install their own memory managers. A few were so picky that they supplied special AUTOEXEC.BAT and CONFIG.SYS files on the program disk.

You can run these programs according to their own requirements by clicking **Specify a new MS-DOS configuration** (Figure 14.18). Windows will let you write new AUTOEXEC.BAT and CONFIG.SYS files which will be read into memory before this DOS program is loaded. In essence, you're leaving Windows behind and giving the program a custom-crafted environment in its place. The proposed text for the system files is fairly intelligent, in that they do things like install support for sound hardware, although this one didn't pick up the real-mode CD driver in our test machine. They also set some Windows-specific environment variables like **tmp**, **temp** and **winbootdir**, but if your target program wants nothing to do with Windows, you can comment those out.

The **Configuration...** button opens a dialog with four more options:

- **Expanded Memory (EMS)** loads EMM386.EXE. Note that by checking this, you can have expanded memory for this particular DOS application *even if it's turned off* in Windows itself.

- **Disk Cache** loads SMARTDRV—presumably something like SmartDrive 4.2 from DOS 6.22—to speed up disk I/O, since you'll blow away VCACHE when you leave Windows.

- **MS-DOS Command Line Editor (Doskey)** enables the handy command stack that lets you repeat commands at the DOS command line by using ↑ and ↓ .

- **Direct Disk Access** gives the program direct file write privileges. ("Boy," we can hear Windows muttering, "don't blame me for anything that happens while I'm gone.")

And now, back to our regularly scheduled explanations ...

# Behind the Curtain

We welcome you to this section and encourage you to use it if you need to know more about memory. It's as straightforward as we could make it, and more technical than we'd prefer it to be. Remember, we also said you could skip it.

## What Are DOS Memory Types?

Windows techniques involved in swapping files to and from memory, as well as management of system resources, are flat-out chicanery. To understand them, you'll need to be familiar with the three types of RAM used by Wintel computers, broadly referred to as *conventional memory, extended memory,* and *expanded memory.*

**Conventional memory** is, technically, the 1 megabyte of RAM that can be addressed by DOS, but more commonly, the user RAM area or first 640KB of this 1MB. The classic mapping of Intel memory is

One paragraph = 16 bytes

One block = 4,096 paragraphs = 64KB

16 blocks = one megabyte; bottom ten blocks user RAM, top six blocks UMA or *Upper Memory Area,* with individual blocks called UMBs or *Upper Memory Blocks.*

**Extended memory** is any RAM in your machine beyond the initial 1 megabyte. You must have at least seven megabytes of extended memory to run Windows 98.

**Expanded memory** is the same physical memory as *extended memory,* but referred to differently because the method of using it is different. Windows 98 doesn't use expanded memory, but DOS applications run from within Windows 98 may need expanded memory.

Now wait a minute; aren't there a couple of holes in there? Yeah—the ones in Intel's and Microsoft's heads!! The 384KB immediately above the user RAM area, and the 64KB right above *that,* are whole worlds of their own … and we might as well dig out the map right away (see Table 14.1).

## Table 14.1  The Layout of Memory Areas

| Name | Range (decimal) | Range (hex) | Used for |
|------|-----------------|-------------|----------|
| **EMS/XMS** | 1024KB up | 100000 up | Extended/expanded memory |
| **HMA** (High Memory Area) | 1024KB–1088KB | 100000–10FFFF | Some of MS-DOS, and translation buffers |
| **UMB F** | 960KB–1024KB | F0000–FFFFF | System BIOS |
| **UMB E** | 896KB–960KB | E0000–EFFFF | Microchannel bus: OS/2 ROM ISA/PCI: Sometimes available |
| **UMB D** | 832KB–896KB | D0000–DFFFF | EMS page frame |
| **UMB C** top half | 800KB–832KB | C8000–CFFFF | Microchannel bus: 8514/a to CBFFF. ISA/PCI: Sometimes available, sometimes ROM |
| **UMB C** bottom half | 768KB–800KB | C0000–C7FFF | VGA ROM, EGA, 8514/a |
| **UMB B** top half | 704KB–768KB | B8000–BFFFF | VGA text mode; less often CGA, EGA, Hercules monochrome |
| **UMB B** bottom half | 704KB–736KB | B0000–B7FFF | VGA, Hercules, MDA monochrome graphics buffer |
| **UMB** (Upper Memory Block) **A** | 640KB–704KB | A0000–AFFFF | Write buffer for VGA adapter RAM |
| **User RAM** | 0KB–640KB | 00000–9FFFF | Application space |

*What's a Hex Address?*  Computer memory locations are often identified by their hexadecimal, or "hex," values. A hex value is a number expressed in base 16, or hexadecimal, rather than decimal base 10 or binary base 2.

Base 16 employs 16 digits; "our" identical 0 through 9, and then A through F, which are equivalent to decimal 10 through 15. Sometimes a lowercase h is placed after a hexadecimal value to avoid confusion with decimal numbers. Table 14.2 compares selected hexadecimal numbers with their corresponding decimal numbers.

The largest single-digit number in hex (F) is equal to decimal 15; the largest double-digit number in hex (FF) is equal to decimal 255; and the largest three-digit number in hex (FFF) is

## Table 14.2  Equivalent Hexadecimal and Decimal Numbers

| Hexadecimal | Decimal | Hexadecimal | Decimal |
|-------------|---------|-------------|---------|
| 0 | 0 | A | 10 |
| 1 | 1 | B | 11 |
| 2 | 2 | C | 12 |
| 3 | 3 | D | 13 |
| 4 | 4 | E | 14 |
| 5 | 5 | F | 15 |
| 6 | 6 | 10 | 16 |
| 7 | 7 | 11 | 17 |
| 8 | 8 | FF | 255 |
| 9 | 9 | 100 | 256 |

equal to decimal 4,095. This allows large numeric values to be expressed with fewer digits, and the "economy" grows as the values get larger. Also, because computer memory is based on multiples of eight, hex is a more convenient numbering system for programmers than the decimal system.

As is often the case in computing, what's easier for programmers can cause grief for the average user. If you need to convert between the two systems, you can use the advanced capabilities of the Windows Calculator; see "Scientific Mode" under "Calculator" in Chapter 5.

**What Is Conventional Memory?** The Methuselah of RAM, conventional memory is found in all PC-compatible computers. The Intel memory mapping scheme, one of technology's enduring bad ideas, had its origins in a CPU somewhat older than the PC itself—the Intel 8080, introduced in 1974. The 8080, an 8-bit chip, powered several early kit computers which were predecessors of the PC.

When Intel introduced its 16-bit processors, the 8086 and 8088, they intended that—in a way that foreshadowed the 386 ten years later—the new chips should be divisible into 8080-compatible virtual machines; sixteen per chip, with 64KB memory each. This was a defensible decision since, at that time, 64KB was a decent amount of memory for a microprocessor-based computer. Unfortunately, it meant that the megabyte of memory addressable by the 8086 and 8088 got broken into sixteen blocks called *segments,* each 64K in size and each with memory addresses that start from zero. In order to know where you absolutely are in the processor's memory map, you need to know two things: where you are in the segment, and which segment you're in. You keep track of which segment you're in with a four-bit number called the *offset,* which calls the first segment 0 (binary 0000) and the last segment 15 (binary 1111). The nicest thing anybody has ever called this scheme is "aggressively non-optimal."

From its beginnings, the original IBM PC contained an 8088 CPU chip, which could address a full megabyte of RAM. But the IBM PCs that were sold from 1981 to 1984 had only 64KB—one segment—of "user RAM," which meant that few people were greatly concerned about the remainder of the PC's memory map. Even when the PC received its first major design upgrade in 1984 (golly, fellas, it's a hard disk!), IBM believed that power users would be more than satisfied with 256K—a quarter-megabyte—of user RAM. Meanwhile, user RAM was growing up from the bottom of the map, video and BIOS RAM were growing down from the top, and ... They collided at the 640K barricade in about 1985, filling the one-megabyte address space. Technically, the entire megabyte is conventional memory; but the 384KB at the top of the map, which isn't directly addressable by DOS applications, is more commonly called *upper memory.*

**What Is Upper Memory?**   The upper memory area is shown in Table 14.1 as Upper Memory Blocks A through F.

When it was first defined, the upper memory area—like most of the rest of the IBM PC memory map—did not contain physical RAM. Instead the region's addresses were used as reference points that specified locations in ROM and RAM on adapter cards plugged into the computer's bus slots, and locations in the computer's BIOS ROM chips on the system motherboard. This is why, in older PC documentation, you sometimes see the upper memory area referred to as the *adapter segment.* Newer systems provide enough physical RAM to make the upper memory area from actual RAM chips; the contents of upper-memory ROM chips are copied into RAM, in a process called *ROM shadowing.* This boosts performance because RAM operates more quickly than ROM. Despite this advantage, ROM shadowing sometimes creates compatibility problems. If you experience memory conflicts, first try temporarily disabling ROM shadowing, to see whether it alleviates the problem.

Strictly speaking, the upper memory area is divided into 24 blocks of 16K each, but it's more convenient to think of it as six blocks of 64K each—the upper memory blocks or UMBs. The UMBs are subunits of the UMA, *Upper Memory Area,* but the two acronyms are often used interchangeably. It's useful to know how your UMBs are used, because Windows can exploit unused memory areas to provide additional conventional memory for DOS sessions. The two tools that Windows 98 provides to examine memory usage are the Device Manager and the Microsoft System Information Tool, both of which we discuss in the next chapter.

**Manual Allocation of Upper Memory.**   In older computers, system crashes and other failures commonly resulted when an adapter card and the Windows system software both tried to use the same area of upper memory. Two things have alleviated this problem; the stringent specifications for Plug and Play hardware, and the fact that Windows 98 handles upper memory more adeptly than previous versions of Windows.

If you have a non-Plug and Play adapter (especially a video card) that required you to use the EMM386.EXE utility to allocate its memory areas manually, you may still have to do that after you upgrade your operating system. Windows 98 no longer installs EMM386.EXE automatically, but it's on the CD-ROM if you still need it.

In the \WIN98 folder of our most recent copy of Windows 98, EMM386.EXE is in the file WIN98_39.CAB, but we can't guarantee its location in the copy that you buy. You can look for it with the System File Checker, or use the FILEINFO utility in the *Windows 98 Resource Kit* to find it, and then extract the file with the EXTRACT tool. Copy EMM386.EXE into your \WINDOWS or \WINDOWS\SYSTEM folder, and then try the settings for EMM*xxxx*= in SYSTEM.INI that worked correctly in your Windows 95 installation.

**What Is Expanded Memory?**    PCs employ two methods of "getting at" memory above the one-megabyte boundary: expanded memory and extended memory. Windows 98 itself uses only extended memory, but many DOS applications use expanded memory, and Windows 98 can provide expanded memory to your DOS applications that require it.

In the early days of single-tasking PCs, a typical user would quickly consume the 640K of user RAM. If more memory was needed for constructing larger spreadsheets, one last frontier held promise: the UMBs, reserved by IBM, but with some portions left unoccupied. DOS programs written before 1985 employed schemes to grab unused slivers of upper memory, but these programs were willing to fight as well as grab, almost guaranteeing a system crash when two or more programs made a rush for the upper frontiers.

In 1985, Lotus Development Corporation and Intel collaborated to break the one-megabyte restriction of DOS with a major development called *expanded memory.* In this scheme, the computer switches four 16K blocks or *pages* of RAM back and forth between conventional memory and the area above one megabyte. These four 16K pages form one 64K *page frame.* A program called an expanded-memory manager referees the switching of the data. Later, the expanded-memory specification was refined twice—once with the collaboration of Microsoft, resulting in a specification called LIM (Lotus-Intel-Microsoft) 3.2, and again with the collaboration of AST (then a leading supplier of add-in memory boards) to provide the final standard, EMS 4.0.

EMS 4.0 provides a maximum of 32 megabytes of expanded memory. Most DOS applications that use expanded memory use EMS 4.0, although some older programs still use LIM 3.2. You can check a DOS application's documentation to find out which version of EMS it uses.

*Expanded Memory and Windows.*    Many DOS applications, such as spreadsheets and CAD software, may force you to allocate expanded memory even though Windows 98 doesn't require it. Windows 98 automatically converts extended memory to expanded memory for DOS programs, with parameters settable through the Memory tab of the MS-DOS Properties sheet, as we've discussed.

Space conflicts can occur because Windows uses 16K of the upper memory area as a buffer that translates DOS and network API calls from protected mode into real mode, which is the only mode DOS understands. All too often, expanded memory page-frame management and this translation buffer compete for an area of upper memory that's too small for both. In this case, Windows will attempt to arbitrate the conflict.

Because Windows 98 already attempts to use all available free areas of upper memory, you probably won't have to use the three lines in SYSTEM.INI'S [386Enh] section that would instruct Windows to statically modify upper-memory allocation: EMMInclude=, EMMPageFrame=, and UsableHighArea=. If no space is available in upper memory, you can use the line

```
NoEMMDriver=TRUE
```

in [386Enh] to tell Windows 98 to disable expanded memory altogether and drop the search for a 64K page frame in upper memory.

***UMB Hardware Conflicts.***　If you're having trouble starting Windows 98, a hardware adapter may be in conflict for space with the translation buffer. To solve this problem, specify that the memory range E000 through EFFF not be used by either expanded memory or the translation table buffer; because no convention applies as to how this area should be used by add-in cards, conflicts can occur and prevent Windows 98 from starting. To exclude this area, add the following line to [386Enh]:

```
EMMExclude=E000-EFFF
```

This line often takes care of the upper-memory conflicts that can prevent Windows 98 from starting. You shouldn't need to run EMM386.EXE for this setting to work properly, because Windows 98 will correctly inherit and interpret static memory allocations from SYSTEM.INI. Nonetheless, as we've said so often in this book, your mileage may vary.

**What Is Extended Memory?**　*Expanded* memory, as an approach to increasing application memory, had a high cost because it used a complex strategy. Bank-switching segments in and out of a page frame located outside of conventional memory consumes software overhead, vitiates performance, and creates conflicts in the upper memory area. But at the time it was developed, no alternative existed that could maintain compatibility with the 8088 and the 8086.

The advent of the '286 and protected mode let memory extend beyond one megabyte and remain continuously addressable, without software tricks that created burdensome overhead. Extended memory, like Captain Picard saying "Make it so," was beautiful in its simplicity. But for many years it had little practical value, because the technology that would allow it to work with DOS—except as a disk cache or a print spooler—had not been developed. Windows 3.0 made extended memory into application memory by introducing Microsoft's **Extended Memory Specification** (XMS), which opened extended memory to Windows programs, and **DOS Protected Mode Interface** (DPMI), which opened extended memory to DOS applications.

The XMS also mandated the first 64K of extended memory as the *High Memory Area* (HMA) which appears to the computer to be part of the system's conventional memory. By default, Windows 98 reserves the HMA for use by DOS code during MS-DOS sessions.

For purposes of using Windows 98, you can consider extended memory as literally an extension of the 640K of conventional memory. In the 32-bit Windows environment, extended memory plays as important a role as does conventional memory—in fact, you can't run any version of 32-bit Windows without at least some extended memory. If part of your system's memory is on an expansion bus card that can be configured either as extended memory or as expanded memory, configure it as extended memory; Windows 98 can use extended memory to emulate any amount of expanded memory your DOS applications may need.

Now for another detour into the baroque: We've mentioned utility programs called DOS extenders, which accessed extended memory and were either sold separately or embedded into applications. Unfortunately, DOS extenders sometimes caused system incompatibilities and crashes which haunted earlier versions of Windows.

***What is VCPI?*** The Virtual Control Program Interface (VCPI), developed by several companies, including Quarterdeck, Phar Lap, and Rational Systems, was one of two common non-Windows software protocols developed to regulate how all applications used extended memory.

VCPI enabled programs that used DOS extenders on 386 systems to run with 386 expanded-memory managers, such as QEMM and 386MAX. Windows 3.0, which did not support the VCPI specifications, suffered from incompatibilities with expanded-memory managers that did support the specifications.

VCPI is incompatible with normal operations of Windows 98 and of most other multitasking operating systems, including Windows NT, OS/2, and UNIX. DOS-extended programs that comply with VCPI cannot run in a Windows 98 DOS session; they must have total control of the PC. 32-bit Windows supports the VCPI protocol, but only in MS-DOS mode.

***What is DPMI?*** DOS Protected Mode Interface (DPMI) was developed as a group effort by Microsoft, Rational Systems, Phar Lap, and several other companies. The DPMI specifications provide DOS applications with a standard protocol for switching the processor into protected mode and gaining access to extended memory. The DPMI standard works with Windows 98, and most applications that use DOS extenders have been upgraded to support the DPMI standard.

## What Is MS-DOS Mode?

The design of a protected-mode, 32-bit operating system, prepared to replace both DOS and Windows in the marketplace, was a Herculean task. Not only would Windows 9*x* have to support the installed base of Windows applications and drivers, it would also have to provide a compatible environment for as many DOS applications as possible. The standard VDM would accommodate most of them, but some DOS applications disdain virtualization and insist on being the only program running on a PC—which was, after all, a privilege they could expect when they were new.

Earlier 32-bit operating systems, such as OS/2 and some versions of Windows NT, met this challenge by providing a dual-boot mechanism. First you loaded DOS onto the PC, then you installed the 32-bit code over it. At your request the 32-bit operating system could reset the machine for DOS and boot into a real DOS environment. Booting between two operating systems is inelegant at best and could be described as downright kludgy, especially if it has to be performed on an unattended computer.

Microsoft's experience with Windows NT drove it to develop a more accessible "pure DOS" environment. The result was MS-DOS mode, a kind of bootless dual-boot in which Windows 98 unloads itself from system memory and replaces itself with a real-mode DOS. Your finicky old DOS program is then free to run amok in the system. Once the program finishes, Windows 98 reloads, and you're back to square one. Even if the program hangs, crashes, or otherwise comes to a bad end, you're no worse for the wear; simply reboot your system, and you're back in Windows.

***Meet the New DOS.*** Don't let point-and-click control of Windows 98's MS-DOS mode fool you. When your PC enters this mode, it really is booting into DOS, and a very good one. Running Windows applications are properly closed with opportunity to save your data, network connections are closed, and online communications sessions are terminated. When you return to the Windows 98 Desktop from MS-DOS mode, you are back from the wars, and you have to restart, reload, and reconnect.

***Choosing and Using MS-DOS Mode.*** When should you use MS-DOS mode? Windows 98 tries to detect and automatically run any program that requires MS-DOS mode, but it doesn't always make the right call. When it doesn't, it's usually because there's a .PIF file in the way that's giving conflicting instructions.

If you have a rogue DOS application that should start in MS-DOS mode, but won't, hunt for its .PIF file. It probably has the same name as the program

## .PIF Rides Again

You mean a *Program Information File?* Didn't we get rid of those in Windows 95? You wish! They've infiltrated your system and are probably camped all over your Desktop, *disguised as Shortcuts.* You heard right—when you make a Shortcut for an MS-DOS application, or even a command prompt, it may look like a .LNK file, but it's really a .PIF file. You can prove it by right-clicking on an MS-DOS Prompt Shortcut and looking at its Properties; its DOS name is MS-DOS~1.PIF.

file, with a .PIF extension, and has to be in the same folder with the program file, or in a folder on your path, or in the \WINDOWS\PIF folder—which is hidden. To make sure your trusty mouse pointer skewers every copy of the file, run its name through **Start Menu\Find Files or Folders**.

When you find the obstructive .PIF file, delete it and double-click the program icon again. Windows will create a new .PIF file that forces the application to use MS-DOS mode. To make the new settings take effect, you may have to double-click the icon in Explorer or My Computer, or type the program name in the Run dialog box; typing the name at an MS-DOS prompt isn't always enough of a jolt.

In general, you should run a DOS program concurrently with other programs only when you're confident it runs reliably in a normal Windows 98 VDM. The type of VDM failure that forces a program to use MS-DOS mode can also hang your entire computer, so it's best to stray on the side of caution.

*You Can't Have Everything.* Few things in life are free, and MS-DOS mode is no exception. The reason this mode works so well is also its undoing: when you're in MS-DOS mode, Windows 98 is no longer loaded, and unfortunately neither are those helpful VxDs, or VCACHE, or any of the 32-bit things you belatedly discover you were taking for granted. To maintain many basic functions—CD-ROM support, for example—you have to use real-mode device drivers. Yes, it's true: to play your favorite game, you need to dive back into the DOS configuration quagmire. Start by clicking **Specify a new MS-DOS configuration** and using the basic DOS real-mode device drivers available through the **Configuration...** button; Windows interprets your requests and adds the appropriate lines to the customized CONFIG.SYS and AUTOEXEC.BAT files. From there, you can hand-hack the files to alter the path, load program-specific drivers, or whatever wizardry is necessary. Remember, you really are booting DOS.

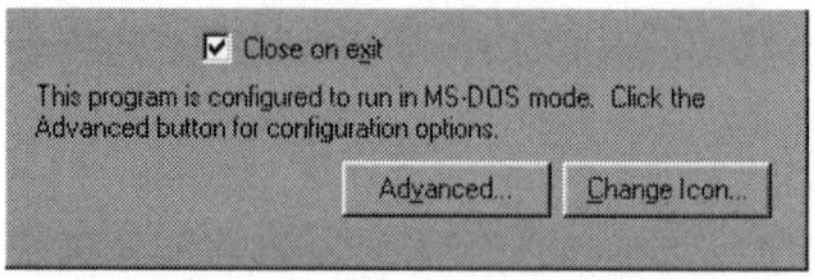

**Figure 14.19**

MS-DOS Mode
Program tab

Once you have the program configured perfectly in DOS, though, you'll
understand what you left behind by
turning your back on Windows.
When you look at the Properties
Program tab, you get this message (Figure 14.19) and—if you've checked **Use
current MS-DOS configuration**—you'll find that **Working**, **Batch file**,
**Shortcut key**, and **Run** are all grayed out. If you're using **Specify a new
MS-DOS configuration**, you get **Working** and **Batch file** back.

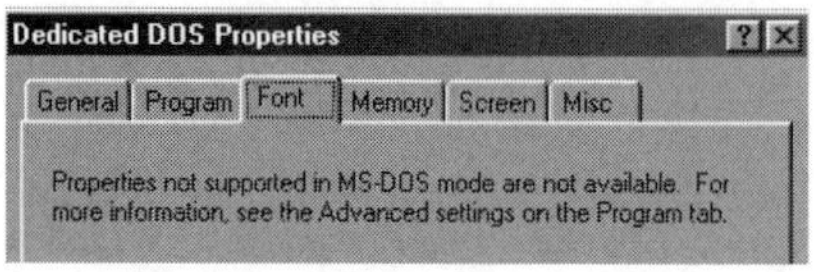

**Figure 14.20**

MS-DOS Mode
other tabs

Meanwhile, the **Font**, **Memory**,
**Screen**, and **Misc** tabs all say this
(Figure 14.20). All in all, we think
you'll decide—as we have—that
configuring a program to run in
MS-DOS mode is acceptable only when there's no alternative.

# Summary

Windows and DOS are still very much intertwined, even now. From
time to time, Windows 98 still makes you delve into the arcane world of
DOS configuration to optimize your PC's operation, and you may have to
edit CONFIG.SYS and AUTOEXEC.BAT files. Microsoft did automate
some features, however; Windows 98 automatically keeps track of configuration information for each DOS program. To access configuration options
for a DOS program, right-click to bring up the program's Properties sheet.
Aggressive configurability, together with universal virtual device drivers
designed to replace obsolete DOS drivers and memory managers, makes
working with Windows' DOS side a less intimidating experience than it has
been since 1990.

# 15

# Tips, Tools, and Troubleshooting

We arrive, finally, at one of the chapters of this book that's the most fun to put together. We hope it's also the most fun to read! Not to mention that, even in these days of relative Windows stability, some of it will save your bacon once in a while. We'll be looking at the little Windows tips, tricks, and secrets that are always greeted with "Aha!"; the tools—greatly improved— that Windows 98 provides to let you examine and analyze your computer's operation; and, finally, some ways that you can save your data, time, and patience when Windows goes wrong.

**Tips**: Tiny timesavers and cool moves are an entire subculture of Windows— so much so that it's impossible to know just how many there are—and one that's expanding while you read. As 32-bitheads, the authors yield to no one, yet time and time again we found ourselves saying "I didn't know Windows would do *that!*" as we collected the tips for this chapter, in a sort of drag-and-doubletake. Some of these, you will grab onto immediately and wonder how you ever lived without; some are cool for their own sake although the possibility of practical use is remote.

A few notes before you dive in:

- Seasoned Web cruisers will recognize that some of these tips originated with Windows 95 or NT 4.0. If a well-known tip is in here, it's because we tested it with Windows 98 and it still worked. (The converse is also true; many of the generally known shortcuts for Windows 95 *don't* work with Windows 98.) We must say, prudently and as usual, that we hope what worked for us works for you.

- The converse of the converse is also true; if you're running Windows 95 or NT 4.0, try our Windows 98 tips and see if they work for you too.

- You'll find we haven't forgotten about DOS, especially DosKey, which remains wonderful. The command-line interface has enduring strengths and, every so often, has to be reintroduced to a new generation of users.

- These tips are for the basic Windows interface and the MS-DOS com- mand prompt. Internet Explorer tips are in the next chapter, "Your Own Private Internet."

**Tools**: Regarding the Windows 98 System Tools, which are much more capable than their counterparts in Windows 95, this chapter finishes the job begun in Chapter 13. The *Optimizing* chapter concentrated on tools you could use to improve performance; this chapter focuses on software repair, debugging, and backup.

**Troubleshooting**: If you've read this far in *The Windows 98 Bible*—which is, as we've pointed out, is only one of the several books we could write about

Windows 98—you realize that this operating system is incredibly, almost incomprehensibly, complex. As a direct consequence, when something goes wrong, just finding the problem (not to mention fixing it) can be a chore of the first order. The possibility of a fatal Windows crash has been considerably diminished by utilities like the System File Checker, Registry Checker, and auto-starting Scandisk—but when it's a computer, anything can happen.

Our Troubleshooting section concentrates on getting you barking up the right tree. It isn't "How to Fix Everything That Can Go Wrong in 32-bit Windows," because we've seen the one of those that Microsoft wrote, and it's three feet thick. What we *can* do, though, is offer a basic correlation between the things that can go wrong, and the first places to look.

# Tips

Here are all the Tips that we could positively make work on the latest version of Windows 98 available as we went to press. We're sure we'll hear about lots more, because in general, people devoted to Windows interface hacks are naturally inclined to spread the word. When more Tips come to us, we'll put them where they'll do you the most good—on the Tips page of `http://www.winbible.com`.

## *Tips*

| | |
|---|---|
| DOS Commands | Why use the Start command to run a program from the command prompt, rather than run it by simply typing in its name? Because the Start command, when you add the name of a program as a parameter, launches a *second* command processor with the program running in it. It's smart enough to run DOS as DOS and Windows as Windows, and let you go back to your original DOS box to keep working. |
| DOS Utility | Most of us know how great DosKey is—and frankly we'd prefer that Windows 98 installed it in command-prompt boxes as a default, the way Windows NT does— but it's a well-kept secret that DosKey's optional parameters make it considerably more useful. The *Windows 98 Resource Kit* spills a few of the beans under the heading "Editing Commands with Doskey and Editing Keys," but not nearly enough; you'd never realize from that, for example, that DosKey is capable of playing back keystroke macros stored in text files. The keys to the kingdom are in DosKey itself; if you type doskey /? at the command line, you'll get a complete list of switches. The text switches have an undocumented terse mode, so that, for example, doskey /history will also work as plain doskey /h. |
| DOS Utility | You can make the Windows-in-DOS **Start** command more powerful by using it to open folders as well as launch programs. If the folder or subfolder is in your Path statement, you won't even need to type the whole path. Try start sendto as an example. |

## *Tips* *(continued)*

| | |
|---|---|
| Interface | You can hit the Caps Lock, Num Lock or Scroll Lock key accidentally and screw up your typing in a flash. If you want a beep to let you know that you've pressed any of these keys, use Windows Setup to install the Accessibility Options (see Appendix B) and step through the Accessibility Wizard to install ToggleKeys. Now you'll get audible confirmation whenever you press any of those keys. |
| Interface | If you open any submenu of the Start Menu, hold down the left mouse button, and *drag* the pointer to the program, document, or Favorite you want to run, that object will launch as soon as you release the mouse button—however deep you are in the submenus. |
| Interface | The problem with running wallpaper is that the title backgrounds are so rarely a good match for it ... but creating a custom color for title backgrounds isn't hard.<br><br>Find your wallpaper file in the \WINDOWS folder and load it into Microsoft Paint. Select the eyedropper tool and pick up a pleasing or prominent color from the wallpaper. Choose **Colors\Edit Colors\Define Custom Colors** and, whoo-ha, the values for the picked-up color are already in the dialog. Copy the numeric values for Red, Green, and Blue into Notepad or something, and close Paint.<br><br>Right-click on the Desktop and choose **Properties**. Click the **Appearance** tab. Click the arrow beside the **Color** list box to expand it, and click **Other**. Double-click the values for Red, Green, and Blue and adjust them to the values you copied from Paint.<br><br>Click **OK** twice. The color of your icon title background will now match the color you picked up from the wallpaper. |
| Interface | Want to find the location of a file in the Start Menu? Right-click on it in the Start Menu, choose **Properties**, click the **Shortcut** tab, click **Find Target**, and you'll jump straight to the file's folder. |
| Interface | If your Recycle Bin is overflowing and you want to recover just a few files from it, remember that you can hold down the Ctrl key and click on names to highlight a discontinuous series of files in any list. After you've selected them, click File\Restore to put them back where they belong; make sure the application they were part of (or whatever) is functional once again, and then empty your Recycle Bin so you won't have these problems. |
| Interface | Everybody knows you can print with drag-and-drop, but have you ever printed with right-click? Open **Control Panel\Printers** or **Start Menu\Settings\Printers**, and Ctrl-drag a copy of your printer icon to your **\Windows\Send To** folder. Now you can right-click any printable file, pick Send To from the Context Menu, and pick the printer from the Send To submenu; the application (like WordPad or Paint) associated with the file type acts as an OLE server to send the file to the printer. You won't believe how fast this is till you try it. |
| Interface | Right-click the Desktop, pick **Properties**, and click the Screen Saver tab. Select **3D Text** in the Screen Saver drop-down list, click the **Settings** button, and under **Display**, click **Text** and type  volcano on the Text line. Tweak the other options, click **OK** on 3D Text Setup and **OK** on Display Properties, and you'll be rewarded with an animated display of the names of famous volcanoes. |

## *Tips*  *(continued)*

| | |
|---|---|
| Interface | To install shortcuts in the Quick Launch toolbar, drag any shortcut, file, or folder icon over to the toolbar, and hover it over any two icons, and a vertical black line will appear to tell you where the shortcut will land. Slide over to your position of choice, drop the shortcut, and it becomes a Quick Launch button. (To remove an item from the Quick Launch toolbar, right-click it and select Delete from the Context Menu.) |
| Interface | A Context Menu shortcut to the **Open With** dialog is the fastest way to change the association of a file type. Left-click on a file icon or Explorer listing to select it, hold down the Shift key, right-click on the file, and you'll see an **Open With...** option that isn't usually there. (Unless you hold down Shift, this option won't appear.) In the **Open With** dialog, choose an application to open files of this type, make sure you've checked **Always use this program to open this type of file**, and click **OK**. |
| Interface | See if you like these two tweaks to make Windows more pleasant to work with: 1. Go to **Control Panel\Mouse**, click the **Pointers** tab, and set **Scheme** to **Windows Inverted**. These cursors look black, but they're actually far more interesting; they're complementary-colored and semi-transparent. (To see what we mean, glide the pointer over the blue title bar of the Mouse Properties dialog, with its white printing.) They're qualitatively more visible than the Windows Standard cursors, even if you don't turn their tails on. 2. Right-click on the Desktop, pick **Properties**, click the **Appearance** tab, drop the **Item** list, click Selected Items, use the arrow to drop the **Color** palette, and select bright red. (If you find bright red a bit garish, pick something more subtle, so long as we make our point that a dark blue highlight is silly.) We also tried bright yellow and liked it a lot; unlike the red, it's a transparent color and doesn't adjust the highlighted font. You may find that these two small changes will help to keep you focused. |
| Interface | Some of the oldest Windows tricks in the book—no, wait, this *is* the book—still work and are especially handy in emergencies. For example, the `Alt` `F4` hotkey still closes every running Windows app, after which you can use `Ctrl` `Esc` to pop up the Start Menu, an arrow key to reach Shut Down and to go to the appropriate button in the Shut Down Windows dialog, and `Enter` to close Windows. So, if you're working away and find yourself suddenly mouseless, you can bail out of Windows using nothing but the keyboard. |
| Interface | If your Start Menu is getting gnarly, you *don't* need to delete superfluous items through Taskbar Properties. Just navigate to the item you want to prune, right-click it and pick Delete. |
| Interface | If you're working at a command prompt and don't feel like typing the long path of a file or folder, you can drag-and-drop the file or folder into the DOS window, and *shazam!* its path appears at the cursor, even if you've already typed something at the prompt and are using the filename as a parameter. (Gotcha: For some reason this shifts the focus off the DOS window, so you'll have to click once in the window before you hit `Enter` on the command prompt.) |

## *Tips* *(continued)*

| | |
|---|---|
| Interface | To hide a Start menu item, navigate your way to the item, right-click on it, and select **Properties**. The default tab is Shortcut, but click **General** and check the **Hidden** checkbox. Click **OK** and it vanishes. Since this works even if you have **View all files** clicked in **View\Folder Options**, how do you get it back? Easy; *right*-click the Start Menu button, click Open, and navigate your way to the item, which will appear as a pale shadow of itself in the Start Menu folder. You can then unhide it through its Properties sheet as usual. |
| Interface | We've all been here—you're working away at a DOS prompt and suddenly need a folder window or an Explorer. Type one of these and hit Enter to get the matching result:<br>explorer  Explorer of the root folder, from anywhere.<br>explorer . Folder window of the current folder.<br>explorer .. Folder window of the folder one level above the current one.<br>   (Mini-tip: Using three dots doesn't extend this in Windows the way it did in some versions of DOS.)<br>explorer /e Explorer of the current folder. |
| Interface | Thanks to the final integration of Internet Explorer with Windows, global settings are easier than ever before. Want all your folders to be set up in exactly the same way? Open one folder, give it the perfect setup, drop the **View** menu, pick **Folder Options** and the **View** tab, and click the **Like Current Folder** button. The confirmation dialog says "(except for toolbars)," but we suppose this means only that toolbars in particular folders will continue to have extra buttons for special purposes. |
| Keyboard | In the same way that you can press Alt Tab to cycle through running programs, you can press Alt Esc to cycle through open windows. The windows will appear in open view the first time you press Alt Esc; each time thereafter, the window on top will be sent to the bottom of the stack and the next one will display. This only works with windows that are currently open on the Desktop; it doesn't open and display minimized windows on the Taskbar. |
| Keyboard | Alt Tab switches you to a new running application. Just release Tab to select. Alt Shift Tab moves backwards through the running applications. |
| Keyboard | Alt Spacebar opens the active window's Control menu. |
| Keyboard | Ctrl Esc opens the Start menu. |
| Keyboard | Print Screen *and* Shift Print Screen *and* Ctrl Print Screen copy a bitmap of the entire screen to the Clipboard. Alt Print Screen copies a bitmap of the active window to the Clipboard. Either way, you can then use Ctrl V to paste the image into Microsoft Paint or, better yet, Paint Shop Pro.<br>   (If you can tell a bitmap from a brickbat, you either have Paint Shop Pro or you need it. Browse to **http://www.jasc.com** for a time-limited demo of the world's best—and best-known—shareware graphics editor.) |
| Keyboard | World's fastest keyboard shortcut for opening the Properties dialog of an MS-DOS command prompt: Alt Spacebar ↑ Enter. You can let up on the Alt key after you hit the spacebar, but you don't have to. (That ↑ move to get from the top of a drop menu to the bottom works in lots of other places, too.) |

## *Tips* *(continued)*

| | |
|---|---|
| Keyboard | If you're in a dialog with multiple tabs, Ctrl Tab moves you one tab to the right, Ctrl Shift Tab moves you one tab to the left. |
| Keyboard | When you choose **Start Menu\Run**, you can use the drop list to select any item you've already used … but if your Run list is fairly long, there's an easier way. Type the first letter of the item you want to use, then press ↑ or ↓ to select an entry. *Note* that this may be a bogus tip; depending on the contents of your Internet Explorer history list, this technique can get URLs mixed in with your Run history. If this disappears from the retail version of Windows, it's a bug, and if not, it's a feature [demented laughter]. |
| Keyboard | You can use the Shift key to expedite closing child windows on your Desktop. For example, if you open **My Computer**, then open **Drive C** within that, and open a folder within that, holding down Shift and clicking the topmost window's title bar Close box will close all windows in the series. It won't close any other open windows, but unlike the **Minimize All Windows** option on the Taskbar Context Menu, it will actually close the target objects rather than minimizing them. |
| Windows Utility | Were you a fan of the old Windows 3.1 Macro Recorder? Did you try to run it in a later version of Windows and marvel at the resulting mess? There's never been a 32-bit upgrade, at least not from Microsoft, which is an obstacle to considerable possibilities for task automation in Windows 98. Luckily, the delightful MacroMagic ($30) and heavy-duty AutoMate ($40) from Unisyn make tremendous replacements. Download time-limited demos from `http://www.unisyn.com` and we'll bet you'll register one or the other. |

# Tools

Briefly put, Windows 98 will tell you more about your computer and its state of health than any other operating system within our experience. The flip side, of course, is that some of the information takes digging to find, and some of it, once found, requires substantial technical understanding. That has less to do with Windows and Microsoft than it does with the fact that, when a computer starts working erratically or not at all, your learning curve suddenly gets a lot steeper.

## Automatic Skip Driver

Default path: `Start Menu\Run\ASD`, but runs automatically

**Automatic Skip Driver** is a tool that prevents crashes at boot-time by skipping any automatically loaded driver that seems to be corrupt or missing. This is a considerable improvement over previous versions of Windows, in which a simple "Bad or missing WHATEVER.VXD" could consume an afternoon while you figured out which file it was, what .INI file it was called from, what directory it should be in, and whether it had been damaged or simply replaced with a weird version by somebody's uncouth application.

ASD lists any and all devices that have failed to start. Once you repair whatever's wrong with it (or them) you can enable any device that ASD has disabled, and Windows will try to use it normally on the next startup.

# Backup

Default path: `Start Menu\Programs\Accessories\System Tools\`
`Backup`

Over the years, as part of their operating systems, Microsoft has supplied backup software that has traditionally been the most frustrating, most counter-intuitive, least useful part of the package. You can kiss those days goodbye! The Microsoft Backup included in Windows 98 is a custom version of Seagate's (formerly Arcada's) workstation backup program, and will turn even an NT user green with envy.

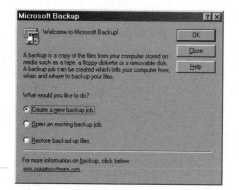

*Figure 15.1*

*Welcome screen*

The backup system is job-based, and the **Welcome** screen (Figure 15.1) gives you the choice of creating a new backup job, opening one that already exists, or restoring files.

**Main Screens.** From the Welcome dialog, make your selection or click **Close** to go directly to the **Backup** screen (Figure 15.2). The major options are:

- Back up all selected files, including all files, if you like.

- Back up files that are new or changed since the last job was run.

- Back up to a wide selection of devices, or to a hard disk file, with or without compression.

- Restore to original or alternate location.

- Restore with tailored relationship between **source** and **target** files.

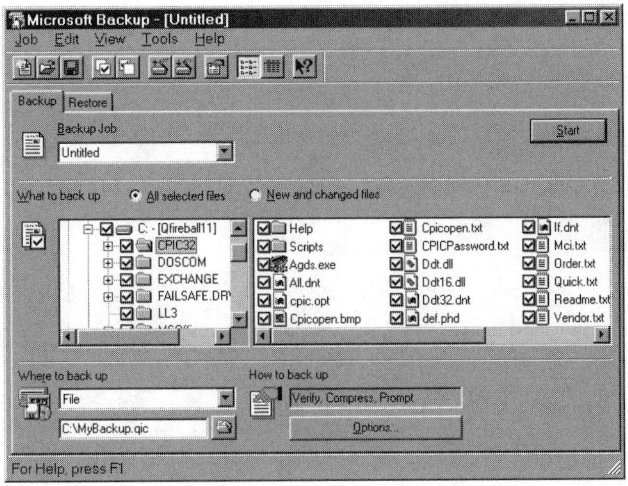

**Figure 15.2**

Backup screen

The **Restore** screen (Figure 15.3) lets you pick what device or file to restore from, what to restore from within that file or device, where to restore files to, and how and whether files from backup should replace files on disk.

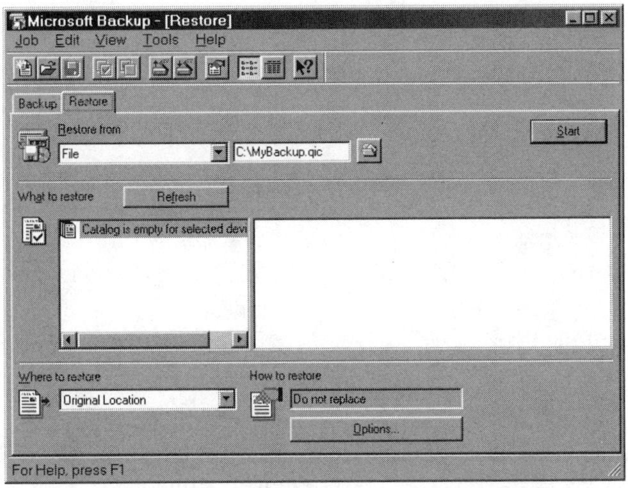

**Figure 15.3**

Restore screen

***Toolbar.*** The Toolbar (Figure 15.4) is common to both main screens and its buttons are: **New Backup Job**, **Open Backup Job**, **Save Job**, **Select items**, **Deselect items**, **Backup Wizard**, **Restore Wizard**, **Job Options**, **List**, **Details**, and **Help**.

**Figure 15.4**

Toolbar

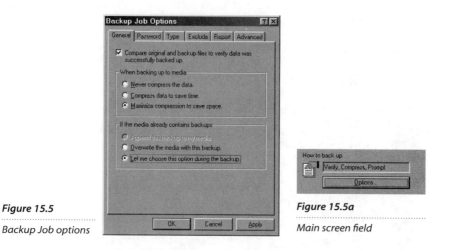

*Figure 15.5*

Backup Job options

*Figure 15.5a*

Main screen field

**Backup Options.**   The **General** tab of the Backup Job Options dialog (Figure 15.5) lets you pick compression options, choose between append and replace, and include a verify pass. The settings in this tab are summarized in the **How to back up** field of the main Backup screen (Figure 15.5a) so that you can see them without clicking **Options**.

The other tabs are:

- **Password** lets you protect the backup file with a password.

- **Type** lets you back up all files, or new and changed files differentially, or new and changed files incrementally. The explanations on the tab are lame and those in the right-click Help slightly less so, but basically, a *differential* backup means backing up anything that's changed since you backed up *everything,* and an *incremental* backup means backing up anything that's changed since you backed up *anything.* The Word from Kip and Fred is: Don't bother with scholastic distinctions. Buy the extra tapes and back up your whole disk every time, because at worst you end up with lots of copies of your files, which (trust us) is not a bad thing. On the other hand, if you're playing circus tricks with file priorities because your whole disk won't fit on one tape, you should be thinking about a new tape drive.

- **Exclude** lets you exclude file types from being backed up. You can pick any number of types to exclude, from a gargantuan list of extensions. If you can possibly think of a kind of file that *isn't* on the list and that you *don't* want to back up, you can define a **Custom type**—but the field accepts only extensions, not file wildcards.

- **Report** lets you pick the data types (files backed up, files not backed up, etc.) to be included in the report available from **Tools\Report\View** or **Tools\Report\Print**. The controls for unattended, invisible-to-user backup are also here.

### You've Got Another Copy

To put it bluntly, **neither Fred nor Kip has ever known a single person who restored the Windows Registry from tape and got away with it**. Unless your disk platters are now aluminum nachos, *always* try to restore the Registry from the most recent .CAB file in \WINDOWS\SYSBCKUP, using the Registry Checker tool. Remember that, if need be, you can restore the .CAB files from tape and let the Registry Checker work from those. If you don't have the .CAB files, you might almost be better off restoring from SYSTEM.1ST in the root folder, which will put your operating system back where it was when you last installed Windows—no pretty prospect, but not as much of a high-wire act as writing SYSTEM.DAT and USER.DAT directly from tape to disk.

We suppose, with a sigh, that there's no harm in checking this box and having your Registry backed up to tape. If you do, though, make darn sure that the matching box on the **Advanced** tab of Restore Options is *not* checked, and that you try other available methods of restoring your Registry before you use the file copies on tape as a last resort.

- **Advanced** means one thing and only one: Do you or do you not want to back up the Registry? Shrieking halt for the Dangerous sidebar, "You've Got Another Copy."

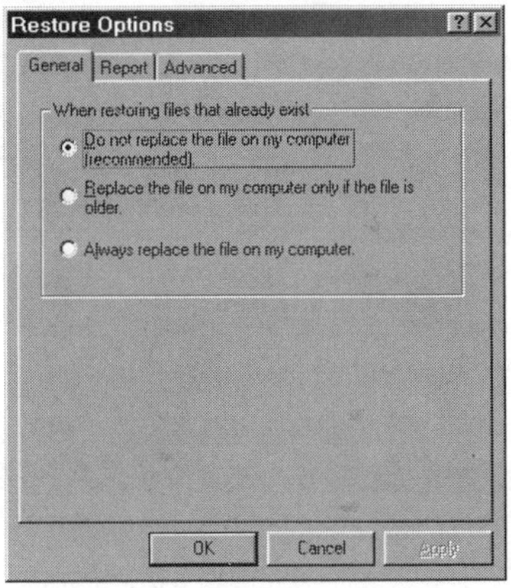

*Figure 15.6*

*Restore Job options*

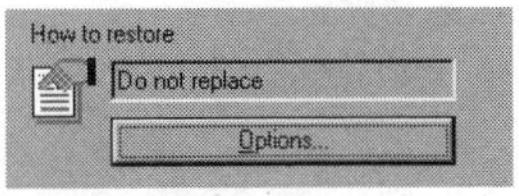

*Figure 15.6a*

*Main screen field*

**Restore Options.**  The **General** tab of the Restore Job Options dialog (Figure 15.6) lets you decide when and if files should be replaced from backup. The setting in this tab is repeated in the **How to restore** field of the main Restore screen (Figure 15.6a) so that you can see it without clicking **Options**.

The other tabs are:

- **Report** lets you pick the data types (files not restored, errors, warnings, etc.) to be included in the report available from **Tools\Report\View** or **Tools\Report\Print**—which is the same report as the Backup report, you're just picking more line items to include in it. The controls for unattended, invisible-to-user restore are also here.

- **Advanced:** see the Danger Zone above.

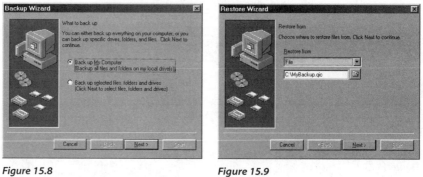

*Figure 15.7*

*Preferences*

**Preferences.** The **Preferences** dialog (Figure 15.7) offers three choices:

- **Show startup dialog...** means the Welcome Screen, and certainly you'll be able to uncheck this after the first few times you use Backup.

- **Back up or restore the Registry...** is, according to Microsoft, "(Recommended)," but we beg to differ! See above.

- **Show the number and size of files...** is a good choice, since it helps you estimate required disk space and time.

*Figure 15.8*

*Backup Wizard*

*Figure 15.9*

*Restore Wizard*

**Wizards.** Yes, on top of all this, you can start Backup and Restore Wizards (Figure 15.8–9) from the Toolbar or from the **Tools** menu.

These work the way most Wizards do—just keep picking the options you want and clicking **Next**.

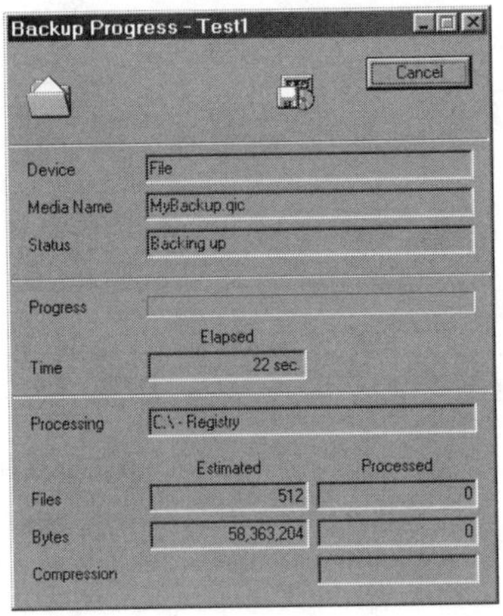

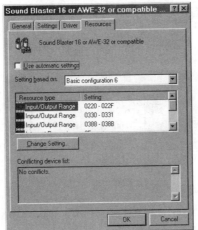

**Figure 15.10**

Backup Progress

**Job Progress.** When you've made your choices and started a backup or restore, this comprehensive Progress dialog (Figure 15.10) will let you know how it's running.

**Summary.** There couldn't be more difference—for the better—between this and prior versions of Microsoft Backup. Extensive features and a well-considered interface would make this a strong contender even as a shrink-wrapped utility. When you're looking at the cost of upgrading to Windows 98, figure Backup as $50 to $70 of the value.

## Basic Configurations

Default path: `Start Menu\Settings\Control Panel\`
`            System Properties\Device Manager\`
`            [devicename]\Properties\Resources`

Microsoft employs a two-pronged strategy to keep your installed devices from getting their setups intertwined beyond repair—and most of us, no doubt, can remember at least one time that happened. *Plug and Play* is an automatic "traffic cop" for devices that play by its rules. For devices that don't play by— or, more likely, don't know—the rules, you can use a template-based setup called *Basic Configurations* (Figure 15.11)

**Figure 15.11**

Example Resources tab

For any given device, Windows offers eight Basic Configurations, which vary in their editability, but are primarily designed to keep conflicts from straying too far out of hand. The **Use automatic settings** box defaults to checked and, if you leave it that way, is likely to minimize device conflicts; but in the days of the Great IRQ Drought (and its lesser-known cousin, the Drying Up of DMA) we can't take that for granted. Therefore, the Basic Configurations are available to let you hand-hack within a system.

Uncheck the box and let's look at the Basic Configurations for COM ports in Table 15-1.

## Table 15.1  Basic Configurations for Serial Ports

| Basic Config | IRQ Setting | Editable | I/O Setting | Editable |
|---|---|---|---|---|
| 0 | 4 | No | 03F8–03FF | No |
| 1 | 4 | Yes | 03F8–03FF | No |
| 2 | 3 | No | 02F8–02FF | No |
| 3 | 3 | Yes | 02F8–02FF | No |
| 4 | 4 | No | 03E8–03EF | No |
| 5 | 4 | Yes | 03E8–03EF | No |
| 6 | 3 | No | 02E8–02EF | No |
| 7 | 3 | Yes | 02E8–02EF | No |
| 8 | Variable | Yes | Variable | Yes |

The pattern manifests itself immediately. Basic Configuration 0, which is the standard configuration for COM1, has both IRQ and address range set immovably to the DOS defaults. This is the setting that in theory is least likely to conflict, so Windows tries to use it first.

If Basic Configuration 0 won't work with your hardware, you can try Basic Configuration 1, which keeps the address range—the parameter most likely to cause conflicts—where it was, but lets you set the IRQ to another value. Then, with Basic Configuration 2, we begin again; that's the "hardwired" configuration for COM2, but if you need to move the IRQ of COM2, you can go to Basic Configuration 3, and so on down the line.

Now, if you have a *lot* of COM ports and need to put one on IRQ5, you'll notice that none of the preset Basic Configurations offers any IRQ but 3 or 4. In that case, you can go to Basic Configuration 8 and set the IRQ to whatever you like.

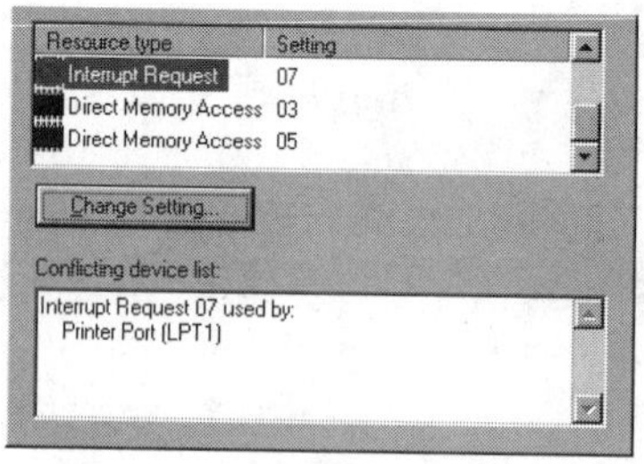

*Figure 15.12*

*Conflicted Device report*

You don't need to go that far. If one of the earlier Basic Configurations suits you "except for one little thing," then use that Basic Configuration and the **Change Setting...** button to move the setting that isn't working. If you produce a device conflict, the blue chip icon under **Resource Type** will be overlaid with the red international "forget this" symbol, and the **Conflicting device list** below it will report the problem (Figure 15.12)

It's certainly still possible to mess up your computer's Resource settings using the Basic Configurations, but it's far less likely than it was under DOS or Windows 3.*x*.

*Figure 15.13*

*Computer Properties dialog, IRQs*

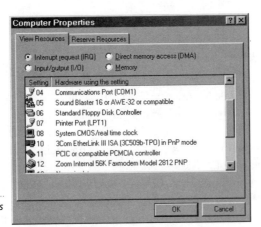

## Device Manager Computer Properties

Default path: **`Start Menu\Settings\Control Panel\System Properties\Device Manager\Computer\Properties`**

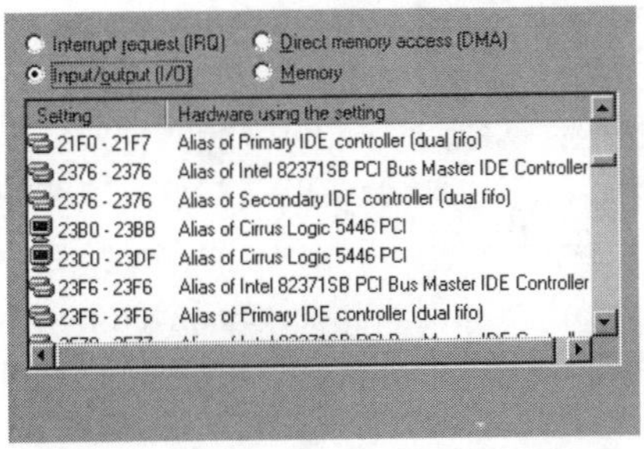

*Figure 15.14*

*Computer Properties dialog, I/O Ranges*

By highlighting the **Computer** entry at the top of the Device Manager tree and clicking the **Properties** button, you can open (oddly enough) the Computer Properties dialog, which gives you a whole pile of system information in four neatly organized stacks (Figure 15.13–15.16):

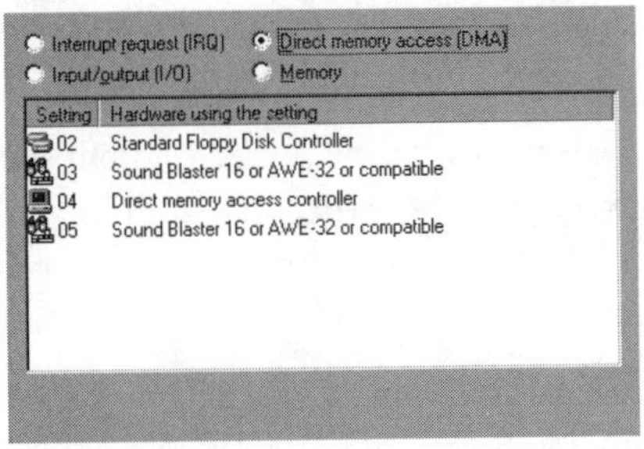

*Figure 15.15*

*Computer Properties dialog, DMA Channels*

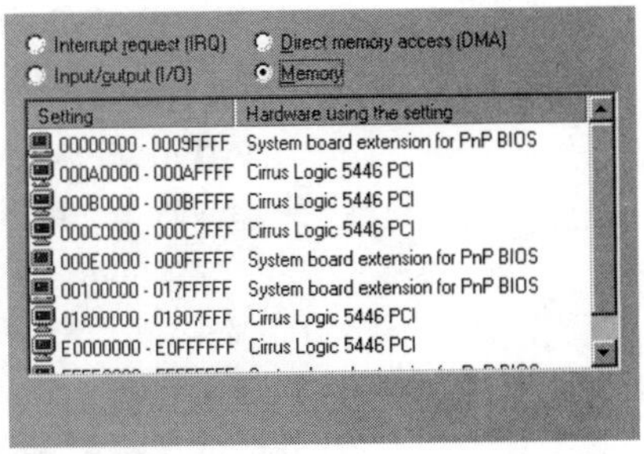

*Figure 15.16*

*Computer Properties dialog, Memory Addresses*

There are two aspects of these four screens that are less desirable than they might be. First, you can't *change* anything from here; this is just the facts. Second, the right-click help isn't particularly context-sensitive. On the other hand, this information is helpful, and the tidy organization makes it more so. Familiarity with the numbers and ranges presented here is a big help when you're custom-setting the Basic Configurations (above).

If you look on the Memory subscreen, though, you'll realize that another walk on the wild side is now paved over. In Windows 95, some of these memory ranges were likely to be flagged "In use by unknown device," which really meant *"Reserved for* use by unknown device," and often meant no device at all. If one was clever and daring, one could then capture that memory range with EMM386.EXE to return it to the overall memory pool. The supremacy of the Plug and Play BIOS has changed all that. As you can see in Figure 15.16, *all* the memory in our test box is under the control of either the Plug and Play BIOS, or the video BIOS. You don't get to pirate away any slivers.

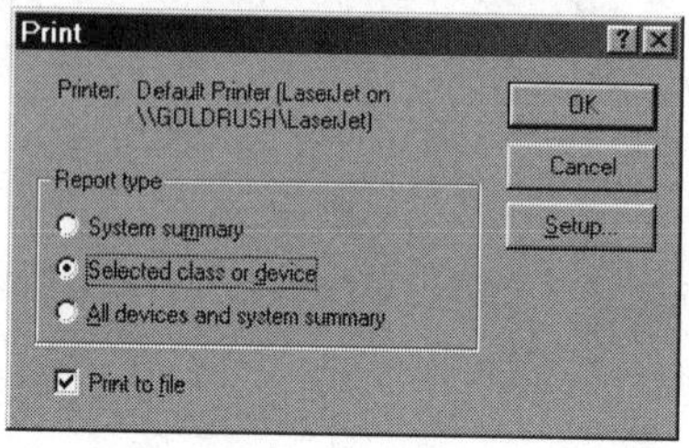

*Figure 15.16a*

*Device Manager Print dialog*

**Device Manager Report.** Just because almost every screen in Windows is saddled with a **Print...** button, don't underestimate the one in Device Manager. With slight effort, you can have a detailed, hardcopy report about any or all of your system's hardware setup; click **Print...** at the foot of the Device Manager tab and choose your report type (Figure 15.16a):

- The **System summary** prints a report organized by IRQs, I/O ports, memory ranges, and DMA channels, with a list of the hardware that uses each resource.

- **Selected class or device** lists resources and drivers used by the device or class you highlighted before you clicked Print.

- **All devices and system summary** prints a system summary and a device report for every piece of hardware that Device Manager considers a separable device. Fill your printer tray before you commit to this one, but it's an education.

- Unfortunately, **Print to file** here creates a file in DOS .PRN format that mixes text and printer control codes for deferred printing; there's no option to output ASCII text and save paper.

 You can get plain text reports with similar scope from the **File\Export** option of the System Information Utility (below).

# Inbox Repair Tool

Default path: `Start Menu\Programs\Accessories\System Tools\`
`Inbox Repair Tool`

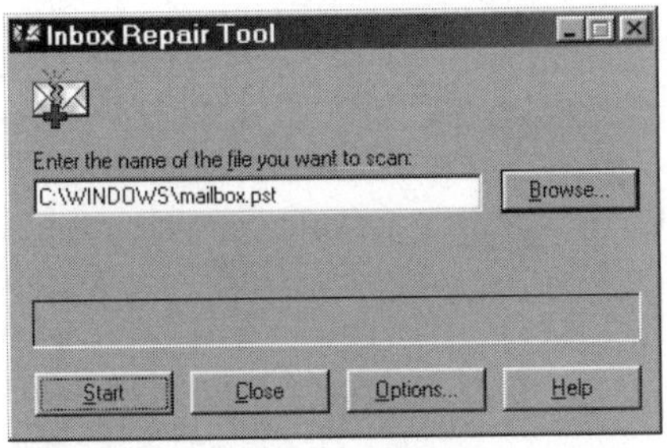

**Figure 15.17**

*Inbox Repair tool*

The **Inbox Repair Tool** (Figure 15.17) repairs your Outlook or Windows Messaging personal folders (*.PST) or your Internet Explorer offline folders (*.OST). As Microsoft tacitly admits, these files have a tendency to become corrupted and are not repairable by hand.

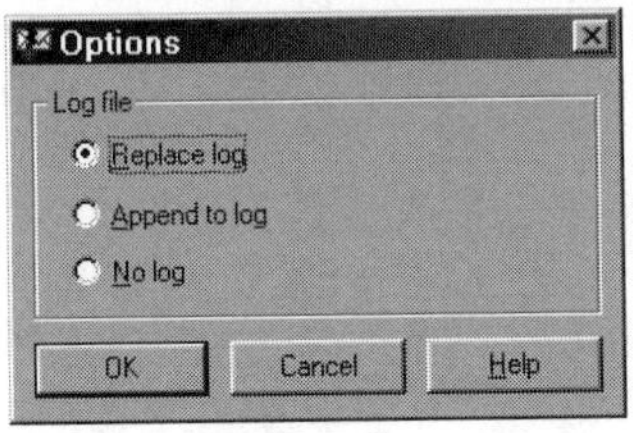

**Figure 15.18**

*Repair Logging options*

**Options.** Click the **Options** button (Figure 15.18) on the main screen to control repair logging. The default is **Replace log**, but as usual we recommend **Append to log**; patterns of repetition in log files can be useful in diagnosing problems, and if you need the disk space, you can always delete \WINDOWS\MAILBOX.LOG.

**Selecting.** Click the **Browse** button to select the file to repair (Figure 15.19), highlight it, and click **Open**.

**Repairing.** Click **Start** on the main screen and your file will be scanned quickly, unless you receive a tremendous number of faxes. When the scan is finished, this report (Figure 15.20) will report errors found, if any, and offer you the option of backing up the file before you repair it.

Click **Details** to review the file's problems; click **Repair** to finish the job.

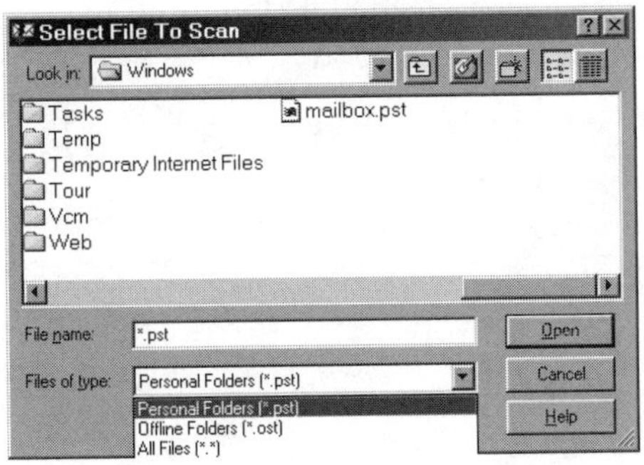

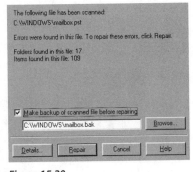

**Figure 15.19**

*Browse box with File type list*

**Figure 15.20**

*Problem report*

# MKCOMPAT (Make Compatible)

Default path: **Start Menu\Run\MkCompat**

We're just telling you about this so you'll know it's here. It helps with Windows 3.x programs *only,* not DOS and not 32-bit Windows.

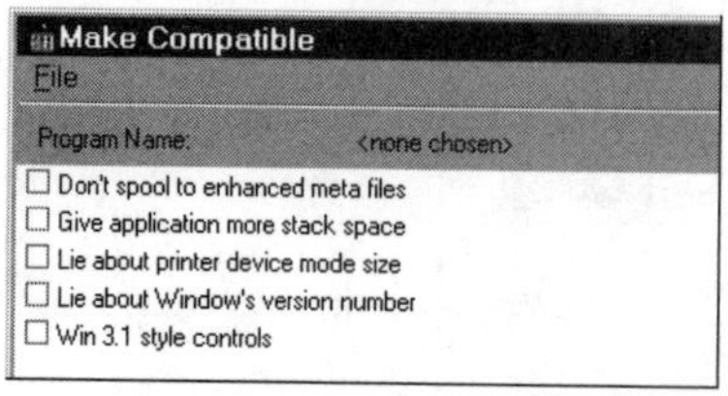

If you have a Win16 program that you desperately must run, *and* it absolutely won't, *but* you might know why, give MKCOMPAT (Figure 15.21) a shot before you grovel to the developer. Pull down **File**, click **Choose Program**, and pick the reluctant app from a Browse box. Some of the checkboxes will disappear because not all of them are applicable to any one program. Then check the rest and see if they help.

We won't even illustrate the **Advanced Options**, but put it this way—if you've ever wanted to ignore discardable segment attributes, lie about SetDIBits validation, or live without a HRGN 1, have fun. Some of MSCONFIG and some of Device Manager might be merely arcane, but this thing is in Sumerian. ("Wait!" Fred exclaims. "It's the dreaded Module Specific Hack!")

# Registry Checker

Default path: **Run\ScanReg**, but runs automatically

The Registry Checker tool, Windows 98's update of the old CFGBACK utility and—to an extent—of the Emergency Recovery Utility (ERU), has three functions:

- It runs automatically when your computer is restarted, and performs any needed repairs in background. It also creates a compressed single-file backup of your Registry, once a day.

- It can be launched from the DOS prompt (Figure 15.22) with the parameters in the screenshot:

**Figure 15.22**

Registry Checker

```
C:\WINDOWS>scanreg /?

Windows Registry Checker

Usage: SCANREG [/<option>]

<option>
    ?           : Displays usage.
    BACKUP      : Backup the registry and related system configuration files.
    RESTORE     : Choose a backup to restore.
    FIX         : Repair the registry.
    COMMENT="<comment>"
                : Adds the specified comment to the CAB file while backing up.
```

- It can be launched from the **\Start Menu\Run** prompt with any of those parameters *except Restore,* which can only be run from a command prompt.

Because Registry Checker serves as the safety net for the Registry itself, we discuss it in more detail in Chapter 17.

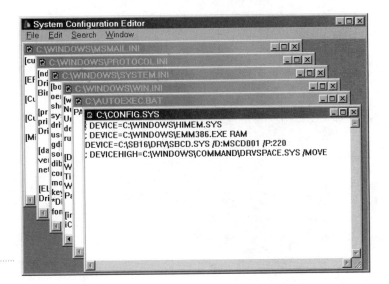

*Figure 15.23*

SysEdit

# SYSEDIT
Default path: `Run\SysEdit`

An invaluable oldie, **SysEdit**—or, to give it its formal title, the System Configuration Editor—lets you open one program and edit all the text files that control your computer (Figure 15.23). Typically these are \AUTOEXEC.BAT and \CONFIG.SYS in the root folder and \WIN.INI, \SYSTEM.INI, \PRO-TOCOL.INI, and \MSMAIL.INI in \WINDOWS. Since most of these are by definition smaller than 64K, you could open them one by one in Notepad, but SysEdit is a lot faster and more convenient to use. Unfortunately, its commands are still Notepad commands, thus at odds with most of the rest of Windows.

SysEdit opens with its windows cascaded, on the assumption that you'll want to pick the title bar of a single file. This is esthetically pleasant but doesn't help when you're saying "Drat, I thought that was in WIN.INI, maybe it's in SYSTEM.INI." When you're perusing more than one file, pull down the **Window** menu and click **Tile**; to edit the file, click the **Maximize** button, and to tile it back into place, click **Restore**.

 It would be handy if the **Search** function worked across all files, but in the version we have, it works haphazardly even in the highlighted file.

Pardon our being nervous, but please don't confuse SYSEDIT, the System Configuration Editor, with REGEDIT, the Registry Editor. If you need to edit the Registry, report to Chapter 17 on the double, and we'll guarantee you're not confining yourself to "Drat."

## System Configuration Utility

Default path: **Start Menu\Run\MSConfig**

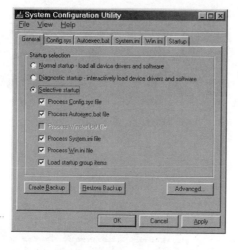

**Figure 15.24**

MSCONFIG

**General Tab.** Think of the System Configuration Utility (Figure 15.24) as SysEdit with major attitude. It's new, shiny, 32-bit, and (as far as we can tell) undocumented.

You can make durable settings in here that would otherwise require you to lunge for function keys while your computer booted. You can kill and revive your Startup group. Oh, and about that **Create Backup** button? Hit it and get an acknowledgement that says, "Your files have been backed up," thanks a lot! It backs up CONFIG.SYS, AUTOEXEC.BAT, WIN.INI and SYSTEM.INI to *.PSS.

**Startup Tab.** The **Startup** tab is probably the only place, and certainly the easiest place, to control loading of the "hidden" Startup items ordinarily loaded by Windows itself (Figure 15.25)

**Figure 15.25**

MSCONFIG Startup tab

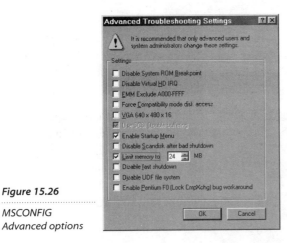

**Figure 15.26**

*MSCONFIG
Advanced options*

**Advanced Options.** The Trouble-shooting options in the **Advanced** dialog (Figure 15.26) are on the same level as the Device Manager File System Properties Troubleshooting options, but totally different and just as dangerous. Some of the checkboxes, like **EMM Exclude...** and **Limit memory to...** are tipoffs that this is a tool for hardware and software—mostly hardware—debugging.

The safest way to run this utility, if you do it without telephone support, is in conjunction with the Troubleshooters in Windows Help, which we discuss later in this chapter.

## System File Checker

Default path: `Start Menu\Programs\Accessories\System Tools\`
`            System File Checker`

A new and true great, the System File Checker (Figure 15.27) would earn its keep if it offered only what you see on the main screen. But there is far more here than the top layer suggests.

**Figure 15.27**

*System File Checker*

On the main screen there are two choices:

- **Scan files for errors** seems to do something like a thorough Scandisk on the system files, then build or update a file information database.

- **Extract one file from installation disk** lets you extract a file from the Windows CD, even if it's embedded in a .CAB file, and without messing with arcane utilities like EXTRACT or CABARC. (We *will* show you how to run EXTRACT, at the end of this section, but we hope you never need it.)

In our original install of the latest version of Windows 98 before press time, System File Checker was *not* installed as part of **Start Menu\System Tools**, which it should have been; but the name of the executable is SFC.EXE, and it's in \WINDOWS\SYSTEM. If you find that your Start Menu is SFC-impaired, you can drag a Shortcut into the Start Menu folder as usual.

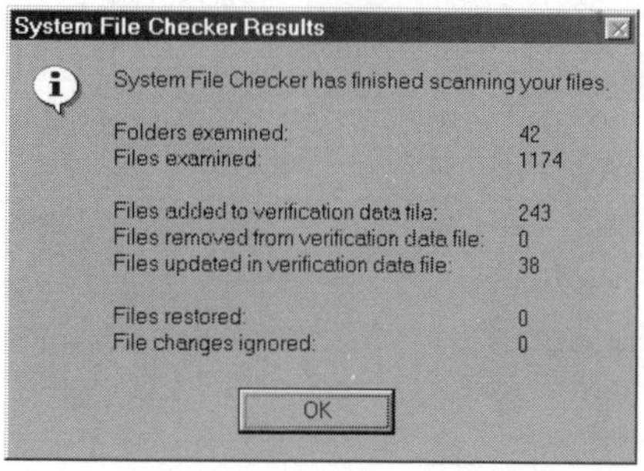

**Scan files.**  Just click **Start**. You'll get a progress bar under **Checking files...**, and a dialog when the scan is finished; click **OK** to end or **Details...** for a report (Figure 15.28)

The "verification data file" referred to in the report is \WINDOWS\DEFAULT.SFC, and contains a lot of information needed to verify file and relational integrity. (To begin with, Windows defines *system file* in such a way that it thinks it has over a thousand of them, which is scary in itself.) We'll say more about this when we discuss the **Advanced** tab.

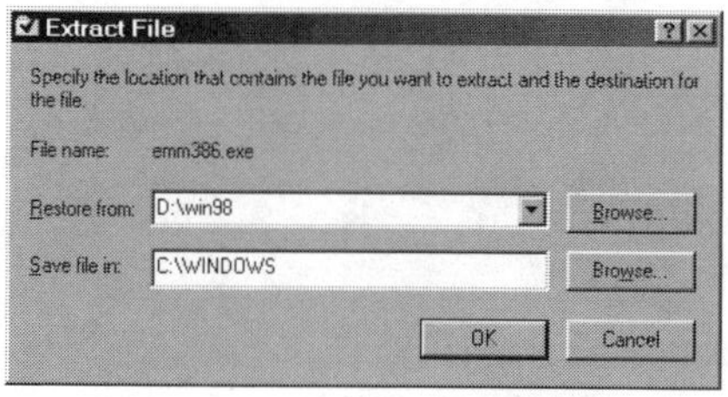

*Figure 15.28*

*System File Checker results*

**Extract one file...**  Click **Extract one file...** and fill in the name of any file on the Windows CD, then click **Start** and you'll get a dialog (Figure 15.29). Make sure that both paths are exactly right, since there's no **Search subfolders** checkbox on the **Restore from** field, and click **OK**.

*Figure 15.29*

*Extract File*

The file may be in the target folder already—for example, if you're extracting a good copy of the file over a damaged one—and, if so, you'll be prompted to either back it up or skip backup (Figure 15.30). If the file contains user information and builds up over time, we recommend that you keep a copy, even if you overwrite it with a Windows default; it may prove helpful when

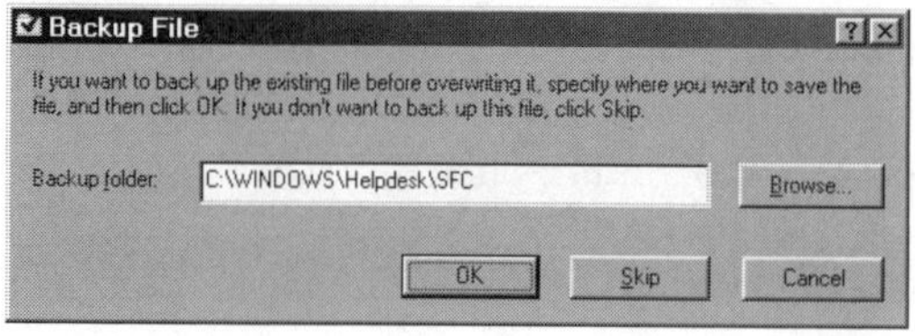

*Figure 15.30*

*Backup File*

you're trying to restore settings. If the file is an .EXE, a .DLL, or any other file that would have had no reason to change since your original Windows installation, then skip it, since there's no reason to leave corrupt or invalid files on your disk.

Click **OK** or **Skip**, and System File Checker will begin finding the file. When it does, you'll be told that the extraction was successful; if it doesn't, you'll be asked to pick a different **Restore from** location and try again.

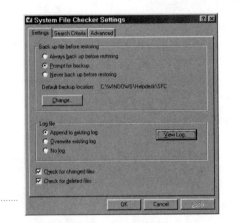

**Figure 15.31**

Settings tab

**Settings.** If you click the **Settings** button, you can get very specific about the way you want System File Checker to operate.

*Settings Tab.* The **Settings** tab (Figure 15.31) is about backing up replaced files, setting the scope of operations, and maintaining logs.

**Back up file before restoring** has three choices and a button:

- **Always back up before restoring** might be overkill. Certainly there are situations in which backing up can save you grief; for example, your version of a particular Windows system file might be newer than the one on your Windows CD, and it's much easier to retrieve a backup from the \SFC folder than it is to figure out where that newer, and now overwritten, copy of the .DLL came from in the first place. Use this option if you don't want to be bothered confirming each file to be backed up; if, after a while, you find that it's sticking you with tons of sludge in your \SFC folder, switch to **Prompt for backup** instead.

- **Prompt for backup** is the best balance, considering that there are some files you'll *always* want to back up and some you'll *never* want to back up, and that you'll probably be able to tell which are which.

- **Never back up before restoring:** Would we in a *million years* tell you to click this? Get real.

- **Change...** lets you browse for a new location for your backup file directory. We can imagine a couple of adept uses for this, like backing up each workstation's system files to a separate subfolder on a network server drive. (In the old phrase, "Only the paranoid survive ... disk crashes.") On the other hand, if you leave it at C:\WINDOWS\HELPDESK\SFC, you and the Microsoft hotline support person will both know where to find it.

**Log file** has three choices and a button:

- **Append to existing log** is the default and we like it, since you'll end up with a system file revision history that could really save your skin. The length of each appended log naturally varies with the number of changed files, but even if you haven't run SFC for a while, one run has a hard time adding more than 20KB.

- **Overwrite existing log** is a shortsighted choice at best.

- Anybody who would check **No log** would grease the rungs of a ladder.

- **View Log...** opens, in Notepad, one of the nicest of the Windows log files—organized by folder, in tabular format, richly commented, and not a cryptic line in it. If you're a standalone user, you'll be more than glad to have this, and any network manager will be dizzy with delight.

*File checks.* The **Check for changed files** and **Check for deleted files** checkboxes, if checked, give you a dialog something like this one (Figure 15.32a)

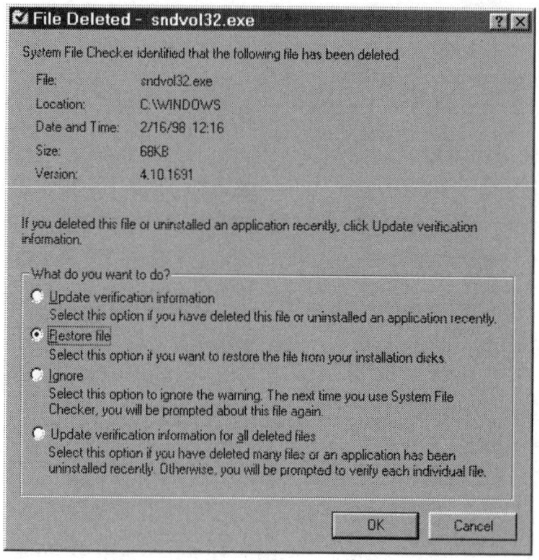

*Figure 15.32a*

*Check Changed or Deleted File dialog*

These dialogs warn you that during the current run of System File Checker, a file or files catalogued in \DEFAULT.SFC (or your designated verification data file) was missing or altered in some way. Four choices are really three:

- **Update verification information** and **...for all deleted files** say to Windows "Look, let's override the verification file with the current file listing on the disk, because I deliberately removed this program or these files, but the verification file doesn't reflect the changes." The verification file then gets updated to match the current folder directories. Click the button at the top to verify every change as it goes by; click the one at the bottom if all changes should be incorporated without any prompting.

- **Restore file** restores a file from the installation disk, but if you're restoring several, you have to confirm the replacements one at a time.

- **Ignore** lets you ignore the warning without changing anything—but only for this file and only for this pass of System File Checker.

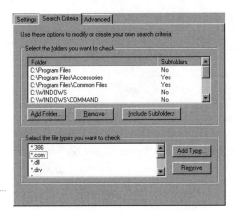

*Figure 15.32b*

*Search Criteria tab*

***Search Criteria Tab.*** The **Search Criteria** tab (Figure 15.32b) lets you reshape the definition of a Windows system file that underlies the System File Checker's operation. If you look carefully here, you'll realize why Windows thinks it has so many system files, but the standard definition isn't unreasonable; for example, checking \PROGRAM FILES but not its subfolders is smart, since many commercial and shareware applications install themselves in subfolders of \PROGRAM FILES, but it obviously isn't productive or necessary to check every one of those folders against a standard reference. Checking \PROGRAM FILES\ACCESSORIES and \PROGRAM FILES\COMMON FILES makes more sense, because Windows largely reserves those subfolders for its own system and utility software. Of the \WINDOWS folders that are checked, the only one that seems superfluous is **\Downloaded Program Files**, which are "reusable" but space-hogging Java and ActiveX controls; it's bad enough to have them hanging around, much less spend time verifying them.

Invoking these options is straightforward; **Add Folder** opens a Browse box, **Add Type** opens a single-line dialog, and any **Remove** asks you for confirmation to remove the folder, type, or subfolder. You can **Include** (all) **Subfolders** of a folder without confirming, but if you want to include some subfolders and not others, you have to select them individually.

When you confirm to Remove a folder, type, or subfolder, you can choose to "keep the information" so that current object entries remain in \DEFAULT.SFC even though that object is no longer checked. This is one way of keeping your \DEFAULT.SFC benchmarked to a particular date and time; another way, of course, is to save a copy and point to it (below)

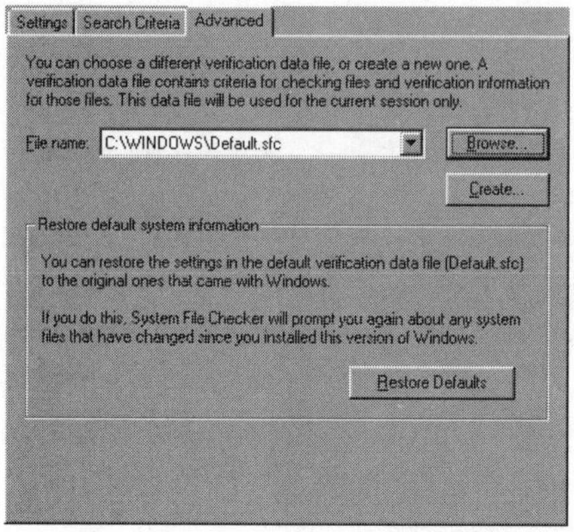

**Figure 15.32c**

Advanced tab

*Advanced Tab.* The **Advanced** tab (Figure 15.32c) gives you tools for verification file management. You can create other verification files (system state files) besides the Windows \DEFAULT.SFC, and choose from among them with the **File name** drop-down list.

Our attitude toward this is that, if you're going to use the System File Checker as a system (or network client) management tool, you should take a few minutes to do it right. As soon as you install Windows, create a verification file called \CURRENT.SFC; use that file for updates, leaving \DEFAULT.SFC as a benchmark. Then, whenever you need a reading on everything that's happened to a particular computer since Windows was installed, you can run a file check against \DEFAULT.SFC rather than against the updated \CURRENT.SFC. If you need more granularity you might create a \MONTHLY.SFC, \WEEKLY.SFC, and so on.

Windows makes this strategy easy. With the **Restore defaults** button, you can "jump" \DEFAULT.SFC back to your Windows installation, by overwriting it with the copy on the Windows CD. If your \DEFAULT.SFC is damaged and you don't want to go back to the dawn of time, there's a backup in the same folder with \DEFAULT.SFC, called \DEFAULT.SF0.

## *What Windows CD?*

Okay. When you bought your computer, you either got a Windows CD or you didn't.

If you *didn't*, here's a tip: Microsoft says that any OEM computer sold without a Windows CD has to have a complete set of the Windows .CAB files installed in a folder called \WINDOWS\OPTIONS\CABS.

If you *did*, the Windows .CAB files are in the \WIN98 folder on the CD, and we fervently recommend that you copy the entire contents to a matching \WIN98 folder on your hard disk—unless your operating system folder is already \WIN98, in which case call it something like \WINCABS.

Now, whenever you're running Add New Hardware or the System File Checker and Windows whistles for the CD, you can point the file scanner to your .CAB file folder instead—insuring that you don't have to dig up the CD, and making the install much faster. Also, if you need to extract files in a total emergency and your CD drive is comatose, you can use the .CAB files on your hard disk and the copy of EXTRACT.EXE on the Windows Emergency Disk to wiggle free of disaster.

**Extract, If You Must.** If you ever need to extract one or more Windows files from a .CAB file and you can't do it with System File Checker, here's how to do it at the command prompt. We'll reproduce the parameter text, and annotate it because some of it doesn't mean what it says.

EXTRACT [/Y] [/A] [/D | /E] [/L *dir*] *cabinet* [*filename* …]

EXTRACT [/Y] *source* [*newname*]

EXTRACT [/Y] /C *source destination*

| | |
|---|---|
| *cabinet* | Cabinet file (contains two or more files). |
| *filename* | Name of the file to extract from the cabinet. Wild cards and multiple filenames (separated by blanks) may be used. |
| *source* | Compressed file (a cabinet with only one file) *Note* that if a single file begins in one .CAB file, completely fills a second one, and ends in a third one, the second .CAB file will appear to DOS to be empty. |
| *newname* | New filename to give the extracted file. If not supplied, the original name is used. |
| /A | Process ALL cabinets. Follows cabinet chain starting in first cabinet mentioned (yeah, right; see below). |
| /C | Copy source file to destination (to copy from DMF disks, which are the compressed Diamond Media Format floppies). |
| /D | Display cabinet directory (use with filename to avoid extract). |
| /E | Extract (use instead of *.* to extract all files). |
| /L *folder* | Location to place extracted files (default is current directory). |
| /Y | Do not prompt before overwriting an existing file. |

This would be fine, except that the /A switch does *not* "follow the cabinet chain starting in [the] first cabinet mentioned." The .CAB files are, in order:

MINI.CAB (the "zeroth" .CAB)

PRECOPY1.CAB and PRECOPY2.CAB

CATALOG3.CAB

BASE4.CAB and BASE5.CAB

NET6.CAB through NET10.CAB

DRIVER11.CAB through DRIVER22.CAB, and

WIN98_23.CAB through WIN98_67.CAB. Your mileage may vary, but we don't imagine that the sequence of the .CAB files in the retail version will be too far off this.

Now, let's say we want to put good old EMM386.EXE in the \WINDOWS folder. First we have to find out what .CAB it's in, and that means getting a directory. So if we take Microsoft's directions as gospel, we can assume that at the command prompt we would type

```
extract /a /d .\win98\mini.cab emm386.exe
```

and EXTRACT would list out all the .CAB files starting with MINI.CAB, until it got to the last one. But no! That reads MINI.CAB *only*. Let's try

```
extract /a /d .\win98\precopy1.cab emm386.exe
```

which reads *only* PRECOPY1.CAB and PRECOPY2.CAB. Keep going with

```
extract /a /d .\win98\catalog3.cab emm386.exe
```

which reads *only* CATALOG3.CAB. Ah, sigh …

```
extract /a /d .\win98\base4.cab emm386.exe
```

which takes off and reads all the .CAB files in order, ending with WIN98_67.CAB; but of course, the location of EMM386.EXE scrolled off the screen before we caught it. Now to discover that, unlike almost *every* other DOS program that produces more than one screenful of output, EXTRACT lacks a /p switch to pause at the foot of each screen. With a sigh for progress we type

```
extract /a /d .\win98\base4.cab emm386.exe|more Enter
```

and, hitting Enter after each -- More --, we reach EMM386.EXE in
WIN98_39.CAB. Eureka! All we need to remember now is that we want
to put this file in C:\WINDOWS and we're not on drive C:, so we point to
the specific .CAB file, ditch the /a switch because we don't need to read
every .CAB file and the /d switch because we don't want a directory this
time, add the /l switch with the copy output path, get rid of the |more because
there's no point in pausing, and the final syntax is

```
extract /l c:\windows .\win98\win98_39.cab emm386.exe Enter
```

If the file is already in the folder, DOS will ask for confirmation with

```
Overwrite c:\windows\emm386.exe (Yes/No/All)?
```

but if you want to forestall that, you can add the /y switch in the original
command line, right after the extract and before the /l.

Now, why go through all this? Because it is possible even for Windows 98,
as spiffy and complex as it is, to crash for lack of one file—or because one
file is corrupt. At some point, Windows should manage to tell you which file
is bogus. When that happens, this is probably your quickest way home:

Boot with your Windows Emergency Disk. (You don't have a Windows
Emergency Disk? My, my. We'll see you in a few minutes.)

Install the real-mode CD-ROM driver.

Finish booting into Safe Mode Command Prompt Only.

Put the Windows 98 CD in the drive, visualize victory, and log over to the CD.

When the CD drive comes up, use the EXTRACT command as outlined
above to overwrite the corrupt file with a fresh copy from the CD.

Boot again. You might come up automatically in GUI Safe Mode because
you didn't boot normally the time before, but with luck, one more boot will
fix that.

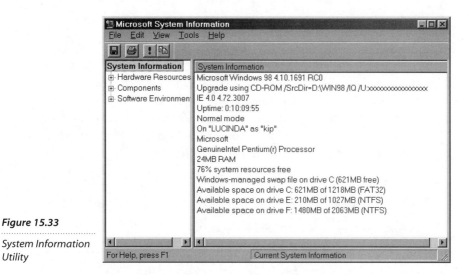

*Figure 15.33*

*System Information
Utility*

# System Information Utility

Default path: **Start Menu\Programs\Accessories\System Tools\
 System Information**

 Where do you go if you want to know everything about your system setup? Well, take the quick tour of Device Manager, SYSEDIT, REGEDIT, and maybe Microsoft Office System Info, with a yellow pad on your knee … or cruise over to System Tools and fire up the Microsoft System Information tool (Figures 15.33–36). All you crave is here.

Besides dividing the system into three segments—**Hardware Resources**, meaning the pool of interrupts, channels and addresses from which all hardware on the bus must draw; **Components**, meaning devices; and **Software**

System Information
 ⊟ Hardware Resources
   — Conflicts/Sharing
   — DMA
   — Forced Hardware
   — I/O
   — IRQs
   — Memory
 ⊞ Components
 ⊞ Software Environment

*Figure 15.34*

*Hardware tree*

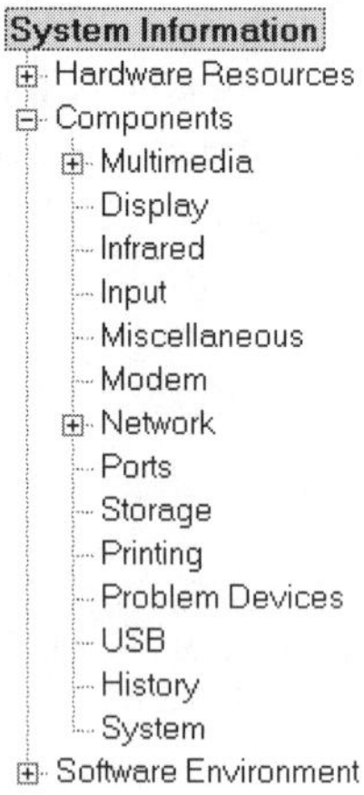

System Information
 ⊞ Hardware Resources
 ⊟ Components
   ⊞ Multimedia
   — Display
   — Infrared
   — Input
   — Miscellaneous
   — Modem
   ⊞ Network
   — Ports
   — Storage
   — Printing
   — Problem Devices
   — USB
   — History
   — System
 ⊞ Software Environment

*Figure 15.35*

*Component tree*

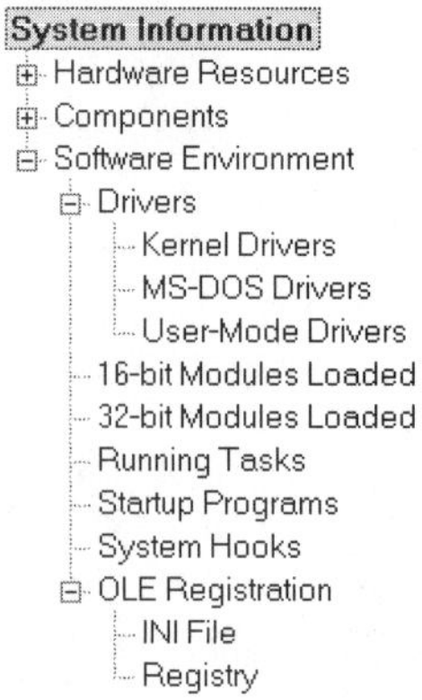

System Information
 ⊞ Hardware Resources
 ⊞ Components
 ⊟ Software Environment
   ⊟ Drivers
     — Kernel Drivers
     — MS-DOS Drivers
     — User-Mode Drivers
   — 16-bit Modules Loaded
   — 32-bit Modules Loaded
   — Running Tasks
   — Startup Programs
   — System Hooks
   ⊟ OLE Registration
     — INI File
     — Registry

*Figure 15.36*

*Software tree*

**Environment**, meaning (it would seem) every block of code resident in memory—the System Information Utility slices its presentation into three dimensions, and lifts itself entirely out of the ordinary.

With the System Information Utility we can examine the cosmos of Windows, and in itself this is nothing very new; we can do the same with REGEDIT or other tools. But with REGEDIT we frown at a murky, star-spattered night sky and wonder if, finally, there is any organization to it, while with the System Information Utility, we sit at the eyepiece of a telescope and bring a confined region into exact focus.

The flip side of this is that, naturally, trying to document the System Information Utility exhaustively would forfeit the whole point. It would be like skimming this whole book the night before a computer-science final, or printing hard copy of HKEY_LOCAL_MACHINE. So let's demonstrate it properly by using it appropriately—as crosshairs on a single component.

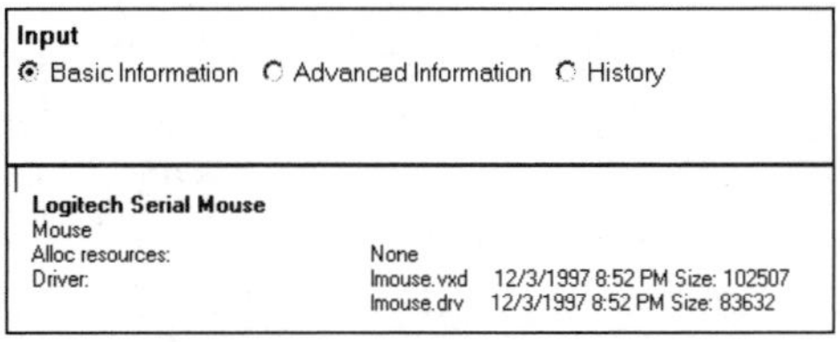

*Figure 15.37*

*Logitech Mouse basic information*

**Basic Information.** Our gray-tailed pointer's device type, allocated resources, and driver filenames, dates, times, and sizes—the filesystem's equivalent of name, rank and serial number. Certainly nothing we haven't seen (or at least looked for) before, but it's convenient to have everything in one place (Figure 15.37).

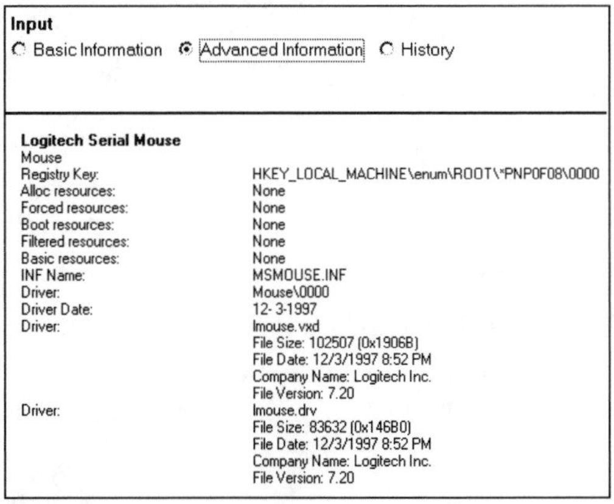

*Figure 15.38*

*Logitech Mouse Advanced information*

**Advanced Information.** One click to the right (Figure 15.38) and the alpha geeks are sprawled and coughing! What in heaven's name is a "filtered resource?" Just as well a mouse doesn't have one. But with the inclusion of the Registry enumerator, we cross a line into serious territory. From now on you won't have to switch windows between REGEDIT and another database viewer, or flip (a grave misnomer) from one part of REGEDIT to another, to examine the overlap between Registry and non-Registry information. Now we begin to understand the greatest strength and purpose of the System Information Utility; its ability to clarify relationships.

Also note the use of statistics culled from whole sheaves of Properties tabs. How do you like having driver version numbers without digging for them? Would it be enlightening to know, for example, that somebody's installation routine had replaced a driver with an older one?

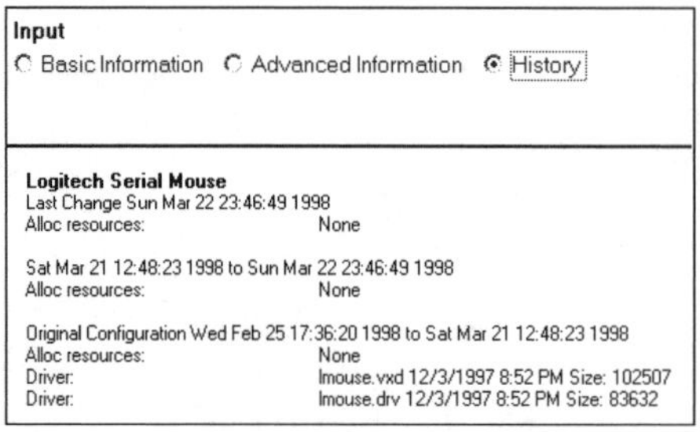

**History.** Here (Figure 15.39) the Utility turns on its axis to examine a dimension, change over time, that could never be examined before. Is this, as it must be, the database that also supplies working knowledge to the System File Checker? We look at what Windows knows and has known, and emerge with new faith that, yes, it all coheres.

*Figure 15.39*

*Logitech Mouse history*

**Output Formats.** The System Information Utility offers a rich selection of output formats. Select a branch of the tree and use **File\Save** to save to MSInfo (*.NFO) format that the Utility can reopen; use **File\Export** to save to ASCII text; or use **File\Print** to send output to the printer. We think that, if you're going for hard copy, you might want to Export first and print a selection—the Export text file for our entire test system (which the Help laughably refers to as a "snapshot") is 230KB, and that's without any formatting. Yo, Microsoft—are you *really* suggesting we fax that to somebody? To you, maybe?

**Tools Menu.** From the **Tools** menu you can run many of the other system interrogation and repair tools, including but not limited to the System File Checker, Registry Checker, Skip Driver Agent, MSCONFIG, and Scandisk.

**System Information and the Registry.** The System Information Utility may be just too ambitious to use routinely. You might end up using it on weekends and Device Manager on weekdays, so to speak. But its very ambition signals a new philosophical departure for Windows.

Until now, the only people who *could* know *everything* about Windows were the REGEDIT commandos, who spoke a strange dialect and necessarily put their computers at risk. And even they settled for the cold comfort of knowing only *anything* about Windows, and not *everything,* because—like all adepts—at last they learned that a fully extended cosmology was unknowable. John Woram, the author of a particularly fine book about the Windows 95 Registry, has said that much of his writing about Windows has fallen into two categories; either it was about the Registry, or it bore some relation to reality. As we'll see in Chapter 17, *this does not imply that the Registry is not real.* The Registry is so real that, without it, 32-bit Windows is demolished; but, in many ways, it resists definable relationship to other real things. This is why Windows experts, like physicists and astronomers, make countless cross-connecting leaps of faith that seem to defy intellectual gravity.

Using the System Information Utility, you can learn in clear progressions the lessons that the Registry would show you opaquely, at best. You can, if you'll pardon the pun, stay in real mode and examine the whole map. System Information, if you need it and can use it, is a revolutionary demystification of the Windows fundamentals.

## Tweak UI

Default path: `Start Menu\Settings\Control Panel\Tweak UI`

Ah, TweakUI! As you slowly realize what this densely packed little grenade is capable of, you'll understand why Microsoft has always professed ambivalence about it—one minute saying "You really should install this, it's so cool," and the next minute saying "This was written by some of our torn-T-shirt crowd in their so-called spare time, and we're giving it away because we'd never have the nerve to sell it." Both statements partake of the truth; neither one does it justice.

If TweakUI (TweakUserInterface) were to shed its cutesy name and be called AutoRegistryHack, its purpose would be clearer. In that vast wildland called the Registry, thousands of key values can be reset to produce tiny changes in the way Windows looks and works. Registry hacks are easily described and understood, among people who know the shorthand, and these cool twiddles got all over the Net … from whence we ourselves collected some of them to put in Chapter 17. This meant lots of people were using REGEDIT, which had to give Microsoft the willies. REGEDIT is nobody's toy.

TweakUI amounts to a truce between patriarchal Microsoft and the black-clad REGEDIT outlaws. It packages the Registry's interface settings in a tabbed dialog that serves up dozens of neatly presented hacks, while it insulates the Registry itself from damage. It retains a roguish flavor and hands over quite a bit of the fun.

Some TweakUI settings can be made to work for multiple users on a single computer, and the right-click Help calls these "per-user settings." If a tweak isn't called a "per-user setting," assume it can only be made to work for a single user.

The layers of TweakUI hide a huge variety of functions. Luckily, the context-sensitive right-click Help is quite good. So, since we can't spare a chapter to devote to this, we're going to present every tab and tell you what we think it's about, but not anatomize every checkbox. Discovery, after all, is at the heart of play.

Some tweaks require you to reboot your computer after they're applied, and some don't. In theory, if the changes will only take effect after a reboot, TweakUI will tell you so. Actually, we find that *most* of the TweakUI hacks need a reboot to work, so if you try clicking **Apply** and then **OK**, and if the tweak still "doesn't take," proceed to Shut-Down-and-Restart.

 And some of them don't work anyway. TweakUI is not "Your mileage may vary;" it's "This may or may not be gasoline."

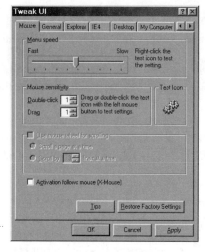

**Mouse Tab.** TweakUI starts with the **Mouse** tab (Figure 15.40) and goes on, and on …

**Mouse** is about the "feel" (the speed, mostly) of the pointer interface. **Menu speed** adjusts a Registry key that has a tremendous range, but in our most recent version of Windows 98, the speed at which the menus expand doesn't seem to vary much— if at all. **Use mouse wheel for scrolling** is grayed out unless you have a Microsoft Intellimouse (or compatible?) with a built-in wheel for screen scrolling; if you do, you can control how many screen lines are scrolled with each "click" of the wheel. TweakUI doesn't offer much here that isn't already in the Intellimouse Control Panel.

**Activation follows mouse**, better known as **X-Mouse**, attempts to welcome immigrants or guest workers into the Windows community. When you're using Windows with a mouse, you have to click on a task's window to bring it into the foreground, also known as "bringing it into focus" or "turning the title bar blue." People accustomed to a rival interface called **X Windows**, which runs on Suns and other UNIX boxes, tend to think this is wacky; for them, the task in focus is the task the mouse pointer is over, and as the mouse pointer slides around the screen, the focus moves with it. If you really like this effect, try checking the box on the General tab called **X-Mouse AutoRaise**, which goes one step further and "floats" the window touched by the pointer to the top of any stack of overlapping windows. We use Suns once in a while and like them, but … we bet you'll try this for half an hour and turn it off. Everything feels too slippery!

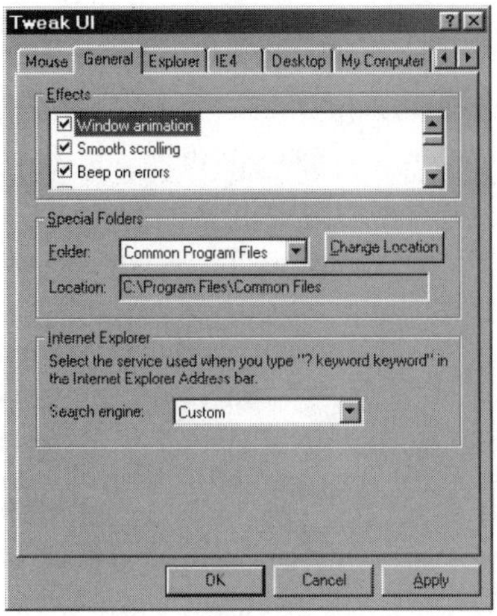

Figure 15.41

TweakUI General
tab

**General Tab.**  The **General** tab (Figure 15.41) is really a "Misc" tab and manages various special effects, custom folder locations, and the way Internet Explorer handles fetches from search engines.

You'll especially like the **Effects** tab if you find the latest Windows scrolling and animation effects distracting, as many people do; you can turn most of them off. **Mouse hot tracking effects**—which should be on the Mouse tab, but TweakUI has minimal consistency—turns off those consarn Tooltips, but only in the operating system, not in applications. And **Menu underlines**, rather than relating to Web browsing as you might think, turns off the underlines under letters that alert you to [Alt]-key shortcuts ... who in their right *mind* ...

**Special folders** lets you move folders that Windows ordinarily expects to find in specific locations, like Program Files, My Documents, Send To, and even the Desktop. We see a lot more wrong than right in principle about this, especially because you might have told Windows about hacking the standard folder hierarchy, and *not* told your applications; but TweakUI doesn't care much about cause and effect.

**Internet Explorer** lets you pick the Internet search engine that gets queried when you type ? *keyword keyword* in the Address Bar. This is truly good, because if you set this to point to your favorite bit-hound, you free up your Home and Search toolbar icons for whatever else you like. (Incidentally, this isn't on the **IE4** tab because—for whatever it's worth in Windows 98—it works in both IE4 and IE3.)

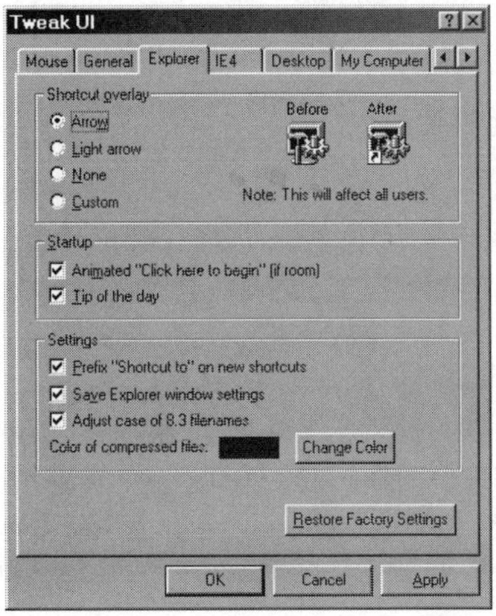

**Explorer Tab.**  **Explorer** (Figure 15.42) is home to one of TweakUI's best-known effects, the muck-with-the-Shortcut hack. It's too bad that, having played with the alternatives, we like the stodgy standard corner arrow best, but: **Light arrow** looks too much like some tiny piece of screen junk that begs to be cleaned off. **None** should be avoided because, if Shortcut icons and file icons

Figure 15.42

TweakUI Explorer
tab

look exactly alike, there's risk of deleting a file when you only meant to delete a Shortcut. And **Custom**, if misused, threatens to paste the identical icon onto every Shortcut. The logic behind the selection of icons in TWEAKUI.CPL is unfathomable; some of them are refugees from SHELL32.DLL.

The two checkboxes in **Startup** are, in our view, tongue-in-cheek. For the ghastly animated Start button cattle-prod, a box that defaults to *checked?* But the Help text that begins "Uncheck the … box to suppress the cheery 'Click here to begin' message …" suggests that the programmer or help author was of the same mind. In any case, there's an easier way to get rid of the Start animation; put *anything* in the Startup group. The **Tip of the day** checkbox is more useful in the real world because, in our experience, new users find those helpful for the first few days.

**Settings** are a much better deal. Thank you, TweakUI, for giving us a way to turn off **Shortcut to…** globally; the boxed-arrow overlay serves the same purpose and doesn't take up screen space. (Icon titles' dirty secret is that, if you have screen fonts set larger than Small and don't edit the defaults, the title can gobble more room than the icon; Figure 15.43 shows an egregious example from Guess Who.)

**Figure 15.43**

[Microsoft®
Network]™ icon,
sign up today!

**Save Explorer window settings** is opaque but useful. Leave this checked to save the state of open folders—or folders opened from within Explorer, at least—when you shut down; uncheck it to close and store folders, leaving the Desktop clean at your next logon. Wouldn't it be nice if your computer would do this to your real desk?

**Adjust case…** actually *preserves* case in the DOS (8.3) names of files that also have long filenames. In other words, **New Folder** turns into **NewFol~1**, not NEWFOL~1.

**Color of compressed files** can give your folder directories an NT-ish look. The crowning touch if you're running DriveSpace and a custom Display Properties Appearance!

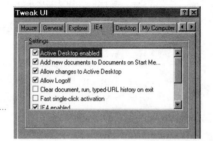

**IE4 Tab.** IE4 (Figure 15.44) allows both major and minor tweaks to the way IE4 operates, many of which are available from other menus, like Active Desktop.

**Figure 15.44**

*TweakUI Internet Explorer 4 tab*

There is one IE4-paranoia item here, **Clear document, run, typed-URL history on exit**, which you may find useful if you … ah … engage in privately motivated Web browsing while at your day job. On the other hand, a checkbox for **Allow logoff** is frightening; imagine a world in which you were on the Net and couldn't leave! Or are we just getting old?

**Desktop Tab.** **Desktop** (Figure 15.45) makes it easier to create icons on the Desktop and in folders.

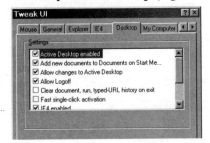

The curious thing about this dialog is TweakUI's contention that some icons not already created by the Windows installation (will an ActiveX cache folder improve your life *that* much?) can be placed in folders, and some only on the Desktop; right-click will gener-

**Figure 15.45**

TweakUI Desktop tab

ally tell you which options are possible for each icon. We'll leave you to play with these, pausing only to note that, if you ask us, most of them don't work.

**My Computer Tab.** **My Computer** (Figure 15.46) *only* controls whether a

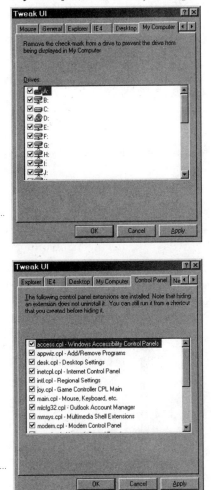

drive is displayed as an icon in My Computer. It gives you a checkbox for each real or imagined drive up to LAST-DRIVE=Z set by IO.SYS. Whether a drive is visible in My Computer has no relation to its mapping or connection in Network Neighborhood.

When you watch My Computer and uncheck one of these boxes for a valid drive, the icon vanishes, poof! (Remember that Registry changes take effect immediately, which is one reason REGEDIT is such a loaded gun.) If you want the icon back, though, you'll have to recheck its box and Restart.

**Figure 15.46**

TweakUI My Computer tab

**Control Panel Tab.** **Control Panel** (Figure 15.47) makes the icon of an installed Control Panel disappear from the Control Panel folder. The .CPL file remains intact and you can still run a concealed Control Panel from any Shortcut you created before you unchecked the box in TweakUI.

Because the checkboxes in TweakUI are sorted by .CPL filename, and the ones in the Control Panel folder are ordered by icon title, you may have to

**Figure 15.47**

TweakUI Control Panel tab

pick around to find what you want. Also, some of the Control Panels in the folder (like Add New Hardware) are missing from the TweakUI list. On the other hand, out of curiosity we checked the nameless TweakUI box for STICPL.CPL, and when we went back into the folder, we had a Control Panel for Scanners and Cameras!

**Network Tab.** **Network** (Figure 15.48) is a way to set up autologon,

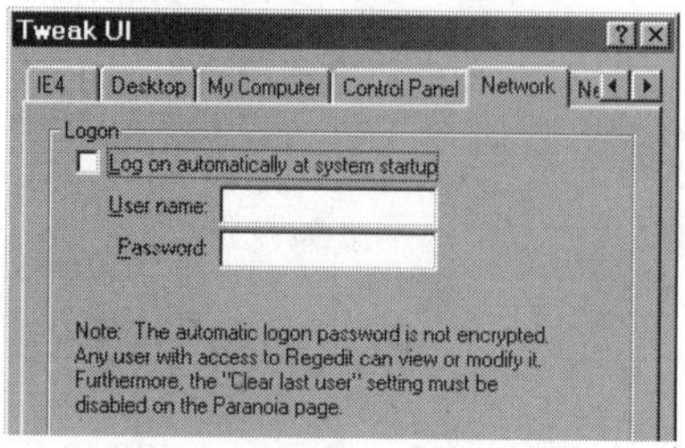

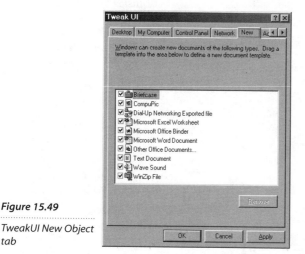

*Figure 15.48*

*TweakUI Logon tab*

and there's not much to add to what the tab says; the **Clear last user** checkbox on the Paranoia tab has to be cleared, and the contents of the **Password** field are sitting as plain text in the **DefaultPassword** subkey of

HKEY_LOCAL_MACHINE\Software\Microsoft\Windows\CurrentVersion\ Winlogon. (If you haven't seen a Registry subkey before, go read Chapter 17, from which you'll emerge with a doctorate in alphabet soup.)

## You're Not Who You Think You Are

*Do not use this autologon procedure on a computer set up for multiple users.* Because the Registry key that gets modified here is in \Windows\CurrentVersion, there's only one copy of it, and only one user can have autologon. Not only that, but the autologon user will override any other user's attempt to log on.

*Figure 15.49*

*TweakUI New Object tab*

**New Tab.** **New** (Figure 15.49) adds to the list of document types (formally, document object types) that can be created with the **New** dialog available from the Desktop Context Menu, the Explorer File menu, and a bunch of other places.

When TweakUI says "Drag in a template" it means "Drag in a blank file of the type you want to add to the dialog."

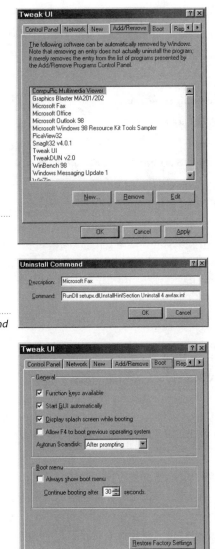

**Add/Remove tab.** Add/Remove
(Figure 15.50) deletes items from the
list, maintained by the Add/Remove
Programs Control Panel, of the
programs that can be automatically
uninstalled. It doesn't delete the
programs themselves.

This will primarily be of interest to
systems administrators who want
to install applications, then deny users
the ability to uninstall them through
Add/Remove Programs. If you've
taken an item off this list, you can use
the **Add** button in TweakUI to put
the list item back so you can run the
uninstall.

The **Edit** button here is interesting
(see Figure 15.51).

This dialog (Figure 15.51) exists primarily to let you edit the list descriptions, but it also gives you the exact
path and parameters used by the
uninstaller when it runs. So far as we
can tell, this is the only source of this
information outside the Registry.

**Boot Tab.** Boot (Figure 15.52) lets
you modify boot-time options, and
this time we'll go through the whole
tab, since many of these switches are
more than useful.

*Figure 15.50*

*TweakUI
Add/Remove tab*

*Figure 15.51*

*Uninstall Command*

*Figure 15.52*

*TweakUI Boot tab*

***Function keys.*** If **Function keys...** is

- *Checked:* After your computer boots past the system BIOS and before the
  Windows splash (logo) screen appears, if you hit F5, startup files will be
  bypassed and your computer will go into GUI Safe Mode. If, at the same
  point, you hit F8, you'll reach the Startup Menu (see "Startup Menu"
  later in this chapter).

- *Unchecked:* These choices are unavailable.

*Start GUI.* If **Start GUI...** is

- *Checked:* Your computer boots into the normal Windows GUI.

- *Unchecked:* Your computer boots into MS-DOS mode. (Tiplet: To go into the GUI from here, you type win Enter. Hey, it's Windows 3.98!)

*Splash screen.* If **Display splash screen...** is

- *Checked:* The Windows splash logo fills the screen from the time DOS processing is finished until the appearance of the password dialog.

- *Unchecked:* Your last DOS commands remain on the screen until the password dialog arrives. This can be handy for diagnostic purposes.

*F4 Dualboot.* If **Allow F4 to boot...** is

- *Checked:* If you hit F4 before the splash screen appears, your computer boots into the operating system from which you upgraded. To quote the peerless right-click Help: "Of course, this assumes that you (1) actually had a previous operating system, and (2) didn't delete any files required by the previous operating system …"

- *Unchecked:* Your computer boots into Windows 98.

*Autorun Scandisk.* Your options for **Autorun Scandisk** after a dirty shutdown are the default **After prompting**, giving you the choice of running Scandisk at boot-time; **Without prompting,** meaning that Scandisk will run automatically after you're notified; and **Never**, meaning skip it. Something is odd here, because **After prompting** and **Without prompting** actually do the same thing, making us wonder if autorunning Scandisk is governed by some Registry setting beyond the reach of TweakUI.

*Boot menu.* If **Always show boot menu** is

- *Checked:* Your computer goes straight from the system BIOS boot into the Startup Menu, where it stays, ticking off the number of seconds set in **Continue booting after...seconds**. During this time you can pick any of the Startup Menu choices.

- *Unchecked:* If you want to go into the Startup Menu, you have to hit F8 as described above.

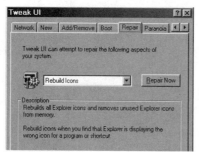

**Repair Tab.** Repair (Figure 15.53) is a "fixer" to be used when the Registry loses its awareness of special exceptions in the interface. Many objects begin generically and are embellished with extra features to suit special

*Figure 15.53*

*TweakUI Repair tab*

purposes; for example, the Temporary Internet Files folder and the REGEDIT screen both start life as Explorer folders and sprout extra columns with special headers.

If certain Registry entries are corrupted, these custom objects revert to their "normal" selves, and you start noticing that features are missing. The context-sensitive text in the **Description** region refers to this state, with hackish vagueness, as the object having "lost its magic." Repairing these defects directly in the Registry would be almost impossibly complex, even if it were a good idea. With TweakUI, you just click and cross your fingers. The Description text is generally accurate; read it carefully before you hit the button.

 One utility in the Repair tab that you should *never* use, or at least not until further notice, is **Repair System Files**. Put it right out of your mind! The "official" repair utility, System File Checker, maintains its backups in \WINDOWS\HELPDESK\SFC, unless you moved that location with the System File Checker Advanced tab. TweakUI maintains a totally separate set of backups in \WINDOWS\SYSBCKUP. Who's to say the two filesets are the same? And if they're not, which one is newer or more correct? ... And if you "repaired" your system files with one utility, didn't like what you got, and tried the other one? ... TweakUI is excellent in many ways, but to repair your system files, stick with System File Checker. We'll bet that, when the Windows 98 final version of TweakUI appears, its functions are clipped so that it and SFC don't overlap.

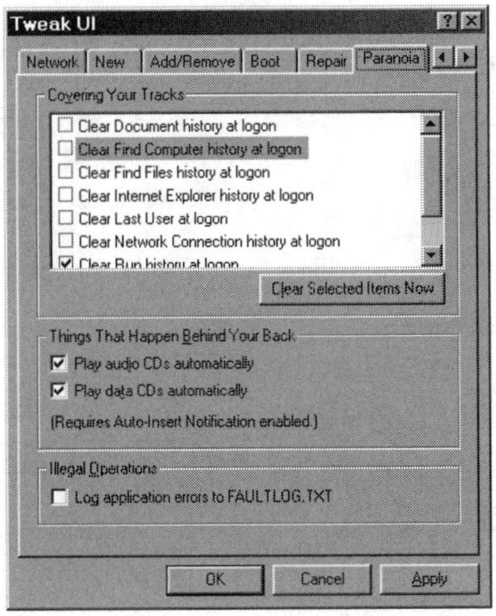

**Paranoia Tab.** Paranoia (Figure 15.54) gave TweakUI its reputation and still may be the most used of all the tabs. It's a guerrilla counter-attack to the astounding amount of user-specific trivia that Windows collects as a byproduct of normal use.

*Covering Your Tracks.* These check-boxes offer to clear most of the log files that Windows keeps to populate drop-down lists. Yes, knowing where you've been is convenient for you, but do you want it to be just as convenient for your boss? Here's what you can wipe out:

**Figure 15.54**

*TweakUI Paranoia tab*

| Clear...history at logon | Location of list |
|---|---|
| Document | Start Menu\Documents, or Recent folder |
| Find Computer | Start Menu\Find\Computer...\Computer Name |
| Find Files | Start Menu\Find\Files or Folders...\Named |
| Internet Explorer | Internet Explorer\Address |
| Last User | Name of last user (not a list) in the System Logon dialog. Again, this box must be cleared if autologon is enabled through the **Network** tab |
| Network Connection | My Computer\Context Menu\Map Network Drive\Path, or Network Neighborhood\Context Menu\Map Network Drive\Path |
| Run | Start Menu\Run...\Open |

All of these changes take effect at the next logon, so that no one who logs on after you can peruse your activity. If even that's not fast enough, hit the **Clear Selected Items Now** button, but what *have* you been up to?

*Things That Happen...* The only place we can imagine paranoia about audio CD's starting automatically is in a horror movie. Otherwise, bring on the Bach fugues! Data CD's starting automatically, though, can be a pain; you're hunting for a CD, you pop open the drive, it's in there, okay, you close the drive, and suddenly the program's giant splat screen is monopolizing your monitor. If you uncheck **Play data CDs...** you can start them manually by double-clicking on them in Explorer.

The **Auto-Insert Notification** that has to be enabled is in Control Panel\System\Device Manager; find your CD-ROM drive (underneath the main **CDROM** key) and double-click on it, pick the **Settings** tab, and check **Auto insert notification**.

*Figure 15.55*

*Sample FAULTLOG.TXT*

```
*****************************************************
Date 03/29/1998 Time 00:44
BADAPP caused a general protection fault
in module BADAPP16.EXE at 0001:0000071b.
Registers:
EAX=00000001 CS=38ef EIP=0000071b EFLGS=00000246
EBX=00000000 SS=38e7 ESP=000022e2 EBP=000022ec
ECX=00580000 DS=38e7 ESI=0000236c FS=0000
EDX=00000000 ES=0000 EDI=000025fe GS=0157
Bytes at CS:EIP:
26 c6 07 00 5f 5e c9 c3 90 c8 04 00 00 56 57 e8
Stack dump:
236c25fe 00000000 231e0000 25fe0381 0108236c
0F1F0004 232034d0 174f0b4f 00000001 0000ffff
00000000 38e7236c 0f1f0000 00f625fe 38e70fe0 10252343
```

*Illegal Operations.* Having put this on the Paranoia tab, they couldn't resist a James Bondish name, but it's useful to leave this box checked. When a program steps on memory and you get a warning dialog, you can click the **Details** button to find out what the fault was, but as soon as you dismiss the dialog, the information is gone.

**Illegal Operations** logs program faults to a file (Figure 15.55) in the \WINDOWS folder that you can peruse to see if, while you're trying to diagnose or repair a program, you can glean any clues from the history of its crashes. This file is also handy to have open in Notepad while you're on the phone to hotline support.

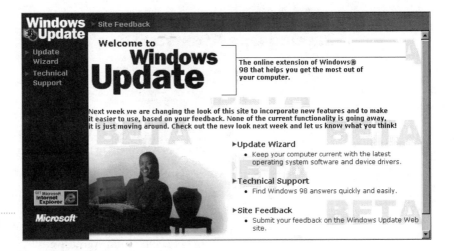

*Figure 15.56*

*Windows Update*
*Welcome screen*

### Update Manager
Default path: `Start Menu\Windows Update`

Windows Update is a Web site, not an application. If you double-click **Start Menu\Windows Update** you'll launch Internet Explorer, pop up the Connect dialog if you're not connected, and bring you to a screen that may look like Figure 15.56.

Click the **Windows Update** link and you'll be brought to a menu-driven selection of automatic setups which will begin with Wizards downloading to your local disk, uncompressing, downloading the remainder of the Update, and patching your local copy of the application ... presumably while ever-vigilant System File Checker watches.

It's difficult to say much about Windows Update because it, like this book, is racing to completion. As we write, the only program you can update through the Web site is Internet Explorer; the site itself, as the screenshot suggests, is evolving almost daily. When the retail distribution of Windows 98 hits the streets, and the update machine begins grinding at full speed, we'll bring you news of its latest developments on the *Windows Bible* Web site, `http://www.winbible.com`.

# Troubleshooting

There is a way to make a Windows Emergency Disk, providing you can boot to any kind of command prompt, and no matter how many of our fervent warnings you ignored in the last several hundred pages. We are not barren of compassion. We want you to get on with your life.

# The Windows Emergency Disk: Making One After You Didn't

Before we dive in here, two caveats remain:

- This procedure makes a disk that is *not exactly, absolutely, 100% comparable* with a real Windows Emergency Disk. Therefore, we cannot guarantee that it will work on your system, not that we would anyway. It works on *our* system and we can't see any reason that it *won't* work on yours.

- This procedure assumes that your computer's CD-ROM drive is properly hitched to a disk controller or motherboard tap, whether it's IDE or SCSI. If your CD-ROM drive is a Mitsumi or similar, and is connected to a sound card, our procedure will not work, because it installs real-mode CD support that is not compatible with your drive. You have a longer row to hoe, because you need to modify your CONFIG.SYS to install device-specific real-mode CD support, probably from the diskettes that came with your sound card; you may end up talking to your sound card's or CD drive's manufacturer, or to Microsoft.

Okay, ready? Find a reasonably fresh 3.5" high-density floppy disk, and try to pick one with no bad sectors, because you don't want to do this twice. Put it in your drive A: At a DOS prompt, which you may have arrived at by booting into Safe Mode Command Prompt Only, type

`format a: /s` Enter

This will put the following files on the disk. (Sizes are approximate, and we're not including file dates and times, which of course will vary with the Windows build you have installed.) The four right-hand columns are file bits set, with H=hidden, S=system, R=read-only, and A=archive.

| File Name | Size (approximate) | File Bits Set: Hidden | System | Read-only | Archive |
|---|---|---|---|---|---|
| COMMAND.COM | 93880 | | | | A |
| DRVSPACE.BIN | 68871 | H | S | R | A |
| IO.SYS | 229558 | H | S | R | A |
| MSDOS.SYS | 9 | H | S | R | A |

Now type c: to get back to drive C:, and

cd\windows\command\ebd [Enter]

to get to the folder where the rest of the Windows Emergency Disk files are. At this prompt, type

copy *.* a: [Enter]

and these files should be copied onto the diskette:

| File Name | Size (approximate) | File Bits Set: Hidden | System | Read-only | Archive |
|-----------|-------------------|-----------------------|--------|-----------|---------|
| ASPI2DOS.SYS | 35,330 | | | | A |
| ASPI4DOS.SYS | 14,386 | | | | A |
| ASPI8DOS.SYS | 37,564 | | | | A |
| ASPI8U2.SYS | 40,792 | | | | A |
| ASPICD.SYS | 29,620 | | | | A |
| AUTOEXEC.BAT | 1,103 | | | | A |
| BTCDROM.SYS | 21,971 | | | | A |
| BTDOSM.SYS | 30,955 | | | | A |
| CONFIG.SYS | 629 | | | | A |
| EBD.CAB | 303,471 | | | | A |
| EXTRACT.EXE | 93,242 | | | | A |
| FDISK.EXE | 63,900 | | | | A |
| FINDRAMD.EXE | 6,855 | | | | A |
| FLASHPT.SYS | 64,425 | | | | A |
| HIMEM.SYS | 33,191 | | | | A |
| OAKCDROM.SYS | 41,302 | | | | A |
| RAMDRIVE.SYS | 12,663 | | | | A |
| README.TXT | 4,419 | | | | A |
| SETRAMD.BAT | 1,416 | | | | A |

You'll also be asked if you want to copy COMMAND.COM, DRVSPACE.BIN, IO.SYS, and MSDOS.SYS, but you can say no—they're already on the diskette. Now, the notes:

If you compare this disk to a "real" Windows Emergency Disk, you'll find you're missing a file called EBD.SYS. It's a zero-byte file, set Hidden, System, Read-only, and Archive; obviously, it's a marker or identifier that says "This is a real Windows Emergency Disk." We're not sure what looks for it or why, but our test system boots fine without it. (Microsoft defines it cutely as a "Utility for the startup disk," but if they've perfected zero-byte utility programs, there are things about DriveSpace that mortals were not meant to know.)

These are not the AUTOEXEC.BAT, CONFIG.SYS, or MSDOS.SYS from your individual computer, but generic copies specifically intended to launch the Windows 98 emergency startup and diagnostic procedure. The Windows Emergency Disk doesn't get you back to the garden; it gets you in through the back door. As soon as you have booted with the Emergency Disk, make every effort to nurse your system back to the point where you can boot off the hard disk.

If you have *any suspicion* that your current emergency was caused by a viral infection, *do not* attempt to go straight back into Windows. Find some up-to-date antiviral software that will allow you to run a scan from the DOS command line. Some of the reinstallations you could do from here would modify the boot sector of your hard disk, and if you happen to have caught a virus that has already modified the boot sector, the combination might render your data inaccessible. As of this writing we haven't heard anything about boot-sector viruses that affect FAT32 partitions, but while the jury is out, we'd recommend that if you've run the FAT32 conversion, you should take precautions every step of the way ... just in case *both* the virus *and* the antiviral software want to modify your boot sector in any way lethal to FAT32.

If getting back into your system involves editing AUTOEXEC.BAT or CONFIG.SYS to load special drivers, remember that the DOS-based text editor EDIT.COM is on the Windows Emergency Disk. You can also use EDIT if you need to edit MSDOS.SYS, but first you'll need to unhide and unprotect it with the command

```
attrib msdos.sys -h -r -s Enter
```

after which you can modify it like any text file, then run

```
attrib msdos.sys +h +r +s Enter
```

to flip the bits back the way they belong. We recommend you modify MSDOS.SYS *only* with close professional supervision. Don't go near IO.SYS with any kind of editor—it's not a text file.

You may need fresh copies of drivers for your older hardware, and we sympathize if you do. Try the Tech Support section of the hardware manufacturer's Web site, and if you get no joy there, browse to Frank Condron's World O'Windows pages, `http://www.worldowindows.com/win95.html` (which may be `/win98.html` by the time you read this) or `http://www.worldowindows.com/drivers.html`.

 **If you try both those sources for a driver and come up dry, try taking the model name and/or model number of your hardware and stuffing them into a search engine. When this works, it works miracles—and it's fast.**

 By now you may think we're insensitive, telling you to go Web browsing while your computer is a smoldering paperweight. Understood, but look: There are only three things that will fix a bad problem with a computer. One is a screwdriver, one is money, and one is another computer. Of those three, which would you rather use?

## The Windows Emergency Disk: Making One Before You Didn't, Meaning Now

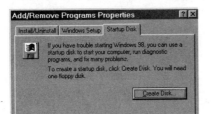

*Figure 15.57*

*Startup Disk tab*

Let's say you're lucky, and you've read the previous section with horrified fascination, because all of that hasn't happened to you yet and you hope it won't. Okay, ready? Find a reasonably fresh 3.5" high-density floppy disk, and try to pick one with no bad sectors, because you don't want a bogus disk. Put it in your drive A: and put your Windows CD in the CD drive. Open **Control Panel\Add/Remove Programs** and click the **Startup Disk** tab (Figure 15.57)

Click **Create Disk**. You'll be prompted to "Insert Disk," which you already did, and warned that existing files on the floppy will be deleted. Click **OK**. A progress bar will begin, and when it reaches 100%, you'll go back to the Startup Disk tab and you can take the diskette out.

While you're labeling that one, make another one. Label it. Write-protect them both. Put one in the diskette stash you keep closest to your computer, and the other one in the Computer Emergency Ziploc that we discussed in Chapter 13.

**If You Don't Have The CD.** If you don't have the Windows 98 CD, this procedure is a bit different. **Open Control Panel\Add/Remove Programs**, click the **Startup Disk** tab, and click **Create Disk**. You'll be prompted to insert the CD (Figure 15.58) thusly:

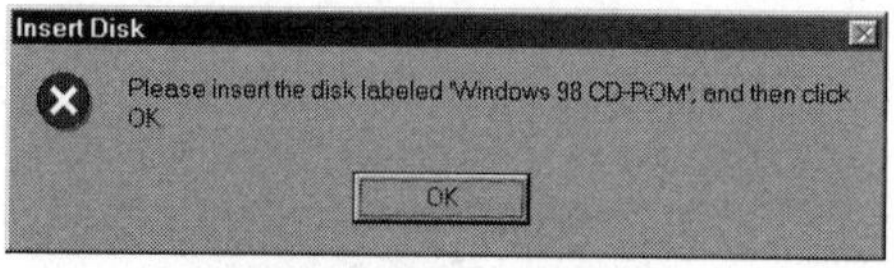

*Figure 15.58*

*Insert CD warning*

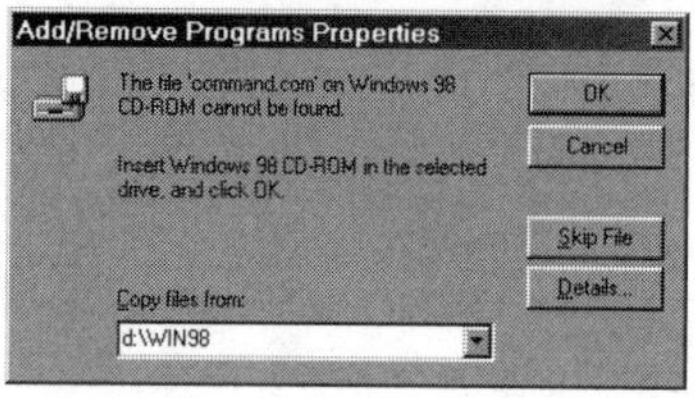

*Figure 15.59*

*Alternate File Location dialog*

Click **OK** and go into the next dialog (Figure 15.59)

In the **Copy files from** field, overwrite whatever's proposed with the name of your Windows installation backup folder, probably called \WINDOWS\OPTIONS\CABS—unless, as discussed, you made it yourself and called it \WIN98 or \WINCABS. Click **OK**.

Windows may complain a couple of times that it can't find a file it needs. The file *is* more than likely to be in one of the .CAB files (mini-tip: WINBOOT.SYS is in PRECOPY2.CAB) and, if you enter the path of your installation backup folder again and click **OK**, the copying may continue. You can also tell Windows to look in \WINDOWS\COMMAND\EBD. Whatever you do, don't click **Skip file** or you'll end up with a bogus disk. After you take the diskette out, proceed as above.

## The Troubleshooters

Default path: **Start Menu\Help\Search tab\keyword troubleshoot\ List Topics\select Topic\Display**

For developers of operating systems and today's humongous applications, technical support is a nightmare from which they know they will never wake up. It takes so much infrastructure! Its underlying database needs to be updated so often and so quickly! It has to be so carefully tailored to the individual user! And it costs a [non-euphemism deleted] fortune and *nobody* wants to pay for it!! (Software purchasers have this irritating idea that they already did, while developers look at their bottom lines and see fiscal hemorrhage.) Recent searches for a less exhausting model have produced all kinds of experiments, of which the Windows 98 Troubleshooters are some of the most interesting.

Making your own computer work is like babysitting for an active toddler. It can be tiring, and bewildering sometimes, and it will take every bit of your attention, but you *can* cope with ninety-five per cent of anything that could ever happen. For the other five per cent, you need immediate communication in real time with an expert, probably someone related by blood to the kid, or the computer. (And we're all related to computers by blood, as you know if you've ever dismantled a cheap case.)

The Troubleshooters, awkwardly stuffed inside the Windows 98 Help, are Microsoft's toolbox to help you take care of the ninety-five per cent. They stick closely to real-world problems and solutions, because they answer the questions that were asked statistically most often in millions of hours of telephone support. If you go through the Troubleshooter that addresses your problem most closely, and it doesn't help, *then* you call Microsoft ... for their typical, remarkably cheerful, slightly plodding, valiant and competent problem-solving. But if the Troubleshooters do their jobs, you'll be on that phone less often, which will save you money, and fewer people will need to *answer* those phones, which will save Microsoft money—at no great cost in customer satisfaction.

Ladies and gentlemen, we give you ... the Troubleshooters.

**Main Screen.** In Windows Help, click the **Search** tab, type in `troubleshoot`, click **List Topics**, click in the Topic pane, type `u`[↓] to get to **Using the Windows 98 troubleshooters**, and click **Display**. If you find the highlighting distracting, you can get rid of it with **Options\Highlighting Off**.

The main screen (Figure 15.60) gives setup and general instructions for using specific Troubleshooters. The directions are dictatorial, but follow them as exactly as possible; you're working with a compact version of what the Microsoft support technician would be looking at if you got Redmond on the phone, so these procedures did not come out of thin air. When you're at ease with the steps to take, click the particular Troubleshooter you need in the Topic pane, and click **Display**.

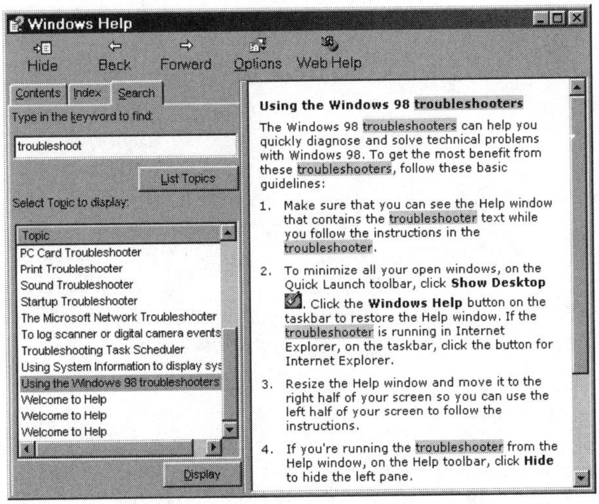


*Figure 15.60*

*Troubleshooter main screen*

**Dial-Up Networking Troubleshooter.** This is really the Modem Troubleshooter, and sends you there.

**Direct Cable Connection Troubleshooter.** … is really the Networking Troubleshooter, and sends you there. We've got crashed communications, and Microsoft thinks we want to play Chutes and Ladders!

**What type of problem are you having?**

- ○ I'm receiving DirectDraw error messages or experiencing video problems.
- ○ My program has stopped responding.
- ◉ Now that I've installed my program, Windows 98 starts only in safe mode.
- ○ I see a black screen or black patches around the cursor.
- ○ I see only vertical lines on my screen.
- ○ I receive the error message: "SetDisplayMode: DDERR_GENERIC."
- ○ I receive the error message: "Error Initializing Directsound."
- ○ The sound is choppy.
- ○ I don't hear sounds anymore.
- ○ I receive the error message: "Ddhelp.exe caused a page fault in module Wstream.dll."
- ○ I receive the error message: "Required.dll is missing. Cannot locate ddraw.dll."
- ○ I receive the error message: "Wsock32.dll file cannot start."
- ○ I receive the error message: "Exception 03h in Msvfw32.dll."

[ Next > ]

**Figure 15.61**

DirectX Troubleshooter

**DirectX Troubleshooter.** DirectX is a multimedia architecture mostly intended to provide graphics and sound for games. It makes heavy demands on your hardware, and also relies on a video addressing technology called DirectDraw, which seems to be in a constant state of flux. Many problems with DirectX arise from obsolete or missing .DLLs, and this Troubleshooter clearly reflects that fact.

**Display Troubleshooter.** Only a few of the buttons on this Troubleshooter are concerned with ordinary still graphics on a single monitor; for everyday issues, you're at least as likely to find recourse on one of the tabs of Display Properties. If, on the other hand, you're running full-motion video or multiple

**Windows 98 Display Troubleshooter**

**What type of problem are you having?**

- ○ Animations stop playing.
- ○ I see garbled or corrupted text.
- ○ I'm having color palette and redraw problems.
- ○ I receive the error message: "Display problems. This program cannot continue."
- ○ I receive the error message: "The specified file cannot be played on the specified MCI device."
- ○ I receive the error message: "Mciavi requires a newer version of the Msvideo.dll."
- ○ I receive the error message: "Invalid Page Fault in Kernel32.dll."
- ○ I receive the error message: "MMVIEWER2 caused a General Protection Fault."
- ○ The screen display is blurry or scrambled when I play videos.
- ○ I can't see anything on the screen of one of my monitors.
- ○ I want to change the desktop settings on one of my monitors or switch the settings of my primary monitor with those of one of my secondary monitors.
- ○ My dialog boxes are not centered.
- ○ Full screen MS-DOS-based programs run only on my primary monitor and I lose operability on my other monitors.
- ○ A new icon has appeared on my taskbar.
- ○ When I attempt to move my mouse pointer to another monitor, it does not appear on that monitor, or it appears on a different monitor.
- ○ How do I disable multi-monitor display after it has been set up?

[ Next > ]

**Figure 15.62**

Display Troubleshooter

monitor support, this Troubleshooter is your primary source of help. Since multiple monitor support is very new, don't be surprised if you end up talking to Microsoft after all.

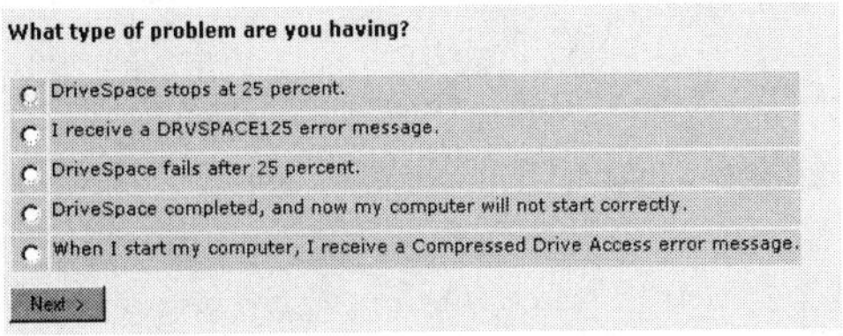

**What type of problem are you having?**

- DriveSpace stops at 25 percent.
- I receive a DRVSPACE125 error message.
- DriveSpace fails after 25 percent.
- DriveSpace completed, and now my computer will not start correctly.
- When I start my computer, I receive a Compressed Drive Access error message.

Next >

*Figure 15.63*

*DriveSpace 3 Troubleshooter*

**DriveSpace 3 Troubleshooter.** Hoo, boy! Talk about automated support we hope we'll never need! But this Troubleshooter seems reasonably comprehensive, although we've seen some error messages from the program itself that we can't find in here. Repairing a compressed volume file is inseparable from fear and trembling, but at least this is a solid discussion of settled technology. You *are* backed up, aren't you?

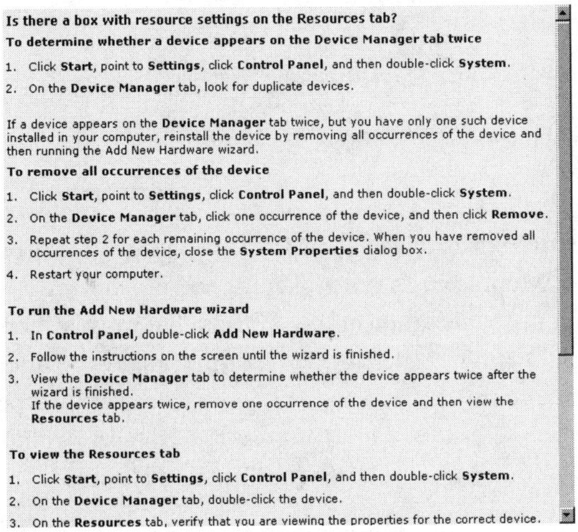

Is there a box with resource settings on the Resources tab?

**To determine whether a device appears on the Device Manager tab twice**

1. Click **Start**, point to **Settings**, click **Control Panel**, and then double-click **System**.
2. On the **Device Manager** tab, look for duplicate devices.

If a device appears on the **Device Manager** tab twice, but you have only one such device installed in your computer, reinstall the device by removing all occurrences of the device and then running the Add New Hardware wizard.

**To remove all occurrences of the device**

1. Click **Start**, point to **Settings**, click **Control Panel**, and then double-click **System**.
2. On the **Device Manager** tab, click one occurrence of the device, and then click **Remove**.
3. Repeat step 2 for each remaining occurrence of the device. When you have removed all occurrences of the device, close the **System Properties** dialog box.
4. Restart your computer.

**To run the Add New Hardware wizard**

1. In **Control Panel**, double-click **Add New Hardware**.
2. Follow the instructions on the screen until the wizard is finished.
3. View the **Device Manager** tab to determine whether the device appears twice after the wizard is finished.
   If the device appears twice, remove one occurrence of the device and then view the **Resources** tab.

**To view the Resources tab**

1. Click **Start**, point to **Settings**, click **Control Panel**, and then double-click **System**.
2. On the **Device Manager** tab, double-click the device.
3. On the **Resources** tab, verify that you are viewing the properties for the correct device.

*Figure 15.64*

*Hardware Conflict Troubleshooter (first text screen)*

**Hardware Conflict Troubleshooter.** Microsoft was gutsy to put so broad a topic into automated Help, but this looks good. Not only is it a quick reference to the Device Manager, the Resources tab, and the Add New Hardware Wizard, but it teaches you to troubleshoot in logical order, which often makes the difference between success and failure. There are also stunts in here, like installing hardware twice and removing it once, that experienced Windows technicians have had up their sleeves for years.

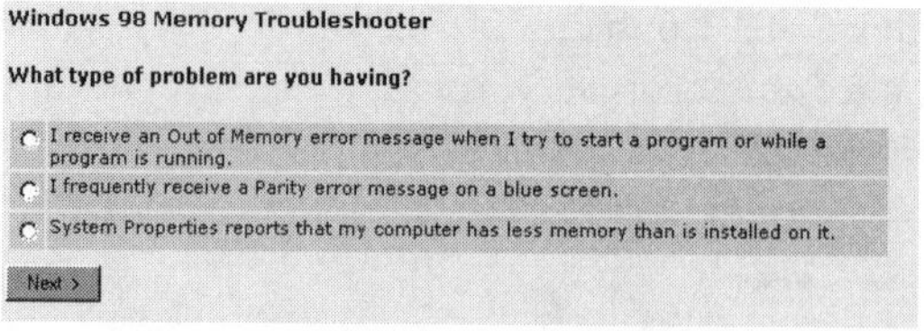

*Figure 15.65*

*Memory Troubleshooter*

**Memory Troubleshooter.** Bullseye. To begin with, this Troubleshooter is candid about hardware memory problems and how they may have arisen. Better yet, it teaches you how to use the nearly-secret MSCONFIG as a diagnostic tool.

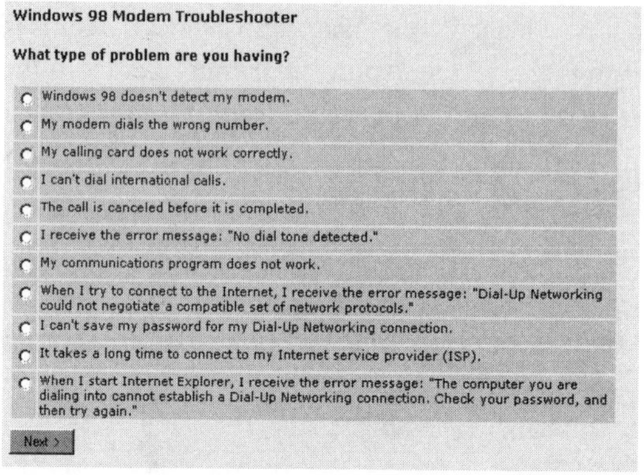

*Figure 15.66*

*Modem Troubleshooter*

**Modem Troubleshooter.** This is called "Modem and Fax Troubleshooter" in the Topics Menu, but as noted, Windows 98 is having a fax identity crisis and the outcome is uncertain. This is the Troubleshooter for Dial-Up Networking, Dialing Properties, the Connect dialog of Internet Explorer, and light treatments of hardware debugging and using HyperTerminal to test communications sessions. Hey, Microsoft! With all your green stuff you couldn't have found us a toll-free number to dial into?

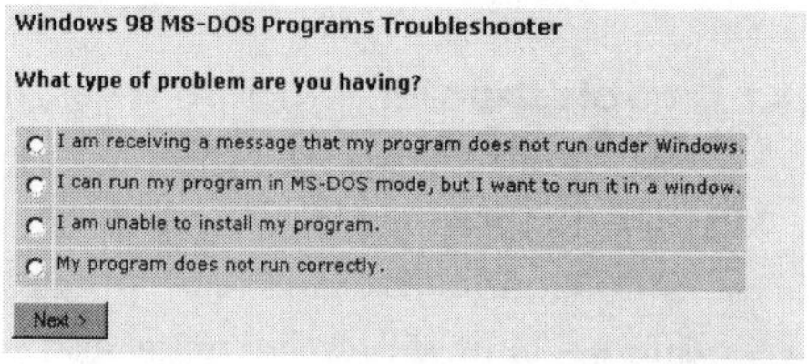

*Figure 15.67*

*MS-DOS Programs Troubleshooter*

**MS-DOS Programs Troubleshooter.** One step off the beach, two steps off the beach … and you're in over your head. As you might guess from the blandly generic top-level queries, this is the Troubleshooter for *all* of the MS-DOS Prompt Properties, MS-DOS Mode, EMS and XMS memory configuration, installation of DOS applications under Windows, launching DOS programs from Windows icons, and on and on. In a couple of places this Troubleshooter concedes defeat, but all in all, we'd certainly rather try DOS configuration this way than plunge into it by hand.

**Network/LAN Troubleshooter.** Very deep, very wide, and about equally concerned with installation (meaning hardware) and operation (meaning software) stumbling blocks, with a very slight nod in the direction of Direct Cable Connection—mostly about a source for high-speed cables. In places, the Networking chapter of this book goes into more detail than the Troubleshooter, and if you're chasing network gremlins you probably want to work with both.

**PC Card (PCMCIA) Troubleshooter.** A straightforward Troubleshooter that walks you through real-mode testing and reinstallation with the Add New Hardware Wizard, to determine whether the problem is with the operating system card and socket services or the card itself.

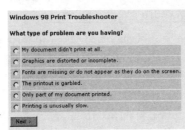

**Print Troubleshooter.** Thank you, Microsoft. What a multitude of sins can be implicit in the plaintive voice on the other end of the phone, saying "My printer is screwing up?" And, with printing *especially,* the only hope of effective debugging is to plod through asking "did that work? … how about that? … how about that?" The most obvious strength of the Troubleshooters, the rigorous decision tree, shows to its best advantage when it faces off against the bizarre behavior of a deranged output device.

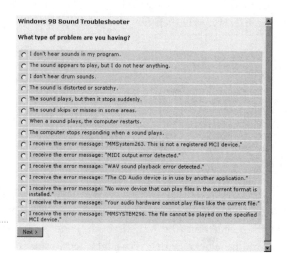

*Figure 15.71*

*Sound Troubleshooter*

**Sound Troubleshooter.** The value of the Sound Troubleshooter becomes apparent when you realize that "trouble with sound" gives you no foothold until you know what *kind* of sound. Like Sinatra, everybody wanted to do it their way, and now *sound* on a lavishly equipped Windows computer means CD audio, FM radio, WAV, MIDI, RealAudio, TV, DVD, MPEG-3, and whatever shows up next week. Like the Print Troubleshooter, the Sound Troubleshooter will sometimes irritate you with its ploddishness, but it has just that much more chance of restoring your prized aural dimension.

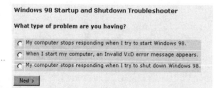

*Figure 15.72*

*Startup Troubleshooter*

**Startup Troubleshooter.** Three specific problem areas, all of them things you would rather not confront:

- **Hang on startup**. The Troubleshooter walks you through starting in Safe Mode, starting in Safe Mode Command Prompt Only, and—one by one—the alternatives that will make your computer yield the secret of its malady.

- **"Invalid VxD" message on startup**. In these days of the universal virtual device driver, the System File Checker, and redundant backups, a VxD crash is about as welcome as a case of cholera in your apartment building. It will also be very unlikely, which is why this option of the Troubleshooter leads you by the hand to … a Registry key.

- **Hang on exit**. Who knew that a damaged Exit Windows sound file could make your system choke at shutdown? Does the world need one that badly? The other likely causes—incompatibility with fast shutdown or power management—are more reasonable, and if none of these solves the problem, you get to play with BOOTLOG.TXT.

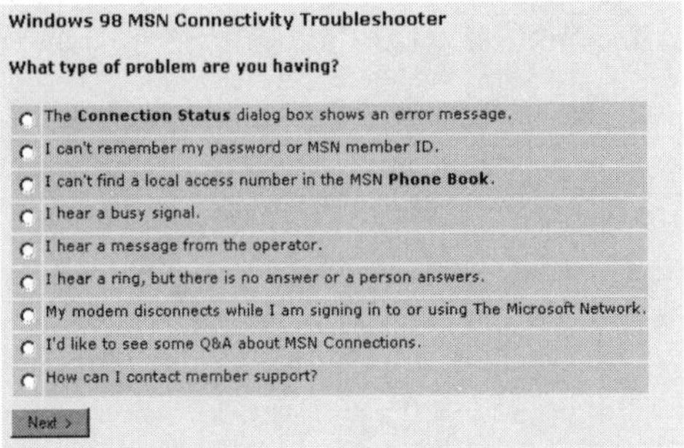

**Windows 98 MSN Connectivity Troubleshooter**

**What type of problem are you having?**

- The **Connection Status** dialog box shows an error message.
- I can't remember my password or MSN member ID.
- I can't find a local access number in the MSN **Phone Book**.
- I hear a busy signal.
- I hear a message from the operator.
- I hear a ring, but there is no answer or a person answers.
- My modem disconnects while I am signing in to or using The Microsoft Network.
- I'd like to see some Q&A about MSN Connections.
- How can I contact member support?

Next >

*Figure 15.73*

MSN Connectivity
Troubleshooter

**MSN Connectivity Troubleshooter.**  If you need it, here it certainly is. For problems like these Microsoft should make house calls! Still, for those who have an online service positioned as a symbiote of an all-conquering operating system, building in the support only makes sense.

# Epilogue: Troublehacking

While we were ramping up to writing this book, we canvassed the Net and realized what a wealth of literature there was on hand-hacking Windows 95— and, to a lesser but still great extent, Windows NT—in the name of quick, effective problem-solving with no need to consult Microsoft's headset-wearing legions. Now, on the eve of Windows 98's release, we wonder: Will the same kind of independent subculture, or even counterculture, spring up around the newest version of 32-bit Windows? From here it's a hard call and a fascinating question.

It's not that Windows 98 is so much more daunting than its forebears. Windows 98 is more feature-rich than Windows 95 and has many more included programs, but we're not sure it's intrinsically more complicated. Even if 98 is more complex than 95, we assure you that NT 4.0 has far more to understand about it than either one. Rather, the users of operating systems may be realizing that—over the years—they've shown an amazing and now less justified tolerance for faults in software. Maybe they're beginning to think that new software, like a new car, should run for months and years on end with only the most trivial maintenance.

So what can we look forward to? Is Windows 98 the miracle operating system with solid-state fuel injection and platinum-tipped plugs, that will put a hundred thousand miles on your mouse without ever stalling in network traffic? Or will the hacker culture decide about Windows 98, as it did about Windows 95, that while Microsoft's tools for operating system support have improved steadily, they're still far too limited to be acceptable?

We'll just have to wait and see what shows up on the Net ...

# 16

# Your Own Private Internet

Some people say that Microsoft is out to own the Internet. Fat chance! Some say that Internet Explorer, Outlook Express, and the rest of the Internet tools in Windows 98 are only Microsoft's way of catching up hastily after having been caught napping by the Net's roaring emergence as a mass medium. Some would have it that Microsoft is only trying to create Web, mail, news, and conferencing software that matches the quality of their applications. To us, these arguments miss the point, which is: Where and how do *you* want to live, work, communicate, shop and chat in cyberspace, and how can Windows 98 help you reach those goals? The Net's far from perfect, and it can be wild and woolly at times—but it's big enough for us all, and *different* for every one of us. Take the Galactic Fred and Kip Tour of the Windows 98 Internet Suite, and you, too, can arrive at Your Own Private Internet.

**Re-Disclaimer.** Remember how we said, back in Chapter 10, "this chapter trades depth of consideration for breadth of outlook?" Well, here we are again. The Internet tools in Windows 98 absolutely deserve a book of their own, which we unfortunately haven't written yet, because Microsoft has gazillions of programmers, and there are only two of us, and we both type slowly.

Therefore, this chapter is not "everything about" the Internet suite. It's the nuts, bolts, tips, and tricks of the core modules:

- Internet Connection Wizard
- Internet Explorer
- Outlook Express

And quick introductions to:

- MS-Chat
- NetMeeting (client side)
- FrontPage Express
- Web Publishing Wizard
- Personal Web Server

As for that other book, Fred is thinking of hiring a typist, and Kip is trying to get some voice-recognition software up to speed. For now, buy this book, and wish us luck.

**About NetShow.** Although the NetShow streaming video/audio applet is definitely part of Microsoft's Internet arsenal, it's not *only* that, and we suspect it may find its widest use in corporate intranets. So we said, "Well, it's streaming video," and put it in Chapter 12—where we urge you to look it up, because it's a cool program.

# Setting Up Your Connection

Most people, ourselves included, find that if we've got Web, mail, and news, our Own Private Internet is well in hand.

Electronic mail is emerging as the killer app of the late nineties—for many people, reason enough to have a computer in and of itself.

What the Web is, we're not sure yet—for the last few years, it's resembled being hit by a truck—but it's transformed the world's awareness of the Net. We've said that Tim Berners-Lee deserves the Nobel Prize, and we'll keep saying it.

Usenet news? Well, it has image problems, and some of them are richly deserved. Two facts remain: It gets a lot of information to a lot of people, many of whom are lonely or scared or desperate and appreciate it very much. And it's one of the oldest and most flavorful parts of Internet history, improbably thriving after all these years. Usenet news may make you cringe, but admit it, you'd miss it if it wasn't there.

So—Let's get linked!

*Figure 16.1*

*Internet Connection Wizard*

## Internet Connection Wizard

If you haven't set up your Internet connection yet, please note this icon on your Desktop (Figure 16.1), scion of Network Neighborhood and Internet Explorer:

Double-click it to this purposeful splash (Figure 16.2) and main (Figure 16.3) screen:

*Figure 16.2*

*ICW splash screen*

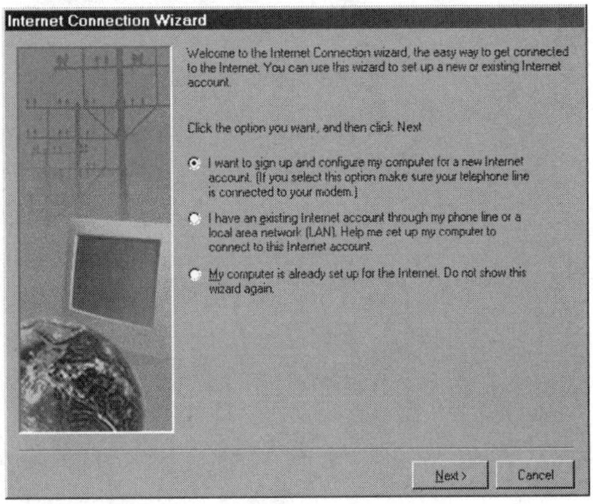

*Figure 16.3*

*ICW main screen*

You have three choices:

- **I want to sign up and configure.** Assumes that there's a modem somewhere in your computer, a phone jack handy in the wall, a piece of twisted-pair in your hand, and a puzzled expression on your face.

- **I have an existing Internet account.** Means you've already contacted the ISP and signed up for your account, but now need to configure your own computer to communicate with the Internet server.

- **My computer is already set up.** Just makes the Wizard go away.

**Signing Up.**  Have you connected your modem to the phone line yet? If not, find the cord (it's probably silver, white, or beige) take the baggie-tie off it, plug one end into the jack marked LINE or TELCO in the back of the modem, and plug the other end into your wall jack. If you have to use the same wall jack for both modem and voice, take the cord from the phone (the one you unplugged from the wall jack) and plug it into the jack marked PHONE in the back of the modem. If the setup you have to do is more complicated than that, refer to the manual that came with the modem.

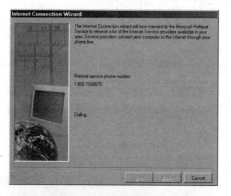

**Figure 16.4**

Logging into provider database

When the modem's ready to dial out, click **Next**. The Wizard uses a toll-free number to connect (Figure 16.4) to a Microsoft-maintained database of Internet providers and then puts up a list of your local providers to select from (Figure 16.5).

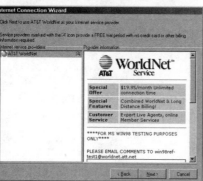

**Figure 16.5**

Provider list

At this writing, the only provider in the Microsoft database is AT&T WorldNet, a technically solid provider with national scope. Whether you should accept Microsoft's recommendations for an Internet service provider (ISP) depends on how many providers contribute their names to this list, which is something we have no way of predicting.

If the ISP list is skimpy, you can also find ISPs who place space ads in the business section of your local paper; or go find a computer with its Web access already set up and browse to `http://www.thelist.internet.com`.

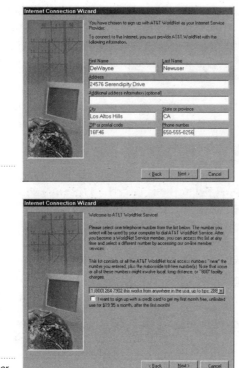

**Figure 16.6**

*Signing up*

**Figure 16.7**

*Selecting a number*

Whatever ISP you pick from the Microsoft database will ask you for information about yourself (Figure 16.6)—probably a billing address at least.

Click **Next**. When the ISP proposes a phone number for your connection, make *sure* it's either a toll-free number or a number that's a local call from your location; you don't want to end up making one payment to your ISP and another one to your phone company every time you connect to the Net. Also remember that not all 800 and 888 numbers are toll-free, or should we say, "facility-charge-free."

Click **Next**. From here the Wizard will send you into Dial-Up Networking to configure your connectoid, so start reading in Appendix C, "Dial-Up Networking Without Tears."

**Existing Account.** This choice assumes you already have Internet connectivity and gives you three options:

- Connect through a phone line. Basically the same as above, but takes advantage of the Dial-Up Networking connectoid you already have established—or lets you set up a new one.

- Connect through an online service. This isn't really a choice; it tells you to open the Online Services folder on your Desktop, double-click on the icon for your commercial service of choice, and follow the onscreen instructions. You will now exit the world of this book, but we're willing to bet you'll be back.

- Connect through a local network. Come with us, please; you have some questions to answer.

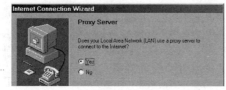

**Figure 16.8**

*Proxy Server dialog*

A *proxy server* is a computer that controls traffic between your local network and the Net, a kind of sentry or gatekeeper. Usually you can have access through a proxy server that's indistinguishable from

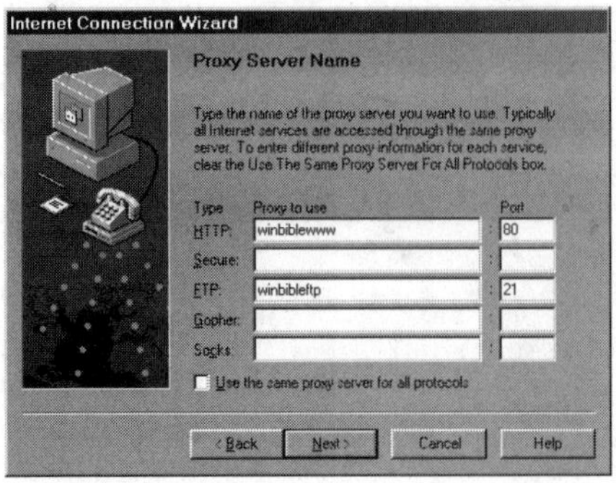

*Figure 16.9*

*Proxy Server name(s)*

the access you would enjoy through a direct connection, but only if you set up the transactions correctly. Let's assume you click **Yes**.

Your network administrator will be able to give you the name and port assignment of your proxy server, and if you work in a department or a small company, you probably only have one; in that case, fill in the top **Proxy to use** and **Port** fields, then check the **Use the same proxy...** checkbox. Consult your sysadmin for further instructions.

If you click **No**, you go into the Set Up Account dialog, which will let you:

- Configure an existing Internet mail account or set up a new one. You'll need information about your SMTP, IMAP, and/or POP3 servers, which you can get from your sysadmin, or your ISP if you're connecting to an external ISP.

- Configure an existing Internet news account or set up a new one. If you're setting up this account on a local network, you probably don't get a full direct Usenet newsfeed, so ask your sysadmin what you do about getting news. You may end up with access to only those newsgroups that directly relate to what you do at work (drat!). If you have no idea what this paragraph means, see "Newsgroups" below, which tries to make Usenet news as meaningful as it ever is.

- Configure a directory account. Ask your ISP or sysadmin for your LDAP (Lightweight Directory Access Protocol) information and for help setting this up.

If you use the Wizard, Windows assumes that you're setting up accounts for Outlook Express, which is the default Windows 98 mail and news client.

# Internet Explorer

This chapter is a quick course (we won't say crash course) in the confident and powerful use of the Microsoft Internet tools. As such it presupposes basic knowledge of Web browsing. If you're uneasy about jumping in here, return to Chapter 3 and the section called "Internetting your Interface," which covers the fundamentals of Internet Explorer's operation, and the relationship between local and Net-wide exploration. Sit in front of your computer, if you like, and make it do the things the book tells you about. Come back here when you're ready.

## Toolbar

The Internet Explorer Toolbar is the key to quick and flexible operation. We concede that if the pull-down menus disappeared, they would be missed; but the more you use IE4, the more you'll rely on pushing buttons. Table 16.1 lists what they all do.

### Table 16.1  Internet Explorer Toolbar

| Title | Function | Hotkey(s) |
|---|---|---|
| Back | Takes you back to the immediate previous Web page, or (with the drop list) to a selected previous Web page | Alt ←, Backspace |
| Forward | Takes you forward to the Web page (or, with the drop list, pages) from which you jumped Back. | Alt →, Shift Backspace |
| Stop | Cut off the data stream now being transferred. | Esc |
| Refresh | Log on to the current Web site and grab another copy of the page currently displayed. | F5 |
| Home | Go to the page defined as your home page (start page) in **View\Internet Options**. | |
| Search | Open a window to your search engine of choice (Figure 16.10). If you haven't chosen one, it takes you to the Microsoft Pick Search Engine page (Figure 16.11). | |
| Favorites | Open the pane with your Favorite links. This is a toggle. | |
| History | Open your Web History organized by week, day, and most recent sites visited. This will be available only if you haven't cleaned your History folder out with the **History** tab of **View\Internet Options**. | |
| Channels | Open a pane listing your available Channel content. Each line item in the Channel pane is a folder containing the individual Channels. | |
| Fullscreen | Maximizes your view of Web content. Other than the Web page you're viewing, the only things you'll see are your Toolbar (without titles) at the top, and a minimal set of controls at the top right. | |
| Print | Print the current Web page on the default printer. (Tip: If the page being displayed has elaborate formatting, don't expect the printed output to look much like the screen.) | |
| Edit | Edit the current Web page in FrontPage Express. | |

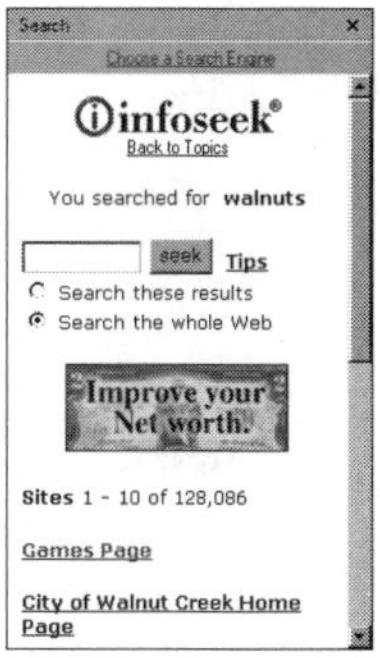

**Figure 16.10**

Search

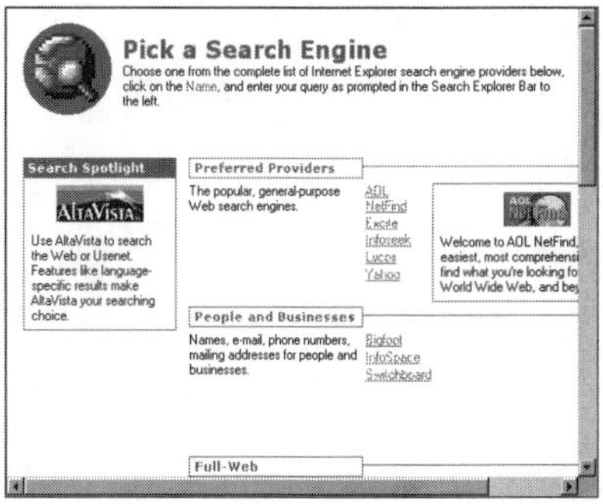

**Figure 16.11**

Pick Search Engine

# Drop Menus

Since Windows Explorer and Internet Explorer are two different expressions of a common interface, and we've already been over the items the two share, we'll just cover what's IE-specific.

**File Menu.**  **File\Open:** Here again, Internet Explorer treats the local computer it's on as an element of the Net—as the local *case* of the Net, if you will—so, from here, you can browse any local drive, any UNC, and any URL. It takes a while to get used to this and, even when you fancy yourself familiar with Internet Explorer, you'll trip over menu items that make you exclaim "I can do that from *here?!*"

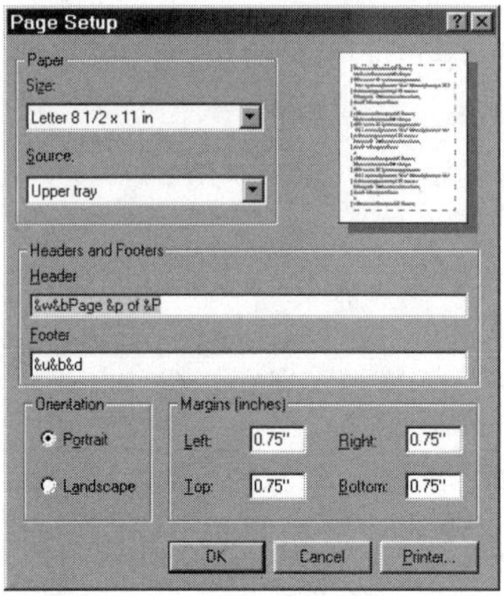

**File\Page Setup:** This is Page Setup for the printer, and as such looks like a Page Setup dialog for a cheap word processor, except for elaborated Header and Footer formatting. Since the document's header and footer are formatted on the fly—that is, they don't occur on the Web page so the output engine has to make them up—you can control how they look. The syntax is:

**Figure 16.12**

*File\Page Setup*

| | |
|---|---|
| **&w** | Window title |
| **&u** | URL |
| **&d** | Short format date |
| **&D** | Long format date |
| **&t** | Time in user-settable format |
| **&T** | Time in forced 24-hour format |
| **&p** | Current page number |
| **&P** | Total number of pages |
| **&&** | Prints a single ampersand |
| **&b** | Center the text immediately after **&b** |
| **&b&b** | Center the text immediately after the first **&b**; right-align the text immediately after the second **&b** |

&d, &D, and &t take the values set for them in Control Panel\Regional Settings.

**File\Send**

**Page by Email...** sends a copy of the page as an HTML document.

**Link by Email...** sends the hyperlink, both as a Shortcut and—for non-Microsoft mail programs that don't like Shortcuts—as hyperlinked plain text. See "Why Microsoft Mail Infuriates People" in the section on Outlook Express.

**Shortcut to Desktop** installs the hyperlink on the local Desktop, and when you click on it, IE acts as an OLE server.

**File\Properties** is a bare-bones Properties General tab except for two special buttons, **Certificates** and **Analyze**. Certificates displays the security certification of the document, if it has any, which it probably doesn't. Analyze nominally checks the HTML of the target document, although we won't swear to it, since no page we've checked has ever displayed an error.

**File\Working Offline:** See below.

**Edit Menu.** Edit\Select All is the foundation for a useful trick. If you want to copy the current Web page as plain text, open a blank file, select the page with `Ctrl``A`, copy it with `Ctrl``C`, and paste it into the blank file with `Ctrl``V`. It's much faster than using **File\Save As...** and **Save As Type**.

**Edit\Page:** Edit the current Web page in FrontPage Express (same as the Toolbar Edit button).

**View Menu.** View\Fonts lets you pick from five display character sizes and several Western and non-Western alphabets, depending on what's installed. (Tip: It helps to have some Unicode sets available. See the discussion of Unicode in Chapter 8, "Fonts.")

**View\Source** pulls up the source of the current page as a Notepad file.

**View\Internet Options:** The biggie, your main configuration dialog. See below.

**Go Menu.** Go\Home Page: Go to the page defined as your home page (same as the Toolbar Home button)

**Go\Channel Guide:** Open your Channels pane (same as the Toolbar Channels button)

**Go\Search the Web:** Go to the Microsoft Search Engine page (same as the Toolbar Search button)

**Go\My Computer:** Jump to My Computer (or whatever you've named it). This is the fastest way from Internet Explorer to your local computer.

**Go\Address Book:** Launch the Windows Address Book. See Chapter 5, "Toys, Games, and Pocketknives."

**Go\Internet Call:** Launch NetMeeting. See below.

**Favorites/Subscriptions Menu.** **Favorites\Add to...:** Add the current page to your Favorites menu or to a folder in it. Whatever you add will appear in Start Menu\Favorites, in the Favorites drop menu, and in the Favorites Toolbar pane. For this and the next three options, see "Favorites and Subscriptions" below.

**Favorites\Organize...:** Manage your hierarchy of Favorites folders. It would seem to us that, in the true spirit of the Explorer interface, this and **Add to...** could profitably be combined, but then we're only tourists.

**Favorites\Manage Subscriptions:** Notice the subtle shift from Favorites to Subscriptions? This is your cue that Internet Explorer's resource management method has gone from passive bookmarking to active content delivery—*if* that's what you want. We still have some doubts about the philosophical implications, but we'll get to those.

**Favorites\Update All Subscriptions:** The triumph of active content, as your hapless computer becomes a binary butterfly net. Of course, you did tell Internet Explorer you wanted the stuff.

Rest of the Favorites\ menu: A duplicate of whatever's on **Start Menu\Favorites**.

**Help Menu.** In the best Internet Explorer tradition, not just **Contents**, **Search**, and **About**, but a real menu full of juicy stuff.

**Help\Contents and Index:** The stuff you think of when you think of Windows Help, except of course that it's in HTML, so it's glacial. Come on—we know the tools are pricey, but can real WINHELP help be *that* hard to develop?

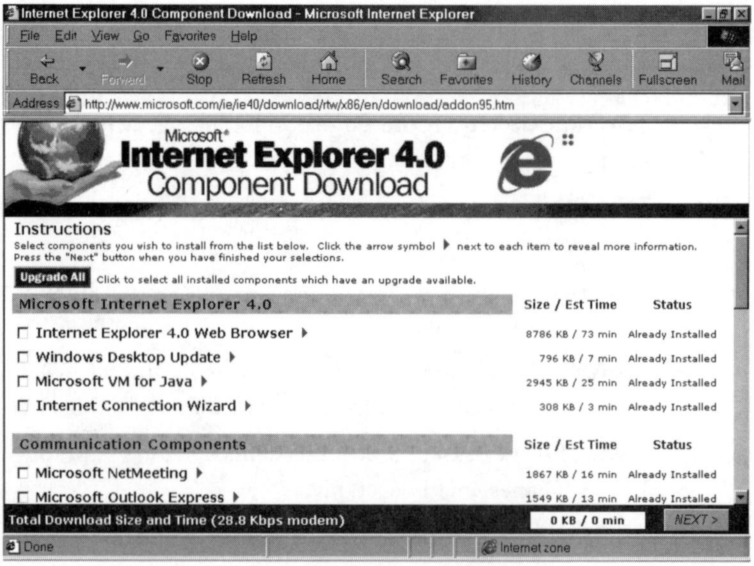

*Figure 16.13*

*Internet Explorer component download site*

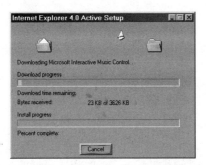

**Figure 16.14**

Active Setup

**Help\Product Updates:** This (Figure 16.13) means updates for Internet Explorer only, which is annoying, but if you want updates for other components you can reach them through Start Menu\Windows Update. Once you select your updates they'll be downloaded and installed by Active Setup (Figure 16.14).

Help\Web Tutorial: This logs on to the Microsoft Personal Computing page about connecting to the Net, browsing with a browser, and setting up a Web site. Since Microsoft seems positively allergic to leaving any of its Web pages alone for more than a week, your mileage may vary.

Help\Online Support: The Microsoft Support Online main page, which might still be orange when you read this. If you invoke it from here, it points to Internet Explorer, but you can use the About list to find support for other Microsoft products … and oh, dear, how many of them there are. We still can't believe they put the Add Active Channel widget on here; if you wanted to be notified every time this page changed, you could never use your computer for anything else.

Help\Microsoft on the Web: We're so grateful to Redmond! How difficult it might have been to find this, if they hadn't given us a hand!

There's your QuickRef, and now for the details.

## Configuring Internet Options

We've often noted Microsoft's somewhat Roman attitude toward Internet links, which can make poking around the Net seem like a stroll through an old-fashioned company town. Hey, it's their operating system, they get to set the defaults. But when you start aggressively creating Your Own Private Internet, you realize that Internet Explorer—like the rest of Windows—is almost unbelievably configurable.

The chrome spaghetti of Internet Explorer is down in the tabs of **View\Internet Options**, which—not to stretch a good thing too far—we might call **TweakII**, for "Tweak the Internet Interface." Like its homeloving cousin TweakUI, the Internet Options dialog offers some settings that you'll find delightful and some you'll never use. But the point is, once again, that there's something for everyone.

*Figure 16.15*

*General tab*

**General Tab.**  The **General** tab is the one you'll use most often, by far.

*Home Page.*  The terminology may be confusing because it talks about the "page to use for your home page," but Microsoft calls the same thing a start page; the page that loads automatically when you open your browser. You can fill in the address by hand; click **Use Current**, which copies the URL of the page you're currently looking at; click **Use Default**, which copies `http://home.microsoft.com`; or click **Use Blank**, which loads a curious thing called **about:blank**. If you view the source of this, it's simply a pair of legal HTML tags, but there's no file with any comparable name on the disk—meaning that you can't embellish your Blank page with rude or cynical statements, the way you could with IE 3.*x*. Of course, if you create your own local page and point to it, the sky's the limit.

*Temporary Internet Files.*  **Temporary Internet Files** is a polite way of saying "browser cache," and you'll find that the files, like the ones in the Recycle Bin, aren't as temporary as all that. Looking at the **Settings** button first, we see that the size of the folder—again like the Recycle Bin—is determined by a percentage of disk volume space. If you do a lot of Web browsing, the contents of the folder often bump against that limit, so Internet Explorer begins throwing the oldest cached files out. You won't miss them.

**Move Folder…** lets you move your graphics-downloads-and-cookies heap from the default, C:\WINDOWS\Temporary Internet Files, to any other folder you like. (The classic rationale is to move a giant folder of non-critical data from a crowded or fast disk to a less crowded or less fast disk.)

The Temporary Internet Files folder has four subfolders in which your browser cache files actually reside. In Windows 95 and NT 4.0 these were called **cache1** through **cache4;** in designing the next round of 32-bit Windows, Microsoft decided that this convention was somehow too obvious, and in Windows 98 they gave the folders (and, worse yet, the contents) random names. To keep the file contents from getting royally confused, Windows maintains a file (several, actually, but we won't get into that) called INDEX.DAT. INDEX.DAT is well protected, though not quite as thoroughly as the Registry .DAT files; it can't be opened directly, and it contains lots of URLs in clear text, interspersed with encrypted headers. Since INDEX.DAT acts as a cache file allocation table, your cache files all seem to be in a single folder, but they're not—when you look in the parent Temporary Internet Files folder, all you're seeing is a bunch of pointers to the URLs that contributed the files in the "real" cache directories below. This is why there are several standard file operations that you can't perform on files in the Temporary Internet Files folder, and why, if you want to save a copy of a file from the cache, your best bet is to drag it to a different folder—where it suddenly becomes a "real" file with normal Properties and a non-random name.

Even so, you can delete these files by hand, more carefully than the Windows automatic deletion will do it. *Most* of the files in the Temporary Internet Files folder will never be used again—but the exceptions are the files named **Cookie:<*yourusername*>@<*sitedomainname*>**. These are files that the Web sites you visit have placed on your disk so that they'll have access to information about you, rather than asking you for it.

Some people find cookies controversial because they don't like the idea of Web sites keeping databases of information about their guests. Part of the point, though, is that the site doesn't keep the information; *you* do, because you've got the cookie. The other advantage for the Web sites is that, if you keep cookies for fifty or a hundred Web sites at a couple of hundred bytes each, the cost to you in disk space is trivial, whereas if a popular site had to store cookies for millions of visitors, it would literally be running extra disks.

We recommend hanging on to cookie files, especially the ones handed to you by favorite sites that you visit frequently. The rest of the files in your browser caches, you can blow away whenever you please, or let Windows do it for you.

**View Files...** shows you the contents of Temporary Internet Files, which are mostly graphics. **View Objects...** shows you the contents of Downloaded Program Files, which are ActiveX and Java controls and classes. You don't need to hang onto these either.

This leaves **Check for newer versions...** which takes a little explaining. The whole point of a browser cache is to speed up Web access by letting you fetch a particular page from your own disk, rather than over the wire from the remote site, whenever it exists in both places. This seamless interleaving of cached local and remote data is one of the reasons we say HTTP is a work of genius. The sticky bit, really a comparatively minor problem, is that while the two copies of the page are disconnected from each other, the one on the Web site may change while the one in the local cache stays the same.

You can get around this by checking the date and time stamps on the two files and, if the one on the Web site is newer than the locally cached copy, downloading the newer one to overwrite the older one. Fine, but how *often* do you check for a newer version? If you check:

**Every visit to the page**, you're sure to have the latest version at all times, but you may add overhead to your browsing that does you no good. If you go to a page, check its version, follow a link away from it, return a few minutes later, and check the version again, it probably hasn't changed in the short time you were gone. If you have a very fast connection, so that you won't notice the delay of an extra comparison, go ahead and click this; if not, keep reading.

**Every time you start Internet Explorer**, you're accepting the default and making a compromise that usually works well. What this says is that when you start IE—that is, between the time you start it and the time you shut it down—each page you visit will be checked against the cache once, but only once. You'll get a *newer* version of the page, but not necessarily the newest one. And if you need the absolutely latest revision (say, you're giving opinions to somebody over the phone while they put up incremental versions of the same page) you can always hit the **Refresh** button on the Toolbar and force the server to hand you the latest copy.

**Never**. Well, like we said, you can hit the **Refresh** button to update the copies in your cache, but you're making work for yourself. We suggest avoiding this if you're surfing with anything faster than a 14.4 modem.

*Figure 16.16*

*Delete Files*

**Delete Files** is simple enough; click the button, click OK, and your cache is out with the trash. This also tosses your cookies, which is one reason not to do it this way. Check **Delete all subscription content** if you want to purge your Subscription folder too (see below).

Tip: If you have as much in your cache folders as most people, you'll click OK here and your computer will be very distracted for a while.

*Figure 16.17*

*History pane*

***History.*** The files in C:\WINDOWS\HISTORY are a record of the URLs you've visited during, by default, the last twenty days. They're organized in the folder the same way they're organized in the Internet Explorer History pane, which is a special folder view (Figure 16.17):

You can delete your Web browsing history with the **Clear History** button. Saving disk space is no reason to do it; the real, or rather "DOS-visible," contents of the folder are a couple of small pointer files. The need to cover your tracks, however, is another matter, and we'll remind you that if privacy is a perennial concern of yours, you can use the Paranoia tab of TweakUI to clear the History cache at every logon. For a less drastic option, use the spin buttons to reduce the cache to fewer days.

On the other hand, if you rely on your History files as an organizational tool and have nothing to fear from the guys with the tightly knotted ties, you can set **Days to keep...** to a maximum of 999. Your History pane may be unwieldy, but you'll absolutely know where you wanted to go today.

***Miscellaneous Options.*** The Miscellaneous options are **Colors**, **Fonts**, **Languages**, and **Accessibility**.

*Figure 16.18*

*Colors dialog*

The **Colors** Dialog sets colors for Web page text, background, and links. **Use Windows colors** defaults to checked, meaning black text on a gray background, but if you need more contrast there's no harm setting **Background** to white. (Remember that any choice you make here will be overridden by color specifications in the page itself. Hardly any decent Web page these days is black on gray, it's so *boring*.)

The **Links** colors are up to you, and you can change them from the standard blue and maroon to anything you find more pleasant or visible. If you check **Use hover color** (in other words, turn the hyperlink a different color when your pointer touches it) the default is red—and this can be very handy if you keep your Web viewing less cluttered by turning off automatic underlining.

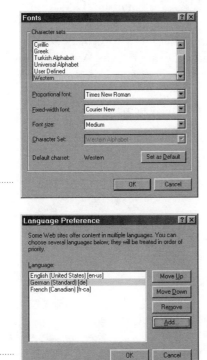

*Figure 16.19*

*Fonts dialog*

*Figure 16.20*

*Languages dialog*

**Fonts** lets you pick a character set— broadly speaking, an alphabet—for your Web viewing, and then implement your character set choice with a proportional font, a fixed font, and one of five font sizes to be the default. The **Character Set** drop-list box will be grayed out unless there's a choice of alphabets for your default, as there is for Central European, Cyrillic, and Greek.

**Languages** lets you install support for reading Web pages in almost any language. Shuffle the languages around until the character set you most need is at the top of the list.

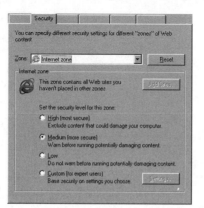

*Figure 16.21*

*Accessibility dialog*

Remember what we said about Web design choices overriding your local preferences for viewing? You can override the override. **Accessibility** lets you set your options in Colors and Fonts, then force all the pages you view to respect your choice of colors, font size, and font style. For more elaborate formatting, you can compel the use of a cascading style sheet (.CSS) file which will let you control any possible formatting. All of these boxes default to unchecked, but don't forget that they're there.

*Figure 16.22*

*Security tab*

**Security Tab.** The **Security** tab recognizes four categories, or "zones," of Web sites (Table 16.2) depending on how likely they are to bomb you with content that damages your computer or data. (Beware the macro virus!) For each zone, you can set one of three standard security levels or create your own.

If a zone is **Based on listed sites**, you can create a log file of URLs (or, presumably, UNCs) that you consider part of that zone. If none of the three preset security levels meets your standard for a particular zone, click **Custom**, click **Settings**, and specify degrees of suspicion for ActiveX controls, Java applets, scripting, downloads, user authentication, form data, IFRAME launches, active installation, drag-and-drop, copy and paste, and channel permissions. *Warning to TweakUI users:* Your nosy nemesis may be using tools of equal potency against you.

## Table 16.2 Security Zones

| Zone | Default Security Level | Based on Listed Sites? |
|---|---|---|
| *Local intranet* | Medium (warn before running potentially damaging content) | Yes |
| *Trusted sites* | Low (do not warn before running content) | Yes |
| *Internet* (everything that's not one of the other three) | Medium | No |
| *Restricted sites* | High (exclude potentially damaging content) | Yes |

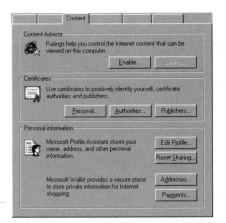

*Figure 16.23*

Content tab

**Content Tab.** The **Content** tab is about three things: Protecting your kids from content that will freak them out or make them act weird; using digital certificates for authentication and security; and storing pre-recorded information that you can give to vendors when you buy stuff over the Net.

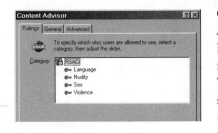

*Figure 16.24*

Content Advisor

***Content Advisor Dialog.*** The Content Advisor dialog, which is passworded, lets you use a ratings service to automatically lock out objectionable sites. The only ratings system that we've seen supplied with Windows 98 is RSAC (Recreational Software Advisory Council), but there may be others available later, which you'll add through the **Advanced** tab. You can also toggle access to restricted or unrated sites.

*Figure 16.25*

Certificate
Authorities

***Certificates.*** Digital certificates are snippets of code, issued by trusted third parties, that attach to downloadable content and vouch for its safety. A complete treatment is outside the scope of this book (*something* has to be) but, historically, the problem has been that valid certificates have come from many issuers and in a huge variety. Because Windows 98 is a forward-looking operating system, and because Microsoft has a vested interest in rising paradigms (like Internet commerce) that need certificates in order to work, you'll find that a computer with Windows 98 on it will happily accept almost any certificate that comes your way.

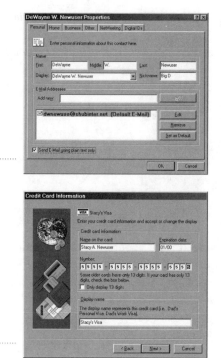

*Personal Information.* This should be called "Personal Gratification," because it's about shopping.

**Edit Profile** stores your name, address, and a bunch of other information in something that looks amazingly like the record template of the Windows Address Book. This information can only be used by Web sites that have permission from you, and **Reset Sharing** revokes those permissions.

**Addresses…** and **Payments…** let you set up credit cards for one-click shopping. *Be very sure you want to do this.* We don't claim to be models of self-discipline, but easy credit gets us in enough trouble when we have to do everything manually, and commercial sites like **Amazon.com** make impulse purchases easy enough without help from an operating system!

**Connection Tab.** The **Connection** tab lets you easily tweak network and connection settings. Everything on this tab exists somewhere else in Windows, but you'd have to dig for it.

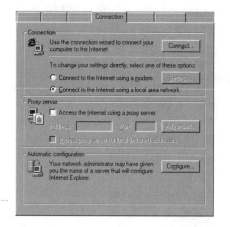

*Connection and Proxy Server.* These shunt you to the Internet Connection Wizard, and you can reach all the LAN settings from here that you can from there. See "Signup Dialog" under "Internet Connection Wizard" earlier in this chapter.

**Figure 16.29**

Automatic
Configuration

***Automatic Configuration.*** In a corporate setting, where many copies of IE4 are running on workstations, you can enforce identical configuration for all of them by using a resource file—which you can think of as a kind of policy file—located on an Internet or intranet server. The right-click Help here is informative but strictly client-side; to find out how to set up the server side of this arrangement, consult the Internet Explorer Administration Kit (IEAK) which, last we looked, was free from Microsoft.

**Figure 16.30**

Configuration Set

After configuration has been set by a resource file, the tab displays an extra message (Figure 16.30)

**Programs Tab.** The **Programs** tab lets you set your Internet defaults for mail, news, teleconferencing, and PIM software. Oddly enough, the drop-down lists contain only the names of Microsoft programs, but we just know the release version will fix that! The **Calendar** field is blank in the screenshot because our test box doesn't have Microsoft Outlook installed.

**Figure 16.31**

Programs tab

**Advanced Tab.** The **Advanced** tab takes care of those few things not covered by the other five. Rather than devote another chapter to a paragraph for each option, we'll gratefully point out that each item in the list has thorough right-click Help.

**Figure 16.32**

Advanced tab

# Favorites and Subscriptions

It would have been more descriptive—and more Windowsy—to call this Active Bookmarks, but never mind the lame name, the idea is attractive.

The problem with the Web has always been, and always will be, keeping up with it. You know the content is out there, but how to find it? Search engines devote more and more power to falling behind. Links pages are cute, but nearly hopeless. In desperation, we resort to flipping through Web sites as if they were cable channels, looking for anything more engaging than static. And yet push carries with it a mute, primal horror, like drowning.

Subscriptions, a kind of push-pull, neatly fill a niche by letting us describe exactly the sites we want to keep up with, then making sure we do. First-generation browser bookmarks made it easier to navigate to sites we wanted to check on regularly; the subscription model makes your computer into an assistant rather than an organizer, saying "Okay, give me the list and I'll check it out." With a lot less fuss than channels or WaveTop, subscriptions can deliver copious, tightly specified information.

**Adding a Favorite/Subscription.** Here's how you subscribe to something:

Pull down the **Favorites** menu and click **Add to Favorites**.

You have three top-level options:

**No, just add...** puts the page's URL in your Favorites folder and makes it accessible with the Favorites Toolbar button.

**Yes, but only...** lets you know when the content of the page is changed, by changing its icon (Figure 16.34a–34b), but the rest is up to you—click on the icon and visit at your leisure.

**Yes, notify...and download...** lets you breathe down a Web site's neck, or whatever they have. You'll be notified of updates (with a choice of methods, as you'll see) and the page will be pulled to your local disk for offline viewing.

Within these options you can customize:

*Figure 16.33*

Add Favorite

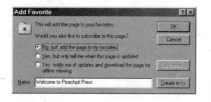

*Figure 16.34a*

URL icon
before update

*Figure 16.34b*

URL icon
after update (the
"gleam" is red)

*Figure 16.35*

Wizard for Notify

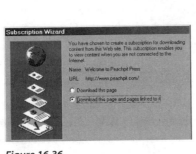

*Figure 16.36*

*Wizard for Notify and Download*

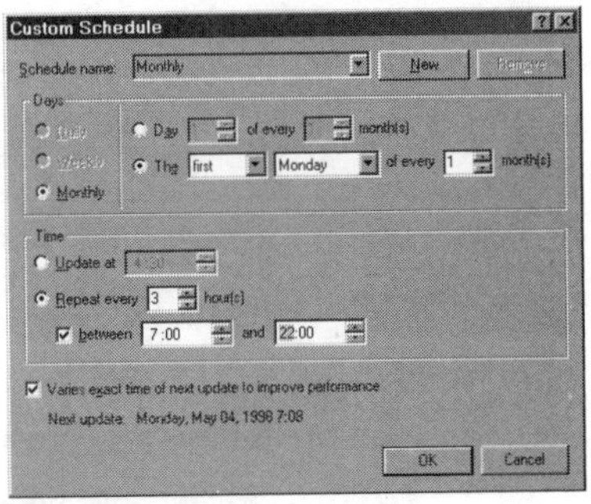

*Figure 16.37*

*Custom Schedule*

We won't go through the whole rigmarole here, but you can choose to:

Be notified of site updates by automatic e-mail.

Query for updates automatically or manually; if automatically, according to a preset schedule, daily, weekly, monthly, weekdays only, between certain hours, etc..

 The checkbox **Varies exact time of next update…** is mesmerizing. To quote from the right-click Help, "Selecting this checkbox increases the likelihood of offsetting the demands other people may make at the same time for the same site." Do Redmond's programmers still have vending machines, or do they drink Coke syrup out of squeeze bottles?

If you download, specify how much depth of linked page levels to pull from the site. The Wizard does caution you about going hog-wild and running out of local disk.

 If you set up scheduled, unattended updates and you use Dial-Up Networking to make your connections, you have to go into **View\Internet Options**, pick the **Connection** tab, click **Connect to the Internet using a modem**, click **Settings…**, and check **Connect automatically to update subscriptions**.

**Organize Favorites.** In marked contrast to Add Favorites, this dialog works as it did in previous versions of Internet Explorer—that is, not much like an Explorer. You can drag-and-drop to a limited extent, but since each pane will only show one level of the tree, you can't expand branches.

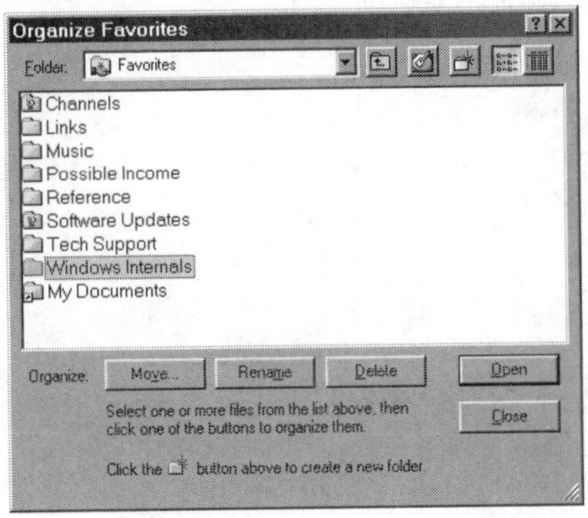

*Figure 16.38*

*Organize Favorites*

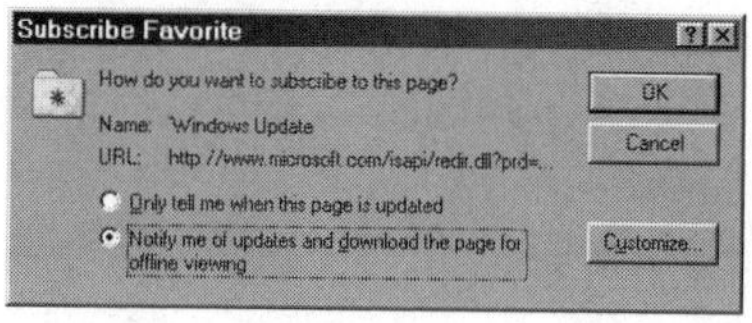

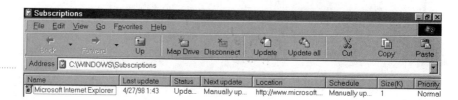

**Figure 16.39**

*Subscribe Favorite*

Also, this is a History folder that keeps statistics—which is a virtue in itself—but the Details view has a column called **Modified** and one called **Last Modified**. With no right-click Help to fall back on, we're left to wonder if they recycled some code once too often.

 Organize Favorites does have one spiffy trick. To convert a Favorite to a Subscription, right-click on any item in a Favorites folder, pick **Subscribe…** from the Context Menu, and complete the **Subscribe Favorite** dialog (Figure 16.39)

**Figure 16.40**

*Subscriptions Explorer*

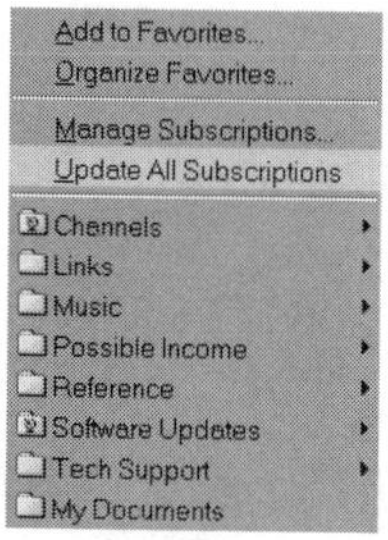

**Manage Subscriptions.** With **Manage Subscriptions** we veer back to the orthodox Explorer interface—with a couple of useful enhancements. There are two new Toolbar buttons: **Update**, which updates the highlighted subscription, and **Update All**, which updates all the subscriptions in the folder at once. On the **View** menu, below Internet Options, **Custom Schedule** gets you to the same Custom Schedule dialog available in Add Subscriptions.

**Figure 16.41**

*Update All Subscriptions on Favorites menu*

**Update All Subscriptions.** Updating your Subscriptions from Internet Explorer's menu is less flexible than doing it from within the Subscriptions folder; you don't get the nice Toolbar buttons, and you can only **Update All**. If you want to update one subscription, use **Manage Subscriptions** to open the Subscriptions folder.

# Working Offline (and Understanding Why)

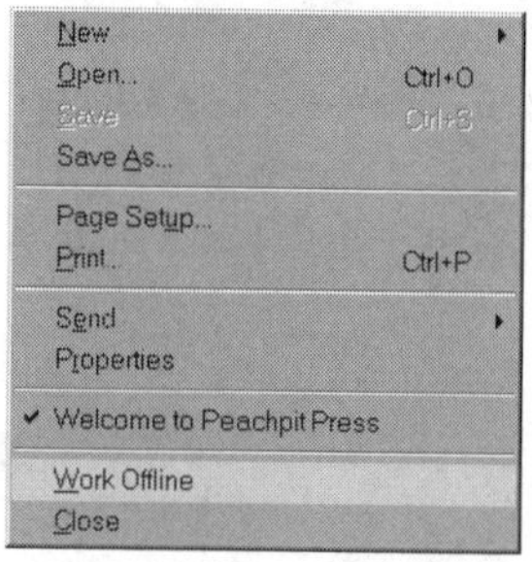

**Figure 16.42**

*Work Offline on File menu*

**Work Offline** (Figure 16.42) is understandable primarily in terms of Subscriptions and unattended pull of Web content.

Like many software developers today, Microsoft envisions a world in which permanent and full-time Net connectivity is a *de facto* standard, at least for those who make it a priority. At the same time, Microsoft "does not ignore" (to use one of their favorite phrases) the brutal practicality of the situation, which is twofold. First, in many parts of the United States, a full-time Net connection is either unavailable or not justifiable economically.

(Pause for a squeak from the gamers' gallery: "But I pay nineteen ninety-five a month and they say I can use it as much as I want!" Uh-huh. You start keeping that connection open 24-seven, and you see how long it takes your ISP to either upgrade your account or start surcharging you.) Second, even if you have all the Net connectivity you can use, you'll find that access to popular Web sites varies tremendously with the time of day. Ever tried to log on to Microsoft Support Online when it was lunch hour anywhere in the continental United States? One reason we wrote this book mostly at night was that, like the mainframe hackers of old, we found fewer obstacles to our work while the rest of the country was asleep. There's never enough bandwidth at the easy times.

The Subscription model of *logon, fetch, and store,* together with the ability to download as many levels of Web content as are useful, introduces a concept we might call "asynchronous pull." For comparison, look at the difference in convenience between e-mail and a phone call. Even leaving out the extreme case of a telemarketer calling during dinner, a phone call can be inconvenient because the calling party makes the implicit assumption that the party called will be ready and willing to talk at the same time; the model is synchronous. By comparison, somebody sends you e-mail when it's easy for them, you read and reply when it's easy for you, in a fundamentally asynchronous model. This is why, in parts of corporate America, an etiquette is developing that prefers e-mail as mainstream communication, reserving the phone for messages that are too urgent to be delayed.

But e-mail is asynchronous while the Web, the Internet's other killer app, is not. It would be interesting to know how many of the Web's theorists pondered that distinction in the early days, before the potential of a totally flooded server became obvious. It wasn't long, in any case, until we all had felt the inarticulate frustration that hits when you're ready for the Web … and the Web ain't ready for you. And without getting too deep into the theory of communications, let's just say that faster modems won't always make this better and might occasionally make it worse.

*Figure 16.43*

URL not offline

Working Offline is a way to *logon* when a Web site's traffic is light, *fetch* home what you said you wanted, and *store* the information until you're ready to look at it. The implementation in IE4 is a first pass, and needs a lot of refinement before it becomes sophisticated. But one dialog is an early clue to a new direction:

The "local 404" in Figure 16.43 says that, although you downloaded material from the site you're currently working with, you're trying to jump to a page that you don't have a local copy of. IE4, faithful to the spirit of the URL (Uniform Resource Locator) replies with "Well, this page isn't on *this* computer, but I can go look for it where the URL says it is." If you hit the **Connect** button, you're working with information distributed—spanned— over your computer and the server.

Doesn't something about this sound familiar? Of course; this is the way the Web has *always* worked, bridging between the server's data structure and the contents of your browser cache files. Local caching was originally a strategy to sidestep problems with performance and bandwidth, but as it matures, it's becoming a true key to cyberspace. Even today, when you're on the Web, you may be pulling files from several servers and not realize it. As your own computer becomes a more active participant in Web browsing, the distinction between "online" and "offline" may be blurred and finally vanish.

Windows 98 and Internet Explorer 4 are not the versions that will get us there. As we mentioned, the current Work Offline option is crude enough that it's not much more than a proof of concept; but we can think of some exciting possibilities if unattended fetches can be more deeply automated. For example, what if the setup for a Subscription could include stroke-and-click macros? (Tip to Microsoft: **Put a 32-bit Windows Macro Recorder** somewhere in the add-on bells and whistles, like Windows Update or a Plus! Pack. Thank you.) Then you could essentially say to Internet Explorer, "At two o'clock tomorrow morning, go to Microsoft Support Online, stick the cursor in the **My question** field, feed in these words, click **Find**, and bring me back what it tells you." As we've implied so often in this book, all the components needed for this exist in principle.

What would you use Subscription pull for, if the implementation had more features? Put your ideas in the guestbook at `http://www.winbible.com`. After all, Windows 2001 is just a few short years away.

## Notes From the Net

Before IE4 became part of Windows 98, it was thoroughly anatomized, abused, discussed, and tire-kicked in one of the most public "public beta" programs in history. (If you downloaded the whole thing, Microsoft should have sent you a Certificate of Appreciation. Personally, we spent the five bucks for the CD.) Naturally, Internet Explorer is a more robust program as a result, but that's not all. A considerable body of knowledge has grown up in IE4's user community, and we're happy to summarize some of it in Table 16.3.

## *Table 16.3  Internet Explorer Tips and Tricks*

| | |
|---|---|
| ***Add Favorites*** | You can add a site to your Favorites folder, even though you've already logged off and closed Internet Explorer, so long as the URL is still in your Address Bar drop-down list.<br><br>    Click on the URL to put it in the Address Bar; then pull down the File menu and pick **Work Offline**. Internet Explorer will open the page from your browser cache. Right-click inside the page, pick **Add to Favorites**, and set up your Favorite or Subscription as we've described earlier. |
| ***Fullscreen*** | Fullscreen by default installs the standard Toolbar across the top of the screen and leaves it visible. No fun! You can add the Address bar and Links bar by right-clicking anywhere on the Toolbar and selecting them; if you like using the menus, you can select Menu Bar too, but with all three selected, the Toolbar gets a bit crowded. For the final touch, right-click again and select **Auto Hide**. Now the toolbar will disappear until your mouse pointer is near the top of the screen. After all, what's Fullscreen for? |
| ***Context Menu and Properties*** | If you right-click the E-icon on the desktop, you can choose Properties and open **Internet Properties** (which is the same dialog as Internet Options from View) without running IE4. You can also launch IE4 as a single pane with **Open**, as a dual pane with **Explore**, or at your home page with **Open Home Page**. |
| ***Cut And Paste URL*** | If a URL appears as plain text in any Windows application, highlight the URL, use Ctrl C to copy it to the Clipboard, start IE4, click in the Address Box and press Ctrl V to paste. If the URL appears as a link in the application, just click it to go directly to the site. |
| ***Change a Link Icon*** | A Link in the Links folder is a Shortcut, and although it's officially an Internet Shortcut, there's nothing special to learn about how it works. For example, you can change its icon in the usual way.<br><br>    Right-click the link you want to change, choose Properties, and pick the **Internet Shortcut** tab; click **Change Icon**, and **Browse**. The default icon source is the odd and sparse selection in URL.DLL, but you can select one of the other icon .DLLs, like SHELL32.DLL. Click **OK** as usual to save your changes.<br><br>    To get the new icon to appear, you have to close IE4 and load it again. |
| ***Local Navigation*** | Remember that Windows treats your hard disk as an extension of the Net and (within limits) vice-versa. You can easily use IE 4 to browse a folder on your local drive, a request it won't even consider unusual. On the other hand, if you use Explorer to browse to a Link or Favorite, Explorer will whistle up Internet Explorer, which will dial your ISP and take you to the selected page.<br><br>    Get used to the idea that Explorer and Internet Explorer are really two instances of the same search capability, each with a different (but appropriate) emphasis. Earlier versions of Windows, starting with Windows for Workgroups, said "Every computer is part of a network, if it wants to be." Windows 98 says "Every computer is part of the Net, *unless* it *doesn't* want to be." |

## Table 16.3 (continued)

| | |
|---|---|
| **Printing** | There are several ways to print a Web page. Click the **Print** button on the toolbar, choose **File\Print**, or press $\boxed{\text{Ctrl}}\boxed{\text{P}}$. Note the special Print dialog with controls for linked documents and frames (Figure 16.44). |
| | You can print a page without loading it by right-clicking on a URL and choosing **Print Target** from the Context Menu. Tip: You won't know how long the page is until it finishes printing. |
| **Shortcut Key** | Assigning a Shortcut key to IE4 can speed up a whole hunk of your life. Right-click on the Start button; choose **Open** from the Context Menu; double-click on **Programs;** double-click on the Internet Explorer program folder. Look for the IE4 icon, right-click on it, choose Properties, and pick the **Shortcut** tab. Set your cursor in the Shortcut Key text box and press $\boxed{\text{E}}$; Ctrl-Alt-E will appear in the text box. Click OK and close the Start Menu window. Now, to open IE4 from the Desktop, just press $\boxed{\text{Ctrl}}\boxed{\text{Alt}}\boxed{\text{E}}$. |
| **Setting a Start Page** | Do you want to make the page you're viewing into your Start page? At the left-hand end of the Address bar, you'll see a little E-icon next to the currently displayed URL. Click and drag it to the icon on the toolbar's Home button. A dialog will ask if you want to make this page your Start page. Click Yes. |
| **Upgrading from IE3** | If, when you upgrade from Internet Explorer 3 to IE4, your ISP information doesn't get updated, don't worry; you get another chance. The first time you run the new version, IE4 will ask you for a provider name. Click **Use Current** and supply any information that the dialogs ask for. |
| | Note: We have *not* tested this independently, but we received it from several trusted sources. |
| **URL Syntax** | When you type a URL into the IE4 Address box, you're probably better off if you enter it without a slash at the end. Some URLs will work with a terminal slash and some won't, but any URL is more likely to work without one. |

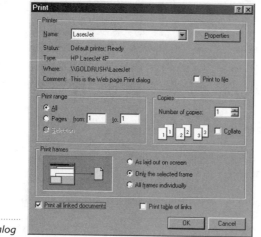

**Figure 16.44**

Internet Print dialog

## Below the Belt

People get very exercised about illicit content on the Net—the Web in particular, since it's so graphic and public, although for sheer salacious overload some of the **alt.*** newsgroups could stack up against anything. As a result, there are scores of Web pages and, probably, half a dozen newsgroups devoted to deploring the cyber-evils that have befallen us. Yes, there is stuff on the Net that will give your child bad dreams, even if she's thirty-three. There is stuff on the Net that would make Caligula wince. This was inevitable. The Net at its beginnings may have been attended by great hopes, but so are we all, and we had no reason to think that as it grew, it would be more moral or more high-minded or disciplined or purposeful than the world itself.

Get to your teenage kid's computer sometime, if it's not also yours, and use some kind of graphics file viewer to dump the browser cache files. You may be startled and discomfited by what you find. But ask yourself how, in the same world with catalog lingerie, *Buford's Beach Bunnies,* and Howard Stern, this could ever have been avoided? And the Net, after all, is so evocative of what Stewart Brand once said about the entire planet: "We can't put it together. It is together." Our computers open us to the Net, for better or worse, just as radios and TV sets open us to the world.

The only way to live on the Net is with a strength of character, as individuals, that we often feel the Net as a whole lacks. Few people today go out into the world—even as children—without some sense of what has merit and what does not, who to make friends with and who to steer clear of. We trust the world itself to provide *some* of that education, but we take it on ourselves to impart at least enough to encourage better judgment. We don't say "I won't teach my child to live in the world, because the world isn't fit to be lived in." We can't say that about the Net either. Browser cache files, in the last analysis, are like the magazines under the mattress; sooner than later, you'll find yourself having a talk about them.

## Summary

Internet Explorer 4, by extending the client-side Windows architecture seamlessly out over the Internet, redefines the Wintel operating system to an extent not seen since the advent of Windows for Workgroups in the early 1990s. It is not perfect by any means—it's a disk hog and a RAM hog, and while it's installing, it plays with your system internals in ways that can create problems for applications. Even so, whether you're an eager at-home novice, a corporate cubicle-dweller, or a seasoned alpha geek, you're likely to find that IE4 does today's best available job of bringing the Net to you and you to it.

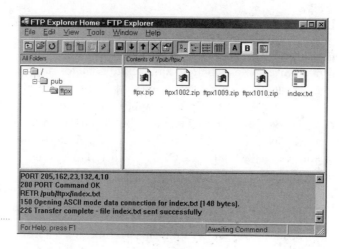

**Figure 16.45**

FTP Explorer

# FTP Explorer (FTPx)

One thing Internet Explorer doesn't do well is FTP transfers. FTP, a holdover from the days when the Net was dominated by UNIX, is the fastest way to get a file (especially a big file) from one point to another, much faster than doing it with any Web browser.

Unfortunately, an elegant FTP solution for 32-bit Windows hasn't been easy to find. Web sites typically use FTP to transfer files, but your browser implements FTP as a task of HTTP, which is much less efficient than it could be. The Windows command-line FTP utility works but is hardly easy to use. Some of the traditional Windows FTP clients offer good transfer rates, but now have outdated interfaces. Can't we have it all? Oh, yes …

Alan Chavis' **FTP Explorer** is just what it sounds like—an FTP client with Explorer-compliant interface, neck-tickling performance, and the ease of use of a pop-top can. As for its tenacity, we used it to download an entire Windows 98 Release Candidate—seven straight hours over a 56K dial-up connection. Intelligence? It can re-establish connections and resume transfers that have been crashed by server faults. You could not ask for more.

**Figure 16.46**

FTPx Setup screen

Browse to **http://www.ftpx.com** and *the real article,* not a demo, is all yours. It's free for personal and educational use; the fee for commercial or corporate use is a modest $30. The Web site suggests voluntary donations toward development costs, as do we, because we want this guy to write more software.

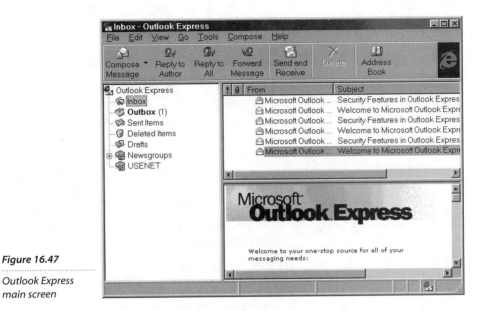

**Figure 16.47**

*Outlook Express main screen*

# Outlook Express

The funny thing about Outlook Express (Figure 16.47) is that it's a teaser applet—Microsoft wants you to get used to Outlook Express and upgrade to Outlook, their full-house mail client, PIM, and calendar manager. We think the "real" Outlook is closer to a busted flush; it's too complicated, it thrashes your hardware without mercy, and it's sloooow. Outlook Express, by contrast, is a nice piece of code—especially for free.

The standard interface is a three-pane window (an architecture well demonstrated by other Internet clients, including Qualcomm's Eudora and Forte's Free Agent) with one window for the folder tree, one for the message list, and one for the current open message. Of course, you can slide the frames of these windows to suit yourself.

## Main Screen Drop Menus

The **Main Screen** drop menus are arduous to describe in depth, because they give you lots of options, because many of those options are found elsewhere in Internet Explorer, and because the menus vary depending on exactly where in Outlook Express you are. We'll confine ourselves in Table 16.4 to the options that are unique to Outlook Express.

### Table 16.4  Outlook Express Menu Options

| | | |
|---|---|---|
| **File** | Save As Stationery | Saves any open HTML file as a mail background. |
| | Folder\Compact and Folder\Compact All | Rewrites mail folders to remove deleted messages and slack space |
| | Import\Address Book | Imports address files from Eudora, Microsoft Exchange, MS-Mail for Windows 3.*x*, Netscape, Netscape Communicator, and in LDIF or comma-separated text |
| | Import\Messages | Imports messages from Eudora, Microsoft Exchange, MS-Mail for Windows 3.*x*, Microsoft Outlook, Windows Messaging, Netscape Mail, or Netscape Communicator |
| | Import\Mail Account Settings | Imports Internet mail account settings from most previously installed mail clients |
| **Edit** | Mark as Read, Mark Thread as Read, Mark All as Read, Mark as Unread | Toggle Inbox messages between read (plain type and icon flap open) and unread (bold type and icon flap closed). A **thread** is a series of messages or postings related by a common subject |
| | Find People | Search the Windows Address Book or standard Internet directory services |
| | Find Text | Find text in the displayed message (not in all highlighted messages, although you can highlight more than one) |
| | Find Message | Search for message with specific sender, recipient, subject, or body text, optionally in specified folders and between specified dates |
| **View** | Columns | Set columns to be displayed, and display order, in folder panes |
| | Sort By | Sort by message features, sort up or down, or group by subject |
| **Tools** | Inbox Assistant, Accounts, Options | See below |
| **Help** | Learn about Microsoft Outlook | Uses Internet Explorer to connect you to a Microsoft Web site for an Outlook tutorial, so you can understand what a backward and self-involved person you are for continuing to run Outlook Express |

# Tools Menu

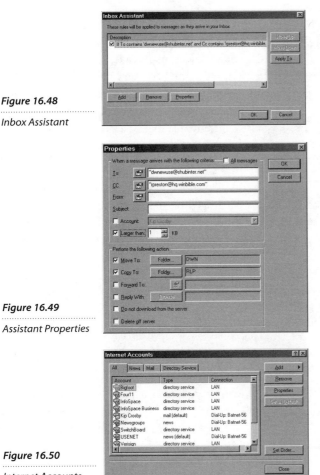

**Figure 16.48**

*Inbox Assistant*

**Figure 16.49**

*Assistant Properties*

**Figure 16.50**

*Internet Accounts*

**Inbox Assistant.**  The **Inbox Assistant** (Figure 16.48) is a front-office mail sorter; it makes sure incoming messages end up in the right folders. The big leap in configurability is the **Apply To...** button, which lets you apply particular sorting rules *to* particular folders.

You'll find enough options in Properties (see Figure 16.49) to keep all your mail organized, to generate replies automagically with forms, and even to prevent giant spam attacks from descending on your hapless server disk.

**Accounts.**  The **Internet Accounts** dialog gives you ordered lists of the accounts—some of which, probably not all of which, will be Dial-Up Networking connectoids—that are your channels to the Net. If the **All** tab is confusing, you can view this broken into lists of news, mail and directory (LDAP) accounts. When you check names against multiple directory services, use the **Set Order...** button to establish the sequence in which the directories will be polled.

There are options worthy of note in the **Advanced** tab of **Mail Properties**, which lets you set parameters you can't set anywhere else in Windows—like server port numbers, SSL locks, server timeouts, and mail delivery options. The **Security** tab here lets you set up digital IDs for e-mail, whereas all other digital IDs are in IE4 Internet Options.

Most, not all, of the remaining switches here have close equivalents in Dial-Up Networking.

**Options.** May we have your attention puh-*leeeze!* It's time for Tweak the Outlook Mail and News Interface—TweakOMNI! Yeah, no kidding.

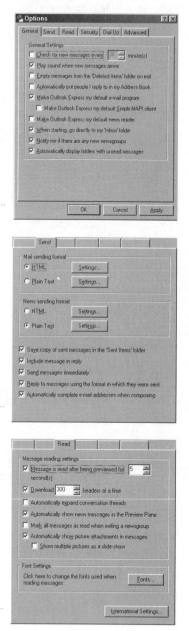

*Figure 16.51*

*General tab*

*Figure 16.52*

*Send tab*

*Figure 16.53*

*Read tab*

***General Tab.*** The **General** tab (Figure 16.51) sets Outlook Express defaults (default news reader, mail reader, etc.). It offers you an OLE link between mail replies and the Windows Address Book, it sets notifications, and it gives you the option of automatically checking mail periodically.

***Send Tab.*** The **Send** tab (Figure 16.52) lets you choose between saving and not saving copies of sent messages; to copy the message into the reply; to send-on-queue or send-on-check; and to match send and receive formats. You can also AutoComplete e-mail addresses the way you can URLs in Internet Explorer.

We have some things to say about the **Sending format** options; see "Why Microsoft Mail Infuriates People."

***Read Tab.*** The **Read** tab (Figure 16.53) sets newsgroup defaults (you mean you can download *more* than 300 headers at a time?!), lets you select mappings of character sets in **Fonts**, and lets you *unmap* them—or something—in the **International Settings** dialog. These last two dialogs have a close relationship that is just too abstruse for our Windows-shattered minds to grasp. Would anybody who's comfortable with this please visit the Web site and leave us a message? We *hate it* when we don't understand things.

**Figure 16.54**

Security tab

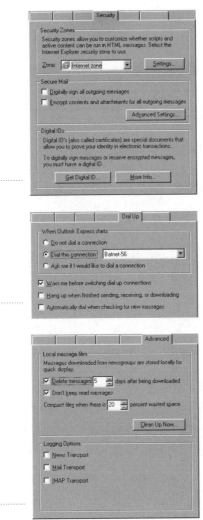

**Figure 16.55**

Dial Up tab

**Figure 16.56**

Advanced tab

*Security Tab.* The **Security** tab, to begin with, carries the **Security Zone**—that is, trusted or restricted site—paradigm of Internet Explorer over to Outlook Express. **Secure Mail** is the "other end" of the mail-encryption utility; whereas the Compose Toolbar will let you digitally sign or encrypt messages one at a time, these checkboxes let you say "Oh, heck, secure them all." **Advanced settings** are the utilities to do it with. And finally, **Digital IDs** gets the digital IDs *for* encrypting your sent mail. We *think* this is the same tab as Digital IDs in Accounts Mail Properties—not the S/MIME one, the other one.

*Dial Up Tab.* The **Dial Up** tab (Figure 16.55) has a bunch of incredibly handy settings: What connection to establish when Outlook Express starts, autodial-on-check, hang up at end of transaction, and warn before switching connectoids. These should really be somewhere more obvious, because novice users will tear their hair trying to find them this deep.

*Advanced Tab.* The **Advanced** tab lets you control local caching of newsgroup postings, and local logging of command traffic with mail and news servers.

## Main Screen Toolbar

The Toolbar for Outlook Express is an Explorer toolbar, but with buttons you don't see elsewhere.

**Figure 16.57**

New Message with Stationery

**Compose Message.** The **Compose Message** button opens a new message. It can be a blank message, or if you like pretty mail—and you know your recipient can accept it, see below—you can use the droplist to select a Stationery background (Figure 16.57).

The new message is a window independent of Outlook Express, which can be minimized while you're working on the message. The dialogs for recipients and subject, when they're not clicked, gently remind you what to enter— one of the touches that makes Outlook Express especially suitable for novice e-mailers.

*Figure 16.58*

*Editing toolbar*

*Compose Toolbars.*  The **Editing** toolbar (Figure 16.58) offers some standard Windows tools and some that are unique to advanced e-mail. The buttons are **Send message**, **Undo**, **Cut**, **Paste**, **Copy**, **Check Names**, **Select Recipients** from the Windows Address Book, **Insert File**, **Insert Signature**, **Digitally sign message**, and **Encrypt message**.

*Figure 16.59*

*Formatting toolbar*

The **Formatting** toolbar (Figure 16.59) will be familiar if you've ever used Microsoft Word, except for the stuff at the right-hand end. The controls are:

- First group: **Font, Font size,** and **Style Tags,** which appear to be standard HTML.

- Second group: **Bold, Italic, Underline,** and **Colors.**

- Third group: **Numbered** paragraphs, **Bulleted** paragraphs, **Decrease** indent, **Increase** indent.

- Fourth group: **Left align, Center,** or **Right align** paragraph.

- Fifth group: Insert **Horizontal line, Hyperlink,** or **Picture.**

**Reply to Author.**  Reply to Author creates a new message to the author of the received message, with a subject that follows up the thread of the original message, and containing a copy of the original message. Tip: Experienced e-mail users, out of respect for bandwidth and their correspondents' time, either delete the copy of the original message or take a minute to trim it back as far as possible. Unless an original message is very short, or must be replied to in incredible detail, returning an entire text to its sender is a mark of either cluelessness or carelessness.

**Reply to All.**  Copy your reply to all recipients of the original message. Think carefully before choosing this option; if you use it when it's not needed, you'll land a lot of superfluous bits in other people's Inboxes.

**Forward Message.** Does exactly the same thing as Reply to Author, except that:

- The **To:** field is blank, for the new recipient.

- The Subject begins with **Fw:** (Forward) instead of **Re:** (Reply)

You'll probably leave more of the original message text in the body than you would with a Reply. It's considered polite to include a brief annotation at the top of the message body—even if it's only "FYI."

**Send and Receive.** Logs on to the connection (whether intranet or Dial-Up Networking) specified in the Accounts dialog, sends the messages from your Outbox, and downloads new mail and puts it in your Inbox.

**Delete.** Moves the highlighted message or messages to the Deleted Items folder. If you're working in the Deleted Items folder, you'll be asked to confirm permanent deletion.

**Address Book.** Opens the Windows Address Book.

**Connect (Root folder).** Makes a connection from a drop-down list of available connectoids.

**Hang Up (Root folder).** Hang up the current connection.

## Newsgroups

The Usenet *newsgroups* are like worldwide, networked computer bulletin boards each devoted to a single topic—theoretically!! In the old days of the ARPAnet, newsgroups were a formal hierarchy for the exchange of mostly technical information. With the Net's explosion they've turned—most people would say degenerated—into the World Wide Watercooler. No matter what you like to chatter aimlessly about, there's a newsgroup for it, or there will be next week; to such an extent that, with all due respect to free speech, this is turning from a feature into a problem. Right this minute, there … ah, *were* about 15,000 newsgroups, and when you're reading this there are more.

If you like living dangerously, you can just subscribe to a random handful of newsgroups and walk in with both guns drawn. For this approach there are only three things you need to know: Writing and sending a message is called *posting,* replying to a message that someone else has posted is called *following up* or *posting a followup,* and vehement criticism of someone else's obnoxious behavior is called *flaming.* You'll survive until you annoy someone who knows enough about the Net to lean on your ISP and get your account taken away. (Yes, it happens; not as often as it should, but more often than you'd think.)

Want to do it right, instead? When you subscribe to newsgroups, start with the two called **news.answers** and **news.announce.newusers**. Read what you find there, and absorb the principle that while Usenet *looks* like supersonic anarchy, there are underlying rules and customs. The rules are meaningful, because they've survived, and nothing arbitrary survives for long on the Net. The customs—which are collectively called "netiquette"—may not have the force of rules, but they quickly make the difference between being welcome and being disdained (or just dissed) in a virtual community.

 **We could go on, but we'll confine ourselves to a few Zen-like tips. If you don't understand some of these, be patient; you will.**

- You're talking to *people.*

- Say to one person what is for one person, and to everyone what is for everyone.

- Find out what crossposting is, and how not to do it, and then don't do it.

- Don't subscribe to more than two or three newsgroups at once. You don't have the time for them, and they probably don't have the time for you, either.

- When you join a new newsgroup, read the traffic for a couple of days before you post anything. It's like walking into a party, except that it lasts forever and no one ever cleans up.

- Keep your .sig short and don't put your phone number in it. Anybody reading the traffic already has your e-mail address and that's bad enough.

- There is Usenet and there is life. There is life in Usenet and there is Usenet in life. Even so they are not the same thing.

**How They Work.** First you decide which newsgroups you might want to look at (*hah!*) so you need to download the current list of newsgroups, using a Dial-Up Networking connectoid to an ISP that has a *news server*—that is, a server that receives the Usenet news feed. Download this list when you have something important to do away from your computer, like eat dinner.

When the list is on your local disk, plan to skim through it and see which newsgroups interest you. What you'll actually be doing is staring goggle-eyed at the arcane and/or bizarre topics that people care enough about to set up newsgroups for, but you're bound to find one or two groups that you want to try out. Highlight each one and *subscribe* to it, which you can do simply by clicking the Subscribe button. Now, in essence, you've told the news server that you want the header of every posting from these groups to be sent to your disk as soon as it arrives. Only the headers of messages are sent because there's no point in sending the (comparatively bulky) bodies of postings you're not interested in reading.

You can look at the list of headers in the Subject pane of Outlook Express, and double-click on each one you want to read. The bodies of the postings will be delivered from the news server. As you follow the meandering, perpetually interrupted conversation, you may decide that you want to use the **Compose Message** button to post a new article, use the **Reply to Group** button to follow up somebody else's posting, or use the **Reply to Author** button to send private e-mail to the poster of an article. (You notice that Microsoft, here as elsewhere, is happy to substitute its own jargon for accepted terminology. This does no harm in intranet usage, but in the context of Usenet it's off-putting.) As the hours go by, people will follow up your postings, send you e-mail about them, and you'll be slowly enmeshed in the sticky tendrils of a newsgroup. How did anything so conceptually simple get so involving?

Well, we're in no position to moralize about newsgroups, so we'll just introduce you to Microsoft's rather attractive toolkit, and leave you to find your own way.

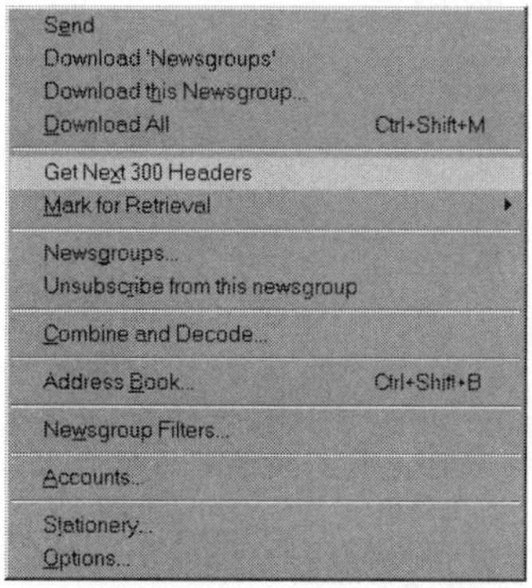

*Figure 16.60*

Tools Menu of newsgroups

**News Drop-Down Menu.** *Downloading.* You can download postings one newsgroup at a time, download all the newsgroups that you subscribe to, or anything in between. Outlook Express will let you download full bodies from subscribed groups, but that uses up disk space quickly; a better choice is to download only headers, peruse them offline, mark the interesting-looking ones for retrieval, and get the bodies the next time you're on.

Volumes of data that are potentially this vast need real-time controls, and that's what **Get Next 300 Headers** is about; no matter how many headers are waiting for you on the server—and it can be thousands if you haven't logged in for a while—you slice off 300 and go through them before you download the next batch. Kip happens to believe that, the more often you find yourself using Get Next 300 Headers, the more likely it is that you're spending too much time on Usenet.

*Encoding/Decoding.* **Combine and Decode** is the client-side tool for retrieving graphics or other binary files from news postings. News, by its nature, is straight ASCII—a point we'll go back to in "Why Microsoft Mail Infuriates People" below. If you want to transmit and receive graphics over Usenet, it has to be encoded as ASCII, posted to the newsgroups, retrieved, and decoded at your end. The process was developed back in the days of universal UNIX and is called uuencode (UNIX-to-UNIX encode) and, on the other side, uudecode.

The one problem with uuencoded graphics is that, as usual with graphics, the files are huge; and habitual Usenet readers have an abiding distaste for large files, which make retrieving news even more laborious than usual. The polite workaround is to encode the files, then split them into small pieces, and make it clear to newsreaders what the pieces are. Therefore, a uuencoded file generally has to be recombined from its pieces before it's decoded.

*Newsgroup filtering*

***Filtering.*** Since there is *no* guarantee of quality in newsgroup traffic—rather the contrary, if you ask us—you'll need some help figuring out which postings you want to read and which you don't. Sometimes the subject is the tip-off, but with a sigh for human nature, we concede that you're more likely to avoid certain *people* than certain topics. The answer is to have a file of criteria for messages that your newsreader will refuse to display. In UNIX this was called a *killfile,* which tells you how high passions ran; Outlook Express calls it **Newsgroup Filtering**, and it looks like Figure 16.61.

**Figure 16.62**

*Filtering Properties*

To add another filter, click the **Add** button and fill out the screen shown in Figure 16.62.

Click **OK**. If you're committed to doing lots of Usenet, carefully crafted filtering will help ensure your peace of mind. This is especially true when you consider that newsgroups are like small medieval city-states; no matter how prosperous and calm they may ordinarily be, they're periodically overrun by packs of coltish, rude barbarians who are viciously determined to talk about Pez dispensers or Australian rules football just when your analysis of Windows NT filesystems was getting somewhere. In a week or two they'll eat up the last of your bandwidth, get disgusted, and leave; in the interim, a good killfile is just the ticket.

# News Toolbar

The News toolbar is a lot like the Mail toolbar—more so than it should be.

**Compose Message.**  As noted, the process is called *posting*.

**Reply to Group.**  Misleading again; the process is called *followup*.

**Reply to Author.**  Send private e-mail to the poster of an article.

**Forward Message.**  Send a copy of an article via e-mail to someone outside the newsgroup.

**Newsgroups.**  Show the list of newsgroups (whether Usenet or intranet) available from a current server.

**Connect.**  Make a connection from a drop-down list of available connectoids.

**Hang Up.**  Hang up the current connection.

**Stop.**  Cut off the disk-inundating flow of postings when you log onto Usenet after going away for the weekend. We *told* you not to subscribe to so many newsgroups.

# Why Microsoft Mail Infuriates People

Sometimes Microsoft acts like a very big frog in a small pond, when it should settle for being a decent-size frog in a great big pond. This tendency is sometimes distasteful, but mostly okay, unless Microsoft's priorities get *you* in trouble. And it is especially not okay when Microsoft makes decisions that get you in trouble and you don't even realize it.

The Microsoft mail architecture provides for a two-part message, which is called "multipart-mixed." The message content is written once in MIME, and then again in HTML. You can use MIME without encoding, or with two different encodings, or not use MIME at all and go to uuencode instead. This is a versatile architecture because PC and Macintosh mail readers will breeze through the MIME-formatted text and see the HTML as a harmless attached file, while anyone who opens the message in a browser will read the message in HTML just as if it were Web content.

MS is pretty chipper about this. "When you use HTML formatting," the Help says, "and the recipient's mail or news program does not read HTML, the message appears as plain text with an HTML file attached. The recipient can view the attached file by opening it in any Web browser." Well, excuse us, but we hear a quite different story!

Since all HTML tags are made up of ordinary keyboard characters, like </A>, a mail client that assumes mail is in plain text will read HTML as text— impenetrable text. If you give a mail message in both HTML and MIME to a text mail reader, the message will be so buried in the formatting that it may be almost impossible to find. Even if the text is discernible, the message will be several times as long as it needed to be. We have several friends, mostly old UNIX hands, who say that if they open a mail message and see a single HTML tag, they delete the message without reading another word. Web-formatted mail is just too inconvenient—and insulting.

Fonts, colors, stationery, vCards, and other techno-fripperies are fine in the cozy universe of PCs, Macs, and … er … PCs. In other words, Microsoft is trying to reposition the Net as a playground for the architectures it supplies software to. Whether this is pardonable pride, shortsightedness, or a fanatical vision of the future, we've never been sure. But the Internet was in full roar when the original IBM PC, the toaster Mac, and even the Apple II were no more than sketches. It disdains to bow its head before the grand visions of a single code-walloper.

When you initiate e-mail, remember to respect your elders. If there is any chance that you're communicating with a computer other than a PC or a Mac, ask about acceptable mail protocols and formatting. If you can't do that before you send mail, send a *short* test message in as close to flat ASCII as you can contrive. ("Hello, world" would pay homage to an appropriate sense of history.) If the message received at the other end is bloated and cryptic, and you're going to be communicating with the target system on a regular basis, go find a flat-ASCII or a UNIX-alike mail program that speaks a dialect you can both understand.

Maybe someday Microsoft will understand why, throughout much of the computing world, the names of its mail programs are bitter curses. While we wait, you at least can act in honor rather than in ignorance. When you send mail with a Microsoft program, but to a computer that may not be running the same program, keep your formatting as plain as possible. When you send mail to a system that isn't a PC or a Mac, *don't* use Outlook or Outlook Express.

Oh, and—now that Rich Text is suddenly defined as HTML, what's going to happen to RTF? Big hint to Redmond: Your original Rich Text Format is one of the few things you ever invented that comes close to being acceptable Internet-wide. Don't walk away from it.

# Chat

If Usenet is the World Wide Watercooler, chat is the World Wide Street Corner—and not in the greatest neighborhood. It's what shock radio would be if you had to type it all. Chat's only saving grace is that, unlike news and mail, it goes away as soon as you type it.

We're going to tell you about some chat software that—oh, the agony of confession!—we happen to like. We're not going to tell you what and what not to do with it.

## Microsoft Chat

MS-Chat is quick, easy cartoon chat. It's not the cutting edge, but it's part of Windows 98, and it's a good way to get your feet wet.

*Figure 16.63*

Chat main screen

When you open up Microsoft Chat, it gives you a four-tab dialog that lets you set up your connection and character, enter your personal info (stick to the minimum) and select a background. If you've used Chat before, it proposes that you go to the last room you were in; if this is your first time, you'll go to the Lobby. Then just pick a server—the default is **mschat.msn.com**—and click **OK** on the **Connect** tab to log on. Incidentally, Microsoft Chat is IRC (Internet Relay Chat) even though it doesn't always look like it.

Microsoft Chat has a rich feature set that can take some digging to get to. If you're new to chat and need background, the Help Topics are generous, and the Help menu also offers a worthwhile set of release notes.

 You can use NetMeeting to conference with your chat partners. Search on **NetMeeting** in the Chat Help.

## Microsoft V-Chat

Microsoft has also developed a much more advanced chat applet, with avatars and all that good stuff, called **V-Chat**. This isn't geared to novices, but it has a feature set that will really take you to town—so to speak.

V-Chat will run with Windows 98, or any other version of 32-bit Windows, but it isn't supplied with them. Get yourself ready for a 4MB download, browse to **http://www.microsoft.com/ie/chat**, and poke around for a V-Chat link—it's there somewhere.

## Mirabilis ICQ

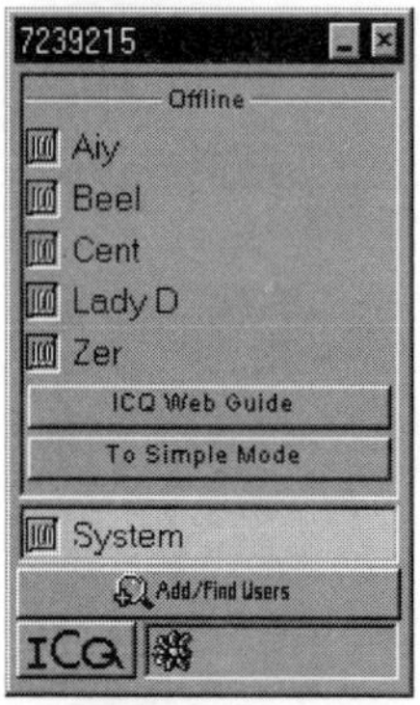

**Figure 16.64**

ICQ Main popup

**Figure 16.65**

ICQ Context menu

It slices, it dices! It's text chat, it's e-mail, it stores and forwards! It's the ingratiating, indescribable ICQ!

ICQ does just about anything you'd want to do over the Net. You can use it as an intercom in your apartment, a phone, a games server, or conference chat. It's available for Windows 98 and 95, Windows 3.1*x*, Windows NT 4.0 and 3.51, PowerMac, 68K Mac, Java, and soon, Windows CE, X Windows, and PalmPilot. That's not counting the custom versions, including one for NetMeeting. And it's free for individual use.

Mirabilis, creator of ICQ, is one of the most aggressively friendly developers we know. Their frequently stated ambition is to bring in more and more platforms, and more and more people, until the whole Net is one big happy ICQ family. All of this has enough attitude and sizzle that it escapes the usual chat sleaziness.

Right now there are about ten million ICQ users, but there's always room for you. Browse to **http://www.icq.com**, **http://www.download.com**, or your fastest TUCOWS mirror and grab yourself a copy.

# NetMeeting

**NetMeeting**, Microsoft's conferencing application, is the world's most ambitious chat applet. It includes H.323 audio and video conferencing, whiteboard, FTP, multipoint capacity, and just about every tool you'd need in a virtual meeting.

**Figure 16.66**

*NetMeeting Server screen*

Clearly the chatting world has taken NetMeeting to its heart—the screen shot shown in Figure 16.66 was taken from public server traffic and demonstrates the usual amount of optimistic trolling—but Microsoft would prefer, and we would concur, that NetMeeting should be seen almost entirely as an industrial-strength business program.

In that context, its demands are acceptable. NetMeeting thinks the latest and greatest hardware is just ducky; it connects to an Internet Locator Server (ILS), which is yet more server capacity you'll have to scrounge up; and it sucks bandwidth like a hot elephant sucks a lake. Even so, having seen what NetMeeting can accomplish, we believe that it's on its way to wide adoption by forward-looking corporations.

NetMeeting isn't immune to the usual head-scratchers that bedevil would-be killer apps. It took a while to figure out, for example, that videoconferencing was problematic unless every participating computer had its monitor set to the same color depth. There have also been interesting problems with some TrueType fonts. We suggest that, while you're evaluating NetMeeting for professional use, you keep close tabs on developments in the Knowledge Base.

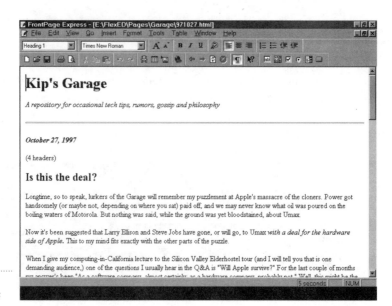

**Figure 16.67**

Local File in
FrontPage Express

# FrontPage Express

FrontPage Express (Figure 16.67) is—surprise!—yet another Microsoft teaser app intended to make us crave the "real thing": the retail version of FrontPage. The problem with this for Microsoft is that FrontPage Express is obviously based on material from previous retail versions (what programmer won't jump at the chance to get more mileage from code that's been thoroughly pounded?), and certainly FrontPage has won its share of awards. So the Web editor supplied free with Windows 98 is almost too good to bother replacing.

**Figure 16.68**

FrontPage Express
toolbars

What's good about it? Mostly the Microsoft common controls (see Figure 16.68).

All the controls on the top toolbar, and half the ones on the bottom, are perfectly familiar from Microsoft Word. Looking further, we spot the Insert Hyperlink from Outlook Express, the Back, Forward, and Refresh from Internet Explorer. No matter how good this program is as a Web editor, the obvious attraction is that you can run it immediately. When the first version of FrontPage arrived along with Windows 95, the concept of an HTML editor with a word processor's controls was new and refreshing. Today it's much less unusual, but it still makes creation and light editing of Web pages a snap.

The one thing about FrontPage that we've always found awkward is the two-piece Editor/Explorer modularity—of which FrontPage Express is basically the Editor half—but even if that's less easy to learn than the rest of the program, it's remarkably powerful once you master it.

So why *should* we buy the full retail FrontPage? Well, with the Express version you only get a few WebBots, with the shrink-wrap version you get a hatful. "Real" FrontPage has many more development tools. It can copy entire sites to servers or act as a server itself. Certainly, if you're the long-suffering guru of a commercial Web site or an intranet, FrontPage has a breadth of capability that makes it worth evaluating. On the other hand, if—like most of us—you mostly need a robust HTML editor and are willing to use exterior utilities for the occasional bout of site management, we'd bet you'll find FrontPage Express a real keeper.

# Web Publishing Wizard

Okay. Supposing you've used FrontPage Express to create all the HTML for your spiffy new Web site, and now it's time to upload it to the server. Microsoft didn't give you those pieces of "real" FrontPage on the Windows CD, and abruptly realizes that you might use a non-Microsoft product, such as WinFTP or the annoyingly meritorious FTP Explorer. So they scrabble around in the bag of controls and classes, and present you with the Web Publishing Wizard! It's not fancy, mind you, but it's absolutely easy and it'll get your site onto the Web. All you need is a previously configured ISP account (it's "previously configured" if you've set up a Dial-Up Networking connectoid for it) some of the setup details for your account, and the name of the folder—ideally just one—with your HTML files and graphics in it. Then just keep clicking **Next**.

*Figure 16.69*

*Web Publishing Wizard*

# Personal Web Server

Since it was Saturday night, you stayed up till two, tweaking and debugging your Web site while you muttered things like, "Why did that whole paragraph just turn into Heading 3?" On Sunday your site got eleven hits, only four of which were from you. Monday at work, during doughnut break, you casually mentioned that you set up a Web site for yourself over the weekend. Now it's after lunch and you're sitting in your boss's office, and he's asking you if you have what it takes to set up a small intranet for the company. He doesn't know the word "intranet," so it takes him longer to say what he means, but that's his drift.

You go back to your office and ponder your two choices. One is to call your ex-significant other, who works for a headhunter, and try for a new job. The other is to go to the software closet, retrieve one of the Windows 98 CDs, go back to your computer and install the Personal Web Server (Figure 16.70).

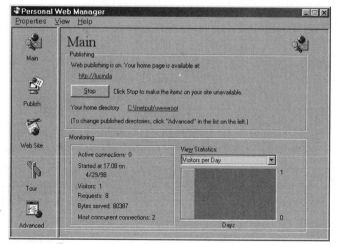

**Figure 16.70**

Personal Web Server
Main tab

## Main Tab

The **Main** tab (Figure 16.70) tells you where your site is set up, monitors request and service statistics, and keeps track of your hits.

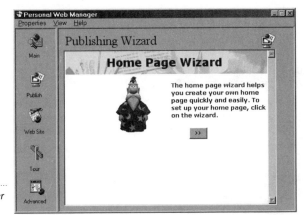

**Figure 16.71**

Personal Web Server
Publish tab

## Publish Tab

The **Publish** tab starts you off with the Home Page Wizard (Figure 16.71) which launches Internet Explorer and lets you construct a page by filling in fields (Figure 16.72)

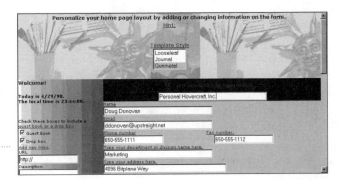

**Figure 16.72**

A home page
template

The generated page is totally bland (Figure 16.73) but if you get something out by five, your boss will be impressed, and you can use FrontPage Express to fix it up later.

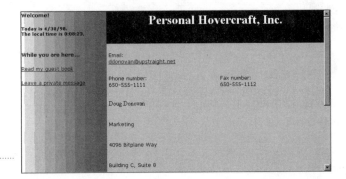

**Figure 16.73**

Hey, it's a start!

*Figure 16.74*

*Security Alert*

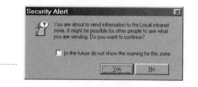

This (Figure 16.74) is the Security Zones monitor sticking its nose in your project. If you have doubts about the security of your intranet, you shouldn't be doing this anyway; otherwise, check the box to make the dialog go away.

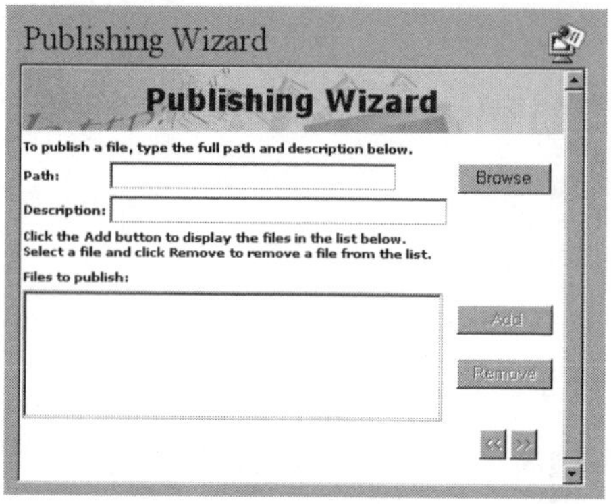


*Figure 16.75*

*Publishing Wizard*

As soon as you have one file for your site, you can begin making a list of files to be "published"—configured on the server-to-be—using the Publishing Wizard (Figure 16.75). To locate the files for you, Personal Web Server loads a special Explorer (Figure 16.76) which calls itself Internet Explorer but looks like a plain Explorer. Maybe they meant Intranet Explorer.

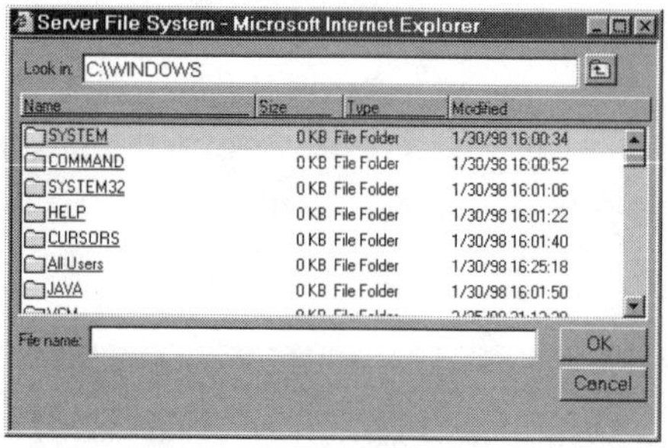


*Figure 16.76*

*Server file system Explorer*

## Web Site Tab

The **Web Site** tab lets you maintain your pages, guestbook, and mail once your site is set up.

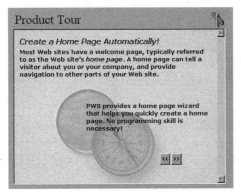

**Figure 16.77**

Personal Web Server
Tour

## Tour Tab

The **Tour**, which is in a position to be a good graphical tutorial, falls short of that and should be called Commercial (Figure 16.77)

## Advanced Tab

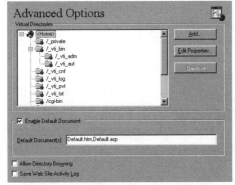

**Figure 16.78**

Personal Web Server
Advanced

If you're the novice that the Tour assumes you are, you'll reach the **Advanced** tab and be in very deep water (Figure 16.78). This isn't as scary as it looks, though; it's mostly where you set aliases for directories. You will need the Help, which launches in Internet Explorer (the real one this time) and is elaborate (Figure 16.79).

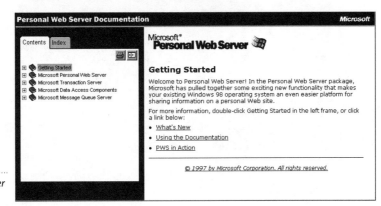

**Figure 16.79**

Personal Web Server
Help

## Gotchas

There are several gotchas here, the most immediate being that on our test system, the version of PWS we had didn't quite run; it froze a few times and put up some Visual Basic errors. However, even when Personal Web Server works, the following are true:

It's not installed with Windows 98 by default. If you go to Start Menu\ Programs\Internet Explorer and click on Personal Web Server, you get a local HTML page explaining how to install it. You need the CD.

You can install it only on the computer you intend to run it from.

It requires 35MB to 70MB of disk space.

Plan to install it on the most powerful computer you have available. While you're setting up a site, along with Personal Web Server, you generally have a copy of Internet Explorer running, and two if you're not careful. Performance is leisurely, to put it politely.

You have Web service, but not FTP. Of course, since an intranet is local, you can always use drive mapping for file transfer, or jury-rig a link to a separate FTP client.

You're only licensed for ten connections to the server.

## Service-level Changes

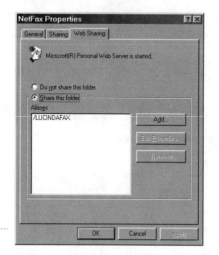

*Figure 16.80*

*Web Sharing tab*

Since Personal Web Server is a server component, it installs as what's called a *service,* rather than as a program or device driver. A service runs whenever the computer is running; you can turn it on and off, but the only way to disable it completely is to uninstall it. Those who manage NT boxes know how this works, but if your whole experience is with Windows 98 and 95, you may never have seen a service.

One characteristic of services is that, since they operate at a low level, their effects can percolate to the surface at any useful point. One manifestation of Personal Web Server (and we're not sure it's the only one) is that objects shared over the physical network can also be shared over the Web-based intranet (Figure 16.80)

### How about NT?

Microsoft, in the PWS Release Notes, points out that if you install Windows NT Workstation and the version of Personal Web Server that comes with it, some limitations will be removed. You're still stuck with a maximum of ten connections. Once again we say: Setting up a small test server with Windows 98 is perfectly okay, but Windows 98 is meant for peer-to-peer use, and if that server site becomes a part of your serious daily life, upgrading to NT Workstation would be prudent.

# Summary

Windows 98 comprises the most elaborate suite of Internet modules and applications you can find from a single vendor today. While some of the applets are of uneven quality, Internet Explorer—the backbone of the suite— is a star. For mail and news, under most circumstances, Outlook Express will give you all the horsepower you need. The clincher is that all the components of Your Own Private Internet are right on the Windows CD.

As you rove the Net, you'll certainly find pointers to other commercial programs and shareware that will enhance your Internet experience. But Windows 98 does a stellar job of getting you up and running; once you install it and try everything, you'll have a whole new idea of possibility and opportunity in cyberspace. If your computer didn't come out of its box with Windows 98 installed, the tools we describe in this chapter offer some of the most important reasons to upgrade.

# 17

# The Windows Registry

The Windows Registry is a central database that contains details about system and program configuration, installed devices, and user preferences. Using the Registry, you can control almost everything about the way Windows 98 runs, looks, and cooperates with Windows applications. The question—one we examine in depth—is whether controlling aspects of Windows' operation directly through the Registry is the preferable method.

The Registry is one of the most complex hierarchies of computer code ever produced. NASA probably launches a Titan missile with fewer lines of code. Even a minimal Windows 98 installation creates a Registry with thousands of entries, which is, in turn, only a small subset of the number of *possible* entries. A look at the Registry might indicate why Microsoft spends $2 billion a year on R&D.

No single chapter, in fact no single *book,* can describe the Registry exhaustively. Renowned authors have tried and, in many cases, conceded failure. We're smart enough to know what we can't get away with, so we're telling you right up front: This chapter introduces you to the Registry and briefly guides you through its key features, principles, and procedures. When you understand the chapter, you'll understand the Registry in general terms, but don't mistake this chapter for a comprehensive tutorial.

# Why Work With the Registry?

Windows maintains the Registry in the background, and you usually won't have to hack it or even look at it. That's the good news. However, sometimes you will need to look at the Registry, and when you pry it open for the first time, it's as if you were watching a bad science-fiction movie in Rumanian without subtitles.

Microsoft doesn't offer much help—and less to you than to your computer. The new Registry maintenance tools in Windows 98, Registry Checker and System File Checker, are designed to run in background and guarantee the Registry's integrity without intervention from you. Registry Checker also backs up your system's two Registry database files once a day. Windows 98 Help says little about the Registry beyond how to back it up to tape or file with the Backup utility, a procedure we have our doubts about anyway (see Chapter 15). The Microsoft utility for manipulating Registry data, REGEDIT, is limited enough to be frustrating and powerful enough to be dangerous.

And the Windows hotline tech support will *not* answer Registry questions. It's as if Microsoft delivered a hearty slap on your shoulder, warned you to back up your Registry before playing with it, and then rode off into the sunset while you yelled, "Wait!"

It's true that you should back up your Registry before you alter it, because if a hosed Registry makes your computer unbootable, your options are few. It's *not* true, however, that the Registry is a sealed box meant to be approached only by programmers and wizards. Knowing what the Registry is and how it works can help you customize your Windows configuration, make you feel more secure about using your computer, and—in an emergency—save you hours of tweaking when you need to restore a crashed Windows setup. And if you happen to be a wizard or a programmer, thorough knowledge of the Registry's internals can make your work much easier. So stick with us for a tour of the arcane files that constitute the nervous system of Windows.

No two Windows setups are exactly alike, except in theory. Each computer has its own Desktop and icon set, installed programs, and peripherals. All these elements fit together in your PC, and when it wakes up in the morning, you expect it to work the same way as when it was shut down the previous night.

As a result, your computer needs to remember a myriad of details about its configuration, even when it's not turned on. Traditionally, this information has been stored in files that the computer reads into its memory every time it boots. The Registry is still just a bunch of files, but because the Windows configuration of any computer or network is so complex, so is the Registry. Some of this complexity is easier to understand if you know the way Windows and its predecessor, MS-DOS, were developed.

## Real Roots: CONFIG.SYS And AUTOEXEC.BAT

Any computer that ever ran MS-DOS has two files in its root directory, usually C:\, that contain configuration information. They're called CONFIG.SYS and AUTOEXEC.BAT, and together, they add everything into memory that gets loaded between the time the computer is turned on and the time that the C:\> prompt appears on the screen. Many people express the difference between the two by saying that "CONFIG.SYS loads drivers, and AUTOEXEC.BAT loads programs," but the truth is a little more complicated. CONFIG.SYS is the first to load and the programs it adds to memory are more tightly keyed into the running copy of the operating system. Usually, if you watch a DOS or Windows 3.*x* computer boot, you *won't* see any messages from the programs added by CONFIG.SYS and you *will* see messages from programs added by AUTOEXEC.BAT. (You will see cryptic messages *about* CONFIG.SYS if it contains any errors.)

These two files accomplished all the configuration that most MS-DOS computers ever needed, because of three strict limitations:

- Very few DOS computers ever ran more than one program at a time.

- Not many DOS computers were combined into networks; when they were, a network operating system (NOS) was installed to handle communications and data sharing among individual computers.

- DOS computers generally used only 640K of RAM.

## Windows 3.x: Out Of The Box

Windows 3.0, 3.1, and 3.11 gradually demolished these roadblocks. Version 3.0 allowed multiple Windows programs to reside in up to 16MB of RAM, and appear in separate windows on the screen, even though only the foreground (or "active") program could be running. Version 3.1 allowed multiple Windows programs to run at the same time and to exchange information while they ran. Version 3.11, often known as Windows for Workgroups (WFW), added limited support for small networks with no need for a separate NOS.

Windows 3.11 also had a binary file called REG.DAT that was mostly used to keep track of data exchanges in background, like OLE transactions. REG.DAT is historically interesting as the direct ancestor of the 32-bit Windows Registry, but was abominably documented by Microsoft—mostly in Help files—and rarely used by programmers.

Windows 3.x needed to keep track of far more information than CONFIG.SYS and AUTOEXEC.BAT could hold. On top of those two files it added a minimum of five more Windows .INI, for "initialization," files: WIN.INI, SYSTEM.INI, CONTROL.INI, PROGMAN.INI, and WINFILE.INI.

- WIN.INI held configuration data for applications, like an expanded AUTOEXEC.BAT.

- SYSTEM.INI held machine settings and priorities for the computer itself, like an expanded CONFIG.SYS.

- CONTROL.INI held settings for the Windows Control Panel.

- PROGMAN.INI held settings for Program Manager.

- WINFILE.INI held settings and preferences for File Manager.

This set of .INI files did its job remarkably well *right after Windows was installed on the computer.* Unfortunately, as time went on some problems surfaced:

Every new program installed on a Windows computer needed to add its own startup information. Some of them appended the information to WIN.INI and SYSTEM.INI. Some of them wrote separate .INI files and placed them in the same directory (folder) with the program. Some wrote separate .INI files and placed them in the Windows directory. Microsoft tried to enforce the distinction that settings affecting *Windows globally* would be added to WIN.INI and settings affecting *only one application* would be confined to a separate .INI file, but this rule was hugely disregarded by third-party programmers and even by Microsoft itself.

Every time a hardware setting was changed on the computer, an appropriate entry was added to the SYSTEM.INI, but generally the old entries weren't deleted. If old and new entries contradicted each other, conflicts had to be unraveled manually.

As each Windows installation grew older and more complex, its WIN.INI and SYSTEM.INI got longer and the computer slowed down.

.INI files were plain text. They could be edited with DOS EDIT or Windows Notepad, often with disastrous results. The (undocumented) maximum size of an .INI file was 64K. If any one .INI file grew larger than about 60K, chunks of it disappeared without warning, and programs malfunctioned for no visible reason.

.INI files accommodated only two levels of information: headings, such as `[386Enh]`, and line items, such as `PerVMFiles=`. Together with the requirement that they had to be text, this gave them a limited ability to pass parameters to Windows.

Under any one heading, several line items could exist with the same name, and the favorite was probably `Device=` in SYSTEM.INI. Thanks to a bug in the way Windows itself modified .INI files, the overlap of these names could create internal errors that were almost incapable of being diagnosed.

Originally developed for standalone computers, .INI files had room for only one set of settings and preferences. If one Windows installation was used by more than one person, its users were constantly tweaking individual settings back and forth, causing frustration, perceived loss of privacy, and poor use of time.

Windows settings on a network had to be updated by editing the .INI files of each individual computer, even when the changes were identical. This made network administration painful and remote network administration almost impossible.

Holding firm to its core belief of "Bigger is better," Microsoft determined to eliminate the pesky and braindead .INI file by crushing it under the weight of a replacement. Luckily, gigabyte disks and dirt-cheap RAM arrived just in time for ...

# The Registry: First Principles

Every 32-bit version of Windows—Win95, Win98, and WinNT 4.0 and 5.0—maintains two large, heavily armored files called SYSTEM.DAT and USER.DAT. These files, together with a special block of RAM we'll discuss later, are collectively called the Registry.

 The Registry management code in Windows 98 has been rewritten internally to be faster than the code in Win95, but REGEDIT and the API calls look substantially the same in both versions. So far as we know, everything in this book about the Win98 Registry should also apply to the Win95 Registry, although we can't guarantee it.

The Registry contains everything that used to be scattered through all the Windows .INI files, plus much, much more. It fixes all the problems that .INI files had, albeit in Microsoft's own very *special* ways.

Every program or preference added to a 32-bit Windows system adds its configuration to the Registry. This means that you know exactly where it is … if you can find it. The only exceptions are 16-bit Windows programs lurking on your disk, which still need .INI files because they know nothing about the Registry, so Win98 hunts for (Microsoft's official phrase is "does not ignore") .INI files when it boots. 32-bit Windows also respects settings in CONFIG.SYS and AUTOEXEC.BAT, and in fact, a fresh 32-bit Windows install creates a CONFIG.SYS and AUTOEXEC.BAT with nothing in them!

When hardware settings are changed on a 32-bit Windows computer, Registry entries automatically change to match, *providing* that the updating process is smart enough to install the new entry under the same subkey as the old one.

The Registry rarely gets much larger when a computer's configuration is changed, because it's gargantuan already. Registry entries of a fresh Win98 installation, if you printed them on your printer, would be almost as thick as this book. Nobody notices, because computers that can run 32-bit Windows have very fast processors.

Registry files can contain both text and binary data. Instead of editing mysterious, unintuitive Win 3.*x* subkeys such as "ActiveAccelerationProfile=3," you can edit straightforward, standardized Registry subkeys such as "{645FF040-5081-101B-9F08-00AA002F954E}\DefaultIcon." The Registry editor, REGEDIT, will be on your Win98 system if you installed Windows from the CD, but not if you installed it from the set of floppies. If you don't have REGEDIT, you can't edit the Registry without destroying it; if you *do,* you must be very, very, very careful. We'll discuss REGEDIT shortly.

Whether the Registry has a maximum size is an open question. The Windows 95 Resource Kit says confidently that "The Registry has no size restriction," but other discussions of the topic—including the Windows NT 4.0 Help file—say that "The total amount of space that can be consumed by registry data ... is restricted by the registry size limit ... a ... universal maximum for registry space." Since the combined size of SYSTEM.DAT and USER.DAT on a fresh Windows 98 install is over 2MB, you probably don't have to worry about overflowing.

Registry information, hierarchical and organized in folders, can accommodate many more than two levels of settings. In fact, a long Registry key can chain so many subfolders that the path to a bottom-level entry can easily be more than one line long. REGEDIT helps by providing an Explorer-like interface with paths that can be easily expanded and collapsed, but tuning up your system's Registry will often require more capability than is possible with REGEDIT. See "Third-Party Registry Tools" at the end of this chapter.

SYSTEM.DAT and USER.DAT, unlike WIN.INI and SYSTEM.INI, don't need to be on the same drive or even the same computer. This feature, if intelligently exploited, can make network setup and maintenance easier.

All things considered, the design and capacity of the Registry mark a vast improvement on the original scattering of .INI files. Fast, flexible, and highly structured, the 32-bit Registry constitutes the armature of Windows now and for the foreseeable future. Unfortunately, it's also so complicated and non-intuitive that even seasoned Windows programmers tend to avoid using it. That's too bad, because if you understand the way the Registry works, you can customize your Windows installation to a degree that most people would never believe possible. So hang on tight.

## Getting a Handle on It

Main headings in the Registry all begin with the abbreviation HKEY, which stands for "Handle to a Key." (The Microsoft programmer who came up with that may have had a few too many of Redmond's free Cokes.) The three most important HKEYs are these:

- HKEY_LOCAL_MACHINE.
- HKEY_USERS.
- HKEY_DYN_DATA.

Collectively, these three keys hold all the data in the Registry. There are also three Registry *alias keys:*

- HKEY_CLASSES_ROOT.

- HKEY_CURRENT_USER.

- HKEY_CURRENT_CONFIG.

If you change anything in an "aliased" key, its "real" equivalent is updated to match automatically.

## The Kingdom of the Keys

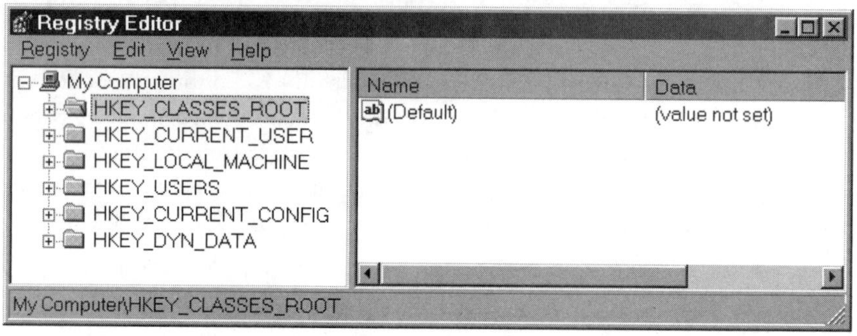

*Figure 17.1*

*The Registry in REGEDIT*

When you open the Registry hierarchy in REGEDIT, all six of these keys will be displayed Explorer-style as subfolders of My Computer. For simplicity's sake, let's discuss them in the order of REGEDIT's display, instead of their order of importance.

HKEY_CLASSES_ROOT holds the same information as HKEY_LOCAL_MACHINE\Software\Classes. This key is a holdover from the Windows 3.*x* Registry and its support of drag-and-drop and OLE. The HKEY_CLASSES_ROOT alias exists for the use of 16-bit programs that accessed the Windows REG.DAT when they were running under Windows 3.*x*; but it's handy for other purposes, as we'll explain.

HKEY_CURRENT_USER holds the same information as HKEY_USERS\ *<logged-on user name>*. If no user is logged on, HKEY_CURRENT_USER is equivalent to HKEY_USERS\.Default, which is mostly a template for new users' settings.

HKEY_LOCAL_MACHINE and its subkeys organize all entries related to your computer's hardware, drivers, and global software settings. All the entries in Device Manager and the whole database that 32-bit Windows uses to install Plug-and-Play hardware are in HKEY_LOCAL_MACHINE. In short, this part of the Registry tells Windows what kind of a computer you have and what's running on it.

HKEY_USERS contains the personal Windows preferences and histories of individual computer users, such as wallpaper, color scheme and desktop fonts, Most Recently Used file lists, and toolbar contents. On a standalone computer with User Profiles turned off, only the .Default user will appear under HKEY_USERS; if the computer is networked, or User Profiles are turned on through the User Profiles tab of Passwords in Control Panel, the current user's Profile will appear in a subfolder named HKEY_USERS\<*logon_name*>, like "HKEY_USERS\ Fred" or "HKEY_USERS\Kip."

HKEY_CURRENT_CONFIG holds the same information as HKEY_LOCAL_MACHINE\Config\<*number of current hardware profile.*> This is almost always HKEY_LOCAL_ MACHINE\Config\0001, because a computer has a single hardware profile unless you've created alternate profiles using the **Hardware Profiles** tab of Control Panel\System. Even Microsoft admits that "there are only a few circumstances in which you may want" to do this.

HKEY_DYN_DATA uses its sub-keys to store the Dynamic Data that reflects the constantly changing state of your computer's hardware configuration. HKEY_DYN_DATA\Config Manager\Enum contains the states of pieces of your system; HKEY_DYN_DATA\PerfStats contains the performance statistics reported by the Windows System Monitor or NT Performance Monitor. Because HKEY_DYN_DATA has to change so quickly, it doesn't really exist on disk, but is maintained in RAM by the Windows kernel; but REGEDIT shows it as a folder hierarchy like all the other HKEYs, and you can poke around in it. You'll find that many of the entries are four pairs of zeroes.

These key handle names take up a lot of room when they're written out over and over again, so from now on we'll abbreviate them according to the standard convention (see Table 17.1), which will not only make the paths look shorter but will help us focus on the right-hand end of the entries, where the action is.

## Table 17.1  Top-Level Key Abbreviations

| | |
|---|---|
| HKEY_CURRENT_CONFIG | HKCC |
| HKEY_CLASSES_ROOT | HKCR |
| HKEY_CURRENT_USER | HKCU |
| HKEY_DYN_DATA | HKDD |
| HKEY_LOCAL_MACHINE | HKLM |
| HKEY_USERS | HKU |

# Safeguarding Registry Data

There will be many times when you want to *look* at your Registry data but be absolutely sure you don't change it accidentally. Unfortunately, this is one place where the REGEDIT that comes with Win98 isn't very reassuring.

Windows NT's industrial-strength REGEDT32 has an option to set the Registry read-only, so that changes are locked out. The simpler REGEDIT in Win95 and Win98, much more like the old Win3.1 version, lacks this, so that you can never be sure you've looked at something without changing it. Therefore, the first thing to learn about the Registry is how to repair or replace it when you mess it up. Luckily, Windows itself provides a selection of tools for the purpose. *Before* you start poking around, use the Registry Checker to make a current backup of your Registry. This handy little tool, the replacement for Windows 95's CfgBack, automatically makes a compressed backup of your Registry data files. Naturally, in true Windows fashion, the files it creates are incompatible with CfgBack's .RBK files, but at least they're plain old .CAB files, which give about four-to-one compression. The only way in which CfgBack was nominally superior was that it would allow nine backup files, whereas the Registry Checker maintains only five.

Unlike CFGBACK, which was so optional that if you wanted to install it you had to go find it on the CD, the Registry Checker installs by default and runs without any help from Scheduled Tasks. Out of pure curiosity we tried to find some way to *prevent* the Registry Checker from doing its stealthy, once-a-day backup, and we couldn't.

## Running Registry Checker

*Figure 17.2*

*Registry Checker results*

We are talking *no major difficulty* here. Registry Checker, phenomenally simpler than CfgBack, has no truck with instructions, filenames, confirmations or progress bars—it's a one-click pony. If you go to the **Start Menu\Run** dialog and type scanreg Enter, you get a few seconds of intense grumbling, followed by what you see in Figure 17.2.

*Figure 17.3*

*Registry Checker process*

If you click **Yes,** you see the lucid and informative screen shown in Figure 17.3.

You see the screen in Figure 17.3 until it tells you it's done—that is, until it has created another .CAB file.

**Registry Checker, Windows, and DOS.** There are two versions of SCANREG. scanreg⌷Enter⌷ in the **Run** dialog launches SCANREGW.EXE; scanreg⌷Enter⌷ at a command prompt launches SCANREG.EXE. Without any switches, this command creates a file, RB★.CAB, which EXTRACT displays like this:

*Figure 17.4*

*Registry Cabinet file structure*

```
Cabinet rb005.cab

03-29-1998 10:43:40p -HR-         159,776 user.dat
03-30-1998  1:11:52a -HR-       2,707,488 system.dat
03-30-1998  1:11:44a A---           9,388 win.ini
03-30-1998  1:11:38a A---           2,372 system.ini
                  4 Files        2,879,024 bytes
```

Notice that SYSTEM.DAT and USER.DAT are, properly, set Hidden and Read-only within the archive. The size of the compressed file is just over 700KB.

The Registry Checker will run automatically at each boot, creating RB★.CAB, until there are five numbered copies, but there shouldn't be more than five; see the note below on SCANREG.INI.

SCANREG can take five parameters in DOS or three in Windows (see Table 17.2).

## Table 17.2  SCANREG Parameters

| | |
|---|---|
| **/BACKUP** | The same as running without a parameter, but you're not queried before the file is created. |
| **/RESTORE** | Restores the Registry from the .CAB file. *This command can only be run in MS-DOS mode.* |
| **/FIX** | Repair the Registry. The purpose of this command is more specialized than you might think; you need it only when you've installed Windows and immediately corrupted the Registry. In that case, you haven't booted yet, so you don't have an RB000.CAB, and if you *do* boot, you'll create that file from the corrupt Registry and make a bad situation worse. From this, and only this, position, run SCANREG /FIX. At any other time, you can assume you have a healthy Registry backup, so run SCANREG /RESTORE. *This command can only be run in MS-DOS mode.* |
| **/COMMENT=** | Appends any comment "between double quotes" to the .CAB file while it's being created. |
| **/?** | Display these options, without running the program. |

**Using Registry Checker to Restore.** If possible, point Explorer to \WINDOWS\SYSBCKUP to make sure that the RB★.CAB files are there. (They'll be in \WINDOWS\SYSBCKUP unless you edited SCANREG.INI to put them somewhere else; see below.) If you have backups that look valid, click the **Start** button, click **Shut Down,** click **Restart in MS-DOS mode,** and click **OK.**

When you boot into MS-DOS mode, you should be at C:\WINDOWS. If you're at the root prompt, type

cd\windows\sysbckup `Enter`

and then

scanreg /restore `Enter`

and the screen in Figure 17.5 will appear.

```
┌─────────────────────────────────────────────────────────────────┐
│                                                                   │
│  Microsoft Registry Checker                                       │
│  ───────────────────────────────────────────────────────────     │
│                                                                   │
│      ┌──────────────────────────────────────────────────┐        │
│      │ 04/01/98 Not Started 10:28:04pm rb005.cab         │ ↑      │
│      │ 04/01/98 Not Started rb004.cab                    │        │
│      │ 04/01/98 Not Started rb003.cab                    │ ▒      │
│      │ 04/01/98 Started     rb002.cab                    │ ↓      │
│      ├──────────────────────────────────────────────────┤        │
│      │         ◀ Restore... ▶    < Cancel >              │        │
│      └──────────────────────────────────────────────────┘        │
│                                                                   │
│                                                                   │
│  ───────────────────────────────────────────────────────────     │
│  Select a cab to restore from.                                    │
│                                                                   │
└─────────────────────────────────────────────────────────────────┘
```

*Figure 17.5*

Registry Checker
Restore

Files marked "Started" are the ones created automatically when the computer booted; files marked "Not Started" are created manually by running SCANREG from Windows or DOS. The file that displays the time as well as the date is the most recent.

 A copy of a reasonably recent RB*.CAB file on a floppy disk might be a prudent thing to keep next to your Windows Emergency Disk in the Computer Emergency Ziploc. If you haven't made an Emergency Disk yet (cries of "shame!") go read the directions in Chapter 15, and do it now. Have a diskette ready.

**SCANREG.INI.** The SCANREG.INI file sets boundaries for the Registry Checker's operation. This is a commented ASCII file and you can edit it in Notepad; the parameters you can set make the Registry Checker more flexible than CfgBack, but not flexible enough for a multiuser computer or network environment. See Table 17.3 for the settings.

So, if you have a typical Windows setup, you can create the CAB files in any folder you like, but the additional files you specify to add to the CAB file have to be in C:\, C:\WINDOWS, or C:\WINDOWS\SYSTEM.

## Table 17.3  SCANREG.INI Options

| | |
|---|---|
| Backup=1 | Registry is backed up at boot time or by request |
| Backup=0 | Boot-time backup is skipped; Registry is backed up by request only |
| Optimize=1 | Registry is optimized before backup |
| Optimize=0 | Optimization is skipped |
| MaxBackupCopies=5 | This should be left at 5. There's no point in having fewer than five backups, but if you have more than five, you can't be sure you'll restore the most recent one; see Microsoft KnowledgeBase article Q182841 at **http://support.microsoft.com**. If that article disappears, Microsoft probably fixed the bug |
| BackupDirectory= | If blank after the equals sign (default) backup will be done to \WINDOWS\SYSBCKUP |
| BackupDirectory=*x:\folder\folder* | Create CAB files in the alternate folder indicated by the path |
| Files=10,*filename,filename* | Add *filename* from *windir* to the CAB file. **windir** environment variable must be set in MSDOS.SYS |
| Files=11,*filename,filename* | Add *filename* from *windir*\SYSTEM to the CAB file. **windir** environment variable must be set in MSDOS.SYS |
| Files=30,*filename,filename* | Add *filename* from *winbootdir* to the CAB file. **winbootdir** environment variable must be set in MSDOS.SYS |
| Files=31,*filename,filename* | Add *filename* from *winbootdir* of a DriveSpace host drive to the CAB file. **winbootdir** environment variable must be set in MSDOS.SYS *Note:* You can specify up to 16 additional files to be included in the backup, beyond the four defaults. |

## Cute Hack: Multiuser Backup

Next question: Where does the Registry Checker get the USER.DAT that it incorporates into RB*.CAB? We think that SCANREG with its default .INI settings backs up the information contained in HKEY_USERS\.Default and doesn't bother with the information in HKEY_USERS\*<logged-on user>* or in any other, latent User Profiles. But SCANREG.INI gives you a way to back them all up.

**Files=10** points to the **windir** directory, but the **Files=*nn*** statements will take parameters that let you fill out the rest of a path. No doubt you can think of several uses for that information; the one that occurs to us is

```
Files=10,profiles\<username1>\user.dat,profiles\<username2>\user.dat ...
```

Microsoft itself says this works. It also says dismissively that backing up USER.DAT(s) is hardly worth the trouble, since 99% of the time it's SYSTEM.DAT and not USER.DAT that gets corrupted. Thanks, but we'll back up anything we can get our hands on.

**Losing Users.** There's no easy fix if USER.DAT and SYSTEM.DAT reside on different computers in a network—with, for example, USER.DAT on the server and SYSTEM.DAT on the local workstation—because SCANREG will only back up Registry data from its local system. The intersection of these two gotchas means that, on most networks, the automatic backup that SCANREG supplies is *not* an adequate safeguard of the Registry. This underscores the axiom that any serious—meaning production—network should include tape backup that makes provision for copying the Registry.

 "Now wait a minute," you're groaning, "in Chapter 15 you said *not* to restore the Registry from tape unless I absolutely had to, and now you're saying that my backups to tape absolutely have to include the Registry files." Yes, but on a standalone single-user computer you can restore your Registry using SCAN-REG /RESTORE, which is easier and far safer than doing it from tape. On a network, a backup tape will be the only copy of your whole Registry when it's time to restore, so you just have to bite the Jolly Rancher. Besides, when you bought the backup device for your network, you did spend the extra money for a reliable DAT or DLT unit … we hope.

 **So you think you're backed up?** If your computer has a tape backup, and you use it regularly, you have a lot less to worry about than most people. The Microsoft Backup software that's installed with Windows backs up the Registry *if* **Back up Windows Registry,** on the **Advanced** tab of the **Backup Job Options** dialog, is checked. Third-party software supplied with tape drives, even when set to "complete backup" or "back up all files," generally *doesn't* make a backup of the Registry unless it's told to. Be sure your settings are correct.

 You may wonder how the Registry can be updated and copied on the fly when both the .DAT and the .DA0 files are set to Read-only and Hidden. After all, you can't alter those files from a DOS prompt. The short answer is that Windows is the operating system, and you're not.

## Using REGEDIT To Back Up

You can use REGEDIT to back up your Registry. Select **Run…** from the Start Menu, type REGEDIT into the Open dialog, and hit OK. Then:

Pull down the **Registry** menu

Select **Export Registry File…**

Under **Export Range** click the **All** button. (It's the default, but make sure it's what you select.)

Windows will propose that you save the information as a .REG file, which is fine, and to the My Documents folder, but it might be more useful to remember that this isn't a document. We suggest saving to \WINDOWS\SYS-BCKUP with a name like FULLREG.REG. The file isn't compressed, so it will be about the size of SYSTEM.DAT plus the USER.DAT of the logged-on user; the one we created on our test machine was just shy of 4MB. Your mileage may vary since, as several Windows 98 beta testers have pointed out, the size of Registry files depends on unpredictable factors like the kind and amount of software you have installed.

## Resorting to SYSTEM.1ST

If your Registry is still corrupt, you are at the last ditch and you have one more option, although it won't be pleasant. In the root directory, C:\, there's a copy of the SYSTEM.DAT file that was created when Windows was *originally* installed, renamed to SYSTEM.1ST. It hasn't been touched since Win98 first hit your disk.

Boot your computer to a command prompt that bypasses the Registry. When the message "Starting Windows 98…" appears, hit the [F8] key and select item 7, "Safe mode command prompt only." You'll be deposited at a C:\> prompt; type:

```
attrib -r -h system.1st [Enter]
cd\windows [Enter]
attrib -r -h system.dat [Enter]
copy \system.1st system.dat [Enter]
attrib +r +h system.dat [Enter]
cd\ [Enter]
attrib +r +h system.1st [Enter]
```

Now reboot again, and you should go into an absolutely clean installation of Windows. This, of course, is a double-edged sword. It *will* work; on the other hand, it doesn't include *any* of USER.DAT or any of the system-level changes—new video card, new printer, whatever—that you made since Windows was first installed. You'll have to open Control Panel and configure all that stuff by hand, but you're still better off than you would be with a non-bootable computer.

 Some Microsoft documentation refers to SYSTEM.1ST as "a copy of the Registry." It would be nice, but don't believe it. SYSTEM.1ST is a copy of HKEY_LOCAL_MACHINE as of the time the Windows Setup program finished executing—period.

Okay. You now know as much as we do about restoring your system's Registry if it happens to take a hit. We're ready for the quick tour.

# The Registry Tree

Now, in REGEDIT, click on the boxed plus-sign to the left of HKLM—remember, that's HKEY_LOCAL_MACHINE—and you'll see something like Figure 17.6.

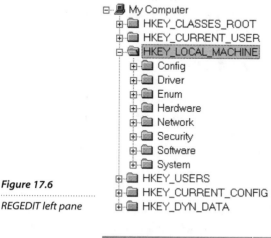

*Figure 17.6*

*REGEDIT left pane*

Yours may not look *exactly* like that. As no two computers running Windows are identical, so no two Registries are identical either. However, since we're not actually going to *edit* the Registry but just look at it, you can use this as an example and follow it as closely as your own configuration will permit.

**VALUE NAMES (Key Names).** On the right-hand side of the screen you'll see a pane divided into two columns, *Name* and *Data* (Figure 17.7).

| Name | Data |
|------|------|
| (Default) | (value not set) |
| Capabilities | 54 00 00 00 |
| Class | "PCMCIA" |
| ClassGUID | "{4d36e977-e325-11ce-bfc1-08002be10318}" |
| ConfigFlags | 00 00 00 00 |
| DeviceDesc | "PCMCIA Card Services" |
| Driver | "PCMCIA\0001" |
| HardwareID | "PCCARD" |
| Mfg | "Microsoft" |

*Figure 17.7*

*Example REGEDIT right pane*

The name is the subkey name. The data is the value of the subkey installed by Windows, whether during Windows Setup, application Setup, Add Hardware, or Plug-and-Play autodetect. There are three Registry data types, and Table 17.4 shows you how to tell them apart.

## Table 17.4  Registry Data Types

| Data Type | Registry Icon | Edit dialog title bar shows | Format | Maximum size |
|-----------|---------------|-----------------------------|--------|--------------|
| String | [ab] | Edit String | `"this is a string"` | 64K |
| Binary | [icon] | Edit Binary Value | 00 00 00 00 ... (hex) See below! | 64K |
| DWORD | [icon] | Edit DWORD Value | Hex string starting with 0x and followed by decimal value in parentheses | Four bytes (32 bits) |

# The Registry's Gotcha: XEH

When you're decoding Binary Values you have to stay alert. In some such keys (maybe, but probably not, all of them) data is presented byte-backward—LSB to MSB—but digit-forward (see Table 17.5).

| Table 17.5  Binary Value Decode | |
|---|---|
| Binary Value format | gh ef cd ab |
| True, decoded hex value | abcdefgh |

DWORD Values in the Registry, on the other hand, are straightforwardly left-to-right … although there is one method of *exporting* DWORD data that puts *it* byte-backward too! (We get into this much more deeply, for better or worse, when we talk about using REGEDIT.)

Evidently Microsoft, not content with the lightweight mystery of expressing all true binary Registry data in hex, makes us jump through the hoop of figuring out which way it's pointing! We suspect that, by invading the Registry at all, we try their patience and they're only reminding us of it. This is obfuscation and, whenever Value data is obviously byte-backward, we're going to flag it with this icon: ⬛.

## Adding Or Modifying Keys

Somewhere, probably locked in a safe in Redmond, are the master copies of two very long lists. The first one is the list of *all valid Registry keynames* for 32-bit Windows. The second is the list of *every valid value* for the usable keys.

The Registry becomes truly frightening when you realize that your Windows system, being one among millions, uses only a small fraction of the set of all *possible* Registry keys and subkeys. If you're brave and skilled in these matters, you can add keys that your system doesn't already use, and some of them will confer amazing benefits. The problem is knowing which of these keys do the things you'd prefer, and worse yet, knowing which ones do anything at all.

For example, in HKCU\Control Panel\Desktop\WindowMetrics, you can add a String key called **MinAnimate** that will let you control window animation—we'll show you how later. If, on the other hand, you create a String key called **EnablePepsi**, it won't turn your computer into a soda machine, and in fact won't do anything but make it a tiny bit slower while Windows puzzles over this weird invalid key. (At least, that's what we *assume*. There are some things that even we won't try at home.)

Similarly, you can add a key called **MenuShowDelay** to HKCU\Control Panel\Desktop that will regulate the speed of your Windows drop-down or pop-up menus, like the Start Menu. Its range of valid values is from 1, much too fast, to 65534, glacial, with a good initial compromise being 200. But what happens if you go wild and set it to 0, or 65535? You just better have a backup copy of your Registry handy in case an unorthodox value freezes your machine.

Again: Don't *create a Registry key* or *reset the value of a key* unless you know that the proposed new key or value will actually be useful!

Quite a few of the values that can be set in HKCU\Control Panel can be set through **Start Menu\Settings\Control Panel** instead, and if you do it the easy way, you know that the values you end up with are valid. Naturally, this only works for changing values of existing keys, since any Control Panel icon and dialog already has a key underneath it. But wait, there's more …

At the top level of most Registry folders you'll find a String key called (Default) whose value is likely to be (value not set). *Don't mess with these.* They assure compatibility with Win16 applications and the Windows 3.*x* REG.DAT. When (Default) is blank, that's what other Registry keys are expecting to find—and Registry keys don't like surprises!

# HKEY_LOCAL_MACHINE: The Subkeys

This is the key about the computer's hardware and software configuration. None of it relates to the logged-on user, so it's stored in SYSTEM.DAT. There are eight subkeys under HKLM (see Table 17.6).

### Table 17.6  HKEY_LOCAL_MACHINE Subkeys

| | |
|---|---|
| **Config** | A roster of configuration profiles for the local computer, beginning with 0001 (usually only 0001, unless User Profiles are enabled) |
| **Desktop Management** | The repository for Microsoft's Desktop Management Interface (DMI) and Windows Management Infrastructure (WMI) device databases. *This key is optional* and not yet fully implemented; see description |
| **Enum** | A roster of basic information on installed hardware devices and protocols |
| **Hardware** | Information on the computer's processor, bus architecture and ports |
| **Network** | Network logon information and username |
| **Security** | Network security and group information and parameters for remote administration |
| **Software** | Software extensions, associations, class ID's, version information and *non-user-specific* configuration |
| **System** | Control database for system boot-up, port mapping, VxD control, device driver loading and priority, Windows services, and OS behavior |

# HKLM\Config

The HKLM\Config subtree contains information about hardware configurations. There can be more than one valid configuration for one computer if, for example, the computer is sometimes connected to a network, docked in a docking station, or attached to a special peripheral. Each alternate configuration is assigned a unique identifier $000n$ which becomes the title of a Config subkey. Configurations are listed under the Hardware Profiles tab in the System option in Control Panel; configuration 0001 is called "Original Configuration." Additional configurations can be called anything you like, and the names get stored in HKLM\System\CurrentControlSet\Control\IDConfigDB as strings called FriendlyName$000n$.

When Windows checks the hardware configuration at boot-time, it makes one of four choices:

- If only configuration 0001 exists, the settings for Config subkey 0001 are used for system configuration.

- If more than one tested configuration exists, Windows uses its best available information to select the appropriate one automatically.

- If the configuration ID is mapped to more than one configuration and Windows cannot distinguish between them automatically, the user is queried for a choice.

- If the user boots the computer after adding new hardware, Windows creates a configuration from scratch with a new ID, and a new Config subkey is added to the Registry. (Yes, it's the Add New Hardware Wizard!)

For each configuration, HKLM\Config maintains four subkeys (see Table 17.7).

## Table 17.7  HKLM\Config Subkeys

| | |
|---|---|
| **Display** | Boot-up configuration for display colors, resolution, and default fonts. All of this can be edited much more easily in the Settings tab of Control Panel\Display Properties |
| **Enum** | Boot-up configuration for Plug and Play or hot-swap hardware |
| **Software** | Settings for Dial-Up Networking or Internet Explorer |
| **System** | Names and configurations of installed printers; but not all the printer information is here, making it advisable to change these settings only through Control Panel\Printers |

 There are *no* network settings in HKLM\Config; all that's in HKLM\Enum\Network or HKLM\Enum\Root\Net.

DesktopManagement is the Registry's repository for Microsoft's Desktop Management Interface (DMI) and Windows Management Infrastructure

## HKLM\DesktopManagement

The subkey of HKEY_LOCAL_MACHINE called DesktopManagement existed in the earliest versions of Windows 98 and had disappeared by the time of Release Candidate 0. **It may or may not exist in the copy of Windows 98 that you're running.** *But,* when we look at what we know about it, we have to assume that this subkey is a Windows wave of the future. It doesn't look like an experiment because it's been developed in too much depth, it adheres to too many standards, and it makes an obvious and clear-cut contribution to management of enterprise-wide computing.

Therefore, in our conviction that DesktopManagement is a key clue to a new direction, we'll tell you what we've been able to dig up. We don't know as much about it as we do about many of the other second-level keys, because it vanished while we were researching it; but, if you'll pardon the potholes, you're welcome to share what we learned.

(WMI) device databases. It contains information on system devices that the *system* wouldn't care about, but the system administrator definitely would—like the manufacturer's name, model number, part number, revision level, support phone number, and the start date and duration of the warranty. This is a distinct improvement over, say, the jumper settings for your IDE controller, which are printed in gray ink on a piece of thin paper the size of an automated-teller chit, somewhere underneath your desk.

Microsoft warns that the DesktopManagement subkey is only one piece—that is, the queryable client-side piece—of a hierarchy that also includes SNMP (Simple Network Management Protocol) and OLE MS (OLE Management Services) as well as, probably, SMS (Systems Management Server). Once all of these are jigsawed together, administrators will be able to monitor, query, configure and inventory the hardware and software that make up their networks. Since all WMI information contained in the Registry is accessible through standard Windows API calls, all this management can be accomplished remotely by jazzy applications of the near future.

Little of this is inherent, though, since—as Microsoft puts it—the DesktopManagement subkey contains the "infrastructure" but not the "instrumentation." In other words, you can examine the information arranged in a useful way, but you don't (yet) have the tools to work with it. If you're interested in developing those tools, you can request the WMI SDK by sending e-mail to `wmi_info@microsoft.com`. Meanwhile, we'll follow the procedure with DesktopManagement that we have with several other keys; we won't dismantle it exhaustively, but we'll dig deep enough to make it clear how it works.

**HKLM\DesktopManagement\Data\1.** Although the purpose of this subkey is obscure because most of its subkeys are numerals, it would seem to comprise client-side tools for checking the integrity of software installations.

Hooking into a library called DMIAPI32.DLL, it can query for the embedded information, name, size, and date of any file, and verify them against (probably embedded) checksums.

If you're in the habit of safeguarding your office copy of Doom by renaming it EXCEL.EXE … those days are over. Sorry.

**HKLM\DesktopManagement\Data\2.**  The hardware side of console-based management uses a library called DESKMGMT.DLL to query physical disks, disk mapping, hard and floppy controllers, input devices, video cards, ports, power management, and accessibility, as well as network adapters, clients, protocols and services.

If you dig into the subkeys of the individual component names, you'll find them generally described in terms of *FRUGroupIndex, OperationalGroupIndex,* or *DeviceGroupIndex.* These keys are totally undocumented anywhere in Microsoft that we've been able to shine our flashlight, and our only insight is that *FRU* is an old, old IBM TLA standing for "Field-Replaceable Unit"—a term given a new lease on life by micros since, of course, few computers go back to the factory in this day of corner-store motherboards and mail-order hard disks.

As we parade down the list of subkeys devoted to hardware items, we stumble over a key innocuously called GeneralInformation which contains six string keys of its own. \,Time and \,TimeZone are reported by DESKMGMT.DLL, \:SystemName is pulled from HKLM\System, and \:SystemPrimaryUserName comes from HKLM\SOFTWARE. But the two remaining keys, \SystemLocation and \SystemPrimaryUserPhone, suggest a more disturbing trend in remote maintenance protocols; the next key logically to be added is \SystemPrimaryUserLocation. If you find this key installed on your computer, use the Paranoia tab of TweakUI to turn it off before hiding out in the utility room with your Game Boy.

Microsoft refers to the subkey space in \DesktopManagement as being ready for "a wealth of information" and you can certainly find good examples in \Data\2\Physical Memory, \Data\2\Partition or \Data\2\Logical Drives. Most of these keys will contain data returned by DESKMGMT.DLL, or simple yes/no answers, or numeric values; but if data is to be selected from a small set of discrete strings, that set may be stored in an Enumerator subkey. Look at \Data\2\SystemCache\Level\Enum for a particularly clean example.

We were unable to research HKLM\DesktopManagement\Install.

**HKLM\DesktopManagement\MIF.**  Here we accommodate heavy corporate environments, running a rich mix of hardware and maybe (horrors!) other OSes than Windows. In 1992 DEC, Hewlett-Packard, IBM, Intel, Microsoft, Novell, SunConnect and SynOptics—like I said, heavy—formed the Desktop Management Task Force (DMTF) and began development of the Desktop Management Interface, an open and consistent set of rules for accessing desktop hardware and software across a LAN. Management Information Files (MIFs) are the agents running on CPUs, LAN adapters, modems, peripherals, and operating systems which discover, and then track, what is installed on the desktop.

Since MIFs adhere to a set of rules developed by a committee with wide-ranging interests, their subkeys don't look much like the rest of the Registry. They're all "string," and they're very wordy. We'll give just one example of a MIF subkey and its Enum, to clarify the principle (see Tables 17.8 and 17.9).

### Table 17.8  HKLM\DesktopManagement\MIF\1\1\6 Subkey

| | |
|---|---|
| Name | "Verify" |
| Type | "ENUM" |
| Access | "Read-Only" |
| Storage | "Common" |
| :Value | "HKEY_LOCAL_MACHINE\DesktopManagement\DATA\1\1\6\Value" |
| Description | "A code that provides a level of verification that the component is still installed and working." |

### Table 17.9  HKLM\DesktopManagement\MIF\1\1\6\ENUM Subkey

| | |
|---|---|
| 0 | "An error occurred; check status code." |
| 1 | "This component does not exist." |
| 2 | "Verification is not supported." |
| 3 | "Reserved." |
| 4 | "This component exists, but the functionality is untested." |
| 5 | "This component exists, but the functionality is unknown." |
| 6 | "This component exists, and is not functioning correctly." |
| 7 | "This component exists, and is functioning correctly." |

## HKLM\Enum

Windows builds its hierarchy of system hardware by using *bus enumerators* to assign string values that accumulate into a tree structure. There are two types of bus enumerators: **Plug and Play,** which run every time you start Windows or click **Refresh** in Device Manager, and **Legacy,** which are for ISA or VLB devices and—for efficiency—run only in Windows Setup and Add New Hardware. (Windows avoids running Legacy enumerators unless it's explicitly told to, because they can hang your computer when they probe for devices.)

The Registry maintains an enumerator for each bus or bus type on the system, such as the ISA bus, PNP bus, SCSI bus, serial bus, or lots of others. The appropriate enumerator:

- Assigns an identification code to each device on its bus.

- Retrieves the device's configuration information directly from the device, if the device has that degree of self-awareness—that is, if it's Plug and Play to any extent.

- Or retrieves the device's configuration information from the Registry, if the device is clueless about itself.

All of this is stored in the HKLM\Enum subtree and can include device type, assigned drive letter, hardware ID, device manufacturer, and some—not all—driver-related information.

Table 17.10 shows which devices are enumerated in typical subkeys. These keys, unless noted, are current as of Windows 98 Release Candidate 1.

### Table 17.10  HKLM\Enum Subkeys

| Subkey | Device Enumeration |
|---|---|
| **BIOS** | Devices embedded in the motherboard (like ports, controllers and sound chips) reported by a Plug and Play BIOS; but see ROOT |
| **DISPLAY** | Video controls, tuning, capture, etc. |
| **ESDI** | ATA, MFM and ESDI fixed disk devices (drives) |
| **FLOP** | Floppy disk devices (drives) |
| **HID** | Human Interface Device. Currently, support for a Universal Serial Bus (USB) device class; will later be used in game hardware, VR, vehicle simulations, smart athletic equipment, and appliance controls. Other keys may be added later for other species. The HID subkey, while important, was *not* in RC0 or RC1, and may have been subsumed to other keys like HKLM\System\CurrentControlSet\Services\Class\HID. |
| **HTREE** | Function unclear; may be reserved for future use. Subkeys, if any, are binary strings HTREE\RESERVED\0\ForcedConfig and ...\ConfigFlags.<br>    A key called HTREE\ROOT\0 is pointed to by HKDD, many times as the Parent of devices in \ConfigManager, but is otherwise unknown in Win98. The HTREE\ROOT key is alive and busy in Windows NT 4.0, and we suppose that its tentative appearance is one sign of the convergence of the two operating systems |
| **INFRARED** | Infrared (IrDA) devices |
| **ISAPNP** | Data port for Plug and Play enumerators on an ISA bus. Subkey ID's are hard-wired to specific device makes and models |

**Table 17.10** (continued)

| Subkey | Device Enumeration |
|---|---|
| **MF** | Multifunction devices, like IDE controller-and-port cards. For MF subkeys, see PCI subkeys, which they resemble. Do not confuse these keys with the \MIF subkeys of DesktopManagement |
| **MONITOR** | Monitor device IDs and descriptions |
| **Network** | Network protocol including TCP/IP, server, and bindings. For adapter info see \ROOT\NET and subkeys of \ISAPNP |
| **PCI** | Internal PCI bridges such as processor-to-bus, and non-PnP embedded devices. The impossible-looking subkeys are *vendor_number&subsystem_number&revision_number*; don't *ever* change one of these, even if, for some arcane reason, you change a value underneath it. (And we can't imagine why you'd do that.) |
| **PCMCIA** | The ClassGUID, ConfigFlags, HardwareID, etc, for PCMCIA Card Services |
| **Root** | Settings, driver names, .INF file locations and other data for PnP and legacy devices with IDs assigned by Windows hardware detection. If the key begins with an asterisk, like *PNP*nnnn,* the device is on the motherboard. Overlap between this key and BIOS is conjectural |
| **SCSI** | SCSI fixed disk devices (drives) and *all* CD-ROM drives and any tape backups not listed under TAPECONTROLLER. Any PCI SCSI host adapter will be listed under PCI, not here |
| **SW** | New and undocumented. Our guess is that these keys are the Registry's provision for real-time data streaming, like teleconferencing, Internet radio, RealAudio and multicasting |
| **TAPECONTROLLER** | New and undocumented. From the key structure, this provides for the type of tape backup device that Y-connects into the floppy controller |

> **Descriptors for physical devices stay in the Registry device tree even after you remove the devices physically, so that, for example, both the monitor you used to have and the one you have now are still described in the Registry. Over time, as you add and remove devices, your Registry gets overgrown and ponderous. Does this sound just like what used to happen with .INI files? Yes, and we think it's one of the problems the Registry Checker tries to alleviate.**

## HKLM\Hardware

Most of the information you think you'll find in the HKLM\Hardware hierarchy is actually maintained "on-the fly" in HKDD\Config Manager\Enum and rebuilt every time Windows starts, or when you click **Refresh** in Device Manager. If you look at **View By Connection** in Control Panel\Device Manager, you'll get a much better idea of what's going on.

The persistent keys in \DeviceMap\SerialComm are for the use of the Windows HyperTerminal applet. The keys under \DESCRIPTION are rudimentary, but obviously the start of something big. We recommend avoiding this key in REGEDIT, mostly because there's argument among Registry gurus as to what it really does.

## HKLM\Network

This set of subkeys governs network access from a workstation, whether to a LAN or to an online service provider. In the default Windows 98 installation, the PrimaryProvider key is filled with a string value of "Microsoft Network", but this will change if the workstation is attached explicitly to another network. The only absolutely necessary keys here are (Default), LMLogon, and UserName, but depending on the specifics of the network installation, many other keys are possible, including ProcessLogonScript, PrimaryProvider, UserProfiles, and DomainLogonMessage. The content of this key is always appropriate to the logged-on user.

Most of these keys can, and should, be created or adjusted through the System Policy Editor, POLEDIT.EXE; if you can't find that on your system, it's in \RESKIT\NETADMIN\POLEDIT on the Windows 98 Resource Kit CD.

If one Win9*x* workstation on your network won't attach to your server, go into HKLM\Network\Logon and make sure that the entry for the PrimaryProvider key is correct!

## HKLM\Security

This key is for network installs only and has the somewhat obscure subkeys seen in Table 17.11.

### *Table 17.11 HKLM\Security Subkey*

| | |
|---|---|
| \Access\Admin\Remote | Name of network admin console |
| \Provider\AddressBook | Network address-book translator DLL |
| \Provider\Address_Server | NT or peer Address server name |
| \Provider\Container | NT Domain server name |
| \Provider\Platform_Type | 00: share-level access control, 01: user-level access control, in Control Panel\Network\Access Control |

## HKLM\SOFTWARE

This subkey ...

- in **\Classes,** stores information about file extensions and matches those extensions with procedures executed by the operating system shell.

- in **\Clients,** stores information about the Microsoft wide-area-network clients: MS-Outlook, the Windows Address Book, NetMeeting, and Outlook Express.

- in **\Description,** stores timing and other information needed when one computer sends procedure and function calls to another computer.

- in other optional folders, stores validation information and working parameters for some applications—especially Microsoft's, but also from a variety of third-party developers.

... contains *no* user-specific data; that's all in HKU\Software or HKCU\Software.

 Remember that HKLM\SOFTWARE\Classes is fully aliased to HKEY_CLASSES_ROOT and that your computer usually employs the alias rather than the actual name.

Throughout this chapter, \SOFTWARE is used to mean HKLM\Software and \Software is used to mean HKU\Software or HKCU\Software. Why? Because it's the only way we can think of to maintain the humongously important distinctions between the two keys.

## Extensions

The (Default)s in filename extension folders are formally called ProgIDs. Keep that term in the back of your mind, because as soon as we nail down a few definitions, we'll need it.

The filename extension information is stored as one subkey of \Classes for each extension or data type, which makes a *whopping* long list. Each subkey contains a string value of the appropriate file type listing, and possibly also a MIME (Multipurpose Internet Mail Extension) Content Type listing, so that for example, the subkey ".gz" has a (Default) of "WinZip" if it's installed— because WinZip is a Windows application that will unpack .gz files—and a Content Type of "application/x-gzip" which is reported to, among other things, your Web browser.

## Data Types

Data types are more involved, because they can be associated with icons as well as executables, so that if you drag them to the Desktop they'll display appropriately.

### *Tracing the Associations of Icons*

Microsoft didn't make it easy to trace the associations of icons. For example, the value of HKLM\SOFTWARE\Classes\AudioCD\DefaultIcon is "C:\WINDOWS\SYSTEM\shell32.dll,40." Huh? This means that the default icon for AudioCD is the forty-first consecutive icon in SHELL32.DLL—forty-first because, naturally, the numbering starts with 0.

You can look at the contents of SHELL32.DLL by right-clicking any Desktop icon, clicking Properties, the Shortcut tab, and Change Icon. The default icon file displayed will be SHELL32.DLL and the icons in the scrolling list will be in numerical order. If SHELL32.DLL doesn't include the icon you want, tell the Change Icon dialog to look in C:\WINDOWS\MORICONS.DLL, C:\WINDOWS\SYSTEM\URL.DLL, or C:\WINDOWS\SYSTEM\PIFMGR.DLL.

Ah, if that were all there was to it! But there are icons associated with negative numbers, which are uniform locators called *icon resource identifiers,* and mean that the icon can still be found even if the DLL containing it is updated; found by the program, that is, not (of course) by you.

## Keeping it Straight: CLSIDs

Of all the techniques that the Registry uses to maintain its network of associations, the most mystifying are CLSIDs—Class Identifiers, globally unique tags generated by a Special Secret Process and permanently attached to each data type. Before we examine a complex data type in detail, we have to understand what a CLSID is, and no, you can't skip the next half-dozen paragraphs.

Let's start with one of the CLSIDs that every 32-bit Windows installation has, the Recycle Bin. Its CLSID is

{645FF040-5081-101B-9F08-00AA002F954E}

The general case of the format is seen in Table 17.12.

### *Table 17.12  Class Identifier Format*

| | |
|---|---|
| Bytes 1–4 (hex digits 1–8) | Randomly generated |
| Bytes 5–6 (hex digits 9–12) | Derived from date and time |
| Bytes 7–16 (hex digits 13–32) | Derived from hardware characteristics of the computer on which the program is being written |

If you're a programmer and you create a data type that relates specifically to your application, you create a CLSID for the data type and hard-wire it to the application. You can do this by running utility programs that are included with the Microsoft developers' toolkits, or you can just ask Microsoft to make a CLSID for you. The theory behind a CLSID is that, because it contains so many random (or, more exactly, unpredictable) numbers, it's what a cryptographer would call a *nonduplicating key*—that is, a key that can be created over and over again without ever coming up twice. Experts tell us that the chances of a duplicate CLSID are infinitesimal, but so are any one person's chances of winning the lottery; see "Twin CLSIDs" below.

The Recycle Bin's CLSID is one subkey of HKLM\SOFTWARE\Microsoft\Windows\CurrentVersion\explorer\Desktop\NameSpace, and has a (Default) of—guess what—string "Recycle Bin." If you delete this key and reboot, the Recycle Bin vanishes from the Desktop.

To *rename* the Recycle Bin, however, your newfound knowledge of its subkey location under HKLM\SOFTWARE won't do a bit of good. Instead, scroll to HKCR\CLSID\{645FF040-5081->}) where the (Default) value is, once again, string "Recycle Bin." Double-click on the (Default) to the right of the [ab] icon, and the **Edit String** dialog opens, displaying the noneditable Value name **(Default)** and the editable, highlighted Value data **Recycle Bin.** If you edit this to **Trash**, close REGEDIT and restart, the title of the Desktop icon Recycle Bin will be Trash.

The title of the *program* Recycle Bin, in its title bar, is still Recycle Bin, and so is its name in the Explorer hierarchy, because both of these data items are somewhere else. See how complicated the Registry can be?

CLSIDs go to great lengths (pardon the pun) to remain unique. At thirty-eight characters each, they take up a lot of space in any discussion of what they do.

Luckily, *most* CLSIDs—not all—are unique in their first eight characters. To save space, we're going to represent the majority of CLSIDs in a short form of eight characters followed by the first hyphen and a right angle bracket, so that "Recycle Bin," for example, will become "{645FF040->}". We'll write out the full CLSID only if we're giving it to you to be inserted into the Registry as a hack, or if it's needed to make the distinction between two nearly identical ones.

There are a *few* CLSIDs that are identical except for either their rightmost digit, or some digit buried in the middle. The ones we can find are in Table 17.13.

These are not the most crucial identifiers in the world, but they are worth watching out for. They're all visibly Microsoft CLSIDs and so probably exist in every Win98 installation; your Registry may have others, depending on

### Table 17.13  Duplicate CLSIDs

| CLSID in HKLM\SOFTWARE\Classes | (Default) |
|---|---|
| {**08B0E5C0**-4FCB-11CF-AAA5-00401C60850**0**} | Java Support for Internet Explorer |
| {**08B0E5C0**-4FCB-11CF-AAA5-00401C60850**1**} | Control for Java |
| {**1B544C22**-FD0B-11CE-8C63-00AA0044B51**E**} | VFW Capture Filter |
| {**1B544C22**-FD0B-11CE-8C63-00AA0044B51**F**} | VFW Capture Filter Property Page |
| {**86F19A00**-42A0-1069-A2E**9**-08002B30309D} | .PIF file property pages |
| {**86F19A00**-42A0-1069-A2E**B**-08002B30309D} | .PIF file handler |
| {**BD96C556**-65A3-11D0-983A-00C04FC29E3**3**} | AdvancedDataControl |
| {**BD96C556**-65A3-11D0-983A-00C04FC29E3**6**} | AdvancedDataSpace |

what third-party software is installed, but it's unlikely. The point is that, when you modify a CLSID, you can *probably* but not *absolutely* rely on the uniqueness of the first eight digits; the wisest precaution is to search in HKLM\SOFTWARE\Classes and check out the whole string.

## Handlers and Properties: SHELL, SHELLNEW and SHELLEX

The likely subkeys of a ProgID include Shell, ShellNew, ShellEx, DefaultIcon, and EditFlags. Their definitions are shown in Table 17.14.

### Table 17.14  ProgID Subkeys

| | |
|---|---|
| SHELL | Description of a file type's actions as listed in its Context menu |
| SHELLNEW | Link to a representation in the Windows File/New menu |
| SHELLEX | Link to a file type's handlers |
| DEFAULTICON | Pointer to the iconDLL and icon associated with a file type by default |
| EDITFLAGS | Toggle bits for editing permissions |

We can understand how these subkeys work by looking at some common, but involved, DOS or Windows file types. Let's begin with .bat, a DOS batch file.

In HKCR, go to the .bat folder, which contains the (Default) "batfile." .bat is the *extension,* and the Default *ProgID* is batfile.

Scroll down to HKCR\batfile. In its own folder, it has two values: a (Default) of string "MS-DOS Batch File," and a binary EditFlags of d0 04 00 00. The

(Default) string of a ProgID is called its *Publicname,* which is used in (among other things) file creation through the New menu; if you create a New batch file, its name until you name and save it is

New MS-DOS Batch File.bat

which Windows creates by pulling a copy of [Publicname][extension] from HKCR, and appending it to "New."

EditFlags is for the true connoisseur of Windows internals. Each of four bytes is expressed as two hex digits, each byte has eight bits, and each bit is a toggle. The lucky thing (for us) is that, at least in any version of 32-bit Windows so far spotted, the last two bytes are undefined—which means Microsoft is saving them for later and won't tell us why. So, when we're decoding the batfile EditFlags, d0 04 00 00, all we have to care about is the d0 04.

 Actually, in a *few* obscure cases, the LSB of the third byte is set, so that EditFlags reads *nn nn* 01 00. See the table below.

You can use your Windows Calculator in Scientific mode to convert hex to binary. Click on the **Hex** button, enter D 0 0 4, and click on the **Bin** button; you get

1101 0000 0000 0100

(split into quartets for easier reading) which means that, of the sixteen possible switches, four are 1's—that is, they're set. Now, what do these do? Look at Table 17.15.

Since the EditFlag for batfile, d0 04h, is 1101 0000 0000 0100 in binary, bits 8, 7, and 5 are on in byte 1, and bit 3 is on in byte 2. Remove is grayed out in File Types; Edit, Remove and Set Default are grayed out in Edit File Type. If you go to View/Options/File Types in Explorer, and then click the **Edit** button, you'll see that exactly these things are true.

Most EditFlags switches are lockouts designed to prevent novices from making changes that might have undesirable or unpredictable results. When you roll your own EditFlags, be cautious as always; stack up your binary string from the bit values above, then use the Windows Calculator to convert it back to the hex expression of the Registry.

 If you change a Registry EditFlags value to 00 00 00 00, you've removed all lockouts and can change any settings you like—*but* this is only safe for ProgIDs that are linked to *extensions*. Zeroing out the EditFlag of a *system* ProgID, like Drive, File, File Folder, or AudioCD, makes it completely vanish from the File Types list. For system ProgIDs, byte 1 bit 2 *must* be set; so the binary for the first byte is 0000 0010, which makes the appropriate EditFlag hex data 02 00 00 00.

## Table 17.15  EditFlags Format

| Byte, L to R | Bit, L to R | Function |
| --- | --- | --- |
| 1 | 8 (MSB) | View/Options/File Types/Edit File Type dialog: Grays out the Remove button. |
| 1 | 7 | View/Options/File Types/Edit File Type dialog: Grays out the Edit button. |
| 1 | 6 | View/Options/File Types/Edit File Type dialog: Grays out the New button. |
| 1 | 5 | View/Options/File Types tab: Grays out the Remove button. |
| 1 | 4 | View/Options/File Types tab: Grays out the Edit button. |
| 1 | 3 | View/Options/File Types tab: Identifies a file type with no associated extension. |
| 1 | 2 | View/Options/File Types tab: Adds the file type if it does not have an associated extension. |
| 1 | 1 (LSB) | Explorer's View/Options/File Types tab: Removes the file type from the master list if it has an associated extension. |
| 2 | 8 (MSB) | View/Options/File Types tab: Grays out the Content Type option. |
| 2 | 7 | Reserved; undocumented. |
| 2 | 6 | View/Options/File Types/Edit File Type dialog: Locks out setting of DDE fields in Edit Action. (Byte 1 bit 1 must be 0) |
| 2 | 5 | View/Options/File Types/Edit File Type dialog: Locks out edits to the command line in Edit Action. (Byte 1 bit 1 must be 0) |
| 2 | 4 | View/Options/File Types/Edit File Type dialog: Locks out edits to an action's description in Edit Action. (Byte 1 bit 1 must be 0) |
| 2 | 3 | View/Options/File Types/Edit File Type dialog: Grays out the Set Default button. |
| 2 | 2 | View/Options/File Types/Edit File Type dialog: Grays out the Change Icon button. |
| 2 | 1 (LSB) | View/Options/File Types/Edit File Type dialog: Locks out edits to a file type's description. |
| 3 | 1 (LSB) | View/Options/File Types/Edit File Type dialog: Clears the Confirm Open checkbox. Uncommon. |

Don't close Edit File Type just yet.

**Associating Commands: The SHELL Key.**  In the Actions dialog of Edit File Type, three actions are listed—Edit, open and print—and **open** is bold-faced. Where are these set? In the SHELL subkey, so flip back to REGEDIT.

To begin with, in the shell folder, (Default) is "", which is an empty string; this means that control, rather than residing with one particular (Default), is taken over by the commands in the subkeys. Shell has three command sub-keys: **edit, open,** and **print.**

The first subkey, **edit,** has a (Default) of "&Edit" which is the <u>E</u>dit that appears in the Context Menu for a batch file. Underneath that, in the command folder, is "C:\WINDOWS\NOTEPAD.EXE %1"—in other words, when <u>E</u>dit is clicked in the right-click menu of any batch file, first substitute the name of the batch file for the %1, then run Notepad, which will open the batch file in Notepad.

The second subkey, **open,** has a (Default) of "" which passes control to the key underneath it, and an EditFlags of 00 00h. Underneath that, in the command folder, is a (Default) of ""%1" %★" Oh, boy, fire up the DOS wayback machine. Click on (Default) to open the Edit String dialog, and the outer pair of quotes are stripped off, leaving the literal key of "%1" %★. Again, the name of the batch file is substituted for the %1, and what <u>O</u>pen in the right-click menu does with a DOS batch file is, actually, run it.

The last subkey, **print,** passes control to the command key underneath it, which is a (Default) of "C:\WINDOWS\NOTEPAD.EXE /p %1", looking remarkably like the command for the **edit** subkey. It isn't, quite, because for execution of the print subkey, Notepad loads, functions as an OLE print server that kicks the file to the printer, and politely vanishes. (You can even make it do this from a DOS box.)

**Some Other SHELL Subkeys.** SHELL is remarkably versatile. Edit, Open and Print may be its commonest and most important subkeys, but there are several others, as you can see in Table 17.16.

### Table 17.16 SHELL Subkeys

| | |
|---|---|
| Config | Configures and launches a screen saver |
| CPLOpen | Adds "Open with Control Panel" to the Context Menu of .CPL files |
| Explore | Opens an Explorer view (side-by-side panes) for the Start Menu, Desktop Folders, the Inbox, and Microsoft Network |
| Find | From My Computer, Drive, and Folder, launches Find All Files. From Network Neighborhood, launches Find Computer |
| Install | Adds "Install" to the Context Menu of .INF and .SCR files |
| OpenAs | Adds "Open with…" to the Context Menu of files of types whose opening applications haven't been defined. After "Always use this program to open this file" is checked, "Open with…" will be replaced by "Open" |
| Play | Opens CDPlayer for audio CD's or files, and Media Player for .AVI files |
| PrintTo | Specifies the application to be used to open a file dropped on a printer |

**Handling Handlers: The SHELLEX Key.** SHELLEX, for *shell extension,* is a subkey that lets programmers add additional functions to a File Type by tying it into a DLL. When viewed in its most global extent this becomes inhumanly complicated, so let's start by considering what it does for batfile—an easy case because the File Type, batfile, is tightly coupled to the file extension, .bat.

The top subkey of batfile\shellex is PropertySheetHandlers. A Property Sheet Handler lets you add tabs to a file's Property Sheets—what you get to by right-clicking on the file and clicking Properties. In the case of batfile, this is accomplished by {86F19A00-42A0-1069-A2E9-08002B30309D}, the CLSID with a (Default) of ".PIF file property pages".

This CLSID has a subkey of InProcServer32, which contains a (Default) of "shell32.dll". So, when OLE invokes the PropertySheet object's handlers, shell32.dll gets called to do the handling.

 Besides InProcServer keys, there are LocalServer and InProcHandler keys, all of which point to DLLs. You can depend on Windows to keep track of which one does what, and if a Server or Handler points to a DLL that's missing or damaged, you'll just get an error message.

**Asterisk Key: Wildcard SHELLEX.** There are document types that *aren't* uniquely identified by a file extension, and the primary type is an OLE object, which can be a Word document, an Excel worksheet, or any number of others. This data type is handled by *\shellex, which is a SHELLEX for files with any extension.

*\shellex has subkeys of ContextMenuHandlers and PropertySheetHandlers. The ContextMenuHandlers subkey BriefcaseMenu points to a CLSID of {85BBD920->} whose InProcServer32 subkey defaults to "syncui.dll". This adds the **Update** function to an object's Context Menu and links in the dynamic library that the Briefcase uses to perform file synchronization. The point here is that only a file in the Briefcase *needs* the **Update** function, so when the file enters the briefcase, it "grows" the extra capability. This is very slick and is, as usual, much more complex on the Registry level than it would seem when you look at the menus and tabs.

In much the same way that **ContextMenuHandlers** adds a function to the menu, **PropertySheetHandlers** adds tabs to the file's Properties sheet. Its two subkeys are:

BriefcasePage, which goes through a CLSID of {85BBD920->} pointing to the same InProcServer32 subkey of "syncui.dll". This adds the Update Status page to an object's Properties page and tells you all you need to know, maybe more, about the properties of the object migrated into the Briefcase relative to its allied object somewhere else in the filesystem.

{3EA48300->}, which in CLSID has a (Default) of "OLE Docfile Property Page," and an InProcServer32 subkey of "docprop.dll". DOCPROP.DLL adds Summary and Statistics tabs to the Properties page of any OLE object, which would otherwise only have a General tab.

On a pristine Win98 system with no third-party software installed, these are the only subkeys of *\shellex. The result is that *any* file—literally "OLE-object-dot-star"—will have these enhancements added to its right-click menu and Properties under the right circumstances.

Other interesting top-level shell extensions are listed in Table 17.17.

### Table 17.17 Top-Level Shell Extensions

| | |
|---|---|
| CopyHookHandler | Used by Directory services to handle copying of files and folders |
| IconHandler | A handler that allows a file type to generate or customize its own icon—for example, the shortcut CLSID, which superimposes the little boxed arrow on the corners of icons for shortcuts |
| DragDropHandler | One method of adding special functions to an object's Context Menu when an object is right-dragged to a folder; Norton Navigator installs its Navigator item |
| DropHandler | Allows data files to receive—that is, incorporate—drag-and-dropped objects when a DropHandler is associated to that data file type's ProgID; Internet Explorer uses a DropHandler tied into SENDMAIL.DLL to process a drag-and-dropped mail message through Outlook |

From these examples it should be clear that you won't have a lot to do with the SHELLEX key unless you're a programmer, but it is quite capable.

**Creating New Objects: The SHELLNEW Key.** SHELLNEW adds items to the File/New menu that are used to create new empty objects, which is fairly straightforward, but SHELLNEW can be an interesting key when it has to make choices. Let's look at what it does for .DOC files. (This assumes you have Microsoft Office or Word installed, but even if you don't, you can follow along with WordPad.)

In HKCR, the .doc key has a ShellEx subkey and also, depending on the file types it needs to accommodate, can have Document.Identifier subkeys of Word.Document.6, Word.Document.8, Word.Document, and Wordpad.Document.1. In English this means a Word 6.0 file, a Word 8.0—that is, Word97—file, a Word 2.0 file, and a WordPad file. The Word 7.0, or Word95, file type isn't needed because the file architecture is the same as Word 6.0.

The ShellEx key is a CLSID, {CC264220->}, and its (Default) is another CLSID, {9DBD2C50->}. The first one of these is associated with a tremendous number of file types and not separately defined in HKCR\CLSID, but its (Default) is string "Summary Info Thumbnail handler (DOCFILES)".

Only when we go down one level to {9DBD2C50->}, which *is* defined in HKCR\CLSID, do we find an InprocServer32 (Default) of "C:\WINDOWS\SYSTEM\THUMBVW.DLL" and a ProgID pointing to a blank document type of Shell.ThumbnailExtract.Docfile. This means that every time Windows needs to generate a thumbnail of any file that it considers a Document, it whistles for THUMBVW.DLL—the ShellEx thumbnail server.

The rest of this is much, much easier. Each file type key has a subkey of ShellNew\FileName, and for the four document types, Table 17.18 lists the associations.

### *Table 17.18  ShellNew File Type Associations*

| Blank document type (Document.Identifier) | ShellNew\FileName subkey |
| --- | --- |
| Word.Document | string "winword2.doc" |
| Word.Document.8 | string "winword8.doc" |
| Word.Document.6 [also 7] | string "winword.doc" |
| Wordpad.Document.1 | string "winword.doc" |

The mystery stands revealed. Windows maintains three blank files—WINWORD.DOC, WINWORD2.DOC, and WINWORD8.DOC—one for each different Word file type. Then, when a Word file is created from the New menu (ShellNew), the FileName subkey points to the appropriate blank file to be copied—whose name, as discussed above, will be "New Microsoft Word Document.doc." This also, incidentally, demonstrates that a WordPad file is a Word 6.0 file; they both start as copies of WINWORD.DOC.

ShellNew has several possible subkeys, and chooses from among them depending on the action that's supposed to follow the click on the **New** menu item. See Table 17.19.

### *Table 17.19  ShellNew File Type Subkeys*

| | |
| --- | --- |
| NullFile | Creates a new, empty file of unspecified type on the Desktop. This takes precedence over … |
| FileName | which creates a copy of the "string" specified file from an original, which is either on the path specified with the filename, or by default in C:\Windows\ShellNew. This takes precedence over … |
| Data | which copies a binary specified value into the header of a new file. (Data, which only creates a file header, is less specific than FileName, which copies a whole file.) Finally, |
| Command | calls an executable when you create a new file. |

And that, amazingly enough, more or less finishes HKLM\SOFTWARE. Actually there's lots more, but if you have a firm grip on the principles outlined above, most of the rest will be self-evident.

## HKLM\System

HKEY_LOCAL_MACHINE\System is where the bare metal—er, silicon—of your computer gets managed. It's a bad dream. It's like a fine old Central European satire about bureaucracy. It verges on the indescribable. And yet it works!

Remember when we mentioned the Secret Master Lists of all valid keys and values? In HKLM\System, you actually get one. It would appear that, when Windows 95 or 98 install, they copy *all* the available driver and service information into a subkey of HKLM\System called CurrentControlSet.

Now: The CurrentControlSet key is an inheritance from previous versions of 32-bit Windows, notably WinNT, in which that keyname actually makes some sense. Windows NT responds to configuration changes by creating up to eight backup Control Sets, and keeping them ready in case you invoke the Hardware Profile/Last Known Good option at boot-time. This is roughly analogous to what Registry Checker accomplishes in Win98.

Win9*x*, however, creates a single Control Set at installation and leaves it pretty much alone afterwards. Why it should then be called the CurrentControlSet is one of those knife-edge, scholastic mysteries that keeps the Windows investigator humble; but Win98 in general is a lot like NT in many ways that aren't immediately obvious, and this is one of them.

CurrentControlSet in its two subkeys, Control and Services, is one of the most voluminous of all Registry keys. (As one quick example, take a look at HKLM\System\CurrentControlSet\InstalledFiles.) While we were researching this chapter we cleverly decided to print out a hard copy, but after about 200 pages the printer ran out of paper. This key—again, so far as we can tell—contains startup and service parameters, not only for every device on your computer, but for every device *that might be* on your computer. Let's consider, for example, one of the keys to be found in the Registry of our humble testbench Win98 installation:

```
[(HKLM...)\CurrentControlSet\Control\MediaResources\mci\videodisc]
Description=PIONEER LaserDisc Device (Media Control)
Driver=mcipionr.drv
Disabled=1
FriendlyName=PIONEER LaserDisc Device (Media Control)
```

No such device exists on this system ... at the moment, which the subkey recognizes through the `Disabled=1`. But if we decide to add one—whether through Plug and Play, or manually through the Add New Hardware Wizard—this subkey is the pointer that will tell the Windows setup procedure which driver is necessary.

Why would Windows copy the full CurrentControlSet to a machine that will, in overwhelming likelihood, use five to ten per cent of it at most? Probably because, to the average Windows user trembling on the brink of the millennium, disk space is *much* cheaper than time. No matter what stunning devices your new fourteen-bay system comes equipped with, the existing Win98 installation will at least *try* to step up to the plate and say "Right!" At worst, the Wizard you're using will tell you it needs to copy a driver off the Windows CD—and will know where to find it.

Naturally, new gizmos will be developed that the existing Windows CD has no drivers for; that's the progression of hardware development. Drivers for unanticipated alphabet soup will arrive either on OEM install diskettes or, more slowly but more comprehensively, within Windows Service Packs.

All of this being so, there's not much point to examining the *entire* CurrentControlSet in detail. Most of it is of interest only to your Windows installation; most of it should never be changed for any reason. But let's skim some of the more interesting functions of the two main subkeys.

**HKLM\System\CurrentControlSet\Control.**  The Control key contains information needed to start systems and subsystems, and to establish the computer's name and location on the network, if there is one. Some of the subkeys are to be found in Table 17.20.

### Table 17.20  \CurrentControlSet\Control Subkeys

| | |
|---|---|
| IDConfigDB | Identification(s) and description(s) for system Hardware Profiles |
| Media Properties, Media Resources | Descriptions and driver information for Win9x built-in multimedia support |
| Nls | Definitions and descriptions for multinational language support |
| PerfStats | Names and descriptions that serve as legends for System Monitor output, and as Value names for HKDD\PerfStats |
| Print | Pointers to network printer handlers, printer drivers, system printer monitors, and system-defined (not hardware) printer ports |
| PwdProvider | Locations of DLLs, user account files, and password caches. Fascinating to look at if only to prove (again) how lame Win9x security really is; but don't edit it or you may lock yourself out |

### Table 17.20 *(continued)*

| | |
|---|---|
| SessionManager\AppPatches | Fixes for apps that give Win9x fits, including Paradox, WordPerfect for Windows 6.1, the Lion King game CD, and—of all things—the Microsoft AntiVirus scanner, among many others. |
| SessionManager\CheckBadApps and \CheckBadApps400 | Two really huge lists of apps that are flaky under Win9x or won't run at all. Includes most of the Norton and Central Point system tools, some versions of XTree, pcAnywhere and Laplink, Stacker, TabWorks, at least one version of Photoshop … and on and on. |
| SessionManager\CheckVerDLLs | A list of DLLs and drivers with data values that Win9x (not *you*) can check to determine if it's about to copy an obsolete DLL over a newer one |
| SessionManager\HackIniFiles | Compatibility strings for the INI files of Windows 3.*x*, Microsoft Bookshelf 94, and QuickTime for Windows. These aren't ever physically written into the file and the switch may actually take place in RAM—Windows is no stranger to self-modifying code |
| SessionManager\Known16DLLs | A list of known 16-bit DLLs and their filenames; if a 16-bit DLL is on this list, Windows will look for it *first* in the \Windows\System folder rather than the app folder |
| SessionManager\KnownDLLs | The list of 32-bit DLLs loaded into memory when Windows starts, needed or not. Use this list and Known16DLLs together to see if an old DLL can be updated by hand |
| SessionManager\WarnVerDLLs | A list of DLLs that may misbehave under Win9x |
| Update | **UpdateMode 00:** Win9x installed on bare metal, **UpdateMode 01:** Win9x installed over previous version of Windows. Installing Win9x over Win 3.*x* is one source of obsolete drivers and DLLs |
| VMM32Files | A list of the formerly independent VXD's compiled into the VMM32 universal virtual device driver. This is not all the VxD's, but a lot of them |

**HKLM\System\CurrentControlSet\Services.** You can learn a lot by looking at these keys, but the consensus among advanced Registry hackers is that you should *never* edit them.

The Services key controls the loading and configuration of drivers, file systems, and interprocess communications. Some of the subkeys are shown in Table 17.21.

### Table 17.21 \CurrentControlSet\Services Subkeys

| | |
|---|---|
| \Arbitrators | Reserves ranges and masks to forestall overlapping of memory addresses, DMA channels, I/O bandwidth and interrupt requests by contending devices. *Don't mess with this key.* Your safe access is through the Resource tabs of device property sheets in Device Manager |
| \Class | *At last!* The entire, legible table of hardware types that Win9*x* supports, and in its subkeys, the settings, descriptions, paths and filenames for what's on *your* computer! |
| \MSNP32 | Authentication and login settings for the Network Provider; see also \Control\PwdProvider |
| \RemoteAccess | Control for various settings and legends that appear in Dial-Up Networking |
| \VxDs | A key for each currently installed VxD with subkeys for configuration parameters. Pretty to look at, but don't touch |

# HKEY_USERS: The Subkeys

HKEY_USERS stores information about users and their preferences. It can store coherent sets of preferences for any number of users—which is why, when you log into a Windows workstation, your Desktop and your applications settings are (or should be) just the way they were when you logged off.

 Examining the values in HKU can be informative; editing them is largely useless. Entries in HKEY_USERS and HKEY_CURRENT_USER should be identical, but when they aren't, the ones in HKCU take precedence, so any entry that you change in HKU will be overridden by the matching entry in HKCU. If you're going to edit, edit HKCU.

## HKU\.Default

Win9*x* maintains the \.Default profile for two reasons:

- To use as a generic logon for any user who doesn't have a User Profile created in the applicable USER.DAT.

- To be copied as the initial data for any user whose User Profile is being set up. See "Multiple Users: The Registry Perspective," below.

 (Default), the top-level compatibility key, and \.Default, the key for the generic set in HKU, have nothing to do with each other.

 Watch that dot! The \.Default key has an initial dot in it; the \<logged-on user> key doesn't. Unless that dot stays where it belongs, Win9*x* will think \Default is a username.

## HKU\.Default: The Subkeys

The subkeys for HKU\.Default are shown in Table 17.22.

### Table 17.22 HKU\.Default Subkeys

| | |
|---|---|
| \AppEvents | The \EventLabels are the names for actions in the scrolling list of Control Panel\Sounds Properties. Actual sound filenames are under Schemes; Win9x installs with two schemes, Windows Default and No Sounds. If an event name has both \.Default and \.Current subkeys, \.Default is the one that was installed originally (which may be blank) and \.Current is whatever it was modified to. Some applets, including Explorer, Sound Recorder and Media Player, can have separate sound schemes |
| \Control Panel | Color schemes, cursor sets, desktop, window metrics, time and date formats, key delay, key speed, mouse speeds and thresholds, power policies (for Control Panel\Power Management Properties sheet) sounds on or off |
| \InstallLocationsMRU | MRU stands for "Most Recently Used." The last five install locations are stored as string keys **a**, **b**, **c**, **d** and **e**; the MRUList key stores the order in which those paths were accessed |
| \keyboard layout | The \preload\1 key here is the same as HKLM\System\CurrentControlSet\Control\Nls\Locale; it's the code number for the national language (keyboard) keyset. This is not the same as the number of the Nls national codepage, which would be too easy |
| \Network | Will only exist if a system is networked and network resources are mapped to local drive letter(s). *Persistent* connections have their *Reconnect at logon* boxes checked; if the boxes are unchecked, the keys are deleted. *Recent* connections are transient connections which were recently established |
| \RemoteAccess | Addresses, network mappings and connection profiling—but not the passwords—for Dial-Up Networking |
| \Software | Discussed under \HKCU for economy of space |

## Multiple Users: The Registry Perspective

When you create a new user through Control Panel\Users, you'll notice that the File Copy dialog really goes bonkers for a couple of minutes. That's because, for each User that you create, Windows installs a complete duplicate of HKU\.Default with all its subkeys.

If you have one user set up on a computer, that user's subkey is HKU\.Default. If you have *more than one user* set up on a computer, each user will have a copy of the \.Default subkey in the Registry, but the only subkeys that show in REGEDIT will be \.Default, \<logged-on user>, and \Software. In effect this means that, in order to change the Registry settings of any user, you have to be logged on as that user, which makes some sense. On the other hand, it raises the frightening probability of subkeys in the Registry that don't appear in REGEDIT.

 **Want to prove that REGEDIT assembles its displayed subkeys on the fly? You can, if you have multiple users set up. Win9x logons aren't case-sensitive. Pick one of your users to log on as, first normally as User, then bizarrely—say, as uSER. After logging on each time, go into REGEDIT and expand HKEY_USERS. You'll find that the name of the \<logged-on user> subkey exactly follows the case of the logon ID you typed! Incidentally, so does the Start Menu item Logoff <logged-on user>..., except that in the Start Menu, the user's name always has the first letter forced to uppercase.**

As we discussed in Chapter 10, the logon security of a Win9x computer is basically nonexistent, unless it's connected to a Windows NT server performing the user management. REGEDIT at least pays lip service to this fact. If you hit Cancel or Esc at the Welcome to Windows dialog to bypass it, the only subkeys displayed in REGEDIT will be \.Default and \Software; all the \<logged-on user> subkeys will be hidden. This is accomplished because, if you have User Profiles enabled, REGEDIT figures out which subkey to display by checking the logged-on user's password against the .PWL file—and if no password is entered, of course, there can't possibly be a match.

# HKEY_DYN_DATA: Windows' Merry-Go-Round

Consider that everything you've learned about the Registry so far has been a description of a static tree, or at least a hierarchy of momentarily static values copied while they were sitting still. Isn't it enough as it stands—pardon the pun—to make you dizzy? Now imagine a sizable chunk of this hierarchy being continuously updated in *real time,* keeping up with every change of state in your hapless box. Ah, the mad tarantella of the transistors, jittering on the red-hot overhang of a torrent of parity errors! It's a wonder the CPU doesn't melt!

Welcome to HKEY_DYN_DATA, one of the most frightening jobs ever performed by a non-military computer. Since you'll never need to edit a value of a key or subkey whose values change in the blink of an electron, we won't go into it very deeply, but you should at least understand how it works.

## HKDD\Config Manager\Enum

HKDD has two subkeys, \Config Manager and \PerfStats. \Config Manager contains a blank (Default) and one subkey, \Enum, which is where the action is.

## \ENUM Hex Subkeys

\Enum has one subkey for each *installed* device on your computer. They are all valid eight-digit hexadecimal numbers that begin with the digit C, decimal 12. On any single computer the first three digits will almost all be the same—on our test machine they're "C29"—but the last five are a mystery. These numbers don't exist anywhere *else* in the Registry, and they vary from one computer to the next.

Each hex key has seven subkeys besides a blank (Default—see Table 17.23).

### Table 17.23  HKDD\Config Manager\Enum Subkeys

| | |
|---|---|
| Allocation | Designates the process that controls the device |
| Child | *new* Child of, that is, device being controlled by, this device. Undocumented |
| HardWareKey | This is the link between \Config Manager and the HKLM hardware tree. See below |
| Parent | *new* Parent of, that is, device controlling, this device. Undocumented |
| Problem | 00 00 00 00: the device is working correctly. *nn* 00 00 00: the device is failing, and *nn* is the Device Manager error code, in hex. See table in Appendix E |
| Sibling | *new* Undocumented |
| Status | Undocumented |

In the Parent, Sibling and Child keys, the Data is broken into the usual four eight-bit pairs, and the "last" pair is always C*n*. Invert the XEH to hex, squish it into a single number, and you'll see it's just a different key from \ConfigManager\Enum. By working all these out you'd map the system hierarchy of devices—which is a bit puzzling in places; the Siblings have non-obvious connections, and many keys have a Parent of HTREE\ROOT\0, which doesn't exist. All will be revealed in time. See Table 17.24.

### Table 17.24  HardWareKey Subkeys

|       | In \ConfigMgr\Enum | [decoded] | In HardWareKey | In HKLM\Enum\Root\*PNPA003\0000 |
|-------|--------------------|-----------|----------------|----------------------------------|
| Key   | C25A58A0           |           | ROOT\*PNPA003\0000 | MKEPanasonic CD-ROM Adapter |
| Child | 50 FA 5A C2        | C25AFA50  | SCSI\MATSHITA… | Matsushita CR-563 CD-ROM drive |

Obviously, much of \Config Manager's information is better organized and presented in the Device Manager than in the Registry. But there's one exception …

## HardWareKey

HardWareKey in \Config Manager overlaps with the device type keys of HKLM\Enum—with the important difference that HKLM\Enum lists every device that was *ever* installed on your computer (a nice way of saying that it doesn't clean itself up) while HKDD lists only those devices that are currently installed and active. Also, HKLM\Enum updates itself variously when you start Windows, run Windows Setup or Add New Hardware, or click **Refresh** in Device Manager; the HardWareKey in HKDD refreshes itself on every clock cycle it can grab, so the HKDD data is fresher. The relationship between the two is that:

If the key in HKLM is

\Enum\subkey1\subkey2\subkey3,

then the HKDD\Config Manager\Enum\C*nnnnnnn*\HardWareKey "string" is

"subkey1\subkey2\subkey3"

So that, for example, if the HKLM key is \Enum\ROOT\*PNP0C01\0000, then HKDD\Config Manager\Enum\C25A5570\HardWareKey is "ROOT\*PNP0C01\0000".

 The \C*nnnnnnn* key is described this way because these keys vary from computer to computer and even change (mostly increment) on the same computer when you upgrade software. The only thing we can be certain of is that no two of them are identical on the same computer at the same time.

## HKDD\PerfStats

PerfStats is something completely different, DYN_DATA running wild. Whereas HKLM\System\CurrentControlSet\Control\PerfStats provides the legends, descriptors and framework for System Monitor—the fixed foot, so to speak—HKDD\PerfStats has the major chore of feeding live, running system data into the graphical interface. There are five subkeys visible in REGEDIT, as shown in Table 17.25.

### Table 17.25  HKDD\PerfStats Subkeys

| | |
|---|---|
| StartSrv | Starting time for polling the server |
| StartStat | Starting time for gathering statistics |
| StatData |  Most current value to be fed to the appropriate graph in System Monitor. |
| StopSrv | Stopping time for polling the server |
| StopStat | Stopping time for gathering statistics |

The Name values of StartSrv and StopSrv show the subsystems that PerfStats is monitoring; the Name values of StartStat and StopStat show the parameters whose values are being gathered.

 StatData, like other formatted live "binary" data, is byte-backward and digit-forward. Example: A typical value for VMM\cpgSwapfileInUse (the bottom subkey in the stack, and one you can easily monitor) is given as follows:

| | |
|---|---|
| In REGEDIT | 00 d0 62 01 |
| Real value in hex | 01 62 d0 00 = 162d000 |
| Value in System Monitor | 162d000h = 23252992 = about 22Mb |

Here's a chance to see a real, live, dynamic Registry key in action:

Open System Monitor, pull down **Edit,** pick **Add Item, Memory Manager,** and **Swapfile in use.**

Open REGEDIT and browse to HKDD\PerfStats\StatData\VMM\cpgSwapfileInUse.

Open Calculator in Scientific mode and click **Hex.** Swap around the Name data in REGEDIT and plug it into Calculator.

Click **Dec.** The decimal value you see will be the one in the Status bar of System Monitor. (If it isn't, go back into REGEDIT and hit F5 .)

Microsoft talks about several places in which the code for Win98 has been significantly sped up over Win95, without being too specific about exact locations. \PerfStats may be one of them. Our own trials and published sources suggest that, when the \PerfStats key of a Win95 Registry is exported to a .REG file, the resulting document will be between 2Mb and 5Mb in size. When \PerfStats is exported on our Win98 computer, the .REG file is 8K—and there's nothing in the file that isn't visible under REGEDIT.

With HKEY_LOCAL_MACHINE, HKEY_USERS, and HKEY_DYN_DATA taken care of, we can proceed to the three "aliased" keys: HKEY_CLASSES_ROOT, HKEY_CURRENT_USER, and HKEY_CURRENT_CONFIG.

# HKEY_CLASSES_ROOT: The Oldie But Goodie

As noted, the HKEY_CLASSES_ROOT key is a complete, simultaneously updated duplicate of HKEY_LOCAL_MACHINE\Software\Classes. The useful thing about HKCR is that its extension, file-type, shell and icon keys are directly below the root, and more accessible if you want to edit them. Any edit you make in HKCR is immediately copied into HKLM\\Software\Classes, where the physical data actually lives.

# HKEY_CURRENT_USER: In the Pilot's Seat

HKCU can be one of three things. If:

- The computer is set up single-user, without Profiles, it's a copy of HKU\.Default.

- The computer is set up with Profiles, but the user hits [Esc] at the logon window, it's still a copy of HKU\.Default. (If the system doesn't know who the user is, it can't pick a profile.)

- The computer is set up with Profiles and the user logs on with the appropriate password from the .PWL file, it's a copy of HKU\<logged-on user>.

HKCU, like HKCR, is copied from the "persistent" data in its master key every time Windows is booted.

## HKCU\Software

Since HKCU is selectively copied from HKU and correlates to the user's logon information, the \Software keys of HKCU contain only *user-dependent* information about installed software, like toolbar settings, window coordinates, plugins, and font selections. User-*independent* information about installed software is stored under HKLM\SOFTWARE, and the two keys are in different cases probably because the distinction is so important.

The tree layout is straightforward. First-level subkeys are the names of software companies, subkeys under those are the names of applications, and subkeys under those are the settings for each program.

The fact that an application is on your system doesn't automatically mean that it's in HKCU\Software, and *vice versa*. Applications programmers who use the Registry for program settings tend to work for companies with a long tradition of Windows development, or companies rich enough to develop separate 16-bit and 32-bit program versions; less sophisticated developers still frequently elect to use .INI files, and the 32-bit Windows boot process is required to take note of them. On the other hand—and unfortunately—Registry keys for an application can hang around after the application itself is gone; the Add/Remove Programs dialog and third-party uninstallers are supposed to prune the Registry when they remove the files and directory structure, but the job they do isn't always perfect.

**The Microsoft Subkey.** It's no surprise that the Microsoft key is the biggest subkey in HKCU\Software for any Win98 machine. Having designed the Registry to begin with, Microsoft's programmers make heavy use of it to enhance the performance of their applications and manage the complex relationships among the apps, applets, wizards and services that make up Windows and the Internet Explorer.

| Name | Data |
|------|------|
| (Default) | (value not set) |
| fSavePageSettings | 0x00000000 (0) |
| fWrap | 0x00000000 (0) |
| iPointSize | 0x0000005a (90) |
| lfCharSet | 0x000000ff (255) |
| lfClipPrecision | 0x00000002 (2) |
| lfEscapement | 0x00000000 (0) |
| lfFaceName | "Terminal" |
| lfItalic | 0x00000000 (0) |
| lfOrientation | 0x00000000 (0) |
| lfOutPrecision | 0x00000001 (1) |
| lfPitchAndFamily | 0x00000031 (49) |
| lfQuality | 0x00000001 (1) |
| lfStrikeOut | 0x00000000 (0) |
| lfUnderline | 0x00000000 (0) |
| lfWeight | 0x00000190 (400) |

*Figure 17.8*

*Notepad subkeys*

Even the humble Notepad has its own Registry key with an amazing number of subkeys, most of which are the comparatively exotic DWORD. Many of these support the full font dialog that 32-bit Notepad offers. **IfFaceName** happens to be set to "Terminal" because we used the old Windows Terminal font in Notepad for Figure 17.5.

Wait a minute. How *can* Notepad offer a Set Font dialog and still produce files that are absolutely clean ASCII? Because there's no need for embedded formatting; all the font settings are in the Registry.

**Other Developers.** Third-party developers, large and small, who pride themselves on their 32-bit Windows programming, add their own keys to HKCU\Software to hold application settings. It's the most Windows-compliant way to store preferences, and it's also the fastest. On our test machine the third-party \Software keys include Creative Labs for its SoundBlaster, IBM for VoiceType dictation software, Intel for the Indeo codec, Kodak for the Windows Messaging image previewer, Netscape for Navigator, Seagate for Microsoft Backup, Somarsoft for the DumpReg Registry browser (see the Third-Party Tools section), Thinking Man Software for the Dimension clock synchronizer, and VDO for the VDOLive video plugin. All of that's aristocracy without a doubt.

# HKEY_CURRENT_CONFIG: The Happening Thing?

If the Registry's internal logic were human-readable, HKCC would be a lot like HKCU; it would describe everything within its purview that was currently true about the system. But HKCC is actually much more like HKLM\Hardware—it doesn't have nearly as many subkeys as you'd expect, and the selection of subkeys is puzzling. This seems to be another key that's evolving, rather than definitive.

HKCC is a straight copy of HKLM\Config\000*n*, the key for the hardware configuration in force; that's almost always 0001, since unless you have something like a docked or undocked laptop, one computer will rarely have more than one configuration. (See "Basic Configurations" in Chapter 15 for more detail on Windows' multiple configurations.)

 When you have more than one hardware configuration available in HKLM\Config, HKCC knows how to select the one that the computer is operating under, but it does *not* tell you which one that is. You can find out by going to Control Panel\Hardware Profiles and looking at the list; assuming you have multiple profiles, they'll be listed in alphabetical order by name, and the one in force will be highlighted.

# REGEDIT: Computer Brain Surgery for the Masses

### You Have Been Warned

 We told you what can happen if you trash your Registry. We told you what steps to take so that, if you do trash it, your computer won't be a doorstop. We told you how to go into MS-DOS mode and restore your Registry from a Registry Checker .CAB file. Go back to the section called "Running Registry Checker" and do a manual backup right now. Then come back here and keep reading.

Finally, having surveyed the inner workings of Windows from a perilous height, we descend into the weird machinery of REGEDIT, winner of the coveted "Best Imitation of Explorer" award from the Windows marketing team. REGEDIT is the samurai sword of Windows; it's well-balanced and physically beautiful, it's carrying around a lot of baggage that you don't know about when you just look at it, and if you learn to use it skillfully, you will attain mastery. If, on the other hand, you misuse it *even slightly,* you may send your computer to the hospital. For this reason, we discuss REGEDIT and its proper use from a somewhat conservative standpoint. We don't want you chewing us out because you did something we told you to and it didn't work.

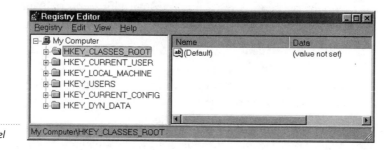

**Figure 17.9**

REGEDIT top level

With all its keys closed—in other words, at the top level—REGEDIT looks like this. You wouldn't expect to find fifty thousand lines of system information in there, would you? But that's the most impressive thing about REGEDIT; it overlays megabytes of data and imposes a structure on it that makes the organization clear, lets you find any item you want and penetrate to it quickly, and makes the information editable.

# Menu Structure

The REGEDIT menu structure looks a lot like an abbreviated Explorer top-bar menu, if we take "Registry" to be a rough equivalent to "File." But although the top-level menu options look remarkably familiar, most of the drop-down menu options are highly specific to Registry manipulation.

**Registry Menu.**  The first thing you'll notice about the Registry menu is that there's no Save option. All Registry edits are saved to disk as soon as they're made, in both the master and the alias keys—for example, in HKEY_CLASSES_ROOT and in HKEY_LOCAL_MACHINE\Software\Classes. (The only exception, of course, is HKEY_DYN_DATA, which is never written to disk at all.) There's no Undo hotkey, either. This makes it doubly important to follow an editing strategy that involves recent backups or exports of Registry branches, because when you're working in REGEDIT your edits become part of the computer's live operating code faster than you can say "Oops!"

Drop-down items are shown in Table 17.26.

## Table 17.26  REGEDIT Registry Menu

| | |
|---|---|
| Import Registry File | Import a file into the Registry that has previously been exported from it. The default is an ASCII text file in a Registry-compatible format and with the extension **.reg**, which Windows refers to as a Registration file.<br>    Opens: An Explorer-type browser of the Windows folder, with a default data type of Registration Files. |
| Export Registry File | Export a Registration file from the Registry to disk, defaulting to the **.reg** format.<br>    Opens: Same as the Import Registry File dialog, with the addition of the Export Range box, giving you the choice of exporting the whole Registry (best for backups) or just the branch that was highlighted when you clicked Export (preferable if you're exporting samples to work with) |
| Connect Network Registry | Connects to the Registry of another computer on the network, providing that computer has Remote Administration enabled and that both computers are running the Remote Registry Service |
| Disconnect Network Registry | As above |
| Print... | Send an ASCII copy of the Registry to the default printer or to a file. The **Print range** box gives you the choice of printing "All" the Registry (if you own stock in a paper company) or just the branch that was highlighted when you clicked (which you'll find useful ninety-nine per cent of the time) |
| Exit | Leave REGEDIT. |

"Print range All" really means "Print HKLM and HKU," ignoring the other "shadow" keys and the humongous HKEY_DYN_DATA. HKLM and HKU together will still run to many hundreds of pages. If you want to print parts of HKCR, HKCU, HKCC or HKDD, you can do it by printing specifically selected branches.

 Watch out for printing HKDD; the printout is likely to be much bigger than what appears in REGEDIT. (Yes, we found out the hard way. We stop at nothing to uncover the ways Windows will bite your ankles.) A better tactic for HKDD is to export the selected branch to a file and then see how big it is before you kick it to the printer.

**Edit Menu.** The Edit menu looks familiar, if rather barebones, but again is quite specific to REGEDIT in the way that it works. Drop-down items are shown in Table 17.27.

## Better Registry Searches

Two techniques can make your Registry searches faster and more accurate:

Since longer Registry keys, and especially CLSIDs, aren't very memorable, it's faster to create exact copies. Go to the first occurrence of the key you want, highlight it, select Edit\Copy Key Name, select Edit\Find, and use Ctrl V to paste the copied key name into the Find What box; then hit Search.

Copy Key Name is useful enough that you're going to wish you had it everywhere, especially since REGEDIT doesn't seem to use Ctrl C for Copy. Unfortunately, if you highlight a Name in the **Value** pane, pull down the **Edit** menu and click **Copy Key Name**, what goes to the Clipboard is … the name of the key you happen to be sitting on in the Key pane.

There's a workaround. Double-click the **Name** field, and if any of the data in the Edit box is highlighted, you can copy *that* with Ctrl C and paste it with Ctrl V as usual. This works with any String data—including CLSIDs!—and with any DWORD, although what you get with a DWORD is the decimal expression from the parentheses at the end.

If you want to copy Binary data, like an EditFlags, you're out of luck; for some reason you can highlight that and *delete* it, but if you highlight it and press Ctrl C, the Clipboard ends up blank.

**Find Options.** The options of the Find dialog are **Look at Keys**, **Look at Values**—meaning Value Names—or **Look at Data**, as well as **Match whole string only**. Train yourself not to ignore these on the way by. Unless you're hunting for a CLSID, you *probably* know whether what you're looking for is a Key in the left pane or a Value or Data in the right pane; and if you adopt the tactic of pasting in copied Key names as find targets, you can routinely restrict Key searches with Match whole string only. Used intelligently, these tricks

## Table 17.27  REGEDIT Edit Menu

| | |
|---|---|
| Modify (in Value pane only) | If the Name field is highlighted, opens the Edit box for that Value, just like double-clicking on the Name field. Grayed out if the Name field is not highlighted |
| New:Key | Creates a key called "New Key #1," ready to be renamed, at the level below the highlighted key, Explorer-style. You can create new keys in any of the "physical" top level keys, even HKCR, HKCU and HKCC, which seems mildly illogical but can be useful. You'll get an error message if you try to create a key in HKDD; be grateful, because if you could, you'd make your computer lie about the contents of memory and that wouldn't be a Good Thing |
| New:String Value | Creates a key called "New Value #1," ready to be renamed, along with the red String icon in the Name column and an empty pair of quotes in the Data column. If you add a String value, don't enclose it in quotes; the Editor will do that |
| New:Binary Value | Creates a key called "New Value #1," ready to be renamed, along with the blue Binary icon in the Name column and the message (zero-length binary value) in the Data column |
| New:DWORD Value | Creates a key called "New Value #1," ready to be renamed, along with the blue Binary icon in the Name column and 0x00000000 (0) in the Data column |
| Delete | All you get is a panel headed "Confirm Key Delete" or "Confirm Value Delete" and with Yes and No buttons, which, to our mind, isn't enough. *Back up keys or values by exporting before you delete them.* Top-level keys can't be deleted.<br><br>If you try to delete a (Default) entry from the Value pane, REGEDIT will let you go through the motions, then pop up an Error panel that says "Unable to delete all specified values." |
| Rename | The highlighted key pops into Rename mode. Again, *export* before you experiment. Top-level keys can't be renamed |
| Copy Key Name | A neat feature that wasn't in the original Win95, but was added to OSR2.*x* and OEM versions. See "Search Tips" below |
| Find... | Find strings, either in the whole Registry or in a selected branch. See "Search Tips" below |
| Find Next | Go to the next occurrence of the string currently set up in Find |

can make your Registry searches two to three times faster than just searching the whole Registry blindly.

 Find will try to help you confine your searches. If you type a string into Find What and use the Look at checkboxes to confine the search, the next time you open the Find box, the same checkboxes will be checked and unchecked.

 When you search the Registry you get a panel that says "Searching the Registry...", but you don't get an animated icon or an hourglass. The clear implication is that a computer scanning the Registry doesn't have machine cycles to waste on frills.

The Find function will only find *strings* in the Registry. This still makes it remarkably useful, because you can use it to search for keys in the Key pane, names in the Value pane, and anything between quotes in the Data column. But you *cannot* use Find to search for binary or DWORD data within the Registry itself, and if you hunt for (say) an EditFlags with Find, it will twirl down through the stack and bounce off the bottom. Amazingly enough, if you're looking for true binary data, the only way to find it is to export the key that includes its location, you hope, open the export file in a text editor and search through it there. For more about this see "Exporting and Importing" below.

**View Menu.** Unless you have some clear preference for controlling REGEDIT through drop-down menus, this one is largely useless. Drop-down items are listed in Table 17.28.

## Table 17.28  REGEDIT View Menu

| | |
|---|---|
| Status Bar | Defaults to On, and that's where you want it, since the Status Bar is generally the only display of the entire path of the Key you're looking at. Otherwise, you can be lost in the depths of HKCR and think you're in HKLM … |
| Split | Places the Split cursor on the borderline between the Key and Value panes. Of interest only if your pointing device is broken |
| Refresh | Refresh the display in the active pane. You can do this quicker with `F5` |

**Help Menu.** The two customary Help options are **Topics** and **About Registry Editor.** Do not expect miracles from REGEDIT.HLP, which is one of the smallest .HLP files in Win98, the same size as the one for the Media Player. Quite a bit of what you do get is paternalistic advice about giving up wild notions of editing the Registry, before you come to grief.

We know you want to edit the Registry. That's why you're here. Unlike Microsoft, we'll tell you to be careful, tell you *how* to be careful, and then leave you alone.

**Context Menu.** Right-clicking in REGEDIT produces a handy and fairly intelligent "from-here" menu that can speed up your editing.

The Key pane Context Menu is basically the Edit drop-down menu—with one addition; if you invoke it from a collapsed key it'll offer to expand, and *vice versa.* The odd exception to this is that, if you click on a *bottom*-level key, instead of offering Collapse it offers a grayed-out Expand.

The Value pane Context Menu offers Modify, Delete, and Rename. Modify on right-click, unlike Modify in drop-down, always *seems* to work, but then produces an error message if the edit would be illegal. Delete on right-click works the same strange way it does in drop-down. Rename plays by the rules.

REGEDIT has some nice keyboard shortcuts that make those gnarly trees easier to manipulate—much easier than scrolling up and down HKCR or CurrentControlSet looking for a handle to collapse the key with (see Table 17.29).

### Table 17.29  REGEDIT Keyboard Shortcuts

| Keyboard | Effect |
|---|---|
| ↓ | Go down one key/subkey |
| ↑ | Go up one key/subkey |
| → | Expand current key; if current key is fully expanded, jump down one key |
| ← | Collapse current key; if current key is fully collapsed, jump up one key |
| Page Up | Jump highlight up one screenful |
| Page Down | Jump highlight down one screenful |
| Home | Jump to My Computer |
| End | Jump to last displayed key |
| Tab | Jump from Key pane to Value pane (toggle) |
| F1 | Help Topics, such as they are |
| F2 | Rename highlighted key |
| F3 | Find or, if a search is in progress, Find Next |
| Alt F4 | Immediate exit, no confirm |
| F5 | Refresh current pane display |
| F6 | Toggle panes, same as Tab |
| F10 | Jump to Menu bar |
| Shift F10 | Toggle Context Menu |

## Exporting and Importing

Live editing of data in the REGEDIT Value pane is okay if all you want to do is tweak single values—which can be handy, as you'll see. But if you want to do serious Registry key manipulation, the best way to do it is by exporting the key, making your edits in plain text, and re-importing the key. You'll have a much better chance of doing it correctly if we lay some groundwork first. (Cries of "You mean all that up there wasn't groundwork?") Patience, please.

**The Great Impostor.** First, realize that the Registry *isn't* the Explorer, even though the two use the same interface as far as possible. Several facts about the Registry should alert you to the distinction (see Table 17.30).

### Table 17.30  Why The Registry Isn't The Explorer

|  | Explorer | Registry |
| --- | --- | --- |
| Rename or delete top-level folders | Yes | No |
| Folder drag-and-drop | Yes | No |
| Subfolders appear in right pane | Yes | No |
| RAM-resident data displayed | No | HKDD |
| Multiple folder structures can be merged | No | Yes |

In short: The Registry looks and works like the Explorer to help you know how to use it, but they aren't much alike underneath the interface.

**Foreign Trade.** When the Registry Menu talks about *Exporting* a file, that's Microspeak for "Saving a copy in a different format without disturbing the source information." When it talks about *Importing* a file, that translates to "Merging appropriately formatted Registry keys and values in plain text with the Registry that lives on your computer." Let's consider Importing first because it's a little more complicated.

### What You Hack, How You Hack

Generally, if you Import the entire Registry, it's because you need to restore from backup, and you have our sympathy. If you're hacking, though, you're probably working only with a single key or part of a key. Remember these three cardinal rules:

*Never try to create part of the Registry tree completely from scratch.* The text and syntax of an import file are very exact. If you try to create one just by keying, you're unlikely to get everything right, and you can—or can't—imagine what will happen if you get something wrong. Export the part of the Registry tree that you mean to change; if you're creating a new key, start with a copy of something that resembles it as closely as possible. This will spare you not only typing, but typos.

*NEVER edit an import file with a word processor, not even WordPad.* Word processors add bizarre characters to regulate text formatting, and you don't see them, but the Registry will; the results are unpredictable and not good. Even if you open Registry keys in a word processor and tell it to save the file as plain text, you can't be sure that you'll get the pristine ASCII you need. Edit import files in Notepad; if (oh, brave soul!) you're reworking a piece of the Registry too big for Notepad, use a programmer's editor that handles bigger files, like TextPad or Brief.

*ALWAYS back up before you hack up.* Go review the instructions for Registry Checker, make yourself a manual .CAB file, and come back here. We can't tell you this too often, and if we could, we would.

**What Replaces What?**   The rules by which an import file overwrites its matching piece of the Registry structure are generous but not lenient (see Table 17.31).

### Table 17.31  Key Overwrite Hierarchy

| Registry before import | Import file | Registry after import |
| --- | --- | --- |
| A | A | A |
| B | B+ | B+ |
| C |  | C |
|  | D | D |

**Case A:** If a key or value exists in the Registry before the file is imported, and the import file contains the *identical* key or value, the new Registry entry will be the same as the old one even though it's physically rewritten.

**Case B:** If a key or value exists in the Registry before the file is imported, and the import file contains the same key or value *updated*, the imported key or value will overwrite the old one.

**Case C:** If a key or value exists in the Registry before the file is imported, and the import file *does not contain* this key or value, the old Registry entry will persist untouched in the physically rewritten key. Keys aren't like files; the overwrite is a selective process rather than all-or-nothing.

**Case D:** If a key or value *does not exist* in the Registry before the file is imported, and the import file brings it in, the Registry will gracefully make room for it and incorporate it.

> If you create an import file that completely replaces (overwrites) an existing Registry key, remember to export the original version of the key and save a copy. That way, if your hacking gives less than ideal results, you can replace your rewritten key with the saved original before your boss even notices. If you have the kind of boss who likes to watch your screen while you're using REGEDIT, encourage him to take up golf.

**Export Format Options.**   The problem with export files is that the ASCII text doesn't look much like the display of keys and values in REGEDIT.

In .REG files—which have to approximate the conventions of the Registry with ASCII—some allowances have to be made for the loss of the graphical tree structure. Examples are shown in Table 17.32.

### Table 17.32  Comparison of REGEDIT and .REG Data

|  | In REGEDIT | In .REG file |
|---|---|---|
| Key | Keyname | "Keyname" |
| Path | "Path1\Path2" | ="Path1\\Path2" |
| String value | "String" | ="String" |
| Binary value | 01 00 00 00 | =hex:01,00,00,00 |
| Single-character binary | "1" | ="1" |
| DWORD value | 0x00000001 (1) | =dword:00000001 |

Some notes are needed here. Path statements in key data use a double back-slash because the single backslash, in a .REG file, is used to denote a branch of the Registry tree itself. (Double backslashes drive partisans of other operating systems, who haven't even resigned themselves to single backslashes, into volcano mode.) Binary data is—correctly, but confusingly—called hex, unless it has only one character, and then it's "string". DWORD, at least called dword, is expressed in hex and sheds the decimal conversion at the end. As a rule of thumb: Anything in double quotes is a string, anything that isn't can be told apart by opening the Edit box in the Value pane.

When we assemble all these data types into an export file—made-up but syntactically accurate—it looks like this:

```
REGEDIT4

[HKEY_LOCAL_MACHINE\Enum\Root\*PNP0C09\0000]
"DeviceDesc"="Hitachi Dangan DVD-RW Drive"
"ConfigFlags"=hex:0a,00,00,00
"INFFileVector"=dword:00000010
"StackPermissions"="1"
```

 The first two lines of an export file are always REGEDIT4 followed by two CR/LF pairs. If this name is altered even slightly—say, to REGEDIT3—the file won't be re-imported into the Registry, *although the Import Registry File menu choice will seem to work correctly.*

Moving downwards, we see the line beginning with a square bracket and HKEY_LOCAL_MACHINE. This is the path of the key that was exported; there's only one such path because this was a bottom-level subkey. If the exported key had had subkeys of its own, there would have been one path for the top-level key and one for each subkey.

DeviceDesc has a string value, and here in a way the export file is more accurate than REGEDIT itself; both the Name and the Data are strings, and they're both in quotes.

ConfigFlags is a binary value and is expressed the way it is in the Value pane, *except for those commas* between bytes. The commas are in the file that's exported (copied) from the Registry and they have to be in the file that's imported (merged) back in, or this key will crash. Incidentally, why is this four-byte data in hex form when it would seem to be perfect for a DWORD? That's up to the programmer of the moment.

INFFileVector is a DWORD and is exported only as a hex value. For clarity, the leading 0x that would *tell* you it's a hex value has been trimmed off. Also note that when you manipulate DWORDs through export/import, you work in hex, whereas through the Edit dialog of the Value pane you can toggle the choice of hex or decimal—which is handy if you don't think in zero through F.

StackPermissions is single-character binary and so, of course, expressed as a string. Actually, this expression is relatively rare compared to 01, which would be stored as pure binary.

Now: If we import this file into a key that looks like Figure 17.10 in REGEDIT:

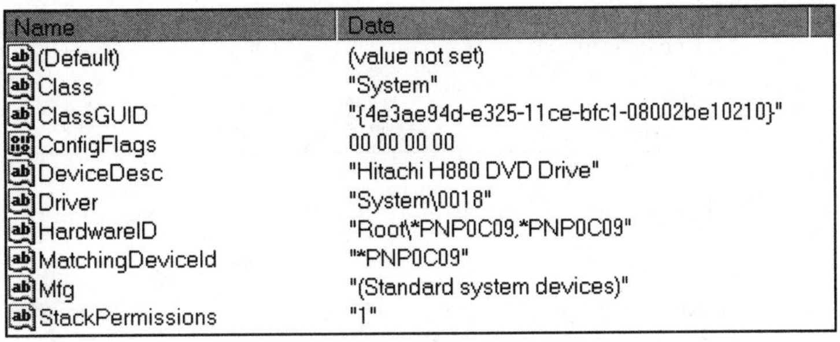

| Name | Data |
|---|---|
| (ab) (Default) | (value not set) |
| (ab) Class | "System" |
| (ab) ClassGUID | "{4e3ae94d-e325-11ce-bfc1-08002be10210}" |
| (bin) ConfigFlags | 00 00 00 00 |
| (ab) DeviceDesc | "Hitachi H880 DVD Drive" |
| (ab) Driver | "System\0018" |
| (ab) HardwareID | "Root\*PNP0C09,*PNP0C09" |
| (ab) MatchingDeviceId | "*PNP0C09" |
| (ab) Mfg | "(Standard system devices)" |
| (ab) StackPermissions | "1" |

*Figure 17.10*

*Existing Registry Key*

and like this in export format:

```
[HKEY_LOCAL_MACHINE\Enum\Root\*PNP0C09\0000]
"Class"="System"
"Driver"="System\\0018"
"Mfg"="(Standard system devices)"
"ConfigFlags"=hex:00,00,00,00
"HardwareID"="Root\\*PNP0C09,*PNP0C09"
"DeviceDesc"="Hitachi H880 DVD Drive"
"ClassGUID"="{4e3ae94d-e325-11ce-bfc1-08002be10210}"
"StackPermissions"="1"
"MatchingDeviceId"="*PNP0C09"
```

**Figure 17.11**

Import Registry File

we click on **Import Registry File** (shown in Figure 17.11).

We navigate to the appropriate directory, double-click on the right file, and what we come out with looks like Figure 17.12.

| Name | Data |
|------|------|
| (Default) | (value not set) |
| Class | "System" |
| ClassGUID | "{4e3ae94d-e325-11ce-bfc1-08002be10210}" |
| ConfigFlags | 0a 00 00 00 |
| DeviceDesc | "Hitachi Dangan DVD-RW Drive" |
| Driver | "System\0018" |
| HardwareID | "Root\*PNP0C09,*PNP0C09" |
| INFFileVector | 0x00000010 (16) |
| MatchingDeviceId | "*PNP0C09" |
| Mfg | "(Standard system devices)" |
| StackPermissions | "1" |

**Figure 17.12**

Registry Key after import

What you see in Figure 17.12 in .REG format looks like this:

| Finished key after importing | Case from table |
|------|------|
| [HKEY_LOCAL_MACHINE\Enum\Root\*PNP0C09\0000] | |
| "Class"="System" | C (not in import file) |
| "Driver"="System\\0018" | C |
| "Mfg"="(Standard system devices)" | C |
| "ConfigFlags"=hex:0a,00,00,00 | B+ (changed by import) |
| "HardwareID"="Root\\*PNP0C09,*PNP0C09" | C |
| "DeviceDesc"="Hitachi Dangan DVD-2 Drive" | B+ |
| "ClassGUID"="{4e3ae94d-e325-11ce-bfc1-08002be10210}" | C |
| "MatchingDeviceId"="*PNP0C09" | C |
| "INFFileVector"=dword:00000010 | D (added by import) |
| "StackPermissions"="1" | A (same in both) |

Hang on! When the file was exported, where was (Default)? Well, *every* Registry key has a (Default), mostly an empty one which won't need to be imported, so empty ones aren't exported. A set, or non-empty, (Default) is exported in a unique format—naturally!—as shown in Table 17.33.

### Table 17.33  Exported (Default) Keys

| Value pane Name | Value pane Data | Export file format |
| --- | --- | --- |
| (Default) | (value not set) | not exported |
| (Default) | "This is a value" | @="This is a value" |

*Watch out for .REG files* lying around loose on your disk. And here's why:

**Associating Registry Files.**  The file type .REG is associated by default with REGEDIT, a truly OLE-aware application.

The .REG type icon is consistent—a little tower of blue bricks superimposed on a document page—but if you're running Small Icons or haven't had enough coffee, it can look like a Word document icon.

**View\Folder Options\View** defaults to "Hide file extensions for known file types," so you don't have that *.reg* to tip you off.

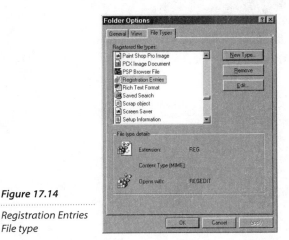

*Figure 17.13*

*Import Warning dialog*

So you click on a .REG file that you think is something else, and the Import Warning Dialog pops up (see Figure 17.13).

Oops!! But it's too true; for .REG files, *to click is to merge.* To guard against this we recommend one or more tactics:

- Keep all your .REG files in a folder called **C:\Registry** or **C:\RegFiles.**

- Disable Merge as the default. Go to View\Folder Options\File Types and scroll to Registration Entries. In the File type details box (Figure 17.14), **Extension:** is REG and **Opens with:** is REGEDIT.

*Figure 17.14*

*Registration Entries File type*

- While you're still in View\Folder Options\File Types\Edit, it's not a bad idea to check "Always show extension." That way you at least won't confuse a .REG file with a .DOC file.

Click **Edit.** You'll see that the Actions options are Edit, **Merge** and Print. Merge, being boldfaced, is the default.

Highlight Edit in the Actions box and click **Set Default** and **Close.** In File type details, Opens with: is now NOTEPAD (see Figure 17.15).

*Figure 17.15*

*Changed association*

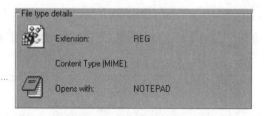

Now, when you click on a .REG file, it'll open in Notepad. Your Context menu looks like Figure 17.16 instead of Figure 17.17.

And, when you really want to Merge a .REG file, the option is just a right-click away.

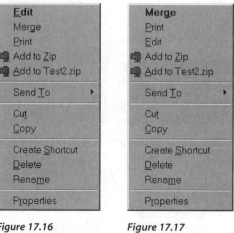

*Figure 17.16*

*Context Menu: Edit default*

*Figure 17.17*

*Context Menu: Merge default*

# Other Ways of Editing the Registry

You now know everything we do about REGEDIT. We'll conclude this chapter with some notes on other ways to modify the Registry, on third-party Registry tools—few as they are—and on a fat bundle of Registry Hacks.

## .INF Files and What They Do (Ouch!)

An .INF file is a tiny, text-based custom setup file for 32-bit Windows hardware or software. When well written, they're concise, quick, and slick.

The Registry Shell key for .INF files adds an Install option to the file's right-click menu. When you click **Install**, it calls a .DLL to set up the gizmo according to the directions—halfway between an .INI file and a script—contained in the .INF file. Developers like these because they're one way of installing hardware or software on a large, far-flung population of computers without a lot of fuss.

**.INFernality.**  But the .INF file, which at first blush looks like a tool to carry out the Registry's will, can actually be turned around and used *to edit the Registry* itself. If you write a section in the file called [DefaultInstall], and within that section add parameters called AddReg or DelReg, then create scripts for those parameters to point to, you can add or delete any desired Registry keys just by right-clicking **Install.**

This is extremely convenient when you need it, and about as dangerous as freshly broken glass. A targeted .INF script can demolish a Registry key while it gives you absolutely no hint of what it's doing. Therefore, in line with our declaration about a conservative approach, we're only telling you that this can be done. If you want to know how to do it, look in John Woram's *Registry Survival Guide* or in the Windows 95 Resource Kit. We assume this information will be available in the Windows 98 Resource Kit, too, but we haven't seen the final version.

 The Windows 98 Resource Kit implies that the AddReg or DelReg parameters can be placed under a section header called [Install]. That won't work—the header has to be [DefaultInstall] for the Registry to be updated correctly. This may be fixed in the release version.

## Registry Script Files: The Thin-Air Way to Go

A Registry script file is the result of sending a portion of the Registry to a text file, not by exporting it through REGEDIT, but by printing it to the FILE: "phantom" printer. (Of course this printer has to be Generic / Text Only or the output will emerge in the printer's language, not yours.)

Registry keys printed to a text printer come out looking *almost* like .REG files, but not quite. Look at these differences:

(.REG file from REGEDIT, abridged)

```
[HKEY_CURRENT_USER\Software\Microsoft\Windows\CurrentVersion\Extensions]
"cal"="calendar.exe ^.cal"
"trm"="terminal.exe ^.trm"
"txt"="notepad.exe ^.txt"
"ini"="notepad.exe ^.ini"
"doc"="C:\\msoffice\\Office\\Winword.exe ^.doc"
"xls"="C:\\msoffice\\Office\\excel.exe ^.xls"
```

(Registry key printed to FILE:, abridged)

```
[HKEY_CURRENT_USER\Software\Microsoft\Windows\CurrentVersion\Extensions]
 cal=calendar.exe ^.cal
 trm=terminal.exe ^.trm
 txt=notepad.exe ^.txt
 ini=notepad.exe ^.ini
 doc=C:\msoffice\Office\Winword.exe ^.doc
 xls=C:\msoffice\Office\excel.exe ^.xls
```

First of all, REGEDIT exports data with strings enclosed in quotes, whereas "printing" doesn't. REGEDIT aligns its data flush left, but "printing" pads it with seven leading spaces, which are a nuisance because you have to get rid of them.

 The kicker, to our way of thinking, is what happens to DWORD:

```
"IfWeight"=dword:00000190 (REGEDIT)
```

```
IfWeight=90,01,00,00 (print to FILE:)
```

Oh, no! Printing to file, DWORD data flips around into the format of "hex" (binary) REGEDIT output! And, believe me, we've only started on the list of things you have to keep in mind when you try to create a Registry script from a text-only print stream; what about converting single to double backslashes? Some experts can make Registry scripts work and work well, but that alone isn't enough reason to turn your back on REGEDIT's flawless automatic formatting. Our advice is to stick with REGEDIT for creating import files, and let it help you however it can.

## TWEAKUI: Registry AutoHack

 Ah, TweakUI! Of the bold and erratic Microsoft PowerToys, created by rebel programmers frustrated with Win95's starchy gloss, TweakUI was the one that millions of users loved and kept. With the release of Windows 98, it sheds its cult status as a hard-to-find download and becomes a tolerated, if not respected, part of the standard installation.

It's a perfectly rational response to an unfortunate contradiction; some of the most useful and customizable features of the Windows interface are buried in the Explorer, Desktop and NameSpace keys and known only by their CLSIDs. TweakUI hauls them into the light of day and makes them work for a living.

TweakUI can add subkeys to the Registry that didn't exist before. For example, the General tab has a checkbox called Window Animation that's checked by default. If you uncheck Window Animation, you turn it off, which is the same effect as creating HKCU\Control Panel\Desktop\WindowMetrics\MinAnimate and setting it to "0". We suggest gaining a thorough knowledge of TweakUI and its effects before you decide that you just *have* to start adding subkeys at the bare metal.

In the following section on Registry Hacks, if a direct Registry edit will produce the same result as a choice in TweakUI, we'll give you the gory details but also flag the hack with our TweakUI icon so that you'll know there's an easy way to do it. Meanwhile, the thorough discussion of TweakUI is in Chapter 15, if you missed it.

## POLEDIT: Bossing the Registry Around

The System Policy Editor, POLEDIT.EXE, is TweakUI's evil twin—it takes toys away. As an end-user, you naturally have to deplore this on principle. But as a network administrator or corporate IS director, should you happen to be one, you'll find POLEDIT as handy as a battery-powered screwdriver.

Underneath HKCU\Software\Microsoft\Windows, there's a galaxy of subkeys that govern access to options in Control Panel or Explorer. The ability to change Network settings, file and print sharing, Display and Printer settings, Password controls, Shell restrictions, and Desktop contents might be something that you—the standalone or small-network user—take for granted as part of the joy of Windows. You the company sysadmin, on the other hand, know that once a network is properly set up, it does not pay to let the people at the workstations poke around too deeply. Very few network users, for example, need a Device Manager tab. Or the Entire Network icon in Network Neighborhood. Or, heaven help us, access to REGEDIT.

System Policy Editor lets you enforce these choices, and many more, on a user-by-user basis without wading around in the sub-basements of HKCU. It doesn't exactly uphold the ideals of Computer Lib, but it's a neat tool and a necessary one that brings TweakUI's level of automation to network client security.

As far as we now know, although the System Policy Editor can be *run* from a computer whose operating system is Windows 98, but it can only be *invoked* on a network that includes at least one computer running Windows NT. We'll therefore discuss it in depth in the **Windows NT 5 Bible,** which you can expect to see in … well, just keep tabs on the Web site.

## Third-Party Registry Tools: Where Hackers Dare

The amount of shareware available to search and manipulate the Registry doesn't hold a candle to the selection of utilities for more mundane tasks. The good news, of course, is that any programmer interested enough to write a Registry utility is probably adept enough to do it right. All four of these have definite merit. *Locations and prices are as of the date of publication* and may change.

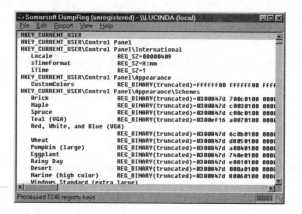

*Figure 17.18*

*DumpReg*

**DumpReg by Somarsoft.**  For the seasoned Registry maniac. DumpReg (see Figure 17.18) runs on both Win98 and WinNT, and lets you perform a full or by-HKEY ASCII output of the Registry to disk, filter to show only keys or data that contain a certain string, show only keys changed since a certain date or time, and print custom reports. Report printing is disabled in the shareware version, which has a voluntary 30-day time limit. Registration is $10 at **www.somarsoft.com**.

**Microsoft RegClean.**  Microsoft's apology for stamping TOP SECRET all over the Registry, now that it's here, is somewhat impressive (see Figure 17.19). It scans and collates the Registry's information, then prowls for errors, creates a tentative set of corrections, then suggests that you Fix Errors or Exit. One pass can understandably take a few minutes. A .REG file of all the corrections and deletions is written into the \Program Files\RegClean directory (if that's where you installed it) as UNDO *<computername>* *<yyyymmdd>* *<hhmmss>*.REG, which you can merge with the Registry in the usual fashion.

 RegClean is not a product for bare-metal enthusiasts. Like many Microsoft applets, it's boringly automatic and gives you absolutely no insight into the correction process, not even putting up a scrolling list of corrections for

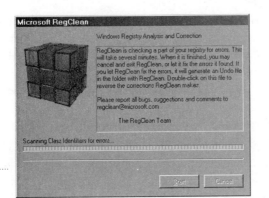

**Figure 17.19**

RegClean in ... action

review. If you have an application installed in a way that doesn't comply with the internal guidelines—whatever they are—running RegClean may corrupt that program's Registry settings, and you will never know how or why. "These types of problems are very rare," says Microsoft's readme soothingly, "but it's a good idea to keep your last UNDO.REG file for at least a few days or so."

RegClean is for Windows 98 and 95 only. If you run it under NT it immediately steps on protected-mode memory and crashes, although without doing any damage that we know of.

The current version of RegClean is 4.1a, which has a reputation for being more stable than earlier ones. RegClean is free (but sometimes hard to find) at **http://www.microsoft.com**, and often available at the larger 32-bit shareware sites.

**Registry Search + Replace by Steven J. Hoek Software Development.** RS+R (see Figure 17.20) lets you establish search and replacement criteria for any Registry data that can be edited from the outside, search

**Figure 17.20**

Registry Search + Replace

remote Registries on appropriately configured networks, run searches from saved profiles, and watch progress indicators. A tool to be used with care and experience, but nothing else gives you the easy control over large-scale Registry manipulation that RS+R does. You can use an evaluation copy 25 times and then register it for $20 at **http://www.pslweb.com**.

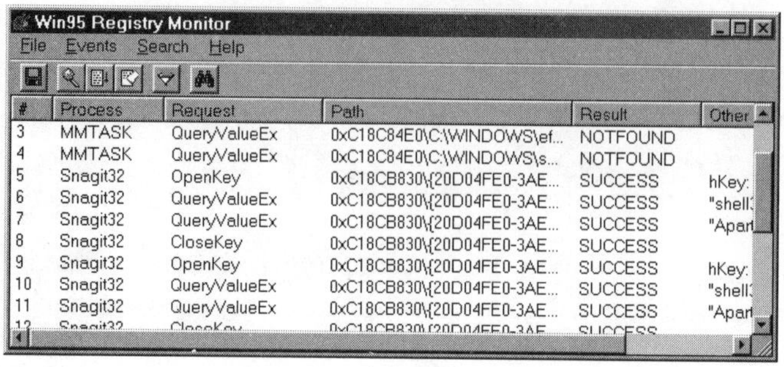

*Figure 17.21*

Regmon

**Regmon by NTInternals** (Mark Russinovich and Bryce Cogswell). In Figure 17.21, we see Regmon bagging the calls from SnagIt while SnagIt captures the window. How recursive can you get?

Regmon is a team of an applet and a device driver that can monitor and display all Registry activity on a system, whether in real time or by saving files. Advanced filtering and search capabilities make it a powerful tool for exploring the way Windows 98 works, seeing how applications use the Registry, or tracking down configuration problems. It can be installed and used *only* on *non-networked* drives. A utility for experts, but no expert would do without it.

Regmon, for Win9*x*, or NTRegmon for several versions of NT, are available free from **http://www.ntinternals.com**.

# Registry Hacks!

You've been so patient! Here, in Table 17.34, for your delectation, are all the interface-related Windows 98 Registry hacks we could find in our travels. Fire up REGEDIT and get going. Not to be repetitive, but *you make use of this information at your own risk*—and we do hope you're backed up.

## Table 17.34  Hacks!

| Target | New feature | Key to edit | Value to edit | Old value | New value | Takes effect |
|---|---|---|---|---|---|---|
| Control Panel | Change descriptor in Date/Time Time Zone | HKLM\SOFTWARE\Microsoft\Windows\CurrentVersion\Time Zones\(your time zone) | Double-click on Value pane Display | (old descriptor) | (new descriptor) | Immediately |
| Control Panel | Delete names of removed apps from Add/Remove Programs list | HKLM\SOFTWARE\Microsoft\Windows\CurrentVersion\Uninstall | Edit, Delete, any desired program key | | | Immediately Add/Remove tab |
| Desktop | Remove Shortcut icon arrows | HKCR\lnkfile, HKCR\piffile | Delete Value IsShortcut | | | On startup Explorer tab |
| Desktop | Remove all icons (*Watch out!!*) | HKCU\Software\Microsoft\Windows\Current Version\Policies\Explorer | Edit, New, DWORD value, NoDesktop | | 1 | On reboot |
| Explorer | Show thumbnail image in mini-icon displayed for .BMP files | HKCR\Paint.Picture\DefaultIcon | (Default) | C:\Progra~1\Access~1\MSPAINT.EXE,1 | %1 | Immediately |
| Explorer Context Menu | Add Quickview for any file type | HKCR\* | Edit, New, Key, Quickview; double-click on (Default) | | * | *Note:* For files that already have Quick View on their Context menus, it may display twice |
| Inbox | Change icon title | HKCR\CLSID\{00020D75->} | (Default) | Inbox | (new name) | Immediately |
| Installation | Recover CD-Key needed for reinstall | HKLM\SOFTWARE\Microsoft\<name of app>\Registration | Double-click on ProductID | Numbers after first hyphen and before last hyphen are CD-Key | | |

*Table 17.34* *(continued)*

| Target | New feature | Key to edit | Value to edit | Old value | New value | Takes effect |
|---|---|---|---|---|---|---|
| Mapping of long filenames into 8.3 | Improve mapping by reducing use of ~# extensions | HKLM\\System\CurrentControlSet\Control\ FileSystem | Edit, New, Binary value, NameNumericTail | | 0 (will read as 00) | On reboot |
| My Computer | Remove drive icons | HKCU\Software\Microsoft\Windows\Current Version\Policies\Explorer | Edit, New, DWORD value, NoDrives | | 3FFFFFF | Immediately; to undo, Delete NoDrives, exit REGEDIT, restart |
| My Computer | Disable Save Settings | HKCU\Software\Microsoft\Windows\Current Version\Policies\Explorer | Edit, New, DWORD value, NoSaveSettings | | 1 | On reboot Explorer tab |
| My Computer | Change icon | HKCR\CLSID\{20D04FE0->} | DefaultIcon | explorer.exe,0 | (new icon) | Immediately |
| My Computer | Change icon title | HKCR\CLSID\{20D04FE0->} | (Default) | My Computer | (new name) | Immediately |
| My Computer Context Menu | Disable Find | HKCR\CLSID\{20D04FE0->}\shell | Delete find key *(export it first!)* | | | Immediately |
| Network Neighborhood | Change icon | HKCR\CLSID\{208D2C60->} | DefaultIcon | shell32.dll,17 | (new icon) | Immediately |
| Network Neighborhood | Change icon title | HKCR\CLSID\{208D2C60->} | (Default) | Network Neighborhood | (new name) | Immediately |
| Network Neighborhood | Remove icon from Desktop | HKCU\Software\Microsoft\Windows\Current Version\Policies\Explorer | Edit, New, DWORD value, NoNetHood | | 1 | On reboot |
| Network Neighborhood | Remove File and Print Sharing from Properties | HKLM\SOFTWARE\Microsoft\Windows\CurrentVersion\Policies\Network | Edit, New, DWORD value, NoFileSharing | | 1 | Immediately. To restore, set NoFileSharing to 0 |

**Table 17.34** *(continued)*

| Target | New feature | Key to edit | Value to edit | Old value | New value | Takes effect |
|---|---|---|---|---|---|---|
| New list in Desktop Context Menu | Remove unwanted type templates | HKCR; Find and Find Again on ShellNew | Right-click and Rename ShellNew to ShellOld | | | Immediately New tab |
| Recycle Bin | Change icon | HKCR\CLSID\ {645FF040->} | DefaultIcon | (Default) shell32.dll,31; Empty, shell32.dll,31; Full, shell32.dll,32 | (new icons) | Immediately |
| Recycle Bin | Change icon title | HKCR\CLSID\ {645FF040->} | (Default) | Recycle Bin | (new name) | Immediately |
| Registration | Change setup info | HKLM\SOFTWARE\ Microsoft\Windows\ CurrentVersion | ProductID, RegisteredOrganization, RegisteredOwner | (old values) | (new values) | Immediately |
| Start Context Menu | Disable Find | HKCR\Directory\ shell\find | Delete find key *(export it first!!)* | | | Immediately |
| Start Context Menu | Disable Explore | HKCR\Folder\ shell\explore | Delete explore key *(export it first!!)* | | | Immediately |
| Start Context Menu | Disable Open | HKCR\Folder\ shell\open | Delete open key *(export it first!!)* | | | Immediately |
| Start Menu | Remove "Click here to begin" arrow | HKCU\Software\ Microsoft\Windows\ Current Version\ Policies\Explorer | Edit, New, Binary value, NoStartBanner | | 01 00 00 00 | On reboot Explorer tab Startup *Or*: Add one application to Startup group |
| Start Menu | Speed up | HKCR\CLSID\ {0021400->} (Default) should be "Desktop" | Edit, New, String Value, MenuShowDelay | | from 1 to 10 | On reboot |

## Table 17.34 *(continued)*

| Target | New feature | Key to edit | Value to edit | Old value | New value | Takes effect |
|---|---|---|---|---|---|---|
| Start Menu | Purge entries on Run list | HKCU\Software\ Microsoft\Windows\ CurrentVersion\ Explorer\RunMRU | Edit, Delete, any desired list entry | | | Immediately<br>Paranoia tab |
| Start Menu | Disable Documents menu | HKCU\Software\ Microsoft\Windows\ Current Version\ Explorer\User Shell Folders | Open name Recent | C:\Windows\ Profiles\<logged-on user>\Recent | C:\Recycle | On reboot; then right-click Recycle Bin, Properties, check "Do not move files…")<br>Paranoia tab |
| Start Menu | Remove Run command | HKCU\Software\ Microsoft\Windows\ Current Version\ Policies\Explorer | Edit, New, DWORD value, NoRun | | 1 | On reboot |
| Startup (stealth) | Launch programs through Registry | HKLM\SOFTWARE\ Microsoft\Windows\ CurrentVersion\ RunOnce | Edit, New, String value, any name | | Name of program to be run (with .exe) | On startup |
| Tips diplayed on Windows startup | Substitute your own text | HKLM\ SOFTWARE\ Microsoft\Windows\ CurrentVersion\ Explorer\Tips | 0 through 47 | Microsoft's tip text | Your tip text | On startup |

# Registry Error Messages:
# Hey, It Happens

You may be startled to learn that the Registry has a really exemplary portfolio of error messages. This isn't exactly common knowledge because: Under ordinary circumstances you'll see them somewhere between rarely and never; The Registry doesn't bother putting up warnings for trivial mistakes, it just goes ahead and makes them; and, given the thoroughness of Microsoft's documentation for REGEDIT and the Registry in general, you can imagine how they deep-sixed the error messages. After all, if you as an end-user ever see a Registry error message, you're far enough out of line that Microsoft certainly has no sympathy for you.

So we'll document the error messages, because this is that kind of book, but we (and you) will be delighted if you never need to look one up. They're in Appendix F, the one part of this book we hope you don't read.

# Summary

The Registry is the thrill-ride park of Windows. If you mess it up, you can definitely hose yourself, although not as royally as you could before Windows 98 introduced the Registry Checker. We advise running SCANREG manually to create a backup file before you manipulate *anything* in the Registry.

Although the Registry contains the ultimate treasure-trove of interface hacks, it's nonetheless true that almost anything you would *want* to hack in the Registry can be fiddled with more easily in the Device Manager, TweakUI, MSCONFIG, or some other dialog. When you edit the Registry directly, you're climbing the stairs in a building with about six elevators.

Why, then, do it? Because when you understand the Registry, you understand Windows in a way otherwise impossible.

# Part 4

## Appendices

# Part 5 At a Glance

# Appendix A

# Windows 98 Installation

In previous versions of this book, installation was a chapter unto itself. We've made considerations of Windows 98's install sequence into an appendix because we think that, under ordinary circumstances, you simply won't need it that much—the install process is easier and more automated than ever before.

Therefore, this appendix is in two sections—if not "easy and difficult," then probably "easy and less easy." The first simply walks you through the Setup process for a single computer, shows you the screens, and explains the few choices you have to make. The second section assumes that you're doing a larger or more complex installation, like a network client installation, and want to automate it by modifying .INF scripts.

# The Easy Way

To install Windows 98 you will, in the real world, need the following:

- A computer with a 486DX2/66 or faster processor and at least 16MB of RAM (see Note 1).

- A CD-ROM drive (see Note 2).

- Between 150 and 325 MB of disk space, depending on how complex your installation will be and whether you want Windows 98 to be uninstallable.

- One to two hours. This will vary according to how fast your computer is, whether you're installing the Windows 98 Upgrade or the full version, what operating system you're upgrading over, and whether you need to use any of the switches (see Table A.2 in the "Starting Setup" section).

- A 3.5-inch floppy disk, freshly formatted on this computer, that passes ScanDisk or CHKDSK with no bad sectors. Format and test it before you start the installation.

**Note 1:** The requirement for a 486DX2/66 or faster processor is Microsoft's *official* position. Some people who tried to install early versions of Windows 98 on 486DX/50-powered computers were stopped at the Setup system check by an error dialog saying that the processor wasn't fast enough; others completed Setup without seeing any such warning, and reported that performance was adequate. If we discover a workaround for this warning, we'll either put it in the "Last Minute" section or post it on the Web site. But, especially with a 486 processor, there is no getting around the minimum 16MB of RAM!

**Note 2:** According to our best information as we go to press, Windows 98 will be available on floppies; to get it, you'll have to buy the retail CD version and send in a coupon from the box, probably with a handling charge.

We'd recommend against going the diskette route, for three reasons:

- If Windows 98 follows the pattern of Windows 95, the diskette version will be little more than the core .CAB files, missing all kinds of extras like the Resource Kit.

- Even the diskette version, on the other hand, will comprise 70 to 90 floppies; do you really want to shuffle that many for the install, and keep track of them afterwards?

- Finally, whereas a properly stored factory-made CD has a shelf life measured in decades, a 3.5 floppy can sprout a bad sector if you look at it cross-eyed. Once again: A new, high-quality, medium-speed IDE CD-ROM drive costs $50 or less, and will install Windows (or anything else) much more quickly than the floppy shuffle.

## The Ideal Install

The ideal install of Windows 98 is probably performed over Windows 95, and you can do the upgrade while you're running Windows. Make sure your CD-ROM drive is set to Autoplay, close all your other running programs, slip in the CD, and the next thing you'll see is this or something like it:

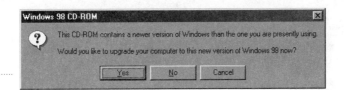

*Figure A.1*

*Click Yes*

**Anti-Virus Boot Warning.** You may also see this (Figure A.2), which is a warning that during the Windows 98 install, Windows will modify the master boot record, and any virus protection you have installed won't like it.

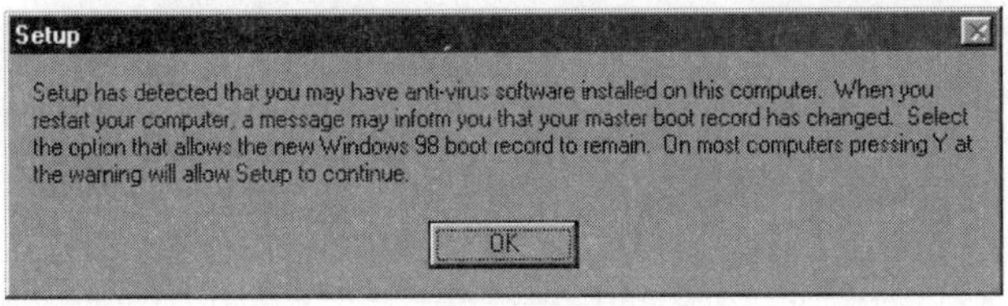

*Figure A.2*

*Anti-Virus Boot warning*

This can happen even if you don't have anti-virus software installed or running, since some newer computers have virus protection in the BIOS, which is one of the chips that provides information to your system while it boots. As the dialog suggests, you can usually bypass it, but if not, you can reboot your computer, go into hardware Setup (which usually involves hitting the ⌐Delete⌐ key before the memory check) and disable the virus check before continuing.

**Close Programs Warning.**  If there are still any other programs running while you upgrade, you'll see the warning in Figure A.3 because Windows, while it's installing, wants a totally free hand with replacing files, but can't overwrite .DLLs or other resource files that are being called by running programs. That's why we cautioned you about this!

*Figure A.3*

*Close programs warning*

**License Agreement.**  You are confronted with the dreaded Microsoft EULA (End-User License Agreement), shown in Figure A.4, which you don't have to read all of, but you do have to click **I accept the agreement** or you go no farther. Click **Next**.

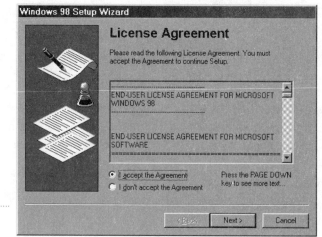

*Figure A.4*

*Dreaded Microsoft EULA*

**Product Key**  Enter the 25-character (up from 10 or 16!) Product Key from the back of the CD's sleeve or jewel box (see Figure A.5).

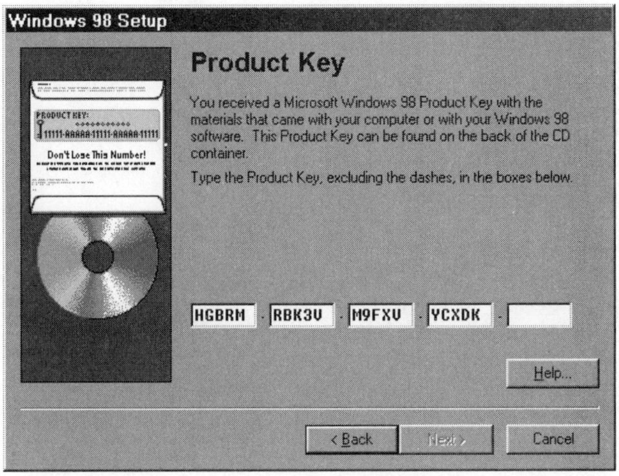

*Figure A.5*
.................
*Product Key*

**Registry Check.**  The system check says it's "initializing" the Registry (see Figure A.6), which it is, if you don't have a Registry already. If you do, it checks the integrity of what's already there. This pass won't fix Registry errors, but if it finds them, you'll be advised to quit Setup and run SCANREG from the command line.

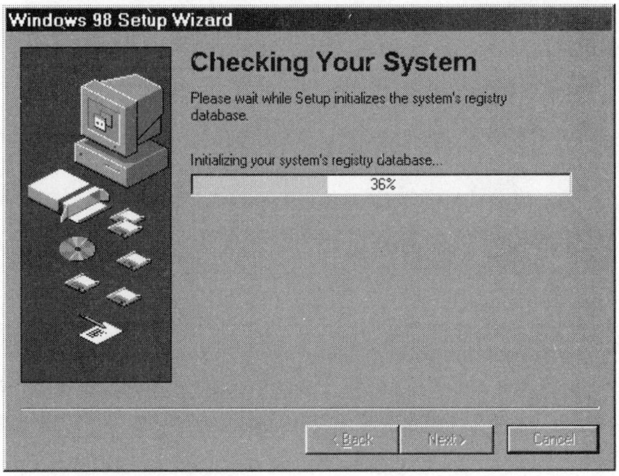

*Figure A.6*
.................
*Registry check*

**Directory Check.**  The installer creates C:\WINDOWS if it doesn't exist and checks for adequate disk space, which it defines according to the type of install being done (see Figures A.7 and A.8).

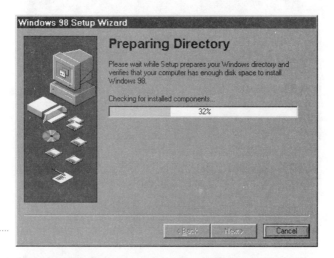

*Figure A.7*

*Creating directory*

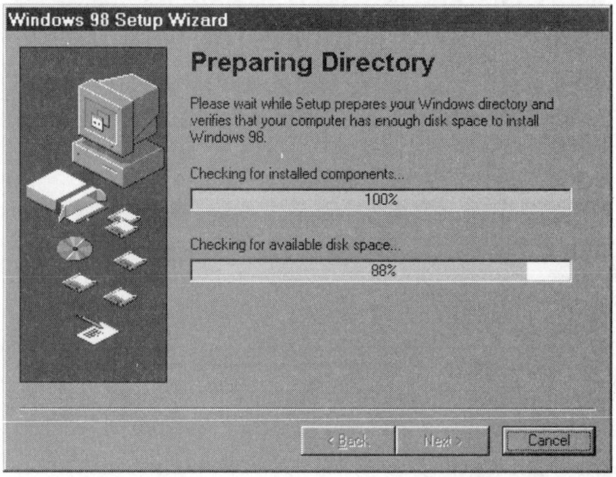

*Figure A.8*

*Checking for disk space*

**Save System Files.**  Microsoft recommends that you save your system files, and so do we (see Figure A.9). There's very little chance that you'll need to back out of Windows 98 and reinstate Windows 95, but—in the words of many a seasoned computer professional—why burn a bridge? And if you're upgrading from DOS, saving your existing system files will allow you to *dual-boot* on startup with the F4 key (see "Preparing for Dualboot" below and

"TweakUI Boot Tab" in Chapter 15). If you're low on disk space and need to delete the backup of your Windows 95 installation, you can always do it *after* you're satisfied that your Windows 98 installation is rock-solid.

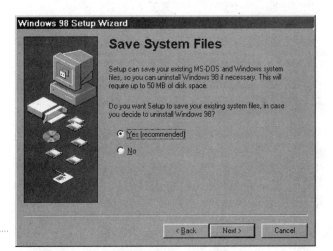

**Your Location.**   This dialog (Figure A.10) is remarkably optimistic, even for Microsoft, since no one has the slightest idea when channel content will become available outside the United States. The more important—if more mundane—purpose of this selection is to pick the country's Regional Settings.

**Startup Disk.** Heads up, *this is important.* Remember that Windows Emergency Disk we've been yammering about ever since the beginning of the book? This is where you make it—your first one, anyway. The progress bar of the dialog box shown in Figure A.11 will get to 20 percent and then you'll be prompted for that diskette we told you to make (Figure A.12).

*Figure A.11*

*Emergency Disk
preparation*

*Figure A.12*

*Emergency Disk
insertion*

You *can* put any junk disk in the drive at this point and let Windows remove the old files, but Setup will quick-format the disk and not report bad sectors, even though they'll be locked out. We prefer to do a full format beforehand with visible results—after all, you have more at stake with your Emergency Disk than with almost any other floppy you own. Put the diskette in the drive, click **OK,** and the dialog will resume (Figure A.13) until Windows tells you the disk is finished (Figure A.14).

Take the diskette out of the drive, click **OK,** and blue skies will be smiling at you (Figure A.15).

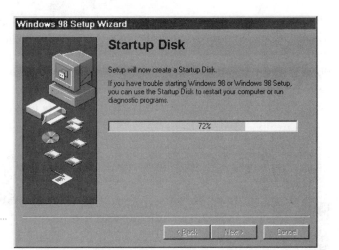

**Figure A.13**

Emergency Disk creation

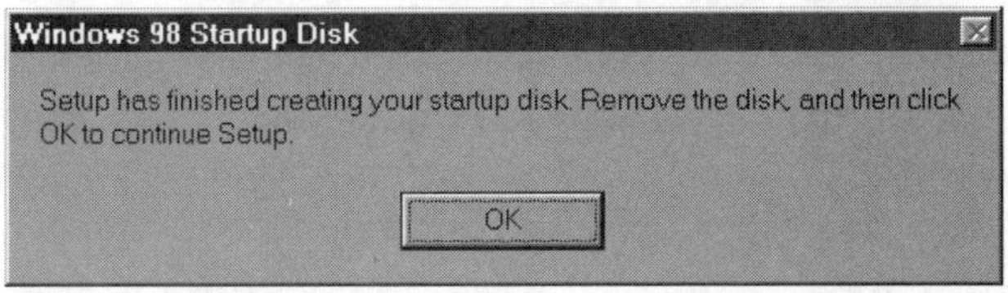

**Figure A.14**

Emergency Disk completion

**Figure A.15**

Blue skies smiling

**File Copy and Configuration.**   At this point you can stay and absorb Microsoft's upbeat message (Figure A.16) or you can pour a glass of something suitable to the season, retire to the porch glider, and see how the orange tree is doing this year, because—in sharp contrast to the versions of old—Windows 98 really doesn't need your help for the next half hour. When you return, assuming everything has gone flawlessly, the Welcome to Windows screen will be waiting for you (Figure A.17).

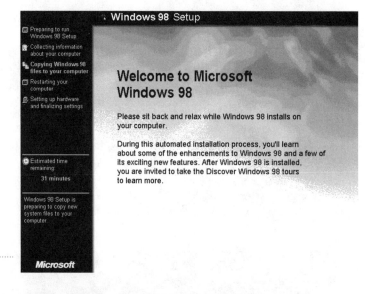

**Figure A.16**

*Upbeat message*

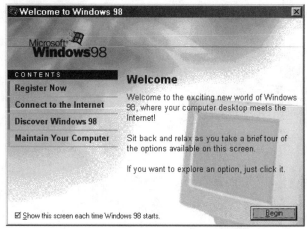

**Figure A.17**

*Welcome to Windows*

Take the tour—Windows 98 is installed on your computer and has a wealth of surprises for you.

## Notes on Upgrading

Microsoft, responding to an alleged upsurge in Windows upgrade piracy, has made it somewhat more involved to install Windows 98 as an upgrade than it was to install previous Windows upgrades.

When you upgraded to Windows 3.*x* or Windows 95, the upgrade installer asked you to insert Setup Disk 1 of your previous version as proof that you were entitled to the upgrade. The Windows 98 upgrade installer, we hear, will ask you to insert several diskettes of your previous version, possibly selected at random.

You can also use a Windows 95 CD for the compliance check, but if you're formatting your hard drive between versions, be sure to back up your real-mode CD-ROM drivers and copy them back; Windows 98's Upgrade Setup will insist on "seeing" the previous version's CD as part of the installation routine, so before you run Setup, your CD drive has to work.

# The Other Way

So much for the ideal, or idyllic, Windows Setup. There are three reasons why your experience with Setup may *not* be like this:

- Windows stumbles over some of your hardware.

- Windows stumbles over some of your software.

- You're configuring something special, like a bunch of network clients, for which the default Setup would be possible but a customized or automated Setup will be more efficient.

In these cases, you'll actually have to know something about the Setup process and the way it works. One of your sources, naturally, will be this appendix. The other will be the remarkably detailed, and unheralded, process documentation called SETUP.TXT.

## SETUP.TXT

SETUP.TXT is a read-only ASCII file located in the \README folder of the Windows 98 CD or, after the installation, in the root folder of your boot drive. We haven't asked to reproduce it here, because it would make this chapter almost twice as long, and because the version you have on your retail Windows CD is newer than anything we could include in this book. We will touch on some of its high points and add our own comments.

## Starting Setup

The Windows 98 Setup programs, libraries, and information files are found on the Windows 98 installation CD–ROM or floppy disks. Setup and the Windows 98 files can be placed on a network and shared directly by several users, or Windows 98 can be installed from the network. Table A.1 lists the files it uses.

### Table A.1  Setup Files

| | |
|---|---|
| **SETUP.EXE** | A protected-mode, 16-bit Windows application with a real-mode stub for command-line installation. You can run Setup from Windows 95, Windows 3.x, or MS-DOS. The switches for setup are shown in Figure A.18 and explained in Table A.2. |
| **SUWIN.EXE** | The protected-mode component called by SETUP.EXE and responsible for calling all DLLs used in Setup. If you get an error message numbered SU*nnnn*, it's from SUWIN.EXE and it's documented in SETUP.TXT. |
| **SETUPX.DLL** | The primary DLL used during the Copy Files phase to perform most of the installation procedures, according to the directions in the .INF files. |
| **NETDI.DLL** | The DLL called to install network services. |
| **SETUP.INF** | The primary reference script for Windows 98, whether you start it from Windows or DOS. The information in this script directs Setup to accommodate your hardware, the configuration of your Windows files, and your existing Desktop (if any) when it installs Windows 98. |
| **SETUPC.INF** | The evil twin of SETUP.INF, this specifies which files are to be kept, which replaced, and which Registry settings changed during an installation or upgrade. The Windows 98 Resource Kit implies in places that this file can be modified for highly arcane hacks, but we personally wouldn't! The /IA and /IB switches below are good examples. |
| **CONTROL.INF** | A mere shadow of what it was under Windows 3.x, this script contains the country-by-country information for Regional Settings. |
| **MSDET.INF** | An almost Registry-like listing of hardware devices that might be detected by Setup, together with estimates of their potential for causing configuration problems. |
| **NETDET.INI** | Detects and accommodates NetWare TSRs in Novell hybrid network installations. (We're not sure whether this file is automatically part of Windows 98; there is no copy in Release Candidate 1. If you need it anyway, you'll find voluminous documentation of it under "Customizing Detection for NetWare Networks" in Chapter 3 of the Resource Kit.) |
| **APPS.INF** | Contains information that Windows 98 uses to create PIFs, and probably .LNK Shortcuts, for applications. |
| **MSBATCH.INF** | The output file of Microsoft Batch 98 from the Windows 98 Resource Kit. By creating this .INF script, you can completely customize Windows 98 installation, then take your Setup from one computer to another to (as only one example) automate network client configuration. Microsoft Batch, which we discuss below, is to Setup what TweakUI is to the Desktop—and you'll never find either one unless you know where to look. |

*Figure A.18*

*Setup switches*

Behind Setup's pretty face, Windows is the perennial creature of mystery. Some switches are documented only at the command line; some switches from older versions of Windows aren't documented at all, but seem to work. They may or may not be case-sensitive, but we've followed the case of the most authoritative source. Table A.2 is as complete as we can make it.

## Table A.2  Setup Switches

| | |
|---|---|
| /? | Provides help on Setup's syntax and command-line switches. Documented in command-line Setup but not in GUI Setup. |
| /C | Instructs Windows 98 Setup not to load the SmartDrive disk cache. Documented in command-line Setup but not in GUI Setup. *Warning:* Use this switch, and the time required to run Setup will triple! If you're using third-party disk caching, see SETUP.TXT. |
| /d | This is an older Windows Setup parameter. In Windows 98, bypasses any installed version of Windows, performs the Registry scan, and launches GUI Setup in VGA mode. Documented only in the Resource Kit. |
| /domainname | Sets the Windows NT Logon Validation of the Client for Microsoft Networks to *domainname.* Documented only in the Resource Kit. |
| /IA | Skips **[AfterProviders]** in SETUPC.INF. Documented only in the Resource Kit. |
| /IB | Skips **[BeforeProviders]** in SETUPC.INF. Documented only in the Resource Kit. |
| /IC | Automatically comments out drivers in boot-time files to force a clean boot. **KeepRMDrives=** in the Registry must equal 0. Documented only in the Resource Kit, and you'd rather do this by hand, anyway. |
| /id | Skips the check for the minimum disk space. |
| /ie | Skips creation of the Emergency Boot Disk. This might be okay if you're re-running Setup right after you made one; otherwise, *no way.* |
| /IF | Forces fast Setup by instructing SETUPX.DLL to draw from a filename cache. Documented only in the Resource Kit. |
| /ih | *Inconsistent.* In GUI setup, claims to skip the Registry check. In the Resource Kit, claims to force ScanDisk to foreground. |
| /iL | Loads the Logitech mouse driver. Use this option if you have a Logitech Series C mouse. Documented in command-line Setup and in the Resource Kit, but not in GUI Setup. |

## Table A.2 *(continued)*

| | |
|---|---|
| */im* | Skips the memory check. Hint: Don't. Windows 98 is picky about memory. Not documented in the Resource Kit. |
| */iN* | Skip all network installation on a networked computer. Documented only in the Resource Kit, and we're not sure it works, either. |
| */iq* | If you skip the ScanDisk pass of Setup (/is), also skips the check for cross-linked files, which is otherwise the default. |
| */IR* | Skip master-boot-record update. We can't be *sure* that this would forestall a conflict with antivirus software that keeps the MBR locked, but it's something to think about. On the other hand, this is exactly the kind of tweak that might cause mystifying compatibility problems long after you've forgotten about using it. Documented only in the Resource Kit. |
| */is* | *Inconsistent.* In GUI setup, claims to skip the routine system check. In command-line help, says "Doesn't run ScanDisk." In the Resource Kit, says "Doesn't run ScanDisk within Windows," which we think is closest to the truth. Not a great idea, but you have to use this switch if you use compression software other than DriveSpace or DoubleSpace—in which case, consult SETUP.TXT *now* to see if the compression you're using is compatible with Windows 98. |
| */it* | Skip check for TSRs that will interfere with Setup if detected. Documented only in the Knowledge Base. |
| */iv* | Skips Microsoft's peppy welcome screens; a distinct plus when you're setting up network workstations. Not documented in the Resource Kit. |
| */IX* | Skips the character-set check. Is this useful for non-English installations? Documented only in the Resource Kit. |
| */IW* | Skips the EULA and goes straight to the Product Key. Documented only in the Resource Kit. This worked for us, but don't be surprised if it's vanished from your copy.... |
| */n* | Runs Setup without a mouse. Documented only in the Knowledge Base. |
| */nostart* | This is an older Windows Setup parameter. If you run it in Windows 98 from the folder where the .CAB files are, it copies a minimal Setup fileset and exits to a command prompt. |
| */p x1;x2;x3....* | Sets options for Setup's detection methods. See "/p Detection Switch Option String Defined" in Knowledge Base article Q128400, "Windows 95 Setup Switches." |
| */T:tempdir* | Specifies the folder into which Setup is to copy its temporary files. If this folder exists, any files in it will be deleted; if it doesn't, it will be created. (*Inconsistent.* The Resource Kit says it has to exist already, in line with what was true for Windows 95.) |
| *<SCRIPTFILENAME>* | Instructs Setup to use the specified script to install Windows 98 automatically; for example, SETUP MSBATCH.INF specifies that Setup should use the settings in MSBATCH.INF. |
| */<SOURCEDIR>* | Lets you specify the source folder of the Windows 98 install files from the command line. This would be lovely if it worked, but we can't find the right syntax. |

# The Setup Process

There are a few steps you can take before starting Setup that may make your life much easier:

- If you're installing on a notebook or laptop, *disable* your Suspend feature. If it takes effect during installation, Setup will crash.

- If you're on a network, be sure your network is operating correctly. Network failures can cause problems with Setup even if you're installing from a local drive.

- If you're using third-party disk caching, consult SETUP.TXT to see if it's compatible with Windows 98. Depending on what you find there, you may want to disable it and let Windows start its native disk caching instead.

- If you're upgrading from Windows 3.*x*, disable 32-bit Disk Access and File Access.

- If you're using third-party display drivers that came with your video card, look in the RELNOTES.DOC file on the Windows CD to make sure they're Windows-compatible. If not, use Device Manager or a comparable utility to set your display to standard VGA (640x480x16) for the installation.

Many third-party extended partitioning schemes or drivers, like Western Digital's EZ-Drive or Ontrack Disk Manager, aren't Windows-compatible unless you have the newest version; this is especially true if you plan to run FAT32. Check with the OEM of your hard drive to see if a current version of the disk manager is available for download. If not, you may want to remove as much data as you can, remove the partitioning software, and restore your old Windows installation before upgrading. If you must reformat the disk, you need a startable copy of MS-DOS, the CD or diskettes for your earlier version of Windows, and a copy of your backup software. See the directions included with your hard disk. Once you upgrade to Windows 98, naturally you won't have such problems.

Copy AUTOEXEC.BAT to AUTOEXEC.OLD and CONFIG.SYS to CONFIG.OLD, then strip down your originals as far as possible. In your CONFIG.SYS, you probably won't need more than statements for FILES=, BUFFERS=, STACKS=, and—very important—your real-mode CD (MSCDEX) support. In your AUTOEXEC.BAT, remove any drivers that your computer doesn't absolutely need in order to run, and make sure that your PATH= statement includes, at a minimum,

```
PATH=C:\WINDOWS;C:\
```

although it may need references to other folders depending on what's loaded by the AUTOEXEC.BAT and CONFIG.SYS.

Remove files you don't need, like browser cache files and Windows .TMP files; then run Defrag. Be especially sure to defragment a drive compressed with DriveSpace or DoubleSpace, because a highly fragmented compressed drive can lie about the amount of space available.

Remove unnecessary TSRs, which can prevent Setup from detecting aspects of your setup correctly. Exceptions to this would be TSRs required to control a hard disk, a CD-ROM, or a network adapter; these usually should remain, since in some cases Windows won't detect the devices if the TSRs are unloaded.

Close unnecessary Windows applications and all DOS windows. Setup restarts the computer several times during the installation process, terminating running Windows applications, and you'd much rather close down programs yourself than have Setup do it. If a DOS session or an application is running, Setup will be interrupted.

Grab the boot disk (probably Setup Disk 1) of whatever operating system you're replacing. You probably won't need it, but if you do, it may be your only way out.

And you *are* backed up, right?

**Getting Going.** When you start Setup, you set Juggernaut in motion. Just because this process is newly streamlined at its surface doesn't mean any less is happening down at the bare metal. You have fewer decisions to make than you did with previous versions of Windows, but the flip-side of that is that you give up some control over your configuration—although you can get that back, and more besides, with MSBATCH.

*Starting From Windows.* If you're upgrading from Windows 95, you can start Setup straight from Windows with the **Start Menu\Run** command, or from Explorer. Just run SETUP.EXE from the root folder of the CD.

*Starting From DOS.* If you're upgrading from Windows 3.1/3.11, Windows 3.0, or OS/2, or for some reason installing over Windows NT, Setup should be started from a command prompt—or from MS-DOS if you can dualboot. Then, of course with the real-mode CD-ROM drivers in memory, log over to the CD's root folder and type setup[Enter].

*Trying To Start From A DOS Box.* If you try to run Setup from a DOS window, it crashes in a mildly amusing way (Figure A.19).

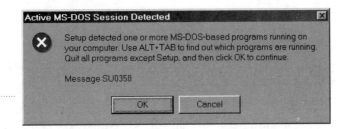

*Figure A.19*

*Setup detecting itself*

Of course, in the process of quitting the active DOS session that Setup finds so repugnant, you'll necessarily quit Setup too.

**Resource Check.**  Regardless of the type of start-up, Setup runs ScanDisk to check for disk problems, then makes sure the platform has a powerful enough CPU and enough memory and disk space, and that the correct version of MS-DOS is running. Setup informs you of any resource shortage, as well as potentially conflicting device drivers. Since Setup can only run efficiently in far more memory than a typical DOS-based system is configured to provide, it's prepared to install an extended-memory specification (XMS) provider, as well as SmartDrive if no disk cache is found.

No matter what operating system Windows 98 is being installed over, it will at least try to run Setup as a GUI, probably in standard VGA mode in 16 colors at a resolution of 640x480. Oversize features and flat-looking surfaces make this mode easily distinguishable from the higher color count and resolution that Windows will try to use if it detects a compatible environment.

**How Long Does It Take?**  The time required to install Windows 98 puts you in a darned-if-you-do, darned-if-you-don't situation. Certainly for those systems with a slower CPU, slower disk, or lower amount of RAM, Setup will take longer. On the other hand, having a fast processor, fast peripherals and lots of memory will not guarantee you speedy Setup, because there are still BIOS features and items of hardware and operating system configuration that can make Setup take longer. About all we can say is that installing from floppies, having a compressed hard disk, and installing over a complex previously existing Windows setup will all make Setup take longer, while disabling disk caching will slow it to a crawl.

On a 486DX2/66 with 16MB of RAM and without SmartDrive, which is probably the worst meaningful case, Setup can take around three hours. On most computers with a Pentium or better processor, though, Setup will take about an hour at most. Even on the fastest and most elaborately equipped Wintel box you can buy today, it's unlikely to finish in less than half an hour.

**Choosing the Location for Windows 98.** Previous versions of Windows asked you, during Setup, where you wanted to locate your new installation. As far as we can find out, Windows 98 doesn't, unless you tell it to. Your choice of folders determines whether you can elect to use your old version of DOS or Windows.

If you choose to install Windows 98 in the same folder as the previous version, Setup moves existing configuration settings in .INI files and file associations from the Registry, if any, into the Windows 98 Registry. All applications and networking settings work automatically in the new Windows 98 environment. Windows 3.*x* Program Manager groups are converted into Windows 98 Start Menu\Programs entries. Some external commands, such as CHKDSK, from the previous version of DOS are removed from the disk.

**Preparation for Dualboot.** You can set up dualboot with Windows 98 and the following operating systems:

- **Windows NT,** providing the two operating systems are installed in separate folders and Windows 98 is running on a FAT16 partition. Win98 won't recognize NTFS and WinNT won't recognize FAT32, and regardless of your feelings about this, it won't change soon. Run Setup by picking MS-DOS or Windows 95 from the NT boot loader selection menu.

- **MS-DOS 5.0** or newer. Install the two operating systems in separate folders.

- **Windows 3.1/3.11** running on top of MS-DOS 5.0 or newer. Install the two operating systems in separate folders.

## Evil Twins

"Windows 98/Windows NT configurations are not recommended," says Microsoft primly. You can do it, but you'll have two Registries and two sets of device drivers, okay? If they get to arguing over who's boss ... misunderstandings are more than likely.

To keep the option of starting your computer either under Windows 98 or under your old version of DOS or Windows, you must use MSBATCH to specify a different folder. Setup installs the Windows 98 files into the new folder and moves the values from .INI files, as well as the Windows 3.*x* REG.DAT if any, into the Windows 98 Registry. Windows 3.*x* program groups are not converted to Windows 98. Also, you may need to reinstall most of your Windows applications before they will function with Windows 98.

Once you have both operating systems successfully installed, you have to change a setting in the MSDOS.SYS control file to enable dualboot. The easiest way to do this is with TweakUI, using the instructions under "F4 Dualboot" in Chapter 15. If you don't have TweakUI installed, here's what to do:

1. After Windows 98 is installed, open the Windows Explorer and select MSDOS.SYS in the root folder of your boot drive. (If your drive is compressed, MSDOS.SYS is on the host drive.)

2. Right-click on the file and select Properties from the Context Menu.

3. Uncheck the System, Hidden, and Read-Only attributes. Click **OK**.

4. Start Notepad or any ASCII editor. Choose **File\Open** and, in the **Files of Type** list, choose **All Documents (\*.\*)**. Navigate to the root folder of the boot drive and pick the MSDOS.SYS file.

5. Find the line that reads **BootMulti=0**. Change the **0** (zero) to a **1** (one).

6. Save the file and exit the editor.

7. Return to Explorer, right-click on the MSDOS.SYS file, pick **Properties,** and recheck System, Hidden, and Read-Only.

8. Click **OK**. Your system is now ready to dual-boot.

To start your computer with the old operating system, press F4 after the initial BIOS check, but before the Windows 98 splash screen appears—which is more difficult than it used to be, because Windows 98 doesn't put up a "Starting Windows 98" message.

 If you need advanced information on this, there's more in Chapter 5 of the Resource Kit.

**Finding Installation Files.**  Setup stores the names of the drive and folder of Windows 98 distribution files in the Registry. The location can be a floppy disk drive, a CD-ROM drive, or a folder on a network server. Windows 98 returns to this location automatically whenever you add a device or additional support files.

Normally, this practice speeds the installation of new files, but it can cause confusion if the device or network folder becomes unavailable. This can happen when you add or remove disk drives or change network settings. If Setup can't find installation files, especially when you start it from DOS, it may not recover. The easiest workaround here is to set the location of the installation files using the **MRU Locations** tab of Microsoft Batch (see below).

**Choosing Installation Type.** Windows Setup running within Windows no longer offers user-selectable installation types. Instead, it queries your computer's BIOS and hardware resources, then decides for itself what components and settings are appropriate—whether, for example, you're installing on a notebook and need Windows' portable-computer options added in. Since this seems a little *too* automated, we remind you that we're testing early releases of Windows 98 and that the retail version of the Setup routine may differ; but for the moment, the only way to select from the Typical, Portable, Compact and Custom installations is to run Setup from the DOS command line.

If you're upgrading over Windows, you may want to go for the easy setup, then add and delete components through Windows Setup after installation.

**Hardware Detection.** During the hardware detection phase, Windows 98 Setup attempts to detect and analyze installed components, hardware devices, and connected peripherals. Setup examines the hardware resources that are available (IRQs, I/O addresses, CPU ports, and DMA lines), identifies the hardware resources used by the installed components, and builds the hardware tree in the Registry which is used by Device Manager and by the System Information Tool.

Setup uses several mechanisms to detect installed hardware. When Windows 98 auto-detects Plug and Play peripherals, they return their own device identification codes. On a computer with a Plug and Play BIOS, Windows 98 also checks for connected Plug and Play peripheral devices connected to the computer. On a non–Plug and Play, or *legacy,* computer, Windows 98 attempts to identify devices by checking for I/O ports and memory addresses known to be used by the hardware. The resources used by any detected Plug and Play devices are added to the Registry, and any required device drivers are installed based on the Registry settings.

Windows 98 uses the same hardware detection procedures during Setup as it uses when you run the Add New Hardware option in the Control Panel, when you use the PCMCIA wizard to enable protected-mode support, and the first time you start a computer in a new docking state. Windows detects components such as ports and processors, and a wide range of standard equipment, such as display adapters, pointing devices, hard-disk controllers, floppy-disk controllers, and network adapters.

**Setup and CONFIG.SYS.** Windows 98 also reads CONFIG.SYS (if you left it active) looking for hints about devices, and steers away from certain resources pointed to by CONFIG.SYS device= entries. For example, the detection process could lock up a fax modem by scanning the I/O ports covered by the driver. Windows can read the device= line in CONFIG.SYS for the equipment, and protect the associated I/O region from disruptive detection.

## Hold It Right There!

During the detection process, lockups can occur when Setup encounters "nonexistent" or "resource-sensitive" equipment. To avoid these lockups, Windows 98 relies on a safe detection method that scavenges hints from configuration files, read-only memory (ROM) strings, and drivers in memory. The process skips detecting any class of equipment for which no hints are found. If hints are found, the detection process polls specific I/O ports for information. Windows loads its detection modules based on information in the MSDET.INF file, which lists the hardware to be detected and points to specific .INF files for each device class (for example, SCSI.INF for SCSI host adapters). Device information from the .INF files is written to the Registry.

**Controlling Detection.** Performing manual hardware detection seems much less possible in Windows 98 than in Windows 95. Given the vast scope of the Windows 98 Hardware Compatibility List, it's a fair bet that Microsoft decided manual detection would rarely, if ever, be necessary. We'll see if they were right, won't we?

By starting Setup from MS-DOS and choosing the Typical or Custom setup, you'll be offered a dialog called **Computer Settings** which makes it possible to configure some—but not much—hardware manually. Your next best option (which consistently works rather well) is to let Setup continue till Windows is installed, go to Device Manager in Control Panel\System, and look for hardware components whose icons include a black exclamation point on a yellow circle. Device Manager knows that any such device is configured incorrectly, and if you look at its Properties, you'll see why. You might need a hand from our Appendix E, "Device Manager Error Codes."

If none of this solves the problem, your last resorts are certain chapters in the Windows 98 Resource Kit—particularly Chapter 30, "Hardware Device Support"—or technical support from the manufacturer of the failing device.

**Setup Logging and Safe Recovery.** Windows 98 Setup creates several log files to help you diagnose a successful or failed installation: BOOTLOG.TXT, DETLOG.TXT, NETLOG.TXT, and SETUPLOG.TXT, plus DETCRASH. LOG if Setup fails. If Setup fails before the hardware detection phase, Windows recovers by reading SETUPLOG.TXT to determine where the system stalled, what to redo, and what to skip. If Setup fails during the hardware detection phase, DETCRASH.LOG will contain information about the detection module that was running and the I/O port or memory resources it was accessing when the failure occurred.

When the detection process finds DETCRASH.LOG, which only Setup can read, Setup automatically invokes Safe Recovery mode to verify all the devices already in the Registry and skips all detection modules up to the failed module.

To make sure installation doesn't fail again, Safe Recovery skips detection and attempted configuration of the failed module; it continues detection starting with the next module. If the detection process is completed successfully, DET-CRASH.LOG is deleted.

***Intrusion and Safe Recovery.*** Safe Recovery also works when the detection process causes a device to quit working (such as a CD-ROM drive or a network connection). Setup recognizes that the detection process was completed successfully and assumes that all the necessary hardware information has been placed in the Registry. During the next run of Setup, the detection process for the device in question is considered completed and is skipped, and Setup continues the installation process.

***Continuing If Setup Stops.*** If the computer freezes during the hardware detection phase of Setup (that is, if you don't see or hear disk activity, and the progress bar does not move for more than 30 seconds), follow these steps:

1. Click on the **Cancel** button to quit Setup.

2. If the computer does not respond to the Cancel button, restart the computer—preferably with its **Reset** button, but if that fails, by turning it off and back on again.

3. Run Setup again. Setup prompts you to use Safe Recovery to recover the failed installation.

4. Click **Use Safe Recovery,** then click **Next.**

5. Repeat your installation choices. Hardware detection runs again, but Setup skips the device that caused the initial failure.

If the computer stops again during the hardware detection process, repeat the above procedure until the hardware detection portion of Setup is completed successfully.

# Rolling Your Own (Installation)

If you install Windows 98 and its accessories with a script, by default you use SETUP.INF. You can do a custom install by overriding SETUP.INF with a homemade script usually called MSBATCH.INF. Table A.3 lists the sections of the MSBATCH.INF file.

 If a value in MSBATCH.INF can be set with Microsoft Batch 3.0—which, if you ask us, is the way you want to do it when possible—we've put a splat ✳ next to its entry.

### Table A.3  Main Sections of MSBATCH.INF

| Section | Description |
| --- | --- |
| [BatchSetup] | Version of MS-Batch, and the date the script was created. |
| [Version] | Windows version signature. |
| [Setup] | Values involved in the setup process. |
| [System] | Values of system settings. |
| [NameAndOrg] | The name and organization of the computer's primary user. |
| [InstallLocationsMRU] | The folders where Setup will look for files. Don't confuse this with the *path*. |
| [OptionalComponents] | Controls for the installation of components like languages and screen savers. |
| [Network] | Controls for network options. |
| [netcard_ID] | Identifiers for NICs (network adapters). |
| [NWLink] | IPX/SPX protocol settings. |
| [NWRedir] | NetWare network client settings. |
| [NWServer] | Novell NetWare network file and printer sharing settings. |
| [VRedir] | Microsoft Network client settings. |
| [VServer] | Microsoft Network file and printer sharing settings. |
| [Printers] | Installable printer settings. |
| [Strings] | Verbose forms of user-defined strings in Setup. |
| [Install] | Settings for Setup File Copy. |

## [BatchSetup] Section

| | |
| --- | --- |
| *Version* | Version of MS-Batch in use. |
| Values | 3.0 for Windows 98; 2.0 for Windows 95; 1.*x* for Windows 3.*x* |
| *SaveDate* | Date of the .INF file's save. |
| Value | *mm/dd/yy*, or according to Regional Settings |

## [Version] Section

| | |
| --- | --- |
| *Signature* | Microsoft internal name for version of Windows in use |
| Value | "$CHICAGO$" for both Windows 98 (4.1) and Windows 95 (4.0) |

## [SETUP] SECTION

The [Setup] section sets parameters for control of the Setup process (see Table A.4). An asterisk (★) after a number indicates a default value.

 *These are not all the parameters that exist.* We've omitted a handful that are, so far as we're concerned, undocumented as well as rare. We make an exception for System=, which is undocumented but seemingly universal.

### Table A.4  Setup Parameters

| **CCP** | Controls whether Windows checks for files from a previous version of Windows during Setup. |
|---|---|
| Values | 0 = Skip this check. |
| | 1* = Make this check. |
| **ChangeDir**☀ | Allows selection of the installation folder. |
| Values | 0* = Installation folder must be C:\WINDOWS. |
| | 1 = Installation folder can be user's choice. |
| **CleanBoot** | Comments out lines in boot-time files to force a boot without drivers. |
| Values | 0 = Disable clean boot. |
| | 1 = Clean boot. Same as setup /IC. |
| **Devicepath**☀ | **Devicepath=1** checks a user-specified installation path for .INF files, rather than looking only in the Windows .INF folder. When the installation source files are in a network folder, means that you can force the use of .INF files you add after Windows installation. |
| | If **Devicepath=1**, the .INF database is rebuilt whenever a network component or device driver is changed. |
| Values | 0* = Check for .INF files only in the Windows folder. |
| | 1 = Add a network folder to the path for finding .INF files. |
| **EBD**☀ | Controls whether a Startup Disk is created during Setup. For unattended installation, consider using **ebd=0** so that the user isn't prompted to insert or remove a floppy disk, and **reboot=0** so that Setup does not attempt to restart the computer while the floppy disk is in the drive. If necessary, you can override this at the command line with /ie. |
| Values | 0 = Skip the Startup Disk. |
| | 1 = Create the Startup Disk. |
| **Express** | If **express=1**, Setup uses settings from MSBATCH.INF and built-in defaults without confirmation. Most of the user interface for Setup is disabled. |
| Values | 0* = Use user-supplied values. |
| | 1 = Use values from MSBATCH.INF. |

### *Table A.4* *(continued)*

| | |
|---|---|
| ***InstallDir*** | Sets the Windows 98 install folder. |
| Value | *foldername* |
| Default | The Windows folder, if there is one. |
| ***InstallType*** | Sets the Windows installation type. |
| Values | 0 = Compact |
| | 1* = Typical |
| | 2 = Portable |
| | 3 = Custom |
| **Network** | Includes or skips the Network module of Setup. |
| Values | 0 = Skip the Network module. Same as **setup /IN**. |
| | 1* = Includes the Network module. |
| **NoDirWarn** | Specifies whether to display a warning if a previous Windows install is located in a folder *other than* C:\WINDOWS. |
| Values | 0* = Do not display the warning. |
| | 1 = Display the warning. |
| **NoPrompt2Boot✳** | Selects automatic or confirmed reboot of PCI and PnP computers after Setup Part 2. |
| Values | 0* = Reboots after confirmation through dialog. |
| | 1 = Reboots automatically. Useful for unattended setup, but may skip some hardware detection. |
| **OptionalComponents** | Specifies whether to parse the [OptionalComponents] list in MSBATCH.INF |
| Values | 0 = Ignore the list. |
| | 1* = Parse the list. |
| **PenWinWarning** | **1** displays a warning if an unknown version of Pen Windows is installed; **0** skips it. |
| **ProductID✳** | The product ID from the Windows 98 CD or Certification of Authenticity can be entered here. |
| Values | *string* |
| Default | None |
| **SaveSUBoot** | With this setting you can save the SUBOOT folder for server-based Setup. |
| Values | 0* = Delete folder. |
| | 1 = Save folder. |

## Table A.4 *(continued)*

| | |
|---|---|
| **ShowEULA**✳ | Specifies whether to show, and force acknowledgment of, the End User License Agreement |
| Values | 0 = Do not show the EULA. Same as **setup /IW**. |
| | 1✳ = Show the EULA. |
| **System** | This has existed in every MSBATCH.INF we've ever seen, almost always set to **System=0**, and we *cannot* find an explanation of it, either within Microsoft or outside. |
| **TimeZone**✳ | Sets the time zone for the computer. |
| Values | Strings from Resource Kit Appendix D. |
| Default | The time zone currently set on the computer. |
| **Uninstall**✳ | Setup can create a compressed backup of previous Windows and MS-DOS system files, used to uninstall Windows 98. |
| Values | 0 = Uninstall options are not settable; uninstall backups are not created. |
| | 1✳ = Uninstall options are displayed and settable. |
| | 5 = Uninstall options are not displayed, but uninstall backups are created. Add a value BackupDir=*path* that specifies a folder to receive the backup files. |
| **VRC**✳ | Tells Setup to overwrite existing files, even if the date of the target file is more recent than the date of the file being copied. |
| Values | 0✳ = Prompt for confirmation before overwriting. |
| | 1 = Overwrite without prompting. |

## [System] Section

The **[System]** section concerns system- and hardware-related items, such as the display, location, and use of Pen Windows. The section contains two types of entries. One type includes parameters that follow the conventions used in the other sections of the MSBATCH.INF file. The second type selects the default item from a group by naming the item or its associated section.

Depending on the details of Setup, the new default may be changed by the user or will be installed automatically by Setup. For example, the following line picks the MicronPnpBIOS14 as the default machine type:

```
Machine=MicronPnpBios14
```

 **Many of these entries can be copied directly from the SETUPLOG.TXT of a computer set up comparably to the one that will run the script.**

**INF Section Entries.**  The following entries are pointers to sections from .INF files; the name of the .INF file matches the section name.

Locale=.*inf_section_name* in LOCALE.INF.

Machine=.*inf_section_name* in MACHINE.INF.

PenWindows=.*inf_section_name* in PENWIN.INF.

Power=.*inf_section_name* in MACHINE.INF or equivalent (for Advanced Power Management support).

Tablet=.*inf_section_name* in PENDRV.INF or equivalent.

**INF Description Entries.**  For the following entries, the entry name matches an .INF description, which must exist.

Display=.*inf_description* in MSDISP.INF or similar file.

Keyboard=.*inf_description* in KEYBOARD.INF. ✳

Locale=.*inf_description* in LOCALE.INF. ✳

Monitor=.*inf_section_name* in MONITOR.INF.

Mouse=.*inf_section_name* in MSMOUSE.INF or similar file.

SelectedKeyboard=.*inf_section_name* in MULTILNG.INF (specifies the keyboard layout).

Two other parameters can be used in the section: *DisplChar* ✳, which sets initial display characteristics, and *MultiLanguage,* which sets the type of installed multilanguage support. The syntax for *DisplChar* is *ColorDepth, x, y* where *ColorDepth* = bits per pixel, $x$ = horizontal resolution, and $y$ = vertical resolution. For details of MultiLanguage, see Appendix D of the Resource Kit.

 If **Express=1**, you cannot override safe detection for network adapters, SCSI controllers, or sound cards, and may need to install support later, through Add New Hardware in Control Panel. To force device installation when **Express=1,** add device entries to the [System] section.

## [NameAndOrg] Section

**[NameAndOrg]** holds user information for Setup and controls the Name and Organization dialog (see Table A.5).

### Table A.5  Name and Organization

| | |
|---|---|
| **Name**✳ | Sets the user name. |
| Values | *string* (default empty) |
| **Org**✳ | Sets the organization or installation name. |
| Values | *string* (default empty) |
| **Display** | Controls the Name and Organization dialog during Setup. |
| Values | 0 = Do not display dialog. |
| | 1* = Display dialog. |

# [InstallLocationsMRU] Section✳

**[InstallLocationsMRU]** specifies a list of folders to appear on separate lines of a drop-down list box, whenever Windows 98 Setup prompts for a path. In this example, Setup offers the user the choice of A:\, C:\, or \\Server\Win98 as the location of files in the list box:

```
[InstallLocationsMRU]
mru1=a:\
mru2=c:\
mru3=\\server\win98
```

# [OPTIONALCOMPONENTS] SECTION✳

**[OptionalComponents]** sets descriptions to appear in the Optional Components dialog of Setup. Each entry in this section is a description enclosed in quotation marks, followed by =1 to install the component, or =0 not to install it. For example, the entries to install HyperTerminal and System Monitor are:

```
[OptionalComponents]
"HyperTerminal"=1
"System Monitor"=1
```

Each description is defined in an .INF file. Many such strings are defined in the Windows 98 standard .INF files; others are contributed by third-party developers. For details of Optional Components, see Appendix D of the Resource Kit.

You can also create this section from a copy of the [OptionalComponents] section in SETUPLOG.TXT from a computer that has all the appropriate-components installed.

## [NETWORK] SECTION

Network parameters belong to six general types:

- Installation parameters

- Network card drivers

- Shared installation parameters

- Computer identification

- Security parameters

- User interface options.

We will only discuss these entries in introductory terms because a thorough treatment, we fear, would necessarily violate Microsoft copyrights on the material. Parameter tables and detailed explanations are in Appendix D of the Resource Kit.

### Installation Parameters

*Clients.* This parameter specifies the network client or clients to be installed. Each client is represented by a list of the device IDs used in the .INF files, not limited to those in the Windows 98 .INF files (NETCLI.INF and NET-CLI3.INF), but including any device IDs listed in an .INF file from another vendor. When you install a third-party client not listed in a Microsoft .INF file, obtain an updated file from the vendor.

**Network Card Drivers.** This parameter specifies the drivers to be installed for network adapters. Device IDs can be from Windows 98 .INF files or an .INF file from another vendor.

NIC device IDs stored as text are being superseded by Plug and Play and, where possible, you should rely on detection in Windows 98 Setup to install the correct driver and define the correct configuration settings.

*Protocols.* Specifies the protocols to be installed. Device IDs can be from Windows 98 .INF files or an .INF file from another vendor. When you install a third-party protocol not listed in a Microsoft .INF file, obtain an updated file from the vendor.

*Default Protocol.* Specifies the default protocol, assigned as LANA 0, which is bound to the NIC or to a specific NIC. If no adapter is specified, the default is the first instance of the named protocol.

*Remove Binding.* Deletes the binding between two devices. This parameter is used to set the precedence of bindings in a Setup script.

*Services.* Specifies the network services to be installed. Device IDs can be from Windows 98 .INF files or an .INF file from another vendor. When you install a third-party protocol not listed in a Microsoft .INF file, obtain an updated file from the vendor. A service listed in a Setup script is subject to verification by the operating system.

The only Windows 98 default service is VServer (File and Printer Sharing for Microsoft Network) if and when peer sharing service for Windows for Workgroups is enabled on the computer. Other valid installable services include the Seagate (Arcada) Backup Exec Agent, the Cheyenne ARCserve Agent, the HP Network Printer Service for Microsoft or NetWare, the Microsoft Network Monitor Agent★, File and Printer Sharing and Microsoft Print Service for NetWare Networks, the Microsoft Remote Registry Service★, and the Microsoft SNMP Agent★. You'll find the starred ones in the \RESKIT\NETADMIN or \TOOLS\NETTOOLS folder of the Resource Kit CD-ROM.

### Computer Identification Information

*Computer Name.* Sets the computer's network name.

*Description.* Provides a description of the computer.

*Workgroup.* Identifies the workgroup of the computer.

### Shared Installation Parameters

*HDBoot (Hard Disk Boot).* Specifies whether a computer running a shared copy of Windows 98 from a server is configured to start from the local hard disk or the network.

*RPLSetup.* Controls whether Setup creates a disk image on the network server for a remote-boot workstation during workstation setup. This parameter is ignored if a corresponding WorkstationSetup value is not defined.

*Workstation Setup.* Specifies whether Setup configures a client computer to run Windows 98 locally or from a shared copy on a server.

*Display Workstation Setup.* Determines whether the Setup user interface appears while Setup installs a shared copy of Windows 98 on a workstation.

### Security Parameters

*Security.* Specifies the type of security and, for user-level security, whether the pass-through validation agent is a server or a domain. Share-level security ignores such validation. These values have no effect if the installed client does not have a security provider.

### User Interface Options

*Display.* Turns the Network Configuration dialogs on or off during Custom Setup.

*Validate NetCard Resources.* Offers (or not) a conflict-resolution wizard to validate NIC resources if a partial configuration or conflict is detected.

## Network Cards Section

The actual name for this section is the network adapter's identifier as defined in the related .INF file. This section sets parameters for a specific network adapter, as defined in the [*netcard*.ndi] sections of .INF files provided with Windows 98.

 Generally, you should let Windows 98 Setup detect the adapter, install the correct driver, and define the correct configuration settings. If, despite it all, you need more information about hand-aligning your network hardware, consult Appendix D of the Resource Kit.

## [MSTCP] Section

This section sets parameters for Microsoft TCP/IP, which we discussed in Chapter 10. For specific values, see the Resource Kit.

## [NWLink] Section

The parameters in the [NWLink] section specify settings for the IPX/SPX protocol.✻

## [NWRedir] Section

These parameters set values for Client for NetWare Networks.✻

## [VRedir] Section

These parameters set redirector values for Client for Microsoft Networks.✻

## [Printers] Section

This section controls the installation of one or more printers during Setup. Each printer has a separate entry comprising a user-defined identifier for the printer, the model name, and the printer port, in the format: PrinterName= *DriverModel,Port*. The model name must be available from an .INF file.

## [Strings] Section

The [Strings] section contains key strings in the form *String_Key=Value,* where *String_Key* is a unique name, and *Value* is the sequence of characters that String_Key should become when it is expanded.

## [Install] Section

The [Install] section sets parameters for copying additional files as part of Windows 98 installation. The format of this section is identical to the format of the [Install] section of general .INF files. If you need to edit the [Install] section directly, we sympathize, and can point you to Appendix D of the Resource Kit but suggest that there's no substitute for experience.

Many of the checkbox options in Microsoft Batch are set by adding entries to the [Install] section. See the section on Microsoft Batch below.

## Choosing a Workgroup with WRKGRP.INI Files

The WRKGRP.INI file specifies a list of workgroups that a user can choose to join. This file also restricts the choices of work group available to a user, reducing the proliferation of work groups on the network. The file can also specify the defaults for a NetWare preferred server or a Windows NT domain on a per-work group basis.

As far as we can tell, WRKGRP.INI control files can be used only on server-based networks with Windows NT or NetWare at the server. Therefore, we won't cover them here, but we will point you to Chapter 3, "Custom Installations," in the Windows 98 Resource Kit.

## Installing Custom DOS Programs

To install custom DOS applications to run with Windows 98, you may need to modify the APPS.INF file, which contains the information for creating PIFs and assigning icons.

**The APPS.INF File.** During installation Setup places the APPS.INF file in the INF folder, and Setup refers to this file when it builds the Start Menu. To add a new DOS application to APPS.INF, you create an entry for the application in the **[PIF98]** section.

Actually, in Windows 98 Release Candidate 1, this section is called **[PIF95]** as it was previously, but we're betting this is one of those details that gets cleaned up at the last minute. If you look in your APPS.INF and this section is still called **[PIF95]**—which it might be, in aid of some obscure backward compatibility— then pretend we said **[PIF95]** from here on down. If backward compatibility stuck us with segmented addressing, it can certainly give us a bogus header.

The entry must be placed in the correct position alphabetically in the list. A section, [*appfile.ext*], that defines the application information and a Title entry for the [Strings] section must also be created. The Title entry must appear in the correct position alphabetically in the [Strings] section. The application section can be inserted anywhere, but customarily lives between [PIF95] and [Strings]. To find out what program is referenced in [*appfile.ext*] you look at the equivalences in [Strings].

 If there are two identical or functionally identical entries in [*appfile.ext*], the syntax becomes [*appfile.ext.n*], where *n* is a decimal number. An identical case is [123.EXE.1] and [123.EXE.2] which are two different versions of Lotus 1-2-3. A functionally identical case is [ZEPHYR.BAT.1] and [ZEPHYR.EXE.2], where Windows uses the appended number to distinguish the two because both files are executable, even though their types are different. This process reaches a lofty plane of absurdity with [INSTALL.EXE.49].

*[PIF98] Section.*  The top section in APPS.INF, **[PIF98],** acts as a master list of settings for MS-DOS applications. Each line in this section corresponds to an entry in APPS.INF that contains information about running a specific application.

Each entry in [PIF98] uses the following syntax:

**appfile**=*%title%,iconfile,iconnumber,setworkdir,  section,otherfile,setpif*

The elements of a [PIF98] entry are listed in Table A.6.

### Table A.6 [PIF98] Syntax

| | |
|---|---|
| **appfile** | The file name, with extension, of the application's executable file. |
| **title** | The name that appears in the application's title bar. Usually the title is a string identifier that appears in the **[Strings]** section of the .INF file and is set to the quoted name of the application. |
| **iconfile** | The file, usually a .DLL, from which to extract the application's icon. |
| **iconnumber** | The number of the desired icon from the icon-extraction table. The default is 0, but that hardly ever happens. |
| **setworkdir** | Automatically sets up the folder containing the executable file as the working folder (0, the default) or prevents Windows from doing so (1). |
| **section** | The name of the corresponding section in APPS.INF that contains details about the application's operation. |
| **otherfile** | A file within a folder, other than the main .EXE, that always installs for this application; used when two *appfile* entries are identical. |
| **setpif** | Allows (0, the default) or prevents (1) the creation of a .PIF file for this application. Optional. |

*[appname.ext] Sections.* Each section block as named by the section parameter in a [PIF98] entry defines parameters, required memory, and other options needed for the .pif file. It also controls which options are enabled or disabled in the .pif file (Table A.14).

The following is an example of the syntax of the section parameter (note that you use commas to separate multiple entries):

```
[WORD.EXE]
LowMem=384
Enable=cwe
Disable=win,bgd,asp
```

## Table A.7  Abbreviations for Enabled and Disabled Entries in the Section Parameter

| Entry | Meaning | Entry | Meaning |
|-------|---------|-------|---------|
| *aen* | Alt Enter | *eml* | EMS memory locked |
| *aes* | Alt Esc | *ems* | EMS memory |
| *afp* | Allow fast paste | *emt* | Emulate ROM |
| *aps* | Alt Print Screen | *exc* | Exclusive mode |
| *asp* | Alt Spacebar | *gmp* | Global memory protection |
| *ata* | Alt Tab | *hma* | Use HMA |
| *awc* | Automatic window | *lml* | Low memory locked conversion |
| *bgd* | Background | *mse* | Mouse |
| *cdr* | CD-ROM | *net* | Network |
| *ces* | Ctrl Esc | *psc* | Print Screen |
| *cwe* | Close on exit | *rvm* | Retain video memory |
| *dit* | Detect idle time | *rwp* | Run Windows applications |
| *dos* | Real mode | *win* | Run in a window |
| *dsk* | Disk lock | *xml* | XMS memory locked |

*[Strings] Section.* The **[Strings]** section contains entries in the same form as entries in the [Strings] section of MSBATCH.INF. The string key is the title from the [PIF98] section, and the value is the name of the application that

appears in the title bar, placed within quotation marks. The entries in this section are alphabetized.

## Customizing Setup Scripts

You can specify custom settings for Windows 98 installations by creating a custom file in .INF format. This Setup script is then used for installation. The default Setup script is stored with the source files on the server. Custom Setup scripts can be stored in users' home folders or in other central locations.

- You can create a custom Setup script in several ways:

- Use the server-based Setup program NETSETUP.EXE to create a script with most of the available custom settings.

- Use the batch Setup program BATCH.EXE to create a script with many settings, including but not limited to the ones marked with ✳. See the section on Microsoft Batch below. The output file in .INF format can be edited by hand, if necessary, to specify all possible custom settings.

- Use the .INF File Generator, INFGEN.EXE, to add and maintain customized scripts.

- Try Richard Fellner's shockingly cool shareware INF-Tool.

***NETSETUP.EXE.*** Use the server-based NETSETUP.EXE to produce a custom script that can be edited with a text editor to create the .INF file. Since NETSETUP adds entries for most sections, and since any changes to this file must be made by hand, this method of creating a script is the most comprehensive but also the most labor-intensive. NETSETUP also offers little help, is cryptic in the way it operates, and temporarily requires about 130MB of server disk space.

NETSETUP, like Microsoft Batch, should be provided on most CD-ROM versions of Windows 98; unfortunately we can't give you a folder path since we don't have a final CD. It may be omitted from some OEM versions.

***.INF Generator.*** The .INF Generator—a free Microsoft .INF Wizard—edits, combines, and adds other Windows 98 features that can be customized through scripts. It's primarily a tool for unattended and multiple installations.

It can be downloaded from many online services and from Microsoft's World Wide Web and FTP sites on the Internet; the filename is usually IG.EXE.

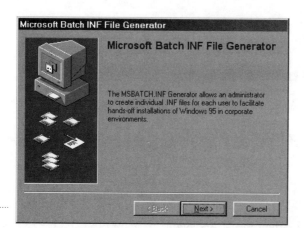

**INFTool.** Although Richard Fellner's **INFTool** (see Figure A.21) is probably the most powerful of all .INF generators—we can't, offhand, find a legal modification that it won't make—the unusually attractive tabbed dialog interface makes it nearly as easy to use as Microsoft Batch. INFTool's abilities go far beyond the scope of this chapter to let you create, for example, fast and compact installation routines to distribute with programs. We would call it an absolute necessity for software developers.

*Figure A.21*

INFTool

Cruise over to **http://www.user.xpoint.at/r.fellner/DL_Inf.htm** to pick up an evaluation copy. If you like it, the price is only US$29—more than a bargain if you use it professionally, inexpensive even if you don't. With programmers like this, Vienna could get as famous for software as for pastry.

***Editing .INF Files By Hand.*** Although you can edit .INF and other Setup script files with any text editor, make sure that you save a file as plain ASCII text by choosing the text (**\*.txt**) option in the File Type list. Some word processors can damage the files, because the programs insert their own formatting information into a file or change the ASCII values of certain characters. (Initialization files and scripts cannot contain characters with ASCII values above 127.)

Windows Notepad edits system files well, because it doesn't change ASCII values or add formatting codes; but Notepad can't edit APPS.INF or other scripts that exceed the puny 60KB Notepad file size limit. You can use Windows 3.1's Write or Windows 95/98's WordPad if you save files with the **Save As Text File** option. If you have upgraded from MS-DOS 5.0 or newer, or you can find a Windows Emergency Disk (hint, hint) you can edit Setup script files safely with EDIT.COM.

To be safe, always make a backup copy of an .INF or script file before you edit it. Discarding mistakes can be easier than trying to fix them.

## TweakINF: Microsoft Batch

Microsoft provides several programs to make .INF file management easier, but of them all, Microsoft Batch is probably the most generally useful (see Figure A.22). Like its more flamboyant cousin, TweakUI, it has a certain entertaining aspect.

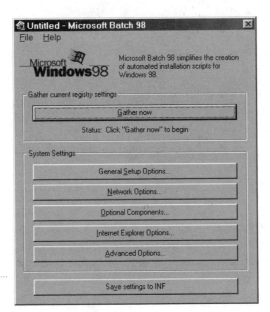

*Figure A.22*

*MS-Batch main menu*

A venerable tool, MS-Batch has gained in stature with every passing version of Windows, and Batch 3.0 is quite muscular. Since you've learned some things about what it will do by reading this much of the chapter, we won't go through its options in great detail, but we will summarize the choices on each tab.

**Gather Settings.** This is a "point-and-shoot" tab that doesn't open; just click it to gather all the current Registry settings that will be included in MSBATCH.INF (see Figure A.23). It only takes a few seconds. Naturally, Batch may add other options to the .INF file by means of [AddReg] statements—see below.

*Figure A.23*

*Gather settings*

**General Setup Options.** See Figure A.24 for General Setup Options.

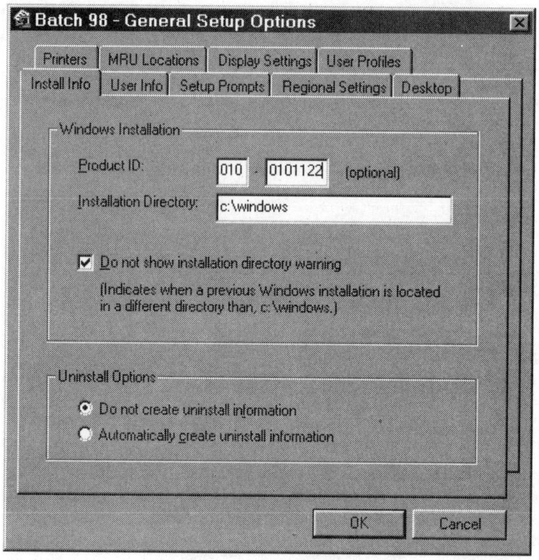

*Figure A.24*

*General Setup
(Install Info tab)*

*Install Info Tab.* Product ID, Windows installation folder, installation folder warning, and uninstall backup creation.

*User Info Tab.* User and company name, and workgroup information.

*Setup Prompts Tab.* Turn off any or all Setup user prompts, so that Setup can finish without user intervention. For unattended installations.

*Regional Settings Tab.* Sets defaults for local Time Zone, keyboard layout, and Regional Settings.

*Desktop Tab.* Lets you remove core Windows icons from the Desktop, delete online services, and suppress the Welcome screen and the Registration Wizard. These settings are modified through Registry keys.

*Printers Tab.* Lets you set the names, driver modules and ports of all printers.

*MRU Locations Tab.* Lets you add Most Recently Used locations for Setup files.

*Display Settings Tab.* Gives access to all the color depth and resolution settings that Windows considers valid, with a warning if you try to enforce settings that the hardware can't handle.

*User Profiles Tab.* Lets you select single or multiple User Profiles as a Setup default, and define the scope of user-dependent default settings.

**Network Options.** You don't get all the options here (see Figure A.25) that you do in Control Panel\Network, but you can set switches so that, if Network Options are included as part of Setup, they require little if any attention.

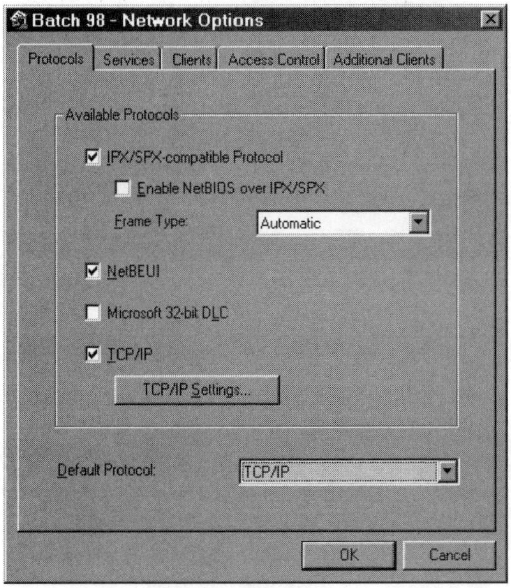

![Batch 98 - Network Options dialog box showing the Protocols tab with Available Protocols: IPX/SPX-compatible Protocol (checked), Enable NetBIOS over IPX/SPX (unchecked), Frame Type: Automatic, NetBEUI (checked), Microsoft 32-bit DLC (unchecked), TCP/IP (checked) with TCP/IP Settings button, and Default Protocol: TCP/IP]

*Figure A.25*

Network Options
(Protocols tab)

*Protocols Tab.* Lets you choose among IPX/SPX, NetBEUI, DLC, and TCP/IP, set a limited range of options, and set default protocol. For TCP/IP you can set IP Address, WINS Configuration, DNS Configuration, and Gateway.

*Services Tab.* Sets up File and Printer Sharing for Microsoft or for NetWare networks, with advertising and browse-mastering options, or turns it off completely.

*Clients Tab.* Incorporates the Client for Microsoft Networks, with optional logon validation by a domain controller, or for NetWare networks, with optional script processing or Directory Service pathing.

*Access Control Tab.* Selects share-level or user-level access control.

*Additional Clients Tab.* Lets you add other supported—Banyan VINES, NetWare NETX Shell, NetWare VLM Shell—or unsupported clients. If you're adding an unsupported client you need the Resource Kit handy.

**Optional Components.** Lets you incorporate Optional Components individually or all at once, clear them all, or reset to defaults (see Figure A.26).

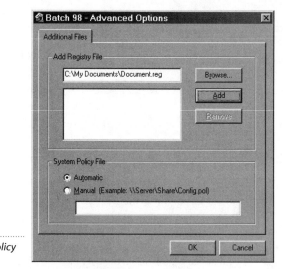

**Figure A.26**

Optional
Components

**Advanced Options.** Adds Registry (.REG) and policy (.POL) files to the [Install] section (see Figure A.27).

**Figure A.27**

Registry and policy
file options

**Save Settings to INF.** Pops up a Browse box with a proposed folder to save your settings into. MSBATCH.INI is the proposed filename, but you can change it (see Figure A.28).

# Summary

Setup of Windows 98 is a multiprogram effort to sniff out the correct hardware, copy and install the correct files, configure the setup, and aid in the migration of programs and settings from an established Windows 3.x installation to Windows 98. The procedure starts when you bring up the Setup program.

Because Setup proceeds according to given scripts, all you have to do to customize Setup is rewrite the scripts. Your best bet is to change MSBATCH.INF, an add-on script that overrides the usual .INF setup files. MSBATCH.INF can be created by hand, edited from samples, or managed by the NETSETUP, Microsoft Batch, .INF Generator, or shareware INFTool programs. Microsoft Batch is the friendliest of these programs for everyday customizing, but the others provide options beyond what Batch makes available.

# Appendix B

# Accessibility Options

One of the great promises of the desktop computer, almost since its beginnings, was that it could make the lives of people with limited vision, limited hearing, or impaired dexterity more productive. The promise was not immediately reasonable and it took longer yet to be fulfilled. Kip remembers a day of trying to configure a computer, for someone who was legally blind, with special DOS drivers that would display characters four times normal size on an EGA monitor. The results were spectacular, but not terribly useful.

In the intervening twelve years, much has changed. We can reconfigure keyboards, install special sound schemes, have the computer render spoken words as text in files, or listen to words spoken from books. A new day's dawning, not only for the disabled but for anyone who might like—let's say—to dictate e-mail. Many fine companies, certainly including Dragon Systems, IBM, and Kurzweil, have worked programming miracles to make today's computers more accessible.

Microsoft is in the thick of the effort, and we look forward to the long-awaited Microsoft Dictation and Microsoft Voice, both of which we've seen work—on videotape—with our brows furrowed in disbelief. We'll have that holodeck yet! But when it comes to accessibility in Windows, there's no need to wait; a startling range of accommodation is right on your Windows CD. It's not installed by default, though, so let's begin by installing it.

# Installing Accessibility Options

To install Accessibility Options:

1. Go to **Control Panel** and double-click **Add/Remove Programs**. Pick the **Windows Setup** tab.

2. Check the **Accessibility** check box. You may need to double-click it to make sure that the checkbox contains a black checkmark on a white background, rather than a black checkmark on a gray background.

3. Click **OK**. This will install both Accessibility Options and Accessibility Tools. You may be prompted to insert the Windows 98 CD into your computer's CD drive.

There are two ways of using the Accessibility options in Windows. One, the **Accessibility Wizard**, takes you through configuration step by step, but only presents some of the available options. The other, **Control Panel\Accessibility Options**, operates with Properties sheets and requires a little more work, but gives you every available choice. Most of the Accessibility settings in Windows 98 can be set either way.

First we'll discuss the ways that each method leads you to the options, then look at the options themselves.

## Accessibility Wizard

Default path: `Start Menu\Programs\Accessories\Accessibility\`
`Accessibility Wizard`

The Accessibility Wizard takes you through a decision tree and presents only the features you need. It also lets you save your settings to a diskette so that you can install them on another computer. Options take effect on the fly so that you don't have to, for example, wait until you finish Setup to get the large type.

**Welcome Screen.**   The initial screen sets font size.

The screen in Figure B.1 lets you set Small Fonts, Large Fonts, or Large Fonts with the Magnifier, so you can read the rest comfortably. We'll discuss the Magnifier lower down, but refer to it now if you think you might need a portion of the screen enlarged.

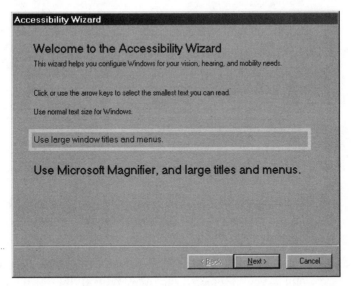

**Figure B.1**

*Accessibility Wizard
Welcome screen*

One mildly confusing point is that, if you select **Use Microsoft Magnifier**... here, you get the very largest titles, which may be too big for your taste. For smaller titles, select **Use large window titles**... on the Welcome screen, and check the **Use Microsoft Magnifier** checkbox on the Text Size screen, which seems like it would do the same thing, but it doesn't. Click **Next**.

**Text Size Screen.** The **Text Size** screen (Figure B.2) confirms your choices.

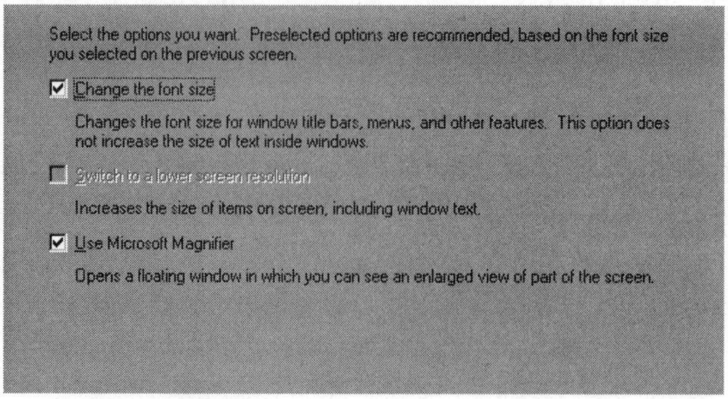

Select the options you want. Preselected options are recommended, based on the font size you selected on the previous screen.

☑ Change the font size

Changes the font size for window title bars, menus, and other features. This option does not increase the size of text inside windows.

☐ Switch to a lower screen resolution

Increases the size of items on screen, including window text.

☑ Use Microsoft Magnifier

Opens a floating window in which you can see an enlarged view of part of the screen.

*Figure B.2*

*Text Size dialog*

**Set Wizard Options.** Click **Next** to reach the object of the exercise, the **Set Wizard Options** dialog, and check the appropriate checkbox:

> **I am blind or have difficulty seeing...** takes you to **Icon Size**, **Size of Window Elements**, and **Color Schemes** (High Contrast)

> **I am deaf or have difficulty hearing...** takes you to **SoundSentry** and **ShowSounds**.

> **I have difficulty using...** takes you to **StickyKeys**, **BounceKeys**, **ToggleKeys**, **Extra Keyboard Help**, **MouseKeys** (two screens), **Mouse Cursor**, **Mouse Button Settings**, **Mouse Speed**, and **Mouse Trails**.

> **I want to set administrative options** takes you to **Automatic Timeouts**, **Default Accessibility Settings**, and **Save Settings to File**.

The **Restore Default Settings** button restores the defaults of any settings changed by these checkboxes, but doesn't alter the font or Magnifier setting you selected on the opening screens.

## Accessibility Options (or Properties)

Default path: `Start Menu\Settings\Control Panel\Accessibility Options`

Well, it's about time they gave us all the clicks and pops! How long did they mean us to get by with that skimpy Wizard? (Juuuust kidding ...)

*Figure B.3*

*Accessibility Options icon*

Accessibility
Options

Whoa! This Properties sheet is backwards; **Keyboard** is the tab that opens with the Properties sheet, and **General** is all the way at the right. Not a ding in the functionality, just worth noticing.

 Almost all the options in the Properties tabs work the same way: click the checkbox to turn on the option, then profile the option with the **Settings** button if there is one. The only exception is **Automatic reset** on the General tab, which is called **Automatic Timeouts** in the Wizard, naturally.

**Keyboard Tab.** The **Keyboard** tab (Figure B.4) takes you to **StickyKeys**, **FilterKeys** (a superset of BounceKeys), **ToggleKeys**, and **Extra Keyboard Help**.

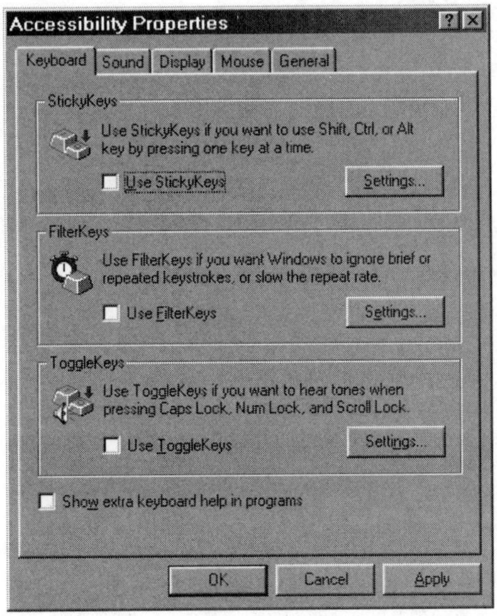

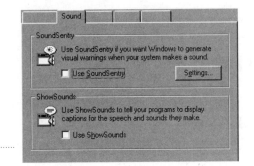

*Figure B.4*

*Keyboard tab*

**Sound Tab.** The **Sound** tab (Figure B.5) takes you to **SoundSentry** and **ShowSounds**.

*Figure B.5*

*Sound tab*

**Display Tab.** The **Display** tab (Figure B.6) takes you to **High Contrast**.

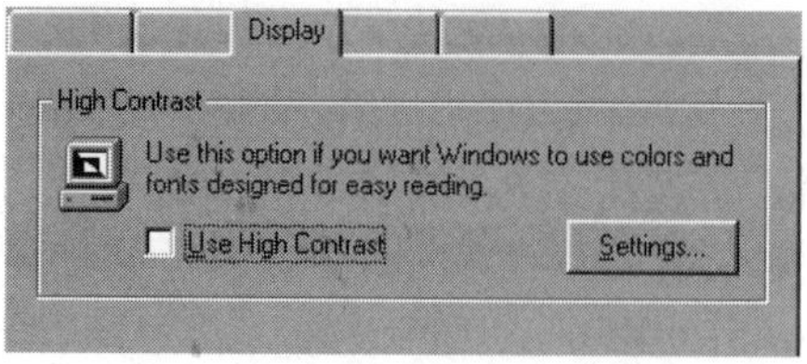

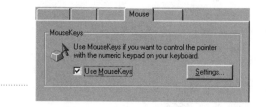

**Mouse Tab.** The **Mouse** tab (Figure B.7) takes you to **MouseKeys**.

*Figure B.7*

*Mouse tab*

**General Tab.** The **General** tab (Figure B.8) takes you to **Automatic reset** (Timeouts), **Notification**, and **SerialKey devices**.

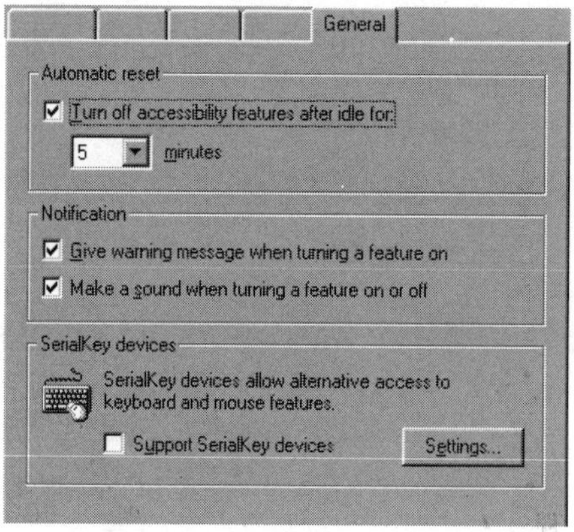

*Figure B.8*

*General tab*

# Option Settings

## Monitoring Status

If you want to monitor the status of your keyboard Accessibility, the enabled options are sitting in the Taskbar next to the clock (Figure B.9). (Shown:

Figure B.10

Status Window

Figure B.9

Status on Taskbar

MouseKeys, FilterKeys, and StickyKeys.) Since they could be more visible, you may want to have them displayed in the Status Window instead. Right-click on any icon in the Taskbar, pick **Show Status Window** from its Context Menu, and the Status Window (Figure B.10) will pop up on your screen.

The Status Window is a mixed blessing. Its two drawbacks are that it's Always, but *always,* On Top, which should be settable, and that it's not resizable. The really neat property is that the icons in it aren't just pictures; you can click on them to get a Settings menu.

## StickyKeys

StickyKeys lets you press keys in succession and produce the effect of pressing them simultaneously. For example, it you want to bring up the Start Menu with the keyboard, you'd ordinarily hold down Ctrl and press Esc. With StickyKeys enabled, this is the sequence of events:

StickyKeys shows in the Taskbar as "unpressed" (Figure B.12a).

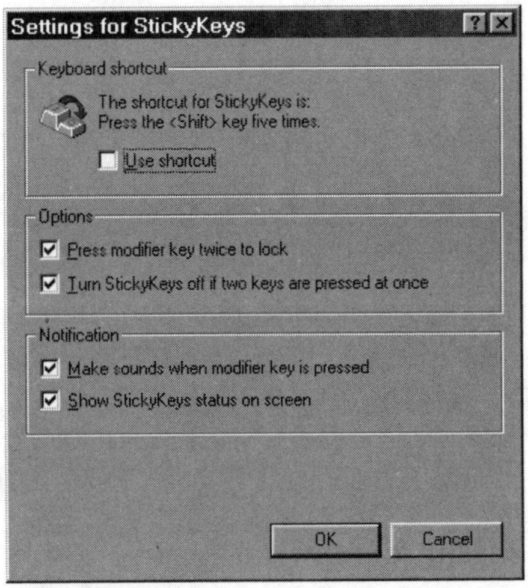

Figure B.11

StickyKeys settings

You press Ctrl and release it. StickyKeys shows in the Taskbar as "Ctrl pressed" (Figure B.12c).

You press Esc which combines with the stored Ctrl to make Ctrl Esc. The Start Menu pops up and, in the Taskbar, StickyKeys returns to "unpressed."

**Settings.** StickyKeys has these settings (Figure B.11):

- **Keyboard shortcut.** If checked, StickyKeys can be turned on by pressing the Shift key five times.

- **Double-lock.** If checked, pressing $\boxed{\text{Shift}}$, $\boxed{\text{Ctrl}}$, or $\boxed{\text{Alt}}$ twice in succession locks it; pressing it a third time unlocks it.

- **Cancel StickyKeys.** If checked, StickyKeys is turned off when two of the keys it modifies (say, $\boxed{\text{Ctrl}}$ and $\boxed{\text{Shift}}$) are pressed at the same time.

- **Notification.** If checked and StickyKeys is enabled, pressing $\boxed{\text{Shift}}$, $\boxed{\text{Ctrl}}$, or $\boxed{\text{Alt}}$ will make a sound.

- **Show status.** If checked and StickyKeys is enabled, its status is displayed in the Taskbar (Figure B.12a–d) or, optionally, in the Status Window.

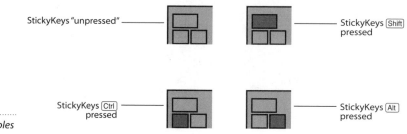

StickyKeys "unpressed" ————————

———————— StickyKeys $\boxed{\text{Shift}}$ pressed

StickyKeys $\boxed{\text{Ctrl}}$ pressed ————

———— StickyKeys $\boxed{\text{Alt}}$ pressed

**Figure B.12**

*StickyKeys examples*

 For detailed information on StickyKeys, BounceKeys, RepeatKeys, and SlowKeys, see the Windows 98 Resource Kit.

## FilterKeys

If you tend to "bounce" on keys or strike keys accidentally, FilterKeys can help by tailoring your keyboard's action and repeat rate to your typing style.

**Figure B.14**

*FilterKeys icon*

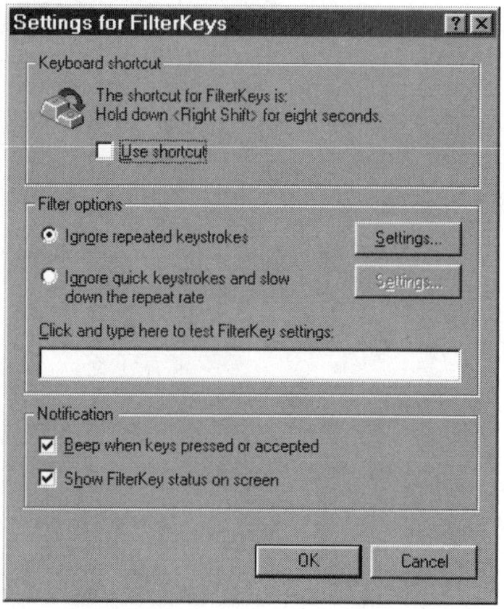

**Settings for FilterKeys**

Keyboard shortcut

The shortcut for FilterKeys is:
Hold down <Right Shift> for eight seconds.

☐ Use shortcut

Filter options

⦿ Ignore repeated keystrokes          Settings...

○ Ignore quick keystrokes and slow          Settings...
down the repeat rate

Click and type here to test FilterKey settings:

Notification

☑ Beep when keys pressed or accepted

☑ Show FilterKey status on screen

OK          Cancel

**Figure B.13**

*FilterKeys settings*

### Settings

- **Keyboard shortcut.** If checked, FilterKeys can be turned on by pressing the [Right Shift] key for eight seconds.

- **Filter options.** If **Ignore repeated keystrokes** is clicked, keystrokes will be ignored if the interval between them is shorter than specified in the Advanced Settings dialog (Figure B.15). The shortest value is 0.5 second; default is 0.7 second; longer values are 1, 1.5, and 2 seconds.

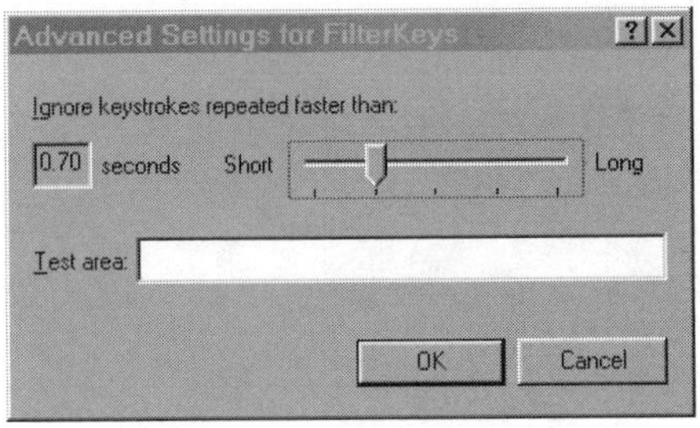

*Figure B.15*

*Advanced key repeat*

If **Ignore quick keystrokes** is clicked, repeat delays and rates in the Advanced Settings dialog (Figure B.16) will override matching values in the Keyboard Control Panel. **Repeat delay** (shortest value 0.3 second; default 0.7 second; maximum 2 seconds) is the length of time a key must be held down before it starts repeating. Repeat can also be turned off. **Repeat rate** (shortest value 0.3 second; default 1 second; maximum 2 seconds) is the interval at which the key will repeat as long as it's held down. **SlowKeys** (shortest value 0; default 1 second; maximum 2 seconds) is the length of time a key must be held down before the keystroke goes to the computer.

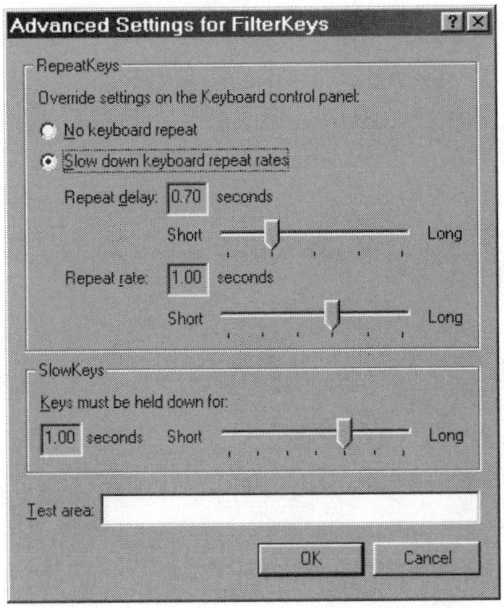

*Figure B.16*

*Advanced key rate*

- **Notification.** If checked and FilterKeys is enabled, pressing any key will make a sound.

- **Show status.** If checked and FilterKeys is enabled, its status is displayed in the Taskbar (Figure B.14) or, optionally, in the Status Window.

## ToggleKeys

If you enable ToggleKeys, your keyboard will chirp when you press [Caps Lock], [Num Lock], and [Scroll Lock].

### Setting

- **Keyboard shortcut.** If checked, ToggleKeys can be turned on by pressing the [Num Lock] key for five seconds.

## Keyboard Help

If this box is checked, certain applications with supplementary Help files will give you extra information about using the keyboard.

## SoundSentry

SoundSentry substitutes visual warnings and cues for the sound cues that applications make.

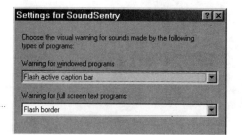

**Settings.** As your warning for windowed programs, you can choose from **Flash active caption bar**, **Flash active window**, **Flash desktop**, or **None**.

As your warning for full-screen text programs, you can choose from **Flash characters**, **Flash border**, **Flash display**, or **None**.

## ShowSounds

ShowSounds displays captions for system sounds and spoken messages. It has no settings; it's either on or off.

## High Contrast

If you check this box, Windows will override the system fonts and colors set in Control Panel with the ones that you select in **Settings for High Contrast**. If you uncheck the box, the settings in Control Panel will be used.

 The implementation of this, unfortunately, is less than perfect. If you check the box for High Contrast, apply the settings, uncheck the box, and apply them again, they may not revert completely to what Control Panel says they should be. We ended up with postmodern purple and sage-green title bars, which were actually refreshing. However, this does underscore the importance of making sure that your preferences in the Appearance tab of Display Properties are saved as a Scheme. If you've been living with 32-bit Windows for years, tweaking your Appearance settings at random, and not saving the result, you'll probably give up on getting your exact settings back—there are too many of them.

**Settings.** High Contrast has these settings (Figure B.19):

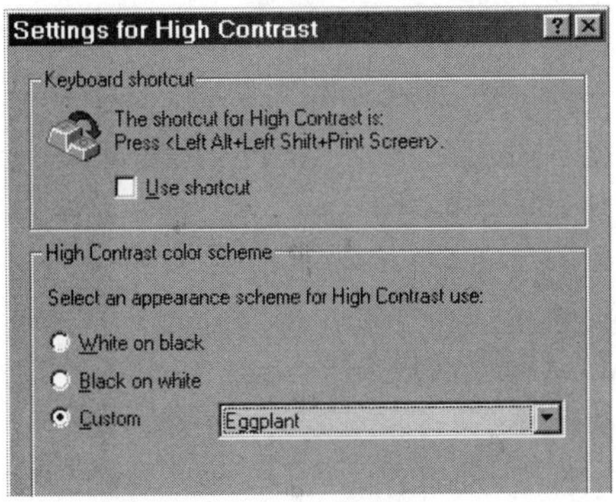

*Figure B.19*

*Settings for High Contrast*

• **Keyboard shortcut.** If checked, High Contrast can be turned on by pressing Left Alt Left Shift Print Screen.

- **Color scheme.** Click the top dot for white on black, the middle dot for black on white, or the bottom dot for your choice of the 27 standard Windows color schemes in Display Properties Appearance.

## MouseKeys

If you check this box, you can use the number pad on the keyboard for mouse control.

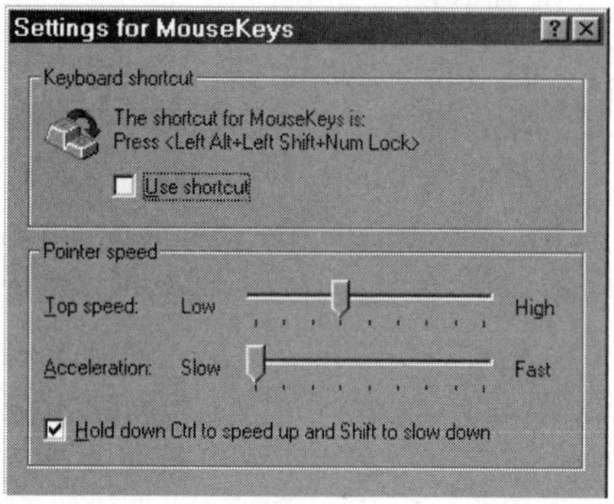

*Figure B.20*

*MouseKeys settings*

*Figure B.21*

*MouseKeys icon (Either button or both may be shaded)*

**Keyboard shortcut.** If checked, MouseKeys can be turned on by pressing Left Alt Left Shift Num Lock.

**Pointer speed\Top speed** governs how quickly the pointer moves when you hold down a direction key and MouseKeys is turned on. This doesn't do you much good unless you know which keys move the pointer. They don't seem to be listed in the Properties sheet but they are listed in the Accessibility Wizard and, of course, here; see below.

**Pointer speed\Acceleration** governs how quickly the pointer accelerates to the speed set by **Top speed.**

**Hold down Ctrl to speed up and Shift to slow down** changes **Acceleration** from fixed to dynamic; you can change it with the Ctrl and Shift keys.

**Use MouseKeys when NumLock is On/Off:** Globally, if you click this On, your keypad is a pointer pad and a cursor pad. If you click it Off, your keypad is a pointer pad and a numeric pad. If your keyboard (like most keyboards today) has a separate, duplicate set of cursor keys, these aren't affected by MouseKeys, so if you want a pointer pad, a numeric pad, and cursor keys, leave this clicked Off.

Because the Shortcut key also toggles the residual state of [Num Lock], this is more complicated than you might think. In other words: Assume that this setting is clicked On, MouseKeys is off, [Num Lock] is on, and you press [Left Alt] [Left Shift] [Num Lock] to turn MouseKeys on. With the same keystrokes you turned [Num Lock] off, so you turned MouseKeys off, again. If you click this setting to Off, you have roughly the same problem in the opposite direction. It would be nicer if the Shortcut key left the underlying state of [Num Lock] alone, but we're not sure that's possible in the hardware.

**Show MouseKey status on screen,** meaning in the Taskbar or the Status Window: Given the above complexity, we recommend this particularly in the case of MouseKeys. Crossover toggling is even worse if you can't see whether MouseKeys is on or off.

Now, the highly intuitive pointer keys—when you look at the pad you'll see what we mean:

| | |
|---|---|
| [←][↑][→][↓] (Arrow) keys | Slide the pointer up, down, left, right |
| [Home], [Pg Up] | Slide the pointer up-left, up-right |
| [End], [Page Down] | Slide the pointer down-left, down-right |
| Keypad-[5] | Select (single-click) |
| two taps of Keypad-[5] | Double-click |
| Gray [+] | Double-click |
| Gray [/] | Keypad-5 is left-click |
| Gray [*] | Keypad-5 is both-click |
| Gray [−] | Keypad-5 is right-click |
| [Ctrl] with [←][↑][→][↓] (Arrow) keys | Jump the pointer up, down, left, right; one jump is about the width specified in Display Properties\Item\Icon Spacing |
| [Control] with [Home], [Pg Up], [End], [Page Down] | Jump the pointer diagonally |
| [Control] with Keypad-[5] | Multiple select |
| [Insert] | Drag lock. If a button is locked, the Taskbar icon shows it as filled, rather than shaded. |
| [Delete] | Drag release |

Frankly, these assignments are slick enough that we can see turning Mouse-Keys on, at times, even when using a pointing device doesn't pose a problem. And that leads us to the big improvement in Windows 98 MouseKeys: You can turn MouseKeys on without turning your mouse or trackball off!

 All the above assumes that your Desktop settings are classic Windows. If you have MouseKeys on, switch to the Active Desktop, and start playing with things like substituting single-click for double-click, you might get some weird interactions. We didn't test every possible keystroke. You can navigate through the Active Desktop by jumping from item to item with ⟨Tab⟩ and ⟨Shift⟩⟨Tab⟩; a one-pixel-wide border appears around the currently selected item.

## General Tab

The **General** tab, as usual, ends up with everything that doesn't fit in a category.

**Automatic reset** (Timeouts) lets you turn off the Control Panel Accessibility features after the computer has been idle for a settable period, from 5 minutes (the default) to 30 minutes in 5-minute steps. This is handy if someone who needs Accessibility is sharing the computer with someone who doesn't.

 If you need user security when you switch users, or if the Accessibility options on a shared computer include some that can't be switched off through Control Panel, you can also make User Profiles for the sharing users, and add Accessibility options as needed. See the material on User Profiles in Chapter 10.

**Notification** shows warnings or plays sounds when you toggle Accessibility features.

**SerialKey.**  SerialKey lets you set the port and baud rate (serial communications rate) for an attached alternative pointing device, like an Eyegaze unit or a head-pointer. These devices encode keystrokes and mouse movements as serial bit streams that can be sent through the port. You have your choice here of COM1 through COM4 and baud rates of 300 to 19,200.

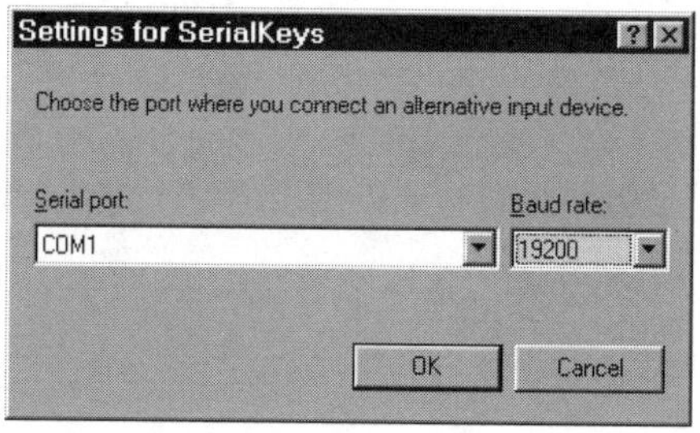

*Figure B.22*

*SerialKey Settings*

# Other Options

There's so much more Accessibility stuff scattered around Windows 98 that, if we might be so bold, it can be hard to remember where it all is. Certainly, remember the **Accessibility** dialog on the General tab of View\Internet Options in Internet Explorer. But there's one more almost undocumented, and really cool, pair of keyboard options:

## LH/RH Dvorak

In **Control Panel\Keyboard\Language\Properties**, at the bottom of the layout list, there are two layouts called **LH Dvorak** and **RH Dvorak**. They look like this:

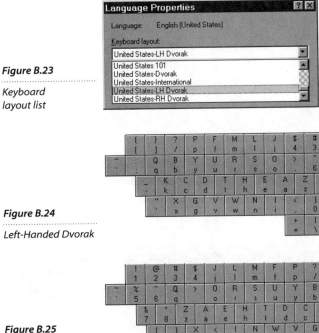

*Figure B.23*

Keyboard layout list

*Figure B.24*

Left-Handed Dvorak

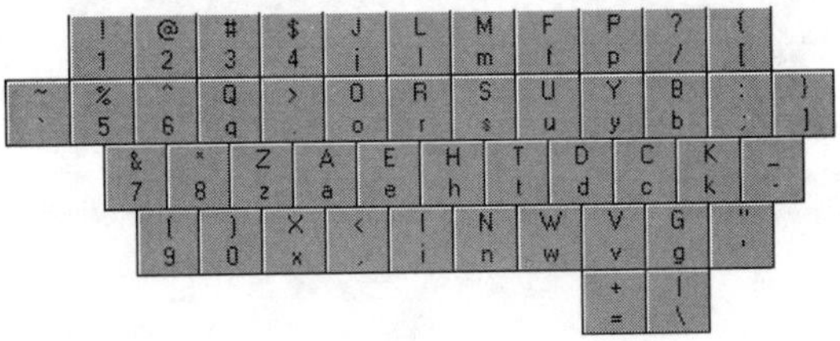

*Figure B.25*

Right-Handed Dvorak

These keyboard layouts, by the self-same Dvorak of the undersung Dvorak keyboard, have been carefully optimized for typing with the left hand only or the right hand only. There is no way to like one-handed typing, but a better layout at least makes it easier. Then again, so does voice recognition software.

# Scalable Interface

You can adjust the sizes of window titles, scroll bars, borders, menu text, and other common controls through the Accessibility Wizard or the **Appearance** tab of Display Properties.

# Customizable Pointer

If you have trouble seeing or following the mouse pointer, you can improve visibility by choosing:

- Pointer size.

- Pointer color.

- Pointer speed.

- Pointer trails.

- Pointer animation.

Some of these options are installed as Windows defaults, and the rest can be installed from the Windows CD. See Appendix H of the Windows 98 Resource Kit for details.

# Magnifier
Default path: **Start Menu\Programs\Accessories\Accessibility\ Magnifier**

Microsoft Magnifier enlarges a portion of the screen display to make it easier to read. Intended for people with limited vision, this is also handy during demos.

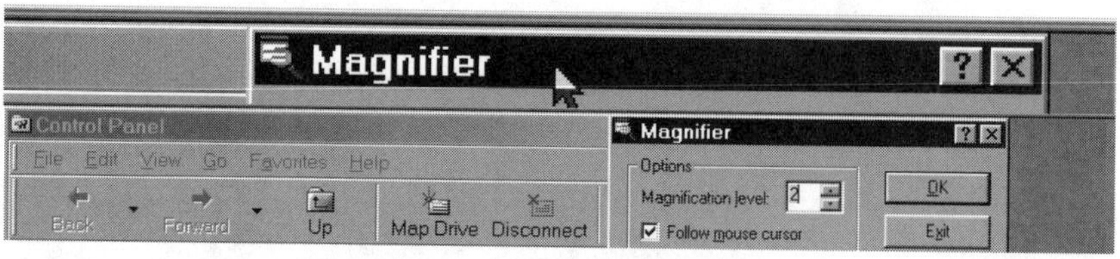

**Figure B.26**

*Magnifier in use*

You can:

- Magnify a region of the screen from one to nine times the standard display size; the default is 2 (Figure B.26). The magnified region is a screenshot; the focus for the cursor, keyboard, and pointer is in the unmagnified region.

- Follow the mouse cursor, the keyboard focus, the text editing focus or any combination of these three.

- Invert colors for contrast.

- Resize and relocate the display area.

### Control Panel

*Magnification Level.* Set magnification level with the spin buttons, or use Win↑ to increase it, Win↓ to decrease it.

*Tracking Options.* Set tracking options with the checkboxes, or use Win Pg Dn to toggle mouse tracking.

*Invert Colors.* Use the checkbox, or toggle colors with Win Pg Up.

**Window Sizing and Position.** For sizing, touch the mouse pointer to the edge of the magnification window. It will become a double-headed arrow; left-click and drag. You can't make the magnifier portion bigger than half the screen.

For positioning, left-click inside the magnified region and drag. It defaults to docking at the top of the screen, but you can dock it at any edge, or break it loose like a floating Toolbar (Figure B.28)

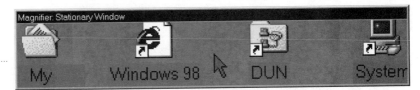

### Magnifier Context Menu

Right-clicking inside the magnified region brings up a Context Menu with three options:

- Open the Magnifier Control Panel.

- Copy the contents of the Magnifier to the Clipboard.

- Exit Magnifier.

### There's More

We've covered the bases, but even now, we haven't considered the full depth of the Accessibility Tools. If you want to know more, browse to **http://www.microsoft.com/enable,** or read Appendix H of the *Windows 98 Resource Kit.*

# Summary

Windows 98 has a huge selection of Accessibility tools, selectable either through the Accessibility Wizard or the Accessibility Options Control Panel. With these, no matter what special circumstances you may face, you can configure a computer to suit yourself as well as possible.

# Appendix C

# Dial-Up Networking without Tears

Dial-Up Networking is definitely one of the coolest parts of Windows—especially Windows 98. Once it's completely configured, it runs flawlessly, gives terrific throughput, and is easy to use. Accomplishing the configuration is the only hard part; the process can be mysterious and, unless you're thoroughly prepared beforehand, frustrating too. The Net has responded by sprouting a crop of shareware utilities that automate the configuration to various degrees; but it's perfectly possible to sail through the process with nothing but a modem, the Windows 98 software, and enough information from your ISP. Assuming you have Windows 98 and the modem, just follow these step-by-step instructions for gratifying results.

# Have You Bought a Modem?

If you're looking for:

**A 56K modem,** find out whether your ISP's connections support the 3Com ("x2") architecture or the Rockwell ("K56flex") architecture, then buy one to match. Your ISP will be glad to tell you which architecture you need, and probably suggest a modem brand, too. (Ours was kind enough to recommend Zoom Telephonics, whose Zoom K56flex Internal is a smooth operator and provides exceptionally robust connections.)

Incidentally, your "56K" modem won't reach out and touch that data rate in the real world. To begin with, regulations on maximum transmission voltage limit download speeds to about 53K even in theory. Also, you're seriously toying with the perceived maximum data rate for analog data transmission over POTS. A well-greased, short-haul ftp connection between "56K" modems will deliver a steady 50K either direction. Using HTTP, which is slower, you'll see 44K to 48K. And to those few of you who retort "I get *much* faster connections than that!" we re-retort that we surveyed a *lot* of people about their reliable data rates.

If you bought a new computer with a modem in it, your situation's reversed— you need to find an ISP that can get along with the type of modem you purchased. The ITU-T standard for 56K communications, V.90, has been set, and this nonsense with dueling modems will soon be over; but just because compatible hardware is available doesn't mean your ISP has it installed.

**An ISDN adapter,** we have no particular recommendation although there are several good ones. Remember that you may have to deal with both an ISDN provider—which is probably your phone company—and an Internet provider.

**An *x*DSL adapter,** they're only available in a few parts of the country and the technology is too unsettled to discuss. We do hear, though, that the monthly teaser rates in the newspaper ads are nowhere *near* the final cost of service.

**Other options,** refer to "Buying and Maintaining Hardware" in Chapter 11, "Data Communications."

# Have You Installed the Modem?

If not, do it now, using the manufacturer's instructions. When you reboot after securing the card in the slot or the cable to the port, Windows should detect it and report its type; almost all the modems you can buy today are Plug and Play. (This means that they're supported by the Windows universal modem driver, but the manufacturer may supply a diskette with an .INF mini-driver updated to wring every molecule of speed out of the hardware chipset. If so, the installation instructions will be in the docs or in a README file on the diskette.)

Having your modem completely installed and tested is a tremendous help when you're configuring Dial-Up Networking, because if the hardware's solid, you can assume that any problem you're having is confined to the software.

**Control Panel\Modems** will tell you that your modem is installed, and the **Diagnostics** tab will tell you whether it's responding correctly. For the procedure, see "Modem Diagnostics" in Chapter 11.

# On The Line to Your ISP

Find out the following things from your ISP.

## What Number Will You Be Dialing in On?

This is important, because it will depend on your modem type. ISPs that support a wide variety of modems usually have at least four phone numbers: one for ISDN, one for 56K, one for 33.6 and 28.8, and one for 28.8 and below. If your ISP supports both 56K architectures, they'll have yet another number.

## What IPs Will You Be Using, or Do You Care?

IPs are the Internet Protocol numbers that every computer on the Internet uses. While your computer is connected to the Net, it needs one (or more) too. An **IP address** is a series of four numbers called **octets**, separated by dots; the smallest possible IP is **0.0.0.0**, and the largest is **255.255.255.255.** (This looks odd, but remember that 255 is FF hex.) Your ISP will assign your computer either a **static IP**, which is a number that the computer keeps and uses for every connection, or a **dynamic IP**, a number that the computer requests from the server as it needs it, so it's different for every connection. If you have a static IP, you need to know what it is; if you have a dynamic IP, you don't, at least not right now.

## What DNS IPs Does Your ISP Use?

The DNS (Domain Name Server) is the computer keeping track of the huge list that correlates domain names, like "winbible.com," with their associated IPs, like "157.24.208.1." Every Internet provider has at least one DNS, and it's standard practice to have two physically identical servers that both provide domain-name service, so that if one goes down (stranger things have happened), the other one goes right on providing and your ISP isn't abruptly a black hole. If you have dynamic IP, then there's an outside chance you'll have dynamic DNS too, but usually your DNS address is fixed even if your IP address moves around. If you have two DNS addresses, they'll be close together.

## What's Your User ID?

Your "user ID" is the part of your personal Internet address that goes before the @ sign. It has to be unique for each ISP, so that two people with the same ISP don't randomly get each other's e-mail, but you get to pick out any (tasteful) ID for yourself that fulfills that requirement.

## What's Your Password?

An ISP password is generally eight characters long, is case-sensitive, and is some horrifically unmemorable mixture of upper- and lower-case letters, numerals, and punctuation marks; an example would be **f!Ke7$Lj**, and you may not get to pick out your own. That being so, it will be even more difficult to remember, so keep it written down on a piece of paper in some place only you know about. Don't keep it on your computer.

# Connectoid Setup

 *Connectoid* is Microsoft-ese for a single Dial-Up Networking connection profile, meaning the icon and all the stuff wrapped up in it.

You now have all the information you'll need to set up a Dial-Up Networking profile, so let's proceed.

Double-click on **My Computer. Dial-Up Networking** (Figure C.1) is one of the standard included objects in the folder.

**Figure C.1**

*Dial-Up Networking*

Dial-Up
Networking

## Connection Wizard

Double-click on **Dial-Up Networking**, then on **Make New Connection.**

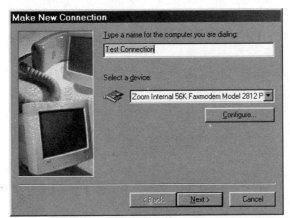

**Figure C.2**

*Make New
Connection Wizard*

Our suggestion for the name of the computer you're dialing would be some form of your provider's name and the speed of the connection, like "Marslink-56." This will be the title of the finished icon or any shortcut you make. Fill it in and Tab to **Select a device**. This should contain the name of the modem you've already set up; your computer may include more than one device that Windows thinks you can use to connect to a network, in which case this will be a drop-down list, so pick the device you'll actually use to make a dial-up connection. For now, leave the **Configure...** dialog alone—you can go back to it later if these settings need changing. Click **Next**.

**Codes and Numbers.** Fill in the area code and the number you want to call; if it's your local area code, you'll get a chance to change this setting later. Check the **Area code** drop-down list to see if the appropriate area code has already been entered in some other dialog. Pick the country code from the drop-down list. Click **Next**.

**Tweaking.** Since the name of the connection is highlighted, you'd think you could edit it here, but you can't! Click **Finish**; you have some more setup to do. Right-click on the new icon and click **Properties.**

# Connectoid Properties

## General Tab

Everything on the **General** tab is, presumably, as you filled it in during configuration. If you filled in your home area code and you don't want the modem to
dial it, uncheck the **Use area code and Dialing Properties** box.

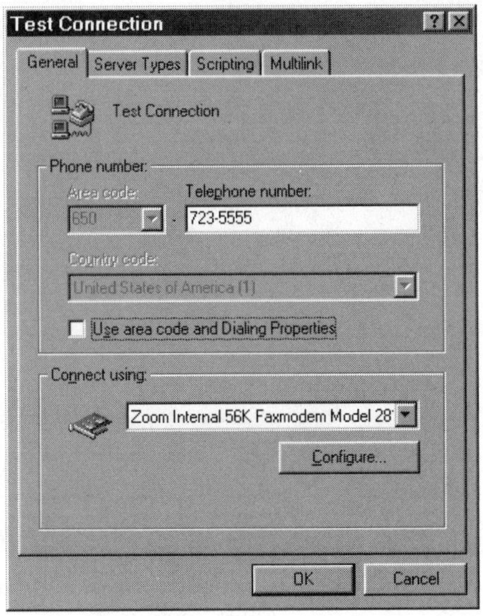

*Figure C.5*

*General tab*

It's too bad that the area code and Dialing Properties are linked this way, since
you probably want to keep your access to Dialing Properties (prefixes, suffixes,
disable-call-waiting, calling card, etc.), but if you uncheck this box, the **Dial
Properties...** button on the main calling dialog is grayed out. If you ask us—
unless your computer is a laptop—you're better off entering a blank area code
on the General tab and keeping the **Use area code...** box checked, so that
Dialing Properties is always available.

## Server Types Tab

This is where your Internet (or intranet) clockwork lives, and where most of
the settings that you got from your ISP (or sysadmin) will be entered.

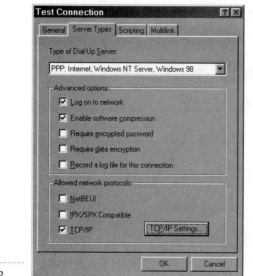

**Figure C.6**

Server Types tab

**Type of Dial-Up Server** follows this table:

| Server type (Protocol) | MS explanation | Meaning in people-talk: You're dialing into a ... |
|---|---|---|
| **CSLIP (TCP/IP)** | UNIX connection with IP header compression | UNIX server with a protocol that's an improvement over SLIP, but not as new as PPP. ISPs with CSLIP are rare, but you may have this on your intranet server; ask your sysadmin. (Tip: You have to scroll the list to see this one.) |
| **NRN (IPX/SPX)** | NetWare Connect, v. 1.0 and 1.1 | DOS intranet server running the Novell NetWare dial-up protocol. If the server is running NetWare components, your computer is too. |
| **PPP (TCP/IP, NetBEUI, IPX/SPX)** | Internet, NT Server, Windows 98 | server running Point-to-Point Protocol, the newest and most versatile UNIX-compatible protocol. Most ISPs now use this, as will any computer running Windows 95, 98, NT 3.51, or 4.0, and configured as a dial-up server. |
| **SLIP (TCP/IP)** | UNIX connection | server running Serial Line Internet Protocol; the oldest and least flexible UNIX dial-up protocol, now fading from commercial use. Don't take this if your ISP offers it. |
| **Win 3.x (NetBEUI)** | WfWg and NT 3.1 | Windows for Workgroups 3.11 or Windows NT 3.1 dial-up server running Remote Access Service (RAS) |

If you change your Server Type while you're connected, the type won't change till you launch your next connection.

### Region: Advanced options

**Log on to network** checkbox: When you connect to the network, if this box is checked, Dial-Up Networking will try to log on. Two things are true:

The host network has to be running a Microsoft operating system, which may be correct if you're dialing into an intranet, but almost certainly isn't (yet) for a commercial ISP. If you log into the network using a separate network layer—the NetWare command-line prompt, for example—you can uncheck this box because you won't need it.

The default dial-up user name and password are the ones you use to log on to Windows, which aren't the right ones for your ISP. Bottom line: For a provider account, uncheck this box.

**Enable software compression** checkbox: Turns on compression for data being sent and received, which can increase throughput by 10% to 30%. So far as we know, you can check this box and leave it checked, because Windows is smart enough to turn on compression only if the server offers compatible compression.

**Require encrypted password** checkbox: Tells Windows to encrypt your password on the fly, so that although you type it in as clear text, the server will receive the encrypted password it's expecting. The server has to be configured to accept encrypted passwords. This option can work with either user-level or share-level security on Microsoft networks or with user-level security on NetWare networks. This box is blank by default.

**Region: Allowed network protocols.** In theory, you should be able to check only the box for the single specific protocol of your sessions with this server, and uncheck the others. In practice, we've encountered some trouble with this habit, but *try it anyway*. If you can get the connectoid to run with only the protocol in use, your connection will originate slightly faster. See "Tuning Your Connectoid" below.

| Check this box ... | if you're connecting to ... |
| --- | --- |
| *NetBEUI* | Any older Windows server or, optionally, any Microsoft server configured to accept it |
| *IPX/SPX Compatible* | Any Novell NetWare server or, optionally, any Microsoft server configured to accept it |
| *TCP/IP* | Any SLIP, CSLIP, PPP, or 32-bit Windows server except Windows NT 3.1—meaning possibly your intranet server, but definitely your ISP |

**TCP/IP Settings.**  Specifically with reference to an ISP:

- You'll probably leave **Server assigned IP address** clicked.

- Most ISPs will require **Specify name server addresses**, and if they do, there will be two of them at least.

- TCP/IP servers overwhelmingly have **DNS** servers; **WINS** compatibility will be confined almost entirely to intranets.

- **Use IP header compression** and **Use default gateway...** are usually both checked.

All of these settings, and particularly the server IP addresses if those are hard-wired, will be on the stapled pages or blurry fax that you get from your ISP. If such materials weren't part of the package, support should be a phone call away. If you end up with nothing but voicemail, think about signing up with a different ISP. *Service* is ISP's middle name, or it should be!

 Howls of outrage from the providers: "Whaddayawant for $19.95/$14.95/$9.95 a month?" Well, if I can't get solutions to my problems, I'm a bonehead for paying even that much – right? Unless you the user are stuck in an area served by only a single ISP, you have every right to sign up with the one that gives you the best support.

**You might not realize how many ISP's there *are* in your area; at this writing there are roughly 5,000 in the United States and Canada. Head for a computer with Web access and browse to http://www.thelist.internet.com. (Thank you, Mecklermedia.)**

**Scripting and Multilink.**  We've never seen an ISP account that would require you to mess with either of these. If you're setting up an intranet account, you may need to visit the **Scripting** tab, but your sysadmin will help you with that.

**Finishing Properties.**  Click **OK.** You're done with Properties and almost finished with Setup. Your new connectoid's icon will appear in the Dial-Up Networking folder. Double-click on it.

# Connect To

## Name and Password

In the Connect To dialog (Figure C.7) fill in your ISP user name. Hit `Tab` and fill in your ISP password. (All you'll see is asterisks.) Check the **Save password** box. Click **Connect**.

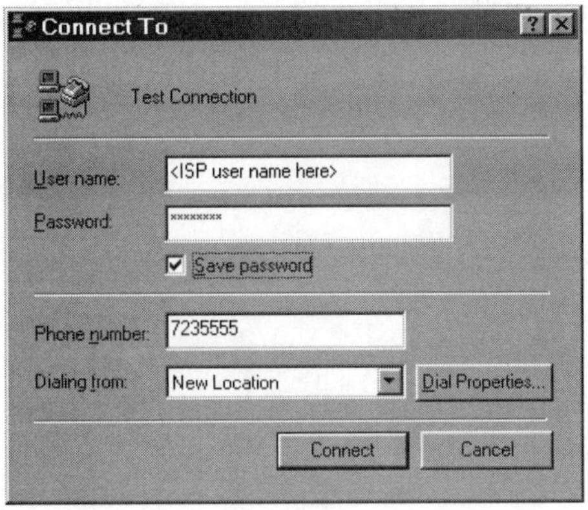

**Figure C.7**

*Connect To dialog*

# Connecting

If all is in readiness, Figure C.8 will appear and you should hear the modem dial out.

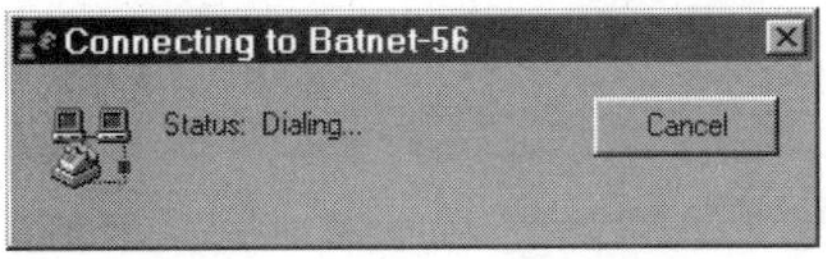

**Figure C.8**

*Dialing advice*

The modem will negotiate with your ISP's modem (Figure C.9) and establish who you are.

**Figure C.9**

*Negotiation advice*

You'll be logged on to your ISP's server and your Internet connection has begun. Fire up Internet Explorer, your FTP or mail client, or whatever Internet application you want to use.

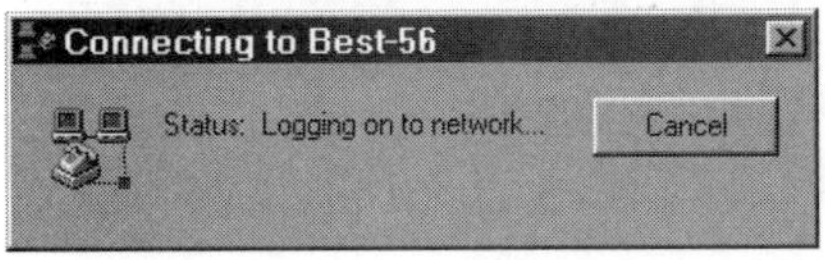

**Figure C.10**

*Logon advice*

## While You're Connected

A small icon of two connected computers (Figure C.11) will appear in your System Tray.

*Figure C.11*

*Connectoid icon*

If you hover your mouse pointer over the icon, you'll get a report (Figure C.12) of connection traffic and speed.

*Figure C.12*

*Connectoid report*

Right-click the icon and you'll get two choices (Figure C.13), **Disconnect** and **Status**, which looks like this (Figure C.14).

*Figure C.13*

*Connectoid context*

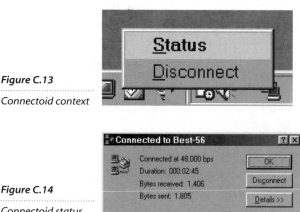

*Figure C.14*

*Connectoid status*

Note that this dialog gives you not only traffic and speed, but the duration of the connection. Finally, if you click **Details** (Figure C.15).

*Figure C.15*

*Connectoid details*

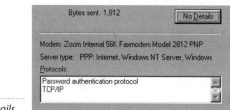

You get information on the modem in use, the server type, and the protocols. Ordinarily, on a standalone computer, this isn't particularly useful. Click **No Details** to get rid of it.

## Are You There Yet?

As in the appendix on Installation, we've just given you an overview of what happens when everything works the way it's supposed to. But would we be giving you the benefit of our whole experience if we didn't describe the things that could go wrong?

**Bring In Da Noize.** All right, so you hit the **Connect** button and something didn't work. Let's assume that you did, as we suggested, run the Modem Diagnostics, so you know the hardware is installed correctly. If your modem is dialing out, but not connecting, the other good free diagnostic tool you have is your ears. So the first question is: While your modem was dialing and negotiating, did you hear anything? You should have.

If you didn't, you need to adjust your modem speaker volume. Unfortunately, you can't do that directly from the connectoid or from Dialing Properties, so go to **Control Panel\Modems**, double-click on the icon, and in the Modems Properties sheet, click the **Properties** button. Slide the **Speaker volume** slider from **Off,** all the way at the left, to the first or second notch. Don't click **OK** yet.

**Check Settings.** While you're here, there are modem settings you should check against the material provided by your ISP. Click the **Connection** tab.

In **Connection preferences,** the most likely values will be the defaults of **Data bits 8**, **Parity None**, and **Stop bits 1**.

In **Call preferences,** you definitely want **Wait for dial tone…** since this is a dial-up connection. **Cancel the call…** should probably be checked, but depending on the speed (or otherwise) with which your ISP's modem pool picks up. Don't bother with **Disconnect a call…** since a competent ISP will cancel a call that hasn't exchanged data for a previously defined number of minutes, without help from you.

Click the Advanced button. Your ISP may have suggested values for **Use error control**, **Required to connect**, **Compress data**, **Use flow control**, and **Extra settings**.

Click **OK** till you're out of Modems Properties.

### The Great Password Bug

 What we're describing here is a cascade of errors that occurred routinely in Windows 95. We haven't been able to reproduce it in Windows 98, but that doesn't mean it can't happen. Just in case this inelegance has survived through one version of Windows to the next, we'll describe what to do about it.

Go back to the Connect To dialog and see if your ISP user name and your password (that is, the asterisks that represent it) are still in their fields.

- **If your name is still there but your password has disappeared:** Windows won't save your password until you make one successful connection with that connectoid. Now that you've checked all your settings, key in your password again and try to connect. If you log on properly and the **Save Password** box is checked, your ID and password should be available from now on.

- **If both your name and your password are grayed out:** Try changing the network name of your computer to your ISP login name. Go to Control Panel\Network, pick the **Identification** tab, and in the **Computer name** field, enter your ISP user name. Click **OK**. Shut down and restart your computer; when you open the connectoid again, enter your password and check the **Save Password** box.

- **If those options are still grayed out:** Use Start Menu\Find Files or Folders to find a file called *<ISPusername>*.PWL. Delete or rename it. Shut down and restart your computer; when you open the connectoid again, recreate your password information.

- **If those options are *still* grayed out:** Use Windows Setup to reinstall Dial-Up Networking. For poorly understood reasons, the second installation is sometimes the charm.

# Tuning Your Connectoid

If your new connectoid is now working fine, a few adjustments will now speed up the logon process. These apply especially if you upgraded to Windows 98 from Windows 95.

Windows 95 Dial-Up Networking connectoids have **Software compression** and **Log On To Network** checked, and NetBEUI, IPX/SPX, and TCP/IP protocols bound to the dial-up adapter.

For an ISP connection, some or most of these are counterproductive. **Log On To Network** means log on to a *Microsoft* network, and saddles your connectoid with the overhead of deciding that the network it's trying to connect to is not a Microsoft network. Uncheck this.

**Software compression** depends on your ISP's system management, but again, if your modem is trying to enforce compression in a way that the other modem doesn't understand, time will be lost. If this option isn't specified on the setup sheet you received from your ISP, call them and find out.

Finally, only TCP/IP should be bound to the dial-up adapter. Windows 98 realizes this, but Windows 95 didn't, and if you upgraded from Windows 95, Windows 98 may have left your old settings intact. To check them:

On the **Configuration** tab of Control Panel\Network, highlight **Dial-Up Adapter**. Click **Properties**.

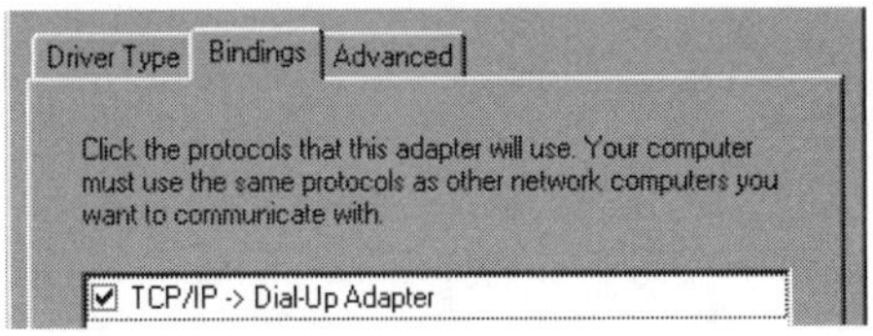

*Figure C.16*

*Bindings tab*

Click the **Bindings** tab and you should see only TCP/IP checked (Figure C.16). If any other protocols appear, uncheck their boxes. Click **OK** on Dial-Up Adapter Properties and **OK** on Network.

# Summary

The process of setting up a TCP/IP Internet connection has been automated to a gratifying degree, as anyone who tried to set one up under Windows 3.*x* or DOS will instantly realize. Even so, a few well-established tips and tricks can spell the difference between success and frustration. If your newly configured Dial-Up Networking connection doesn't succeed the first time, follow the steps in this section; if they don't help, call your ISP and discuss the problem.

# Appendix D

# The *Windows 98 Resource Kit*

In this Appendix, we were going to give an executive summary of the *Windows 98 Resource Kit*. Then we saw one! Now the best we can do is recommend it and point you at it.

The *Windows 98 Resource Kit* could as easily be called the *Windows 98 Advanced Manual*. With nearly 1,600 pages and a CD crammed into *one* paperback book, it's the size of a small cinderblock and practically needs casters to be portable. Microsoft Press hasn't released a price on the definitive edition, but the Beta Release is $70 list and $40 to $50 street. There are times we have to stand in awe of Microsoft; first they made a profitable business out of beta software, now they've started selling beta documentation.

It remains true that the *Resource Kit* scrupulously fills two needs. First, it's a Windows manual that—in many senses—picks up with the technical arcana and deep waters at (largely) the points where this book leaves off. We hope you're glad that you've purchased the *Windows 98 Bible,* and we tried to pack as much into a thousand pages as we possibly could, but if you get to the point of simply needing greater depth on a certain topic, we unhesitatingly recommend the *Resource Kit.* (At the same time, if you'll pardon us saying so, the *Resource Kit* doesn't meet the needs of the beginning and intermediate Windows user nearly as well as our book does. It's tense, it's dense, it's outline-ish, and it presupposes a ton of general knowledge about 32-bit Windows.)

"Now hang on," we can hear you saying. "So I've got your book and I've got the *Resource Kit*, which makes twenty-six hundred pages, or about four years' worth of bedtime reading. Will I know everything about Windows 98 that I need to?" Actually you won't, because the Windows 98 Plus! Pack hasn't appeared in semi-public yet, and you're a little light on the Internet components, since we haven't written that book. Here we have a computer operating system for retail consumers that needs documentation the size of a small encyclopedia. Is this a Good Thing? In light of our previous remarks about Windows' being unknowable in its uttermost extent, we're obviously wondering, ourselves. On the other hand, since the facts render it a moot point, you're better off knowing more than knowing less about Windows.

# *Resource Kit* **Applets**

The other side of the *Resource Kit*, though, is not a topic of philosophical debate—it's flat-out cool. The included utilities and applets, more than ever before, do things that you may have waited for since you began running Windows. So what we *will* do here, to help you decide whether the *Resource Kit* is worth its price, is list the included software and briefly describe its abilities. We devote more detail the the stars among them after the table.

| | | |
|---|---|---|
| *Adapter Card Help* | W98CARD.HLP | A dedicated help file for SCSI adapters, NICs and sound cards, with troubleshooting tips. If you've ever had two legacy cards at war, you know what a blessing this is. |
| *Animated Cursor Editor* | ANIEDIT.EXE | See stars (pp. 912–917). |
| *Batch File Input* | CHOICE.EXE | A command-line utility that lets you choose from a set of options while a batch file runs. |
| *Batch File Wait* | SLEEP.EXE | SLEEP takes the argument *nnnn*, which is the decimal number of seconds to pause before executing the next command in a batch file.. |
| *cat* | CAT.EXE | A workalike of UNIX cat, near-equivalent to the DOS TYPE command, but will work with multiple files. |
| *chmod* | CHMODE.EXE | A workalike of UNIX chmod, near-equivalent to the DOS ATTRIB command, but also works with sets of files. |
| *Clip* | CLIP.EXE | A command-line utility that reads the data stream intended for a display, printer, or other peripheral and sends it to the Clipboard. |
| *Clipboard Buffer Tool* | CLIPSTOR.EXE | An unobtrusive little box that contains multiple text buffers to be pasted into the Clipboard; a configurable and much more convenient replacement for the Clipbook Viewer. |
| *Clipboard Organizer* | CLIPTRAY.EXE | More permanent and elaborate than ClipStor. See Chapter 4 for our rave about this. |
| *Code Page Changer* | CHDOSCP.EXE | A drop-list box that lets you change the MS-DOS code page, changing the display of fonts in some DOS programs running under Windows. The **About** button would be handier if it told you about the code page, not the program. |

| | | |
|---|---|---|
| ***Compound File Layout Tool*** | DFLAYOUT.EXE | A *compound file* is any one of several types of Windows document files, including Microsoft Word .DOC files. Depending on how they're organized internally, they can contain wasteful slack space; this optimizes them and makes them smaller, for transmission over the Net or intranet. |
| ***Daylight Savings Time Utility*** | TIMEZONE.EXE | Sets the start date and time and the end date and time of DST at the computer's site, for variations that the standard table doesn't cover. |
| ***Default Printer Tool*** | DEFPTR.EXE | See stars (pp. 912–917). |
| ***Dependency Walker*** | DEPENDS.EXE | See stars (pp. 912–917). |
| ***Disk Space Checker*** | FREEDISK.EXE | A command-line utility that takes a specified amount of disk space and tells you whether or not you have it available. If run in a batch file, will provide an errorlevel. |
| ***Duplicate File Finder*** | DUPFINDER.EXE | Finds duplicate files at about a thousand a minute, returns information including their checksum, and offers to send the offenders to the Recycle Bin. Very nice. |
| ***Error Code Converter*** | TRANSLATE.EXE | At the command line, translates standard Win32 numeric error codes into the text equivalents displayed in the GUI dialogs. |
| ***Executable Type Finder*** | EXETYPE.EXE | Tells you what operating system and processor you need to run a particular executable. One of the tools you can use to diagnose a program that won't run. |
| ***Expand for Windows*** | EXPAND.EXE | An expander, with some switches, for files that have been compressed by COMPRESS. |
| ***File and Folder Compare*** | WINDIFF.EXE | A GUI utility that shows differences between contents of folders, or within files, including line-by-line comparison. Can also be run from the command line with switches. |
| ***File Batch Processor*** | FORFILES.EXE | A command-line utility that lets you select multiple files or folders as the targets (arguments) of a batch file, running the batch file repeatedly. |
| ***File Compress*** | COMPRESS.EXE | A utility that compresses single or multiple files, to be uncompressed with EXPAND. Handy for software distribution. |
| ***File Locator*** | WHERE.EXE | A powerful network file finder. |

| | | |
|---|---|---|
| ***File Type Associator*** | ASSOCIATE.EXE | A command-line utility that lets you create custom associations between file types and the programs that open them. |
| ***FileVer*** | FILEVER.EXE | A command-line utility that returns the exact build of a binary file, which can be a lifesaver if its date and time have been changed. |
| ***FileWise*** | FILEWISE.EXE | A version information tool for validating progressive build deltas and CD burns. If you know what we just said, you'll know you want this. |
| ***Hardware Compatibility List*** | HCL.HLP | A giant (10MB) cascading HTML file that tells you exactly what hardware has been tested and found compatible with Windows 98. Updates are available from a Web site. |
| ***Image Editor*** | IMAGEDIT.EXE | See stars (pp. 912–917). |
| ***Internet Explorer Profile Manager*** | PROFMGR.EXE | A tool to customize user settings, not unlike Microsoft Batch, but for Internet Explorer. Invaluable for centralized administration of Internet access. |
| ***Job Time Logger*** | LOGTIME.EXE | A command-line utility that logs the start and finish times of programs running in a batch file, and appends them to a log file. |
| ***Link Check Wizard*** | CHECKLINKS.EXE | A utility that lists all the dead Shortcuts on your system and lets you select which ones to remove. |
| ***Logging Copy*** | MCOPY.EXE | A command-line utility that works like the DOS COPY command, but logs the output detail to a file. Handy for remote admin. |
| ***ls*** | LS.EXE | A workalike of UNIX ls, near-equivalent to the DOS DIR command, but with lots more switches. |
| ***Microsoft Batch 3.0*** | BATCH.EXE | A fabulous tweaker for Windows Setup. See Appendix A. |
| ***Minitel Emulation Files*** | MINITEL.TTF | Two TrueType fonts that you can use to give HyperTerminal the "look and feel" of a Minitel (French national intranet) terminal. |
| ***Multi-File Text Editor*** | LIST.EXE | One rather wishes this were a licensed version of Vern Buerg's shareware LIST, but no such luck. A rudimentary DOS-box multi-file editor. |

| | | |
|---|---|---|
| ***Multiple Language Boot*** | WINBOOT.EXE | GUI utility for installing, and multi-booting with, versions of Windows in different languages. Comes with some cautions about being unsupported, but will be very useful if it works right. |
| ***mv*** | MV.EXE | A workalike of UNIX mv, near-equivalent to the vanished DOS MOVE command; a file mover. Will rename files on reboot. |
| ***Network Monitor*** | NETMON.EXE | A NetBIOS-compatible installable service to sniff network packets and gather statistics about them; can be used as a trouble-shooter for Remote Access as well as for networks. Windows 98 gets more like NT every day … |
| ***Network Signal Listener*** | WAITFOR.EXE | Automates timed signaling between computers on a network. |
| ***Now*** | NOW.EXE | Like MS-DOS ECHO with a date and time stamp; just the thing for sending job progress reports to a screen or log file. |
| ***OLE/COM Object Viewer*** | OLEVIEW.EXE | See stars (pp. 912–917). |
| ***Performance Optimizer*** | WINALIGN.EXE | Optimizes performance of executables by aligning their sections on *x86*-compatible memory page boundaries. If this causes problems, it can generally be reversed. |
| ***qgrep*** | QGREP.EXE | A workalike of UNIX qgrep, a highly sophis-ticated string search utility. |
| ***Regina REXX*** | REXX.EXE; REXX.DOC | In the arguments of long ago about the comparative merits of Windows NT and OS/2, one of the OS/2 cappers was always "Yeah, but REXX is fabulous." Now Windows has a REXX of its own, one of the world's most robust scripting languages. |
| ***Registry Backup*** | CFGBACK.EXE | The Registry backup utility that was replaced by Registry Checker, but gives you somewhat more control than the newer program. |
| ***Registry Compare*** | COMPREG.EXE | A command-line utility that lets you com-pare two Registry keys, which can be on two different computers. Primarily meant for sys-tem administration using Remote Registry Service. |
| ***Registry grep*** | SRCHREG.EXE | A Registry string searcher, much more powerful than the Find command in REGEDIT, and with color-coded output. |

| | | |
|---|---|---|
| *Registry Manipulator* | REG.EXE | A command-line utility that uses parameters like QUERY, ADD, UPDATE and (brr!) DELETE to modify Registry keys, on your local computer if you like, but primarily for remote admin. A target pistol with no safety. |
| *Remote Registry Services* | REMOTREG | A dedicated channel (to run on both computers) that lets an administrator modify the remote machine's Registry with REGEDIT and POLEDIT. |
| *rm* | RM.EXE | A workalike of UNIX rm, roughly combining the functions of the DOS DEL, ERASE, and RD commands. Includes file permissions and will delete files on reboot. |
| *Search Tool* | FINDSTR.EXE | A text string finder with switches that make it much more versatile than Start Menu Find. |
| *SET for Windows* | WINSET.EXE | Like the DOS SET command and with the same syntax, but can set, remove or report on variables in the Windows global environment. |
| *System File Information* | FILEINFO.EXE | See stars (pp. 912–917). |
| *System Policy Editor* | POLEDIT.EXE | A management utility that can set security levels for users, computers, or workgroups by selectively overriding the global values set in the Registry. For network administrators *only*, and don't mess with this unless you are one. |
| *System Stress Tester* | CREATEFILE.EXE | A command-line utility (it won't work from the Start Menu) that creates any size file full of zeroes, to use up disk space quickly for program or system testing. |
| *System Tray Utility* | QUIKTRAY.EXE | See stars (pp. 912–917). |
| *TextViewer* | TEXTVIEW.EXE | A GUI file viewer and editor for text, .INI and .INF files, HTML, and source code. Might be great when they get it right; the current version doesn't show the file path in the title bar, has no Help, and seems to have a file size limit of about 40KB … not again! … |
| *Time This* | TIMETHIS.EXE | A utility to time the execution of a command, that can be used interactively or in a batch file. |
| *Time Zone Utility* | TZEDIT.EXE | Edits everything—name, abbreviations, offset, start and end date and time, and bias—about the Time Zone screens that appear in Control Panel\Date and Time. |

| | | |
|---|---|---|
| ***touch*** | TOUCH.EXE | A workalike of UNIX touch, near-equivalent to Michael J. Mefford's TOUCH.COM, but will also create zero-byte files. |
| ***TweakUI*** | TWEAKUI.CPL | We discuss this clever and indispensable, ah … personal trainer in Chapter 15. |
| ***USB Device Troubleshooter*** | USBVIEW.EXE | A utility to poll the system's USB (Universal Serial Bus) ports and return the device configurations. |
| ***UUDecode/UUEncode Utility*** | UUCODE.EXE | A 32-bit GUI utility to translate binary files into mail-attachable text, then regenerate the binary at the receiving end. |
| ***vi*** | VI.EXE | A workalike of UNIX vi, one of the world's quirkiest text editors, very fast once learned because most of the commands are single letters. |
| ***wc*** | WC.EXE | A workalike of UNIX wc, which counts the number of characters, words, or lines in a file or files. |
| ***Windows Boot Editor*** | BOOTEDIT.EXE | See stars (pp. 912–917). |

## Animated Cursor Editor

With AniEdit you can create and edit animated cursors, as well as icons in the standard 32x32 and mini 16x16 sizes. This is a capable program in itself, but extends its reach considerably by working hand in glove with the Image Editor (below). For developers, an easy path to that extra bit of flash; for the rest of us, major fun.

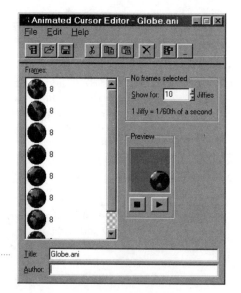

*Figure D.1*

*Animated Cursor Editor*

## Default Printer Tool

This minimalist drop-box saves you from going into Control Panel\Printers and pawing through drop menus until you find **Set as Default**. Lots of people these days seem to be sending output to two or more printers, and you couldn't make it much easier than this. As a bonus, it minimizes to the System Tray and you can actually tell *its* icon apart from the printer-spooler icon.

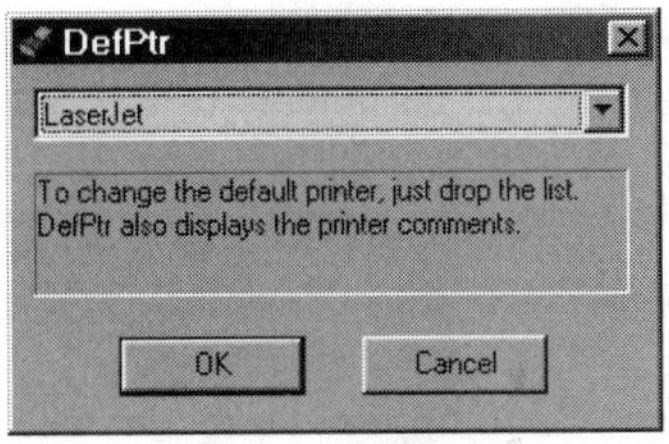

**Figure D.2**

*Default Printer tool*

## Dependency Walker

If you don't know what this is for, you'll be scratching your head. If you *do,* you will fall to your knees and thank … whoever you habitually thank from that position. For the first time—outside of pricey programmers' toolkits—a utility that tells you which libraries and other files are loaded when you start a Windows executable, and what the relationship among them is. Not only a boon to code grinders, the Dependency Walker becomes a formidable diagnostic tool if one of your Windows apps starts crashing for lack of a file.

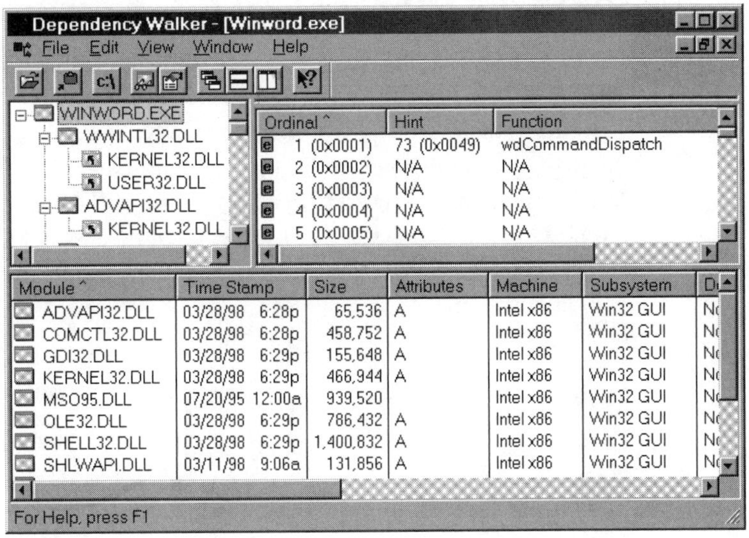

**Figure D.3**

*Dependency Walker*

## Image Editor

The Image Editor's obvious family relationship to Microsoft Paint makes it easy to use; but we also have the rational extensions that make it possible to edit icons. The copy we have is an authentic beta, with a 3.10 version number and no Help file, so we'll have to wait and see if the real thing fulfills its promise.

*Figure D.4*

*Image Editor*

## OLE/COM Object Viewer

The Object Viewer, like the Dependency Walker, is something you'll either never need—or *really* need. It defines all the COM and OLE object models in terms of their Registry class information, their Implementation paths, and their activation. You can set up system-wide DCOM defaults, diagnose ActiveX controls, and insert OBJECT tags into HTML documents. Aren't you glad the interface has a Novice mode? But we would have given a lot for this while we were writing Chapter 17, up to our ankles in CLSIDs scribbled on Post-It notes.

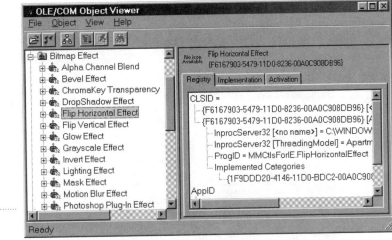

**Figure D.5**

*OLE/COM Object Viewer*

## Quick Tray

The concept of Quick Tray couldn't be simpler, although we suspect the clockwork took some doing. Click **Add,** browse to a program you want to quick-launch, and select it; it appears in the **Application** window with its icon and full path. Do that as many times as you like, and click **Close.**

**Figure D.6**

*Quick Tray setup*

**Figure D.7**

*System Tray with Quick Tray*

In your System Tray you'll see an icon for Quick Tray and one for each program you installed in it. This is majorly spiffy and our only reservation is that, what with the Start button, our permanently overloaded Taskbar, the Links bar, the *other* Quick Launch, and now a burgeoning System Tray ... we'll need trifocals to see all the icons.

## System File Information

There's no frustration quite like having a Web page blandly tell you "Builds of this driver later than 3.41.1109 can conflict with versions of CTL3D32.DLL earlier than 4.0.1330 if your color depth is set to High Color or True Color and your RAMDAC clock rate > 83MHz ..." C'mon, *scream time!* The *Resource Kit* can't fix your chipset, but System File Information will do you one big favor; tell you which file you've got, right here and now. Just select it alphabetically by name or extension, highlight it, click **Display File Information,** and:

Everything you could want to know about the file, including a description of what the heck it is. (Tip: Anything you can't find out here is probably in the System Information Utility.) The beta only supplies information for Internet Explorer 3.*x,* but we're told the release copy will handle all of Windows 98 including IE4.

# Windows Boot Editor

With the Windows Boot Editor, you can customize and diagnose the startup routine of your computer. Some of these switches duplicate settings in TweakUI but are easier to reach here.

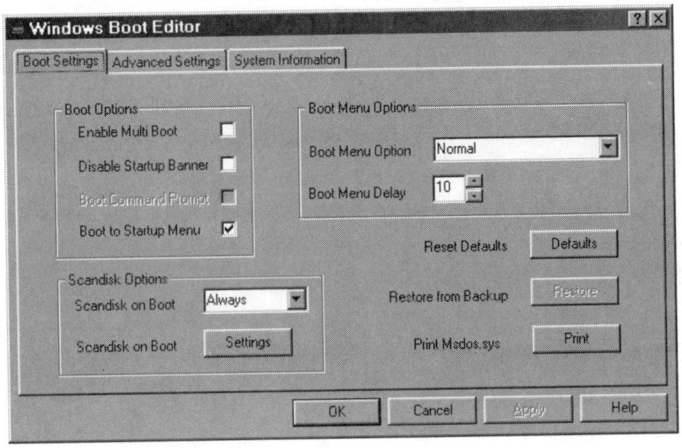

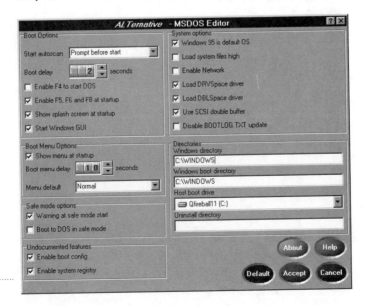

*Figure D.10*

Windows Boot Editor

# A Nice Alternative

The *Resource Kit*'s Boot Editor gets a run for no-money from **MSDOS Editor 98** by Arjan van de Logt's ALTernative Productions in the Netherlands. It's fast, flexible, free, and all on one screen rather than tabbed. The two applets have slightly different approaches, but Arjan's effort has a lot to recommend it. If editing MSDOS.SYS has ever crossed your mind, download this from `http://www.tomb.demon.nl/alt/index.htm` and share our satisfaction.

*Figure D.11*

MSDOS Editor 98

## Other Programs

Other potentially interesting software, in the *Resource Kit* folder of the CD but not in the Overview, includes Microsoft Voice, Microsoft Dictation, NetShow, the Microsoft Management Console, the Windows Scripting Host with a bunch of VBScript and JScript samples, the KiXtart logon processor, and the Remote Printer Service. What did it always say on the front covers of those thick, rainy-day books for kids—"Hours of fun for everyone?" The *Windows 98 Resource Kit* has to be considered the modern adult equivalent, and we urge you to round out your 32-bit Windows library with it.

# Summary

Since the time, many versions back, when the first *Resource Kit*s appeared, they've grown in stature and scope with each release. In 1998 it's fair to say that, without the *Resource Kit*, Windows isn't really Windows.

This *Resource Kit* points in two fundamental directions, equally important, but toward distinct audiences. For the *standalone user,* it packs more functions and more fun onto the Desktop, trying to second-guess your musing of "Wouldn't it be nice …" with a parade of applets and extensions longer than the options list of a car you can't afford. For the *network user* and *network administrator,* it makes Windows flat-out easier to live with when you're scrambling to service your seats. We haven't attained Zero Admin Windows and—sorry, Redmond—we may never, but Windows 98 with the *Resource Kit* at least knows what you're going through and tries to have answers.

That said, we have one complaint. Solitaire, Minesweeper, FreeCell and Hearts are childhood memories of our younger colleagues; now that a full copy of Windows spans a couple of CDs, surely Microsoft could find room for a good new game or two.

# Appendix E

# Device Manager Error Codes

The error codes that Device Manager generates can be fairly cryptic. To unravel error codes, follow these steps:

1. Double-click Control Panel\System.

2. Click the **Device Manager** tab and **View devices by type**.

3. Double-click a device type to see the devices in that category. Any device with a problem will have its icon partly obscured with either a red X, or a black exclamation point on a yellow circle.

4. Double-click the device. In its Properties, click the General tab if necessary. The Device Status box will show an error message followed by a code number in parentheses.

**As a general principle, if you're using Device Manager to poke around for problems to solve by editing the Registry, be sure to close Device Manager before you open the Registry Editor. If you try to examine the same hardware key with both programs at once, you get a cryptic error message in REGEDIT. See Appendix F.**

Decimal values are from the Device Manager Device Status box. Hex values are from the leftmost bytepair of the HKEY_DYN_DATA\Config Manager\ Enum\Problem key, when that isn't 00.

Look up the code number in the following humongous table.

| Decimal | Hex | Explanation |
|---|---|---|
| Code 1 | 01h | Your computer hasn't had a chance to configure this device. Use Remove in Device Manager to remove it, then add it back in with Control Panel\Add New Hardware. |
| Code 2 | 02h | The device loader (DevLoader) failed to load this device. Use Remove in Device Manager to remove it, then add it back in with Control Panel\Add New Hardware. |
| Code 3 | 03h | Your computer has run out of memory. Use Remove in Device Manager to remove the device, then add it back in with Control Panel\Add New Hardware. |
| Code 4 | 04h | There's a bug in the .inf file for this device. Use Remove in Device Manager to remove it, then add it back in with Control Panel\Add New Hardware. If this error code appears again, try to get an updated .inf file from the hardware manufacturer. |
| Code 5 | 05h | The device failed because it requested a resource type that doesn't have an arbitrator. Use Remove in Device Manager to remove it, then add it back in with Control Panel\Add New Hardware. |
| Code 6 | 06h | This device is conflicting with another device. See the section "Troubleshooting Device Conflicts with Device Manager" below. |

| Decimal | Hex | Explanation |
|---------|-----|-------------|
| *Code 7* | 07h | This device can't be configured by Windows' installation routines. If it works correctly, you don't need to do anything. If it doesn't work correctly, use Remove in Device Manager to remove it, then add it back in with Control Panel\Add New Hardware. If it still doesn't work correctly, try to get an updated driver from the hardware manufacturer or the Microsoft Software Library. |
| *Code 8* | 08h | The device loader (DevLoader) is missing, or the device's .inf file is pointing to a missing or invalid file. Use Remove in Device Manager to remove it, then add it back in with Control Panel\Add New Hardware. If this error code appears again, try to get an updated .inf file from the hardware manufacturer. |
| *Code 9* | 09h | The Registry information for this device is invalid. Use Remove in Device Manager to remove it, then add it back in with Control Panel\Add New Hardware. If this error code appears again, try to get updated registry settings from the hardware manufacturer. |
| *Code 10* | 0Ah | The device is missing, or not working right, or failed to start. Make sure the device is attached or seated correctly; if it's an external device, make sure that the cable is fully engaged, or if it's an internal device, that the card is plugged into its slot and bolted down. If all of this doesn't work, try to get an updated driver from the hardware manufacturer or the Microsoft Software Library. |
| *Code 11* | 0Bh | The device failed. Use Remove in Device Manager to remove it, then add it back in with Control Panel\Add New Hardware. If it still fails, there may be a hardware fault. |
| *Code 12* | 0Ch | A resource arbitrator failed. This happens to software-configurable devices that aren't attached to a resource, that can't find a resource (if, for example, all the interrupts are in use), or that request a resource currently in use by another device that won't release it. See the section "Troubleshooting Device Conflicts with Device Manager" below. |
| *Code 13* | 0Dh | This device's driver is corrupt or buggy. Use Remove in Device Manager to remove it, then add it back in with Control Panel\Add New Hardware. |
| *Code 14* | 0Eh | This device has a problem that might clear up if you reboot your computer. Shut down Windows, turn off your computer, and turn it back on. |
| *Code 15* | 0Fh | This device's resources are overlapping with another device's resources and Windows can't resolve the conflict. See the section "Troubleshooting Device Conflicts with Device Manager" below. |
| *Code 16* | 10h | The device and its resources were not completely detected. Go to Device Manager, right-click on the device, pick the Resources tab, uncheck Use Automatic Settings if it's checked, click Change Settings and enter the settings manually. (Try this only if you understand your system's address ranges and IRQ's pretty well.) |

| Decimal | Hex | Explanation |
| --- | --- | --- |
| *Code 17* | 11h | This device is a multiple-function device and the .inf file for it is allocating resources to the functions incorrectly. Use Remove in Device Manager to remove it, then add it back in with Control Panel\Add New Hardware. If this error code appears again, try to get an updated .inf file from the hardware manufacturer. |
| *Code 18* | 12h | This device needs to be reinstalled, and you will never know why. Use Remove in Device Manager to remove it, then add it back in with Control Panel\Add New Hardware. |
| *Code 19* | 13h | The registry returned an unknown result for this device. Use Remove in Device Manager to remove it, then add it back in with Control Panel\Add New Hardware. |
| *Code 20* | 14h | VxD Loader (Vxdldr) returned an unknown result; you probably have the wrong version of the device driver for your version of Windows. Use Remove in Device Manager to remove the device, then add it back in with Control Panel\Add New Hardware, and if Windows asks you if you want to use the driver already on the system, click No. If, after you install a fresh copy of the driver, this error still occurs, try to get an updated driver from the hardware manufacturer or the Microsoft Software Library. |
| *Code 21* | 15h | This device has a problem that might clear up if you reboot your computer. Shut down Windows, turn off your computer, and turn it back on. |
| *Code 22* | 16h | The device is disabled; enable it. Go to Control Panel\System\Device Manager; double-click the device. In the Device Usage box, check Enable in this hardware profile, click OK, click Close, and shut down and restart your computer. |
| *Code 23* | 17h | Communication broke down between the device loader and Windows. Use Remove in Device Manager to remove the device, then add it back in with Control Panel\Add New Hardware. |
| *Code 24* | 18h | The device was not found; either it's missing or it's not responding. Make sure the device is attached or seated correctly; if it's an external device, make sure that the cable is fully engaged, or if it's an internal device, that the card is plugged into its slot and bolted down. |
| *Code 25* | 19h | This code occurs during the first reboot in Windows Setup. You will never see it or need to do anything about it. |
| *Code 26* | 1Ah | A device failed to load, or the device driver file is corrupt or obsolete. Use Remove in Device Manager to remove it, then add it back in with Control Panel\Add New Hardware. If it still doesn't work correctly, try to get an updated driver from the hardware manufacturer or the Microsoft Software Library. |

| Decimal | Hex | Explanation |
|---------|-----|-------------|
| **Code 27** | 1Bh | The Registry's description of appropriate resources for a device conflicts with the configuration information in the .inf file. Use Remove in Device Manager to remove the device, then add it back in with Control Panel\Add New Hardware. |
| **Code 28** | 1Ch | This device was not installed completely. Highlight the device in Device Manager, click Properties and the Driver tab, and then Update Driver to start the Device Driver Wizard. |
| **Code 29** | 1Dh | This device does not and cannot work properly with Windows and has been disabled at the operating-system level. You may be able to enable or disable the device in your computer's CMOS setup, which Windows can't reach. If the device can't be configured in CMOS you'll probably have to upgrade it. |
| **Code 30** | 1Eh | Two devices are requesting an IRQ that can't be shared. The most likely case is that a PCI or EISA SCSI controller, which can share an IRQ, is contending with a real-mode device driver that wants the whole IRQ and that Windows can't control or disable.<br><br>    In Device Manager, right-click Computer, select Properties, click View Resources and click Interrupt request (IRQ). Devices that have hardware IRQs latched will be displayed in order by IRQ; the contended one will show a black exclamation point on a yellow circle. Open SYSEDIT or a DOS box, look in CONFIG.SYS or AUTOEXEC.BAT for a real-mode driver using the contended IRQ. If you find it, comment it out, save the file, shut down Windows and reboot the computer; then navigate to the computer's Properties sheet again and the yellow circle should be gone. Then call the manufacturer or look on the Web for a protected-mode driver for the legacy device. |

If you need more information than this, log onto **http://www.microsoft.com** and browse to Knowledge Base article Q133240.

# Appendix F

# Registry Error Messages

Let's just say that we hope you never need these. We've never needed most of them ourselves. Nonetheless, if one ever pops up, far better to have this list handy than to live or die in ignorance. Registry error messages fall into four broad categories:

- Trivial and misleading

- Important, but misleading

- Trouble

- Big trouble

 These are listed in alphabetical order, without regard to where they may occur. The really serious ones are flagged with this icon. Before you go messing around in here, read *all of* Chapter 17, if you haven't.

 means that this error message will appear only when you run REGEDIT from a command prompt.

 Not all of these error messages have been confirmed in Windows 98, but all are known to exist in some version of 32-bit Windows. Conversely, and unfortunately, we've probably never seen some error messages that exist in Windows 98 but not in Windows 95. We have only our own research and the literature to rely on; if you know how secretive Microsoft is about the Registry in general, you won't be surprised that they're stone-faced about the error messages.

| | |
|---|---|
| Backup cannot find this file | Occurs during file comparison if Microsoft Backup is set to verify. This is an opaque way of saying that the automatic Registry backup files HKLM-BACK and HKUBACK, which were created during the backup, were erased when it closed, and the verify pass can't find them. This is normal. |
| Cannot create key: Error while opening the key My Computer. | You tried to create a new key directly under My Computer, that is, a key on the same level as HKLM, HKU, and the other top-level keys. You can't do that. |
| Cannot edit (whatever). Error writing the value's new contents. | You were probably trying to edit values in the Value Pane of HKDD, which are maintained in RAM by the system and can't be edited. |
| Cannot edit (whatever): Error reading the value's contents. | You're trying to edit a key in REGEDIT while Device Manager is open and pointing to that same key, so it's locked. Minimize REGEDIT, exit the Device Manager, go back into REGEDIT, pick View\Refresh, and try the edit again. |

| | |
|---|---|
| **DOS** Cannot export <path>*filename.ext*: Error creating the file. | Be absolutely sure that <path>*filename.ext* is typed correctly and, incidentally, that the file doesn't already exist. If it does, the new file will be saved over the old one, which is too close for comfort when you're dealing with Registry data you might want. |
| **DOS** Cannot export <path>*filename.ext*: The specified key name does not exist. | You tried to export a nonexistent key. Good trick! But the message *does* exist … |
| Cannot find a device that may be needed to run Windows. The windows registry or SYSTEM. INI file refers tothis device file, but the device no longer exists. If you deleted *filename.vxd* Press any key to continue. | First, search SYSTEM.INI for *filename.vxd*. If you find a line in [386Enh] that reads device= *filename . vxd*, do a Start Menu Find on that file, starting at \Windows. If it isn't in your \Windows\ System folder, it probably got clobbered, so hunt up another copy.<br><br>    If there *is* no *filename.vxd* in [386Enh], go into REGEDIT, highlight HKLM\System\CurrentControl-Set\Services\VxD, and do a Find on *filename.vxd* with only the Data box checked. If you find it in a subkey, export the subkey to a file, then delete it from the Registry. Either you'll never hear of *file-name.vxd* again, in which case you had a bogus Registry key, or some app will tell you that it needs *filename.vxd*, in which case you hunt up another copy, add it to your \Windows\System folder, and import the Registry key from the saved file. (Take good care of that file, or you'll have to reinstall the program to recover the Registry key. We've been through this.) |
| Cannot find a device that may be needed to run Windows. The windows registry or SYSTEM. INI file refers to this device file, but the device no longer exists. If you deleted Press any key to continue. | Note that no filename is specified. Go into REGEDIT, highlight HKLM\System\CurrentControlSet\ Services\VxD, and do a Find on StaticVxD with only the Value box checked. As each occurrence is highlighted, look for a zero-byte ("") string in the Data column, and when you find it, delete the subkey that contains it. |
| Cannot import <path>\\*filename.REG:* Error accessing the registry. | Either you're trying to import into a key that's maintained by the system, like HKDD, which is illegal, or you're trying to import into a damaged key, in which case export the key to a temporary file, delete it, and then do the import. |
| Cannot import <path>\\*filename.REG:* The specified file is not a registry script. You can import only registry files. | Either the file you're trying to import isn't a real Registry export file, or it's damaged. Open the .REG file in Notepad and check it against the format under "Export Format Options" in Chapter 17, especially the header. |

| | |
|---|---|
| Cannot open DefaultIcon: Error while opening key. | You're probably trying to look at HKCR\AutoRun\ *(number)*\DefaultIcon, but the particular CD in your drive doesn't have an embedded icon. Click OK, remove the CD, hit F5 , and the key should vanish along with the message. |
| **DOS** Cannot open *filename.ext:* Error opening the file. The previous registry has been restored. | Whether *filename.ext* is real, phantom, or damaged, Windows has freaked out and replaced your Registry from the root directory backup file. You may be in for some surprises. |
| Cannot open HKEY_CLASSES_ROOT: Error while opening key. | Hit F5 or pull down View and click Refresh, then look for the boxed + to the left of the HKCR folder. If it's not there, one of two things is true: <br> *HKLM\SOFTWARE\Classes exists.* Open it and see if it looks all right. If so, shut down with Start Menu, Shut Down..., Restart. HKCR should be rebuilt from HKLM\SOFTWARE\Classes when your computer reboots. <br> *HKLM\SOFTWARE\Classes does not exist or is damaged.* Import a copy of the key, if you've got one handy, or restore the Registry using the techniques discussed in Chapter 17; then reboot and HKCR should be rebuilt. |
| Cannot rename *keyname:* Error while renaming key. | If you're trying to rename a key in HKDD, you can't. This error message has been *rumored* to appear when renaming subkeys of other top-level keys, but we've never seen it happen and we don't know what it means when it does. Try calling Microsoft ☺. |
| Cannot rename *keyname:* The specified key name already exists. Type another name and try again. | You can't have two subkeys with the same name under the same key. How much coffee are you drinking? |
| Cannot rename *keyname:* The specified key name contains illegal characters. | The character you tried to put in the key was most likely a backslash. If REGEDIT is objecting to any other odd character, it's probably odd enough to be fairly obvious. |
| Cannot rename *keyname:* The specified key name is too long. Type a shorter name and try again. | Sorry, only 255 characters maximum per keyname. |
| Connecting *X:* to \\*(computer name)*\ *(folder or filename).* | This is only for your information on startup, but if you get another error message after this one, there may be a problem. |

| | |
|---|---|
| Disable Registry editing tools | Run the System Policy Editor—if it's not on your system, it's on the Windows 98 CD in \admin\app-tools\poledit—and double-click on the appropriate User icon; then go to \System\Restrictions\ Disable Registry editing tools and clear the checkbox. If you still can't access REGEDIT, yell loudly for your administrator.<br><br>If you *are* the administrator: REGEDIT can be re-enabled by running a homemade .INF file or .REG file that are beyond the scope of this book, but are detailed in Woram's *Registry Survival Guide*. |
| Display: There is a problem with your display settings. The adapter type is incorrect, or the current settings do not work with your hardware. | This may appear when you reboot Windows after a REGEDIT session, and it means that you mistweaked something. Fix it either in REGEDIT or in Control Panel\Display\Settings. |
| Display: Your display adapter is not configured properly. To correct the problem, click OK to start the Hardware Installation wizard. | Windows may have restored your SYSTEM.DAT file from your SYSTEM.1ST file, without warning. If so, your computer's configuration is at ground zero, and you have work to do. Read Chapter 17 *now*. |
| **DOS** Error accessing the registry: The file may not be complete. | You're trying to import a .REG file so big that Windows can't supply enough conventional memory. Abandon the edit, close all other programs (or reboot in Safe Mode) and try to import it again. |
| Error accessing the system registry. You should restore the Registry now and restart your computer. (....) this backup copy may not contain all the information recently added to your system. | You would seem to have two choices; the tyrannical button that says "Restore from Backup and Restart," or the Close button in the top corner. The Close button doesn't work, so click the other one, cancel some appointments, and get coffee. |
| Error in *filename.ext*. Missing entry: (whatever) | Check three things in this order:<br>• Your Startup folder, to see if anything looks pertinent.<br>• The LOAD= and RUN= lines in WIN.INI.<br>• With a sigh, into REGEDIT for a look at HKLM\ SOFTWARE\Microsoft\Windows\CurrentVersion\ Run; search the Data column for *filename.ext*. When you find it, look for an incorrect trailing switch or parameter, and make sure it's right. You might have to reinstall. |

| | |
|---|---|
| Error occurred while trying to remove *application_name.* Uninstallation has been canceled. | If you got this in Add/Remove Programs when you tried to remove an application, it means the Uninstaller file is already missing, probably along with more of the app—like, maybe you deleted the folder and didn't tell the Registry about it. You could try to excise all the bits and scraps from your Software keys, but the simplest thing to do is open the Add/Remove tab of TweakUI, remove the program name from the list, and forget about the rest. |
| Errors occurred during this operation. Do you want to view them now? | See "Backup cannot find this file." |
| Fatal exception 0E has occurred at 0028: *xxxxxxxxx* in VxD VMM(06) +*xxxxxxxx* | If this happens once, restore your Registry from backup. If it happens again with the new files, try to guess the name of the malfunctioning program from the information about the VxD. If you can live without this program, uninstall it; if you can't, call its tech support and hope they know what you're talking about. |
| Invalid (or damaged, unrecognizable, etc.) diskette. | During the installation of this software, Windows may have overwritten the diskette's OEM name field with unrelated stuff of its own; now the application doesn't recognize this diskette as being the right one, although it is. If you know how to use DEBUG, ask the manufacturer for the contents and location of the OEM name field, and hex-patch the diskette. If you don't, ask the manufacturer for a new diskette. |
| **DOS** Invalid switch. | This is a REGEDIT message. Typing REGEDIT /? [Enter] at a DOS prompt will list out the valid switches. |
| Modem is busy or not responding. | If this happens repeatedly and other tactics don't fix it (you've checked the cable, of course?) go into HKLM\System\CurrentControlSet\Services\Class\Modem\0000, assuming 0000 is the number of the running Profile. Then: Look at DriverDesc and make sure this is the modem you're working with. If not, go to Control Panel\Modems, uninstall the wrong modem and install the right one. If DriverDesc is okay: Open the Settings subkey of 0000. Find the subkeys FlowControl_Hard, InactivityTimeout, and SpeedNegotiationOn, or as many of these as you have. Edit each one and delete the value, whatever it may be, but leave the keys. As soon as you exit REGEDIT you may have to reboot your computer, your modem or both—modem settings are exceptionally sticky. |

| | |
|---|---|
| MS-DOS Prompt. One or more programs did not close. Quit your other programs, and then try again. | First, make sure that all DOS apps are closed. If they are, ignore this, shut down normally, and it probably won't bother you again. |
| | If it does, go to the Startup folder in Start Menu, open the Shortcut Properties for any DOS-based programs, click the Program tab and make sure the Close on exit box is checked. |
| Networking: The following error occurred while reconnecting *X:* to \\*(network computer name)*\*(share name)*. The share name was not found. Be sure you typed it correctly. Do you want to restore this connection next time you log on? | Clicking on Yes will delete a subkey of HKCU\Network\Persistent, and the next time Windows starts, the system will try to restore this connection automatically. If you think this problem is temporary or obvious, click No, leave the subkey in place, fix the problem, and reboot; the dialog will come up again, you can click Yes, and the connection will be automatic from then on. |
| New Hardware Found. | If this is phantom, it can be a symptom of Registry corruption. Click Cancel until you back completely out of the New Hardware dialog, click Yes at the prompt to restart, and hunt down the Registry problem. |
| **DOS** Parameter format not correct. | Type REGEDIT /? and review the switches. |
| Program Not Found: Windows cannot find *filename.exe*. The program is needed for opening files of type '*type description*'. Repair the… Registry data. | Open HKCR and highlight the *.ext* subkey that matches the file extension corresponding to '*type description*'; note the contents of the (Default) of the highlighted key. Search HKCR for the subkey with that name, and go down to its Shell\Open\Command; look at the name of the associated executable, and check it against Explorer. If the name in the Registry is wrong, edit the Command key. If the name in the Registry is right, do a Start Menu Find on the file, and either drag it into the right folder or replace it from backup. |
| Program Not Found: Windows cannot find *filename.exe*. The program is needed for opening files of type '*type description*'. Find the… *filename.exe* file. | Use Start Menu Find or the Explorer to look for *filename.exe*. If it doesn't exist, and you know where it should go, you may have to download or expand another copy. |
| Program Not Found: Windows cannot find *filename.exe*. The program is needed for opening files of type '*type description*'. Enter path… to the *filename.exe* file. | When you enter the filename, it gets inserted into the [programs] section of WIN.INI, which takes precedence over any conflicting Registry entry. This is quick and easy, but it's a workaround that "fixes" your Registry problem by ignoring it. To fix the problem instead of the symptom, refer to **Repair the … Registry** data below. |

| | |
|---|---|
| Properties for this item are not available. | If this shows up when right-click Properties is selected, a subkey is missing that relates to either the item itself, a supporting DLL, or a supporting .CPL (Control Panel) file. The easiest thing to do is reinstall the program. |
| REGEDIT.EXE is not a valid Win32 application. | This is file damage to REGEDIT. Rename REGEDIT.EXE to REGEDIT.OLD, expand a new copy of REGEDIT.EXE into the Windows directory, make sure it works, and delete REGEDIT.OLD. |
| Registry "Replace" function failed internally. Look for hidden files. | We're not sure this message still exists, but if you see it or something like it, it means that the Registry Checker's restore function failed. Call Microsoft, not us. |
| Registry Editor: Registry editing has been disabled by your administrator. | Talk to your administrator. |
| Registry File was not found. Registry services may be inoperative for this session. | If this message still exists, either the Registry Checker's restore function failed, or SYSTEM.DAT is no longer in your FAT. Call Microsoft. |
| Registry Problem | This is the title bar for all Registry error dialogs. Glance at it to be sure that what you have is a Registry error and not something else. |
| Registry/configuration error. Choose Safe mode, to start Windows with a minimal set of drivers. | This message may appear on startup, or Windows may start in Safe mode automatically. If a Registry Problem dialog box appears, check this list for the source of the damage and try to repair it.<br><br>When you restart after the repair, Windows may start in Safe mode again because the last termination was abnormal; it may also corner you into a complete run of ScanDisk. Once this is over, exit Windows and try to start again normally. If this sequence repeats itself, your only choices are to restore the Registry from backup—which may not work—or to reinstall Windows. |
| Restrictions: This operation has been canceled due to restrictions in effect on this computer. Please contact your system administrator. | Sounds like a great idea. *If this happens on startup:* Restrictions are preventing items in your Startup group from loading. Restart and hold down the Ctrl key to bypass the Startup group. |
| Setup cannot find the files on *X:\* from which you originally installed the product. If this is a network server, make sure that the server is still available. | This happens when you try to uninstall a program through Add/Remove Programs, and either the server has vanished, or the letter of the CD drive on the local computer has changed. If the former, re-connect to the server; if the latter, try to shuffle your drive letters until the CD drive has the same letter it did before. Then run the uninstall again. |

| | |
|---|---|
| Setup Error 544: Setup is unable to open the data file *<path>filename.stf;* run Setup again from where you originally ran it. | This may be followed by a Setup Error 723 and the warning that "Setup was not completed successfully." The real Registry fix for this is complex; installing again (and then uninstalling, if that's what you were after) is probably easier. |
| Sharing. There are *x* user(s) connected to your computer. Shutting down your computer will disconnect them. Do you want to continue? | This is a perfectly polite message when it's real. The point here is that, when you exit Windows after running REGEDIT or the System Policy Editor, you may get this warning even when it's not true. Depending on how sure you are that no one else is connected, click Yes and exit right away, or click No, launch the Net Watcher applet to confirm that all connections are down, and then Shut Down and click Yes. |
| Shortcut, Problem with (whatever) | Warnings of malfunctioning Shortcuts are one sign that Windows may have restored your SYSTEM.DAT file from your SYSTEM.1ST file, rather than your most recent backups. If so, your computer's configuration is at ground zero; read Chapter 17 *now.* |
| System Error: Windows cannot read from drive A: If this is a network drive, make sure the network is working. If it is a local drive, check the disk. | Check the true state of drive A:. If this message is patently wrong, the Registry may be damaged, and clicking Cancel will put you straight into the Setup Wizard User Info screen. Try to run Registry Checker. |
| System Setting Change: To finish restoring your registry, you must restart your computer. Do you want to restart your computer now? | This should trigger a normal restart. If you click Yes at the end of a REGEDIT session and immediately get *another* error message, you may need to try a DOS-level Registry Checker restore from backup over the current SYSTEM.DAT and USER.DAT. If you click No, Windows may drop into Safe mode, and the consequences are unpredictable. |
| There is not enough memory to load the registry, or the registry is corrupted. Some devices may not function properly (DOS screen). | This may have nothing to do with memory. If the next things you see are a password prompt and a warning that *You have not logged on at this computer before…,* click No and proceed to work on the other problems, which you will almost certainly have. |
| Too many parameters. | This can happen not only for the reason given, but because one parameter is *incomplete.* Look over what you typed. |
| Topic does not exist. Contact your application vendor for an updated Help file(129). | This is a bug in CFGBACK Help and you'll only see it if you're running CFGBACK from the Windows 98 Resource Kit. |

| | |
|---|---|
| Unable to delete all specified values. | You'll get this:<br>    Whenever you try to delete a (Default) Value, which can't be deleted. To get rid of a surplus key in which (Default) is the only value, delete the whole key.<br>    Whenever you try to delete anything in HKDD. |
| Unable to determine your network address. The UUID generated is unique to this computer only. It should not be used on another computer. | One of the most arcane Registry error messages, this pops up when you run UUIDGen, the Microsoft CLSID generating utility, on a computer with no network adapter. It can probably be ignored. |
| **DOS** Unable to open registry (1,016)-*<path>filename.ext.* | REGEDIT simply couldn't find *<path>filename.ext,* and did nothing. What (1,016) may mean, we have no idea. |
| **DOS** Unable to open registry (14)-System.dat. | This is REGEDIT asking for more conventional memory than Windows can provide—the same message as "Error accessing the registry: The file may not be complete." |
| Windows could not restore your registry. Either a disk error occurred, or no valid backup copy of the Registry exists. Use a utility such as ScanDisk to check your hard disk for errors, and then reinstall Windows. If you continue without reinstalling, you may lose data. | Hold your horses and read that carefully. *Before* you run ScanDisk, boot into Safe Mode Command Prompt Only and try to run Registry Checker manually. If it succeeds and you restart correctly, you can run ScanDisk with a sigh of relief. Only if this message appears a second time will you be forced to think about (ugh) reinstalling Windows.<br>    If Registry Checker doesn't succeed, or if your RB*.CAB files in \WINDOWS\SYSBCKUP contain Registry versions that are also damaged, then reinstalling Windows is the destiny of your next few hours. |
| Windows encountered an error while backing up the system registry. Make sure you have enough space on the drive for three copies of the file C:\WINDOWS\SYSTEM.DAT [or USER.DAT]. This error should not cause any loss of information, but if space is not made on the drive you may experience additional problems. Please fix the problem, and then restart your computer. | How much free disk space do you have? If it's more than about 30MB, disk space isn't the problem, but memory might be; a corrupt device driver can eat free memory faster than Pac-Man eats dots. Boot into Safe mode, and if that solves the problem—because the device drivers were bypassed—then track down the bad driver and replace it.<br>    If you click OK on this dialog and most of the stuff instantly vanishes from your Desktop, it means that Windows just replaced SYSTEM.DAT with a copy of SYSTEM.1ST. Check the date and time of your SYSTEM.DAT and restore over it with Registry Checker, if possible. |

| | |
|---|---|
| You are about to backup over a previous backup. Do you want to proceed? | This is a bug if it appears during a Restore; ignore it and click Yes. We're not sure this message exists in Windows 98 at all. |
| You have chosen to replace your current configuration with the backed-up one. Restore selected Configuration? | This is just CFGBACK being extra-careful, and you can't blame it. |
| You have not logged on at this computer before. Would you like this computer to retain your individual settings for use when you log on here in the future? | This message can appear, confusingly enough, when the Registry is damaged, but also the first time you log on after a REGEDIT session. Either way, click No, and poke around for other signs of trouble; but it's most likely that the message is simply wrong. |

# Appendix G

# Driving a Legacy Printer

We offer here a short (believe it or not) tutorial in how to configure the Windows 98 Generic/Text Only printer driver so that it supports any legacy printer you might want to print to. We want to emphasize, before you dig in, that crafting this driver is a last resort and may be frivolous use of your time. Please go through the following steps:

# Are You There Yet?

Look in your printer manual for names of compatible printers, then check the Add New Printer Wizard hardware list for the names of any printer compatible with yours. Return here *only* if you're absolutely sure that Windows 98 doesn't support anything like your printer.

Rummage through your old diskettes for any hint of a Windows 95 or Windows 3.1 driver that might still work; try to install it with the Have Disk option. If it works, stick with it. If it doesn't, keep reading.

Consider an upgrade to a printer guaranteed Windows-compatible. We're not advocating new-hardware mania here; a used, but newer, printer from the classified ads might be much less expensive than the frustration you're about to go through.

Still hanker to set up your own minidriver? Here we go.

## Secretly Compatible Printers

Printer manufacturers want you to believe that the printer you bought is unique and special. You may like it, but under the plastic shell it has a lot in common with other printers of the same type! If the Windows device table

| If you have this printer type ... | Try this stock Windows driver ... |
|---|---|
| Parallel (Centronics) laser | Hewlett-Packard LaserJet Series II or Series III, see note below table |
| Serial laser, non-PostScript, Canon CX or SX engine ("write-black") | Hewlett-Packard LaserJet, LaserJet Plus, or early Canon laser |
| Serial laser, non-PostScript, Ricoh "write-white" engine (e. g., original AST TurboLaser) | You may be out of luck. Try contacting the manufacturer, or see if a Windows 3.1 driver will work |
| Serial laser, PostScript | Apple LaserWriter or LaserWriter Plus |

| If you have this printer type ... | Try this stock Windows driver ... |
| --- | --- |
| Ink-jet | Canon BubbleJet BJ-10e or BJ-30, or Hewlett-Packard DeskJet, or try contacting the manufacturer |
| 24-pin dot matrix | Epson LQ-1500, IBM Proprinter X24, or Panasonic KX-P1124 |
| Nine-pin dot matrix | Epson FX-80, IBM Proprinter, or Panasonic KX-P1081. For a wide-carriage printer, try Epson FX-100 |
| Daisywheel | Ingenuity required. See if a Windows 3.1 driver will work; if not, start with a copy of the Generic / Text Only driver, read "Sample Command Sets" below, grab the manual, and get ready for some fun |

and the printer's documentation don't give specific names of compatible printers, try this list.

These are worth trying, but not guaranteed, and even if they "sort of" work, will produce the occasional odd artifact—especially if a printer is paired with a driver that calls the wrong internal character set. (A nine-pin dot-matrix printer, for example, may print a single slash or zero in any line that should be blank.) Only you know how long you want to spend tweaking drivers before you go shopping for a printer.

### Parlez-vous PCL?

The LaserJet Series II uses version 4 of HP PCL, the Hewlett-Packard Printer Control Language. If you happen to know that your printer emulates PCL 5, you can install the driver for the LaserJet Series III (which supports scalable PCL 5 fonts), although the Series II driver also works just fine.

# Escape Codes

The Generic/Text Only driver included with Windows 98 can become a limited minidriver for almost any printer, providing you know the hardware escape codes (control codes). You must also, as the Help makes clear, enter the information in one of the legal formats.

Designing printer control codes always involves a problem. The printer driver can be happily pumping text to the printer, and suddenly, in the middle of the string, a word is boldfaced, or underlined, or put in a different font. The printer has to receive a command in the middle of the text string, and recognize it instantly. "Instantly" in the context of a data stream means "in the length of one character."

The universal convention has been to use the **Escape** character—otherwise known as $\boxed{\text{Esc}}$, $^{\textbf{E}}\textbf{C}$, **1Bh**, or "**chr(27)**"—as a red flag to the printer, saying "Execute this next glob, don't print it." The $\boxed{\text{Esc}}$ character and the characters immediately after it are interpreted as the command, and when the stream goes back to being printable text, the printer automagically starts printing it. Sometimes, when one byte is enough for a command, an older printer will use a $\boxed{\text{Ctrl}}$ character, like $\boxed{\text{Ctrl}}\boxed{\text{R}}$—which actually is one byte. ("Control" characters are called that because they were in-stream commands, or "controls," on old Teletype machines.)

The Windows Generic/Text Only driver Properties sheet gives you two customizable tabs that make up a basic minidriver. *Device Options* includes the following fields:

- Begin print job and End print job are both almost always Reset.

- Paper size, in an older printer that isn't a laser, is probably stated as Form Length.

- Paper source, for a laser, is likely to be your choice of Tray or Manual feed; for anything other than a laser, it's irrelevant unless you're dealing with one of the comparatively rare dot-matrix printers or daisywheels that has both a tractor and a sheet feeder. This is less useful than it might be, because—since it gives you only one command, rather than "Paper source on" and "Paper source off"—you'll be able to pick one paper feed mechanism or the other, but not to switch between them.

- We'll get to Extended character mapping as soon as we're done with escape codes.

*Fonts* includes the following fields:

- **Select 10 cpi** is probably in your printer manual as **Pica on.**

- **Select 12 cpi** is probably in your printer manual as **Elite on.**

- **Select 17 cpi** is often called **Compressed on.** The smallest font size available, unlike Pica or Elite, varies; for Epson, Diablo and Qume printers and compatibles it's usually 15 cpi, and for IBM dot-matrix printers and Hewlett-Packard LaserJets and compatibles it's usually between 16.5 and 17 cpi.

- **Double wide on** is largely confined to dot-matrix printers. LaserJets and compatibles call it **Expanded.** You can fake it with a daisywheel by setting the printer's pitch to Pica and installing an Elite printwheel.

- **Bold on** bolds the font. LaserJets and true compatibles have about seven stroke weights on the bold side of Normal; the one simply called **Bold** is usually the middle one.

- **Underline on,** in the printer configuration table below, is the setting for fixed underline. Any printer new enough to cope with a floating underline is probably new enough to have its own Windows driver. Whether you get a continuous or a word-wide underline depends on the printer.

- **Double wide off, Bold off,** and **Underline off** set the font back to Normal. Even though they all do the same thing, they usually have different codes.

## What You Get Is What You Get

You don't have a lot of flexibility concerning what you put in these fields. It's tempting, for example, to decide that **Italic** would be more useful than **Double wide**, and try to sneak the codes for Italic into the Double-wide fields. Unfortunately, so far as we can tell, you can trick the printer into doing that, but there's no way to make your applications understand the trick.

Also, if you have multiple printers installed with the Generic driver running one of them—for example, a laser and a daisywheel—the Windows font formatting box will obstinately insist that the daisywheel can use your installed soft (TrueType or PostScript) fonts, even though it can't.

 Given that Windows 98 supplies minidrivers for over a thousand printers, we can't imagine having more than one printer that needed a Generic driver, but who are we to tell you what to do with your computer? It is our sad duty to inform you, however, that you can't install two copies of the Generic driver— at least not the way you probably want to. The stopper is in the dialog that begins "A driver is already installed for this printer...." and gives you the choice of **Keep existing driver** or **Replace existing driver.** If you **Keep existing driver,** you can easily install two copies, but—woops!—they'll have the same settings in Device Options and Fonts, so they won't be much use for two different printers. If you **Replace existing driver,** you'll get halfway through the installation and be told that it can't continue because UNIDRV.DLL is in use. This presumably means that the file is locked by the current default printer, and the Wizard tries to install another copy from the distribution disk, but can't. The cherry on top was that, after the Wizard crashed in mid-create, we couldn't access a printer till we rebooted the computer. The only way to run more than one printer with the Generic driver is to set up multiple models through **Add new model...** and then, each time you print, choose a printer through the Device Options tab of Properties. It's better than nothing but we'd have to call it a nuisance.

## Entering Escape Codes

When you enter control codes in these fields, you have to abide by Microsoft's "clearly" presented rules in the Help, which we will quote directly:

You can specify control codes in symbol characters, control-letter sequences, or decimal digits. If your printer manual specifies control codes using ASCII mnemonics or hexadecimal numbers, you must convert them. To enter the control code, press (Enter) on your keyboard and then enter the code.

This gets merely complicated for *escape* codes, like the ones that drive an HP LaserJet, and more complicated for *control* codes that you occasionally see in things like IBM Proprinters. Here's an example of each:

| In the manual | Data type | What you type | Legal format |
|---|---|---|---|
| $E_C$&k0S | Symbol chars | (Esc)&k0S | Yes |
| 27 38 107 48 83 | Decimal digits | (Esc) 38 107 48 83 | Yes |
| 1B 26 6B 30 53 | Hex digits | | No |

| In the manual | Data type | What you type | Legal format |
|---|---|---|---|
| Double-headed vertical arrow | Symbol chars | (Alt)(NumPad)0018 | Yes |
| ^R | Control-letter | (Ctrl)R | Yes |
| 18 | Decimal digits | 18 | Yes |
| DC2 | Mnemonic | | No |
| 15 | Hex digits | | No |

Our advice is: Stick to (Esc) *string* for the escape codes, stick to (Ctrl) *letter* for the control codes, and have an ASCII table handy. We hear you whimpering "How do I know whether a numeric sequence is hex or decimal?" and: It might say so in the docs. If not, any sequence including any of the letters A through F is hex. If neither of the above, you'll have to figure it out from context, or try it both ways.

**Extended Character Mapping**   In the Generic driver there are three mapping options: *TTY custom, Code page 437,* and *Code page 850.* For the last two, see "Code Pages" below.

**TTY custom** lets you custom-map the top half of eight-bit ASCII—that is, the characters between binary 10000000 (decimal 128, hex 80) and 11111111 (decimal 255, hex FF). Whereas the *bottom* half of eight-bit ASCII—characters 0 through 127—has a standard definition, the *top* half varies from printer to printer and has been used, for example, by Epson dot-matrix printers for italics, by IBM dot-matrix printers for graphics characters, and by HP LaserJets for the accented letters found in Romance and Germanic languages.

In many standard eight-bit symbol sets, characters 128 through 159 (or most of them) are empty positions. These positions only fill up when character sets are expanded with graphics characters.

In the **On screen** scrolling list, the number to the left of the equals sign is the decimal ASCII value; the character to the right is that value's mapping in the character set known as Windows 3.0 Latin 1, or Hewlett-Packard PCL 9U. If you highlight any line in the scrolling list, in the **On printer** field, the character will appear that's mapped to that value in the driver. Usually it's nothing fancy, since generic printers rarely add flourishes like umlauts, accents or tildes.

You can edit the contents of this field, though; in fact, you can map any character to any ASCII value you please, although that doesn't guarantee the printer will print it. The way to print the characters in the printer's firmware, even though you may not be able to reproduce them from the keyboard—if, for example, they're single- and double-line box graphics—is to use the Alt key and the numeric keypad. For example, you can highlight the value 242 in the **On screen** scrolling list, tab over to the **On printer** field, and enter Alt Num Pad 0242; the **On printer** field will fill with <242>, and whatever the printer's firmware thinks an ASCII 242 is, by golly, that's what the printer will print.

Defining all 128 of the high-order ASCII characters this way would be incredibly tedious, so we think you may be interested in what comes next.

# Code Pages

The other two options in **Character Mapping,** *Code page 437* and *Code page 850,* are predefined character sets included with Windows. There are others—including the 32-bit Windows default, Code Page 1252—but these are the two compatible with the Generic driver.

Code page 437 looks like this:

| | | | | | | | |
|---|---|---|---|---|---|---|---|
| Ç 128 Ccedil 00C7 | É 144 Eacute 00C9 | á 160 aacute 00E1 | ░ 176 blk14 2591 | └ 192 2514 | ╨ 208 2568 | α 224 alpha 03B1 | ≡ 240 equiv 2261 |
| ü 129 uuml 00FC | æ 145 aelig 00E6 | í 161 iacute 00ED | ▒ 177 blk12 2592 | ┴ 193 2534 | ╤ 209 2564 | ß 225 szlig 00DF | ± 241 plusmn 00B1 |
| é 130 eacute 00E9 | Æ 146 AElig 00C6 | ó 162 oacute 00F3 | ▓ 178 blk34 2593 | ┬ 194 252C | ╥ 210 2565 | Γ 226 Gamma 0393 | ≥ 242 ge 2265 |
| â 131 acirc 00E2 | ô 147 ocirc 00F4 | ú 163 uacute 00FA | │ 179 2502 | ├ 195 251C | ╙ 211 2559 | π 227 pi 03C0 | ≤ 243 le 2264 |
| ä 132 auml 00E4 | ö 148 ouml 00F6 | ñ 164 ntilde 00F1 | ┤ 180 2524 | ─ 196 2500 | ╘ 212 2558 | Σ 228 Sigma 03A3 | ⌠ 244 2320 |
| à 133 agrave 00E0 | ò 149 ograve 00F2 | Ñ 165 Ntilde 00D1 | ╡ 181 2561 | ┼ 197 253C | ╒ 213 2552 | σ 229 sigma 03C3 | ⌡ 245 2321 |
| å 134 aring 00E5 | û 150 ucirc 00FB | ª 166 ordf 00AA | ╢ 182 2562 | ╞ 198 255E | ╓ 214 2553 | µ 230 micro 00B5 | ÷ 246 divide 00F7 |
| ç 135 ccedil 00E7 | ù 151 ugrave 00F9 | º 167 ordm 00BA | ╖ 183 2556 | ╟ 199 255F | ╫ 215 256B | τ 231 tau 03C4 | ≈ 247 ap 2248 |
| ê 136 ecirc 00EA | ÿ 152 yuml 00FF | ¿ 168 iquest 00BF | ╕ 184 2555 | ╚ 200 255A | ╪ 216 256A | Φ 232 PHgr 03A6 | ° 248 deg 00B0 |
| ë 137 euml 00EB | Ö 153 Ouml 00D6 | ⌐ 169 2310 | ╣ 185 2563 | ╔ 201 2554 | ┘ 217 2518 | Θ 233 Theta 0398 | • 249 2219 |
| è 138 egrave 00E8 | Ü 154 Uuml 00DC | ¬ 170 not 00AC | ║ 186 2551 | ╩ 202 2569 | ┌ 218 250C | Ω 234 Omega 03A9 | · 250 middot 00B7 |
| ï 139 iuml 00EF | ¢ 155 oslash 00F8 | ½ 171 frac12 00BD | ╗ 187 2557 | ╦ 203 2566 | █ 219 block 2588 | δ 235 delta 03B4 | √ 251 radic 221A |
| î 140 icirc 00EE | £ 156 pound 00A3 | ¼ 172 frac14 00BC | ╝ 188 255D | ╠ 204 2560 | ▄ 220 lhblk 2584 | ∞ 236 infin 221E | ⁿ 252 207F |
| ì 141 igrave 00EC | ¥ 157 yen 00A5 | ¡ 173 iexcl 00A1 | ╜ 189 255C | ═ 205 2550 | ▌ 221 258C | ø 237 phis 03C6 | ² 253 sup2 00B2 |
| Ä 142 Auml 00C4 | ₧ 158 20A7 | « 174 laquo 00AB | ╛ 190 255B | ╬ 206 256C | ▐ 222 2590 | ε 238 epsi 03B5 | ■ 254 squf 25A0 |
| Å 143 Aring 00C5 | ƒ 159 fnof 0192 | » 175 raquo 00BB | ┐ 191 2510 | ╧ 207 2567 | ▀ 223 uhblk 2580 | ∩ 239 cap 2229 | □ 255 nbsp 00A0 |

*Figure G.1*

*Code page 437*

This symbol set is also known as **PC-8,** and Hewlett-Packard PCL calls it Symbol Set 10U. The advantage of this code page is the inclusion of full single, double, and mixed-line box graphics, a modest set of Greek letters, and some math operators.

Code page 850 looks like this:

| | | | | | | | |
|---|---|---|---|---|---|---|---|
| Ç 128 Ccedil 00C7 | É 144 Eacute 00C9 | á 160 aacute 00E1 | ░ 176 blk14 2591 | └ 192 2514 | ð 208 eth 00F0 | Ó 224 Oacute 00D3 | - 240 shy 00AD |
| ü 129 uuml 00FC | æ 145 aelig 00E6 | í 161 iacute 00ED | ▒ 177 blk12 2592 | ┴ 193 2534 | Ð 209 ETH 00D0 | ß 225 szlig 00DF | ± 241 plusmn 00B1 |
| é 130 eacute 00E9 | Æ 146 AElig 00C6 | ó 162 oacute 00F3 | ▓ 178 blk34 2593 | ┬ 194 252C | Ê 210 Ecirc 00CA | Ô 226 Ocirc 00D4 | ‗ 242 2017 |
| â 131 acirc 00E2 | ô 147 ocirc 00F4 | ú 163 uacute 00FA | │ 179 2502 | ├ 195 251C | Ë 211 Euml 00CB | Ò 227 Ograve 00D2 | ¾ 243 frac34 00BE |
| ä 132 auml 00E4 | ö 148 ouml 00F6 | ñ 164 ntilde 00F1 | ┤ 180 2524 | ─ 196 2500 | È 212 Egrave 00C8 | õ 228 otilde 00F5 | ¶ 244 para 00B6 |
| à 133 agrave 00E0 | ò 149 ograve 00F2 | Ñ 165 Ntilde 00D1 | Á 181 Aacute 00C1 | ┼ 197 253C | ı 213 inodot 0131 | Õ 229 Otilde 00D5 | § 245 sect 00A7 |
| å 134 aring 00E5 | û 150 ucirc 00FB | ª 166 ordf 00AA | Â 182 Acirc 00C2 | ã 198 atilde 00E3 | Í 214 Iacute 00CD | µ 230 micro 00B5 | ÷ 246 divide 00F7 |
| ç 135 ccedil 00E7 | ù 151 ugrave 00F9 | º 167 ordm 00BA | À 183 Agrave 00C0 | Ã 199 Atilde 00C3 | Î 215 Icirc 00CE | þ 231 thorn 00FE | ¸ 247 cedil 00B8 |
| ê 136 ecirc 00EA | ÿ 152 yuml 00FF | ¿ 168 iquest 00BF | © 184 copy 00A9 | ╚ 200 255A | Ï 216 Iuml 00CF | Þ 232 THORN 00DE | ° 248 deg 00B0 |
| ë 137 euml 00EB | Ö 153 Ouml 00D6 | ® 169 reg 00AE | ╣ 185 2563 | ╔ 201 2554 | ┘ 217 2518 | Ú 233 Uacute 00DA | ¨ 249 uml 00A8 |
| è 138 egrave 00E8 | Ü 154 Uuml 00DC | ¬ 170 not 00AC | ║ 186 2551 | ╩ 202 2569 | ┌ 218 250C | Û 234 Ucirc 00DB | · 250 middot 00B7 |
| ï 139 iuml 00EF | ø 155 oslash 00F8 | ½ 171 frac12 00BD | ╗ 187 2557 | ╦ 203 2566 | █ 219 block 2588 | Ù 235 Ugrave 00D9 | ¹ 251 sup1 00B9 |
| î 140 icirc 00EE | £ 156 pound 00A3 | ¼ 172 frac14 00BC | ╝ 188 255D | ╠ 204 2560 | ▄ 220 lhblk 2584 | ý 236 yacute 00FD | ³ 252 sup3 00B3 |
| ì 141 igrave 00EC | Ø 157 Oslash 00D8 | ¡ 173 iexcl 00A1 | ¢ 189 cent 00A2 | ═ 205 2550 | ¦ 221 brvbar 00A6 | Ý 237 Yacute 00DD | ² 253 sup2 00B2 |
| Ä 142 Auml 00C4 | × 158 times 00D7 | « 174 laquo 00AB | ¥ 190 yen 00A5 | ╬ 206 256C | Ì 222 Igrave 00CC | ¯ 238 macr 00AF | ■ 254 squf 25A0 |
| Å 143 Aring 00C5 | ƒ 159 fnof 0192 | » 175 raquo 00BB | ┐ 191 2510 | ¤ 207 curren 00A4 | ▀ 223 uhblk 2580 | ´ 239 acute 00B4 | 255 nbsp 00A0 |

*Figure G.2*

*Code page 850*

This symbol set is also known as **PC-850 Multilingual,** and the PCL name for it is Symbol Set 12U. The single and double-line box graphics remain—in the same positions as 437—but the mixed-line graphics, most of the Greek letters, and most of the math operators are gone. In their positions, you'll find additional accented and special alphabetic characters for European languages.

For the sake of completeness, here's 1252:

| | | | ° 0176 deg 00B0 | À 0192 Agrave 00C0 | Ð 0208 ETH 00D0 | à 0224 agrave 00E0 | ð 0240 eth 00F0 |
|---|---|---|---|---|---|---|---|
| 0128 | 0144 | 0160 nbsp 00A0 | | | | | |
| 0129 | ' 0145 lsquo 2018 | ¡ 0161 iexcl 00A1 | ± 0177 plusmn 00B1 | Á 0193 Aacute 00C1 | Ñ 0209 Ntilde 00D1 | á 0225 aacute 00E1 | ñ 0241 ntilde 00F1 |
| , 0130 lsquor 201A | ' 0146 rsquo 2019 | ¢ 0162 cent 00A2 | ² 0178 sup2 00B2 | Â 0194 Acirc 00C2 | Ò 0210 Ograve 00D2 | â 0226 acirc 00E2 | ò 0242 ograve 00F2 |
| ƒ 0131 fnof 0192 | " 0147 ldquo 201C | £ 0163 pound 00A3 | ³ 0179 sup3 00B3 | Ã 0195 Atilde 00C3 | Ó 0211 Oacute 00D3 | ã 0227 atilde 00E3 | ó 0243 oacute 00F3 |
| „ 0132 ldquor 201E | " 0148 rdquo 201D | ¤ 0164 curren 00A4 | ´ 0180 acute 00B4 | Ä 0196 Auml 00C4 | Ô 0212 Ocirc 00D4 | ä 0228 auml 00E4 | ô 0244 ocirc 00F4 |
| … 0133 hellip 2026 | • 0149 bull 2022 | ¥ 0165 yen 00A5 | µ 0181 micro 00B5 | Å 0197 Aring 00C5 | Õ 0213 Otilde 00D5 | å 0229 aring 00E5 | õ 0245 otilde 00F5 |
| † 0134 dagger 2020 | – 0150 ndash 2013 | ¦ 0166 brvbar 00A6 | ¶ 0182 para 00B6 | Æ 0198 AElig 00C6 | Ö 0214 Ouml 00D6 | æ 0230 aelig 00E6 | ö 0246 ouml 00F6 |
| ‡ 0135 Dagger 2021 | — 0151 mdash 2014 | § 0167 sect 00A7 | · 0183 middot 00B7 | Ç 0199 Ccedil 00C7 | × 0215 times 00D7 | ç 0231 ccedil 00E7 | ÷ 0247 divide 00F7 |
| ˆ 0136 02C6 | ˜ 0152 02DC | ¨ 0168 uml 00A8 | ¸ 0184 cedil 00B8 | È 0200 Egrave 00C8 | Ø 0216 Oslash 00D8 | è 0232 egrave 00E8 | ø 0248 oslash 00F8 |
| ‰ 0137 permil 2030 | ™ 0153 trade 2122 | © 0169 copy 00A9 | ¹ 0185 sup1 00B9 | É 0201 Eacute 00C9 | Ù 0217 Ugrave 00D9 | é 0233 eacute 00E9 | ù 0249 ugrave 00F9 |
| Š 0138 Scaron 0160 | š 0154 scaron 0161 | ª 0170 ordf 00AA | º 0186 ordm 00BA | Ê 0202 Ecirc 00CA | Ú 0218 Uacute 00DA | ê 0234 ecirc 00EA | ú 0250 uacute 00FA |
| ‹ 0139 lsaquo 2039 | › 0155 rsaquo 203A | « 0171 laquo 00AB | » 0187 raquo 00BB | Ë 0203 Euml 00CB | Û 0219 Ucirc 00DB | ë 0235 euml 00EB | û 0251 ucirc 00FB |
| Œ 0140 OElig 0152 | œ 0156 oelig 0153 | ¬ 0172 not 00AC | ¼ 0188 frac14 00BC | Ì 0204 Igrave 00CC | Ü 0220 Uuml 00DC | ì 0236 igrave 00EC | ü 0252 uuml 00FC |
| 0141 | 0157 | 0173 shy 00AD | ½ 0189 frac12 00BD | Í 0205 Iacute 00CD | Ý 0221 Yacute 00DD | í 0237 iacute 00ED | ý 0253 yacute 00FD |
| 0142 | 0158 | ® 0174 reg 00AE | ¾ 0190 frac34 00BE | Î 0206 Icirc 00CE | Þ 0222 THORN 00DE | î 0238 icirc 00EE | þ 0254 thorn 00FE |
| 0143 | Ÿ 0159 Yuml 0178 | ¯ 0175 macr 00AF | ¿ 0191 iquest 00BF | Ï 0207 Iuml 00CF | ß 0223 szlig 00DF | ï 0239 iuml 00EF | ÿ 0255 yuml 00FF |

*Figure G.3*

Code page 1252

## Code Page Compatibility

If you're lucky, your printer's manual will mention code page 437 or 850 by number and claim to be compatible with it. In that case, just go to **Device Options\Character mapping,** click the appropriate **Code page** button, and you're home free. There's a chance, though, that your printer's character set is sort of like *both* fixed pages but doesn't conform fully to either one. (Tip: Since most Epson printers use positions above 127 for an English italic font, the top half of their symbol set isn't much like either 437 *or* 850. Sorry.) In that case, our advice is to try both code pages and see which one you like better … or at least which one you can use more effectively.

It would be nice if you could click the button for 437 or 850, load that mapping into the **On printer** dialog, and edit the incompatible characters one by one till you had them exactly right. No such luck; as soon as you click on either one of the fixed code pages, **On screen** and **On printer** are grayed out.

If being this deep in code pages and symbol sets strums a chord in your soul—and you don't already have an HP LaserJet—you still need a copy of the manual for any LaserJet Series II, III, or 4. You don't have to buy it new; any beat-up example from a nerdy garage sale will be fine. The appendices to the manuals for PCL 4 and PCL 5 are the best references for this information that you'll find, short of some expensive specialized book on the subject.

# Sample Command Sets

Finally, as a sort of Help page for the Device Options and Fonts tabs of the Generic driver, we present the full Properties command set—which is nowhere near the whole command set, but it's all you can use—for four significant printers:

- Epson FX-80, the "most generic" dot-matrix printer.

- IBM Proprinter, the "other most generic" dot-matrix printer; most nine-pin, and some 24-pin, dot-matrix printers will emulate one or the other of these.

- Qume Sprint-11, the "most generic" daisywheel printer; these codes should drive almost any Qume or Diablo daisywheel and some others.

- HP LaserJet with PCL 4, the "most generic" laser printer; these codes should drive almost any non-PostScript laser built between 1985 and 1990, although you may have to flip a switch (or add an escape code to **Begin job**) to toggle on HP emulation.

All codes are in formats legal for the Properties sheet tabs; (symbols) are Microsoft's "control-letter sequences" and (decimal) are Microsoft's "decimal digits." In the decimal codes it would also be possible to represent <ESC> as **27,** but the Help says to use the [Esc] key, so why fight it? See Tables G.1 and G.2.

## Table G.1  Properties Sheet Codes: Epson and IBM (Dot-Matrix Printers)

| Properties sheet | Epson (symbols) | Epson (decimal) | IBM (symbols) | IBM (decimal) | Ignore spaces in (symbols) columns |
|---|---|---|---|---|---|
| Begin job | [Esc] @ | [Esc] 64 | [Esc] @ | [Esc] 64 | Initialize |
| End job | [Esc] @ | [Esc] 64 | [Esc] @ | [Esc] 64 | Initialize |
| Paper size | [Esc] ( c | [Esc] 40 99 | [Esc] C 66 | [Esc] 67 54 54 | page format |
| Paper source | See docs | See docs | See docs | See docs | |
| Select 10 cpi | [Esc] P | [Esc] 80 | [Ctrl] R | 18 | Elite off/ Pica (10) on |

## Table G.1 *(continued)*

| Properties sheet | Epson (symbols) | Epson (decimal) | IBM (symbols) | IBM (decimal) | Ignore spaces in (symbols) columns |
|---|---|---|---|---|---|
| Select 12 cpi | [Esc] M | [Esc] 77 | [Esc] : | [Esc] 58 | Elite (12) on |
| Select 17 cpi | | | [Ctrl] O | 15 | Compressed (16.7) on |
| Select 17 cpi | [Esc] g | [Esc] 103 | | | (15) width on (use for 15) |
| Double-width on | [Esc] W 1 | [Esc] 87 49 | [Esc] W 1 | [Esc] 87 49 | |
| Double-width off | [Esc] W 0 | [Esc] 87 48 | [Esc] W 0 | [Esc] 87 48 | |
| Bold on | [Esc] E | [Esc] 69 | [Esc] E | [Esc] 69 | |
| Bold off | [Esc] F | [Esc] 70 | [Esc] F | [Esc] 70 | |
| Underline on | [Esc] - 1 | [Esc] 45 49 | [Esc] - 1 | [Esc] 45 49 | |
| Underline off | [Esc] - 0 | [Esc] 45 48 | [Esc] - 0 | [Esc] 45 48 | |

## Table G.2 Properties Sheet Codes: Qume (Daisywheel) and HP LaserJet

| Properties sheet | Qume Sprint-11 (symbols) | Qume Sprint-11 (decimal) | HP LaserJet (symbols) | HP LaserJet (decimal) | Ignore spaces in (symbols) columns |
|---|---|---|---|---|---|
| Begin job | [Esc][Ctrl] Z I | [Esc] 26 73 | [Esc] E | [Esc] 69 | Initialize |
| End job | [Esc][Ctrl] Z I | [Esc] 26 73 | [Esc] E | [Esc] 69 | Initialize |
| Paper size | [Esc] F (See docs) | [Esc] 70 | [Esc] &l2A | [Esc] 38 108 50 65 | page format |
| Paper source | See docs | See docs | See docs | See docs | |
| Select 10 cpi | SW1 OFF, SW2 OFF | leave field empty | [Esc] &k0S | [Esc] 38 107 48 83 | Elite off/Pica (10) on |
| Select 12 cpi | SW1 ON, SW2 OFF | leave field empty | [Esc] &k4S | [Esc] 38 107 52 83 | Elite (12) on |
| Select 17 cpi | SW1 OFF, SW2 ON | leave field empty | | | (15) width on (use for 15) |
| Select 17 cpi | | | [Esc] &k2S | [Esc] 38 107 50 83 | Compressed (16.7) on |
| Double-width on | printwheel | leave field empty | [Esc] (s24S | [Esc] 40 115 50 52 83 | |
| Double-width off | printwheel | leave field empty | [Esc] (s0S | [Esc] 40 115 48 83 | |
| Bold on | [Esc] K | [Esc] 75 | [Esc] (s3B | [Esc] 40 115 51 66 | |
| Bold off | [Esc] M | [Esc] 77 | [Esc] (s0B | [Esc] 40 115 48 66 | |
| Underline on | [Esc] I | [Esc] 73 | [Esc] &d0D | [Esc] 38 100 48 68 | |
| Underline off | [Esc] J | [Esc] 74 | [Esc] &d@ | [Esc] 38 100 64 | |

# Summary

We've dissected these drivers so that you can use these control-code sets as a starting point when you hand-roll a minidriver for a printer that runs *almost,* but not quite, like one of the above. Run your printer with these codes, see what it does wrong, and hope that the changes you need to make will actually fit in the fields of the Properties tabs. If, in the course of your research, you discover that your printer runs correctly with the Epson, IBM, or HP driver, we encourage you to go ahead and use it; any real Windows minidriver will access more of the printer's feature set than a driver you make yourself. Unfortunately, the Generic driver is your only hope (we think) for the Qume/Diablo printer, because no daisywheel minidrivers ship with Windows 98.

If you experiment with this material and find out something important that we haven't covered, please let us know by browsing to `http://www.winbible.com` and posting the details to the guestbook. Good luck, and thanks!

# Appendix H

# At the Last Minute

Well, thanks, everybody. Thanks for reading *The Windows 98 Bible,* thanks for buying it, and thanks for giving us a reason to write it.

Naturally, with the release of Windows 98 only a few weeks away, we're engulfed in a blizzard of rumors—and some developments that are more than rumors. We could keep wedging new details into the chapters, and we have been, but it's in the nature of books that eventually they have to end, so they can get printed. Fun's over. Time for bed. The last version of Windows 98 we tested was Release Candidate 2, and the most recent details or afterthoughts are on these pages. From now on, new information that comes to us will appear at *The Windows 98 Bible* Web site, `http://www.winbible.com`.

# Chapter 3: Navigating Windows 98

**End of the Channel Bar.** There are rumors that at some point, whether in the retail version of Windows 98 or in some patch available from Windows Update, the Channel Bar is going to vanish and be replaced by some other display of targeted content. So all those Web sites that installed the "Add Active Channel" button now get to take it off? "We're waiting for the latest orders from Redmond, Major, but until we get them...."

# Chapter 5: Toys, Games, and Pocketknives

**Windows 98 Plus! Pack.** We stumbled over a preliminary specification for the Windows 98 Plus! Pack and were not surprised to learn that it addresses several deficiencies we complain about. This is not a final spec, your mileage may vary.

- A full version of Network Associates' **McAfee VirusScan** to be installed in the Windows 98 Maintenance Wizard. You get six months of free updates.

- **File Cleaner** is an improvement to Windows 98 Disk Cleanup that makes more and better suggestions about files to delete.

- **Start Menu Cleaner** removes broken links and empty folders from the Start Menu. Wasn't this originally supposed to be part of Windows 98 itself?

- **Compressed Folders** is a powerful archiver that provides "up to 90%" compression while it lets you drag and drop, view, and run files from a compressed folder. This sounds better than DriveSpace and more like Windows NT compression.

- A pack of **PLUS! 98 Themes,** naturally, some of which have improved 3D effects.

- **Deluxe CD Player** uses CDDB (see Chapter 12) to put CD title, artist and track information into playlists. Feeling the heat, Redmond?

- **Picture It! Express** lets you adjust brightness, contrast and tint, crop or soften edges, and fix red-eye in digital photos. Whether it's as useful as Paint Shop Pro or Kai's Photo Soap, we shall see, but a digital editor's a good thing to have.

- Two new games: **Lose Your Marbles** from SegaSoft, and an "intense" two-deck variation of classic Solitaire called **Spider Solitaire.**

Street price of the Windows 98 Plus! Pack is expected to be $35.

# Chapter 7: Of Displays, Mice, and Keyboards

**Iiyama VisionMaster Pro.** Monitors now are at an awkward stage of development. Prices of 17" monitors become ever more attractive, but the true devotee of multimedia and Total Immersion Hack might lust after something bigger. The problem is that tank-like 21" monitors are too big to fit in many of the places where monitors have to live—and besides, they cost a bundle.

In Chapter 7 we recommended Iiyama (Idek) as one of the premier makers of high-quality, high-resolution monitors. While we were writing the Multimedia chapter a while later, we were privileged to work with an Iiyama VisionMaster Pro 450—a 19" monitor scarcely bigger than many seventeen-inchers, and with a street price of only $700 to $800. Its flat screen, exceptional color saturation, and ultra-fine .22-millimeter dot pitch make icons seem to levitate over the desktop, DVD look like movie film, and paint programs respond as never before. This is literally the finest monitor we've seen that costs less than thousands of dollars, and we urge you to look at the VisionMaster Pro before you purchase any monitor in its price range.

# Chapter 12: Multimedia

**About .MP3 Files.** Our cheerful friend (the one with the red plastic navel ring and the obnoxious cat) was reading the Multimedia chapter and said, "Hey! You can't write about media and not write about .MP3 files. What are we supposed to do about them? Windows won't play 'em, right?"

Right, actually—neither Sound Recorder nor the DirectShow player will play back .MP3 (MPEG Level 3 Audio) files. This was probably deliberate on Microsoft's part, and we were avoiding the issue because that whole scene is so … rancid. But since it is possible that you might have some legitimately obtained .MP3 files on your system, and need to play them back, since, after all, it happened to us, and certainly we're above reproach, there's a fine shareware player called WINAMP written by some guys at least one of whom is in Arizona. You can check this out at `http://www.winamp.com` or `http://www.nullsoft.com`, and remember: don't play .MP3 and drive.

**WaveTop and Advanced Power Management.** Press reports of WaveTop have disclosed that, because the server sets the schedule for content delivery, the browser's cable connection has to be permanently "live" to avoid missing updates. This would be fine, except that WaveTop can't push its content to a sleeping or suspended computer, so—as of now—you've got your choice between WaveTop and Advanced Power Management. If you're of the opinion that computers should be fully powered all the time anyway, this doesn't affect you, but if not, it's a problem.

Microsoft is working with WavePhore to deliver a patch for this, and it may be incorporated in the Windows 98 retail version. If it doesn't make that deadline, look for it on Windows Update.

**WebTV Improvements.** When we installed Release Candidate 2 of Windows 98, WebTV for Windows had better performance—it's still slow but not glacial. Also, after we reinstalled the new build, the sound worked. Now, if they'd just get the sound level out of Volume Control Line-In and into the TV controls, where it belongs.…

# Chapter 13: Optimizing Windows 98 Resources

**Kingston TurboChip 233.** In "Upgrade CPUs" and "The Alternative," we were less than enthusiastic about upgrading your computer by swapping in a new CPU. Let us remember that the computer industry does three things superbly; build computers, push envelopes, and make liars out of journalists.

Kingston Technology, whose hardware memory we've liked for years, has announced that in June they'll ship a drop-in upgrade chip, the TurboChip 233, for $300 list. According to Kingston product manager Raymond Wang, this chip will work in any Socket 5 or Socket 7 system and includes its own on-board voltage regulator. Wang says the product is meant to upgrade 75-, 100-, and 133-MHz Pentium systems to the level of a Pentium 233 MMX.

Our general lukewarmth about CPU swaps is unabated, but any time you can double or triple your system's CPU speed with $300 and half an hour.... We'll try to keep you up to date on this one.

# Chapter 14: Windows 98 and DOS

**DOS Game Support.** We suspect that the DOS game support in Windows 98 has improved significantly from previous releases. Our benchmark "tough DOS game," Disney's *Stunt Island*—which in its time was legendary both for its graphics and for the demands it made on your system—would never run in *any* version of Windows 95. It runs fine in Windows 98 Release Candidate 1, although without any sound, but with more tweaking we may fix even that.

We'll keep you posted, and we'd like you to keep us posted, on how well Windows 98 does with the great gnarly games of the past. After all, they're paid for and they're still fun.

See you on the Web site! Remember, that's **http://www.winbible.com** !

# Appendix I

# System Benchmark Information

The system benchmark information pertinent to comparative disk testing in the "Faceoff!" section of Chapter 13 is published at the request of Ziff-Davis Laboratories. These tests were performed without independent verification by Ziff-Davis, and Ziff-Davis makes no representation or warranty as to the results.

Test software used was the Business Disk WinMark® module of WinBench® 98 version 1.0. WinBench is a registered trademark or trademark and WinMark is a trademark of Ziff-Davis, Inc., in the United States and other countries.

The computer used for this test is homemade and using a single Intel Pentium® processor with a clock rate of 120 MHz and a level-2 cache of 256 KB. System BIOS is Award Modular v4.51PG. System RAM is 24 MB.

The hard disk subsystem comprises a Quantum Fireball 1080 EIDE disk with 128 KB of hardware cache on-backplane, driven by an embedded Intel 82371SB PCI Bus Master IDE controller. Disk cache in main RAM is allocated by the operating system as available. Installed file systems for testing were FAT16, FAT32, and DriveSpace 3, according to the test being run.

The graphics adapter in use is an ATI All-in-Wonder PCI with an ATI Mach64/ Rage II+ chipset and 4 MB VRAM. The graphics adapter driver file is Microsoft ATI_M64.DRV build 4.10.00.1691. Resolution and depth are 800 x 600 x 16 bpp.

The CD-ROM drive is an MKE CR-563 (4x) driven by the CD-ROM drive control logic of a Creative Labs Sound Blaster 16 multimedia card. CD-ROM Windows RAM cache is 1238 KB allocated by the operating system.

Operating system in use for the tests was Windows 98 build 4.10.1691.

All products used in the test were shipping versions available to the general public.

Once again, we thank Ziff-Davis Laboratories for making this test suite freely available and consenting to publication of its benchmark results.

# Index